Great Problems in

European Civilization

Great Problems in

Contributors

Crane Brinton, *Harvard University*
R. V. Burks, *Radio Free Europe*
Peter Charanis, *Rutgers University*
Evalyn A. Clark, *Vassar College*
Stewart C. Easton, *Formerly of The City College of New York*
Myron P. Gilmore, *Harvard University*
James L. Godfrey, *University of North Carolina*
E. Harris Harbison, *Princeton University*
David Herlihy, *University of Wisconsin*
Harry H. Kimber, *Michigan State College*
Lowell Ragatz, *The Ohio State University*
Kenneth M. Setton, *University of Wisconsin*
John Hall Stewart, *Western Reserve University*
Henry R. Winkler, *Rutgers University*
John B. Wolf, *University of Minnesota*
Norman P. Zacour, *Franklin and Marshall College*

EUROPEAN CIVILIZATION

SECOND EDITION

Editors

Kenneth M. Setton, UNIVERSITY OF WISCONSIN

Henry R. Winkler, RUTGERS UNIVERSITY

Prentice-Hall, Inc., *Englewood Cliffs, N. J.*

Prentice-Hall International, Inc., *London*
Prentice-Hall of Australia, Pty., Ltd., *Sydney*
Prentice-Hall of Canada, Ltd., *Toronto*
Prentice-Hall of India (Private) Ltd., *New Delhi*
Prentice-Hall of Japan, Inc., *Tokyo*

Great Problems in European Civilization, Second Edition
Kenneth M. Setton and Henry R. Winkler

© 1954, 1966 by Prentice-Hall, Inc., *Englewood Cliffs, N.J.*

Current printing (last digit):
10   9   8   7   6   5   4   3   2   1

Library of Congress Catalog Card No.: 66–11190

Printed in the United States of America
C-36461

Preface

Continued demand for this book and our desire to improve it have led to this second edition. All chapters have been carefully reviewed, and most of them have been thoroughly revised. Two chapters are entirely new. We have also brought the book up to date.

The contributors to this volume believe that neither the general reader nor the student of history should be shielded from the facts of history, for they are the facts of life. History is not a cut-and-dried series of memorable names and dates, a mere succession of laws, institutions, and the like. It is not just a chronicle of court scandal and intrigue. It is the study of the continuous stream of human experience. The problems in this volume represent great landmarks in this long journey of mankind.

Experienced and highly trained historians have set the problems for us in this volume; they have asked the questions and supplied the material for answers pro and con. They have given us no answers, however, and have attempted no conclusions. They have tried to give us material on both sides, and on more sides still when the question cannot be resolved into alternatives. Only readers who will not think for themselves will complain that they have not been supplied with the answers. Inquiring minds will seek their own answers, and this volume has been designed to help them.

All the present readings are focused upon certain great problems, themselves a source of perennial fascination, and central to the history of European civilization. The spotlight is put upon these problems and shifted from side to side to broaden our view of them as we seek to understand them; if understanding of these problems is not everywhere easy, achievement of such understanding is enormously worthwhile, for these problems have supplied the pattern of much of contemporary civilization. Letters and speeches, documents and historical writings, newspapers and other sources are excerpted and organized for study or even perusal by the reader. The effort has been to assist every man to be his own historian, for every man is a historian. He cannot escape it.

The boy who finds a bundle of his grandmother's love letters in the attic becomes a historian as he reads them. His curiosity moves him to historical research: he wants to find out what a stately old lady of his acquaintance was up to, fifty years ago. There are at least two general types of questions which we put to the sources. The first are simple questions. When was Caesar or Napoleon or Stalin born? What is the date of this treaty or that, and what are its provisions? When did the war begin? Who was the king's last mistress? The answers to these questions are sometimes interesting, sometimes entertaining, but in themselves they are rarely important. The other questions are far less simple. How do you explain the phenomenal victory of Christianity over all its rivals and opponents in the early centuries of its existence? What is the validity of the historical concept of the Renaissance? What are the causes of the Protestant Movement? Was it Reformation or chiefly Revolt? How has industrialization molded the structure of modern society? How has communism achieved such strength as to place democracy and freedom of thought and enterprise in jeopardy? What caused the quick disintegration of the settlement at Versailles which helped to build the road to World War II? What has capitalism meant in the history of European peoples? Every reader will grant that these are far more important questions than the first sort posed. We have not lacked answers to important questions. If anything, we have had too many answers from historians and theologians, popular writers and publicists, and from almost everyone who has found an audience. Sometimes we come to the conclusion that the historian is a person who can ask the big questions but cannot answer them, at least not to another historian's satisfaction. The great problems of history are subjects of unending controversy. We have attempted here to present a selection of materials for the thoughtful reader to consider, in the hope that he may thus broaden his own understanding of the past as well as the present, for his future will be built upon both.

As in the first edition, we have incurred obligations which we are happy to acknowledge, most notably to Miss Margaret C. Nolan, who solved a hundred problems for us, to Miss Mary C. Hendrickson, who checked all the proofs of the first half of the book with painstaking care, and to Mrs. Jane L. Burks, who typed the revisions of the second half with equal attention and accuracy.

If the present edition proves as useful both to teachers and students as the first obviously did, the editors and contributors will regard their expenditure of time and effort as well worthwhile.

K.M.S.
H.R.W.

Acknowledgments

*In the preparation of this volume, the editors and
contributors have been placed under obligation, which is
hereby acknowledged with thanks, to the following publishers,
individuals, and others who have allowed them the use of
materials from the books and other sources indicated.*

Académie royale de Belgique
Henri Pirenne, *Les Périodes de l'histoire sociale du capitalisme.*

George Allen & Unwin, Ltd.
Friedrich Engels, *The Condition of the Working-Class in England
in 1844;* J. A. Hobson, *Imperialism;* and Wilhelm Roepke, *The
Solution of the German Problem.*

Appleton-Century-Crofts
William Godwin, *An Equiry Concerning Political Justice and Its
Influence on General Virtue and Happiness,* ed. R. A. Preston.

Beacon Press
Franz H. Mautner and Henry Hatfield, *The Lichtenberg Reader.*

G. Bell & Sons, Ltd.
H. Butterfield, *The Statecraft of Machiavelli.*

Basil Blackwell & Mott, Ltd.
Geoffrey Barraclough, *Papal Provisions;* and Lucan, *Bellum Civile,*
ed. A. E. Housman.

Geoffrey Bles, Ltd.
Nicholas Berdyaev, *The Origin of Russian Communism,* trans.
R. M. French.

Cambridge University Press
W. A. Pantin, *The English Church in the Fourteenth Century.*

The Catholic University of America Press
Fathers of the Church, trans. Thomas B. Falls.

The Clarendon Press
H. A. L. Fisher, *Studies in History and Politics;* and Walter
Ullman, *Journal of Theological Studies.*

Columbia University Press
Sebastian Castellio, *Concerning Heretics,* trans. R. H. Bainton;
Grover Clark, *The Balance Sheets of Imperialism; Correspondence
of Pope Gregory VII,* trans. Ephraim Emerton; Marsilius of

Padua, *The Defender of the Peace,* ed. A. Gewirth; Odo of Deuil, *De perfectione Ludovici VII in orientem,* ed. and trans. Virginia Gingerick Berry; Robert of Clari, *The Conquest of Constantinople,* trans. Edgar Holmes McNeal; William of Tyre, *A History of Deeds Done Beyond the Sea,* trans. Emily Atwater Babcock and August C. Krey; and Earle M. Winslow, *The Pattern of Imperialism.*

Crowell-Collier Educational Corporation

Nicolaus Copernicus, *Revolutions of the Heavenly Bodies;* and Sir Isaac Newton, Preface to the *Philosophiae Naturalis Principia Mathematica,* trans. Andrew Motte.

Crown Publishers

Marquis de Sade, *Dialogue Between a Priest and a Dying Man,* trans. Samuel Putnam.

The John Day Company, Inc.

James Burnham, *The Struggle for the World.*

J. M. Dent & Sons, Ltd.

The Memoirs of the Crusades by Villehardouin and de Joinville, trans. Sir Frank Marzials.

Duell, Sloane and Pearce, Inc.

The Complete Jefferson, ed. S. K. Padover.

E. P. Dutton & Co., Inc.

Memoirs of the Crusades by Villehardouin and de Joinville, trans. Sir Frank Marzials; Jean Jacques Rousseau, *The Social Contract and Discourses,* trans. G. D. H. Cole; and *The Works of Liudprand of Cremona,* trans. F. A. Wright.

Wm. B. Eerdmans Publishing Co.

Martin Luther, *The Bondage of the Will,* trans. Henry Cole.

The Folio Society Limited

Voltaire's England, ed. Desmond Flower.

Fortress Press

Heinrich Boehmer, *Road to Reformation: Martin Luther to Year 1521,* trans. J. W. Doberstein and T. G. Tappert; and Preserved Smith, *Luther's Correspondence.*

The Free Press of Glencoe

Robert Owen, *A New View of Society.*

Gyldendalske Boghandel Nordisk Forlag

J. Plessner, *L'Émigration de la campagne à la ville libre de Florence au XIIIe siècle.*

Hafner Publishing Co., Inc.

Aristotle, *Constitution of Athens,* trans. K. von Fritz and E. Knapp.

Harvard University Press

From the Loeb Classical Library: Dion Cassius, *Roman History,* trans. E. Cary; Eusebius, *Ecclesiastical History,* trans. J. E. L. Oulton and H. J. Lawlor; Isocrates, *Panegyricus,* trans. G. Norlin; *Res Gestae Divi Augusti,* trans. F. W. Shipley; Plutarch, *Aristides,* trans. B. Perrin; Suetonius, *The Lives of the Caesars,* trans. J. C. Rolfe; St. Basil of Caesarea, *To Young Men, On Pagan Literature,* trans. R. J. Deferrari and M. R. P. McGuire; Tertullian, *Apology,* trans. Peter Holmes; Velleius Paterculus, *History of Rome,* trans. F. W. Shipley; Joseph A. Schumpeter, *Imperialism and Social Classes,* trans. Heinz Norden, ed. Paul M. Sweezy.

B. Herder Book Company

Hartmann Grisar, *Martin Luther: His Life and Work,* trans.
F. J. Eble; and *Canons and Decrees of the Council of Trent,* ed.
H. J. Schroeder.

Her Majesty's Stationery Office

A European Free Trade Area.

Houghton Mifflin Company

E. L. Higgins, *The French Revolution as Told by Contemporaries.*

International Publishers

Maximilien Robespierre, *Speeches: Voices of Revolt;* and
Diderot: Interpreter of Nature, trans. Jean Stewart and Jonathan
Kemp, ed. Jonathan Kemp.

The Johns Hopkins Press

Jeremy Bentham, *The Handbook of Political Fallacies,* ed. Harold A.
Larrabee; and *An Economic Survey of Ancient Rome,* ed. T. Frank.

Journal of the History of Ideas

Ernst Cassirer, *Some Remarks on the Question of the Originality
of the Renaissance;* and Lynn Thorndike, *Renaissance or
Prenaissance.*

The Kenyon Review

Erwin Panofsky, *Renaissance and Renascences.*

Kessing's Publications Limited

Kessing's Contemporary Archives.

Alfred A. Knopf, Inc.

Frederick L. Schuman, *The Nazi Dictatorship.*

Librairie Armand Colin

J. E. Spenlé, *La Pensée allemande de Luther à Nietzsche.*

Librairie Droz

Louis Le Roy, *Considérations sur l'histoire universelle.*

The Macmillan Company

Parker T. Moon, *Imperialism and World Politics;* and John Hall
Stewart, *A Documentary Survey of the French Revolution.*

Macmillan & Co., Ltd.

Keith Feiling, *The Life of Neville Chamberlain.*

Methuen & Co., Ltd.

Desiderius Erasmus, *Enchiridion Militis Christian;* and G. B.
Grundy, *A History of the Greek and Roman World.*

Francis Morgan Nichols

The Epistles of Erasmus, trans. Francis Morgan Nichols.

Martinus Nijhoff, Publisher

Erasmi Opuscula, ed. W. K. Ferguson.

Oxford University Press

Niccolò Machiavelli, *The Prince;* Arnold Toynbee, *The World
and the West;* and D. Whitelock, *English Historical Documents,*
Vol. I.

Penguin Books, Ltd.

V. G. Childe, *What Happened in History.*

Frederick A. Praeger, Inc.

Theodore Draper, *Castro's Revolution—Myths and Realities.*

Presses universitaires de France

J. Lestocquoy, *Les Villes de Flandre et d'Italie sous le gouvernment des patriciens (XIe-XVe siècles)*.

Princeton University Press

R. V. Burks, *The Dynamics of Communism in Eastern Europe;* Desiderius Erasmus, *The Praise of Folly,* trans. H. H. Hudson; August C. Krey, *The First Crusade;* Georges Lefebvre, *The Coming of the French Revolution;* Louis Le Roy, *De la Viscissitude ou Variété des choses en l'universe;* and *Theodosian Code and Novels,* trans. C. Pharr.

G. P. Putnam's Sons

E. B. Hall, *Voltaire in His Letters;* Adolph Hausrath, *Treitschke: His Doctrine of German Destiny and of International Relations,* trans. Leila Vennewitz; Klaus Mehnert, *Peking and Moscow;* and Heinrich von Treitschke, *Germany, France, Russia and Islam.*

Random House, Inc.

Jacob Burckhardt, *The Age of Constantine the Great,* trans. M. Hadas; and Niccolò Machiavelli, *The Discourses.*

Routledge & Kegan Paul, Ltd.

The Alexiad of the Princess Anna Comnena, trans. Elisabeth A. S. Dawes; and *The Works of Liudprand of Cremona,* trans. F. A. Wright.

Charles Scribner's Sons

Alphonse Aulard, *The French Revolution,* trans. Bernard Miall; Pierre Gaxotte, *The French Revolution,* trans. Walter Alison Phillips; Jacques Maritain, *Three Reformers;* and Paul van Dyke, *Ignatius Loyola.*

The Slavonic and East European Review

Manifesto of the First Slavonic Congress, trans. William Beardmore.

Staples Press, Ltd.

Antony van Leeuwenhoek and His "Little Animals," ed. Clifford Dobell.

University of California Press

Galileo Galilei, *Dialogue Concerning the Two Chief World Systems —Ptolemaic and Copernican,* trans. Stillman Drake.

University of Chicago Press

Petrarch's Letters to Classical Authors, trans. Mario E. Cosenza.

University of Michigan Press

Nicholas Berdyaev, *The Origin of Russian Communism,* trans. R. M. French.

University of Wisconsin Press

A. A. Vasiliev, *History of the Byzantine Empire.*

The Viking Press, Inc.

The Age of Reason Reader, ed. Crane Brinton.

A. P. Watt & Sons

John Buchan, *Augustus;* and H. G. Wells, *The Outline of History.*

George Weidenfeld & Nicholson, Ltd.

Marquis de Condorcet, *A Sketch for a Historical Picture of the Human Mind,* trans. June Barraclough.

The Westminster Press

Roland H. Bainton, *The Travail of Religious Liberty.*

Contents

A. The Nature of Athenian Imperialism. 1. As a Benefit to All
Greece. (a) The Ideal Beginnings: The Just Tax Assessments of Aris-
tides. (b) The Ideal of the Empire: Funeral Speech of Pericles. (c)
Advantages of the Empire for the Allies. 2. Athens as the Exploiter of
Greece. (a) The League as an Athenian Preserve. (b) The League as
a Means of Enriching Athens. (c) Athens as Exploiter of the Rich for
Benefit of the Poor. (d) How Athens Controlled Her Empire—A
Modern Summary. B. The Athenian Attitude Toward the Political
Freedom of Others. 1. As Preservers of Greek Liberties. (a) The
Kindness and Humanity of the Athenian Empire. (b) Imperial De-
fense as a Benefit for Allies. 2. As Destroyers of Greek Liberties. (a)
Severe Exactions and Refusal to Permit Secession. (b) An Ally's View
of Athenian Domination. (c) Wanton Aggression Against a Neutral.
C. Limitations on Athenian Democracy. (a) Women and Slaves. (b)
Erosion of Civil Liberties under Impact of War.

A. The Achievement of Augustus. 1. Public Statement of Augustus
Himself a Year Before His Death. 2. Tacitus Reports Opposing Views
in His Time (About A.D. 120). 3. Opinion of the Ancient World.
(a) View of a Faithful Imperial Officer. (b) View of an Early Third-
century Historian. (c) The Biographer of the Caesars. 4. Varying
Opinion of Posterity. (a) The Eighteenth-century Rationalist. (b) A
Twentieth-century Professional Historian. (c) A Modern Administrator. B. Did the Principate Degenerate into a Tyranny under Tiberius?
1. Opinion of the Ancient World. (a) The Official View: Tiberius as a

at the Time. 2. As Reported by Robert the Monk. 3. As Reported by Balderic of Bourgueil. 4. As Reported by Guibert of Nogent. D. Urban's Letter to the Assembling Crusaders, December, 1095. E. Anna Comnena on the First Crusade. F. Skutariotes on the Rôle of the Emperor Alexius in the Origin of the First Crusade.

A. Odo of Deuil on the French Attitude Toward Constantinople During the Second Crusade. B. John Cinnamus on the Second Crusade. C. William of Tyre on the Massacre of the Latins in Constantinople in 1182. D. Nicetas Choniates on the Capture of Thessalonica by the Normans in 1185.

A. Villehardouin on the Diversion of the Fourth Crusade. B. Robert of Clari on the Diversion of the Fourth Crusade. C. Nicetas Choniates on the Fourth Crusade. D. Views of Modern Historians Concerning the Diversion of the Fourth Crusade. 1. A. A. Vasiliev. 2. H. Grégoire.

DAVID HERLIHY, *University of Wisconsin*

A. What Was the Status of the Free Peasant in Late Antiquity and the Barbarian Age? 1. Roman Imperial Legislation Concerning the Colonus. (a) Emperor Constantine Forbids Coloni to Leave the Soil, 30 October 332. (b) Emperors Gratian, Valentinian and Theodosius Forbid the Harboring of Escaped Coloni, 25 October 386. (c) An Unknown Emperor Requires that Escaped Coloni Be Denounced. (d) Emperors Valentinian and Valens Forbid Coloni to Alienate Property, 27 January 365. (e) Emperors Arcadius and Honorius [395–408] Forbid Coloni to Bring Law Suits Against Their Lords. 2. Inscriptions from Roman North Africa Concerning the Coloni. (a) From the Inscription of Ain-el-Djemala: The Procurators of Emperor Hadrian Confirm the Right of Coloni to the Permanent Use of Lands Improved by Them, A.D. 116–117. (b) From the Inscription of Suk-el-Khmis: Emperor Commodus Forbids Arbitrary Exactions from the Coloni, A.D. 180–183. 3. From the Tablettes Albertini: Coloni in Vandal North Africa Sell Lands Without Their Lord's Permission, 5 April 493(?). B. What Happened to the Carolingian Freeman? 1. The Plight of the Freeman as Reflected in Carolingian Capitularies. (a) Charlemagne Regulates the Status of Freemen Who, Out of Poverty, Become Serfs of the Church, 787(?). (b) Charlemagne Complains that His Officials Are Oppressing the People, 787(?). (c) Charlemagne Complains of the Oppression by the Powerful, 805. (d) Charlemagne

13 IMPERIALISTIC RIVALRIES BEFORE WORLD WAR I   452

LOWELL RAGATZ, *The Ohio State University*

14 THE ADVANCE OF COMMUNISM   488

R. V. BURKS, *Radio Free Europe*

1

Freedom and Tyranny in the Ancient World

STEWART C. EASTON

Formerly of The City College of New York

I. Greece: The Athenian Love of Freedom—Fact or Myth?

We are accustomed to look back to the Athenians as the founders of democracy, and as the first people to make freedom an ideal. Yet clearly there were limitations on Athenian democracy. It excluded all who were not citizens, and the freedom of those who were citizens of foreign states was not always respected. A great deal of Athenian history is occupied with wars, not all of which were in self-defense. This first chapter will therefore be concerned with the question of how far the Athenians were really lovers of freedom, or whether the limitations were so serious that they have no right to the praise so frequently lavished upon them. Their cultural achievements will be taken for granted in this chapter; it is only their attitude toward freedom that will be considered here.

In the latter part of the sixth century B.C. the Persians established a great empire in Western Asia which spread as far as the Aegean Sea. In the process they swallowed up the flourishing coastal cities of Asia Minor which were populated by Greeks. In 499 B.C. these cities revolted against Persia and appealed to the mainland Greeks for aid. The Athenians, almost alone among the Greeks, responded. Their expeditionary force landed in Asia Minor, burned one of the Persian capitals, and won some other minor victories. But it soon returned home without having made any serious inroads into Persian power.

Darius I, the powerful Persian monarch, was determined to punish the Greeks for their presumption. In 490 B.C. he sent a naval expedition against Athens, but after being defeated in the battle of Marathon, it returned to Persia, and Darius, who died soon afterwards, bequeathed his project of revenge to his son Xerxes. The latter, after collecting a huge and motley army, began a full-scale invasion of Greece by land and sea. The Greeks, however, were by now better prepared. The Athenians had built a fleet, and were able to persuade the Spartans and their allies to join in the common defense of the country. The result was the rout of the Persian forces in the campaigns of 480 and 479 B.C., although during the war Athens herself was sacked and burned.

The Athenians realized that Persia was not damaged beyond repair. At any time she could renew the assault. They therefore proposed to the other Greeks that a permanent defensive alliance be formed. The Spartans, however, refused to cooperate, with the result that the Athenians went ahead without them. Under the leadership of Aristides, they succeeded in organizing the Confederation of Delos, composed of almost all the islands in the Aegean, Athens herself, and a few of the mainland cities. Some of the allies provided ships to the common pool, but the majority merely furnished money, with which the Athenians built and equipped the ships. The Confederation was entirely successful in policing the Aegean and preventing the resurgence of Persian power in that area.

The Confederation was, of course, a highly profitable enterprise for the Athenians. But its very success caused murmurs among the allies. Was it really necessary, they asked, to keep such a substantial navy in being? The Persian danger seemed to have receded. Could they not be relieved of some of the financial burden? The Athenians retorted by raising the assessments whenever they found it necessary, while they refused to permit secession, using the confederate fleet against those members who tried to regain their independence. Finally, under the leadership of Pericles, the Athenians began to adopt an aggressive imperial policy beyond the confines of the Aegean, still using the fleet which had been built, but for entirely different purposes. When one such expedition suffered a resounding defeat at the hands of the Persians and Phoenicians in the Mediterranean Sea off Egypt, Samos, a big island in the Confederation, at this time friendly to Athens, suggested that the treasury of the League, hitherto kept in Delos, a tiny island sacred to Apollo, should be moved to Athens for greater safety. The League meekly consented, and thereafter the Confederation was an Athenian Empire in all but name. There was no further check upon her imperial ambitions, as long as she could force her allies to pay the ever increasing tax assessments that she levied upon them.

Pericles, with the constant support of the Athenian democracy, now embarked on an expansionist policy, interfering with the internal government of the cities in the Empire, attempting by threats and promises to seduce allies of the Spartans, members of the rival Peloponnesian League, away from Sparta and into the Athenian Empire, even engaging in minor wars for the purpose. At last the exasperated Spartans, urged thereto especially by the Corinthians, trade rivals of the Athenians, undertook a preventive war, which lasted, with short intervals of truce, for 27 years. In 404 B.C. the Spartans, aided by Persian money and ships, utterly defeated the Athenians, and the Persians, thus brought back into Greek politics, became the virtual arbiters of Greece for most of the fourth century, even though they made no further attempt at military conquest. It was, therefore, possible to claim that the Athenian Empire had been the sole bulwark against Persian intervention, and with its destruction the enemy of all the Greeks had been once more permitted a foothold in the Greek world.

The facts are undisputed. But there has always been a difference of opinion, in the ancient as well as in the modern world, as to whether the Athenians were justified in their imperialism, or whether they merely exploited their Empire for their own benefit, taking advantage of their domination of the free Confederation to fasten an imperial system upon their unwilling partners, making them no longer partners but slaves—while accompanying their imperialism with protestations of their love of freedom and their devotion to democracy. There can be no doubt that the economic advantages of the Empire made possible the flowering of culture in fifth-century Athens, but was the price paid too high? Were the Athenians truly lovers of freedom, as their apologists claimed, or was this freedom an exclusive thing of benefit only to themselves? Indeed, how deep did their own commitment prove to be when the leadership of Pericles was removed and party strife was renewed under the impact of a long war?

Among the writers from whose works selections appear below, it is noticeable that none of those who were contemporary with the events described condones the excesses of imperialism. Thucydides in reporting the Funeral Oration of Pericles gives expression to the ideal as it was conceived by the great statesman. In other passages in his history he makes it clear that he regards the demagogic successors of Pericles as responsible for the degradation of the ideal. Of the two writers of the next century Isocrates, the Athenian, makes a typical patriotic defense of his city's policy, whereas the resident alien Aristotle explains the economic motives behind Athenian imperialism without comment. Posterity has been divided in its opinions. When modern writers have, like Zimmern, a great admiration for the achievements of Athens during the age of her Empire, they tend to gloss over her excesses. Others, like Grundy, argue that the Empire itself on balance proved in some respects beneficial to its members, even though they resented it. Both points of view are represented here.

A. The Nature of Athenian Imperialism

1. AS A BENEFIT TO ALL GREECE

(a) The Ideal Beginnings: *The just tax assessments of Aristides*

Plutarch was a Greek historian, biographer, and moralist of the second century A.D., or some six hundred years after the events he describes. He had access, however, to many sources lost to us, and in general his history, when capable of being checked, has for the most part been found to be reasonably accurate. However, his bias as moralist and biographer seems sometimes to have led him to make judgments on the characters he describes which would not be sustained by modern, and probably indeed, not by some ancient historians. The following account of Aristides the incorruptible should be contrasted with the much earlier account given by Aristotle (2 [b] below), although Aristotle himself was not contemporary with the events and is not necessarily free from bias. The critical modern reader should always be awake to the necessity of discounting personal bias in historians, especially when the historian lived close to the events he describes and was still suffering from their political consequences.

The Hellenes used to pay a kind of contribution for the war even during the period when the Spartans held the leadership, but now they desired to be assessed city by city. So they asked the Athenians for Aristides, and commissioned him to inspect their territories and revenues, and then to fix the assessments, according to the worth and ability to pay of each member.

And yet, though he thus became controller of so much power, and though, in a sense, Hellas put all her property in his sole hands, poor though he was when he started on his mission, he came back from it poorer still. He fixed the money assessments in accordance with purity and justice, and at the same time he earned the gratitude and satisfied the needs of all concerned. Indeed, as in antiquity people used to sing the praises of the Age of Kronos—the Golden Age—so now did the Athenian allies all praise the tariff of Aristides, calling it a piece of wonderful good fortune for all Hellas, especially since, after a short time, it was doubled and even trebled.

For Aristides taxed them only to the extent of four hundred sixty talents. But Pericles must have added almost a third to this, for Thucydides says that when the war began the Athenian revenue was six hundred talents from the allies. Then, after the death of Pericles, the demagogues increased it little by little so that in the end the total amounted to thirteen hundred talents, not so much because of the excessive expenses of the long and constantly changing war, but because they incited the people to spend money on spectacular entertainments, and the erection of statues and the building of temples.

Plutarch, *Aristides,* 24, adapted from the translation by B. Perrin, *Plutarch's Lives,* Loeb Classical Library (Cambridge, Mass.: Harvard University Press, 1914), II, 287–89.

(b) The Ideal of the Empire: *The funeral speech of Pericles*

At the end of the first year of the Peloponnesian War, Pericles delivered the customary public eulogy of those who had fallen in battle. The speech which Thucydides puts in his mouth is one of the most justly famed speeches of all history. Pericles takes the occasion to praise the city of Athens for which these men had died, and the ideal of the open friendly city, the "School of Hellas," has provided posterity with a picture of Athens of this period which has too often been accepted without question as truth. Perhaps it is better to regard it as the ideal of Thucydides, and possibly of Pericles; and though no ideal has ever been better stated, the other side of the picture, as depicted also by Thucydides, should not be forgotten in the quest for the fifth-century reality.

I shall begin with our ancestors; it is both just and proper that they should have the honor of the first mention on an occasion like the present. They lived in this country without a break in the succession from generation to generation, and they handed it down free to the present time by their deeds of valor. And if our more remote ancestors deserve praise, so much the more do our own fathers, who added to their inheritance the empire which we now possess, and spared no pains to be able to leave their acquisitions to us of the present generation. Finally, there are few parts of our territories that have not been increased by those of us here who are still in the prime of life, who consolidated our power throughout the greater part of the Empire and secured the city's complete independence in war and peace. I do not wish to say more about the battles fought by us and our fathers which gave us our possessions, or of the courage with which we withstood both barbarians and Greeks at home; for they are well known to you. But I would rather speak of the spirit in which we faced them, the kind of government and customs which gave rise to our greatness. . . .

Our government does not follow the laws of neighboring states; we are an example to others rather than imitators. Our constitution is a democracy, favoring the many rather than the few. Our laws secure equal justice for all in private disputes, while talent in every branch of endeavor is welcomed and honored; in such matters we pay no attention to social standing but only to merit, and this same spirit is carried over into our ordinary relations with one another. Poverty does not prevent any man from attaining office in the state if he is able to serve it. We do not watch each other jealously, nor do we resent it when others do as they please; we do not give each other black looks and angry words, nor indulge in those minor pinpricks which annoy, even if they do no actual harm. We are open and friendly in our private relations, and yet in public life we keep strictly to our laws. We pay reverence where it is due, and we are obedient to those in authority over us, paying especial attention to those laws which protect the oppressed and to the unwritten laws which we should be ashamed to break.

And yet ours is no city for work alone. Nowhere else can be found such opportunities for refreshing of the spirit. All the year round are games and sacrifices, and there is beauty in our public buildings to cheer the heart and delight the eye every day. And the city is so large and powerful that the wealth of all the world flows into it; to the Athenian the fruits of other countries are as familiar as those of his own.

Our military policy is different from that of our enemies. We fling the gates of our city open to the world. We do not deport foreigners, nor do we ever prevent them from observing what they will, even at the cost of revealing what our enemies might be able to use against us; for we do not trust so much in our material means of defense as in the spirit of our citizens. . . .

We love beauty without extravagance,

we love wisdom without being effeminate. Wealth is not for us a means of ostentation, but an opportunity for further achievements; for us poverty is not something which disgraces us to admit, though it is a real disgrace to make no effort to overcome it. Our citizens pay attention to both public and private duties. They do not become so absorbed in their private affairs that they have no time left for the city. We differ from other states in that we look upon those who take no part in public affairs as useless rather than merely quiet; we debate carefully and in person on all political matters, and then come to a decision, for we do not think that full discussion impedes a decision. On the contrary we think that without discussion our deeds are doomed to failure.

We are famous for being adventurous in action while at the same time thoughtful before action, in this respect differing from those who are only bold when they are ignorant, and lose their élan when they give themselves time to think. Surely the bravest men are those who know clearly what is before them, the glory and the danger equally, and yet do not hesitate to go forward to meet what is in store for them. In doing good, again, we differ from other people. We do not win friends by accepting favors from them, but rather by conferring them. This makes us more reliable as friends. We are creditors rather than debtors, and thus anxious to cement our friendly relations by doing kindnesses. If they do not respond with the same friendliness this can only be because they do not feel that they are giving their services spontaneously, but only because they owe it to us as a debt. Alone among mankind we benefit others not out of self-interest but because we believe firmly and fearlessly in freedom.

In short, I claim that as a city we are the school of Hellas, and that our citizens, man for man, are unequalled for their independence of spirit, versatility, and readiness to meet any emergency in complete self-reliance.

This is no idle boast. It is a fact borne out by the supremacy won for us by our customs. No other city of the present time, when tested in action, is found to be greater than her reputation; no other is so powerful that it is no shame to be defeated by her, and no indignity to be dependent upon her. The signs and evidence of her supremacy are great and visible for all to see; and posterity will be astonished, as all mankind is already today. We need no Homer or other poet to tell of our deeds and praise us; he would give a momentary pleasure only— while the truth itself is sufficient for us. Over every sea and into every land our pioneers have forced their way, and,

whether they were welcomed or resisted, they have built themselves an everlasting memorial of their settlement.

This, then, is the city for which these men, resolved not to lose her, nobly fought and died; and we who survive would naturally wish to spend ourselves in service to her. And if I have spent much time in praising her I only wished to show how great is our stake in her, far greater than for those who have no such inheritance. . . . Words cannot magnify the deeds these men have done. . . .

Thucydides, *The History of the Peloponnesian War*, II, 36–42, freely adapted from the translation by R. Crawley (New York: E. P. Dutton & Co., Inc., 1876).

(c) *Advantages of the Empire for the allies*

The Athenians in order to rebuild their city and decorate it with their artistic masterpieces drew upon the money of the League, which had been entrusted to them. Elsewhere Professor Zimmern has gone into great detail in explaining the care which Pericles took to obtain the most for this money, and implying that it was well spent for such a cause. In the following extract the same writer explains the advantages the Empire held for the "allies," even though they may have had no interest in the beautification of Athens for which they were paying.

Thus the allies had, without knowing it, slipped into financial centralization and established the first Greek imperial exchequer. Moreover, it was centralization of a peculiarly insidious kind, for the predominant partners, and especially Athens, who did most of the work and bore the chief responsibility, did not contribute a penny to the costs.

Who controlled the spending of the money? Officially, of course, the allies themselves. For this purpose they elected representatives to a parliament at Delos, which, like the Ecclesia or any other city assembly, was to discuss and decide upon matters of policy. But in practice little importance attached to its deliberations, for its executive officers, the Athenian

generals, were themselves responsible to their own sovereign people; so if the two sovereigns decided differently, a deadlock would ensure. The imperial parliament therefore could do little more than ratify, or, if it wished to be zealous, anticipate, the decisions of the Athenians. . . .

But side by side with the new military alliance, Athens set to work to establish a network of commercial treaties between herself and each individual member of the league. This she was able to do, not merely because of her newly won prestige, but because of the acknowledged excellence of the Solonian laws and institutions under which she lived. These formed a natural starting point for a process of unification; and as there were scores and hundreds of different forms of law and custom and procedure in use among her allies, such a process could not but be felt as a convenience. . . .

Let us look first at the sphere of civil jurisdiction. The motto of the alliance was Freedom. Athens was engaged, not only in clearing the seaboard of Persians, but in clearing the sea itself of pirates and evildoers. This was a duty which had devolved, from time immemorial, upon the chief seapower of the Aegean. . . . So Athens stood, not only for freedom from the barbarian, but for freedom of intercourse and freedom of trade; and it was to the interest of the allies to encourage her in promoting them. To police the Aegean with her triremes was only the first step. It was an obvious corollary to add to traders' convenience by simplifying the procedure in business disputes. Athens was able, therefore, to insert in her treaties a provision that all disputes arising out of business contracts entered into at Athens must be tried by Athenian law before Athenian judges. This was accepted as early as 466 by Chios, one of the most independent of the allies. Smaller states acquiesced in still greater encroachments on their sovereign jurisdiction; and in cases of revolt or disturbance, when opportunity arose for a clean sweep, they might wake up to discover that it had almost entirely disappeared....

In the criminal sphere the process of unification was slower, for here the sovereign tradition was more tenacious and intimate. Even the tiniest island liked to manage its own murderers. On the other hand, Athens was all the more anxious to interfere, for she needed authority to protect her own adherents and put down mutineers. We cannot trace the development in detail. It seems to have begun with interference in cases where loss of citizen rights was involved. Athens was called in, as Rome and so many ambitious suzerains have been called in since, as the champion of a minority when party strife had become acute. Thus Athens interfered at Erythrae in 455–50 to protect the "democrats" against a party favorable to Persia. She seized the opportunity to give the city a new constitution, enforced and defended by a garrison on the citadel. The new government had to swear not to repeal the sentence of banishment against "those who had fled to the Persians" without the consent, not only of the people of Erythrae, but of the Athenians.... In other words, Athens, not only by her garrison, but also by her civil jurisdiction, enforced the maintenance of the *status quo*. Her double hold is emphasized by the mention, side by side with the commandant of the garrison, of "Overseers," imperial civil servants appointed by the Home Government, but paid by the allies,

to watch and report on the state of affairs of the cities. This shows how easy it was for Athens, with her overwhelming military predominance, to steal on from position to position....

Thus Athens had gradually formed herself, whether her pupils liked it or not, to be "an education to Greece." The process was so gradual and the control so wisely exercised, that the allies could not easily put their hand on any particular cause of complaint.... The Athenian courts did their work well. The advantage of having a sensible code to deal with was too great to be despised. Moreover, surely it was worth the expense to have a fortnight in the capital and to see how the imperial money was being laid out on the Acropolis. So the lawcourts brought sightseers; the Parthenon and the great Vestibule proved the best of advertisement; and the waggoners and the lodging-house keepers found their own businesses more profitable than sitting still and listening hard for their day's pay in the courts. It is not surprising on the whole, though the fact remains to their credit, that the Athenians were able to boast, without fear of contradiction, before a hostile assembly, of the impartiality of their justice.... For Athens took her own duties, as she took everything, very seriously, and did her best, in an imperfect world, however complicated the problem, to mete out fair decisions....

Athens had thus become recognized as a model state; and Greece was in the mood to adopt or imitate her ways in small things as in great. We can see this in the rapid spread of Athenian weights and measures and the Athenian coinage, or of systems arranged so as to work in with them. Athens was standardizing Greek coinage as she was unifying Greek law. She did not, of course, compel her allies to use only Attic money, or money coined on the Attic standard. But she naturally preferred that contributions should be paid in it; and there were many indirect ways by which she could encourage it. It was only decent to pay Apollo, and later Athena, in the coinage they preferred to see.... Attic silver began to be used not only in the Confederacy, but all over Greece and among distant barbarians. . . .

Athenian influence was thus spreading, as Pericles realized, far beyond the Aegean and the confines of the Empire. Her traders were moving east and west, finding their way into every land and every sea . . . for this also was part of the imperial mission—to mix freely with all mankind and to give of their best to men and nations. Friendships were knit and alliances made with Greek, and even with barbarian powers without a thought of the Persians or the original object of the league. . . . In the course of a generation freedom had changed its meaning; and Pericles did not feel ashamed to make a convention with the national enemy [Persia], or even to receive for the league and put away in its exchequer the contributions of Carians and Lycians. Athens had now become an Empire just like

Persia or Assyria, and she did not blush to receive tribute from her inferiors. Indeed she needed it for the fulfilment of the work she had to do; and Pericles, like Darius, was determined to see that she should secure and keep it. Already in 454, when nearly the whole Athenian fleet had been destroyed in Egypt and the Aegean was for a moment exposed to pirates and Phoenicians, it was thought wiser to remove the treasury of the allies from Delos to Athens. Ostensibly this meant no more than a change of banker, Athena taking the place of Apollo. But, practically, the result was to remove it once and for all from the control of the Confederate parliament, and to make everyone see and feel, what they had known in their hearts long ago, that it was the money of Athens, with which she could do what she liked. The world is still blessing her for what she did with it.

A. Zimmern, *The Greek Commonwealth,* 5th ed. (Oxford: The Clarendon Press, 1931), pp. 188–94.

2. ATHENS AS THE EXPLOITER OF GREECE

(a) *The League as an Athenian preserve*

The remainder of the extracts in this section will put the case against the Athenians. The first is taken from Plutarch. It will be remembered that Plutarch was a moralist writing several hundred years after the events. He points out briefly the effect of the possession of Empire on the allies, by implication blaming them for their acquiescence in Athenian imperialism.

The allies of the Athenians now began to be weary of war and military service, anxious to have some repose and look after their agriculture and commerce. For they saw their enemies driven out of the country, and no longer feared new aggression from them. They continued to pay the taxes at the rate they were assessed, but

they ceased sending men and ships as they had done before. . . . Cimon . . . forced no man to go who was not willing, but he accepted money and unmanned vessels from those who wished to be excused from military service, and permitted them to yield to the temptation of staying at home and attending to their private affairs. Thus they lost their military habits, and became, through their folly and new taste for luxury, unwarlike farmers and traders; while Cimon, putting large numbers of Athenians on board his galleys, thoroughly disciplined them in his expeditions, and before long he had made them supreme over their own paymasters. The allies, whose laziness supported them while they sailed around everywhere, acquiring military and naval skills incessantly, began to fear and flatter them, finding themselves after a time no longer allies, but against their will tributaries and slaves. . . .

Plutarch, *Cimon,* II, trans. A. H. Clough, *Plutarch's Lives* (Boston: Little, Brown & Co., 1889), III, 213–14.

(b) *The League as a means of enriching Athens*

Aristotle, writing some 120 years after the founding of the Confederacy, did not hold the same view of the disinterestedness of Aristides. He seems to have regarded the whole Confederacy as deliberately planned for the enrichment of Athens at the expense of the allies.

At this time Aristides the son of Lysimachus, and Themistocles the son of Neocles were the leaders of the people. The latter had greatest renown for military skill, while the former was famous as a statesman and as the most upright man of his time. For this reason they used the one as a general, the other as a counselor. . . . It was Aristides who first assessed the contribution to be paid to the allied cities in the third year after the battle of Salamis. . . .

When the Athenian state was growing in self-confidence and in the accumulation of much wealth, he advised the Athenians to seize the leadership and to give up their residence in the countryside to come to live in the city. For they would all have their livelihood there, some by participating in military expeditions, some by doing garrison service, and in this way they would keep hold of the "leadership." They followed this advice and placed themselves in control of the empire, and from then on they got into the habit of treating their allies, with the exception of Chios, Lesbos, and Samos as if they were their masters. These three they used as guards of the Athenian empire and . . . left their constitutions untouched and allowed them to rule over whatever subjects they happened to have.

They also made it possible for the masses to live comfortably, as Aristides had proposed. For out of the income derived from the contributions made by the allies and from internal levies more than twenty thousand persons were maintained. For there were six thousand judges, sixteen hundred bowmen, twelve hundred cavalrymen, five hundred Councilmen, five hundred guards of the dockyards, plus fifty guards on the Acropolis, about seven hundred state officials at home and about seven hundred abroad. In addition when later they went to war, there were twenty-five hundred heavy armed soldiers, twenty guard ships, and other ships carrying the guardians, that is, two thousand men chosen by lot. Finally there were the Prytaneum [certain persons were honored by being entertained at public expense in the Prytaneum or City Hall, as a reward for some exceptional service to the city], the orphans, and the jail-keepers. All these persons received their livelihood from the state.

Aristotle, *Constitution of Athens*, 23–24, trans. K. von Fritz and E. Kapp (New York: Hafner Publishing Co., Inc., 1950), pp. 93–94.

(c) *Athens as exploiter of the rich for benefit of the poor*

The unknown writer of the following passage which is contemporary with the Empire itself is usually known as the Old Oligarch. It is not certain whether he was a disgruntled aristocrat (the usual view) or whether he was a sophist who composed his short treatise as an exercise in rhetoric. The burden of his complaint is that the richer classes both in Athens and in the Empire are exploited for the benefit of the poor, for whom the Empire was a valuable source of income and employment.

To speak next of the allies, when Athenian envoys go out and slander and vent their hatred on the upper classes, this is done because the ruler cannot help being hated by those whom he rules, but if wealth and respectability were to be dominant in the subject cities, the Athenians could hardly expect to hold their power for very long. So the upper classes are punished with infamy, robbed of their money, driven from their homes, and put to death, while the lower classes are given special honors. On the other hand, upper class Athenians protect, as far as they can, the upper class in the allied cities, because that is to the interest of their own class here. It may be urged that in the matter of might and power the real strength of Athens lies in the ability of the allies to contribute their quota of money; but to the democratic mind it is manifestly an even greater advantage for individual Athenians to lay their hands on the wealth of the allies, leaving them only enough to cultivate their estates and live upon them, but not powerful enough to entertain treasonable designs upon Athens.

Some people seem to think it a mistaken policy for the Athenians to make their allies come to Athens to have their lawsuits tried. But it is obvious what a number of advantages the Athenian people derive from this. The court fees pay them a regular salary throughout the year; they can look after the affairs of the allied states without stirring from home and without the expense of naval expeditions. And they can give their decisions in favor of their own democratic partisans, and thus ruin their opponents. While if these cases were tried at home, it would be the very friends of the Athenians who would be destroyed out of hatred for Athens. Moreover, the democracy gains the following advantages from hearing the cases involving the allies at Athens. There is the one per cent tax levied at the Peiraeus, the rooming house owner makes a nice profit, and so does the owner of animals and slaves to be let out on hire. Heralds and criers do better owing to the presence of the allies at Athens, and finally we should remember that if the allies did not have to come to Athens themselves for their lawsuits only such Athenians as visited them would be held in honor, dignitaries like generals, trierarchs and ambassadors; while, as it is, every single individual among the allies is compelled to flatter the people of Athens because he knows that it is not a casual group of judges who will try his case, but the sovereign people themselves, for this is the law and custom at Athens. He is made to behave like a suppliant in the courts of justice. When some juryman comes into court he has to shake his hand. So the allies find themselves more and more in the position of slaves to the Athenian democracy.

Anonymous [Pseudo-Xenophon], *The Constitution of the Athenians*, 14–18, trans. Stewart Easton.

(d) *How Athens controlled her Empire—a modern summary*

In the following extract a specialist in ancient history summarizes the case for and against the Athenians and their Empire.

The solution [of Athenian economic problems] was absolutely dependent on the tribute which came in from the now subject states; for it was that which rendered it possible to keep the great fleet in commission, and formed, too, the basis of the economic policy of Pericles when the war died away. The Athenian democrat came to regard himself as absolutely dependent on that tribute. A new theory was created to justify its use, namely, that it was paid to Athens as guarantor of the peace of the Aegean; and that if she managed to maintain that peace at an expenditure which did not absorb the tribute income, then the balance saved was her own to do with as she liked. Hence in his later years Pericles used it for the beautifying of Athens with intent to employ the unemployed, and for various other objects designed to the same end.

It must be recognized, however, that the tribute levied was not a heavy burden on the individual states; it was, in fact, a somewhat cheap price to pay for safety against Persia. But the allies did not look at it in that way, for they supposed the danger from Persia to have passed away for ever and ever, while in any case they resented the appropriation of the surplus by Athens instead of the assessment being reduced in time of peace. . . .

In many other respects the hand of Athens lay heavy on her subjects. Even the tribute was assessed by her, though there is no reason to suppose that she abused a right she had probably arrogated from the now effete council of the old league. Constitutions were dictated to various subject states—to how many is not known—a more or less necessary measure in a political world where the oligarch hated his democratic fellow-citizen far more than he did the oligarch of even a hostile state. Still, in some of the states Athens tolerated oligarchies, for, though they might be hostile to Athens both as a democracy and as a ruling power, yet the small numbers of those responsible for the government made them more easy to control in respect to Athenian interests. The fragmentary inscriptions which survive show the constitutions imposed on some of the subject states to have been democratic in form but oligarchic in character. In form they appear to be copies of the constitution of Athens itself; but in fact they are very different. The Council [*Boule*] which controlled the business brought before the Assembly of the people is in these constitutions a body with far greater powers than those of the Council at Athens, for it is put in a position to control the policy of the state. It was not freely elected, for an Athenian officer was present at the selection of nominees, and could exclude from the list anyone who was suspected of disloyalty to Athens, so that it consisted of a personnel packed in the Athenian interest. An Assembly of all the citizens of one of the subject states would almost certainly contain a large anti-Athenian majority, so unpopular was the rule of Athens. So the government, in name a democracy, was really a philo-Athenian minority banded together under the form of a democratic Council.

But Athens had to protect the philo-Athenian minorities in the subject cities in another way also. A philo-Athenian brought before the popular court of his own state on any charge could hardly escape condemnation by the anti-Athenian majority. And so Athens withdrew all cases involving the death penalty or the loss of civil rights to her own courts. To her subjects this seemed high-handed dealing; but in point of fact it made for justice. Cases involving charges of disloyalty to the empire were naturally tried at Athens. But undoubtedly one of the most unpopular features of Athenian control was the presence of Athenian officials, either overseers or commanders of garrisons, in the allied states, with what were evidently large powers of control over the local government. Athenian garrisons were not likely to be popular in the cities in which they were planted, all the more so as they were probably sent only to those of known or suspected disloyalty.

Such are the main features of the organization of the empire, an organization plainly designed to bind it hand and foot to Athenian rule.

G. B. Grundy, *A History of the Greek and Roman World* (London: Methuen & Co., Ltd., 1926), pp. 174–76.

B. The Athenian Attitude Toward the Political Freedom of Others

1. AS PRESERVERS OF GREEK LIBERTIES

In the years after the Peloponnesian War, when Athens was no longer dominant in Greece, Athenians looked back to the period of their supremacy as a kind of Golden Age, and some idealized it in order to point the contrast with their present decadence. In the *Panegyric*, Isocrates, a professional orator and speech writer, tries to persuade his readers to undertake again the leadership in Greece, this time for the purpose of getting rid of the intolerable influence of Persia in Greek affairs. In the process he praises the period of the Confederacy when Persia was kept at her proper distance. Each of the next two passages is taken from this speech.

(a) *The kindness and humanity of the Athenian Empire*

So public spirited were they that even in their party struggles they opposed one another, not to see which faction should destroy the other and rule over the remnant, but which should outstrip the other in doing something good for the state. . . . In the same spirit they governed their relations with other states. They treated the Hellenes with consideration and not with insolence, regarding it as their duty to command them in the field but not to tyrannize over them, desiring rather to be addressed as leaders than as masters, and rather to be greeted as saviors than reviled as destroyers; they won the Hellenic cities to themselves by doing kindness instead of subverting them by force, keeping their word more faithfully than men now keep their oaths, and thinking it right to abide by their covenants as by the decrees of necessity; they exulted less in the exercise of power than they gloried in living with self-control, thinking it their duty to feel toward the weaker as they expected the stronger to feel toward themselves; and while they regarded their home cities as their several places of abode, yet they considered Hellas to be their common fatherland.

Isocrates, *Panegyricus* (c. 380 B.C.), 79–81, trans. G. Norlin, Loeb Classical Library (Cambridge, Mass.: Harvard University Press, 1928), I, 167–69.

(b) *Imperial defense as a benefit for allies*

Now up to this point I am sure that all men would acknowledge that our city has been the author of the greatest number of blessings, and that she should in fairness be entitled to the hegemony. But from this point on some take us to task, urging that after we succeeded to the sovereignty of the sea we brought many evils upon the Hellenes; and, in these speeches of theirs, they cast it in our teeth that we enslaved the Melians [see 2 c below] and destroyed the people of Scione. I, however, take the view, in the first place, that it is no sign that we ruled badly if some of those who were at war with us are shown to have been severely disciplined, but that a much clearer proof that we administered the affairs of our allies wisely is seen in the fact that among the states which remained our loyal subjects not one experienced these disasters. In the second place, if other states had dealt more leniently in the same circumstances, they might reasonably censure us; but since that is not the case, and it is impossible to control so great a multitude of states without disciplining those who offend, does it not follow that we deserve praise because we acted so harshly in the fewest possible cases, and were yet able to hold our dominion for the greatest length of time?

But I believe that all men are of the opinion that those will prove the best leaders and champions of the Hellenes under whom in the past those who yielded obedience have fared the best. Well, then, it will be found that under our supremacy the private households grew most prosperous and that the commonwealths also became greatest. For we were not jealous of the growing states, nor did we engender confusion among them by setting up conflicting polities side by side, in order that faction might be arrayed against faction and both might court our favor. On the contrary, we regarded harmony among our allies as the common boon of all, and therefore we governed all the cities under the same laws, deliberating about them in the spirit of allies, not of masters; guarding the interests of the whole confederacy but leaving each member of it free to direct its own affairs; supporting the people but making war on despotic powers, considering it an outrage that the many should be subject to the few, that those who were poorer in fortune but not inferior in other respects should be banished from the offices . . ., that furthermore in a fatherland which belongs to all in common some should hold the place of master, others of aliens, and that men who are citizens by birth should be robbed by law of their share in the government.

It was because we had these objections, and others besides, to oligarchies that we established the same polity in the other states as in Athens itself—a polity which I see no need to extol at greater length, since I can tell the truth about it in a word: They continued to live under this regime for seventy years, and during this time they experienced no tyrannies, they were free from the domination of the barbarians, they were untroubled by internal factions, and they were at peace with all the world.

On account of these services it becomes all thinking men to be deeply grateful to us, much rather than to reproach us because of our system of colonization; for we sent our colonies into the depopulated states for the protection of their territories and not for our own aggrandisement. And here is proof of this: We had in proportion to the number of our citizens a very small territory, but a very great empire; we possessed twice as many ships of war as all the rest combined, and these were strong enough to engage double their number; at the very borders of Attica lay Euboea, which was not only fitted by her situation to command the sea but which also surpassed all the islands in her general resources, and Euboea lent itself more readily to our control than did our own country; besides, while we knew that both among the Hellenes and among the barbarians those are regarded most highly who have driven their neighbors from their homes and have so secured for themselves a life of affluence and ease [an allusion to the Spartans who lived from the labor of conquered Messenians], nevertheless none of these considerations tempted us to wrong the people of the islands. On the contrary, we alone of those who have obtained great power suffered ourselves to live in more straitened circumstances than those who were reproached with being our slaves. And yet, had we been disposed to seek our own advantage, we should not, I imagine, have set our hearts on the territory of Scione (which as all the world knows, we gave over to our Plataean refugees), and passed over this great territory which would have enriched us all.

Isocrates, *Panegyricus,* 100–109, trans. G. Norlin, Loeb Classical Library (Cambridge, Mass.: Harvard University Press, 1928), I, 181–89.

2. AS DESTROYERS OF GREEK LIBERTIES

(a) *Severe exactions and refusal to permit secession*

The darker side of Athenian imperialism is drawn entirely from the pages of the contemporary Thucydides who describes without comment just what it meant for the islanders to live under Athenian rule and be unable to escape it. The first extract tells what happened to the Naxians when, having decided the Persian danger was over and that they would like to discontinue their contribution, they became the first of the allies to secede.

After this Naxos left the confederacy [466 B.C.] and a war ensued, and she had to return after a siege; this was the first instance of the engagement being broken by the subjugation of an allied city, a precedent which was followed by that of the rest in the order which circumstances prescribed. Of all the causes of defection, that connected with the arrears of tribute and vessels, and with failure of service, was the chief; for the Athenians were very severe and exacting, and made themselves offensive by applying the screw of necessity to men who were not used to and indeed not disposed to any continuous labor. In some other respects the Athenians were not the old popular rulers they had been at first; and if they had more than their fair share of service, it was correspondingly easy for them to reduce any that tried to leave the confederacy. For this the allies had themselves to blame; the wish to avoid service making most of them arrange to pay their share of the expense in money instead of in ships, and so to avoid having to leave their homes. Thus while Athens was increasing her navy with the funds which they contributed, whenever the allies revolted they found themselves without resources or experience for war. . . .

Thucydides, *The History of the Peloponnesian War,* I, 99–100, adapted from the translation by R. Crawley (1876).

(b) *An ally's view of Athenian domination*

When the Peloponnesian War broke out and the Spartans invaded Attica, the island of Lesbos revolted, led by the chief city Mitylene. The Mitylenians petitioned the Spartans to take them into their alliance. Thucydides has put into the mouths of the envoys from Mitylene the growing disillusionment of the allies with Athenian imperial policy.

Justice and honesty will be the first topics of our speech, especially as we are asking for alliance, because we know that there can never be any solid friendship between individuals, or union between communities that is worth the name, unless the parties be persuaded of each other's honesty.... Between ourselves and the Athenians alliance began when you withdrew from the Median [Persian] War, and they remained to finish the business. But we did not become allies of the Athenians for the subjugation of the Hellenes, but allies of the Hellenes for their liberation from the Mede, and as long as the Athenians led us fairly we followed them loyally. But when we saw them relax their hostility to the Mede, and try to compass the subjection of the allies, then our apprehensions began. As we were, however, unable to unite and defend ourselves, on account of the number of confederates who had votes, all the allies were enslaved except ourselves and the Chians, who continued to send our contingents as independent and nominally free. However we could no longer feel confidence in Athens as a leader when we looked at the examples we have mentioned; it seemed unlikely that she would refrain from reducing us to the same condition once she had enslaved our fellow confederates, as long as she had the power to do so. Had we all remained independent we might have trusted her not to make any violent change; but since most of the allies were her subjects they would resent our independence in contrast to their own submission, and especially since they daily grew more powerful while we became poorer. Now the only safe basis for an alliance is mutual fear; a would-be aggressor is deterred by the fact that the odds are not in his favor. The only reason they left us independent was because they thought that by specious words and political manipulations they could gain empire without having to fight for it...and, in addition, the system of voting made it possible for them to lead the stronger states against the weaker first, and leave the stronger states to the last when they would have lost their natural allies and be unable to defend themselves. But if they had begun with us, while all the states were still independent and commanding their own resources, and there was still a center to rally around, they would have found the task of subjugation more difficult. Moreover our navy still gave them some apprehension; it was always possible that it might unite with you or with some other power and become dangerous to Athens. For a time the flattery which we paid to the common people and their leaders also helped us to maintain our independence. But we did not expect to be able to continue this policy once war broke out, when we considered how they had treated others.

How then could we put any trust in such friendship or freedom as this? We accepted each other against our inclination; fear made them pay court to us in war, as we paid court to them in peace. Instead of sympathy, the usual basis of confidence, we were afraid, fear keeping us to the alliance more than friendship; and it was certain that as soon as one or the other of us felt that we could break faith with impunity we should do so. You should not therefore condemn us for making the break first instead of waiting for them to strike the first blow.... If we could resist their plots and afford to wait for them, then we should be indeed their equals and under no necessity to become their subjects. But the initiative was always theirs, not ours, so we ought clearly to be able to be free to take steps in our own defense....

You should not think that this is a

case of endangering yourselves for a country which is not yours. Lesbos may appear far off, but when help is wanted she will be found near enough. It is not in Attica that the war will be decided, as some imagine, but in the countries by which Attica is supported; and the Athenian revenue is drawn from the allies and will become larger still if they reduce us; since not only will no other state revolt, but our resources will be added to theirs, and we shall be treated worse than those that were enslaved before. . . .

Thucydides, *The History of the Peloponnesian War,* III, 10–14, freely adapted from the translation by R. Crawley (1876).

(c) *Wanton aggression against a neutral*

In 416 occurred the classic case of wanton Athenian aggression against the island of Melos, populated by relatively unsophisticated Dorians who had never formed part of the Confederation. This was the case for which even Isocrates felt impelled to apologize, explaining it but unable whole-heartedly to defend it (see 1 b above).

The Athenians also made an expedition against the island of Melos, with thirty ships of their own, six Chian and two Lesbian vessels, one thousand six hundred heavy infantry, three hundred archers, and twenty mounted archers from Athens, and about one thousand five hundred heavy infantry from the allies and the islanders. The Melians are a colony of Lacedaemon that would not submit to the Athenians like the other islanders, and at first remained neutral and took no part in the struggle, but afterwards upon the Athenians using violence and plundering their territory, assumed an attitude of open hostility. Cleomedes. . .and Tisias. . .the generals, encamping in their territory with the above armament before doing any harm to their land, sent envoys to negotiate. These the Melians did not bring before the people but bade them state the object of their mission to the magistrates and the few; upon which the Athenian envoys spoke as follows:

Athenians. . . . Supposing you refrain from making any set speech, but tell us whatever you do not like, and let us settle that before proceeding further. Does this proposition suit you?

Melians. There is nothing the matter with quietly instructing each other as you propose. But your military preparations are so far advanced that we can see you are here to be judges in your own cause, and that all we can reasonably expect from this negotiation is war, if we prove to have right on our side and refuse to submit, and, in the contrary case, slavery.

Athenians. If you are merely going to talk about your forebodings for the future, and have no intention of consulting about the safety of your state on the basis of realities, then we might as well stop now; otherwise we will continue.

Melians. Surely it is natural and excusable for men in our position to consider and talk about more things than one. As you say, the question in this conference is the matter of the safety of our country. We are ready to proceed in the way you propose if it is agreeable to you.

Athenians. For ourselves we shall not trouble you with specious pretenses. We shall not explain how we have a right to Empire because we overthrew the Mede, nor shall we pretend that we are now attacking you because of any wrong you have done us. We shall not bother to make a long speech which would not convince you. And we hope that you, in return, will not try to influence us by saying that you refrained from joining the Spartans even though you are their colonists, nor by telling us you have done us no wrong. Try to be practical, keeping in mind what we both really feel. You know as well as we that there is no question of right and wrong except when power is equal. That is the way the world is—the strong do what they can, while the weak suffer what they must.

Melians. Since you won't permit us to speak about right, and we must only speak of interest, we think it *expedient* that you should not destroy what is our common protection, namely the privilege of being allowed in danger to invoke what is fair and right, and even to make use of arguments which may not be strictly valid but are current usage. You are just as much interested in this as we or anyone else; for your fall would be a signal for the heaviest vengeance, and an example for the world to meditate upon.

Athenians. We are not frightened by the possible end of our Empire if it should come about. . . . In any case it is a risk we are prepared to take. We shall now proceed to show you that we have come here in the interests of our Empire, while at the same time for the preservation of your country. We wish to exercise that Empire over you, and see you preserved for the good of us both.

Melians. How could it be as good for us to serve as for you to rule?

Athenians. Because you would have the advantage of submitting before the worst has befallen you; and we should gain by not destroying you.

Melians. So you won't consent to let us be neutral, friends and not enemies, but allies of neither side?

Athenians. No, for our allies would think our friendship for you to be a sign of our weakness, while if you are our enemies, this is a sign of our power.

Melians. Do your subjects think it just to put those who have nothing to do with you in the same category as people who are mostly your own colonists, or conquered rebels?

Athenians. As far as right goes, they think one has as much of it as the other. But they think that if anyone maintains his independence it is only because he is strong, and we only refrain from molesting them because we are afraid. So, if we reduce you to subjection our own security is increased. You are islanders, and weak, so it is more important than ever that you should not be able to baffle the masters of the sea.

Melians. Since we are debarred from talking about justice, and you have invited us to consider your interest, wouldn't our suggested policy give you a greater security? How can you avoid making enemies of all neutrals who will see what you are doing to us and conclude that some day or another you will attack them? So you make more enemies than you have already, and force others to become so who would otherwise never have thought of it. . . . If you risk so much to keep your Empire, and your subjects risk so much to get rid of your yoke, wouldn't it be cowardly and shameful for us to submit before we have tried anything?

Athenians. Not if you are well advised. The contest is unequal. The reward of honor and the penalty of shame are beside the point. It is a simple matter of preservation, and not resisting those who are far stronger than you.

Melians. But we know that it is not always numbers which decide the fortune of war. To submit is to yield to despair, while action at least gives us some chance to stand erect.

Athenians. Those who have abundant resources can afford to indulge in hope; at least they may be spared utter ruin. But hope is naturally extravagant, and people don't see it for what it is until they have staked everything upon it and been ruined. It prevents them from taking the proper precautions. Don't you be so hopeful, but remember you are weak and your whole existence depends upon a single chance. And please don't be like those crude people who abandon such security as human men can still give them, who, when visible hopes fail them, turn to the invisible, to prophecies and oracles, and other such inventions that delude men with hopes to their destruction.

Melians. You may be sure that we have no illusions about the difficulty of defending ourselves against your power and fortune, unless the terms be equal. But we trust that the gods may grant us fortune as good as yours, since we are just men fighting against unjust, and that what we lack in power will be made up by our alliance with the Spartans, who are bound, if only for very shame, to come to the aid of their kinsmen. So our confidence is not altogether irrational.

Athenians. When you speak of the favor of the gods, we may as fairly hope for that as you; neither our pretensions nor our conduct is in any way contrary to what men believe of the gods or practise among themselves. Of the gods we believe and of men we know, that by a necessary law of their nature they rule wherever they can. We were not the first to make this law or to act upon it; we found it existing before us, and it will continue to exist after us. All we do is make use of it, well aware that you would do the same if you had the power. So as far as the gods are concerned we are not afraid, nor do we fear that we shall be at a disadvantage. But when we come to your notion about the Spartans, and your belief that they will for very shame come to help you, we bless your simplicity but do not envy you your folly. When their own interests or their country's laws are at stake they are the worthiest men alive. We could say much about their conduct towards others; but if we may put it in a nutshell, no people are more apt to consider what is agreeable to be also honorable, and what is expedient to be just. This kind of thinking does not augur well for your safety which you are counting on so unreasonably.... Only with numerous allies do they venture to attack a neighbor. Is it likely that they will cross the sea to protect an island while we are masters of the sea?

Melians. But they would have others to send.... The Cretan sea is a wide one, and it is not always so easy for the masters of the sea to intercept others.... And even if the Spartans miscarried in this, they would fall upon your land and upon your allies.... And instead of fighting for places which don't belong to you, you will have to fight for your own confederacy and your own country.

Athenians. Some day they might make such a diversion, but they will learn, as others before them, that the Athenians

never once have withdrawn from a siege from fear of anyone.... But we are struck by the fact that...in all this discussion your strongest arguments depend upon hope and the future, and your actual resources are too scanty, as compared with those arrayed against you, for you to come out victorious.... Surely you will not let yourself be fooled by the idea of being disgraced, a fatal delusion in the face of unmistakable danger. From fear of that seductive word, too many men are enslaved by the phrase in such a way as to fall wilfully into hopeless disaster. Such error is more disgraceful than any disgrace that comes by misfortune. If you are well advised you will avoid this error, and not think it dishonorable to submit to the greatest city in Hellas, when it makes you the modest offer of becoming its tributary ally, without ceasing to enjoy the country that belongs to you; nor when you have a choice between war and security, will you be so blinded as to choose the worse.... Think over the matter then once again, and remember that it is for your country that you are consulting, and that you have only one. Upon this one deliberation depends its prosperity or ruin.

The Athenians now withdrew from the conference; and the Melians, left to themselves, came to the decision corresponding to the stand they had maintained during the conference, and answered, "Our resolution, Athenians, is the same as it was at first. We will not in a moment deprive of freedom a city that has been inhabited these seven hundred years; but we put our trust in the fortune by which the gods have preserved it till now, and in the help of men, that is, of the Spartans; and so we will try to save ourselves. Meanwhile we invite you to allow us to be friends to you, and foes to neither party...."

The Athenian envoys now returned to the army; and the Melians showing no signs of yielding, the generals at once began hostilities...and besieged the place....

The next winter the Spartans intended to invade the Argive territory, but arriving at the frontier found the sacrifices for crossing unfavorable and went back again.... About the same time the Melians again took another part of the Athenian lines which were but feebly garrisoned. Reinforcements afterwards arriving from Athens in consequence,... the siege was now pressed vigorously; and some treachery taking place inside, the Melians surrendered at discretion to the Athenians, who put to death all the grown men whom they took, and sold the women and children for slaves, and subsequently sent out five hundred colonists and inhabited the place themselves....

Thucydides, *The History of the Peloponnesian War*, VI, 86–116, freely adapted from the translation by R. Crawley (1876).

C. Limitations on Athenian Democracy

(a) *Women and slaves*

After the panegyrics on Athenian democracy recorded above, it is well also to be reminded that such democracy as there was did not benefit everyone in Athens. As the following extract from another economic historian suggests, the Athenian democrats were only an "exceptionally large diversified ruling class," and it was by no means a government by and for the whole people.

Fifth-century Athens thus provides the first adequately documented example of a thorough-going popular government. Its popular character must not be exaggerated. In the first place women had no place in public life. The wives of citizens were almost as completely secluded as women in Mohammedan countries today, and at law were in a worse position than their Assyrian and Babylonian sisters. Secondly, citizenship was now a hereditary privilege from which resident aliens were rigidly excluded. Yet on Gomme's estimate these included a tenth of the total population and comprised most of the craftsmen and manufacturers. Finally industry was based on slavery; even the small farmer generally owned a slave or two, and the majority of the employees in mines and factories and even the policemen were slaves. Though citizens did work on their farms, ply crafts, take on small contracts for public works, work as wage laborers for fellow citizens and even in mines, they secured leisure for politics and culture largely at the expense of their wives, of aliens who had no share in the government and of slaves who had no rights whatever.

Moreover the revenues of Athens which paid magistrates, jurors and assemblymen were swollen by two exceptional sources. The richest silver mines in the Aegean lay in Attica at Laurion; exploited mainly by slaves under local contractors, they yielded a rich harvest of royalties to the state. Secondly, Athens was an imperial city, nourished by the tribute of subjects. It is true that the Athenian Empire began as a league of free cities against Persia. The tribute was a substitute for the ships that the allies had originally equipped and manned for the common defense. But after 450 B.C. the allies felt themselves subjects and tried to rebel; the imperial people were diverting some of their contributions to the adornment of Athens and their own support.

Thus the Athenian "people" was in a sense only an exceptionally large diversified ruling class. The appearance of economic democracy had been achieved not so much by an even distribution of the wealth it produced as by using the proceeds of exploitation to relieve the poverty of its poorer sections. When external supplies were cut off by the loss of the empire, the conflict of poor and rich broke out again in violence. In the sequel Athens lost her full autonomy and returned to a moderate oligarchy with foreign support in the late fourth century.

V. G. Childe, *What Happened in History* (London: Penguin Books, Ltd., 1942), pp. 207–208.

(b) *Erosion of civil liberties under impact of war*

By the year 406 B.C. the Athenians were close to final defeat in the Peloponnesian War. The expedition to Sicily had failed and the Spartan fleet, aided by Persian money, was pressing them hard. Conon, the chief Athenian admiral, hemmed in by the Spartan fleet, was able to get news to Athens of his plight, whereupon the Athenians impressed every able-bodied person, slave or freeman, into service and fitted out a relief expedition, which won a brilliant and unexpected victory, but at the cost of more than twenty ships (the battle of Arginusae). The Athenian admirals, hoping to complete the rout of the enemy, pursued them, leaving two captains of triremes to pick up the dead and wounded. Prevented from fulfilling this task by a sudden storm, they tried to protect themselves from the charge of having failed in their duty by accusing the admirals. Amid scenes of emotion in the Assembly the admirals who had returned to Athens were put to death, without having been given any serious opportunity to defend themselves individually. Tried as a group, they were executed as a group, in spite of the protests of a few courageous men, including Socrates, who insisted that the procedure was illegal. There follows an extract from the account of the trial by Xenophon. It should be noted that under the Athenian constitution if anyone arose in the Assembly who declared that any proposed action was illegal or unconstitutional, the proposer had to submit to a trial before a jury, and no action could be taken until he had been acquitted. The extract reveals the manner in which mob fury was able to overcome procedural safeguards.

Then came the festival of the Apaturia, with its family gatherings of fathers and kinsfolk. Accordingly the party of Theramenes [one of the captains deputed to pick up the wounded] procured numbers of people clad in black apparel and close-shaven, who were to go in and present themselves before the public assembly in the middle of the festival, as relatives, presumably, of the men who had perished; and they persuaded Callixenus to accuse the generals in the senate [the *Boule*,

where legislation was prepared for submission to the Assembly or Ecclesia, made up of all the citizens]. The next step was to convoke the assembly, when the senate laid before it the proposal just passed by their body at the instance of Callixenus, which ran as follows: "Seeing that both the parties to this case, the prosecutors of the generals on the one hand, and the accused themselves in their defense on the other, have been heard in the late meeting of the assembly; we propose that the people of Athens now record their votes one and all, by their tribes; ... and the public crier in the hearing of each tribe proclaim the mode of voting as follows: "Let everyone who finds the generals guilty of not rescuing the heroes of the late sea fight deposit his vote in urn No. 1. Let him who is of the contrary opinion deposit his vote in urn No. 2. Further, in the event of the aforesaid generals being found guilty, let death be the penalty. ..."

Now there came forward in the assembly a man, who said that he had escaped drowning by clinging to a meal tub. The poor fellows perishing around him had commissioned him, if he succeeded in saving himself, to tell the people of Athens how bravely they had fought for their fatherland, and how the generals had left them there to drown.

Presently Euryptolemus, the son of Peisianax, and others served notice of indictment on Callixenus, insisting that his proposal was unconstitutional, and this view of the case was applauded by some members of the assembly. But the majority kept crying out that it was monstrous if the people were to be hindered by any stray individual from doing what seemed to them right. And then Lyciscus, embodying the spirit of those cries, formally proposed that if these persons would not abandon their actions, they should be tried by the same votes along with the generals: a proposition to which the mob gave vociferous assent; and so these were compelled to abandon their summonses. Again, when some of the Prytanes [committees chosen by lot to manage the council and assembly affairs for a tenth of the year each] objected to putting a resolution to the vote which was in itself unconstitutional, Callixenus again got up and accused them in the same terms, and the shouting began again. "Yes, summon all who refuse," until the Prytanes, in alarm, all agreed with one exception to permit the voting. This obstinate dissentient was Socrates, the son of Sophroniscus, who insisted that he would do nothing except in accordance with the law. After this Euryptolemus rose and spoke on behalf of the generals. . . .

[After arguing that all the generals could not be equally guilty and that there were already suitable laws on the statute book under which they could be tried, he demanded:]

"Do you imagine that you may be robbed of the power of life and death over whom you please, should you condescend to a legal trial? But that you are safe if you take shelter behind an illegality, like the illegality of Callixenus, when he worked upon the senate to propose to this assembly to deal with the accused by a single vote? But consider, you may actually put to death an innocent man, and then repentance will one day visit you too late. Bethink you how painful and unavailing remorse will then be, and more particularly if your error has cost a fellow-creature his life. What a travesty of justice it would be if in the case of a man like Aristarchus, who first tried to destroy the democracy and then betrayed Oenoe to our enemy the Thebans, you granted him a day for his defense, consulting his wishes and conceded to him all the other benefits of the law; whereas you are now proposing to deprive of these same privileges your own generals, who in every way conformed to your views and defeated your enemies. Do not you, of all men, I implore you, men of Athens, act thus. Why, these laws are your own, to them beyond all else you owe your greatness. Guard them jealously;

in nothing, I implore you, act without their sanction."

[After explaining the circumstances of the case, and that one of the generals on trial was in fact a man who was himself rescued from a sinking ship, he ends his speech with an appeal:]

"Once more I beg you, men of Athens, to accept your victory and your good fortune, instead of behaving like the desperate victims of misfortune and defeat. Recognize the finger of divine necessity; do not incur the reproach of stony-heartedness by discovering treason where there was only powerlessness, and condemning as guilty those who were prevented by the storm from carrying out their instructions. Nay! You will better satisfy the demands of justice by crowning these conquerors with wreaths of victory than by punishing them with death at the instigation of wicked men."

At the conclusion of his speech Euryptolemus proposed as an amendment that the prisoners should...be tried each separately, as against the proposal of the senate to try them all by a single vote.

At the show of hands the tellers gave the majority in favor of the amendment of Euryptolemus; but upon the application of Menecles, who took formal exception to this decision, the show of hands was gone through again, and now the verdict was in favor of the resolution of the senate. At a later date the balloting was made, and by the votes recorded the eight generals were condemned, and the six who were in Athens were put to death.

Not long after, repentance seized the Athenians, and they passed a decree authorizing the public prosecution of those who had deceived the people.... Callixenus was one of these committed for trial...but all subsequently effected their escape before the trial...Callixenus eventually came back at the time of the amnesty..., only to die of hunger, an object of universal detestation.

Xenophon, *Hellenica*, I, 7, trans. H. G. Dakyns (New York: The Macmillan Company, 1890).

II. Rome: The Early Principate—An Effort to Preserve The Republic, or a Disguised Tyranny?

Rome had been a self-governing republic for many centuries before Julius Caesar became permanent dictator in 46 B.C. Two years later Caesar was murdered by embittered republicans. Personal grievances may have predominated in the minds of the conspirators; but at least Brutus, and probably several of the others, were genuinely convinced that he intended to destroy the Republic and replace it by one-man rule.

Nearly forty years earlier Sulla had held a position of similarly unquestioned supremacy, but he had resigned his dictatorship after handing over the leadership in the state to a reformed Senate; the Senate, however, had long before ceased to be competent to run the empire which had been won by Roman arms, and now had lost confidence in itself. One-man rule was probably inevitable in the situation of the time, and to hindsight no possible alternative appears. But the die-hard republicans, and perhaps a majority of Roman citizens, had by no means yet accepted the inevitable. The title of king was detested by Romans who remembered their ancient domination by the Etruscans, and no better title had yet been devised. Though some Romans may have been prepared to accept the position, few indeed could have been happy about the name. So Caesar was murdered, and the murderers proclaimed the restoration of the Republic and of liberty.

Yet there was no true restoration of the Republic. After the conspirators had been defeated, there was an uneasy alliance between Caesar's chief general, Mark Antony, and his designated heir, Octavian Caesar. When the issue of supremacy was ultimately decided by civil war and Octavian emerged the master of the Roman world, the problem was in no way solved. Probably more Romans had grown accustomed to the idea that the Republic had gone forever, but the institutions suitable for the new Roman one-man government had not yet been devised.

Octavian, who now accepted the title of Augustus, a title which conferred increased dignity but no power, and had for the most part previously been used of gods, was the true founder of the new imperial Roman state which has been called the Roman Empire—a misleading title for modern students, since the great bulk of the Roman possessions had been acquired under the Republic. Concerned with the problem of how to make his government legitimate and at the same time effective, he conceived the idea of assuming a few important republican powers for life. These gave him the real control of the state, though he called himself only a *princeps,* or chief citizen. He took the *proconsulare imperium* and the *tribunicia potestas*—the imperium, or military power, of a proconsul, and the civil power of a tribune, which included the right to introduce and veto legislation. Later he assumed the power of a censor, which entitled him to draw up the census of citizens and purge the ranks of the Senate, and the title of *pontifex maximus,* or chief priest, which permitted him to reform the religion. With these powers his rule was unchallenged, and he bequeathed his position intact to Tiberius, his chosen successor, by having the Senate bestow the two principal powers upon Tiberius before his own death.

There have always been varying opinions on the nature of the rule of Augustus. Was it a barely disguised tyranny, or was it, as he claimed himself, an honest attempt to restore such of the dead Republic as was possible, and give back power to the Senate and people? Was he a hypocrite, giving away the forms and shadow of power, while he retained the substance in his own hands, intentionally bamboozling the people, though concealing the fact by consummate craft? Or was he at least a genuine republican who tried to steer a middle path between the dictatorship of Julius Caesar and the anarchy of the last days of the Republic, a man who did not care for power, tried to use it as little as possible, but was forced to reform the Republic for its own good, even though the ultimate result was its abolition?

If Augustus himself was not a tyrant, and did not abuse his power, was then Tiberius the ruler who transformed the disguised monarchy into an undisguised tyranny? Many of the ancient Romans thought so; and yet even his bitterest enemies and critics admit that he was an admirer of the old Republic, and he had in earlier years at least maintained the old republican virtues of simplicity, frugality and honesty, permitted criticism of himself and his policies, and wished to avoid the task that fell to him as the successor of the divine Augustus.

The two problems that follow are closely connected. The first concerns the nature of the character and rule of Augustus, and the second asks similar questions about Tiberius. The two problems may suggest to the reader certain reflections on the nature of power, and the difficulties involved in trying to exercise it indirectly, and the inevitable pressures that beset its holders. Since none of the writers, ancient or modern, is able to adopt a totally impartial attitude, the selections may help the reader to realize the fallibility and transience of moral judgments upon public characters. John Buchan, twentieth-century imperial administrator, and Edward Gibbon, professional liberal after the manner of the eighteenth-century Enlightenment, are neither more nor less subjective in their judgments than the ancients who lived and suffered under the immediate successors of the founders of their Empire, and who were vitally interested in how they had fallen away from the old ideals of republican liberty.

A. The Achievement of Augustus

1. PUBLIC STATEMENT OF AUGUSTUS HIMSELF A YEAR BEFORE HIS DEATH

In A.D. 13 Augustus prepared a bare statement of his achievements since becoming *princeps*, and had it engraved on bronze tablets which were to be set up in front of his mausoleum. Though these tablets have disappeared, many copies were made, the most perfect of which is the *Monumentum Ancyranum*, an inscription chiseled on the walls of a temple at Ancyra (Ankara) in modern Turkey. The account contains, of course, exactly what Augustus wished to be believed about himself by posterity, and is therefore of first-rate historical interest, whatever may be the opinion held about the nature of his achievements: each word is carefully chosen, and none is wasted.

In my sixth and seventh consulships, when I had extinguished the flames of civil war, after receiving by universal consent the absolute control of affairs, I transferred the republic from my own control to the will of the senate and the Roman people. For this service on my part I was given the title of Augustus by decree of the senate, and the doorposts of my house were covered with laurels by public act, and a civic crown was fixed above my door, and a golden shield was placed in the Curia Julia whose inscription testified that the senate and the Roman people gave me this in recognition of my valor, my clemency, my justice, and my piety. After that time I took precedence of all in rank, but of power I possessed no more than those who were my colleagues in any magistracy.

Res gestae divi Augusti, 34, trans. F. W. Shipley, Loeb Classical Library (Cambridge, Mass.: Harvard University Press, 1924), pp. 399–401.

2. TACITUS REPORTS OPPOSING VIEWS IN HIS TIME (ABOUT A.D. 120)

Tacitus, considered by many to be by far the greatest of Rome's historians, had been forced to endure the outright tyranny of a later Emperor, Domitian, an account of which he gives movingly in his *Agricola.* A sentimental republican, he was yet enough of a realist to recognize that the Empire in his own time had become established, and that it was now too late to restore the republican regime. But the recognition of this fact did not prevent him from yearning after the lost days of freedom, and devoting considerable attention especially to the tyrannies of Tiberius, whom he seems to have regarded as the real destroyer of Roman liberties, as will be seen from later extracts. In this first extract from Tacitus, the historian merely records the two views held in his time about Augustus, without stating his personal preference. This is a common procedure in his work, for he was evidently trained as an orator, and had a natural or acquired interest in human psychology. Frequently his pictures are unfair, but they are always vivid and thoughtful.

When, after the destruction of Brutus and Cassius, there was no longer any army of the Commonwealth, when...even the Julian faction had only Caesar left to lead it, then, dropping the title of triumvir, and giving out that he was a Consul, and was satisfied with a tribune's authority for the protection of the people, Augustus won over the soldiers with gifts, the populace with cheap corn, and all men with the sweets of repose, and so grew greater by degrees, while he concentrated in himself the functions of the Senate, the magistrates, and the laws. He was wholly unopposed, for the boldest spirits had fallen in battle or in the proscription, while the remaining nobles, the readier they were to become slaves, were raised the higher by wealth and promotion, so that, aggrandized by revolution, they preferred the safety of the present to the dangerous past. Nor did the provinces dislike that condition of affairs, for they distrusted the government of the Senate and the people, because of the rivalries between the leading men and the rapacity of the officials, while the protection of the laws was unavailing, as they were continually deranged by violence, intrigue, and finally by corruption.... At home all was tranquil, and there were magistrates with the same titles; there was a younger generation, sprung up since the victory of Actium, and even many of the older men had been born during the civil wars. How few were left who had seen the republic!

Thus the State had been revolutionized, and there was not a vestige left of the old sound morality. Stripped of equality, all looked up to the commands of a sovereign without the least apprehension for the present....

On the day of the funeral...sensible men spoke variously of his life with praise and censure. Some said "that dutiful feeling towards a father, and the necessities of the State in which laws then had no place, drove him into civil war, which can neither be planned nor conducted on any right principles.... The only remedy for his distracted country was the rule of a single man. Yet the State had been organized under the name neither of a kingdom nor a dictatorship, but under that of a prince. The ocean and remote rivers were the boundaries of the empire; the legions, provinces, fleets, all things were linked together; there was law for the citizens;

there was respect shown to the allies. The capital had been embellished on a grand scale; only in a few instances had he resorted to force, simply to secure general tranquillity."

It was said, on the other hand, "that filial duty and State necessity were merely assumed as a mask. It was really from a lust for sovereignty that he had excited the veterans by bribery...and turned against the State the arms with which he had been entrusted against Antonius. Citizens were proscribed, lands divided, without so much as the approval of those who executed these deeds....No doubt there was peace after all this, but it was a peace stained with blood; there were the disasters of Lollius and Varus, the murders at Rome of the Varros, Egnatii, and Julii....No honor was left for the gods when Augustus chose to be himself worshipped with temples and statues, like those of the deities, and with flamens and priests. He had not even adopted Tiberius as his successor out of affection or any regard for the State, but, having thoroughly seen his arrogant and savage temper, he had sought glory for himself by a contrast of extreme wickedness...."

Tacitus, *Annals,* trans. A. J. Church and W. J. Brodribb, I, 2–4, 8–10 (New York: Modern Library, Inc., 1942), pp. 3–5, 9–11.

3. OPINION OF THE ANCIENT WORLD

(a) *View of a faithful imperial officer*

Velleius Paterculus was an officer in the imperial army under both Augustus and Tiberius. He has no nostalgia for the lost republic, and seems to have had no doubts about the excellence of the new regime which put an end to the anarchy of the last days of the republic. He wrote a brief history of Rome which became fuller as he reached his own times. There is thus a fairly extensive account of Augustus, and the work closes with a eulogy of Tiberius in his earlier years as *princeps,* an extract from which will appear in the next section. The history is not apparently written to order, to please an imperial patron, but out of a genuine enthusiasm. Its value, therefore, is considerable in that it describes Augustus and Tiberius from the point of view of a loyal, if perhaps too uncritical, supporter of their rule.

There is nothing that man can desire from the gods, nothing that the gods can grant to a man, nothing that wish can conceive or good fortune bring to pass, which Augustus on his return to the city did not bestow upon the republic, the Roman people, and the world. The civil wars were ended after twenty years, foreign wars suppressed, peace restored, the frenzy of arms everywhere lulled to rest; validity was restored to the laws, authority to the courts, and dignity to the senate. The power of the magistrates was reduced to its former limits, with the sole exception that two were added to the existing eight praetors. The old traditional form of the republic was restored. Agriculture returned to the fields, respect to religion, to mankind freedom from anxiety, and to each citizen his property rights were now assured. Old laws were usefully amended, and new laws passed for the general good; the revision of the senate, while not too drastic, was not lacking in severity. The chief men of the state who had won triumphs and held high office were at the invitation of Augustus induced to adorn the city. In the case of the consulship only, Caesar was not able to have his way, but was obliged to hold that office consecutively until the eleventh time in spite of his frequent efforts to prevent it; but the dictatorship which the people persistently offered him, he as stubbornly refused.

Velleius Paterculus, *History of Rome,* II, 89, trans. F. W. Shipley, Loeb Classical Library (Cambridge, Mass.: Harvard University Press, 1924), pp. 237–39.

(b) *View of an early third-century historian*

Dion Cassius was a Roman administrator and historian who wrote in the first quarter of the third century A.D. He was able to use for his history contemporary sources which are now lost to us, and, although of course he had no first-hand knowledge of the period, he makes some attempt to criticize his sources and to come to his own opinion. The following extract is taken from the eulogy of Tiberius on his predecessor as reported by Dion, together with Dion's own comments on the reign of Augustus.

After these achievements and when by kindness he had allayed all that remained of factional discord and by generosity had moderated the victorious soldiery, he might on the strength of this record and of the weapons and the money at his command have been indisputably the sole lord of all, as indeed he had become by the very course of events. Nevertheless he refused; and like a good physician who takes in hand a disease-ridden body and heals it, he first restored to health and then gave back to you the whole body politic. . . . He possessed all your armies, whose numbers you know; he was master of all your funds, so vast in amount; he had no one to fear or suspect, but might have ruled alone with the approval of all; yet he saw fit not to do this, but laid the army, the provinces, and the money at your feet.

You [i.e., the Roman people], on your part, acted well and prudently, when you withheld your assent and did not permit him to retire to private life; for you know well that a democracy could never accommodate itself to interests so vast, but that the leadership of one man would be the most likely to conserve them, and so refused to return to what was nominally independence but really factional discord; and making choice of him whom you had tested by his actual deeds and approved, you constrained him for a time at least to be your leader. And when you had thus proved him far better than before, you

compelled him for a second, third, fourth and fifth time to continue in the management of affairs. And this was but fitting, for who would not choose to be safe without trouble, to be prosperous without danger, to enjoy without stint the blessings of government while escaping the life of constant anxiety for its maintenance?. . . .

As regards the members of the senate, he did not take away from them the right to cast lots for the governorship of provinces, but even offered them additional prizes as a reward for excellence, nor in connection with the senate's decrees did he do away with their privilege of voting, but even added safeguards for their freedom of speech. From the people he transferred matters difficult of decision to the strict jurisdiction of the courts, but preserved to them the dignity of the elections; and at these elections he inculcated in the citizens the love of honor rather than the love of party strife, and eliminating the element of greed from their office-seeking, he put in its place the regard for reputation. . . .

[After reporting the remainder of the eulogy along the same lines, Dion Cassius then comments:]

Real grief was not in the hearts of many at the time, but later was felt by all. For Augustus had been accessible to all allies, and was accustomed to aid many persons in the matter of money. He showed great honor to his friends, and delighted exceedingly when they frankly spoke their opinions. . . . Not only for these reasons did the Romans greatly miss him, but also because by combining monarchy with democracy he preserved their freedom for them, and at the same time he established order and security, so that they were free alike from the license of a democracy and from the insolence of a tyranny, living at once in a liberty of moderation and in a monarchy without terrors; they were subjects of royalty yet not slaves, and citizens of a democracy yet without discord. If any of them remembered his former deeds in the course of the civil wars, they attributed them to the pressure of cares, and they thought it fair to seek his real disposition in what he did after he was in undisputed possession of the supreme power; for this, in truth, afforded a mighty contrast. Anybody who examines his acts in detail can establish this fact; but summing them all up briefly I may state that he put an end to all the factional discord, transformed the government in a way to give it the greatest power, and vastly strengthened it. ... Though the people understood all this during his lifetime, they nevertheless realized it more fully after he was gone. For when they found his successor Tiberius a different sort of man, they yearned for him who was gone. ...

Dion Cassius, *Roman History,* LVI, 39–41, 43–45, trans. E. Cary, Loeb Classical Library (Cambridge, Mass.: Harvard University Press, 1942), VII, 87–91, 99–103.

(c) *The biographer of the Caesars*

Suetonius, who wrote the *Lives of the Twelve Caesars,* is an unsatisfactory biographer for want of a critical faculty and for want of insight into the character of his subjects. Yet he has his uses as a historian since he had access to a considerable wealth of source material, especially some of the imperial archives; and his flat recitation of facts gives far less of an impression of bias than the interpretative records of Tacitus. Suetonius lacks sympathy for his subjects, but he also seems to lack equally any antipathy. Where his sources repeat gossip he faithfully does the same. Thus to him Tiberius was a tyrant, with a few redeeming features, while Augustus was the model of an enlightened monarch. These were no doubt the stereotypes prevalent in his own day (the middle of the second century A.D.). He considers the constitutional problem not at all, and he shows no interest in the question of whether human freedom had met its greatest check or had been restored. He catalogues the achievements of Augustus, without troubling to distinguish between the important and the trivial, and he attempts no summary. His value therefore for us lies in the revealing anecdotes which we can interpret for ourselves. A brief selection of these follows, the choice having been made for the light they throw upon the methods of Augustus in either preserving freedom or disguising tyranny.

He twice thought of restoring the republic; first immediately after the overthrow of Antony, remembering that his rival had often made the charge that it was his fault that it was not restored; and again in the weariness of a lingering illness, when he went so far as to summon the magistrates and the Senate to his house, and submit an account of the general condition of the empire. Reflecting, however, that as he himself would not be free from danger if he should retire, so too it would be hazardous to trust the State to the control of the populace, he continued to keep it in his hands; and it is not easy to say whether his intentions or their results were the better. His good intentions he not only expressed from time to time, but put them on record as well in an edict in the following words: "May it be my privilege to establish the State in a firm and secure position, and enjoy therefrom the rewards of which I am ambitious, that of being called the author of the best possible government, and of carrying with me when I die the hope that the foundations which I have laid for the State will remain unshaken." And he realized his hope by making every effort to prevent any dissatisfaction with the new regime. ...

When the people did their best to force the Dictatorship upon him he knelt down, threw off his toga from his shoulders, and with bare breast begged them not to insist. He always shrank from the title of Lord [*Dominus*—the title used by a slave for the master] as reproachful and insulting. When the words "O just and gracious Lord!" were uttered in a farce at which he was a spectator and all the people sprang to their feet and applauded as if they were said of him, he at once checked their unseemly flattery by look and gesture, and on the following day sharply reproved them in an edict. After that he would not suffer himself to be addressed by that term even by his children or his grandchildren either in jest or earnest, and he forbade them to use such flattering terms even amongst themselves. He did not if he could help it leave or enter any city or town except in the evening or at night, to avoid disturbing anyone by the obligations of ceremony. In his consulship he commonly went through the streets on foot, and when he was not Consul, generally in a closed litter. His morning receptions were open to all, including even the Commons, and he met the requests of those who approached him with great affability.... He exchanged social calls with many, and did not cease to attend all their anniversaries until he was well on in years....

As he was delivering a speech in the Senate someone said to him, "I did not understand," and another, "I would contradict you if I had an opportunity." Several times when he was rushing from the House in anger at the excessive bickerings of the disputants, some shouted after him, "Senators ought to have the right of speaking their mind on public affairs.".... Yet for all that no one suffered for his freedom of speech or insolence. Even when some infamous libels against him were scattered in the Senate house he was neither disturbed nor gave himself great trouble to refute them. Without trying to discover the authors, he merely proposed that those who henceforth under a false name published notes or verses defamatory of anyone should be called to account....

Whenever he took part in the election of magistrates, he went the round of the tribes with his candidates and appealed for them in the traditional manner. He also cast his own vote in his tribe, as one of the people. When he gave testimony in court, he was most patient in submitting to questions and even to contradiction.... He never recommended his sons for office without adding, "If they be worthy of it.".... He wished his friends to be prominent and influential in the State, but to be bound by the same laws as the rest and equally liable to prosecution.... He secured the acquittal of no more than one man, and then by entreaty, making a successful appeal to the accuser in the presence of the jurors....

How much he was beloved for his admirable conduct in all these respects it is easy to imagine. I say nothing of decrees of the Senate, which might seem to have been dictated by necessity or by awe.... The whole body of citizens with a sudden unanimous impulse proffered him the title of Father of the Country; first the commons, by a deputation sent to Antium, and then, because he declined it, again at Rome as he entered the theatre;... the Senate afterwards in the House, not by a decree or by acclamation, but through Valerius Messala. He speaking for the whole body said: "Good fortune and divine favor attend thee and thy house, Caesar Augustus; for thus we feel that we are praying for lasting prosperity for our country and happiness for our city. The Senate in accord with the people of Rome hails thee Father of thy Country." Then Augustus, with tears in his eyes, replied as follows (and I have given his exact words, as I did those of Messala): "Having attained my highest hopes, Fathers of the Senate, what more have I to ask of the immortal gods than that I may retain this same unanimous approval of yours to the very end of my life?"

Suetonius, *The Lives of the Caesars*, II, 28, 52–58, trans. J. C. Rolfe, Loeb Classical Library (Cambridge, Mass.: Harvard University Press, 1913), I, 165, 207–15.

4. VARYING OPINION OF POSTERITY

The modern world has by no means been as unanimous on the virtues of the rule of Augustus as were the ancients. Much appears to have depended upon the circumstances of the time of writing. In days when peace seems a rare blessing, the achievements of Augustus rank high in the opinion of mankind; in days when war seems remote, as in the days of Gibbon, the historian can permit himself the luxury of deploring the loss of freedom: in days when we are threatened by dictators any man who in the past had any share in the establishment of one-man rule is suspect and his motives impugned. On the other hand, modern imperial administrators have always admired the deftness of his touch and his sure political sense as well as his administrative abilities. Historians with a liking for the dramatic and an admiration for the strong man of action have tended to depreciate Augustus by comparison with the great Julius Caesar. So we have to make allowance for personal prejudice even though Augustus died nearly two thousand years ago, and his empire collapsed a few hundred years later. No history, it seems, is ever quite dead, and there is still room for difference of opinion.

(a) *The eighteenth-century rationalist*

Edward Gibbon, eighteenth-century English historian, posed as a disillusioned skeptic. He greatly admired the Roman Empire especially in the second century of its existence. It was his considered view that the bulk of mankind had never been so happy as under the Good Emperors (A. D. 96–180). Yet even he was not greatly impressed by Augustus, the Empire's founder.

The tender respect of Augustus for a free constitution which he had destroyed, can only be explained by an attentive consideration of the character of that subtle tyrant. A cool head, an unfeeling heart, and a cowardly disposition prompted him, at the age of nineteen, to assume the mask of hypocrisy, which he never afterwards laid aside. . . . His virtues, and even his vices, were artificial; and according to the various dictates of his interest, he was at first the enemy, and at last the father of the Roman world. When he framed the artful system of the imperial authority, his moderation was inspired by his fears. He wished to deceive the people by an image of civil liberty, and the armies by an image of civil government.

The death of Caesar was ever before his eyes. He had lavished wealth and honors on his adherents; but the most favored friends of his uncle were in the number of the conspirators. The fidelity of the legions might defend his authority against open rebellion; but their vigilance could not secure his person from the dagger of a determined republican; and the Romans, who revered the memory of Brutus, would applaud the memory of his virtue. Caesar had provoked his fate as much by the ostentation of his power as by his power itself. The consul or the tribune might have reigned in peace. The title of king had armed the Romans against his life. Augustus was sensible that mankind is governed by names; nor was he deceived in his expectations, that the senate and people would submit to slavery, provided they were respectfully assured that they still enjoyed their ancient freedom. A feeble senate and enervated people cheerfully acquiesced in the pleasing illusion, as long as it was supported by the virtue, or even the prudence, of the successors of Augustus. . . .

The insolence of the armies inspired Augustus with fears of a still more alarming nature. The despair of the citizens could only attempt what the power of the soldiers was, at any time, able to execute. How precarious was his own authority over men whom he had taught to violate every social duty! He had heard their seditious clamors; he dreaded their calmer moments of reflection. One revolution had been purchased by immense rewards; but a second revolution might double those rewards. The troops professed the fondest attachment to the house of Caesar; but the attachments of the multitude are capricious and inconstant. Augustus summoned to his aid whatever remained in those fierce minds of Roman prejudices; enforced the rigor of discipline by the sanction of law; and interposing the majesty of the senate between the emperor and the army, boldly claimed their allegiance, as the first magistrate of the republic. . . .

E. Gibbon, *History of the Decline and Fall of the Roman Empire* (1787), ed. J. B. Bury (London: Methuen & Co., Ltd., 1896), I, 71–72.

(b) *A twentieth-century professional historian*

The book from which the next extract is taken is an interesting one. Ronald Syme in his introduction states clearly that it is his view that it "is surely time for some reaction from the traditional and conventional view of the period. Much that has recently been written about Augustus is simply panegyric, whether ingenuous or edifying. Yet it is not necessary to praise political success or to idealize the men who win wealth and honors through civil war." Such a statement disarms criticism, especially when it is coupled with the admission that his design has "imposed a pessimistic and truculent tone, to the almost complete exclusion of the gentler emotions and the domestic virtues." Syme claims to be a realist, and he has had the benefit of the researches of numerous specialists who have delved into the family records of the ancient Romans. His picture and judgment must be treated with respect, even if he has not said the last word yet on the subject.

In his sixth and seventh consulates C. Julius Caesar Octavianus went through a painless and superficial transformation. The process was completed in a session of the Senate on January 13th, 27 B.C., when he solemnly announced that he resigned all powers and all provinces to the free disposal of the Senate and People of Rome. Acclamation was drowned in protest. The senators adjured him not to abandon the Commonwealth that he had preserved. Yielding with reluctance to these manifestations of loyalty and patriotism, the master of the whole world consented to assume a special commission for a period of ten years, in the form of proconsular authority over a large *provincia,* namely Spain, Gaul, and Syria. That and nothing more. For the rest, proconsuls were to govern the provinces as before, but responsible only to the Senate; the Senate, People, and magistrates were to resume the rightful exercise of all their functions.

Three days later the Senate again met, eager and impatient to render thanks, to confer honors upon the saviour of the State. . . . A new name was devised, ex-

pressing veneration of more than mortal due. A veteran politician, the consular L. Munatius Plancus, proposed the decree that conferred on Caesar's heir the appellation of Augustus. Nothing was left to chance in preparing these exemplary manifestations. The ruler had taken counsel with his friends and allies—and perhaps with neutral politicians. They knew what they were about. In name, in semblance and in theory the sovereignty of Senate and People had been restored. . . .

The Romans as a people were possessed by an especial veneration for authority, precedent and tradition, by a rooted distaste for change unless change could be shown to be in harmony with ancestral custom, "mos majorum," which in practice meant the sentiments of the oldest living senators. . . . Yet the memory of the past reminded the Romans that change had come, though slow and combated. Rome's peculiar greatness was due not to one man's genius or to one age, but to many men and the long process of time. Augustus sought to demonstrate a doctrine—Roman history was a continuous and harmonious development. Augustus himself, so he asserted, accepted no magistracy that ran contrary to the "mos majorum." He did not need to. As it stood, the Roman constitution would serve his purpose well enough. It is therefore no paradox to discover in the Principate of Augustus both the institutions and the phraseology of Republican Rome. The historical validity of the inferences derived therefrom is another question. . . .

Certain precedents of the recent past were so close as to be damaging. Pompeius Magnus governed Spain in absence through his legates. . . . But Pompeius was sinister and ambitious. That *princeps* did not cure, but only aggravated the ills of the Roman State. Very different was Augustus, a "salubris princeps" [healthy *princeps*] for as such he would have himself known. Not only that. The whole career of Pompeius was violent and illicit . . . it would not do to revive such memories. . . . Seeking to establish continuity with a legitimate government, Caesar's heir foreswore the memory of Caesar; in the official conception, the Dictatorship and the Triumvirate were blotted from record. This meant a certain rehabilitation of the last generation of the Republic, which in politics is the Age of Pompeius. In his youth Caesar's heir, the revolutionary adventurer, won Pompeian support by guile and coolly betrayed his allies, overthrowing the Republic and proscribing the Republicans; in his mature years the statesman stole their heroes and their vocabulary.... On the whole, better to say nothing of Caesar, or for that matter of Antonius, save as criminal types. The power and domination of Augustus was in reality far too similar to that of the Dictator to stand even a casual reminder, let alone pointed and genuine comparison. The claims of the Divine Julius, the glories of Trojan descent and the obsession with Romulus, prevalent for some years in the aftermath of Actium, gradually recede and lose ground just as the victory itself, on quieter reflection an uncomfortable matter, is no longer fervently advertised.

A purified Pompeius or a ghostly and sanctified Cato were not the only victims of the Civil Wars who could be called up and enlisted in the service of the revived Republic. Cicero might be remunerative for every purpose; and the blame of his proscription was profitably laid upon Antonius, dead and disgraced.... In so far as Cicero had a political program, he advocated the existing order, reformed a little by return to ancient practices but not changed, namely the firm concord of the propertied classes, and the traditional distinction in function and standing between the different classes in society. Such was also the opinion of Augustus, for the Revolution had now been stabilized. Neither the Princeps nor any of his adherents desired change and disturbance.... Augustus labored to conserve the new order, announcing it as his dearest wish to be known as the "originator of the best state.".... Only ghosts and words were called up to comfort the living and confound posterity....

It is time to turn from words and theories. Only a robust faith can discover authentic relics of Cicero in the Republic of Augustus; very little attention was paid to him at all.... Augustus proudly dispensed with support of precedents—he claimed to be unique.... Names might change; Augustus was none the less a revolutionary leader who won supreme power through civil war.... To retain power, however, he must base his rule upon general consent, the support of men of property, and the active co-operation of the governing class. To that end he modified the forms of the constitution to fit his policy, his policy to harmonize with Roman sentiment....

His rule was personal—and based ultimately upon a personal oath of allegiance rendered by Rome, Italy and the West in 32 B.C., subsequently by the other regions of the Empire. Caesar Augustus possessed indefinite and tremendous resources, open or secret—all that the *principes* in the last generation held, but now stolen from them and enhanced to an exorbitant degree; and he was Divi filius [son of the god] destined for consecration in his turn. The plebs of Rome was Caesar's inherited clientèle. He fed them with doles, amused them with games, and claimed to be their protector against oppression. Free elections returned—that is to say, a grateful people would unfailingly elect the candidates whom Caesar in his wisdom had chosen, with or without formal commendation. He controlled the armies of the Roman People, in fact though not in law, and provided from his own pocket the bounty for the legionaries when they returned from service. Augustus was by far the wealthiest man in the Empire, ruling Egypt as a king and owing account of it to no man; he coined in silver and gold in the provinces; and he spent his money with ostentation and for power. The military colonies in Italy and abroad were a network of his armed and devoted garrisons. Towns in Italy and the provinces knew him as their founder or their patron; kings, tetrarchs, and dynasts over the wide empire were in his portion as allies and clients. A citizen and magistrate to the senators, he was *imperator* to the legions, a king and a god to the subject populations. Above all, he stood at the head of a large and well organized political party as the source and fount of patronage and advancement.

Such was Caesar Augustus. . . . Yet it would be an elementary error to fancy that the ceremony of January 13th was merely a grim comedy devised to deceive the ingenuous or intimidate the servile. On the contrary, the purified Senate, being in a majority the partisans of Augustus, were well aware of what was afoot. To secure the domination of the Caesarian party, the consolidation of the Revolution and the maintenance of peace, it was necessary that the primacy of Caesar's heir should be strengthened and perpetuated. Not, however, under the fatal name of dictator or monarch. On all sides prevailed

a conspiracy of decent reticence about the gap between fact and theory. . . .

It has been maintained in recent times that Augustus not only employed Republican language but intended that the Republican constitution should operate unhampered—and that it did, at least in the earlier years of his presidency. Augustus' purpose was just the reverse. He controlled government and patronage, especially the consulate, precisely after the manner of earlier dynasts, but with more thoroughness and without opposition. This time the domination of a faction was to be permanent and unshaken; the era of rival military leaders had closed.

The choice of means did not demand deep thought or high debate in the party councils. Augustus took what he deemed necessary for his designs, the consulate and a group of military provinces. Definition of powers and extent of *provincia* might later be modified how and when he pleased. One thing could never change, the source and origin of his domination. . . .

R. Syme, *The Roman Revolution* (Oxford: The Clarendon Press, 1939), pp. 313–25.

(c) *A modern administrator*

John Buchan was a man of many sides. By way of the law, publishing, and the writing of novels and biographies he was elected to the British Parliament in 1927 and finally, with the title of Lord Tweedsmuir, became Governor-General of Canada, where his tenure of office was a marked success. The author of three political biographies, he was in no sense a professional historian, but was greatly interested in the problems involved in the exercise of power and its relationship to human freedom (his best-known biography is probably *Cromwell*). His picture of Augustus neglects those aspects of his rule emphasized in the previous extract, but on the other hand it takes very seriously Augustus' desire to preserve what was worth preserving from the republican tradition of freedom and self-government. Since politics must consider both the desirable and the practicable, the truth may be that Syme and Buchan are both in part right, and the two extracts do not con-

tradict each other, though each emphasizes a different aspect of Augustus' work.

The twin principles of the new system were, first, that the reality of power should remain in the hands of Augustus, and, second, that such a central control should be given a constitutional façade. This meant that any scheme must be accepted and ratified by what remained of the mechanism of the Republic. He had been living on real, but for the most part, irregular, grants of authority; these must be relinquished and a new dispensation established on a basis of strict legality. His former powers had enabled him to clear the ground, but something different was needed before he could build. The new authority might be extraordinary and beyond precedent, but it must spring from the traditional sources, the Senate and the People. He was beginning to see what the ultimate form of the Roman polity must be, but he had no intention of presenting it as a clean-cut and fully articulated scheme. He would start with the rudiments, and guide the evolution on the lines he desired. He was a statesman, not a political theorist.

First for his name, since the head of the state must have a title. "Imperator," to which Julius had inclined, he unhesitatingly rejected. . . . As a term of daily use it smacked too much of dictatorship and the sword. . . . The word "princeps" as adopted by Augustus, was a popular appellation. . . and it is best translated "First Citizen",—first citizen and principal servant. . . . It combined diverse loyalties and aroused no antagonisms. Wiser than Julius, Augustus. . . recognized that names have a dangerous potency.

His next step was to decide upon the precise form which his authority should take. He must have the reality of power, but he must dress it in a cunning constitutional habit. He knew well the antiquarian propensities of his countrymen, and their passion for the minutiae of constitutionalism, and he was prepared to indulge it to the full so far as theory was concerned, provided that in practice he had the guiding of the state. His concern was less with abstract authority than with function. There was no such thing as a Roman constitution, for under the Republic the polity had always been insensibly changing, and if he set out to restore the Republic in full he would have found no general agreement as to what that Republic meant. His business, therefore, was to interweave his personal "auctoritas" with institutions which still had a strong appeal to the Roman mind, but, since these institutions were not clean cut and rigid, he could subtly adapt them in the interweaving. His task was not that of the lawyer, but of the practical statesman; the logic which guided him was not of paper but of facts.

His first step was simple. To begin with at any rate, he must hold the main office, the consulship, hold it in the old fashion by annual election. That would give him the dignity of the traditional head of the Roman state, and the handicap of colleagueship could be got over by the selection of the right kind of colleague. But the consulship alone was not enough. The kernel of his authority lay in his command of the chief—and, but for the Parthian, the only—army in the world. How was this command to be legitimated? Only by the grant of the "imperium proconsulare," so that he would be at once consul and proconsul. This was a departure from normal republican practice, but it was not without precedent, for in 52 B.C. the double office had been held by Pompey, and Pompey was still dear to conservative sentiment. . . .

But the imperium of a proconsul was not valid in the city of Rome, and in any case some authority was needed which should bring him more closely into touch with the people and conceal the truth that his ultimate power lay in the command of the army. The popular office of tribune was closed to him as a patrician, but already he had been granted many of the tribune's privileges. Now he must be invested with the others, for the key of his new policy was to acquire the power without the office. . . . The military imperium was the actual basis of his authority, but the tribunician power was at once its popular coloring and the source of its moral appeal.

There was another power which he must possess before he could deal with the hardest part of his problem, the status of the Senate. He must have some of the rights of the censor. . . for the taking of a census—neglected since 70 B.C.—and the revision of the Senate and the whole class system, he must have an *ad hoc* authority. . . . With a Senate purged and reduced in numbers and a purified aristocracy he was now ready for his great step—the division of the burden of empire between the Senate and himself. He had no need to concern himself greatly with the popular Assemblies. In theory the supreme legislative organ. . .they had become dull inorganic things, without individuality or prestige. But the Senate was a different matter. It was the very heart and soul of the Republic, and had still in the popular eye the glamor of ancient dignity and long descent. Having revived the distinction of its membership by expelling the low-born element introduced by Julius and Antony, he could ally himself with it in the business of government. His intention was to restore all of the Republic that would work; the Republic meant nothing without the Senate. . . . The Senate should reign like a modern constitutional monarch, and it should be permitted to govern up to the full limit of its capacity. . . .

Augustus. . .had no illusions about the temporary nature of the constitution which he was about to offer to the people. It was a trial trip, a provisional arrangement strictly limited in duration, a structure which might have to be profoundly modified. The fundamental principles, which he was careful not to emphasize unduly, he did indeed believe to be essential, but the details were to be largely a matter of slow evolution and adjustment. He was summoning Rome to a partnership in a great experiment and taking her frankly into his confidence. . . . There was no figure which for a moment could compare with his in authority. More important, there was no political creed passionately held which might be an obstacle to his own. Doctrinaire republicanism had sunk almost out of sight; it had become less a dogma than a lingering sentiment, which he was ready to conciliate because he himself shared it. . . .

Did he or did he not restore the Republic? The question is really without meaning, though it has occasioned a wealth of misplaced ingenuity. What republic? That of the old simple city-state? But no antiquarian piety could have brought that to life again, for it would have meant the reduction of the Roman people to a manageable size, the abolition of the system which made rank depend on office, a return to the [earlier citizen] army, and the restoration of primitive manners and morals. No Roman of any class would have accepted such a revolution. Does the question concern the resto-

ration of civic liberty? Then let us be careful in our definitions. The Roman "libertas" was never the Greek "eleutheria"; it was not freedom unfettered but freedom from arbitrary rule, and did not involve an atomic self-sufficiency, but could be as well, or better, attained as part of a greater whole. . . .

Augustus preserved whatever of the republican institutions still had vitality, and adapted them to a new executive purpose. . . . Of the legal sovereignty in the narrower sense there could be no doubt. It resided, as in republican days, in the Senate and the People. In theory these were supreme; all the powers of the Princeps emanated from them, and what they had granted they could withdraw. This right of resumption was emphasized by the limitation of the grant to ten years. . . . The Princeps was a magistrate in the traditional sense, with an extraordinary jurisdiction established in the republican way after sound republican precedents.

But the legal aspect was not the only, or the most vital, one. In effect Augustus had a status which the laws could not limit. . . . The logic of facts was to make this high command endure for life, since any change was unthinkable. He was resolved not to let slip those reins of power, and Rome was not less resolved, and it was therefore certain that time would increase and not diminish his influence. The old institutions, though Augustus had all the will in the world to preserve them, were bound to wither in the shadow of the new. He summoned the energies of the past to legitimize the future, but these energies were already half exhausted. If all his powers had republican precedents their combination in the hands of one man was a novelty, in one man of extraordinary administrative genius. Not all his constitutional probity and antiquarian zeal could put life into dying things. The mechanism of the small city-state could not long be combined with the mechanism required by a vast empire. . . .

A great scholar has reproached him because he "willed the impossible and set up the impermanent;" but what he willed was tentative, a thing the feasibility of which was left to the test of time, and the taunt of impermanence is idle in the case of an institution which endured for centuries and is still part of the framework of the modern world.

John Buchan, *Augustus* (Boston: Houghton Mifflin Company, 1937), pp. 133–41, 149–52, 162. By permission of the Tweedsmuir Trustees and Hodder & Stoughton Ltd.

B. Did the Principate Degenerate into a Tyranny under Tiberius?

The ancient sources, as we have seen, unanimously approved of Augustus, though Tacitus records adverse opinions held of him by some unnamed Romans. It was left for modern historians to attempt to discount the ancient tradition. In the case of Tiberius, Augustus' successor, the best historical tradition is almost equally unanimous against him, though some historians mention redeeming features of his rule. It is true that Velleius Paterculus, who had served under him, offers a much criticized eulogy of his master; but even Velleius might have changed his opinion if he had lived to see the end of the reign. Since his narrative ends before the fall of the praetorian prefect Sejanus and the subsequent treason trials (which will be referred to below), we cannot use him as a satisfactory witness for the defense.

There can, then, be no doubt of the ancient tradition that Tiberius was a suspicious tyrant. Our problem therefore is to assess the value of this tradition, and see whether it is justified. The unanimity of the sources makes the task of rehabilitation exceptionally difficult, and perhaps gratuitous, since the tradition may have represented the truth. Perhaps it would never have been attempted had not the narrative of Tacitus presented such obvious discrepancies, and had not the prejudice of Tacitus himself been apparent to anyone who reads him even for the first time. He records the reluctance of Tiberius to accept the throne, and at once explains it as window-dressing; he records dignified and humane statements of the *princeps,* and then suggests that they were but fair words concealing his true thoughts. Above all the picture of the licentious monster, aged nearly 80, disporting himself on the fair island of Capri in horrible orgies, seems utterly at variance with what we can bring ourselves to believe possible for an old, weary, and embittered ruler, betrayed by those he had trusted, fearful of assassination, and hated by all. Does such a man in the evening of his life, on one of the most beautiful and peaceful islands of the world, suddenly recover vitality enough for such orgies, and would he be tempted to indulge in them? The picture simply does not fit. Nor can we easily believe that from the beginning of his reign he was always the same tyrant, but put on the mask of a lover of freedom reluctantly compelled to be a monarch, throwing off the mask only after the fall of Sejanus. Could the truth be that he was frightened as well as embittered by the conspiracy, and either by desire for vengeance or in panic, or even in the genuine belief that the state could only be preserved by such means, resorted to the treason trials? And that his voluntary seclusion on the island of Capri was simply the longed-for asylum of a tired old man who knew himself to be hated in Rome?

If these things are so, then Tiberius cannot truly be called a tyrant. By using informers he set a bad precedent for later rulers to follow, but the conspiracy was no fake. The punishments he meted out were severe, but not unjustified where guilt was proved. And even if the innocent suffered sometimes with the guilty, this is not unknown in other, less dangerous, times. This is the line of argument adopted by those who would rehabilitate him.

Again the problem is insoluble. But it will reveal the difficulty of coming to a final decision in historical inquiries. The last two extracts, one of considerable length, will suggest the kind of work that can still be done in rehabilitating the reputation of one whom the author feels to have been unjustly maligned; and it will show the methods that can be used by modern historians to break up the formidable case for the prosecution presented by one of the greatest historians of antiquity.

1. OPINION OF THE ANCIENT WORLD

(a) The Official View: *Tiberius as a just and efficient ruler*

There is no reason to suppose that the work of Velleius was in any way sponsored by Tiberius, or that the following eulogy was anything other than the genuine opinion of an imperial servant who had fought under Tiberius and admired him both as general and *princeps*. As noted earlier, however, the history was written prior to the treason trials that followed the fall of Sejanus.

Who would undertake to tell in detail the accomplishments of the past sixteen years?... Credit has been restored in the forum, strife has been banished from the forum, canvassing for office from the Campus Martius, discord from the senate-house; justice, equity, and industry, long buried in oblivion, have been restored to the state; the magistrates have regained their authority, the senate its majesty, the courts their dignity; rioting in the theater has been suppressed; all citizens have either been impressed with the wish to do right, or have been forced to do so by necessity. Right is now honored, evil is punished; the humble man respects the great but does not fear him, the great has precedence over the lowly but does not despise him. When was the price of grain more reasonable, or when were the blessings of peace greater? The *pax augusta*, which has spread to the regions of the west and to the bounds of the north and of the south, preserves every corner of the world safe from the fear of brigandage.... Fair play has now precedence over influence, and merit over ambition, for the best of emperors teaches his citizens to do right by doing it, and though he is greatest among us in authority, he is still greater in the example which he sets...

Velleius Paterculus, *History of Rome*, II, 126, trans. F. W. Shipley, Loeb Classical Library (Cambridge, Mass.: Harvard University Press, 1924), pp. 317–19.

(b) The Sensational Biographer: *Tiberius as hypocrite*

Far different is the picture provided by Suetonius, who adopts the traditional view discussed earlier. But even Suetonius, though he devotes the bulk of his biography to the sensational details of the later part of his reign, nevertheless concedes Tiberius some merit during the earlier years. Both aspects of his narrative are included in the following selection.

Though Tiberius did not hesitate at once to assume and to exercise the imperial authority, surrounding himself with a guard of soldiers, that is, with the actual power and the outward sign of sovereignty, yet he long refused the title, at one time with barefaced hypocrisy upbraiding his friends who urged him to accept it, saying that they did not realize what a monster the empire was, at another by evasive answers and calculating hesitancy keeping the Senators in suspense when they implored him to yield, and fell at his feet. Finally, some lost patience, and one man cried out in the confusion: "Let him take it or leave it!" Another openly voiced the taunt that others were slow in doing what they promised but that he was slow to promise what he was already doing. At last, as though on compulsion, and complaining that a wretched and burdensome slavery was being forced upon him, he accepted the empire, but in such fashion as to suggest the hope that he would one day lay it down. His own words were: "Until I come to the time when it may seem right to you to grant an old man some repose"....

Once relieved of fear, he at first played a most unassuming part, almost humbler than that of a private citizen. Of many high honors he accepted only a few of the more modest.... He so loathed flattery that... if any one in conversation or a set speech spoke of him in too flattering terms, he did not hesitate to interrupt him to take him to task, and to correct his language on the spot.... More than that, he was self-contained and patient in the face of abuse and slander, and of lampoons on himself and his family, often asserting that in a free country there should be free speech and free thought. When the Senate on one occasion demanded that cognizance be taken of such offenses and those guilty of them, he said: "We have not enough spare time to warrant involving ourselves in more affairs. If you open this loophole you will find no time for any other business. It will be an excuse for laying everybody's quarrels before you." A most unassuming remark of his in the Senate is also a matter of record: "If so and so criticizes me I shall take care to render an account of my acts and words; if he persist I shall return him in kind." All this was the more noteworthy because in addressing and in paying his respects to the Senators individually and in a body he himself almost exceeded the requirements of courtesy....

He even introduced a semblance of free government by maintaining the ancient dignity and powers of the Senate and the magistrates. For there was no matter of public or private business so small or so great that he did not lay it before the Senators, consulting them about revenues and monopolies, constructing and restoring public buildings, even about levying and disbanding the soldiers.... He always entered the House alone. Once when he was taken there in a litter because of illness he dismissed his attendants at the door. When certain decrees were passed contrary to his expressed opinion, he did not even remonstrate.... Once when the Senate was divided and the act might pass by the difference of a few votes he went over to the side of the minority, but not a man followed him.... He himself actually rose in the presence of the Consuls, and made way for them in the street....To the governors who recommended burdensome taxes for his provinces, he wrote in answer that it was the part of a good shepherd to shear his flock, not skin it....

For two whole years after becoming Emperor he did not set foot outside the gates. But after being bereft of both his sons...he retired to Campania, and... after traversing Campania...he went to Capri, particularly attracted to that island because it was accessible by only one small beach, being everywhere else girt with sheer cliffs of great height and by deep water.....

Having gained the license of privacy, and being as it were out of sight of the citizens, he at last gave free rein at once to all the vices which he had for a long time ill concealed. Of these I shall give a detailed account from the beginning. [There follows an account of perversions and unnatural vices which were no doubt the common gossip of Rome, though they strain modern credulity.] His cruel and coldblooded character was not completely hidden even in his boyhood.... But it grew still more noticeable after he became Emperor, even at the beginning, when he was still courting popularity by a show of moderation. When a funeral was passing by and a jester called aloud to the corpse to let Augustus know that the legacies which he had left to the people were not yet being paid, Tiberius had the man haled before him, ordered that he receive what was due him, and then be put to death.... He did so many other cruel and savage deeds under the guise of strictness and improvement of the public morals, but in reality rather to gratify his natural instincts, that some resorted to verses to express their detestation of the present ills and a warning against those to come.... After the death of Sejanus he was more cruel than ever, which showed that his favorite was not wont to egg him on, but on the contrary gave him the opportunities which he himself desired....

It is a long story to run through his acts of cruelty in detail. It will be enough to mention the forms that they took, as samples of his barbarity. Not a day passed without an execution, even days that were sacred and holy, for he put some to death even on New Year's Day. Many were accused and condemned with their children, and even by their children. The relatives of the victims were forbidden to mourn for them. Special rewards were voted the accusers and sometimes even the witnesses. The word of no informer was doubted. Every crime was treated as capital, even the utterance of a few simple words. A poet was charged with having slandered Agamemnon in a tragedy, and a writer of history of having called Brutus and Cassius the last of the Romans. The writers were at once put to death and their works destroyed, although they had been read with approval in public some years before in the presence of Augustus himself. . . .

Many things go to show, not only how hated and execrable he was all this time, but also that he lived a life of extreme fear and was even exposed to insult. . . . His anxiety of mind became torture because of reproaches of all kinds from every quarter, since every single one of those condemned to death heaped all kinds of abuse upon him, either to his face or by handbills placed in the Senators' seats at the shows. By these, however, he was most diversely affected, now through a sense of shame desiring that they all be concealed and kept secret, sometimes scorning them and producing them of his own accord and giving them publicity. Why, he was even attacked by Artabanus, King of the Parthians, who charged him in a letter with the murder of his kindred and other bloody deeds, and with shameless and dissolute living, counseling him to gratify the intense and just hatred of the citizens as soon as possible by a voluntary death.

At last in utter self-disgust he all but admitted the extremity of his wretchedness in a letter which began thus: "If I know what to write to you, Fathers of the Senate, or how to write it, or what to leave unwritten at present, may all gods and goddesses visit me with more utter destruction than I feel that I am daily suffering." . . .

Suetonius, *The Lives of the Caesars,* III, 24–32, 38–42, 57–67, trans. J. C. Rolfe, Loeb Classical Library (Cambridge, Mass.: Harvard University Press, 1914), pp. 329–41, 349–51, 71–89.

(c) The Roman Senatorial Historian: *Tiberius as Rome's first tyrant*

The historical work of Tacitus is an even more severe indictment of Tiberius than the biography of Suetonius, since he is obviously a more thoughtful man. Yet his prejudice is also evident, since, although he records words and deeds which might bear a contrary interpretation, as seen in the third selection below, they do not affect his judgment of Tiberius' character, and he attributes them to hypocrisy when he troubles to make any comment upon them. Note, however, that the third selection is the earliest in time.

(i) His Disgust with His Self-Imposed Task

Much of what I have related and shall have to relate, may perhaps, I am aware, seem petty trifles to record. . . . My labors are circumscribed and inglorious; peace wholly unbroken or but slightly disturbed, dismal misery in the capital, an emperor careless about the enlargement of the empire, such is my theme. Still it will not be useless to study those at first sight trifling events out of which the movements of vast changes often take their rise.

All nations and cities are ruled by the people, the nobility, or by one man. . . . Now after a revolution, when Rome is nothing but the realm of a single despot, there must be good in carefully noting and recording this period, for it is but few who have the foresight to distinguish right from wrong, or what is sound from what is hurtful, while most men learn wisdom from the fortunes of others. Still, though this is instructive, it gives little pleasure. Descriptions of countries, the various incidents of battles, glorious deaths of great generals, enchain and refresh a reader's mind. I have to present in succession the merciless biddings of a tyrant, incessant prosecutions, faithless friendships, the ruin of innocence, the same causes issuing in the same results, and I am everywhere confronted by a wearisome monotony in my subject matter.

Tacitus, *Annals*, IV, 32–33, trans. A. J. Church and W. J. Brodribb (New York: Modern Library, Inc., 1942), pp. 162–63.

(ii) The Reign of Terror

Former alarms then returned, as there was a charge of treason against Considius Proculus. While he was celebrating his birthday without fear, he was hurried before the Senate, condemned and instantly put to death. . . . Pompeia Macrina too was sentenced to banishment. Her husband Argolicus and her father-in-law Laco, leading men of Achaia, had been ruined by the Emperor. Her father likewise, an illustrious Roman knight, and her brother, an ex-praetor, seeing their doom was near, destroyed themselves. It was imputed to them as a crime that their great grandfather Theophanes of Mitylene had been one of the intimate friends of Pompey the Great, and that after his death Greek flattery had paid him divine honors. Sextus Marius, the richest man in Spain, was next accused of incest with his daughter, and thrown headlong from the Tarpeian rock. To remove any doubt that the vastness of the man's wealth had proved his ruin, Tiberius kept his gold mines for himself, though they were forfeited to the State. Executions were now a stimulus to his fury, and he ordered the death of all who were lying in prison under accusation of complicity with Sejanus. There lay, singly or in heaps, the unnumbered dead, of every age and sex, the illustrious with the obscure. Kinsfolk and friends were not allowed to be near them, to weep over them, or even to gaze on them too long. Spies were set around them, who noted the sorrow of each mourner and followed the rotting corpses, till they were dragged to the Tiber, where, floating or driven on the bank, no one dared to burn them or to touch them. The force of terror had utterly extinguished the sense of human fellowship, and, with the growth of cruelty, pity was thrust aside. . . .

Rome meanwhile being a scene of ceaseless bloodshed, Pomponius Labeo, . . . governor of Moesia, severed his veins and let his life ebb from him. His wife Paxaea emulated her husband. What made such deaths eagerly sought was dread of the executioner, and the fact too that the condemned, besides forfeiture of their property, were deprived of burial, while those who decided their fate themselves, had their bodies interred, and their wills remained valid. The emperor, however, argued in a letter to the Senate that it had been the practice of our ancestors, whenever they broke off an intimacy, to forbid the person their house, and so put an end to friendship. This usage he himself revived in Labeo's case, but Labeo, being pressed by charges of maladministration in his province and other crimes, had screened his guilt by bringing odium on another, and had groundlessly alarmed his wife, who, though criminal, was still free from danger. . . .

Though three years had elapsed since the destruction of Sejanus, neither time, nor intreaties, nor sated gratifications, all which have a soothing effect on others, softened Tiberius, or kept him from punishing doubtful or forgotten offenses as most flagrant and recent crimes. . . .

Tacitus, *Annals*, VI, 18–19, 29, 38, *ibid.*, pp. 204–5, 210, 218.

(iii) Contrary Instances: Justice and Humanity of Tiberius

Not satisfied with judicial proceedings in the Senate, the emperor would sit at one end of the praetor's tribunal, but so as not to displace him from the official seat. Many decisions were given in his presence, in opposition to improper influence and the solicitations of great men.

This, though it promoted justice, ruined freedom. Pius Aurelius, for instance, a senator, complained that the foundations of his house had been weakened by the pressure of a public road and aqueduct, and he appealed to the Senate for assistance. He was opposed by the praetors of the treasury, but the emperor helped him, and paid him the value of his house, for he liked to spend money on a good purpose, a virtue which he long retained, when he cast off all others. To Propertius Celer, an ex-praetor, who sought because of his poverty to be excused from his rank as a senator, he gave a million sesterces, having ascertained that he had inherited his poverty. He bade others, who attempted the same, prove their case to the Senate, as from his love of strictness he was harsh, even where he acted on right grounds. Consequently everyone else preferred silence and poverty to confession and relief. . . .

Cornelius Dolabella, by way of carrying flattery yet further, sharply censured the morals of Silanus, and then moved that no one of disgraceful life and notorious infamy should be eligible for a province, and that of this the emperor should be the judge. "Laws, indeed," he said, "punish crimes committed; but how much more merciful would it be to individuals, how much better for our allies, to provide against their commission."

The emperor opposed the motion. "Although," he said, "I am not ignorant of the reports about Silanus, still we must decide nothing by hearsay. Many a man has behaved in a province quite otherwise than was hoped or feared of him. Some are roused to higher things by great responsibility; others are paralyzed by it. It is not possible for a prince's knowledge to embrace everything, and it is not expedient that he should be exposed to the ambitious schemings of others. Laws are ordained to meet facts, inasmuch as the future is uncertain. It was the rule of our ancestors that, whenever there was first an offense, some penalty should follow. Let us not revolutionize a wisely devised and ever approved system. Princes have enough burdens, and also enough power. Rights are invariably abridged, as despotism increases; nor ought we to fall back on imperial authority, when we can have recourse to the laws."

Tacitus, *Annals*, I, 75; III, 69, *ibid.*, pp. 49–50, 130–40.

2. CRITICISM OF ANCIENT OPINION BY A MODERN HISTORIAN

(a) *"Reign of terror" an invention of Tacitus*

It seems desirable to devote some space to the consideration of the reasons why Tacitus held so firmly to the view that the last years of Tiberius were a reign of terror, and of the literary devices by which he has impressed this picture on his readers.

It is probable that he originally derived his conception of a terror from the tradition concerning Tiberius which was current in his day. . . . I have elsewhere pointed out some reasons for thinking that Tacitus, instead of making a careful study of the whole reign before beginning his work, examined and compared his various sources for the two or three years which he intended to treat in a single book, and that, as soon as this study was completed, he forthwith wrote the book, and then took up the investigations preliminary to the next. Thus, when he began, he had only a vague and general knowledge of the events of his reign, and he assumed that they would be found to harmonize with the legendary character of Tiberius. What he learned in gathering material for the first books of the *Annals* compelled him to admit that for some years Tiberius had shown himself a wise and able ruler, but this difficulty was easily overcome by the help of that hypocrisy which seems to have been attributed to Tiberius by tradition. There was, therefore, nothing in the early part of the reign which could force Tacitus to modify his preconceived ideas, and all that was necessary was to let the reader see through the mask worn by the emperor. This Tacitus accomplished by numerous comments, innuendoes, and anticipations, and, as he wrote, the picture which he was drawing became so vivid in his mind that it completely dominated his imagination. When finally he reached the sixth book and with it the dreadful climax for which he had from the first been preparing the reader and himself, he was no longer capable of weighing evidence fairly. Since a reign of terror was a logical necessity if his portrait was to stand, it only remained for him to present the facts in such a way that they would make what he thoroughly believed to be the right impression on the reader. If enough victims could not be found, he explained the deficiency by the assumption that previous historians had wearied of the monotonous catalogue of executions and suicides, and exerted himself the more to make up for the inadequacy of his material by the dexterous use of rhetoric. [The author then goes on to analyze the passage on p. 38, where Tiberius ordered the death of all those who were still lying in prison. He comments:]

This is a powerful and vivid description, but Tacitus himself supplies the proof that strict accuracy has been sacrificed to effect. He asserts that all who were in prison as accomplices of Sejanus were put to death, and we are, therefore, surprised to learn of the execution in prison of Sextius Paconianus in 35 A.D. (two years later). Tacitus said he had been imprisoned after the fall of Sejanus.... Aside from this it is very strange that such a massacre as is here described should have escaped the notice of Dio and Suetonius. The latter merely states incidentally that as many as twenty persons...were put to death on one day. The "untold number" of Tacitus thus shrinks very considerably.... The truth of the matter can not be determined with certainty, but perhaps the best guess at what happened is that Tiberius ordered the immediate execution of some twenty persons then in prison under sentence of death. Why they had not been already executed we do not know, but it is possible that some of them had been spared in the hope that they could give important information to the government....

In A.D. 34 Tacitus has no such golden opportunity, and is compelled to use considerable ingenuity. He begins with an account of the Egyptian phoenix and then continues his reign of terror with the remark that at Rome the slaughter continued and that Pomponius Labeo opened his veins, his wife following his example [p. 38]. If Tacitus had at once added that Labeo was accused of maladministration in Moesia and other crimes, the proper effect would hardly have been achieved, so he follows the suicide of Labeo with some general comments on the motives for suicide.... The proper atmosphere having now been created, the charges may now safely be stated. The statement, however, is introduced by the words, "But Tiberius declared in letters to the senate," as though the emperor, unsatisfied with the death of his victim, had maliciously sought to blacken his memory. In this way our sympathy is enlisted for Labeo without any assertion of his innocence on the part of Tacitus. Then follows a confused account of the prosecution and suicide of Scaurus, so contrived that, although Tacitus attributes the responsibility to Macro [the praetorian prefect], we are yet left with the impression that Scaurus was somehow a victim of Tiberius, whom he had angered by some lines in a tragedy he had written. Another touch is added when, having to record the banishment of three informers, Tacitus begins by saying that even *they* were punished if the opportunity offered. By these means he has succeeded in placing the events of the year in a wholly false perspective. The reasons given for suicide are adequate only if those accused were guilty or if they had no hope of a fair hearing. But immediately after the fall of Sejanus several who faced a trial before the senate were acquitted, and we have no grounds for thinking that an acquittal had become impossible since that time. If Labeo and Scaurus were guilty there was nothing horrible in their fate, and in the case of the informers it is clear that Tacitus is ready for Tiberius whatever he may do; if he punishes the delators [informers] it shows how bloodthirsty he was, and, if he spares them it shows the same thing. . . .

The narrative of Tacitus for the next year (A.D. 35) reveals the rhetorical method even more plainly. He begins by putting together the events of two eastern campaigns and apologizes for this violation of chronology by saying that he has done so to give his readers some relief from the record of domestic calamities, for, although three years had passed since the death of Sejanus, neither time nor prayers nor satiety, which soften other men [cf. p. 38], had any effect on Tiberius, who continued to punish old and uncertain offenses as if they had been recent and serious. The suicide of Trio is then briefly told and the four other cases for the year dismissed in a few lines. This brevity of treatment robs them of most of their effectiveness, but Tacitus makes up for this by his concluding comment: "Tiberius," he says, "heard of these things, not across a strait of the sea, as formerly, or by the hands of messengers from a distance, but so close to the city

that he could answer the dispatches from the Consuls on the same day, or with only a night intervening, and almost see with his own eyes the blood streaming through men's houses, or the hands of the executioner." The force of this passage is as remarkable as its irrelevance, for the proximity of Tiberius to Rome cannot increase his wickedness if he was guilty of murdering the innocent. However, Tacitus does not say that any of the victims were innocent, and it can hardly be doubted that he would have done so if he could. The rhetorical machinery is very evident at this point. The introductory remarks on the implacability of Tiberius naturally lead us to expect something horrible, we are then hurried past the facts, and by a lurid picture at the close we are left with the impression, if we do not stop to think, that the events so narrated were very horrible indeed.

It is unnecessary to give further examples of the literary devices by which Tacitus has succeeded in persuading the world that during the last years of his reign Tiberius was a ferocious tyrant, wallowing in blood. A careful reading of the sixth book of the *Annals* will show that the whole picture of the Tiberian terror is derived from the rhetorical setting in which the facts are presented and not from the facts themselves. . . .

F. B. Marsh, *The Reign of Tiberius* (Oxford: The Clarendon Press, 1931), pp. 284–88.

(b) *A summing up of Tiberius by the same historian*

Tacitus . . . told the truth as he saw it and was scrupulous in matters of detail. . . . Thus in the end, while, on the one hand, by his literary genius he was able to stamp his portrait of Tiberius on the minds of men for centuries, on the other, he supplied the materials for a more impartial and sober judgment. . . .

Whether such a man as Tacitus has pictured could exist at all we need not discuss. That Tiberius was not such a man the record seems to prove beyond reason-

able doubt. Most of the charges against him are refuted by the facts; he did not nurse the law of treason but struggled steadily against its extension; he did not encourage delation, but punished false accusers to the last; he was not cruel or bent upon a stern severity. For years his government was singularly lenient, and even in his last years the number of his victims seems very small when we consider what had passed and the real danger of his isolated position. Tacitus will have it that his gloomy temper led him to brood over his resentments for years, and then break out in sudden vengeance, yet in every case where this charge is made, the supposed victim of these old grudges had been guilty of some fresh offense. That he forgave his enemies cannot be asserted, but there is nothing in the record to prove he was implacable or vindictive. That he was suspicious there is exceedingly little to show. Augustus in his last days warned Tiberius of several possible pretenders to the throne; one of them, Cn. Piso, was trusted in an important post; another, Manius Lepidus, was honored and respected till his death; a third, L. Arruntius, was allowed to live unmolested until the emperor himself was dying, and the Romans believed that the "suspicious tyrant" was ignorant of his fate. . . .

Nor is the charge of hypocrisy any better sustained. It seems to have been based chiefly on the emperor's bearing in the senate, which was misunderstood by a later generation, and perhaps in some degree by contemporaries as well. At the accession of Tiberius the republican forms still possessed some vitality and he was sincerely anxious to preserve the independence of the senate. With this object in view he was forced on many occasions to hide his real feelings and opinions under ambiguous phrases for fear of influencing unduly the decisions of the conscript fathers. Tacitus tells us that while his language was usually guarded even to hesitation so that his words seemed to struggle forth with difficulty, yet when he acted mercifully he spoke with readiness and fluency. The historian is somewhat puzzled by the contrast and fails to see the obvious explanation, namely, that, when Tiberius intervened in the proceedings by virtue of his imperial prerogatives, he bore himself naturally, since it was impossible to disguise his interference. By the time of Tacitus the senate had become accustomed to the open and constant assertion of the imperial authority, and it was easy for those who disliked the memory of Tiberius to construe his attempts to respect the freedom of that body as evidence of hypocrisy.

The real faults of Tiberius seem to have been quite different. A Roman of the old school, he had little sympathy with the prevailing tendencies of the generation in which he lived, and ignored too much the smaller arts of popularity. A blunt soldier, he found the part of princeps as designed by Augustus an irksome and difficult one to play. He lacked the genial tact which had enabled his predecessor to smooth over and disguise unpleasant realities and to keep up agreeable fictions. He hated flattery and strove to maintain the independence of the senate, but disposing as he did of the patronage of the empire, he could accomplish little. In his heart he despised his contemporaries, and took too little pains to conceal his feelings. On several occasions he failed to realize, or wilfully ignored, the effect of his conduct on the public mind, as, for example, when he absented himself from the funeral of Germanicus. Whatever his reasons for leaving Rome, his long seclusion at Capri was a serious blunder, since it destroyed the illusion on which the principate was based. His blind confidence in Sejanus seems to show a real lack of discernment; perhaps it indicates that, although Tiberius was a shrewd judge of ability, he had little insight into character. . . .

Certainly the emperor cannot reasonably be blamed for punishing those who had been guilty of real crimes in connection with the long series of intrigues of which Sejanus was the instigator. The record seems to prove that Tiberius tried to secure justice and did not intentionally oppress the innocent. There is nothing to show that there was any fundamental change in either his character or his conduct; if in the last years of his reign there were more suicides and executions, the most simple and natural explanation is that many crimes had come to light, and that the isolated position of the emperor led to more frequent conspiracies. Yet the number who suffered was small, and if there was terror in Rome it was due rather to the guilty consciences of those who escaped than to the cruelty of Tiberius.

Yet it cannot be denied, that, in spite of his ability and his good intentions,

Tiberius failed in his role of princeps, and that the constitution of Augustus broke down in his hands. For this failure he was not wholly or even chiefly responsible, but it is impossible not to feel that a man of greater tact and more winning manners might have reconciled the feuds in the imperial family, or at least have kept them within bounds, and that Tiberius committed a grave blunder in not dealing more promptly and firmly with the question of the succession. Sejanus was certainly the evil genius of the emperor, and but for him the reign might have had a happier ending. . . . As a result of his blind confidence in an unscrupulous minister, Tiberius, as princeps, was defeated in most of his aims. He tried to maintain the independence of the senate, but he left it more subservient than ever; he sought to restrain delation, but it steadily developed, and even if he was not himself a tyrant, it was under him that the apparatus of the later tyranny took shape; he made a sincere effort to preserve the republican monarchy of Augustus, but it was transformed into the despotism of the later Caesars, and it was this last fact, which, perhaps, contributed most to blast his memory.

Ibid., pp. 221–27.

2

The Triumph of Christianity

KENNETH M. SETTON

University of Wisconsin

To the historian the most astonishing aspect of the early history of the Church is the rapidity with which Christianity spread. The new religion appeared at a singularly opportune time, as the first historian of the Church, Eusebius of Caesarea, emphasized in the early fourth century, in his oration *In Praise of the Emperor Constantine* (chap. xv, 4):

> One universal power, the Roman Empire, arose and flourished, while the enduring and implacable hatred of nation against nation was now removed; and as the knowledge of one God, and one way of religion and salvation, even the doctrine of Christ, was made known to all mankind; so at the same time, the entire dominion of the Roman Empire being vested in a single sovereign, profound peace reigned throughout the world. And thus, by the express appointment of the same God, two roots of blessing, the Roman Empire and the doctrine of Christian piety, sprang up together for the benefit of men.

A number of important reasons can be advanced to help explain the Christian success. First of all, Christianity was born, during the reigns of the Emperors Augustus and Tiberius, into a world at peace: travel and communication were easy. Next, the popular Greek of the day, the *koiné,* the language of the New Testament, was spoken almost universally in the cities of the Levant and the seaboard towns of the whole Mediterranean. Before this time, a belief in the gods of the Graeco-Roman pantheon had been basic to the civic life of the ancient city-state, and these gods had been served by civic colleges of priests. Religion and affairs of state had been indissolubly connected, and the ancient gods and the city-states had lost their vitality together. With the passing of the independence of the (Greek) city-states, and with the subsequent emergence of the large territorial monarchies in the Hellenistic age, men's yearnings for recognition as individuals, the human desire to feel important in society, could no longer be satisfied by participation in the now insignificant affairs of the city-states. Alexander the Great and the intellectuals around him talked of the brotherhood of man; horizons had been broadened far beyond the walls of any small group of city-states; and the universalist philosophies of Stoicism and Epicureanism gained many adherents. Then, as the city-states and the Hellenistic monarchies were drawn into the world government of the Roman Empire, the pagan cults gradually went down before the inexorable triumph of Christianity.

The way had been well prepared for Christianity. The gospel traveled rapidly along the Roman roads and the sea lanes of the Mediterranean, from city to city, and all roads led to Rome, where our interest chiefly lies.

But if there were factors deep within the changing culture of the Graeco-Roman world which thus assisted the growth of Christianity, there were at least three forces militating against the new religion: 1) the competition which Christianity faced in the eastern "mystery cults"; 2) the Roman government's persecution of Christians for their refusal to worship the Emperor; and 3) the growth of heretical sects within Christianity, as Greek rationalist philosophy and science made their impact upon the doctrines of the new faith. Of these three obstacles to its development, Christianity had the most to fear from heresy, for it challenged authority within the Church and gave rise to doctrinal strife.

It is easy to exaggerate the extent of the competition furnished to Christianity by the oriental "mystery cults." Contrary to the impression created by several modern textbooks, these salvationist cults were never really dangerous competitors of Christianity. The Romans and westerners in general were by and large prejudiced against the worship of Cybele (and her consort Attis), the "Great Mother of the Gods" from Asia Minor. The worship of Isis (and her consort Osiris), from Egypt, always kept the mark and individuality of the land of its origin; there was little connection among the Isiac congregations throughout the Roman world; and although the cult of Isis employed the Greek language, its appeal was chiefly to Egyptians. There were, it is true, many worshippers of Isis in Rome, but they were chiefly recruited from the large Egyptian colony in the city. The Syrian divinities, such as Astarte, enjoyed even less success than those of Asia Minor and Egypt, for their devotees remained socially isolated, usually kept their Semitic dialects, often practiced sacred prostitution (a fertility rite), and even made sacrifice of human beings. The oriental cults lacked content and ethical teaching; for the most part ignored the character of the initiate; and held out salvation to their devotees chiefly in half-magical rites and secret mystical experiences; they failed to possess and even to reach the whole of men's lives; and so they could easily compromise with the worship of the Roman Emperor.

These cults and others, especially Mithraism, caused the early fathers of the Church much anxiety, but never the fear of defeat. Mithraism, the Hellenized worship of the Persian god of light Mithras, was widespread among soldiers, especially those of eastern origin, and some sixty little chapels dedicated to Mithras have been identified by archaeologists in Rome. Mithraism was a form of sun worship, especially popular in the Empire in the third century, but it is very doubtful that it was ever a serious competitor to Christianity, once the new religion had reached its stride. Modern scholarship increasingly tends to the belief, contrary to another textbook cliché that Christianity constantly borrowed the practices of the mystery cults, that in actual fact the latter probably borrowed more heavily from Christianity!

Christianity had more to fear from persecution, for its failure to subscribe to the Emperor cult, but even here the "blood of the martyrs was the seed of the Church." Each successive text in the history of persecution attests in its way the rapid growth of the early Church. In A.D. 64, when Nero sought to throw blame for the great fire in Rome upon the Christians, "a vast multitude was convicted" (Tacitus, *Annals*, XV, 44). About the year 112 the younger Pliny, then governor of the province of Bithynia, sought the advice of the Emperor Trajan concerning Christians in his province, "especially on account of the number of those endangered, for many persons of every age and of every class in society, and of both sexes, are and will be brought into danger [by charges that they are Christians]. The contagion of this superstition has spread not only through the cities but also through the towns and countryside as well. . . . But it is easy to see what a host of people could be set right if they were given a chance of repentance!" (Pliny's *Letters*, X, 96.) But Christians did not repent for the faith. Their numbers increased, and they were inclined to avoid an active participation in the affairs of the world.

Until the Roman destruction of Jerusalem in A.D. 70, the three chief centers of Christianity had been Jerusalem, Caesarea (in Palestine), and Antioch, "and it was in Antioch that the disciples were first called 'Christians' " (Acts, 11:26). After A.D. 70 the chief centers were Antioch, Ephesus, and Rome, although about the beginning of the third century Alexandria eclipsed Ephesus in importance. Antioch and Alexandria were the homes of two vigorous and opposing schools of Christian doctrine. Antioch, in Syria, close to the scenes forever associated with the birth, life, and crucifixion of Christ, clung to its view of the "Jesus of history," and tended toward the heresy of adoptionism, i.e. that Jesus, of human birth, was adopted into the Godhead, and was thus divine. The Antiochene School was of a concrete, practical, and ethical bent, inclined to a literal interpretation of the Scriptures. The Alexandrian School, less familiar with the scenes and homely facts of Jesus' life, inclined to the heresy of docetism, i.e. that Jesus was actually God, a *phantasma* of a man, and only "seemed" to be a human being (from the Greek *dokein*, "to seem"). This school was inclined to abstraction, mysticism, theology, and was moved by the "Christ of experience." Alexandrian theologians saw allegories everywhere in the Scriptures.

Although many early, influential, and persistent heretical groups were unconnected with either the Antiochene or Alexandrian schools of Christian thought, some of the chief heresies in the early history of Christianity did arise in the one school or the other. Antioch and Alexandria were both Greek cities during the Roman Empire; they were the homes of Greek theologians who read and pondered not only the religious heritage of Israel, but also the philosophy of Greece. These theologians sought the synthesis of the truths of revelation and of nature, but their different interpretations only served to point up the apparent conflicts between Christianity and Greek philosophy and science. Must the latter be rejected to preserve the integrity of the Christian faith? During the first two generations after Christ, and even longer, there was a tendency among Christians to reject the world, and many Christians looked for the almost immediate second coming of Christ and the establishment of the Kingdom of God. In the middle of the second century, for example, Justin Martyr wrote in his first defense of Christianity to the Emperor Antoninus Pius, "Having heard that we are looking forward to a kingdom, you Emperors have wrongly assumed that we refer to a kingdom of men, like yours, whereas we mean the kingdom of God!" (*Apol.* I, 11).

Early Christians commonly avoided participation in either local or imperial government; tending strongly to pacifism, they often resisted service in the army; they were in the world, but they sought not to be of it. Generations later this contrast between the kingdom of God and that of men was to receive its most abundant and philosophic treatment in St. Augustine's contrast between the City of God (*Civitas Dei*) and that on Earth (*Civitas terrena*). But what was the Christian educator, in actual fact, to do with the scientific and cultural inheritance of the pagan past? Should it be retained or abandoned? If retained, how should it be modified? Was Tertullian right? Did Athens have nothing in common with Jerusalem? We find the following advice in a third-century Christian source (*Didascalia Apostolorum*, iii, ed. R. H. Connolly, Oxford, 1929, p. 13):

Avoid completely heathen books! For what have you to do with strange words or laws or false prophecies, which are a ready source of error for unsteady minds? For what do you lack in the word of God that you should betake yourself to these heathen tales? If you wish to read histories, you have the Book of Kings; if you wish to read philosophy and poetry, you have the Prophets in whom you will find a greater understanding of all poetry and philosophy, for their wisdom and words are those of the Lord, Who alone is truly wise. If you want books of songs, you have the Psalms; if you want to read about the beginning of the world's formation, you have Genesis; if you want to read of laws and precepts, you have the law of the Lord in all its glory. From all such things, therefore, which are alien to you and the work of the devil, do keep yourself entirely apart.

Was this sound advice? The question was a serious one for the Church under the Roman Empire. This is Problem 1, the conflict of the old pagan and the new Christian thought, and the student will find some of the pros and cons in the texts collected below.

There was a severe persecution of Christians under the Emperors Decius and Valerian (A.D. 250–260), which closed with Gallienus' recognition of Christianity as a legal religion in the year 260–261 (Eusebius,

Eccl. Hist., VII, 13). From this time on there was little persecution for almost half a century, but final peace did not come to the Church until after the last great persecution, from A.D. 303 to 311, under Diocletian and Galerius, after which Christianity was never again seriously molested by the state. By the early fourth century Christians had become very numerous, and the historian Eusebius refers thus to the numbers enrolled in the ranks of Christendom on the eve of the Galerian persecution: "And how could one fully describe those assemblies thronged with countless men, and the multitudes that gathered together in every city, and the famed concourses in the places of prayer; by reason of which... [Christians] were no longer satisfied with the buildings of olden time, and would erect from the foundations churches of spacious dimensions throughout all the cities? And as these things went forward with the times, and day by day increasingly grew mightier, no envy could stop them, nor was any evil spirit able to cast its spell or hinder them by human devices, so long as the divine and heavenly hand was sheltering and guarding, as a worthy object, its own people" (Eusebius, *Ecclesiastical History*, VIII, 1, 5–6, trans. J. E. L. Oulton and H. J. Lawlor, Loeb Classical Library, II [1932], 253).

During the later years of the Galerian persecution in the East there was tension, and finally civil war, in the West. After deriving no advantage from eight years of persecution, Galerius acknowledged his failure, and issued his famous edict of toleration on 30 April, 311, the interesting text of which will be found below. Eighteen months after this the Emperor Constantine crushed his rival Maxentius in the battle of the Milvian Bridge, just outside the city of Rome, on 28 October, 312, and immediately thereafter the "conversion" of Constantine became apparent to all the world. The conversion of Constantine has been one of the more highly controversial problems in the history of the Church in the critical fourth century: it began the long and difficult history of the relation of the Christian Church to the Christian state. Not without reason, therefore, have some of the chief historians of the last two generations written scores of books and articles on this subject. But when we ask of these historians why Constantine became a Christian, they give us very different answers although they all derive these answers from the same sources! Some scholars have claimed that Constantine was chiefly motivated by political opportunism (thus Niebuhr and Burckhardt, Duruy and Bouché-Leclercq, Otto Seeck, Th. Brieger, and Ed. Schwartz). But what did Constantine stand to gain? Christians were more numerous in the East, but he was Emperor in the West. Christians had never been distinguished by their numbers and service in the army, but he had been made Emperor and maintained in his position by the army.

Other scholars have held that Constantine's conversion was sincere, whether the result of a devoted search for truth or merely of fear and a gross superstition (thus Maurice and Lot, Piganiol, Alföldi, and N. H. Baynes). Pagan contemporaries recognized that Constantine claimed divine assistance in his victory, and the Roman Senate inscribed these words on the triumphal Arch of Constantine, which still stands between the Roman Forum and the Colosseum: "To the Emperor Caesar Flavius Constantinus, the greatest, pious, fortunate Augustus, because by the inspiration of Divinity and by greatness of mind, he avenged with his forces the commonwealth with just arms both on the tyrant and on all his party, the Senate and the Roman people have dedicated this triumphal Arch." Less than a year after the battle of the Milvian Bridge a pagan orator thus addressed Constantine in the summer of 313: "Certainly you have some secret understanding, O Constantine, with that divine mind, which has delegated the care of us to lesser gods, and deigns to manifest itself to you alone" (from the ninth Imperial Panegyric, chap. 3). What was the nature of Constantine's "conversion"? What was his attitude towards the Christian Church? This is Problem 2. The student may seek answers in the sources given below, especially in Constantine's own official correspondence.

Until the year 313, when Christianity finally received official recognition for all time, Christian writers had pleaded for religious freedom and toleration, and had assailed persecuting Emperors as evil tyrants and violators of the very souls of men; with the triumph of their faith, however, Christians became persecutors in their turn, and in the later fourth and early fifth centuries the pagan cults and mysteries were largely destroyed. The final victory of Christianity may be studied in the religious edicts of the Theodosian Code (book XVI, title 10, laws 10–25): pagan rites and sacrifices were prohibited; the cults suppressed, and the privileges of their priests revoked; pagans were debarred from civil and military service; scorn was cast upon veneration of "images made by the work of mortals and destined to suffer the ravages of time"; provision was sometimes made for the destruction of temples— until finally there were laws enough to suppress "any pagans who survive although we now believe that there are none" (C. Th. XVI, 10, 22). The student may read this imperial legislation in favor of Christianity and on the destruction of paganism in the translation of the Code prepared under the supervision of Clyde Pharr, *The Theodosian Code*, Princeton University Press, 1952.

There were many diversities of thought and practice throughout the early Church, and a correct or orthodox understanding of the data of the faith as provided by the New Testament and the tradition of the Apostles was especially sought by the Church in Rome, where one of the earliest large Christian communities had been formed. When St. Paul wrote his Epistle to the Romans (A.D. 58 or a little later), the Church in Rome had been in existence, and he had been wanting to visit it, "for many years" (Rom. 15:24). The Church of Rome came to be of particular importance in the newly emerging Christendom, and whoever would seek to understand something of the triumph of Christianity must pay especial attention to the early history of this Church. The Bishop of Rome achieved a position of pre-eminence in western European society from the fourth century on. The fact that Rome had for generations been the capital of the Empire certainly enhanced the prestige of the Roman See. It was not, however, on this political accident that its Bishop was to base his claim to authority, but rather on the early tradition that the Church in Rome had been founded by St. Peter (and also by St. Paul): "Thou art Peter, and upon this rock [*petra*] I will build my Church . . . , and I will give thee the keys of the kingdom of heaven" [Matthew, 16:18–19]. The pope came to be regarded as the "heir of St. Peter," with all that the concept of inheritance implied in the Roman law.

Actually the Petrine foundation of the Church of Rome rests rather more on dogmatic than on historical fact. If St. Peter, however, wrote the First Epistle which has come down to us under his name, we appear to have at least evidence of his presence in Rome: "The Church which is at Babylon [i.e. Rome]...greets you...." (1 Peter, 5:13). Of Paul's presence in Rome we have the testimony of Acts, 28:11–30, which informs us of his residence in the city "for two full years...in his own hired lodging." (The first clear assertion, however, that the Church of Rome was thus of dual apostolic foundation comes in a letter of Bishop Dionysius of Corinth, about A.D. 170, quoted in Eusebius' *Ecclesiastical History,* II, 25, 8.) What was the nature, then, of authority within the Church of Rome during the first century of its existence? We come to the problem of the episcopacy in the early Roman Church, "that most tangled of all questions" (J. T. Shotwell and L. R. Loomis, *The See of Peter,* New York, 1927, p. 59). Some attention must be given to this tangled question, however, if we are to understand the background of the growth of papal power. The more important facts and sources are noted below, in the introduction to Problem 3, which is concerned with the establishment of papal supremacy over the Western Church.

Any office which St. Peter had held, if not his merits, could be inherited. Nevertheless, it cannot be shown explicitly from the New Testament that Christ intended St. Peter to have a successor, and that (if He did) the successor should be bishop or pope of Rome. But since Peter obviously had successors as bishop of Rome, and the Church continued from one generation to the next as the corporate body of those baptized as Christians, there had to be some authority to maintain both doctrine and discipline. If in Matt. 16:18–19 Christ implicitly provided for successors to Peter—"and upon this rock I will build my Church"—did Peter ever designate a successor to himself? Preceding the so-called *Clementine Homilies* is an interesting letter (of the early third century) which purports to have been written by St. Clement to St. James in Jerusalem, and which represents Peter as stating before the Christian community in Rome: "I impart to him [Clement] the authority of binding and loosing in order that whatever he [Clement] will decide upon earth, will be approved in heaven...."

What is surprising is not that we should have to wait so long for a text of such specificity, but that it should come so early, within five generations or so of Peter's death, i.e. within the lifetime of various members of the Church of Rome whose grandparents could have known Peter. Although the interpretation of this letter is more than a little complicated by the fact that Linus and Cletus are recorded in the early tradition as bishops of Rome between Peter and Clement I, it was often cited from the later fourth century as proof of the Roman bishops' succession to both the spiritual and jurisdictional powers of Peter (for the general background see Walter Ullmann, *Principles of Government and Politics in the Middle Ages* [New York, 1961], pp. 38–45).

Christian theology was itself like the corporate body of the Church, an organic and integrated whole. Neither the discernment of doctrinal truth nor the norms of ecclesiastical discipline could be left for pronouncement to the individual members of the Christian commonwealth. A special knowledge and a special relationship to the Church were necessary for the definition of dogma. Elaboration of the liturgy also required a well-trained clergy.

Despite persecution the Church of Rome grew enormously, always increasing in influence and in authority, during the first two centuries of its existence. At the close of the reign of the Emperor Decius (A.D. 251), a letter of Pope Cornelius tells us that, in the Church of Rome, "there are 46 presbyters, 7 deacons, 7 sub-deacons, 42 acolytes, 52 exorcists, readers and door-keepers, and more than 1,500 widows and persons in distress..." (quoted in Eusebius, *Eccl. Hist.*, VI, 43, 11). These figures have been interpreted as indicating that the Church of Rome must have had some 30,000 adherents by the middle of the third century. Almost one hundred years later we have striking evidence of the increased prestige of the Church of Rome when in the year 343 the western bishops, who had assembled at the Council of Sardica (the modern Sofia), agreed that if a bishop believed himself unjustly dealt with in an ecclesiastical trial conducted by his fellow bishops or superiors, he might appeal his case, for retrial, to the Bishop of Rome. This is the first general acknowledgment of the appellate jurisdiction of the Roman See.

Three quarters of a century later, in the year 417, the great Pope Innocent I wrote to a council of African bishops, who had just condemned the Pelagian heresy, commending the bishops' wisdom in appealing for support to the Roman See. The Fathers of the Church had rightly decreed, wrote the Pope, "that whatever is done, even in the most distant and remote provinces, must not be regarded as final unless it has come to the notice of this See, so that it may be confirmed as a just pronouncement by the full authority of this See, for in this way other churches may understand what to teach..." (*Ep.* XXIX). Finally, in 445 the Emperor Valentinian III not only acknowledged but himself helped to establish, by an imperial edict, the supremacy of the Roman papacy over the whole of western Christendom. Concerning the edict of Valentinian, B. J. Kidd has written: "The result of this enactment was...to rivet a papal autocracy on the Western Empire by the whole force of the Civil Law....It is the crowning proof that the papacy at Rome—as distinct from the primacy of the Apostolic See in Christendom—is the creation of the State" (*A History of the Church to A.D. 461*, III [1922], 358–59). But in remonstrance against this point of view, J. W. C. Wand has replied: "He would be blind to the facts of history who did not realize that in one respect at least this was a great gain. It was the prestige of the Papacy more than any other single factor which tamed the barbarian and preserved for future generations the best elements of the ancient civilisation in the West" (*A History of the Early Church to A.D. 500*, London, 1937, pp. 237–38). Here is Problem 3, the establishment of papal supremacy over the western Church; here it would be easy to cull pros and cons from the works of modern historians, but we are more interested in the evidence of the sources. Was the establishment of papal authority the gradual but deliberate recognition by western Christendom of what was believed to be the will of God or was it the result of historical accident and development?

I.   The Conflict of the Old Pagan and the New Christian Thought

The character of western civilization would be determined to no small extent by the Christians' acceptance or rejection of the cultural legacy of the pagan past. But it remained to be seen to what extent Christians would be influenced by Graeco-Roman rationalist philosophy, literary traditions, Greek canons of beauty in art and architecture, Roman law and government, and so on.

A. Christianity and the State

1.

Before we study some of the conflicting opinions entertained by Christian writers concerning the value, or lack thereof, of pagan culture, perhaps we ought first to seek at least some small knowledge of the attitude of cultivated pagans and of the imperial government towards Christianity. Our sources are very limited for the first century of Christian history. Perhaps the most illuminating text is the letter which the younger Pliny (Gaius Plinius Secundus), then governor of the Roman province of Bithynia (in Asia Minor), wrote to the Emperor Trajan in A.D. 112:

It is my solemn rule, Sire, to refer to you all matters about which I am doubtful, for who can better direct my indecision or instruct my ignorance? I have never been present at trials of Christians. Therefore I do not know either what to look for nor the extent of the punishment to be inflicted in such cases. ... In the meantime I have followed this method in dealing with those who have been denounced to me as Christians. I have asked them whether they were Christians. In the event of confession I have repeated the question a second and even a third time, threatening with death those who persisted; and if they still persisted [in professing Christianity], I ordered them to be executed. For I had no doubt at all that, whatever this thing might be which they were confessing, such contumacy and unbending obstinacy should certainly be punished. There were others of like madness whom I ordered to be sent to Rome, because they were Roman citizens [just

as St. Paul had "appealed to Caesar" before the Roman governor Festus in Acts, 25: 6–12].

Soon, by the very fact of investigation, as usually happens, several more cases were brought to light. An anonymous accusation was placed before us: it contained many names of alleged Christians. I thought it best to discharge those who denied that they were or had ever been Christians when they repeated after me an invocation to the gods, and made supplication with incense and wine to your image, which I had ordered to be produced for this purpose, together with the statues of the gods, besides which they cursed Christ, and none of these things, it is said, can those who are really Christians be forced to do. Some persons named by the informer admitted they were Christians, and then denied it; other said they had been, but had withdrawn from the sect, some three years ago, some many years ago, and at least one twenty-five years ago! They all worshipped both your image and the statues of the gods, and they reviled Christ.

They maintained, however, that this had been the sum total of their mistake or guilt, that they had been accustomed on a set day to come together before dawn and, all together, to sing a hymn to Christ as to a god, and that they bound themselves by an oath, not for the purpose of some crime, but not to commit theft, robbery, or adultery, nor to betray a trust, nor to deny a deposit when called upon to return it to its owner. But when such rites as these were over, they said it was their custom to depart, and to come together later on to take food, but ordinary and harmless food [early Christians were sometimes accused of cannibalism!], but even this practice they had given up after my edict by which in accordance with your instructions I had forbidden secret associations. Hence I believed it the more necessary to find out the truth, and by torture, from two women slaves, who were called "deaconesses." *But I found nothing else than a depraved, immoderate superstition* [the Roman gentleman's dictum on Christianity!].

Therefore I have delayed the investigation, and I have come to you for advice. The matter has seemed to me well worth your consideration, especially on account of the number of those imperilled. . . .

[To this the Emperor Trajan replied:]

You have followed the method you should, my dear Secundus, in looking into the cases of those denounced to you as Christians. It is impossible to set up a rule of universal application which may result in a fixed form of action in such cases. Christians are not to be sought out;

if they are informed against and found guilty, however, they must be punished; but with this provision, that a person who has denied he is a Christian, and has made the fact manifest in the proper way, i.e. by making supplication to our gods, even though he may have been suspect in the past, is to receive pardon for repentance. Accusations made anonymously ought not to receive attention on any charge; for this sets the worst kind of precedent, and is not in keeping with the character of our reign.

Pliny, *Letters*, X, 96–97, trans. K. M. Setton.

2.

The search for rules of universal application was, however, the animating principle of the Roman law. Trajan's position was untenable. Less than a century after this, the early church father Tertullian (fl. A.D. 200) easily put his finger upon the flaw in the judicial procedure which Trajan had prescribed against Christians:

When Plinius Secundus was governing his province and had condemned some Christians and driven others from their steadfastness, and still the sheer numbers concerned worried him as to what he ought to do thereafter, he consulted the Emperor Trajan. He asserted that, apart from an obstinacy that refused to sacrifice, he had learnt nothing about the Christian mysteries—nothing beyond meetings before dawn to sing to Christ and to God [*sic*], and to band themselves together in discipline, forbidding murder, adultery, dishonesty, treachery, and the other crimes. Trajan replied in a rescript that men of this kind were not to be sought out, but if they were brought before Pliny they must be punished. What a decision!

how inevitably entangled! He says they must not be sought out, implying they are innocent; and he orders them to be punished, implying they are guilty. He spares them and rages against them; he pretends not to see and punishes. Why cheat yourself with your judgment? If you condemn them, why not hunt them down? If you do not hunt them down, why not also acquit them? . . .

. . . You do not deal with us in accordance with your procedure in judging criminals. If the other criminals plead Not guilty, you torture them to make them confess; the Christians alone you torture to make them deny. Yet if it were something evil, we should deny our guilt, and you would use torture to force us to confess it. . . .

A man shouts, "I am a Christian." He says what he is. You, sir, wish to hear what he is *not*. Presiding to extort the truth, you take infinite pains in our case, and ours alone, to hear a lie. . . . Clearly, when others deny, you do not readily believe them; if we have denied, you at once believe us. . . .

Tertullian, *Apology*, 2, trans. T. R. Glover, Loeb Classical Library [Cambridge, Mass.: Harvard University Press, 1931], pp. 11 ff.

B. *What Has Athens to do with Jerusalem?*

Tertullian's main point is well taken despite his special pleading. Before the conversion of Constantine the relations of Church and state were rather simple: the Church was a voluntary association of intractable people to whom it was sound policy for the state to be hostile. Under persecution Christians tended to withdraw from society which was, of course, very largely pagan, but there were necessarily serious limits to this withdrawal. Education was as important to the Christian community as to pagan society at large. Ancient education was for the most part literary and philosophical; the schools of the Roman Empire were the products of centuries of pagan culture. Almost all the Fathers who oppose the Greek (and Latin) classics and philosophy do so on the grounds of their error and lack of truth, their immorality and frivolity. Those who defend them do so on the grounds of their utility as an intellectual and moral preparation for the study of Holy Scripture. The classics are not defended on the grounds of their beauty as literature.

Justin Martyr, in the middle of the second century, was a philosopher, having been a Stoic, an Aristotelian, a Pythagorean, and a Platonist in turn; converted to Christianity, he became an ardent defender of the new religion, but he remained a philosopher to the day he finally died for the faith he had adopted. On the other hand Tertullian had been a lawyer, and was very well read, but he saw no usefulness in pagan letters and in philosophy, which the Christian experience had shown, in his opinion, to be merely the seedbed of heresy. To Clement (fl. A.D. 200), head of the catechetical school of Alexandria, pagan philosophy had been necessary for the larger truths of Christianity:

Before the advent of the Lord, philosophy was necessary to the Greeks for righteousness, and now it becomes conducive to piety, being a kind of preparatory training to those who attain to faith through understanding. God is the cause of all good things; but of some primarily, as of the Old and the New Testaments; and of others by consequence, as philosophy. Perhaps, too, philosophy was given to the Greeks directly and primarily until the Lord should call them. Philosophy was thus a preparation, paving the way for him who is perfected in Christ. The way of truth is therefore one, but into it, as into a perennial river, streams flow from all sides. As all the branches of study contribute to philosophy, which is their mistress, so also philosophy itself co-operates in the acquisition of wisdom. Philosophy is the study of wisdom, and wisdom is the knowledge of things divine and human, and of their cause also. Philosophy is characterized by investigation into truth and the nature of things—this is the truth of which the Lord Himself said, "I am the truth" [John 14: 6]. But as we say that a man can be a believer without learning, so also we assert that it is impossible for a man without learning to comprehend the things which are declared in the faith. But to adopt what is well said, and not to adopt the reverse, is caused not simply by faith, but by faith combined with knowledge.

Adapted from Clement, *Stromateis* or *Miscellanies*, I, 5, 6.

This was the chief Christian argument in defense of pagan learning. Pagan literature was to receive its classic defense at the hands of St. Basil of Caesarea in his essay *To Young Men, On Pagan Literature,* of which a few passages are given below. Although St. Augustine, in the *City of God,* "attempts with more than ordinary diligence to tear up and eradicate depraved and ancient opinions hostile to the truth of piety, which the long-continued error of the human race has fixed deeply in unenlightened minds" (from preface to bk. VII), he nevertheless shares St. Basil's view as to the general utility of pagan thought, and expresses a high respect for Plato and his successors.

But there were other prominent fathers of the Church, such as Epiphanius of Salamis (in eastern Cyprus), and Lucifer of Cagliari (in Sardinia), who were consistently hostile to the pagan classics and to pagan thought, and St. Gregory of Nazianzus and St. John Chrysostom give frequent expression to an unfriendly attitude toward pagan philosophy and letters. Sometimes Chrysostom is moved to a violent denunciation of the gross superstitions and immoralities of pagan religious legends and literature, as in his fifth *Homily on Titus* (in the *Nicene and Post-Nicene Fathers,* XIII, 535 ff). Nevertheless, Chrysostom wrote with a conscious artistry which reveals no inconsiderable study of the classical models. The fathers long debated and never solved the problem of whether, in general, to read or not to read the pagan classics and philosophy, but many of them were fascinated by the apparent pagan anticipation of some of the truths of Christian doctrine. It was as St. Paul himself had said, as he spoke to the Athenians from the hill of Areopagus: "For in Him we live and move and have our being, as indeed some of your own poets have said!" (Acts 17, 28).

1. "SEE THAT NO ONE BEGUILE YOU THROUGH PHILOSOPHY..."

Here is a denial by Tertullian of the value of pagan philosophy to the Christian. On the involved and ill-understood philosophical "system of Valentinus," with its concept of the *enthymesis*, to which Tertullian alludes, the student may consult the brilliant chapter of F. C. Burkitt, "Pagan Philosophy and the Christian Church," in the *Cambridge Ancient History*, XII (1939), 469–73.

For it is philosophy which is the material of the world's wisdom, the rash interpreter of the nature and the dispensation of God. Indeed heresies are themselves instigated by philosophy. From this source came the Aeons, and I know not what infinite forms, and the trinity of man in the system of Valentinus, who was of Plato's school. From the same source came Marcion's better god, with all his tranquillity: he came of the Stoics. Then, again, the opinion that the soul dies is held by the Epicureans; while the denial of the restoration of the body is taken from the aggregate school of all the philosophers; also, when matter is made equal to God, then you have the teaching of Zeno; and when any doctrine is alleged touching a god of fire, then Heraclitus comes in. The same subject-matter is discussed over and over again by the heretics and the philosophers. The same arguments are involved. Whence comes evil? Why is it permitted? What is the origin of man? and in what way does he come? Besides the question which Valentinus has very lately proposed—

Whence comes God? Which he settles with the answer: from *enthymesis* ["conception"] and *ektroma* ["abortion"]! Unhappy Aristotle! who invented for these men dialectics, the art of building up and pulling down, an art so evasive in its propositions, so farfetched in its conjectures, so harsh in its arguments, so productive of contentions—embarrassing even to itself, retracting everything, and really treating of nothing! Whence spring those "fables and endless genealogies" [1 Tim. 1, 4], and the "unprofitable questions" [cf. Tit. 3, 9], and "words which spread like a cancer" [2 Tim. 2, 17]?

From all these, when the apostle would restrain us, he expressly names *philosophy* as that which he would have us be on our guard against. Writing to the Colossians, he says, "See that no one beguile you through philosophy and vain deceit, after the tradition of men, and contrary to the wisdom of the Holy Ghost" [Col. 2, 8]. He had been at Athens, and had in his interviews (with the philosophers) become acquainted with that human wisdom which pretends to know the truth, while it only corrupts it, and is itself divided into its own manifold heresies, by the variety of its mutually repugnant sects.

What indeed has Athens to do with Jerusalem? What concord is there between the Academy and the Church? what between heretics and Christians?

Our instruction comes from the "porch of Solomon," who had himself taught that "the Lord should be sought in simplicity of heart" [Book of Wisdom, 1, 1]. Away with all attempts to produce a mottled Christianity of Stoic, Platonic, and dialectic composition! We want no curious disputation after possessing Christ Jesus, no inquisition after enjoying the gospel! With our faith, we desire no further belief. For this is our first belief, that there is nothing which we ought to believe besides.

Tertullian, *On the Prescription of Heretics*, 7, adapted from the translation of Peter Holmes, *Ante-Nicene Fathers*, III, 246.

2. ST. JOHN CHRYSOSTOM ON THE SUPERIORITY OF THP CHRISTIAN RUSTIC OVER THE PAGAN PHILOSOPHER

In the following sermon, one of the twenty-one *Homilies on the Statues*, preached during Lent in 387, St. John Chrysostom asserts that the simple country folk who have come into the city of Antioch to attend a religious festival are of higher virtue and display a greater wisdom than the pagan philosophers.

These [country folk] are our philosophers, and theirs the best philosophy, exhibiting their virtue not by their outward appearance, but by their mind. The pagan philosophers are in character no wise better than those who are engaged on the stage, and in the sports of actors; and they have nothing to show beyond the threadbare cloak, the beard, and the long robe! But these, quite on the contrary, bidding farewell to staff and beard, and the other accoutrements, have their souls adorned with the doctrines of the true philosophy, and not only with the doctrines, but also with the real practice. And were you to question any one of these, who live a rustic life at the spade and plough, as to the dogmas respecting which the pagan philosophers have discoursed an infinite deal, and have expended a multitude of words, without being able to say anything sound, one of these would give you an accurate reply from his store of wisdom. And not only is this to be wondered at, but they confirm the credibility of these doctrines by their actions. For of the fact that we have an immortal soul, and that we shall hereafter render an account of what we have done here, and stand before a fearful Tribunal, their minds are at once thoroughly persuaded, and they have also regulated their whole course of life by such hopes as these; and have become superior to all worldly show, instructed as they have been by the sacred Scriptures, that "all is vanity, yea, vanity of vanities," and they do not greedily long for any of those things which seem to be so splendid. These too know how to philosophize concerning God, even as God hath deter-

mined; and if, taking one of them, you were now to bring forward some pagan philosopher... , and then open the books of the ancient philosophers, and go through them, and institute an enquiry by way of parallel as to what these now answer, and the others in their day philosophically advanced, you would see how much wisdom belonged to the former, and how much folly to the philosophers. For while some of these would aver that the things existing were destitute of a providence, and that the creation did not have its origin from God; that virtue was not sufficient for itself, but stood in need of wealth, and nobility, and external splendor, and other things still more ridiculous; and while these [simple Christians], on the other hand, would discourse wisely respecting Providence, respecting the future Tribunals of judgment, respecting the creative power of God, bringing forth all things out of nothing, as well as respecting all other points, although at the same time they were entirely destitute of worldly schooling; who could but learn from hence the power of Christ, which hath proved these unlearned and simple persons to be as much wiser than those, who make so much boast of their wisdom, as men of discretion are seen to be in comparison to little children? For what harm can result to them from their simplicity in regard to learning, when their thoughts are full of much wisdom?

And what advantage have those philosophers from this learning, when the understanding is devoid of right thoughts? It were just as if one should have a sword that had its hilt of silver, whilst the blade was weaker than the vilest lead. For truly these philosophers have their tongue decked out with words and names, but their understanding is full of mere weakness and good for nothing. Not so with our "philosophers," but quite the reverse. Their understanding is full of spiritual wisdom and their mode of life is a transcript of their doctrines. Amongst these there are no luxurious women; there are no ornaments of dress, nor colors, nor paints; but all such corruption of manners is discountenanced. Hence the population under their charge are the more readily trained to sobriety, and the law which Paul gave, when he directed that food and covering should be had, and nothing more be sought after, they most rigidly observe. Amongst them, there are no perfumed unguents to fascinate the senses; but the earth bringing forth herbs prepares for them a varied fragrance of flowers, above all the skill of perfumers. For this reason, their bodies as well as souls enjoy a sound state of health, inasmuch as they have banished all luxury of diet, and driven off all the evil floods of drunkenness; and they eat just as much as suffices for subsistence. Let us then not despise them because of their outward appearance, but let us admire their minds. For of what advantage is the external habit, when the soul is more wretchedly clad than any beggar! The man ought to be praised and admired, not for dress, nay more, not even for his bodily form, but for his soul. Lay bare the soul of these men, and you will see its beauty, and the wealth it possesses, in their words, in their doctrines, and in the whole system of their manners!

Let the Gentiles then be ashamed, let them hide their heads, and slink away on account of their philosophers, and their wisdom, wretched as it is beyond all folly! For the philosophers that have been amongst them in their lifetime have hardly been able to teach their doctrines to a very few, who can easily be numbered; and when any trifling peril overtook them, they lost even these. But the disciples of Christ, the fishermen, the publicans, and the tentmakers, in a few years brought over the whole world to the truth; and when from that time, ten thousand perils have been constantly arising, the preaching of the Gospel was so far from being put down, that it still flourishes and increases; and they taught simple people, tillers of the ground, and occupied with cattle, to be lovers of wisdom. Such are the persons, who besides all the rest, having deeply rooted in them that love which is the source of all good things, have hastened to us, undertaking so long a journey, that they might come and embrace their fellow members.

St. John Chrysostom (d. 407), *Homily XIX on the Statues,* 3–5, adapted from the translation in the *Nicene and Post-Nicene Fathers,* IX, 465–66.

3. JUSTIN MARTYR ON THE DIVINE INSPIRATION OF THE PAGAN PHILOSOPHERS

While Justin Martyr deplores the error, immorality, and frivolity of some of the pagan classics, he emphasizes, in the famous doctrine of the "spermatic Logos," that all truth is derived from the same divine source, and might be expressed by Socrates as well as by Plato. Christ was the Logos (or "Word"), the creative reason of God, which had sown the seed, hence "spermatic," of understanding in the pre-Christian philosophers as well as in the Christian teachers of Justin's own day. The pre-Christian philosophers were clearly worth reading:

Beyond doubt, therefore, our teachings are more noble than all human teaching, because Christ, who appeared on earth for our sakes, became the whole Logos, namely, Logos and body and soul. Everything that the philosophers and legislators discovered and expressed well, they accomplished through their discovery and contemplation of some part of the Logos. But, since they did not have a full knowledge of the Logos, which is Christ, they often contradicted themselves. And those who were born before Christ assumed human nature were dragged into law courts as irreligious and meddling persons, when they tried in human narrowness to think out and prove things by reason. Socrates, the most ardent of all in this regard, was accused of the very crimes that are imputed to us. They claimed that he introduced new deities and rejected the state-sponsored gods. But what he did was to ostracize Homer and the other poets, and to instruct men to expel the evil demons and those who perpetrated the deeds narrated by the poets; and to exhort men by meditation to learn more about God who was unknown to them, saying: "It is not an easy matter to find the Father and Creator of all things, nor, when He is found, is it safe to announce Him to all men." Yet our Christ did all this through His own power. There was no one who believed so much in Socrates as to die for his teaching, but not only philosophers and scholars believed in Christ, of whom even Socrates had a vague knowledge (for He was and is the Logos who is in every person, and who predicted things to come first through the prophets and then in person when He assumed our human nature and feelings, and taught us these doctrines), but also workmen and men wholly uneducated, who all scorned glory, and fear, and death. Indeed, this is brought about by the power of the ineffable Father, and not through the instrumentality of human reason. . . .

When I learned of the evil camouflage which the wicked demons had thrown around the divine doctrines of the Christians to deter others from following them, I had to laugh at the authors of these lies, at the camouflage itself, and at the popular reaction. I am proud to say that I strove with all my might to be known as a Christian, not because the teachings of Plato are different from those of Christ, but because they are not in every way similar; neither are those of other writers, the Stoics, the poets, and the historians. For each one of them, seeing, through his participation of the seminal Divine Word, what was related to it, spoke very well. But they who contradict themselves in important matters evidently did not acquire the unseen [that is, heavenly] wisdom and the indisputable knowledge. The truths which men in all lands have rightly spoken belong to us Christians. For we worship and love, after God the Father, the Word who is from the Unbegotten and Ineffable God, since He even became Man for us, so that by sharing in our sufferings He also might heal us. Indeed, all writers, by means of the engrafted seed of the Word which was implanted in them, had a dim glimpse of the truth. For the seed of something and its imitation, given in proportion to one's capacity, is one thing, but the thing itself, which is shared and imitated according to His grace, is quite another.

Justin Martyr (fl. A.D. 150), *Second Apology*, 10, 13, trans. Thomas B. Falls, *Saint Justin Martyr* (New York: Fathers of the Church, Inc., 1948), pp. 129–30, 133–34.

4. ST. BASIL THE GREAT'S DEFENSE OF CLASSICAL GREEK LITERATURE

First, then, as to the learning to be derived from the poets, that I may begin with them, inasmuch as the subjects they deal with are of every kind, you ought not to give your attention to all they write without exception; but whenever they recount for you the deeds or words of good men, you ought to cherish and emulate these and try to be, as far as possible, like them; but when they treat of wicked men, you ought to avoid such imitation, stopping your ears no less than Odysseus did, according to what those same poets say, when he avoided the songs of the Sirens [cf. Homer, *Odyssey*, XII, 37 ff.]. For familiarity with evil words is, as it were, a road leading to evil deeds. On this account, then, the soul must be watched over with all vigilance, lest through the pleasure the poets' words give we may unwittingly accept something of the more evil sort, like those who take poisons along with honey.

We shall not, therefore, praise the poets when they revile or mock, or when they depict men engaged in amours or drunken, or when they define happiness in terms of an over-abundant table or dissolute songs. But least of all shall we give attention to them when they narrate anything about the gods, and especially when they speak of them as being many, and these too not even in accord with one another. For in their poems brother is at feud with brother, and father with children, and the latter in turn are engaged in truceless war with their parents. But the adulteries of gods and their amours and their sexual acts in public, and especially those of Zeus, the chief and highest of all, as they themselves describe him, actions which one would blush to mention of even brute beasts—all these we shall leave to the stage-folk.

These same observations I must make concerning the writers of prose also, and especially when they fabricate tales for the entertainment of their hearers. And we shall certainly not imitate the orators in their art of lying. For neither in courts of law nor in other affairs is lying befitting to us, who have chosen the right and true way of life, and to whom refraining from litigation has been ordained in commandment. But we shall take rather those passages of theirs in which they have praised virtue or condemned vice.... And just as in plucking the blooms from a rose-bed we avoid the thorns, so also in garnering from such writings whatever is useful, let us guard ourselves against what is harmful....

And since it is through virtue that we must enter upon this life of ours, and since much has been uttered in praise of virtue by poets, much by historians, and much more still by philosophers, we ought especially to apply ourselves to such literature. For it is no small advantage that a certain intimacy and familiarity with virtue should be engendered in the souls of the young, seeing that the lessons learned by such are likely, in the nature of the case, to be indelible, having been deeply impressed on them by reason of the tenderness of their souls. Or what else are we to suppose Hesiod had in mind when he composed these verses which are on everybody's lips, if he were not exhorting young men to virtue?—that "rough at first and hard to travel, and full of abundant sweat and toil, is the road which leads to virtue, and steep withal." There-

fore it is not given to everyone to climb this road, so steep it is, nor, if one essays to climb it, easily to reach the summit. But when once one has come to the top he is able to see how smooth and beautiful, how easy and pleasant to travel it is, and more agreeable than that other road which leads to vice, which it is possible to take all at once from near at hand, as this same poet has said. For to me it seems that he has narrated these things for no other reason that to urge us on to virtue and to exhort all men to be good, and to keep us from becoming weak and cowardly in the face of the toils and desisting before reaching the end. And assuredly, if anyone else has sung the praise of virtue in terms like Hesiod's, let us welcome his words as leading to the same end as our own. Moreover, as I myself have heard a man say who is clever at understanding a poet's mind, all Homer's poetry is an encomium of virtue, and all he wrote, save what is accessory, bears to this end....

It was for this reason indeed, as it seems to me, that Solon said this with respect to the rich: "But we will not exchange with them our virtue for their wealth, since the one abides always, while riches change their owners every day." And similar to these words are those of Theognis also in which he says that God, whomsoever he means indeed by this term, inclines the scale for men at one time this way, at another that way, now to be rich, but now to have nothing.

And furthermore, the sophist from Ceos, Prodicus, somewhere in his writings uttered a doctrine kindred to these others regarding virtue and vice; therefore we must apply our minds to him also, for he is not a man to be rejected. His narrative runs something like this, so far as I recall the man's thought, since I do not know the exact words, but only that he spoke in general to the following effect, not employing metre. When Heracles was quite a young man and was nearly of the age at which you yourselves are now, while he was deliberating which of the two roads he should take, the one leading through toils to virtue, or the easiest, two women approached him, and these were Virtue and Vice. Now at once, although they were silent, the difference between them was evident from their appearance. For the one had been decked out for beauty through the art of toiletry, and was over-flowing with voluptuousness, and she was leading a whole swarm of pleasures in her train; now these things she displayed, and promising still more than these she tried to draw Heracles to her. But the other was withered and squalid, and had an intense look, and spoke quite differently; for she promised nothing dissolute or pleasant, but countless sweating toils and labours and dangers through every land and sea. But the prize to be won by these was to become a god, as the narrative of Prodicus expressed it; and it was this second woman that Heracles in the end followed.

And almost all the writers who have some reputation for wisdom have, to a greater or less degree, each to the best of his power, discoursed in their works in praise of virtue. To these men we must hearken and we must try to show forth their words in our lives; for he in truth who confirms by act his devotion to wis-dom, which among others is confined to words, "He alone has understanding, but the others flit about as shadows. . . ."

As to the passages in literature, then, which contain admonitions of excellent things, let us accept this procedure. And since the virtuous deeds, likewise, of the men of old have been preserved for us, either through an unbroken oral tradition or through being preserved in the words of poets or writers of prose, let us not fail to derive advantage from this source also. For example, a certain fellow, a market-lounger, kept railing at Pericles, but he paid no attention; he kept it up all day long, giving Pericles a merciless dressing of abuse, but the latter took no heed of it. Then, when it was already evening and dark, though the man was scarcely desist-ing, Pericles escorted him home with a light, lest his own schooling in philosophy be utterly brought to naught.

Again, a certain man, having become enraged against Eucleides of Megara,

threatened him with death and took oath upon it; but Eucleides took a counter-oath, to the effect that verily he would appease the man and make him put aside his wrath against him. How very valuable it is that an example of this kind should be recalled to memory by a man who is on the point of being held in the grip of a fit of passion! For one must not put a simple-minded trust in the tragedy when it says "Against enemies anger arms the hand," but, on the contrary, we should not permit ourselves to be aroused to anger at all; but if this is not easy to achieve, we should at least apply reason to our anger as a sort of curb and not allow it to be carried too far beyond the bounds.

But let us bring our discussion back again to the examples of virtuous deeds. A certain man kept striking Socrates, son of Sophroniscus, full in the face, falling upon him unmercifully; yet he did not oppose, but permitted the wine-mad fellow to satiate his rage, so that his face was presently swollen and bruised from the blows. Now when the man ceased striking him, Socrates, it is said, did nothing ex-cept inscribe on his own forehead, like the name of the sculptor on a statue, "So-and-so (naming the man) made this," and only to that extent avenged himself. Since these examples tend to nearly the same end as our own precepts, I maintain that it is of great value for those of your age to imitate them. For this example of Socrates is akin to that precept of ours—that to him who strikes us on the cheek, so far from aveng-ing ourselves upon him, we should offer the other cheek also. And the example of Pericles or Eucleides is akin to the precept that we should submit to those who perse-cute us and gently suffer their anger; and this other one—that we should pray for blessings for our enemies instead of curs-ing them. For whoever has been instructed in these examples beforehand cannot after that distrust those precepts as utterly im-possible to obey. I should not pass over the example of Alexander, who, when he had taken prisoner the daughters of Darius, although it had been testified to him that they possessed a marvellous beauty, did not think it fitting even to look upon them, judging it to be disgraceful for one who had captured men to be vanquished by women. Indeed, this example tends to the same purport as that well-known precept of ours—that he who looks upon a woman to enjoy her, although he does not commit adultery in act, yet in truth, because he has received the desire into his soul, is not free of guilt. . . .

But, in a single word, the body in every part should be despised by everyone who does not care to be buried in its pleasures, as it were in slime; or we ought to cleave to it only in so far as we obtain from it service for the pursuit of wisdom, as Plato advises, speaking in a manner somewhat similar to Paul's when he admonishes us to make no provision for the body unto the arousing of concupiscences [cf. Rom. 13, 14]. Or in what way do those differ, who are solicitous how the body may be as well off as possible, but overlook the soul, which is to make use of it, as utterly worthless, from those who are much concerned about their implements but neglect the art which uses them for its work? Hence we must do quite the opposite—chastise the body and hold it in check, as we do the violent chargings of a wild beast, and by smiting with reason, as with a whip, the disturbances engendered by it in the soul, calm them to sleep; instead of relaxing every curb upon pleasure and suffering the mind to be swept headlong, like a charioteer by unmanageable horses riotously running at large. . . .

But although we Christians shall doubtless learn all these things more thoroughly in our own literature, yet for the present, at least, let us trace out a kind of rough sketch, as it were, of what virtue is according to the teaching of the pagans. For by those who make it their business to gather the benefit to be derived from each source many accretions from many sides are wont to be received, as happens to mighty rivers.

St. Basil of Caesarea (d. 379), *To Young Men, On Pagan Literature*, 4–7, 9–10, trans. R. J. Deferrari and M. R. P. McGuire, *The Letters of St. Basil*, Loeb Classical Library (Cambridge, Mass.: Harvard University Press, 1934), IV, 387 ff.

5. ST. AUGUSTINE ON THE SUPERIORITY OF CHRISTIAN THEOLOGY OVER PAGAN PHILOSOPHY

1. We shall require to apply our mind with far greater intensity to the present question than was requisite in the solution and unfolding of the questions handled in the preceding books [of the *City of God*]; for it is not with ordinary men, but with philosophers that we must confer concerning the theology which they call natural. For it is not like the fabulous, that is, the theatrical; nor the civil, that is, the urban, theology: the one of which displays the crimes of the gods, whilst the other manifests their criminal desires, which demonstrates them to be rather malign demons than gods. It is, we say, with philosophers we have to confer with respect to this theology,—men whose very name, if rendered into Latin, signifies those who profess the love of wisdom.

Now, if wisdom is God, who made all things, as is attested by the divine authority and truth, then the philosopher is a lover of God. But since the thing itself, which is called by this name, exists not in all who glory in the name,—for it does not follow, of course, that all who are called philosophers are lovers of true wisdom,—we must needs select from the number of those with whose opinions we have been able to acquaint ourselves by reading, some with whom we may not unworthily engage in the treatment of this question. For I have not in this work undertaken to refute all the vain opinions of the philosophers, but only such as pertain to theology, which Greek word we understand to mean an account or explanation of the divine nature. Nor, again, have I undertaken to refute all the vain theological opinions of all the philosophers, but only of such of them as, agreeing in the belief that there is a divine nature, and that this divine nature is concerned about human affairs, do nevertheless deny that the worship of the one unchangeable God is sufficient for the obtaining of a blessed life after death, as well as at the present time; and hold that, in order to obtain that life, many gods, created, indeed, and appointed to their several spheres by that one God, are to be worshipped.

2. As far as concerns the literature of the Greeks, whose language holds a more illustrious place than any of the languages of the other nations, history mentions two schools of philosophers, the one called the Italic school, originating in that part of Italy which was formerly called Magna Graecia; the other called the Ionic school, having its origin in those regions which are still called by the name of Greece. The Italic school had for its founder Pythagoras of Samos, to whom also the term "philosophy" is said to owe its origin. For whereas formerly those who seemed to excel others by the laudable manner in which they regulated their lives were called sages, Pythagoras, on being asked what he professed, replied that he was a philosopher, that is, a student or lover of wisdom; for it seemed to him to be the height of arrogance to profess oneself a sage.

The founder of the Ionic school, again, was Thales of Miletus, one of those seven who were styled the "seven sages," of whom six were distinguished by the kind of life they lived, and by certain maxims which they gave forth for the proper conduct of life. Thales was distinguished as an investigator into the nature of things; and, in order that he might have successors in his school, he committed his dissertations to writing. That, however, which especially rendered him eminent was his ability, by means of astronomical calculations, even to predict eclipses of the sun and moon. He thought, however, that water was the first element of things, and that of it, all the elements of the world, the world itself, and all things which are generated in it, ultimately consist. Over all this work, however, which, when we consider the world, appears so admirable, he set nothing of the nature of divine mind. To him succeeded Anaximander, his pupil, who held a different opinion concerning the nature of things; for he did not hold that all things spring from one principle, as Thales did, who held that principle to be water, but thought that each thing springs from its own proper principle. These principles of things he believed to be infinite in number, and thought that they generated innumerable worlds, and all the things which arise in them. He thought, also, that these worlds are subject to a perpetual process of alternate dissolution and regeneration, each one continuing for a longer or shorter period of time, according to the nature of the case; nor did he, any more than Thales, attribute anything to a divine mind in the production of all this activity of things.

Anaximander left as his successor his disciple Anaximenes, who attributed all the causes of things to an infinite air. He neither denied nor ignored the existence of gods, but, so far from believing that the air was made by them, he held, on the contrary, that they sprang from the air. Anaxagoras, however, who was his pupil, perceived that a divine mind was the productive cause of all the things which we see, and said that all the various kinds of things, according to their several modes and species, were produced out of an infinite matter consisting of homogeneous particles, but by the efficiency of a divine mind. Diogenes, also, another pupil of Anaximenes, said that a certain air was the original substance of things out of which all things were produced, but that it was possessed of a divine reason without which nothing could he produced from it.

Anaxagoras was succeeded by his disciple Archelaus, who also thought that all things consisted of homogeneous particles, of which each particular thing was made, but that those particles were pervaded by a divine mind, which perpetually energized all the eternal bodies, namely, those particles, so that they are alternately united and separated. Socrates, the master of Plato, is said to have been the disciple of

Archelaus; and on Plato's account it is that I have given this brief historical sketch of the whole history of these schools.

3. Socrates is said to have been the first who directed the entire effort of philosophy to the correction and regulation of manners, all who went before him having expended their greatest efforts in the investigation of physical, that is, natural phenomena. However, it seems to me that it cannot be certainly discovered whether Socrates did this because he was wearied of obscure and uncertain things, and so wished to direct his mind to the discovery of something manifest and certain, which was necessary in order thus to obtain a blessed life,—that one great object toward which the labor, vigilance, and industry of all philosophers seem to have been directed,—or whether (as some yet more favorable to him suppose) he did it because he was unwilling that minds defiled with earthly desires should essay to raise themselves upward to divine things. For he saw that the causes of things were sought for by them,—which causes he believed to be ultimately reducible to nothing else than the will of the one true and supreme God,—and on this account he thought they could only be comprehended by a purified mind; and therefore that all diligence ought to be given to the purification of the life by good morals, in order that the mind, delivered from the depressing weight of lusts, might raise itself upward by its native vigor to eternal things, and might, with purified understanding, contemplate that nature which is incorporeal and unchangeable light, where live the causes of all created natures.

It is evident, however, that he hunted out and pursued, with a wonderful pleasantness of style and argument, and with a most pointed and insinuating urbanity, the foolishness of ignorant men, who thought that they knew this or that,—sometimes confessing his own ignorance, and sometimes dissimulating his knowledge, even in those very moral questions to which he seems to have directed the whole force of his mind. And hence there arose hostility against him, which ended in his being calumniously impeached, and condemned to death. Afterwards, however, that very city of the Athenians, which had publicly condemned him, did publicly bewail him, —the popular indignation having turned with such vehemence on his accusers, that one of them perished by the violence of the multitude, whilst the other only escaped a like punishment by voluntary and perpetual exile.

Illustrious, therefore, both in his life and in his death, Socrates left very many disciples of his philosophy, who vied with one another in desire for proficiency in handling those moral questions which concern the chief good [*summum bonum*]....

4. But, among the disciples of Socrates, Plato was the one who shone with a glory which far excelled that of the others, and who not unjustly eclipsed them all. By birth an Athenian of honorable parentage, he far surpassed his fellow-disciples in natural endowments, of which he was possessed in a wonderful degree.... For, as Plato liked and constantly affected the well-known method of his master Socrates, namely, that of dissimulating his knowledge or his opinions, it is not easy to discover clearly what he himself thought on various matters, any more than it is to discover what were the real opinions of Socrates.

We must, nevertheless, insert into our work certain of those opinions which he expresses in his writings, whether he himself uttered them, or narrates them as expressed by others, and seems himself to approve of,—opinions sometimes favorable to the true religion, which our faith takes up and defends, and sometimes contrary to it, as, for example, in the questions concerning the existence of one God or of many, as it relates to the truly blessed life which is to be after death. For those who are praised as having most closely followed Plato, who is justly preferred to all the other philosophers of the Gentiles, and who are said to have manifested the greatest acuteness in understanding him, do perhaps entertain such an idea of God as to admit that in Him are to be found the cause of existence, the ultimate reason for the understanding, and the end in reference to which the whole life is to be regulated. Of which three things, the first is understood to pertain to the natural, the second to the rational, and the third to the moral part of philosophy. For if man has been so created as to attain, through that which is most excellent in him, to that which excels all things,—that is, to the one true and absolutely good God, without whom no nature exists, no doctrine instructs, no exercise profits,—let Him be sought in whom all things are secure to us, let Him be discovered in whom all truth becomes certain to us, let Him be loved in whom all becomes right to us.

5. If, then, Plato defined the wise man as one who imitates, knows, loves this God, and who is rendered blessed through fellowship with Him in His own blessedness, why discuss the other philosophers? It is evident that none come nearer to us than the Platonists. To them, therefore, let that fabulous theology give place which delights the minds of men with the crimes of the gods; and that civil theology also, in which impure demons, under the name of gods, have seduced the peoples of the earth given up to earthly pleasures, desiring to be honored by the errors of men, and by filling the minds of their worshippers with impure desires, exciting them to make the representation of their crimes one of the rites of their worship, whilst they themselves found in the spectators of these exhibitions a most pleasing spectacle,—a theology in which whatever was honorable in the temple was defiled by its mixture with the obscenity of the theater, and whatever was base in the theater was vindicated by the abominations of the temples.... Let these two theologies, then, the fabulous and the civil, give place to the Platonic philosophers, who have recognized the true God as the author of all things, the source of the light of truth, and the bountiful bestower of all blessedness.

6. The Platonists, then, whom we see not undeservedly exalted above the rest in fame and glory, have seen that no material body is God, and therefore they have transcended all bodies in seeking for God. They have seen that whatever is changeable is not the most high God, and therefore they have transcended every soul and all changeable spirits in seeking the supreme.

7. Then, again, as far as regards the doctrine which treats of that which they call logic, that is, rational philosophy, far be it from us to compare them with those who attributed to the bodily sense the faculty of discriminating truth and thought, that all we learn is to be measured by their untrustworthy and fallacious rules. Such were the Epicureans, and all of the same school. Such also were the Stoics, who ascribed to the bodily senses that expertness in disputation which they so ardently love, called by them dialectic, asserting that from the senses the mind conceives the notions [*ennoiai*] of those things which they explicate by definition. And hence is developed the whole plan and connection of their learning and teaching.

I often wonder, with respect to this, how they can say that none are beautiful but the wise; for by what bodily sense have they perceived that beauty, by what eyes of the flesh have they seen wisdom's comeliness of form? Those, however, whom we justly rank before all others, have distinguished those things which are conceived by the mind from those which are perceived by the senses, neither taking away from the senses anything to which they are competent, nor attributing to them anything beyond their competency. And the light of our understandings, by which all things are learned by us, they have affirmed to be that self-same God by whom all things were made.

8. The remaining part of philosophy is morals, or what is called by the Greeks *ethiké*, in which is discussed the question concerning the chief good,—that which will leave us nothing further to seek in order to be blessed, if only we make all our actions refer to it, and seek it not for the sake of something else, but for its own

sake. Therefore it is called the end, because we wish other things on account of it, but itself only for its own sake. This beatific good, therefore, according to some, comes to a man from the body, according to others, from the mind; and, according to others, from both together. For they saw that man himself consists of soul and body; and therefore they believed that from either of these two, or from both together, their well-being must proceed, consisting in a certain final good, which could render them blessed, and to which they might refer all their actions, not requiring anything ulterior to which to refer that good itself.

This is why those who have added a third kind of good things, which they call extrinsic,—as honor, glory, wealth, and the like,—have not regarded them as part of the final good, that is, to be sought after for their own sake, but as things which are to be sought for the sake of something else, affirming that this kind of good is good to the good, and evil to the evil. Wherefore, whether they have sought the good of man from the mind or from the body, or from both together, it is still only from man they have supposed that it must be sought. But they who have sought it from the body have sought it from the inferior part of man; they who have sought it from the mind, from the superior part; and they who have sought it from both, from the whole man. Whether, therefore, they have sought it from any part, or from the whole man, still they have only sought it from man; nor have these differences, being three, given rise only to three dissentient sects of philosophers, but to many. For diverse philosophers have held diverse opinions, both concerning the good of the body and the good of the mind, and the good of both together.

Let, therefore, all these give place to those philosophers who have not affirmed that a man is blessed by the enjoyment of the body, or by the enjoyment of the mind, but by the enjoyment of God,—enjoying Him, however, not as the mind does the body or itself, or as one friend enjoys another, but as the eye enjoys light, if, indeed, we may draw any comparisons between these things. But what the nature of this comparison is, will, if God help me, be shown in another place, to the best of my ability.

At present it is sufficient to mention that Plato determined the final good to be to live according to virtue, and affirmed that he only can attain to virtue who knows and imitates God,—which knowledge and imitation are the only cause of blessedness. Therefore he did not doubt that to philosophize is to love God, whose nature is incorporeal. Whence it certainly follows that the student of wisdom, that is, the philosopher, will then become blessed when he shall have begun to enjoy God. For though he is not necessarily blessed who enjoys that which he loves (for many are miserable by loving that which ought not to be loved, and still more miserable when they enjoy it), nevertheless no one is blessed who does not enjoy that which he loves. For even they who love things which ought not to be loved do not count themselves blessed by loving merely, but by enjoying them. Who, then, but the most miserable will deny that he is blessed, who enjoys that which he loves, and loves the true and highest good? But the true and highest good, according to Plato, is God, and therefore he would call him a philosopher who loves God; for philosophy is directed to the obtaining of the blessed life, and he who loves God is blessed in the enjoyment of God.

9. Whatever philosophers, therefore, thought concerning the supreme God, that He is both the maker of all created things, the light by which things are known, and the good in reference to which things are to be done; that we have in Him the first principle of nature, the truth of doctrine, and the happiness of life,—whether these philosophers may be more suitably called Platonists, or whether they may give some other name to their sect; whether, we say, that only the chief men of the Ionic school, such as Plato himself, and they who have well understood him, have

thought thus; or whether we also include the Italic school, on account of Pythagoras and the Pythagoreans, and all who may have held like opinions; and, lastly, whether also we include all who have been held wise men and philosophers among all nations who are discovered to have been and taught this, be they Atlantics, Libyans, Egyptians, Indians, Persians, Chaldeans, Scythians, Gauls, Spaniards, or of other nations,—we prefer these to all other philosophers, and confess that they approach nearest to us.

10. For although a Christian man instructed only in ecclesiastical literature may perhaps be ignorant of the very name of Platonists, and may not even know that there have existed two schools of philosophers speaking the Greek tongue, to wit, the Ionic and Italic, he is nevertheless not so deaf with respect to human affairs as not to know that philosophers profess the study, and even the possession, of wisdom. He is on his guard, however, with respect to those who philosophize according to the elements of this world, not according to God, by whom the world itself was made; for he is warned by the precept of the apostle, and faithfully hears what has been said, "Beware that no one deceive you through philosophy and vain deceit, according to the elements of the world"....

It is from the one true and supremely good God that we have that nature in which we are made in the image of God, and that doctrine by which we know Him and ourselves, and that grace through which, by cleaving to Him, we are blessed. This, therefore, is the cause why we prefer these to all the others, because, whilst other philosophers have worn out their minds and powers in seeking the causes of things, and endeavoring to discover the right mode of learning and of living, these, by knowing God, have found where resides the cause by which the universe has been constituted, and the light by which truth is to be discovered, and the fountain at which felicity is to be drunk.

All philosophers, then, who have had these thoughts concerning God, whether Platonists or others, agree with us. But we have thought it better to plead our cause with the Platonists, because their writings are better known. For the Greeks, whose tongue holds the highest place among the languages of the Gentiles, are loud in their praises of these writings; and the Latins, taken with their excellence, or their renown, have studied them more heartily than other writings, and, by translating them into our tongue, have given them greater celebrity and notoriety.

St. Augustine (d. 430), *City of God,* VIII, 1–10, adapted from the translation of Marcus Dods, *Nicene and Post-Nicene Fathers,* II, 144–51.

II. What Prompted Constantine the Great to Turn to Christianity?

A. Two Modern Judgments

1.

When the Emperor Constantine turned to Christianity, the long and troubled history of the relations of the Christian Church to the Christian state began. The problem of the "conversion" of Constantine to Christianity has been much discussed and disputed. It is a problem of high significance with many implications. From a very large secondary literature two opposing points of view are presented in the following selections from two well-

known studies of Constantine. In the first, the Swiss historian Jacob Burckhardt (1818–1897) depicts Constantine as a cold-blooded political opportunist who sought to employ Christianity to serve his own purposes.

Constantine's historical memory has suffered the greatest misfortune conceivable. That pagan writers must be hostile to him is obvious and would do him no damage in the eyes of posterity. But he has fallen into the hands of the most objectionable of all eulogists, who has utterly falsified his likeness. The man is Eusebius of Caesarea and the book his *Life of Constantine.* The man who with all his faults was always significant and always powerful is here presented in the guise of a sanctimonious devotee; in point of fact his numerous misdeeds are amply documented in a number of passages. Eusebius' equivocal praise is basically insincere. He speaks of the man but really means a cause, and that cause is the hierarchy, so strongly and richly established by Constantine. Furthermore, to say nothing of the contemptible style, there is a consciously furtive mode of expression, so that the reader finds himself treading concealed traps and bogs at the most vital passages. The reader who notices these hazards in time may be easily misled into putting the worst possible construction upon what has been withheld from him.

The introduction [to Eusebius' *Life of Constantine*] is ecstatic enough: "When I gaze in spirit upon this thrice-blessed soul, united with God, free of all mortal dross, in robes gleaming like lightning and in ever radiant diadem, speech and reason stand mute, and I would willingly leave it to a better man to devise a worthy hymn of praise." Would that had been the case! If we only possessed instead the description of a reasonable pagan like Ammianus, we should come infinitely closer to the great historical phenomenon which was the man Constantine, even though his moral character might not have emerged unsullied. Then we could perhaps see clearly what we can now only surmise, namely, that virtually throughout his life Constantine never assumed the guise of or gave himself out as a Christian but kept his free personal convictions quite unconcealed to his very last days. . . .

Eusebius is no fanatic; he understands Constantine's secular spirit and his cold and terrible lust for power well enough and doubtless knows the true causes of the war [with Licinius in 323] quite precisely. But he is the first thoroughly dishonest historian of antiquity. His tactic, which enjoyed a brilliant success in his own day and throughout the Middle Ages, consisted in making the first great protector of the Church at all costs an ideal of humanity according to his lights, and above all an ideal for future rulers. Hence we have lost

the picture of a genius in stature who knew no moral scruple in politics *and regarded the religious question exclusively from the point of view of political expediency.* [Constantine] found it advisable to attach himself more closely to the Christians after this war, and. . . the elevation of Christianity to the position of state religion was thus consummated. But Constantine was a more honorable man than Eusebius; he rather allowed these events to transpire than intervened actively on their behalf, and as regards his own personal conviction, he enjoined definite beliefs upon his subjects as little as did Napoleon in his concordat. . . .

Attempts have often been made to penetrate into the religious consciousness of Constantine and to construct a hypothetical picture of changes in his religious convictions. Such efforts are futile. In a genius driven without surcease by ambition and lust for power there can be no question of Christianity and paganism, of conscious religiosity or irreligiosity; such a man is essentially unreligious, even if he pictures himself standing in the midst of a churchly community. Holiness he understands only as a reminiscence or as a superstitious vagary. Moments of inward reflection, which for a religious man are in the nature of worship, he consumes in a different sort of fire. World-embracing plans and mighty dreams lead him by an easy road to the streams of blood of slaughtered armies. . . . Men argue from Constantine's zealous Christian edicts, even from an address of the Emperor "to the assembly of the saints," an expression impossible on the lips of a non-Christian. But this address, it may be remarked in passing, was neither composed by Constantine nor ever delivered; and in writing the edicts Constantine often gave the priests a free hand [but how can Burckhardt be sure of this?]. And Eusebius, though all historians have followed him, has been proven guilty of so many distortions, dissimulations, and inventions that he has forfeited all claim to figure as a decisive source [Is this not too strong?]. It is a melancholy but very understandable fact that none of the other spokesmen of the Church, as far as we know, revealed Constantine's true position, that they uttered no word of displeasure against the murderous egoist who possessed the great merit of having conceived of Christianity as a world power and of having acted accordingly. We can easily imagine the joy of the Christians in having finally obtained a firm guarantee against persecution, but we are not obliged to share that elation after a millennium and a half.

Jacob Burckhardt, *The Age of Constantine the Great*, trans. Moses Hadas (London: Routledge & Kegan Paul, Ltd., 1949), pp. 260–61, 283, 292–93.

2.

With Burckhardt's dogmatic certainty one may contrast the view of Norman H. Baynes, who is fully prepared to accept the possibility that Constantine's conversion was sincere.

No student of the Middle Ages can evade Constantine: he is one of the few inescapable figures in European history and one of the most intractable. To take man's past and demonstrate its inherent logic is a fascinating pursuit—to prove to one's own satisfaction that the past could not have been otherwise than it was, being a necessary development from that which had gone before, this is gratifying to man, for he can thus look back upon human history and regard it as in a sense his own creation and can then praise its creator. In this reconstruction of the past, however, difficulties are at times caused by the interposition in the stream of history of outstanding personalities which resist rationalization and remain unexpected and embarrassing. One of these personalities is Constantine the Great. To my mind, at least, all attempts to explain away Constantine as the natural outcome of the previous history of Rome have failed completely. Constantine can only be satisfactorily interpreted in terms of the *Zeitgeist* if the *Zeitgeist* is arbitrarily fashioned in the likeness of Constantine. The more closely Constantine's life and achievement are studied, the more inevitably is one driven to see in them an erratic block which has diverted the stream of human history. It may be true that by A.D. 311 the imperial policy of persecution of the Christians had been proved a failure—Galerius, the instigator of that policy, had publicly confessed its futility—but this failure could not carry with it the implications that it was the duty of a Roman Emperor so far to disavow Rome's past as himself to adopt the faith professed by perhaps one-tenth of his subjects. Constantine presents to the student of history so interesting a problem precisely because he is an intractable individual, because he was not merely the creation of the past, but marked in himself a new beginning which was in such large measure to determine the future of the Roman world.

The representations attempted by modern scholars of the convictions and aims of Constantine have been so diverse that at times it is hard to believe that it is one and the same emperor that they are seeking to portray. As students of history we protest energetically that a man can only be rightly understood if he be regarded against the background of his world, that he can only be fairly judged in the light of the standards and the values of the society in which he lived; and then, having formulated the principle, we straightway forget it. We write our biographies in terms of the thought of our own day and impose upon another age the standards with which we are familiar. Burckhardt began his famous chapter upon Constantine and the Christian Church with the remark: "In the case of a man of genius, whose ambition and love of power refuse him a moment's peace, there can be no question of Christianity or paganism, of conscious religion or irreligion. Such a man even when he persuades himself that he has his place in an ecclesiastical community, is essentially unreligious." The issue is thus, you observe, pre-judged, and the answer to the problem cannot be for an instant in doubt. . . .

Or again, consider Otto Seeck as he discusses the authenticity of documents attributed by Eusebius to Constantine: the belief that the divine will had punished those emperors who had persecuted the Christians and preserved those who had not enforced the edicts of persecution is, he notes, common to Lactantius, Eusebius, and the documents purporting to represent the thought of Constantine; the idea was in many men's minds. "Why then should we be surprised if the good Constantine in his turn repeats the same trivialities" [says Seeck]. Trivialities? But what if a man really believes that God does actively, consistently, intervene in human affairs, that victory and defeat, prosperity and adversity are alike in His gift?—and what if that man is the ruler of the Roman world? Is that belief then insignificant? is it not rather of supreme moment? So hard it is to think ourselves back into a world which is not our own!

And there remains a yet subtler danger: we may imagine that we have discovered the key to a personality, and then we persuade ourselves that it will open every lock. And yet it is surely but rarely that every secret door of thought and motive in human life will yield to a single master-key. Life is not so simple as that. Eduard Schwartz has done as much as any scholar in our day to advance the study of the reign of Constantine; in his book, *The Emperor Constantine and the Christian Church,* he has found the Open Sesame to the understanding of the reign in Constantine's resolution to exploit in his own interest the organization which gave to the Christian Church its corporate strength: through alliance with the Church Constantine sought to attain victory and the sole mastery of the Roman world. The emperor's toleration sprang from his desire that pagan and Christian alike should be conscious that they depended upon him alone. "Never," writes Schwartz, "has an emperor so triumphed over the Church as did Constantine in and through the Council of Nicaea"; the victory lay with the emperor's "diabolical cleverness." The one man who opposed Constantine was Athanasius, and in that contest of wills Greek met Greek; for the opposition of Athanasius was inspired not by zeal for the true faith, not by any passion for the independence of the Church, but by the pride of a hierarch in the authority of his patriarchate. The master-key in this analysis which Schwartz has given us of the personalities of Constantine and Athanasius is thus "Der Wille zur Macht" [i.e. "the will to power"]. But it may be doubted whether so extreme a simplification can do justice to the complexity of human convictions and human motives. The solution would appear rather to be imposed upon the evidence than to arise from a patient study of the documents themselves.

Norman H. Baynes, "Constantine and the Christian Church," *Proceedings of the British Academy,* XV (1929), 341–44.

B. The Evidence of Constantine's Letters

1.

Shortly after Constantine's victory over his rival Maxentius in the battle of the Milvian Bridge (28 October 312), he wrote the following letter to Anulinus, the proconsul of Africa, ordering the restoration of property to the Church. This letter was written late in the year 312, about seven months before the so-called Edict of Milan. All the documents which follow appear to be genuine.

Greetings, Anulinus, our most honored Sir. It is the consequence of our love of goodness that whatever belongs to another by right we are not only not unwilling but we are even anxious to restore, most honored Anulinus. Therefore we wish that, when you receive this letter, you restore immediately to the churches whatever of those things which belonged to the Catholic Church of the Christians in the several cities as well as in other places have found their way into the possession of citizens or of other persons. For we have decided that whatever these same churches owned before shall be returned to them as their just due. Since therefore your Excellency perceives that the tenor of this our command is most explicit, make haste that there be restored as soon as possible to the churches all the things which belonged to them of right, whether gardens, houses, or anything else whatsoever, so that we may learn that you have rendered the most attentive obedience to this our command. Farewell, most honored and beloved Anulinus.

Eusebius, *Eccl. Hist.*, X, 5, 15–17, trans. K. M. Setton.

2.

About the same time as the preceding letter was addressed to Anulinus, Constantine wrote also to Caecilian, the Bishop of Carthage, granting subsidies from the imperial treasury to the Christian Church in North Africa, and affording the Church the official protection of the state against heresy.

Constantine Augustus to Caecilian, Bishop of Carthage. Forasmuch as it has been our pleasure in all provinces, namely the African, the Numidian and the Mauretanian, that something be contributed for expenses to certain specified ministers of the lawful and most holy Catholic religion, I have dispatched a letter to Ursus, our esteemed finance-minister of Africa, and have notified him that he be careful to pay over to your Grace three thousand *folles* [a sum of uncertain value, but equal to many tens of thousands of dollars]. Do you, therefore, when you have secured delivery of the aforesaid sum of money, give orders that this money be distributed among all the above-mentioned persons in accordance with the schedule sent to you by Hosius [Bishop of Cordova]. But if, after all, you find that there is something lacking for the fulfilment of this my purpose in respect to them all, you should ask without any hesitation for whatever you find to be necessary from Heraclides, our fiscal procurator. For indeed when he was here I gave him orders that if your Grace should ask any money from him, he should be careful to pay it over without any scruple.

And since I have learned that certain persons of unstable mind [i.e. the Donatists in North Africa] are desirous of turning aside the laity of the most holy and Catholic Church by some vile method of seduction, know that I have given such commands to Anulinus, the proconsul, and moreover to Patricius, the Vicar of Africa, when they were here, that they should give due attention to all other matters and especially to this, and not suffer such an occurrence to be overlooked; therefore if you observe any such persons continuing in this madness, do not hesitate to go to the above-mentioned officials and bring this matter before them, so that, as I commanded them when they were here, they may turn these people from their error. May the divinity of the great God preserve you for many years.

Eusebius, *ibid.*, X, 6, 1–5, adapted from trans. J. E. L. Oulton and H. J. Lawlor, Loeb Classical Library (Cambridge, Mass.: Harvard University Press, 1932), II, 461, 463.

3.

Early in the year 313 Constantine wrote again to Anulinus on behalf of the Church in North Africa, this time granting the clergy immunity from enforced services to the state (such services being called *liturgies*): "Already in Constantine's thought the Catholic priests through their priesthood are maintaining the fortunes of Rome: this is more than mere tolerance" [N. H. Baynes].

Greetings, Anulinus, most honored Sir. Since from many facts it appears that disregard of divine worship, by which the highest reverence for the most holy and heavenly [power] is preserved, has brought great dangers upon the state, and that its lawful restoration and preservation have bestowed the greatest good fortune on the Roman name and singular prosperity on all the affairs of mankind (for it is the Divine Providence which bestows these blessings): it has seemed good that those men who, with due holiness and constant observance of this law, bestow their services on the performance of divine worship, should receive the rewards of their own labors, most honored Anulinus. Wherefore it is my wish that those persons who, within the province committed to you, in the Catholic Church over which Caecilian presides, bestow their service on this holy worship—those whom they are accustomed to call clerics—should once for all be kept absolutely free from all public burdens [*liturgies*], that they be not drawn away by any error or sacrilegious fault from the worship which they owe to the Divinity, but rather without any hindrance serve to the utmost their own law. For when they render supreme service to the Deity, it seems that they confer incalculable benefit on the affairs of state. Farewell, most honored and esteemed Anulinus.

Eusebius, *ibid.*, X, 7, 1–2, adapted from trans. Oulton and Lawlor, *op. cit.*, II, 463, 465.

4.

Constantine Augustus to Aelafius. Since it had already come to my attention, some time before this, that in our province of Africa many persons in a mad furor, with vain accusations against one another, had begun to differ in their observance of the most holy Catholic law, I decided, in order to do away with dissension of this kind, that there should appear in person [for judgment] in Rome both Caecilian, the Bishop of Carthage, against whom in particular all [the Donatists] have more than once brought action before me, and some of his opponents also, who had imagined that there were certain charges to be made against Caecilian.

[The opponents of Caecilian were eventually called Donatists, after their energetic leader Donatus "the Great." They were adjudged heretics, their heresy being the contention that a sacrament was invalid if administered by an unworthy priest. The chief charge against Caecilian was that his consecration as bishop of Carthage was invalid, because it had been performed by a bishop who had, it was alleged by the Donatists, betrayed the faith during the great persecution of Diocletian and Galerius. The imperial commission which the Emperor Constantine had intended to have investigate the case against Caecilian was transformed, at the request of Bishop Miltiades of Rome, into a church council, which declared for Caecilian against his Donatist accusers. The latter, however, refused to accept the decision of the council, and appealed therefrom to Constantine himself, who reluctantly summoned a large council to meet at Arles in the south of France on 1 August of the next year (A.D. 314) to go over the matter again. In the present letter, therefore, Constantine instructed Aelafius, the chief governor of Africa, to dispatch, by the imperial post service, Caecilian and certain of his chosen supporters, together with a representative group of his Donatist opponents, to Arles, in order that this larger body of the clergy, with imperial sanction, might make a final adjudication of the case against Caecilian. Constantine concluded his letter to Aelafius with an expression of personal anxiety, of great interest and importance to the student who seeks to depict Constantine's attitude toward Christianity and the Church:]

Since I am assured that you are also a worshipper of the supreme God, I confess to your Excellency that I consider it absolutely wrong that we should pass over in insincerity quarrels and altercations of this kind, whereby perhaps the supreme divinity may be moved not only against the human race, *but even against me myself* (!), to whose care He has, by His celestial will, entrusted rule over all earthly affairs—and yet, if angered, He may decree otherwise than up to now! For then, and only then, shall I be able truly and most fully to feel secure and always to hope for the greatest prosperity and good fortune from the ever ready kindness of the most powerful God, when I shall see all men, in the proper cult of the Catholic religion, venerate the most holy God with hearts joined like brothers in their worship.

Constantine, *Epistle to Aelafius*, trans. K. M. Setton, from Karl Ziwsa, ed., *S. Optati Milevitani libri VII*, Vienna, 1893 (*Corpus scriptorum ecclesiasticorum latinorum*, vol. XXVI), appendix, pp. 204, 206.

5.

To the bishops assembled at the Council of Arles (A.D. 314), to which reference is made in the preceding document, the Emperor Constantine sent the letter which follows, in condemnation of the Donatists. In seeking to evaluate Constantine's attitude toward Christianity, note both the general tone of the letter and such references as those to "our God" and to Christ, whose judgment he awaits.

Constantine Augustus to the Catholic Bishops, his dearest brethren, greetings. The eternal and revered and incomprehensible goodness of our God by no means permits that mankind should stray too long in the darkness, nor does it allow that the hated wishes of certain people should so far prevail as not to open up the path to salvation through its own most glorious light and cause conversion to the rule of truth. I have learned this from many examples which I can illustrate from my own experience. For in the beginning there were in me things which seemed quite removed from truth; I certainly did not think that the power in heaven could see into the secrets which I carried in my heart. What fortune, then, should these things which I have mentioned have caused to be allotted to me? Obviously one overflowing with all manner of evil! But Almighty God, who sits in the very watchtower of heaven, has made me gifts that I did not deserve. They can be neither described nor counted, these things which God in his heavenly kindness has bestowed upon me, his servant! Most holy bishops of the Savior Christ, my dearest brethren, I rejoice therefore, especially do I rejoice, that finally by the very justice of your decision you have recalled to a better hope and fortune these people [the Donatists], whom the evil purpose of the devil, with sinister power of persuasion, seemed to have turned aside from the glorious light of the Catholic law....

But your just decision has been of no avail with these people [the Donatists]. ...What force of evil persists in their hearts! ... They ask me to judge, I who myself await the judgment of Christ, and I reply, as is the truth, that the judgment of bishops ought to be regarded as if the Lord Himself were sitting in judgment. These people have no right to any observance or to any judgment except what they have been taught by Christ's own teaching.... What is to be done with these detractors of the law, who renouncing the judgment of heaven have believed that they should seek judgment of me? Do they think thus so little of Christ the Savior?...Go now and return to your own sees, and bear me in your memories that our Savior may ever have mercy upon me.... I have directed my men to bring these evil deceivers of religion into my court from now on in order that they may be kept there and may see something worse than death provided for them. I have also dispatched letters addressed to the Vicar of Africa to the effect that he should send at once to my court as many as he may find who share this madness, lest they should be guilty of any further offenses under the clear light of our God which could call down upon us the grievous wrath of the Divine Providence. May Almighty God keep you safe for all time, in answer to your prayers and to my own, my dearest brethren.

Constantine, *Epistle to the Catholic Bishops*, trans. K. M. Setton, from K. Ziwsa, *op. cit.*, pp. 208–10.

C. "In This Sign Conquer!"

The following passage, which recounts Constantine's alleged vision of the sign of the cross in the heavens, with the exhortation to "conquer in this," is taken from Eusebius of Caesarea's *Life of Constantine*. Historians have taken the account seriously as a miracle; regarded the cross of light as a parahelion, or other strange but natural phenomenon; considered the whole affair as merely the product of an overwrought imagination; and scoffed at the text as being a later interpolation. Lactantius, *On the Deaths of Persecutors*, 44, describes Constantine as having had this manifestation of divine support merely in a dream rather than in an actual vision. However, the events related here are alleged to have occurred shortly before the Battle of the Milvian Bridge.

Constantine, being convinced, however, that he needed some more powerful aid than his military forces could afford him, on account of the wicked and magical enchantments which were so diligently practiced by the tyrant [Maxentius], sought divine assistance, deeming the possession of arms and a numerous soldiery of secondary importance, but believing the co-operating power of Deity invincible and not to be shaken. He considered, therefore, on what God he might rely for protection and assistance. While engaged in this enquiry, the thought occurred to him, that, of the many emperors who had preceded him, those who had rested their hopes in a multitude of gods, and served them with sacrifices and offerings, had in the first place been deceived by flattering predictions, and oracles which promised them all prosperity, and at last had met with an unhappy end, while not one of their gods had stood by to warn them of the impending wrath of heaven; while one alone who had pursued an entirely opposite course, who had condemned their error, and honored the one Supreme God during his whole life [namely, Constantius Chlorus, the father of Constantine], had found him to be the Savior and Protector of his empire, and the Giver of every good thing. Reflecting on this, and well weighing the fact that they who had trusted in many gods had also fallen by manifold forms of death, without leaving behind them either family or offspring, stock, name, or memorial among men: while the God of his father had given to him, on the other hand, manifestations of his power and very many tokens: and considering farther that those who had already taken arms against the tyrant, and had marched to the battle-field under the protection of a multitude of gods, had met with a dishonorable end (for one of them [Galerius] had shamefully retreated from the contest without a blow, and the other [Severus], being slain in the midst of his own troops, became, as it were, the mere sport of death); reviewing, I say, all these considerations, he judged it to be folly indeed to join in the idle worship of those who were no gods, and, after such convincing evidence, to stray from the truth; and therefore felt it incumbent on him to honor his father's God alone.

Accordingly he called on Him with earnest prayer and supplications that He would reveal to him who He was, and stretch forth His right hand to help him in his present difficulties. And while he was thus praying with fervent entreaty, a most marvelous sign appeared to him from heaven, the account of which it might have been hard to believe had it been related by any other person. But since the victorious emperor himself long afterwards declared it to the writer of this history, when he was honored with his acquaintance and society, and confirmed his statement by an oath, who could hesitate to accredit this account, especially since the testimony of aftertime has established its truth? He said that about noon, when the day was already beginning to decline, he saw with his own eyes the sign of a cross of light in the heavens, above the sun, and bearing the inscription CONQUER BY THIS. At this sight he himself was struck with amazement, and his whole army also, which followed him on this expedition, and witnessed the miracle.

He said, moreover, that he doubted within himself what the import of this apparition could be. And while he continued to ponder and reason on its meaning, night suddenly came on; then in his sleep the Christ of God appeared to him with the same sign which he had seen in the heavens, and commanded him to make a likeness of that sign which he had seen in the heavens, and to use to it as a safeguard in all engagements with his enemies.

At dawn of day he arose, and communicated the marvel to his friends: and then, calling together the workers in gold and precious stones, he sat in the midst of them, and described to them the figure of the sign he had seen, bidding them represent it in gold and precious stones. And this representation I myself have had an opportunity of seeing.

Now it was made in the following manner. A long spear, overlaid with gold, formed the figure of the cross by means of a transverse bar laid over it. On the top of the whole was fixed a wreath of gold and precious stones; and within this, the symbol of the Savior's name, two letters indicating the name of Christ by means of its initial characters, the letter P [the Greek letter Rho] being intersected by X [the Greek letter Chi] in its center: and these letters the emperor was in the habit of wearing on his helmet at a later period. From the cross-bar of the spear was suspended a cloth, a royal piece, covered with a profuse embroidery of most brilliant precious stones; and which, being also richly interlaced with gold, presented an indescribable degree of beauty to the beholder. This banner was of a square form, and the upright staff, whose lower section was of great length, bore a golden half-length portrait of the pious emperor and his children on its upper part, beneath the sign of the cross, and immediately above the embroidered banner.

The emperor constantly made use of this sign of salvation as a safeguard against every adverse and hostile power, and commanded that others similar to it should be carried at the head of all his armies.

These things were done shortly afterwards. But at the time above specified, being struck with amazement at the extraordinary vision, and resolving to worship no other God save Him who had appeared to him, he sent for those who were acquainted with the mysteries of His doctrines, and enquired who that God was, and what was intended by the sign of the vision he had seen.

They affirmed that He was God, the only begotten Son of the one and only God: that the sign which had appeared was the symbol of immortality, and the trophy of that victory over death which He had gained in time past when sojourning on earth. They taught him also the causes of His advent, and explained to him the true account of His incarnation. Thus he was instructed in these matters, and was impressed with wonder at the divine manifestation which had been presented to his sight. Comparing, therefore, the heavenly vision with the interpretation given, he found his judgment confirmed; and, in the persuasion that the knowledge of these things had been imparted to him by divine teaching, he determined thenceforth to devote himself to the reading of the inspired writings.

Moreover, he made the priests of God his counselors, and deemed it incumbent on him to honor the God who had appeared to him with all devotion. And after this, being fortified by well-grounded hopes in Him, he hastened to quench the threatening fire of tyranny.

Eusebius of Caesarea, *Life of Constantine*, I, chaps. 27–32, adapted from the translation in the *Nicene and Post-Nicene Fathers*, 2nd series, I, 489–91.

D. The Edict of Galerius

The Edict of Galerius, to which attention is called in the Introduction, was issued on 30 April, 311, shortly before its author's death.

A translation follows of the text as preserved in the Greek version of Eusebius.

And Galerius, wrestling with terrible misfortunes, was conscience-stricken for the cruel deeds he had perpetrated against the godly. Collecting, therefore, his thoughts, he first openly confessed to the God of the universe; then he called those around him, and commanded them without delay to cause the persecution against Christians to cease, and by an imperial law and decree to urge them to build their churches and to perform their accustomed rites, offering prayers on the Emperor's behalf. Action immediately followed his word, and imperial ordinances were promulgated in each city, containing the recantation of the [persecution edicts] of our time, after this manner:

"The Emperor Caesar Galerius Valerius Maximianus Invictus Augustus, Pontifex Maximus...to the people of the provinces, greeting:

"Among the other measures that we frame for the use and profit of the state, it had been our own wish formerly that all things should be set to rights in accordance with the ancient laws and public order of the Romans; and to make provision for this, namely, that the Christians also, such as had abandoned the persuasion of their own ancestors, should return to a sound mind; seeing that through some reasoning they had been possessed of such self-will and seized with such folly that, instead of following the institutions of the ancients, which perchance their own forefathers had formerly established, they made for themselves, and

were observing, laws merely in accordance with their own disposition and as each one wished, and were assembling various multitudes in divers places:

"Therefore when a command of ours soon followed to the intent that they should betake themselves to the institutions of the ancients, very many indeed were subjected to peril, while very many were harassed and endured all kinds of death; and since the majority held to the same folly, and we perceived that they were neither paying the worship due to the gods of heaven nor honoring the god of the Christians; having regard to our clemency and the invariable custom by which we are wont to accord pardon to all men, we thought it right in this case also to extend most willingly our indulgence: That Christians may exist again and build the houses in which they used to assemble, always provided that they do nothing contrary to order. In another letter we shall indicate to the judges how they should proceed. Wherefore, in accordance with this our indulgence, they will be bound to beseech their own god for our welfare, and that of the state, and their own; that in every way both the well being of the state may be secured, and they may be enabled to live free from care in their own homes."

Such is the character of this edict in the Latin tongue, translated into Greek as well as may be.

Eusebius, *Eccl. Hist.*, VIII, 17, 1–11, trans. Oulton and Lawlor, *op. cit.*, II, 317, 319, 321.

E. The So-Called "Edict of Milan"

When Constantine and Licinius met at Milan in February of 313, three or four months after Constantine's victory at the Milvian Bridge, they agreed upon a policy of freedom for all religions in the Empire. Very likely a text was agreed upon for promulgation by Licinius when he returned to the East (whence he had come to render Constantine assistance, if needed, against Maxentius). Apparently no "Edict of Milan" was ever issued; it was not necessary. Constan-

tine's religious policy in the West had already been laid down, and his attitude toward Christianity sufficiently defined, in the letters to Anulinus and Caecilian, given above. In 1891 the German scholar Otto Seeck first asserted that no Edict of Milan was ever issued, and this opinion has in general been adopted by Norman Baynes, Henri Grégoire, and Erich Caspar. However, when Licinius went back to the East, he sent the rescript which historians have improperly called the "Edict of Milan" to the governor (*praeses*) of Bithynia on 15 June, 313, as we learn from Lactantius, *On the Deaths of Persecutors*, chap. 48, where we also have a Latin version, but not the official text, of this document preserved.

But come, let us now quote also the translations made from the Latin of the imperial ordinances of Constantine and Licinius. . . .

"In our watchfulness in days gone by that freedom of worship should not be denied, but that each one according to his mind and purpose should have authority given him to care for divine things in the way that pleased him best, we had given orders that both to the Christians [and to all others liberty should be allowed] to keep to the faith of their own sect and worship. But inasmuch as many and various conditions seemed clearly to have been added in that rescript, in which such rights were conceded to the same persons, it may be that perchance some of them were shortly afterwards repelled from such observance.

"When I, Constantine Augustus, and I, Licinius Augustus, had come under happy auspices to Milan, and discussed all matters that concerned the public advantage and good, among the other things that seemed to be of benefit to the many,—or rather, first and foremost—we resolved to make such decrees as should secure respect and reverence for the Deity; namely, to grant both to the Christians and to all the free choice of following whatever form of worship they pleased, to the intent that all the divine and heavenly powers that be might be favorable to us and all those living under our authority. Therefore with sound and most upright reasoning we resolved on this counsel: that authority be refused to no one whomsoever to follow and choose the observance or form of worship that Christians use, and that authority be granted to each one to give his mind to that form of worship which he deems suitable to himself, to the intent that the Divinity may in all things afford us his wonted care and generosity. It was fitting to send a rescript that this is our pleasure, in order that when those conditions had altogether been removed, which

were contained in our former letters sent to your Excellency, concerning the Christians, those things also which seemed to be wholly unfortunate and foreign to our clemency might be removed, and that now each one of those who were possessed of the same purpose—namely, to observe the Christians' form of worship—should observe this very thing, freely and simply, without any hindrance. Which things we have resolved, to signify in the fullest manner to your Excellency, to the intent that you may know that we have granted to these same Christians free and unrestricted authority to observe their own form of worship. And when you perceive that this has been granted unrestrictedly to them by us, your Excellency will understand that authority has been given to others also, who wish to follow their own observance and form of worship—a thing clearly suited to the peacefulness of our times—so that each one may have authority to choose and observe whatever form he pleases. This has been done by us, to the intent that we should not seem to have detracted in any way from any rite or form of worship.

"And this, moreover, with special regard to the Christians, we resolve: That their places, at which it was their former wont to assemble, concerning which also in the former letter dispatched to your Excellency a definite ordinance had been formerly laid down, if any should appear to have bought them either from our treasury or from any other source—that they should restore them to these same Christians without payment or any demand for compensation, setting aside all negligence and doubtfulness; and if any chance to have received them by gift, that they should restore them with all speed to these same Christians: provided that if either those who have purchased these same places or those who have received them by gift request our generosity, let them approach the prefect of the district, to the intent that through our kindness thought may be taken for them also. All which things must be handed over to the corporation of the Christians by your zealous care immediately and without delay.

"And inasmuch as these same Christians had not only those places at which it was their wont to assemble, but also are known to have had others, belonging not to individuals among them, but to the lawful property of their corporation, that is, of the Christians, all these, under the provisions of the law set forth above, you will give orders to be restored without any question whatsoever to these same Christians, that is, to their corporation and assembly; provided always, of course, as aforesaid, that those persons who restore the same without compensation, as we have mentioned above, may look for indemnification, as far as they are concerned, from our generosity.

"In all these things, you should use all the diligence in your power for the above-mentioned corporation of the Christians, that this our command may be fulfilled with all speed, so that in this also, through our kindness, thought may be taken for the common and public peace. For by this method, as we have also said before, the divine care for us, which we have already experienced in many matters, will remain steadfast. . . . And that the form which this our enactment and generosity takes may be brought to the knowledge of all, it is fitting that this which we have written be set forth by your order and published everywhere, and brought to the knowledge of all, to the intent that the enactment which embodies this our generosity may escape the notice of no one."

Eusebius, *ibid.*, X, 5, 1–14, II, 445 ff.

F. Constantine's Declaration to the World

Constantine and Licinius ruled the Empire together for a decade, but in A.D. 323 there broke out between them a war, which "is represented as a religious war in the history of Eusebius, and I see no reason to doubt that such was its character in the eyes of Constantine" (Baynes). Just as after the defeat of Maxentius, Constantine wrote the letters to Anulinus and Caecilian, so now after the defeat of Licinius he repeated his avowal of Christianity. Eusebius writes:

And now that through the powerful aid of God his Savior, all nations owned their subjection to the emperor's authority, he openly proclaimed to all the name of Him to whose bounty he owed all his blessings, and declared that He and not himself, was the author of his past victories. This declaration, written both in the Latin and Greek languages, he caused to be transmitted through every province of the empire. Now the excellence of his style of expression may be known from a perusal of his letters themselves, which were two in number; one addressed to the churches of God; the other to the heathen. The latter of these I think it well to insert here, as connected with my present subject, in order on the one hand that a copy of this document may be recorded as a matter of history, and thus preserved to posterity, and on the other that it may serve to confirm the truth of my present narrative. It is taken from an authentic copy of the imperial statute in my own possession; and the signature in the emperor's own handwriting attaches as it were the impress of truth to the statement I have made. . . .

"And now, with such a mass of impiety oppressing the human race, and the commonwealth in danger of being utterly destroyed, as if by the agency of some pestilential disease, and therefore needing powerful and effectual aid; what was the relief, and what the remedy which the Divinity devised for these evils? (And by Divinity is meant the one who is alone and truly God, the possessor of almighty and eternal power: and surely it cannot be deemed arrogance in one who has received benefits from God, to acknowledge them in the loftiest terms of praise.)

I myself, then, was the instrument whose services He chose, and esteemed suited for the accomplishment of His will. Accordingly, beginning at the remote Britannic ocean, and the regions where, according to the law of nature, the sun sinks beneath the horizon, through the aid of divine power I banished and utterly removed every form of evil...in the hope that the human race, enlightened through my instrumentality, might be called to a due observance of the holy laws of God, and at the same time our most blessed faith might prosper under the guidance of His almighty hand.

"I said, under the guidance of His hand; for I would desire never to be forgetful of the gratitude due to His grace. Believing, therefore, that this most excellent service had been confided to me as a special gift, I proceeded as far as the regions of the East, which, being under the pressure of severe calamities, seemed to demand still more effectual remedies at my hands. At the same time I am most certainly persuaded that I myself owe my life, my every breath, in short, my very inmost and secret thoughts, entirely to the favor of the Supreme God."...

Eusebius, *Life of Constantine*, II, chaps. 23, 28–29, from *Nicene and Post-Nicene Fathers*, 2nd series, I, 506–7.

III. The Problem of Papal Supremacy over the Western Church

The problem of how the Pope in Rome became recognized as supreme pontiff over the Western Church, and laid claim to authority also over the Eastern Churches, must start with the question of the organization of the early churches in general and of that of Rome in particular. This question is complicated by the apparent disagreement of some important early sources, and also by the difficulty of deciding to what extent "church order," or government, was (and is) assumed to be of divine or apostolic institution, and to what extent it simply grew up in response to administrative necessity. How, then, was the early Church of Rome governed? At least two contemporary sources seem to indicate that this church was presided over by a board of senior members called "overseers" [*episkopoi*, bishops] and "elders" [*presbyteroi*, priests], with little or no distinction between them. Other sources would, however, lead us to believe that the Church of Rome was in fact presided over by a single person, a "monarchical bishop," being thus under "mon-episcopal rule."

Some scholars have believed that, until well into the second century A.D., rule by a board of elders or presbyters prevailed in the Churches of Rome, Corinth, and Philippi, although the rule of a single bishop, or "mon-episcopacy," was common in Asia Minor and Syria before the close of the first century. Other texts suggest, however, and other scholars affirm, a mon-episcopal organization in the

Church of Rome, even in the later first century A.D., in direct descent from its apostolic foundation by Sts. Peter and Paul. Hence has come the "Petrine" theory of the papacy, to the effect that the Bishop of Rome received (and still wields) the authority of St. Peter, according to the famous text in St. Matthew, 16:18–19, which will be quoted several times in the pages which follow.

The two chief sources which seem to show that the Church of Rome was governed by a board of elders, rather than by a single bishop, are: 1) the so-called First Epistle of St. Clement, to the Corinthian Church (about A.D. 96), and 2) an early apocalypse, or work of visions, called *The Shepherd* of Hermas, written sometime between A.D. 100 and 140. These two texts are rather difficult to interpret, owing to the fact that some other early evidence appears not to be in accord with them. Another early work, *The Didaché*, or *Teaching of the Twelve Apostles*, also written between A.D. 100 and 140, appears to show the bishops and deacons at a time when they are just coming into their own as two different grades of clergy (presbyters are not mentioned in the *Didaché*), but are still regarded as of less importance in the Christian community than "the prophets and teachers," of whom St. Paul speaks (cf. 1 Cor. 12, 28). Thus we read in *The Didaché*, 15: "Elect therefore for yourselves bishops and deacons who are worthy of the Lord, men gentle and without avarice, men tried and true, for they also minister to you the ministry of the prophets and teachers. Do not, then, hold them in too low esteem, for these men have been and are to be honored among you together with the prophets and teachers."

In the Second Vision of *The Shepherd*, the Church appears to Hermas in the guise of an old woman, and directs him to "tell *those who rule the Church* [*of Rome*] that they are to direct their paths in righteousness...," and makes other references to "the elders who are set over the Church" (chaps. 1–2, 4). *The Shepherd* also makes reference, in its Third Vision, chap. 5, to "the apostles and overseers [*episkopoi*, bishops] and teachers and ministers [*diakonoi*, deacons], who went their way according to the holiness of God, and did their overseeing and teaching and ministering in pure and holy fashion for the elect of God, and some of whom are dead and others are still living, and since they always agreed with one another, they both kept peace among themselves and listened to one another." These passages have been interpreted as proving that a "presbyterian" board presided over the Church of Rome.

A. *The Evidence of St. Clement of Rome*

The following passage from St. Clement's *Epistle to the Corinthians* is the first clear statement of the doctrine of apostolic succession, but note that the succession appears to be collegiate or "presbyterian," i.e. through the bishops and deacons as a group or governing board, rather than a mon-episcopal succession, i.e. through an individual. Observe the use of the plural "bishops and deacons." Clement seems to have written this letter, about A.D. 96, for the Church of Rome, to the Church of Corinth, protesting "that the steadfast and ancient Church of the Corinthians, because of one or two persons, has risen up against the presbyters" (chap. 47, 6), and deposed some of them; but the presbyters should be restored to their office, for their removal had been contrary to the intentions of Christ and the Apostles: the Corinthian congregation was not the source of the presbyters' authority, *which came from Christ through the Apostles*, and therefore the con-

gregation could not remove divinely appointed presbyters:

The Apostles presented the Gospel to us from the Lord Jesus Christ. Jesus the Christ [i.e. the Anointed, the "Messiah"] was sent from God. The Christ then is from God, and the Apostles from the Christ. Both therefore came in due accord with the will of God. Having thus received their commands and having been fully assured by the Resurrection of our Lord Jesus Christ, and having placed their trust in the word of God, they went forth with full certainty of the Holy Spirit, announcing the glad tidings that the Kingdom of God was about to come. Throughout the country districts, then, and throughout the cities, they appointed their successors, having tested them in the Spirit, to be bishops and deacons [*episkopoi* and *diakonoi*, i.e. overseers and ministers] of those who were to receive the faith. And this was not at all new, because of old there had been written of bishops and deacons —as the Scripture says somewhere—"I will establish their bishops in righteousness and their deacons in faith" [cf. Isaiah, 60:17?].

And our Apostles knew through our Lord Jesus Christ that there would be strife for the title of bishop. For this reason, therefore, since they had received full knowledge in advance, they appointed the aforesaid, and afterwards added the provision that, if these should fall asleep [i.e. die], other approved men should succeed to their duties. Thus we believe it is not right to remove from their duties those appointed by the Apostles, or by other notable men after them with the agreement of the entire Church, for they have done their duty to the flock of Christ blamelessly, in humbleness of spirit, with peace and without seeking profit, as all have borne witness these many years.

Clement of Rome (A.D. 96), *Epistle to the Corinthians*, 42, 44, trans. K. M. Setton.

B. *"The Church is Founded upon the Bishops!"*

Other early sources, however, are not easily reconciled with the evidence of the First

Epistle of Clement and *The Shepherd* of Hermas. Texts from Ignatius of Antioch (A.D. 112), Hegesippus (about A.D. 165), and Irenaeus of Lyon (fl. A.D. 185) show clearly the importance of the bishop from the early second century, and the texts from Hegesippus and Irenaeus seem to show a "monarchical" episcopal succession in Rome. Irenaeus, furthermore, glorifies "that tradition, derived from the Apostles, of the very great, the very ancient, and universally known Church founded and organized at Rome by the two most glorious Apostles Peter and Paul..., for it is a matter of necessity that every church should agree with this Church, on account of its pre-eminent authority...." (*Against Heresies*, III, 3). Two generations after Irenaeus, the famous St. Cyprian, Bishop of Carthage (A.D. 248–258), gave a classic statement of the establishment of the episcopal office (as he saw it) and of the central position occupied by the monarchical bishop within the Church:

Our Lord, whose precepts and admonitions we ought to observe, in establishing the office of bishop and the organization of his Church, speaks thereof in the Gospel, and says to Peter: "Thou art Peter, and upon this rock I will build my Church, and the gates of hell shall not prevail against it. And I will give unto thee the keys of the kingdom of heaven; and whatsoever thou shalt bind on earth shall be bound in heaven; and whatsoever thou shalt loose on earth shall be loosed in heaven" (Matt. 16, 18–19). Thence, with the passage of time, as bishop has succeeded bishop, the episcopal office and the organization of the Church have come down to us, so that the Church is founded upon the bishops, and every act of the Church is controlled by these same officers. Therefore, since this has been ordained by the divine law, I am amazed that certain persons have thus presumed to write me with such audacity as to send on their letters in the name of the Church itself, "while the Church," they say, "consists of the bishop and the clergy and all those who are steadfast in the faith!"

St. Cyprian, Bishop of Carthage (A.D. 248–258), *Epistle XXXIII* (also numbered XXVI and XXVII), in J.-P. Migne, *Patrologia Latina,* IV, 305–6, trans. K. M. Setton.

C. St. Cyprian on the Independence of All Bishops Within the Church

Although Cyprian of Carthage believed, as we have seen above, "that the Church is founded upon the bishops," he also believed that all bishops were equal in rank and authority. The Church of the middle of the third century was much exercised by the question whether baptism received at the hands of a schismatic or a heretic was valid. Cyprian believed that there was no salvation outside the Church, and that heretics and schismatics were outside the Church. Therefore, heretical baptism was an evil farce, and was no baptism at all. Those who wished to enter the true Church must thus receive true baptism, which washed away all sin, and without which the penitent's soul was forever imperilled. Rebaptism, however, was contrary to the ancient practice of the Church, and so was strongly objected to by Bishop Stephen of Rome (254–256). Stephen apparently believed, if we may state his view in rather later terms, that defect neither of doctrine nor of character rendered invalid any sacrament administered by a properly ordained priest, however far the latter may have deviated into heresy or schism.

Stephen was vigorous and tactless in his opposition to Cyprian's view, which was shared by most of the Church in Africa; he removed a number of bishops and their churches from communion with the Roman See, which aroused great animus against him, especially in Africa and in Asia Minor. The question of the rebaptism of those who had received baptism at the hands of heretics was taken up by a council of eighty-seven African bishops at Carthage under the presidency of Cyprian in the year 256, at which council Cyprian began the proceedings, after the reading of some letters, with this address, emphasizing the equality and independence of all bishops within the Church:

You have heard, my dearly beloved colleagues, what Jubaianus, our fellow bishop, has written to me...concerning the unlawful and profane baptism of heretics, as well as what I wrote in answer to him, decreeing, to wit, what we have once and again and frequently determined, that heretics who come into the Church must be baptized and sanctified by the baptism of the Church. Moreover, another letter of Jubaianus has also been read to you, wherein, replying, in accordance with his sincere and religious devotion, to my letter, he has not only acquiesced in what I said, but, confessing that he had been instructed thereby, he has returned thanks for it.

It remains that upon his same matter each of us should bring forward what we think, judging no man, nor rejecting any one from the right of communion, if he should think differently from us. For neither does any of us set himself up as a bishop of bishops [an allusion to what Cyprian regards as an unwarranted assumption of power by the Bishop of Rome], nor by tyrannical terror does any compel his colleague to the necessity of obedience; since every bishop, according to the allowance of his liberty and power, has his own proper right of judgment, and can no more be judged by another than he himself can judge another.

But let us all wait for the judgment of our Lord Jesus Christ, who is the only one that has the power both of preferring us in the government of His Church, and of judging us in our conduct there.

Seventh Council of Carthage, trans. adapted from *Ante-Nicene Fathers*, V, 565.

D. The Opposition of Bishop Firmilian to the See of Rome

Cyprian's view of the equality and independence of bishops was shared not only by the African bishops present at the Council of Carthage, but also by the eastern bishops; it was at this time that one of the latter, Firmilian of Caesarea in Cappadocia, wrote Cyprian a well-known letter, of which parts are given below.[1]

Firmilian to Cyprian, his brother in the Lord, greeting. We have received by Rogatian, our beloved deacon, the letter sent by you which you wrote to us, well-beloved brother; and we gave the greatest thanks to the Lord, because it has happened that we who are separated from one another in body are thus united in spirit, as if we were not only occupying one country, but inhabiting together one and the self-same house. . . .

We may in the present matter give thanks to Stephen [the Bishop of Rome] that it has now happened through his unkindness that we receive the proof of your faith and wisdom. But although we have received the favor of this benefit on account of Stephen, certainly Stephen has not done anything deserving of kindness and thanks. . . . But let these things which were done by Stephen be passed by for the present, lest, while we remember his audacity and pride, we bring a more lasting sadness on ourselves from the things that he has wickedly done. . . .

Since the messenger sent by you was in haste to return to you, and the winter season was pressing [A.D. 256], we have replied what we could to your letter. And indeed, as respects what Stephen has said, as though the apostles forbade those who come from heresy to be baptized, and delivered this also to be observed by their successors, you have replied most abundantly that no one is so foolish as to believe that the apostles delivered this, when it is even well known that these heresies themselves, execrable and detestable as they are, arose subsequently. . . .

But they who are at Rome do not observe those things in all cases which are handed down from the beginning, and vainly pretend the authority of the apostles: this any one may know also from the fact that concerning the celebration of Easter, and concerning many other sacraments of divine matters, he may see

---

[1] Although Firmilian also agreed with Cyprian's views concerning baptism, we are not concerned with this problem: suffice it to say that the wiser views of the Bishop of Rome finally prevailed (in the West, at the Council of Arles in 314).

there are some diversities among them, and that all things are not observed among them alike, which are observed at Jerusalem, just as in very many other provinces also many things are varied because of the difference of places and people. And yet on this account there is no departure at all from the peace and unity of the Catholic Church, such as Stephen has now dared to make [i.e. no one bishop and no one see could arrogate to itself the authority of the Apostles Peter and Paul], breaking the peace against you, which his predecessors have always kept with you in mutual love and honor, even herein defaming Peter and Paul, the blessed Apostles, as if the very men delivered this who in their epistles execrated heretics, and warned us to avoid them. Whence it appears that this tradition is human which maintains heretics, and asserts that the latter have baptism, which belongs to the Church alone.... [Firmilian distorts the argument of Stephen, seeking to reduce it to absurdity.]

And in this respect I am justly indignant at the open and manifest folly of Stephen, in that he who so boasts of the place of his episcopate and contends *that he holds the succession of Peter,* on whom the foundation of the Church was laid, should introduce many other rocks and establish many new churches, maintaining that there is baptism in them by his authority. For they who are baptized, without doubt, make up the number of the Church.... Stephen, who announces that he holds by succession the throne of Peter, is stirred with no zeal against heretics, when he concedes to them, not a moderate, but the very greatest power of grace....

This indeed you Africans are able to say against Stephen, that when you knew the truth you forsook the error of custom. But we join custom to truth, and to the Romans' custom we oppose custom, but the custom of truth, holding from the beginning that which was delivered by Christ and the Apostles. Nor do we remember that this at any time began among us, since it has always been ob-

served here, that we have known but one Church of God, and have accounted no baptism holy except that of the holy Church....

Consider with what want of judgment you dare to blame those who strive for the truth against falsehood [Firmilian now writes as though addressing Stephen directly.].... For how much strife and how many dissensions you have stirred up throughout the churches of the whole world! Moreover, how great sin you have heaped up for yourself, when you cut yourself off from so many flocks! For it is yourself that you have cut off! Do not deceive yourself, since he is really the schismatic who has made himself an apostate from the communion of ecclesiastical unity. For while you think that all may be excommunicated by you, you have alone excommunicated yourself from all, and not even the precepts of an Apostle have been able to mould you to the rule of truth and peace....

How carefully has Stephen fulfilled these salutary commands and warnings of the Apostle, keeping in the first place lowliness of mind and meekness! For what is more lowly or meek than to have disagreed with so many bishops throughout the whole world, breaking peace with each one of them in various kinds of discord: at one time with the Easterners, as we are sure is not unknown to you; at another time with you who are in the South, from whom he received bishops as messengers so patiently and meekly as not to receive them even to the speech of common conference; and, even more, so unmindful of love and charity as to command the whole brotherhood that no one should receive them into his house, so that not only peace and communion, but also shelter and hospitality were denied to them when they came. This is to have kept the unity of the Spirit in the bond of peace, to cut himself off from the unity of love, and to make himself a stranger in all things to his brethren, and to rebel against the sacrament and the faith with the madness of contumacious discord!...

And yet Stephen is not ashamed to

afford patronage to such [heretics] in opposition to the Church, and for the sake of maintaining heretics to divide the brotherhood, and in addition to call Cyprian "a false Christ, a false apostle, and a deceitful worker." Stephen, conscious that all these characters are in himself, has been in advance of you by falsely charging another with those things which he himself ought deservedly to hear. We all bid you, for all our sakes, with all the bishops who are in Africa, and all the clergy, and all the brotherhood [of Christendom], farewell; that, constantly of one mind, and thinking the same thing, we may find you united with us even though afar off.

Firmilian of Caesarea, *Epistle to Cyprian*, 1–3, 5–6, 17, 19, 24–26, in Cyprian, *Epistles*, no. 74, trans. adapted from *Ante-Nicene Fathers*, V. 390–97.

E. The Council of Sardica and the Right of Appeal to the Bishop of Rome

In contrast to the foregoing statements of Cyprian and Firmilian, in opposition to the ever increasing authority and influence of the Roman See within the Church, the student will find in the document which follows one of the first great markers along the road which leads to the final establishment of papal supremacy over the western Church.

In A.D. 343 a church council met at Sardica, the modern Sofia, to consider certain questions relating to the doctrine of the Council of Nicaea. The western bishops at the council affirmed the Nicene doctrine, but the eastern bishops opposed it, and withdrew to Philippopolis where they held a small council of their own. The western bishops, according to the Roman tradition of the text, passed the following canons recognizing the appellate jurisdiction of the Roman See. There is no doubt, however, as to the authenticity of these canons.

Canon 3. Bishop Hosius [of Cordova] said: "And it is necessary to add this: that no bishop should pass from his own province into another province in which there are bishops, unless he should happen to have been invited by his brethren, so that we may not appear to be closing the gates of love. And yet we must also make this provision: that if in any province, any bishop bring suit against his brother and fellow bishop, neither one of them is to call in bishops, as arbitrators, from another province. But if any bishop appears to have had the decision in any case go against him improperly, and believes that he does not have a bad cause, but rather a good one, so that the decision should be reviewed, then, if it seems best to you all, let us honor the memory of the Apostle Peter, and agree that letters be written to Julius, the Bishop of Rome [337–352], by those who have tried the case, so that the trial may be reopened, if it should seem necessary, by the neighboring bishops, and let Bishop Julius himself appoint arbitrators. Nevertheless, if he is not able to advise that the case is of such sort that it requires a second trial, then the first settlement of the case shall not be undone, but shall thereby be confirmed.

"Are you all in agreement with this?"

The synod replied: "We are!"

Canon 4. Bishop Gaudentius [of Naissus, now Nish] said: "We must add, if you please, to this decision of true sanctity, which you have just passed, that if any bishop has been deposed by the judgment of those bishops who are his neighbors, and declares that he has something to add in the matter of his defense, let no other bishop be established in his see [*cathedra*] before the Bishop of Rome has been apprised of the case and rendered his judgment."

Canon 5. Bishop Hosius said: "Let it be agreed, then, that if any bishop has been accused, and the assembled bishops of that region have removed him from office, and he, as it were, seeks refuge in appeal to the blessed Bishop of the Roman Church, and wishes the latter to hear him, then if the Bishop of Rome thinks it right that the investigation of the matter should be renewed, let him decide to write to those fellow bishops of the accused, who are close to his province, in order that they may conduct a careful and exact inquiry into all aspects of the case, and render a decision in the affair in accord with what they believe to be the truth. But if anyone should think it worthwhile that his case should be heard still once more, and if by his entreaty he should prevail upon the Bishop of Rome to send presbyters from his own staff, then it shall be in the power of that Bishop, if he believes and decides that it is right, to send such presbyters to render judgment together with the bishops; and those who are thus sent from Rome are to have the authority of the one from whom they have been sent. Well, we have agreed this is to be done. But if the Bishop of Rome thinks that the neighboring bishops are sufficient for hearing the case and rendering a decision concerning the bishop in question, he shall do whatever seems to be best in the great wisdom of his judgment."

The bishops answered: "We approve of what has been said!"

The Council of Sardica (A.D. 343), Canons 3–5, trans. K. M. Setton, from Heinrich Denzinger, *Enchiridion symbolorum*, 28th ed. by C. Rahner (Freiburg and Barcelona, 1952), sections 57b-d, pp. 33–35.

F. St. Jerome to Pope Damasus

The following selection from a letter which St. Jerome addressed to Pope Damasus (A.D. 367–384), from the East about A.D. 376, illustrates clearly Jerome's high reverence for the See of Rome, "for this, I know, is the rock on which the Church is built."

Since the East, shattered as it is by the long standing feuds subsisting between its peoples, is bit by bit tearing into shreds the seamless garment of the Lord, "woven from the top throughout," since the foxes are destroying the vineyard of Christ, and since among the broken cisterns that hold no water it is hard to discover "the sealed fountain" and "the garden inclosed," I think it my duty to consult the chair of Peter, and to turn to a church whose faith has been praised by Paul. I appeal for spiritual food to the church whence I have received the garb of Christ. The wide space of sea and land that lies between us cannot deter me from searching for "the pearl of great price." "Wheresoever the body is, there will the eagles be gathered together." Evil children have squandered their patrimony; you alone keep your heritage intact. The fruitful soil of Rome, when it receives the pure seed of the Lord, bears fruit an hundredfold; but here the seed corn is choked in the furrows and nothing grows but darnel or oats. In the West the Sun of righteousness is even now rising; in the East, Lucifer, who fell from heaven, has once more set his throne above the stars. "Ye are the light of the world," "ye are the salt of the earth," "ye are vessels of gold and of silver." Here are vessels of wood or of earth, which wait for the rod of iron, and eternal fire.

Yet though your greatness terrifies me, your kindness attracts me. From the priest I demand the safe-keeping of the victim, from the shepherd the protection due to the sheep. Away with all that is overweening; let the state of Roman majesty withdraw. My words are spoken to the successor of the fisherman, to the disciple of the cross. As I follow no leader save Christ, so I communicate with none but your blessedness, that is with the chair of Peter. For this, I know, is the rock on which the church is built! This is the house where alone the paschal lamb can be rightly eaten. This is the ark of Noah, and he who is not found in it shall perish when the flood prevails. But since by reason of my sins I have betaken myself to this desert which lies between Syria and the uncivilized waste, I cannot, owing to the great distance between us, always ask of your sanctity the holy thing of the Lord.

St. Jerome, Ep. XV, to Pope Damasus, trans. W. H. Fremantle, *Nicene and Post-Nicene Fathers*, 2nd series, VI, 18.

G. The Authority of the Roman See under Pope Leo the Great

In the early fifth century the western provinces of the Empire were overrun by the Vandals, Visigoths, and other barbarians. After the death of the Emperor Theodosius I (395) and his general Stilicho (408) Roman government was never again strong in the West. Roman administration faltered and finally failed; the towns declined still further; there was an increased localization of markets; and the imperial government at Ravenna lost effective touch with the provinces. As civil institutions failed, ecclesiastical institutions grew in strength; the Church took over many of the functions of the State. By the time of Pope Leo I (440–461) the Petrine theory of the papacy had reached the conclusion of the first period of its development. On Leo's concept of the pope as the "heir of St. Peter," of great importance when viewed under the light of Roman law, see Walter Ullmann, "Leo I and the Theme of Papal Primacy," in *The Journal of Theological Studies*, new series, XI (1960), 25–51. After gaining recognition of its authority in doctrinal matters, the papacy had gone on to achieve a position of supremacy in the entire polity of the western Church. There were still dissenting voices, but now they were fewer and weaker than they had been in earlier generations. In 445 the Emperor Valentinian III recognized the authority of the Pope over the western Church.

It is certain that the only protection both for us and for our Empire lies in the favor of God on high, and in order to earn this favor we must above all support the Christian faith and its revered religion. Since moreover the merit of St. Peter, who stands first in renown among bishops, has confirmed the primacy of the Apostolic See, as has the importance of the city of

Rome, and also the authority of the holy synod, let no man's presumption make an unlawful attack upon the authority of this See. For peace will be preserved in churches everywhere only if all Christendom acknowledges its ruler. Although these principles have been observed without violation up to now, Hilary, Bishop of Arles [who had challenged the good judgment and authority of Pope Leo I], as we have learned from the faithful report of that venerable man, Pope Leo of Rome, has attempted certain unlawful undertakings with bold daring and unwarranted presumption, and in consequence of this the most wretched tumult has assailed the churches north of the Alps [Hilary having been primate of the Church in Gaul].... By such audacious acts [as those of which Hilary has been guilty] confidence in our reign is diminished, and reverence for it is outraged. Not only therefore must we dispel such an attitude, which is in itself a great offense, but lest a disturbance, however slight, should arise among the churches, or religious discipline seem to be relaxed in some way, this do we decree by a law in perpetuity: that nothing is to be attempted either by the bishops of Gaul or by those of other provinces contrary to ancient custom, without the authority of the venerable Pope of the Eternal City. But whatever the authority of the Apostolic See has established or shall establish is to be taken as law for these bishops and for all others, so that whenever a bishop has been summoned to appear before the tribunal of the Roman Pope, and has failed to do so, he is to be forced to make such appearance by the governor of the province in which he resides.

Letter of Valentinian III to Aetius, dated 8 July, 445, in Migne, *Patr. Lat.*, LIV, 637–38, trans. K. M. Setton.

H. The Voice of Pope Leo the Great

1.

...And from Christ's overruling and eternal protection we have received the support of the Apostles' aid also, which

assuredly does not cease from its operation: and the strength of the foundation on which the whole superstructure of the Church is reared is not weakened by the weight of the temple that rests upon it. For the solidity of that faith which was praised in the chief of the Apostles is perpetual: and as that remains which

Peter believed in Christ, so that remains which Christ instituted in Peter. For when, as has been read in the gospel lesson [for today], the Lord had asked the disciples whom they believed Him to be amid the various opinions that were held, and the blessed Peter had replied, saying, "Thou art the Christ, the Son of the living God," the Lord said, "Blessed art thou, Simon Bar-Jona, because flesh and blood hath not revealed it to thee, but my Father, which is in heaven. And I say unto thee, that thou art Peter, and upon this rock will I build my Church, and the gates of hell shall not prevail against it. And I will give unto thee the keys of the kingdom of heaven. And whatsoever thou shalt bind on earth, shall be bound in heaven; and whatsoever thou shalt loose on earth, shall be loosed also in heaven."

The dispensation of Truth therefore abides, and the blessed Peter persevering in the strength of the Rock, which he has received, has not abandoned the helm of the Church, which he undertook. For he was ordained before the rest in such a way that from his being called the Rock, from his being pronounced the Foundation, from his being constituted the Doorkeeper of the kingdom of heaven, from his being set as the Umpire to bind and to loose, whose judgments shall retain their validity in heaven, from all these mystical titles we might know the nature of his association with Christ. And still today he more fully and effectually performs what is entrusted to him, and carries out every part of his duty and charge in Him and with Him, through Whom he has been glorified. And so if anything is rightly done and rightly decreed by us, if anything is won from the mercy of God by our daily supplications, it is of his work and merits whose power lives and whose authority prevails in his See. For this, dearly-beloved, was gained by that confession, which, inspired in the Apostle's heart by God the Father, transcended all the uncertainty of human opinions, and was endued with the firmness of a rock, which no assaults could shake. For throughout the Church Peter daily says, "Thou art the Christ, the Son of the living God," and every tongue which confesses the Lord, accepts the instruction his voice conveys.

Leo the Great, *Third Sermon*, 2–3, trans. C. L. Feltoe, in *Nicene and Post-Nicene Fathers*, 2nd series, XII, 117.

2.

The so-called Second Ecumenical Council of Constantinople in 381 declared, in its third canon, that "the Bishop of Constantinople shall have the prerogative of honor after the Bishop of Rome, *because Constantinople is the New Rome*." The twenty-eighth canon of the famous Council of Chalcedon in 451 was still more explicit: "For the Fathers rightly granted privileges to the throne of Old Rome, because it was the royal city, and the 150 most religious bishops, moved by the same considerations, gave equal privileges to the most holy throne of New Rome [in 381], judging with good reason that the city which is honored with the sovereignty and the Senate, and also enjoys equal privileges with old imperial Rome, should in ecclesiastical matters also be magnified as she is, and rank next after her...." But the Roman See claimed its prerogative not "because it was the royal city," but because of its foundation by St. Peter, "and upon this rock [*petra*] I will build my Church." A see is apostolic if founded by an apostle; no canon of a church council can alter historical fact; the mere political preeminence of a city did not bestow upon the see in that city ecclesiastical superiority over other sees (for Constantinople claimed jurisdiction over much of the eastern Church). The three letters which follow are worthy of careful study; they set forth papal views of the position of the Roman See, its relation to the See of Constantinople, and hence to other sees. (Anatolius, mentioned below, was Patriarch of Constantinople.)

To Marcianus Augustus.... Let the city of Constantinople have, as we desire, its high rank, and under the protection of God's right hand, long enjoy your Clemency's rule. Yet things secular stand on a different basis from things divine: and there can be no sure building save on that rock which the Lord has laid for a foundation. He that covets what is not his due, loses what is his own. Let it be enough for Anatolius that by the aid of your piety and by my favour and approval he has obtained the bishopric of so great a city. Let him not disdain a city which is royal, though he cannot make it an Apostolic See; and let him on no account hope that he can rise by doing injury to others. For the privileges of the churches determined by the canons of the holy Fathers, and fixed by the decrees of the Nicene Synod, cannot be overthrown by any unscrupulous act, nor disturbed by any innovation. And in the faithful execution of this task by the aid of Christ I am bound to display an unflinching devotion; for it is a charge entrusted to me, and it tends to my condemnation if the rules sanctioned by the Fathers and drawn up under the guidance of God's Spirit at the Synod of Nicaea for the government of the whole Church are violated with my connivance (which God forbid), and if the wishes of a single brother have more weight with me than the common good of the Lord's whole house.

Leo the Great, *Epistle 104*, 3, trans. Feltoe, *op. cit.*, p. 75.

3.

To Pulcheria Augusta. ...Let [Anatolius, Patriarch of Constantinople] realize what a man he has succeeded, and expelling all the spirit of pride let him imitate the faith of Flavian [his predecessor], the modesty of Flavian, the humility of Flavian, which has raised him to a confessor's glory. If he will shine with his virtues, he will merit all praise, and in all quarters he will win an abundance of love not by seeking human advancement but by deserving divine favor. And by this careful course I promise he will bind my heart also to him, and the love of the Apostolic See, which we have ever bestowed on the church of Constantinople, shall never be violated by any change. Because if sometimes rulers fall into errors through want of moderation, yet the churches of Christ do not lose their purity. In keeping with your own piety [he is writing to the Empress], we declare invalid the assents of the bishops [see below], since they are inconsistent with the provisions of the holy canons composed at Nicaea, and by the authority of the blessed Apostle Peter we annul them absolutely, for we obey in all ecclesiastical cases the laws which the Holy Spirit established, through the 318 bishops [at Nicaea], for the peaceful observance of all priests, so that even if a much greater number were to pass a decree different from theirs, whatever was opposed to their pronouncement would have to be disregarded.

Leo the Great, *Epistle 105*, 3, revised from translation of Feltoe, *op. cit.*, p. 77.

4

As the student now reads the final source herewith presented to illustrate "the triumph of Christianity," he may again contemplate the question with which our general Introduction closed. Was the establishment of papal authority the gradual but deliberate recognition by western Christendom of what was believed to be the will of God, or was it the result of historical accident and development?

To Bishop Anatolius [Patriarch of Constantinople]. ...Your purpose is in no way whatever supported by the written assent of certain bishops given, as you allege, 60 years ago [at the Council of Constantinople in 381], and never brought to the knowledge of the Apostolic See by your predecessors; and this transaction, which from its outset was doomed to fall through and has now long done so, you now wish to bolster up by means that are too late and useless, namely, by extracting from the brethren an appearance of consent which their modesty from very weariness yielded to their own injury. Remember what the Lord threatens him with, who shall have caused one of the little ones to stumble, and get wisdom to understand what a judgment of God he will have to endure who has not feared to give occasion of stumbling to so many churches and so many priests. For I confess that I am so fast bound by love of the whole brotherhood that I will not agree with any one in demands which are against his own interests, and thus you may clearly perceive that my opposition to you, beloved, proceeds from the kindly intention to restrain you, by sounder counsel, from disturbing the universal Church. The rights of provincial primates may not be overthrown nor metropolitan bishops be defrauded of privileges based on antiquity. The See of Alexandria may not lose any of that dignity which it merited through St. Mark, the evangelist and disciple of the blessed Peter, nor may the splendor of so great a church be obscured by another's clouds, Dioscorus [recently deposed Patriarch of Alexandria] having fallen through his own persistence in impiety. The church of Antioch too, in which first at the preaching of the blessed Apostle Peter the Christian name arose, must continue in the position assigned to it by the Fathers, and being set in the third place [by the sixth canon of the Council of Nicaea] must never be lowered therefrom. For the See is on a footing different from that of its holders, and each individual's chief honor is his own integrity. And since that does not lose its proper worth in any place, how much more glorious must it be when placed in the magnificence of the city of Constantinople, where many priests may find both a defence of the Fathers' canons and an example of uprightness in observing you? In thus writing to you, brother, I exhort and admonish you in the Lord, laying aside all ambitious desires in order to cherish a spirit of love....

Leo the Great, *Epistle 106*, 5–6, adapted from translation of Feltoe, *op. cit.*, p. 79.

3

Byzantium
and the West

PETER CHARANIS

Rutgers University

The year A.D. 476 is generally taken by historians of the West as marking the end of the Roman Empire, because in that year the barbarian Odovacar put an end to the imperial office in Italy. But the Empire had been broken up already. Long before 476 the Vandals had established themselves in North Africa and the Visigoths in Spain, while the Burgundians had settled in the Rhone valley. Not long after 476 the Frank Clovis made his appearance, and conquered Gaul, while the Ostrogoth Theodoric broke into Italy where, supported by his people, he set himself up as king. Meanwhile Britain had been abandoned to the Anglo-Saxons. The Roman Empire was no more.

But this was true of the West only. The eastern half of the Empire, consisting of Egypt, Syria and Palestine, Asia Minor and the major part of the Balkan peninsula, did not succumb to the barbarians. The East had by now become the center of power. Constantinople, founded by Constantine the Great (d. 337) and patterned to some extent after Rome, had been dedicated as the new capital of the Empire in 330. After Constantine the Great, and especially after the death of Theodosius I (d. 395), there was an emperor at Constantinople and another in Italy, but the former was usually in a stronger position than the latter. Constantinople outstripped Rome in population, wealth, and political activity. It became also a great cultural center. The emperor who resided there represented, along with his colleague in Italy, the Roman imperial tradition. In surviving the barbarian flood which inundated the West and brought to an end the imperial office in Italy, Constantinople and the East preserved the continuity of that tradition. This is the Empire which modern historians generally call "Byzantine" and sometimes "Greek": "Byzantine" because Constantinople occupied the site of the old Greek city of Byzantium and was sometimes itself called Byzantium; "Greek" because of its Greek character, at least in language.

The Byzantine Empire is one of the great empires in history. It endured for over a thousand years. Down to about the middle of the eleventh century it was the center of civilization in Christendom. It preserved the thought and literature of antiquity; it developed new forms of art; it held back the barbarians. It produced great statesmen, soldiers, and diplomats, as well as reformers and renowned scholars. Its missionaries, aided by its diplomats and sometimes by its armies, spread the gospel among the pagan tribes, especially the Slavs, who dwelt along its frontiers and beyond. As a Czech historian has put it, Byzantium "moulded the undisciplined tribes of Serbs, Bulgars, Russians, Croats even, and made nations out of them; it gave to them its religion and institutions, taught their princes how to govern, transmitted to them the very principles of civilization—writing and literature."[1] Throughout its long period of existence all, of course, was not triumph and glory. In its internal life acts of treachery and cruelty, revolts, social and religious strife, were not uncommon. There were times when it suffered serious military reverses and losses in territory. But at no time, except perhaps during the last phase of its declining years, was it an insignificant force. It finally succumbed to the Turks in 1453. Among the factors which brought about its end, the antagonism and hostility which developed between Greeks and Latins were not the least significant.

In the centuries which followed the disintegration of the Roman power in the West, Byzantium and the West went through divergent developments. There were, to begin with, some important differences between the two. There was the difference in language: Greek in Byzantium, Latin in the West. There was the difference in ethnic composition with all its cultural implications. The West was Latin and Germanic; Byzantium and the regions under its influence, especially after Egypt and Syria were lost to the Arabs, were Greek, Slavic, and Armenian. More differences developed as the two regions evolved under different historical conditions. The West came to be broken up into numerous feudatories with no, or hardly any, central organization; Byzantium remained a great Empire with a well established administrative system. The West derived its living almost entirely from agriculture; Byzantium drew its wealth from commerce and industry in addition to agriculture. The West had almost no cities; Byzantium had such great urban centers as Constantinople and Thessalonica. The West had forgotten Greek, and Byzantium was contemptuous of Latin. A Byzantine emperor in the ninth century described Latin as a "barbarous

---

[1] F. Dvorník, *Les Slaves, Byzance et Rome au IXᵉ Siècle* (Paris, 1928), p. ii.

and Scythian" language. The Byzantines, proud of their superior culture, referred to the Westerners as barbarians, "children of darkness," in the words of a Byzantine patriarch. The Latins, not understanding the subtleties of Byzantine diplomacy, considered the Greeks treacherous and unfaithful. A Western ambassador, sent to Constantinople by the German emperor in the tenth century, scribbled on the wall of his quarters:

> "Trust not the Greeks; they live but to betray;
> Nor heed their promises, whate'er they say.
> If lies will serve them, any oath they swear,
> And when it's time to break it feel no fear."[2]

Two developments in particular contributed in giving rise to, and intensifying, the antagonism between Byzantium and the West. One was the revival of the Roman imperial title in the West in the year 800. The Byzantines never quite became reconciled to this development. At times, under the force of circumstance, they might yield to the extent of recognizing the title of Emperor, but at no time would they concede that a barbarian king of the West could represent the Roman imperial tradition. This point is well illustrated by a passage taken from the work of Liudprand of Cremona, the ambassador of the German emperor to whom reference has already been made.[3] An "embassy," writes Liudprand, "came from the apostolic and universal Pope John with a letter asking Nicephorus 'the emperor of the Greeks' to conclude an alliance and firm friendship with his beloved and spiritual son Otto, 'august emperor of the Romans.' If you ask me why these words, and manner of address, which to the Greeks seem sinful audacity, did not cost the bearer his life..., I cannot answer. The Greeks abused the sea, cursed the waves.... 'The audacity of it!' they cried, 'to call the universal emperor of the Romans, the one and only Nicephorus, the great, the august, "emperor of the Greeks," and to style a poor barbaric creature "emperor of the Romans!" O sky! O earth! O sea! What shall we do with these scoundrels and criminals?' " The rivalry of the two Empires over the possession of certain territories in southern Italy contributed to their antagonism, but the question of the imperial title always remained a fundamental issue. "Do you want a greater scandal," said the Byzantine Emperor Nicephorus to Liudprand, "than that he [Otto of Germany] should call himself Emperor and claim for himself provinces belonging to our Empire? Both these things are intolerable; and if both are insupportable, that especially is not to be borne, nay, not to be heard of, that he calls himself Emperor."[4]

The other development was the separation of the Churches. This more than anything else gave expression to the psychological and cultural differences which had grown up between Byzantium and the West. The break did not take place all at once; it was long in coming, but the Church in Byzantium and the Church in the West never really understood each other. Except for the last years of its existence the Byzantine Empire was not an ethnically homogeneous unit. Within its

---

[2] F. A. Wright, trans., *The Works of Liudprand of Cremona* (New York: E. P. Dutton & Co., Inc. and Routledge & Kegan Paul, Ltd., 1930), p. 270.
[3] *Ibid.*, pp. 263–64.
[4] *Ibid.*, p. 249.

borders were different peoples representing different but well-established cultural traditions. As a consequence differences of opinion, taking a theological form, often developed. The Byzantine Church, in dealing with these differences, usually took into account the realities of the situation. This point of view Rome never really understood, and her intervention to bring about solutions on her own conditions often led to the disruption of relations with Byzantium. Thus, in the fifth century the question over the nature of Christ led to a schism between Rome and Byzantium which lasted for almost 40 years. In the eighth century the dispute over the problem of the worship of images led to another schism. This schism was one of the factors which prompted the papacy to seek the cooperation of the Franks, a cooperation which had as a consequence the revival of the imperial title in the West. And again in the ninth century the intervention of the papacy in a dispute which arose in the Byzantine Church over the designation of a new patriarch in Constantinople had as a consequence another schism—the famous Photian schism. Much in this schism has been shown by modern scholarship to be legendary, but its historical significance as a contributory factor in the final and permanent separation of the two Churches can hardly be overestimated.

The permanent separation of the two Churches is associated with events of the eleventh century. For reasons not quite clear, a break in the relations between Rome and Constantinople occurred sometime after 1009. An attempt made some years later to re-establish relations ended in failure, and then in 1054 a new crisis was produced. The crisis was provoked by the Byzantine patriarch, Cerularius, who viewed with alarm the activities of the papacy in southern Italy, a region where the Church of Byzantium had jurisdictional interests. But the violence of the quarrel was due to the obstinacy and arrogance of Cardinal Humbert, who headed the papal delegation sent to Constantinople in an effort to settle the differences which existed between the two Churches. Humbert and Cerularius excommunicated each other, and the Churches were further apart than ever before. Involved in the quarrel were the different liturgical usages of the two Churches and their difference in creed—the problem of the *filioque*—but the fundamental issue was the question of the supremacy of the papacy. The arrogance with which Cardinal Humbert insisted upon this point completely alienated the Byzantines. The papal delegates, writes the Catholic scholar Jugie, "had wished...to act in Constantinople as they would have acted in a city of the West. And they did not notice that in Constantinople they cut the figures of arrogant strangers with insupportable airs."[5] The quarrel of 1054 is generally regarded by scholars as the beginning of the permanent separation of the two Churches.

The divergent developments, and the consequent antagonisms which one notices in the relations between Byzantium and the West, had not yet, up to the end of the eleventh century, created an unbridgeable chasm between the two sections of Christendom. Intercourse between them was not always unfriendly. At times princes of the West cooperated militarily with the emperor of Constantinople; there were marriage alliances. Even the relations between the Churches might be best

---

[5] Martin Jugie, *Le Schisme byzantin* (Paris, 1941), p. 218.

described, despite the schisms which separated them at times, as indifferent rather than hostile. The bitter quarrel of 1054 itself was not regarded as ending all hope of reconciliation. One hundred years later, however, this was no longer true. A Byzantine historian wrote toward the end of the twelfth century: "Between us and the Latins a bottomless gulf of enmity has established itself; we cannot unite our souls and we entirely disagree with each other although we keep up our external relations and often live in the same house." "The Latins," wrote another Greek writer, "consider that the world is not big enough to hold both the Greeks and themselves." This state of affairs was brought about largely, if not entirely, by the Crusades.

I. The Problem of the Origin of the First Crusade

The question of the origin of the First Crusade, and with it the crusading movement, despite the voluminous literature that exists on the subject, still remains a problem. The facts themselves are clear enough. In 1071 the Seljuk Turks, already converted to Islam when they made their appearance, inflicted a disastrous defeat upon the Byzantines in a place, located deep in Asia Minor, called Mantzikert. For reasons associated primarily with the internal conditions of their Empire, the Byzantines were not able to recover from this defeat, and it was not long before the Seljuks overwhelmed virtually all Asia Minor. Three years after Mantzikert we find Pope Gregory VII urging the faithful of the West to go to the assistance of the Greeks, and some months later, writing to the German Emperor Henry IV, that he was organizing an expedition of 50,000 men in response to the appeals of the Greeks, whose Church, he said, wanted to reunite itself with Rome. He stated further that, if possible, he would command this expedition himself and would go as far as Jerusalem. The expedition contemplated by Gregory VII, of course, never took place. In the spring of 1095 at a church council held at Piacenza, in which Pope Urban II participated, Greek ambassadors representing the Byzantine Emperor Alexius are said to have been present and to have appealed for help against the Seljuks. It is further said that Pope Urban urged those present to go to the assistance of the Greeks. During the summer of 1095 Urban toured France, and in November of the same year attended the Council of Clermont, where he made what is described as an eloquent appeal, urging the faithful to launch an expedition whose ultimate objective should be the liberation of Jerusalem. The First Crusade, and with it the beginning of the crusading movement, followed.

The question which now arises is this: What prompted Urban to make his appeal for this expedition at the time he did, and what did he hope to accomplish besides the alleged objective of liberating Jerusalem? The question has been answered variously by the different historians who have studied the problem. But let the student himself, by studying the sources at his disposal, come to his own conclusion. In studying these sources, however, he should keep in mind several things relating to conditions which existed in western Europe at the time. He should remember that the papacy was in the midst of the Investiture Struggle (see Chapter 4) whose outcome was still in doubt; that the peace and truce of God, which the Church had proclaimed in order to check the widely prevalent private warfare, had not yet succeeded; that the Church had already sanctioned the wars of the Christians against the Moslems in Spain and in Sicily; that numerous pilgrimages were taking place to the Holy Land; that western warriors were eager to seek their fortunes whenever opportunities offered themselves. He should remember also that the mercantile class which was now rising in western Europe, especially in Italy, was ready to push its interests in the Near East where trade and commerce had been thriving for centuries.

The sources themselves are scanty, a fact which explains to a large extent why the origin of the First Crusade is still a problem. We have brought together virtually all of them. Among the Latin sources we include: (1) three letters of Pope Gregory VII, urging the West to go to the assistance of Byzantium and, in one of them, broaching the possibility of liberating Jerusalem; (2) the reference to the presence of Byzantine ambassadors at the

Council of Piacenza as it is reported by the Latin chronicler Bernold who, if not present himself at Piacenza, must have derived his information from his bishop who had been there; (3) the speech which Urban II delivered at Clermont as it was recorded some years later by four chroniclers, two of whom, Robert the Monk and Balderic of Bourgueil, say that they were present at Clermont, while the other two, Fulcher of Chartres and Guibert of Nogent, were probably also there; and (4) the letter which Urban II wrote toward the end of December, 1095, to the assembling crusaders. Among the Greek sources, there are only two of any significance. One is the account of Anna Comnena in which she relates the coming of the crusaders to Constantinople and gives her own version of the cause of the crusade. Anna wrote the *Alexiad*—the title of her book (on her father Alexius)—some years after the First Crusade, but she was the daughter of the Byzantine Emperor Alexius and, as a consequence, must have had access to important sources of information. It must be pointed out, however, that in matters pertaining to the relations of her father with the West she is not always well informed. The other is a passage drawn from a Greek world chronicle written in the thirteenth century by a Byzantine ecclesiastic, Theodore Skutariotes. The passage, of course, is not contemporary with the event to which it refers, but, as the chronicle of Skutariotes as a whole is known to derive from good sources, it deserves serious consideration.

These are virtually all the sources that bear upon the problem of the origin of the First Crusade.

A. The Appeal of Gregory VII on Behalf of the Greeks

1. LETTER TO COUNT WILLIAM OF BURGUNDY, FEBRUARY 2, 1074

Gregory...to Count William of Burgundy, greeting...

Your Prudence may remember how affectionately the Roman Church received your Mightiness not long since and how greatly it enjoyed your visit. Nor can you in decency forget the promise which you made to God before the tomb of Peter, chief of the Apostles, in the presence of our venerable predecessor, Pope Alexander, and of an innumerable company of bishops, abbots and people of many nations, that whenever necessary your force would not be lacking if it were called for in defense of the property of St. Peter.

Wherefore, remembering the noble repute of your honor, we beg and require of your prudence and your zeal that you bring together a military force to protect the freedom of the Roman Church and if need be that you come hither with your army in the service of St. Peter. We beg you also to send this same summons to the count of St. Giles, father-in-law of Richard, prince of Capua, and to Amadeus, son of Adelaide of Turin, and others whom you know to be loyal to St. Peter and who made the same promise with hands upraised to Heaven. If we decide to send a definite reply to Your Prudence, send back word to us by the same messenger, who will relieve us of all doubts. And let that same messenger of yours come by the way of the countess Beatrice; who, with her daughter and her son-in-law, Duke Godfrey of Lorraine, is promoting this enterprise.

We are not, however, trying to bring together this force of fighting men for the sacrifice of Christian blood, but in order that our enemies, learning of the expedition, may fear to join battle and be the more easily won over to the right side. We are hoping also that another advantage may come from this, namely, that when the Normans are pacified we may cross over to Constantinople in aid of the Christians who, oppressed by frequent attacks of the Saracens, are urging us eagerly to reach out our hands to them in succor. The troops we have with us are sufficient against those Normans who are in rebellion against us. And be assured that you and all who shall join you in this undertaking will receive a double—nay, as we believe, a manifold—reward from Peter and Paul, chiefs of the Apostles.

The Correspondence of Pope Gregory VII, trans. Ephraim Emerton (New York: Columbia University Press, 1932), pp. 22–23.

2. The Summons to the Faithful to Defend Constantinople, March 1, 1074

Gregory...to all who are willing to defend the Christian faith, greeting....

We desire to make known to you that the bearer of these presents upon his recent return from beyond the seas visited us at the threshold of the Apostles. From him, as also from many others, we have learned that a people of the pagans have been pressing hard upon the Christian empire, have cruelly laid waste the country almost to the walls of Constantinople and slaughtered like sheep many thousand Christians. Wherefore, if we love God and acknowledge ourselves to be Christians, we ought to be deeply grieved by the wretched fate of that great empire and the murder of so many followers of Christ. But it is not enough to grieve over this event; the example of our Redeemer and the duty of brotherly love demand of us that we should set our hearts upon the deliverance of our brethren. For as he offered his life for us, so ought we to offer our lives for our brothers. Be it known, therefore, that we, trusting in the mercy of God and in the might of his power, are preparing in every possible way to carry aid to the Christian empire as soon as may be, by God's help. We adjure you, by the faith in which you are united [to them] in the adoption of the sons of God, and by authority of St. Peter, prince of the Apostles, to be stirred with compassion by the wounds and the blood of your brethren and the peril of the empire and willingly to offer your powerful aid to your brethren in the name of Christ.

Whatever decision you may make in this matter by God's mercy, pray report it to us without delay by trustworthy messengers.

Ibid., pp. 25–26.

3. Letter to Henry IV, Setting Forth Gregory's Plan for an Offensive Against the Turks, December 7, 1074

Gregory...to the glorious King Henry, greeting...

If God would grant by some act of his grace that my thoughts might lie open before you, I know beyond a doubt that no person could separate you from my sincere affection. But even as it is, I have entire confidence in his mercy, that it shall one day become clear that I am truly devoted to you. For to this I am directed by the common law of all Christian men; to this the majesty of empire and the mild sway of the Apostolic See impel me; so that if I do not love you as I ought, I am trusting in vain in the mercy of God through the merits of St. Peter.

But since I desire to labor day and night in the Lord's vineyard, through many dangers even unto death, I will always strive with God's help to preserve a sacred and merited affection not only towards you whom God has placed at the summit of earthly affairs and through whom many may be led either to wander from the path of rectitude or to observe the faith of Christ, but also toward the least among Christians. For he who should try to approach the marriage feast of the king without this wedding garment will suffer a monstrous disgrace. Alas! Those who are daily plotting to sow discord between us pay no attention to these truths, that with these nets prepared at the Devil's prompting they may catch their own advantage and conceal their own vices by which they are madly calling down upon themselves the wrath of God and of St. Peter. I therefore warn and exhort you, my best beloved son, to turn your ear away from them and listen without reserve to those who seek not their own but the things that are of Jesus Christ and who do not set their own honor or profit above righteousness, so that through their counsel you may not forfeit the glory of this life, but may gain with confidence the life that is in Christ Jesus.

Further, I call to your attention that the Christians beyond the sea, a great part of whom are being destroyed by the heathen with unheard-of slaughter and are daily being slain like so many sheep, have humbly sent to beg me to succor these our brethren in whatever ways I can, that the religion of Christ may not utterly perish in our time—which God forbid! I, therefore, smitten with exceeding grief and led even to long for death—for I would rather stake my life for these than reign over the whole earth and neglect them— have succeeded in arousing certain Christian men so that they are eager to risk their lives for their brethren in defense of the law of Christ and to show forth more clearly than the day the nobility of the sons of God. This summons has been readily accepted by Italians and northerners, by divine inspiration as I believe— nay, as I can absolutely assure you—and already fifty thousand men are preparing, if they can have me for their leader and prelate, to take up arms against the enemies of God and push forward even to the sepulcher of the Lord under his supreme leadership.

I am especially moved toward this undertaking because the Church of Constantinople, differing from us on the doctrine of the Holy Spirit, is seeking the fellowship of the Apostolic See, the Armenians are almost entirely estranged from the Catholic faith and almost all the Easterners are waiting to see how the faith of the Apostle Peter will decide among their divergent views. For it is the call of our time that the word of command shall be fulfilled which our blessed Savior deigned to speak to the prince of the Apostles: "I have prayed for thee that thy faith fail not: and when thou art converted, strengthen thy brethren." And because our fathers, in whose footsteps we, though unworthy, desire to walk, often went to those regions for the strengthening of the Catholic faith, we also, aided by the prayers of all Christian men, are under compulsion to go over there for the same faith and for the defense of Christians— provided that the way shall be opened with Christ as our guide—for the way of man is not in his own hand, and the steps of a man are ordered by the Lord.

But, since a great undertaking calls for the aid and counsel of the great, if God shall grant me to begin this, I beg you for your advice and for your help according to your good pleasure. For if it shall please God that I go, I shall leave the Roman Church, under God, in your hands to guard her as a holy mother and to defend her for his honor.

Advise me at the earliest possible moment of your pleasure in this matter and what your divinely inspired judgment may determine. If I did not have better hopes of you than many suppose, these exhortations would be in vain. But since there is perchance no man whom you can completely trust in regard to the sincerity of my affection for you, I leave to the Holy Spirit, which can do all things, to show you in its own way what I ask of you and how great is my devotion to you, and may it in the same way so dispose your heart toward me that the desires of the wicked may come to naught and those of the righteous may increase. These two desires are keeping incessant watch upon us two— though in different ways—and are fighting according to the wishes of those from whom they proceed.

May Almighty God, from whom cometh every good thing, cleanse you from all your sins by the merits and the authority of the blessed Apostles Peter and Paul, and make you to walk in the way of his commandments and lead you into life eternal.

Ibid., pp. 56–58.

B. Bernold on the Byzantine Embassy at the Council of Piacenza

There arrived at this council [Council of Piacenza, March, 1095] an embassy from the emperor of Constantinople which humbly beseeched Our Lord, the Pope, and all the faithful of Christ to procure for him some help against the pagans for the defense of our holy church which the pagans had already destroyed in his territories. The pagans had rendered themselves masters of his territories as far as the walls of the city of Constantinople. Our Lord the Pope, therefore, urged many to furnish this aid, even engaging them to promise under oath to go there with the consent of God and bring to this same emperor, to the best of their power, their most faithful aid against the pagans.

Bernold, *Chronicon, Monumenta Germaniae historica, SS., V,* 462, trans. Peter Charanis.

C. The Speech of Urban II at the Council of Clermont, November 27, 1095

1. THE VERSION OF FULCHER OF CHARTRES INCLUDING HIS DESCRIPTION OF CONDITIONS IN WESTERN EUROPE AT THAT TIME

In the year of our Lord 1095, in the reign of the so-called Emperor Henry in Germany and of King Philip in France, throughout Europe evils of all kinds waxed strong because of vacillating faith. Pope Urban II then ruled in the city of Rome. He was a man admirable in life and habits, who always strove wisely and energetically to raise the status of Holy Church higher and higher....

But the devil, who always desires man's destruction and goes about like a raging lion seeking whom he may devour, stirred up to the confusion of the people a certain rival to Urban, Wibert by name. Incited by the stimulus of pride and supported by the shamelessness of the aforesaid Emperor of the Bavarians, Wibert attempted to usurp the papal office while Urban's predecessor, Gregory, that is Hildebrand, was the legitimate Pope; and he thus caused Gregory himself to be cast out of St. Peter's. So the better people refused to recognize him because he acted thus perversely. After the death of Hildebrand, Urban, lawfully elected, was consecrated by the cardinal bishops, and the greater and holier part of the people submitted in obedience to him. Wibert, however, urged on by the support of the aforesaid Emperor and by the instigation of the Roman citizens, for some time kept Urban a stranger to the Church of St. Peter; but Urban, although he was banished from the Church, went about through the country, reconciling to God the people who had gone somewhat astray. Wibert, however, puffed up by the primacy of the Church, showed himself indulgent to sinners, and exercising the office of pope, although unjustly, amongst his adherents, he denounced as ridiculous the acts of Urban. But in the year in which the Franks first passed through Rome on their way to Jerusalem, Urban obtained complete papal power everywhere, with the help of a certain most noble matron, Matilda by name, who then had great influence in the Roman state. Wibert was then in Germany. So there were two Popes; and many did not know which to obey, or from which counsel should be taken, or who should remedy the ills of Christianity. Some favored the one; some the other. But it was clear to the intelligence of men that Urban was the better, for he is rightly considered better who controls his passions, just as if they were enemies. Wibert was Archbishop of the city of Ravenna. He was very rich and revelled in honor and wealth. It was a wonder that such riches did not satisfy him. Ought he to be considered by all an exemplar of right living who, himself a lover of pomp, boldly assumes to usurp the sceptre of Almighty God? Truly, this office must not be seized by force, but accepted with fear and humility.

What wonder that the whole world was a prey to disturbance and confusion? For when the Roman Church, which is the source of correction for all Christianity, is troubled by any disorder, the sorrow is communicated from the nerves of the head to the members subject to it, and these suffer sympathetically. This Church, indeed, our mother, as it were, at whose bosom we were nourished, by whose doctrine we were instructed and strengthened, by whose counsel we were admonished, was by this proud Wibert greatly afflicted. For when the head is thus struck, the members at once are sick. If the head be sick, the other members suffer. Since the head was thus sick, pain was engendered in the enfeebled members; for in all parts of Europe peace, goodness, faith, were boldly trampled under foot, within the church and without, by the high, as well as by the low. It was necessary both that an end be put to these evils, and that, in accordance with the plan suggested by Pope Urban, they turn against the pagans the strength formerly used in prosecuting battles among themselves. . . .

He saw, moreover, the faith of Christendom greatly degraded by all, by the clergy as well as by the laity, and peace totally disregarded; for the princes of the land were incessantly engaged in armed strife, now these, now those quarrelling among themselves. He saw the goods of the land stolen from the owners; and many, who were were unjustly taken captive and most barbarously cast into foul prisons, he saw ransomed for excessive sums, or tormented there by the three evils, starvation, thirst, and cold, or allowed to perish by unseen death. He also saw holy places violated, monasteries and villas destroyed by fire, and not a little

human suffering, both the divine and the human being held in derision.

When he heard, too, that interior parts of Romania were held oppressed by the Turks, and that Christians were subjected to destructive and savage attacks, he was moved by compassionate pity; and, prompted by the love of God, he crossed the Alps and came into Gaul. He there called a council at Clermont in Auvergne, which council had been fittingly proclaimed by envoys in all directions. It is estimated that there were three hundred and ten bishops and abbots who bore the crozier. When they were assembled on the day appointed for the council, Urban, in an eloquent address full of sweetness, made known the object of the meeting. With the plaintive voice of the afflicted Church he bewailed in a long discourse the great disturbances which, as has been mentioned above, agitated the world where faith had been undermined. Then, as a supplicant, he exhorted all to resume the fullness of their faith, and in good earnest to try diligently to withstand the deceits of the devil, and to raise to its pristine honor the status of Holy Church, now most unmercifully crippled by the wicked.

"Dearest brethren," he said, "I, Urban, invested by the permission of God with the papal tiara, and spiritual ruler over the whole world, have come here in this great crisis to you, servants of God, as a messenger of divine admonition. I wish those whom I have believed good and faithful dispensers of the ministry of God to be found free from shameful dissimulation. For if there be in you any disposition or crookedness contrary to God's law, because you have lost the moderation of reason and justice, I shall earnestly endeavor to correct it at once, with divine assistance. For the Lord has made you stewards over His family, that you provide it with pleasant-tasting meat in season. You will be blessed, indeed, if the Lord shall find you faithful in stewardship. You are also called shepherds; see that you do not the work of hirelings. Be true shepherds and have your crooks always in your hands. Sleep not, but defend everywhere the flock committed to your care. For if through your carelessness or neglect the wolf carries off a sheep, doubtless you will not only lose the reward prepared for you by our Lord, but, after having first been tortured by the strokes of the lictor, you will also be savagely hurled into the abode of the damned. In the words of the gospel, 'Ye are the salt of the earth'! But, it is asked, 'If ye fail, wherewith shall it be salted?' Oh, what a salting! Indeed, you must strive by the salt of your wisdom to correct this foolish people, over-eager for the pleasures of the world, lest the Lord find them insipid and rank, corrupted by crimes at the time when He wishes to speak to them. For if because of your slothful performance of duty He shall discover any worms in them, that is to say any sins, He will in contempt order them to be cast forthwith into the abyss of uncleanness; and because you will be unable to make good to Him such a loss, He will surely banish you, condemned by His judgment, from the presence of His love. But one that salteth ought to be prudent, foresighted, learned, peaceful, watchful, respectable, pious, just, fair-minded, pure. For how can the unlearned make others learned, the immodest make others modest, the unclean make others clean? How can he make peace who hates it? If anyone has soiled hands, how can he cleanse the spots from one contaminated? For it is written, 'If the blind lead the blind, both shall fall into the pit.' Accordingly, first correct yourselves, so that without reproach you can then correct those under your care. If, indeed, you wish to be the friends of God, do generously what you see is pleasing to Him.

"See to it that the affairs of Holy Church, especially, are maintained in their rights, and that simoniacal heresy in no way takes root among you. Take care lest purchasers and venders alike, struck by the lash of the Lord, be disgracefully driven through narrow ways into utter confusion. Keep the Church in all its orders entirely free from the secular power; have given to God faithfully one-tenth of the fruits of the earth, neither selling them, nor withholding them. Whoever lays violent hands on a bishop, let him be considered excommunicated. Whoever shall have seized monks, or priests, or nuns, and their servants, or pilgrims, or traders, and shall have despoiled them, let him be accursed. Let thieves and burners of houses and their accomplices be excommunicated from the church and accursed. Therefore, we must consider especially, as Gregory says, how great will be his punishment who steals from another, if he incurs the damnation of hell who does not distribute alms from his own possessions. For so it happened to the rich man in the Gospel, who was punished not for stealing anything from another, but because, having received wealth, he used it badly.

"By these evils, therefore, as I have said, dearest brethren, you have seen the world disordered for a long time, and to such a degree that in some places in your provinces, as has been reported to us (perhaps due to your weakness in administering justice), one scarcely dares to travel for fear of being kidnapped by thieves at night or highwaymen by day, by force or by craft, at home or out of doors. Wherefore, it is well to enforce anew the Truce, commonly so-called, which was long ago established by our holy fathers, and which I most earnestly entreat each one of you to have observed in his diocese. But if any one, led on by pride or ambition, infringes this injunction voluntarily, let him be anathema in virtue of the authority of God and by the sanction of the decrees of this council."

When these and many other things were well disposed of, all those present, priests and people alike, gave thanks to God and welcomed the advice of the Lord Pope Urban, assuring him, with a promise of fidelity, that these decrees of his would be well kept. . . .

But the Pope added at once that another trouble, not less, but still more grievous than that already spoken of, and even the very worst, was besetting Christianity from another part of the world. He said: "Since, O sons of God, you have promised the Lord to maintain peace more earnestly than heretofore in your midst, and faithfully to sustain the rights of Holy Church, there still remains for you, who are newly aroused by this divine correction, a very necessary work, in which you can show the strength of your good will by a certain further duty, God's concern and your own. For you must hasten to carry aid to your brethren dwelling in the East, who need your help, which they often have asked. For the Turks, a Persian people, have attacked them, as many of you already know, and have advanced as far into the Roman territory as that part of the Mediterranean which is called the Arm of St. George; and, by seizing more and more of the lands of the Christians, they have already often conquered them in battle, have killed and captured many, have destroyed the churches, and have devastated the kingdom of God. If you allow them to continue much longer, they will subjugate God's faithful yet more widely.

"Wherefore, I exhort with earnest prayer—not I, but God—that, as heralds of Christ, you urge men by frequent exhortation, men of all ranks, knights as well as foot-soldiers, rich as well as poor, to hasten to exterminate this vile race from the lands of your brethren, and to aid the Christians in time. I speak to those present; I proclaim it to the absent; moreover, Christ commands it. And if those who set out thither should lose their lives on the way by land, or in crossing the sea, or in fighting the pagans, their sins shall be remitted. This I grant to all who go, through the power vested in me by God. Oh, what a disgrace, if a race so despised, base, and the instrument of demons, should so overcome a people endowed with faith in the all-powerful God, and resplendent with the name of Christ! Oh, what reproaches will be charged against you by the Lord Himself if you have not helped those who are counted, like yourselves, of the Christian faith! Let those who have been accustomed to make private war against the faithful carry on to a successful issue a war against infidels, which ought to have been begun ere now. Let those who for a long time have been robbers now become soldiers of Christ. Let those who once fought against brothers and relatives now fight against barbarians, as they ought. Let those who have been hirelings at low wages now labor for an eternal reward. Let those who have been wearing themselves out to the detriment of body and soul now labor for a double glory. On the one hand will be the sad and poor, on the other the joyous and wealthy; here the enemies of the Lord; there His friends. Let no obstacle stand in the way of those who are going, but, after their affairs are settled and expense money is collected, when the winter has ended and spring has come, let them zealously undertake the journey under the guidance of the Lord."

August C Krey, *The First Crusade. The Accounts of Eye-Witnesses and Participants* (Princeton: Princeton University Press, 1921), pp. 24–30. (The translation used is Krey's.)

2. AS REPORTED BY ROBERT THE MONK

. . ."O race of Franks, race from across the mountains, race chosen and beloved by God—as shines forth in very many of your works—set apart from all nations by the situation of your country, as well as by your Catholic faith and the honor of the Holy Church! To you our discourse is addressed, and for you our exhortation is intended. We wish you to know what a grievous cause has led us to your country, what peril, threatening you and all the faithful, has brought us.

"From the confines of Jerusalem and the city of Constantinople a horrible tale has gone forth and very frequently has been brought to our ears; namely, that a race from the kingdom of the Persians, an accursed race, a race utterly alienated from

God, a generation, forsooth, which has neither directed its heart nor entrusted its spirit to God, has invaded the lands of those Christians and has depopulated them by the sword, pillage, and fire; it has led away a part of the captives into its own country, and a part it has destroyed by cruel tortures; it has either entirely destroyed the churches of God or appropriated them for the rites of its own religion. They destroy the altars, after having defiled them with their uncleanness. They circumcise the Christians, and the blood of the circumcision they either spread upon the altars or pour into the vases of the baptismal font. When they wish to torture people by a base death, they perforate their navels, and, dragging forth the end of the intestines, bind it to a stake; then with flogging they lead the victim around until his viscera have gushed forth, and he falls prostrate upon the ground. Others they bind to a post and pierce with arrows. Others they compel to extend their necks, and then, attacking them with naked swords, they attempt to cut through the neck with a single blow. What shall I say of the abominable rape of the women? To speak of it is worse than to be silent. The kingdom of the Greeks is now dismembered by them and deprived of territory so vast in extent that it cannot be traversed in a march of two months. On whom, therefore, is the task of avenging these wrongs and of recovering this territory incumbent, if not upon you? You, upon whom above other nations God has conferred remarkable glory in arms, great courage, bodily energy, and the strength to humble the hairy scalp of those who resist you.

"Let the deeds of your ancestors move you and incite your minds to manly achievements; likewise, the glory and greatness of King Charles the Great, and his son Louis, and of your other kings, who have destroyed the kingdoms of the pagans, and have extended in these lands the territory of the Holy Church. Let the Holy Sepulchre of the Lord, our Saviour, which is possessed by unclean nations, especially move you, and likewise the holy places, which are now treated with ignominy and irreverently polluted with filthiness. Oh, most valiant soldiers and descendants of invincible ancestors, be not degenerate, but recall the valor of your forefathers!

"However, if you are hindered by love of children, parents, and wives, remember what the Lord says in the Gospel, 'He that loveth father, or mother more than me, is not worthy of me.' 'Every one that hath forsaken houses, or brethren, or sisters, or father, or mother, or wife, or children, or lands for my name's sake shall receive an hundred-fold and shall inherit everlasting life.' Let none of your possessions detain you, no solicitude for your family affairs, since this land which you inhabit, shut in on all sides by the sea and surrounded by mountain peaks, is too narrow for your large population; nor does it abound in wealth; and it furnishes scarcely food enough for its cultivators. Hence it is that you murder and devour one another, that you wage war, and that frequently you perish by mutual wounds. Let therefore hatred depart from among you, let your quarrels end, let wars cease, and let all dissensions and controversies slumber. Enter upon the road to the Holy Sepulchre; wrest that land from the wicked race, and subject it to yourselves. That land which, as the Scripture says, 'floweth with milk and honey' was given by God into the possession of the children of Israel.

"Jerusalem is the navel of the world; the land is fruitful above others, like another paradise of delights. This the Redeemer of the human race has made illustrious by His advent, has beautified by His presence, has consecrated by suffering, has redeemed by death, has glorified by burial. This royal city, therefore, situated at the center of the world, is now held captive by His enemies, and is in subjection to those who do not know God, to the worship of the heathen. Therefore, she seeks and desires to be liberated and does not cease to implore you to come to her aid. From you, especially, she asks succor, because, as we have already said, God has conferred upon you, above all nations, great glory in arms. Accordingly, undertake this journey for the remission of your sins, with the assurance of the imperishable glory of the kingdom of heaven."

When Pope Urban had said these and very many similar things in his urbane discourse, he so influenced to one purpose the desires of all who were present that they cried out, "God wills it! God wills it!" When the venerable Roman pontiff heard that, with eyes uplifted to heaven he gave thanks to God and, with his hand commanding silence, said:

"Most beloved brethren, today is manifest in you what the Lord says in the Gospel, 'Where two or three are gathered together in my name there am I in the midst of them.' Unless the Lord God had been present in your minds, all of you would not have uttered the same cry. For, although the cry issued from numerous mouths, yet the origin of the cry was one. Therefore I say to you that God, who implanted this in your breasts, has drawn it forth from you. Let this then be your battle-cry in combat, because this word is given to you by God. When an armed attack is made upon the enemy, let this one cry be raised by all the soldiers of God: 'God wills it! God wills it!'

Ibid., pp. 30–33.

3. AS REPORTED BY BALDERIC OF BOURGUEIL

...."We have heard, most beloved brethren, and you have heard what we cannot recount without deep sorrow—how, with great hurt and dire sufferings our Christian brothers, members in Christ, are scourged, oppressed, and injured in Jerusalem, in Antioch, and the other cities of the East. Your own blood-brothers, your companions, your associates (for you are sons of the same Christ and the same Church), are either subjected in their inherited homes to other masters, or are driven from them, or they come as beggars among us; or, which is far worse, they are flogged and exiled as slaves for sale in their own land. Christian blood, redeemed

"And we do not command or advise that the old, or the feeble, or those unfit for bearing arms, undertake this journey; nor ought women to set out at all without their husbands, or brothers, or legal guardians. For such are more of a hindrance than aid, more of a burden than an advantage. Let the rich aid the needy; and, according to their means, let them take with them experienced soldiers. The priests and clerks of any order are not to go without the consent of their bishops; for this journey would profit them nothing if they went without such permission. Also, it is not fitting that laymen should enter upon the pilgrimage without the blessing of their priests.

"Whoever, therefore, shall determine upon this holy pilgrimage and shall make his vow to God to that effect and shall offer himself to Him as a living sacrifice, holy, acceptable unto God, shall wear the sign of the cross of the Lord on his forehead, or on his breast. When, having truly fulfilled his vow, he wishes to return, let him place the cross on his back between his shoulders. Such, indeed, by two-fold action will fulfil the precept of the Lord, as He commands in the Gospel, 'He that doth not take his cross and follow after me, is not worthy of me.'"...

by the blood of Christ, has been shed, and Christian flesh, akin to the flesh of Christ, has been subjected to unspeakable degradation and servitude. Everywhere in those cities there is sorrow, everywhere misery, everywhere groaning (I say it with a sigh). The churches in which divine mysteries were celebrated in olden times are now, to our sorrow, used as stables for the animals of these people! Holy men do not possess those cities; nay, base and bastard Turks hold sway over our brothers. The blessed Peter first presided as Bishop at Antioch; behold, in his own church the Gentiles have established their superstitions, and the Christian religion, which they ought rather to cherish, they have basely shut out from the hall dedicated to God! The estates given for the support of the saints and the patrimony of nobles set aside for the sustenance of the poor are subject to pagan tyranny, while cruel masters abuse for their own purposes the returns from these lands. The priesthood of God has been ground down into the dust. The sanctuary of God (unspeakable shame!) is everywhere profaned. Whatever Christians still remain in hiding there are sought out with unheard of tortures.

"Of holy Jerusalem, brethren, we dare not speak, for we are exceedingly afraid and ashamed to speak of it. This very city, in which, as you all know, Christ Himself suffered for us, because our sins demanded it, has been reduced to the pollution of paganism and, I say it to our disgrace, withdrawn from the service of God. Such is the heap of reproach upon us who have so much deserved it! Who now serves the church of the Blessed Mary in the valley of Josaphat, in which church she herself was buried in body? But why do we pass over the Temple of Solomon, nay of the Lord, in which the barbarous nations placed their idols contrary to law, human and divine? Of the Lord's Sepulchre we have refrained from speaking, since some of you with your own eyes have seen to what abominations it has been given over. The Turks violently took from it the offerings which you brought there for alms in such vast amounts, and, in addition, they scoffed much and often at your religion. And yet in that place (I say only what you already know) rested the Lord; there He died for us; there He was buried. How precious would be the longed-for, incomparable place of the Lord's burial, even if God failed there to perform the yearly miracle! For in the days of His Passion all the lights in the Sepulchre and round about in the church, which have been extinguished, are relighted by divine command. Whose heart is so stony, brethren, that it is not touched by so great a miracle? Believe me, that man is bestial and senseless whose heart such divinely manifest grace does not move to faith! And yet the Gentiles see this in common with the Christians and are not turned from their ways! They are, indeed, afraid, but they are not converted to the faith; nor is it to be wondered at, for a blindness of mind rules over them. With what afflictions they wronged you who have returned and are now present, you yourselves know too well, you who there sacrificed your substance and your blood for God.

"This, beloved brethren, we shall say, that we may have you as witness of our words. More suffering of our brethren and devastation of churches remains than we can speak of one by one, for we are oppressed by tears and groans, sighs and sobs. We weep and wail, brethren, alas, like the Psalmist, in our inmost heart! We are wretched and unhappy, and in us is that prophecy fulfilled; 'God, the nations are come into thine inheritance; thy holy temple have they defiled; they have laid Jerusalem in heaps; the dead bodies of thy servants have been given to be food for the birds of the heaven, the flesh of thy saints unto the beasts of the earth. Their blood have they shed like water round about Jerusalem, and there was none to bury them.' Woe unto us, brethren! We who have already become a reproach to our neighbors, a scoffing, and derision to them round about us, let us at least with tears condole and have compassion upon our brothers! We who are become the scorn of all peoples, and worse than all, let us bewail the most monstrous devastation of the Holy Land! This land we have deservedly called holy in which there is not even a foot-step that the body or spirit of the Saviour did not render glorious and blessed; which embraced the holy presence of the mother of God, and the meetings of the apostles, and drank up the blood of the martyrs shed there. How blessed are the stones which crowned you, Stephen, the first martyr! How happy, O, John the Baptist, the waters of the Jordan which served you in baptizing the Saviour! The children of Israel, who were led out of Egypt, and who prefigured you in the crossing of the Red Sea, have taken that land by their arms, with Jesus as leader;

they have driven out the Jebusites and other inhabitants and have themselves inhabited earthly Jerusalem, the image of celestial Jerusalem.

"What are we saying? Listen and learn! You, girt about with the badge of knighthood, are arrogant with great pride; you rage against your brothers and cut each other in pieces. This is not the (true) soldiery of Christ which rends asunder the sheepfold of the Redeemer. The Holy Church has reserved a soldiery for herself to help her people, but you debase her wickedly to her hurt. Let us confess the truth, whose heralds we ought to be; truly, you are not holding to the way which leads to life. You, the oppressors of children, plunderers of widows; you, guilty of homicide, of sacrilege, robbers of another's rights; you who await the pay of thieves for the shedding of Christian blood—as vultures smell fetid corpses, so do you sense battles from afar and rush to them eagerly. Verily, this is the worst way, for it is utterly removed from God! If, forsooth, you wish to be mindful of your souls, either lay down the girdle of such knighthood, or advance boldly, as knights of Christ, and rush as quickly as you can to the defence of the Eastern Church. For she it is from whom the joys of your whole salvation have come forth, who poured into your mouths the milk of divine wisdom, who set before you the holy teachings of the Gospels. We say this, brethren, that you may restrain your murderous hands from the destruction of your brothers, and in behalf of your relatives in the faith oppose yourselves to the Gentiles. Under Jesus Christ, our Leader, may you struggle for your Jerusalem, in Christian battle-line, most invincible line, even more successfully than did the sons of Jacob of old—struggle, that you may assail and drive out the Turks, more execrable than the Jebusites, who are in this land, and may you deem it a beautiful thing to die for Christ in that city in which He died for us. But if it befall you to die this side of it, be sure that to have died on the way is of equal value, if Christ shall find you in His army. God pays with the

same shilling, whether at the first or eleventh hour. You should shudder, brethren, you should shudder at raising a violent hand against Christians; it is less wicked to brandish your sword against Saracens. It is the only warfare that is righteous, for it is charity to risk your life for your brothers. That you may not be troubled about the concerns of tomorrow, know that those who fear God want nothing, nor those who cherish Him in truth. The possessions of the enemy, too, will be yours, since you will make spoil of their treasures and return victorious to your own; or empurpled with your own blood, you will have gained everlasting glory. For such a Commander you ought to fight, for One who lacks neither might nor wealth with which to reward you. Short is the way, little the labor, which, nevertheless, will repay you with the crown that fadeth not away. Accordingly, we speak with the authority of the prophet: 'Gird thy sword upon thy thigh, O mighty one.' Gird yourselves, everyone of you, I say, and be valiant sons; for it is better for you to die in battle than to behold the sorrows of your race and of your holy places. Let neither property nor the alluring charms of your wives entice you from going; not let the trials that are to be borne so deter you that you remain here."

And turning to the bishops, he said, "You, brothers and fellow bishops; you, fellow priests and sharers with us in Christ, make this same announcement through the churches committed to you, and with your whole soul vigorously preach the journey to Jerusalem. When they have confessed the disgrace of their sins, do you, secure in Christ, grant them speedy pardon. Moreover, you who are to go shall have us praying for you; we shall have you fighting for God's people. It is our duty to pray, yours to fight against the Amalekites. With Moses, we shall extend unwearied hands in prayer to Heaven, while you go forth and brandish the sword, like dauntless warriors, against Amalek."

As those present were thus clearly informed by these and other words of this kind from the apostolic lord, the eyes of some were bathed in tears; some trembled, and yet others discussed the matter. However, in the presence of all at that same council, and as we looked on, the Bishop of Puy, a man of great renown and of highest ability, went to the Pope with joyful countenance and on bended knee sought and entreated blessing and permission to go. Over and above this, he won from the Pope the command that all should obey him, and that he should hold sway over all the army in behalf of the Pope, since all knew him to be a prelate of unusual energy and industry. . . .

Ibid., pp. 33–36.

4. AS REPORTED BY GUIBERT OF NOGENT

. . ."If among the churches scattered about over the whole world some, because of persons or location, deserve reverence above others (for persons, I say, since greater privileges are accorded to apostolic sees; for places, indeed, since the same dignity which is accorded to persons is also shown to regal cities, such as Constantinople), we owe most to that church from which we received the grace of redemption and the source of all Christianity. If what the Lord says—namely, 'Salvation is from the Jews—,' accords with the truth, and it is true that the Lord has left us Sabaoth as seed, that we may not become like Sodom and Gomorrah, and our seed is Christ, in whom is the salvation and benediction of all peoples, then, indeed, the very land and city in which He dwelt and suffered is, by witness of the Scriptures, holy. If this land is spoken of in the sacred writings of the prophets as the inheritance and the holy temple of God before ever the Lord walked about in it, or was revealed, what sanctity, what reverence has it not acquired since God in His majesty was there clothed in the flesh, nourished, grew up, and in bodily form there walked about, or was carried about; and, to compress in fitting brevity all that might be told in a long series of words, since there the blood of the Son of God, more holy than heaven and earth, was poured forth, and His body, its quivering members dead, rested in the tomb. What veneration do we think it deserves? If, when the Lord had but just been crucified and the city was still held by the Jews, it was called holy by the evangelist when he says, 'Many bodies of the saints that had fallen asleep were raised; and coming forth out of the tombs after His resurrection, they entered into the holy city and appeared unto many,' and by the prophet Isaiah when he says, 'It shall be His glorious sepulchre,' then, surely, with this sanctity placed upon it by God the Sanctifier Himself, no evil that may befall it can destroy it, and in the same way glory is indivisibly fixed to His Sepulchre. Most beloved brethren, if you reverence the source of that holiness and glory, if you cherish these shrines which are the marks of His foot-prints on earth, if you seek (the way), God leading you, God fighting in your behalf, you should strive with your utmost efforts to cleanse the Holy City and the glory of the Sepulchre, now polluted by the concourse of the Gentiles as much as is in their power.

"If in olden times the Maccabees attained to the highest praise of piety because they fought for the ceremonies and the Temple, it is also justly granted you, Christian soldiers, to defend the liberty of your country by armed endeavor. If you, likewise, consider that the abode of the holy apostles and any other saints should be striven for with such effort, why do you refuse to rescue the Cross, the Blood, the Tomb? Why do you refuse to visit them, to spend the price of your lives in rescuing them? You have thus far waged unjust wars, at one time and another; you have brandished mad weapons to your mutual destruction, for no other reason than covetousness and pride, as a result of which you have deserved eternal death and sure damnation. We now hold out to you wars which contain the glorious reward of martyrdom, which will retain that title of praise now and forever.

"Let us suppose, for the moment, that Christ was not dead and buried, and had never lived any length of time in Jerusalem. Surely, if all this were lacking, this fact alone ought still to arouse you to go to the aid of the land and city—the fact that 'Out of Zion shall go forth the law and the word of Jehovah from Jerusalem!' If all that there is of Christian preaching has flowed from the fountain of Jerusalem, its streams, whithersoever spread out over the whole world, encircle the hearts of the Catholic multitude, that they may consider wisely what they owe such a well-watered fountain. If rivers return to the place whence they have issued only to flow forth again, according to the saying of Solomon, it ought to seem glorious to you to be able to apply a new cleansing to this place, whence it is certain that you received the cleansing of baptism and the witness of your faith.

"And you ought, furthermore, to consider with the utmost deliberation, if by your labors, God working through you, it should occur that the Mother of churches should flourish anew to the worship of Christianity, whether, perchance, He may not wish other regions of the East to be restored to the faith against the approaching time of the Antichrist. For it is clear that Antichrist is to do battle not with the Jews, not with the Gentiles; but, according to the etymology of his name, he will attack Christians. And if Antichrist finds there no Christians (just as at present when scarcely any dwell there), no one will be there to oppose him, or whom he may rightly overcome. According to Daniel and Jerome, the interpreter of Daniel, he is to fix his tents on the Mount of Olives; and it is certain, for the apostle teaches it, that he will sit at Jerusalem in the Temple of the Lord, as though he were God. And according to the same prophet, he will first kill three kings of Egypt, Africa, and Ethiopia, without doubt for their Christian faith. This, indeed, could

not at all be done unless Christianity was established where now is paganism. If, therefore, you are zealous in the practice of holy battles, in order that, just as you have received the seed of knowledge of God from Jerusalem, you may in the same way restore the borrowed grace, so that through you the Catholic name may be advanced to oppose the perfidy of the Antichrist and the Antichristians—then, who can not conjecture that God, who has exceeded the hope of all, will consume, in the abundance of your courage and through you as the spark, such a thicket of paganism as to include within His law, Egypt, Africa, and Ethiopia, which have withdrawn from the communion of our belief? And the man of sin, the son of perdition, will find some to oppose him. Behold, the Gospel cries out, 'Jerusalem shall be trodden down by the Gentiles until the times of the Gentiles be fulfilled.' 'Times of the Gentiles' can be understood in two ways: Either that they have ruled over the Christians at their pleasure, and have gladly frequented the sloughs of all baseness for the satisfaction of their lusts, and in all this have had no obstacle (for they who have everything according to their wish are said to have their time; there is that saying: 'My time is not yet come, but your time is always ready,' whence the lustful are wont to say 'you are having your time'). Or, again, 'the times of the Gentiles' are the fulness of time for those Gentiles who shall have entered secretly before Israel shall be saved. These times, most beloved brothers, will now, forsooth, be fulfilled, provided the might of the pagans be repulsed through you, with the co-operation of God. With the end of the world already near, even though the Gentiles fail to be converted to the Lord (since according to the apostle there must be a withdrawal from the faith), it is first necessary, according to the prophecy, that the Christian sway be renewed in those regions, either through you, or others, whom it shall please God to send before the coming of Antichrist, so that the head of all evil, who is to occupy there the throne of the kingdom, shall find some support of the faith to fight against him.

"Consider, therefore, that the Almighty has provided you, perhaps, for this purpose, that through you He may restore Jerusalem from such debasement. Ponder, I beg you, how full of joy and delight our hearts will be when we shall see the Holy City restored with your little help, and the prophet's, nay divine, words fulfilled in our times. Let your memory be moved by what the Lord Himself says to the Church: 'I will bring thy seed from the East and gather thee from the West.' God has already brought our seed from the East, since in a double way that region of the East has given the first beginnings of the Church to us. But from the West He will also gather it, provided He repairs the wrongs of Jerusalem through those who have begun the witness of the final faith, that is the people of the West. With God's assistance, we think this can be done through you.

"If neither the words of the Scriptures arouse you, nor our admonitions penetrate your minds, at least let the great suffering of those who desired to go to the holy places stir you up. Think of those who made the pilgrimage across the sea! Even if they were more wealthy, consider what taxes, what violence they underwent, since they were forced to make payments and tributes almost every mile, to purchase release at every gate of the city, at the entrance of the churches and temples, at every side-journey from place to place: also, if any accusation whatsoever were made against them, they were compelled to purchase their release; but if they refused to pay money, the prefects of the Gentiles, according to their custom, urged them fiercely with blows. What shall we say of those who took up the journey without anything more than trust in their barren poverty, since they seemed to have

nothing except their bodies to lose? They not only demanded money of them, which is not an unendurable punishment, but also examined the calluses of their heels, cutting them open and folding the skin back, lest, perchance, they had sewed something there. Their unspeakable cruelty was carried on even to the point of giving them scammony to drink until they vomited, or even burst their bowels, because they thought the wretches had swallowed gold or silver; or, horrible to say, they cut their bowels open with a sword and, spreading out the folds of the intestines, with frightful mutilation disclosed whatever nature held there in secret. Remember, I pray, the thousands who have perished vile deaths, and strive for the holy places from which the beginnings of your faith have come. Before you engage in His battles, believe without question that Christ will be your standard-bearer and inseparable fore-runner."

The most excellent man concluded his oration and by the power of the blessed Peter absolved all who vowed to go and confirmed those acts with apostolic blessing. He instituted a sign well suited to so honorable a profession by making the figure of the Cross, the stigma of the Lord's Passion, the emblem of the soldiery, or rather, of what was to be the soldiery of God. This, made of any kind of cloth, he ordered to be sewed upon the shirts, cloaks, and *byrra* of those who were about to go. He commanded that if anyone, after receiving this emblem, or after taking openly this vow, should shrink from his good intent through base change of heart, or any affection for his parents, he should be regarded an outlaw forever, unless he repented and again undertook whatever of his pledge he had omitted. Furthermore, the Pope condemned with a fearful anathema all those who dared to molest the wives, children, and possessions of these who were going on this journey for God....

Ibid., pp. 36–40.

D. Urban's Letter to the Assembling Crusaders, December, 1095

Urban, bishop, servant of the servants of God, to all the faithful, both princes and subjects, waiting in Flanders; greeting, apostolic grace, and blessing.

Your brotherhood, we believe, has long since learned from many accounts that a barbaric fury has deplorably afflicted and laid waste the churches of God in the regions of the Orient. More than this, blasphemous to say, it has even grasped in intolerable servitude its churches and the Holy City of Christ, glorified by His passion and resurrection. Grieving with pious concern at this calamity, we visited the regions of Gaul and devoted ourselves largely to urging the princes of the land and their subjects to free the churches of the East. We solemnly enjoined upon them at the council of Auvergne (the accomplishment of) such an undertaking, as a preparation for the remission of all their sins. And we have constituted our most beloved son, Adhemar, Bishop of Puy, leader of this expedition and undertaking in our stead, so that those who, perchance, may wish to undertake this journey should comply with his commands, as if they were our own, and submit fully to his loosings or bindings, as far as shall seem to belong to such an office. If, moreover, there are any of your people whom God has inspired to this vow, let them know that he (Adhemar) will set out with the aid of God on the day of the Assumption of the Blessed Mary, and that they can then attach themselves to his following.

Ibid., pp. 42–43.

E. Anna Comnena on the First Crusade

Before he had enjoyed even a short rest, he [the Emperor Alexius] heard a report of the approach of innumerable Frankish armies. Now he dreaded their arrival for he knew their irresistible manner of attack, their unstable and mobile character and all the peculiar natural and concomitant characteristics which the Frank retains throughout; and he also knew that they were always agape for money, and seemed to disregard their truces readily for any reason that cropped up. For he had always heard this reported of them, and found it very true. However, he did not lose heart, but prepared himself in every way so that, when the occasion called, he would be ready for battle. And indeed the actual facts were far greater and more terrible than rumour made them. For the whole of the West and all the barbarian tribes which dwell between the further side of the Adriatic and the pillars of Heracles, had all migrated in a body and were marching into Asia through the intervening Europe, and were making the journey with all their household. The reason of this upheaval was more or less the following. A certain Frank, Peter by name, nicknamed Cucupeter,[1] had gone to worship at the Holy Sepulchre and after suffering many things at the hands of the Turks and Saracens who were ravaging Asia, he got back to his own country with difficulty. But he was angry at having failed in his object, and wanted to undertake the same journey again. However, he saw that he ought not to make the journey to the Holy Sepulchre alone again, lest worse things befall him, so he worked out a cunning plan. This was to preach in all the Latin countries that "the voice of God bids me announce to all the counts in France that they should all leave their homes and set out to worship at the Holy Sepulchre, and to endeavor whole-heartedly with hand and mind to deliver Jerusalem from the hand of the Hagarenes." And he really succeeded. For after inspiring the souls of all with his quasi-divine command

---

[1] Peter of the Cowl.

he contrived to assemble the Franks from all sides, one after the other, with arms, horses and all the other paraphernalia of war. And they were all so zealous and eager that every highroad was full of them. And those Frankish soldiers were accompanied by an unarmed host more numerous than the sand or the stars, carrying palms and crosses on their shoulders; women and children, too, came away from their countries. And the sight of them was like many rivers streaming from all sides, and they were advancing towards us through Dacia generally with all their hosts. . . .

The incidents of the barbarians' approach followed in the order I have described, and persons of intelligence could feel that they were witnessing a strange occurrence. The arrival of these multitudes did not take place at the same time nor by the same road (for how indeed could such masses starting from different places have crossed the straits of Lombardy all together?). Some first, some next, others after them and thus successively all accomplished the transit, and then marched through the continent. Each army was preceded, as we said, by an unspeakable number of locusts; and all who saw this more than once recognized them as forerunners of the Frankish armies. When the first of them began crossing the straits of Lombardy sporadically the Emperor summoned certain leaders of the Roman forces, and sent them to the ports of Dyrrachium and Valona with instructions to offer a courteous welcome to the Franks who had crossed, and to collect abundant supplies from all the countries along their route; then to follow and watch them covertly all the time, and if they saw them making any foraging-excursions, they were to come out from under cover and check them by light skirmishing. These captains were accompanied by some men who knew the Latin tongue, so that they might settle any disputes that arose between them.

Let me, however, give an account of this subject more clearly and in due order. According to universal rumour Godfrey, who had sold his country, was the first to start on the appointed road; this man was very rich and very proud of his bravery, courage and conspicuous lineage; for every Frank is anxious to outdo the others. And such an upheaval of both men and women took place then as had never occurred within human memory, the simpler-minded were urged on by the real desire of worshipping at our Lord's Sepulchre, and visiting the sacred places; but the more astute, especially men like Bohemund and those of like mind, had another secret reason, namely, the hope that while on their travels they might by some means be able to seize the capital itself, looking upon this as a kind of corollary. And Bohemund disturbed the minds of many nobler men by thus cherishing his old grudge against the Emperor. Meanwhile Peter, after he had delivered his message, crossed the straits of Lombardy before anybody else with eighty thousand men on foot, and one hundred thousand on horseback, and reached the capital by way of Hungary. For the Frankish race, as one may conjecture, is always very hot-headed and eager, but when once it has espoused a cause, it is uncontrollable.

The Alexiad of the Princess Anna Comnena, trans. Elizabeth A. S. Dawes (London: Routledge & Kegan Paul, Ltd., 1928), pp. 248–50.

F. Skutariotes on the Rôle of the Emperor Alexius in the Origin of the First Crusade

Skutariotes writes that Alexius was ready to take the offensive against the Turks and continues:

Having considered, therefore, that it was impossible for him alone to undertake the battle on which everything depended, he recognized that he would have to call on the Italians as allies and he effected this with considerable cunning, adroitness and deeply laid planning. For finding a pretext in the fact that this nation considered unbearable the domination of

Jerusalem and the life-giving Sepulchre of Our Saviour Jesus Christ by the Persians [the Turks are meant] and seeing therein a heaven-sent opportunity, he managed, by dispatching ambassadors to the bishop of Old Rome and to those whom they call kings and rulers of those parts [i.e., the West], and by the use of appropriate arguments, to prevail over not a few of them to leave their country and succeeded in directing them in every way to the task. That is the reason why many of them, numbering thousands and tens of thousands, having crossed the Ionian Sea, reached Constantinople with all speed. And, having exchanged assurances and oaths with them, he advanced towards the east. With the aid of God and their alliance and by his own efforts he speedily expelled the Persians from Roman territories, liberated the cities and restored his sway in the East to its former glory. Such was this emperor: great in the conception of plans and the doing of deeds.

Peter Charanis, "A Greek Source on the Origin of the First Crusade," *Speculum,* XXIV (1949), 93. (Trans. Peter Charanis.)

II. The Secularization of the Crusades and the Antagonism Between Greeks and Latins

The First Crusade was a military success. The crusading armies had met at Constantinople where, following an understanding with the Byzantine emperor, they began their march through Asia Minor. This was in late April, 1097; in little more than two years the expedition reached its military goal. On July 15, 1099, Jerusalem fell into the hands of the crusaders.

The conquered territories in Syria and Palestine were organized into feudal principalities under the general suzerainty of the king of Jerusalem, himself one of the leaders of the crusade. These states, planted in a hostile world, loosely organized and often fighting against each other, required constant reinforcements from the West. The Moslems, who never accepted the loss of these territories, were a continuous threat, and the Byzantines were not friendly. The reason for the enmity of the Byzantines was the principality of Antioch. Up to 1085 Antioch had belonged to the Byzantine Empire and, as the leaders of the crusade while in Constantinople had promised to restore to the Empire whatever territories had belonged to it, the Byzantines had expected that Antioch would be returned to them. But Antioch was not returned; instead, it was granted to Bohemond, leader of the Norman contingent of southern Italy, who had previously campaigned against the Byzantine Empire. The Byzantines refused to accept this and sought to regain Antioch by force. Bohemond and his successors fought back and also carried on, at times with the open support of the papacy, intensive propaganda against Byzantium in the West. Thus developed the feeling in the West that, as the Greeks were treacherous, the way to prevent them from injuring the Latins, was to destroy their Empire. The Greeks in the meantime came to look upon the crusading expeditions as really aiming at their Empire. These sentiments manifested themselves in connection with the Second Crusade (1147–1149) and raised the question of the secularization of the crusading movement. Two passages, one taken from the work of Odo of Deuil, the chaplain of the French King Louis VII, whom he accompanied to the East in connection with the Second Crusade, and the other, from the Byzantine historian, John Cinnamus, also a contemporary, will introduce the reader to this problem. Both of these passages have been reproduced.

The antipathy and distrust between Greeks and Latins shown by these passages increased as the twelfth century progressed and led to violence and bloodshed, which in turn widened the chasm between the two peoples. Two incidents in particular stand out in this development: the massacre of the Latins in Constantinople in 1182 and the sack of Thessalonica by the Normans of southern Italy in 1185. The two passages which have been chosen to introduce the student to this problem are taken from the Latin historian William of Tyre, a native of the kingdom of Jerusalem, who finished about the year 1183 a general history of the crusades and the kingdom of Jerusalem, and from the Byzantine historian Nicetas Choniates, whose great history, covering the period from 1118 to 1206, was completed before 1210. The first describes the massacre of the Latins in 1182; the second gives the reaction of the Greeks to the sack of Thessalonica in 1185.

A. Odo of Deuil on the French Attitude Toward Constantinople During the Second Crusade

Although the Greeks furnished us no proof that they were treacherous, I believe that they would not have exhibited such unremitting servitude if they had had good intentions. Actually, they were concealing the wrongs which were to be avenged after we crossed the Arm [i.e. the Bosporus]. . . .

Distrusting their pledge, scorning their favors, and foretelling the injuries which we afterwards endured, the bishop of Langres, however, urged us to take the city. He proved that the walls, a great part of which collapsed before our eyes, were weak, that the people were inert, that by cutting the conduits the fresh water supply could be withdrawn without delay or effort. He, a man of wise intellect and saintly piety, said that if that city were taken it would not be necessary to conquer the others, since they would yield obedience voluntarily to him who possessed their capital. He added further that Constantinople is Christian only in name, not in fact, and, whereas for her part she should not prevent others from bringing aid to Christians, her emperor had ventured a few years previously to attack the prince of Antioch. He said: "First he took Tarsus and Mamistra and numerous strongholds and a broad expanse of land, and, after expelling the Catholic bishops in the cities and replacing them with heretics, he besieged Antioch. And although it was his duty to ward off the nearby infidels by uniting the Christian forces, with the aid of the infidels he strove to destroy the Christians. Nevertheless, God, who knows, judges, and avenges such things as these, willed that he should wound himself with a poisoned arrow and end his shameful life as the result of that slight wound. How-

ever, just as the present ruler, the heir of that lamentable crime, keeps for himself the ecclesiastical domains and other property which his father acquired by wickedness, just so he gazes longingly at the rest of the territory which his father wanted and already has exacted the prince's homage and, setting up one altar against another, has established his own patriarch in the city, scorning Peter's patriarch. Let it be your decision whether you ought to spare the man under whose rule the cross and sepulcher of Christ are not at all safe and after whose destruction nothing would be hostile to them."

When the bishop had finished speaking, his remarks found favor with some. Many with whom he did not find favor, however, replied with words such as the following: "Without knowledge of the law we cannot judge about their good faith. The fact that he attacked Antioch was evil, but he could have had justifiable reasons which we do not know. It is certainly true that the king recently conferred with the pope and that he was not given any advice or command concerning this point. He knows, and we know, that we are to visit to Holy Sepulcher and, by the command of the supreme pontiff, to wipe out our sins with the blood or the conversion of the infidels. At this time we can attack the richest of the Christian cities and enrich ourselves, but in so doing we must kill and be killed. And so, if slaughtering Christians wipes out our sins, let us fight. Again, if harboring ambition does not sully our death, if on this journey it is as important to die for the sake of gaining money as it is to maintain our vow and our obedience to the supreme pontiff, then wealth is welcome; let us expose ourselves to danger without fear of death."

Such was their contention, and the supporters of each side defended themselves ably. Nevertheless, I believe that the bishop would have won out if the Greeks had not gained the upper hand more by treachery than by force.

Odo of Deuil, *De profectione Ludovici VII in orientem,* ed. and trans. by Virginia Gingerick Berry (New York: Columbia University Press, 1948), pp. 67, 69–73.

B. John Cinnamus on the Second Crusade

And now began the problem of the West. For the Germans and the Franks, the nation of the Gauls and all the peoples who dwell around old Rome, the Brittii and the Brittani and generally the entire force of the West put themselves on the move. Their pretext was that they were going to cross over into Asia from Europe, fight the Turks whom they encountered, get possession of the temple in Palestine and view the Holy Places. Their real reason, however, was to occupy at the first assault the land of the Romans [i.e. Byzantines] and plunder everything in sight. Their army was beyond number. When the emperor had learned that they had arrived very near the Hungarian border he sent ambassadors to them, Demetrius Macrembolites and Alexander, an Italian by descent who had come over to the emperor because, as a count of the Italian city of Gravina, he had been divested of his office...by the tyrant of Sicily. He ordered them to make proof of the intentions of the [Westerners] and if they had not come to do injury to the Romans, to confirm this matter by oath. When the ambassadors came to the leaders of these barbarians, they spoke as follows: "The waging of undeclared war against those who have done no wrong is neither just nor in other respects proper especially for men who claim to be of splendid lineage and to possess overwhelming power. For when they are victorious, should this happen, their victory is not won with valor, and when they are defeated, they are judged to have run risks not for virtue. Neither the one nor the other of these things is praiseworthy. As for you, you will not be permitted at all to pass over the land of the Romans before you have given pledges to the emperor that you will do no harm. And so, unless you intend to swear falsely, why do you not wage war openly? For to attack the Romans straightway will indeed be dangerous for you, but to carry the war against them with perjury will be much more so, since you will have to fight against God and the might of the Romans. But if in truth you are friendly and have no design of deceit, then confirm the matter by oath. You will then be permitted out of friendship to go through the land of the great emperor and will get a reception as is proper and other kindness." The ambassadors said these things and they, gathering in the tent of Conrad, the king of the Germans, for he held the place of pre-eminence among the nations of the West, said that they had not come to do any injury to the Romans and that, if it were necessary to confirm this by oath, they were disposed to do so most readily. Their expedition was directed to Palestine and against the Turks who were plundering Asia. As this was acceptable to the Romans, they put their words into deed.

John Cinnamus, *Historia* (Bonn, 1836), pp. 67–68, trans. Peter Charanis.

C. William of Tyre on the Massacre of the Latins in Constantinople in 1182

While these events were taking place in our part of the Orient, an important change occurred in the empire of Constantinople. This resulted most unfortunately for the entire Latin race and brought upon them unheard-of affronts and enormous loss. For the evils long since conceived by false and perfidious Greece travailed and "brought forth falsehood." For on the death of Manuel, that most happy emperor of illustrious memory, his son Alexius, a boy scarcely thirteen years old, succeeded to the throne, both by his father's will and by hereditary right. He was under his mother's guardianship, however, and the affairs of the empire were administered by Alexius, the *protosebastos*, son of the elder brother of the dead emperor. The principal nobles and the people of that city accordingly felt that an opportunity had come to carry into effect the evil designs which they had formed against our people.

During the reign of Manuel, beloved of

God, the Latins had found great favor with him—a reward well deserved because of their loyalty and valor. The emperor, a great-souled man of incomparable energy, relied so implicitly on their fidelity and ability that he passed over the Greeks as soft and effeminate and intrusted important affairs to the Latins alone. Since he held them in such high esteem and showed toward them such lavish generosity, men of the Latin race from all over the world, nobles and men of lesser degree as well, regarded him as their great benefactor and eagerly flocked to his court. As the result of this eager deference, his affection toward the Latins increased more and more, and he was constantly improving their status.

The Greek nobles, especially the near kindred of the emperor, and the rest of the people as well, naturally conceived an insatiable hatred toward us, and this was increased by the difference between our sacraments and those of their church, which furnished an additional incentive to their jealousy. For they, having separated insolently from the church of Rome, in their boundless arrogance looked upon everyone who did not follow their foolish traditions as a heretic. It was they themselves on the contrary, who deserved the name of heretics, because they had either created or followed new and pernicious beliefs contrary to the Roman church and the faith of the apostles Peter and Paul against which "the gates of hell shall not prevail."

For these and other reasons they had for a long time cherished this hatred in their hearts and were ever seeking an opportunity, at least after the death of the emperor, to destroy utterly the hated race of the Latins, both in the city and throughout the entire empire, that in this way they might satisfy their inexorable animosity.

...They summoned Andronicus the Elder, a cousin of the late emperor, from Pontus, where he was ruling, that he might assist them in their wicked plot to drive Alexius, the *protosebastos*, from the control of affairs in the realm....

Thus summoned, Andronicus came to the city bringing with him large forces of barbarian troops. He encamped along the Hellespont in full sight of the city and took possession of all Bithynia. Certain powerful nobles who had been sent against him to resist his attempts traitorously deserted to his side. First and most important among these were Andronicus Angelus, commander of the troops which had been dispatched against him, and Alexius Megalducas, commander in chief of the fleet, both kinsmen of the emperor. The desertion of those who had gone over to Andronicus thus openly weakened the cause of our people greatly as did also the fact that many other notable men and a great many citizens as well showed their partisanship for Andronicus no longer secretly but in public. They longed to see him enter the city and in every possible way helped to hasten the time of his crossing.

The conspiracy continued to gain strength; the *protosebastos* was seized, blinded, and horribly mutilated. This change of affairs spread consternation among the Latins, for they feared that the citizens would make a sudden attack upon them; in fact they had already received warning of such intention from certain people who had private knowledge of the conspiracy. Those who were able to do so, therefore, fled from the wiles of the Greeks and the death which threatened them. Some embarked on forty-four galleys which chanced to be in the harbor, and others placed all their effects on some of the many other ships there.

The aged and infirm, however, with those who were unable to flee, were left in their homes, and on them fell the wicked rage which the others had escaped. For Andronicus, who had secretly caused ships to be prepared, led his entire force into the city. As soon as they entered the gates these troops, aided by the citizens, rushed to that quarter of the city occupied by the Latins and put to the sword the little remnant who had been either unwilling or unable to flee with the others. Although but few of these were able to fight, yet they resisted for a long time and made the enemy's victory a bloody one.

Regardless of treaties and the many services which our people had rendered to the empire, the Greeks seized all those who appeared capable of resistance, set fire to their houses, and speedily reduced the entire quarter to ashes. Women and children, the aged and the sick, all alike perished in the flames. To vent their rage upon secular buildings alone, however, was far from satisfying their unholy wickedness; they also set fire to churches and venerated places of every description and burned, together with the sacred edifices, those who had fled thither for refuge. No distinction was made between clergy and laymen, except that greater fury was displayed toward those who wore the honorable habits of high office or religion. Monks and priests were the especial victims of their madness and were put to death under excruciating torture.

Among these latter was a venerable man named John, a sub-deacon of the holy Roman church, whom the pope had sent to Constantinople on business relating to the church. They seized him and, cutting off his head, fastened it to the tail of a filthy dog as an insult to the church. In the midst of such frightful sacrilege, worse than parricide, not even the dead, whom impiety itself generally spares, were suffered to rest undisturbed. Corpses were torn from the tombs and dragged through the streets and squares as if the insensate bodies were capable of feeling the indignities offered them.

The vandals then repaired to the hospital of St. John, as it is called, where they put to the sword all the sick they found. Those whose pious duty it should have been to relieve the oppressed, namely the monks and priests, called in footpads and brigands to carry on the slaughter under promise of reward. Accompanied by these miscreants, they sought out the most secluded retreats and the inmost apartments of homes, that none who were hiding there might escape death. When such were discovered, they were dragged out with violence and handed over to the executioners, who, that they might not work without pay, were given the price of blood for the murder of these wretched victims.

Even those who seemed to show more consideration sold into perpetual slavery among the Turks and other infidels the fugitives who had resorted to them and to whom they had given hope of safety. It is said that more than four thousand Latins of various age, sex, and condition were delivered thus to barbarous nations for a price.

In such fashion did the perfidious Greek nation, a brood of vipers, like a serpent in the bosom or a mouse in the wardrobe evilly requite their guests—those who had not deserved such treatment and were far from anticipating anything of the kind; those to whom they had given their daughters, nieces, and sisters as wives and who, by long living together, had become their friends.

William of Tyre, *A History of Deeds Done Beyond the Sea,* trans. Emily Atwater Babcock and August C. Krey (New York: Columbia University Press, 1943), II, 461–65.

D. Nicetas Choniates on the Capture of Thessalonica by the Normans in 1185

Thus the city of Thessalonica, having held out for a short while, fell...into the hands of the enemy. Its fall was followed by an endless array of woes surpassing those of tragedy. Every house was abandoned. No building, no alley, no cave could offer safety from the hands of the murderers. The humblest prayers, the most subdued gestures were not able to give rise to pity. Everything was treated by the sword. And only the blows which carried away lives could check the furor of the soldiers. Churches offered no asylum and the protection of the images of the saints was of no avail. For the barbarians, confounding things divine and human, were not awed so as to respect the deity and offered no asylum to those who had fled to the churches. When they spared a life and satisfied themselves by taking the goods, they felt that they were doing a favor. But this too befell those who had fled to the churches: they were stifled to death by the congestions caused by the enormous crowds that sought refuge there. The barbarians carried their violence to the altars, massacring the conquered as if they were victims. For, as they took no heed of God and insulted the divine objects, how could they be expected to spare human beings? They plundered the sacred offerings, laid defiled hands and shameless eyes on things forbidden to be touched and seen. This was strange, indeed, but stranger still were the unholy acts which they committed against the sacred images of Christ and the saints. These they knocked down to the ground, trampled them with their feet, tore off in whatever manner they could their precious decorations and threw the rest on the crossroads to be trodden by the passers-by, or used them as fuel to cook their food. But the most profane and ill-sounding to the ear of the faithful was this, that some of them climbed upon the altars...and danced thereon singing obscene native barbarian songs. Then they exposed their shameful parts and sprinkled the holy places with their urine.... Finally the chiefs intervened and put a stop to all this.

But this was not the end of the calamities for the people of Thessalonica. For although the killing had stopped the day after the city was captured, those who escaped were oppressed with so many afflictions that they were driven to death preferring that to life.... Now, others,

too, when victors in war, treat the vanquished with abuse and no pity and in such other ways as the arrogance of victory may inspire. But the Latins, when they have vanquished and subjugated their adversaries, become an unbearable and indescribable evil. When their captive is a Roman who is not dressed like them and does not speak their language, they consider him an enemy of God who must drink the entire chalice of His wrath. For Latin inhumanity in its outrages against captives is like the ferocity of a viper, or a lion or a dragon when they fall upon their prey. It does not yield to either prayers or tears and is not brightened by wheedling words.... It is deaf to harmony and song and if charmed for the moment it soon goes back to its natural state....

There is no nation which gives itself so naturally to wrath as that of the Latins. Their hatred for the Romans surpasses even that which that ancient serpent, the plotter against mankind, had conceived and spewed out long ago. The land on which we dwell and enjoy the fruit thereof these most accursed Latins compare to Paradise and the desire with which they burn to possess it ever makes them ill-disposed toward our race and architects of evil for it. They hate as the bitterest enemies even when under the necessity of the moment they pretend friendship. Their speech, even if courteous and gentle, conceals in it javelins and double-edge daggers. Between them and us a bottomless gulf of enmity has established itself; we cannot unite our souls and we entirely disagree with each other, although we keep up our external relations and often live in the same house.

Nicetas Choniates, Historia (Bonn, 1835), pp. 387–92, trans. Peter Charanis.

III. The Problem of the Diversion of the Fourth Crusade

What made the chasm which had come to separate Greeks and Latins virtually unbridgeable was the Fourth Crusade (1202–1204). This expedition was to go by sea and its ultimate objective was Egypt. The crusaders, however, did not see Egypt; instead

they captured Constantinople and partitioned the Byzantine Empire.

Was the capture of Constantinople by the Fourth Crusade the fortuitous result of a series of events or was it deliberately planned? Historians still disagree as to the answer. To introduce the student to this problem we have chosen three important contemporary texts. One is the account of Geoffrey of Villehardouin. The other is taken from the work of Robert of Clari, and the third from the Byzantine historian Nicetas Choniates. Villehardouin was one of the chief leaders of the Fourth Crusade, and participated in the making of the important decisions. Robert was a simple knight, but he was a participant of the expedition and does not seem to be uninformed. Nicetas was a Byzantine functionary who was well acquainted with the problems which existed in the relations between Byzantium and the West, particularly Venice. The student should remember that Venice, which had obtained important commercial privileges in the Byzantine Empire, was disturbed by recent attempts of the Byzantine emperors to curtail these privileges. She resented, in particular, the granting of similar privileges to her commercial rivals, Pisa and Genoa. He should remember also that Boniface of Montferrat, the military commander of the expedition, had important connections in Byzantium and, as a consequence, he may have had personal political ambitions. We have also included two passages from modern scholars to illustrate the divergent views to which the problem of the diversion of the Fourth Crusade has given rise.

A. Villehardouin on the Diversion of the Fourth Crusade

Now give ear to one of the greatest marvels, and most wonderful adventures that you have ever heard tell of. At that time there was an emperor in Constantinople, whose name was Isaac, and he had a brother, Alexius by name, whom he had ransomed from captivity among the Turks. This Alexius took his brother the emperor, tore the eyes out of his head, and made himself emperor by the aforesaid treachery. He kept Isaac a long time in prison, together with a son whose name was Alexius. This son escaped from prison, and fled in a ship to a city on the sea, which is called Ancona. Thence he departed to go to King Philip of Germany, who had his sister for wife; and he came to Verona in Lombardy, and lodged in the town, and found there a number of pilgrims and other people who were on their way to join the host.

And those who had helped him to escape, and were with him, said: "Sire, here is an army in Venice, quite near to us, the best and most valiant people and knights that are in the world, and they are going oversea. Cry to them therefore for mercy, that they have pity on thee and on thy father, who have been so wrongfully dispossessed. And if they be willing to help thee, thou shalt be guided by them. Perchance they will take pity on thy estate." And Alexius said he would do this right willingly, and that the advice was good.

Thus he appointed envoys, and sent them to the Marquis Boniface of Montferrat, who was chief of the host, and to the other barons. And when the barons saw them, they marvelled greatly, and said to the envoys: "We understand right well what you tell us. We will send an envoy with the prince to King Philip, whither he is going. If the prince will help to recover the land oversea, we will help him to recover his own land, for we know that it has been wrested from him and from his father wrongfully." So were envoys sent into Germany, both to the heir of Constantinople and to King Philip of Germany. . . .

A fortnight after came to Zara the Marquis Boniface of Montferrat, who had not yet joined, and Matthew of Montmorency, and Peter of Bracieux, and many another man of note. And after another fortnight came also the envoys from Germany, sent by King Philip and the heir of Constantinople. Then the barons, and the Doge of Venice assembled in a palace where the Doge was lodged. And the envoys addressed them and said: "Lords, King Philip sends us to you, as does also the brother of the king's wife, the son of the Emperor of Constantinople.

" 'Lords,' says the king, 'I will send you the brother of my wife; and I commit him into the hands of God—may He keep him from death!—and into your hands. And because you have fared forth for God, and for right, and for justice, therefore you are bound, in so far as you are able, to restore to their own inheritance those who have been unrighteously despoiled. And my wife's brother will make with you the best terms ever offered to any people, and give you the most puissant help for the recovery of the land oversea.

" And first, if God grant that you restore him to his inheritance, he will place the whole empire of Romania in obedience to Rome, from which it has long been separated. Further, he knows that you have spent of your substance, and that you are poor, and he will give you 200,000 marks of silver, and food for all those of the host, both small and great. And he, of his own person, will go with you into the land of Babylon, or, if you hold that that will be better, send thither 10,000 men, at his own charges. And this service he will perform for one year. And all the days of his life he will maintain, at his own charges, five hundred knights in the land oversea, to guard that land.'

"Lords, we have full power," said the envoys, "to conclude this agreement, if you are willing to conclude it on your parts. And be it known to you, that so favourable an agreement has never before been offered to any one; and that he that would refuse it can have but small desire of glory and conquest."

The barons and the Doge said they would talk this over; and a parliament was called for the morrow. When all were assembled, the matter was laid before them.

Then arose much debate. The abbot of Vaux, of the order of the Cistercians, spoke, and that party that wished for the dispersal of the host; and they said they would never consent: that it was not to fall on Christians that they had left their homes, and that they would go to Syria.

And the other party replied: "Fair lords, in Syria you will be able to do nothing; and that you may right well perceive by considering how those have fared who abandoned us, and sailed from other ports. And be it known to you that it is only by way of [Egypt] or of Greece, that the land oversea can be recovered, if so be that it ever is recovered. And if we reject this covenant we shall be shamed for all time."

There was discord in the host, as you hear. Nor need you be surprised if there was discord among the laymen, for the white monks of the order of Citeaux were also at issue among themselves in the host. The abbot of Loos, who was a holy man and a man of note, and other abbots who held with him, prayed and besought the people, for pity's sake, and the sake of God, to keep the host together, and agree to the proposed convention, in that "it afforded the best means by which the land oversea might be recovered;" while the abbot of Vaux, on the other hand, and those who held with him, preached full oft, and declared that all this was naught, and that the host ought to go to the land of Syria, and there do what they could.

Then came the Marquis of Montferrat, and Baldwin Count of Flanders and Hainault, and Count Louis, and Count Hugh of St. Pol, and those who held with them, and they declared that they would enter into the proposed covenant, for that they should be shamed if they refused. So they went to the Doge's hostel, and the envoys were summoned, and the covenant, in such terms as you have already heard, was confirmed by oath, and by charters with seals appended.

And the book tells you that only twelve persons took the oaths on the side of the Franks, for more (of sufficient note) could not be found. Among the twelve were first the Marquis of Montferrat, the Count Baldwin of Flanders, the Count Louis of Blois and of Chartres, and the Count of St. Pol, and eight others who held with them. Thus was the agreement made, and the charters prepared, and a term fixed for the arrival of the heir of Constantinople; and the term so fixed was the fifteenth day after the following Easter.

Memoirs of the Crusades by Villehardouin and De Joinville, trans. Sir Frank Marzials (New York: Everyman's Library, E. P. Dutton & Co., Inc., and J. M. Dent & Sons, Ltd., 1933), pp. 17–18, 22–24.

B. Robert of Clari on the Diversion of the Fourth Crusade

In the meantime, while the crusaders and the Venetians were staying there that winter, the crusaders bethought them that they had spent a great deal. And they talked with one another and said that they could not go to [Cairo] or to Alexandria or to Syria, because they had neither provisions nor money for going there. For they had spent nearly everything, on the long delay they had made as well as on the great price they had given for the hire of the fleet. So they said they could not go, and if they went they would not be able to do anything, because they had neither money nor provisions to maintain themselves.

The Doge of Venice saw right well that the pilgrims were in sore straits, and he spoke to them and said: "Lords, in Greece there is a land that is very rich and plenteous in all good things. If we could have a reasonable excuse for going there and taking provisions and other things in the land until we were well restored, it would seem to me a good plan. Then we should be well able to go oversea." Then the marquis rose and said: "Lords, last year at Christmas I was in Germany at the court of my lord the emperor. There I saw a youth who was brother to the wife of the emperor of Germany. This youth was the son of the emperor Isaac of Constantinople, whose brother had taken the empire of Constantinople from him by treason. Whoever could get hold of this youth," said the marquis, "would be well able to go to Constantinople and get provisions and other things, for this youth is the rightful heir. . . ."

When the marquis had told the pilgrims and the Venetians that whoever had this youth, of whom we have just spoken, would have a good excuse for going to Constantinople and getting provisions, then the crusaders had two knights right well and finely equipped and sent them to Germany for this youth to come to them. And they sent him word that they would

help him gain his rights. When the messengers came to the court of the emperor of Germany, there where the youth was, they told him the message they had been charged to tell. When the youth heard this, and learned the offer which the high men of the crusaders had made to him, he was very glad and made great joy over it. And he was very gracious to the messengers and he said that he would consult with the emperor his brother-in-law. When the emperor heard it, he said to the youth that this was a fine chance that had come to him and that he was greatly in favor of his going to them. And he said that he would never get anything of his heritage unless it should be by the help of God and of the crusaders.

The youth knew well that the emperor was giving him good counsel, and he arrayed himself the finest he could and went off with the messengers. Now before the youth and the messengers were come to Zara, the fleet had gone on to the island of Corfu, because Easter was already past; but when the fleet set out to go there they left two galleys behind to wait for the messengers and the youth. So the pilgrims stayed at the island of Corfu until the youth and the messengers should come. When the youth and the messengers came to Zara, they found these two galleys that had been left for them, and they put to sea and went on until they came to Corfu where the fleet was. When the high men saw the youth coming they all went to meet him, and they greeted him and did great honor to him, and when the youth saw the high men honoring him so and saw all the fleet that was there, he was glad as no man ever was before. Then the marquis came forward and took the youth and led him away to his tent.

When the youth was there, then all the high barons and the Doge of Venice assembled at the tent of the marquis, and they talked of one thing and another, until finally they asked him what he would do for them if they made him emperor and made him wear the crown in Constantinople, and he answered them that he would do whatever they wanted. So they parleyed until he said he would give the host two hundred thousand marks and would maintain the fleet a year longer at his own cost and would go oversea with them with all his forces and would keep ten thousand men in the land oversea at his own cost all the days of his life and would give provisions for a whole year to all those who should leave Constantinople to go oversea.

Then all the barons of the host were summoned and the Venetians. And when they were all assembled, the Doge of Venice rose and spoke to them. "Lords," said the Doge, "now we have a good excuse for going to Constantinople, if you approve of it, for we have the rightful heir." Now there were some who did not at all approve of going to Constantinople. Instead they said: "Bah! what shall we be doing in Constantinople? We have our

pilgrimage to make, and also our plan of going to [Cairo] or Alexandria. Moreover, our navy is to follow us for only a year, and half of the year is already past." And the others said in answer: "What shall we do in [Cairo] or Alexandria, when we have neither provisions nor money to enable us to go there? Better for us before we go there to secure provisions and money by some good excuse than to go there and die of hunger. Then we shall be able to accomplish something. Moreover, he offers to come with us and to maintain our navy and our fleet a year longer at his own cost." And the marquis of Montferrat was more at pains to urge them to go to Constantinople than anyone else who was there, because he wanted to avenge himself for an injury which the emperor of Constantinople who was then holding the empire had done to him.

Robert of Clari, *The Conquest of Constantinople,* trans. Edgar Holmes McNeal (New York: Columbia University Press, 1936), pp. 45–46, 57–59.

C. Nicetas Choniates on the Fourth Crusade

The Venetians, recalling their old alliance with the Romans, were not able to endure that the friendship of the latter was now transferred to the Pisans. They gradually alienated themselves and looked for an opportunity for revenge. They were embittered also because the emperor Alexius [Alexius III Angelus] out of avarice had not yet paid to them the 20,000 pieces of gold which were still due to them from the fifteen pounds of gold [105,000 gold pieces] which the emperor Manuel had agreed to pay them at the time he had confiscated the property of the Venetians in the empire. But another source of evil and not the least was Enrico Dandolo, their duke, who was aged and blind, but for the Romans the most inimical and insidious man. Proud and shrewd, he called himself the most prudent among the prudent and had a madness for glory greater than any other man. When he pondered over the wrongs which his compatriots had suffered when the Angeli

brothers ruled [1185–1203] and before them, during the reign of Andronicus [1183–1185] and that of Manuel [1143–1180], he felt such a desire for vengeance that he preferred to die than not to avenge these wrongs. But because he knew that any undertaking against the Romans by his people alone would rebound against his head, he sought to obtain other accomplices, people with whom he could share his secrets and whom he knew to have implacable hatred for the Romans and envy for their felicity. Time brought him these accomplices. Certain noble toparchs who had set out to go to Palestine were won over by him to join as fellow-conspirators in a common enterprise against the Romans. These toparchs were Boniface, Marquis of Montferrat; Baldwin, Count of Flanders; Henry [Hugh], Count of St. Pol; and Louis, Count of Blois. There were, besides, many others, daring warriors and in stature as tall as their spears.

Three entire years were consumed in Venice in the creation of a fleet. In the end they built one hundred and ten light ships (*dromones*) for the transport of the cavalry and sixty long ones. They gathered, besides, about seventy very big round ships of which one exceeded the others in size by so much that they called it World (*Cosmos*). On these they put one thousand cavalry clad in full armor and thirty thousand infantry including bowmen.

Now as the fleet was about to depart there supervened another evil for the Romans. This was the arrival of Alexius, son of Isaac Angelus, who came to the fleet with letters from the pope of Old Rome and the king of Germany, Philip, in which they said to the corsairs that they would do them a great favor if they received Alexius and restored him to his paternal throne. The corsairs, thinking that the presence of Alexius would give them a good pretext for their piratical expedition and quench their avarice with heaps of money, received the young man. Now Alexius, who was not so much young in years as he was in wit, caught by adroit and crafty men, made promises on oath which were beyond his power to fulfill. Not only did he promise to give them the heaps of money which they asked, but also to participate in the expedition against the Saracens with Roman troops and thirty ships. And, what is more important and most absurd, he agreed to accept the Latin deviations from the faith and the innovations concerning the privileges of the pope, and to change the old customs of the Romans.

Nicetas Choniates, *Historia* (Bonn, 1835), pp. 713–15, trans. Peter Charanis.

D. Views of Modern Historians Concerning the Diversion of the Fourth Crusade

1. A. A. VASILIEV

Many scholars have devoted much attention to the problem of the Fourth Crusade. Their chief attention has been turned to the causes of the change of direction of the crusade. One party of scholars explained the whole unusual course of the crusading enterprise by accidental circumstances and were the followers of the so-called "theory of accidents." An opposing group of scholars saw the cause of the change in the premeditated policy of Venice and Germany and became the partisans of the so-called "theory of premeditation."

Until about 1860 no dispute on that problem had existed because all historians had depended mainly on the statements of the chief western source of the Fourth Crusade and a participant in it, the French historian Geoffrey de Villehardouin. In his exposition the events of the crusade progressed simply and accidentally: not having vessels, the crusaders hired them at Venice and therefore assembled there; after having hired the vessels they could not pay the Republic of St. Mark the full amount fixed and were forced to support the Venetians in their strife with Zara; then followed the coming of the prince Alexius, who inclined the crusaders against Byzantium. Thus, there was no question of any treason of Venice nor of any complicated political intrigue.

In 1861, for the first time, a French scholar, Mas-Latrie, author of the very well-known history of the island of Cyprus, accused Venice, which had important commercial interests in Egypt, of making a secret treaty with the sultan of Egypt and thereupon skillfully forcing the crusaders to abandon the original plan of the expedition upon Egypt and to sail against Byzantium. Then the German historian, Karl Hopf, seemed definitely to prove the treason of the Venetians towards the Christian task, stating that the treaty between Venice and the sultan of Egypt was concluded on the 13th of May, 1202. Although Hopf produced no text of the treaty and did not even indicate where this text was to be found, the authority of the German scholar was so great that many scholars adopted his standpoint without any doubt. But it was shown soon after that Hopf had no new document in his hands at all and that his date was quite arbitrary. A French scholar, Hanotaux, who a little later investigated this problem, refuted the theory of Venetian treason and, consequently, "the theory of premeditation." But he thought that if the Venetians were the chief instigators of the change of direction of the Fourth Crusade, they had obvious motives: the desire to subdue Zara, which had revolted; the wish to restore their candidate to the Byzantine throne, to revenge themselves on Byzantium for the sympathy Alexius III had given the Pisans, and, possibly, the hope to obtain some profit, if the Empire fell to pieces. The theory of Hopf at the present time is considered refuted. If the Venetians can be really accused of treason, they become traitors not because of a secret treaty with the Muslims, but exclusively because they had in view their commercial interests in the Byzantine Empire.

But the followers of "the theory of premeditation" did not confine themselves to the attempt to prove the fact of the treason of Venice. In 1875 a new motive was brought forward by a French scholar, Count de Riant, who tried to prove that the chief instigator of the change of direction of the Fourth Crusade was not Dandolo, but the king of Germany, Philip of Swabia, son-in-law of the deposed Isaac Angelus. In Germany a skillful political intrigue had been woven which was to direct the crusaders upon Constantinople. Boniface of Montferrat fulfilled Philip's plans in the East. In the change of direction of the crusade Riant sees one of the episodes of the long struggle between the papacy and the Empire. By his leading role in the crusade Philip humiliated the pope and falsified his conception of the crusade; welcoming the restored Byzantine Emperor as an ally, Philip might hope to be successful in his strife with the pope and with his rival in Germany, Otto of Brunswick. But a blow was struck to Riant's theory by an investigation of Vasilievsky, who showed that the flight of the prince Alexius to the West took place

not in the year 1201, as all the historians believed, but in 1202, so that for a complicated and long-conceived political intrigue "Philip was left neither place nor time; thus the German intrigue may be proved as illusive as the Venetian." The accurate investigation of a Frenchman, Tessier, on the basis of examination of contemporary sources, refuted the theory of the German sovereign's role and returned to the acknowledgment of the great significance of the narrative of Villehardouin, that is to say, to the prevailing standpoint before 1860, "the theory of accidents." Tessier said that the Fourth Crusade was a French crusade, and the conquest of Constantinople was an achievement neither Germanic nor Venetian, but French. Of Riant's premeditation theory there remains only the fact that Philip of Swabia took part in the change of direction of the crusade and, like Henry VI, claimed the Eastern Empire; but the sources do not justify affirming the existence of a leading and subtle plan on Philip's part on which could depend the destiny of the whole Fourth Crusade.

At the end of the nineteenth century a German historian, W. Norden, definitely refuting "the theory of premeditation" and agreeing essentially with "the theory of accidents," endeavored to investigate the latter more deeply, discussed the problem of the Fourth Crusade in the light of the political, economic, and religious relations between the West and East, and tried to elucidate the inner connection between the Fourth Crusade and the history of the previous hundred and fifty years.

To sum up: in the complicated history of the Fourth Crusade there were in action various forces originating in the motives of the pope, Venice, and the German king in the West, as well as forces originating in the external and internal conditions of Byzantium in the East. The interplay of these forces created an exceedingly complex phenomenon which is not entirely clear, in some details, even at the present day. "This," said the French historian Luchaire, "will never be known, and science has something better to do than interminably to discuss an insoluble problem." Grégoire has recently even gone so far as to proclaim that "there is really no problem of the Fourth Crusade."

But among all the plans, hopes, and complications it remains clear that over all prevailed the firm will of Dandolo and his unyielding determination to develop the trade activity of Venice, to which the possession of the eastern markets promised limitless wealth and a brilliant future. Moreover, Dandolo was greatly alarmed by the growing economic power of Genoa, which at that time, in the Near East in general and in Constantinople in particular, began to gain a strong foothold. The economic competition between Venice and Genoa must also be taken into consideration when the problem of the Fourth Crusade is discussed. Finally the unpaid debt of Byzantium to Venice for the Venetian property seized by Manuel Comnenus may also have had something to do with the diversion of the Fourth Crusade.

A. A. Vasiliev, *History of the Byzantine Empire, 324–1453* (Madison: University of Wisconsin Press, 1952), pp. 456–59.

2. H. GRÉGOIRE

To a Byzantinist, there can be no doubt about the fact that the course ultimately taken by the so-called Fourth Crusade, the capture of Constantinople, and the partition of the Byzantine Empire was *not* the fortuitous result of a series of unforeseen and surprising events. On the contrary, I have always been convinced, and I see that my learned colleague Professor Ostrogorsky in his excellent history of Byzantium is convinced likewise, that the "diversion" of that expedition, the détournement, as I prefer to say in allusive and ironical French, had been intended from the beginning, or rather from the moment when Boniface of Montferrat was elected to succeed Count Thibault of Champagne. Some critics call this view "la théorie byzantine." I must protest against such an expression, which seems to hint at a bias, at a tendency to look at things from the standpoint of a Byzantine. Now, the Byzantine point of view as expressed, for instance, by Nicetas Choniates, is that the capture of Constantinople fulfilled the wish of the Pope. We have no "national" bias at all. We simply try to write history, connecting as much as possible Western and Eastern affairs, Western and Eastern sources. To us, of course, the character of Boniface de Montferrat alone supplies a strong presumption in favor of the preconceived plan of conquest. But the scope of this article is limited. It is only to show that an overwhelming bulk of evidence, Latin—or French—and Greek, proves that the responsible leader of the Crusade knew, from the outset, "where he was going."

...The testimony of Robert de Clari...affords so admirable a confirmation of all the other texts that we must remind the reader of that definite, clear-cut statement, according to which Boniface declared to the crusaders, at the end of 1202 or the beginning of 1203, that he had met young Alexius at Christmas of the preceding year, thus in December, 1201, at the court of Philip of Swabia, in Germany—three months after Boniface of Montferrat had been elected as the Generalissimo of the Holy War. I shall refrain today from repeating what that choice meant. Instead, I advise those who would still be in doubt to read Usseglio's splendid book on the Montferrat family, one of the most important contributions ever made to our Byzantine studies by a non-Byzantinist. Boniface was the son of a man who had enjoyed the intimate friendship of the Byzantine Emperors. He was the brother of two Caesars of Byzantium, Rainer and Conrad. Those men were looked upon in Byzantium as epic heroes. One of the most "genuine" features of Robert de Clari's vivid narration is his perfect acquaintance with those Byzantine connections of the Montferrats. There are a few confusions in his account of Conrad's "geste," but nothing really "legendary," as has often been contended in order to disparage him.

Really, there is no problem of the Fourth Crusade. As soon as Alexius the Younger, the pretender, succeeded in reaching Italy and Germany and in appearing at the Court of Philip of Swabia, his brother-in-law and brother of Henry VI, who died as he was about to carry out the Norman plan of the conquest of the Eastern Empire, Boniface of Montferrat, the leader elect of the Crusade, saw himself sitting on the Imperial throne, which his two brothers had well-nigh occupied and which he missed himself, not because of the opposition of the Pope, who hated the "Swabian" and did not trust the Montferrat, but because of the shrewd Doge of Venice.

Henri Grégoire, "The Question of the Diversion of the Fourth Crusade," *Byzantion,* XV (Boston: The Byzantine Institute, Inc., 1941), 158, 166.

4

Medieval Society : Peasant, Lord, and Townsman

DAVID HERLIHY

University of Wisconsin

The social history of the Middle Ages marks the emergence of a society at once radically different from that of the Ancient World and clearly related to our own. It is not too much to say that Europe by 1200 had acquired the "social physiognomy" which in large measure she was to retain up to the French Revolution, and in some respects even beyond. This chapter is an examination of the social position and social development of three of the classes which by 1200 were clearly differentiated within European society and which subsequently played a major role in medieval and modern European history. They are the peasants, the lords, and the townsmen.

In the period of the late Roman Empire and the early Middle Ages, the great slave-run villa of Antiquity was being replaced as the basic unit of agricultural production by the single-family peasant farm. It would be hard to exaggerate the human or economic importance of this fundamental change. In a human sense, the lot of the medieval peasant, even as a serf, was far superior to that of the landless slave of Antiquity. The medieval serf usually inherited and inhabited his own farm, and he and his heirs gained direct benefit from improvements they made upon it. Usually too, he retained a moral right to a portion of its produce. Economically as well, the early medieval peasant economy ultimately proved itself superior to the slave system of Antiquity. In time it succeeded in producing that abundance of food essential for further economic and cultural progress, and did this without the great human cost the slave system had extracted.

The social position of the medieval peasant can best be evaluated by reconstructing the obligations he owed to the lord of his land or his person, and the rights, if any, he possessed to his farm and its produce. In Part I, these obligations and rights are examined for three periods of the Middle Ages: the period of the late Empire and the barbarian kingdoms, the period of Carolingian Europe, and the twelfth century. The student is asked to apply to the sources specific questions as to what the peasant owed the lord and what, if any, were the limitations of the lord's prerogatives over him. In point of fact, these three periods illustrate the progress and decline of medieval serfdom: from the loosely exerted lordship of the late Roman and barbarian ages, through the rigorous and systematic serfdom of the Carolingian manor, to the clear beginnings of peasant emancipation already evident in the late twelfth century.

Above the peasant a new aristocracy was also taking shape in the early Middle Ages. The German freeman had been both a fighter and a farmer, though he fought more enthusiastically than he farmed. But his social position was being undermined by a basic change in military technology in the early Middle Ages: the growing importance in battle of the heavily armed horseman, the prototype of the medieval knight. By the Carolingian age, fighting had become a highly skilled, expensive, and hence exclusive, profession. The great proportion of freemen, unable to afford the new equipment or master the skills required by it, slipped back into the ranks of full-time cultivators, of peasants and serfs. Conversely, those relatively few freemen able and rich enough to master the arts of mounted shock combat became specialized as a new warrior aristocracy, distinguished from their fellows by the fact that they fought and didn't work.

Within that new aristocracy, social and political relations were coming to be defined by a complex of personal and property bonds traditionally described by the name feudalism. The student should note that feudalism in this sense did not directly involve the serfs, who, since they were not freemen, were not able to enter into the free contract which created the authentic feudal bond. Feudalism was not, in other words, a system of economic organization but a system of society and of government. And only the warrior and clerical aristocracies directly participated in it.

The feudal bond linked freemen by both a personal relationship, called vassalage, and a property relationship created by the fief. Part II examines the development of this feudal bond for three phases of its history: the prototypes of feudal institutions and practices in Roman and Germanic societies, the use made of those institutions by the Carolingian rulers, and the matured feudalism of the twelfth and thirteenth centuries. By the time of the Merovingian period, our sources show clearly the existence of institutions which undoubtedly were the prototypes of both vassalage and fief tenure. These institutions are as yet, however, largely "domestic," in the sense that they bound together not the king and the distant great princes of his realm but a local strongman and the members of his immediate household or the poorer freemen living near him. The Carolingian state attempted to utilize these hitherto spontaneously developing institutions to strengthen its own authority. Still, the feudalism, if such we may call it, of the Carolingian state remained incomplete and unsystematic. The Carolingian state, in its basic constitutional principles, was a curious amalgam of German tribal kingship, Roman imperial reminiscences, and the new institutions of political feudalism.

After the period of chaos accompanying the disintegration of the Carolingian Empire in the late ninth and tenth centuries, new efforts at political reorganization got under way in the late eleventh and particularly in the twelfth centuries. The rise of feudal principalities, particularly precocious in the northwest of Europe (Normandy, England, the Ile-de-France, Flanders, and so forth), introduced a new sort of systematic feudalism. In these principalities, the feudal relationship, which had first developed spontaneously as a link between private persons, was consciously applied in defining the relationship between the feudal prince and his subjects. The advantage of this reconstitution of political bonds on a feudal model was that it gave to princely authority a precise content and clear prerogatives, which the vigorous princes of the age were not slow to exploit. The much vaguer notions of German tribal kingship and even of Carolingian rulership more easily allowed opposition, as they left the exact prerogatives of princely authority obscure and disputable. Feudalism was not, in other words, a kind of legalized anarchy against which strong rulers had to contend, but a body of institutions and practices which strong rulers could and did utilize in their own interest. Political absolutism was, to be sure, incompatible with the continuing feudal insistence on the mutual rights and obligations of both ruler and ruled; but political chaos was not possible either, as long as the contractual obligations were mutually respected and enforced. The emergence of the feudal principalities was a great victory for social and political order.

By the late eleventh and twelfth centuries, medieval society was also witnessing the appearance of an entirely new class, composed of men who lived not by farming or fighting, but by buying and selling. The origins of what was to become the European bourgeoisie or middle class is one of the most difficult problems of medieval social history. Because townsmen were so new, the sources illuminating their origins are particularly scarce and ambiguous. Part III accordingly presents three interpretations by recent historians on the background and motivations of these pioneers of a new way of life. As an illustration of the position of the townsmen in medieval society, their points of friction with the old feudal authorities, and their agitation for greater autonomy, this part also presents an account of a dispute between the burghers of Vézelay in north-central France and their feudal lord, the abbot of Vézelay, in 1137. This source should offer some indication of the economic activities and interests, and the political aspirations, of these townsmen at an early stage in their history.

This last part, along with the others, should also illustrate a primary problem of method in medieval social history. Medieval social changes do not stem from a directed evolution, and there are limitations on what we can learn about them through studying public laws or the interventions of government. The appearance and the passing of certain institutions which involved the great mass of Western Europe's population must be studied through private records and transactions of the type this chapter contains. These sources will illustrate the difficulties that confront the social historian of the Middle Ages; perhaps they may also show the fascination of his work.

I. The Peasant

A. What Was the Status of the Free Peasant in Late Antiquity and the Barbarian Age?

In the period of the late Empire and even after its fall in the West, the free peasant settled on another's land was called a *colonus*. What was his status? Was he already a serf? Was medieval serfdom an outgrowth of late-Roman conditions, and the medieval manor a direct continuation of the Roman villa? To reconstruct the status of the *colonus*, we have three principal kinds of sources: Roman imperial legislation concerning him, inscriptions regulating the status of *coloni* on particular estates, and private transactions involving *coloni*. The information these sources provide is, however, often quite divergent, if not flatly contradictory. According to Roman imperial legislation, he was already a serf, virtually without rights before his lord; but our other sources give a quite different picture. In seeking to arrive at a balanced assessment, the student should consider not only what the following sources say, but what kind of documents they are, and how representative they could have been of actual conditions.

1. ROMAN IMPERIAL LEGISLATION
   CONCERNING THE COLONUS

The first four imperial "constitutions" (laws) given below were preserved in the Theodosian, the last in the Justinian Code. The Theodosian Code was particularly influential in the Latin West in the early Middle Ages,

and the "Interpretations" also given below were added to the Code by Latin jurists between 438 and 506 A.D. These imperial regulations are important not only for what they reveal concerning the contemporary legal status of the *coloni*, but also because they served as a kind of juridical model for serfdom in the early Middle Ages.

(a) *Emperor Constantine forbids coloni to leave the soil, 30 October, 332*

Emperor Constantine Augustus to the Provincials.

Any person in whose possession a colonus that belongs to another is found not only shall restore the aforesaid colonus to his birth status (*origo*) but also shall assume the capitation tax for this man for the time that he was with him.

(1) Coloni also who meditate flight must be bound with chains and reduced to a servile condition, so that by virtue of their condemnation to slaves they shall be compelled to fulfill the duties that befit freemen. . . .

Interpretation: If any person should knowingly retain in his own household a colonus that belongs to another, he shall first restore the man himself to his owner and he shall be compelled to pay his tribute for as long a time as the man was with him. But the colonus himself who was unwilling to be what he had been born shall be reduced to slavery.

The Theodosian Code and Novels, trans. C. Pharr (Princeton: Princeton University Press, 1952), 5.17.1, pp. 115–16.

(b) *Emperors Gratian, Valentinian, and Theodosius forbid the harboring of escaped coloni, 25 October, 386*

Emperors Gratian, Valentinian, and Theodosius Augustuses to Cynegius, Praetorian Prefect.

If any person through solicitation should receive a colonus belonging to an-

other or by concealment should harbor him, he shall be compelled to pay six ounces of gold for him if he is a colonus belonging to a private person, and a pound of gold if he is a colonus belonging to an imperial patrimonial estate. . . .

Interpretation: If any person should either solicit or harbor a colonus that belongs to another and if by his solicitation he should receive a man that belongs to a private person, he shall pay to the man's owner six ounces of gold; if he should solicit and detain a fiscal colonus, he shall be compelled to pay a pound of gold.

Ibid., 5.17.1, p. 116.

(c) *An unknown emperor requires that escaped coloni be denounced*

...to Florentius, Count of the Sacred Imperial Largesses.

But if a master should know that the slave or colonus of another person (provided that he belongs to Our region) is dwelling in his house or on his land and should not present such slave or colonus to the judges or if he should be admonished by the master of the fugitive and should neglect to consign the slave or colonus to him, he shall incur a fine as an unjust holder of property.

Ibid., 5.17.3, p. 116.

(d) *Emperors Valentinian and Valens forbid coloni to alienate property, 27 January, 365*

Emperors Valentinian and Valens Augustuses to Clearchus, Vicar of Asia.

There is no doubt that coloni do not have the right to alienate the fields they cultivate, to the extent that even if they have any belongings of their own, they may not transfer them to others without the advice and knowledge of their patrons....

Interpretation: Coloni are held obligated to their owners in all things, to such an extent that without the knowledge of their owners they may not presume to alienate either any of the land or any of their own personal property.

Ibid., 5.19.1, p. 117.

(e) *Emperors Arcadius and Honorius [395–408] forbid coloni to bring law suits against their lords*

Although coloni who owe at least a rent are free in relation to those to whom their tribute has not made them subject, they are still bound, as it were, by a kind of slavery to those to whom they owe yearly payments and the obligations of their status. Therefore it is not to be tolerated that they should presume to bring suit against their lords, from whom certainly neither they nor their possessions many be removed. Henceforth we take away the right of anyone to attack the name of his lord in court. And let them know that all their possessions belong to him to whom they belong. It has frequently been decreed, that no colonus may sell or in any other way alienate any of his possessions without the knowledge of the lord of the property. How then can he stand in equal right against the person of his lord? For the laws do not intend that he own even his own possessions in his own right. They admit the right of acquiring only, not of transferring, and intend that he acquire and possess for the lord....

Supplied from the Codex Justinianus, 11.50.2, in *Theodosiani Libri XVI,* ed. T. Mommsen and P. Meyer (Berlin, 1954), p. 241, trans. D. Herlihy.

2. INSCRIPTIONS FROM ROMAN NORTH AFRICA CONCERNING THE COLONI

The harsh imperial regulations binding the *coloni* to the soil and limiting their rights have helped give the late Empire the reputation of a police state. We do not know how effectively these laws were enforced, and other sources suggest that, *in fact,* the status of the *coloni* was not entirely unfavorable. The following two inscriptions from Roman North Africa are in the form of petitions presented by *coloni* to imperial procurators or to the emperor himself and the responses given by them. While the inscriptions do not represent general laws affecting all African *coloni*, they probably reflect accurately what their real status was. The Lex Manciana mentioned in No. 1 may refer to an edict of T. Curtilius Mancia, proconsul of Africa ca. A.D. 70–72. This edict perhaps extended to that province the same favorable terms governing resettlement already obtaining in Italy. A *saltus* was a great estate, and the *conductores* mentioned were men who leased them from the government and organized their production.

(a) From the inscription of Ain-el-Djemala: *The procurators of Emperor Hadrian confirm the right of coloni to the permanent use of lands improved by them, A.D. 116–117*

[Petition of the *coloni*] . . .we ask, procurators, that you. . .grant us those fields which are swampy and wooded, that we may plant them to olive groves and vines in accordance with the Lex Manciana, on the terms applying to the neighboring saltus Neronianus.

[Response of the procurators] Since our Caesar in the untiring zeal with which he constantly guards human needs has ordered all parts of the land which are suitable for olives or vines, as well as for grain, to be cultivated, therefore by the grace of his foresight the right is given to all to enter upon those parts of said land which are included in the surveyed units of the saltus Blandianus and Udensis, together with those sections of the saltus Lamianus and Domitianus, which border upon the saltus Tuzritanus, and which are not exploited by the lessors [*conductores*]; and to those who shall have entered upon said fields the right is given of possessing and enjoying the produce, and of leaving the same to an heir, a right which is derived from both the Lex Hadriana concerning virgin soil and [the Lex Hadriana] concerning fields which have remained untilled for ten consecutive years; nor [shall there be] from the saltus Blandianus and Udensis greater shares of produce [demanded as rent than that which is customary]. . . .

> *Corpus Inscriptionum Latinarum,* VIII (Berlin, 1881), No. 25942, heavily excerpted and based upon the translation in R. Haywood, "Roman Africa," *An Economic Survey of Ancient Rome,* ed. T. Frank, IV (Baltimore: Johns Hopkins University Press, 1938), pp. 95–96.

(b) From the inscription of Suk-el-Khmis: *Emperor Commodus forbids arbitrary exactions from the coloni,* A.D. *180–183*

[Petition of the *coloni* of the estate Saltus Burunitanus] . . .we ask, therefore, most sacred Emperor, that you succor us; that the right which, in accordance with the clause of the Lex Hadriana, as it has been written above [cf. No. 1a above], has been limited, continue to be limited with reference to procurators and especially to the *conductor,* namely the right of increasing the shares [for rent in kind], or the tasks [for rent in manual labor], or the teams [for the latter service]; that the conditions remain as in the commentaries of the procurators, which are deposited in your archive of the district of Carthage;

that we owe not more than two days' work per year of plowing, two of cultivating, two of harvesting; and that there may be no dispute: inasmuch as this has been established in the *forma perpetua* inscribed upon bronze and has been recognized by all our neighbors on every side, and has been confirmed by the commentaries of the procurators, that is, six days' work [per year]. So that through the kindliness of your majesty, we your rural workers, born and raised on your estates, may no longer be harassed by the *conductores* of the imperial estates. . . .

[Response of the Emperor] The Emperor Caesar Marcus Aurelius Commodus Antoninus Augustus Sarmaticus Germanicus Maximus to Lurius Lucullus and others whom it may concern. In view of the law and of my decision, procurators shall not demand more than thrice two days' work [per year] lest any unjust exaction be made by you, in violation of the *forma perpetua.* . . .

Corpus Inscriptionum Latinarum, No. 10570, based on the translation in Haywood, *op. cit.,* p. 98.

3. FROM THE TABLETTES ALBERTINI: COLONI IN VANDAL NORTH AFRICA SELL LANDS WITHOUT THEIR LORD'S PERMISSION, 5 APRIL, 493(?)

The *Tablettes Albertini* are a collection of forty-five wooden tablets recording some thirty-four private transactions drawn up between the years 493–496 during the period of Vandalic rule in North Africa. They are among our earliest medieval collection of private acts, and the picture they give of the status of the *coloni* bears little resemblance to that suggested by the imperial legislation, still technically in force. The following sale shows that *coloni* residing on another man's land were apparently able to sell it without their lord's permission. Can this be reconciled with the imperial constitutions cited above? Can any conclusions be drawn from this document as to whether the *coloni* were in fact bound to the soil?

In the year of the lord king Gutha-bondus, April 5. Leporius, Coia his wife, Silbanianus and Victorinus, the brothers of Leporius, the undersigned, in the presence of the undersigned [witnesses] sell pieces of fields in various places with their [boundary] designations. These pieces are the property [*literally:* under the lordship] of Flavius Geminus Catulinus, perpetual priest, and his children. That is: [five pieces of land are designated with their boundaries]. All these above mentioned fields this day Geminius Cresconius and Cresconia his wife have purchased from Iulius Leporius, Coia his wife, Silbanianus, and Victorinus for one gold solidus and 100 gold folles of good alloy. Iulius Leporius, Coia his wife, Silbanianus, and Victorinus have taken the one solidus and 100 folles to themselves and have received them from Geminius Cresconius and Cresconia the purchasers. They agree that nothing further is owed beyond the said price. [The purchaser] or his heirs forever may have, hold and possess [the said fields] and if anyone should say that one of the same fields is his or should bring suit, then [the sellers] shall return that much money or its equivalent or as much as it may be worth. Geminius Cresconius and Cresconia the purchasers have stipulated and the sellers have promised. Done on [the estate] Fundus Tuletianus on the above-mentioned day and year. I Montius [the notary] at the request of Leporius, Coia his wife, Silbanianus, and Victorinus, the sellers, who are ignorant of letters have made their mark on this instrument dictated by them. As given above, they have made the sale and have agreed to it and have accepted and received the full price and ask the witnesses to subscribe. [Witnesses listed.]

Tablettes Albertini. Actes privés de l'époque vandale. ed. C. Courtois, *et al.* (Paris, 1952), No. 3, p. 218, trans. D. Herlihy.

B. What Happened to the Carolingian Freeman?

While Roman imperial legislation, as accepted by the Middle Ages, did provide a juridical model for medieval serfdom, this does not mean that serfdom was already characteristic of the rural population in late Roman times. On the contrary, the evidence from North Africa shows that the organiza-tion of great properties was extremely loose, and the rights actually enjoyed by the *coloni* upon them remarkably generous. The *colonus* or freeman, even if he inhabited another's land, used the land as he wished under easy terms and could even sell it without seeking the lord's permission. Not until about 750, until the early Carolingian period in fact, do our sources give substantial evidence of the appearance of a new kind of great property, which imposed a high level of discipline upon the peasants living upon it and demanded from them heavy rents and labor services. The rise of the true manor in the early Carolingian period means that a great proportion of freemen were losing the favorable status they had enjoyed even as *coloni* and were sinking into actual serfdom. The following selections from Carolingian sources should permit the student to judge the forces which led many freemen to prefer the status of a serf upon a great estate to that of a man technically free but actually exposed to numerous risks and dangers.

1. THE PLIGHT OF THE FREEMAN
   AS REFLECTED IN CAROLINGIAN
   CAPITULARIES

The following excerpts are from the capitularies or public laws and directives issued by the Merovingian and Carolingian kings. They are significant not only for the specific regulations contained in them but also for the indirect information they provide concerning the plight of the freeman and the efforts

of the "powerful" to deprive him of his land and reduce him to the status of a serf.

(a) *Charlemagne regulates the status of freemen who, out of poverty, become serfs of the Church, 787 (?)*

(5) Neither the count nor any of his officials should force or compel to perform any public or private service the slaves, the half-free [*aldiones*], or old or new leaseholders who have removed themselves from the public land not fraudulently or dishonestly but solely because of poverty and need, and who are cultivating the land of the Church or have received it for cultivation. Rather their patron or lord should determine what ought justly to be done by them. If, however, they are accused of any crime, the bishop should first be constrained, and he through his advocate, and they should do justice according to the law and according to the legal status of the individual persons....

Capitularia Regum Francorum, ed. A. Boretius, I (Hanover, 1883), No. 93, p. 196, trans. D. Herlihy.

(b) *Charlemagne complains that his officials are oppressing the people, 787 (?)*

(6) We have also heard that the agents of the count, some public officials, and even some of the more powerful vassals of the counts are accustomed to demand as a favor grants and collections, some as if needed for their food and others [without this pretext]. Through these or other tricks they have also come to demand from the people labor services, harvesting, plowing, sowing, hoeing, carting,

drying, and other similar services, not only from ecclesiastical [dependents] but from the rest of the people. We think that the people ought justly to be relieved of these things, because in some places the people have been so oppressed by them that many, unable to bear it, have slipped away by flight from their lords or patrons and their lands have been reduced to a desert. On the other hand, we by no means prohibit from giving aid the stronger or richer persons who out of mutual love and from their own free will wish to do so.

Ibid., p. 197, trans. D. Herlihy.

(c) *Charlemagne complains of the oppression by the powerful, 805*

(15) Concerning freemen who wish to give themselves to the service of God, let them not do this before asking our permission. This for the reason that we have

heard that some of them have been led to this not out of devotion but in order to flee the army or other royal service, and others do it for the sake of profiting from those who desire their possessions. This we prohibit.

(16) Concerning the oppression of

poor freemen, let them not be oppressed dishonestly and unjustly by the powerful, so that under duress they sell or give up their possessions. We reiterate here what we ordered above concerning freemen, lest perchance their relatives should be unjustly disinherited and the royal service should be reduced, and the heirs themselves should through want be turned into beggars, thieves, or criminals. We have also commanded that freemen should not be summoned too frequently to court sessions, unless as we have ordered in another capitulary.

Ibid., No. 44, p. 125, trans. D. Herlihy.

(d) *Charlemagne complains that churchmen are oppressing the people, 811*

(5) We may also ask: Has he truly left the world who daily and continuously increases his possessions by any manner or means, through persuasion, by mentioning the happiness of the celestial kingdom, and through threats, by mentioning the eternal punishment of hell? Has he left the world who under the name of God or of a particular saint despoils both rich and poor, persons by nature simple, ignorant and naïve, of their possessions and disinherits their legitimate heirs? Has he left the world who in this way forces many persons to commit outrages and crimes because of the poverty to which they have been reduced? Those who do not receive but have lost their paternal inheritance to another almost by necessity commit robberies and thefts.

(6) We ask again: How has he abandoned the world, who induced by greed brings men to perjured and false testimony, in order to acquire the possessions of someone else? How has he abandoned the world, who seeks out an advocate or an unjust and God-defying, cruel, and avaricious provost [judge] and considers, in seeking possessions, not how, but how much?

(7) What is to be said concerning those who, as if for the love of God and His saints, martyrs, or confessors, carry bones and relics of holy bodies from place to place, there construct new basilicas, and strongly urge whomever they can to surrender their possessions to them. . . .

Ibid., No. 72, p. 163, trans. D. Herlihy.

(e) From the Capitulary on Military Affairs, 811: *The securities of serfdom*

(3) [The poor freemen] also say that the bishop, abbot, count, judge, or hundredman [i.e. a local judicial official] seek the chance to condemn [in court] the poor man who does not wish to give up his possessions to them and to force him to go forever into the army. Thus impoverished whether he wishes to do so or not, he gives up or sells his possessions. Others, however, who have given up [their possessions] remain at home without worry of anyone.

(4) [The poor freemen complain] that bishops, abbots, counts and even abbesses leave their own freemen at home as servants; these are falconers, hunters, toll collectors, provosts, deacons, and other servants who receive the imperial agents [*missi*] and their followers.

(5) Others also say, that they oppress those poorer people and force them to go into the army, and allow to go home those who have something to give.

(7) There are also others who say that they are the "men of Pippin" or the "men of Louis," and then they profess to go to the service of their lords when the other men of the district have to go into the army.

(8) There are also those who remain and say that their lords are staying home and that they have to go with their lords, whatever the command of the lord em-

peror may be. There are others who for that reason commend themselves to some lords, who they know are not going into the army.

Ibid., No. 73, p. 165, trans. D. Herlihy.

2. THE CAROLINGIAN MANOR

The Carolingian age seems to have brought a considerable extension of serfdom, as many former freemen became full-time cultivators bound by heavy obligations to their estate or manor. It also brought a systematization of serfdom. This does not mean that there was ever a servile status common to the entire empire. Rather the obligations of the Carolingian serf varied enormously from region to region. Still, within the limitations of each manor, the obligations of the servile residents were being defined and rendered uniform within certain broad categories. The following sources should provide an idea of the organization of the Carolingian great property and the obligations of the serfs resident upon it.

(a) *An estate described in the Bavarian Laws (before 750)*

The following excerpt from the Bavarian Laws seems to have been in origin a royal directive concerning the administration of a manor which was later incorporated into the laws in order to serve as a model for the administration of church lands in that area. Its interest is that it is one of the oldest of the Merovingian-Carolingian manorial records. The student should note that the obligations are still primarily based on the personal status of the peasant, whether he be a *colonus* (i.e. freeman) or serf (*servus*). This basis of determining obligations should be compared with a later manorial survey given in (b) below. The reference to spring wheat is also interesting, as it probably shows a recognition of the value of the new three-field system of crop rotation (winter wheat, spring wheat, fallow). The Carolingian manor, while it had its oppressive features, was undoubtedly a center of considerable technical progress in agriculture.

On the *coloni* and slaves [*servi*] of the Church, how they should serve and what tribute they should render.

The rent is set according to the estimate of the judge [i.e. steward]. The judge should see to it that [the *colonus*] gives according to what he possesses. Out of thirty modia [measure of grain] he should give three, and should pay the grazing tax according to the custom of the region. He should plow, sow, inclose fields of legal size, being four rods wide, forty rods long, the rod having ten feet. He should collect, carry and store [the harvest]; he should inclose a meadow of one arpent, dry, collect and cart [the hay]. In regard to spring grain, each inhabitant should sow [land to the size] of the planting of two modia [of seed], and collect and store the harvest. He should plant vineyards, inclose them, hoe the earth [around the vines], pare, prune, and harvest them. Let them [*sic*] pay a bundle of linen, and from the bees ten containers of honey; they should give four chickens and fifteen eggs. They should provide horses for messengers or should themselves go when they are commanded. They should provide carting services to a distance of fifty leagues; they should not be menaced [into doing] more. They should undertake reasonable services for the maintenance of the manor houses, the hay bins, the granges and fences, or when necessary they should altogether construct them. For the lime furnace, when it is nearby, fifty men should provide the wood or stone; when it is distant, one hundred men should be required. And, when necessary, the lime should be brought to the city or village.

The slaves of the Church should pay rent according to their holdings. However, he [*sic*] should labor three days each week on the lord's land, but on three he should work for himself. If however his lord should provide them [*sic*] with oxen or other things to possess, he should perform as much service as is imposed upon him according to his ability. However, you should oppress no man.

Lex Baiuariorum I, 13, *Monumenta Germaniae historica, Legum sectio* I, *Leges nationum germanicarum*, V², p. 289, trans. D. Herlihy.

(b) *An estate of the Bishop of Augsburg, ca. 810*

At its maturity, the Carolingian manor was characteristically divided into two parts, the lord's own lands or demesne and the servile farms (*mansi*) upon which lived the families of the dependent cultivators. The *mansi* were classified as free or servile, and the obligations differentiated accordingly. The status of the land, in other words, and not primarily the status of the peasants, sets the weight of obligations. "Free" peasants could inhabit servile *mansi*, and vice versa. What importance has this shift in the basis of rent collecting from persons to the land?

The following description of an estate is preserved in a capitulary, where it was intended to serve as a model for drawing up inventories of the possessions of churches. Only the latter paragraphs dealing with lands are here translated.

(7) We have found in the same place [the island Staffelsee in the diocese of Augsburg] a manor [*curtis*] and a lord's house, with other buildings belonging to the above church. There belong to the manor 740 units of arable land which can be plowed in a day [*iurnales*] and meadowland from which 610 cartloads of hay can be collected.

Of grain we have found nothing, except 30 cartloads which we have given to the household servants. They are provided for up to St. John's Mass [27 December] and are 72. Of malt, [we found] 12 modia.

One tame horse, 26 head of cattle, 20 cows, one bull, 61 smaller animals, 5 calves, 87 sheep, 14 lambs, 17 he-goats, 58 she-goats, 12 kids, 40 pigs, 50 piglets, 63 birds, 50 chickens, 17 beehives.

Of fat, we found 20 bacons along with sausages, 27 pieces of suet, one swine killed and hung, 40 cheeses.

Of honey, one-half siccle; of butter, 2 siccles; of salt, 5 modia; of soap, 3 siccles.

Five mattresses with feathers, 3 bronze pots, but 6 iron pots, 5 small containers, one iron lamp, 17 vats bound in iron, 10 scythes, 17 sickles, 7 axes, 10 goat skins, 26 sheep skins, one net for fishing.

There is also a workshop, in which are 24 women; there we have found 5 light woolen cloths with 4 linen cloths and 5 shirts. There is also a mill; it returns 12 modia every year.

(8) There belong to the same manor 23 free, inhabited *mansi*. Of these there are 6 of which each returns every year 14 modia of grain, 4 pigs, one measure of linen, 10 eggs, one sestarius of linseed, one sestarius of lentils, 5 weeks of work each year, the plowing of three iurnales [of land], the drying of one cart load of hay in the lord's field and the carting of it [to the lord's barn]. Each also does messenger service. Of the other free *mansi*, there are 6 of which each plows each year 2 iurnales, sows and brings in, and dries in the lord's meadow 3 cartloads and brings them in. Each of these gives 2 weeks' work, and every 2 provides for the army one bull when they themselves do not go into the army; each rides wherever commanded. And there are 5 *mansi* which give every year 2 cattle, and ride wherever commanded. There are 4 *mansi* which plow each year 9 iurnales, sow and bring in, and dry in the lord's meadow 3 cartloads and bring them in. Each gives 6 weeks' labor yearly, does service in bringing wine, manures one iurnalis of the lord's land and provides 10 cartloads of wood. And there is one *mansus* which plows each year 9 iurnales, sows, and brings in; dries 3 cartloads in the lord's fields and brings them in; does service, provides a horse; gives 5 weeks' work each year.

There are 19 inhabited servile *mansi*, of which each gives each year one pig, 5 chickens, 10 eggs, nourishes 4 of the lord's piglets, plows half a field, works each week

3 days, does service, provides a horse. His wife makes one shirt and one light wool cloth, prepares malt, and bakes bread.

(9) There are in addition 7 manors belonging to this bishopric, which we have not described in detail here, but we give the total. The bishopric of Augsburg has in total 1006 free inhabited *mansi* and 35 deserted *mansi;* 421 servile inhabited *mansi* and 45 deserted. Between free and servile inhabited *mansi* there are 1427, and 80 are deserted.

Brevium exempla ad describendas res ecclesiasticas et fiscales, Capitularia, op. cit.
No. 128, p. 251, trans. D. Herlihy.

C. What Freed the Medieval Serf?

One of the great problems of medieval social history is the gradual decline and disappearance of serfdom in Western Europe without any public laws or emancipation proclamations abolishing it. The rigorous serfdom of the Carolingian age was disappearing in France, Italy, northern Spain, and western Germany clearly by the twelfth century, and somewhat later in England. Simultaneously, the highly disciplined manorial organization was giving way to more modern forms of agricultural organization. The cultivation of the lord's demesne was largely abandoned, the serf was transformed into a free tenant holding his land in lease, and the lord was becoming a *rentier* and not an actual cultivator. These changes progressed at different paces in different parts of Europe, but by the twelfth century their direction was unmistakable. What were the forces behind this slow but momentous transformation in the medieval countryside?

1. EMPEROR OTTO III COMPLAINS OF THE BREAKDOWN OF MANORIAL DISCIPLINE, 996–1002

The Carolingian manor was nothing if not a highly disciplined community of peasants, but that discipline was in a period of disorders hard to maintain and difficult to restore once it was lost. The following constitution of Emperor Otto III is reflective of conditions both in Italy and Germany.

We must do much deliberating, since the great men of our kingdom, lay and ecclesiastical, rich and poor, great and small, are continuously complaining that they cannot obtain from their serfs and their own men the appropriate service due them. Some serfs state falsely that they are free, because their lords, as often happens, cannot prove the servitude which they are dishonestly seeking to avoid through custom and lack of proof. Still others strive to attain the honor of liberty, because, as by chance happens, their lords, impeded by various affairs, have ignored them for a long time, and the accustomed service has not been required of them. Nor do these serfs let fall a single word indicative of their service owed. Taking advantage of this situation, they contend that they are free and proclaim that they have lived under the law and custom of liberty, because they have not for some time been required to fulfill the accustomed service. For this reason it has pleased our imperial authority:

(1) If a serf out of a desire for liberty should call himself free, the lord, if it seems better to him because of the difficulty of insidious proof, may decide the contest [by combat] either through himself or a champion. However, the serf may himself advance a champion, if he is sick or if age should prevent him from fighting.

(2) If, however, the serf is not recognizable because of any omission, by this our edict with God's will to be valid forever, we decree that henceforth everyone should pay at 1 December one penny of public money, whether to his lord or to his minister appointed to this office, in order to show the condition of his servitude.

(3) The sons and daughters of serfs should begin to pay this prescribed tax indicative of servitude in the twenty-fifth year of their age at the set interval. And no grant of [further] time should abolish servitude.

(4) If any serf of the Church should neglect to observe this our edict, he should

be fined half of all his goods and remain subject to the condition of servitude. The serf of the Church shall never be allowed to pass out of servitude. Not even the heads of churches may emancipate him.

We altogether forbid that serfs of the churches should become free, and those who have become free by any pretense we order returned to the ownership and service of the churches.

Monumenta Germaniae historica, Legum sectio IV, *Constitutiones et acta publica imperatorum et regum,* I, No. 21, pp. 47–48, trans. D. Herlihy.

2. KING LOUIS VI OF FRANCE EMANCIPATES A SERF, *1114*

Piety was a factor in the emancipation of serfs, and the following charter is typical of hundreds in the twelfth century. Many emancipations were made to permit serfs to marry the serfs of another lord, and such marriages come to obtain a surprising frequency in the twelfth century. This may remotely reflect a breakdown of manorial isolation and exclusiveness. The Carolingian manor tended to be a self-sufficient unit, socially as well as economically. By the twelfth century, however, with better communications and more vigorous trade, that self-sufficiency and exclusiveness was breaking down. The pressures to permit a greater physical mobility of the population were mounting, and they aided the erosion of manorial discipline.

On the manumission of Sancelina. The events of this world, because they have a temporal end, are easily destroyed by the wind of oblivion unless they are impressed in the memory of letters. Therefore, I, Louis by the grace of God king of the French, make known to those present and to come that, for the benefit of my soul and for the peace of the souls of our predecessors, we do altogether absolve a certain serf of ours, responsible for due service to us, by the name of Sancelina, the daughter of Ascho, from the bonds of the said servitude. Giving her to perpetual liberty so that, as if born from free parents, from now on she may have the right and permission to marry whom she may wish and of making a marriage with a man of Blessed Mary. We shall not because of this [marriage] rescind her liberty but she shall remain forever altogether undisturbed. That this may remain firm and unshaken, we have ordered it to be confirmed by written letters and by the impression of our seal. . . .

Cartulaire de l'église Notre-Dame de Paris, ed. B. Guérard, I (Paris, 1850), No. 7, p. 449, trans. D. Herlihy.

3. A SERF BUYS HIS FREEDOM

Because the serf always had a moral right to his property and to a portion of his produce, he had had the chance to save enough money to buy his own freedom. However, the expanding trade in the twelfth century doubly facilitated such purchased emancipations. The growth of urban markets gave the serf unprecedented opportunities to sell his produce. Also, revived commerce and new luxuries made the lords often eager to grant freedom in return for hard cash.

A certain Giroardus, a serf of Saint-Père of Chartres, freed by Abbot Eustachius with the consent of the monks, gave to the monastery that fisc or fief which he held from the monastery, also adding ten pounds of money. [Witnesses listed.]

Cartulaire de l'abbaye de Saint-Père de Chartres, ed. B. Guérard, II (Paris, 1840), No. 37, p. 294, trans. D. Herlihy.

4. A SERF IS FREED IN RETURN FOR THE LAND HE HELD, 1159–1170

One of the paradoxes of serfdom is that the serf's moral right to the land he held severely restricted the lord's own freedom of action with respect to his estates. The lord could not dislodge a serf, rearrange his lands, introduce new methods of cultivation, or raise the level of rent without the serf's consent.

In the twelfth century, as the growth of towns and trade created new markets for agricultural products, serfdom was widely becoming an encumbrance to agricultural managers interested in more rational systems of cultivation. Many lords found the free use of land more valuable than the ownership of serfs, but to gain that free use they had to free the serfs. The following charter is illustrative of this paradoxical situation.

Let everyone know that we have emancipated Andreas and his wife and children under this condition, that he give back to us our enclosure, which is called "of Engelardus," and which he held under a life-time lease. For not using sane judgment, but trying to defend it for himself as hereditary property, he brought [against us] many complaints. Disturbed by the injuries of this man, we preferred to let him go free from the yoke of our servitude rather than bear any longer his wickedness and perverse complaints. So coming to our chapter with his wife and sons and friends and neighbors, before everyone he abandoned our enclosure altogether and forever which he had possessed, under this condition, that we free him with the said wife and sons. Also, before everyone, he confirmed by oath that neither he nor his heirs would raise up later any more complaint, and that also the children, when they came of age, would swear at our request. If however they should wish to raise any complaint about this, they would return to their former servitude.

Ibid., II, No. 182, p. 396, trans. D. Herlihy.

5. THE CONSTITUTION OF A "NEW VILLAGE," 1214

If, in many of the older parts of Europe, free use of the land was becoming more valuable to the lord than the ownership of serfs, in the frontier areas labor was at a premium, and the terms it could command extraordinarily liberal. The late eleventh and twelfth centuries were an age of considerable colonization of new lands, both within Europe and along her eastern and southern frontiers. Within Europe, lords vied with one another in the creation of "free" or "new" villages. In the interest of attracting colonists without which their land would be worthless, the lords held out very favorable terms, which could not help but influence beneficially the harsher conditions of serfs in the older centers of cultivation. The following Belgian charter is typical of the liberal terms of settlement offered to the inhabitants of a new village. Note the characteristic absence of any obligation in labor. Note too the provision that a serf who resides in the village a year and a day would be free. This provision was typical also of many northern cities, giving rise to the aphorism *Standtluft macht frei,* "city air makes one free." The chapter numbers in the following document have been added.

In the name of the Father and of the Son and of the Holy Spirit, Amen. . . . Let it be known to the memory of those present and to come that Yolende, countess of Aulchoire and of Namur, with the consent of her husband Count Pierre and of Philippe her son has established Neuf-Ville, close to Namur, free from evil laws.

(1) The house lots are of one length [figure omitted] and thirty feet in width. Each household shall pay [yearly] two shillings and four capons in two payments, on the martyrdom of St. Stephen [26 December] and the rest on the feast of St. John the Baptist [24 June].

(2) If sons or daughters should succeed those invested, they should inherit the patrimony without investiture [i.e. without inheritance tax]. If however a brother should succeed a brother, or a sister a sister, or a cousin a cousin, he shall give for investiture as much as he gives in rent for hereditary right.

(3) No one of the serfs of the count shall live in the said village. If however a serf of anyone should remain there for one year and a day, not recalled according to right and law, he shall remain free, paying only the head tax due.

(4) The said village shall be under the disposition of judges (*veridici*) elected by the council of the village. [There fol-

lows a list of punishments to be imposed for various crimes.]

(5) If anyone should not wish to remain in the said village, having sold his home and all his belongings, he shall go away a freeman without payment.

(6) If anyone of those living there should find a debtor of his possessions within the territory [ban] of the village, he shall hold him and his belongings through the justice of the mayor and the judges until he be adequately satisfied with him for that for which he complains. Let it be further known that if anyone guilty of robbery should be captured within the territory of the village, he shall answer for the robbery there. If it should happen that someone should flee from the village of Namur to Neuf-Ville for the sake of easier justice, he should be surrendered to the officials of the count.

(7) [Regulations concerning the use of a near-by meadow and forest.]

(8) The said Neuf-Ville is entirely exempt from all aids, *mortmain,* [inheritance tax] and obligations of guarding the castle. The men shall however serve the count in arms, so that, setting forth with the count, they can return to their homes the same day. If it should happen that a villager there dies without a [direct] heir, the count shall have the *mortmain.*

(9) [Regulations concerning the pasturing of pigs in the forest.]

(10) It is also determined that to whatever market within the land of the count the men of Neuf-Ville should come, they should be free of all taxes which are customarily demanded from sellers or buyers.

(11) No stewards or judges of the count of Namur shall be permitted to bring to his justice the men of the above mentioned Neuf-Ville.

(12) Whenever any villager should for a year and a day hold a lot [without building a house], he shall no longer enjoy its possession, unless by will of the count.

(13) [Regulations concerning the village bakeries and breweries.]

This was ordered in the year 1214 from the incarnation of the Lord. And there was placed the wax seal of the said Yolende.

Cartulaire de la commune de Namur, ed. J. Bornet and S. Bormans (Namur, 1876), Nos. 5–6, trans. D. Herlihy.

6. THE BISHOP OF HAMBURG GIVES GOOD TERMS TO DUTCH COLONISTS, 1106

One phase of the surge of colonizing activity in the Middle Ages was the movement of settlers to the East, the famous *Drang nach Osten* which, between 800 and 1300, tripled the area of German settlement in Europe. Here also, the terms offered to those willing to colonize the new Eastern lands were remarkably favorable, as the following charter, granted by Frederick, bishop of Hamburg, illustrates.

Frederick, by the grace of God bishop of the church of Hamburg, to all the faithful in Christ, present and future, perpetual blessing. We wish to make known to all a certain agreement which certain men living on the other side of the Rhine, called Hollanders, have made with us. These men came to our majesty, beseeching that we grant them for cultivation lands at present uncultivated, marshy and useless to our people. We have therefore considered with the advice of our faithful that this would benefit ourselves and our successors and have granted their petition. This agreement has been made, that from each farm of the said land they should give us each year a penny. Lest discord should later arise among the people, we have thought it necessary to set the size of the farms, which are to be 720 royal rods in length and 30 in width. We also give the streams flowing through the land. They agreed to give a tithe according to our decree, that is, from the fruits of the land the eleventh sheaf of grain, the tenth lamb, and similarly for pigs, goats, and geese. Also, they should give the tenth measure of honey and of linen. For every colt they should pay one penny on St. Martin's day [11

November] and for every calf a half-penny. In ecclesiastical matters they promised to obey in all things, according to the decrees of the holy fathers, canon law, and the customs of the church of Utrecht. Lest they suffer injustice from foreign judges, they agreed that they would pay two marks every year from one hundred farms, so that they themselves could decide their own disputes. If they cannot settle the more important cases, they shall refer them to the bishop's audience. If they take him with them to decide the case, each party will support him as long as he remains through this arrangement, that two-thirds of the profit of the court should go to them and one-third to the bishop. We have given permission to construct churches wherever they think suitable. To these churches we have conceded a tithe of the tithes of these churches expressly for the support of the priest who will serve God there. Nonetheless, the parishioners of the single churches promise that they shall give to their churches one farm as endowment for the support of the priest. The names of the men who came to make and confirm this agreement are these. . . .

Bremisches Urkundenbuch I, No. 21, reprinted in *Deutsches Bauerntum,* I (Vienna, 1940), No. 40, p. 87, trans. D. Herlihy.

II. The Lord

A. What Were the Antecedents of Feudalism in Roman and Germanic Society?

Feudalism as a system of society and government grew out of the spontaneous efforts of European peoples to create order and find security under the chaotic conditions of life prevalent up to the eleventh or twelfth century. But in seeking to find a new basis for social order, those peoples made use of practices and institutions that had existed for centuries among both the Germanic and Latin races of Europe. The following source selections will illustrate both the Germanic and Roman antecedents for the two basic institutions of feudalism, vassalage and fief tenure. The student should examine them carefully, note the nature of the bonds created by them, and how this so-called "domestic" feudalism differed from the developed political feudalism of the high Middle Ages.

1. TACITUS DESCRIBES THE COMITATUS AMONG THE GERMANS, A.D. 98

Tacitus, a Roman historian of the first century after Christ, wrote a famous description of the Germanic tribes, and among their institutions mentioned a practice by which young warriors associated themselves with an established fighter or "chief." This association is called the *comitatus* ("following"), and in many of its features it is strikingly similar to later feudal vassalage. Like vassalage, the *comitatus* was rooted in a kind of contract which established a personal bond between two freemen. Note that the chief was expected to feed his follower, but there is yet no relationship in land between them. The bond between chief and follower was emotionally strong but juridically very vague. The Germanic follower, unlike the later vassal, would be in continuous personal attendance upon his lord; hence the reason for considering the *comitatus* a form of "domestic" vassalage.

(13) . . . The dignity of chieftain is bestowed even on mere lads whose descent is eminently illustrious or whose fathers have performed signal services to the public. They associate themselves, however, with those of mature strength who have already been declared capable of service. Nor do they blush to be seen in the rank of followers. For the state of companionship [*comitatus*] itself has its several degrees, determined by the judgment of him whom they follow. And there is a great emulation among the followers as to who shall gain the highest place in the favor of their chief; and among the chiefs as to who shall excel in the number and valor of his followers. It is their dignity, their strength, to be always surrounded with a large body of select youths. This is an ornament in peace and a bulwark in war. And not in his own country alone, but

among the neighboring states, the fame and glory of each chief consists in being distinguished for the number and bravery of his companions. Such chiefs are courted by embassies and distinguished by presents. Often by their reputation alone they decide the outcome of a war.

(14) In the field of battle, it is disgraceful for the chief to be surpassed in valor. It is disgraceful for the followers not to equal their chief, but it is reproach and infamy during a whole succeeding life to retreat from the field surviving him. To aid and protect him and to place their own gallant actions to the account of his glory is the first and most sacred obligation. The chiefs fight for victory, and the followers for their chief. If their native country be long sunk in peace and inaction, many of the young nobles repair to some other state then engaged in war. For apart from the fact that repose is unwelcome to their race and toils and perils afford them a better opportunity of distinguishing themselves, they are unable without war and violence to maintain a large train of followers. The follower requires from the liberality of his chief the warlike steed and the bloody and conquering spear. And in place of pay, he expects to be supplied with a table, homely indeed, but plentiful. The funds for this munificence must be found in war and rapine.

> Tacitus, *Germania*, Chaps. 13–14. Adapted from the Oxford translation in *The Germany and the Agricola of Tacitus* (New York: David McKay Co., Inc., 1897), pp. 33–35.

2. SALVIAN DESCRIBES PATRONAGE AMONG THE ROMANS, CA. A.D. 440

The work of the Roman historian Salvian, *On the Governance of God,* is a protracted condemnation of Roman morals and social practices. One of the institutions he singles out for criticism is Roman patronage. The following description of poor people placing themselves under the protection of the rich and powerful shows that among the Romans too a kind of proto-vassalage was developing. Again, however, the system of patronage involves poor freemen obviously in need, not, as in later vassalage, the great princes of the realm.

Can I wonder that not all the poor and needy [Roman] taxpayers [flee to the Germans], for there is only one reason why they do not do this. They cannot take with them their few possessions, houses, and families. Therefore, because they are unable to do what they would prefer to do, they do the one thing they can. They deliver themselves to the more powerful men to secure defense and protection. They make themselves subjects of the wealthy and, as it were, pass under their ownership and authority. I would not consider this a seriously deplorable act, but I would rather be thankful for the generosity of the powerful men to whom the poor surrender themselves, if the powerful did not traffic in these patronages, if their "defense of the poor," as they call it, sprang from humanity and not from avarice. But this is the wicked and bitter part of it, that the poor are despoiled by the very law by which they are supposed to be protected, that the powerful defend the poor in order to rob them, that they defend the miserable in order to make them more miserable by defending them. For all those who are supposed to be protected surrender almost all their property to their defenders even before they are accorded protection. The result is that, for the fathers to gain protection, the sons lose their inheritance. The protection of the parents is purchased by the impoverishment of their sons. Look at the kind of help and patronage the powerful are providing: they give to themselves, but nothing to their protegeés.

> Salvian, *De Gubernatione Dei,* V, 8. *Monumenta Germaniae historica, Auctores antiquissimi,* I, 62, trans. D. Herlihy.

3. A MEROVINGIAN COMMENDATION

The following model contract, from a book of formulas redacted at Tours in northern France about 600, shows that the systems of patronage described by Salvian persisted even after the fall of the Roman Empire in the West. The act is technically called a commendation. The fact that the following document is a formula suggests that commendations must have been fairly common. Why?

Who commends himself under the power of another. To the magnificent lord _____, I _____. As it is known to all that I have nothing with which to feed or clothe myself, therefore I have beseeched your piety, and your benevolence has allowed me, that I might deliver and commend myself to your protection [*mundoburdum*]. This I have done with these con-ditions. You are to help and aid me both with food and clothing, to the extent that I shall be able to serve you and merit well of you, and as long as I shall live, I am to give to you service and obedience in keeping with my free status. And for all of my life I shall not have the power of withdrawing myself from your power and protection, but all the days of my life I am to remain under your power or protection. Therefore it is agreed that, if one of us should wish to withdraw himself from these agreements, he should pay _____ shillings to his fellow and this agreement should remain in force; whence it is agreed that they are to draw up mutually and confirm two written documents of one tenor. And this they have done.

Formulae turonenses, No. 43. *Monumenta Germaniae historica, Formulae*, I, 158, trans. D. Herlihy.

4. THE "MYSTIQUE" OF VASSALAGE

It must be emphasized that commendation and the personal bond that derived from it created not so much a legal as a moral, quasi-familial relationship. The vassal was supposed to love his lord, and his lord was to love him in return. Their relationship involved a really emotional commitment which some historians call the "mystique" of vassalage. The following chapter from a capitulary of the Carolingian king Pippin the Short, redacted ca. 758–768, shows that he considered the bonds of vassalage more sacred than those of marriage.

(9) If anyone by unavoidable necessity should flee into another duchy or province or should follow his lord, to whom he may not deny faith, and his wife, when she is able, should not wish to follow him for love of her relatives or possessions, she is to remain forever unmarried for all the time that her husband whom she did not follow shall live. But her husband, who through necessity flees into another place, if he is not able to abstain, can take another wife with penitence.

Capitularia, op. cit., I, No. 16, p. 41, trans. D. Herlihy.

5. FROM KING ATHELSTAN'S LAWS ISSUED AT GRATELY: VASSALAGE IN ANGLO-SAXON ENGLAND, 924–939

Anglo Saxon England has a peculiar interest in the study of feudal institutions, as it presents an almost pure example of a Germanic proto-feudalism unaffected by the strong Latin influences on the Continent. The following selections from the Laws of Athelstan give a good idea of Anglo-Saxon lordship. Note the characteristic absence of any property relationship. The Laws are also interesting since they reveal an early effort by the king to utilize the bonds of vassalage for the support of public order.

(2) Concerning lordless men. And we pronounced about those lordless men, from whom no justice can be obtained, that one should order their kindred to fetch back such a person to do justice and to find him a lord in public meeting.

(2.1) And if they then will not, or cannot, produce him on that appointed day, he is then to be a fugitive afterwards, and he who encounters him is to strike him down as a thief.

(2.2) And he who harbors him after that, is to pay for him with his *wergild* or to clear himself by an oath of that amount.

(3) Concerning the refusal of justice. The lord who refuses justice and upholds his guilty man, so that the king is appealed to, is to repay the value of the goods and 120 shillings to the king. . . .

(4) Concerning treachery to a lord. And we have pronounced concerning treachery to a lord, that he [who is accused] is to forfeit his life if he cannot deny it or is afterwards convicted at the three-fold ordeal.

(22) And no one is to receive the man of another man, without the permission of him whom he served before.

(22.1) If anyone does so, he is to give back the man and pay the fine for disobedience to the king.

(22.2) And no one is to dismiss his man who has been accused, before he has rendered justice.

English Historical Documents, I (*c. 500–1042*), ed. D. Whitelock (London: Oxford University Press, 1955), No. 35, pp. 381–82.

6. A MEROVINGIAN "PRECARIUM"

Merovingian (and Anglo-Saxon) vassalage apparently involved only a personal, not a property, bond between the lord and his man. However, Merovingian sources do reveal a kind of land grant which seems to have served as a model for the later fief and hence ultimately provided the second great pillar for the developed feudal system. This was the ecclesiastic *precarium* or *beneficium.* The Church was canonically forbidden to alienate her lands. However, churchmen often wished to make grants to laymen in reward for past, or in expectation of future, services. Unable to give the land in full title, they could still grant the use of the land while technically retaining eminent ownership. Because a layman often formally "prayed for" or requested the grant, it was called a *precarium;* because it was considered as a "favor" to the layman, it was also called a *beneficium.* The *precarium* thus established a temporary, nonhereditary and conditional form of land tenure, as the layman retained the use, not the ownership, of the land and held it only so long as he fulfilled certain conditions. The *precarium* is therefore juridically very close to the later fief, which was similarly in essence a form of temporary, nonhereditary, and conditional land tenure. The following example of a Merovingian *precarium* is from the Formulas of Tours.

To the venerable lord _____, rector of the church of _____, and to all the congregation there established, I _____. At my petition you have willingly determined that you should authorize me to keep with right of usufruct your villa located in the district of _____, in the county of _____, in the place called _____, with all improvements pertaining or belonging to it. This you have done. With this provision, that I am not allowed either to sell it anywhere or donate it or in any way alienate it, but I shall hold it and make use of it with your permission as long as your decree should remain in effect. Wherefore I have agreed to pay to you so much silver every year at the feast of Saint _____ . Also, after my death, you and the agents of the church of _____ may recall into your power and ownership that said possession in its integrity and completeness, whatever belongs or pertains to it, with everything upon it and whatever is left there at my death, without waiting for it to be formally transferred or consigned by judges and without my heirs reclaiming it. And if it should happen that I or any of my heirs or any person presumes to raise any lawsuit against this tenancy or any claim or defiance, he should not obtain what he seeks and, what is more, should pay 100 shillings to him against whom he should bring suit. Although the property should be held by me for a period of many years, this tenancy should not prejudice you, but [the contract] should remain as firm as if it were renewed every five years with a stipulation joined, and should remain inviolate for all time.

Formulae turonenses, No. 7. *Formulae, op. cit.,* p. 159, trans. D. Herlihy.

B. What Was the Role of Feudal Institutions in the Carolingian State?

Carolingian rulers were aware of the peculiar kind of personal relationship created by commendation and the peculiar kind of land tenure represented by the *precarium*. They sought to utilize both institutions in the organization of their own society and government in a variety of ways which the following sources will partially illustrate. While it would be hard to characterize the Carolingian state as "feudal," it did initiate the effort to apply feudal principles as a means of constructing a stable society and a fairly efficient government.

1. KING PIPPIN RECEIVES THE HOMAGE OF DUKE TASSILO OF BAVARIA, 757

The following submission of the duke of Bavaria to King Pippin of the Franks is one of our earliest descriptions of the act of homage, by which a vassal-lord relationship was created. The characteristic gesture in this as in later acts of homage was the *immixio manuum*. The vassal joined his hands and placed them within the hands of his lord. Frequently but not always an oath was also required, and the following citation is our first example of an oath of vassalage. The passage is also significant because it shows the extension of the concept of vassalage from the domestic applications of the Merovingian period into the realm of public law. That concept was here being used to define the nature of the relationship between the king and one of the greatest princes of his realm.

King Pippin held his court assembly in Compiègne with the Franks. There came the duke of the Bavarians, Tassilo, commending himself in vassalage by hands. He swore many uncountable oaths, placing his hands on the relics of saints, and he promised to King Pippin and the above-mentioned sons, Lord Charles and Carloman, faith as a vassal ought to do with the right mind and firm devotion that a vassal ought to have towards his lord.

Annales regni Francorum, ed. F. Kurze, Monumenta Germaniae historica, Scriptores rerum germanicarum in usum scholarum (Hanover, 1895), p. 14, trans. D. Herlihy.

2. CHARLEMAGNE MAKES LORDS RESPONSIBLE FOR THEIR VASSALS, 810

The following brief chapter from a capitulary shows that Charlemagne welcomed an extension of vassalage, as it provided an additional means of assuring proper service. Lords could be made responsible for the behavior of their men, and the state in turn could rely upon this form of social solidarity to supervise and control its members.

(17) Let everyone compel his inferiors, that they should obey better and better and agree to imperial commands and orders.

Capitularia, op. cit., I, No. 64, p. 153, trans. D. Herlihy.

3. CHARLEMAGNE REGULATES THE RELATIONSHIP OF LORD AND VASSAL, 801–813 (?)

(8) If any vassal should wish to abandon his lord, he may do so if he can prove against him one of these crimes: first, if his lord should have sought unjustly to reduce him to slavery; second, if the lord plotted against his life; third, if the lord committed adultery with the wife of his vassal; fourth, if with drawn sword he voluntarily attacked him to kill him; fifth, if, after the vassal commended his hands into his, the lord could provide defense and did not do so. Whichever of these five [crimes] the lord should have committed against his vassal, the vassal may abandon him.

Capitularia, op. cit., I, No. 104, 215, trans. D. Herlihy.

4. CHARLES THE BALD ENCOURAGES THE EXTENSION OF VASSALAGE, 847

Historians long disputed whether Charles in the following capitulary was ordering or simply expressing a desire that every freeman in his kingdom find himself a lord. The latter interpretation seems correct, but the passage still shows the interest of the Carolingians in extending the bonds of vassalage.

(2) We wish that every free man in our realm select the lord whom he prefers, us or one of our faithful.

(3) We also command that no man abandon his lord without just cause, nor should anyone receive him, unless as was the custom at the time of our ancestors.

(5) And we wish that a man of any one of us [referring to his brothers Lothar and Louis the German], in no matter whose kingdom he should be, should go with his lord into the army or to perform other services. But if that kind of invasion of the realm should occur which is called *Landwehr* (may it not happen!), then all the people of the realm should go together to repel it.

Capitularia, op. cit., II, No. 204, p. 71, trans. D. Herlihy.

5. THE PRECARIUM VERBO REGIS

The Carolingian rulers also made use of the ecclesiastical *precarium* or benefice as a means of buttressing their state. First among the Carolingians, Charles Martel (714–741) began the practice of "ordering" bishops and abbots to grant from their lands benefices to his soldiers. By this means a good part of the church lands was turned to the support of the army. The *precarium verbo regis,* as this form of forced grant was called, is important juridically, as it seems to form the bridge between the exclusively ecclesiastical *precarium* and the lay fief. In the following capitulary, Charlemagne, in response to protests from churchmen concerning the loss of ecclesiastical land, attempted to make the laymen who held them responsible for some support to the Church as well. The capitulary dates from 779, but the words in parentheses are glosses added by Lombard judges before 830.

(14) Concerning the possessions of the churches (which up to the present laymen have held in benefice by order of the lord king). Let them continue to hold them, unless by order of the lord king they should be restored to the churches. (And if) up to the present a tithe and a ninth have been paid (to the church) let it be continued, and (moreover) let one shilling be paid (to those churches) for every fifty households, one-half shilling for every thirty, one tremisse [one-third shilling] for every twenty. (And whoever up to the present has paid a different rent, let him continue to do as he did before.) And if up to the present (no rent) has been paid, and the possession belongs to a church, let it be responsible for a rent, and where the possessions are not responsible, let a rent be prescribed for them. And let there be a distinction between *precaria* made by the lord king's order and those which (bishops and abbots and abbesses by their own will and judgment) make. (It should be permitted them, whenever they should see fit, to receive back the possessions which they gave out in benefice on behalf of the church, to assure that every man should faithfully and firmly serve in God's cause and God's honor.)

Capitularia, op. cit., I, No. 20, p. 47, trans. D. Herlihy.

C. How Did the Relationship of Lord and Vassal Change in the "Second Feudal Age"?

The basic institutions of feudalism thus seem rooted in ancient practices of Roman and Germanic societies, and the Carolingian state was already attempting to utilize them to further public order. The effort failed, as in the ninth and tenth centuries invasions and internal troubles wrecked the Carolingian Empire. By 1050, however, a new period of political reconstruction had begun, first evident not so much in the empire and large kingdoms, but in geographically restricted regions or small kingdoms such as Normandy and England. So transformed do feudal institutions become after 1050 that some historians, notably Marc Bloch, have felt it necessary to call this period a "second feudal age," clearly distinct from the centuries preceding it. The new feudalism is characterized not only by a tight association of vassalage and fief but by a growing emphasis on the property bond at the expense of the personal. Feudal society at this period becomes clearly a society based on land tenure. Simultaneously as the personal, quasi-familial element wanes, the bonds of feudalism come to be ever more the object of precise legal definition. The obligations often considered typical of feudalism—forty days of knights' service a year, special aids at special events or "incidents," and so forth —are typical only of the kind of precise, lawyers' feudalism coming to prevail in this second feudal age. An example of legal feudalism is provided here through the "Book of Customs" of the north Italian city of Milan (1216–1224). It is typical of the numerous compilations of feudal customs and law produced as the work of systematizing feudal obligations progressed.

This systematization of the feudal relationship, emphasizing more the property than the personal bond, offered the princes of the period an effective means of strengthening the constitutions of their states. By construing all the subjects of their state as their vassals, and all the land as their fiefs, an effective ruler could, with the aid of his lawyers, impose precise obligations upon his subjects. Feudalism, in other words, provided the essential concepts for defining the relationship between ruler and ruled. And the feudal principalities based upon those concepts, in spite of considerable weaknesses, still proved more stable and more lasting than any other medieval state or constitutional system that had existed before.

1. COUNT WILLIAM OF FLANDERS RECEIVES HOMAGE FROM HIS VASSALS AND INVESTS THEM WITH THEIR FIEFS AT BRUGES, 1127

The following description of the ceremonies of homage and investiture performed at the court of Bruges shows the close association of vassalage and fief tenure and the acts by which they were created in the period of matured feudalism.

On Thursday, the seventh of April, acts of homage were again performed to the count. They were done in this fashion, to assure him faith and surety. First they performed acts of homage as follows: The count asked if [the prospective vassal] wished to become completely his man, and he answered: "I do wish it." With hands joined and inclosed by the hands of the count, they were united by a kiss. In the second place, he who had done homage gave to the spokesman [*prolocutor*] of the count [a pledge of] faith in these words: "I promise in my faith that I shall be faithful from now on to Count William and that I shall fully observe my homage to him with good faith and without deceit." In the third place he swore the same on the relics of the saints. Finally, by the staff which the count was holding in his hand, he gave the investitures to all those who had with this agreement promised surety and homage and at the same time had made the oath.

De multra, traditione et occisione gloriosi Karoli, comitis Flandriarum, ed. H. Pirenne, in *Histoire du meurtre de Charles le Bon* (Paris, 1891), p. 89, trans. D. Herlihy.

2. THE LAW OF THE FIEF IN THE MILANESE "BOOK OF CUSTOMS," 1216–1224

Among the compilations of regional feudal practices which had become quite common throughout Europe from the twelfth century, the "Book of Customs" of the Italian city of Milan is distinguished for the clarity of its presentation, undoubtedly reflecting the good training of the lawyers who redacted it.

Northern Italy was in fact particularly precocious in reducing feudal customs to a clear juridic system, and hence provides a good example of a phenomenon common to the whole of Europe. The following selection is from Chapter 24, "On Fiefs." Note that the suggested etymology of the word "fief" is fanciful.

(2) Let us see therefore what a fief or benefice is, whence it is named, how it is

constituted, over what things, to whom, how, and by whom it can be given and how conceded.

(3) A fief is nothing other than a benefice [favor]. A benefice, as Seneca defines it, is a benevolent action giving joy to the recipients. It is called "fief" from the faith which the vassal must give to his lord and the lord to his vassal, as we shall discuss below.

(4) A fief or benefice is constituted over things of the soil or adhering to the soil, or over those things which are reckoned as movables, as when it is determined to give something from the treasury or storehouse.

(5) A fief is constituted by a prior investiture. This investiture is properly called "[the act of taking] possession." It is however wrongly called investiture when by a spear or staff or other corporeal thing the lord invests his vassal with any benefice in the presence of the peers of his court (if he has any) or through a properly attested writ. According to our customs, investiture may be legitimately proved by suitable witnesses if there is any doubt about it.

(6) A benefice may be given or conferred by a prince (of which there is no doubt), by a duke, margrave, landgrave, count, captain, valvassor, castellan, or other citizen or townsman; this is according to our custom, although among others the contrary may be found expressed.

(7) Today no new fief may be given or conceded from the archbishop or abbot, because by oath they are prevented from doing this. It is allowable for them, however, to invest old fiefs.

(8) [The named persons must be over twenty years to confer a fief.]

(9) A fief or benefice may be given or conceded to a duke, margrave, landgrave, count, captain, valvassor, castellan, citizen or townsman, a free peasant and a serf, especially with the knowledge of the one who makes the investiture. If he is ignorant, an investiture done to a serf shall be invalid in our judgment.

(10) The investiture of which we have been speaking may be done and received by the principal person or by his agent.

(11) It should however be known that investiture precedes fealty. But after the investiture the vassal must swear fealty, unless the fief should have been acquired with the agreement that the vassal would not do fealty, which agreement had come between the lord and the vassal.

(12) Investiture may be done concerning a future fief, which at some [later] time will be open to the lord. That investiture will finally be valid and in effect, when that fief should be open to the lord or his heir. These things obtain when he [at present] invested with the fief should consent. . . .

Liber consuetudinum Mediolani anni MCCXVI–XXIV, ed. E. Besta and G. L. Barni (Milan, 1949), p. 119, trans. D. Herlihy.

3. THE OBLIGATIONS OF FEALTY ACCORDING TO THE MILANESE "BOOK OF CUSTOMS"

(1) Because we have mentioned fealty, we shall briefly consider the form of the oath of fealty, which is set by old law and tradition. "I, _____ , swear that from now on I shall be a faithful man or vassal to my lord; nor shall I reveal to his detriment anything which he has revealed to me under the name of fealty." In these words many things are contained, which it is difficult to insert here.

(2) If however he is a domestic vassal, that is, his servant who swears not because he has a fief from him to whom he swears but because he is under the jurisdiction of him to whom he swears, this is added in the oath: "I shall guard his life, limb, mind, and his right honor."

(3) However, other vassals swear to their lords fealty and secrecy and right council according to what obtained in ancient law, as we said above.

(4) But they should not swear against all men, because in every oath the reverence owed the prince must be excepted. If the vassal has a prior lord, the vassal should except the fealty that belongs to him.

(5) When investiture has been done followed by fealty, as said above, the lord is compelled to bring the vassal into possession of the fief. And if he delays to do this, he must give full indemnity to the vassal.

(6) But if he should give as a fief the property of another person or property mortgaged to another person and it should be taken from the vassal, the lord is compelled, after legitimate complaint, to give another property equally good, whether the lord did or did not know that he had given the property of another or mortgaged property as a fief.

(7) The vassal possesses this power over property invested as a fief, that he may claim it from any possessor at all and refuse another's summons. And he may rightly demand and retain services due [from the property].

(9) We have seen what is a fief and how it is constituted and over what possessions and how and by whom it may be given and to whom conceded. Now let us see how it may be lost.

A benefice is lost in many ways: by accident if the vassal should die without heir or relative on his father's side, in which case the fief perishes and the property given in fief returns to the lord. A fief is lost also by the fault of the vassal, if for a year and a day he does not seek investiture from his lord, and this according to the law of the Lord Frederick [Barbarossa, 1152–1190].

However, in our custom the vassal does not lose his fief although for a long time he does not seek investiture from his lord. But if the vassal is summoned three times by the peers of the court to serve the lord and to swear fealty and he does not come but contemptuously remains for a year and a day, he can lose his fief through [court] decision.

(10) The fief is also lost by sale or seizure with the knowledge of the vassal and reverts to the lord who did not agree to the sale. . . .

(16) A fief or benefice is also lost through ingratitude, for example, if a vassal shows himself ungrateful toward his lord. The cases of ingratitude can be gathered from the new custom and old laws and ancient customs of fiefs, through which sons are excluded from the inheritance of relatives and gifts given are revoked and a benefice or fief is lost. But since nature is hurriedly producing new forms, the discrete and circumspect judge should diligently learn if any other causes of ingratitude may emerge by which a benefice could be revoked. This however should be noted: If a vassal should perform or plot assault, death, capture, or grave damage of property against his lord or should not inform his lord about these things; if he should have sexual intercourse with his wife or daughter-in-law or sister; if he should attack with force the village in which his lord is, place or put impious hands upon his lord, ambush his lord with poison or sword, desert him in battle, or refuse the service for which the fief was given; if he should be a betrayer of his lord and his lord suffer grave damage from it; if he should not free his imprisoned lord when he is able—by all the above-mentioned causes let him know that he shall be deprived of his fief. For both natural and civil reason convinces that by the above ways the fief ought to be lost. . . .

(21) But if anyone not having sons should enter a religious house or take the religious habit and become a monk or lay brother, he loses his fief and shall not retain any of the fruit to be taken from it for the time of his life. The same holds if anyone takes holy orders.

Ibid., Chap. 25, trans. D. Herlihy.

4. FEUDAL CONCEPTS IN THE SERVICE OF PRINCES

The following excerpt from the assize of King Amaury of the Latin Kingdom of Jerusalem (1162) illustrates how princes were

attempting to utilize the concepts of feudalism to strengthen their own authority. Here King Amaury requires that the rear vassals of his kingdom accept him as their "liege," i.e. primary lord, and be responsible to him at the risk of losing their lands. The application of feudal principles depended of course for its success on how much actual power the prince could wield. Still, the effort alone shows that in no sense could feudalism be considered equivalent to anarchy.

That the [rear] vassals of the vassals of the chief lord [i.e. the king] of the kingdom do liege homage to the chief lord of the kingdom according to the assize, for the fiefs which they hold of these vas-

sals.... If the king wishes to have the fealty of the people who are living in cities, in castles, and in burgs for that which they hold of him, they should all swear fealty, and they should be bound by that fealty for that for which the [rear] vassals of these vassals are bound, in accordance with the liege homage done by the assize to the chief lord....

Cited by J. L. LaMonte, *Feudal Monarchy in the Latin Kingdom of Jerusalem* (Cambridge, Mass.: Mediaeval Academy of America, 1932), p. 21, trans. D. Herlihy.

III. The Townsman

A. What Were the Origins of the Medieval Townsmen?

From the later eleventh century, towns and the bourgeoisie that inhabited them became an ever more important factor in the social and political world of Europe. How did it happen that a group of men were willing and able to break with the predominantly agricultural activities of the early medieval world and begin the development of a new commercial economy? Historians have long argued over the issue, and they tend to divide according to what they consider was the most important factor in the formation of the new merchant class. For the Belgian historian Henri Pirenne, that factor was primarily psychological incentive, and that incentive could be found only among those segments of medieval society, the proletarians in fact, who had no vested interest in keeping things as they were. Only the penniless, the landless wanderers and foot-loose adventurers had nothing to lose in undertaking new enterprises. Pirenne's argument forms part of a larger theory of economic and social change by which he also sought to explain other major economic departures: the commercial expansion of the sixteenth century and the industrial revolution of the eighteenth and nineteenth. In all these great turning points, argued Pirenne, the innovators were exactly those who had no vested interest in the old ways of doing things, for they alone had the pioneering incentive.

But what resources had these proletarians? What was their initial capital? Pirenne believed that this "primitive accumulation"

could be attributed to luck; the wandering proletarian might have accidentally struck upon a lost treasure, or found the opportunity to rob some wealth and even to earn it. But other historians have been reluctant to concede that luck or accident could have equipped a substantial number of the new townsmen with their essential capital. Moreover, Pirenne's studies were principally concerned with northern towns, and he himself was aware that his theories had only limited application to Italy, southern France, and Spain. In our second selection, a Danish scholar, Johannes Plesner, argues from an investigation of urban immigration in thirteenth-century Florence that those who left the countryside were not at all the landless proletarians but property owners, often substantially so. This rendered the late medieval or Renaissance Italian town the counterpart of the ancient *civitas,* which had served as the center of the agricultural as well as the commercial life of the region.

Are different origins of the urban classes then to be sought in Italy as distinct from the North? In a recent study, Abbé Jean Lestocquoy has aimed at a synthesis, focusing on what he has called the "patriciate," i.e. the great urban families of both Italy and Flanders. As the selection below shows, he veers considerably away from Pirenne's enterprising proletarians. The tendency of both Plesner and Lestocquoy to emphasize the wealth in land possessed by the townsmen before their immigration to the city solves the problem of initial capital. Already fairly substantial citizens in their rural homes, they had the means to invest in commerce. But Pirenne's principal point remains unanswered: had they the incentive? Or is the psychological orientation of the Belgian historian's views a legitimate one? To give the reader a chance to evaluate for himself the status of the bourgeoisie in an early phase of its history, the last part of this section contains the record of a dispute between the burghers of Vézelay and their feudal lord. From it something of both the economic interests of the burghers and their political aspirations may be learned.

1. THE "FOOT-LOOSE ADVENTURERS" OF HENRI PIRENNE

Landed wealth, in effect, did not make the slightest contribution to the economic activity which, after the disasters of the Norman invasions in the north and the pillages of the Saracens on the Mediterranean shores began to stir towards the end of the tenth century and the beginning of the eleventh. European towns are the daughters of commerce and industry. The bourgeoisie appears to us from its origins as a class of uprooted people. But it is at the same time an essentially commercial class, and we need adduce no further proof of this than the identification up to the beginning of the twelfth century of the word *mercator* [merchant] and the word *burgensis* [townsman].

What resources did these pioneers of commerce, these emigrants in search of the means of subsistance, bring with them into the nascent towns? Almost always, nothing but the strength of their arms, the force of their will, the clarity of their intelligence. Agricultural life continued to be the normal life, and the holders of the soil could not have had at the beginning any idea of abandoning their tenures in order to run the risks of a new life in the town. As for selling one's land in order to secure liquid capital after the manner of modern farmers, that would have been an act of which no one at that time could even have dreamed. Therefore, we must search out the ancestors of the bourgeoisie above all among the mass of wanderers who floated through society, living from day to day from the charities of monasteries, hiring themselves out at the time of harvest, joining armies in times of war and not refraining even from pillage or from rapine if they had the chance. That there might have been among them some rural artisans, some professional porters, disposing of a little property, can be admitted without difficulty. But it remains no less true that, save for rare exceptions, it was poor people who in the towns founded the first commercial fortunes of the Middle Ages. In other words, liquid capital was constituted independently of all influence of landed capital. [The townsmen] were at the beginning only parvenus, incited to action by the transformations of society, unhampered either by custom or routine, having nothing to lose and so much the more audacious in their pursuit of profit.

Condensed from H. Pirenne, "Les Périodes de l'histoire sociale du capitalisme," *Bulletin de l'Académie royale de Belgique. Classe des Lettres.* V (1914), 258–99, trans. D. Herlihy.

2. THE LANDED IMMIGRANTS OF JOHANNES PLESNER

As a result of these present studies, it may definitely be affirmed that the belief, unassailable up to the present, in the grandiose but legendary event by which in the thirteenth century the land changed owners, conquered at the price of blood and usury by a bourgeoisie originally destitute of land, is about to be abandoned. In studying the question closely, we naturally find some commercial people who seem to have been personally strangers in the rural parishes where their farms were found. But this type, which should have predominated over all the others if the theories of the historians were acceptable, fades to sporadic appearances in comparison with the regularity with which another type becomes evident—a type forming a stratification so clear and sharply defined, that with reason it may be called "strata" in the archeological or geological sense.

These strata are not found in the countryside but in the town. There we find almost exclusively families, great and small, who were old and landed and who in successive waves at different epochs emigrated to the town. These were people who continued to be peasants or rural nobles; they did not abandon their land but constantly supervised its cultivation and enlarged it by new purchases. They remained in the town and they engaged in the specifically urban professions, commercial or industrial, but the basis of their existence and of their business was the incomes from leases in wheat, oil, wine, etc., which were regularly furnished them by their leaseholders. For the epoch of the free town, the fundamental fact is not that the land changed owners, which naturally occurred in certain isolated cases.

The fundamental fact is this: that families owning lands emigrated as in antiquity to their town and there increased their wealth by the exercise of urban professions. In these natural tendencies we must discern the true renaissance, the renaissance of the *civitas* that is authentic right down to the cells of the structure. The medieval townsman, from the highest class of society to the humblest artisan, is a social type resembling the citizen of the ancient city. He does not resemble either the mercantile bourgeois or feudal nobles of other countries. Social structure thus explains why the culture of the free Italian town, which is to say the "Renaissance," never carried the imprint of a socially limited horizon, whether of the merchant or artisan, the courtier or peasant or rural noble.

J. Plesner, *L'Emigration de la campagne à la ville libre de Florence au XIIIe siècle* (Copenhagen: Gyldendalske Boghandel, 1934), pp. 214–15, trans. D. Herlihy.

3. THE ORIGINS OF THE "PATRICIATE" ACCORDING TO ABBÉ LESTOCQUOY

What was the patriciate? It was a fraction of the townspeople, often the richest but about all the most powerful for having laid hands upon the government of the city. Whence came these patricians? Or rather, whence came their wealth? This is certain enough. In Venice it might be the possession of salt flats, at Genoa or Florence the possession of lands. In Flanders, it could be a mill. Or else there is the secondary employment as an official, of the customs at Siena or of the Abbey of Saint-Vaast at Arras, or in the entourage of the count of Flanders. And those usurers

who multiply to the point of worrying general councils from 1139—why would they not be at the origin of some families?

Patrician families have a local origin not far from the city: the small ports of the Adriatic for Venice, the surrounding countryside for Florence or Arras. And if we must evidently admit that the towns recruited their inhabitants in the countryside (and all investigations show that it is a matter of a proximate countryside, within a radius of thirty kilometers [eighteen miles]), the arrival in the city was far from being the signal for a lightninglike rise. In almost all cases, the ancestors of the patricians are recognizable as persons of middle importance.

Condensed from J. Lestocquoy, *Les Villes de Flandre et d' Italie sous le gouvernment das patriciens (XIe–XVe siècles)* (Paris: Presses Universitaires de France, 1952), pp. 242 ff.

B. The Quarrel Between the Abbot and the Burghers of Vézelay, 1137

The following document is typical of many which record disputes between growing towns and their feudal overlords from the eleventh

century. Does the document show, as Pirenne argued, that the burghers were an exclusively mercantile class? What powers of their lord, the abbot, were they seeking to restrict and control?

Our complaints against the burghers and of the burghers against us [Brother

Alberic, Abbot of Vézelay] were of this sort:

(1) We complained that the burghers did not fully pay the tithes of wine and grain; they paid little or nothing of the tithes of other things, such as sheep and lambs, calves and pigs and so forth, which are called "first fruits."

(2) We complained that the lodges which, according to ancient custom, we take for the service of visitors who come to Vézelay on Easter and the feast of St. Mary Magdalen have been leased by the burghers against our prohibition to pilgrims and merchants. For this reason we have often been forced to lease other houses with our own money.

(3) We have against them another quarrel, that they do not pay the quit-rent on vineyards, neither when nor how much nor what they ought.

(4) There was another complaint against them concerning the marks [units of weight], according to which the money changers, against ancient custom, sell and buy. They are of different weight [than the traditional].

(5) We said that from each man owning meadows in the district of Vézelay, we should have one measure of grass as often as it was found in the meadow.

(6) There was a complaint as to what [services] are due (which by another name are called *corvées*) from which fields pertaining to the tables of the abbot and the brothers. The fields are held by both burgesses and peasants.

(7) There was also a complaint concerning fishing in the waters of the Masot.

(8) We also complained that, while we were expecting to make peace and concord, the burghers again made a conspiratorial confederation against us and our church, and even joined to themselves peasants from many of our villas in that conspiracy.

The complaint of the burghers was:

(1) When they died without legitimate heirs of sons or daughters, we took both their movable and immovable possessions. They also complained that we were unwilling to permit that they should make their brothers, sisters, or other relatives their heirs.

(2) They also complained that we did not permit them to donate any land or vines (held from us in quit-rent) to the sick who are called lepers.

(3) They complained that burial and due [liturgical] service was denied to the dead until the relatives and friends of the deceased paid us the obligations [due us]. There was also complaint that we were leasing the tables of the money changers and merchants for more than our predecessors had charged.

(4) They complained also that we did not allow them to set up stalls and displays or any such thing without paying.

(5) Also they complained about the *taille* [a tax] which is customarily collected after Christmas both from burghers and from peasants. They said that four men, whom they would elect from among themselves, should accompany the deacon and the provost when the said tax was being collected, and the collection should be made according to their advice, and the worth of each person should be considered both among the burghers and the peasants according to their wealth, that is, one should be assessed more and the other less. They said that these four elected would do this only this one year, and in another year [four] others, and thus the men would change from year to year.

(6) They complained that a larger quit-rent was being demanded of them from their vines than what they were accustomed to pay.

(7) They also complained that we had placed forests out of bounds which should be in common.

(8) They also complained that we did injury to our peasants of [the villa] Saint-Pierre and of our other villas, and they wanted that we do justice through them.

Condensed from the *Cartulaire général de l'Yonne*, ed. M. Quantin (Auxerre, 1854), No. 186, trans. D. Herlihy.

5

Political Authority
in the Later Middle Ages

NORMAN P. ZACOUR

Franklin and Marshall College

The major issues of political power in medieval Europe are frequently portrayed against a background of that stormy conflict between spiritual and temporal authority, the echoes of which may still be heard. This dualism of "church and state" has become a familiar theme in the historical treatment of the Middle Ages. The theme is an attractive one—all the more so to those who accept the modern doctrine of the separation of church and state—and it has come to dominate much of the discussion about ultimate political authority in the medieval West. In its welcome suggestion, however, of two separate spheres of human activity, secular and spiritual, it sometimes leads to serious distortion.

We must continually remind ourselves that Christian society in the Middle Ages was assumed to be one and indivisible, a single corporate body embracing all Christians from prince to peasant, whose end was salvation, and whose direction therefore had to accord with the ideals of Christianity. Given all this it was important to know who, priest or prince, was to decide what the ideals of the Christian life were and was to judge how they were to be pursued, for it was a medieval commonplace that a single body demands a single head. It was on this assumption that, for a long time, conflicting theories of political authority were built. As the assumption changed—as the unitary conception of the world gave way to pluralism—the conflicts became sharper, more violent. The problems which are examined below all have to do, directly or indirectly, with the way western Europe, in rejecting a unified society in favor of a multiplicity of sovereign states, deprived the papacy of the role it claimed as functional head of Christendom.

At the outset the question seemed relatively clear, even if the answer tended to be elusive. It has recently been put thus (by Walter Ullmann, *The Growth of Papal Government in the Middle Ages* [London, 1955], p. 11):

Who—that is the basic problem—was to govern, that is, to direct and orientate the corporate union of Christians—the emperor, because he was emperor, or the pope because he was successor of St. Peter?...The emperors... viewed [the corporate union of Christians] as the Roman body politic, as a mere empire, within which Christianity was indeed of paramount importance and for this very reason demanded imperial control. If we keep in mind that Christianity seizes the whole of man and cannot, by its very nature, be confined to certain departmental limits...we shall perhaps grasp the intrinsic force of papal ideology and the strength of imperial resistance. In brief, who was functionally qualified to define the doctrine, purpose and aim underlying the corporate union of all Christians, to direct that body according to its underlying purpose or aim—emperor or pope?

From the point of view of the papacy the answer was self-evident. The governor of Christian society was Christ. He would hardly have established his church without providing for its continued direction, and had obviously not intended, when he transmitted his power to the apostle Peter, that it should end there. In the words "Thou art Peter, and upon this rock I will build my church," there was an implied provision for Peter's successors, the popes, in whose hands, it was said, lay the ultimate government of Christian society. Pope Innocent IV, himself a noted canon lawyer of the thirteenth century, put it quite bluntly:

Christ the son of God, while in the world, was lord of Nature from eternity, and by the law of Nature could depose and sentence to damnation emperors and any others, inasmuch as they were persons he had created, had endowed with natural and free gifts, and had conserved in their being. For this same reason his vicar can do so, for he would not seem to have been a wise Lord (though I speak with reverence) if he had not left such a unique vicar who had power to do all this. His vicar was Peter...and the same must be said of Peter's successors, since the same absurdity follows if, after the death of Peter, Christ had left humankind, which he had created, bereft of the rulership of a single person. (Innocent IV, *apparatus quinque librorum decretalium,* Bk. II, Tit. XXVII, Chap. 27.)

Christ was both priest and king. The pope was the vicar of Christ. It was his overriding responsibility to work for the salvation of the world. He alone could ensure the reign of Christian justice.

It followed, of course, that such great responsibilities demanded means adequate to their fulfillment which came in time to be defined as a plenitude, a fullness, of power—*plenitudo potestatis*. There could be no limit to papal jurisdiction even in the "temporal" sphere, since no human act, political or otherwise, could avoid the possibility of sinful behavior, wherein only the priest could intervene and had a duty to do so. In this respect the distinction between "spiritual" and "temporal" lost much of its force.

This is not to say that the papacy laid claim to the immediate government of the Christian community. Secular authorities—imperial, royal, feudal, civic—had an important function in assisting in the divine work of salvation by defending and cooperating with the Church. As early as A.D. 494 Pope Gelasius I, in a letter to the Byzantine emperor which future popes were fond of quoting, distinguished between the spiritual and secular rulership of the Christian world:

There are two things, august emperor, by which this world is chiefly ruled, the sacred authority [*auctoritas*] of the pontiffs and the royal power [*potestas*]. In these, the weight of the priests is so much the greater as it is they who will render account at the day of judgment for [the conduct of] those kings of men.

His careful use of the words *auctoritas* and *potestas*, authority and power, words which in Roman law had clear meanings—the former expressing final, supreme authority, the latter delegated or proximate authority; the former indivisible, the latter shared by many—seems to imply a firm idea of papal superiority; but it certainly also provided for the place of secular government, itself a divine gift, as a cooperating agency in the work of the Church.

In subsequent centuries the Gelasian theory received much elaboration and support, among others from Isidore of Seville in the seventh century whose works were widely read and were greatly influential in the Middle Ages:

The princes of the world sometimes occupy the summits of power in the church, in order to defend ecclesiastical discipline by their power. But in the church these powers would not be needed if they did not have to impose by the fear of discipline that which the priests are powerless to effect by exhortation. (*Sentences*, III, 51, in Migne, *PL* 83, 723.)

So secular government is a necessary evil only. If priests could have prevailed without princes then God need not have created princes. This is only another way of saying with St. Augustine that man is by nature sinful and that political organization is therefore necessary and unavoidable. As such, however, it exists as an arm of the Church, to serve the purposes of the Christian life, subordinate to ecclesiastical direction.

It took centuries for this view of society and government to prevail. There were several obstacles to overcome. First there was "Caesaropapism," the theocratic monarchy of the Byzantine emperors, which embraced a view of society much the same as that of the papacy, but saw the emperor rather than the pope as the divinely instituted agent of God's will, and relegated the Church and its hierarchy to a position subordinate to the imperial dignity. Caesaropapism held in check the papal claims to ultimate jurisdiction; and even when, in the eighth century, the papacy finally broke with Constantinople, and thought to find in the king of the Franks the secular power which would defend the papacy, would aid in the divine mission of the Church, and would rule in accordance with Christian justice as defined in Rome, it found in fact that it had exchanged one master for another—closer, more effective, equally demanding. Charlemagne (d. 814), king of the Franks, crowned emperor by Pope Leo III on Christmas Day, 800, treated the church as an agency of the crown, and while he always accorded to Rome a position of primacy within the Church, he never conceded to it jurisdiction over society at large. He saw his own role in much the same light as did the emperors of Byzantium theirs, legislated in liturgical and doctrinal matters, was an active governor of the Church, insisted on approving the decrees of church synods—was, in effect, the supreme head of an empire which he equated with western Christendom, often to the discomfort of the pope. In a letter to Pope Leo, written for him by the scholar Alcuin, Charlemagne clearly defined their respective functions:

It is for us [meaning himself] with the aid of divine piety, to defend by force of arms the Holy Church of Christ everywhere from the attack of pagans and the devastation by infidels from without, and from within to fortify it with the knowledge of the catholic faith. It is for you, holy father, to aid our arms with hands upraised to God like Moses, that by your intercession the Christian people under God's leadership and grace may always conquer everywhere the enemies of his holy name, and the name of our lord Jesus Christ may shine throughout the whole world. (Alcuin, Ep. 93, *Epistolae Karolini aevi*, II, ed. E. Dümmler, *MGH., Epp.*, IV, 137–38.)

This is a complete reversal of roles: the king not only defends the church physically but even ensures the right teaching of the faith; the pope is now merely the helper, aiding by intercession and prayer.

The second obstacle, ecclesiastical authority, arose from the general conviction, obstinately opposed by the papacy, that kings were different from ordinary laymen, that they were holy and sacred. The primitive sources of this idea were many; by the Middle Ages it was fully confirmed by the ceremony of royal consecration and the anointing of the monarch with holy oil. The royal person, emperor or king, thus entered into the ranks of the clergy, so to speak, enjoying a religious rank and veneration that no other lay person had. He was the Lord's anointed. The idea of sacred kingship enormously strengthened theocratic government in the West and gave to monarchy a sanction for its claim to autonomous rule under God.

Third, the ideas of theocratic government and the sacredness of kings were dominant at a time when the Church lacked administrative unity and central direction, and churches of Europe were dominated by secular authorities and under lay control—when, in other words, the institution of the "proprietary church" was prevalent. This institution developed as a result of the foundation or usurpation of religious establishments by lay lords who retained legal proprietary interests in them, installed the priests or monks, laid down rules governing their duties, regulated their collection of tithes, endowed the establishments with their own lands, often reaped for themselves much of the income, and finally transmitted the proprietary churches and monasteries to their heirs along with their other offices, rights, and properties. This practice spread throughout Europe, bringing churches into close dependence upon local political authorities and making it all but impossible for the development of a papal government of a united Church.

Finally, political conditions which might have allowed the realization of papal ideas of hierarchical government did not exist for many centuries. A unified Christian society remained for long an unrealizable ideal and the peace which was a cornerstone of that unity a noble dream. The papacy, for all its grand conception of a united Christian community, was for centuries immersed in local struggles in Italy, pitifully subservient to whatever secular ruler would give aid. Little wonder, then, that with the revival of the Roman Empire in the West by the German kings, the latter would look on the papacy as on any other imperial bishopric, an instrument in the hands of the German crown.

What all this came to was the fact that the papacy could not control the Church itself, without which papal authority in the world would remain an idle boast. For the papacy to rule the visible Church effectively it would be necessary to destroy local ecclesiastical dependence on lay authority. In Germany, where the emperors controlled all the important churches and monasteries and where the integrity of the state depended upon the loyalty of the ecclesiastics to the emperor, this would amount to the destruction of the basis of royal power, an immense revolution. Pope Gregory VII (1073–1085) began it in earnest almost as soon as he was elected to the papal office.

The grounds for an attack on the lay control of the Church had been prepared by a series of church reforms of such abuses as the sale of church offices (simony), the general moral decadence among many of the clergy, especially the prevalence of clerical marriages which had no sanction in canon law, and the investiture of clergy with their offices by lay lords, a practice repugnant because it was symbolic of the demoralizing lay dominion over the Church. This attack began as a reform of monasteries under the leadership of the Benedictine house of Cluny, but soon spread throughout the Church at large, often ironically enough encouraged by pious laymen including the German emperors themselves. When, therefore, Pope Gregory legislated against simony, clerical marriage, and the investiture of clergy by laymen, he was responding to imperative moral demands of the time. But he was also giving expression to traditional papal views of the independence and superiority of the ecclesiastical state. In doing so he attacked the very basis of royal authority in Germany and, by implication, elsewhere. From this time forward secular political authority was thrown on the defensive against papal claims.

In the circumstances there would be many occasions for tension and turmoil. The success of those who followed Gregory VII in the papal office came mainly at the expense of the German emperors and led to greater papal control of the Church with an accompanying increase in papal administrative and judicial activities. In the meantime the feudal monarchies which were emerging in the West began a constant search for greater autonomy. As the empire declined, these—especially France and England—grew stronger and more centralized, taking the place of the empire in the arena with the papacy. The ultimate problem of these monarchies was to find a rationale for their existence and activity, still limited by the now historical demand of the papacy that all secular authority cooperate in the work of the Church. Relations grew more strained with the increasing centralization both of these monarchies and of the Church in Rome, which itself was taking on many of the attributes of a state.

A fruitful source of friction was the matter of "papal provisions." The old practice of the popes of recommending worthy clerics for church offices (benefices), with attached sources of income (prebends), had gradually grown into a right to confer benefices and prebends with little or no regard to the wishes of the patron of the local church in question, whether king, noble, bishop, cathedral chapter, or monastery. It was in part a means whereby the papacy could meet the expenses of an ever growing bureaucracy. What the pope gained, however, others lost. Kings and princes everywhere were also faced with the problem of meeting the costs of an increasingly expensive administrative staff and looked for an easy solution to the appointment of their servants to church benefices. Further, the system inevitably led to abuses since many did not take up residence in their new appointments but merely collected the annual income. Finally, the fees and other costs involved in obtaining benefices led to a growing concern over a system which by its very magnitude seemed to amount to the sale of church offices. But could the highly developed Church with its far-flung activities in education, the military crusades, the administration of justice, the guardianship of public morality, to say nothing of the worship of God, abandon the practice of supervising and controlling appointments to church offices without abandoning its leadership of the Church itself? Here is our first problem.

Underlying this tension respecting papal provisions was the basic conflict between the theory of a unified Christian society with the pope at its head, directing, guiding, judging, and punishing, and the existence of increasingly independent monarchies. The former postulated a united Christendom; the latter revealed disunity and division. And there could be no doubt that the loyalties of individuals were swinging more and more to the latter. Where were the advocates of secular authority to find a new theory of political society to fit the facts? This is the second problem.

All this led to an increasing attack on papal authority in the secular sphere. But the attack did not stop there. Current legal and constitutional ideas growing out of the examination of contemporary corporate institutions such as universities, episcopal churches, guilds, town corporations, feudal government, and even the papacy itself, tended to emphasize the rights of members of the corporation concerned to participate in their own government. The student need only remind himself of the growth of parliament. Applied specifically to the papacy, this meant a greater drive on the part of churchmen to share the papal authority, the *plenitudo potestatis*. The college of cardinals made an ambitious attempt in this direction but, moved by oligarchical ideas, hesitated to allow any further distribution of power. However, during the crisis of the Great Schism which the cardinals brought on (1378–1417), there emerged the view that the final evidence of God's will would be found, not in one person, nor in a few, but in the church at large, expressed in church councils representative of all Christendom— that far from the pope ruling the Church the Church should rule the pope, now reduced from absolute head to executive director. These ideas are considered as our third problem.

This Conciliar Movement, as it is called, ultimately failed, but not before it had helped to lay the grounds for a later revolt against papal authority in the sixteenth century of such proportions as to shatter all illusions of a unified Christian society. By the end of the Middle Ages the assumptions about society and government upon which papal dominion had been based were no longer universally held. As a result the papacy found itself faced not only by opposition from without but by rebellion from within—opposition not merely to its temporal claims but to its supremacy within the Church itself. In the process the ideal of a single corporate society, directed to a final, ultimate end, was rejected. Why this should have been—indeed, whether this must always be—the reader may try to answer for himself.

I. *The Problem of Papal Provisions*

During the thirteenth century many new sources of revenue were gradually being developed by the papacy in its search to support the increasing administrative and judicial burdens which were among the fruits of power and growth. One of these was the "services," payments made by churchmen who had been appointed to their benefices by the pope—who had received, in other words, a "papal provision." The services came to be paid by those who had received a benefice bringing in a minimum annual income of 100 florins, and went toward the salaries of the officials and clerks of the papal court, the college of cardinals, and the papal treasury.

These services had developed out of the old practice of giving presents to the pope and to the papal officials when a churchman was confirmed in his new appointment. Gradually the voluntary gift became a regular fee with fixed rates. And for those whose benefices were not rich enough to support the payment of services it became customary to levy "annates" or "first fruits"—a portion of the first year's revenue of the benefice.

During the same period the papacy began to enlarge the number of benefices which could be granted only by the pope. This meant an increase in the "services." But there were certainly more reasons for such extension than merely the search for additional revenue. In fact the impetus for papal appointment to benefices came from outside the papacy, from those who sought in papal authority a stronger claim to their office than could be found elsewhere. Also in many cases it was probably true that the papacy could exhibit a greater dis-

interestedness in its appointments than could be expected in the ordinary course of events, where local appointments at all levels of the Church were subject to political and private pressures, where kings ensured that their servants were rewarded at the expense of the Church, and where noble families often turned churches into private preserves for their high-born offspring and relatives. Then, too, papal provisions supported higher education throughout Europe, for this was the way that university scholars, who might have had short shrift at the hands of the laity and the local hierarchy, were assured a source of regular income and were drawn into the service of the Church upon graduation.

However, when the popes began in more systematic fashion to reserve more and more benefices for their own disposal it was inevitable that local interests would suffer and that opposition would grow. The pope claimed that the disposition of all church offices was theoretically his; in practice, however, he tended to exploit the custom that he could dispose of those benefices which "fell vacant" when the holder was in Rome itself—at first minor benefices, then all benefices; at first those vacated by death, then those vacated by all other causes: resignation, transfer, etc.; at first those vacated at the papal court itself, then those vacated anywhere on the way to or from, or in the vicinity of, that place where the court might be at the time.

It was perhaps inevitable that, as the papacy began to dispose of more church offices, there would follow a growing clamor for papal favors which gave moralists much to deplore. Then, too, a growing sense of national self-consciousness in the fourteenth century led to sharp criticisms of this manifestation of church centralization. For example, the hostility between France and England which led to the Hundred Years' War, coupled with the fact that the papacy was held by a succession of French popes in Avignon who were believed to favor the French cause, made the continued centralization of papal administration seem all the more destructive of England's independence.

The effect of resistance to papal provisions would be to limit the authority of the papacy. The attack on papal administrative procedures would soon lead to a questioning of the basis for papal government of the church. Was the problem of papal provisions a moral one, such that the only solution was to destroy papal control over the Church, and place it in the hands of secular authorities to the betterment of Christianity? Or was the problem a political one, for the simple reason that rulers could not achieve autonomy without restricting, and eventually expelling, papal authority within their national churches?

A. Papal Reservations

In the fourteenth century, after the disastrous struggle between Pope Boniface VIII (1294–1303) and King Philip IV of France (1295–1314), the papacy came to be located in the city of Avignon in Provence, where it remained from 1309 to 1378. During this time the popes, kept out of Italy and Rome by conditions of civil war and political chaos, found themselves cut off from large sources of revenue and at the same time committed to a policy of reconquest and pacification in central Italy which placed a large strain on papal resources. Further, in a constant effort to keep western Christendom unified and at peace the papacy tried over and over to launch crusades to the East, an expensive business without, as it happened, much to show for it. In the circumstances hitherto sporadic rev-

enues were made more systematic and the papacy developed, as efficiently as possible, a whole range of ecclesiastical taxes in order to finance its far-flung and expensive enterprises. The "reservations" of church offices was one of many such methods.

1. POPE CLEMENT IV RESERVES MINOR BENEFICES VACANT AT THE ROMAN COURT, 1265

Although the full disposition of churches, parsonages, dignities, and other ecclesiastical benefices is known to belong to the Roman pontiff, so that he not only can confer them by law when vacant, but indeed can grant a right to those that will fall vacant in the future; nevertheless ancient custom has specially reserved to other Roman pontiffs the bestowal of churches, parsonages, dignities, and benefices falling vacant "at the apostolic see." We, therefore, finding this a praiseworthy custom, and approving it by apostolic authority, and moreover desiring it to be observed inviolably, do ordain, by that same authority, that no one other than the Roman Pontiff may presume to confer upon any person or persons the churches, dignities, parsonages, and benefices which happen hereafter to be vacant at that same see, no matter what authority in the matter he may be strengthened with, whether their election, provision, or collation may belong to him by right of ordinary authority, or he has received a general or even special letter under any form of words about their provision (unless there has been granted him special and express authority by the highest pontiff himself on the conferring of those [benefices] vacant in the Roman court). For we decree it invalid and void if it should be done or attempted otherwise.

Sext., Lib. IV, Tit. IV, Cap. II, in E. Friedberg, *Corpus iuris canonici* (Leipzig, 1881), II, 1021, trans. N. P. Zacour.

2. POPE BONIFACE VIII EXTENDS THE SCOPE OF VACANCIES (AFTER 1295)

We declare, by the present edict, that the statute of our predecessor Pope Clem-

ent [IV], of happy memory, regarding benefices vacant at the apostolic see which ought not to be conferred by anyone other than the Roman Pontiff, holds for benefices which legates or nuncios of this see, or anyone else, coming to the Roman court or else leaving it, are known to have, if it happens that they die in places neighboring the court, just as though they died in the very place where the court was situated. The same holds for any member of the court...who dies in a neighboring place.... Places neighboring to the court may be defined as those which are not more than two days' distant [i.e., about 40 miles].... When it happens that the court is transferred from one place to another, if members of the court either on the way... or remaining sick in the place where the court has departed from, should there be freed from human affairs, the aforesaid statute extends to their benefices, no matter how far away from the court may be the place where they died.

Sext., Lib. III, Tit. IV, Cap. XXXIV, *ibid.*, 1031, trans. N. P. Zacour.

3. POPE CLEMENT V NOW INCLUDES THE MAJOR BENEFICES, 1305

Although the caution of discretion should be exercised in the disposition of worldly goods, especially so that they may be distributed in a fitting and praiseworthy manner; nevertheless in ecclesiastical things it should be our purpose to ensure more carefully that ecclesiastical persons be appointed on the basis of merit, according to the condition and status of the persons, for their own usefulness and the praise of the divine name, since according to canonical sanctions there is nothing that hinders the church of God more than that unworthy persons are elevated to the rule of souls. Moved, therefore, by this consideration, we at this time by apostolic authority reserve to the provision, collation, and disposition of ourself and this See, the church of Bordeaux especially,[1] from which (though undeservedly) we were recently raised to this state of the highest apostolate, and the monastery of the Holy Cross of Bordeaux, of the order of St. Benedict, vacant through the death of the late brother William of Bonbio, its abbot; and, in general,[2] patriarchal, archiepiscopal, episcopal churches, monasteries, priories and whatever benefices with stalls or places in churches without jurisdiction, dignities, or offices, of whatever order and condition they may be, as well as canonries, prebends, churches with or without cure of souls and every other ecclesiastical benefice called by any name whatsoever which are known to be vacant at the apostolic see at the present time and which happen to become vacant in the future during the whole time of our pontificate ...notwithstanding the constitutions of Clement IV and Boniface VIII, Roman pontiffs, our predecessors....

Extravag. Commun., Lib. III, Tit. II, Cap. III, *ibid.*, 1258, trans. N. P. Zacour.

B. The Search for Office

The pressures on the popes to make appointments frequently came from outside the papal court. Englishmen were often scolded by compatriots for seeking office from the papacy and paying the requisite fees. But the practice continued to increase and not infrequently the king of England, whose rights were supposed to be violated by papal provisions, himself wrote to the pope to recommend some servant or other for papal appointment. Especially, however, requests continued to pour into the papal court from the universities on behalf of their graduates.

1. ADAM MURIMUTH SCORNS PAPAL APPOINTMENTS

This year, just after Christmas [1343], Anthony, bishop of Norwich, died, and forthwith the prior and convent of

---

[1] This is called a "special reservation" as contrasted with the "general reservation" to follow.
[2] Here follows the "general reservation."

Norwich in concord elected Master William Bateman, dean of Lincoln, at that time present in the court of Rome; but hearing of the said bishop's death he arranged to be sent by the pope to the king of England and to have the said bishopric conferred upon himself, since he preferred to have it granted by the pope than through the aforesaid election. And coming around the feast of the Purification [2 Feb., 1344] to the king, who was in London at the time with his council, he promised to do much on their behalf at the papal court, and so finally got from the king the temporal goods of the said bishopric.... He returned to the [papal] court, got himself consecrated there and a procuration granted for his travels *viz.*, 4 florins a day going to England, while there, and returning to the court before his consecration, and 8 florins after consecration; the execution and levy of this was committed to the archbishop and to the dean of St. Paul's, London, who levied one obol per mark on all incomes of parish churches.... And so, as always, the church of England is burdened. In fact, the said

bishop of Norwich arranged for the pope to bestow the deanery of Lincoln, now vacant since his own coronation, on Master John Offord, archdeacon of Ely, keeper of [the King's] privy seal, and immediately a certain cardinal sought to have the archdeaconry of Ely conferred upon himself. And so, as always, benefices of this kingdom are transferred to foreigners.

In this same year, a little before Quadragesima, Thomas bishop of Hereford died [Jan. 11, 1344], and on the first day of Quadragesima [Feb. 12] Master John Trillek was elected, and was confirmed immediately afterward by the archbishop of Canterbury. Notwithstanding this, the pope bestowed the same bishopric on him in order that he could get the common and private services, just as he did from many other elected candidates, wishing in the usual way to squeeze the English. I have written all this so that thereby one can see how great is the inconstancy, the idleness, and the dangerous tolerance of the English, and how great the greed of the Romans.

Adae Murimuth continuatio chronicarum, ed. E. M. Thompson (London: Oxford University Press, 1889), Rolls series, 93, pp. 156–58, trans. N. P. Zacour.

2. OXFORD UNIVERSITY WRITES TO THE COLLEGE OF CARDINALS (1335 OR 1338) IN SUPPORT OF PAPAL PROVISIONS FOR UNIVERSITY GRADUATES

Since in the sight of the apostolic dignity the world trembles, the universe is filled with dread, and every kind of human venture is hushed, it is not to be wondered at if our insignificance is all the more struck with terror in approaching such sublimity, in pouring out our prayers before the same, or in submitting our less agreeable petitions. Because, therefore, we see that this does not accord with our unimportance, we beg your lordships that you may graciously ensure that our petitions and prayers, which we have hardly dared to submit to the apostolic loftiness, may be the more favorably heard, supported by your benign paternal patronage. And so, pressed by our great poverty, we seek a boon of our lord the highest pontiff, that certain masters of our University, in our judgment worthy and honorable, endowed not with cents but with sense, renowned not for their wealth but for their deeds and good morals, be promoted to ecclesiastical benefices. We are confident of achieving a more favorable success in this if your lordships, who share the dominion of the word with the said most holy vicar of Christ, may deign to intercede on our behalf.

H. E. Salter, W. A. Pantin, and H. G. Richardson, *Formularies Which Bear on the History of Oxford, c. 1204–1420,* Oxford Historical Society, new series, Vol. IV (1942), I, 93, No. 10, trans. N. P. Zacour.

C. The Complaints

Papal provisions struck hardest at the inherited and traditional rights of local church patrons, especially bishops and nobles. These had a large vested interest in the disbursement of church patronage, seriously threatened by papal reservations. The rights especially of the bishops were increasingly limited by the crown, which often cooperated with the papacy in sharing the distribution of church taxes. The laity were even more outspoken against papal provisions which were a direct blow against their pocket as well as their pride.

1. AN ENGLISH BISHOP'S GENTLE COMPLAINT TO CLEMENT VI (1342)

When I see on all sides the disturbances of kings and kingdoms, from which the Church Militant and its Ruler cannot hope to be free, I must confess I am not a little anguished within and weighed down with weariness without. For suffering together with the Head, I hope also likewise to be consoled with it. For I am weak with those that are weak, and on fire with those that are scandalized; and there is added to the grief of my wounds, whenever I hear my fellow-servants murmuring against the master of the household of God [i.e. the Pope]. Lately, indeed, on the Ides of October I was present in the Council of the province of Canterbury held in London, where among other things, if I may say so by your leave, no small wonder arose at the burdensome and hitherto unknown multitude of apostolic [papal] provisions. For it was

said that from now onwards prelates, both greater and lesser, indiscriminately, without distinction of estate or person, will never be able to provide for the well-deserving or necessary servants of their churches or of themselves. What has perhaps added to the astonishment at these novelties is the fact that there is no doubt that many better and more worthy men have stayed at home, doing their own duty, or in the service of others,—more than all those other ambitious men who have flown to the Roman Curia. Nor was there lacking displeasure as well as wonder among my brethren, inasmuch as from now onwards they will scarcely be able to find useful and skilled cooperators in the pastoral office, since all hope of reward is taken away. Moreover this was the chief and almost the only thing that many found commendable in Benedict XII of good memory, namely that he did not burden any churches or prelates. Let your holy discretion therefore see and judge concerning these matters, having had experience of like cases. And if by chance, while you are bent on unaccustomed and arduous business at the beginning of your rule, you find yourself overcome by the surreptitious action or importunity of claimants or petitioners, pray think in your heart of your fellow servants and brethren in Christ, among whom you have been made the first-born. And moreover forgive me, the least of your servants, if, as truth is my witness, out of a pure heart I speak directly to my lord, since charity alone urges me.

Grandisson, Reg. I, III, in W. A. Pantin, *The English Church in the Fourteenth Century* (London: Cambridge University Press, 1955), pp. 70–71.

2. A LETTER FROM THE BARONS OF FRANCE TO THE COLLEGE OF CARDINALS, 1302

He who at present presides over the government of the church has made, and still makes every day by his willful ordinances, confirmations and grants of bishoprics and archbishoprics and other noble benefices of the kingdom, and has done this for large sums of money with

which he has burdened the benefices, so that it happens that the little people who are subject to them are burdened and taxed; for otherwise they could not pay the exactions levied upon them by unknown and untrustworthy persons and such like, and the many, such as children and many others, who are not worthy to hold church benefices, and who do not take up residence in the churches where their benefices are, or even go there. Thus the churches are deprived of service due to them, and the intentions of those who founded the churches are frustrated, for alms are neglected, charity forgotten, and the revenues usually going to the churches taken away. The churches are therefore so degraded and prostrated that there is hardly anyone to serve in them, and the bishops cannot give benefices to noble clergy and other well-born, educated persons in their dioceses, by whose ancestors the churches have been founded; and a bad example is thus set before all the people. Respecting the new pensions, the outrageous and unusual "services," the various exactions and extortions, and the damaging novelties, the estate general of the church is quite silent. He has deprived the sovereign bishops of the power to do that which belongs to them because of their office and which they are accustomed to do. Yet this morsel does not suffice him, but the granting of benefices, which our lord the King and our ancestors founded and which belong to him and to us and have in all times belonged to his and to our predecessors, he forbids to us, and wishes to draw them to himself out of great greed in order to get greater exactions and greater "services." All this we cannot and will not suffer henceforth in any manner, no matter what the consequence to ourselves; and even if we, or some of us, might put up with it, our said lord the King will not tolerate it in the least, nor will the common people of the kingdom.

P. Dupuy, *Histoire du différend d'entre le pape Boniface VIII et Philippes le Bel roy de France* (Paris, 1655), p. 61, trans. N. P. Zacour.

3. LETTER FROM THE ENGLISH PARLIAMENT TO POPE CLEMENT VI, 18 MAY, 1343

To the most holy father in God, lord Clement.... We all in full deliberation, by common assent, hereby make known in lively manner to your holiness that the noble kings of England and our progenitors and predecessors and we...have ordained and established, founded and endowed, within the kingdom of England churches, cathedrals, collegiate churches, abbeys, and priories, and other various religious houses, and in them have ordained, and to the prelates and governors of the said places have given lands, possessions, patrimonies, franchises, advowsons, and the patronage of dignities, prebends, offices, churches, and other various benefices, to the end and with the intention that the care and government of such benefices be given to those by whom the service of God and the Christian faith may be honored, increased, and embellished.... And we make known to your holiness that by various reservations, provisions, and collations by your predecessors, apostles of Rome, and by yourself, most holy father, more extensively in your time than usual, to various persons, strangers, of different nations, and to some who are our enemies, having no knowledge of the language nor of the conditions of those whose government and care ought to pertain to them, and to others who are unsuitable, there come to pass the following perils and mischiefs: The souls of the parishioners are in danger; the service of God destroyed; alms are withdrawn; hospitalities impoverished; churches and their buildings decayed; charity restrained; and the cure of souls and the government which pertains to this brought to nothing; the devotion of the people reduced; honorable people of the country carried off; strangers banished against the intent and devotion of the founders. These errors, faults, perils, and shortcomings, holy father, we cannot and ought not suffer or endure. We therefore humbly request that...it please you to withdraw all such reservations, provisions, and collations....

Adae Murimuth continuatio chronicarum, op. cit. pp. 138 ff., trans. N. P. Zacour.

4. POLITICAL PROPAGANDA

In France an institution comparable to the English parliament only came into existence in the early fourteenth century. This was the Estates General, summoned by Philip IV in his struggle with Pope Boniface VIII in an effort to arouse public opinion against the pope. National feeling was now a weapon of some effectiveness, witness the story put about that Boniface had said that he "would rather be a dog or an ass than a Frenchman"—a piece of propaganda bound to arouse strong national resentment. But especially, the king's ministers caused to be circulated two forged documents designed to the same end. They purported to be an exchange of letters between the king and the pope.

Boniface, bishop, servant of the servants of God, to Philip, King of the Franks. Fear God, and observe his commands. We wish you to know that you are subject to us in spiritual and temporal matters. No granting of benefices and prebends belongs to you. If you have the custody of any church vacancies, you are to preserve their incomes for those who will fill them; if you have granted any away, we decree such a grant void; and whatever in fact has been so granted we hereby revoke. Those who believe otherwise, we judge to be heretics.

Philip, by the grace of God King of the Franks, to Boniface who makes himself out as the highest pontiff, little or no greeting.

May your greatest simplicity know that in temporal matters we are not subject to anyone; that the granting of vacant churches and prebends belongs to us by royal law, to make their incomes ours; grants made by us and to be made by us have been valid in the past and will be valid in the future, and we shall staunchly defend their possessors against all; those who believe otherwise we judge to be fools and madmen.

Dupuy, *Histoire du différend, op. cit.,* p. 44, trans. N. P. Zacour.

D. Modern Views

1. EXTORTIONS OF THE AVIGNON POPES

As the Church had grown wealthy in every land Kings and Popes competed with one another to have a share in its revenues. Gregory VII had laboured to deliver the Church from the power of the temporal rulers, and his attempt was so far successful as to establish a compromise. The Church was to have the show of independence, the State was to have the practical right of nominating to important offices. The claims of the Chapters to elect to bishoprics were nominally unimpaired, but the royal influence was generally supreme. Still the Chapters were equally amenable to the pope and to the king, and might exercise their right according to the dictation of either. Gradually the King and the Pope arrived at a practical understanding as to the division of spoil. If the offices of the Church were to furnish salaries for the King's ministers, they must also supply revenues to the head of the Church. At times the Pope's authority was exercised to order a rebellious Chapter to accept the King's nominee; at times the Royal authority supported the Pope's request, that the Chapter in their election should provide for one of the Pope's officials. Thus the Chapters, placed between two fires, tended to lose even the semblance of independence, while in this alliance with the Crown, the Papacy soon gained the upper hand. Armed with spiritual power and claiming obedience as the head of the Church, the Pope cloaked his usurpations under the show of right, and extended his claims to smaller benefices, which were in the gift of the King or private patrons. It was but a further extension of this principle when John XXII reserved to himself all benefices vacated by promotion made by the Pope, and afterwards extended his reservation to the most lucrative posts in chapters, monasteries and collegiate Churches. Monstrous as were these claims, they met with no decided opposition. The frequency of disputes about elections, and the consequent appeals to the Pope, had practically given him the decision of the validity of ecclesiastical appointments. His assumed power of granting dispensations from canonical disabilities made him a useful means of overstepping inconvenient barriers. The Pope had been allowed so much authority to act as the instrument of the selfish interest of kings, that they had nothing to urge when he began to use his powers shamelessly in his own behalf. Clement VI provided for his nephews and his Court at the expense of Christendom, and said, with a laugh, that his predecessors had not known how to be Popes. Besides provisions, reservations, and dispensations, he demanded large fees for the confirmation of all episcopal elections, and succeeded in wresting from the bishops many of their rights over the inferior clergy. Chief of these were the revenues of benefices during a vacancy, which arose from the extension of feudal reliefs to ecclesiastical holdings. Bishops, as protectors of benefices, disposed of their revenues when they were vacant, and this claim tended to become a regular tax of half a year's revenue paid by the presentee on his succession. The Papacy in its turn took this right from the bishops and claimed it for itself. Moreover, the Pope imposed tithes from time to time on clerical revenues; sometimes for his own use, sometimes granting them to princes on the specious pretext of a crusade. A vast system of Papal extortion was gradually developed, partly from the fault of churchmen, who too readily brought their quarrels to the Pope's tribunals, partly from the short-sighted policy of kings and princes, who found in an alliance with the Pope an easy means of helping themselves to ecclesiastical revenues. Papal aggression could not have grown unless it had been welcomed in its beginnings; and those who used the Pope's interference to serve their own ends had no strong ground for repelling the Pope when he used his powers in his own behalf. Cries went up throughout Christendom, but it was long before the cries were more than utterances of despair.

M. Creighton, *A History of the Papacy During the Period of the Reformation,*
I (London: Longmans, Green & Company, Ltd., 1892), pp. 45–47.

2. IN DEFENSE OF PROVISIONS

Papal intervention in the bestowal of ecclesiastical benefices is a phenomenon which earlier ages had not known. It stands out among the many acts of prerogative and authority, which the popes of the twelfth and thirteenth centuries began to exercise, as that which had least ground in tradition or in theory. In other directions, direct papal action may have appeared as the culmination of age-long traditions and gradually accumulated tendencies. The right to the disposal of all ecclesiastical benefices, on the other hand, which Clement IV formulated in his famous decretal of 27 August, 1265, had actually been acquired by the papacy less through theoretical justification or a legal qualification of the rights of others, than through practical exercises during the course of the immediately preceding century. Papal provisions belong to the ages of ecclesiastical centralization, and are one of the most obvious examples of the way in which that centralization worked.

Both from the political and from the purely ecclesiastical point of view, no sphere of papal administration was more radically challenged in the fourteenth and fifteenth centuries than the combined system of provisions and reservations. After generations of unmitigated condemnation from the standpoint of morality, religion, politics and government, opinion is slowly swinging round in favour of the fourteenth century papacy. Virtues—such as the immense administrative vigour of a pope like John XXII—are being brought to light; supposed vices and weaknesses—such as political subservience—are being questioned and former judgements reconsidered. But the work of rehabilitation has stopped short at provisions. Much may be palliated, much explained: they remain as an unquestioned evil amidst much which was fundamentally sound. They are the morbid sore on the body of the medieval church, which led to its final decay. "We can admit that the popes of Avignon deserve no reproach in regard to their attitude towards the princes of Europe," wrote Fierens, the Belgian historian of provisions and one of the most balanced critics of the fourteenth century church, "that they supported dogma and devoted their energies to the conversion of the heathen: the main fact still remains that, through their beneficial policy, and through the fiscal policy which is bound up with it, they brought the moral and religious integrity of Europe to a state of calamity. And this evil is so great that no services rendered in any other domain are sufficient to efface it."

A judgment such as this is in itself a striking testimony to the importance—if only to the tragic and ill-famed importance—of papal provisions. Precisely because of their central position in the whole question of church reform, their history—above all in the crucial years of the fourteenth century—demands the closest critical attention. . . .

For the maintenance of aristocratic and family influence in the [cathedral] chapters, . . . no question was more important than the control of admission. Thus we find that during the thirteenth century, if not before, not only was the bishop forced step by step to surrender his rights in regard to the creation of canons —a constitutional issue of some magnitude which seems to have been fought out in all countries of Europe—but also the old system of canonical election was supplanted in most collegiate churches by a procedure of simple nomination, in accordance with which each canon in turn was able to name a new member of the chapter. "The results of such a procedure are self-evident. A family which had once obtained a firm foothold in the chapter was able to maintain its position for centuries, since

the canons naturally gave first consideration to the claims of their relatives in the nomination of new members." Thus there grew up a practice of family connexions and nepotism, the extension and ramifications of which only become obvious when the detailed history of individual chapters is subjected to independent treatment. Next to family, however, rank was the chief consideration with the electors. The rapid decline in the number and size of aristocratic families in the later Middle Ages, combined with the ever more stringent regulation and ever increasing exclusiveness of the qualifications demanded from candidates for places in collegiate churches, sooner or later made it impossible for the aristocratic families resident within a diocese to provide enough members to fill the local chapters. In these circumstances, rather than allow families of inferior standing to fill the vacant places, the canons recruited their ranks from distant dioceses. The 352 canons of Cologne during the fourteenth and fifteenth centuries sprang from, in all, thirty dioceses; not a third belonged to the diocese, only about two-fifths to the province of Cologne; the rest were recruited from such distant parts as Utrecht, Bremen, Ratzeburg, Meissen, Freising, Constance, Geneva and Arras.

Thus whatever we think of the papal policy of transferring clerks from one diocese to another by means of provisions —a policy the effects of which have certainly been exaggerated—it is clear that the popes were doing little that the canons themselves had not done, or were not at any moment prepared to do. From time to time, and in some countries more than others, there may have been real objection to providees on account of their nationality; but it is obvious that local considerations did not weigh heavily on the nominators to canonries; they showed no desire to confine membership of the chapter to those with a knowledge of and an interest in local affairs, and where they raised objections to papal providees questions of class were more likely to be at issue, except in times of high political tension, than the question of nationality. Thus, even if provisions were often used to further family interests and connexions, it is generally admitted that papal intervention, in counteracting the growing spirit of exclusiveness and nepotism and introducing new elements into the chapters, exercised a salutary influence in cathedral and collegiate churches. Even the Italians and other foreigners appointed by the papacy, for the very reason that they usually won admittance only because they were able to lay claim to a higher class of education and university training than that possessed by the scions of noble families who formed the majority in most chapters, cannot be condemned as an unjustifiable burden. [In connection with the diocese of Constance,] "anyone who works through the list of providees will not be disposed to deny the fact that altogether outstanding people appear among them. Candidates who have not reached the statutory age or are marked out by illegitimate birth, are unable to obtain admission, even when persons of high rank lend them their support. From the time of Benedict XII onwards it can be shown that the majority of providees had studied at the famous universities of Bologna, Padua, Paris, or Prague, and had distinguished themselves in their studies. Others again were in the service of cardinals, bishops or temporal magnates, or had been appointed as collectors by the papal Treasury or as ambassadors by secular princes. Considered as a whole, it was certainly not indifferent material which was brought into the cathedral chapter at Constance in virtue of papal provisions."

Such a judgment as this cuts right across the old-fashioned estimate of provisions as an instrument of papal greed and unscrupulous materialism, and unqualified, uneducated upstarts. It cuts across the theory that they were used above all to the detriment of poor but worthy clerks, who had acquired a suitable education but not the necessary influence for a benefice, and were exercised by constant and shameless pressure at the expense of the episcopal right of collation; for talent and personal merit were more sure of recognition in the Roman court than in the provinces, and the episcopal right of collation was destroyed, not by the papacy, but by the growing pretensions of the chapters of collegiate churches and of lay patrons during the thirteenth and fourteenth centuries.

Geoffrey Barraclough, *Papal Provisions: Aspects of Church History Constitutional, Legal and Administrative in the Later Middle Ages* (Oxford: Basil Blackwell & Mott, Ltd., 1935), pp. 4–5, 16–18, 54–58.

II. The Secular State

On what basis could papal claims be refuted? That was the problem of the rising feudal kingdoms, made difficult by the success of the papacy in the secular sphere. A conservative defense, as we shall see, might resort to the old theocratic view that the papacy and the church were subordinate to the monarch and that the monarch owed his position to God directly, who alone had the power to judge his acts. The trouble with this argument was that it still relied on divine grace as a sanction for royal authority. This left the way open for the intervention of the pope as the divinely appointed dispenser of that grace and the sole mediator between God and man. In an atmosphere saturated with the idea that all Christendom was a single corporate society it was difficult to avoid the conclusion that such a society demanded a single head functionally qualified to direct it, and it became increasingly difficult to use old arguments of divine authority to refute the divine claims of a divine papacy.

But new conditions provided new arguments. The emergence of strong monarchies in France, England, Sicily and elsewhere, their growing political cohesiveness and their subsequent rivalries and wars posed a threat to Christian unity. Monarchs benefited from ideas derived from the renewed study of Roman law which assisted in recreating the concept of political sovereignty and locating it in the person of the king who, within his kingdom, stood above the law like the emperors of old and answered to no one but God alone.

This was especially strengthened by the revival of Aristotle during the thirteenth century which worked something of a revolution in political thought hitherto dominated by ideas inherited from St. Augustine. The Augustinian view had held that man must be governed as a punishment for sin—specifically, the original sin of Adam. Although man in a presinful state of nature was free and equal, his fall had introduced inequalities and brought his animality to the fore. Political power, the domination of one man by another, was therefore necessary not only as a punishment for sin but especially as a means of bringing redemption to the sinner. Furthermore such political power, if its purpose of redemption was to be realized, would have to be submitted to the service of the intermediaries of redemption, i.e. the priesthood. To those who read their St. Augustine it followed that the king should be subject to the Church.

But the revival of Aristotle brought a change, introducing the ancient idea of man as a political animal by nature for whom social life was a condition of nature. Man must live in society; society by its very existence demands government; such government can only be justified if it aims at the common good of those governed. The ancient Greek philosophers had recognized this and had insisted that in social and political life lay one of the deepest needs of human nature. These ideas steadily gained currency in the thirteenth and fourteenth centuries, serving to undermine the traditional views which lay at the basis of papal and ecclesiastical authority. The Aristotelian notion of man as a political unit, and man's government as a natural thing rather than an affliction to be suffered because of sin, gave to the growing national monarchies a philosophical basis which owed nothing to divine grace. Roman law and ancient philosophy combined to give ambitious kings new grounds for independent action: the utility of state, the necessity of state or, as it was often put, the common good.

Finally another current, bearing no relation to those just mentioned, would yet reinforce them. The "mystical body of the church," a phrase which had for long been used as a synonym for the corporate church whose head was the vicar of Christ in Rome, now began to be interpreted in such a fashion as to imply a distinct opposition between the mystical body and the visible corporational body. The new interpretation saw the true church as a mystical society of only those predestined to salvation. Such a church no longer needed corporational or juridical forms —neither administration, nor court, nor hierarchy, nor head save Christ alone.

A. The Norman Anonymous

The excerpt which follows is taken from a remarkable series of tracts written in the early twelfth century in response to the swift expansion of papal claims and papal authority. The author, an unknown cleric, probably of Rouen in Normandy, raised secular authority above the priestly office and thus, by inference, the royal power above the papal. In doing so he summed up in a bold and vigorous manner the traditional ideas of sacred kingship widely current up to his time as a defense against papal claims to superiority.

These two persons [king and priest], we read in the Old Testament, have been consecrated by the anointment of holy oil and sanctified by divine blessing so that they take on the appearance and place of Christ the Lord in ruling their people, and mirror forth his image in the sacrament of consecration. For upon this anointment and divine blessing, the spirit of the Lord and God-making perfection leapt into them, by which they took on the figure and image of Christ. This changed them into other men, so that each in his own person was another man and was changed in spirit and perfection. . . .

And so in each we recognize a twin person—one person by nature, the other by grace; one person in his manhood, the other in spirit and perfection; one person by which, through the condition of nature, he conformed with other men, the other by which, through the distinction of deification and the power of the sacrament of consecration, he excelled all others. In the one person, to be sure, he was a complete man by nature; in the other, he was, through grace, a christ, that is a God-man. . . . It was common to both the king and the priest to be a christ of the Lord, although in the holy scriptures you can find the king called a christ of the Lord more frequently and more particularly than the priest. . . .

King and priest are both anointed with holy oil; each has the spirit of sanctification and the virtue of benediction; each has the name of God and Christ in common, and the common character for which this name is appropriate. For if they have not this character they would be falsely called by this name. But they have it truly, and are sharers of it, not by nature, but by grace, since only Christ the son of God and the son of man has this both by grace and nature. For nature is God, and is made divine by no one. Nature is sacred, and is made sacred by no one. Since king and priest, the image and figure of Christ who is God and man, were both complete men, each was made completely divine and sacred, then, by the grace of anointment and the consecration of the blessing. . . . Since, therefore, both priest and king are god and christ of the Lord by grace, whatever each does or performs according to this grace he now does not do as a man but as a god and a christ of the Lord. And whatever is done in him is not done in a man but in a god and a christ of the Lord. And whatever the king requires of or grants to the bishopric, or the priest requires of or grants to the kingdom, is not done by a man, but by a god and a christ of the Lord. If we wish to confess the truth, the king can rightly be called a priest, and the priest a king, inasmuch as each is a christ of the Lord. . . .

Indeed, the priest prefigured one nature in Christ, man's nature; the king the other, God's nature; the king prefigured the higher nature, by which he is equal to God the father; the priest, the lower nature which is less than the Father. For the priest prefigured that Christ would suffer unto death and would give himself as an offering and "a sacrifice to God for a sweet smelling savour" [Eph. 5: 2]. But the king prefigured that Christ would reign

forever and would sit alone on the heavenly throne "above all principality, and power, and might, and dominion" [Eph. 1: 21], and that he would be crowned in glory and honor, and be set above all the works of God. . . .

Now let us turn to the New Testament, for here too priests and kings are made sacred with holy oil. . . . In spirit each is God and Christ, and in his office each is the figure and image of God and Christ, the priest of Christ the priest, the king of Christ the king. The priest is of the lower office and nature, that is of the human office and nature; the king is of the higher, that is the divine, office and nature. . . . Christ's kingship comes from a divine eternity. . . his priesthood from his assumption of humanity. . . . As king he created all, ruled all, and in his governance saved men and angels both; as priest he has redeemed men only, that they might reign with him. This is why he was made a priest, and offered himself as a sacrifice, so that he might make men partakers of his kingdom and sharers of his royal power. For everywhere in the scriptures he promises to the faithful a kingdom of heaven, but nowhere a priesthood of heaven. It appears therefore that in Christ the royal power is greater and more eminent than the priestly power, to the same extent as his divinity is greater and more eminent than his humanity.

It is therefore considered by some that among men the royal power is greater and more esteemed than the priestly power, and the king is greater and more esteemed than the priest, being a reflection and copy of the greater and the more esteemed of Christ's two natures. . . .

The king's power is God's power. God wields it by nature, the king by grace. Hence, the king is God and Christ, though by grace, and whatever he does is done not by a mere man but, through grace, by one who has been made God and Christ.

Norman Anonymous, Tract IV, in *MGH, Lib. de Lite,* III, 652–67, trans. N. P. Zacour.

B. The Papal Bull Unam Sanctam, 1302

Here is a clear, unequivocal statement by Pope Boniface VIII respecting the authority of the Roman pontiff. It was prompted by the controversy between Boniface and King Philip IV of France, but it is made in general terms and expresses ideas which had long been commonplace to advocates of papal superiority.

We are constrained by the compulsion of faith to believe and to hold that there is one holy, catholic, and apostolic church, in which we firmly believe and which we unreservedly own. Outside of her there is neither salvation nor remission of sins, as the bridegroom proclaims in the Canticles: "My dove, my undefiled is but one; she is the choice one of her mother, she is the choice one of her that bare her" [Song of Solomon 6:9], which represents one mystic body whose head is Christ, and Christ's head is God. In this church is one Lord, one faith, one baptism. Indeed, in the time of the flood there was one ark of Noah, prefiguring the one church, finished in one cubit [Gen. 6:16], and having one helmsman and master, namely Noah. We read that all things existing on the earth outside the ark were destroyed. This church we venerate as the only one, as the Lord said through the prophet: "Deliver my soul from the sword; my darling from the power of the dog" [Ps.22:20]. He prayed at the same time for his soul (that is, for himself as the head), and for his body. He called this body the one church because of the oneness of the bridegroom, the faith, the sacraments, and the charity of the church. This is that seamless tunic of the Lord which was not rent but was parted by lot. Therefore there is one body of the one and only church, and one head—not two heads, as of a monster. The head is Christ, Christ's vicar Peter, and Peter's successor. For the Lord said to Peter: "Feed my sheep." He said "my" sheep, not "these" or "those" sheep; sheep in general, not particular sheep. From this it is known that all sheep were entrusted to him. If, therefore, the Greeks or anyone else say that they were not entrusted to Peter and to his successors, they necessarily admit that they are not Christ's sheep. For the Lord says in the gospel of John that there is one fold and only one shepherd [John 10:16] in whose power, we are taught by the words of the gospel, are two swords, the spiritual and the temporal. For when the apostles said: "Behold here are two swords" [Luke 22:38] (that is, two swords in the church, since it was the apostles who were speaking), the Lord did not reply that it was too many, but that it was enough. Certainly he who denies that the temporal sword is under the control of Peter misunderstands the Lord when he said: "Put up thy sword into the sheath" [John 18:11]. Therefore each sword, the spiritual and the material, is in the power of the church. The former is to be used by the church, the latter for the church; the one by the hand of the priest, the other by the hand of kings and knights, but at the command and with the forbearance of the priest. Moreover, it is fitting that one sword be subjected to the other, and that temporal authority be subjected to spiritual power, for as the apostle says: "There is no power but of God; the powers that be are ordained of God" [Rom. 13:1]. But they would not be ordained, that is arranged in order, if one sword were not under the other, and the lower, so to speak, brought to its highest end by the other. For according to the blessed Dionysius, it is the divine law that the lowest is brought to the highest through the intermediate. According to the law of the universe all things are not arranged on a level and without hierarchy, but rather the lowest is ordered by the intermediate, the inferior by the superior. And we must all the more admit that the spiritual power surpasses the worldly power both in dignity and honor, just as spiritual things are superior to temporal things. We see quite clearly that this is so from the giving of tithes, their benediction, their sanctification, from the recognition of such authority, and from the governance of these things. For the truth bears witness, that the spiritual power must establish temporal power, and must judge it if it is not good.

Thus the prophecy of Jeremiah concerning the church and the power of the church is borne out: "See, I have this day set thee over the nations and over the kingdoms, to root out, and to pull down, and to destroy, and to throw down, to build, and to plant" [Jer. 1:10]. Therefore, if the temporal power errs, it will be judged by the spiritual power; if the spiritual power errs, the lesser will be judged by the greater; and if the greatest spiritual power errs, it will be judged by no man, but by God alone. For the apostle says: "But he that is spiritual judgeth all things, yet he himself is judged of no man" [I Cor. 2:15]. For this authority, though it may be given to man and wielded by man, is not human, but rather divine, given by divine word to Peter—a rock strengthened to him and his successors in Christ himself whom he had confessed. The Lord said to Peter: "Whatsoever thou shalt bind," etc. [Matt. 16:19]. Whosoever therefore resists this power thus ordained of God resists the ordination of God, unless there be two first causes or beginnings, as Manicheus claims and which we judge to be false and heretical, for Moses says that God created heaven and earth not in beginnings, but in the beginning. We therefore declare, say, affirm, and pronounce that it is altogether necessary for salvation for every human creature to be subject to the Roman pontiff.

Dupuy, *Histoire du différend,* op. cit., pp. 54–56, trans. N. P. Zacour.

C. Roman Law and the Common Good

1. THE KING IS SOVEREIGN

Truly the king is sovereign over all and has of right the general care of all his kingdom. He can therefore make whatever laws he wishes for the common good, and whatever he orders must be obeyed. And so there is no one beneath him so great that he cannot be hailed into the king's court for default of the law or false judgment and for any matter affecting the interests of the king.

No one can make a new regulation with the force of law, or establish new markets, or new customs, other than the king or kingdom of France, except in times of necessity—for each baron in times of need can require his subjects not to withhold their goods from markets, but the barons cannot make new markets, or new customs, without the permission of the king. But the king can do so when he pleases and when he sees that it is to the common good, just as we see every day when the king grants a new custom to some towns or to some barons who are bound to him or are his subjects, to remake a bridge, or road, or monastery, or some other public service. In every such case the king has authority, but no one other than the king.

Philippe de Beaumanoir, *Coutumes de Beauvaisis,* 1043, ed. A. Salmon, II (Paris, 1900), 24–25, trans. N. P. Zacour.

2. THE KING IS EMPEROR

All within the confines of his kingdom belongs to the lord king [of France], at least with respect to protection, high justice, and lordship; and indeed just as much with respect to proprietary rights over all goods, movable and immovable, in his kingdom, which the same lord king can give, take, and use on the grounds of public utility and defense of his kingdom. Further, the lord king is emperor in his kingdom, and can rule as an emperor over land and sea, and reigns as an emperor over all the peoples of his kingdom; and indeed all prelates and clerics are in temporal things bound by his laws, edicts, and constitutions.

Mémoire relatif au Paréage de 1307 (Documents historiques sur le Gévaudan), I (Mende, 1896), 521, trans. N. P. Zacour.

D. Theology and the Common Good

St. Thomas Aquinas, a member of the Dominican Order and the greatest theologian of the Middle Ages, adressed himself to a whole range of theological and philosophical problems in his *Summa Theologiae*. Aquinas' great contribution lay in his fusion of the knowledge gained from the renewed study of Aristotle with the traditional tenets of Christianity. Although Aquinas resisted ideas diminishing the stature of the papacy, we find him propounding the view, derived from Aristotle, that society is a natural organism requiring a single ruler who would govern in the interests of the common welfare. In the hands of later writers this idea would be developed to exclude papal temporal authority.

Whether in the state of innocence man would have dominated man.

1. It seems that man in a state of innocence would not have dominated man. For Augustine says in the *City of God*, 19, at the beginning: "God did not wish man, who was given reason, and made in his own image, to dominate anything other than irrational creatures—not man over man, but man over cattle."

2. Further, that which is inflicted as a penalty for sin, would not have existed in a state of innocence. But that man be subject to man was introduced as a penalty for sin; for it was said to the woman [Eve] after her sin "Thou shalt be under thy husband's power" as it is said in Genesis, 3:16. Therefore, in a state of innocence man would not have been subject to man.

3. Further, subjection is opposed to liberty. But liberty is one of the chief goods which would not have been lacking in a state of nature, when "nothing was lacking that good will could desire" as Augustine says, in the *City of God*, 14. Therefore, man would not have dominated man in a state of innocence.

But, on the contrary: the condition of man in a state of innocence was not worthier than the condition of the Angels. But among the Angels some rule over others; whence indeed one group is called

the order of *Dominations*. Therefore it was not against the dignity of the state of innocence that man dominate man.

I reply, by saying that lordship may be understood in two senses—in one way, according as it is opposed to servitude; and so one is called a lord to whom someone is subjected, such as a slave—in another way, lordship is understood accordingly as it commonly refers to any kind of subject. And so he who has the office of governing and directing free men can be called lord. If lordship is accepted in the first sense, man would not have dominated man in a state of innocence; but if in the second sense, man would have dominated man in a state of innocence. The reason for this is because the slave differs from the free man in this way, that the free man is at his own disposal, but the slave is ordered to another. Therefore, anyone dominates anyone as a slave when he rules him for himself as lord, for his, the lord's, own utility. And since each is desirous of his own good; and in consequence it is grievous that that good which ought to be his he must cede to another; therefore such dominion must result in a penalty to him who is subjected, so that such dominion of man over man could not have existed in a state of innocence. But one dominates another who is a free man when he directs him to his own good, that is the good of him who is directed, or to the common good; and such dominion of man over man would have existed in a state of innocence for two reasons. First, since man is a social animal by nature. Hence man in a state of innocence would have lived in a society. But a social life cannot exist among many persons if someone does not preside who might lead it to the common good. For many lead in many directions, but one in one direction. And therefore Aristotle says at the beginning of the *Politics* that whenever many are directed to a single end, there is always found one as head and director. Secondly it would have been inconvenient for one man to have superiority of knowledge and justice, except that this might lead to the utility of all.

St. Thomas Aquines, *Summa Theologiae*, I, xcvi, 4, trans. N. P. Zacour.

E. The Separation of Ecclesiastical and Secular Authority

John of Paris (d. 1306), a supporter of the doctrines of the fellow Dominican St. Thomas Aquinas, wrote his treatise *On Royal and Papal Power* in reply to works of the time which supported papal authority in secular affairs. That the priestly "dignity" is superior is not doubted; but Aristotelian ideas of the state led John to support an independent secular authority.

What is royal rule, and whence does it come?

Concerning this first question, it ought to be known that "kingdom" properly so-called can be defined thus: the kingdom is a government of a large number of people, directed in all respects by a single person toward the common good. In this description the word "government" is used as a general classification, but "government of a large number of people" is only one of a species of governments whereby people might rule themselves, either by natural instinct as among brute animals, or by their reason as with those who lead a solitary life. I say "in all respects" rather than "privately" which is not complete and is adequate only for a short time and does not serve all aspects of life as does the city-state, according to Aristotle's *Politics*. The words "directed toward the common good" are used in contrast to the species of government of an oligarchy, tyranny, and democracy, where the ruler seeks his own good alone, especially in a tyranny. The words "by a single person" are opposed to the species of government called aristocracy, that is a rulership of magnates, where a few enjoy dominion because of their ability, which some define as a government according to wise counsel or senatorial decree. "By a single person" is also opposed to the species of government called polycracy where the people rule through plebiscites. For he is not king who does not rule alone, as the Lord said through Ezekiel: "And I will set up one shepherd over them" [Ezek. 34:23]. Such a government, moreover, derives from natural law and the law of nations.

For since man is a political or civil animal by nature, as it says in the *Politics,* which is revealed, so Aristotle says, by the nourishment, garments, and protection which man cannot provide for himself alone, and by the speech by which he communicates with others, all of which things are characteristic of man alone, it is necessary to man that he live in a community, and it is necessary to such a community that it provide for life. "Community" in this sense is not the community of the household or the village, but rather of the city-state or the kingdom, for in a household or village alone there are not to be found all those things necessary to nourishment, clothing, and protection needed for the whole of life, as they may be found in the city-state or kingdom. Moreover, if each seeks what he himself wants, the entire community is divided and fragmented if it is not ordered for the common good by someone who is responsible for the common good, just as man's body would pass away if there were not some common force in the body serving the common good of all its members. On account of this Solomon says, in *Proverbs* [11: 14]: "Where no counsel is, the people fall." This, then, is necessary, for what is private and what is common are not the same things. Men differ over private things, but they unite in what is common. Divisions come from diverse causes; therefore what is needed, for more than that which promotes the private good of each, is that there be something which promotes the common good of the many....

Whether kingship or priesthood is first in dignity.

...What comes later in time is usually first in dignity, as the perfect is to the imperfect, and as the ultimate is to that which only approaches the ultimate. And therefore we say that the priestly power is greater than the royal power and that it is pre-eminent in dignity, since we have always found that that to which pertains the highest end is more perfect and better than, and directs, that to which pertains a lower end. For the kingdom is established that the community live together according to virtue, as was said, and this is directed to a lower end than the other, which is the enjoyment of God, the care of such righteousness being given to Christ whose vicars and ministers are the priests. And therefore the priestly power is worthier than the secular power. . . .

Still, if the priest is greater than the prince in dignity in an absolute sense, it is not true that he is greater in all things. For the lesser secular power is not related to the greater spiritual power as though it were derived from it, as a proconsul is related to an emperor who is greater than he is in all things since his power was derived from him; but is related as is the power of the head of a family to a military general, where neither power is derived from the other, but both from a superior authority. And therefore in some things, namely in temporal things, the secular power is greater than the spiritual power. Nor in this respect is the one subjected to the other since it does not originate from it, but both originate directly from one supreme power, the divine power. Therefore the lower is not subject to the higher in all things. . . .

John of Paris, *On Royal and Papal Power,* in Dom Jean Leclercq, O.S.B., *Jean de Paris et l'ecclésiologie du xiiie siècle* (Paris, 1942), pp. 176–77, 183–84, trans. N. P. Zacour.

F. The New State

Marsiglio of Padua, a supporter of the Emperor Louis the Bavarian against the papacy, completed his treatise *Defender of the Peace* by 1324. He was an Italian by birth, and from his experience of Italian city-states and their political life he probably derived many of his ideas, especially that the "legislator," the source of all law, was to be identified with the community. As an Italian he resented the papacy upon which he cast all blame for Italian disunity and war. But what is most clearly evident in his work is the deep influence of Aristotle on his political thought.

The last remaining task of this discourse is to infer from our previous findings the causes of tranquillity and of its opposite in the city or state. Tranquillity is the good disposition of the city or state, whereby each of its parts can perform the functions appropriate to it in accordance with reason and its establishment. . . . These are the mutual association of the citizens, their intercommunication of their functions with one another, their mutual aid and assistance, and in general the power, unimpeded from without, of exercising their proper and common functions, and also the participation in common benefits and burdens according to the measure appropriate to each.

On the other hand, from whatever has essentially impeded the action of this ruling part of the state there will emerge, as from an efficient cause, intranquillity or discord. A sufficient conception of the general character of this cause, as well as of the many species and modes by which it is varied and the usual actions from which they emerge, was provided by Aristotle in the fifth book of his *Civil Science,* which we have called the *Politics.* There is, however, a certain unusual cause of the intranquillity or discord of cities or states, a cause which arose upon the occasion of the effect produced by the divine cause in a manner different from all its usual action in things; and this effect, as we recall having mentioned in our introductory remarks, could not have been discerned either by Aristotle or by any other philosophers of his time or before.

This cause has for a long time been impeding the due action of the ruler in the Italian state, and is now doing so even more; it has deprived and is still depriving that state of peace or tranquillity, and of all the above-mentioned goods which follow thereon; it has vexed it continually with every evil, and has filled it with almost every kind of misery and iniquity. In accordance with our original aim, we must determine the specific nature of this cause which is such a singular impediment because of its customarily hidden malignity. Hence we must recall what we said in Chapter VI: that the son of God, one of the three divine persons, true

God, assumed a human nature to redeem the sin of our first parents and the consequent fall of the whole human race. Long after the time of Aristotle, he became a true man, being at the same time God; called Jesus Christ, he is worshipped by faithful Christians. This Christ, blessed son of God, at once God and man in the same person, lived among the Jewish people, from whom he drew his fleshly origin. He began to teach and did teach the truth of what men must believe, do, and avoid in order to attain eternal life and avoid misery. Because of having finally suffered and died from the malice and insanity of the Jews under Pontius Pilate, vicar of Caesar, he rose up from the dead on the third day after his death and ascended the heavens. Earlier, however, while he was still living a corruptible life, he selected, for the salvation of the human race, certain colleagues for the ministry of teaching the truth; these men are called apostles, and Christ commanded them to preach throughout the entire world the truth which he had taught and in which he had instructed them. So in Matthew, Chapter 28, he said to them after his resurrection: "Go ye therefore and teach all nations, baptizing them in the name of the Father, the Son, and the Holy Ghost, teaching them to observe all things whatsoever I have commanded you." By these apostles, whose names are well enough known among faithful Christians, and by certain other men, Christ wanted the evangelic law to be written, and so it was written, by their utterances as by certain instruments immediately moved and directed by divine virtue. Through this law, we should be able to comprehend the commands and counsels of eternal salvation in the absence of Christ and the apostles and evangelists. Also, in this law, Christ established and made known the sacraments which wash away original and actual sin, which produce and conserve divine grace, which recover it when it is lost, and which ordain the ministers of this law.

Christ also first ordained the aforementioned apostles as the teachers of this law and as ministers of the sacraments according to it, bestowing on them through the Holy Ghost the authority of this ministry, which authority is called "priestly" by faithful Christians. Through this authority he bestowed on these same men and on their successors in this office, and on no others, the power, under the form of certain words said by them collectively or individually, of transubstantiating bread and wine into his true body and blood. Together with this he granted them the authority to bind and loose men from sins, which is usually called the power of the keys, as well as the power of appointing other men in their place with the same authority. This authority the apostles also bestowed upon certain men, or God did it through the apostles when they prayed and laid their hands on other men. These others also received the power of so doing; and so they then did, and are doing, and will continue to do until the end of the world. . . .

But besides this there is a certain other authority which was given to priests by man in order to avoid scandal after the number of priests had multiplied. This latter authority is the preeminence of one among them over the others in directing them in the proper performance of divine worship in the temple, and in ordering or distributing certain temporal things which were established for the use of the aforesaid ministers. . . . This authority is not given immediately by God, but rather through the will and mind of men, like the other offices of the state.

And so, having thus repeated and made somewhat clear the origin of ecclesiastic ministers, and the efficient cause of their office, we must now note further that among the aforesaid apostles of Christ there was one named Simon, also called Peter, who first received from Christ the promise of the authority of the keys. . . .

Because of the prerogative which this disciple or apostle seemed to have over the others, inasmuch as he was given the keys before the others through the aforementioned words of the Scripture and certain other words spoken to him alone by Christ, which will also be mentioned below, some of the bishops who succeeded him in the apostolic or episcopal seat at Rome, especially after the time of the

Roman emperor Constantine, declared and assert that they are over all the other bishops and priests in the world, with respect to every kind of jurisdictional authority. And some of the more recent Roman bishops make this claim not only with regard to bishops and priests, but even with regard to all the rulers, communities, and individuals in the world. . . .

Later bishops of the Romans. . .assumed for themselves this universal coercive jurisdiction over the whole world under the all-embracing title "plenitude of power," which they assert was granted by Christ to St. Peter and to his successors in the episcopal seat of Rome, as vicars of Christ. For Christ, as they truly say, was "king of kings and lord of lords," and of all persons and things; yet from this there does not follow what they wish to infer, as will appear with certainty in our subsequent discussions. The meaning of this title among the Roman bishop, therefore, is that just as Christ had plenitude of power and jurisdiction over all kings, princes, communities, groups, and individuals, so too do those who call themselves vicars of Christ and of St. Peter have this plenitude of coercive jurisdiction, limited by no human law.

An evident sign that the Roman bishops intend this title of plenitude of power to have the meaning which we have stated is that a certain Clement, the fifth Roman bishop of that name, uses it in this way in a certain edict or decretal of his *On the Sentence and the Thing Judged,* in the seventh book, in regard to Henry VII, of divine memory, the most recent emperor of the Romans. And that this is the meaning which the Roman bishops intend this title to have is also clearly shown to us by the belligerent attack of Boniface VIII against Philip the Fair of bright memory, the king of the French, and then by the subsequent decretal of the same Boniface [*Unam sanctam*]. . . . In this decretal, he declares that it must be believed to be necessary for eternal salvation that "every human creature" be subject in coercive jurisdiction to the Roman pontiff.

This wrong opinion of certain Roman bishops, and also perhaps their perverted desire for rulership, which they assert is owed to them because of the plenitude of power given to them, as they say, by Christ—this is that singular cause which we have said produces the intranquillity or discord of the city or state. With this opinion, therefore, and perhaps also with what we have called a desire for ruling, the Roman bishop strives to make the Roman ruler subject to him in coercive or temporal jurisdiction whereas that ruler neither rightly ought to be, nor wishes to be subject to him in such judgment. From this there has arisen so much strife and discord that it cannot be extinguished without great effort of souls and bodies and expenditure of wealth.

For the office of coercive rulership over any individual, of whatever condition he may be, or over any community or group, does not belong to the Roman or any other bishop, priest, or spiritual minister, as such. And this was what Aristotle held with respect to the priesthood in any law or religion, when he said in the fourth book of the *Politics*: "Hence not all those who are elected or chosen by lot are to be regarded as rulers. Consider the priests in the first place. These must be regarded as different from the political rulers," etc.

Alan Gewirth, *Marsilius of Padua, The Defender of the Peace,* II (New York: Columbia University Press, 1956), 89–96.

G. The Mystical Church

John Wyclif (1324–1384), a noted English critic of many of the ecclesiastical practices of his day, was led from a criticism of papal practices to an eventual denial of papal headship of the church and many of the traditional articles of Catholic faith. In particular, he viewed the mystical body of the Church not as a community of all nominal believers, but rather as comprising only those predestined to eternal salvation. Such a view rejected the

Church as a corporation, and therefore left no room for a governor.

1. The Church is the bride of Christ, and has three parts. The first part is the state of bliss, with Christ as head of the Church, and contains the angels and the blessed men who are now in heaven. The second part consists of the saints in purgatory; these do not sin anew, but purge themselves of their old sins. We err in praying for these saints. Since they have all died in body, Christ's words may be applied—let us seek Christ while we live, and let the dead bury the dead. The third part of the Church comprises the true men who are now alive, who shall be saved [i.e. are predestined to salvation] in the hereafter, and who live this life of Christian men here below....This third part is called the Church Militant....The head of this Church is Christ, both God and man. And this Church is mother to each man that shall be saved, and contains no person other than those men that shall be saved....And so while we struggle here below, and know not whether we shall be saved, we know not whether we are members of the holy Church....But as each man hopes that he shall be saved, so he must suppose that he is a member of holy Church, and therefore he should love holy Church and worship it as his mother.... No pope that now lives [this was written during the Schism, when there were two claimants to the papal throne] knows whether he is a member of the Church or a limb of the fiend, to be damned with Lucifer.

Select English Works of John Wyclif, ed. T. Arnold (Oxford, 1871), III, 339, adapted by N. P. Zacour.

2. It may be concluded that no pope with his collection of cardinals is absolutely necessary to wield the headship of the holy church of God, other than Christ. First, it is apparent that every such person [as the pope] may possibly fall into mortal sin and be damned....Again, God freely gives his grace to a certain Christian, constituting with him, as with one of his limbs, a single mystical body; no individual person is needed for such an inflowing of grace; therefore no person of the Roman church is needed as a mediator absolutely necessary to the running of the church. Again, Christ the Head, with his law, is sufficient unto himself for the governance of his bride [the mystical church], and so no other man is needed as a bridegroom.

De civili dominio, XLIII, ed. R. L. Poole, (London, 1885) I, 380, trans. N. P. Zacour.

III. The Conciliar Movement

The long stay of the papacy in Avignon (1309–1378) and the strong French character of the papal court while there aroused resentment not only among the English, who suspected papal support of the French enemy, but especially among the Italians, who looked upon the desertion of historic Rome and the neglect of Italy as a disaster and scorned the northern "barbarians" who kept the papacy away from its natural home. The popes of Avignon were not impervious to the criticisms and were moved especially by the appeals of such outstanding figures in the fourteenth century as the poet Petrarch and St. Catherine of Siena. They were also increasingly concerned about the problem of either pacifying Italy or losing control there forever, and this too seemed to demand their presence in Rome. Furthermore southern France was becoming overrun by mercenary soldiers released from the French-English campaigns, and Avignon was no longer the secure haven it once was. As a result of all this Pope Urban V transferred the papacy to Rome in 1367 but so despaired of the situation there that in September, 1370, he returned to Avignon where he shortly died. His successor, Gregory XI, was persuaded to try again, but again the papal determination to remain in Rome broke before the difficulties of the local political situation, the lack of facilities and amenities, and the persuasiveness of French cardinals anxious to return to the banks of the Rhone. But Gregory died before he could leave Rome. The cardinals thus found themselves faced with the necessity of electing a new pope while still on the banks of the Tiber.

Usually the college elected one of its own members. Occasionally, however, no cardinal was able to get the necessary two-thirds majority. In 1378, because most of the cardinals were French, there might have been no problem in electing one of them had the French not been divided into two parties, making it impossible to agree. This meant going outside the College of Cardinals for the next pope. Another complication was the very evident desire of the populace for a pope who was a Roman, or at least an Italian, and the cardinals were faced with many demonstrations in the streets and demands, not to say threats, made by city spokesmen. The cardinals finally elected Bartolommeo Prignani, the archbishop of Bari, who had been in the service of the papal court for many years, was well known to all the cardinals, and was an Italian.

If the cardinals thought that they had elected a complacent pope they had a rude shock coming to them. Urban VI, as the new pope called himself, took seriously many of the complaints against the luxurious life of the ecclesiastical hierarchy; but he was head-strong, lacked self-control, had little sense of proportion, and soon revealed himself to those who had elected him as a serious menace. The cardinals, a small oligarchical group of prince-ly persons most of whom were related to the great houses of France, were aghast at Urban's language and conduct, his crude outbursts against themselves and their mode of life, his unmeasured accusations of corruption and avarice, even his physical violence, as when in a private consistory he leaped up from his seat in a fury and made for one of the cardinals to attack him. The cardinals soon withdrew from Rome and in September 1378, after declaring that Urban's election had not been valid because of the coercive rioting and violence in Rome at the time, and that the papal throne was thus still vacant, proceeded to elect the French cardinal, Robert of Geneva, as Pope Clement VII. Clement promptly led his court back to Avignon; Urban created a new College of Cardinals and stayed in Italy. Europe was confronted now with two popes and two papal courts.

While the cardinals justified their step on the ground that Urban was not true pope, careful examination does little to support their views. In fact the college had taken the momentous step of trying to depose and re-place a pope—momentous because it was a direct onslaught on that complete papal authority which had been virtually an article of faith for so long. How had they come to this? Were others ready for it? If the pope did not rule the church, who did? In the next decades, as the church fell apart into two factions or "obediences" each with its own pope, thought-ful men everywhere, both lay and ecclesiastic, addressed themselves to the problem of final authority in the church.

A. The Cardinals Seek to Share Papal Authority

Innocent VI was elected in 1352. In a decree issued soon after his election he described what went on in the conclave. The direction in which the cardinals were moving, and the progress they had already made, is obvious.

Recently, when the apostolic see was vacant through the death of our predecessor Pope Clement VI of happy memory, our venerable brethren the cardinals of the holy Roman church, of whose number we were then one, came together in Avignon in the apostolic palace, where our said predecessor had died, in order to treat of those matters pertaining to the election of a Roman pontiff. They agreed upon a document the tenor of which we have caused to be appended to this one word for word, and then some of them took an unconditional oath (and we and certain others took the oath with this condition, namely, if and insofar as such a document conformed with law), that the one of the cardinals who, as it should happen, might be elected to the papacy, should keep in-violable all the contents of that document, and that on the same day on which occurs his manifest election he should declare that he will faithfully preserve each and all of those contents and will maintain the oaths as valid and binding upon them. Afterwards, however, when we, though of insufficient merits, were called to this office by divine direction, we reconsidered all the aforesaid. We realized that, although these cardinals did what they did with good intentions, and although it seemed to some that we ought to preserve those oaths outlined above as binding upon them, nevertheless, by the prohibitive regulations of our predecessors, Popes Gregory X and Clement V, of happy memory (by which it is warned that the cardinals during a vacancy in the Roman see cannot immerse themselves in any business except what has to be done to provide [a pope] for the Roman church, with the exception of only certain matters, regarding which, however, there is no mention in this document), the cardinals are quite unable to proceed to such affairs. We considered carefully that that document is known to redound undoubtedly to the diminution and prejudice of the plenitude of power granted from the lips of God to the Roman pontiff alone, since through this same document great and perpetual prejudice manifestly threatens the aforesaid see as long as the Roman pontiff is deprived of this power and, while he is restricted by certain man-made rules and limits, his power is confined. We also perceived that it is rash and mad among Catholics to maintain or to claim that the Roman pontiff, the successor of Peter and the vicar of Jesus Christ, is not called and chosen in plenitude of power, which power indeed he would not have if he depended on the agreement, the judgment, or the support of others; and that those oaths, uncanonical and indeed rash, which not only in the Roman church but indeed in every other church inflict prejudice and injury, ought to be ruled on. We have been led to this decision, after mature deliberation with certain of these same cardinals and several scholars and other legal experts on these and other considerations, in order to dispel every scruple and doubt in this matter: by the tenor of these presents, we declare by apostolic authority that those same cardinals were unable whatsoever to make such a declaration in this document, and its entire effect has been and is quite without force or moment whatever. And we or our successors as Roman pontiffs or those cardinals have not been and are not now obliged or bound in any way whatsoever to observe those aforesaid oaths. Now the tenor of the said document is as follows:

In full deliberation held for the public good all the cardinals, without exception, have agreed to the following.

First, that the pope who is to be elected by divine providence at no time at all for any reason whatsoever may proceed to create cardinals except in the manner outlined hereunder, namely, that he may not create or make any cardinals until the number of present cardinals drops to sixteen, after those who were above the number sixteen have been borne off from their midst; then he may elevate as many as will appear will increase the number up to twenty and no more, counting in the group of twenty the aforesaid sixteen or fewer, if by chance fewer remain. The pope must create and ordain the cardinals to be created with the advice and consent of all the cardinals then existing, or two thirds of them, with the exception that to the extant number now existing, or perchance fewer, the pope may if he wishes add two cardinals upon the advice of all his brethren [the cardinals] or a majority of them.

Further, the pope may not proceed to the deposition or the arrest of the person of any cardinal without the advice and unanimous consent of all his brethren, nor may he proceed to his excommunication, or any ecclesiastical censure, or the deprivation of his voice in consistory or his right to a portable chapel, nor deprive cardinals or suspend them from their benefices without the consent of all the brethren or two thirds of them.

Further, the pope may not in any way place his hands on the goods of any cardinals whatsoever, be they alive or dead.

Further, the pope may not alienate provinces, cities, castles, or other lands of the Roman church, either in fief or in emphyteusis, nor may he grant any for payment, and where it is expedient that such alienation or concession be made on just and reasonable grounds, he may proceed to such with the advice and consent of all his brethren or two thirds of them.

Further, the College of Cardinals ought to receive and to hold as of their right half of all the fruits, returns, incomes, revenues, fines, and taxes and all other gifts and emoluments coming to the Roman church in all the provinces, lands and places of the Roman church, as is specified more fully in the Privilege of Pope Nicholas IV of happy memory.

Further, both in the Roman court and in the lands and provinces of the Roman church, the higher officers managing temporal matters are to be appointed and dismissed on the advice and consent of all the Cardinals or a majority of them, just as it is known to appear in the said Privilege or constitution of the aforesaid lord Pope Nicholas IV.

Further, no one related to the Roman pontiff by blood or marriage is to be appointed to the office of marshal of the Roman court and rector of the lands or provinces of the Roman church.

Further, the pope may not concede tithes, nor parts of tithes, nor other subsidies to any king or prince or anyone else in their kingdoms, provinces or lands; he will not reserve them to his [financial] chamber without the advice and consent of all his brethren or at least two thirds of them, and then only for just and reasonable cause.

Further, the pope may not prevent to the cardinals, all and singly, a free voice in advising and consenting in the matters at hand.

Further, all the lord cardinals who are here have to swear that he of the said cardinals who is elected to the papacy by divine approval will observe the aforesaid diligently and inviolably; and he who is elected to the papacy, whether it is a cardinal or any other who will have been elected and received by the cardinals, is to promise on that very day to observe faithfully all and singly the aforesaid, and hold the foregoing oath as valid.

Further if any doubt respecting the foregoing arises or comes up, or appears to the pope, the lord pope has to clarify it with the advice and consent of at least two thirds of the cardinals.

Reg. Vat. 210, fols. 2r–3r, in Pierre Gasnault and M. H. Laurent, eds., *Innocent VI: Lettres secrètes et curiales,* I, fasc. 2 (Paris, 1960), 137–38 (no. 435), trans. N. P. Zacour.

B. We Want a Roman!

On the death of Gregory XI in 1378 while in Rome, the election of his successor was complicated by the strong local desire for a Roman or at least an Italian pope. This was expressed in a relatively mild form in the following address by an official of the city to the conclave of cardinals.

Most reverend Fathers...the sacred [Roman] people for seventy years and more have, like orphans, been without the highest pontiff and pastor. This City is the head of all Christianity according to the ordination of the blessed apostles Peter and Paul, to whom Jesus Christ gave the keys of the kingdom of heaven, saying: "Thou art Peter and upon this rock I will build my Church." Therefore, since the said apostles made and ordained this city as the foundation of the entire Christian faith, we see no popes sanctified except those who come among the said holy people, just as our lord Pope Urban V, who visited them; and lord Gregory [XI], who now has ended his life, and is sanctified, as we firmly believe, since he visited this holy people. God truly does many miracles through him. Therefore we beg you...to elect a Roman pope, for you will find many great clergy, noble, wise, and worthy of governing in the office of pope. But if you do not wish to do this, then seek [a candidate] from Italy; it would be quite remarkable if you do not find a worthy pope there. If you do this you will give great consolation to the sacred people of Rome and indeed to all Italy. If you don't, you can be sure, my reverend lords, that first all we officials will be killed, and then certainly all of you, for you can hear clearly the clamoring mob saying "We want a Roman pope, we want a Roman! or at least an Italian, at least an Italian!"

E. Baluze, *Vitae paparum Avenionensium,* ed. G. Mollat, I, 444, trans. N. P. Zacour.

C. The Cardinals Know Best

The election of two popes in 1378, and the division of western Christendom into two "obediences," dismayed many contemporaries. As it became increasingly evident that neither claimant to the papal throne would give way to the other, the "way of the council," long debated, won more and more supporters. This idea threatened the papal headship of the church; it also threatened the influence of the cardinals, who feared the extension of ultimate authority among representatives of all Christendom. Pierre Sortenac, the cardinal of Viviers (d. 1390 in Avignon), reveals here his great distrust of a council (1380).

First is shown the impossibility of convocation [of a council] because of the wars and dissensions raging everywhere throughout Christianity.

Further, since every king thinks himself an emperor in his own kingdom, each wants the location of the council in his own kingdom, nor do the clergy of one kingdom want to go to another, especially to one in enmity to their own, as is obvious in the example of France and England, and several others. So they could never agree on a place. Meanwhile the church would continue to fall apart more and more.

Further, who will convoke this council? If it is said the emperor will, this cannot be, since in truth today's emperor may not really be such. And supposing that he was, other kings would not obey him since they all think themselves his equal within their own kingdom.

Further, who will preside in this council? Who will establish it as a council? I don't see who can. And if no one presides, what good can come of such a council when there will be such a multitude without a head? Assuredly, none; since where there is a multitude, there is confusion.

Further, a council does not have the power of judging who may be pope, since no law or decretal has conceded such to it. And so it can happen that it might make a pope from no pope, and no pope from a pope.

Further, there are many nations which in no way wish to be informed of the true facts, but proceed in accord with their own desires: such as the Germans, the Hungarians, and most of the Italians. . . .

Further, since nations are divided in this schism, some for one, others for the other, if they come together in this matter, they will only confirm their prejudices, and so withdraw in discord. In which case the schism would be forever rooted.

If the council is to be decisive, or judicative, the above words regarding a general council apply. If it is only declarative, then first it is necessary to record the true facts. Therefore it is proper that equal information from each side and not from one alone, be provided—and from the cardinals, who alone can know the true facts.

Further, to know and to judge of this matter pertains to the cardinals, who during a vacancy in the holy see have to provide a pope and present him to the people, and the people receive him whom the cardinals present. . . .It is vain, therefore, to summon a council either general or particular.

Further, all faithful men look to the cardinals in this matter. For the cardinals have true jurisdiction, since they alone can well and surely judge in the matter, since they know the truth of the facts and the law, and may proceed on their own.

E. Baluze, *Vitae paparum Avenionensium,* ed. G. Mollat, IV, 207–9, trans. N. P. Zacour.

D. The Church Is the Council

The pressure to heal the Schism became too great to withstand and cardinals from both colleges broke away and summoned a council to meet in Pisa in 1409. To dispose of both claimants and elect a third required justification of the general council as an agency of the universal church superior to the papacy itself. Jean Gerson (1362–1429), chancellor of the University of Paris, was one of many who helped to define the new constitutional role of the council. The following is taken from what appears to be an outline of a treatise which Gerson wrote in late 1408 or early 1409, just before the Council of Pisa.

The third article will discuss the summoning of a council not expressly called or approved by the pope, either because there is no pope, or because there is doubt as to who is pope, or because he stubbornly denies or culpably neglects the need of Christendom; and therefore by the failure of the pope, the aforesaid convocation of the universal church, representative of it and acting on its behalf, can and ought to be held. And in this article there will be six conclusions.

First conclusion. Although customarily the universal church ought to be convoked [in a council] by the authority of the pope, nevertheless, without his consent, some one or more of the faithful can, for cause, effect a legal and authentic congregation representing the universal church.

Second conclusion. Even if the pope disapproves or forbids it, the summoning of all the faithful in one body, when the utility of the faith or the church requires it, pertains to the faithful and catholic cardinals, by law or de facto.

Third conclusion. Lacking pope or cardinals, either through death or because of their culpable neglect, the authority to summon the Christian religion [i.e. the council] devolves upon the catholic bishops.

Fourth conclusion. By Christian law as it stands, the bishops as a body cannot go astray as regards will or understanding, nor is it at all possible, under Christ's law, for them all collectively to disappear by death or to fall into heresy.

Fifth conclusion. It ought to be believed as a matter of certain faith that the corporation of all the Christian bishops cannot err in matters of faith and cannot be defiled by schism.

Sixth conclusion. That multitude which cannot err is not merely the multitude of the faithful, including men and women, children and adults.

The fifth article will determine what the universal church can do when summoned [in council], whether with the pope's consent, or without (either because there is no pope, or the pope obstinately refuses to the prejudice of Christendom), in the matter of declaring and determining the truths of the faith necessary or useful for the conduct of the universal church, in which there will be twelve conclusions.

First conclusion. It is not possible, under the existing law of Christ, for the general council, the universal church duly congregated, to err in defining the truths of the faith necessary or useful for the conduct of the church.

Second conclusion. The pope can err in matters of faith; but it is not possible for the pope in the church council to pronounce errors in matters of faith.

Third conclusion. Where matters of faith are to be dealt with, or the state of the universal church, such as the present schism, as touching the whole state of the church, the pope must use the council of the church and of the bishops.

Fourth conclusion. The council of the church, which the pope must use in defining in binding fashion the truths of the faith or those things needful to the conduct of the church, is the universal church, and the church of Rome, and the church of Paris, and is the council of all and singular the true churches of Christ, conjointly and individually.

Fifth conclusion. The council, acting on behalf of the universal church, cannot err in determining faith and morals for the conduct of the universal church.

Sixth conclusion. The council, acting on behalf of the universal church, cannot err according to law, not only because it represents the universal church, but because it holds this special privilege from Christ.

Seventh conclusion. The authority of deciding on matters of faith or on those things necessary or useful for the conduct of the universal church pertains in different fashion to the pope and to the rest of the church canonically summoned in council.

Eighth conclusion. Although all the aforesaid components of the church may be in error, nevertheless this does not mean that the church in universal and true council will pronounce errors in questions of faith.

Ninth conclusion. If, upon the legal convocation made for the common good by the church principals beneath the rank of the pope because of his damnable neglect and culpable failure, or his legal or practical impotence, there turns up only four, this does not mean that they will pronounce errors in questions of faith.

Tenth conclusion. Just as the universal council has the singular right to deal with matters which ought to be believed by the faithful, explicit or necessary for the conduct of the church, either as preferable or required, so the multitude of the faithful individually are drawn by the Holy Spirit to a determinative or authoritative agreement through the council.

Eleventh conclusion. Above all it must be guarded against lest, in the ecclesiastical community, particular decisions in matters of faith or in matters necessary for salvation may be made from which disagreements and division ensue.

Twelfth conclusion. The council summoned without the express call of the pope, since there is none who wishes or is able to do so, is sufficiently endowed to pronounce a true judgment on every possible question touching upon the rule of Christians.

The ninth article will disclose the sufficiency of the sacrosanct church by reason of the offices instituted in it not by mere man but directly by Jesus Christ, and to be instituted until the world's end. And there will be ten conclusions in it [Conclusions two and ten are missing].

First conclusion. Until the end of the world there will always be someone or some group established by divine designation to receive from God special enlightenment for the usefulness of the church at large.

Third conclusion. Those offices and gifts have not been bestowed as a free gift in the church militant by the canonical law of a pure man.

Fourth conclusion. They are established by the man Christ, or with the consent or authority of a pure man, as officers sufficient to the end of the world toknow, enunciate, and confirm all truth necessary or useful for the conduct of the church, or for the edification of the faithful and the termination of whatever doubts have arisen or will arise on the conduct of Christianity.

Fifth conclusion. The exercise of these offices in serving the church according to the ranks assigned to them by the man Christ does not depend on the consent, call, or authority of the pope.

Sixth conclusion. With the two popes, contending with one another out of malice, excluded from the council of the universal church, the council is said to be sufficiently endowed by Christ, in and of itself, to determine usefully how Christianity ought to conduct itself in the matter of the present schism.

Seventh conclusion. The aforesaid officers, in the exercise of their office, receive God, who inspires them and acts through them.

Eighth conclusion. In that most sacred council to be celebrated in March [1409, the council of Pisa], in which the faith and the state of the universal church will be dealt with, all Catholic Christians ought to be received who wish to attend.

Ninth conclusion. The church, lawfully and canonically assembled without the express consent of the pope, since there is none, is indeed established by the man Christ for pronouncing to the faithful all the truths necessary to the conduct of the church....

De auctoritate concilii, ed. Z. Rueger, *Revue d'histoire ecclésiastique*, LIII (1958), 785–87, trans. N. P. Zacour.

E. The Council Triumphant

The Council of Pisa only succeeded in making matters worse, by deposing the two existing popes and electing a third. Since the other two refused to recognize the council, there were now three claimants. A second council, at Constance in 1414, finally settled the Schism by obtaining the withdrawal of two of the disputants, ignoring the third whose claims were later abandoned, and electing Pope Martin V, who was recognized throughout the church. In the process, however, the theory of conciliar superiority was refined and enacted into law, and arrangements were made for the subsequent meetings of councils to supervise the rule of the church.

1. THE CONCILIAR EDICT "SACROSANCTA"

This holy synod of Constance, constituting a general council, lawfully assembled in the Holy Spirit for the ending of the Schism and the union and reformation of the Church of God in head and members, to the praise of Almighty God, in order that it may pursue more readily, securely, and freely the union and reformation of the Church of God, ordains, defines, enacts, and declares the following:

First, it declares that being lawfully assembled in the Holy Spirit, constituting a general council and representing the Catholic Church, it holds its authority directly from Christ, whom all persons of every, even papal, rank or dignity are bound to obey in those things pertaining to faith, the ending of the Schism, and the reformation of the said Church in head and members.

Further, it declares that whosoever, of any position, rank, or dignity, even papal, contumaciously refuses to obey the mandates, statutes, ordinances, or regulations enacted or to be enacted by this holy synod, or by any other general council lawfully assembled, on the aforesaid matters or other things pertaining to them, shall, unless he repents, be subject to deserved punishment and shall be duly punished even, where necessary, through recourse to other aids of the law.

G. D. Mansi, *Sacrorum conciliorum nova et amplissima collectio,* XXVII (Venice, 1784), 590, trans. N. P. Zacour.

2. THE CONCILIAR EDICT "FREQUENS"

The frequent meeting of general councils is the best means of tilling the Lord's field; it roots out the brambles, thorns, and thistles of heresies, errors and schisms, corrects deviations, reforms the deformed, and brings the vineyard of the Lord to bear fruit of a most copious fertility. The neglect of councils sows and nourishes the seeds of the aforesaid; the memory of times past and consideration of the present make this evident. Therefore, by this perpetual edict, we establish, decree and ordain that henceforth general councils be held, so that the first may meet in the five years immediately following upon the end of this council, the second in seven years immediately following upon the end of that council, and thenceforward every ten years perpetually, in those places which the pope, in the last month of each council, with the approval and consent of the council (or failing him, the council itself) is required to establish and designate. Thus through a certain continuity either a council may always be in session or planned for at the end of a given period. The pope, on the advice of his brethren the cardinals of the Holy Roman Church, may shorten that [intervening] period for reasons of emergency, but he may not lengthen it on any account. He may not change the place designated for the holding of a future council except out of manifest necessity. If by chance some reason arises because of which it seems necessary for the place to be changed—such as sieges, wars, epidemics, and the like—then the pope, with the signed consent of his aforesaid brethren or two thirds of them, may substitute another place, suitable, nearby, and within the same nation, for that first designated; unless the same or a like obstacle is present throughout the entire nation, in which case he can convoke the council to some other suitable and nearby place of another nation. To this place the prelates and others who are usually summoned to council may be required to proceed as if that place had been designated from the outset. The pope may be required legally and solemnly to publish and announce the change of place or the shortening of the period between councils a year before the date fixed for the council, so that the prelates can convene at the appropriate time to attend the council.

C. J. Hefele and H. Leclercq, *Histoire des conciles,* VII, i (Paris, 1916), 459–60, trans. N. P. Zacour.

F. The End of Conciliarism

The Council of Constance dealt with more than the Schism, for there were many who saw in the council an instrument of long overdue church reform. But they were disappointed with what was done by the new pope, and a later council at Basel (which met from 1431 to 1449) soon fell to quarreling with the papacy and ultimately attempted the election of a rival pope. This was a fatal slip which discredited the entire movement and allowed the papacy to regain its superiority within the church. With the advent of Pope Pius II (1458–1464), who as a young man had been an active conciliarist at Basel, the movement was ended, but not before it had taken its toll of a papacy once held to be supreme and of the idea of a single corporate society which the papacy had symbolized.

A detestable corruption, unheard of in earlier times, has grown up in our own age, with the result that some, imbued with the spirit of rebellion, do presume, not from desire for saner counsel but to evade the consequence of the sins they have committed, to appeal to a future council from the Roman pontiff, vicar of Jesus Christ, to whom it was said in the person of St. Peter "Feed my sheep," and "whatsoever thou shalt bind on earth shall be bound in heaven."

Desirous, therefore, of driving out from the church of Christ this pestilential stench, of looking to the safety of the sheep committed to us, and of repelling every matter of scandal from the sheepfold of our Savior, we condemn these appeals as mistaken and abominable.

H. Denzinger, *Enchiridion symbolorum* (Freiburg, 1955), p. 267, trans. N. P. Zacour.

6

The Meaning
of the Renaissance

MYRON P. GILMORE

Harvard University

The historian, like other people who try to interpret human experience past or present, makes use of general concepts as well as collections of particular facts. Among these general concepts are our ideas of causation, of development or regression, of change or continuity, upon all of which we draw when we define periods and mark important turning points in any historical sequence. More than most such periodizations in the history of Europe the age of the Renaissance has depended for its meaning on the shifting content of the general hypotheses about history expressed or implied in the work of successive generations of historians. The Renaissance is in other words an abstraction, and it is an abstraction less immediately and obviously related to a series of particular events than most of the other familiar terms by which we identify particular epochs. We speak for example of the age of the French Revolution. Scholars have debated and will debate every aspect of the causes and consequences of the series of events which we call the Revolution, but no one has ever denied that the Revolution took place, unless it be that English bishop who satirized the higher critics of the Bible by writing historic doubts on the existence of Napoleon Bonaparte. Yet there are historians of repute who maintain that there is no historical reality corresponding to the conventional conception of the Renaissance, and that it would improve our understanding of the past to eliminate the term altogether from our vocabulary.

This is a more extreme position than it is possible to take about even such debated terms as the Reformation and the Industrial Revolution. After all Luther tacked up his 95 theses on October 31, 1517, and the success of Hargreaves' spinning jenney can be measured from a definite time and place, but the student who seeks to find for the Renaissance a comparable specific event on the real or symbolic significance of which there is an equal amount of general agreement will seek in vain. If we are to avoid the unhappy results of misplaced concreteness and escape being the victims of our own metaphors, it is of the first importance to be aware of the fact that different kinds of discourse are appropriate to different levels of generalization. We cannot—or at least should not—personify the Renaissance nor treat it as an event like Magna Carta or the Declaration of Independence. It is in reality a concept which historians use to describe a stage in the history of the European mind, and changes in intellectual history can seldom if ever be described in the same kind of language as may be used for a revolutionary act or the introduction of a new technology. Any inward and spiritual change of great magnitude is of course accompanied and followed by outward and visible signs in every field of human activity, but the particular events that are regarded as characteristic manifestations of the Renaissance will vary with the descriptions of more elusive transformations in the attitudes, tastes, and convictions of individual men and women.

Our first problem must therefore be concerned with some of the definitions of the Renaissance proposed by its greatest historians. In the elaboration of the concept that has become familiar in textbooks and in common parlance, the historical writing of the nineteenth century occupies the most important place, for it was in that century that there emerged a notion of the Renaissance as a period which saw a sharp break with the medieval past and the beginning of the modern world. Earlier writers had distinguished the fifteenth and early sixteenth centuries in Italy as an age of literary and artistic achievement. Voltaire for example in his *Siècle de Louis XIV* placed Medicean Italy alongside Periclean Greece, Augustan Rome and the France of Louis XIV as the four great ages in the history of human culture, and long before Voltaire, men had spoken of a "rebirth" of literature, law, painting, architecture, and scholarship, and located these phenomena in Italy in the age of humanism roughly beginning with Petrarch. In spite of this periodization in the history of culture, it was left to the nineteenth century, the most historically minded of epochs, to define the Renaissance in a deeper and broader significance as a period which saw a decisive change in all departments of human activity and in the human spirit itself, marking the end of the Middle Ages and the beginning of the Modern World.

In this emphasis by the great nineteenth-century historians on a break in continuity there lies a paradox. For one of the great preoccupations of nineteenth-century thought was the idea of development: the present was to be explained by the past. The past must be understood in all its uniqueness, but at the same time a historical explanation was a complete explanation and even a justification for the present. While Darwin explored the origin of species in the tremendously enlarged framework of geological time, those who directed their attention to the achievements of *Homo sapiens* studied the links between modern parliamentary institutions and the customs of the Germanic tribes. The interpretation of the Renaissance as a decisive break in continuity—an epoch of transcendent significance standing as it were outside time, and marking the birth of the modern world—presents the strongest possible contrast to those evolutionary ideas which were developed and applied to so many areas of historical investigation. It was almost as if men felt themselves oppressed by the weight of historical development, imprisoned by necessity, and sought to affirm in the concept of the Renaissance the possibility of a historical miracle, *a sudden transformation* which had no satisfactory explanation in terms of antecedent causes and which violated the ordinary laws of continuity, founding, as Lord Acton said, "a new order of things."

In contrast twentieth-century scholarship reacting against this view has frequently depreciated the importance of the Renaissance and emphasized the continuities between medieval and modern history. Many medieval historians have pointed out that the modern world owes more to the institutions of the Middle Ages than to those of the Renaissance. Such "revisionists" as Professor Lynn Thorndike have furthermore insisted that the very concept of a Renaissance as a rebirth is a logical absurdity when applied to the course of human history.

The more comprehensive modern interpretations of the Renaissance whether "pro" or "contra" have commonly attempted to measure its significance for us by looking back over a long perspective. The very conflicts created by this attempt have produced another kind of evaluation of the Renaissance which shifts the emphasis from hindsight to contemporary opinion. If we cannot decide what the Renaissance was "in reality," we can at least ask ourselves what the "men of the Renaissance" thought about themselves and their own cultural achievement. If people believed they were living in a period of significant change of direction, this may not be evidence of actual change by any retrospective standard of measurement, but it is at least a basis on which a defensible periodization can be constructed. Our second problem is therefore concerned with the kind of generalizations that may be made about a period by those of its thinkers and writers who showed themselves most aware of the relationship between their own age and the past. The selection of excerpts included here is necessarily very limited and arbitrary, but it may serve to raise questions of interest and importance. What was the attitude of a man like Petrarch toward the classical past? How far did representative scholars think of their work as a "restoration" or "rebirth"? Did the artist look upon the great achievements in painting, sculpture, and architecture with the same kind of judgments as were used by the men of letters when they evaluated the present and the past? To what extent can we discover a "common denominator" underlying quite different kinds of creative activity? How did men estimate the effects of such innovations as printing, gunpowder, and the new aids to navigation, and how did their consciousness of these things affect the idea of their age as a restoration of antiquity?

Such questions as these obviously cannot be answered by perusing a small selection of texts ranging in time from Petrarch to beyond the middle of the sixteenth century, and including not only one or two authors who are particularly representative of their time, but others who are so great as to transcend it. Nevertheless even these few texts may serve to focus the problem and to indicate the variety of possibilities inherent in any attempt to describe the significance of an age as it appeared to contemporary eyes.

General estimates of the Renaissance as an epoch in European intellectual history have always been closely related to the analysis of the importance of the work of certain of the greatest creative individuals whose achievement has come to symbolize the larger aspects of the period. This relationship, which is of course the basis for the discussion of the "spirit" of any age, is, in the case of the Renaissance, intensified precisely because so many of the characterizations of this age have turned on the meaning of "individualism." Among the eponymous heroes of the age of the Renaissance no names are more frequently mentioned than those of Machiavelli and Erasmus. The last problems in this section attempt to present some of the evidence for the conflicting interpretations of the significance of these great figures. In moving from the problems of describing and evaluating an age as a whole to that of analyzing the work of a single man, the field of observation is narrowed, but many of the fundamental questions remain. The Renaissance like the Middle Ages before it frequently appealed to the analogy between the microcosm and the macrocosm. The one has reflected the other in historical writing at least as often as in metaphysics. In the long run a revision in our judgment about a Machiavelli or an Erasmus is likely to lead to a revision in our judgment about the Renaissance as a whole.

I. What Do Modern Historians Mean by the Renaissance ?

The following selections are intended to indicate the range of opinions on the meaning and significance of the age of the Renaissance judged as a whole. They consist of short passages, taken on the whole from much longer works, but representing the most comprehensive commitments of their respective authors.

The great French historian, Jules Michelet, devoted a large part of his life to an eloquent and passionate *History of France,* the hero of which was in fact the spirit of the French people through the ages. The seventh volume of this work entitled *The Renaissance* appeared in 1855. In its opening pages Michelet with characteristic exuberance declared that the Renaissance was nothing less than the discovery of the world and of man. With this famous phrase he became the first historian to attribute to the period a universal significance.

The second of the passages from the same work shows Michelet capturing the drama of the invasion of Italy by the army of Charles VIII in 1494, and endowing this event with a crucial and almost apocalyptic quality. Henceforward 1494 became like 1492 and 1453 one of the dates most often accepted as symbolically marking the beginning of modern times.

The Swiss historian Jacob Burckhardt published in 1860 *The Civilization of the Renaissance in Italy.* This classic work gave to subsequent generations their idea of the Renaissance. Accepting Michelet's general conclusion, Burckhardt refined it and analyzed its application to Italy in the period from Giotto to Michelangelo. The selections given here, including the analysis of individualism and the significance of the revival of antiquity, illustrate the way in which Burckhardt developed his descriptive categories.

At the end of the nineteenth century Lord

Acton was Regius Professor of Modern History at the University of Cambridge. The dramatic description of the break in continuity which marked the beginning of the modern period is taken from his posthumously published lectures.

Against these views of earlier students of the period must be placed the conclusions of twentieth-century scholars. Here there are included the judgments on the Renaissance of Lynn Thorndike (a historian of science), Ernst Cassirer (a historian of philosophy), and Erwin Panofsky (a historian of art).

A. Michelet

1. THE MEANING OF THE RENAISSANCE

The lovely word Renaissance means to those who care for beauty only the advent of a new art and the free development of the imagination. To the scholar it is the renovation of classical studies; to the lawyer the light that began to be cast on the disorder and chaos in our old customary laws.

Is this all there is to be said? Through the fogs of theological battles, the *Orlando*, the arabesques of Raphael, the nymphs of Jean Goujon continue to beguile the whims of fashion. Three very different types of mind, the artist, the priest, and the skeptic might be willing to agree on such a description of the significance of this great age. The skepticism of Montaigne was all that Pascal could see in it, and Bossuet was in agreement when he wrote his *History of the Variations of the Protestant Churches*.

According to this interpretation a mighty revolutionary force, complex, extensive and profound, issued in nothing. So great an effort of the human will remained without result. What could be more discouraging for human thought?

These prejudiced views, however, forget but two little things which characterize this age more than all the preceding periods: the discovery of the world and the discovery of man.

The sixteenth century in its proper interpretation extends from Columbus to Copernicus, from Copernicus to Galileo, from the discovery of the earth to the exploration of the heavens.

In this period Man rediscovered himself. While Vesalius and Servetus revealed the bases of life, Luther and Calvin, Dumoulin and Cujas, Rabelais, Montaigne, Shakespeare, and Cervantes penetrated its moral mysteries. Mankind therefore sounded the depths of human nature and began to base itself on justice and reason. Skeptics came to the aid of faith and the boldest of all reached the point of inscribing on the portico of his Temple of the Will: "Enter to build here a profound faith."

And deep indeed were the foundations on which the new faith was supported at a time when the identity between a rediscovered antiquity and the modern age began to be recognized, when the newly discovered East extended its hands to our western civilization and when in due course began the happy reconciliation of the members of the human family.

J. Michelet, *Histoire de France*, IX, "La Renaissance" (Paris, 1879), 7–9, adapted, trans. M. P. Gilmore.

2. THE SIGNIFICANCE OF THE FRENCH
   INVASION OF ITALY IN 1494

On the thirty-first of December at three o'clock in the afternoon the army of Charles VIII entered Rome and the passage of its marching files was prolonged far into the night by the light of torches. The Italians viewed not without terror this

sudden appearance of France and glimpsed among these barbarians the results of an art, an entirely new organization for warfare, the existence of which they had not previously suspected.

...Although the army had boasted sixty thousand men at the crossing of the Alps, it had detached various units all along its route and now at Rome amounted to hardly more than thirty thousand. But this was the very heart of the army, the most vigorous and the best armed; by detaching the weak and the laggards it had become still more formidable.

...Surrounding the king there marched with the Swiss guard three hundred archers and two hundred knights wearing gold and purple and clothed in massive armour.

There followed in rapid succession thirty-six bronze cannon, each weighing thousands of pounds, then long culverins and about a hundred falconets. Each of these pieces was drawn not by oxen in the Italian manner but by a lively team of six horses with mobile gun-carriages which

Ibid., pp. 125–29.

B. Burckhardt

1. THE ITALIAN STATE AND THE INDIVIDUAL

In the Middle Ages both sides of human consciousness—that which was turned within as that which was turned without—lay dreaming or half awake beneath a common veil. The veil was woven of faith, illusion, and childish prepossession, through which the world and history were seen clad in strange hues. Man was conscious of himself only as member of a race, people, party, family, or corporation—only through some general category. In Italy this veil first melted into air; an *objective* treatment and consideration of the state and of all the things of this world became possible. The *subjective* side at the same time asserted itself with corresponding emphasis; man became a spiritual *individual,* and recognized himself as such. In the same way the Greek had once distinguished himself from the barbarian, and the Arabian had felt himself an individual at a time when other Asiatics knew themselves only as members of a race. It will not be difficult to show that this result was owing above all to the political circumstances of Italy.

In far earlier times we can here and

in combat were detached from their fore-carriages and were immediately ready for action.

All this was to be seen in the light of the torches reflected on the walls of the Roman palaces and in the depths of the long streets with fantastic silhouettes larger than life, sinister and mournful in their effects. Everyone sensed that this was a great revolution which amounted to more than the passage of a single army and that there would emerge from this event not only the ordinary tragedies of war but a general and decisive change even in the realm of customs and ideas. The Alps were lowered forever.

there detect a development of free personality which in Northern Europe either did not occur at all, or could not display itself in the same manner. The band of audacious wrongdoers in the tenth century described to us by Liudprand, some of the contemporaries of Gregory VII, and a few of the opponents of the first Hohenstaufen, show us characters of this kind. But at the close of the thirteenth century Italy began to swarm with individuality; the charm laid upon human personality was dissolved; and a thousand figures meet us, each in its own special shape and dress. Dante's great poem would have been impossible in any other country of Europe, if only for the reason that they all still lay under the spell of race. For Italy the august poet, through the wealth of individuality which he set forth, was the most national herald of his time. . . . The Italians of the fourteenth century knew little of false modesty or of hypocrisy in any shape; not one of them was afraid of singularity, of being and seeming unlike his neighbours.

Despotism, as we have already seen, fostered in the highest degree the individuality not only of the tyrant or condottiere himself, but also of the men whom he protected or used as his tools—the secretary, minister, poet, and companion.

These people were forced to know all the inward resources of their own nature, passing or permanent; and their enjoyment of life was enhanced and concentrated by the desire to obtain the greatest satisfaction from a possibly very brief period of power and influence.

But even the subjects whom they ruled over were not free from the same impulse. Leaving out of account those who wasted their lives in secret opposition and conspiracies, we speak of the majority who were content with a strictly private station, like most of the urban population of the Byzantine empire and the Mohammedan states. No doubt it was often hard for the subjects of a Visconti to maintain the dignity of their persons and families, and multitudes must have lost in moral character through the servitude they lived under. But this was not the case with regard to individuality; for political impotence does not hinder the different tendencies and manifestations of private life from thriving in the fullest vigour and variety. Wealth and culture, so far as display and rivalry were not forbidden to them, a municipal freedom which did not cease to be considerable, and a Church which, unlike that of the Byzantine or of the Mohammedan world, was not identical with the State—all these conditions undoubtedly favoured the growth of individual thought, for which the necessary leisure was furnished by the cessation of party conflicts. The private man, indifferent to politics, and busied partly with serious pursuits, partly with the interests of a *dilettante,* seems to have been first fully formed in these despotisms of the fourteenth century. Documentary evidence cannot, of course, be required on such a point. The novelists, from whom we might expect information, describe to us oddities in plenty, but only from one point of view and insofar as the needs of the story demand. Their scene, too, lies chiefly in the republican cities.

In the latter, circumstances were also, but in another way, favourable to the growth of individual character. The more frequently the governing party was changed, the more the individual was led to make the utmost of the exercise and enjoyment of power. The statesmen and popular leaders, especially in Florentine history, acquired so marked a personal character, that we can scarcely find, even exceptionally, a parallel to them in contemporary history, hardly even in Jacob van Arteveldt.

...An acute and practised eye might be able to trace, step by step, the increase in the number of complete men during the fifteenth century. Whether they had before them as a conscious object the harmonious development of their spiritual and material existence, is hard to say; but several of them attained it, so far as is consistent with the imperfection of all that is earthly. It may be better to renounce the attempt at an estimate of the share which fortune, character, and talent had in the life of Lorenzo il Magnifico. But look at a personality like that of Ariosto, especially as shown in his satires. In what harmony are there expressed the pride of the man and the poet, the irony with which he treats his own enjoyments, the most delicate satire, and the deepest goodwill!

When this impulse to the highest individual development was combined with a powerful and varied nature, which had mastered all the elements of the culture of the age, then arose the 'all-sided man'—'l'uomo universale'—who belonged to Italy alone. Men there were of encyclopaedic knowledge in many countries during the Middle Ages, for this knowledge was confined within narrow limits; and even in the twelfth century there were universal artists, but the problems of architecture were comparatively simple and uniform, and in sculpture and painting the matter was of more importance than the form. But in Italy at the time of the Renaissance, we find artists who in every branch created new and perfect works, and who also made the greatest impression as men. Others, outside the arts they practised, were masters of a vast circle of spiritual interests.

...The fifteenth century is, above all, that of the many-sided men. There is no biography which does not, besides the chief work of its hero, speak of other pursuits all passing beyond the limits of dilettantism. The Florentine merchant and statesman was often learned in both the classical languages; the most famous humanists read the ethics and politics of Aristotle to him and his sons; even the daughters of the house were highly educated. It is in these circles that private education was first treated seriously. The humanist, on his side, was compelled to the most varied attainments, since his philological learning was not limited, as it now is, to the theoretical knowledge of classical antiquity, but had to serve the practical needs of daily life. While studying Pliny, he made collections of natural history; the geography of the ancients was his guide in treating of modern geography, their history was his pattern in writing contemporary chronicles, even when composed in Italian; he not only translated the comedies of Plautus, but acted as manager when they were put on the stage; every effective form of ancient literature down to the dialogues of Lucian he did his best to imitate; and besides all this, he acted as magistrate, secretary, and diplomatist— not always to his own advantage.

Jacob Burckhardt, *The Civilization of the Renaissance in Italy,* trans. S. G. C. Middlemore (New York: The Macmillan Company, 1890), pp. 129–31, 134–36.

2. THE REVIVAL OF ANTIQUITY

We must insist upon it, as one of the chief propositions of this book, that it was not the revival of antiquity alone, but its union with the genius of the Italian people, which achieved the conquest of the western world. The amount of independence which the national spirit maintained in this union varied according to circumstances. In the modern Latin literature of the period, it is very small, while in plastic art, as well as in other spheres, it is remarkably great; and hence the alliance between two distant epochs in the civilization of the same people, because concluded on equal terms, proved justifiable and fruitful. The rest of Europe was free either to repel or else partly or wholly to accept the mighty impulse which came forth from Italy. Where the latter was the case we may as well be spared the complaints over the early decay of mediæval faith and civilization. Had these been strong enough to hold their ground, they would be alive to this day. If those elegiac natures which long to see them return could pass but one hour in the midst of them, they would gasp to be back in modern air. That in a great historical process of this kind flowers of exquisite beauty may perish, without being made immortal in poetry or tradition, is undoubtedly true; nevertheless, we cannot wish the process undone. The general result of it consists in this—that by the side of the Church which had hitherto held the countries of the West together (though it was unable to do so much longer) there arose a new spiritual influence which, spreading itself abroad from Italy, became the breath of life for all the more instructed minds in Europe. The worst that can be said of the movement is, that it was anti-popular, that through it Europe became for the first time sharply divided into the cultivated and uncultivated classes. The reproach will appear groundless when we reflect that even now the fact, though clearly recognised, cannot be altered. The separation, too, is by no means so cruel and absolute in Italy as elsewhere. The most artistic of her poets, Tasso, is in the hands of even the poorest.

The civilization of Greece and Rome, which, ever since the fourteenth century, obtained so powerful a hold on Italian life, as the source and basis of culture, as the object and ideal of existence, partly also as an avowed reaction against preceding tendencies—this civilization had long been exerting a partial influence on mediæval Europe, even beyond the boundaries of Italy. The culture of which Charles the Great was a representative was, in face of the barbarism of the seventh and eighth centuries, essentially a Renaissance, and could appear under no other form. Just as in the Romanesque architecture of the North, beside the general outlines inherited from antiquity, remarkable direct imitations of the antique also occur, so too monastic scholarship had not only gradually absorbed an immense mass of materials from Roman writers, but the style of it, from the days of Eginhard onwards, shows traces of conscious imitations.

But the resuscitation of antiquity took a different form in Italy from that which it assumed in the North. The wave of barbarism had scarcely gone by before the people, in whom the former life was but half effaced, showed a consciousness of its past and a wish to reproduce it. Elsewhere in Europe men deliberately and with reflection borrowed this or the other element of classical civilization; in Italy the sympathies both of the learned and of the people were naturally engaged on the side of antiquity as a whole, which stood to them as a symbol of past greatness. The Latin language, too, was easy to an Italian, and the numerous monuments and documents in which the country abounded facilitated a return to the past. With this tendency other elements—the popular character which time had now greatly modified, the political institutions imported by the Lombards from Germany, chivalry and other northern forms of civilization, and the influence of religion and the Church—combined to produce the modern Italian spirit, which was destined to serve as the model and ideal for the whole western world.

Ibid., pp. 171–73.

3. THE DISCOVERY OF MAN

To the discovery of the outward world the Renaissance added a still greater achievement, by first discerning and bringing to light the full, whole nature of man.

This period, as we have seen, first gave the highest development to individuality, and then led the individual to the most zealous and thorough study of himself in all forms and under all conditions. Indeed, the development of personality is essentially involved in the recognition of it in oneself and in others. Between these two great processes our narrative has placed the influence of ancient literature, because the mode of conceiving and representing both the individual and human nature in general was defined and coloured by that influence. But the power of conception and representation lay in the age and in the people.

The facts which we shall quote in evidence of our thesis will be few in number. Here, if anywhere in the course of this discussion, the author is conscious that he is treading on the perilous ground of conjecture, and that what seems to him a clear, if delicate and gradual, transition in the intellectual movement of the fourteenth and fifteenth centuries, may not be equally plain to others. The gradual awakening of the soul of a people is a phenomenon which may produce a different impression on each spectator. Time will judge which impression is the most faithful.

Ibid., p. 308.

C. Lord Acton

1. THE BREAK IN CONTINUITY

...I describe as Modern History that which begins four hundred years ago, which is marked off by an evident and intelligible line from the time immediately preceding, and displays in its course specific and distinctive characteristics of its own. The modern age did not proceed from the medieval by normal succession, with outward tokens of legitimate descent. Unheralded, it founded a new order of things, under a law of innovation, sapping the ancient reign of continuity. In those days Columbus subverted the notions of the world, and reversed the conditions of production, wealth, and power; in those days Machiavelli released government from the restraint of law; Erasmus diverted the current of ancient learning from profane into Christian channels; Luther broke the chain of authority and tradition at the strongest link; and Copernicus erected an invincible power that set for ever the mark of progress upon the time that was to come. There is the same unbound originality and disregard for inherited sanctions in the rare philosophers as in the discovery of Divine Right, and the intruding Imperialism of Rome. The like effects are visible everywhere, and one generation beheld them all. It was an awakening of new life; the world revolved in a different orbit, determined by influences unknown before. After many ages persuaded of the headlong decline and impending dissolution of society, and governed by usage and the will of masters who were in their graves, the sixteenth century went forth armed for untried experience, and ready to watch with hopefulness a prospect of incalculable change.

That forward movement divides it broadly from the older world; and the unity of the new is manifest in the universal spirit of investigation and discovery which did not cease to operate, and withstood the recurring efforts of reaction,

until, by the advent of the reign of general ideas which we call the Revolution, it at length prevailed. This successive deliverance and gradual passage, for good and evil, from subordination to independence is a phenomenon of primary import to us, because historical science has been one of its instruments. If the Past has been an obstacle and a burden, knowledge of the Past is the safest and surest emancipation. And the earnest search for it is one of the signs that distinguish the four centuries of which I speak from those that went before. The Middle Ages, which possessed good writers of contemporary narrative, were careless and impatient of older fact. They became content to be deceived, to live in a twilight of fiction, under clouds of false witness, inventing according to convenience, and glad to welcome the forger and the cheat. As time went on, the atmosphere of accredited mendacity thickened, until, in the Renaissance, the art of exposing falsehood dawned upon keen Italian minds. It was then that History as we understand it began to be understood, and the illustrious dynasty of scholars arose to whom we still look both for method and material. Unlike the dreaming prehistoric world, ours knows the need and the duty to make itself master of the earlier times, and to forfeit nothing of their wisdom or their warnings, and has devoted its best energy and treasure to the sovereign purpose of detecting error and vindicating entrusted truth.

Lord Acton, *Lectures on Modern History*, eds. John Neville Figgis and Reginald Vere Laurence (London: Macmillan & Co., Ltd., 1906), pp. 3–5.

2. THE CLASSICAL REVIVAL

Next to the discovery of the New World, the recovery of the ancient world is the second landmark that divides us from the Middle Ages and marks the transition to modern life. The Renaissance signifies the renewed study of Greek, and the consequences that ensued from it, during the century and a half between Petrarca and Erasmus. It had survived, as a living language, among Venetian colo-

nists and Calabrian monks, but exercised no influence on literature.

The movement was preceded by a Roman revival, which originated with Rienzi [in the middle of the fourteenth century]. Rome had been abandoned by the Papacy, which had moved from the Tiber to the Rhone, where it was governed by Frenchmen from Cahors, and had fallen, like any servile country, into feudal hands. Rienzi restored the Republic, revived the self-government of the city, the memories attached to the Capitol, the inscriptions, the monuments of the men who ruled the world. The people, no longer great through the Church, fell back on the greatness which they inherited from ancient times. The spell by which the Tribune directed their patriotism was archæology. In front of the Capitoline temple, near the Tarpeian rock and the She-Wolf's cave, he proclaimed their rights over the empire and the nations; and he invited the people of Italy to a national parliament for the restoration of Italian unity and of the ancient glory and power of Rome. Patriotism, national independence, popular liberty, all were founded on antiquarian studies and the rhetorical interpretation of the fragments of the Lex Regia.

The political scheme of Rienzi failed, but it started a movement in the world of thought deeper and more enduring than State transactions. For his ideas were adopted by the greatest writer then living, and were expounded by him in the most eloquent and gracious prose that had been heard for a thousand years. Petrarca called the appearance of the patriotic Tribune and rhetorician the dawn of a new world and a golden age. Like him, he desired to purge the soil of Italy from the barbaric taint. It became the constant theme of the humanists to protest against the foreign intruder, that is, against the feudal noble, the essential type of the medieval policy. It is the link between Rienzi, the dreamer of dreams, and the followers of Petrarca.

Boccaccio had already spoken of the acceptable blood of tyrants.

But the political influence of antiquity, visible at first, made way for a purely literary influence. The desire for good Latin became injurious to Italian, and Petrarca censured Dante for his error in composing the *Divine Comedy* in the vulgar tongue. He even regretted that the *Decamerone* was not written in Latin, and refused to read what his friend had written for the level of uneducated men. The classics became, in the first place, the model and the measure of style; and the root of the Renaissance was the persuasion that a man who could write like Cicero had an important advantage over a man who wrote like Bartolus or William of Ockham; and that ideas radiant with beauty must conquer ideas clouded over with dialectics. In this, there was an immediate success. Petrarca and his imitators learnt to write excellent Latin. Few of them had merit as original thinkers, and what they did for erudition was done all over again, and incomparably better, by the scholars who appeared after the tempest of the Reformation had gone down. But they were excellent letter writers. In hundreds of volumes, from Petrarca to Sadolet and Pole, we can trace every idea and mark every throb. It was the first time that the characters of men were exposed with analytic distinctness; the first time indeed that character could be examined with accuracy and certitude.

Ibid., pp. 171–73.

D. Thorndike's Case Against the Renaissance

Legacies from the past? Yes. Inheritances from previous periods? Yes. Survivals? Yes. Resemblances to our forebears? Yes. Reformations? Perhaps. Reactions? Unfortunately. But no rebirths and no restorations!

Books and works of art are about all that remain to us of the past. The latter are all too soon sadly altered, and their

restoration, whether by some German professor or by a Thorwaldsen or Viollet-le-Duc, only makes them less like what they originally were. Books remain less changed by the lapse of time, but even their text may become corrupt, or the meaning of the very words they use alter in the interim. The humanists of the so-called Italian Renaissance had only a bookish knowledge of antiquity; they failed almost as dismally as have Mussolini and his Fascists to make the reality of ancient

Rome live again. If, even in our own day, all the resources of the art of history aided by archaeology can give us only a faint and imperfect idea of the past, how can we expect actual renaissances of it or recognize them as such, if they were to occur? At the age of sixty I am perhaps more like myself at the age of twenty than I am like anyone else. But I couldn't possibly put myself back into the frame of mind that I had then. I have a dim recollection of it; my present state of mind is an outgrowth of it; that is all. A girl of eighteen, dressed up in the clothes which her grandmother wore when a girl of eighteen, may look more like her grandmother as she was then than her grandmother herself does now. But she will not feel or act as her grandmother felt and acted half a century or more ago. Much more tenuous is the connection between distant historical periods, and much less likely is it that historians can successfully venture upon glittering generalities about them. Who can evoke from the past more than a wraith, a phantasy, a specter, which murmurs, like the ghost in *Hamlet*, "Historian, remember me!"

...The concept of the Italian Renaissance or Prenaissance has in my opinion done a great deal of harm in the past and may continue to do harm in the future. It is too suggestive of a sensational, miraculous, extraordinary, magical, human and intellectual development, like unto the phoenix rising from its ashes after five hundred years. It is contrary to the fact that human nature tends to remain much the same in all times. It has led to a chorus of rhapsodists as to freedom, breadth, soaring ideas, horizons, perspectives, out of fetters and swaddling clothes, and so on. It long discouraged the study of centuries of human development that preceded it, and blinded the French *philosophes* and revolutionists to the value of medieval political and economic institutions. It has kept men in general from recognizing that our life and thought is based more nearly and actually on the middle ages than on distant Greece and Rome, from whom our heritage is more indirect, bookish and sentimental, less institutional, social, religious, even less economic and experimental.

But what is the use of questioning the Renaissance? No one has ever proved its existence; no one has really tried to. So often as one phase of it or conception of it is disproved, or is shown to be equally characteristic of the preceding period, its defenders take up a new position and are just as happy, just as complacent as ever.

You may break, you may shatter the
  vase, if you will,
But the scent of the roses will hang
  round it still.

Still lingers the sweet perfume of the Renaissance; still hovers about us the blithe spirit of the Prenaissance.

Lynn Thorndike, "Renaissance or Prenaissance?" *Journal of the History of Ideas,* IV (1943), 65–66, 74.

E. Cassirer on the Originality of the Renaissance

Our controversy as to the originality of the Renaissance and as to the dividing-line between the "Renaissance" and the "Middle Ages" seems to me in many ways rather a "logical" dispute than one about the historical facts. Ideas like "Gothic," "Renaissance," or "Baroque" are ideas of historical "style." As to the meaning of these ideas of "style" there still prevails a great lack of clarity in many respects. They can be used to *characterize* and *interpret* intellectual movements, but they express no actual historical facts that ever existed at any given time. "Renaissance" and "Middle Ages" are, strictly speaking, not names for historical periods at all, but they are concepts of "ideal types," in Max Weber's sense. We cannot therefore use them as instruments for any strict division of periods; we cannot inquire at what temporal point the Middle Ages "stopped" or the Renaissance "began." The actual historical facts cut across and extend over each other in the most complicated manner.

Nevertheless the distinction itself has a real meaning. What we can express by it, and what alone we intend to express, is that from the beginning of the fifteenth century onward the *balance* between the particular forces—society, state, religion, church, art, science—begins to shift slowly. New forces press up out of the depths and alter the previous equilibrium. And the character of every culture rests on the equilibrium between the forces that give it form. Whenever therefore we make any comparison between the Middle Ages and the Renaissance, it is never enough to single out particular ideas or concepts. What we want to know is not the particular idea as such, but the importance it possesses, and the strength with which it is acting in the whole structure. "Middle Ages" and "Renaissance" are two great and mighty streams of ideas. When we single out from them a particular idea, we are not doing what a chemist does in analyzing the water of a stream or what a geographer does in trying to trace it to its source. No one denies that these are interesting and important questions. But they are neither the only nor the most important concern of the *historian of ideas*.

The historian of ideas knows that the water which the river carries with it changes only very slowly. The same ideas are always appearing again and again, and are maintained for centuries. The force and the tenacity of tradition can hardly be over-estimated. From this point of view we must acknowledge over and over again that there is nothing new under the sun. But the historian of ideas is not asking primarily what the *substance* is of particular ideas. He is asking what their *function* is. What he is studying—or should be studying—is less the *content* of ideas than their *dynamics*. To continue the figure, we could say that he is not trying to analyze the drops of water in the river, but that he is seeking to measure its width and depth and to ascertain the force and velocity of the current. It is all *these* factors that are fundamentally altered in the Renaissance: the dynamics of ideas has changed.

Ernst Cassirer, "Some Remarks on the Question of the Originality of the Renaissance," *Journal of the History of Ideas*, IV (1943), 54–55.

F. Panofsky

1. THE SENSE OF HISTORY

In sum, the Italian Renaissance looked upon classical antiquity from a historical distance; therefore, for the first time, as upon a totality removed from the present; and therefore, for the first time, as upon an ideal to be longed for instead of a reality to be both utilized and feared. The pre-Gothic Middle Ages had left antiquity unburied, and alternately galvanized and exorcized its body. The Renaissance stood weeping at its grave and tried to resurrect its soul. And in one fatally auspicious moment it succeeded. This is why the mediaeval concept of The Antique was so concrete and, at the same time, so incomplete and distorted; whereas the modern one is, in a sense, abstract but more comprehensive and consistent. And this is why the mediaeval revivals were real but transitory whereas the Italian, or main, Renaissance was, in a sense, academic but permanent. Resurrected souls are somewhat intangible but they have the advantage of being immortal and omnipresent. Therefore the rôle of classical antiquity in the modern world is a little elusive but, on the other hand, pervasive—and changeable only with a change in the form of our civilization as such.

...One of the leading anti-Renaissancists has recently dismissed the relevance of the *"rinascimento dell' antichità"* by the following simile: "A girl of eighteen, dressed up in the clothes which her grandmother wore when a girl of eighteen, may look more like her grandmother as she was then than her grandmother herself looks now. But she will not feel or act as her grandmother did half a century ago." Taking up this simile, we may answer: If this girl decides to adopt the clothes of her grandmother for good and wears them all the time in the serious conviction that they are more appropriate and becoming than those she used to wear before, this very decision not only induces but actually presupposes a change in her whole personality and way of life—a change not sufficient to make her a duplicate of her grandmother (which no one has claimed to be true of the Renaissance period in relation to classical antiquity), but basic enough to make her "feel and act" quite differently from the way she did as long as she believed in slacks and polo shirts.

Erwin Panofsky, "Renaissance and Renascences," *The Kenyon Review*, VI (1944), 228–29, 229–30.

2. MIDDLE AGES AND RENAISSANCE

If one wants to perceive, at one glance, the difference between the Middle Ages and the Renaissance one may compare Sebastian Brant's *Fools' Ship* of 1494 with Erasmus of Rotterdam's *Praise of Folly* of 1512. Brant, without a trace of tolerance or irony, inveighs against more than a hundred kinds of human folly, firmly convinced that he is right and that everybody else is wrong. Erasmus also ridicules human folly. But he, the most intelligent man of the century, does this by pretending to speak in the name of Folly herself. Whatever is said must therefore be interpreted as his opinion as well as hers. In one of the chapters Erasmus—or Folly—thus assails, apparently as grimly serious as Brant, the foolishness of old women still going to drinking parties, still using make-up, still hiring gigolos, still removing hair from the strangest places. But what is the conclusion? "Such capers are laughed at by everyone, and with good reason, as being the silliest in the world. Yet the old ladies are satisfied with themselves, and in the meantime they swim in

pleasure and anoint themselves all over with honey; they are happy, in a word, by courtesy of me. And as for the people who find it all too ridiculous, I want them to mull over the question whether it is not better to lead this sort of honeyed life in folly than to look for a rafter, as the phrase goes, suitable for a hanging." Folly, then, first attacks foolishness and then defends it. Being Folly, her attack should really mean justification and her defense the opposite. But since she speaks in the name of Erasmus as well as in her own it also works out the other way: the attack may be serious but no less serious would then be the defense—the insight into the fact that "to be engrossed in folly, to err, to be deceived, not to know" is simply "to live as a man."

In an ironical double-twist like this there does appear a humanism—and a humanity—utterly foreign to the Middle Ages. In the Middle Ages reason could question faith and faith could question reason. But reason could not question itself and yet emerge with wisdom—even though Robert Grosseteste had a telescope.

Ibid., pp. 234–35.

II. What Was the Attitude of the " Men of the Renaissance " Toward Their Own Place in History?

The second problem turns from the modern analysis of the Renaissance to the various meanings of the concept of "rebirth" or "restoration" as that concept was used in the contemporary sources.

In the following excerpts Petrarch's Letter to Livy and Bruni's account of his own time illustrate with different emphases the intensity of the nostalgic longing among the early humanists for the recovery of the classical world. Bruni's recollections in particular bear witness to the strength of the feeling that the achievement of his generation marked an epoch in intellectual history. Modern historians recognize that there is much that is exaggerated in this account. It is not true, for example, that Greek literature had been unknown in Italy for 700 years. Yet the belief of Bruni and others like him that they were bringing a whole culture to new birth is a fact of the first importance. Vasari, the biographer of the Italian artists, writing in the sixteenth century, relies on this same metaphor of a rebirth to characterize the artistic achievement of the period.

Erasmus, Rabelais, and Dolet lived in northern Europe at a time when the results of humanist scholarship had been more widely diffused. The selections taken from their writing illustrate a much more comprehensive interpretation of the idea of restoration. Not only literature and art are "reborn" but medicine, law, science, theology, and, most important of all for Erasmus, Christian piety. Furthermore the restoration of the old is now inseparably connected with the birth of the new. In Dolet's eloquent statement the revival of good literature is bound to be accompanied by a social and political improvement. With Louis LeRoy, who published his *Considerations on Universal History* in 1567 and his *Vicissitude or Variety of Things in the Universe* ten years later, we reach the point of self-conscious questioning about the balance between innovation and tradition and a willingness to recognize those achievements of his own age which were entirely unknown to the ancients.

A. *Petrarch's Letter to Titus Livy*

I should wish (if it were permitted from on high) either that I had been born in your age or you in ours; in the latter case our age itself, and in the former I personally should have been the better for it. I should surely have been one of those pilgrims who visited you. For the sake of seeing you I should have gone not merely to Rome, but indeed, from either Gaul or Spain I should have found my way to you as far as India. As it is, I must fain be content with seeing you as reflected in your works—not your whole self, alas, but that portion of you which has not yet perished, notwithstanding the sloth of our age. We know that you wrote one hundred and forty-two books on Roman affairs. With what fervor, with what unflagging zeal must you have labored; and of that entire number there are now extant scarcely thirty.

Oh, what a wretched custom is this of willfully deceiving ourselves! I have said "thirty," because it is common for all to say so. I find, however, that even from these few there is one lacking. They are twenty-nine in all, constituting three decades, the first, the third, and the fourth, the last of which has not the full number of books. It is over these small remains that I toil whenever I wish to forget these regions, these times, and these customs. Often I am filled with bitter indignation against the morals of today, when men value nothing except gold and silver, and desire nothing except sensual, physical pleasures. If these are to be considered the goal of mankind, then not only the dumb beasts of the field, but even insensible and inert matter has a richer, a higher goal than that proposed to itself by thinking man. But of this elsewhere.

It is now fitter that I should give you thanks, for many reasons indeed, but for this in especial: that you so frequently caused me to forget the present evils, and transferred me to happier times. As I read, I seem to be living in the midst of the Cornelii Scipiones Africani, of Laelius, Fabius Maximus, Metellus, Brutus and Decius, of Cato, Regulus, Cursor, Torquatus, Valerius Corvinus, Salinator, of Claudius, Marcellus, Nero, Aemilius, of Fulvius, Flaminius, Attilius, Quintius, Curius, Fabricius, and Camillus. It is with these men that I live at such times and not with the thievish company of today among whom I was born under an evil star. And O, if it were my happy lot to possess your entire works, from what other great names would I not seek solace for my wretched existence, and forgetfulness of this wicked age! Since I cannot find all these in what I now possess of your work, I read of them here and there in other authors, and especially in that book where you are to be found in your entirety, but so briefly epitomized that, although nothing is lacking as far as the number of books is concerned, everything is lacking as regards the value of the contents themselves.

Pray greet in my behalf your predecessors Polybius and Quintus Claudius and Valerius Antias, and all those whose glory your own greater light has dimmed; and of the later historians, give greeting to Pliny the Younger, of Verona, a neighbor of yours, and also to your former rival Crispus Sallustius. Tell them that their ceaseless nightly vigils have been of no more avail, have had no happier lot, than yours.

Farewell forever, matchless historian!

Written in the land of the living, in that part of Italy and in that city in which I am now living and where you were once born and buried, in the vestibule of the Temple of Justina Virgo, and in view of your very tombstone; on the twenty-second of February, in the thirteen hundred and fiftieth year from the birth of Him whom you would have seen, or whose birth you could have heard, had you lived a little longer.

Petrarch's Letters to Classical Authors, trans. Mario E. Cosenza (University of Chicago Press, copyright 1910 by the University of Chicago), pp. 100–103, adapted.

B. Leonardo Bruni on the History of His Own Time

I have decided to discuss in this little book in brief compass the men who excelled in Italy during my own time as well as the general condition of public affairs and of intellectual life. For I feel that I have an obligation to this age of mine to give some notice of it to posterity whatever it may turn out to have been. If only the men of earlier generations who had some skill in writing had done the same thing, we should not now find ourselves in such a profound darkness of ignorance. To me indeed the times of Cicero and Demosthenes seem much more familiar than the period of sixty years ago. For those famous men shed such a flood of light on their own age that even after so long a time has elapsed it may be seen almost as if it were placed before our eyes. An incredible ignorance, however, depressed and concealed the centuries which came after. Moreover I note that Plato in an earlier age had the same diligence and when we read his books and letters we acquire an almost living and breathing picture of his times. For he tells us in such a way about the studies of his youth and his desire of realizing a republic and the revolutions of the times and his own journeys into Sicily and these confusing struggles of Dionysius and Dio and the final ruin of both that he seems to have wished to commend to immortality the knowledge of these things. I wish that others had been moved to do the same thing so that everyone might have left us an equally celebrated knowledge and recollection of his own age. But I think that although no one lacked the will to do this the greater number lacked the knowledge of how to write. For literature unless it is clear and elegant cannot shed light on the affairs of which it treats nor extend their memory far into the future. Therefore what I desire in others I am now about to try to present to our descendants so that if by chance they care to read, some knowledge of our times may not be lacking.

...During the intervals of this war it was remarkable how much the cult of letters developed in Italy, for then for the first time there began to be attained a knowledge of Greek which for seven hundred years had ceased to be current among our people. Chrysoloras of Byzantium, a man of a noble house and most skilled in literature, brought back to us the knowledge of Greek. When his country was besieged by the Turks, he had first come to Venice by sea, but soon after when his reputation had spread, warmly invited and besought and influenced by the offer of a public salary, he came to Florence to present his learning to the young.

I was at that time studying the civil law although not unacquainted with other disciplines. For I was by nature inflamed by the love for learning and I had spent no small amount of time on dialectic and rhetoric. For this reason on the advent of Chrysoloras I went through a period of indecision since I concluded it would be disgraceful to desert the study of the civil law and yet thought it a kind of crime to pass over such a great opportunity for learning Greek. I frequently said to myself with youthful emotion: "Can you thus betray yourself and deprive yourself when you have the opportunity to give your attention to Homer and Plato and Demosthenes and the other poets and philosophers and orators about whom such great and wonderful qualities are reported, and it is not only an opportunity to read them but to become imbued with their marvelous teaching. Can you pass over an opportunity thus offered to you by Providence? For seven hundred years no one in Italy has known Greek literature and yet we admit that all our learning derives from it. What a useful tool for further learning, what an opportunity for fame, what an enrichment of pleasure will be yours from the knowledge of this language? There are great numbers of doctors of the civil law and you will never lack an opportunity of learning it, but this man is the one and only doctor of Greek literature and if he is removed from the scene there may afterwards be found no one from whom you could learn." Convinced by this reasoning I surrendered myself to Chrysoloras with such a great ardor for learning that what I had learned when awake during the day I turned over in my mind again when asleep at night.

Leonardo Aretino, *Rerum suo tempore gestarum commentarius,* in Muratori, *Raccoltà degli storici italiani,* XIX, part iii (Città di Castello, 1914), 420, 431–32, trans. M. P. Gilmore.

C. Vasari

1. THE DECLINE AND RESTORATION OF THE ARTS

But as fortune, when she has raised either persons or things to the summit of her wheel, very frequently casts them to the lowest point, whether in repentance or for her sport, so it chanced that, after these things, the barbarous nations of the world arose, in divers places, in rebellion against the Romans; whence there ensued, in no long time, not only the decline of that great empire, but the utter ruin of the whole, and more especially of Rome herself, when all the best artists, sculptors, painters, and architects, were in like manner totally ruined, being submerged and buried, together with the arts themselves, beneath the miserable slaughters and ruins of that much renowned city.

...But infinitely more ruinous than all other enemies to the arts...was the fervent zeal of the new Christian religion which, after long and sanguinary combats, had finally overcome and annihilated the ancient creeds of the pagan world, by the frequency of miracles exhibited, and by the earnest sincerity of the means adopted; and ardently devoted, with all diligence, to the extirpation of error, nay, to the removal of even the slightest temptation to heresy, it not only destroyed all the wondrous statues, paintings, sculptures, mosaics, and other ornaments of the false pagan deities, but at the same time extinguished the very memory, in casting down the honours, of numberless excellent ancients, to whom statues and other monuments had been erected, in public places, for their virtues, by the most virtuous times of antiquity. Nay, more than this, to build the churches of the Christian faith, this zeal not only destroyed the most renowned temples of the heathens, but, for the richer ornament of St. Peter's, and in addition to the many spoils previously bestowed on that building, the tomb of Hadrian, now called the castle of St. Angelo, was deprived of its marble columns, to employ them for this church, many other buildings being in like manner despoiled, and which we now see wholly devastated. And although the Christian religion did not effect this from hatred to these works of art, but solely for the purpose of abasing and bringing into contempt the gods of the Gentiles, yet the result of this too ardent zeal did not fail to bring such total ruin over the noble arts, that their very form and existence was lost. Next, and that nothing might be wanting to the completion of these misfortunes, the rage of Totila was aroused against Rome [in the sixth century], and having first destroyed her walls, he devastated her most noble and beautiful edifices, giving the whole city to fire and the sword, after having driven forth all the inhabitants, so that, during eighteen days, no living soul was to be found within the city; paintings, statues, mosaics, and all other embellishments, were so entirely wasted and destroyed by these means, that all were deprived, I do not say of their beauty and majesty only, but of their very form and being. The lower rooms of palaces and other edifices being adorned with pictures, statues, and various ornaments, all these were submerged in the fall of the buildings above them, and thence it is that, in our day, so many admirable works have been recovered: for the immediate successors of those times, believing all to be totally ruined, planted their vines on the site, when these chambers remained buried in the earth; the rooms thus buried were named "grottoes" by the moderns who discovered them, while the paintings found in them were called "grotesque."

...The best works in painting and sculpture, remaining buried under the ruins of Italy, were concealed during the same period, and continued wholly unknown to the rude men reared amidst the more modern usages of art, and by whom no other sculptures or pictures were produced, than such as were executed by the remnant of old Greek artists. They formed images of earth and stone, or painted monstrous figures, of which they traced the rude outline only in colour. These

artists—the best as being the only ones— were conducted into Italy, whither they carried sculpture and painting, as well as mosaic, in such manner as they were themselves acquainted with them; these they taught, in their own coarse and rude style, to the Italians, who practised them, after such fashion, as I have said, and will further relate, down to a certain period. The men of those times, unaccustomed to works of greater perfection than those thus set before their eyes, admired them accordingly, and, barbarous as they were, yet imitated them as the most excellent models. It was only by slow degrees that those who came after, being aided in some places by the subtlety of the air around them, could begin to raise themselves from these depths; when, towards 1250, Heaven, moved to pity by the noble spirits which the Tuscan soil was producing every day, restored them to their primitive condition. It is true that those who lived in the times succeeding the ruin of Rome, had seen remnants of arches, colossi, statues, pillars, storied columns, and other works of art, not wholly destroyed by the fires and other devastations; yet they had not known how to avail themselves of this aid, nor had they derived any benefit from it, until the time specified above. And the minds then awakened, becoming capable of distinguishing the good from the worthless, and abandoning old methods, returned to the imitation of the antique, with all the force of their genius, and all the power of their industry.

...Thus much I have thought it advisable to say respecting the first commencement of sculpture and painting, and may perhaps have spoken at greater length than was here needful; but this I have done, not so much because I was carried on by my love of art, as because I desire to be useful and serviceable to the whole body of artists, for they, having here seen the manner in which art proceeded from small beginnings, until she attained the highest summit, and next how she was precipitated from that exalted position into the deepest debasement; and considering that it is the nature of art, as of human existence, to receive birth, to progress, to become old, and to die, may thus more perfectly comprehend and follow the progress of her second birth to the high perfection which she has once more attained in these our days. I have further thought, that if even it should chance at any time, which may God forbid, that by the neglect of men, the malice of time, or the will of Heaven, which but rarely suffers human things to remain long without change, the arts should once again fall into their former decay, these my labours, both what has been said and what yet remains to be said, should they be found worthy of a more happy fortune, may avail to keep those arts in life, or may at least serve as an incentive to exalted minds to provide them with more efficient aids and support, so that, by my own good intentions, and the help of such friends, the arts may abound in those facilities, of which, if it be permitted to speak the truth freely, they have ever been destitute even to this day.

Giorgio Vasari, *Lives of the Most Eminent Painters, Sculptors, and Architects,* trans. Margaret E. Foster (London: G. Bell & Sons, Ltd., 1876), I, 20–23, 30–31, 32–33.

2. THE ACHIEVEMENT OF GIOTTO

The gratitude which the masters in painting owe to Nature—who is ever the truest model of him who, possessing the power to select the brightest parts from her best and loveliest features, employs himself unweariedly in the reproduction of these beauties—this gratitude, I say, is due, in my judgment, to the Florentine painter, Giotto, seeing that he alone—although born amidst incapable artists, and at a time when all good methods in art had long been entombed beneath the ruins of war—yet, by the favour of Heaven, he, I say, alone succeeded in resuscitating art, and restoring her to a path that may be called the true one. And it was in truth a great marvel, that from so rude and inapt an age, Giotto should have had strength to elicit so much, that the art of design, of which the men of those days had little, if any, knowledge, was, by his means, effectually recalled into life.

Ibid., pp. 93–94.

D. Erasmus

It is no part of my nature, most learned Wolfgang, to be excessively fond of life; whether it is, that I have, to my own mind, lived nearly long enough, having entered my fifty-first year, or that I see nothing in this life so splendid or delightful, that it should be desired by one who is convinced by the Christian faith, that a happier life awaits those who in this world earnestly attach themselves to piety. But at the present moment I could almost wish to be young again, for no other reason but this, that I anticipate the near approach of a golden age; so clearly do we see the minds of princes, as if changed by inspiration, devoting all their energies to the pursuit of peace. The chief movers in this matter are Pope Leo, and Francis, King of France.

There is nothing this king does not do or does not suffer, in his desire to avert war and consolidate peace; submitting, of his own accord, to conditions which might be deemed unfair, if he preferred to have regard to his own greatness and dignity, rather than to the general advantage of the world; and exhibiting in this, as in everything else, a magnanimous and truly royal character. Therefore, when I see that the highest sovereigns of Europe, Francis of France, Charles the Catholic King, Henry of England and the Emperor Maximilian have set all their warlike preparations aside, and established peace upon solid, and as I trust adamantine foundations, I am led to a confident hope, that not only morality and Christian piety, but also a genuine and purer literature may come to renewed life or greater splendour; especially as this object is pursued with equal zeal in various regions of the world, —at Rome by Pope Leo, in Spain by the Cardinal of Toledo, in England by Henry, eighth of the name, himself not unskilled in Letters, and among ourselves by our young king Charles. In France King Francis, who seems as if he were born for this object, invites and entices from all countries men that excel in merit or in learning. Among the Germans the same object is pursued by many of their excellent princes and bishops, and especially by Maximilian Caesar, whose old age, weary of so many wars, has determined to seek rest in the employments of peace, a resolution more becoming to his own years, while it is fortunate for the Christian world. To the piety of these princes it is due, that we see everywhere, as if upon a given signal, men of genius are arising and conspiring together to restore the best literature.

Polite letters, which were almost extinct, are now cultivated and embraced by Scots, by Danes and by Irishmen. Medicine has a host of champions; at Rome Nicolas of Leonice; at Venice Ambrosius Leo of Nola, in France William Cop, and John Ruelle, and in England Thomas Linacre. The Imperial Law is restored at Paris by William Budé, in Germany by Udalric Zasy; and Mathematics at Basel by Henry of Glaris. In the theological sphere there was no little to be done, because this science has been hitherto mainly professed by those who are most pertinacious in their abhorrence of the better literature, and are the more successful in defending their own ignorance as they do it under pretext of piety, the unlearned vulgar being induced to believe, that violence is offered to Religion, if any one begins an assault upon their barbarism. For in the presence of an ignorant mob they are always ready to scream and excite their followers to stone-throwing, if they see any risk of not being thought omniscient. But even here I am confident of success, if the knowledge of the three languages continues to be received in schools, as it has now begun. For the most learned and least churlish men of the profession do in some measure assist and favour the new system; and in this matter we are especially indebted to the vigorous exertions of James Lefèvre of Etaples, whom you resemble not only in name, but in a number of accomplishments.

The humblest part of the work has naturally fallen to my lot. Whether my contribution has been worth anything, I cannot say; at any rate those who object to the world regaining its senses, are as angry with me, as if my small industry had had some influence, although the work was not undertaken by me with any confidence that I could myself teach anything magnificent; but I wanted to construct a road for other persons of higher aims, so that they might be less impeded by pools and stumbling-blocks in carrying home those fair and glorious treasures.

The Epistles of Erasmus from his earliest letters to his fifty-first year Arranged in Order of Time, trans. Francis Morgan Nichols (London: Longmans, Green & Company, Ltd., 1904), II, 505–8.

E. Rabelais: *Gargantua's Letter to Pantagruel*

Now it is that the minds of men are qualified with all manner of discipline, and the old sciences revived which for many ages were extinct. Now it is that the learned languages are to their pristine purity restored, viz., Greek, without which a man may be ashamed to account himself a scholar, Hebrew, Arabic, Chaldaean, and Latin. Printing likewise is now in use, so elegant and so correct that better cannot be imagined, although it was found out but in my time by divine inspiration, as by a diabolical suggestion on the other side was the invention of ordnance. All the world is full of knowing men, of most learned schoolmasters, and vast libraries; and it appears to me as a truth, that neither in Plato's time, nor Cicero's, nor Papinian's, there was ever such convenience for studying as we see at this day there is. Nor must any adventurer henceforward come in public, or present himself in company, that hath not been pretty well polished in the shop of Minerva. I see robbers, hangmen, freebooters, tapsters, ostlers, and such like, of the very rubbish of the people, more learned now than the doctors and preachers were in my time.

What shall I say? The very women and children have aspired to this praise and celestial manner of good learning. Yet so it is that, in the age I am now of, I have been constrained to learn the Greek tongue—which I contemned not like Cato, but had not the leisure in my younger years to attend the study of it—and take much delight in the reading of Plutarch's Morals, the pleasant Dialogues of Plato, the Monuments of Pausanias, and the Antiquities of Athenaeus, in waiting on the hour wherein God my Creator shall call me and command me to depart from this earth and transitory pilgrimage. Wherefore, my son, I admonish thee to employ thy youth to profit as well as thou canst, both in thy studies and in virtue. Thou art at Paris, where the laudable examples of many brave men may stir up thy mind to gallant actions, and hast likewise for thy tutor and pedagogue the learned Epistemon, who by his lively and vocal documents may instruct thee in the arts and sciences.

I intend, and will have it so, that thou learn the languages perfectly; first of all the Greek, as Quintilian will have it; secondly, the Latin; and then the Hebrew, for the Holy Scripture's sake; and then the Chaldee and Arabic likewise, and that thou frame thy style in Greek in imitation of Plato, and for the Latin after Cicero. Let there be no history which thou shalt not have ready in thy memory; unto the prosecuting of which design, books of cosmography will be very conducible and help thee much. Of the liberal arts of geometry, arithmetic, and music, I gave thee some taste when thou wert yet little, and not above five or six years old. Proceed further in them, and learn the remainder if thou canst. As for astronomy, study all the rules thereof. Let pass, nevertheless, the divining and judicial astrology, and the art of Lullius, as being nothing else but plain abuses and vanities. As for the civil law, of that I would have thee to know the texts by heart, and then to confer them with philosophy.

Now, in matter of the knowledge of the works of nature, I would have thee to study that exactly, and that so there be no sea, river, nor fountain, of which thou dost not know the fishes; all the fowls of the air; all the several kinds of shrubs and trees, whether in forests or orchards; all the sorts of herbs and flowers that grow upon the ground; all the various metals that are hid within the bowels of the earth; together with all the diversity of precious stones that are to be seen in the orient and south parts of the world. Let nothing of all these be hidden from thee. Then fail not most carefully to peruse the books of the Greek, Arabian, and Latin physicians, not despising the Talmudists and Cabalists; and by frequent anatomies get thee the perfect knowledge of the other world, called the microcosm, which is man. And at some hours of the day apply thy mind to the study of the Holy Scriptures; first in Greek, the New Testament, which is the Epistles of the Apostles; and then the Old Testament in Hebrew. In brief, let me see thee an abyss and bottomless pit of knowledge; for from henceforward, as thou growest great and becomest a man, thou must part from this tranquillity and rest of study, thou must learn chivalry, warfare, and the exercises of the field, the better thereby to defend my house and our friends, and to succour and protect them at all their needs against the invasion and assaults of evildoers.

François Rabelais, *Five Books of the Lives, Heroic Deeds and Sayings of Gargantua and his Son Pantagruel,* trans. Thomas Urquhart and Peter Antony Motteux (London: Lawrence and Bullen, Ltd., 1892), I, 191–93.

F. Dolet

...But I wish to congratulate the state of literature in our times which is so happily and so remarkably flourishing for the study of literature today is everywhere fostered by such great efforts that nothing is lacking to attain the glory of antiquity except the ancient liberty of their men of genius and their opportunity to pursue the arts with general approbation.... A hundred years ago the struggle with barbarism and want of eloquence was continuous and bitter and the victory often in doubt because of the great strength and power of the barbarians, yet the ranks of virtue finally triumphed. The first to make a breach in the defences of the barbarians was Lorenzo Valla, aided by a group of his contemporaries. But this first attack was made by the light-armed troops and it was a matter of distant conflict rather than hand-to-hand fighting. Although their ranks had been opened and attacks had broken through, yet the power of the barbarians had not been sufficiently disturbed. In the end the efforts of Lorenzo Valla and his companions against barbarism which had been almost frustrated by the leaders of the barbarian horde were sustained by Angelo Poliziano, Ermolao Barbaro, Pico della Mirandola, Volaterra, Caelius Rhodiginus, Sabellicus, Critinus, Filelfo, Marsilio Ficino, and that whole generation of illustrious men who, combining their forces and recouping their losses sent against the barbarians those whom we have just listed. These men were sufficiently well-instructed and strongly motivated to defeat barbarism. Thus the shafts of good literature descended on the remaining ranks of the barbarians first from Italy, then from Germany, Britain, Spain and France. The crested helmets of the enemy were cast down, their hands were bound and they were finally led prisoners into captivity.... Now all the cities of Europe are freed from this horrid monster. Litera-

ture is everywhere cherished as highly as it has ever been, the study of all the arts is flourishing. By their regard for literature men are brought back to the study so long neglected of the good and the true. Now men can learn to know themselves and now those who have been heretofore in darkness and wretchedly blind to all things stand in a universal light. Now they seem truly to differ from the beasts by reason of their minds which have been so diligently cultivated by the arts and by reason of the eloquence of their speech which has been so accurately developed. Have I not reason therefore to congratulate the study of letters which has both recovered its pristine glory and blessed the life of man with so many good things (which is its true mission)? If we could only extinguish the envy which certain men educated barbarously and without discipline still bear towards literature and the educated, what then would be lacking to the happiness of this age? But at last the authority of such men begins to decline and a new generation is growing up well and properly instructed in the dignity of letters. This generation will cast out the enemies of literature from their positions of importance and it will enter upon public office and be admitted to the councils of kings; it will undertake the management of affairs and administer all things wisely. Among all those who receive the benefit of its improved status, literature will warn against those things which are to be avoided and will generate a love of virtue, ordering that those who are studious and observant of virtue, justice and equity be everywhere received by kings, indeed that they be regarded and retained as kings themselves, further, that flatterers, sycophants, panderers to pleasure, with whom the halls of kings abound, be avoided like poison and banished. What more would would Plato himself then ask for the felicity of his Republic?

Etienne Dolet, *Commentaria Linguae Latinae,* I (Lyons, 1536), art. "litterae," trans. M. P. Gilmore.

G. LeRoy on the Idea of Progress

1. THE INNOVATIONS OF THE RENAISSANCE

...During the last hundred years not only have things come to light which were previously covered with the darkness of ignorance but also many other things have become known which were entirely unknown to the ancients: new seas, new lands, innovations in the ways of men, habits, laws and customs, new herbs... trees...minerals, new inventions have been found, like those of printing, artillery and the use of the compass and sextant for navigation...ancient languages have been restored....When we consider all this we ought to endure more calmly the calamities which have come and still come upon this age....Some people think that men are progressively diminishing and that human affairs are always going from bad to worse. If this had been so during the long time that the world has lasted we should all have been completely annihilated and there would no longer be anything of value among us.

LeRoy, *Considérations sur l'histoire universelle* (Paris, 1567), translated from the selection quoted in G. Atkinson, *Les Nouveaux horizons de la Renaissance française* (Geneva: Librairie, 1935), pp. 404–5.

2. THE BASIS OF COMPARISON

Having discussed briefly the excellence of this age we shall now compare it with the most illustrious of the preceding periods in the matters of arms, artillery, military leaders, armies, battles, sieges, empires and other states, travels by land and by sea, discoveries of unknown lands, wealth, manners and learning; to determine in what respect this age is superior or inferior or equal.... For five hundred years the Venetians and Genoese have been masters of the Mediterranean and they have fought bitterly one against the other to determine with whom this mastery should remain. The Venetians in the end had the best of it and are still very powerful there. In the Ocean the Portuguese and Castilians by their skill, science and sureness of navigation hold the first place in this field, having surpassed the Tyrians, Egyptians, Phoenicians, Rhodians, Romans, Carthaginians, and people of Marseilles and Brittany and all others who have ever attempted long voyages or the discovery of previously unknown lands, since they surrounded the whole earth by their navigation. And this was a thing the ancients never did nor knew how to do nor dared to undertake.

LeRoy, *De la Vicissitude ou variété des choses en l'univers*, selections with an introduction by Blanchard W. Bates (Princeton: Princeton University Press, 1944), p. 35.

III. The Problem of Understanding Machiavelli

Few reputations in the history of literature have had as lively and controversial a history as that of Machiavelli. On the one hand there is the scheming villain of the Elizabethans, the figure who symbolizes the wickedness and corruption of Italy under the Borgias forever associated in the popular mind with a society in which men rid themselves of their enemies by such means as the poisoned ring or the stab in the back. On the other hand, there is the patriot who gave years of service to the Florentine signory and admired the institutions of republican Rome. Scholars have debated and still debate the intentions of Machiavelli in his two major works, *The Prince* and the *Discourses on the First Decade of Livy*, and they have tried also to separate Machiavelli from Machiavellianism.

The first selection included here is Machiavelli's own statement of what he is trying to do, taken from the opening of the *Discourses*. Here speaks the man who proposes to use the remote history of republican Rome as a source of generalizations which will not only enable men to increase their understanding but also to improve their present situation. Granting that Machiavelli was a retrospective sociologist, the question may be asked whether history or sociology came first, that is, whether Machiavelli evolved a political program and then turned to history to find evidence in support of it, or on the contrary went to history first to see what "lessons" it could teach. This passage contains one of his most important statements on this question.

Turning from the problems of method to those of the content of his political program, one of the most debated issues has been Machiavelli's relation to nationalism. The Italian Risorgimento made him one of its heroes and saluted him as a prophet of the unification of Italy. On the other hand it has been maintained that his program was really founded on the city-state like Florence and its expansion, that he had no real scheme for bringing the various powers of Italy into union, and that his nationalistic appeals are no more than the reiteration of an already old tradition descending from Dante and Petrarch. The famous last chapter of *The Prince*, which is Machiavelli's most eloquent appeal for the liberation of all Italy, is given below.

What is the relationship between *The Prince* and the *Discourses*? Is there a fundamental inconsistency between the two books or can their differences be explained by the fact that *The Prince* was written in a special set of circumstances for a particular political purpose, whereas the *Discourses* reflect Machiavelli's ideal? Was he really in favor of a kind of dictator, or did he believe that the will of the community should be recognized? There is no sound method of attempting to answer these questions short of a thorough study of all of Machiavelli's writings, but some acquaintance with the nature of the real or apparent conflicts which have produced problems of interpretation may be gained from the two chapters given below. The first is from the *Discourses* and deals with the religion of the Romans; the second is from *The Prince* on whether princes should keep faith.

Finally two estimates by modern commentators who differ widely in their judgment on Machiavelli's morality are included in this section.

A. Machiavelli's Methods and Aims

Although the envious nature of men, so prompt to blame and so slow to praise, makes the discovery and introduction of any new principles and systems as dangerous almost as the exploration of unknown seas and continents, yet, animated by that desire which impels me to do what may prove for the common benefit of all, I have resolved to open a new route, which has not yet been followed by anyone, and may prove difficult and troublesome, but may also bring me some reward in the approbation of those who will kindly appreciate my efforts.

And if my poor talents, my little experience of the present and insufficient study of the past, should make the result of my labors defective and of little utility, I shall at least have shown the way to others, who will carry out my views with greater ability, eloquence, and judgment, so that if I do not merit praise, I ought at least not to incur censure.

When we consider the general respect for antiquity, and how often—to say nothing of other examples—a great price is paid for some fragments of an antique statue, which we are anxious to possess to ornament our houses with, or to give to artists who strive to imitate them in their own works; and when we see, on the other hand, the wonderful examples which the history of ancient kingdoms and republics presents to us, the prodigies of virtue and of wisdom displayed by the kings, captains, citizens, and legislators who have sacrificed themselves for their country,—when we see these, I say, more admired than imitated, or so much neglected that not the least trace of this ancient virtue remains, we cannot but be at the same time as much surprised as afflicted. The more so as in the differences which arise between citizens, or in the maladies to which they are subjected, we see these same people have recourse to the judgments and the remedies prescribed by the ancients. The civil laws are in fact nothing but decisions given by their jurisconsults, and which, reduced to a system, direct our modern jurists in their decisions. And what is the science of medicine, but the experience of ancient physicians, which their successors have taken for their guide? And yet to found a republic, maintain states, to govern a kingdom, organize an army, conduct a war, dispense justice, and extend empires, you will find neither prince, nor republic, nor captain, nor citizen, who has recourse to the examples of antiquity! This neglect, I am persuaded, is due less to the weakness to which the vices of our education have reduced the world, than to the evils caused by the proud indolence which prevails in most of the Christian states, and to the lack of real knowledge of history, the true sense of which is not known, or the spirit of which they do not comprehend. Thus the majority of those who read it take pleasure only in the variety of the events which history relates, without ever thinking of imitating the noble actions, deeming that not only difficult, but impossible; as though heaven, the sun, the elements, and men had changed the order of their motions and power, and were different from what they were in ancient times.

Wishing, therefore, so far as in me lies, to draw mankind from this error, I have thought it proper to write upon those books of Titus Livius that have come to us entire despite the malice of time; touching upon all those matters which, after a comparison between the ancient and modern events, may seem to me necessary to facilitate their proper understanding. In this way those who read my remarks may derive those advantages which should be the aim of all study of history; and although the undertaking is difficult, yet, aided by those who have encouraged me in this attempt, I hope to carry it sufficiently far, so that but little may remain for others to carry it to its destined end.

Niccolò Machiavelli, *The Prince and The Discourses* (New York: Modern Library, Inc., 1940), pp. 103–5.

B. Machiavelli and Nationalism:

[Exhortation to Liberate Italy from the Barbarians: to the Medici]

Having now considered all the things we have spoken of, and thought within myself whether at present the time was not propitious in Italy for a new prince, and if there was not a state of things which offered an opportunity to a prudent and capable man to introduce a new system that would do honour to himself and good to the mass of the people, it seems to me that so many things concur to favour a new ruler that I do not know of any time more fitting for such an enterprise. And if, as I said, it was necessary in order that the power of Moses should be displayed that the people of Israel should be slaves in Egypt, and to give scope for the greatness and courage of Cyrus that the Persians should be oppressed by the Medes, and to illustrate the pre-eminence of Theseus that the Athenians should be dispersed, so at the present time, in order that the might of an Italian genius might be recognized, it was necessary that Italy should be reduced to her present condition, and that she should be more enslaved than the Hebrews, more oppressed than the Persians, and more scattered than the Athenians; without a head, without order, beaten, despoiled, lacerated, and overrun, and that she should have suffered ruin of every kind.

And although before now a gleam of hope has appeared which gave hope that some individual might be appointed by God for her redemption, yet at the highest summit of his career he was thrown aside by fortune, so that now, almost lifeless, she awaits one who may heal her wounds and put a stop to the pillaging of Lombardy, to the rapacity and extortion in the Kingdom of Naples and in Tuscany, and cure her of those sores which have long been festering. Behold how she prays God to send some one to redeem her from this barbarous cruelty and insolence. Behold her ready and willing to follow any standard if only there be some one to raise it. There is nothing now she can hope for but that your illustrious house may place itself at the head of this redemption, being by its power and fortune so exalted, and being favoured by God and the Church, of which it is now the ruler. Nor will this be very difficult, if you call to mind the actions and lives of the men I have named. And although those men were rare and marvellous, they were none the less men, and each of them had less opportunity than the present, for their enterprise was not juster than this, nor easier, nor was God more their friend than He is yours. Here is a just cause; *"iustum enim est bellum quibus necessarium, et pia arma ubi nulla nisi in armis spes est."*[1] Here is the greatest willingness, nor can there be great difficulty where there is great willingness, provided that the measures are adopted of those whom I have set before you as examples. Besides this, unexampled wonders have been seen here performed by God, the sea has been opened, a cloud has shown you the road, the rock has given forth water, manna has rained, and everything has contributed to your greatness, the remainder must be done by you. God will not do everything, in order not to deprive us of free will and the portion of the glory that falls to our lot.

It is no marvel that none of the before-mentioned Italians have done that which it is to be hoped your illustrious house may do; and if in so many revolutions in Italy and so many warlike operations, it always seems as if military capacity were extinct, this is because the ancient methods were not good, and no one has arisen who knew how to discover new ones. Nothing does so much honour to a newly-risen man than the new laws and measures which he introduces. These things, when they are well based and have greatness in them,

render him revered and admired, and there is not lacking scope in Italy for the introduction of every kind of new organization. Here there is great virtue in the members, if it were not wanting in the heads. Look how in duels and in contests of a few the Italians are superior in strength, dexterity, and intelligence. But when it comes to armies they make a poor show; which proceeds entirely from the weakness of the leaders, for those that know are not obeyed, and every one thinks that he knows, there being hitherto nobody who has raised himself so high both by valour and fortune as to make the others yield. Hence it comes about that for so long a time, in all the wars waged during the last twenty years, whenever there has been an entirely Italian army it has always been a failure, as witness first Taro, then Alexandria, Capua, Genoa, Vailà, Bologna, and Mestri.

If your illustrious house, therefore, wishes to follow those great men who redeemed their countries, it is before all things necessary, as the true foundation of every undertaking, to provide yourself with your own forces, for you cannot have more faithful, or truer and better soldiers. And although each one of them may be good, they will united become even better when they see themselves commanded by their prince, and honoured and favoured by him. It is therefore necessary to prepare such forces in order to be able with Italian prowess to defend the country from foreigners. And although both the Swiss and Spanish infantry are deemed terrible, nonetheless they each have their defects, so that a third method of array might not only oppose them, but be confident of overcoming them. For the Spaniards cannot sustain the attack of cavalry, and the Swiss have to fear infantry which meets them with resolution equal to their own. From which it has resulted, as will be seen by experience, that the Spaniards cannot sustain the attack of French cavalry, and the Swiss are overthrown by Spanish

---

[1] "War is just for those to whom it is necessary, and arms are pious where there is no hope except in arms."

infantry. And although a complete example of the latter has not been seen, yet an instance was furnished in the battle of Ravenna, where the Spanish infantry attacked the German battalions, which are organized in the same way as the Swiss. The Spaniards, through their bodily agility and aided by their bucklers, had entered between and under their pikes and were in a position to attack them safely without the Germans being able to defend themselves; and if the cavalry had not charged them they would have utterly destroyed them. Knowing therefore the defects of both these kinds of infantry, a third kind can be created which can resist cavalry and need not fear infantry, and this will be done by the choice of arms and a new organization. And these are the things which, when newly introduced, give reputation and grandeur to a new prince.

This opportunity must not, therefore, be allowed to pass, so that Italy may at length find her liberator. I cannot express the love with which he would be received in all those provinces which have suffered under these foreign invasions, with what thirst for vengeance, with what steadfast faith, with what love, with what grateful tears. What doors would be closed against him? What people would refuse him obedience? What envy could oppose him? What Italian would withhold allegiance? This barbarous domination stinks in the nostrils of every one. May your illustrious house therefore assume this task with that courage and those hopes which are inspired by a just cause, so that under its banner our fatherland may be raised up, and under its auspices be verified that saying of Petrarch:

Valour against fell wrath
Will take up arms; and be the combat
    quickly sped!
For, sure, the ancient worth,
That in Italians stirs the heart, is not
    yet dead.

Ibid., pp. 94–98. Reprinted by permission of Oxford University Press, London.

C. The "Strong Man" and the Community

1. OF THE RELIGION OF THE ROMANS

Although the founder of Rome was Romulus, to whom like a daughter, she owed her birth and her education, yet the gods did not judge the laws of this prince sufficient for so great an empire, and therefore inspired the Roman Senate to elect Numa Pompilius as his successor, so that he might regulate all those things that had been omitted by Romulus. Numa, finding a very savage people, and wishing to reduce them to civil obedience by the arts of peace, had recourse to religion as the most necessary and assured support of any civil society; and he established it upon such foundations that for many centuries there was nowhere more fear of the gods than in that republic, which greatly facilitated all the enterprises which the Senate or its great men attempted. Whoever will examine the actions of the people of Rome as a body, or of many individual Romans, will see that these citizens feared much more to break an oath than the laws; like men who esteem the power of the gods more than that of men. This was particularly manifested in the conduct of Scipio and Manlius Torquatus; for after the defeat which Hannibal had inflicted upon the Romans at Cannae many citizens had assembled together, and, frightened and trembling, agreed to leave Italy and fly to Sicily. When Scipio heard of this, he went to meet them, and with his drawn sword in hand he forced them to swear not to abandon their country. Lucius Manlius, father of Titus Manlius, who was afterwards called Torquatus, had been accused by Marcus Pomponius, one of the Tribunes of the people. Before the day of judgment Titus went to Marcus and threatened to kill him if he did not promise to withdraw the charges against his father; he compelled him to take an oath, and Marcus, although having sworn under the pressure of fear, withdrew the accusation against Lucius, And thus these citizens, whom neither the love of country nor the laws could have kept in Italy, were retained there by an oath that had been forced upon them by compulsion; and the Tribune Pomponius disregarded the hatred which he bore to the father, as well as the insult offered him by the son, for the sake of complying with his oath and preserving his honour; which can be ascribed to nothing else than the religious principles which Numa had instilled into the Romans. And whoever reads Roman history attentively will see in how great a degree religion served in the command of the armies, in uniting the people and keeping them well conducted, and in covering the wicked with shame. So that if the question were discussed whether Rome was more indebted to Romulus or to Numa, I believe that the highest merit would be conceded to Numa; for where religion exists it is easy to introduce armies and discipline, but where there are armies and no religion it is difficult to introduce the latter. And although we have seen that Romulus could organize the Senate and establish other civil and military institutions without the aid of divine authority, yet it was very necessary for Numa, who feigned that he held converse with a nymph, who dictated to him all that he wished to persuade the people to; and the reason for all this was that Numa mistrusted his own authority, lest it should prove insufficient to enable him to introduce new and unaccustomed ordinances in Rome. In truth, there never was any remarkable lawgiver amongst any people who did not resort to divine authority, as otherwise his laws would not have been accepted by the people; for there are many good laws, the importance of which is known to the sagacious lawgiver, but the reasons for which are not sufficiently evident to enable him to persuade others to submit to them; and therefore do wise men, for the purpose of removing this difficulty, resort to divine authority. Thus did Lycurgus and Solon, and many others who aimed at the same thing.

The Roman people, then, admiring the wisdom and goodness of Numa, yielded in all things to his advice. It is true that those were very religious times, and the people with whom Numa had to deal were very untutored and superstitious, which made it easy for him to carry out his designs, being able to impress upon them any new form. And doubtless, if anyone wanted to establish a republic at the present time, he would find it much easier with the simple mountaineers, who are almost without any civilization, than with such as are accustomed to live in cities, where civilization is already corrupt; as a sculptor finds it easier to make a fine statue out of a crude block of marble than out of a statue badly begun by another. Considering then all these things, I conclude that the religion introduced by Numa into Rome was one of the chief causes of the prosperity of that city; for this religion gave rise to good laws, and good laws bring good fortune, and from good fortune results happy success in all enterprises. And as the observance of divine institutions is the cause of the greatness of republics, so the disregard of them produces their ruin; for where the fear of God is wanting, there the country will come to ruin, unless it be sustained by the fear of the prince, which may temporarily supply the want of religion. But as the lives of princes are short, the kingdom will of necessity perish as the prince fails in virtue. Whence it comes that kingdoms which depend entirely upon the virtue of one man endure but for a brief time, for his virtue passes away with his life, and it rarely happens that it is renewed in his successor, as Dante so wisely says:—

" 'T is seldom human wisdom descends
    from sire to son;
Such is the will of Him who gave it,
That at his hands alone we may implore the boon."

The welfare, then, of a republic or a kingdom does not consist in having a prince who governs it wisely during his lifetime, but in having one who will give it such laws that it will maintain itself even after his death. And although untutored and ignorant men are more easily persuaded to adopt new laws or new opinions, yet that does not make it impossible to persuade civilized men who claim to be enlightened. The people of Florence are far from considering themselves ignorant and benighted, and yet Brother Girolamo Savonarola succeeded in persuading them that he held converse with God. I will not pretend to judge whether it was true or not, for we must speak with all respect of so great a man; but I may well say that an immense number believed it, without having seen any extraordinary manifestations that should have made them believe it; but it was the purity of his life, the doctrines he preached, and the subjects he selected for his discourses, that sufficed to make the people have faith in him. Let no one, then, fear not to be able to accomplish what others have done, for all men (as we have said in our Preface) are born and live and die in the same way, and therefore resemble each other.

Ibid., pp. 145–49.

2. IN WHAT WAY PRINCES MUST KEEP FAITH

How laudable it is for a prince to keep good faith and live with integrity, and not with astuteness, every one knows. Still the experience of our times shows those princes to have done great things who have had little regard for good faith, and have been able by astuteness to confuse men's brains, and who have ultimately overcome those who have made loyalty their foundation.

You must know, then, that there are two methods of fighting, the one by law, the other by force: the first method is that of men, the second of beasts; but as the first method is often insufficient, one must have recourse to the second. It is therefore necessary for a prince to know well how to use both the beast and the man. This was covertly taught to rulers by ancient writers, who relate how Achilles and many others of those ancient princes were given to Chiron the centaur to be brought up and educated under his discipline. The parable of this semi-animal, semi-human teacher is meant to indicate that a prince must know how to use both natures, and that the one without the other is not durable.

A prince being thus obliged to know well how to act as a beast must imitate the fox and the lion, for the lion cannot protect himself from traps, and the fox cannot defend himself from wolves. One must therefore be a fox to recognize traps, and a lion to frighten wolves. Those that wish to be only lions do not understand this. Therefore, a prudent ruler ought not to keep faith when by so doing it would be against his interest, and when the reasons which made him bind himself no longer exist. If men were all good this precept would not be a good one; but as they are bad, and would not observe their faith with you, so you are not bound to keep faith with them. Nor have legitimate grounds ever failed a prince who wished to show colourable excuse for the nonfulfillment of his promise. Of this one could furnish an infinite number of modern examples, and show how many times peace has been broken, and how many promises rendered worthless, by the faithlessness of princes, and those that have been best able to imitate the fox have succeeded best. But it is necessary to be able to disguise this character well, and to be a great feigner and dissembler; and men are so simple and so ready to obey present necessities, that one who deceives will always find those who allow themselves to be deceived.

I will only mention one modern instance. Alexander VI did nothing else but deceive men, he thought of nothing else, and found the occasion for it; no man was ever more able to give assurances, or affirmed things with stronger oaths, and no man observed them less; however, he always succeeded in his deceptions, as he well knew this aspect of things.

It is not, therefore, necessary for a

prince to have all the above-named qualities, but it is very necessary to seem to have them. I would even be bold to say that to possess them and always to observe them is dangerous, but to appear to possess them is useful. Thus it is well to seem merciful, faithful, humane, sincere, religious, and also to be so; but you must have the mind so disposed that when it is needful to be otherwise you may be able to change to the opposite qualities. And it must be understood that a prince, and especially a new prince, cannot observe all those things which are considered good in men, being often obliged, in order to maintain the state, to act against faith, against charity, against humanity, and against religion. And, therefore, he must have a mind disposed to adapt itself according to the wind, and as the variations of fortune dictate, and, as I said before, not deviate from what is good, if possible, but be able to do evil if constrained.

A prince must take great care that nothing goes out of his mouth which is not full of the above-named five qualities, and, to see and hear him, he should seem to be all mercy, faith, integrity, humanity, and religion. And nothing is more necessary than to seem to have this last quality, for men in general judge more by the eyes than by the hands, for everyone can see, but very few have to feel. Everybody sees what you appear to be, few feel what you are, and those few will not dare to oppose themselves to the many, who have the majesty of the state to defend them; and in the actions of men, and especially of princes, from which there is no appeal, the end justifies the means. Let a prince therefore aim at conquering and maintaining the state, and the means will always be judged honourable and praised by every one, for the vulgar is always taken by appearances and the issue of the event; and the world consists only of the vulgar, and the few who are not vulgar are isolated when the many have a rallying point in the prince. A certain prince of the present time, whom it is well not to name, never does anything but preach peace and good faith, but he is really a great enemy to both, and either of them, had he observed them, would have lost him state or reputation on many occasions.

Ibid., pp. 63–66. Reprinted by permission of Oxford University Press, London.

D. Two Modern Views of Machiavelli

1. DEFENSE OF MACHIAVELLI'S INTENTION

There is, in one of the startling chapters of *The Prince,* an opening sentence which has seemed to many the confirmation of Machiavelli's cynicism. It is on the subject of faith in princes. The first half pays lip-service to the virtue of keeping one's word, and then his terrible *nevertheless* steps in to point to the reality: "Still the experience of our times shows those princes to have done great things who have had little regard for good faith, and have been able by astuteness to confuse men's brains and who have ultimately overcome those who have made loyalty their foundation." This is, indeed, one of those texts on which it is customary to base the attack not only on Machiavelli, but on the Italian Renascence as well: so pagan, and ergo, so wicked, how could it reckon in terms of keeping faith? ... And those whose business it is to blacken the Renascence have been quick to follow up the issue. So neat, so symmetrical a position: the Italians were corrupt (it was Machiavelli's own word for them) because they had abandoned the Age of Faith, so that their punishment came at the hands of the incorrupt; at the hands of those who, presumably, still lived in the Age of Faith, and of faith. Does not Alexander VI come later in the chapter as a concrete example of faithlessness? All that is most convenient for those who like the ready-made in pictures, or who have the cause of medievalism at heart. But it is precisely because of this that the background of the *Legations* is essential to any comprehension of the ideas current in Machiavelli's mind at the time he wrote *The Prince*. When we know that background is it not clear that it is Florence who built on loyalty, and that it is Florence who has gone down before the faithlessness of Charles VIII, Louis XII, Ferdinand of Aragon, and Maximilian, to keep the list short? This chapter which has given so much offense to the moralists north of the Alps has an opposite function to the one always lent to it. It is not Machiavelli codifying Italian corruption for the use of would-be despots. Once more, there would be little use his codifying formulas that had led to defeat as a recipe for securing success.... The praise that he gives to the virtue of keeping faith is quite sincere; but the bitterness arises from the fact that the policy of keeping faith has proved inadequate.

J. H. Whitfield, *Machiavelli* (Oxford: Basil Blackwell & Mott, Ltd., 1947), pp. 60–61.

2. MACHIAVELLI'S IMMORALITY

Above all, there is Machiavelli's most curious statement on the subject of morality, a thesis which appears in Chapter XV of *The Prince;* and this contains an assertion which, because it is vague, will cover everything. It is more important in that the author points out that in his case in particular his opinion differs from that of his contemporaries. It is the thesis that in the world a man must behave as other people behave; and that if he allows his conduct to be guided by the thought of what men *ought* to do, this will conduce rather to his ruin than to his advantage or preservation. In itself the statement might be meaningless, and on one construction indeed, might be regarded as innocuous. A man can scarcely be accused of any great immorality if he accepts the standards of his time and consents to live as the world lives. The thesis might prove, however, more pointed and more dangerous if it implied that men should take as their standard of conduct the morality of their day conceived at its worst; and it is important to note in this respect that Machiavelli had a remarkably low view of human nature. He does not recommend us to break a treaty merely when we think that the other party is going to break it; he says that since men are wicked the other party may always be presumed to be about to break it. And his whole attitude is more significant if we note that this is a thesis concerning general conduct; it is not conditioned by any reference to the safety or even the welfare of the state. It would have been expressed in different terms if it had meant that everything is allowable which is intended for the public good. Finally it is based on the simple fact that the wicked have prospered and the loyal have been defeated. We may account for the attitude by historical circumstances, we may befog the question with mystical interpretations, but in Machiavelli the doctrine "live as the world lives" is the ordinary vulgar doctrine that morality does not pay; its only purport is the reduction of the conduct of good men to the standards of that of the worst, and it is difficult to see how an invitation to immorality could have been expressed in other terms or placed on a more comprehensive basis. Just as the tendency of Machiavelli's system was to make men more consistent and scientific in their political cunning, so the effect—the very intention—of his remarks on morality was to clear the path for the more general acceptance of the kind of statecraft that he had to teach.

H. Butterfield, *The Statecraft of Machiavelli* (London: G. Bell & Sons, Ltd., 1940), pp. 110–13.

IV. Erasmus and the Christian Inheritance

The figure of Erasmus of Rotterdam dominated the intellectual world of his time and has ever since been regarded as symbolizing the mighty achievements of Renaissance scholarship. His work is intimately related to both the Reformation and the Counter-Reformation, and many men who began by being his disciples found themselves on opposing sides when the lines of the great sixteenth-century battle were drawn. Yet, if we ask ourselves to what extent Erasmus was a Christian and what kind of Christian, the answers are not altogether simple. No man did more to exalt the noblest of the pagan philosophers (Saint Socrates, pray for us), and no man did more to hold up to ridicule and scorn the abuses and even some of the uses of the Christian Church as he found it. On the other hand, he provided the first Greek Testament, devoted a lifetime to restoring a direct knowledge of the early texts of Christianity, and left eloquent and moving exhortations to the pious life. He has been accused of being in effect a pagan, of being a Lutheran before Luther, and of being a renegade to the Reform which he had helped to make possible. He died in communion with the Roman Church, but although he had been offered a cardinal's hat by Paul III, many of his works were put on the Index by Paul IV. In him we see changes of emphasis and new tensions in the relation between the classic and Christian traditions, and many of the arguments about the religious or "pagan" character of the Renaissance are focused in the attempt to evaluate his convictions.

The first selections included here illustrate the kind of attack Erasmus directed at contemporary religious practices. The first passage is taken from one of the so-called *Colloquies*, dialogues which Erasmus had written originally for an instructional manual in Latin but which he had continued because they served as dramatic vehicles for the expression of his own views. The interlocutors in the *Shipwreck* discuss the behavior of a ship's company and crew under the threat of imminent death, and the contrast between simple trust in God and the elaborate invocation of the saints. The second selection is from the most famous of Erasmus' works, *The Praise of Folly,* and contains Folly's indictment of the theologians. This is followed by an excerpt from the dialogue called *Julius Exclusus* which Erasmus never acknowledged but which he very probably wrote. Here Pope Julius II is represented as excluded from heaven because of the scandalous contrast between his behavior and his pretensions.

The second section presents some characteristic statements of Erasmian piety. The first is from the *Enchiridion,* a manual of Christian practice for the layman written by Erasmus in 1501. The second is the eloquent statement of what Erasmus called the philosophy of Christ contained in one of the prefaces to the edition of the New Testament which he published in 1516.

A. The Erasmian Critique of Church and Theology

1. THE INVOCATION OF SAINTS: ADOLPH AND ANTHONY

ADOL. The Mariners striving in Vain with the Storm, at length the Pilot, all pale as Death comes to us.

ANT. That Paleness presages some great Evil.

ADOL. My Friends, says he, I am no longer Master of my Ship, the Wind has got the better of me; all that we have now to do is to place our Hope in God, and every one to prepare himself for Death.

ANT. This was cold Comfort.

ADOL. But in the first Place, says he, we must lighten the Ship; Necessity requires it, tho' 'tis a hard Portion. It is better to endeavour to save our Lives with the Loss of our Goods, than to perish with them. The Truth persuaded, and a great many Casks of rich Merchandize were thrown over-Board.

ANT. This was casting away, according to the Letter.

ADOL. There was in the Company, a certain *Italian,* that had been upon an Embassy to the King of *Scotland.* He had a whole Cabinet full of Plate, Rings, Cloth, and rich wearing Apparel.

ANT. And he, I warrant ye, was unwilling to come to a Composition with the Sea.

ADOL. No, he would not; he had a Mind either to sink or swim with his beloved Riches.

ANT. What said the Pilot to this?

ADOL. If you and your Trinkets were to drown by yourselves, says he, here's no Body would hinder you; but it is not fit that we should run the Risque of our Lives, for the Sake of your Cabinet: If you won't consent, we'll throw you and your Cabinet into the Sea together.

ANT. Spoken like a Tarpawlin.

ADOL. So the *Italian* submitted, and threw his Goods over-Board, with many a bitter Curse to the Gods both above and below, that he had committed his Life to so barbarous an Element.

ANT. I know the *Italian* Humour.

ADOL. The Winds were nothing the less boisterous for our Presents, but by and by burst our Cordage, and threw down our Sails.

ANT. Lamentable!

ADOL. Then the Pilot comes to us again.

ANT. What, with another Preachment?

ADOL. He gives us a Salute; my Friends, says he, the Time exhorts us that every one of us should recommend himself to God, and prepare for Death. Being ask'd by some that were not ignorant in Sea Affairs, how long he thought the Ship might be kept above Water, he said, he could promise nothing, but that it could not be done above three Hours.

ANT. This was yet a harder Chapter than the former.

ADOL. When we had said this, he orders to cut the Shrouds and the Mast down by the Board, and to throw them, Sails and all, into the Sea.

ANT. Why was this done?

ADOL. Because, the Sail either being gone or torn, it would only be a Burden, but not of Use; all our Hope was in the Helm.

ANT. What did the Passengers do in the mean Time?

ADOL. There you might have seen a wretched Face of Things; the Mariners, they were singing their *Salve Regina*, imploring the Virgin Mother, calling her the Star of the Sea, the Queen of Heaven, the Lady of the World, the Haven of Health, and many other flattering Titles, which the sacred Scriptures never attributed to her.

ANT. What has she to do with the Sea, who, as I believe, never went a Voyage in her Life?

ADOL. In ancient Times, *Venus* took Care of Mariners, because she was believ'd to be born of the Sea, and because she left off to take Care of them, the Virgin Mother was put in her Place, that was a Mother, but not a Virgin.

ANT. You joke.

ADOL. Some were lying along upon the Boards, worshipping the Sea, pouring all they had into it, and flattering it, as if it had been some incensed Prince.

ANT. What did they say?

ADOL. O most merciful Sea! O most generous Sea! O most rich Sea! O most Beautiful Sea, be pacified, save us; and a Deal of such Stuff they sung to the deaf Ocean.

ANT. Ridiculous Superstition! What did the rest do?

ADOL. Some did nothing but spew, and some made Vows. There was an *Englishman* there, that promis'd golden Mountains to our Lady of *Walsingham,* so he did but get ashore alive. Others promis'd a great many Things to the Wood of the Cross, which was in such a Place; others again, to that which was in such a Place; and the same was done by the Virgin *Mary,* which reigns in a great many Places, and they think the Vow is of no Effect, unless the Place be mentioned.

ANT. Ridiculous! As if the Saints did not dwell in Heaven.

ADOL. Some made Promises to become *Carthusians.* There was one who promised he would go a *Pilgrimage* to St. *James* at *Compostella,* bare Foot and bare Head, cloth'd in a Coat of Mail, and begging his Bread all the Way.

ANT. Did no Body make any Mention of St. *Christopher?*

ADOL. Yes, I heard one, and I could

not forbear laughing, who bawling out aloud, lest St. *Christopher* should not hear him, promised him, who is at the Top of a Church at *Paris,* rather a Mountain than a Statue, a wax Taper as big as he was himself: When he had bawl'd out this over and over as loud as he could, an Acquaintance of his jogg'd him on the Elbow, and caution'd him: Have a Care what you promise, for if you should sell all you have in the World, you will not be able to pay for it. He answer'd him softly, lest St. *Christopher* should hear him, you Fool, says he, do you think I mean as I speak, if I once got safe to Shore, I would not give him so much as a tallow Candle.

ANT. O Blockhead! I fancy he was a *Hollander.*

ADOL. No, he was a Zealander.

ANT. I wonder no Body thought of St. *Paul,* who has been at Sea, and having suffered Shipwreck, leapt on Shore. For he being not unacquainted with the Distress, knows how to pity those that are in it.

ADOL. He was not so much as named.

ANT. Were they at their Prayers all the While?

ADOL. Ay, as if it had been for a Wager. One sung his *Hail Queen;* another, *I believe in God.* There were some who had certain particular Prayers not unlike

magical Charms against Dangers.

ANT. How Affliction makes Men religious! In Prosperity we neither think of God nor Saint. But what did you do all this While? Did you not make Vows to some Saints?

ADOL. No, none at all.

ANT. Why so?

ADOL. I make no Bargains with Saints. For what is this but a Bargain in Form? I'll give you, if you do so and so; or I will do so and so, if you do so and so: I'll give you a wax Taper, if I swim out alive; I'll go to *Rome,* if you save me.

ANT. But did you call upon none of the Saints for Help?

ADOL. No, not so much as that neither.

ANT. Why so?

ADOL. Because Heaven is a large Place, and if I should recommend my Safety to any Saint, as suppose, to St. *Peter,* who perhaps would hear soonest, because he stands at the Door; before he can come to God Almighty, or before he could tell him my Condition, I may be lost.

ANT. What did you do then?

ADOL. I e'en went the next Way to God the Father, saying, *Our Father which art in Heaven.* There's none of the Saints hears sooner than he does, or more readily gives what is ask'd for.

The Colloquies of Erasmus, trans. N. Bailey (London, Reeves and Turner, 1878), I, 276–80.

2. THE THEOLOGIANS

Perhaps it were better to pass over the theologians in silence, and not to move such a Lake Camarina, or to handle such an herb, *Anagyris foetida,* as that marvelously supercilious and irascible race. For they may attack me with six hundred arguments, in squadrons, and drive me to make a recantation; which if I refuse, they will straightway proclaim me an heretic. By this thunderbolt they are wont to terrify any toward whom they are ill-disposed. No other people are so loth to acknowledge my favors to them; yet the divines are bound to me by no ordinary obligations. They are happy in their self-

love, and as if they already inhabited the third heaven they look down from a height on all other mortal creatures as on creatures that crawl on the ground, and they come near to pitying them. They are protected by a wall of scholastic definitions, arguments, corollaries, implicit and explicit propositions; they have so many hideaways that they could not be caught even by a net of Vulcan; for they slip out on their distinctions, by which also they cut through all knots as easily as with a double-bitted axe from Tenedos; and they abound with newly invented terms and prodigious vocables. Furthermore, they explain as pleases them the most arcane matters, such as by what method the world was founded and set in order, through what conduits original sin has been passed down along the generations, by what means, in what measure, and how long the perfect Christ was in the Virgin's womb, and how accidents subsist in the Eucharist without their subject.

But those are hackneyed. Here are questions worthy of the great and (as some call them) illuminated theologians, questions to make them prick up their ears—if ever they chance upon them. Whether divine generation took place at a particular time? Whether there are several sonships in Christ? Whether this is a possible proposition: God the Father hates the Son? Whether God could have taken upon Himself the likeness of a woman? Or of a devil? Or of an ass? Of a gourd? Of a piece of flint? Then how would that gourd have preached, performed miracles, or been crucified? Also, what would Peter have consecrated if he had administered the sacrament while Christ's body hung upon the Cross? Also whether at that moment Christ could be said to be a man? And whether after the resurrection it will be forbidden to eat and drink? (Now, while there is time they are providing against hunger and thirst!) These finespun trifles are numberless, with others even more subtle, having to do with instants of time, notions, relations, accidents, quiddities, entities, which no one can perceive with his eyes unless, like Lynceus, he can see in blackest darkness things that are not there.

We must put in also those hard sayings, contradictions indeed, compared to which the Stoic maxims which were called paradoxes seem the merest simplicity. For instance: it is less of a crime to cut the throats of a thousand men than to set a stitch on a poor man's shoe on the Lord's day; it is better to choose that the universe should perish, body, boots, and breeches (as the saying is), than that one should tell a single lie, however inconsequential. The methods our scholastics pursue only render more subtle these subtlest of subtleties; for you will escape from a labyrinth more quickly than from the

tangles of Realists, Nominalists, Thomists, Albertists, Occamists, Scotists,—I have not named all, but the chief ones only. But in all these sects there is so much learning and so much difficulty that I should think the apostles themselves must needs have the help of some other spirit if they were to try disputing on these topics with our new generation of theologues.

Paul could exhibit faith; but when he said, "Faith is the substance of things hoped for, the evidence of things not seen," he did not define it doctorally. The same apostle, though he exemplified charity supremely well, divided and defined it with very little logical skill in his first epistle to the Corinthians, Chapter 13. And no doubt the apostles consecrated the Eucharist devoutly enough; but suppose you had questioned them about the *terminus a quo* and the *terminus ad quem,* or about transubstantiation—how the body is in many places at once, the difference between the body of Christ when in heaven, when on the Cross, when in the sacrament of the Eucharist, about the point when transubstantiation occurs (seeing that the prayer effecting it is a discrete quantity having extension in time)—they would not have answered with the same acuteness, I suggest, with which the sons of Scotus distinguish and define these matters. The apostles knew the mother of Jesus, but who among them has demonstrated philosophically just how she was kept clear from the sin of Adam, as our theologians have done? Peter received the keys, received them from One who did not commit them to an unworthy person, and yet I doubt that he ever understood— for Peter never did attain to subtlety—that a person who did not have knowledge could have the key to knowledge. They went about baptizing everywhere, and yet they never taught what is the formal, the material, the efficient, and the final cause of baptism, nor is mention made by them that it has both a delible character and an indelible one. They worshipped, to be sure, but in spirit, following no other teaching than that of the Gospel, "God is a spirit and they that worship Him must worship

Him in spirit and in truth." It seems never to have been revealed to them that a picture drawn with charcoal on a wall ought to be worshipped with the same worship as Christ himself—at least if it is drawn with two fingers outstretched and the hair unshorn, and has three sets of rays in the nimbus fastened to the back of the head. For who would comprehend these things if he had not consumed all of thirty-six years upon the physics and metaphysics of Aristotle and the Scotists?

Desiderius Erasmus, *The Praise of Folly,* trans. from the Latin, with an essay and commentary, by H. H. Hudson (Princeton: Princeton University Press, 1941), pp. 77–81.

3. JULIUS II EXCLUDED FROM HEAVEN: JULIUS, HIS TUTELARY SPIRIT, AND SAINT PETER

JULIUS. What's the trouble here? Won't the doors open? The lock must have been changed or at least tampered with.

SPIRIT. Perhaps you haven't brought the right key, for this door will never be opened by the same key as you use for your money-box. So why haven't you brought both keys here, for this one that you have is the key of power not of knowledge?

JULIUS. This is the only one I ever had and I see no need of another as long as I have this.

SPIRIT. Nor indeed do I except that in the meantime we are shut out.

JULIUS. I am getting very angry. I will beat down these gates. Hey, someone in there, open this door at once! What is the matter? Will no one come? Why does the porter dally like this? No doubt he's snoring and probably drunk.

SPIRIT. (As always he judges everyone else by himself!)

SAINT PETER. It's a good thing we have adamantine doors here; otherwise this man would have broken in. He must be some giant or satrap, a conqueror of cities. But, O immortal God, what a stench! I will not open the door at once, but by looking out of this little barred window find out what kind of a monster this may be. Who are you and what do you want?

JULIUS. Open as quickly as you can. If you had done your duty, you ought to have come out to meet me with all the pomp due an emperor.

SAINT PETER. Spoken imperiously enough. But first explain to me who you are.

JULIUS. As if you could not see for yourself!

SAINT PETER. See? Indeed I see a strange and hitherto unknown, not to say monstrous, spectacle.

JULIUS. Unless you are wholly blind, you must recognize this key even if you don't know the golden oak. And you see the triple crown and the pallium gleaming with gems and with gold.

SAINT PETER. Indeed I see a key silvered all over although it is only one and very different from those keys which Christ as the true pastor of the Church once gave over to me. And how should I recognize this proud crown? No barbarian tyrant ever wore such a one still less anyone who demanded to be admitted here. Nor does this pallium in the least move me who have always scorned and despised gold and gems as rubbish. But what is this? I see everywhere on key and crown and pallium the signs of that most wicked rogue and impostor Simon [Magus] who shares my name but not my way of life, and whom I long ago turned out of the temple of Christ.

JULIUS. If you are wise you will put aside this joking, for, in case you don't know, I am Julius the Ligurian and you will surely recognize the two letters P.M. if you learned to read at all.

SAINT PETER. I believe they stand for "Pestis Maxima" [Supreme Plague].

SPIRIT. Ha ha ha! How this soothsayer has hit the nail on the head!

JULIUS. No, "Pontifex Maximus" [Supreme Pontiff].

SAINT PETER. If you were three times

"Maximus" and more even than Mercury Trismegistus, you would not come in here unless you were also "optimus," that is holy [*sanctus*].

JULIUS. If in fact it matters at all to be called "sanctus," you who are delaying opening the doors for me have passed the bounds of impudence since you during so many centuries have been called only "sanctus," while no one has ever called me anything but "sanctissimus." And there are six thousand bulls...in which I am not only named "most sacred lord" but am described by the very name of holiness itself, not *sanctus,* so that I did whatever I pleased.

SPIRIT. Even indulging in drunkenness.

JULIUS. They said that that made the sanctity of the most sacred lord Julius.

SAINT PETER. Then ask admission of those flatterers who made you most sacred and let them give you happiness who gave you sanctity. Although you think this is a question of no concern, will you be called "sanctus" whether you are or not?

JULIUS. I am exasperated. If I were only permitted to live, I should envy you neither that sanctity nor that felicity.

SAINT PETER. O what a revelation of a "most sacred mind"! Although I have now for some time been inspecting you from all sides, I notice in you many signs of impiety and none of holiness. And what does this strange crowd so very unpontifical want for itself? You bring some twenty thousand with you nor do I see anyone in such a great mob who has the countenance of a Christian. I see the loathsome dregs of men, smelling of nothing but brothels, drink-shops and gunpowder. It seems to me that hired robbers or rather infernal skeletons have rushed hither from hell to make war on heaven. Also the more I contemplate you yourself, the less do I see any vestige of an apostle. In the first place what kind of monster are you who, although you wear outside the garments of a priest, underneath bristle and clink with a covering of bloody armor? In addition to this how savage are your eyes, how stubborn your mouth, how threatening your brow and how haughty and arrogant your glance! It is shameful to have to say and at the same time disgusting to see that no part of your body is not defiled by the signs of your unrestrained and abominable lust. Not to speak of the fact that you always belch and smell of inebriation and drunkenness and indeed seem to me to have just vomited. This is so truly the condition of your whole body that you seem withered, wasted, and broken not so much by age and disease as by drunkenness.

SPIRIT. How graphically he has depicted him in all his colors.

SAINT PETER. Although I see that you have long been threatening me with your look, yet I cannot keep back what I feel. I suspect that you are that most pestilential heathen Julius returned from hell to make sport of me.

Erasmi Opuscula, ed. W. K. Ferguson (The Hague: Martinus Nijhoff, 1933), pp. 65–68, trans. M. P. Gilmore.

B. The Erasmian Affirmation

1. AGAINST THE EVIL OF IGNORANCE

But inasmuch as faith is the only gate unto Christ, the first rule must be that thou judge very well both of him and also of scripture given by his spirit, and that thou believe not with mouth only, not faintly, not negligently, not doubtfully, as the common rascal of Christian men do: but let it be set fast and immovable throughout all thy breast, not one jot to be contained in them that appertaineth not greatly unto thy health. Let it move thee nothing at all that thou seest a great part of men so live, as though heaven and hell were but some manner of tales of old wives, to fear or flatter young children withal: but believe thou surely and make no haste, though the whole world should be mad at once, though the elements should be changed, though the angels should rebel: yet verity cannot lie, it cannot but come which God told before should come. If thou believe he is God, thou must needs believe that he is true also, and on this wise think without wavering, nothing to be so true, nothing to be so sure, and without doubt of the things which thou hearest with thine ears, which thou presently beholdest with thine eyes, which thou handlest with thy hands, as those things be true which thou readest in the scriptures, that God of heaven, that is to say verity, gave by inspiration, which the holy prophets brought forth, and the blood of so many martyrs hath approved: unto which now so many hundred years the consent of all good men hath agreed and set their seals: which Christ here being in flesh, both taught in his doctrine and expressly represented or counterfeited in his manners and living. Unto which also miracles bear witness, the devils confess and so much believe, that they quake and tremble for fear. Last of all which be so agreeable unto the equity of nature, which so agree between themselves, and be everywhere like themselves, which so ravisheth the minds of them that attend, so moveth and changeth them. If these so great tokens agree unto them alone, what devil's madness is it to doubt in the faith? Yea of those things past thou mayst easily conjecture what shall follow: how many and great things also, how incredible to be spoken did the prophets tell before of Christ: which of these things came not to pass? Shall he in other things deceive which in them deceived not? In conclusion, the prophets lied not, and shall Christ the Lord of prophets lie? If with this and such other like cogitations thou often stir up the flame of faith, and then fervently desire of God to increase thy faith, I shall marvel if thou canst be any long time an evil man. For who is all together so unhappy and full of mischief that would not depart from vices, if so be he utterly believed, that with these momentary pleasures, beside the unhappy vexation of conscience and mind, are purchased also eternal punishments: on the other side, if he surely believed for this temporal and little wordly vexation to be rewarded or recompensed to good men an hundred fold joy of pure conscience presently: and at the last life immortal.

Erasmus, *Enchiridion Militis Christiani* [*The Manual of the Christian Knight*], English trans. (London: Methuen & Co., Ltd., 1905), Chap. IX, 115–17.

2. THE PHILOSOPHY OF CHRIST

...In this epoch of ours when men turn their attention with such eagerness to studies, each according to his choice, the philosophy of Christ is the only one to be scorned by some although they are Christians, to be neglected by the mass of men and discussed but without warmth not to say hypocritically by very few. Yet in all the other sciences which human industry has produced there is nothing so hidden and abstruse that the keeness of the intellect has not discovered it, nothing so difficult that an immense effort has not conquered it. What brings it about that we do not embrace this philosophy alone with the eagerness which it deserves although we profess to call ourselves Christians? Platonists, Pythagoreans, Academics, Stoics, Cynics, Peripatetics, and Epicureans have a profound knowledge of the dogmas of their own sects or at least have memorized them; on behalf of these they engage in combat and would prefer to give their lives rather than to desert the inheritance of their founders. But why should we not show a similar devotion to Christ, the author of our being and our leader? Who would not think it a betrayal on the part of a man who professed himself an Aristotelian not to know what that philosopher thought about the causes of thunder, origins of matter or infinity? Yet these are not things the knowledge or ignorance of which renders us happy or unhappy. Shall not we who have been brought in so many ways to the knowledge of Christ and drawn to him by so many sacraments regard it as a base betrayal to deny his dogmas which offer to all men an assured felicity? And how can anyone charge here that we exaggerate when the impious madness of some has reached the point of wanting to compare Christ with Zeno or Aristotle and his doctrine with what I can only call as politely as possible their little precepts. Let them attribute as much as they can or as much as they like to the leaders of their sects; in reality Christ is the only doctor to come to us from heaven, he is the only one to teach the certain truth, since he is himself eternal wisdom; as the unique author of human salvation he alone has taught the things necessary for salvation and he alone perfectly realized in practice what he taught and was able to show forth in reality what he had promised.

...I strongly dissent from those who are unwilling to have the Scriptures translated into the vernacular and read by the ignorant, as if Christ taught so complicated a doctrine that it can hardly be understood even by a handful of theologians or as if the arcanum of the Christian religion consisted in its not being known. It is perhaps reasonable to conceal the mysteries of kings but Christ seeks to divulge his mysteries as much as possible. I should like to have even the most humble women read the Evangel and the Epistles of St. Paul. And these ought also to be translated into all languages so that they might be read and known not only by Scots and Irishmen but also by Turks and Saracens. The first step is certainly to know the Scriptures in whatever manner. Although many will mock at them some will be captivated. Would that the ploughboy recited something from them at his ploughshare, that the weaver sang from them at his shuttle and that the traveller whiled away the tedium of his journey with their tales, indeed would that the converse of Christian men were drawn from them, for we are on the whole what our daily discourse reveals us to be. Let each attain what he can and express what he can. Let him who is behind not envy him who is ahead and let the leader encourage the follower without making him despair. Why should we restrict to a few a profession which is common to all? For since baptism in which the first profession of the philosophy of Christ is made is equally common to all Christians, since they share alike the other sacraments and finally the supreme reward of immortality, it is not fitting that the possession of dogma be relegated to those few whom we call theologians or monks. Although these latter constitute only a minute proportion of the Christian people nevertheless I could wish that they conform more closely to what they hear. For I fear lest there be found among the theologians those who are far from deserving this title, who discourse of earthly not of divine things and among the monks who profess poverty and contempt for the world you may find instead even more of the world. To me he is truly a theologian who teaches not with syllogisms and contorted arguments but with compassion in his eyes and his whole countenance, who teaches indeed by the example of his own life that riches are to be despised, that the Christian man must not put his faith in the defenses of this world but depend entirely on heaven, that he is not to return an injury for an injury, that he is to pray well for those who pray badly and do his best for those who deserve ill, that all good men ought to love and cherish each other as members of the same body and evil men tolerated if they cannot be corrected. Those who lose their goods, who are despoiled of their possessions, who mourn,—these are not to be pitied for they are the blessed and death is even to be desired by the pious for it is the passage to immortality. If anyone inspired by the spirit of Christ preaches things of this kind, if he inculcates, urges, invites, encourages, then he is a true theologian even if he should be a ditch digger or a weaver.

... For that which is especially according to nature easily comes into the minds of all. And what else is the philosophy of Christ which he himself calls a re-birth *(renascentia)* but a restoration of a nature which was originally created good?

From the text of "Paraclesis," in *D. Erasmus Roterodamus Ausgewählte Werke,* eds. Hajo and Annemarie Holborn (Munich: C. H. Beck'sche, 1933), pp. 140–41, 142, 145, trans. M. P. Gilmore.

7

Protestant and Catholic

E. HARRIS HARBISON

Princeton University

The Protestant Revolt and the Catholic Reformation in the sixteenth century were vast and complex historical movements with origins
which lay deep in the economic, political, and intellectual conditions
of the preceding centuries. The historical consequences of the two
movements were as various and wide-ranging as their causes. But it is
well to remember that each began in the inner religious consciousness
of individual human beings, and that each was primarily a religious
movement.

The chapter which follows considers the Protestant and Catholic
reform movements from within, so to speak, through the thoughts of
the leaders on both sides: their appeals, their confessions, their
reasoned arguments, and their impassioned propaganda. The words
come from an age in which the relation of man to God and salvation
of the soul from eternal damnation were profoundly important concerns of most intellectuals as well as of ordinary people. To understand
the problems suggested by the selections, therefore, requires a strenuous
effort of the historical imagination. The reader must attempt to get
inside men of four centuries ago who were convinced that the questions
how a man is "saved," whether man has "free will" or not, and where
a Christian must look for religious "authority," are crucially important.

For a modern Christian, of course, such language is not hard to understand. But even those today who have lost touch with all religion are aware that individuals still undergo "conversion" (to or away from one ideology or another of the age), that "free will vs. determinism" is still a disturbing question to scientists, philosophers, and statesmen, and that our world is just as distraught as was the sixteenth century over the clash of apparently irreconcilable "authorities" (ideologies of nation, race, or class). The thought-world of Luther and Loyola is remote from us, but their problems remind us of ours since many of them were and are perennial human concerns.

Three main questions are outlined below.

(1) What actually happened to Martin Luther in his room in the tower of the Augustinian Friary at Wittenberg some time in 1512 or 1513? And what happened to Ignatius of Loyola at Manresa some ten years later in 1522? An obvious difficulty presents itself here: neither man wrote down an account of his experience at the time (as Pascal did a century later), and perhaps religious "conversion" is indescribable in any case. But the peculiarities of Luther's experience to a large extent determined the later beliefs and practices of Protestants, and the peculiarities of Loyola's experience were responsible for many of the tenets of the Order he founded, and even for some of the general tendencies of the Catholic Reformation, or "Counter-Reformation" as Ranke called it. It is important, therefore, to puzzle out as accurately as possible what the similarities and differences were in the two religious "conversions" to which the religious upheaval of the sixteenth century can be traced. To this end, the most important documents relating to Luther's experience are given, followed by several sharply contrasting modern interpretations. Loyola's account of his conversion concludes the section.

(2) Careful study of these two conversion experiences will suggest the second main question: Why did most Protestants believe so strongly in predestination and Catholics in free will? What was the religious and psychological stake in the controversy, and why did men literally slit each other's throats over it? It is one of the strangest paradoxes of historical experience that *both* the belief in predestination and the belief in free will can stimulate vigorous and dynamic movements— as the history of the Puritans (who believed in predestination) and of the Jesuits (who believed in free will) appears to prove. In the long run, which is the greater spur to action on the stage of history: belief that the individual is the helpless instrument of irresistible super-natural power, or belief that this power is helpless without the free and willing cooperation of the self-determined individual? How is the historian to explain the heat of the controversy, and what is its long-range significance?

(3) The argument over free will leads naturally into the more crucial argument over religious authority. Granted (as everyone did grant in the sixteenth century) that all power is of God, how does God actually make known His will to men? Through the visible, historical institution known as the Church, centered at Rome and headed by the Pope? Or rather through the Old and New Testaments considered as the direct revelation of the divine will? Or is it through man's reason, the divine gift which distinguishes human beings from beasts? Or through direct, intimate experience of God, through the "inner light,"

through mystical experience, intuition, or "conscience"? These were the four main answers: Church, Bible, reason, and individual intuition or conscience. Generally the Protestants held to the Bible and conscience, the Catholics to the Church and reason, but like all generalizations this is far too simple, as careful reading of the documents given below will suggest. Were there only two main positions on religious authority, or was there a wide spectrum of opinions? How did different individuals combine two or more of the four main answers suggested, and why? Why were "reasonable" positions on the question apparently so difficult to maintain?

In answering this last question, one very important broad fact must be constantly borne in mind: it occurred to almost no one on either side of the bitter religious controversy of the sixteenth century that there could be some truth on both sides. Truth was one and indivisible. Like the totalitarians of a later day, Lutherans, Calvinists, and Catholics could hardly ever entertain the idea that their opponents might be possessed of a fraction of the truth; the fight would have to be fought out to a finish. The few who did envisage the possibility of irreconcilable believers agreeing to disagree and yet living peaceably with each other were lonely voices crying in the wilderness.

I. The " Conversion " Experiences of Luther and Loyola

[MARTIN LUTHER]

The facts concerning the background of Luther's "conversion" upon which historians are generally agreed are the following: Martin Luther (1483–1546) entered the Order of Augustinian Friars in 1505 at the age of twenty-one. He was a conscientious monk—zealous, if not overzealous, in the performance of his duties. At the same time he became increasingly troubled by a sense of guilt, which no amount of confession or ascetic practices could alleviate. The popular theology of his day tended to emphasize the importance in salvation of "good works," i.e. the sacramental and monastic practices, such as penance or pilgrimage, universally recognized throughout the Church as practices pleasing to God. The particular scholastic theology which he had been taught—Nominalism—emphasized the power, majesty, and inscrutability of God's will. Luther was terror-stricken by the recurring thought that nothing which he as a human being and sinner might do could possibly please God and win His forgiveness.

Then something happened. While working up lectures on the Bible for his students at Wittenberg, probably in the winter of 1512–13 (the date is disputed), the true meaning of what St. Paul had insisted upon—that God considers not men's "works" but their "faith" —flooded in upon him. Undoubtedly, the way to this illumination had been prepared by his reading, thinking, and personal contacts for months or years before, but as he looked back upon it, it came suddenly. Notice carefully the dates of the selections that follow: only a few of them are really contemporary with the event. What weight is to be given to later reminiscences in such a case? What really happened to Luther? What did he mean when he insisted over and over throughout the rest of his life that a man is "justified" by "faith alone," and not by "works"? Why did this become a slogan subversive of the whole medieval ecclesiastical system?

A. A Tract of 1533

Certain it is, I was a pious monk and followed the rule of my order so strictly that I could say, if ever a monk got to heaven by his monkery, I should certainly have got there. All my fellow-monks who knew me will bear me out. If I had kept on any longer, I should have killed myself with vigils, prayers, reading, and other work.

Martin Luthers Werke: Kritische Gesamtausgabe. (Weimar, 1883 ff), XXXVIII, 143. Hereafter cited as *WA*. Translation of this and the next five selections by E. Harris Harbison.

B. A Sermon of 1539

In the monastery we had enough to eat and drink, but the heart and conscience suffered pain and martyrdom, and the greatest suffering is that of the soul. I was often frightened by the name of Jesus, and when I looked upon him hanging on the cross, he seemed to me like a flash of lightning. When I heard his name mentioned, I would rather have heard the Devil named, for I thought that I would have to do good works until Christ became friendly and gracious to me because of them. In the monastery I thought not about women nor money nor wealth, but my heart troubled and writhed, worrying how I might make God gracious to me. For I had fallen from the faith, and it left me no way but to think that I had offended God and that I would have to appease Him with my good works. But thank God we once more have His Word, which pictures and points out Christ as our righteousness.

WA, XLVII, 589–90.

C. A Conversation of 1533

I often confessed to Staupitz [Vicar-General of the Augustinian Friars, Luther's monastic order], not about women, but about my really knotty problems. He used to say, "I don't understand." That was fine comfort! If I went to someone else, I got the same answer. In fact, no confessor wanted to know about my problems. So I thought, "No one has this temptation but you!" So I became like a dead body. At last Staupitz, seeing how sad and downcast I was, leaned over to me at table [one day] and asked, "Why are you so sad?" I replied, "Ah, what will become of me?" He said, "You don't realize how necessary all this is to you. Without it nothing good will come of you." He didn't understand. He thought I was learned, and that unless tempted, I would become proud.

WA, Tischreden, I, 240 (no. 518).

D. Preface to Luther's Collected Works, 1545

[While working on the Psalms] I was absorbed by a passionate desire to understand Paul in his Epistle to the Romans. Nothing stood in my way but that one expression, "The justice of God is revealed in the Gospel" (Romans 1:17). For I hated those words, "the justice of God," because I had been taught to understand them in the scholastic sense as the formal or active justice whereby God, who is righteous, punishes unrighteous sinners. I was in the frame of mind of feeling that although I was living a blameless life as monk, I was still a sinner with a troubled conscience before God, and I had no confidence that I could appease Him by my efforts. I did not love—nay, I hated the righteous God who punishes sinners, and I murmured with unbridled resentment, if not with unspoken blasphemy, against Him, saying, "As if it were not enough for miserable sinners who are eternally lost through original sin to be afflicted with every kind of calamity through the law of the Ten Commandments, without God's adding woe to woe through the Gospel and even threatening us with His justice and wrath in the Gospel." Thus I raged, my conscience wild and disturbed. Still I kept hammering away at those words of Paul, wishing passionately to know what he meant.

After I had pondered the problem for days and nights, God took pity on me and I saw the inner connection between the two phrases, "The justice of God is revealed in the Gospel" and "The just shall live by faith." Then I began to understand that this "justice of God" is the righteousness by which the just man lives through the free gift of God, that is to say "by faith"; and that the justice "revealed in the Gospel" is the passive justice of God by which He takes pity on

us and justifies us by our faith, as it is written, "The just shall live by faith." Thereupon I felt as if I had been born again and had entered Paradise through wide-open gates. Immediately the whole of Scripture took on a new meaning for me. I raced through the Scriptures, so far as my memory went, and found analogies in other expressions: "the work of God," i.e. what God works in us; "the strength of God," by which He gives us strength; "the wisdom of God," by which He makes us wise; "the power of God," 'the blessing of God," "the glory of God."

Whereas the expression "justice of God" had filled me with hate before, I now exalted it as the sweetest of phrases with all the more love. And so this verse of Paul's became in truth the gate to Paradise for me.

WA, LIV, 185–86.

E. A Conversation of 1532

These words, "the just" and "the justice of God," were a flash of lightning in my consciousness. The moment I heard them I was terribly frightened: if God is just, then He will punish. But thank God, once when I was turning these words over in my mind in the heated room in this tower [another version adds, "in which was the monks' latrine"]—"the just shall live by faith," "the justice of God"—

it soon occurred to me that if we must be "justified by faith" and if the "justice of God" must save all those who have faith, then it will not be as a reward to us but by the free mercy of God. This raised up my spirit. For the justice of God is what justifies and saves us through Christ. And so these words became more pleasing to me. The Holy Spirit revealed the meaning of this passage to me in this tower.

WA, Tischreden, III, no. 3232c.

F. Lecture Notes on the Psalms, 1513–1515

What our scholastic theologians call the act of penance—that is, to be displeased with oneself, to detest, condemn, and accuse oneself, to wish to avenge, punish, and chastise oneself, and in effect to hate evil and be wroth with oneself—this in one word the Scripture calls justification. Therefore so long as we fail to condemn ourselves before God, we cannot rise and be justified. . . . The justification

of God will never rise in us unless our own justification first falls and perishes utterly. . . . Otherwise God's justice would be mocked and Christ would have died in vain. This is the argument of that very profound theologian, the Apostle Paul—an argument unknown in the highest degree to our theologians today, in practice if not in theory. For Paul wants to be found in Christ, with no justification of his own. He calls himself the first of sinners—a great and happy point of pride. For the more sin abounds [he says], the more God's grace and justice abounds in us. That is, the less justification we have of our own, the more we judge and curse and detest ourselves, the more abundantly God's grace flows into us.

WA, III, 31.

G. Letter to Staupitz, May 30, 1518

I remember, reverend Father, among those happy and wholesome stories of yours, by which the Lord used wonderfully to console me, that you often mentioned the word *poenitentia*, whereupon, distressed by our consciences and by those torturers who with endless and intolerable precept taught nothing but what they called a method of confession, we received you as a messenger from Heaven, for penitence is not genuine save when it begins from the love of justice and of God, and this which they consider the end and consummation of repentance is rather its commencement.

Your words on this subject pierced me like the sharp arrows of the mighty, so that I began to see what the Scriptures had to say about penitence, and behold the happy result: the texts all supported and favored your doctrine, in so much that, while there had formerly been no word in almost all the Bible more bitter to me than *poenitentia* (although I zealously simulated it before God and tried to express an assumed and forced love), now no word sounds sweeter or more pleasant to me than that. For thus do the commands of God become sweet when we understand that they are not to be read in books only, but in the wounds of the sweetest Saviour.

After this it happened by the favor of the learned men who taught me Hebrew and Greek that I learned [from Erasmus' edition of the New Testament in Greek, note on Matthew 3:2] that the Greek word is *metanoia* from *meta* and *noun*, i.e. from "afterwards" and "mind," so that penitence or *metanoia* is "coming to one's right mind, afterwards," that is, comprehension of your own evil, after you had accepted loss and found out your error. This is impossible without a change in your affections. All this agrees so well with Paul's theology, that, in my opinion, at least, nothing is more characteristically Pauline.

Then I progressed and saw that *metanoia* meant not only "afterwards" and "mind," but also "change" and "mind," so that *metanoia* means change of mind and affection. . . .

Sticking fast to this conclusion, I dared to think that they were wrong who attributed so much to works of repentance that they have left us nothing of it but formal penances and elaborate confession. They were seduced by the Latin, for *poenitentiam agere* means rather a work than a change of affection and in no wise agrees with the Greek.

When I was glowing with this thought, behold indulgences and remissions of sins began to be trumpeted abroad with tremendous clangor, but these trumpets animated no one to real struggle. In short, the doctrine of true repentance was neglected, and only the cheapest part of it, that called penance, was magnified. . . .As I was not able to oppose the fury of these preachers, I determined modestly to take issue with them and to call their theories in doubt, relying as I did on the opinion of all the doctors and of the whole Church, who all say that it is better to perform the penance than to buy it, that is an indulgence. . . .This is the reason why I, reverend Father, who always love retirement, have unhappily been forced into the public view. . . .

Preserved Smith, *Luther's Correspondence* (Philadelphia: Fortress Press, 1913), I, 91–93.

H. A Tract of 1520

Lo! my God, without merit on my part, of His pure and free mercy, has given to me, an unworthy, condemned, and contemptible creature, all the riches of justification and salvation in Christ, so that I no longer am in want of anything, except of faith to believe that this is so. For such a Father, then, who has over-whelmed me with inestimable riches of His, why should I not freely, cheerfully, and with my whole heart, and from voluntary zeal, do all that I know will be pleasing to Him and acceptable in His sight? I will therefore give myself, as a sort of Christ, to my neighbour, as Christ has given himself to me; and will do nothing in this life except what I see will be needful, advantageous, and wholesome for my neighbour, since by faith I abound in all good things in Christ.

Luther, *On Christian Liberty* (1520), in Henry Wace and C. A. Buchheim, eds., *Luther's Primary Works* (London: Hodder & Stoughton, Ltd., 1896), pp. 281–82.

Naturally modern historians still differ sharply in interpreting the preceding docu-ments, although there is much on which all are agreed. To Catholic historians, Luther was unbalanced and "abnormal," a "heretic" in the literal sense of one who seizes upon a single aspect of truth and blows it up out of all proportion to its significance. The trouble, they insist, was with Luther, not with the Catholic tradition on salvation, although there admittedly were abuses in practice. To Prot-estant historians, Luther was essentially "nor-mal," in a badly mechanized ecclesiastical sys-tem which was offering salvation in exchange for "good works"—and cash. The trouble was with the Church, not with Luther. Moderate historians of both persuasions and some of neither are able to see the tragic conflict of personal and institutional standards involved, and to point out the truth on both sides. But it is not easy to reconcile the following twen-tieth-century interpretations of Luther's ex-perience. Can it be done at all?

I. Grisar: A Moderate Roman Catholic Account

In none of his other Epistles does St. Paul penetrate so deeply into the questions of grace, justification, and election, as in his magnificent Epistle addressed to the Christians of Rome. Luther believed that this profound Epistle furnished the thread that would lead him out of his labyrinth. Disregarding the tradition of the Church concerning the meaning of the Epistle, he buried himself in its contents and brooded over its many mysterious expressions. For him the sacred document was to become the subject-matter of academic lectures with entirely new ideas. How often may he not have wandered up and down the venerable corridors of the monastery meditating on the significance of the words of the Apostle. His emaciated form may have become animated, his deep-set eyes may have flashed, as he imagined to dis-cover in the Epistle to the Romans the desired solution of his problems. With ever-increasing confidence he imputed to the Apostle the ideas to which he was urged for the sake of the supposed quiet-ing of his scruples. Simultaneously, an arsenal of new weapons against the self-righteous Pharisees within the Church seemed to open itself to him. . . .

The ancient Church, above all things, upheld the freedom of the human will to do good. She steadfastly maintained that God wills the salvation of all men without exception and to this end offers them the necessary grace, with which men should freely cooperate. Baptism makes a man a child of God by virtue of sanctifying grace; but the inclination to evil remains through no fault of his own, provided he does not consent to sin. Concupiscence is diminished by the means of grace offered by the Church. If any one has been seduced into committing mortal sin, he may confidently hope to regain the state of grace through the merits of the death of Christ, provided he submits to penance and resolves to amend his life. Mere faith in the application of the merits of Christ is not sufficient. Actual grace assists man to be converted and to persevere in doing good. . . .

Luther, with the Epistle to the Romans in his hand, proclaimed that man was not free to do good; that all his efforts were sinful, because evil concupiscence dwelled in his soul; that God did everything in him, governing him as the rider governs his steed. He did not differentiate between natural and supernatural good. Christ, he said, has fulfilled the law for me and atoned for every weakness and sin. Through His righteousness the believing and trustful sinner is covered, apart from his own works and his own righteousness. He remains a sinner as before, but is justified by the imputation of the justice of Christ and necessarily brings forth good works through the infinite causality of God, just as trust in God is imparted to the hesitating only through the divine omnipotence.

Hartmann Grisar, *Martin Luther: His Life and Work,* trans. F. J. Eble (St. Louis: B. Herder Book Co., 1935), pp. 71, 73.

J. Maritain: A Militant Roman Catholic Analysis

From his own witness and the studies of Denifle and Grisar I note here two things in the inner life of Brother Martin [Luther].

First, he seems to have sought in the spiritual life chiefly what authors call sensible consolations, and to have been desperately attached to that experimental savouring of piety, that assurance in feeling, which God sends to souls to draw them to Himself, but takes from them when He wills, and which are only means. For Luther, on the other hand, the whole point was to *feel* oneself in a state of grace —as if grace itself were an object of sensation! . . .

Second, and as a result of the same vicious disposition, he relied on his own strength to arrive at Christian virtue and perfection, trusting his own efforts, in his penances, in the works of his will, far more than in grace. Thus he practiced the very Pelagianism [emphasis on man's will] with which he was to charge Catholics, from which he himself was never really to be free. In his spiritual life he was, in practice, a Pharisee relying on his works, as his scrupulous fidgetiness shows. . . .

Is it then that in the decisive moment of his crisis he falls into some grave outward sin? We do not think so. But inwardly he fell; he despaired of grace.

When a man begins to know the wounds and wretchedness of the sons of Adam, the serpent whispers in his ear: "Be content to be what you are, spoiled angel, misbegotten creature; your business is to do ill, since your every being is bad." A spiritual temptation preeminently. Luther makes that act of perverse resignation; he gives up the fight; he declares that the fight is impossible. Submerged by sin on all sides, or by what he thinks to be sin, he lets himself go with the tide. And he comes to the practical conclusion: *Concupiscence cannot be conquered.* . . .

Concupiscence Luther identified with original sin. Original sin is always in us, ineffaceable; it has made us radically bad and corrupted us in the very essence of our nature. God commanded the impossible when He gave us His law. But now Christ has paid for us and His justice redeems us. *He* is just instead of us. Justification is wholly exterior to us and we are still sin to our very bones: it infuses no new life into us, it simply covers us as with a cloak. There is nothing for us to do to be saved. On the contrary, to want to cooperate with the divine action is a lack of faith, a denial of the Blood of Christ, and damnation.

From henceforth "Heaven opens." Good-bye to torments and remorse! Absolute uselessness of works; salvation by faith alone, that is through confidence in Christ. "Sin courageously, believe more firmly than ever" [says Luther] and you will be saved....One might say that that immense disaster for humanity, the Protestant Reformation, was only the effect of an interior trial which turned out badly in a monk who lacked humility.

Reprinted from Jacques Maritain, *Three Reformers* (New York: Charles Scribner's Sons, 1929), pp. 6–13 *passim*.

K. Boehmer: A Protestant Interpretation

If we ask what that decisive hour produced, Luther himself gives us the answer: a new insight and a new sense of life. The new insight is reflected in the argument to Psalm 31, probably written on the same day: "Concerning the means of true repentance, that sins are remitted, not by any works, but alone by the mercy of God without any merit." But this sentence still does not clearly express what is, in the last analysis, treated of here; namely, not merely the conditions of the forgiveness of sin, but rather the nature of God and His gracious will toward us. However, he was always of the opinion that in this he had uttered nothing new, but had "only restored the Holy Gospel again." In reality, in this, the head and heart of his message, he is not an innovator but a renovator. Therefore of all the names that his or later generations have invented to characterize his unique position in the history of the Christian religion and religion in general, none fits him so well as the name *Reformer,* which was coined especially for him.

In the first place, this term clearly expresses that he was not the founder of a new religion, nor even that he was one of those many well-meaning, alleged renovators of "true" Christianity who think that they can restore original Christianity by an external, mechanical imitation of primitive Christian ordinances for congregational life, or by a literal, verbal application of primitive Christian doctrines. He was rather the rediscoverer and reviver of what was essential and specifically Christian in primitive Christianity. This is evangelical faith in God, or, to put it in another way, the Gospel of the grace of God in Christ.

In the second place, this name is also very fortunate in that it fixes and symbolizes in the simplest manner the significant distinction which exists between Luther's religious self-consciousness and the self-consciousness of most other great personalities in the history of religion, Christian and non-Christian. If there is anything that is characteristic of the latter, it is the consciousness of being a bearer and instrument of a special revelation which is believed to have been received in visions, dreams, and other ecstatic experiences and confirmed by miracles and signs. Luther never had such ecstatic experiences. Nevertheless, he never doubted that the "insight" which had made him a reformer had been "given to him by the Holy Ghost," or "revealed" to him. The suddenness with which this "insight" emerged, after days of agonizing thought and search, and the profound emotion and the feeling of being liberated which accompanied it certainly contributed toward strengthening him in this conviction. But it is unquestionable that his conviction was confirmed by the impression that God had been especially near to him in that moment; and that it was corroborated by the certainty that "his teaching was not his but rather the true, pure Word of God," and that he had received it not in visions and dreams, but in a completely normal state of mind. For in his opinion visions and dreams are always very dubious and delusive, dependent upon the temperament and disposition of the individual who has them, often caused by evil spirits, never equal in value to the Gospel even when they are genuine, and, for that matter, no longer necessary to Christianity now that it possesses the Gospel....

As is shown in a classical manner by the ecstatic experiences of Loyola, visions, auditions, and inspirations...almost never have a single meaning, and like all visionary complexes are not easily retained in their original form. "Insights," however, always have a single meaning and are not easily altered.... Naturally, this frequently results in the "insights" being handed down as a mere formula, appropriated merely by rote and not inwardly assimilated. On the other hand, it also means that they reach much wider circles, that they may be readily translated into action, indeed that they can actually change the face of the whole world without their originator having moved a finger.

Heinrich Boehmer, *Road to Reformation: Martin Luther to the Year 1521*, trans. J. W. Doberstein and T. G. Tappert (Philadelphia: Fortress Press, 1946), pp. 111–12, 115–16.

[IGNATIUS LOYOLA]

Boehmer's interpretation of the significance of Luther's experience suggests comparison with the experience of Ignatius of Loyola (1491–1556), founder of the Society of Jesus or Jesuit Order (1540). Loyola was a Spaniard of the lesser nobility, with romantic sensibilities and courtly ambitions, apparently headed for a humdrum career in camp and court. This never came about, for a French cannon ball shattered his leg at Pampluna in May, 1521 (a month after Luther defied the assembled Diet at Worms). During a long and painful convalescence, he found none of his favorite chivalric romances to read and so devoured a life of Christ and legends of the saints. What if he should become a saint instead of a knight? The romantic idea was translated into action shortly after he was able to walk again. He determined to become a soldier of Christ and dedicated himself to the Virgin as a knight to his Lady. But like Luther, he soon went through the valley of doubt, as the following account makes clear. It is his "Confessions," dictated during the closing years of his life to a friend, Father Gonzalez de Camara. Some 30 years separate the account itself from the events described, which took place at Manresa in Spain in 1522. As in the case of Luther, what confidence is to be placed in such reminiscences? How did Loyola's experience differ from Luther's, and what might this difference mean for any future movements founded by the two men?

L. Ignatius of Loyola's Account of His Conversion

The 24th of March, 1522, the eve of Our Lady, as secretly as possible he [Loyola] gave to a poor man all his clothes and put on the clothes he longed for and went to kneel before the altar of Our Lady, and now there and now on foot, staff in hand, passed the whole night, and left for Barcelona at daybreak. In order not to be recognized he went, not by the direct road where he would find many people who would know him and show him honour, but by a roundabout way to a town called Manresa; where he determined to stay in a hospital some days and note down some things which he took with him very carefully and in which he found much consolation....

But he began to be much troubled by scruples. Because, even though the general confession which he had made in Montserrat had been made very carefully and all in writing, nevertheless it seemed to him sometimes that he had not confessed some things, and that idea afflicted him very much because, though he confessed this idea itself, he found no inward satisfaction. And so he began to seek out spiritual men who might aid these scruples of conscience but nothing helped him, and at last a doctor of theology, who was preaching in the church of Manresa, a very spiritual man, told him one day in confession to write everything he could recollect. He did it and after confession his scruples of conscience came back, so that he was in great tribulation and although he knew that these things caused him great loss and that it would be well for him to free himself from them, he could not. He thought sometimes that there might be a cure in having his confessor order him in the name of Jesus Christ not to confess again any things in his past life and he wanted to have his confessor so order him, but he had not the boldness to say it to his confessor. But the confessor, without being told, ordered him not to confess anything in his past life unless it was a very clear, distinct sin in his memory. He did not profit at all by that order and remained troubled. At that time he lived in a room which the Dominican monks had given him in their convent and kept up his daily seven hours of prayer on his knees, rising always at midnight, and all other exercises of the spirit, but in all these he found no cure for the scruples of his conscience and many months passed in torment. And once, when he was in great tribulation because of them, he took to prayer and in his fervour called aloud on God, saying, "Help me, O Lord, for I find no help in man nor in any other creature; though if I thought I could find help no work would seem too great for me. Show me, Lord, where to find help, because, even though it should be necessary to follow a little dog in order that he might lead me to the remedy, I would do it."

Possessed by these thoughts there came to him many times with great force, the temptation to throw himself into a large opening there was in his room close to the place where he prayed. But realizing that it was a sin to kill himself, he began to say aloud, "Lord, I will not do anything which is an offense to Thee," repeating those words many times. And there came to his memory the story of a saint who, to obtain from God something he much desired, went many days without food until he obtained it. And thinking of that a good while, at last he made up his mind to do it, saying to himself, that he would neither eat nor drink until God provided for him or he saw himself near to death: because if he saw himself so far *in extremis* that if he did not eat he must die, he determined that then he would beg bread and eat it. (This was a foolish plan, for in truth how could he in the very article of death either beg or eat bread?) That happened on a Sunday after he had communed and the whole week he persevered

without putting anything in his mouth and without giving up his accustomed exercises, even going to divine services and praying on his knees at midnight, etc. But when the next Sunday arrived when it was necessary to go to make his confession, as he was wont to tell his confessor very much in detail what he had done, he told him also how in that week he had eaten nothing. The confessor told him to break his fast: and although he found himself still with force, nevertheless he obeyed his confessor and found himself that day free from his scruples of conscience. But the third day, which was a Tuesday, while he was praying he commenced to remember his sins and as if he were threading beads, he kept on passing in thought from sin to sin of his past life and it seemed to him that he was obliged to confess them again. But at the end of these thoughts there came to him disgust with the life he led and impulses to leave it. And with that, it pleased God that he awoke as if out of sleep. And as he already had some experience in the diversity of spirits by the lessons which God had given him, he began to regard the way in which that spirit had come and so determined very clearly not to confess any more anything of his past life, and so from that day on he remained free from those torments of conscience; holding it for certain that our Lord had freed him by His mercy.

Aside from his seven hours of prayer he occupied himself in aiding the souls of some who came to him seeking help in spiritual things and all the rest of the day not occupied in these two things, he gave to meditation on the things of God and what he had read and heard. But when he came to go to bed, often great spiritual consolation came to him and intimations of divine things which made him lose a large share of the time destined for sleep— which was not much. And considering this, he thought that he had a certain time set aside for communion with God and in addition the rest of the day. And by this road he came to doubt if those intimations came from the good spirit, and he came to the conclusion that it was better to neglect them and sleep the hours allotted to sleep. And he did so. He still persevered in his determination to eat no meat and was so firm in it that he had no thought of changing it in any way. One day when he got up in the morning there appeared to him meat ready to be eaten; as if he saw it with his bodily eyes without any wish to eat meat preceding the appearance of it. And there came to him, at the same moment, a strong assent of his will to eat meat for the future. And though he recalled his former determination, he could not doubt that he ought to eat meat. Afterwards his confessor said he wondered if it was not a temptation, but he (Ignatius) examining the whole matter carefully, could not doubt that it was a sign.

In those days God was treating him like a boy in school, teaching him; and this because of his rudeness and gross mind, either because there was no one to teach him or because of the firm will which had been given him by God Himself for His service. At all events he clearly judged and has always judged that God was so teaching him. First if he doubted it he would think he was sinning against the divine majesty and then it can be seen by the five following points.

He was very much devoted to the Holy Trinity and offered prayer every day to the three persons separately. And offering prayer to the most Holy Trinity the thought came to him "How would it be to offer four prayers to the Trinity?" But the thought gave him little or no trouble as a thing of small importance. And standing one day praying the hours of Our Lady on the steps of the monastery, his understanding began to be raised as if he saw the most Holy Trinity as the three keys of an organ and that with so many tears and sobs that he could not restrain them. And, taking part that morning in a procession, he could not until dinner time keep back the tears, nor, after dinner, cease to talk about the Trinity: and that with much joy and consolation, so that all his life the impression remained with him to feel great devotion in offering prayer to the most Holy Trinity.

Once he saw in his understanding with great spiritual joy the way in which God had created the world, because he seemed to see a white thing from which issued rays and from that God made light. But he would not know how to explain these things, nor does he remember entirely well everything about that information which at that time God was impressing on his soul.

Also at Manresa, where he stayed almost a year after he began to be consoled by God and saw the fruit of his efforts to help souls, he gave up those extremes which he had before practiced and cut his nails and hair [which had been uncut]. One day when he was in the church of the monastery hearing mass and the body of Our Lord was raised, he saw, with the inner eyes, so to speak, rays of light which came from above. And although he cannot after so long a lapse of time explain it well, nevertheless what he saw clearly with the understanding was how Our Lord Jesus Christ was in that most Holy Sacrament.

On many occasions and for a long time when in prayer he saw with the interior eyes the humanity of Christ and the figure which appeared to him was like a white body, neither very big nor very small, but he could not see any distinction of members. He saw that in Manresa many times. If he should say twenty or forty he would not dare to judge that it was a falsehood. Another time he saw it when he was in Jerusalem and again when he was journeying near Padua. He also saw Our Lady in a similar form without distinguishing the parts of her body. Those things which he has seen gave so much confirmation to his faith that he has often thought within himself that if he had not read the scriptures which teach us those things of the faith, he would determine to die for them solely because of what he has seen.

Once he went to a church which stood a little more than a mile from Manresa which was called, I think, St. Paul, and the road runs next to the river. And walking and saying his prayers, he sat down for a little with his face toward the river. And thus sitting the eyes of his understanding began to open and, without seeing any vision, he understood and knew many things—as well spiritual things as things of the faith and things in the realm of letters and that with a brightness of illustration so great that they seemed to him entirely new things. And the details of what he then understood cannot be explained though they were many. All that can be said is that he received a clarity in his understanding of such a sort that in all the reasoning of his life up to the age of more than sixty-two years, collecting all the help he had received from God and all he has known and joining them into one, it does not seem to him that he has gained as much from all these advantages as from that single illumination when he sat by the river.

And that left him with an understand-ing so enlightened that it seemed to him he was another man and that he had an intellect different from the one he had before. And after this had lasted for some time, he went on his knees before a road-side cross which stood nearby to give thanks to God and there appeared to him the vision [of a serpent] which had ap-peared to him many times but which he had never understood; the thing of which it has been said before that it appeared very beautiful with many eyes. But he saw plainly, being before the cross, that the thing had not as beautiful a colour as usual. And he recognized very clearly, with a powerful assent of the will, that it was the devil and since, although for a long time the devil continued to appear to him often, he, as a sign of contempt, drove him away with a pilgrim staff he always carried in his hand.

Reprinted from Paul Van Dyke, *Ignatius Loyola* (New York: Charles Scribner's Sons, 1926), pp. 36, 39–44. Original in *Scripta de Sancto Ignatio de Loyola* (Madrid, 1904), I, 47–55.

II. Free Will vs. Predestination

Reflection on the preceding selections will suggest that Luther and Loyola thought quite differently about the relative part which *his own will*, as distinguished from God's, had played in the process of his conversion. What was there in Luther's experience to induce him to emphasize God's power and his own helplessness? Did this logically imply a theology of "predestination" and the elimina-tion of "free will"? Why might Loyola be more inclined to defend "free will"?

Enough has been said to suggest that the Protestant and Catholic positions on the question grew to a large extent out of personal religious experience. But the question of free will was already expounded before Luther began to wrestle with his soul in the monastery. Humanists had been rereading Greek and Roman arguments about the problem. On the whole these humanists thought highly of man, his reason, his good-ness, and his will. They were in conscious revolt against the more sombre view of man held by medieval thinkers: they tended to emphasize man's freedom. To one who had

gone through such a shattering conversion experience as Luther, such an optimistic view of human nature was almost blasphemous: unaided by God, man was utterly helpless except to sin.

It is for this reason that the great humanist Erasmus (1469?–1536) deliberately chose the issue of free will when he finally decided that he must break with Luther (1524). The Reformer's gloomy view of human nature went against the grain of the humanist's belief in the dignity, rationality, and freedom of man, qualified though such a belief was by trust in God's grace. Luther saw the importance of the issue and struck back at Erasmus (1525) in a large book which turned out to be the closest thing to a systematic exposition of his theology which he ever wrote. Sir Thomas More (1478–1535), humanist and close friend of Erasmus, saw the problem more specifically from the point of view of the Church, as did Loyola and the fathers of the Church assembled at the Council of Trent (1545–7, 1551–2, 1562–3). John Calvin (1509–1564) summed up the case for predestination with the hard legal logic which convinced so many thousands of his readers of God's majesty and man's misery.

What, if anything, is at stake in this controversy in terms of human happiness and understanding?

A. Erasmus Attacks Luther (1524)

What shall I say of the prodigal son? How could he have wasted his share of the inheritance had it not been his to do with as he pleased? But what he had, he held of his father; and we, too, remember that all our natural qualities are so many gifts of God. Besides, he enjoyed his share even when it was in his father's possession, and then it was in safer hands. What does it mean, then—his departure from his father after suddenly having demanded his share? Quite simply, to give oneself credit for one's natural qualities, and to use them, not in obeying the commandments of God, but in satisfying carnal lusts. And what means the hunger of the prodigal son? It is the sickness by which God directs the mind of the sinner towards self-knowledge, self-hatred, and regret for having left his Father. What is the meaning of the son's inner questioning, when he envisions confession and return? It is the human will adapting itself to the motivating grace that is also called, as we have said, "prevenient" grace. What about this Father who goes before his son on the way? It is the grace of God, which allows our will to do the good when we have determined to do it.

Besides, I ask, what merit could a man claim for himself who is indebted to Him from whom he received natural intelligence and free will for all he can do with these faculties? And yet God considers it meritorious in us not to turn our soul from His grace, and to enlist our talents in His service. That is enough to show that we make no mistake in attributing something to man, although we refer all his works to God as to their author: it is from Him, in fact, that man derives the power of making his strivings one with the operations of divine grace. . . . [The divine wisdom assists man] as guide and advisor, just as an architect directs his workman, draws his plans for him, explains the reason for them, corrects his faulty beginnings, and bolsters him if he loses courage: the work is attributed to the architect, without whose aid nothing would have been created, but no one pretends that the worker and pupil were worthless. What the architect is to his pupil, grace is to our will. That is why Paul writes to the Romans (Chapter 8: 26): "Even so His Spirit cometh to aid our weakness." Now no one calls a person who does nothing weak; that term, rather, is applied to him who lacks strength sufficient to accomplish what he undertakes; in the same sense, you do not say that some one helps you when he does everything. Now Scripture continually speaks of aid, support, succour, shelter. In order for there to be aid, the person aided has to do something. You would not say that the potter helps the clay to become a pot, or that the carpenter aids the axe in making a stool.

That is why, when our opponents declare that man can do nothing without the grace of God, therefore there are no good works by men, we confront them with this proof, which I believe more probable, that men can do everything with the aid of grace, therefore all human works can be good. As many passages as there are in Holy Scripture which mention succour, there are an equal number to establish free will, and they are countless; and I shall carry the day without any possible disagreement if the matter is judged by the number of proofs. . . .

In my opinion, similarly, free will could be preserved while completely avoiding this flagrant confidence in our own merits and the other dangers seen by Luther, without even considering those which we have cited above, and while retaining the main advantages of the Lutheran teaching. This is what the doctrine means to me which attributes to grace all the first inspiration which enflames the soul, but which leaves to the human will, when it is not devoid of divine grace, a certain place in the unfolding of the drama. Now since this drama has three parts, the beginning, the development, and the fulfilment, we give the two extremities to grace and let free will enter only into the development. Thus two causes collaborate in the same given action, divine grace and the human will; but grace is the principal cause, the will a secondary one which could do nothing without the first, while grace is sufficient in itself—thus fire burns by its natural virtue, although God is the essential cause which sustains its action, without which the fire would lose all its power, if God happened to withdraw his support....

But why, we are asked, leave a place for free will? In order to have something with which justly to accuse the impious who by their own decision stand outside divine grace; to acquit God of the false charges of cruelty or injustice; to drive despair or arrogance far from us; to inspire us to effort. These are the reasons which have led almost all writers to admit free will; but it would remain ineffective without the perpetual aid of the grace of God, which justly prevents us from pride. But still it will be said: what good, then, is free will, if it can do nothing by itself? I shall only reply, And what would be the use of man himself and all his faculties, if God acted on him as the potter on the clay, or even as He might act on a pebble?

Erasmus, *De Libero Arbitrio* (1524), in J. Clericus, ed., *Desiderii Erasmi Roterodami Opera Omnia* (Lugduni Batavorum, 1703–1706), IX, 1240, 1244, 1248, trans. Brice M. Clagett.

B. Luther Replies to Erasmus (1525)

You [Erasmus] alone in pre-eminent distinction from all others, have entered upon the thing itself; that is, the grand turning point of the cause; and have not wearied me with those irrelevant points about popery, purgatory, indulgences, and other like baubles, rather than causes, with which all have hitherto tried to hunt me down,—though in vain. You, and you alone, saw what was the grand hinge upon which the whole turned, and therefore you attacked the vital part at once; for which, from my heart, I thank you....

The human will is, as it were, a beast between [God and Satan]. If God sit thereon, it wills and goes where God will: as the Psalm saith, "I am become as it were a beast before thee, and I am continually with thee." (Ps. 73:22–23.) If Satan sit thereon, it wills and goes as Satan will. Nor is it in the power of its own will to choose, to which rider it will run, nor which it will seek; but the riders themselves contend, which shall have and hold it....

God is that Being, for whose will no cause or reason is to be assigned, as a rule or standard by which it acts; seeing that, nothing is superior or equal to it, but it is itself the rule of all things. For if it acted by any rule or standard, or from any cause or reason, it would be no longer the will of God. Wherefore, what God wills is not therefore right, because He ought or ever was bound so to will; but on the contrary, what takes place is therefore right, because He so wills. A cause and reason are assigned for the will of the creature, but not for the will of the Creator; unless you set up, over Him, another Creator....

As to myself, I openly confess, that I should not wish "free-will" to be granted me, even if it could be so, nor anything else to be left in my own hands, whereby I might endeavour something towards my own salvation. And that, not merely because in so many opposing dangers, and so many assaulting devils, I could not stand and hold it fast (in which state no man could be saved, seeing that one devil is stronger than all men); but because, even though there were no dangers, no conflicts, no devils, I should be compelled to labour under a continual uncertainty, and to beat the air only. Nor would my conscience, even if I should live and work to all eternity, ever come to a settled certainty, how much it ought to do in order to satisfy God. For whatever work should be done, there would still remain a scrupling, whether or not it pleased God, whether He required any thing more; as is proved in the experience of all those who believe in works, and as I myself learned to my bitter cost, through so many years of my own experience.

But now, since God has put my salvation out of the way of *my* will, and has taken it under *His own,* and has promised to save me, not according to my working or manner of life, but according to His own grace and mercy, I rest fully assured and persuaded that He is faithful, and will not lie, and moreover great and powerful, so that no devils, no adversities can destroy Him, or pluck me out of His hand.

"No one (saith He) shall pluck them out of My hand, because My Father which gave them Me is greater than all" (John, 10:27–28). Hence it is certain, that in this way, if all are not saved, yet some, yea, many shall be saved; whereas by the power of "free-will," no one whatever could be saved, but all must perish together. And moreover, we are certain and persuaded, that in this way, we please God, not from the merit of our own works, but from the favour of His mercy promised unto us; and that, if we work less, or work badly, He does not impute it unto us, but, as a Father, pardons us and makes us better.

Martin Luther, *The Bondage of the Will* (1525), trans. Henry Cole (Grand Rapids, Mich.: W. B. Eerdmans Publishing Co., 1931), pp. 74, 231, 384–85, 391. Original in *WA,* XVIII, 551 ff.

C. Sir Thomas More Criticizes Luther (1528)

Every man that any faith hath, and any manner knowledge of Christian belief, may well and surely perceive that Luther and all his offspring, with all those that favour and set forth his sect, be very limbs of the devil, and open enemies to the faith of Christ. And not only to the faith and manhood of our Saviour Christ, but also against the Holy Ghost and the Father Himself, and utterly against all goodness of the Godhead, as those that wretchedly lay all the weight and blame of our sin to the necessity and constraint of God's ordinance, affirming that we do no sin of ourself by any power of our own will but by the compulsion and handiwork of God. And that we do not the sin ourself, but that God doth the sin in us Himself. And thus these wretched heretics, with this blasphemous heresy alone, lay more villainous rebuke to the great majesty of God, than ever any one ribald laid unto another.

For who was there ever that laid unto another all the particular evil deeds of any one other man, where these ribalds lay to the charge and blame of God all the malice and mischiefs, from the first fault to the last, that ever was wrought or thought by man, woman or devil? And by this give they [to] wretches great boldness to follow their foul affections as things after their opinion more verily wrought in them by God than the best minds be in good men, and that it were therefore in vain for them to resist their sinful appetites. And if they shall be damned, yet they say it shall be long ere they feel it. For Luther saith that all souls shall sleep and feel neither good nor bad after this life till doomsday. And then they that shall be damned, shall be damned, he saith, for no deserving of their own deeds but for such evil deeds as God only forced and constrained them unto and wrought in them Himself, using them in all those evil deeds but as a dead instrument, as a man heweth with an hatchet; and that God shall damn all that shall be damned for His own deeds only which Himself shall have done in them; and, finally, for his own pleasure because it liked him not to choose them as he did his chosen people. Whom they say that he chose in such wise before the beginning of the world, that they can never sin.

The Dialogue Concerning Tyndale by Sir Thomas More (1528), W. E. Campbell, ed. (London: Eyre & Spottiswoode, Ltd., 1927), pp. 279–80.

D. Loyola Warns Those Who Attack Free Will

Although it is very true that no one can be saved unless he is predestined and has faith and grace, there is great need for caution in the way we speak and write about all this. We ought not to speak much about predestination as a matter of course; but if mention is made of it at some time in some way, we should speak so that ordinary people may not fall into any error and say, as sometimes they do, "If I am going to be saved or lost, the question is already settled, and whether I do good or evil, there can be no other outcome"; and therefore becoming paralyzed, they neglect the good works which lead to their salvation and to the spiritual profit of their souls. . . . So we may speak of faith and grace so far as we can with the help of God, for the greater praise of His divine majesty, but not in such a way nor in such terms, especially in these perilous times of ours, that good works and free will shall receive any detriment or come to be considered of no account.

Ignatius of Loyola, "Rules for the true understanding which we should have of the Church Militant," Nos. 14, 15, 17, *Monumenta Ignatiana* (2nd series), *Exercitia Spiritualia* (Madrid, 1919), 556–60, trans. E. Harris Harbison.

E. Calvin Reasserts Predestination (1559)

Indeed, God asserts his possession of omnipotence, and claims our acknowledgment of this attribute; not such as is imagined by sophists, vain, idle, and almost asleep, but vigilant, efficacious, operative, and engaged in continual action; not a more general principle of confused motion, as if he should command a river to flow through the channels once made for it, but a power constantly exerted on every distinct and particular movement. For he is accounted omnipotent, not because he is able to act, yet sits down in idleness, or continues by a general instinct the order of nature originally appointed by him; but because he governs heaven and earth by his providence, and regulates all things in such a manner that nothing happens but according to his counsel. For when it is said in the Psalms, that he does whatsoever he pleases, it denotes his certain and deliberate will. For it would be quite insipid to expound the words of the Prophet in the philosophical manner, that God is the prime agent, because he is the principle and cause of all motion; whereas the faithful should rather encourage themselves in adversity with this consolation, that they suffer no affliction, but by the ordination and command of God, because they are under his hand. But if the government of God be thus extended to all his works, it is a puerile cavil to limit it to the influence and course of nature. And they not only defraud God of his glory, but themselves of a very useful doctrine, who confine the Divine providence within such narrow bounds, as though he permitted all things to proceed in an uncontrolled course, according to a perpetual law of nature; for nothing would exceed the misery of man, if he were exposed to all the motions of the heaven, air, earth, and waters. . . .

Predestination, by which God adopts some to the hope of life, and adjudges others to eternal death, no one, desirous of the credit of piety, dares absolutely to deny. But it is involved in many cavils, especially by those who make foreknowledge the cause of it. We maintain, that both belong to God; but it is preposterous to represent one as dependent on the other. When we attribute foreknowledge to God, we mean that all things have ever been, and perpetually remain, before his eyes, so that to his knowledge nothing is future or past, but all things are present; and present in such a manner, that he does not merely conceive of them from ideas formed in his mind, as things remembered by us appear present to our minds, but really beholds and sees them as if actually placed before him. And this foreknowledge extends to the whole world, and to all the creatures. Predestination we call the eternal decree of God, by which he has determined in himself, what he would have to become of every individual of mankind. . . .

In conformity, therefore, to the clear doctrine of the Scripture, we assert, that by an eternal and immutable counsel, God has once for all determined, both whom he would admit to salvation, and whom he would condemn to destruction. We affirm that this counsel, as far as concerns the elect, is founded on his gratuitous mercy, totally irrespective of human merit; but that to those whom he devotes to condemnation, the gate of life is closed by a just and irreprehensible, but incomprehensible, judgment. . . .

These things will amply suffice for persons of piety and modesty, who remember that they are men. But as these virulent adversaries are not content with one species of opposition, we will reply to them all as occasion shall require. Foolish mortals enter into many contentions with God, as though they could arraign Him to plead to their accusations. In the first place they inquire, by what right the Lord is angry with his creatures who had not provoked him by any previous offence; for that to devote to destruction whom he pleases, is more like the caprice of a tyrant than the lawful sentence of a judge; that men have reason, therefore, to expostulate with God, if they are predestinated to eternal death without any demerit of their own, merely by his sovereign will. If such thoughts even enter the minds of pious men, they will be sufficiently enabled to break their violence by this one consideration, how exceedingly presumptuous it is only to inquire into the causes of the Divine will; which is in fact, and is justly entitled to be, the cause of every thing that exists. For if it has any cause, then there must be something antecedent, on which it depends; which it is impious to suppose. For the will of God is the highest rule of justice; so that what He wills must be considered just, for this very reason, because He wills it. When it is inquired, therefore, why the Lord did so, the answer must be, Because He would. But if you go

further, and ask why He so determined, you are in search of something greater and higher than the will of God, which can never be found. Let human temerity, therefore, desist from seeking that which is not, lest it should fail of finding that which is. This will be a sufficient restraint to any one disposed to reason with reverence concerning the secrets of his God. Against the audaciousness of the impious, who are not afraid openly to rail against God, the Lord will sufficiently defend himself by his own justice, without any vindication by us, when, depriving their consciences of every subterfuge, he shall convict them and bind them with a sense of their guilt. Yet we espouse not the notion of the Romish theologians concerning the absolute and arbitrary power of God, which, on account of its profaneness, deserves our detestation. We represent not God as lawless, who is a law to himself; because, as Plato says, laws are necessary to men, who are the subjects of evil desires; but the will of God is not only pure from every fault, but the highest standard of perfection, even the law of all laws. . . .

Wherefore some people falsely and wickedly charge God with a violation of equal justice, because, in his predestination, he observes not the same uniform course of proceeding towards all. If he finds all guilty, they say, let him punish all alike; if innocent, let him withhold the rigour of justice from all. But they deal with him just as if either mercy were forbidden to him, or, when he chooses to show mercy, he were constrained wholly to renounce justice. What is it that they require: if all are guilty, that they shall suffer the same punishment. We confess the guilt to be common, but we say, that some are relieved by Divine mercy. They say, Let it relieve all. But we reply, Justice requires that he should likewise show himself to be a just judge in the infliction of punishment. When they object to this, what is it but attempting to deprive God of the opportunity to manifest his mercy, or to grant it to him, at least, on the condition that he wholly abandon his justice?

John Calvin, *Institutes of the Christian Religion*, trans. John Allen, 6th American ed. (Philadelphia: The Westminster Press, 1930), I, 185; II, 144–45, 149, 165.

III. The Problem of Authority

The medieval theory of the authority of the pope in the Church and of the Church in human society is clearly summarized in the papal bull *Unam Sanctam* (1302). Luther did not challenge this authority until six or seven years after his conversion experience. In 1517 he attacked corruptions in the doctrine of indulgences in 95 Theses. Unexpectedly and immediately, he was applauded by thousands of his fellow Germans. The papacy saw the danger but handled it clumsily. In three years of disputing and negotiating Luther was driven step by step to see the full implications of his belief that man is saved by faith, not by works. As his position became more and more revolutionary, he was officially condemned by ecclesiastical authority; and as he was condemned, he appealed first to a future pope who might be better informed, then to a General Council, finally in effect to the Bible and his own conscience. He had raised the problem of religious authority in a way more pregnant with danger to the Church than any heretic had done for over a thousand years.

In 1520 Luther openly broke with the papacy in a pamphlet from which selections are given below. A year later he defied the demand of the highest authorities in Church and State at the Imperial Diet of Worms that he recant his views—in words which rang throughout Europe. Humanists like Erasmus, who had greeted Luther's attack on indulgences with enthusiasm, were shocked. Erasmus' subtle mind saw the difficulties and dangers in Luther's appeal to the Bible and to individual judgment. As a professional scholar, Erasmus valued reason, and he had a high regard for the authority of the early Church Fathers. His friend, Sir Thomas More, saw the problem more from the point of view of the Church, the divine institution founded by Christ to continue His authority. The Council of Trent finally settled the issue of the interpretation of Scripture for Roman Catholics. No one stated the belief in the virtues of obedience to ecclesiastical authority with more warmth and conviction than Loyola, writing in the closing years of his life to the members of his Order in Portugal. It remained for Calvin to state the argument for the sole authority of Scripture more sharply than it had ever been stated before, and for his erstwhile pupil and later incisive critic, Sebastian Castellio (1515–1563), to attack Calvin's argument from a point of view still Christian and Protestant, but suggestive of the skepticism and tolerance of a later age.

In reading what follows, it is important to notice the key words which betray an author's cast of mind or point of view. What are these words? What is at stake in the argument? What modern parallels suggest themselves?

A. Luther Challenges the Authority of the Roman Church (1520–21)

The Romanists have, with great adroitness, drawn three walls round themselves, with which they have hitherto protected themselves, so that no one could reform them, whereby all Christendom has fallen terribly.

Firstly, if pressed by the temporal power, they have affirmed and maintained that the temporal power has no jurisdiction over them, but, on the contrary, that the spiritual power is above the temporal.

Secondly, if it were proposed to admonish them with the Scriptures, they objected that no one may interpret the Scriptures but the Pope.

Thirdly, if they are threatened with a council, they pretend that no one may call a council but the Pope.

Thus they have secretly stolen our three rods, so that they may be unpunished, and intrenched themselves behind these three walls, to act with all the wickedness and malice, which we now witness. . . .

Let us, in the first place, attack the first wall [that the temporal power has no jurisdiction over the spiritual]:

It has been devised that the Pope, bishops, priests, and monks are called the *spiritual estate;* princes, lords, artificers, and peasants are the *temporal estate.* This is an artful lie and hypocritical device, but let no one be made afraid by it, and that for this reason: that all Christians are truly of the spiritual estate, and there is no difference among them, save of office alone. As St. Paul says (1 Cor. 12), we are all one body, though each member does its own work, to serve the others. This is because we have one baptism, one Gospel, one faith, and are all Christians alike; for baptism, Gospel, and faith, these alone make spiritual and Christian people.

As for the unction by a Pope or a bishop, tonsure, ordination, consecration, and clothes differing from those of laymen—all this may make a hypocrite or an anointed puppet, but never a Christian or a spiritual man. Thus we are all consecrated as priests by baptism....

Therefore a priest should be nothing in Christendom but a functionary; as long as he holds his office, he has precedence of others; if he is deprived of it, he is a peasant or a citizen like the rest. Therefore a priest is verily no longer a priest after deposition. But now they have invented *caractère indélébiles,* and pretend that a priest after deprivation still differs from a simple layman. They even imagine that a priest can never be anything but a priest —that is, that he can never become a layman. All this is nothing but mere talk and ordinance of human invention.

It follows, then, that between laymen and priests, princes and bishops, or, as they call it, between spiritual and temporal persons, the only real difference is one of office and function, and not of estate....

Now see what a Christian doctrine is this: that the temporal authority is not above the clergy, and may not punish it. This is as if one were to say the hand may not help, though the eye is in grievous suffering. Is it not unnatural, not to say unchristian, that one member may not help another, or guard it against harm? Nay, the nobler the member, the more the rest are bound to help it. Therefore I say, Forasmuch as the temporal power has been ordained by God for the punishment of the bad and the protection of the good, therefore we must let it do its duty throughout the whole Christian body, without respect of persons, whether it strike Popes, bishops, priests, monks, nuns, or whoever it may be....

The second wall is even more tottering and weak: that they alone pretend to be considered masters of the Scriptures; although they learn nothing of them all their life. They assume authority, and juggle before us with impudent words, say that the Pope cannot err in matters of faith, whether he be evil or good, albeit they cannot prove it by a single letter. That is why the canon law contains so many heretical and unchristian, nay unnatural laws; but of these we need not speak now. For whereas they imagine the Holy Ghost never leaves them, however unlearned and wicked they may be, they grow bold enough to decree whatever they like. But were this true, where were the need and use of the Holy Scriptures? Let us burn them, and content ourselves with the unlearned gentlemen at Rome, in whom the Holy Ghost dwells, who, however, can dwell in pious souls only. If I had not read it, I could never have believed that the devil should have put forth such follies at Rome and find a following....

Therefore it is a wickedly devised fable —and they cannot quote a single letter to confirm it—that it is for the Pope alone to interpret the Scriptures or to confirm the interpretation of them. They have assumed the authority of their own selves. And though they say that this authority was given to St. Peter when the keys were given to him, it is plain enough that the keys were not given to St. Peter alone, but to the whole community. Besides, the keys were not ordained for doctrine or authority, but for sin, to bind or loose; and what they claim besides this from the keys is mere invention....

Only consider the matter. They must needs acknowledge that there are pious Christians among us that have the true faith, spirit, understanding, word, and mind of Christ; why then should we reject their word and understanding, and follow a pope who has neither understanding nor spirit? Surely this were to deny our whole faith and the Christian Church. Moreover, if the article of our faith is right, "I believe in the holy Christian Church," the Pope cannot alone be right; else we must say, "I believe in the Pope of Rome," and reduce the Christian Church to one man, which is a devilish and damnable heresy. Besides that, we are all priests, as I have said, and have all one faith, one Gospel, one Sacrament; how then should we not have the power of discerning and judging what is right or wrong in matters of faith?... Balaam's ass was wiser than the prophet. If God spoke by an ass against a prophet, why should He not speak by a pious man against the Pope?

The third wall falls of itself, as soon as the first two have fallen....

When need requires, and the pope is a cause of offence to Christendom, in these cases whoever can best do so, as a faithful member of the whole body, must do what he can to procure a true free council. This no one can do so well as the temporal authorities, especially since they are fellow-Christians, fellow-priests, sharing one spirit and one power in all things, and since they should exercise the office that they have received from God without hindrance, whenever it is necessary and useful that it should be exercised....

As for their boasts of their authority, that no one must oppose it, this is idle talk. No one in Christendom has any authority to do harm, or to forbid others to prevent harm being done. There is no authority in Church but for reformation. Therefore if the Pope wished to use his power to prevent the calling of a free council, so as to prevent the reformation of the Church, we must not respect him or his power; and if he should begin to excommunicate and fulminate, we must despise this as the doings of a madman, and, trusting in God, excommunicate and repel him as best we may....

And now I hope the false, lying spectre will be laid with which the Romanists have long terrified and stupefied our consciences. And it will be seen that, like all the rest of us, they are subject to the temporal sword; that they have no authority to interpret the Scriptures by force without skill; and that they have no power to prevent a council, or to pledge it in accordance with their pleasure, or to bind it beforehand, and deprive it of its freedom; and that if they do this, they are verily of the fellowship of anti-Christ and the devil, and have nothing of Christ but the name.

Martin Luther, *To the Christian Nobility of the German Nation* (1520), in Henry Wace and C. A. Buchheim, eds., *Luther's Primary Works, op. cit.*, pp. 162–75, *passim.*

[Closing words at the Diet of Worms, April 18, 1521]:...Since your Majesty and your lordships ask for a simple reply, I shall give you one without horns and without teeth: unless I am convinced by the evidence of the Scriptures or by plain reason—for I do not accept the authority of the Pope or the councils alone, since it is established that they have often erred and contradicted themselves—I am bound by the Scriptures I have cited and my conscience is captive to the Word of God. I cannot and will not recant anything, for it is neither safe nor right to go against conscience. I can do no other. Here I stand. God help me. Amen. [The words "I can do no other. Here I stand" are not in the earliest accounts of what Luther said.]

WA, VII, 838, trans. E. Harris Harbison.

B. Erasmus on the Difficulties of Biblical Authority

Not that I do not know that the whole source and vein of Christian philosophy is hidden in the Gospel and the Epistles. But the strange and often confused terms, the metaphors and oblique figures of speech, hold so much difficulty that we must often perspire with effort before we understand the meaning. In my opinion it would be best if some men of both piety and learning were assigned the task of distilling from the purest sources of the Evangelists and the Apostles and from the most approved interpreters the essence of the whole philosophy of Christ—as simply as is compatible with scholarship, as briefly as is compatible with clarity. Let those things which have to do with faith be summed up in as few articles as possible. Let those which have to do with conduct be set down also in few words and in such

a way that men may know that the yoke of Christ is pleasant and easy, not painful; that their forebears are fathers, not tyrants —pastors, not pirates; and that they themselves are called to salvation, not to slavery. They are human beings, after all; their hearts are not iron or adamant. They can melt, they can be won by kindnesses, as even the beasts. And the most effective agent is Christian truth. . . .

Erasmus to Paul Volz, August 14, 1518, P. S. Allen, ed., *Opus Epistolarum Desiderii Erasmi Roterodami* (Oxford: The Clarendon Press, 1913), III, 365–66, trans. E. Harris Harbison.

I take so little pleasure in dogmatizing that I should rather rank myself with the sceptics, whenever I am justified in so doing by the inviolable authority of Holy Scripture and by the decisions of the Church, to which I always submit my judgment quite willingly, whether or not I understand the reasons for what she decrees. And this temper of mind appears to me preferable to that of certain others, who, narrowly attached to their own views, never let anyone deviate from them in anything, and who violently twist all the texts of Scripture in support of the position they have embraced once and for all. . . .

Here it will be objected: "Why the need of interpretation, when Scripture itself is perfectly clear?" But if it is as clear as all that, why, over the centuries, have such eminent men been blind on so important a point, as our opponents contend? If Scripture is without obscurity, why was there need for prophecies in apostolic times? That, I shall be told, was a gift of the Holy Spirit. But I should like to know whether, just as the gift of healing and the gift of tongues have ceased, this divine gift has not ceased also. And if it has not ceased, we must seek to learn to whom it could have passed. If it has passed to merely anyone at all, then every interpretation will be uncertain; if it has been received by no one, since today so many obscurities still torment the learned, no interpretation will be more certain. If I

maintain that it resides in the successors of the apostles, it will be objected that over the centuries many men have succeeded the apostles who nevertheless had none of the apostolic spirit. And yet, everything else being equal, it will be sought in them, for it is more probable that God has infused His Spirit in those to whom He has given holy orders; just as we believe that grace is more clearly given to the baptized than to the unbaptized.

But, as we must, we shall admit no less than the possibility that the Spirit may actually reveal to some humble and illiterate person truths withheld from a host of learned men, as when Christ thanked His Father for the things He made known to the simple, to those whom the world thought mad—things he had hidden from the wise and the judicious, from the knowledge of scribes, Pharisees, and philosophers. And perhaps Dominic, perhaps Francis [the thirteenth-century saints], were the kind of madmen who are allowed to follow their inspirations. But if Paul, in the day when this gift of the Spirit was in its full vigor, already warns men to check on whether these inspirations really come from God, what must we do in our worldly age? By what standard shall we judge opinions? By learning? But there are none but master scholars in both parties. By conduct? On both sides, likewise, there are only sinners. But we find the chorus of saints all on the same side, defending free will. I am told, it is true, "They were nothing but men." But I only meant to compare men with one another, never with God. I am asked, what does the majority prove, with regard to spiritual insight? I answer, what does the minority prove? I am asked, how can a bishop's mitre be of use in understanding Holy Scripture? I answer, what good is a mantle or cowl? Again, how can philosophical studies make it easier to understand Holy Writ? And I reply, what use is ignorance? And again, how is the comprehension of texts connected with the meeting of a council, where it might be that no member had received the Spirit of God? I answer, what then is the value of private pseudo-councils of a few individuals, where there is only too clearly no possessor of the Spirit?

Do we remember this plea of Paul's, "Don't ask for proof that Christ lives in me"? Then the apostles were only believed to the extent to which their miracles confirmed their teaching. These days, on the contrary, anyone at all demands credence just because he declares he is filled with the spirit of the Gospel. Because the apostles drove out serpents, cured the sick, brought the dead to life, and gave the gift of tongues by the laying on of hands, men decided to believe, and not without difficulty, the paradoxes they taught. And today, when we see new teachers declaring things that common sense cannot even class as paradoxes, we have not yet seen one of them capable of curing a lame horse. And would to Heaven that, if they cannot work miracles, some of them would at least show the purity and simplicity of apostolic life, which to us, poor latecomers, would be miraculous enough!

I am not speaking specifically of Luther, whom I have never met and whose works give me a confused impression, but of certain others whom I have known more closely. It is they who in biblical controversies reject the interpretation of the Fathers which we suggest to them, they who cry unrestrainedly, "The Fathers were only men!" If they are asked what criterion can be used to establish the true interpretation of Scripture, since there are only men on both sides, they rely on the revelations of the Spirit. But if they are asked why the Spirit should favor them rather than those whose miracles have shone forth throughout the world, they answer as if the Gospel had disappeared from the earth thirteen centuries ago. If you insist that their life be worthy of the Spirit, they retort that they are justified by faith, not by works. If you require miracles, they tell you that the time for them has long passed, and that there is no longer any need for them, now that the Scriptures are fully clarified. And then if you doubt that Scripture is clear precisely on the point where so many great minds have erred, you fall back into the same vicious circle.

Besides, if we admit that he who possesses the Spirit is sure of understanding the Scriptures, how shall I be certain of what he has seen only partially? What shall I do when several learned men bring me different interpretations, each one swearing all the time that he has the Spirit? Especially, if we add that the Spirit does not reveal all truth to them fully, even he who has the Spirit can go wrong, and err on some point.

These are my objections to those who so easily reject the traditional interpretation of the Holy Books, and who propose their own as if it had plummeted from Heaven. Finally, assuming that the Spirit of Christ could have left His people in error on some secondary point without immediate repercussions on human salvation, how can we admit that for thirteen hundred years He abandoned His Church to error, and that in all the host of holy people not one could reveal to the Church that truth which, our recent arrivals pretend, constitutes the heart of all the Gospel teaching?

But to finish this matter: whatever others may arrogate to themselves is their own affair; as for me, I claim for myself neither wisdom nor sanctity, and I take no pride in my intellect, but I shall simply and carefully set forth the views which capture my allegiance. If any one wishes to teach me, I shall not meet the truth with a closed mind.

Erasmus, *De Libero Arbitrio* (1524), in J. Clericus, ed., *Desiderii Erasmi Roterodami Opera Omnia* (Lugduni Batavorum, 1703–1706), IX, 1215, 1219–20, trans. Brice M. Clagett.

C. Sir Thomas More Defends and Defines the Church (1528)

And therefore is Holy Scripture, as I said, the highest and the best learning that any man can have, if one take the right way in the learning.

It is, as a good holy saint saith, so marvellously tempered, that a mouse may wade therein, and an elephant be drowned therein. For there is no man so low but if he will seek his way with the staff of his faith in his hand, and hold that fast and search the way therewith, and have the old holy fathers also for his guides, going on with a good purpose and a lowly heart, using reason and refusing no good learning with calling of God for wisdom, grace and help, that he may well keep his way and follow his good guides, then shall he never fall in peril, but well and surely wade through and come to such end of his journey as himself would well wish. But surely if he be as long as Longyus, and have an high heart and trust upon his own wit as he doth, look he never so lowly, that setteth all the old holy fathers at nought, that fellow shall not fail to sink over the ears and drown. And of all wretches worst shall he walk that, forcing little of the faith of Christ's church, cometh to the scripture of God to look and try therein whether the church believe aright or not. For either doubteth he whether Christ teach his church true, or else whether Christ teacheth it at all or not. And then he doubteth whether Christ in his words did say true when he said he would be with his church till the end of the world. And surely the thing that made Arius, Pelagius, Faustus, Manichaeus, Donatus, Eluidius and all the rabble of the old heretics to drown themselves in those damnable heresies, was nothing but high pride of their learning in scripture, wherein they followed their own wits and left the common faith of the catholic church, preferring their own gay glosses before the right catholic faith of all Christ's church, which can never err in any substantial point that God would have us bounden to believe. And therefore, to end where we began, whoso will not unto the study of scripture take the points of the catholic faith as a rule of interpretation, but, of diffidence and mistrust, study to seek in scripture whether the faith of the church be true or not, he cannot fail to fall in worse errors and far more jeopardous than any man can do by philosophy, whereof the reasons and arguments in matters of our faith have nothing in like authority. . . .

And finally—to put out of question which is Christ's very [i.e. true] church, since it is agreed between us and granted through christendom and a conclusion very true that by the church we know the scripture—which church is that by which ye know the scripture?

Is it not this company and congregation of all these nations that, without factions taken and precision from the remnant, profess the name and faith of Christ? By this church know we the scripture; and this is the very church; and this hath begun at Christ and hath had him for their head, and saint Peter his vicar, after him, the head under him, and always since, the successors of him continually—and have had his holy faith, and his blessed sacraments, and his holy scriptures delivered, kept, and conserved therein by God and his holy spirit. And albeit some nations fall away, yet likewise as how many boughs soever fall from the tree— though they fall more than be left thereon —yet they make no doubt which is the very tree, although each of them were planted again in another place and grew to a greater than the stock he came first of; right so, while we see and well know that all the companies and sects of heretics and schismatics—how great soever they grow—came out of this church that I spake of, we know evermore that the heretics be they that be severed, and the church the stock that all they came out of. And since that only the church of Christ is the vine that Christ spake of in the gospel, which he taketh for his body mystical; and that every branch severed from that tree loseth his lively nourishing, we must needs well know that all these branches of heretics fallen from the church —the vine of Christ's mystical body— seem they never so fresh and green, be yet indeed but witherlings that wither and shall dry up, able to serve for nothing but for the fire.

W. E. Campbell, ed., *The Dialogue Concerning Tyndale by Sir Thomas More* (1528) (London: Eyre & Spottiswoode, Ltd., 1927), pp. 102–3. 143–44.

D. The Council of Trent Defines the Relation of Church and Scripture (1546)

...Following the examples of the orthodox Fathers, [the Council] receives and venerates with a feeling of piety and reverence all the books both of the Old and New Testaments, since one God is the author of both; also the traditions, whether they relate to faith or to morals, as having been dictated either orally by Christ or by the Holy Ghost, and preserved in the Catholic Church in unbroken succession. ...

[The Council], considering that not a little advantage will accrue to the Church of God if it be made known which of all the Latin editions of the sacred books now in circulation is to be regarded as authentic, ordains and declares that the old Latin Vulgate Edition, which, in use for so many hundred years, has been approved by the Church, be in public lectures, disputations, sermons and expositions held as authentic, and that no one dare or presume under any pretext whatsoever to reject it.

Furthermore, to check unbridled spirits, it decrees that no one relying on his own judgment shall, in matters of faith and morals pertaining to the edification of Christian doctrine, distorting the Holy Scriptures in accordance with his own conceptions, presume to interpret them contrary to that sense which holy mother Church, to whom it belongs to judge of their true sense and interpretation, has held and holds, or even contrary to the unanimous teaching of the Fathers, even though such interpretations should never at any time be published. Those who act contrary to this shall be made known by the [bishops] and punished in accordance with the penalties prescribed by the law. (Fourth Session, Decrees concerning the Scriptures.)

H. J. Schroeder, ed., *Canons and Decrees of the Council of Trent* (St. Louis: B. Herder Book Co., 1941), pp. 17–19.

E. Calvin Insists upon the Sole Authority of Scripture (1559)

There has very generally prevailed a most pernicious error, that the Scriptures have only so much weight as is conceded to them by the suffrages of the Church; as though the eternal and inviolable truth of God depended on the arbitrary will of men. For thus, with great contempt of the Holy Spirit, they inquire, Who can assure us that God is the author of the Scriptures? Who can with certainty affirm, that they have been preserved safe and uncorrupted to the present age? Who can persuade us that this book ought to be received with reverence, and that expunged from the sacred number, unless all these things were regulated by the decisions of the Church? It depends, therefore (say they), on the determination of the Church, to decide both what reverence is due to the Scripture, and what books are to be comprised in its canon. Thus sacrilegious men, while they wish to introduce an unlimited tyranny under the name of the Church, are totally unconcerned with what absurdities they embarrass themselves and others, provided they can extort from the ignorant this one admission, that the Church can do every thing. But, if this be true, what will be the condition of those wretched consciences, which are seeking a solid assurance of eternal life, if all the promises extant concerning it rest only on the judgment of men? Will the reception of such an answer cause their fluctuations to subside, and their terrors to vanish? Again, how will the impious ridicule our faith, and all men call it in question, if it be understood to possess only a precarious authority depending on the favor of men!

But such cavillers are completely refuted even by one word of the Apostle. He testifies that the Church is "built upon the foundation of the apostles and prophets." If the doctrine of the prophets and apostles be the foundation of the Church, it must have been certain, antecedently to the existence of the Church. Nor is there any foundation for this cavil, that though the Church derive its origin from the Scriptures, yet it remains doubtful what writings are to be ascribed to the prophets and apostles, unless it be determined by the Church. For if the Christian Church has been from the beginning founded on the writings of the prophets and the preaching of the apostles, wherever that doctrine is found, the approbation of it has certainly preceded the formation of the Church; since without it the Church itself had never existed. It is a very false notion, therefore, that the power of judging of the Scripture belongs to the Church, so as to make the certainty of it dependent on the Church's will. Wherefore, when the Church receives it, and seals it with her suffrage, she does not authenticate a thing otherwise dubious or controvertible, but,

knowing it to be the truth of her God, performs a duty of piety, by treating it with immediate veneration. But with regard to the question, How shall we be persuaded of its divine original, unless we have recourse to the decree of the Church? this is just as if any one should inquire, How shall we learn to distinguish light from darkness, white from black, sweet from bitter? For the Scripture exhibits as clear evidence of its truth, as white and black things do of their color, or sweet and bitter things of their taste....

The testimony of the Spirit is superior to all reason. For, as God alone is a sufficient witness of himself in his own word, so also the word will never gain credit in the hearts of men, till it be confirmed by the internal testimony of the Spirit. It is necessary, therefore, that the same Spirit, who spake by the mouths of the prophets, should penetrate into our hearts, to convince us that they faithfully delivered the oracles which were divinely intrusted to them....

Without this certainty, better and stronger than any human judgment, in vain will the authority of the Scripture be either defended by arguments, or established by the consent of the Church, or confirmed by any other supports; since, unless the foundation be laid, it remains in perpetual suspense. Whilst, on the contrary, when, regarding it in a different point of view from common things, we have once religiously received it in a manner worthy of its excellence, we shall then derive great assistance from things which before were not sufficient to establish the certainty of it in our minds. For it is admirable to observe how much it conduces to our confirmation, attentively to study the order and disposition of the Divine Wisdom dispensed in it, the heavenly nature of its doctrine, which never savours of any thing terrestrial, the beautiful agreement of all the parts with each other, and other similar characters adapted to conciliate respect to any writings.

John Calvin, *Institutes of the Christian Religion*, trans. John Allen, *op. cit.*, I, 75–77, 79, 81.

F. Sebastian Castellio Upholds Sense and Reason (c.1563)

All sects hold their religion according to the Word of God and say that it is certain.... Calvin says that his is certain, and they, theirs. He says they are wrong and wishes to be judge, and so do they. Who shall be judge? Who made Calvin the arbiter of all the sects, that he alone should kill? He has the Word of God and so have they. If the matter is certain, to whom is it certain? To Calvin? But why does he then write so many books about manifest truth? There is nothing unknown to Calvin. He talks as if he might be in paradise and writes huge tomes to explain what he says is absolutely clear.

In view of all this uncertainty we must define the heretic simply as one with whom we disagree. And if, then, we are going to kill heretics, the logical outcome will be a war of extermination, since each is sure of himself. Calvin would have to invade France and other nations, wipe out cities, put all the inhabitants to the sword, sparing neither sex nor age, not even the babes and the beasts. All would have to be burned save Calvinists, Jews, and Turks, whom he excepts.

Sebastian Castellio, *Contra libellum Calvini*...[composed c. 1562, pub. in Holland, 1612], H, p. 125, trans. R. H. Bainton, *The Travail of Religious Liberty* (Philadelphia: The Westminster Press, 1951), pp. 114–15. Copyright 1951 by W. L. Jenkins. Used by permission.

All the Christian sects are agreed as to the authority [of Scripture]. The question is not whether Scripture is true, but how it is to be understood. All agree that it is true but contend as to the meaning. Learned men have not been so blind as to debate for centuries about matters which are perfectly plain....

Now since Scripture is obscure on controverted points...we must consider where lies the plain incontrovertible and unshakable truth. Then when this is discovered we can see which side of the controversy accords with Scripture and with the plain incontrovertible truth as above determined, for this must decide. Nor is there doubt that a double support is preferable to a single. I am thinking of the support of sense and intellect. These are the instruments of judging....

When men have been persuaded to shut their eyes and reject the evidence of the senses of the body and of the mind, to believe words, though all the senses refute the words, then nothing is so absurd, impossible, or false as not to be accepted. Why not believe that the white which you see is not white?...That what you perceive with the mind is not what you perceive? And then do we wonder that such monstrous errors survive until now among those who are persuaded of the like, or that today such stubborn controversies flourish among theologians? When each adheres tenaciously to words and words disagree, how can you decide if the judgment of the senses is rejected?...One says that you must eat Christ's flesh to be saved, and he has the plain words of Christ, "Except ye eat the flesh of the Son of Man," etc. Another denies that Christ's flesh profits a man for salvation and he, too, cites the plain words of Christ, "The flesh profiteth nothing." What will you do?...

I will fight with all my might against this monster [of literalism]. If I cannot kill it I hope at least to wound it severely.

We must make it clear, however, that in denying what is contrary to the senses we do not deny that which is above the senses. There is a vast distinction. In human and divine things we say that those matters are above the senses, which cannot be perceived by the senses, for example the questions what God is and whether He created the world; in how many days He made it; whether the souls of men sleep with their bodies, to rise with them....

I never find that Christ did anything contrary to the senses and intellect, and rightly, for the senses and intellect are the works of the Father, and Christ came to destroy not the works of the Father, but of the devil. No wonder then that he did not deprive men of sense and intellect. . . .

Reason is, so to speak, the daughter of God. She was before letters and ceremonies, before the world was made; and she is after letters and ceremonies, and after the world is changed and renewed she will endure and can no more be abolished than God Himself. Reason, I say, is a sort of eternal word of God, much older and surer than letters and ceremonies, according to which God taught His people before there were letters and ceremonies, and after these have passed away He will still so teach that men may be truly taught of God. According to reason Abel, Enoch, Noah, and Abraham and many others lived before the letters of Moses, and after these many have lived and will continue to live. According to reason Jesus Christ himself, the Son of the living God, lived and taught. They are the same, for reason is a sort of interior and eternal word of truth always speaking. By reason Jesus refuted the Jews who placed greater trust in letters and ceremonies. Reason worked upon the Sabbath day and taught the Jews that they might remove a sheep from the ditch on the Sabbath without offense. . . .

Let us hold to this very general rule: if any statement either in profane or sacred authors is of such a kind that, unless taken figuratively, it clearly runs counter to reason or the senses, then it must be taken figuratively and so interpreted as to be reconcilable with reason and the senses. This rule will be incredibly useful in solving many problems.

Sebastian Castellio, *De Arte Dubitandi et Confidendi, Ignorandi et Sciendi* [composed 1563], Elisabeth Feist, ed., in *Per la storia degli eretici italiani del secolo xvi in Europa* (Rome, 1937), Book I, chaps. 22–25 [trans. R. H. Bainton, *Concerning Heretics* (New York: Columbia University Press, 1935), pp. 293–97], and Book II, chap. 41, trans. E. Harris Harbison.

8

Seventeenth-Century Europe:
Politics and Science

JOHN B. WOLF

University of Minnesota

I. The Problem of Government

Seventeenth-century European men were responsible for two very important developments in the civilization of the West. In the realm of politics they brought into existence the military, bureaucratic police-state which created the first standing armies on European soil since the days of the Romans, and gave new prestige and power to government. In the realm of knowledge they overthrew what remained of Aristotle's authority and established both a new design of the universe and a new philosophy in what may well have been one of the most revolutionary developments of all time.

The century between the deaths of Henry IV (1610) and Louis XIV (1715) saw the emergence of the bureaucratic state as the central agency of government. For over a thousand years European political society had been loosely organized, with the realities of power largely in the hands of men who ruled the towns and villages rather than in the central authority of the king. The economic, technical, and military development, as well as the legal and administrative machinery, had been inadequate to support any really strong central authority. Thus, even though his predecessors for several hundred years had been working to strengthen the monarchy, Henry IV was often quite unable to

254

enforce obedience to his commands, and at the same time was very careful not to encroach upon the authority of local governments. Since the royal authority in France was more fully developed than that of most of the rest of Europe, this meant, in effect, that the traditional authorities on the land and in the towns of Europe still could and did act like quasi-independent powers.

A century later Louis XIV, the grandson of Henry IV, with an army of 400,000 men and a complex administrative and police machine that reached into the villages and towns alike, ruled the kingdom of France. The local traditional authorities in the towns and on the land were either broken or tamed; they had to recognize the power of the central government. The revolution that is implied in this contrast within France occurred elsewhere in Europe more or less in the same way. The Hapsburg lands in central Europe in 1610 were decentralized to a point that implied practically complete abdication of power by the central authority. When Leopold I died in 1705, the government in Vienna was already the central authority for the Danubian Monarchy, ruling a multinational state by a complex bureaucratic organization. On a smaller scale the same alteration in the locus of power occurred in Sweden, Denmark, Brandenburg-Prussia, and, after 1700, in Spain and in some of the Italian states. This was the dramatic political revolution of the seventeenth century.

It is, of course, impossible adequately to discuss a problem of this magnitude in a short essay. We should note, however, that the characteristic institutions that forced the rise of the bureaucratic administrative machine were the standing army and the standing navy. Up to the seventeenth century, princes relied upon feudal levies, the "free companies" of condottieri, and their palace guards for military power. Even a great king like the ruler of France did not possess military powers greater than many of his subjects. Louis XIII (1610–43), for example, made war on relatively even terms against coalitions of his barons, the city of La Rochelle, the Huguenot towns of the south, and the Protestants in Navarre. He had difficulty assembling an army stronger than the ones available to either Huguenots or noblemen. By the end of the seventeenth century, however, all over Europe there were armies of professional soldiers wearing the king's coat, supplied and fed from the king's storehouse, paid by the king's treasury, and ruled by the king's war minister. The time was past when a great baron or a city could defy the royal authority with military power.

In a way this appearance of standing armies was a return of the Roman legions to the Continent, and it is undoubtedly related to the same economic forces that had allowed the government of Rome to guard the frontier and to keep the peace with the professional soldiers. When the monetary economy gave way to one of sustenance and barter, the Roman soldiers and the Roman bureaucracy disappeared, for the absolute *sine qua non* for a standing army is money that can be collected by taxation. By the seventeenth century the extension of trade and manufacturing, lubricated by gold and silver from the new world, had re-established a monetary economy in most of Europe. It is probably not surprising that soldiers reappeared at the same time, for soldiers and sailors can protect commerce and society, and therefore trade will carry the burden of their support.

At the same time the political rivalries between the communities of Europe that had been building up for a century or more emerged as full-blown problems unrelated to the religious issues that had beclouded them in the preceding century. The rise of bureaucratic governments interested in extending the empire of taxation, and concerned with problems of strategic defenses, colonial rivalries, and commercial competition, as well as with the dynastic interests of the monarch, led to the conception of policy based upon reason of state. The treaties of Westphalia (1648), Pyrenees (1659), Nijmwegen (1678), and Ryswick (1697) successively mark the rise of the idea that the state has a reason of its own, and therefore its central government has need of power to implement it.

Actually, of course, in the second half of the seventeenth century, the preponderant power of France forced the rest of Europe to reorganize both politically and militarily to avoid falling under French domination. Louis XIV probably made his most important contribution to the historical process of his age not in France, but in the neighboring states that had to reorganize to meet his power.

One must be careful not to simplify so complex a problem as the emergence of the bureaucratic state. It was not only the great increase of commerce and a monetary economy, and the emergence of the idea of reason of state. Indeed, one should consider changes in the art of warfare, the development and expansion of legal conceptions, the religious rebellion that had placed princes at the head of state churches, and perhaps a host of other lesser forces that contributed to the process. For several hundred years, princes had been striving consciously or unconsciously to enlarge the power of their central administration. The chief instruments of this process had always been the bourgeois figures trained in law, finance, or administration who entered the royal government. These "men of the pen" in contrast to the "men of the sword" had every interest in seeing the king's government strong. The seventeenth century saw an acceleration of the process. All over Europe learned graduates of the law schools or men trained in the counting houses entered governmental service, and in the second half of the century these men came to predominate in the royal councils. When the "men of the pen" crowded the noblemen and princes of the blood from the benches around the king's council table, the bureaucratic centralized monarchy had arrived.

Naturally such a development of centralized bureaucracy did not occur without protest. In England, in France, in Hungary, and in many other states this protest took the form of armed rebellion. In France rebellious noblemen and Huguenots challenged Louis XIII's government time and again. The tenacity of the King and the genius of his great minister, Richelieu, brought victory to the royal arms, but when both the King and the Cardinal were dead, the forces of opposition again tried to rebel. These revolts, called the Fronde (1649–52), failed as much because of disunion in the camp of the opposition as because of the skill of the Cardinal Mazarin, the first minister of the regency government. The English civil war that led to the execution of Charles I and the creation of a new government made the middle years of the century even more turbulent in England than they were in France. In Brandenburg-Prussia, in Sweden, in Russia and elsewhere, the revolts came in the second half of the century. The results were nearly everywhere the same. In most of the continental states the king's government was triumphant; both nobles and townsmen were brought to heel. In England the central authority emerged as the real power in the kingdom, but its direction came to be controlled by Parliament rather than by an absolute king. Nonetheless, the rise of the English treasury and of the admiralty bespeaks the victory of the centralizing forces in society. Poland is the striking example of the state in which this centralizing process failed to achieve a victory. The Polish kingdom was left so weak and disorganized that the partitions of the eighteenth century were the inevitable results. Obviously the form of the political process demanded conformity of development in the various states of Europe; failure to create a centralized bureaucratic government invited disaster.

A revolution such as this one naturally required rationalization to make it acceptable to men. The political theorist explains what is happening in politics and in a measure helps to establish the pattern of the process. He also presents a measure of the civilization that he represents, for the political theorist picks up arguments in his environment and, by his assumptions, indicates what his society believes to be true beyond all need of questioning. Thus the theorist provides an excellent mirror in which we can see the political process as well as the intellectual climate of an era. The following selections have been chosen to bring out the rationale that men developed to explain the political developments of their age.

The great moral question that rulers and theorists alike had to face involved the relationship between the power or "might" to establish a government and rule a people, and the authority or "right" to conduct that rule. Political theorists of the Graeco-Roman era as well as of the Christian Middle Ages had almost universally condemned the exercise of naked power as tyranny and despotism. Thus men nourished in the classical tradition (as European men of culture were) had to find "right" or authority for the exercise of power. The first three selections illustrate three different approaches to this question.

The first selection, by Thomas Hobbes, brutally bases power and authority upon a necessity that he finds in the nature of man and society. Hobbes is a product of the scientific thought of his century. He pushes aside legal and theological argument and stands firmly upon a theory of psychology and society that made him both one of the most read and one of the most unpopular theorists of his age. To many of his contemporaries his frank materialism and cynical realism about men's motives, as well as his scarcely concealed rejection of Christianity, seemed monstrous and insupportable. No political philosopher after Hobbes, however, could afford to ignore the problem that *The Leviathan* posits. Like most medieval and Renaissance theorists, and, for that matter, political thinkers of the next hundred years, Hobbes assumes the medieval legal formula of the contract as the basic legal principle of society. This was the natural form for a political theory in the seventeenth century just as the idea of evolution and emergence provides a frame for theorists of our day. His analysis of the contract, however, is made dependent upon his conception of man and society rather than upon any medieval legalism. The student should be sure to understand how Hobbes has combined both power and authority in the hands of the Leviathan and given sanctity to the situation.

The second selection is from the works of the great Bishop of Meaux, Jacques Bénigne Bossuet. It was written for the instruction and edification of the Dauphin, the son of Louis XIV. The Bishop's solution is much less complex than that of the English materialist. He saw the world through the eyes of the Bible, St. Augustine, and St. Thomas, and he himself was convinced that order and authority were essential for society. Louis' government, therefore, was good, and both Louis' power and his authority were the gift and the institution of God. The Divine Right theory never found a more eloquent protagonist than Bossuet, but by the time that he propounded it, the process of history was already making kings into the first servants of states, and Divine Right was on the verge of becoming an ornamental anachronism to which men gave only lip service. Nonetheless, in Bossuet's pages we find seventeenth-century Europe's testimony to its religious faith just as Hobbes manifests its growing materialism.

The third selection is a justification for the English Revolution of 1688. John Locke ably states the Whig case that a king must obey the law or forfeit the throne. Both power and authority, according to Locke, are derived from the people who delegate power to kings but who can never give up their authority or right to anyone. Thus, as long as princes obey the law, that is, satisfy the people, they are allowed to rule, but the people do not thereby surrender their right to change rulers if princes abuse their power. Locke has been hailed as the theorist of modern constitutionalism. Indeed, the men who made the revolutions in Europe and America at the end of the eighteenth century were certainly inspired by his thinking. It must be noted, however, that neither Locke nor the men who made the English Revolution of 1688 had any intention of disrupting royal authority; they merely wanted to be sure that the king did not act arbitrarily and beyond the law. In reality the Revolution of 1688 is well within the form of the political process of the seventeenth century, for Parliament willingly strengthened the central authority to achieve its ends in war, and thereby gave England the most effective government in Europe. The "democratic" tendencies inherent in Locke's argument did not manifest themselves until almost a century after his death.

A. By What Right Does Government Exist?

1. THOMAS HOBBES' "LEVIATHAN"

Educated at Oxford and a frequent visitor to the Continent, Thomas Hobbes (1588–1679) was one of the most important political theorists of all time. He was acquainted with Bacon, Gassendi, Campanella, Descartes, Galileo, and many others who were giving the western mind a new orientation through sci-

ence. He himself was never more than an amateur in the natural sciences, but his attempt to place political philosophy on a scientific basis made him one of the first modern political theorists. Obviously Hobbes was attacking the violence and the anarchy that accompanied the English civil wars, but even more, he was attempting to establish a secure intellectual basis for the government of his king. His materialistic premises and his rigorous logic made him one of the most controversial figures of the age.

[13.] *Of the natural condition of mankind as concerning their felicity and misery*

...in the nature of man, we find three principal causes of quarrel. First, competition; secondly, diffidence; thirdly, glory.

The first, maketh men invade for gain; the second, for safety; and the third, for reputation. The first use violence, to make themselves masters of other men's persons, wives, children, and cattle; the second, to defend them; the third, for trifles, as a word, a smile, a different opinion, and any other sign of undervalue, either direct in their persons, or by reflection in their kindred, their friends, their nation, their profession, or their name.

Hereby it is manifest, that during the time men live without a common power to keep them all in awe, they are in that condition which is called war; and such a war, as is of every man, against every man. For war consisteth not in battle only, or the act of fighting; but in a tract of time, wherein the will to contend by battle is sufficiently known; and therefore the notion of *time* is to be considered in the nature of war; as it is in the nature of weather. For as the nature of foul weather lieth not in a shower or two of rain; but in an inclination thereto of many days together: so the nature of war, consisteth not in actual fighting; but in the known disposition thereto, during all the time there is no assurance to the contrary. All other time is peace.

Whatsoever therefore is consequent to a time of war, where every man is enemy to every man; the same is consequent to the time, wherein men live without other security, than what their own strength, and their own invention shall furnish them withal. In such condition, there is no place for industry, because the fruit thereof is uncertain: and consequently no culture of the earth; no navigation, nor use of the commodities that may be imported by sea; no commodious building; no instruments of moving, and removing, such things as require much force; no knowledge of the face of the earth; no account of time; no arts; no letters; no society; and which is worst of all, continual fear, and danger of violent death; and the life of man, solitary, poor, nasty, brutish, and short.

It may seem strange to some man, that has not well weighed these things; that nature should thus dissociate, and render men apt to invade, and destroy one another: and he may therefore, not trusting to this inference, made from the passions, desire perhaps to have the same confirmed by experience. Let him therefore consider with himself, when taking a journey, he arms himself, and seeks to go well accompanied; when going to sleep, he locks his doors; when even in his house he locks his chests; and this when he knows there be laws, and public officers, armed, to revenge all injuries shall be done him; what opinion he has of his fellow-subjects, when he rides armed; of his fellow citizens, when he locks his doors; and of his children, and servants, when he locks his chests. Does he not there as much accuse mankind by his actions, as I do by my words? But neither of us accuse man's nature in it. The desires, and other passions of man, are in themselves no sin. No more are the actions, that proceed from those passions, till they know a law that forbids them: which till laws be made they cannot know: nor can any law be made, till they have agreed upon the person that shall make it.

The passions that incline men to peace, are fear of death; desire of such things as are necessary to commodious living; and a hope by their industry to obtain them. And reason suggesteth convenient articles of peace, upon which men may be drawn to agreement. These articles, are they, which otherwise are called the Laws of Nature: whereof I shall speak more particularly in the two following chapters.

[14.] *Of the first and second natural laws, and of contracts*

The Right of Nature, which writers commonly call *jus naturale*, is the liberty each man hath, to use his own power, as he will himself, for the preservation of his own nature; that is to say, of his own life; and consequently, of doing anything, which in his own judgment, and reason, he shall conceive to be the aptest means thereunto.

By Liberty, is understood, according to the proper signification of the word, the absence of external impediments: which impediments, may oft take away part of a man's power to do what he would; but cannot hinder him from using the power left him, according to his judgment, and reason shall dictate to him.

A Law of Nature, *lex naturalis*, is a precept or general rule, found out by reason, by which a man is forbidden to do that, which is destructive of his life, or taketh away the means of preserving the same; and to omit that, by which he thinketh it may be best preserved. For though they that speak of this subject, use to confound *jus*, and *lex, right* and *law:* yet they ought to be distinguished; because Right consisteth in liberty to do, or to forbear; whereas Law, determineth, and bindeth to one of them: so that law, and right, differ as much, as obligation, and liberty; which in one and the same matter are inconsistent.

And because the condition of man, as hath been declared in the precedent chapter, is a condition of war of every one against every one; in which case every one is governed by his own reason; and there is nothing he can make use of, that may not be a help unto him, in preserving his life against his enemies; it followeth, that in such a condition, every man has a right to every thing; even to one another's body. And therefore, as long as this natural right of every man to every thing endureth, there can be no security to any man, how strong or wise soever he be, of living out the time, which nature ordinarily alloweth men to live. And consequently it is a precept, or general rule of reason, *that every man ought to endeavour peace, as far as he has hope of obtaining it; and when he cannot obtain it, that he may seek, and use, all helps, and advantages of war.* The first breach of which rule, containeth the first, and fundamental law of nature; which is, *to seek peace, and follow it.* The second, the sum of the right of nature; which is, *by all means we can, to defend ourselves.*

From this fundamental law of nature, by which men are commanded to endeavour peace, is derived this second law; *that a man be willing, when others are so too, as far forth, as for peace, and defence of himself he shall think it necessary, to lay down this right to all things; and be contented with so much liberty against other men, as he would allow other men against himself.* For as long as every man holdeth this right, of doing any thing he liketh; so long are all men in the condition of war. But if other men will not lay down their right, as well as he; then there is no reason for any one, to divest himself of his: for that were to expose himself to prey, which no man is bound to, rather than to dispose himself to peace. This is that law of the Gospel; *whatsoever you require that others should do to you, that do ye to them.* And that law of all men *quod tibi fieri non vis, alteri ne feceris.*

To *lay down* a man's *right* to any thing, is to *divest* himself of the *liberty,* of hindering another of the benefit of his own right to the same. For he that renounceth, or passeth away his right, giveth not to any other man a right which he had not before; because there is nothing to which every man had not right by nature: but only standeth out of his way, that he may enjoy his own original right, without hindrance from him; not without hindrance from another. So that the effect which redoundeth to one man, by another man's defect of right, is but so much diminution of impediments to the use of his own right original.

Right is laid aside, either by simply renouncing it; or by transferring it to another. By *simply* Renouncing; when he cares not to whom the benefit thereof redoundeth. By Transferring; when he intendeth the benefit thereof to some certain person, or persons. And when a man hath in either manner abandoned, or granted away his right; then is he said to be Obliged, or Bound, not to hinder those, to whom such right is granted, or abandoned, from the benefit of it . . . : and that such hindrance is Injustice, and Injury, as being *sine jure;* the right being before renounced, or transferred. So that *injury,* or *injustice,* in the controversies of the world, is somewhat like to that, which in the disputations of scholars is called *absurdity.* For as it is there called an absurdity, to contradict what one maintained in the beginning: so in the world, it is called injustice, and injury, voluntarily to undo that, which from the beginning he had voluntarily done. The way by which a man either simply renounceth, or transferreth his right, is a declaration, or signification, by some voluntary and sufficient sign, or signs, that he doth so renounce, or transfer; or hath so renounced, or transferred the same, to him that accepteth it. And these signs are either words only, or actions only; or, as it happeneth most often, both words, and actions. And the same are the Bonds, by which men are bound, and obliged: bonds, that have their strength, not from their own nature, for nothing is more easily broken than a man's word, but from fear of some evil consequence upon the rupture. . . .

The mutual transferring of right, is that which men call Contract. . . . One of the contractors may deliver the thing contracted for on his part, and leave the other to perform his part at some determinate time after, and in the meantime be trusted; and then the contract on his part is called Pact, or Covenant: or both parts may contract now, to perform hereafter: in which cases, he that is to perform in time to come, being trusted, his performance is called *keeping of promise,* or faith; and the failing of performance, if it be voluntary, *violation of faith.*

When the transferring of right, is not mutual: but one of the parties transferreth, in hope to gain thereby friendship, or service from another, or from his friends; or in hope to gain the reputation of charity, or magnanimity; or to deliver his mind from the pain of compassion; or in hope of reward in heaven; this is not contract, but Gift, Free-Gift, Grace: which words signify one and the same thing. . . .

If a covenant be made, wherein neither of the parties perform presently, but trust one another; in the condition of mere nature, which is a condition of war every man against every man, upon any reasonable suspicion, it is void: but if there be a common power set over them both, with right and force sufficient to compel performance, it is not void. For he that performeth first, has no assurance the other will perform after; because the bonds of words are too weak to bridle men's ambition, avarice, anger, and other passions, without the fear of some coercive power; which in the condition of mere nature, where all men are equal, and judges of the justness of their own fears, cannot possibly be supposed. And therefore he which performeth first, does but betray himself to his enemy; contrary to the right he can never abandon, of defending his life, and means of living.

But in a civil estate, where there is a power set up to constrain those that would otherwise violate their faith, that fear is no more reasonable; and for that cause, he which by the covenant is to perform first, is obliged so to do.

The cause of fear, which maketh such a covenant invalid, must be always something arising after the covenant made; as some new fact, or other sign of the will not to perform; else it cannot make the covenant void. For that which could not hinder a man from promising, ought not to be admitted as a hindrance of performing.

He that transferreth any right, transferreth the means of enjoying it, as far as lieth in his power. As he that selleth land, is understood to transfer the herbage, and whatsoever grows upon it: nor can he that sells a mill turn away the stream that drives it. And they that give to a man the right of government in sovereignty, are understood to give him the right of levying money to maintain soldiers; and of appointing magistrates for the administration of justice.

The force of words being, as I have formerly noted, too weak to hold men to the performance of their covenants;

there are in man's nature, but two imaginable helps to strengthen it. And those are either a fear of the consequence of breaking their words; or a glory, or pride in appearing not to need to break it. This latter is a generosity too rarely found to be presumed on, especially in the pursuers of wealth, command, or sensual pleasure; which are the greatest part of mankind. The passion to be reckoned upon is fear; whereof there be two very general objects: one, the power of spirits invisible; the other, the power of those men they shall therein offend. Of these two, though the former be the greater power, yet the fear of the latter is commonly the greater fear. The fear of the former is in every man, his own religion: which hath place in the nature of man before civil society. The latter hath not so; at least not place enough, to keep men to their promises; because in the condition of mere nature, the inequality of power is not discerned, but by the event of battle. So that before the time of civil society, or in the interruption thereof by war, there is nothing can strengthen a covenant of peace agreed on, against the temptations of avarice, ambition, lust, or other strong desire, but the fear of that invisible power, which they every one worship as God; and fear as a revenger of their perfidy. All therefore that can be done between two men not subject to civil power, is to put one another to swear by the God he feareth. . . .

[18.] *Of the rights of sovereigns by institution*

A *commonwealth* is said to be *instituted*, when a *multitude* of men do agree, and *covenant, every one*, with every one, that to whatsoever *man*, or *assembly of men*, shall be given by the major part, the *right* to *present* the person of them all, that is to say, to be their *representative;* every one, as well he that *voted for it*, as he that *voted against it*, shall *authorize* all the actions and judgments, of that man, or assembly of men, in the same manner, as if they were his own, to the end, to live peaceably amongst themselves, and be protected against other men.

From this institution of a commonwealth are derived all the *rights*, and *faculties* of him, or them, on whom sovereign power is conferred by the consent of the people assembled.

First, because they covenant, it is to be understood, they are not obliged by former covenant to anything repugnant hereunto. And consequently they that have already instituted a commonwealth, being thereby bound by covenant, to own the actions, and judgments of one, cannot lawfully make a new covenant, amongst themselves, to be obedient to any other, in any thing whatsoever, without his permission. And therefore, they that are subject to a monarch, cannot without his leave cast off monarchy, and return to the confusion of a disunited multitude; nor transfer their person from him that beareth it, to another man, or other assembly of men: for they are bound, every man to every man, to own, and be reputed author of all, that he that already is their sovereign, shall do, and judge fit to be done: so that any one man dissenting, all the rest should break their covenant made to that man, which is injustice: and they have also every man given the sovereignty to him that beareth their person; and therefore if they depose him, they take from him that which is his own, and so again it is injustice. Besides, if he that attempteth to depose his sovereign, be killed, or punished by him for such attempt, he is author of his own punishment, as being by the institution, author of all his sovereign shall do: and because it is injustice for a man to do anything, for which he may be punished by his own authority, he is also upon that title, unjust. And whereas some men have pretended for their disobedience to their sovereign, a new covenant, made not with men, but with God; this also is unjust: for there is no covenant with God, but by mediation of somebody that representeth God's person; which none doth but God's lieutenant, who hath the sovereignty under God. But this pretence of covenant with God is so evident a lie, even in the pretenders' own consciences, that it is not only an act of an unjust, but also of a vile and unmanly disposition.

Secondly, because the right of bearing the person of them all, is given to him they make sovereign, by covenant only of one to another, and not of him to any of them; there can happen no breach of covenant on the part of the sovereign; and consequently none of his subjects, by any pretence of forfeiture, can be freed from his subjection. That he which is made sovereign maketh no covenant with his subjects beforehand, is manifest; because either he must make it with the whole multitude, as one party to the covenant; or he must make a several covenant with every man. With the whole, as one party, it is impossible; because as yet they are not one person: and if he make so many several covenants as there be men, those covenants after he hath the sovereignty are void; because what act soever can be pretended by any one of them for breach thereof, is the act both of himself, and of all the rest, because done in the person, and by the right of every one of them in particular. Besides, if any one, or more of them, pretend a breach of the covenant made by the sovereign at his institution; and others, or one other of his subjects, or himself alone, pretend there was no such breach, there is in this case, no judge to decide the controversy; it returns therefore to the sword again; and every man recovereth the right of protecting himself by his own strength, contrary to the design they had in the institution. It is therefore in vain to grant sovereignty by way of precedent covenant. The opinion that any monarch receiveth his power by covenant, that is to say, on condition, proceedeth from want of understanding this easy truth, that covenants being but words and breath, have no force to oblige, contain, constrain, or protect any man, but what it has from the public sword; that is, from the united hands of that man, or assembly of men that hath the sovereignty, and whose actions are avouched by them all, and performed by the strength of them all, in him united. But when an assembly of men is made sovereign; then no man imagineth

any such covenant to have passed in the institution; for no man is so dull as to say, for example, the people of Rome made a covenant with the Romans, to hold the sovereignty on such or such conditions; which not performed, the Romans might lawfully depose the Roman people. That men see not the reason to be alike in a monarchy, and in a popular government, proceedeth from the ambition of some, that are kinder to the government of an assembly, whereof they may hope to participate, than of monarchy, which they despair to enjoy.

Thirdly, because the major part hath by consenting voices declared a sovereign; he that dissented must now consent with the rest; that is, be contented to avow all the actions he shall do, or else justly be destroyed by the rest. For if he voluntarily entered into the congregation of them that were assembled, he sufficiently declared thereby his will, and therefore tacitly covenanted, to stand to what the major part should ordain: and therefore if he refuse to stand thereto, or make protestation against any of their decrees, he does contrary to his covenant, and therefore unjustly. And whether he be of the congregation, or not; and whether his consent be asked, or not, he must either submit to their decrees, or be left in the condition of war he was in before; wherein he might without injustice be destroyed by any man whatsoever.

Fourthly, because every subject is by this institution author of all the actions, and judgments of the sovereign instituted; it follows, that whatsoever he doth, it can be no injury to any of his subjects; nor ought he to be by any of them accused of injustice. For he that doth anything by authority from another, doth therein no injury to him by whose authority he acteth: but by this institution of a commonwealth, every particular man is author of all the sovereign doth: and consequently he that complaineth of injury from his sovereign, complaineth of that whereof he himself is author; and therefore ought not to accuse any man but himself; no nor himself of injury; because to do injury to one's self, is impossible. It is true that they that have sovereign power may commit iniquity, but not injustice, or injury in the proper signification.

Fifthly, and consequently to that which was said last, no man that hath sovereign power can justly be put to death, or otherwise in any manner by his subjects punished. For seeing every subject is author of the actions of his sovereign; he punisheth another for the actions committed by himself.

And because the end of this institution is the peace and defense of them all; and whosoever has right to the end, has right to the means; it belongeth of right, to whatsoever man, or assembly that hath the sovereignty, to be judge both of the means of peace and defense, and also of the hindrances, and disturbances of the same; and to do whatsoever he shall think necessary to be done, both beforehand, for the preserving of peace and security, by prevention of discord at home, and hostility from abroad; and, when peace and security are lost, for the recovery of the same. And therefore,

Sixthly, it is annexed to the sovereignty, to be judge of what opinions and doctrines are averse, and what conducing to peace; and consequently, on what occasions, how far, and what men are to be trusted withal, in speaking to multitudes of people; and who shall examine the doctrines of all books before they be published. For the actions of men proceed from their opinions; and in the well-governing of opinions, consisteth the well-governing of men's actions, in order to their peace, and concord. And though in matter of doctrine, nothing ought to be regarded but the truth; yet this is not repugnant to regulating the same by peace. For doctrine repugnant to peace can no more be true, than peace and concord can be against the law of nature. It is true, that in a commonwealth, where by the negligence, or unskilfulness of governors, and teachers, false doctrines are by time generally received; the contrary truths may be generally offensive. Yet the most sudden, and rough bursting in of a new truth,

that can be, does never break the peace, but only sometimes awake the war. For those men that are so remissly governed, that they dare take up arms to defend, or introduce an opinion, are still in war; and their condition not peace, but only a cessation of arms for fear of one another; and they live, as it were, in the precincts of battle continually. It belongeth therefore to him that hath the sovereign power, to be judge, or constitute all judges of opinions and doctrines, as a thing necessary to peace; thereby to prevent discord and civil war.

Seventhly, is annexed to the sovereignty, the whole power of prescribing the rules, whereby every man may know, what goods he may enjoy, and what actions he may do, without being molested by any of his fellow-subjects; and this is it men call *propriety*. For before constitution of sovereign power, as hath already been shown, all men had right to all things; which necessarily causeth war: and therefore this propriety, being necessary to peace, and depending on sovereign power, is the act of that power, in order to the public peace. These rules of propriety, or *meum* and *tuum*, and of *good, evil, lawful*, and *unlawful* in the actions of subjects, are the civil laws; that is to say, the laws of each commonwealth in particular; though the name of civil law be now restrained to the ancient civil laws of the city of Rome; which being the head of a great part of the world, her laws at that time were in these parts the civil law.

Eighthly, is annexed to the sovereignty, the right of judicature; that is to say, of hearing and deciding all controversies, which may arise concerning law, either civil, or natural; or concerning fact. For without the decision of controversies, there is no protection of one subject, against the injuries of another; the laws concerning *meum* and *tuum* are in vain; and to every man remaineth, from the natural and necessary appetite of his own conservation, the right of protecting himself by his private strength, which is the condition of war, and contrary to the end for which every commonwealth is instituted.

Ninthly, is annexed to the sovereignty, the right of making war and peace with other nations, and commonwealths; that is to say, of judging when it is for the public good, and how great forces are to be assembled, armed, and paid for that end; and to levy money upon the subjects, to defray the expenses thereof. For the power by which the people are to be defended, consisteth in their armies; and the strength of an army, in the union of their strength under one command; which command the sovereign instituted, therefore hath; because the command of the *militia*, without other institution, maketh him that hath it sovereign. And therefore whosoever is made general of an army, he that hath the sovereign power is always generalissimo.

Tenthly, is annexed to the sovereignty, the choosing of all counsellors, ministers, magistrates, and officers, both in peace and war. For seeing the sovereign is charged with the end, which is the common peace and defense, he is understood to have power to use such means, as he shall think most fit for his discharge.

Eleventhly, to the sovereign is committed the power of rewarding with riches, or honour, and of punishing with corporal or pecuniary punishment, or with ignominy, every subject according to the law he hath formerly made; or if there be no law made, according as he shall judge most to conduce to the encouraging of men to serve the commonwealth, or deterring of them from doing disservice to the same.

Lastly, considering what value men are naturally apt to set upon themselves; what respect they look for from others; and how little they value other men; from whence continually arise amongst them, emulation, quarrels, factions, and at last war, to the destroying of one another, and diminution of their strength against a common enemy; it is necessary that there be laws of honour, and a public rate of the worth of such men as have deserved, or are able to deserve well of the commonwealth; and that there be force in the hands of some or other, to put those laws in execution. But it hath already been shown, that

not only the whole *militia*, or forces of the commonwealth; but also the judicature of all controversies, is annexed to the sovereignty. To the sovereign therefore it belongeth also to give titles of honour; and to appoint what order of place, and dignity, each man shall hold; and what signs of respect, in public or private meetings, they shall give to one another.

These are the rights, which make the essence of sovereignty; and which are the marks, whereby a man may discern in what man, or assembly of men, the sovereign power is placed, and resideth. For these are incommunicable, and inseparable. The power to coin money; to dispose of the estate and persons on infant heirs; to have præemption in markets; and all other statute prerogatives, may be transferred by the sovereign; and yet the power to protect his subjects be retained. But if he transfer the *militia*, he retains the judicature in vain, for want of execution of the laws: or if he grant away the power of raising money; the *militia* is in vain; or if he give away the government of doctrines, men will be frighted into rebellion with the fear of spirits. And so if we consider any one of the said rights, we shall presently see that the holding of all the rest will produce no effect, in the conservation of peace and justice, the end for which all commonwealths are instituted. And this division is it, whereof it is said, *a kingdom divided in itself cannot stand:* for unless this division precede, division into opposite armies can never happen.

[21.] *Of the liberty of subjects*

Liberty, or freedom, signifieth, properly, the absence of opposition; by opposition, I mean external impediments of motion; and may be applied no less to irrational, and inanimate creatures, than to rational. For whatsoever is so tied, or environed, as it cannot move but within a certain space, which space is determined by the opposition of some external body, we say it hath not liberty to go further. And so of all living creatures, whilst they are imprisoned, or restrained, with walls, or chains; and of the water whilst it is kept in by banks, or vessels, that otherwise would spread itself into a larger space, we use to say, they are not at liberty, to move in such manner, as without those external impediments they would. But when the impediment of motion, is in the constitution of the thing itself, we use not to say; it wants the liberty; but the power to move; as when a stone lieth still, or a man is fastened to his bed by sickness.

And according to this proper, and generally received meaning of the word, a Freeman, *is he, that in those things, which by his strength and wit he is able to do, is not hindered to do what he has a will to.* But when the words *free,* and *liberty,* are applied to any thing but bodies, they are abused; for that which is not subject to motion is not subject to impediment: and therefore, when it is said, for example, the way is free, no liberty of the way is signified, but of those that walk in it without stop. And when we say a gift is free, there is not meant any liberty of the gift, but of the giver, that was not bound by any law or covenant to give it. So when we *speak freely,* it is not the liberty of voice, or pronunciation, but of the man, whom no law hath obliged to speak otherwise than he did. Lastly, from the use of the word *free-will,* no liberty can be inferred of the will, desire, or inclination, but the liberty of the man; which consisteth in this, that he finds no stop, in doing what he has the will, desire, or inclination to do.

But as men, for the attaining of peace, and conservation of themselves thereby, have made an artificial man, which we call a commonwealth; so also have they made artificial chains, called *civil laws,* which they themselves, by mutual covenants, have fastened at one end, to the lips of that man, or assembly, to whom they have given the sovereign power; and at the other end to their own ears. These bonds, in their own nature but weak, may nevertheless be made to hold, by the danger, though not by the difficulty of breaking them.

In relation to these bonds only it is,

that I am to speak now, of the *liberty* of *subjects.* For seeing there is no commonwealth in the world, wherein there be rules enough set down, for the regulating of all the actions, and words of men; as being a thing impossible: it followeth necessarily, that in all kinds of actions by the laws praetermitted, men have the liberty, of doing what their own reasons shall suggest, for the most profitable to themselves. For if we take liberty in the proper sense, for corporal liberty; that is to say, freedom from chains and prison; it were very absurd for men to clamour as they do, for the liberty they so manifestly enjoy. Again, if we take liberty, for an exemption from laws, it is no less absurd, for men to demand as they do, that liberty, by which all other men may be masters of their lives. And yet, as absurd as it is, this is it they demand; not knowing that the laws are of no power to protect them, without a sword in the hands of a man, or men, to cause those laws to be put in execution. The liberty of a subject, lieth therefore only in those things, which in regulating their actions, the sovereign hath praetermitted: such as is the liberty to buy, and sell, and otherwise contract with one another; to choose their own abode, their own diet, their own trade of life, and institute their children as they themselves think fit; and the like.

Nevertheless we are not to understand, that by such liberty, the sovereign power of life and death, is either abolished, or limited. For it has been already shown, that nothing the sovereign representative can do to a subject, on what pretence soever, can properly be called injustice, or injury; because every subject is author of every act the sovereign doth; so that he never wanteth right to any thing, otherwise, than as he himself is the subject of God, and bound thereby to observe the laws of nature. . . .

The liberty, whereof there is so frequent and honourable mention, in the histories, and philosophy of the ancient Greeks, and Romans, and in the writings, and discourse of those that from them have received all their learning in the politics, is not the liberty of particular men; but the liberty of the commonwealth: which is the same with that which every man then should have, if there were no civil laws, nor commonwealth at all. And the effects of it also be the same. For as amongst masterless men, there is perpetual war, of every man against his neighbour; no inheritance, to transmit to the son, nor to expect from the father; no propriety of goods, or lands; no security; but a full and absolute liberty in every particular man: so in states, and commonwealths not dependent on one another, every commonwealth, not every man, has an absolute liberty, to do what it shall judge, that is to say, what that man, or assembly that representeth it, shall judge most conducing to their benefit. But withal, they live in the condition of a perpetual war, and upon the confines of battle, with their frontiers armed, and cannons planted against their neighbours round about. The Athenians, and Romans were free; that is, free commonwealths: not that any particular men had the liberty to resist their own representative. . . . There is written on the turrets of the city of Lucca in great characters at this day, the word LIBERTAS; yet no man can thence infer, that a particular man has more liberty, or immunity from the service of the commonwealth there, than in Constantinople. Whether a commonwealth be monarchical, or popular, the freedom is still the same.

To come now to the particulars of the true liberty of a subject; that is to say, what are the things, which though commanded by the sovereign, he may nevertheless, without injustice, refuse to do; we are to consider, what rights we pass away, when we make a commonwealth; or, which is all one, what liberty we deny ourselves, by owning all the actions, without exception, of the man, or assembly, we make our sovereign. For in the act of our *submission*, consisteth both our *obligation*, and our *liberty;* which must therefore be inferred by arguments taken from thence; there being no obligation on any man, which ariseth not from some act of his own; for

all men equally are by nature free. And because such arguments, must either be drawn from the express words, *I authorize all his actions,* or from the intention of him that submitteth himself to his power, which intention is to be understood by the end for which he so submitteth; the obligation, and liberty of the subject, is to be derived, either from those words, or others equivalent; or else from the end of the institution of sovereignty, namely, the peace of the subjects within themselves, and their defense against a common enemy.

First therefore, seeing sovereignty by institution, is by covenant of every one to every one; and sovereignty by acquisition, by covenants of the vanquished to the victor, or child to the parent; it is manifest, that every subject has liberty in all those things, the right whereof cannot by covenant be transferred. I have shown before in the 14th chapter, that covenants, not to defend a man's own body, are void. Therefore,

If the sovereign command a man, though justly condemned, to kill, wound, or maim himself; or not to resist those that assault him; or to abstain from the use of food, air, medicine, or any other thing, without which he cannot live; yet hath that man the liberty to disobey.

If a man be interrogated by the sovereign, or his authority, concerning a crime done by himself, he is not bound, without assurance of pardon, to confess it; because no man. . .can be obliged by covenant to accuse himself.

Again, the consent of a subject to sovereign power, is contained in these words, *I authorize, or take upon me, all his actions;* in which there is no restriction at all, of his own former natural liberty: for by allowing him to *kill* me, I am not bound to kill myself when he commands me. It is one thing to say, *kill me, or my fellow, if you please;* another thing to say, *I will kill myself, or my fellow.* It followeth therefore, that

No man is bound by the words themselves, either to kill himself, or any other man; and consequently, that the obligation a man may sometimes have, upon the command of the sovereign to execute any dangerous, or dishonourable office, dependeth not on the words of our submission; but on the intention, which is to be understood by the end thereof. When therefore our refusal to obey, frustrates the end for which the sovereignty was ordained; then there is no liberty to refuse: otherwise there is.

Upon this ground, a man that is commanded as a soldier to fight against the enemy, though his sovereign have right enough to punish his refusal with death may nevertheless in many cases refuse, without injustice; as when he substituteth a sufficient soldier in his place: for in this case he deserteth not the service of the commonwealth. And there is allowance to be made for natural timorousness; not only to women, of whom no such dangerous duty is expected, but also to men of feminine courage. . . .

To resist the sword of the commonwealth, in defense of another man, guilty, or innocent, no man hath liberty; because such liberty, takes away from the sovereign, the means of protecting us; and is therefore destructive of the very essence of government. . . .

As for other liberties, they depend on the silence of the law. In cases where the sovereign has prescribed no rule, there the subject hath the liberty to do, or forbear, according to his own discretion. And therefore such liberty is in some places more, and in some less; and in some times more, in other times less, according as they that have the sovereignty shall think most convenient. . . .

If a monarch, or sovereign assembly, grant a liberty to all, or any of his subjects, which grant standing, he is disabled to provide for their safety, the grant is void; unless he directly renounce, or transfer the sovereignty to another. For in that he might openly, if it had been his will, and in plain terms, have renounced, or transferred it, and did not; it is to be understood it was not his will, but that the grant proceeded from ignorance of the repugnancy between such a liberty and the sovereign power; and therefore the sovereignty is still retained; and consequently all those powers, which are necessary to the exercising thereof; such as are the power of war, and peace, of judicature, of appointing officers, and councillors, of levying money, and the rest named in the 18th chapter.

The obligation of subjects to the sovereign, is understood to last as long, and no longer, than the power lasteth, by which he is able to protect them. For the right men have by nature to protect themselves, when none else can protect them, can by no covenant be relinquished. The sovereignty is the soul of the commonwealth; which once departed from the body, the members do no more receive their motion from it. The end of obedience is protection; which, wheresoever a man seeth it, either in his own, or in another's sword, nature applieth his obedience to it, and his endeavour to maintain it. And though sovereignty, in the intention of them that make it, be immortal; yet is it in its own nature, not only subject to violent death, by foreign war; but also through the ignorance, and passions of men, it hath in it, from the very institution, many seeds of a natural mortality, by intestine discord. . . .

Thomas Hobbes, *Leviathan* (1651) *passim.*

2. BOSSUET'S POLITICS DRAWN FROM THE HOLY SCRIPTURES

One of the greatest orators of seventeenth-century France, Jacques Bénigne Bossuet (1627–1704), bishop of Meaux and tutor to Louis XIV's son, the dauphin, was perhaps the most important Catholic thinker of Louis' court. His numerous sermons, theological treatises, and historical studies entitle him to the position of leader of the conservative party in the France of his day.

[BOOK I]

I. *Man is made to live in society*

1st Proposition: Men have only one real goal and one real object, which is God. "Hear O Israel: The Lord our God is one Lord. Thou shalt love the Lord thy God with thy whole heart, and with thy whole soul, and with thy whole strength" (Deut. 6:4, 5).

2nd Proposition: The love of God obliges men to love one another. "...we ought to love each other because we ought all to love the same God who is our common father."

3rd Proposition: All men are brothers. First of all they are all children of the same God. "All you are brethren and call none your father upon earth; for one is your father in heaven" (Matt. 23:8, 9). Those we call fathers and from whom we are descended according to the flesh do not know who we are. God alone knows us from all eternity.

5th Proposition: Each man has need of other men. If we are all brothers, all made in the image of God and equally his children, we need to take care of each other, and it is not without reason that it is written, "And He gave to every one of them commandment concerning his neighbor" (Ecc. 17:12).

II. *From the general society of mankind is born civil society*

III. *To form nations and unite peoples it was necessary to establish government*

[BOOK II]

I. *Who has held authority since the beginning of the world?*

1st Proposition: God is the true king. A great king recognized this, since he spoke thus in the presence of all his people: "...Blessed are Thou, O Lord, the God of Israel, our father from eternity to eternity....Thine are riches and Thine is glory; Thou hast dominion over all" (1 Par. 29:10, 12). "The Empire of God is eternal, from that comes that he is called the King of the Centuries" (Apoc. 15:3).

7th Proposition: Monarchy is the most common, the oldest, and the most natural form of government. The people of Israel subjected themselves to monarchy as being the universally accepted government. "Make us a king, to judge us, as all nations have" (1 Sam. 8:5). If God was irritated it was because up till then He had governed this people himself, and that He was their true king. That is why He said to Samuel: "...for they have not rejected thee, but Me, that I should not reign over them" (1 Sam. 8:7).

Indeed this form of government is so natural that one finds it first of all with all peoples.... Rome began that way, and it finally returned to it as its natural state....

8th Proposition: Monarchical government is the best.

If it is the most natural, it is consequently the most durable, and from that also the strongest. It is thus most opposed to division which is the essential evil of states and the most certain cause of their ruin.... "Every kingdom divided against itself shall be made desolate and every city or house divided against itself shall not stand." (Matt. 12:25) We have seen that Our Savior has followed in this sentence the natural progress of government....

[BOOK III]

II. *Royal authority is sacred*

1st Proposition: God establishes kings as His ministers, and reigns by them over His people. We have already seen that all power comes from God. St. Paul says: "For he [the prince] is God's minister to thee for good. But if thou do that which is evil, fear: for he beareth not the sword in vain: For he is God's minister, an avenger to execute wrath upon him that doeth evil" (Romans 13:4). Princes act then as ministers of God and His lieutenants on the earth. It is by them that He exercises His empire. "And now you say that you are able to withstand the kingdom of the Lord which He possesseth by the sons of David" (2 Par. 13:8). It is by that that we have seen that the royal throne is not the throne of a man, but the throne of God Himself. "He hath chosen Solomon my son, to sit upon the throne of the kingdom of the Lord over Israel" (1 Par. 28:5). And again: "Solomon sat on the throne of the Lord." (*Ibid.* 29:23)

2nd Proposition: The person of kings is sacred. It follows from all that the person of kings is sacred and that to attempt to murder a king is a sacrilege. God has anointed them by His prophets with a sacred unction, just as he has anointed the pontiffs and His altars. But even without the exterior application of unction, they are sacred by their profession; as representatives of the divine majesty, deputized by Providence to exercise His designs. It is thus that God called Cyrus His anointed one: "Thus saith the Lord to My anointed Cyrus whose right hand I have taken hold of, to subdue nations" (Is. 45:1).

3rd Proposition: One owes obedience to the prince by the principles of religion and of conscience. St. Paul, after having said that the prince is the minister of God, concludes thus: "Wherefore ye must needs be subject: not only for wrath but also for conscience' sake" (Romans 13:5). That is why "Servants be obedient to them that are your lords, not serving to the eye, as it were pleasing to men, but as servants of Christ, doing the will of God from the heart" (Ephes. 6:5–6). And again: "Servants obey in all things your masters according to the flesh, not serving to the eye, as pleasing to men, but in simplicity of heart fearing God. Whatsoever you do, do it with good heart: as to the Lord and not to men: knowing that you shall receive of the Lord the reward of inheritance, serve ye the Lord Christ" (Coloss. 3:22–24).

If the apostle spoke thus of servitude, an estate contrary to nature, what ought we to think of the legitimate subjugation to princes, and to the magistrates, protectors of public liberty?

4th Proposition: Kings ought to respect their own power and employ it only for public good. Their power coming from on high, as it has been said, they ought not to believe that they receive it to be used at their own discretion, but rather that they ought to make use of it with fear and restraint as a thing that comes to them from God, and of which God will demand of them an accounting.

[BOOK IV]

The royal authority is absolute

1st Proposition: The prince owes no account to any person for that which he orders. "I observe the mouth of the king and the commandments of the oath of God. Be not hasty to depart from his face and do not continue in an evil work. For he will do all that pleaseth him; and his word is full of power. Neither can any man say to him: Why dost thou so? He that keepeth the commandments shall find no evil" (Eccles. 8:2–5). Without this absolute authority, he could neither effect the good nor suppress the evil: it is necessary that his power be such that no one could hope to escape him. . . .

This doctrine is confirmed by St. Paul: "Wilt thou then not be afraid of power? Do that which is good" (Rom. 13:3).

2nd Proposition: When the prince has judged, there is no other judgment.

Sovereign judgments are attributed to God. And Josaphat established judges to judge the people. "You do not exercise the judgment of man but of the Lord" (2 Par. 19:6). Ecclesiasticus says: "Judge not against a judge" (Eccl. 8:17). It is necessary to obey princes as justice itself, otherwise there is neither order nor goal in affairs. They are gods, and participate in some fashion in the divine independence. "I have said: You are gods and all of you the sons of the most high" (Psl. 81:6).

Bishop de Bossuet, *Politics Drawn from the Holy Scriptures,* trans. John B. Wolf, from *Oeuvres complètes de Bossuet,* vol. XVI (Paris, 1838).

3. JOHN LOCKE'S STUDY OF CIVIL GOVERNMENT

Principal theorist for the Whig party, John Locke (1632–1704) undoubtedly deserves a primary place in the annals of revolutionary though. He was attached as a tutor to the fortunes of one of the great Whig families—Shaftesbury—sharing both its exile and its triumph in the Revolution of 1688. The *Two Treatises on Government,* of which the selection below is a part, was his defense of that Revolution. It proved to be so telling an argument that Locke has inspired the thought and action of revolutionary figures in Europe and the Americas from his day until our own, when Marxian justifications have supplanted his ideas in some parts of the world.

[CHAPTER I]

...Political power, then, I take to be a right of making laws, with penalties of death, and consequently all less penalties for the regulating and preserving of property, and of employing the force of the community in the execution of such laws, and in the defence of the commonwealth from foreign injury, and all this only for the public good.

[CHAPTER II: OF THE STATE OF NATURE]

To understand political power aright, and derive it from its original, we must consider what state all men are naturally in, and that is, a state of perfect freedom to order their actions, and dispose of their possessions and persons as they think fit, within the bounds of the law of Nature, without asking leave or depending upon the will of any other man.

A state also of equality, wherein all the power and jurisdiction is reciprocal, no one having more than another, there being nothing more evident than that creatures of the same species and rank, promiscuously born to all the same advantages of Nature, and the use of the same faculties, should also be equal one amongst another, without subordination or subjection, unless the lord and master of them all should, by any manifest declaration of his will, set one above another, and confer on him, by an evident and clear appointment, an undoubted right to dominion and sovereignty.

...The state of Nature has a law of Nature to govern it, which obliges every one, and reason, which is that law, teaches all mankind who will but consult it, that being all equal and independent, no one ought to harm another in his life, health, liberty or possessions; for men being all the workmanship of one omnipotent and infinitely wise Maker; all the servants of one sovereign Master, sent into the world by His order and about His business; they are His property, whose workmanship they are, made to last during His, not one another's pleasure. And, being furnished with like faculties, sharing all in one community of Nature, there cannot be supposed any such subordination among us that may authorize us to destroy one another, as if we were made for one another's uses, as the inferior ranks of creatures are for ours. Every one as he is bound to preserve himself, and not to quit his station wilfully, so by the like reason, when his own preservation comes not in competition, ought he as much as he can to preserve the rest of mankind, and not unless it be to do justice on an offender, take away or impair the life, or what tends to the preservation of the life, the liberty, health, limb, or goods of another.

And that all men may be restrained from invading others' rights, and from doing hurt to one another, and the law of Nature be observed, which willeth the peace and preservation of all mankind, the execution of the law of Nature is in that state put into every man's hands, whereby every one has a right to punish the transgressors of that law to such a degree as may hinder its violation. For the law of Nature would, as all other laws that concern men in this world, be in vain if there were nobody that in the state of Nature had a power to execute that law, and thereby preserve the innocent and restrain offenders; and if any one in the state of Nature may punish another for any evil he has done, every one may do so. For in that state of perfect equality, where naturally there is no superiority of jurisdiction of one over another, what any may do in prosecution of that law, every one must needs have a right to do....

Besides the crime which consists in violating the law, and varying from the right rule of reason, whereby a man so far becomes degenerate, and declares himself to quit the principles of human nature and to be a noxious creature, there is commonly injury done, and some person or other, some other man, receives damage by his transgression; in which case, he who hath received any damage has (besides the right of punishment common to him, with other men) a particular right to seek reparation from him that has done it. And any other person who finds it just may also join with him that is injured, and assist him in recovering from the offender so much as may make satisfaction for the harm he hath suffered.

From these two distinct rights (the one of punishing the crime, for restraint and preventing the like offence, which right of punishing is in everybody, the other of taking reparation, which belongs only to the injured party) comes it to pass that the magistrate, who by being magistrate hath the common right of punishing put into his hands, can often, where the public good demands not the execution of the law, remit the punishment of criminal offences by his own authority, but yet cannot remit the satisfaction due to any private man for the damage he has received. That he who hath suffered the damage has a right to demand in his own name, and he alone can remit. The damnified person has this power of appropriating to himself the goods or service of the offender by right of self-preservation, as every man has a power to punish the crime to prevent its being committed again, by the right he has of preserving all mankind, and doing all reasonable things he can in order to that end. And thus it is that every man in the state of Nature has a power to kill a murderer, both to deter others from doing the like injury (which no reparation can compensate) by the example of the punishment that attends it from everybody, and also to secure men from the attempts of a criminal who, having renounced reason, the common rule and measure God hath given to mankind, hath, by the unjust violence and slaughter he hath committed upon one, declared war against all mankind, and therefore may be destroyed as a lion or a tiger, one of those wild savage beasts with whom men can have no society nor security. And upon this is grounded that great law of Nature, "Whoso sheddeth man's blood, by man shall his blood be shed."

To this strange doctrine—viz., That in the state of Nature every one has the executive power of the law of Nature—I doubt not but it will be objected that it is unreasonable for men to be judges in their own cases, that self-love will make men partial to themselves and their friends; and, on the other side, ill-nature, passion, and revenge will carry them too far in punishing others, and hence nothing but confusion and disorder will follow, and that therefore God hath certainly appointed government to restrain the partiality and violence of men. I easily grant that civil government is the proper remedy for the inconveniences of the state of Nature, which must certainly be great where men may be judges in their own case, since it is easy to be imagined that he who was so unjust as to do his brother an injury will scarce be so just as to condemn himself for it. But I shall desire those who make this objection to remember that absolute monarchs are but men; and if government is to be the remedy of those evils which necessarily follow from men's being judges in their own cases, and the state of Nature is therefore not to be endured, I desire to know what kind of government that is, and how much better it is than the state of Nature, where one man commanding a multitude has the liberty to be judge in his own case, and may do to all his subjects whatever he pleases without the least question or control of those who execute his pleasure?

[CHAPTER III: OF THE STATE OF WAR]

The state of war is a state of enmity and destruction; and therefore declaring by word or action, not a passionate and hasty, but sedate, settled design upon another man's life puts him in a state of war with him against whom he has declared such an intention, and so has exposed his life to the other's power to be taken away by him, or any one that joins with him in his defence, and espouses his quarrel; it being reasonable and just I should have a right to destroy that which threatens me with destruction; for by the fundamental law of Nature, man being to be preserved as much as possible, when all cannot be preserved, the safety of the innocent is to be preferred, and one may destroy a man who makes war upon him, or has discovered an enmity to his being, for the same reason that he may kill a wolf or a lion, because they are not under the ties of the common law of reason, have no other rule but that of force and violence, and so may be treated as a beast of prey, those dangerous and noxious creatures that will be sure to destroy him whenever he falls into their power.

And hence it is that he who attempts to get another man into his absolute power does thereby put himself into a state of war with him; it being to be understood as a declaration of a design upon his life. For I have reason to conclude that he who would get me into his power without my consent would use me as he pleased when he had got me there, and destroy me too when he had a fancy to it; for nobody can desire to have me in his absolute power unless it be to compel me by force to that which is against the right of my freedom—*i.e.* make me a slave. To be free from such force is the only security of my preservation, and reason bids me look on him as an enemy to my preservation who would take away that freedom which is the fence to it; so that he who makes an attempt to enslave me thereby puts himself into a state of war with me. He that in the state of Nature would take away the freedom that belongs to any one in that state must necessarily be supposed to have a design to take away everything else, that freedom being the foundation of all the rest; as he that in the state of society would take away the freedom belonging to those of that society or commonwealth must be supposed to design to take away from them everything else, and so be looked on as in a state of war.

[CHAPTER VII: OF POLITICAL OR CIVIL SOCIETY]

Man being born, as has been proved, with a title to perfect freedom and an uncontrolled enjoyment of all the rights and privileges of the law of Nature, equally with any other man, or number of men in the world, hath by nature a power not only to preserve his property—that is, his life, liberty, and estate, against the injuries and attempts of other men, but to judge of and punish the breaches of that law in others, as he is persuaded the offence deserves, even with death itself, in crimes where the heinousness of the fact, in his opinion, requires it. But because no political society can be, nor subsist, without having in itself the power to preserve the property, and in order thereunto punish the offences of all those of that society, there, and there only, is political society where every one of the members hath quitted this natural power, resigned it up into the hands of the community in all cases that exclude him not from appealing for protection to the law established by it. And thus all private judgment of every particular member being excluded, the community comes to be umpire, and by understanding indifferent rules and men authorised by the community for their execution, decides all the differences that may happen between any members of that society concerning any matter of right, and punishes those offences which any member hath committed against the society with such penalties as the law has established; whereby it is easy to discern who are, and are not, in political society together. Those who are united into one body, and have a common established law and judicature to appeal to, with authority to decide controversies between them and punish offenders, are in civil society one with another; but those who have no such common appeal, I mean on earth, are still in the state of Nature, each being where there is no other, judge for himself and executioner; which is, as I have before showed it, the perfect state of Nature.

And thus the commonwealth comes by a power to set down what punishment shall belong to the several transgressions they think worthy of it, committed amongst the members of that society (which is the power of making laws), as well as it has the power to punish any injury done unto any of its members by any one that is not of it (which is the power of war and peace); and all this for the preservation of the property of all the members of that society, as far as is possible. But though every man entered into society has quitted his power to punish offences against the law of Nature in prosecution of his own private judgment, yet with the judgment of offences which he has given up to the legislative, in all cases where he can appeal to the magistrate, he has given up a right to the commonwealth to employ his force for the execution of the judgments of the commonwealth whenever he shall be called to it, which, indeed, are his own judgments, they being made by himself or his representative. And herein we have the original of the legislative and executive power of civil society, which is to judge by standing laws how far offences are to be punished when committed within the commonwealth; and also by occasional judgments founded on the present circumstances of the fact, how far injuries from without are to be vindicated, and in both these to employ all the force of all the members when there shall be need.

Wherever, therefore, any number of men so unite into one society as to quit every one his executive power of the law of Nature, and to resign it to the public, there and there only is a political or civil society. And this is done wherever any number of men, in the state of Nature, enter into society to make one people one body politic under one supreme government: or else when any one joins himself to, and incorporates with any government already made. For hereby he authorises the society, or which is all one, the legisla-

tive thereof, to make laws for him as the public good of the society shall require, to the execution whereof his own assistance (as to his own decrees) is due. And this puts men out of a state of Nature into that of a commonwealth, by setting up a judge on earth with authority to determine all the controversies and redress the injuries that may happen to any member of the commonwealth, which judge is the legislative or magistrates appointed by it. And wherever there are any number of men, however associated, that have no such decisive power to appeal to, there they are still in the state of Nature.

And hence it is evident that absolute monarchy, which by some men is counted for the only government in the world, is indeed inconsistent with civil society, and so can be no form of civil government at all. For the end of civil society being to avoid and remedy those inconveniences of the state of Nature which necessarily follow from every man's being judge in his own case, by setting up a known authority to which every one of that society may appeal upon any injury received, or controversy that may arise, and which every one of the society ought to obey, wherever any persons are who have not such an authority to appeal to, and decide any difference between them there, those persons are still in the state of Nature. And so is every absolute prince in respect of those who are under his dominion. . . .

For he that thinks absolute power purifies men's blood, and corrects the baseness of human nature, need read but the history of this, or any other age, to be convinced to the contrary. . . .

[CHAPTER VIII: OF THE BEGINNING OF POLITICAL SOCIETIES]

Men being, as has been said, by nature all free, equal and independent, no one can be put out of this estate and subjected to the political power of another without his own consent, which is done by agreeing with other men, to join and unite into a community for their comfortable, safe, and peaceable living, one amongst another, in a secure enjoyment of their properties, and a greater security against any that are not of it. This any number of men may do, because it injures not the freedom of the rest; they are left, as they were, in the liberty of the state of Nature. When any number of men have so consented to make one community or government, they are thereby presently incorporated, and make one body politic, wherein the majority have a right to act and conclude the rest.

For, when any number of men have, by the consent of every individual, made a community, they have thereby made that community one body, with a power to act as one body, which is only by the will and determination of the majority. For that which acts any community, being only the consent of the individuals of it, and it being one body, must move one way, it is necessary the body should move that way whither the greater force carries it, which is the consent of the majority, or else it is impossible it should act or continue one body, one community, which the consent of every individual that united into it agreed that it should; and so every one is bound by that consent to be concluded by the majority. And therefore we see that in assemblies empowered to act by positive laws where no number is set by that positive law which empowers them, the act of the majority passes for the act of the whole, and of course determines as having, by the Law of Nature and reason, the power of the whole.

And thus every man, by consenting with others to make one body politic under one government, puts himself under an obligation to every one of that society to submit to the determination of the majority, and to be concluded by it; or else this original compact, whereby he with others incorporates into one society, would signify nothing, and be no compact if he be left free and under no other ties than he was in before in the state of Nature. For what appearance would there be of any compact? What new engagement if he were no farther tied by any decrees of the society than he himself thought fit and

did actually consent to? This would be still as great a liberty as he himself had before his compact, or any one else in the state of Nature, who may submit himself and consent to any acts of it if he thinks fit.

For if the consent of the majority shall not in reason be received as the act of the whole, and conclude every individual, nothing but the consent of every individual can make anything to be the act of the whole, which, considering the infirmities of health and avocations of business, which in a number though much less than that of a commonwealth, will necessarily keep many away from the public assembly; and the variety of opinions and contrariety of interests which unavoidably happen in all collections of men, it is next impossible ever to be had. . . .

[CHAPTER XIII: OF THE SUBORDINATION
OF THE POWERS OF THE
COMMONWEALTH]

Though in a constituted commonwealth standing upon its own basis and acting according to its own nature—that is, acting for the preservation of the community, there can be but one supreme power, which is the legislative, to which all the rest are and must be subordinate, yet the legislative being only a fiduciary power to act for certain ends, there remains still in the people a supreme power to remove or alter the legislative, when they find the legislative act contrary to the trust reposed in them. . . .

It may be demanded here, what if the executive power, being possessed of the force of the commonwealth, shall make use of that force to hinder the meeting and acting of the legislative, when the original constitution or the public exigencies require it? I say, using force upon the people, without authority, and contrary to the trust put in him that does so, is a state of war with the people, who have a right to reinstate their legislative in the exercise of their power. For having erected a legislative with an intent they should exercise the power of making laws, either at certain set times, or when there is need of it, when they are hindered by any force from what is so necessary to the society, and wherein the safety and preservation of the people consists, the people have a right to remove it by force. In all states and conditions the true remedy of force without authority is to oppose force to it. The use of force without authority always puts him that uses it into a state of war as the aggressor, and renders him liable to be treated accordingly. . . .

[CHAPTER XVIII: OF TYRANNY]

As usurpation is the exercise of power which another hath a right to, so tyranny is the exercise of power beyond right, which nobody can have a right to; and this is making use of the power any one has in his hands, not for the good of those who are under it, but for his own private, separate advantage. When the governor, however entitled, makes not the law, but his will, the rule, his commands and actions are not directed to the preservation of the properties of his people, but the satisfaction of his own ambition, revenge, covetousness, or any other irregular passion. . . .

May the commands, then, of a prince be opposed? May he be resisted, as often as any one shall find himself aggrieved, and but imagine he has not right done him? This will unhinge and overturn all polities, and instead of government and order, leave nothing but anarchy and confusion.

To this I answer: That force is to be opposed to nothing but to unjust and unlawful force. Whoever makes any opposition in any other case draws on himself a just condemnation, both from God and man. . . .

[CHAPTER XIX: OF THE DISSOLUTION OF GOVERNMENT]

He that will, with any clearness, speak of the dissolution of government, ought in the first place to distinguish between the dissolution of the society and the dissolution of the government. That which makes the community, and brings men out of the loose state of Nature into one politic society, is the agreement which every one has with the rest to incorporate and act as one body, and so be one distinct commonwealth. The usual, and almost only way whereby this union is dissolved, is the inroad of foreign force making a conquest upon them. For in that case (not being able to maintain and support themselves as one entire and independent body) the union belonging to that body, which consisted therein, must necessarily cease, and so every one return to the state he was in before, with a liberty to shift for himself and provide for his own safety, as he thinks fit, in some other society.

This being usually brought about by such in the commonwealth, who misuse the power they have, it is hard to consider it aright, and know at whose door to lay it, without knowing the form of government in which it happens. Let us suppose, then, the legislative placed in the concurrence of three distinct persons:— First, a single hereditary person having the constant, supreme, executive power, and with it the power of convoking and dissolving the other two within certain periods of time. Secondly, an assembly of hereditary nobility. Thirdly, an assembly of representatives chosen, *pro tempore,* by the people. Such a form of government supposed, it is evident:

First, that when such a single person or prince sets up his own arbitrary will in place of the laws which are the will of the society declared by the legislative, then the legislative is changed. For that being, in effect, the legislative whose rules and laws are put in execution, and required to be obeyed, when other laws are set up, and other rules pretended and enforced than what the legislative, constituted by the society, have enacted, it is plain that the legislative is changed. Whoever introduces new laws, not being thereunto authorised, by the fundamental appointment of the society, or subverts the old, disowns and overturns the power by which they were made, and so sets up a new legislative.

Secondly, when the prince hinders the legislative from assembling in its due time, or from acting freely, pursuant to those ends for which it was constituted, the legislative is altered. . . .

Thirdly, when, by the arbitrary power of the prince, the electors or ways of election are altered without the consent and contrary to the common interest of the people, there also the legislative is altered. For if others than those whom the society hath authorised thereunto do choose, or in another way than what the society hath prescribed, those chosen are not the legislative appointed by the people.

Fourthly, the delivery also of the people into the subjection of a foreign power, either by the prince or by the legislative, is certainly a change of the legislative, and so a dissolution of the government. For the end why people entered into society being to be preserved one entire, free, independent society, to be governed by its own laws, this is lost whenever they are given up into the power of another.

Why, in such a constitution as this, the dissolution of the government in these cases is to be imputed to the prince is evident, because he, having the force, treasure, and offices of the State to employ, and often persuading himself or being flattered by others, that, as supreme magistrate, he is incapable of control; he alone is in a condition to make great advances towards such changes under pretence of lawful authority, and has it in his hands to terrify or suppress opposers as factious, seditious, and enemies to the government; whereas no other part of the legislative, or people, is capable by themselves to attempt any alteration of the legislative without open and visible rebellion, apt enough to be taken notice of, which, when it prevails, produces effects very little different from foreign conquest. Besides, the prince, in such a form of government, having the power of dissolving the other parts of the legislative, and thereby rendering them private persons, they can never, in opposition to him, or without his concurrence, alter the legislative by a law, his consent being necessary to give any of their decrees that sanction. But yet so far as the other parts of the legislative any way contribute to any attempt upon the government, and do either promote, or not, what lies in them, hinder such designs, they are guilty, and partake in this, which is certainly the greatest crime men can be guilty of one towards another.

There is one way more whereby such a government may be dissolved, and that is: When he who has the supreme executive power neglects and abandons that charge, so that the laws already made can no longer be put in execution; this is demonstratively to reduce all to anarchy, and so effectively to dissolve the government. For laws not being made for themselves, but to be, by their execution, the bonds of the society to keep every part of the body politic in its due place and function; when that totally ceases, the government visibly ceases, and the people become a confused multitude without order or connection. Where there is no longer the administration of justice for the securing of men's rights, nor any remaining power within the community to direct the force, or provide for the necessities of the public, there certainly is no government left. Where the laws cannot be executed it is all one as if there were no laws, and a government without laws is, I suppose, a mystery in politics inconceivable to human capacity, and inconsistent with human society.

In these, and the like cases, when the government is dissolved, the people are at liberty to provide for themselves by erecting a new legislative differing from the other by the change of persons, or form, or both, as they shall find it most for their safety and good. For the society can never, by the fault of another, lose the native and original right it has to preserve itself, which can only be done by a settled legislative and a fair and impartial execution of the laws made by it. But the state of mankind is not so miserable that they are not capable of using this remedy till it be too late to look for any. To tell people they may provide for themselves by erecting a new legislative, when, by oppression, artifice, or being delivered over to a foreign power, their old one is gone, is only to tell them they may expect relief when it is too late, and the evil is past cure. This is, in effect, no more than to bid them first be slaves, and then to take care of their liberty, and, when their chains are on, tell them they may act like free men. This, if barely so, is rather mockery than relief, and men can never be secure from tyranny if there be no means to escape it till they are perfectly under it; and, therefore, it is that they have not only a right to get out of it, but to prevent it.

There is, therefore, secondly, another way whereby governments are dissolved, and that is, when the legislative, or the prince, either of them act contrary to their trust.

For the legislative acts against the trust reposed in them when they endeavour to invade the property of the subject, and to make themselves, or any part of the community, masters or arbitrary disposers of the lives, liberties, or fortunes of the people.

The reason why men enter into society is the preservation of their property; and the end why they choose and authorise a legislative is that there may be laws made, and rules set, as guards and fences to the properties of all the society, to limit the power and moderate the dominion of every part and member of the society...what I have said here concerning the legislative in general holds true also concerning the supreme executor, who having a double trust put in him, both to have a part in the legislative and the supreme execution of the law, acts against both, when he goes about to set up his own arbitrary will as the law of the society. He acts also contrary to his trust when he employs the force, treasure, and offices of the society to corrupt the representatives and gain them to his purposes, when he openly preengages the electors, and prescribes, to their choice, such whom he has, by solicitations, threats, promises, or otherwise, won to his designs, and employs them to bring in such who have promised beforehand what to vote and what to enact. Thus to regulate candidates and electors, and new model the ways of election, what is it but to cut up the government by the roots, and poison the very fountain of public security? For the people having reserved to themselves the choice of their representatives as the fence to their properties, could do it for no other end but that they might always be freely chosen, and so chosen, freely act and advise as the necessity of the commonwealth and the public good should, upon examination and mature debate, be judged to require. This, those who give their votes before they hear the debate, and have weighed the reasons on all sides, are not capable of doing. To prepare such an assembly as this, and endeavour to set up the declared abettors of his own will, for the true representatives of the people, and the law-makers of the society, is certainly as great a breach of trust, and as perfect a declaration of a design to subvert the government, as is possible to be met with.... What power they ought to have in the society who thus employ it contrary to the trust [which] went along with it in its first institution, is easy to determine; and one cannot but see that he who has once attempted any such thing as this cannot any longer be trusted.

To this, perhaps, it will be said that the people being ignorant and always discontented, to lay the foundation of government in the unsteady opinion and uncertain humour of the people, is to expose it to certain ruin; and no government will be able long to subsist if the people may set up a new legislative whenever they take offence at the old one. To this I answer, quite the contrary. People are not so easily got out of their old forms as some are apt to suggest. They are hardly to be prevailed with to amend the acknowledged faults in the frame they have been accustomed to. And if there be any original defects, or adventitious ones introduced by time or corruption, it is not an easy thing to get them changed, even when all the world sees there is an opportunity for it. This slowness and aversion in the people to quit their old constitutions has in the many revolutions which have been seen in this kingdom, in this and former ages, still kept us to, or after some interval of fruitless attempts, still brought us back again to our old legislative of king, lords and commons; and whatever provocations have made the crown be taken from some of our princes' heads, they never carried the people so far as to place it in another line.

But it will be said this hypothesis lays a ferment for frequent rebellion. To which I answer:

First, no more than any other hypothesis. For when the people are made miserable, and find themselves exposed to the ill usage of arbitrary power, cry up their governors as much as you will for sons of Jupiter, let them be sacred and divine, descended or authorised from Heaven; give them out for whom or what you please, the same will happen. The people generally ill treated, and contrary to right, will be ready upon any occasion to ease themselves of a burden that sits heavy upon them. They will wish and seek for the opportunity, which in the change, weakness, and accidents of human affairs, seldom delays long to offer itself. He must have lived but a little while in the world, who has not seen examples of this in his time. . . .

Secondly, I answer, such revolutions happen not upon every little mismanagement in public affairs. Great mistakes in the ruling part, many wrong and inconvenient laws, and all the slips of human frailty will be borne by the people without mutiny or murmur. . . .

Thirdly, I answer, that this power in the people of providing for their safety anew by a new legislative when their legislators have acted contrary to their trust by invading their property, is the best fence against rebellion, and the probablest means to hinder it. For rebellion being an opposition, not to persons, but authority, which is founded only in the constitutions and laws of the government: those, whoever they be, who, by force, break through, and, by force, justify their violation of them, are truly and properly rebels. For when men, by entering into society and civil government, have excluded force, and introduced laws for the preservation of property, peace, and unity amongst themselves, those who set up force again in opposition to the laws, do *rebellare*—that is, bring back again the state of war, and are properly rebels, which they who are in power, by the pretence they have to authority, the temptation of force they have in their hands, and the flattery of those about them being likeliest to do, the properest way to prevent the evil is to show them the danger and injustice of it who are under the greatest temptation to run into it. . . .

The end of government is the good of mankind; and which is best for mankind, that the people should be always exposed to the boundless will of tyranny, or that the rulers should be sometimes liable to be opposed when they grow exorbitant in the use of their power, and employ it for the destruction, and not the preservation, of the properties of their people?

Nor let any one say that mischief can arise from hence as often as it shall please a busy head or turbulent spirit to desire the alteration of the government. It is true such men may stir whenever they please, but it will be only to their own just ruin and perdition. For till the mischief be grown general, and the ill designs of the rulers become visible, or their attempts sensible to the greater part, the people, who are more disposed to suffer than right themselves by resistance, are not apt to stir. The examples of particular injustice or oppression of here and there an unfortunate man moves them not. But if they universally have a persuasion grounded upon manifest evidence that designs are carrying on against their liberties, and the general course and tendency of things cannot but give them strong suspicions of the evil intention of their governors, who is to be blamed for it? Who can help it if they, who might avoid it, bring themselves into this suspicion? Are the people to be blamed if they have the sense of rational creatures, and can think of things no otherwise than as they find and feel them? And is it not rather their fault who put things in such a posture that they would not have them thought as they are? I grant that the pride, ambition, and turbulency of private men have sometimes caused great disorders in commonwealths, and factions have been fatal to states and kingdoms. But whether the mischief hath oftener begun in the people's wantonness, and a desire to cast off the lawful authority of their rulers, or in the rulers' insolence and endeavours to get and exercise an arbitrary power over their people, whether oppression or disobedience gave the first rise to the disorder, I leave it to impartial history to determine. . . .

That subjects or foreigners attempting by force on the properties of any people may be resisted with force is agreed on all hands; but that magistrates doing the same thing may be resisted, hath of late been denied: as if those who had the greatest privileges and advantages by the law had thereby a power to break those laws by which alone they were set in a better place than their brethren; whereas their offence is thereby the greater, both as being ungrateful for the greater share they have by the law, and breaking also that trust which is put into their hands by their brethren.

Whosoever uses force without right— as every one does in society who does it without law—puts himself into a state of war with those against whom he so uses it, and in that state all former ties are cancelled, all other rights cease, and every one has a right to defend himself, and to resist the aggressor. This is so evident that Barclay himself—that great assertor of

the power and sacredness of kings—is forced to confess that it is lawful for the people, in some cases, to resist their king, and that, too, in a chapter wherein he pretends to show that the Divine law shuts up the people from all manner of rebellion. Whereby it is evident, even by his own doctrine, that since they may, in some cases, resist, all resisting of princes is not rebellion. . . .

To conclude. The power that every individual gave the society when he entered into it can never revert to the individuals again, as long as the society lasts, but will always remain in the community; because without this there can be no community—no commonwealth, which is contrary to the original agreement; so also when the society hath placed the legislative in any assembly of men, to continue in them and their successors, with direction and authority for providing such successors, the legislative can never revert to the people whilst that government lasts; because, having provided a legislative with power to continue forever, they have given up their political power to the legislative, and cannot resume it. But if they have set limits to the duration of their legislative, and made this supreme power in any person or assembly only temporary; or else when, by the miscarriages of those in authority, it is forfeited; upon the forefeiture of their rulers, or at the determination of the time set, it reverts to the society, and the people have a right to act as supreme, and continue the legislative in themselves or place it in a new form, or new hands, as they think good.

John Locke, *Of Civil Government* (1689), *passim*.

II. The Scientific Revolution

The origins of the intellectual movement that overthrew the authority of Aristotle reach deeply into the European past, but for purposes of simplification we must start with Copernicus, an astronomer who became dissatisfied with the cosmology of his day and struck out to find a more viable system. By the sixteenth century the description of the cosmos had become unbelievably complex; for two centuries or more, astronomers attempted to adjust to observed facts in the sky the system that had been described by Ptolemy in the second century of the Christian era: the result was an ever-increasing complexity of movements that failed to explain the system as it seemed to function. Copernicus, armed with the suggestion provided by a Greek philosopher —that the sun might well be the center of the entire universe—set about to explain the planetary movements with this hypothesis. He did not spend much time observing the skies; Copernicus was a mathematician-astronomer, and Ptolemy's star tables were all that he really needed to work out his heliocentric solar system. His great achievement was the establishing of the postulate that the sun was the center of the system and that the earth, like the other planets, revolved in orbits about it. The tone and the method of his work were more closely akin to the Greek philosophers than to a modern astronomer, and while he did postulate the sun as the center, he also made many other assumptions that were far from the mark. Copernicus argued that his system was a simpler explanation for the movements of the planets; neither he nor any of his contemporaries ever believed that man would actually prove that it was the true and only explanation.

In the two generations following Copernicus, his postulate of a heliocentric universe bore great fruit. The first important contributor was a Danish astronomer named Tycho Brahe. Brahe was an observer. He built astronomical instruments for measuring the angles of the planets and set about to make a new set of star tables to replace those of the ancients which were obviously faulty. His observations were so carefully and accurately made that his student and assistant, Johann Kepler, was able to use them in calculating his three laws of planetary movement: (1) that the orbit of the planet (Mars) is an ellipse with the sun as the center of one of the foci; (2) that the speed of movement of the planet changes, and that it is describable in terms of geometry, and (3) that the time required for a complete orbit is related to the radius of the orbit and also describable in mathematical terms. Kepler seemed to prove what some men suspected, namely that the universe was a machine and that it was governed by number; he also provided mathematical evidence of the heliocentric postulate. About the same time that Kepler developed the laws of planetary motion, Galileo made a telescope which allowed him to see the satellites of Jupiter, the imperfections on the moon, and the phasing of the planets. For anyone who was willing to look, here was evidence of the sun-centered system.

It was no small thing to pull the earth loose from its traditional place as the solid center of all things and send it spinning around the sun as simply another planet. Nor is it surprising that conservatives in the churches, the universities, and the streets objected to this reduction of man and his planet to insignificance. Galileo, as everyone knows, was brought before the Inquisition and forced to recant, but the stars in the skies and the new instruments in the hands of men worked against the traditionalists.

The period was one in which learned men came to assume that the world was a machine, and that number was the key to knowledge. Mathematicians devised new tools: trigonometry, logarithms, analytical geometry, and finally, at the end of the century, the calculus. At the same time, instrument makers developed scales, thermometers, clocks, barometers, pumps, telescopes, and microscopes that allowed men to measure, weigh, and take the temperature of the earth and find numbers that could be analyzed. The conservatives could rail at the emergence of a mechanistic world so foreign to that of Aristotle, but the arguments of their opponents were buttressed by evidence that could not be brushed aside. The conservatives could continue to ask of the world the question "Why?" and "For what purpose?"; the new men were content to ask "How does it work?" and as the seventeenth century grew old, their question came to be the only one that seemed important.

The greatest triumph of the new science came with the publication of Isaac Newton's *Principia* in 1687. With the astronomical observations and discoveries and the new insight into the laws of mechanics as his arsenal, and with the new mathematical tool (fluxions or calculus) which he had himself invented, Newton was able to demonstrate that the orbit of the moon proved that the satellite was falling toward the earth at a speed which showed that the moon was subject to the same force that controlled the falling of bodies on the earth. He then went on to demonstrate that the force of gravity could be used to explain the movement of the entire solar system. The time-space machine of the universe stood revealed. Three generations of mathematicians, astronomers, and physicists had piled up evidence that Newton's genius had fixed in a system. It was unquestionably the most astonishing and remarkable achievement of the human mind.

While the scientists were remaking the cosmos and reinterpreting the natural world, the philosophers had to fit these discoveries into a philosophical system. A new cosmology demanded new explanations. René Descartes is the man most usually associated with the new philosophy. Starting with the idea that the world was discoverable by man ("I think; therefore I am"), Descartes proceeded to mark out a new approach to knowledge. His world was a machine, and everything in it with the exception of God and of the soul of man was mechanical and subject to mathematical analysis. He rejected the logic of Aristotle for that of Euclid: his was an age of geometry, and one found truth through theorems and postulates that were demonstrated as a geometer proves his laws. It was Descartes who gave the age its sign: *l'esprit géometrique*. Fontenelle, one of his most distinguished followers, was to say that after Descartes, any book, be it on morals, philosophy, theology, or history, would be better if it were written by the hand of a geometer. Thus the new science entered all aspects of men's thoughts, and gave a new foundation for the future explanations of the world and man and God.

The first item dealing with the scientific revolution is the dedication of Copernicus' *On the Revolutions of the Heavenly Bodies*. It is dedicated to the pope and the author was obviously anxious not to displease defenders of the traditional beliefs. Nonetheless, it is evident that Copernicus believed that he had a better explanation for the movements in the skies than that provided by a geocentric hypothesis. The next item is a cut from Galileo's *Dialogue Concerning the Two Chief World Systems*. Here we see Salviati, Sagredo, and Simplicio struggling with the problems presented by the conflict between Aristotle and the new science. Galileo is discursive in his style, but it soon becomes clear that poor Simplicio, with his slavish following of Aristotle, is the buffoon of the drama. Since the English translation of this book runs to more than four hundred pages, it will be obvious to the reader that this cut can do little more than give an insight into the spirit and the method of the work. Unfortunately, Kepler's writings do not allow an easy reproduction; they bristle with mathematics, and become obscure to anyone not completely familiar with the problems they discuss.

Selections from Descartes' *Discourse on Method* will introduce the student (see Chapter 9) to the famous postulate "I think; therefore I am," and provide insight into Descartes' method of argument. He had to prove the existence of God before he could proceed with his work. Descartes himself relied heavily upon St. Thomas Aquinas and Aristotle, but his successors tended to repudiate both these earlier thinkers and, in effect, made Descartes responsible for much of the anti-Christian thought of the eighteenth century.

The next two pieces deal with the work of Newton. The preface to the *Principia* should be compared with the one written by Copernicus almost a century and a half earlier. Newton shows none of the anxiety or uncertainty of the sixteenth-century astronomer. Fontenelle's *Eulogy on Newton* is interesting both as a statement of the early eighteenth-century conception of Newton's work and as a comparison of the methodologies of Descartes and Newton. Fontenelle was one of the continental savants who had at first been reluctant to accept Newton's idea of a universe held together by the mysterious force of gravity; it seemed almost to be a superstition rather than a possible explanation for the "world-machine." However, before Newton's death, the idea of an empty universe held together by the force of gravity acting at enormous distances had become the common belief of learned men, and in this piece Fontenelle freely accepts Newton's great discovery as the explanation for the world-machine.

The last piece by Antony van Leeuwenhoek does not fit into the schema of the others. The man with the microscope could not contribute to the geometric pattern of a mechanical world; he was in the company of men who attempted to understand the earth and its living inhabitants without realizing that the earth was fantastically old, and without a chemistry that could give insight into many of its processes. Thus these naturalists were condemned to the role of taxonomists and observers. In that role Leeuwenhoek's discoveries of the micro-world were important and significant. This description of a drop of rainwater and the "animalcules" that inhabited it is a classic.

A. Nicolaus Copernicus' Dedication on the Revolutions of the Heavenly Bodies to Pope Paul III, 1543

Nicolaus Copernicus (1473–1543) was born near Thorn in Poland-Prussia, studied at the universities of Cracow, Bologna, Padua, and Ferrara. He was widely recognized as an astronomer and mathematician, and lectured at Rome as well as in his native Poland. The book *On the Revolutions of the Heavenly Bodies,* which is the basis of his subsequent reputation, was published after his death in 1543. The dedication, herewith reproduced, provides interesting insights into both the mind of the author and the era in which this book was written.

I can easily conceive, most Holy Father, that as soon as some people learn that in this book which I have written concerning the revolutions of the heavenly bodies, I ascribe certain motions to the Earth, they will cry out at once that I and my theory should be rejected. For I am not so much in love with my conclusions as not to weigh what others will think about them, and although I know that the meditations of a philosopher are far removed from the judgment of the laity, because his endeavor is to seek out the truth in all things, so far as this is permitted by God to the human reason, I still believe that one must avoid theories altogether foreign to orthodoxy. Accordingly, when I considered in my own mind how absurd a performance it must seem to those who know that the judgment of many centuries has approved the view that the Earth remains fixed as center in the midst of the heavens, if I should, on the contrary, assert that the Earth moves; I was for a long time at a loss to know whether I should publish the commentaries which I have written in proof of its motion, or whether it were not better to follow the example of the Pythagoreans and of some others, who were accustomed to transmit the secrets of Philosophy not in writing but orally, and only to their relatives and friends.... Therefore, when I considered this carefully, the contempt which I had to fear because of the novelty and apparent absurdity of my view, nearly induced me to abandon utterly the work I had begun.

My friends, however, in spite of long delay and even resistance on my part, withheld me from this decision. First among these was Nicolaus Schonberg, cardinal of Capua, distinguished in all branches of learning. Next to him comes my very dear friend, Tidemann Giese, bishop of Culm, a most earnest student, as he is, of sacred and, indeed, of all good learning. The latter has often urged me, at times even spurring me on with reproaches, to publish and at last bring to the light the book which had lain in my study not nine years merely, but already going on four times nine. Not a few other very eminent and scholarly men made the same request, urging that I should no longer through fear refuse to give out my work for the common benefit of students of Mathematics. They said I should find that the more absurd most men now thought this theory of mine concerning the motion of the Earth, the more admiration and gratitude it would command after they saw in the publication of my commentaries the mist of absurdity cleared away by most transparent proofs. So, influenced by these advisors and this hope, I have at length allowed my friends to publish the work, as they had long besought me to do.

But perhaps Your Holiness will not so much wonder that I have ventured to publish these studies of mine, after having taken such pains in elaborating them that I have not hesitated to commit to writing my views of the motion of the Earth, as you will be curious to hear how it occurred to me to venture, contrary to the accepted view of mathematicians, and well-nigh contrary to common sense, to form a conception of any terrestrial motion whatsoever. Therefore I would not have it unknown to Your Holiness, that the only thing which induced me to look for another way of reckoning the movements of the heavenly bodies was that I knew that mathematicians by no means agree in their investigations thereof. For, in the first place, they are so much in doubt concerning the motion of the sun and the moon, that they cannot even demonstrate and prove by observation the constant length of a complete year; and in the second place, in determining the motions both of these and of the five other planets, they fail to employ consistently one set of first principles and hypotheses, but use methods of proof based only upon the apparent revolutions and motions. For some employ concentric circles only; others, eccentric circles and epicycles; and even by these means they do not completely attain the desired end. For, although those who have depended upon concentric circles have shown that certain diverse motions can be deduced from these, yet they have not succeeded thereby in laying down any sure principle, corresponding indisputably to the phenomena. These, on the other hand, who have devised systems of eccentric circles, although they seem in great part to have solved the apparent movements by calculations which by these eccentrics are made to fit, have nevertheless introduced many things which seem to contradict the first principles of the uniformity of motion. Nor have they been able to discover or calculate from these the main point, which is the shape of the world and the fixed symmetry of its parts; but their procedure has been as if someone were to collect hands, feet, a head, and other members from various places, all very fine in themselves, but not proportionate to one body, and no single one corresponding in its turn to the others, so that a monster rather than a man would be formed from them. Thus in their process of demonstration which they term a "method," they are found to have omitted something essential, or to have included something foreign and not pertaining to the matter in hand. This certainly would never have happened to them if they had followed fixed principles; for if the hypotheses they assumed were not false, all that resulted therefrom would be verified indubitably. Those things which I am saying now may be obscure, yet they will be made clearer in their proper place.

Therefore, having turned over in my mind for a long time this uncertainty of the traditional mathematical methods of calculating the motions of the celestial bodies, I began to grow disgusted that no more consistent scheme of the movements of the mechanism of the universe, set up for our benefit by that best and most law-abiding Architect of all things, was agreed upon by philosophers who otherwise investigate so carefully the most minute details of this world. Wherefore I undertook the task of rereading the books of all the philosophers I could get access to, to see whether any one ever was of the opinion that the motions of the celestial bodies were other than those postulated by the men who taught mathematics in the schools. And I found first, indeed, in

Cicero, that Niceta perceived that the Earth moved; and afterward in Plutarch I found that some others were of this opinion, whose words I have seen fit to quote here, that they may be accessible to all:

"Some maintain that the Earth is stationary, but Philolaus the Pythagorean says that it revolves in a circle about the fire of the ecliptic, like the sun and moon. Heraklides of Pontus and Ekphantus the Pythagorean make the Earth move, not changing its position, however, confined in its falling and rising around its own center in the manner of a wheel."

Taking this as a starting point, I began to consider the mobility of the Earth; and although the idea seemed absurd, yet because I knew that the liberty had been granted to others before me to postulate all sorts of little circles for explaining the phenomena of the stars, I thought I also might easily be permitted to try whether by postulating some motion of the Earth, more reliable conclusions could be reached regarding the revolution of the heavenly bodies than those of my predecessors.

And so, after postulating movements, which, farther on in the book, I ascribe to the Earth, I have found by many and long observations that if the movements of the other planets are assumed for the circular motion of the Earth and are substituted for the revolution of each star, not only do their phenomena follow logically therefrom, but the relative positions and magnitudes both of the stars and all their orbits, and of the heavens themselves, become so closely related that in none of its parts can anything be changed without causing confusion in the other parts and in the whole universe. Therefore, in the course of the work I have followed this plan: I describe in the first book all the positions of the orbits together with the movements which I ascribe to the Earth, in order that this book might contain, as it were, the general scheme of the universe. Thereafter in the remaining books, I set forth the motions of the other stars and of all their orbits together with the movement of the Earth, in order that one may see from this to what extent the movements and appearances of the other stars and their orbits can be saved, if they are transferred to the movement of the Earth. Nor do I doubt that ingenious and learned mathematicians will sustain me, if they are willing to recognize and weigh, not superficially, but with that thoroughness which Philosophy demands above all things, those matters which have been adduced by me in this work to demonstrate these theories. In order, however, that both the learned and the unlearned equally may see that I do not avoid anyone's judgment, I have preferred to dedicate these lucubrations of mine to Your Holiness rather than to any other, because, even in this remote corner of the world where I live, you are considered to be the most eminent man in dignity of rank and in love of all learning and even of mathematics, so that by your authority and judgment you can easily suppress the bites of slanderers, albeit the proverb hath it that there is no remedy for the bite of a sycophant. If perchance there shall be idle talkers, who, though they are ignorant of all mathematical sciences, nevertheless assume the right to pass judgment on these things, and if they should dare to criticise and attack this theory of mine because of some passage of scripture which they have falsely distorted for their own purpose, I care not at all; I will even despise their judgment as foolish. For it is not unknown that Lactantius, otherwise a famous writer but a poor mathematician, speaks most childishly of the shape of the Earth when he makes fun of those who said that the Earth has the form of a sphere. It should not seem strange then to zealous students, if some such people shall ridicule us also. Mathematics are written for mathematicians, to whom, if my opinion does not deceive me, our labors will seem to contribute something to the ecclesiastical state whose chief office Your Holiness now occupies; for when not so very long ago, under Leo X, at the Lateran Council the question of revising the ecclesiastical calendar was discussed, it then remained unsettled, simply because the length of the years and months, and the motions of the sun and moon were held to have been not yet sufficiently determined. Since that time, I have given my attention to observing these more accurately, urged on by a very distinguished man, Paul, bishop of Fossombrone, who at that time had charge of the matter. But what I may have accomplished herein I leave to the judgment of Your Holiness in particular, and to that of all other learned mathematicians; and lest I seem to Your Holiness to promise more regarding the usefulness of the work than I can perform, I now pass to the work itself.

Nicolaus Copernicus' Dedication on the *Revolutions of the Heavenly Bodies,* in *The Harvard Classics,* **XXXIX** (New York: The Crowell-Collier Publishing Co., 1938), 52–57.

B. Galileo Galilei's Dialogue Concerning the Two Chief World Systems—Ptolemaic and Copernican, 1632

Galileo Galilei (1564–1642) was one of the founders of the experimental method. Born in Pisa, educated in Italian universities, Galileo taught and lectured at Pisa, Rome, and Padua. His discovery of the laws of the pendulum, of falling bodies, and his statement of the problems of mechanics place him in the forefront of the great thinkers of the world. His telescope was important in the establishment of the heliocentric universe; his pen was even more important in the popularization of the new science.

Galileo introduces three interlocutors into this Dialogue—Salviati, Sagredo, and Simplicio.

SALV. Yesterday we resolved to meet today and discuss as clearly and in as much detail as possible the character and the efficacy of those laws of nature which up to the present have been put forth by the partisans of the Aristotelian and Ptolemaic position on the one hand, and by the followers of the Copernican system on the other. Since Copernicus places the earth among the movable heavenly bodies, making it a globe like a planet, we may well begin our discussion by examining the Peripatetic steps in arguing the impossibility of that hypothesis; what they are, and how great is their force and effect. For this it is necessary to introduce into nature two substances which differ esssentially. These are the celestial and the elemental, the former being invariant and eternal; the latter, temporary and destructible. This argument Aristotle treats in his book *De Caelo,* introducing it with some discourses dependent upon certain general assumptions, and afterwards confirming it by experiments and specific demonstrations. Following the same method, I shall first propound, and then freely speak my opinion, submitting myself to your criticisms—particularly those of Simplicio, that stout champion and defender of Aristotelian doctrines.

The first step in the Peripatetic arguments is Aristotle's proof of the completeness and perfection of the world. For, he tells us, it is not a mere line, nor a bare surface, but a body having length, breadth, and depth. Since there are only these three dimensions, the world, having these, has them all, and, having the Whole, is perfect. To be sure, I much wish that Aristotle had proved to me by rigorous deductions that simple length constitutes the dimension which we call a line, which by the addition of breadth becomes a surface; that by further adding altitude or depth to this there results a body, and that after these three dimensions there is no passing farther —so that by these three alone, completeness, or, so to speak, wholeness is concluded. Especially since he might have done so very plainly and speedily.

SIMP. What about the elegant demonstrations in the second, third, and fourth texts, after the definition of "continuous"? Is it not there first proved that there are no more than three dimensions, since Three is everything, and everywhere? And is this not confirmed by the doctrine and authority of the Pythagoreans, who say that all things are determined by three—

beginning, middle, and end—which is the number of the Whole? Also, why leave out another of his reasons; namely, that this number is used, as if by a law of nature, in sacrifices to the gods? Furthermore, is it not dictated by nature that we attribute the title of "all" to those things that are three, and not less? For two are called "both," and one does not say "all" unless there are three.

You have all this doctrine in the second text. Afterwards, in the third we read, *ad pleniorem scientiam,* that All, and Whole, and Perfect are formally one and the same; and that therefore among figures only the solid is complete. For it alone is determined by three, which is All; and, being divisible in three ways, it is divisible in every possible way. Of the other figures, one is divisible in one way, and the other in two, because they have their divisibility and their continuity according to the number of dimensions allotted to them. Thus one figure is continuous in one way, the other in two; but the third, namely the solid, is so in every way.

Moreover, in the fourth text, after some other doctrines, does he not clinch the matter with another proof? To wit: a transition is made only according to some defect; thus there is a transition in passing from the line to the surface, because the line is lacking in breadth. But it is impossible for the perfect to lack anything, being complete in every way; therefore there is no transition beyond the solid or body to any other figure.

Do you not think that in all these places he has sufficiently proved that there is no passing beyond the three dimensions, length, breadth, and thickness; and that therefore the body, or solid, which has them all, is perfect?

SALV. To tell you the truth, I do not feel impelled by all these reasons to grant any more than this: that whatever has a beginning, middle, and end may and ought to be called perfect. I feel no compulsion to grant that the number three is a perfect number, nor that it has a faculty of conferring perfection upon its possessors. I do not even understand, let alone believe, that with respect to legs, for example, the number three is more perfect than four or two; neither do I conceive the number four to be any imperfection in the elements, nor that they would be more perfect if they were three. Therefore it would have been better for him to leave these subtleties to the rhetoricians, and to prove his point by rigorous demonstrations such as are suitable to make in the demonstrative sciences. . . .

SIMP. Oh, there is no doubt whatever that the earth is more perfect the way it is, being alterable, changeable, etc., than it would be if it were a mass of stone or even a solid diamond, and extremely hard and invariant. But to the extent that these conditions bring nobility to the earth, they would render less perfect the celestial bodies, in which they would be superfluous. For the celestial bodies—that is, the sun, the moon, and the other stars, which are ordained to have no other use than that of service to the earth—need nothing more than motion and light to achieve their end.

SAGR. Has nature, then, produced and directed all these enormous, perfect, and most noble celestial bodies, invariant, eternal, and divine, for no other purpose than to serve the changeable, transitory, and mortal earth? To serve that which you call the dregs of the universe, the sink of all uncleanness? Now to what purpose would the celestial bodies be made eternal, etc., in order to serve something transitory, etc. Take away this purpose of serving the earth, and the innumerable host of celestial bodies is left useless and superfluous, since they have not and cannot have any reciprocal activities among themselves, all of them being inalterable, immutable, and invariant. For instance, if the moon is invariant, how would you have the sun or any other star act upon it? The action would doubtless have no more effect than an attempt to melt a large mass of gold by looking at it or by thinking about it. Besides, it seems to me that at such times as the celestial bodies are contributing to

the generations and alterations on the earth, they too must be alterable. Otherwise I do not see how the influence of the moon or sun in causing generations on the earth would differ from placing a marble statue beside a woman and expecting children from such a union.

SIMP. Corruptibility, alteration, mutation, etc., do not pertain to the whole terrestrial globe, which as to its entirety is no less eternal than the sun or moon. But as to its external parts it is generable and corruptible, and it is certainly true that generations and corruptions are perpetual in those parts, and, as perpetual, that they require celestial and eternal operations. Therefore it is necessary that celestial bodies be eternal.

SAGR. This is all very well, but if there is nothing prejudicial to the immortality of the entire terrestrial globe in the corruptibility of its superficial parts, and if this generability, corruptibility, alterability, etc., give to it a great ornament and perfection, then why can you not and should you not likewise admit alterations, generations, etc., in the external parts of the celestial globes, adding these as an ornament without diminishing their perfection or depriving them of actions; even increasing those by making them operative not only upon the earth but reciprocally among themselves, and the earth also upon them?

SIMP. This cannot be, because the generations, mutations, etc. which would occur, say, on the moon, would be vain and useless, and *natura nihil frustra facit*.[1]

SAGR. And why should they be vain and useless?

SIMP. Because we plainly see and feel that all generations, changes, etc., that occur on earth are either directly or indirectly designed for the use, comfort, and benefit of man. Horses are born to accommodate men; for the nutriment of horses, the earth produces hay and the clouds water it. For the comfort and nourishment of men are created herbs, cereals, fruits, beasts, birds, and fishes. In

---

[1] "Nature does nothing in vain."

brief, if we proceed to examine and weigh carefully all these things, we shall find that the goal toward which all are directed is the need, the use, the comfort and the delight of men. Now of what use to the human race could generations ever be which might happen on the moon or other planets? Unless you mean that there are men also on the moon who enjoy their fruits; an idea which if not mythical is impious.

SAGR. I do not know nor do I suppose that herbs or plants or animals similar to ours are propagated on the moon, or that rains and winds and thunderstorms occur there as on the earth; much less that it is inhabited by men. Yet I still do not see that it necessarily follows that since things similar to ours are not generated there, no alterations at all take place, or that there cannot be things there that do change or are generated and dissolve; things not only different from ours, but so far from our conceptions as to be entirely unimaginable by us.

I am certain that a person born and raised in a huge forest among wild beasts and birds, and knowing nothing of the watery element, would never be able to frame in his imagination another world existing in nature differing from his, filled with animals which would travel without legs or fast-beating wings, and not upon its surface alone like beasts upon the earth, but everywhere within its depths; and not only moving, but stopping motionless wherever they pleased, a thing which birds in the air cannot do. And that men lived there too, and built palaces and cities, and traveled with such ease that without tiring themselves at all they could proceed to far countries with their families and households and whole cities. Now as I say, I am sure that such a man could not, even with the liveliest imagination, ever picture to himself fishes, the ocean, ships, fleets, and armadas. Thus, and more so, might it happen that in the moon, separated from us by so much greater an interval and made of materials perhaps much different from those on earth, substances exist and actions occur which are not merely remote from but completely beyond all our imaginings, lacking any resemblance to ours and therefore being entirely unthinkable. For that which we imagine must be either something already seen or a composite of things and parts of things seen at different times; such are sphinxes, sirens, chimeras, centaurs, etc.

SALV. Many times have I given rein to my fancies about these things, and my conclusion is that it is indeed possible to discover some things that do not and cannot exist on the moon, but none which I believe can be and are there, except very generally; that is, things occupying it, acting and moving in it, perhaps in a very different way from ours, seeing and admiring the grandeur and beauty of the universe and of its Maker and Director and continually singing encomiums in His praise. I mean, in a word, doing what is so frequently decreed in the Holy Scriptures; namely, a perpetual occupation of all creatures in praising God.

SAGR. These are among the things which, speaking very generally, could be there. But I should like to hear you mention those which you believe cannot be there, as it must be possible for you to name them more specifically.

SALV. I warn you, Sagredo, that this will be the third time we have thus strayed imperceptibly, step by step, from our principal topic, and we shall get to the point of our argument but slowly if we make digressions. Therefore it will perhaps be good if we defer this matter, along with others we have agreed to put off until a special session.

SAGR. Please, now that we are on the moon, let us go on with things that pertain to it, so that we shall not have to make another trip over so long a road.

SALV. As you wish. To begin with the most general things, I believe that the lunar globe is very different from the terrestrial, although in some points conformity is to be seen. I shall speak first of their resemblances and then of differences.

The moon certainly agrees with the earth in its shape, which is indubitably spherical. This follows necessarily from its disc being seen perfectly circular, and from the manner of its receiving light from the sun. For if its surface were flat, it would all become covered with light at once, and likewise would all be deprived of light in an instant; not first the part directed toward the sun and then successively the following parts, so that the whole apparent disc is illuminated at opposition but not before. And on the other hand the contrary would occur if the visible surface were concave; that is, illumination would commence at the part opposite to the sun.

In the second place, it is itself dark and opaque like the earth, by which opacity it is fitted to receive and reflect the light of the sun; for if it were not so, it could not do this.

Third, I hold its material to be very dense and solid, no less than the earth's, of which a sufficiently clear proof to me is the unevenness of the major parts of its surface, evidenced by the many prominences and cavities revealed by the aid of the telescope. The prominences there are mainly very similar to our most rugged and steepest mountains, and some of them are seen to be drawn out in long tracts of hundreds of miles. Others are in more compact groups, and there are also many detached and solitary rocks, precipitous and craggy. But what occur most frequently there are certain ridges [*argini*] (I shall use this word because no more descriptive one occurs to me), somewhat raised, which surround and enclose plains of different sizes and various shapes, but for the most part circular. In the middle of many of these there is a mountain in sharp relief, and some few are filled with a rather dark substance similar to that of the large spots that are seen with the naked eye; these are the largest ones, and there are a very great number of smaller ones, almost all of them circular.

Fourth, just as the surface of our globe is divided into two chief parts—the land and the sea—so in the lunar disc we see a sharp distinction between the brighter areas and the less bright. I believe that the appearance of the earth illuminated by the sun would be very similar to this for one who could see it from the moon or from some similar distance, and that the surface of the seas would appear darker, and that of the land brighter.

Fifth, as from the earth we see the moon now completely lighted, now half, now more, now less, sometimes sickle-shaped and sometimes completely invisible (that is, when it is beneath the sun's rays so that the part which faces the earth remains darkened), just so would the illumination made by the sun on the face of the earth be seen from the moon, with precisely the same period and the same alterations of shape. Sixth, . . .

SAGR. Hold on a minute, Salviati. I understand perfectly well that for anyone on the moon the illumination of the earth would be similar, in its various shapes, to that which we discover in the moon. . . .

SALV. To get back to our original discussion, I state that the sixth agreement between the moon and the earth is that just as the moon supplies us with the light we lack from the sun a great part of the time, and by reflection of its rays makes the nights fairly bright, so the earth repays it by reflecting the solar rays when the moon most needs them, giving a very strong illumination—as much greater than what the moon gives us, it would seem to me, as the surface of the earth is greater than that of the moon.

SAGR. Stop there, Salviati, and allow me the pleasure of showing you how from just this first hint I have seen through the cause of an event which I have thought about a thousand times without ever getting to the bottom of it.

You mean that a certain baffling light which is seen on the moon, especially when it is horned, comes from the reflection of the sun's light from the surface of the earth and the sea; and this light is seen most clearly when the horns are the thinnest. For at that time the luminous part of the earth that is seen from the moon is greatest, in accordance with your conclusion a little while ago that the luminous part of the earth shown to the moon is always as great as the dark part of the moon which is turned toward the earth. Hence when the moon is thinly horned and consequently in large part shadowy, the illuminated part of the earth seen from the moon is large, and so much the more powerful is its reflection of light.

SALV. That is exactly what I meant. Really, it is a great pleasure to talk with discriminating and perceptive persons, especially when people are progressing and reasoning from one truth to another. For my part I more often encounter heads so thick that when I have repeated a thousand times what you have just seen immediately for yourself, I never manage to get it through them.

SIMP. If you mean being unable to show them so that they understand it, that is a great surprise to me; I am sure that if they did not understand it from your explanation they would not understand it from anyone's, since yours seems to me very clear in its expression. But if you mean not having persuaded them so that they believe it, I am not at all surprised, for I must confess myself one of those who understand your reasoning without being satisfied by it. For me, there remain many difficulties in this and in parts of others of your six analogies....

Of the resemblances you have set forth in order to draw a parallel between the earth and the moon, I find that I can admit without misgivings only the first one and a couple of others. I admit the first, that is, the spherical shape, though even in this there is a difficulty; for I consider the moon's sphere to be as smooth and polished as a mirror, whereas that of this earth that we touch with our hands is very rough and rugged. But this matter of the irregularity of the surface comes considerably into one of the other correspondences you have set forth, and so I reserve what I have to say until we get to that.

That the moon is opaque and dark in itself, as you say in your second analogy, I admit only as to the first attribute of opacity, which the solar eclipses assure me of. For if the moon were trans-parent, the sky would not become as dark as it does in a total eclipse of the sun. Transparency of the lunar globe would permit a refracted light to pass through as do the densest clouds. But as to the darkness, I do not believe that the moon is entirely without light, like the earth. On the contrary, that brightness which is observed on the balance of its disc outside of the thin horns lighted by the sun I take to be its own natural light; not a reflection from the earth, which is incapable of reflecting the sun's rays by reason of its extreme roughness and darkness.

In your third parallel, I agree with you in one part and disagree in another. I concur in judging the body of the moon to be very solid and hard like the earth's. Even more so, for if from Aristotle we take it that the heavens are of impenetrable hardness and the stars are the denser parts of the heavens, then it must be that they are extremely solid and most impenetrable.

SAGR. What excellent stuff, the sky, for anyone who could get hold of it for building a palace! So hard, and yet so transparent!

SALV. Rather, what terrible stuff, being completely invisible because of its extreme transparency. One could not move about the rooms without grave danger of running into the doorposts and breaking one's head.

SAGR. There would be no such danger if, as some of the Peripatetics say, it is intangible; it cannot even be touched, let alone bumped into.

SALV. That would be no comfort, inasmuch as celestial material, though indeed it cannot be touched (on account of lacking the tangible quality), may very well touch elemental bodies; and by striking upon us it would injure us as much, and more, as it would if we had run against it.

But let us forsake these palaces, or more appropriately these castles in the air, and not hinder Simplicio....

SIMP. Back to our purpose. I reply that I consider the moon more solid than the earth, not for the reason you already gave, of the roughness and ruggedness of its surface, but on the contrary from its being suited to receive a polish and a lustre superior to that of the smoothest mirror, as observed in the hardest stones on earth. For thus must be its surface in order to make such a vivid reflection of the sun's rays. The appearances you speak of, the mountains, rocks, ridges, valleys, etc., are all illusions. I have heard it strongly maintained in public debates against these innovators that such appearances belong merely to the unevenly dark and light parts of which the moon is composed inside and out. We see the same thing occur in crystal, amber, and many perfectly polished precious stones, where, from the opacity of some parts and the transparency of others, various concavities and prominences appear to be present.... I concede that the surface of the terrestrial globe, seen from a distance, would have two different appearances, one lighter and the other darker, but I consider that the differences would fall out in reverse of what you say. I believe that the surface of the water would appear shining because it is smooth and transparent, while that of the land would remain dark by reason of its opacity and roughness, these being badly suited for the reflection of sunlight.... I think it most false that the moon can receive light from the earth, which is completely dark, opaque, and unfit to reflect sunlight as the moon reflects it so well to us. And as I have said, I consider the light which is seen over the rest of the face of the moon (outside the horns brightly illuminated by the sun) to be the moon's own proper and natural light, and it would be quite a feat to make me think otherwise....

SALV. If I have rightly understood so far as you have answered, it seems to me that there remain in dispute between you and me certain properties which I have made common to the moon and the earth, and they are these: You consider the moon to be as polished and smooth as a mirror and, as such, fitted to reflect the sunlight, and the earth, on the other hand, because of its roughness, as having no power to make a similar reflection. You concede the moon to be solid and hard; you deduce

this from its being polished and smooth, and not from its being mountainous. As to its appearing mountainous, you assign as a cause its parts being more and less opaque and clear. And finally you believe that the secondary light of the moon is its own, and not reflected from the earth— although it seems that you do not deny some reflection from our seas, which are smooth of surface....

We are inquiring, Simplicio, whether in order to produce a reflection of light similar to that which comes to us from the moon, it is necessary that the surface from which the reflection comes shall be as smooth and polished as a mirror, or whether a rough and ill-polished surface, neither smooth nor shiny, may not be better suited. Now if two reflections should come to us, one brighter than the other, from two surfaces situated opposite to us, I ask you which of the two surfaces you believe would look the lighter to our eyes, and which the darker?

SIMP. I think without any doubt that the surface which reflected the light more brilliantly would look lighter to me, and the other darker.

SALV. Now please take that mirror which is hanging on the wall, and let us go out into that court; come with us, Sagredo. Hang the mirror on that wall, there, where the sun strikes it. Now let us withdraw into the shade. Now, there you see two surfaces struck by the sun, the wall and the mirror. Which looks brighter to you; the wall, or the mirror? What, no answer?

SAGR. I am going to let Simplicio answer; he is the one who is experiencing the difficulty. For my part, from this small beginning of an experiment I am persuaded that the moon must indeed have a very badly polished surface.

SALV. Tell me, Simplicio; if you had to paint a picture of that wall with the mirror hanging on it, where would you use the darkest colors? In depicting the wall or the mirror?

SIMP. Very clever, my dear sir; and is this the best experiment you have to offer? You have placed us where the reflection from the mirror does not strike. But come with me a bit this way; no, come along.

SAGR. Perhaps you are looking for the place where the mirror throws its reflection?

SIMP. Yes, sir!

SAGR. Well, just look at it—there on the opposite wall, exactly as large as the mirror, and little less bright than it would be if the sun shone there directly.

SIMP. Come along, then, and look at the surface of the mirror from there, and then tell me whether I should say it is darker than that of the wall.

SAGR. Look at it yourself; I am not anxious to be blinded, and I know perfectly well without looking that it looks as bright and vivid as the sun itself, or little less so.

SIMP. Well, then, what do you say? Is the reflection from a mirror less powerful than that from a wall? I notice that on this opposite wall, which receives the reflection from the illuminated wall along with that of the mirror, the reflection from the mirror is much the brighter. And I see likewise that from here the mirror itself looks very much brighter to me than the wall.

SALV. You have got ahead of me by your perspicacity, for this was the very observation which I needed for explaining the rest. You see the difference, then, between the reflections made by the surface of the wall and that of the mirror, which are struck in exactly the same way by the sun's rays. You see how the reflection that comes from the wall diffuses itself over all the points opposite to it, while that from the mirror goes to a single place no larger than the mirror itself. You see likewise how the surface of the wall always looks equally light in itself, no matter from what place you observe it, and somewhat lighter than that of the mirror from every place except that small area where the reflection from the mirror strikes; from there, the mirror appears very much brighter than the wall. From this sensible and palpable experiment it seems to me that you can very readily decide whether the reflection which comes here from the

moon comes like that from a mirror, or like that from a wall; that is, whether from a smooth or a rough surface.

SAGR. If I were on the moon itself I do not believe that I could touch the roughness of its surface with my hand more definitely than I now perceive it by understanding your argument. The moon, seen in any position with respect to the sun and to us, always shows the surface exposed to the sun equally bright. This effect corresponds precisely with that of the wall, which seen from any place appears equally bright; it conflicts with that of the mirror, which from one place alone looks luminous and from all others dark. Besides, the light that comes to me from the reflection of the wall is weak and tolerable in comparison with that from the mirror, which is extremely strong and little less offensive to the eyes than the primary and direct rays of the sun. It is in just such a way that we can calmly contemplate the face of the moon. If that were like a mirror, appearing as large as the sun because of its closeness, it would be of an absolutely intolerable brilliance, and would seem to us almost as if we were looking at another sun.

SALV. Please, Sagredo, do not attribute to my demonstration more than belongs to it. I am about to confront you with a fact that I think you will find not so easy to explain. You take it as a great difference between the moon and the mirror that the former yields its reflections equally in all directions, as the wall does, while the mirror sends its reflection to one definite place alone. From this, you conclude that the moon is like the wall and not like the mirror. But I tell you that this mirror sends its reflection to one place alone because its surface is flat, and since reflected rays must leave at equal angles with incident rays, they have to leave a plane surface as a unit toward one place. But the surface of the moon is not flat, it is spherical; and the rays incident upon such a surface are found to be reflected in all directions at angles equal to those of incidence, because of the infinity of slopes which make up a spherical surface. Therefore the moon can send its reflections everywhere and need not send them all to a single place like those of a plane mirror.

SIMP. This is exactly one of the objections which I wanted to make.

SAGR. If it is one of them, then you must have others; but let me tell you that so far as this first one is concerned, it seems to me to be not so much for you as against you.

SIMP. You have called it obvious that the reflection made by that wall is as bright and luminous as that of the moon, whereas I think it trifling in comparison with the moon's. For "in this matter of illumination, one must look for and define the sphere of activity." Who doubts that celestial bodies have greater spheres of activity than our transitory mortal elements? And as to that wall, is it after all anything more than a bit of earth; dark, and unfit to illumine?

SAGR. Here again I believe that you are quite mistaken. But I return to the first point raised by Salviati, and tell you that in order to make an object appear luminous, it is not sufficient for the rays of the illuminating body to fall upon it; it is also necessary for the reflected rays to get to our eyes. This is to be clearly seen in the case of the mirror, upon which no doubt the rays of the sun are falling, but which nevertheless does not appear to be bright and illuminated unless we put our eyes in the particular place where the reflection is going. . . .

I merely smile, but believe me, I am hardly able to keep from laughing, because I am reminded of a situation that I witnessed not many years ago together with some friends of mine, whom I could name to you for that matter.

SALV. Perhaps you had better tell us about it so that Simplicio will not go on thinking your mirth was directed at him.

SAGR. I'll be glad to. One day I was at the home of a very famous doctor in Venice, where many persons came on account of their studies, and others occasionally came out of curiosity to see some anatomical dissection performed by a man who was truly no less learned than he was a careful and expert anatomist. It happened on this day that he was investigating the source and origin of the nerves, about which there exists a notorious controversy between the Galenist and Peripatetic doctors. The anatomist showed that the great trunk of nerves, leaving the brain and passing through the nape, extended on down the spine and then branched out through the whole body, and that only a single strand as fine as a thread arrived at the heart. Turning to a gentleman whom he knew to be a Peripatetic philosopher, and on whose account he had been exhibiting and demonstrating everything with unusual care, he asked this man whether he was at last satisfied and convinced that the nerves originated in the brain and not in the heart. The philosopher, after considering for awhile, answered: "You have made me see this matter so plainly and palpably that if Aristotle's text were not contrary to it, stating clearly that the nerves originate in the heart, I should be forced to admit it to be true."

SIMP. Sir, I want you to know that this dispute as to the source of the nerves is by no means as settled and decided as perhaps some people like to think.

SAGR. Doubtless it never will be, in the minds of such opponents. But what you say does not in the least diminish the absurdity of this Peripatetic's reply; who, as a counter to sensible experience, adduced no experiment or argument of Aristotle's, but just the authority of his bare *ipse dixit*.

SIMP. Aristotle acquired his great authority only because of the strength of his proofs and the profundity of his arguments. Yet one must understand him, and not merely understand him, but have such thorough familiarity with his books that the most complete idea of them may be formed, in such a manner that every saying of his is always before the mind. He did not write for the common people, nor was he obliged to thread his syllogisms together by the trivial ordinary method; rather, making use of the permuted method, he has sometimes put the proof of a proposition among texts that seem to deal with other things. Therefore one must have a grasp of the whole grand scheme, and be able to combine this passage with that, collecting together one text here and another very distant from it. There is no doubt that whoever has this skill will be able to draw from his books demonstrations of all that can be known; for every single thing is in them.

SAGR. My dear Simplicio, since having things scattered all over the place does not disgust you, and since you believe by the collection and combination of the various pieces you can draw the juice out of them, then what you and the other brave philosophers will do with Aristotle's texts, I shall do with the verses of Virgil and Ovid, making centos of them and explaining by means of these all the affairs of men and the secrets of nature. But why do I speak of Virgil, or any other poet? I have a little book, much briefer than Aristotle or Ovid, in which is contained the whole of science, and with very little study one may form from it the most complete ideas. It is the alphabet, and no doubt anyone who can properly join and order this or that vowel and these or those consonants with one another can dig out of it the truest answers to every question, and draw from it instruction in all the arts and sciences. Just so does a painter, from the various simple colors placed separately upon his palette, by gathering a little of this with a bit of that and a trifle of the other, depict men, plants, buildings, birds, fishes, and in a word represent every visible object, without any eyes or feathers or scales or leaves or stones being on his palette. Indeed, it is necessary that none of the things imitated nor parts of them should actually be among the colors, if you want to be able to represent everything; if there were feathers, for instance, these would not do to depict anything but birds or feather dusters.

SALV. And certain gentlemen still living and active were present when a doctor lecturing in a famous Academy, upon hearing the telescope described but not yet having seen it, said that the invention was taken from Aristotle. Having a text fetched, he found a certain place where the reason is given why stars in the sky can be seen during daytime from the bottom of a very deep well. At this point the doctor said: "here you have the well, which represents the tube; here the gross vapors, from whence the invention of glass lenses is taken; and finally here is the strengthening of the sight by the rays passing through a diaphanous medium which is denser and darker."

SAGR. This manner of "containing" everything that can be known is similar to the sense in which a block of marble contains a beautiful statue, or rather thousands of them; but the whole point lies in being able to reveal them. Even better we might say that it is like the prophecies of Joachim or the answers of the heathen oracles, which are understood only after the events they forecast have occurred.

SALV. And why do you leave out the prophecies of the astrologers, which are so clearly seen in horoscopes (or should we say in the configurations of the heavens) after their fulfillment?

SAGR. It is in this way that the alchemists, led on by their madness, find that the greatest geniuses of the world never really wrote about anything except how to make gold; but in order to tell this without revealing it to the vulgar, this fellow in one manner and that one in another have whimsically concealed it under various disguises. And a very amusing thing it is to hear their comments upon the ancient poets, revealing the important mysteries hidden behind their stories— what the loves of the moon mean, and her descent to the earth for Endymion; her displeasure with Acteon; the significance of Jupiter's turning himself into a rain of gold, or into a fiery flame; what great secrets of the art there are in Mercury the interpreter, in Pluto's kidnapings, and in golden boughs.

SIMP. I believe, and to some extent I know, that the world does not lack certain giddy brains, but their folly should not redound to the discredit of Aristotle, of whom it seems to me you sometimes speak with too little respect. His antiquity alone, and the mighty name he has acquired among so many men of distinguished mind, should be enough to earn him respect among all the learned.

SALV. That is not quite how matters stand, Simplicio. Some of his followers are so excessively timid that they give us occasion ... to think less of him. Tell me, are you so credulous as not to understand that if Aristotle had been present and heard this doctor who wanted to make him inventor of the telescope, he would have been much angrier with him than with those who laughed at this doctor and his interpretations? Is it possible for you to doubt that if Aristotle should see the new discoveries in the sky he would change his opinions and correct his books and embrace the most sensible doctrines, cast-

ing away from himself those people so weak-minded as to be induced to go on abjectly maintaining everything he had ever said? Why, if Aristotle had been such a man as they imagine, he would have been a man of intractable mind, of obstinate spirit, and barbarous soul; a man of tyrannical will who, regarding all others as silly sheep, wished to have his decrees preferred over the senses, experience, and nature itself. It is the followers of Aristotle who have crowned him with authority, not he who has usurped or appropriated it to himself. And since it is handier to conceal oneself under the cloak of another than to show one's face in open court, they dare not in their timidity get a single step away from him, and rather than put any alterations into the heavens of Aristotle, they want to deny out of hand those that they see in nature's heaven.

From Galileo Galilei, *Dialogo...sopra i due massimi sistemi del mondo, Tolemaico e Copernicano*, trans. Stillman Drake, *Galileo Galilei: Dialogue Concerning the Two Chief World Systems—Ptolemaic and Copernican* (Berkeley: University of California Press, 1953), pp. 9–111, *passim*.

C. Isaac Newton's Preface to the Principia Mathematica, *1686*

Sir Isaac Newton (1643–1727), although known most widely for his *Principia* in which he showed that the universe was held together by a basic physical law, is also famous for his studies of optics and his mathematics. Few men are ever "immortal" in their own lifetimes as Newton was; the name of this scientist and philosopher, nearly universally recognized before his death, is the veritable symbol of the scientific revolution.

Since the ancients ... made great account of the science of mechanics in the investigation of natural things; and the moderns, laying aside substantial forms and occult qualities, have endeavored to subject the phenomena of nature to the laws of mathematics, I have in this treatise cultivated mathematics so far as it regards philosophy. The ancients considered mechanics in a twofold respect; as rational, which proceeds accurately by demonstration, and practical. To practical mechanics

all the manual arts belong, from which mechanics took its name. But as artificers do not work with perfect accuracy, it comes to pass that mechanics is so distinguished from geometry, that what is perfectly accurate is called geometrical; what is less so is called mechanical. But the errors are not in the art, but in the artificers. He that works with less accuracy is an imperfect mechanic: and if any could work with perfect accuracy, he would be the most perfect mechanic of all; for the description of right lines and circles, upon which geometry is founded, belongs to mechanics. Geometry does not teach us to draw these lines, but requires them to be drawn; for it requires that the learner should first be taught to describe these accurately, before he enters upon geometry; then it shows how by these operations problems may be solved. To describe right lines and circles are problems, but not geometrical problems. The solution of these problems is required from mechanics; and by geometry the use of them, when so solved, is shown; and it is the glory of geometry that from those few principles, fetched from without, it is able to produce so many things. Therefore geometry is founded in mechanical practice, and is nothing but that part of universal mechanics which accurately proposes and demonstrates the art of measuring. But since the manual arts are chiefly conversant in the moving of bodies, it comes to pass that geometry is commonly referred to their magnitudes, and mechanics to their motion. In this sense rational mechanics will be the science of motions resulting from any forces whatsoever, and of the forces required to produce any motions, accurately proposed and demonstrated. This part of mechanics was cultivated by the ancients in the five powers which relate to manual arts, who considered gravity (it not being a manual power) no otherwise than as it moved weights by those powers. Our design, not respecting arts, but philosophy, and our subject, not manual, but natural powers, we consider chiefly those things which relate to gravity, levity, elastic force, the resistance of fluids, and the like forces, whether attractive or impulsive; and therefore we offer this work as mathematical principles of philosophy; for all the difficulty of philosophy seems to consist in this—from the phenomena of motions to investigate the forces of nature, and then from these forces to demonstrate the other phenomena; and to this end the general propositions in the first and second book are directed. In the third book we give an example of this in the explication of the system of the World; for by the propositions mathematically demonstrated in the first book, we there derive from the celestial phenomena the forces of gravity with which bodies tend to the sun and the several planets. Then, from these forces, by other propositions which are also mathematical, we deduce the motions of the planets, the comets, the moon, and the sea. I wish we could derive the rest of the phenomena of nature by the same kind of reasoning from mechanical principles; for I am induced by many reasons to suspect that they may all depend upon certain forces by which the particles of bodies, by some causes hitherto unknown, are either mutually impelled towards each other, and cohere in regular figures, or are repelled and recede from each other; which forces being unknown, philosophers have hitherto attempted the search of nature in vain; but I hope the principles here laid down will afford some light either to that or some truer method of philosophy.

In the publication of this work, the most acute and universally learned Mr. Edmund Halley not only assisted me with his pains in correcting the press and taking care of the schemes, but it was to his solicitations that its becoming public is owing; for when he had obtained of me my demonstrations of the figure of the celestial orbits, he continually pressed me to communicate the same to the Royal Society, who afterwards, by their kind encouragement and entreaties, engaged me to think of publishing them. But after I had begun to consider the inequalities of the lunar motions, and had entered upon some other things relating to the laws and measures of gravity, and other forces; and the figures that would be described by bodies attracted according to given laws; and the motion of several bodies moving among themselves; the motion of bodies in resisting mediums; the forces, densities, and motions of mediums; the orbits of the comets, and such like; I put off that publication till I had made a search into those matters, and could put out the whole together. What relates to the lunar motions (being imperfect) I have put all together in the corollaries of proposition 66, to avoid being obliged to propose and distinctly demonstrate the several things there contained in a method more prolix than the subject deserved, and interrupt the series of the several propositions. Some things, found out after the rest, I chose to insert in places less suitable, rather than change the number of the propositions and the citations. I heartily beg that what I have here done may be read with candor; and that the defects I have been guilty of upon this difficult subject may be not so much reprehended as kindly supplied, and investigated by new endeavors of my readers. [Cambridge, Trinity College, May 8, 1686.]

Sir Isaac Newton, Preface to the *Philosophiae Naturalis Principia Mathematica,* trans. Andrew Motte, in The Harvard Classics, **XXXIX** (New York: The Crowell-Collier Publishing Co., 1938), 150–52.

D. Fontenelle's Elogium of Sir Isaac Newton

Bernard le Bovier de Fontenelle (1657–1757) was the "perpetual secretary" of the French Academy of Science; he was also a facile writer whose popularizations of science and eulogies of the great men of his era furnish excellent insights into the mentality and ideas of this period. When nearly a hundred years old, Fontenelle met a young friend who said "But, Sir, death has overlooked you!" to which Fontenelle replied "Sh-h-h-h-h!"—with a finger on his lips. His charm and his learning were both impressive.

Sir Isaac Newton, who was born at Woolstrope in the county of Lincoln, on Christmas day in the year 1642, descended from the elder branch of the family of Sir John Newton, Baronet. The manor of Woolstrope had been in his family near 200 years. The Newtons came thither from Westby in the same county, but originally from Newton in Lancashire. Sir Isaac's mother, whose maiden name was Hannah Ascough, was likewise of an ancient family; she married again after his father's death.

When her son was twelve years old she put him to the free-school at Grantham; from whence she removed him some years after, that he might be accustomed betimes to look into his affairs, and to manage them himself. But she found him so careless of such business, and so taken up with his books, that she sent him again to Grantham, that he might be at liberty to follow his inclinations; which he farther indulged by going to Trinity College in Cambridge, where he was admitted in 1660, being then eighteen years of age.

In learning Mathematicks he did not study Euclid, who seemed to him too plain and too simple, and not worthy of taking up his time; he understood him almost before he read him, and a cast of his eye upon the contents of the Theorems was sufficient to make him master of them. He advanced at once to the Geometry of Descartes, Kepler's *Opticks,* etc., so that we may apply to him what Lucan said of the Nile, whose head was not known by the Ancients,

> *Arcanum Natura caput non prodidit ulli,*
>
> *Nec licuit populis parvum te, Nile, videre:*[1]
>
> *Nature conceals thy infant Stream with care,*
>
> *Nor lets thee, but in Majesty appear.*

It is certain that Sir Isaac had made his great discoveries in geometry, and laid the foundation of his two famous pieces the *Principia* and the *Opticks* by the time that he was twenty-four years of age. If those beings that are superior to man have likewise a progression in knowledge, they fly whilst we creep, and leap over those *mediums* by which we proceed slowly and with difficulty from one truth to another that has a relation to it.

Nicholas Mercator, who was born in Holstein, but spent most of his time in England, published in 1668 his *Logarithmotechnia,* in which he gave the quadrature of the hyperbola by an infinite series. This was the first appearance, in the learned world, of a series of this sort, drawn from the particular nature of the

---

[1] Lucan, *Bellum civile,* X, 295–6, ed. A. E. Housman (Oxford: Basil Blackwell & Mott, Ltd., 1926), p. 314.

curve, and that in a manner very new and abstracted. The famous Dr. Barrow, then at Cambridge, where Mr. Newton, who was about twenty-six years of age, resided, recollected that he had met with the same thing in the writings of that young gentleman, and there not confined to the hyperbola only, but extended by general forms to all sorts of curves, even such as are mechanical, to their quadratures, their rectifications and their centers of gravity, to the solids formed by their rotations, and to the superficies of those solids; so that supposing their determinations to be possible, the series stopt at a certain point, or at least their sums were given by stated rules: But if the absolute determinations were impossible, they could yet be infinitely approximated which is the happiest and most refined method of supplying the defects of human knowledge that man's imagination could possibly invent. To be master of so fruitful and general a theory was a mine of gold to a geometrician, but it was a greater glory to have been the discoverer of so surprizing and ingenious a system. So that Sir Isaac finding by Mercator's book that he was in the way to it, and that others might follow in his track, should naturally have been forward to open his treasures, and secure the property, which consisted in making the discovery. But he contented himself with his treasure which he had found, without regarding the glory. He himself says in a letter of the *Commercium epistolicum, that he thought Mercator had entirely discovered the secret, or that others would discover it before he was of an age to write himself.* He without any concern suffered that to be taken from him, from which he might propose to himself abundance of glory, and flatter himself with the most pleasing expectations. He waited with patience till he was of a fit age to write, or to make himself known to the world, though he was already capable of the greatest things.

His manuscript upon infinite series was communicated to none but Mr. Collins, and the Lord Brounker, both learned in that way. And even this had not been done, but for Dr. Barrow, who would not suffer him to indulge his modesty so much as he desired.

This manuscript was taken out of the author's study in the year 1669, entitled, *The method which I formerly found out,* etc., and supposing this *formerly* to mean no more than three years, he must then have discovered this admirable theory of his series when he was not twenty-four years of age; but what is still more, this manuscript contains both the discovery and method of fluxions, or those *infinitely small quantities,* which have occasioned so great a contest between M. Leibniz and him, or rather between Germany and England; of which I have given an account in 1716, in the Elogium upon M. Leibniz; and tho' it was in the Elogium of M. Leibniz, the impartiality of an historian was so exactly kept that there now remains nothing new to be said of Sir Isaac Newton. It was there particularly observed *that Sir Isaac was undoubtedly the inventor, that his glory was secure, and that the only question was, whether M. Leibniz did take this notion from him.* All England is convinced that he did take from him, tho' the Royal Society have not declared so in their determination, but only hinted it at most. However Sir Isaac Newton was certainly the first discoverer, and that too by many years. M. Leibniz on the other side was the first that published the method, and if he did take it from Sir Isaac, he at least resembled Prometheus in the fable, who stole fire from the Gods to impart it to mankind.

In 1687 Sir Isaac at length resolved to unveil himself and shew what he was, and accordingly the *Philosophiae Naturalis Principia Mathematica* appeared in the world. . . .

There are two theories which chiefly prevail in the *Principia,* that of the central power, and that of the resistance which mediums make to motion, both almost entirely new, and treated of according to the sublime geometry of the author. We can never touch upon either of these subjects without having Sir Isaac before us, without repeating what he has said, or following his track, and if we endeavour'd to disguise it, what skill could prevent Sir Isaac Newton's appearing in it?

The relation between the revolutions of the heavenly bodies and their distances from the common center of those revolutions, found out by Kepler, prevails throughout the whole celestial system. If we suppose, as it is necessary, that a certain force hinders these great bodies from pursuing, above an instant, their natural motion in a straight line from West to East, and continually draws them towards a center; it follows, by Kepler's rule, that this force, which will be central or rather centripetal, will act differently upon the same body according to its different distances from that center, and this in the reciprocal proportion of the squares of those distances; that is, for instance, if a body be at twice the distance from the center of its revolution, the action of the central force upon it will be four times weaker. It appears that Sir Isaac set out from hence when he entered upon his physicks of the world in general: We may likewise suppose or imagine that he first considered the moon, because the earth is the center of her motion.

If the moon should lose all her impulse or inclination to move from West to East in a straight line, and if nothing but the central power remained which forces her towards the center of the earth, she would then only obey that power, only follow its directions, and move in a straight line towards that center. The velocity of her motion being known, Sir Isaac demonstrates from that motion that in the first minute of her descent she would fall 15 Paris feet: her distance from the earth is 60 semi-diameters of the earth, therefore when the moon comes to the surface of the earth, the action of the force which brought her thither will be encreased as the square of 60, that is, it would be 3600 times stronger; so that the moon in her last minute would fall 3600 times 15 feet.

Now if we suppose that the force which would have acted upon the moon is the same which we call gravity in terrestrial bodies, it will follow from the system of Galileo that the moon, which at the surface of the earth would have fallen 3600 times 15 feet in a minute, should likewise have fallen 15 feet in the first 60th part, or in the first second of that minute. Now it is known by all experiments, and they only can be made at small distances from the surface of the earth, that heavy bodies fall 15 feet in the first second of their fall: Therefore as to the velocity of their fall they are exactly in the same condition, as if having made the same revolution round the earth that the moon doth and at the same distance, they should happen to fall by the mere force of their gravity; and if they are in the same condition as the moon, the moon is in the same condition as they, and is only moved each instant towards the earth by the same gravity. So exact an agreement of effects, or rather this perfect identity can proceed from nothing else but the causes being the same.

It is true that in the system of Galileo, which is here followed, the gravity is equal, and the central force of the moon is not so, even in the demonstration that has just been given; but gravity may well not discover its inequality, or rather, it only appears equal in all our experiments, because the greatest height from which we can observe bodies falling is nothing in comparison of 1500 leagues, the distance which they all are from the center of the earth. It is demonstrated that a cannon bullet shot horizontally describes, in the hypothesis of equal gravity, a parabolic line, terminated at a certain point, where it meets with the earth, but if it was shot from an height considerable enough to make the inequality of the action of its gravity perceptible, instead of a parabola it would describe an ellipsis, of which the center of the earth would be one of the foci, that is, it would perform exactly what the moon doth.

If the moon hath gravity like terrestrial bodies, if she is moved towards the earth by the same power, by which they are moved; if, according to Sir Isaac's expression, she gravitates towards the earth, the same cause acts upon all the rest of that wonderful concourse of heavenly bodies; for all nature is one and the same, there is everywhere the same disposition, everywhere ellipses will be described by bodies, whose motions are directed to a body placed in one of their foci. The satellites of Jupiter will gravitate towards Jupiter, as the moon gravitates towards the earth; the satellites of Saturn towards Saturn, and all the planets together towards the sun.

It is not known in what gravity consists. Sir Isaac Newton himself was ignorant of it. If gravity acts only by impulse, we may conceive that a block of marble falling, may be pushed towards the earth, without the earth being in any manner pushed towards it; and in a word all the centers to which the motions caused by gravity have relation, may be immoveable. But if it acts by attraction the earth cannot draw the block of marble, unless the block of marble likewise draw the earth, why then should that attractive power be in some bodies rather than others? Sir Isaac always supposes the action of gravity in all bodies to be reciprocal and in proportion only to their bulk; and by that seems to determine gravity to be really an attraction. He all along makes use of this word to express the active power of bodies, a power indeed unknown, and which he does not take upon him to explain; but if it can likewise act by impulse, why should not that clearer term have the preference? for it must be agreed that it is by no means possible to make use of them both indifferently, since they are so opposite. The continual use of the word attraction supported by great authority, and perhaps too by the inclination which Sir Isaac is thought to have had for the thing itself, at least makes the reader familiar with a notion exploded by the Cartesians, and whose condemnation had been ratified by all the rest of the philosophers; and we must now be upon our guard, lest we imagine that there is any reality in it, and so expose ourselves to the danger of believing that we comprehend it.

However all bodies according to Sir Isaac gravitate towards each other, or attract each other in proportion to their bulk: and when they revolve about a common center, by which consequently they are attracted, and which they attract, their attractive powers are in the reciprocal proportion of their distances from that center, and if all of them together with their common center revolve round another center common to them, and to others, this will again produce new proportions, which will become strangely complex. Thus each of the five satellites of Saturn gravitate towards the other four, and the other four gravitate towards it; all the five gravitate towards Saturn, and Saturn towards them; all together gravitate towards the sun, and the sun again towards them. What an excellent geometrician must he have been to separate such a chaos of relations! the very undertaking seems rashness; and we cannot without astonishment conceive that from so abstracted a theory, composed of so many separate theories, all very difficult to handle, such necessary conclusions should arise, and all conformable to the approved axioms of astronomy.

Sometimes these conclusions even foretell events, which the astronomers themselves had not remarked. It is asserted, and more especially in England, that when Jupiter and Saturn are nearest, which is at 165 millions of leagues distance, their motions have no longer the same regularity as in the rest of their course; and the system of Sir Isaac at once accounts for it, which cannot be done by any other system. Jupiter and Saturn attract each other with greater force, because they are nearer; and by this means the regularity of the rest of their course is very sensibly disordered; nay, they go farther still, and determine the quantity and the bounds of this irregularity.

The motion of the moon is the least regular of any of the planets, the most exact tables are sometimes wrong, and she makes certain excursions which could not before be accounted for,...*the Moon ...at last...is subdued by this new sys-*

tem. All the irregularities of her course are there shewn to proceed from a necessity by which they are foretold. It is difficult to imagine that a system in which they take this form should be no more than a lucky conjecture; especially if we consider this but as a small part of a theory, which with the same success comprehends an infinite number of other solutions. The ebbing and flowing of the tyde so naturally shews itself to proceed from the operation of the moon upon the sea, combined with that of the sun, that the admiration which this phenomenon used to raise in us seems to be lessened by it.

The second of these two great theories, upon which the *Principia* chiefly runs, is that of the resistance of *mediums* to motion, which must enter into the consideration of all the chief phenomena of nature, such as the motions of the celestial bodies, of light and sound. Sir Isaac, according to his usual method, lays his foundations in the most solid proofs of geometry, he considers all the causes from which resistance can possibly arise; the density of the medium, the swift motion of the body moved, the magnitude of its superficies, and from thence he at last draws conclusions which destroy all the vortices of Descartes, and overturn that immense celestial edifice, which we might have thought immoveable. If the planets move round the sun in a certain medium whatever it be, in an aetherial matter which fills up the whole, and which notwithstanding its being extremely subtil, will yet cause resistance as is demonstrated, whence comes it then that the motions of the planets are not perpetually, nay instantly lessened? but besides this, how can comets traverse those vortices freely every way, sometimes with a tendency absolutely opposite to theirs, without receiving any sensible alteration in their motions, tho' of never so long a continuance? whence comes it that these immense torrents whirling round with almost incredible velocity, do not instantly destroy the particular motion of any body, which is but an atom in comparison of them, and why do they not force it to follow their course? The

celestial bodies do then move in a vast vacuum, unless their exhalations and the rays of light which together from a thousand different mixtures, should mingle a small quantity of matter with the almost infinite immaterial spaces. Thus attraction and vacuum banished from physicks by Descartes, and in all appearance forever, are now brought back again by Sir Isaac Newton, armed with a power entirely new, of which they were thought incapable, and only perhaps a little disguised.

These two great men, whose systems are so opposite, resembled each other in several respects; they were both geniuses of the first rank, both born with superior understandings, and fitted for the founding of empires in knowledge. Being excellent geometricians, they both saw the necessity of introducing geometry into physicks; For both founded their physicks upon discoveries in geometry, which may almost be said of none but themselves. But one of them taking a bold flight, thought at once to reach the fountain of all things, and by clear and fundamental ideas to make himself master of the first principles; that he might have nothing more left to do, but to descend to the phenomena of natures as to necessary consequences; the other more cautious, or rather more modest, began by taking hold of the known phenomena to climb to unknown principles; resolved to admit them only in such manner as they could be produced by a chain of consequences. The former sets out from what he clearly understands, to find out the causes of what he sees; the latter sets out from what he sees, in order to find out the cause, whether it be clear or obscure. The self-evident principles of the one do not always lead him to the causes of the phenomena as they are; and the phenomena do not always lead the other to principles sufficiently evident. The boundaries which stopped two such men in their pursuits through different roads, were not the boundaries of their understanding, but of human understanding itself.

While Sir Isaac was composing his

great work, the *Principia,* he had also another in hand, as much an original and as new; which, though by the title it did not seem so general, is yet as extensive by the manner in which he has treated that particular subject. *This work* was his *Opticks, or treatise of Light and Colours,* which first appeared in the year 1704, after he had been making the necessary experiments for thirty years together.

It is no small art to make experiments exactly. Every matter of fact which offers itself to our consideration is complicated with so many others, which either compound or modify it, that without abundance of skill they cannot be separated; nay without an extraordinary sagacity, the different elements that enter into the composition can hardly be guessed at. The fact therefore to be considered must be resolved into the different ones of which it is composed; and they themselves are perhaps composed of others; so that if we have not chosen the right road, we may sometimes be engaged in endless labyrinths. The principles and elements of things seem to have been concealed from us by nature, with as much care as the causes, and when we attain to the discovery of them, it is a sight entirely new and unexpected.

What Sir Isaac Newton aims at quite through his *Opticks,* is the anatomy of light; this expression is not too bold since it is no more than the thing itself. By his experiments, the smallest ray of light that is conveyed into a dark room, and which cannot be so small, but that it is yet compounded of an infinite number of other rays, is divided and dissected in such manner, that the elementary rays of which it is composed, are separated from each other, and discover themselves every one tinged with its particular colour, which after this separation can no more be altered. The first total ray before the dissection, is white, and this whiteness arose from all the particular colours of the primitive rays. Separating these rays is so difficult, that when Mariotte undertook it upon the first news of Sir Isaac's experiments, he miscarried in the attempt, even

he who had such a genius for experiments, and had been so successful on many other subjects.

No primitive coloured rays could be separated, unless they were such by their nature, that in passing through the same medium, or through the same glass prism, they are refracted at different angles, and by that means separate when they are received at proper distances. This different refrangibility of rays, red, yellow, green, blue, purple, and all other colours infinite in number, a property which was never before suspected, and to which we could hardly be led by conjecture, is the fundamental discovery of Sir Isaac Newton's treatise. The different refrangibility leads us to the different reflexibility. But there is something more; for the rays which fall at the same angle upon a surface are refracted and reflected alternately, with a kind of play only distinguishable to a quick eye, and well assisted by the judgment of the observer. The only point, the first idea of which does not entirely belong to Sir Isaac Newton, is, that the rays which pass near the extremities of a body without touching it, do somewhat turn from a straight line, which is called inflection. But the whole together forms a body of opticks so perfectly new, that we may henceforward look upon that science as almost wholly owing to this author.

That he might not confine himself to these bare speculations, which are sometimes unjustly styled idle, he gave us the design of a telescope by reflection, which was not thoroughly put in execution 'till a long time after. It has here been experienced that one of these telescopes but 2 foot and a half long, had as good an effect as a tolerable common telescope of 8 or 9 feet, which is a very extraordinary advantage, and the whole improvement of it will probably be better known hereafter.

One advantage of this book, equal perhaps to that of the many new discoveries with which it abounds, is that it furnishes us with an excellent model of proceeding in experimental philosophy. When we are for prying into nature, we ought to examine her like Sir Isaac, that is, in as accurate and importunate a manner. Things that almost hide themselves from our enquiries, as being of too abstracted a nature, he knows how to reduce to calculation, though such calculations might elude the skill of the best geometricians, without that dexterity which was peculiar to himself; and the use which he makes of his geometry, is as artful as the geometry itself is sublime....

Attraction is the governing principle in this short plan of physicks; that property which is called the *hardness* of bodies, is the mutual attraction of their parts, which closes them together, and if they are of such a figure as that whole surfaces are capable of being, everywhere joined, without leaving any void spaces, the bodies are then perfectly hard. Of this kind there are only certain small bodies, which are primitive and unalterable, and which are the elements of all other bodies. *Fermentations,* or chemical *effervescences,* whose motion is so violent, that they may sometimes be compared to storms, are the effects of this powerful attraction, which acts upon small bodies only at small distances.

He conceives in general, that attraction is the active principle of everything in nature, and the cause of all motion. If a certain degree of motion that is once given to any thing by the hand of God, did afterwards only distribute itself according to the laws of percussion, it appears that it would continually decrease in its motion by contrary percussions, without ever being able to recover itself, and the universe would very soon fall into such a state of rest, as would prove the destruction of the whole. The power of attraction, which always subsists and is not weakened by being exerted, is a perpetual spring of action and life. It may likewise happen that the effects of this power may at length combine in such a manner, as that the system of the universe may be disordered, and require, according to Sir Isaac's expression, *a hand to repair it.*

He declares very freely that he lays down this attraction, only as a cause which he knows not, and whose effects he only considers, compares and calculates; and in order to avoid the reproach of reviving the *occult qualities* of the Schoolmen, he says, that he establishes none but such qualities as are *manifest* and very visible by their phenomena, but that the causes of these qualities are indeed *occult,* and that he leaves it to other philosophers to search into them; but are they not properly causes which the Schoolmen call *occult qualities;* since their effects are plainly seen? besides, could Sir Isaac think that others would find out these *occult causes* which he could not discover? with what hopes of success can any other man search after them? ...

It was Sir Isaac Newton's peculiar happiness, to enjoy the reward of his merit in his life-time, quite contrary to Descartes, who did not receive any honors until after his death. The English do not respect great geniuses the less for being born amongst them; and so far are they from endeavouring to depreciate them by malicious criticisms, so far from approving the envy which attacks them, that they all conspire to raise them; and that great degree of liberty which occasions their differences in the most important points, does not hinder them from uniting in this. They are all very sensible how much the glory of the *understanding* should be valued in a state, and whoever can procure it to their country becomes extremely dear to them. All the learned men of a nation, which produces so many, placed Sir Isaac at their head by a kind of unanimous applause, they acknowledged him for their chief and their master: not so much as one opposer did appear, nay they would not even have admitted of a moderate admirer. His philosophy has been adopted throughout England, it prevails in the Royal Society, and in all the excellent performances which have come from there; as if it had been already made sacred by the respect of a long series of age. In short he was reverenced to so great a degree that death could not procure him new honours, and he himself saw his own *apotheosis.* Tacitus who has reproached the Romans with their extreme indifference for the great men of their nation, would certainly have given the English the quite contrary character. In vain would the Romans have excused themselves by pretending that great merit was no more than what was common amongst them. Tacitus would have told them that it never was so, or that we should even endeavour to make it so by the honour we annex to it.

In 1703, Sir Isaac Newton was chosen President of the Royal Society, and continued so without any interruption until the time of his death, for the space of 23 years; a singular example, and one from which they could fear no ill consequences hereafter. Queen Anne knighted him in 1705, a title of honour which at least serves to shew that his name had reached the throne, to which the most celebrated names do not always arrive. . . .

From Fontenelle, *The Elogium of Sir Isaac Newton* (London, 1728), pp. 3–24, *passim*.

E. Antony van Leeuwenhoek's Observations on Rainwater (October 9, 1676)

While most of the scientists were professors at a university (Copernicus, Galileo, Newton, and others), Antony van Leeuwenhoek (1632–1723) was a cloth merchant and an official of his native town of Delft. His achievement was first the manufacture of microscopes that allowed him to see the micro-universe in mold, a drop of water, a bit of semen, or the scrapings from a tooth, and secondly, an accurate description of his findings. The postulate of a mechanical universe, however, proved not to be useful for the study of biological materials; nonetheless, Leeuwenhoek's findings were highly respected by his own generation as well as by posterity.

In the year 1675, about half-way through September (being busy with studying air, when I had much compressed it by means of water), I discovered living creatures in rain, which had stood but a few days in a new tub, that was painted blue within. This observation provoked me to investigate this water more narrowly; and especially because these little animals were, to my eye, more than ten thousand times smaller than the animalcule which Swammerdam has portrayed, and called by the name of Water-flea, or Water-louse, which you can see alive and moving in water with the bare eye.

Of the first sort that I discovered in the said water, I saw, after divers observations, that the bodies consisted of 5, 6, 7, or 8 very clear globules, but without being able to discern any membrane or skin that held these globules together, or in which they were inclosed. When these animalcules bestirred themselves, they sometimes stuck out two little horns, which were continually moved, after the fashion of a horse's ears. The part between these little horns was flat, their body else being roundish, save only that it ran somewhat to a point at the hind end; at which pointed end it had a tail, near four times as long as the whole body, and looking as thick, when viewed through my microscope, as a spider's web. At the end of this tail there was a pellet, of the bigness of one of the globules of the body; and this tail I could not perceive to be used by them for their movements in very clear water. These little animals were the most wretched creatures that I have ever seen; for when, with the pellet, they did but hit on any particles or little filaments (of which there are many in water, especially if it hath but stood some days), they stuck intangled in them; and then pulled their body out into an oval, and did struggle, by strongly stretching themselves, to get their tail loose; whereby their whole body then sprang back towards the pellet of the tail, and their tails then coiled up serpentwise, after the fashion of a copper or iron wire that, having been wound close about a round stick, and then taken off, kept all its windings. This motion, of stretching out and pulling together the tail, continued; and I have seen several hundred animalcules, caught fast by one another in a few filaments, lying within the compass of a coarse grain of sand.

I also discovered a second sort of animalcule, whose figure was an oval; and I imagined that their head was placed at the pointed end. These were a little bit bigger than the animalcules first mentioned. Their belly is flat, provided with divers incredibly thin little feet, or little legs, which were moved very nimbly, and which I was able to discover only after sundry great efforts, and wherewith they they brought off incredibly quick motions. The upper part of their body was round, and furnished inside with 8, 10, or 12 globules: otherwise these animalcules were very clear. These little animals would change their body into a perfect round, but mostly when they came to lie high and dry. Their body was also very yielding: for if they so much as brushed against a tiny filament, their body bent in, which bend also presently sprang out again; just as if you stuck your finger into a bladder full of water, and then, on removing the finger, the inpitting went away. Yet the greatest marvel was when I brought any of the animalcules on a dry place, for I then saw them change themselves at last into a round, and then the upper part of the body rose up pyramid-like, with a point jutting out in the middle; and after having thus lain moving with their feet for a little while, they burst asunder, and the globules and a watery humor flowed away on all sides, without my being able to discern even the least sign of any skin wherein these globules and the liquid had, to all appearance, been inclosed; and at such times I could discern more globules than when they were alive. This bursting asunder I figure to myself to happen thus:

imagine, for example, that you have a sheep's bladder filled with shot, peas, and water; then, if you were to dash it apieces on the ground, the shot, peas, and water would scatter themselves all over the place.

Furthermore, I discovered a third sort of little animals, that were about twice as long as broad, and to my eye quite eight times smaller than the animalcules first mentioned: and I imagined, although they were so small, that I could yet make out their little legs, or little fins. Their motion was very quick, both roundabout and in a straight line.

The fourth sort of animalcules, which I also saw a-moving, were so small, that for my part I can't assign any figure to them. These little animals were more than a thousand times less than the eye of a full-grown louse (for I judge the diameter of the louse's eye to be more than ten times as long as that of the said creature), and they surpassed in quickness the animalcules already spoken of. I have divers times seen them standing still, as 'twere, in one spot, and twirling themselves round with a swiftness such as you see in a whip-top a-spinning before your eye; and then again they had a circular motion, the circumference whereof was no bigger than that of a small sand-grain; and anon they would go straight ahead, or their course would be crooked.

Furthermore, I also discovered sundry other sorts of little animals; but these were very big, some as large as the little mites on the rind of cheese, others bigger and very monstrous. But I intend not to specify them; and will only say, that they were for the most part made up of such soft parts, that they burst asunder whenever the water happened to run off them.

Clifford Dobell, ed., *Antony van Leeuwenhoek and His 'Little Animals"* (London: Staples Press, Ltd., 1932), pp. 117–22.

9

The Enlightenment:
A New World-View

CRANE BRINTON

Harvard University

That life for all mankind here on this earth can be better—that *all* can be happier, richer, better adjusted—is, at least as a generally shared belief or hope among the mass of mankind, only a few centuries old. Many, perhaps most, Americans hardly realize how new this belief is. Yet the confident statement of Adlai Stevenson in a campaign speech of 1952, "Progress is what happens when inevitability yields to necessity. And it is an article of the democratic faith that progress is a basic law of life," is a statement that would have been incomprehensible to his own ancestors half a dozen generations back.

Let us, in a deliberate simplification we may hope later to complicate and qualify, contrast in broad lines the traditional Judaeo-Christian world-view of the nature of the universe and man's destiny in it with this new world-view of the eighteenth-century Enlightenment.

The traditional view, enshrined in the Book of Genesis, held that an omnipotent Creator had made this planet the center of the universe and had made man in His own image the center of a dramatic struggle between good and evil. The creation, according to the seventeenth-century Archbishop Ussher, took place in 4004 B.C.

The men of the Enlightenment, as a culmination of several centuries of scientific study of astronomy, physics, and mathematics, had by 1780 or so come to believe that the earth was only a minor planet, that on it life, including human life, was many thousands of years old, and that, as for a God who created it, the word of a great eighteenth-century French scientist, Laplace, might stand: "I have no need for *that* hypothesis."

More important perhaps, the traditional Judaeo-Christian view held that man, by nature a bewildering mixture of good and evil, was condemned on this earth to much irremediable suffering, but could, if he were true to his religious upbringing, hope for salvation and eternal happiness in another and quite different world, which men called heaven. By contrast, the view of the fully Enlightened of the late eighteenth century was that man, though at the moment capable of doing evil through ignorance and bad environmental conditions (for example, corruption by wealth and privilege, or corruption by poverty and degradation), is by nature good and reasonable and therefore is capable, under conditions the Enlightened could hope by universal education and by political, social, and economic reforms to bring about, of attaining happiness here and now, on this earth. Heaven and hell, the Christian drama of redemption, were to the fully Enlightened "superstitions" that hindered human development.

Finally, though in such long and firmly held traditional beliefs as Christian Scholasticism, the human faculty of "reason" was held to be of great importance; such reason was always held to need the bolstering of "faith"; and faith, unlike reason, did not depend for its hold on men, for its *validity,* on confirmation by logic and/or experimentation and verification as, say, the scientist understands these latter terms.

Now one of the great problems we face in understanding the eighteenth century—and our own twentieth century, which is, the historian must believe, in very important ways and beliefs affected by the Enlightenment of the eighteenth century—is how far the above simplification corresponds to the facts. Certainly one of the writers whom we cite below, the French *philosophe* Condorcet, came very near to believing in the perfectibility of all men, came at least to hint at what has been called the doctrine of "natural salvation," the belief that all men may ultimately attain personal immortality in this flesh, on this earth. Yet for the most part, believers in the new doctrines of progress, the natural goodness and/or reasonableness of man, the possibility of successful "pursuit of happiness" for all, did not go to Condorcet's extreme, did in fact compromise, did qualify their new beliefs and retained many of the old ones. The reader should for the writings that follow constantly ask himself the question: How much of this seems contrary to traditional Judaeo-Christian beliefs, how much of it seems congruous with such beliefs, or at least to develop "naturally" or "logically" from such beliefs?

A central problem about the world-view of the Enlightenment, or, to point up the problem sharply, of its "ideology" is one we cannot attempt to resolve from the material here presented. This is the problem of whether the world-view of the Enlightenment followed from, was "caused by," material, economic, concrete changes in the whole human situation or whether this world-view itself helped produce exactly these changes. In mid-twentieth century, the true Communist believer is trained to hold that all world-views (except perhaps those of communism?) are mere "superstructure," mere reflections of changes in the "mode of production" and the "class structure." The ideas of the eighteenth-century Enlightenment thus become, for the Marxist, merely ideas inevitably produced by commercial capitalism and the "bourgeoisie."

We repeat, the excerpts which follow will not in themselves enable the reader to answer this question of "ideology" versus "reality"— which may well be an unanswerable question. But the reader should keep in mind the fact that Marxism itself is a direct derivation of eighteenth-century Enlightenment in its extreme anti-Christian form. The material that follows should, however, give a reader the opportunity to consider many more manageable problems, and in particular, as we have noted, the many problems of the interrelation of the old and the new, the Christian and the Enlightened, the pessimistic or "realistic" and the optimistic view of "human nature," the role of reason in human affairs, the very foundations of our democratic faith "that all men are created equal, that they are endowed by their Creator with certain unalienable Rights, that among these are Life, Liberty and the pursuit of Happiness."

I. Reason : Deduction or Observation and Experiment ?

One of the great reproaches made against the thinkers of the Enlightenment is that they thought in long chains of deduction, as do mathematicians. It is claimed that, though they gave lip service to the careful experiments and observations of natural science, they did not really recognize the dangers of thinking without frequent refreshing returns to the earth of facts, of sense data. We begin with an excerpt from the seventeenth-century French philosopher René Descartes, in which this "rationalistic" mathematical method of reasoning is clearly stated. Descartes is one of the important intellectual sources of the Enlightenment. His influence, especially on the Continent, was perhaps greater than that of the scientist Newton. In Descartes men found clearly stated, not only the logic of mathematical reasoning, but the basic theme of the Enlightenment: think it out for yourself, regardless of what your parents, your teachers, your priests have told you, regardless of Authority and Tradition. Our other selections suggest how different indeed were men's interpretation of "reason"; we have first the practical English reformer Bentham, seeking to reveal the "hidden persuaders" of the 1790s, then two Frenchmen, Voltaire, symbol for the whole Enlightenment, and Denis Diderot, one of the subtlest and most

imaginative of the French *philosophes*, a writer whose reputation has risen greatly in our own century. Do these thinkers advocate an oversimple, mathematical approach to the problems of human relations? Is man for them a mere thinking machine?

A. Descartes. Right Reason, 1637

Good sense is better distributed than anything in the world; for each thinks himself so well provided therewith, that as a rule even those who are the most difficult to satisfy with regard to everything else, do not desire more of it than they already have. This does not show that every one deceives himself; it testifies rather to the fact that the power of judging well and of distinguishing the true from the false, which is properly that which we call good sense, or reason, is naturally equal in all men. And thus the diversity of our opinions is not because some are more reasonable than others, but only because we conduct our thought by different ways, and do not all consider the same things. For it is not sufficient that the understanding be good—the thing is to apply it well. The greatest minds are capable of the greatest vices as well as of the greatest virtues, and those who proceed but slowly can advance much further, if they follow the right road, than those who hasten in the wrong direction.

For my own part, I have never presumed that my understanding was in any way more perfect than that of most people: indeed, I have often wished that my thought were as quick, or my imagination as exact and vivid, or my memory as comprehensive or as ready, as those of others. And I know no qualities but these which make for the perfection of the mind, for inasmuch as reason or sense is the only thing which renders us human and distinguishes us from animals, I would believe that it is quite complete in every individual, and follow herein the common opinion of the philosophers, who say that there are variations only as regards accidentals, and not between the forms and natures of individuals. . . .

Above all, I took pleasure in mathematics, because of the certainty and evidence of their reasons, but I did not yet remark their true use; and thinking that they served the mechanical arts alone, I was surprised that since their foundations were so firm and solid, nothing more lofty had been built upon them. So, on the other hand, I compared the writings of ancient pagans who treated of morals to very superb and magnificent palaces built only on sand and mud, for they highly exalted the virtues and made them appear estimable above all existing things, but they did not sufficiently teach how to know them, and often that which they call by so fine a name is only insensibility, or pride, or despair, or parricide. . . .

I could in nowise approve those blundering and restless persons who, being called neither by birth nor fortune to the management of public affairs, are always devising some new reformation. And if I thought that this writing contained the least thing which could make me suspected of this folly, I should be very sorry to permit its publication. My design never extends further than the endeavour to reform my own thoughts, and to build on ground which is wholly mine. If, since my work

has pleased me, I here show you its plan, it is not because I wish to counsel anyone to imitate it. Those to whom God has allotted more of His grace would perhaps have loftier designs, but I much fear that this one is already but too hard for many. Even the resolve to free oneself from all opinions formerly accepted and believed is not an example which every man ought to follow, and the world is almost solely made up of two classes of minds for whom it is by no means expedient,—to wit, of those who, thinking themselves cleverer than they are, cannot refrain from precipitating their judgments, and have not patience enough to conduct all their thoughts methodically, so that if they once took the liberty of doubting the principles they have received, and of escaping from the beaten track, they would never be able to keep to the path they ought to follow in order to proceed more directly, and would remain astray all their life; and those who, having sufficient reason or modesty to judge that they are less capable of distinguishing the true from the false than others by whom they might be instructed, ought much rather to content themselves with following the opinions of those others than seek better for themselves. . . .

I do not know whether I ought to discuss with you the earlier of my meditations, for they are so metaphysical and so out of the common that perhaps they would not be to everyone's taste; and yet, in order that it may be judged whether the bases I have taken are sufficiently firm, I am in some measure constrained to speak of them. I had remarked for long that, in conduct, it is sometimes necessary to follow opinions known to be very uncertain, just as if they were indubitable, as has been said above: but then, because I desired to devote myself only to the research of truth, I thought it necessary to do exactly the contrary, and reject as absolutely false all in which I could conceive the least doubt, in order to see if afterwards there did not remain in my belief something which was entirely indubitable. Thus, because our senses sometimes deceive us, I wanted to suppose that nothing is such as they make us imagine it; and because some men err in reasoning, even touching the simplest matters of geometry, and make paralogisms, and judging that I was as liable to fail as any other, I rejected as false all the reasons which I had formerly accepted as demonstrations; and finally, considering that all the thoughts which we have when awake, can come to us also when we sleep, without any of them then being true, I resolved to feign that everything which had ever entered into my mind was no more true than the illusions of my dreams. But immediately afterwards I observed, that while I thus desired everything to be false, I, who thought, must of necessity be something; and remarking that this truth, *I think, therefore I am,* was so firm and so assured that all the most extravagant suppositions of the sceptics were unable to shake it, I judged that I could unhesitatingly accept it as first principle of the philosophy I was seeking.

Then, examining attentively what I was, and seeing that I could feign that I had no body, and that there was no world or any place where I was, but that nevertheless I could not feign that I did not exist, and that, on the contrary, from the fact that I thought to doubt of the truth of other things, it followed very evidently that I was; while if I had only ceased to think, although all else which I had previously imagined had been true, I had no reason to believe that I might have been, therefore I knew that I was a substance whose essence or nature is only to think, and which, in order to be, has no need of any place, and depends on no material thing; so that this I, that is to say, the soul by which I am what I am, is entirely distinct from the body, and even easier to know than the body, and although the body were not, the soul would not cease to be all that it is.

After that I considered generally what is requisite to make a proposition true and certain; for since I had just found one which I knew to be so, I thought that I ought also to know in what this certainty consisted. And having remarked that there is nothing at all in this, *I think, therefore I am,* which assures me that I speak the truth, except that I see very clearly that in order to think it is necessary to exist, I judged that I might take it as a general rule, that the things which we conceive very clearly and very distinctly are all true, and that there is difficulty only in seeing plainly which things are that we conceive distinctly.

René Descartes, *Discourse on Method and Metaphysical Meditations* (London: Walter Scott Publishing Co., Ltd., n. d.), pp. 2–3, 9, 17–19, 37–39.

B. Bentham. On Political Fallacies, [1802] 1824

Sec. 3. Relation of Fallacies to Vulgar Errors

Vulgar error is the name given to an opinion which, being thought to be false, is considered in itself only, and not with a view to any consequences which it may produce. It is termed vulgar with respect to the multitude of persons by whom it is supposed to be entertained. *Fallacy* is applied to discourse in any shape considered as having a tendency, with or without design, to cause any erroneous opinion to be embraced, or, through the medium of some erroneous opinion already entertained, a pernicious course of action to be engaged in or persevered in. Thus to believe that the persons who lived in early or old times were, because they lived in those times, wiser or better than those who live in later or modern times, is a vulgar error; but to employ that error in the endeavor to cause pernicious practices and institutions to be retained is a fallacy.

Most of those who employed the term fallacy originally, considered deception not merely as a more or less probable consequence of such arguments, but as the end aimed at by at least some of their utterers. The thirteen arguments enumerated by Aristotle to which his Latin commentators gave the name of *fallaciae* (from *fallere*, to deceive), were undoubtedly regarded by him as instruments of deception, since on every occasion on which they are mentioned by him, the intent to deceive is either directly asserted or assumed.

Sec. 4. Political Fallacies the Subject of this Work

The present work confines itself to the examination and exposure of only one class of fallacies: those relating to the adoption or rejection of some measure of government, whether of legislation or of administration. The latter pair are so intimately connected that for our purposes they needed not be distinguished from one another.

Under the name of a *Treatise on Political Fallacies* this work will possess the character and effect of a manual on the art of government, having for its practical object and tendency the introduction of such features of good government as remain to be introduced, and their perpetuation by means of that instrument, reason, which alone will be productive of any useful effect.

Now there are two ways in which the instrument of reason can be employed in this endeavor. The first and more direct is by showing positively, with respect to each measure proposed, in what ways and with what consequences it is likely to accomplish the end which it professes to have in view. The second and less direct is by pointing out the irrelevancy, and thus anticipating and destroying the persuasive force of such deceptious arguments as are likely to be used in dissuading men from supporting it.

Of these two different but harmonizing modes of applying this same instrument of reason to its several purposes, the more direct is that of which a sample has been before the public since 1802 in the collection of unfinished papers of legislation published at Paris in French by M. Dumont, but for whose labors it would scarcely, in the author's lifetime at least, have seen the light. To exhibit the less direct, but in its application the more extensive use, is the business of the present work.

To give existence to good arguments was the object of the former work; to provide for the exposure of bad ones is the object of the present one—to provide for the exposure of their real nature, and hence for the destruction of their pernicious force. Sophistry is a hydra of which, if all the necks could be exposed, the force would be destroyed. In this work they have been diligently looked out for, and in the course of it the principal and most active of them have been brought in view.

Sec. 5. Classification of Fallacies

So numerous are the instruments of persuasion which the present work will expose in the character of fallacies that to enable the mind to obtain any tolerably satisfactory command of the subject a scheme of classification is altogether indispensable. To frame such a classification with perfect logical accuracy would be an undertaking requiring more time than either author or editor has been able to spare. An imperfect classification, however, being preferable to no classification at all, the author [Bentham] adopted several principles of division into classes. One was the situation of the utterers of fallacies, especially in a legislative body such as a parliament: the fallacies of the *Ins;* the fallacies of the *Outs;* and *Either-side* fallacies. Another principle relates to the quarter to which the fallacy applies itself in the persons on whom it is designed to operate: fallacies of *the affections;* fallacies of *the judgment;* and fallacies of *the imagination.*

To the several clusters of fallacies marked out by this principle, a Latin affix expressive of the faculty or affection aimed at, was attached, not for ostentation, but for prominence, impressiveness, and hence for clearness. Thus we have arguments 1. *Ad verecundiam* (to modesty); 2. *Ad superstitionem* (to superstition); 3. *Ad amicitiam* (to friendship); 4. *Ad metum* (to fear); 5. *Ad odium* (to hatred); 6. *Ad invidentiam* (to envy); 7. *Ad quietem* (to rest); 8. *Ad socordiam* (to weakmindedness); 9. *Ad superbiam* (to pride); 10. *Ad judicium* (to judgment); and 11. *Ad imaginationem* (to fancy). In the same manner, John Locke has employed Latin names to distinguish four kinds of argument: *Ad verecundiam, Ad ignorantiam, Ad hominem,* and *Ad judicium.*

M. Dumont, who some few years ago published a translation, or rather a *redaction,* of a considerable portion of the present work, divided the fallacies into three classes according to the particular object to which each class appeared to be immediately applicable. Some of them he supposed destined to repress discussion altogether; others to postpone it; and still others to perplex, when discussion could no longer be avoided. The first class he called the fallacies of *authority,* the second, fallacies of *delay,* and the third, fallacies of *confusion,* adding to the name of each the Latin affix which indicated the faculty or affection to which it was chiefly addressed.

The present editor has preferred Dumont's arrangement to that pursued by the author, and with some little variation he has adopted it in this volume. In addition to the immediate object of each class of fallacies, he has considered the subject-matter of each, with a view to placing all the fallacies that are similar in subject-matter in the same class. The classes he has arranged in the order in which the enemies of improvement may be expected to resort to them according to the emergency of the moment:

First, the fallacies of *authority,* including laudatory personalities, the subject-matter of which is authority in various shapes, and the immediate object to repress, on the ground of the weight of such authority, all exercise of the reasoning faculty.

Secondly, the fallacies of *danger,* including vituperative personalities, the subject-matter of which is the suggestion of danger in various shapes, and the object to repress altogether, on the ground of such danger, the discussion of a proposed measure.

Thirdly, the fallacies of *delay,* the subject-matter of which is the assigning of reasons for delay in various shapes, and the object, to postpone such discussion, with a view to eluding it altogether.

Fourthly, the fallacies of *confusion,* the subject-matter of which consists chiefly of vague and indefinite generalities, while the object is to produce, when discussion can no longer be avoided, such confusion in the minds of the hearers as to incapacitate them for forming a correct judgment on the question at issue.

In this classification, imperfections will be found, the removal of which (should it be practicable and worth the trouble) must be left to some more expert hand. The classes are not in every instance sufficiently distinct from each other; yet, imperfect as the classification is, it is to be hoped that the reflecting reader will not find it altogether without use.

Jeremy Bentham, *The Handbook of Political Fallacies,* Harold A. Larrabee, ed. (New York: Harper Torchbooks, 1962), pp. 5–9. Reprinted by permission of the Johns Hopkins University Press, Baltimore.

C.   *Voltaire. On Locke, 1733*

Perhaps there never was a more sage, a more methodical genius, never a more accurate logician, than Locke; yet he was by no means a great mathematician. He could never submit to the fatigue of calculations, nor endure the dry and barren nature of mathematical truths, which do not at first present the mind with any sensible image; and no man was ever a more decisive evidence, that it is possible to have a geometrical mind, without the assistance of geometry. Before his time, great philosophers had decided positively in what the soul of man consisted. But as they knew nothing at all about the matter, they were, just as might be expected, all of different opinions.

In Greece, the cradle both of arts and errors, and in which the strength and weakness of the human mind have been so strikingly displayed, men reasoned, as we ourselves do now, upon the subject of the soul. The divine Anaxagoras—to whom an altar was raised, for having taught mankind that the sun was larger than the Peloponnesus, that snow was black, and that the heavens were composed of stone— asserted that the soul was an aerial spirit, but nevertheless immortal. Diogenes, a different man from him who became a cynic, after having been a dealer in base coin, asserted, that the soul was a portion of the very substance of God himself; an idea which was, at least, brilliant and dazzling. Epicurus composed it of parts, like the body. Aristotle, who has been explained in innumerable ways, because he was utterly unintelligible, believed, if we refer for his belief to some of his disciples, that the understanding of all men was one and the same substance. The divine Plato, master of the divine Aristotle—and the divine Socrates, master of the divine Plato, pronounced the soul corporeal and eternal. The demon of Socrates had undoubtedly informed him what it was. There are, indeed, people who pretend that a man who boasted of having a familiar genius, must inevitably have been a little foolish, or a little knavish; but such people are extremely difficult to please.

With respect to our fathers of the church, many in the early ages thought the human soul, and angels, and God himself, corporeal. The world improves and refines every day. St. Bernard, according to the confession of Father Mabillon, taught, on the subject of the soul, that after death it did not see God, in heaven, but communed solely with the humanity of Jesus Christ. For this once, he was not believed upon his word; and, indeed, the adventure of the crusade had rather discredited his oracles. Numberless schoolmen appeared afterwards upon the stage in pompous succession, such as the irrefragable doctor, the subtle doctor, the angelic doctor, the

seraphic doctor, and the cherubic doctor, all of whom were perfectly confident they understood the nature of the human soul, but at the same time always spoke about it as if they wished no one else should understand it. Our own countryman, Descartes—born to detect the errors of antiquity, but unfortunately also to substitute his own in their room, and urged on by that spirit of system which blinds the strongest understandings—conceived he had demonstrated that the soul was the same thing as thought; as matter, according to him, is the same thing as extension. He affirms strongly, that a man always thinks, and that the soul arrives in the body provided with a whole stock of metaphysical notions, acquainted with God, with space and infinity, in possession of all sorts of abstract ideas, full, in short, of beautiful and sublime knowledge, which, most unluckily, it totally forgets immediately on its departure from the mother's womb. Father Malebranche, of the Oratory, in his sublime illusions, does not admit the doctrine of innate ideas; but he had no doubt but that we saw in God everything, and that God, if we may so express it, was in fact our soul.

After so many random reasoners had been thus forming what might have been called the Romance of the Soul, a sage appears who has modestly presented us with the history of it. Mr. Locke has developed human reason to man, just as a skillful anatomist explains the springs and structure of the human body. He avails himself of all the light that can be derived from natural philosophy; he sometimes ventures to speak affirmatively; but he also ventures to express doubt. Instead of displaying definitions of what we are little or not at all acquainted with, he examines, step by step, what we wish to be acquainted with. He begins with an infant at its birth; he follows slowly and cautiously the progress of its understanding; and he sees what it has in common with brutes, and what it has above them. He consults particularly his own testimony—the evidence of consciousness. "I leave those," says he, "who are better informed on the subject than myself, to discuss whether the soul exists before, or not until after the organization of the body; but I acknowledge it has fallen to my lot to have one of those heavy and inert souls which do not always think; and I am even unfortunate enough to conceive, that it may very possibly be no more necessary that the soul should be always thinking, than that the body should be always in motion."

With regard to myself, I pride myself in being on this subject as simple as Mr. Locke. No one can ever induce me to believe that I am always thinking, and I feel no more disposed than he was, to imagine that a few weeks after my conception I was a very knowing soul, acquainted with a thousand things which I forgot on being born; and that I have to no purpose whatever possessed, while in the womb, invaluable stores of information, which abandoned me the instant I really wanted them, and which I have never since been able to recover.

Locke, after having destroyed innate ideas; after having wisely renounced the vanity of believing that man always thinks; having well established the principle, that all our ideas are derived to us through the senses; having examined our simple and analysed our compound ideas; having followed the human mind through all its operations; having pointed out the imperfections of the various languages employed by mankind, and the abuse we make of words almost every moment of our lives—Locke, I say, at last considers the extent, or rather the nothingness, of human knowledge. It is in this chapter that he ventures modestly to observe:— "We shall, perhaps, never be capable of

knowing, whether a being purely material thinks or not." This judicious and guarded observation was considered by more than one divine, as neither more nor less than a scandalous and impious declaration, that the soul is material and mortal. Some English devotees, after their usual manner, sounded the alarm. The superstitious are in society what poltroons are in an army—they both feel and excite causeless terror. The cry was that Mr. Locke wished to overturn religion: the subject, however, had nothing to do with religion at all; it was purely a philosophical question, and perfectly independent of faith and revelation. It was only necessary to examine, without acrimony or heat, whether there is any contradiction in say—'Matter may think, and God may communicate thought to matter.' But theologians too often begin with passionately charging the man who does not join in their opinion with blaspheming or insulting God. . . .

Every philosopher is destined to endure reviling and calumny. For one man capable of replying with reason, there are a hundred who have nothing to advance but abuse, and every one pays with the money which he possesses. My ears are every day dinned and wearied with the exclamations —'Locke denies the immortality of the soul; Locke destroys morality'; and what is surprising, if anything could surprise, is that out of all those who in this manner bring accusations against the morality of Locke, there are very few indeed that have ever read him, fewer still that have understood him, and none whom it is not our duty to wish possessed of such virtues as were possessed by that great man, who so truly merited the epithets of wise and good.

Desmond Flower, ed., *Voltaire's England* (London: The Folio Society Limited, 1950), pp. 175–79.

D. Diderot. The Interpretation of Nature, 1754

VII. So long as things are only in our understanding, they are our opinions; these are notions which can be true or false, granted or denied. They take on con-

sistency only by being related to externally existing things. This connection is made either by an uninterrupted chain of reasoning, which is connected at one end with observation and at the other with experiment; or by a series of experiments dispersed at intervals along the chain of reasoning, like weights along a thread suspended by its two ends. Without these weights the thread would be the sport of the slightest motion of the air.

VIII. One may compare ideas which have no foundation in nature, to those forests of the North whose trees have no roots. It needs only a breath of wind, only a small fact, to overturn a whole forest of trees and of ideas.

IX. Men are disturbed to feel how severe are the laws of the investigation of truth, and how limited is the number of our means. Everything is reduced to a return from the senses to reflection, and from reflection to the senses; to turn into oneself and to turn outwards again, ceaselessly; it is the labour of the bee. Much country has been covered in vain, if a load of wax is not brought back to the hive. A useless accumulation of wax has been made if it is not known how to make a comb of it.

X. But, unfortunately, it is easier and quicker to consult oneself than to consult nature. Also, reason is inclined to dwell within itself, and instinct to spread outward. Ceaselessly instinct goes, observing, tasting, touching, listening and there would be perhaps more experimental physics to be learnt by studying animals than by following a course of lectures by a professor. There is no deception in their behaviour. They proceed to their ends without caring about what surrounds them; if they surprise us, it is not in the least their intention. Astonishment is the first effect of some great phenomenon: it is the task of philosophy to dissipate this. In a course of experimental philosophy, it is a question of sending the student away more enlightened and not more puzzled. To pride oneself about the phenomena of nature, as if one were the author of them oneself, is to imitate the stupidity of that editor of the *Essais*, who could not hear the name of Montaigne without blushing. A great lesson which there is often occasion to give, is the confession of one's insufficiency. Is it not better to gain the confidence of others by the sincerity of a "I know nothing about it," than to babble words

and excite pity for oneself, by trying to explain everything? He who freely admits that he does not know the things of which he is ignorant, disposes me to believe that what he undertakes to make me admit is correct.

XI. Astonishment often comes from supposing several marvels where there is only one; from imagining in nature as many particular acts as there are phenomena, while perhaps it has ever produced but a single act. It seems, even, that if it had been under the necessity of producing several acts, the different results of these acts would have been isolated; that there would have been collections of phenomena independent of one another, and that the general connection of things, of which philosophy supposes the continuity, would be broken at several places. The absolute independence of a single fact is incompatible with the idea of the whole; and without the idea of the whole, no more philosophy....

XIV. I represent to myself the vast body of science as a large area strewn with dark places and with illuminated places. Our labours should have as their aim, either to extend the limits of the lighted places, or to multiply the number of centers of illumination. The latter is for the creative genius; the other for the wisdom which improves, develops, amplifies.

XV. We have three principal means: the observation of nature, thought and experiment. Observation collects the facts, thought combines them, and experiment verifies the result of the combination. The observation of nature must be assiduous, the thinking must be profound and the experiment must be exact. One rarely sees these methods combined. And creative geniuses are not common....

XXIII. We have distinguished two kinds of philosophy, the experimental and that based on reasoning. The former has its eyes bandaged, walks always feeling its way, grasps whatever falls into its hands and finds precious things in the end. The other gathers these precious things, and tries to make a torch of them; but this pretended torch has up to the present served it less well than the gropings of its rival, and this must be so. Experiment multiplies its actions infinitely, it is ceaselessly in action, it is busy seeking phenomena all the time that reasoning uses in seeking analogies. Experimental philosophy knows neither what will come nor will not come out of its labours; but it works on without relaxing. The philosophy based on reasoning, on the contrary, weighs possibilities, makes a pronouncement and stops short. It boldly said: "light cannot be decomposed": experimental philosophy heard, and held its tongue in its presence for whole centuries; then suddenly it produced the prism, and said, "light can be decomposed."

Jonathan Kemp, ed., *Diderot: Interpreter of Nature,* in *Selected Writings,* trans. Jean Stewart and Jonathan Kemp (New York: International Publishers, 1943), pp. 43–47.

II. Religion in the Enlightenment: God and Nature

Organized Christianity was one of the great targets for the critical thought of the Enlightenment. To many of the thinkers of the eighteenth century, Christianity was an "unnatural" and therefore harmful superstition, its miracles unconfirmed by their "modern" science, its dogmas unreasonable, its whole structure dedicated to maintaining existing evil society. "Revelation" they denied as a valid criterion of truth. They sought for what they called a "natural" in contrast with a "revealed" religion. But their actual range of religious opinion was great. Some sought to retain Christianity purified of its "superstitions," but with its ethics and much of its theology intact. These men are *theists.* Others sought to create a new religion, based on the orderly universe Newton had made familiar to their generation, a universe in which Nature was deified as a kind of Supreme Being. These men are *deists,* who believe in what a critic has called the "clockmaker God"—a God who has made the universe, including man, and has set it in motion, but who never interferes with its running according to the laws he made for it. Voltaire was a deist, at least for practical purposes. Jean Jacques Rousseau was a deist of more serious turn. Finally, there are the *atheists,* men who maintain that all we can know is the material universe, and that if there is a God who began everything, we cannot possibly know anything at all about him, and had better give up talking about him. Atheism was actually a most unpopular doctrine in the eighteenth century, and its open profession illegal almost everywhere. One of its earliest and most outright advocates was the French physician La Mettrie, whose *L'Homme Machine (Man a Machine)* was published in 1748. Though legally banned almost everywhere, the book circulated, as did most banned books, quite freely among the educated public throughout the Europe of the Enlightenment. *Man a Machine* is, however, packed with allusions to writers ancient and modern, and any excerpt would require too many explanatory footnotes for our use. We take instead to represent the atheist's position a short dialogue by the Marquis de Sade, who was quite as outspoken as La Mettrie. Finally, we have in the concluding section of Condorcet's *Sketch for a Historical Picture of the Human Mind* a secularist substitute for Christianity. Our excerpt gives the picture of a possible—indeed probable—heaven on earth. The reader must not, however, forget that Christianity was very much alive in this eighteenth century. The century of the Enlightenment saw the birth of a great Protestant sect, the Methodists, led by John Wesley (1703–1791). Actually, are any of these men really *skeptics?* Are they not, even the secularists, even Voltaire, believers in some kind of organized and knowable universe in which man can feel at home?

A. Voltaire. "On the Soul and God," 1770

Monseigneur, the royal family of Prussia has excellent reasons for not wishing the annihilation of the soul. It has more right than anyone to immortality.

It is very true that we do not know any too well what the soul is: no one has ever seen it. All that we do know is that the eternal Lord of nature has given us the power of thinking, and of distinguishing virtue. It is not proved that this faculty survives our death: but the contrary is not proved either. It is possible, doubtless, that God has given thought to a particle to which, after we are no more, He will still give the power of thought: there is no inconsistency in this idea.

In the midst of all the doubts which we have discussed for four thousand years in four thousand ways, the safest course is to do nothing against one's conscience. With this secret, we can enjoy life and have nothing to fear from death.

There are some charlatans who admit no doubts. We know nothing of first principles. It is surely very presumptuous to define God, the angels, spirits, and to pretend to know precisely why God made the world, when we do not know why we can move our arms at our pleasure.

Doubt is not a pleasant condition, but certainty is an absurd one.

What is most repellent in the *System of Nature* [of Holbach]—after the recipe to make eels from flour—is the audacity with which it decides that there is no God, without even having tried to prove the impossibility. There is some eloquence in the book: but much more rant, and no sort of proof. It is a pernicious work, alike for princes and people:

"Si Dieu n'existait pas, il faudrait l'inventer," [If God did not exist, it would be necessary to invent him.]

But all nature cries aloud that He does exist: that there *is* a supreme intelligence, an immense power, an admirable order, and everything teaches us our own dependence on it.

From the depth of our profound ignorance, let us do our best: this is what I think, and what I have always thought, amid all the misery and follies inseparable from seventy-seven years of life.

Your Royal Highness has a noble career before you. I wish you, and dare prophesy for you, a happiness worthy of yourself and of your heart. I knew you when you were a child, monseigneur: I visited you in your sick room when you had smallpox: I feared for your life. Your father honoured me with much goodness: you condescend to shower on me the same favours which are the honour of my old age, and the consolation of those sufferings which must shortly end it. I am, with deep respect, etc.

Letter to Frederick William, Prince of Prussia, in E. B. Hall [S. G. Tallentyre, *pseud.*] *Voltaire in His Letters* (New York: G. P. Putnam's Sons, 1919), pp. 232–33.

B. Rousseau. The Deist Position, 1762

The first causes of motion do not exist in matter; bodies receive from and communicate motion to each other, but they cannot originally produce it: The more I observe the action and reaction of the powers of nature acting on each other, the more I am convinced that they are merely effects; and we must ever recur to some volition as the first cause: for to suppose there is a progression of causes to infinity, is to suppose there is no first cause at all. In a word, every motion that is not produced by some other, must be the effect of a spontaneous, voluntary act. Inanimate bodies have no action but motion; and there can be no real action without volition. Such is my first principle. I believe, therefore, that a *Will* gives motion to the universe, and animates all nature. This is my first article of faith.

In what manner volition is productive of physical and corporeal action I know not, but I experience within myself that it is productive of it. I *will* to act, and the action immediately follows; I *will* to move my body, and my body instantly moves; but, that an inanimate body lying at rest, should move itself, or produce motion, is incomprehensible and unprecedented. The *Will* also is known by its effects and not by its essence. I know it as the cause of motion; but to conceive matter producing motion, would be evidently to conceive an effect without a cause, or rather not to conceive any thing at all.

It is no more possible for me to conceive how the will moves the body, than how the sensations affect the soul. I even know not why one of these mysteries ever appeared more explicable than the other. For my own part, whether at the time I am active or passive, the means of union between the two substances appear to me absolutely incomprehensible. Is it not strange that the philosophers have thrown off this incomprehensibility, merely to confound the two substances together, as if operations so different could be better explained as the effects of one subject than of two.

The principle which I have here laid down, is undoubtedly something obscure; it is however intelligible, and contains nothing repugnant to reason or observation. Can we say as much of the doctrines of materialism? It is very certain that, if motion be essential to matter, it would be inseparable from it; it would be always the same in every portion of it, incommunicable, and incapable of increase or diminution; it would be impossible for us even to conceive matter at rest. Again, when I am told that motion is not indeed essential to matter, but necessary to its existence, I see through the attempt to impose on me by a form of words, which it would be more easy to refute, if more intelligible. For, whether the motion of matter arises from itself, and is therefore essential to it, or whether it is derived from some external cause, it is not further necessary to it than as the moving cause acting thereon: so that we still remain under the first difficulty.

General and abstract ideas form the source of our greatest errors. The jargon of metaphysics never discovered one truth; but it has filled philosophy with absurdities, of which we are ashamed as soon as they are stripped of their pompous expressions. . . .

I believe therefore, that the world is governed by a wise and powerful *Will.* I see it, or rather I feel it; and this is of importance for me to know. But is the world eternal, or is it created? Are things derived from one self-existent principle, or are there two or more, and what is their essence? Of all this I know nothing, nor do I see that it is necessary I should. In proportion as such knowledge may become interesting I will endeavor to acquire it: but further than this I give up all such idle disquisitions, which serve only to make me discontented with myself, which are useless in practice, and are above my understanding.

You will remember, however, that I am not dictating my sentiments to you, but only explaining what they are. Whether matter be eternal or only created, whether it have a passive principle or not, certain it is that the whole universe is one design, and sufficiently displays one intelligent agent: for I see no part of this system that is not under regulation, or that does not concur to one and the same end; viz. that of preserving the present and established order of things. That Being, whose will is his deed, whose principle of action is in himself,—that Being, in a word, whatever it be, that gives motion to all parts of the universe, and governs all things, I call GOD.

J. J. Rousseau, *Profession of Faith of a Savoyard Vicar,* trans. Olive Schreiner (New York: Peter Eckler, 1889), pp. 15–16, 17–18, 28–30, 35.

C. De Sade. The Atheist Position, 1782

THE PRIEST. Now that you have come to that fatal moment when the veil of illusion is rent only to permit straying man a sight of the cruel picture of his errors and his vices, do you not repent, my child, the many misdemeanors you have been led to commit through weakness and human fragility?

THE DYING MAN. Yes, my friend, I repent.

THE PRIEST. Ah, then, profit from that

happy remorse by obtaining from Heaven, during the brief interval that remains to you, a general absolution of your sins, and remember that it is only through meditation on the most blessed Sacrament of penitence that it will be possible for you to obtain the gift of eternal life.

THE DYING MAN. I do not understand you, any more than you have understood me.

THE PRIEST. What!

THE DYING MAN. I told you that I repented.

THE PRIEST. I heard you.

THE DYING MAN. Yes, but without understanding.

THE PRIEST. What do you mean...?

THE DYING MAN. Just this.... Since I have been created by nature with very lively tastes, with very strong passions, and have been placed in this world for the sole purpose of giving myself over to, and satisfying, those tastes and passions, and since these consequences of my having been created are, merely, necessities in keeping with the first designs of nature, or, if you prefer, essential corollaries to her plans for me, the whole being in accordance with her own laws, I repent not having sufficiently recognized her omnipotence, and the only remorse I feel has to do with the mediocre employment I have made of those faculties (criminal according to you, wholly natural according to me) which she gave me for her own service: I have, at times, resisted her, and for this I am penitent. Blinded by the absurdities of your doctrines, I have combatted, for the sake of those doctrines, the violence of those desires which I received by an inspiration a good deal more divine, and this I repent: I have reaped only flowers, when I might have gathered an ample harvest of fruits...there you have the just cause of my regret; please do me the honor not to suppose there is any other cause.

THE PRIEST. Oh, where are those errors, those sophistries of yours, leading you? You impute to the thing created all the power of the Creator, and this unfortunate tendency, which leads you astray is,

though you will not see it, simply the result of that corrupt Nature which you endow with omnipotence.

THE DYING MAN. My friend, it appears to me your dialectic is as false as your mind itself. I wish you would either reason more justly or leave me to die in peace. What do you mean by "creator," and what do you understand by "corrupt nature"?

THE PRIEST. The Creator is the master of the universe; it is He who has made everything, created everything, and who preserves everything, as the simple consequence of His omnipotence.

THE DYING MAN. He's quite a chap, upon my word! Ah, well, tell me, then, why it is that this fellow, who is so powerful, still has created, according to you, a Nature that is corrupt.

THE PRIEST. What merit would men have had, if God had not left them a free choice, and if they had not encountered, upon the earth, the possibility either of doing good or of avoiding evil?

THE DYING MAN. And so, that god of yours must do everything crosswise, solely for the purpose of tempting, or of proving, his creature? He did not know his own creature, then? He doubted the result?

THE PRIEST. He undoubtedly knew what the result would be, but He wished to leave man the merit of choice.

THE DYING MAN. Of what use was that, since he knew what the choice would be? Why, if he is all-powerful, as you say —why did he not keep man in the right path and force him to choose the good?

THE PRIEST. Who can fathom the immense and infinite wisdom of God towards man, and who can understand all that we behold?

THE DYING MAN. The one who simplifies things, my friend, the one, above all, who does not multiply causes in order to confuse effects the more. What need have you of a second difficulty, when you cannot explain the first; and since it is possible that Nature alone has done all that you attribute to your god, why must you go seeking a master for her? The cause of what you do not understand is, it may be, the simplest thing in the world. Perfect your physics, and you will understand Nature better; purify your reason, banish your prejudices, and you will have no need of that god of yours.

THE PRIEST. Poor fellow!...I have arms to fight you, but I see clearly that you are an atheist, and since your heart refuses the infinite and authentic proofs we every day receive of the existence of the Creator, I have nothing more to say to you. One does not give light to a blind man.

THE DYING MAN. My friend, you must grant me one point: the blinder of us is surely the one who puts a bandage over his eyes, not the one who snatches the bandage away. You build up, you invent, you multiply; as for me, I destroy, I simplify. You pile error upon error, while I combat all errors. Which is the blinder of the two?

THE PRIEST. You have no belief whatever, then, in God?

THE DYING MAN. None. And for a very simple reason, namely, that it is utterly impossible for me to believe what I do not understand. Between comprehension and faith, there should be a direct relation; comprehension is the first food of faith: where there is no comprehension, faith is dead, and those who, in such a case, pretend to have faith, are self-imposters. I defy you, yourself, to believe in the god you preach to me—because you cannot demonstrate him to me, because the power is not in you to define him for me, because, in short, you do not understand him. And since you do not understand him, you are unable to furnish me with any reasonable argument. In a word, whatever is beyond the limits of the human mind is a chimera or a futility, and your god can be only one or the other of these things. In the former case, I should be a fool to believe in him; in the later, an imbecile. My friend, prove to me the inertia of matter, and I will grant you your creator; prove to me that Nature is not sufficient to herself, and I will permit you to assume that she must have a master. Until that time, look for nothing

from me: I only yield to evidence, and I receive evidence only through my senses: where they stop, my faith is powerless. I believe in the sun because I see it; I conceive it to be the unifying center of all the inflammable material in Nature; its periodical revolution pleases, without astonishing, me. It is an operation of physics, as simple, possibly, as that of electricity, but one which is not permitted us to understand. What need have I to go further? When you shall have built me a scaffolding for your god above all that, shall I be any the further along, and will it not require quite as much effort to understand the workman as to define the work? As a consequence, you do me no service by setting up your edifying chimera; you have troubled my mind, but you have not enlightened it, and I owe you nothing but hatred as compensation. Your god is a machine which you have manufactured to serve your own passions; it moves at their direction, but when it interferes with my own passions, grant me the right to overthrow it. And so, at the moment when my weakened soul has need of philosophic calm, please do not come to terrify it with your sophistries, which frighten without convincing, which irritate without improving. This soul, my friend, is what Nature has willed it should be, that is to say, the result of those organs and their needs which she has been pleased to create for me. And since she has equal need of virtues and of vices, when it has pleased her to impel me to the former, she has done so; when she would impel me to the latter, she does it by inspiring in me certain desires; and I, likewise, have surrendered to these. Do not seek beyond her laws for the sole cause of all human inconsistency; and in her laws, look for no other principles than her own volition and her own needs.

THE PRIEST. Then everything in the world is inevitable.

THE DYING MAN. Assuredly....

THE PRIEST. If you are off on that foot, it seems to me there is little use in speaking to you of religion.

THE DYING MAN. Why not? Nothing

amuses me like evidence of the excessive fanaticism and imbecility of which men can be guilty on this score; there are, for me, some mistakes so prodigious that the contemplation of them, however horrible the picture, is always interesting. Answer my questions frankly, and above all, banish egotism. If I were so weak as to permit myself to be taken in by those ridiculous beliefs of yours concerning the fabled existence of a being who makes religion necessary, under what form should you advise me to render him my tribute of worship? Would you have me adopt the dreams of Confucius rather than the absurdities of Brahma? Should I adore the great serpent of the Africans, the star of the Peruvians or Moses' god of armies? What sect of Mahomet would you have me join, or which of the Christian heresies would, in your eyes, be preferable? Look well to your answer.

THE PRIEST. Can there be any doubt about my answer?

THE DYING MAN. There you have the perfect egotist.

THE PRIEST. No. It is merely because I love you as much as I do myself that I advise you in accordance with what I believe.

THE DYING MAN. We must love ourselves very little if we listen to such errors.

THE PRIEST. Ah, who could be so blind as not to be convinced by the miracles of our divine Redeemer?

THE DYING MAN. One who sees in him only the most ordinary of all knaves and the shallowest of impostors.

THE PRIEST. *Ye Gods! Who hear him, yet do not strike him dead!*

THE DYING MAN. No, my friend, all is at peace, because that god of yours, whether divine impotence or divine reason, or all that you would have him be—though I do not for a moment admit his existence, except out of condescension toward you or, if you prefer, to lend myself the better to your narrow views—because, I say, that god, if he did exist, as you are foolish enough to believe, would never, to convince us of his existence, have adopted means so ridiculous as those your Jesus supposes.

Marquis de Sade, *Dialogue Between a Priest and a Dying Man,* ed. Maurice Heine, trans. Samuel Putnam (Chicago: Pascal Covici, Publishers, Inc., 1927), pp. 33–50, *passim.* Reprinted by permission of Crown Publishers, Inc.

D. Condorcet. The Perfectibility of Man, 1794

The Tenth Stage:

The Future Progress of the Human Mind

If man can, with almost complete assurance, predict phenomena when he knows their laws, and if, even when he does not, he can still, with great expectation of success, forecast the future on the basis of his experience of the past, why, then, should it be regarded as a fantastic undertaking to sketch, with some pretence to truth, the future destiny of man on the basis of his history? The sole foundation for belief in the natural sciences is this idea, that the general laws directing the phenomena of the universe, known or unknown, are necessary and constant. Why should this principle be any less true for the development of the intellectual and moral faculties of man than for the other operations of nature? Since beliefs founded on past experience of like conditions provide the only rule of conduct for the wisest of men, why should the philosopher be forbidden to base his conjectures on these same foundations, so long as he does not attribute to them a certainty superior to that warranted by the number, the constancy, and the accuracy of his observations?

Our hopes for the future condition of the human race can be subsumed under three important heads: the abolition of inequality between nations, the progress of equality within each nation, and the true perfection of mankind. Will all nations one day attain that state of civilization which the most enlightened, the freest and the least burdened by prejudices, such as the French and the Anglo-Americans, have attained already? Will the vast gulf that separates these peoples from the slavery of nations under the rule of monarchs, from the barbarism of African tribes, from the ignorance of savages, little by little disappear?

Is there on the face of the earth a nation whose inhabitants have been debarred by nature herself from the enjoyment of freedom and the exercise of reason?

Are those differences which have hitherto been seen in every civilized country in respect of the enlightenment, the resources, and the wealth enjoyed by the different classes into which it is divided, is that inequality between men which was aggravated or perhaps produced by the earliest progress of society, are these part of civilization itself, or are they due to the present imperfections of the social art? Will they necessarily decrease and ultimately make way for a real equality, the final end of the social art, in which even the effects of the natural differences between men will be mitigated and the only kind of inequality to persist will be that which is in the interests of all and which favours the progress of civilization, of education, and of industry, without entailing either poverty, humiliation, or dependence? In other words, will men approach a condition in which everyone will have the knowledge necessary to conduct himself in the ordinary affairs of life, according to the light of his own reason, to preserve his mind free from prejudice, to understand his rights and to exercise them in accordance with his conscience and his creed; in which everyone will become able, through the development of his faculties, to find the means of providing for his needs; and in which at last misery and folly will be the exception, and no longer the habitual lot of a section of society?

Is the human race to better itself, either by discoveries in the sciences and the arts, and so in the means to individual welfare and general prosperity; or by progress in the principles of conduct or practical morality; or by a true perfection of the intellectual, moral, or physical faculties of man, an improvement which may result from a perfection either of the instruments used to heighten the intensity of these faculties and to direct their use or of the natural constitution of man?

In answering these three questions we shall find in the experience of the past, in the observation of the progress that the sciences and civilization have already made, in the analysis of the progress of the human mind and of the development of its faculties, the strongest reasons for believing that nature has set no limit to the realization of our hopes.

If we glance at the state of the world today we see first of all that in Europe the principles of the French Constitution are already those of all enlightened men. We see them too widely propagated, too seriously professed, for priests and despots to prevent their gradual penetration even into the hovels of their slaves; there they will soon awaken in these slaves the remnants of their common sense and inspire them with that smouldering indignation which not even constant humiliation and fear can smother in the soul of the oppressed. . . .

The time will therefore come when the sun will shine only on free men who know no other master but their reason; when tyrants and slaves, priests and their stupid or hypocritical instruments, will exist only in works of history and on the stage; and when we shall think of them only to pity their victims and their dupes; to maintain ourselves in a state of vigilance by thinking on their excesses; and to learn how to recognize and so to destroy, by force of reason, the first seeds of tyranny and superstition, should they ever dare to reappear amongst us.

In looking at the history of societies we shall have had occasion to observe that there is often a great difference between the rights that the law allows its citizens and the rights that they actually enjoy, and, again, between the equality established by political codes and that which in fact exists amongst individuals: and we shall have noticed that these differences were one of the principal causes of the destruction of freedom in the ancient republics, of the storms that troubled them, and of the weakness that delivered them over to foreign tyrants.

These differences have three main causes: inequality in wealth; inequality in status between the man whose means of subsistence are hereditary and the man whose means are dependent on the length of his life, or, rather, on that part of his life in which he is capable of work; and, finally, inequality in education.

We therefore need to show that these three sorts of real inequality must constantly diminish without, however, disappearing altogether: for they are the result of natural and necessary causes, which it would be foolish and dangerous to wish to eradicate; and one could not even attempt to bring about the entire disappearance of their effects without introducing even more fecund sources of inequality, without striking more direct and more fatal blows at the rights of man.

It is easy to prove that wealth has a natural tendency to equality, and that any excessive disproportion could not exist, or at least would rapidly disappear, if civil laws did not provide artificial ways of perpetuating and uniting fortunes; if free trade and industry were allowed to remove the advantages that accrued wealth derives from any restrictive law or fiscal privilege; if taxes on covenants, the restrictions placed on their free employment, their subjection to tiresome formalities, and the uncertainty and inevitable expense involved in implementing them did not hamper the activity of the poor man and swallow up his meagre capital; if the administration of the country did not afford some men ways of making their fortune that were closed to other citizens; if prejudice and avarice, so common in old age, did not preside over the making of marriages; and if in a society enjoying simpler manners and more sensible institutions, wealth ceased to be a means of satisfying vanity and ambition, and if the equally misguided notions of austerity, which condemn spending money in the cultivation of the more delicate pleasures, no longer insisted on the hoarding of all one's earnings.

Let us turn to the enlightened nations of Europe, and observe the size of their present populations in relation to the size of their territories. Let us consider, in agriculture and industry, the proportion that holds between labour and the means of subsistence, and we shall see that it would be impossible for those means to be kept at their present level, and consequently for the population to be kept at its present size, if a great number of individuals were not almost entirely dependent for the maintenance of themselves and their family either on their own labour or on the interest from capital invested so as to make their labour more productive. Now both these sources of income depend on the life and even on the health of the head of the family. They provide what is rather like a life annuity, save that it is more dependent on chance; and in consequence there is a very real difference between people living like this and those whose resources are not at all subject to the same risks, who live either on revenue from land, or on the interest on capital, which is almost independent of their own labour.

Here then is a necessary cause of inequality, of dependence and even of misery, which ceaselessly threatens the most numerous and most active class in our society.

We shall point out how it can be in great part eradicated by guaranteeing people in old age a means of livelihood produced partly by their own savings and partly by the savings of others who made the same outlay, but who die before they need to reap the reward, or, again, on the same principle of compensation, by securing for widows and orphans an income which is the same and costs the same for those families which suffer an early loss and for those which suffer it later; or again by providing all children with the capital necessary for the full use of their labour, available at the age when they start work and found a family, a capital which increases at the expense of those whom premature death prevents from reaching this age. It is to the application of the calculus to the probabilities of life and the investment of money that we owe the idea of these methods which have already been successful, although they have not been applied in a sufficiently comprehensive and exhaustive fashion to render them really useful, not merely to a few individuals, but to society as a whole, by making it possible to prevent those periodic disasters which strike at so many families and which are such a recurrent source of misery and suffering.

We shall point out that schemes of this nature, which can be organized in the name of the social authority and become one of its greatest benefits, can also be the work of private associations, which will be formed without any real risk, once the principles for the proper working of these schemes have been widely diffused and the mistakes which have been the undoing of a large number of these associations no longer hold terrors for us. . . .

So we might say that a well-directed system of education rectifies natural inequality in ability instead of strengthening it, just as good laws remedy natural inequality in the means of subsistence, and just as in societies where laws have brought about this same equality, liberty, though subject to a regular constitution, will be more widespread, more complete, than in the total independence of savage life. Then the social art will have fulfilled its aim, that of assuring and extending to all men enjoyment of the common rights to which they are called by nature.

The real advantages that should result from this progress, of which we can entertain a hope that is almost a certainty, can have no other term than that of the absolute perfection of the human race; since, as the various kinds of equality come to work in its favour by producing ampler sources of supply, more extensive education, more complete liberty, so equality will be more real and will embrace everything which is really of importance for the happiness of human beings.

It is therefore only by examining the progress and the laws of this perfection that we shall be able to understand the extent or the limits of our hopes.

No one has ever believed that the mind can gain knowledge of all the facts of nature or attain the ultimate means of precision in the measurement, or in the analysis of the facts of nature, the relations between objects and all the possible combinations of ideas. Even the relations between magnitudes, the mere notion of quantity or extension, taken in its fullest comprehension, gives rise to a system so vast that it will never be mastered by the human mind in its entirety, that there will always be a part of it, always indeed the larger part of it, that will remain forever unknown. People have believed that man can never know more than a part of the objects that the nature of his intelligence allows him to understand, and that he must in the end arrive at a point where the number and complexity of the objects that he already knows have absorbed all his strength so that any further progress must be completely impossible.

But since, as the number of known facts increases, the human mind learns how to classify them and to subsume them under more general facts, and, at the same time, the instruments and methods employed in their observation and their exact measurement acquire a new precision; since, as more relations between various objects become known, man is able to reduce them to more general relations, to express them more simply, and to present them in such a way that it is possible to grasp a greater number of them with the same degree of intellectual ability and the same amount of application; since, as the mind learns to understand more complicated combinations of ideas, simpler formulae soon reduce their complexity; so truths that were discovered only by great effort, that could at first only be understood by men capable of profound thought, are soon developed and proved by methods that are not beyond the reach of common intelligence. If the methods which have led to these new combinations of ideas are ever exhausted, if their application to hitherto unsolved questions should demand exertions greater than either the time or the capacity of the learned would permit, some method of a greater generality or simplicty will be found so that genius can continue undisturbed on its path. The strength and the limits of man's intelligence may remain unaltered; and yet the instruments that he uses will increase and improve, the language that fixes and determines his ideas will acquire greater breadth and precision, and, unlike mechanics, where an increase of force means a decrease of speed, the methods that lead genius to the discovery of truth increase at once the force and the speed of its operations.

Therefore, since these developments are themselves the necessary consequences of progress in detailed knowledge, and since the need for new methods in fact only arises in circumstances that give rise to new methods, it is evident that, within the body of the sciences of observation, calculation and experiment, the actual number of truths may always increase, and that every part of this body may develop, and yet man's faculties be of the same strength, activity and extent.

If we apply these general reflections to the various sciences, we can find in each of them examples of progressive improvement that will remove any doubts about what we may expect for the future. We shall point out in particular the progress that is both likely and imminent in those sciences which prejudice regards as all but exhausted. We shall give examples of the manner and extent of the precision and unity which could accrue to the whole system of human knowledge as the result of a more general and philosophical application of the sciences of calculation to the various branches of knowledge. We shall show how favourable to our hopes would be a more universal system of education by giving a greater number of people the elementary knowledge which could awaken their interest in a particular branch of study, and by providing conditions favourable to their progress in it; and how these hopes would be further raised if more men possessed the means to devote themselves to these studies, for at present even in the most enlightened countries scarcely one in fifty of the people who have natural talents receives the necessary education to develop them; and how, if this were done, there would be a proportionate increase in the number of men destined by their discoveries to extend the boundaries of science.

We shall show how this equality in education and the equality which will come about among the different nations would accelerate the advance of these sciences whose progress depends on repeated observations over a large area; what benefits would thereby accrue to mineralogy, botany, zoology and meteorology; and what a vast disproportion holds in all these sciences between the poverty of existing methods, which have nevertheless led to useful and important new truths, and the wealth of those methods which man would then be able to employ.

We shall show how even the sciences in which discovery is the fruit of solitary meditation would benefit from being studied by a greater number of people, in the matter of those improvements in detail which do not demand the intellectual energy of an inventor but suggest themselves to mere reflection.

If we turn now to the arts, whose theory depends on these same sciences, we shall find that their progress, depending as it does on that of theory, can have no other limits; that the procedures of the different arts can be perfected and simplified in the same way as the methods of the sciences; new instruments, machines and looms can add to man's strength and can improve at once the quality and the accuracy of his productions, and can diminish the time and labour that has to be expended on them. The obstacles still in the way of this progress will disappear, accidents will be foreseen and prevented, the insanitary conditions that are due either to the work itself or to the climate will be eliminated.

A very small amount of ground will be able to produce a great quantity of supplies of greater utility or higher quality; more goods will be obtained for a smaller outlay; the manufacture of articles will be achieved with less wastage in raw materials and will make better use of them. Every type of soil will produce those things which satisfy the greatest number of needs; of several alternative ways of satisfying needs of the same order, that will be chosen which satisfies the greatest number of people and which requires least labour and least expenditure. So, without the need for sacrifice, methods of preservation and economy in expenditure will improve in the wake of progress in the arts of producing and preparing supplies and making articles from them.

So not only will the same amount of ground support more people, but everyone will have less work to do, will produce more, and satisfy his wants more fully.

With all this progress in industry and welfare, which establishes a happier proportion between men's talents and their needs, each successive generation will have larger possessions, either as a result of this progress or through the preservation of the products of industry; and so, as a consequence of the physical constitution of the human race, the number of people will increase. Might there not then come a moment when these necessary laws begin to work in a contrary direction; when, the number of people in the world finally exceeding the means of subsistence, there will in consequence ensue a continual diminution of happiness and population, a true retrogression, or at best an oscillation between good and bad? In societies that have reached this stage, will not this oscillation be a perennial source of more or less periodic disaster? Will it not show that a point has been attained beyond which all further improvement is impossible, that the perfectibility of the human race has after long years arrived at a term beyond which it may never go?

There is doubtless no one who does not think that such a time is still very far from us; but will it ever arrive? It is impossible to pronounce about the likelihood of an event that will occur only when the human species will have necessarily acquired a degree of knowledge of which we can have no inkling. And who would take it upon himself to predict the condition to which the art of converting the elements to the use of man may in time be brought?

But even if we agree that the limit will one day arrive, nothing follows from it that is in the least alarming as far as either the happiness of the human race or its indefinite perfectibility is concerned. If we consider that, before all this comes to pass, the progress of reason will have kept pace with that of the sciences, and that the absurd prejudices of superstition will have ceased to corrupt and degrade the moral code by its harsh doctrines instead of purifying and elevating it, we can assume that by then men will know that, if they have a duty towards those who are not yet born, that duty is not to give them existence but to give them happiness; their aim should be to promote the general welfare of the human race or of the society in which they live or of the family to which they belong, rather than foolishly to encumber the world with useless and wretched beings. It is, then, possible that there should be a limit to the amount of food that can be produced, and, consequently, to the size of the population of the world, without this involving that untimely destruction of some of those creatures who have been given life, which is so contrary to nature and to social prosperity....

Organic perfectibility or deterioration amongst the various strains in the vegetable and animal kingdom can be regarded as one of the general laws of nature. This law also applies to the human race. No one can doubt that, as preventive medicine improves and food and housing become healthier, as a way of life is established that develops our physical powers by exercise without ruining them by excess, as the two most virulent causes of deterioration, misery and excessive wealth, are eliminated, the average length of human life will be increased and a better health and a stronger physical constitution will be ensured. The improvement of medical practice, which will become more efficacious with the progress of reason and of the social order, will mean the end of infectious and hereditary diseases and illnesses brought on by climate, food, or working conditions. It is reasonable to hope that all other diseases may likewise disappear as their distant causes are discovered. Would it be absurd, then, to suppose that this perfection of the human species might be capable of indefinite progress; that the day will come when death will be due only to extraordinary accidents or to the decay of the vital forces, and that ultimately the average span between birth and decay will have no assignable value? Certainly man will not become immortal, but will not the interval between the first breath that he draws and the time when in the natural course of events, without disease or accident, he expires, increase indefinitely? Since we are now speaking of a progress that can be represented with some accuracy in figures or on a graph, we shall take this opportunity of explaining the two meanings that can be attached to the word *indefinite*.

In truth, this average span of life, which we suppose will increase indefinitely as time passes, may grow in conformity either with a law such that it continually approaches a limitless length but without ever reaching it, or with a law such that through the centuries it reaches a length greater than any determinate quantity that we may assign to it as its limit. In the latter case such an increase is truly indefinite in the strictest sense of the word, since there is no term on this side of which it must of necessity stop. In the former case it is equally indefinite in relation to us if we cannot fix the limit it always approaches without ever reaching, and particularly if, knowing only that it will never stop, we are ignorant in which of the two senses the term *indefinite* can be applied to it. Such is the present condition of our knowledge as far as the perfectibility of the human race is concerned; such is the

sense in which we may call it indefinite.

So, in the example under consideration, we are bound to believe that the average length of human life will forever increase unless this is prevented by physical revolutions; we do not know what the limit is which it can never exceed. We cannot tell even whether the general laws of nature have determined such a limit or not.

But are not our physical faculties and the strength, dexterity and acuteness of our senses, to be numbered among the qualities whose perfection in the individual may be transmitted? Observaion of the various breeds of domestic animals inclines us to believe that they are, and we can confirm this by direct observation of the human race.

Finally may we not extend such hopes to the intellectual and moral faculties? May not our parents, who transmit to us the benefits or disadvantages of their constitution, and from whom we receive our shape and features, as well as our tendencies to certain physical affections, hand on to us also that part of the physical organization which determines the intellect, the power of the brain, the ardour of the soul or the moral sensibility? Is it not probable that education, in perfecting these qualities, will at the same time influence, modify and perfect the organization itself? Analogy, investigation of the human faculties and the study of certain facts, all seem to give substance to such conjectures, which would further push back the boundaries of our hopes.

These are the questions with which we shall conclude this final stage. How consoling for the philosopher, who laments the errors, the crimes, the injustices which still pollute the earth, and of which he is often the victim, is this view of the human race, emancipated from its shackles, released from the empire of fate and from that of the enemies of its progress, advancing with a firm and sure step along the path of truth, virtue and happiness! It is the contemplation of this prospect that rewards him for all his efforts to assist the progress of reason and the defence of liberty. He dares to regard these strivings as part of the eternal chain of human destiny; and in this persuasion he is filled with the true delight of virtue and the pleasure of having done some lasting good, which fate can never destroy by a sinister stroke of revenge, by calling back the reign of slavery and prejudice. Such contemplation is for him an asylum, in which the memory of his persecutors cannot pursue him; there he lives in thought with man restored to his natural rights and dignity, forgets man tormented and corrupted by greed, fear, or envy; there he lives with his peers in an Elysium created by reason and graced by the purest pleasures known to the love of mankind.

Marquis de Condorcet, *Sketch for a Historical Picture of the Human Mind,* trans. June Barraclough (London: George Weidenfeld and Nicolson, Ltd., 1955), pp. 173–202.

III. Man in Nature and in Society

The men of the Enlightenment found their own society seriously deficient, and in need of reform. But did they, as so many of their later critics have maintained, believe that man had once, in a primitive savage state, before art, law, and the sciences had corrupted him, been happy and good? Did they believe in the natural goodness of man even in their own day, if he could only go back to the simple life, if he could only rely on his heart instead of his head? Rousseau in his first work, *A Discourse on the Arts and Sciences* (1750), certainly concluded that the progress of the arts and sciences had been accompanied by a moral decadence; and in his second, *A Discourse on the Origin of Inequality* (1755), he maintained that the physical (i.e. "natural") inequalities among men were relatively unimportant in comparison with the social and economic (i.e. "unnatural") inequalities the growth of civilization had produced. Primitivism—the belief that men were better and happier in days of old, or in parts of the world as yet untouched by European civilization—was a doctrine in the air of the Enlightenment. But do the following excerpts suggest that this primitivism was unchallenged among the men of the Enlightenment? As to man's own nature, did these thinkers again oversimplify, making man by nature free, equal, and virtuous, corrupted only by society, by "environment," by arrangements made by unenlightened men and presumably therefore alterable by enlightened men? Rousseau and Diderot are joined by Claude Helvetius, author of the materialistic study *De l'Esprit,* and Thomas Jefferson to help us cope with these questions. We also cite from two specimens of a very eighteenth-century literary form, the aphorism, witty, skeptical, "realistic," surely the reverse of naïve primitivism.

Franklin we all know; George Christoph Lichtenberg (1742–1799) was a German scientist and man of letters. As a final touch, we give a very famous quotation from the polished verse of Alexander Pope (1688–1744). Does this last sound like simple optimism about human nature?

A. Rousseau. Good Man and Bad Civilization, 1755

If the reader thus discovers and retraces the lost and forgotten road, by which man must have passed from the state of nature to the state of society; if he carefully restores, along with the intermediate situations which I have just described, those which want of time has compelled me to suppress, or my imagination has failed to suggest, he cannot fail to be struck by the vast distance which separates the two states. It is in tracing this slow succession that he will find the solution of a number of problems of politics and morals, which philosophers cannot settle. He will feel that, men being different in different ages, the reason why Diogenes could not find a man was that he sought among his contemporaries a man of an earlier period. He will see that Cato died with Rome and liberty, because he did not fit the age in which he lived; the greatest of men served only to astonish a world which he would certainly have ruled, had he lived five hundred years sooner. In a word, he will explain how the soul and the passions of men insensibly change their very nature; why our wants and pleasures in the end seek new objects; and why, the original man having vanished by degrees, society offers to us only an assembly of artificial men and factitious passions, which are the work of all these new relations, and without any real foundation in nature. We are taught nothing on this subject, by reflection, that is not entirely confirmed by observation. The savage and the civilised man differ so much in the bottom of their hearts and in their inclinations, that what constitutes the supreme happiness of one would reduce the other to despair. The former breathes only peace and liberty; he desires only to live and be free from labour; even the *ataraxia* [imperturbability] of the Stoic falls far short of his profound indifference to every other object. Civilised man, on the other hand, is always moving, sweating, toiling and racking his brains to find still more laborious occupations: he goes on in drudgery to his last moment, and even seeks death to put himself in a position to live, or renounces life to acquire immortality. He pays his court to men in power, whom he hates, and to the wealthy, whom he despises; he stops at nothing to have the honour of serving them; he is not ashamed to value himself on his own meanness and their protection; and, proud of his slavery, he speaks with disdain of those, who have not the honour of sharing it. What a sight would the perplexing and envied labours of a European minister of State present to the eyes of a Caribean! [sic] How many cruel deaths would not this indolent savage prefer to the horrors of such a life, which is seldom even sweetened by the pleasure of doing good! But, for him to see into the motives of all this solicitude, the words *power* and *reputation*, would have to bear some meaning in his mind; he would have to know that there are men who set a value on the opinion of the rest of the world; who can be made happy and satisfied with themselves rather on the testimony of other people than on their own. In reality, the source of all these differences is, that the savage lives within himself, while social man lives constantly outside himself, and only knows how to live in the opinion of

others, so that he seems to receive the consciousness of his own existence merely from the judgment of others concerning him. It is not to my present purpose to insist on the indifference to good and evil which arises from this disposition, in spite of our many fine works on morality, or to show how, everything being reduced to appearances, there is but art and mummery in even honour, friendship, virtue, and often vice itself, of which we at length learn the secret of boasting; to show, in short, how, always asking others what we are, and never daring to ask ourselves, in the midst of so much philosophy, humanity and civilisation, and of such sublime codes of morality, we have nothing to show for ourselves but a frivolous and deceitful appearance, honour without virtue, reason without wisdom, and pleasure without happiness. It is sufficient that I have proved that this is not by any means the original state of man, but that it is merely the spirit of society, and the inequality which society produces, that thus transform and alter all our natural inclinations.

I have endeavoured to trace the origin and progress of inequality, and the institution and abuse of political societies, as far as these are capable of being deduced from the nature of man merely by the light of reason, and independently of those sacred dogmas which give the sanction of divine right to sovereign authority. It follows from this survey that, as there is hardly any inequality in the state of nature, all the inequality which now prevails owes its strength and growth to the development of our faculties and the advance of the human mind, and becomes at last permanent and legitimate by the establishment of property and laws. Secondly, it follows that moral inequality, authorised by positive right alone, clashes with natural right, whenever it is not proportionate to physical inequality; a distinction which sufficiently determines what we ought to think of that species of inequality which prevails in all civilised countries; since it is plainly contrary to the law of nature, however defined, that children should command old men, fools wise men, and that the privileged few should gorge themselves with superfluities, while the starving multitude are in want of the bare necessities of life.

J. J. Rousseau, "A Discourse on the Origin of Inequality," in *The Social Contract*, trans. G. D. H. Cole, Everyman's ed. (New York: E. P. Dutton & Co., Inc., n. d.), pp. 236–38.

B. Helvetius. Men Are Alike, 1773

RECAPITULATION

After having in the Introduction to this work said a few words on its importance, and on the ignorance of mankind relative to the true principles of education, and lastly, of the dryness of the subject, and the difficulty of treating it, I have examined,

SECTION I

"Whether education, necessarily different in different men, be not the cause of that inequality of understandings hitherto attributed to the unequal perfection of their organs."

To this purpose I have inquired at what age the education of man begins, and who are his instructors.

I see that man is the pupil of every object which surrounds him, of all the positions in which chance has placed him, in short, of every incident that happens to him.

That these objects, positions, and incidents are not exactly the same for any two persons, and consequently no two receive the same instructions.

That if it were possible for two men to have the same objects before their eyes, these objects not striking them at the precise moment when their minds are in the same situation, will not, in consequence, excite in them the same ideas: therefore the pretended uniformity of instruction received, either in the schools or in the paternal house, is one of those suppositions whose impossibility is proved by facts, and by the influence that chance, independent of instructors, has, and always will have, on the education of childhood and youth.

These matters settled, I consider the extreme extent of the power of chance, and I examine,

Whether illustrious men do not frequently owe to it their taste for a particular sort of study, and consequently their talents and their success in that study.

If the science of education can be perfected without restraining the bounds of the empire of chance.

If the contradictions at present perceived among all the precepts of education, do not extend the empire of chance.

If these contradictions, of which I have given some examples, ought not to be regarded as effects of the opposition that is found between the religious system and that of the public prosperity.

If religions might not be rendered less destructive of the national felicity, and founded on principles more conformable to the general interest.

What those principles are.

If they might not be established by an intelligent prince.

If among the false religions there are not some whose worship has not been less opposite to the welfare of society, and consequently to the improvement of the science of education.

If after these several examens, and on the supposition that all men have an equal aptitude to understanding, the mere difference in their education ought not to produce a difference in their ideas and their talents. From whence it follows, that the inequality in understanding cannot be regarded, in men commonly well organized, as a demonstrative proof of their unequal aptitude to acquire it.

I have examined,

SECTION II

"If all men, commonly well organized, have not an equal aptitude to understanding?"

...It results, that as the greater or less fineness of the senses does not at all change the proportion in which objects strike us, all men, commonly well organised, have an equal aptitude to understanding.

To augment proofs of this important truth, I have added a demonstration of it in the same section, by another series of propositions. I have shewn that the most sublime ideas, once simplified, are, by the consent of all philosophers, reducible to this clear proposition, *that white is white, and black is black.*

That every truth of this kind is comprehensible by all understandings; and that therefore there is not any one, how great and general soever it may be, which clearly represented, and disengaged from the obscurity of words, cannot be equally conceived by all men commonly well organised. Now to be equally able to comprehend the highest truths, is to have an equal aptitude to understanding. Such is the conclusion of the second section.

SECTION III

The object of this section is an inquiry concerning the causes to which the inequality of understandings is to be attributed.

These causes are reducible to two.

The one is the unequal desire that men have to knowledge.

The other, the diversity of positions in which chance places them; a diversity from which results that of their instruction, and their ideas. To shew that it is to these two causes only we ought to refer the difference and inequality of understandings, I have proved that most of our discoveries are the gifts of chance.

That these same gifts are not granted to all.

This distribution however is not so unequal as imagined.

That in this respect chance is less neglectful of us, than we are, if I may use the expression, neglectful of chance.

That in fact all men commonly well organised have an equal power of understanding, but that power is dead in them, when not put in action by some passion, such as the love of esteem, glory, etc.

That men owe to such passions only the attention proper to fecundate the ideas offered to them by chance.

That without passions their minds might be, so to say, regarded as perfect machines, whose movement is suspended till the passions put them in action.

From whence I conclude, that the inequality of understandings in men is the produce of chance, and of the unequal vivacity of their passions....

Claude Helvetius, *A Treatise on Man,* trans. W. Hooper (London: B. Law, 1777), II, 443–52.

C. Diderot. Men Are Not Alike, ca. 1774

[Text of Helvetius] Page 154.—*Are men of different opinion on the same question? This difference is always due to the fact that either they do not understand one another, or they do not have the same objects before them, or they do not give to the question itself the necessary interest.*

[Comment of Diderot] This is not all, and men's arguments have a breeding place perhaps more fertile than any of those noted above.

However well organized two heads might be, it is impossible for the same ideas to be equally evident in one as in the other. I do not think that this principle can be refuted.

Therefore it is impossible for the same reasoning to appear equally conclusive to both.

One line of reasoning, tying in with the chain of ideas of one of the disputants, will appear evident to him. The other disputant, if only because he would have to admit several errors if this reasoning, which does not tie in with or even thwarts his chain of ideas, were true, naturally will be inclined to think it false.

[Text of Helvetius] Page 155.—*All men are born with equality of understanding.*

[Comment of Diderot] All men are born without understanding; they have it neither false nor just: it is the experience of the things of life that disposes them toward justness or falseness.

He who has always made bad use of his senses will have false understanding.

He who, mediocrely educated, thinks he knows all, will have false understanding.

He who, carried away by self-sufficiency and hastiness, is hurried in his judgments, will have false understanding.

He who attaches too much or too little importance to certain things will have false understanding.

He who dares pronounce himself on a question which exceeds the capacity of his natural talent will have false understanding.

There is nothing so rare as logic: an infinity of men lack it, almost all women have none at all.

He who is subject to prejudices will have false understanding.

He who is obstinate out of conceit, out of a desire to be different, or out of inclination for paradoxes, will have false understanding.

And he who trusts his reason too much and he who trusts it too little will have false understanding.

All interests, all prejudices, all passions, all vices, all virtues are capable of perverting the understanding.

Thence I conclude that equality of understanding is in every respect a figment of the imagination. . . .

CHAPTER II

Page 13.—*Is man good or evil at birth?*

If one can give the name of good only to him who has done good, and the name of evil only to him who has done evil, then assuredly man, at birth, is neither good nor evil. I will say as much of understanding and of stupidity.

But does man bring with him at birth organic and natural tendencies to say and do foolish things, to harm himself and his fellow-men, to listen to or disregard the advices of his parents, to diligence or laziness, to justice or anger, to respect or despise laws? Only he who in his life has never seen two children nor has ever heard them cry in their cradles can doubt this. Man is born nothing, but every man is born with a special aptitude for something.

"M. Helvetius, you are a hunter, I think?"

"Yes, I am one."

"Do you see that little dog?"

"The one with the twisted legs, the low and long body, the pointed muzzle and the paws and hide spotted with fire?"

"Yes. What is he?"

"He is a basset hound; this species has good scent, high spirits, courage: he will thrust himself in the burrow of a fox, at the risk of emerging with torn ears and sides."

"And this other one?"

"He is a brach hound. He is an indefatigable animal: his hard and bristling fur permits him to plunge into thorny and thick bushes; he stops the partridge, he bays the hare, he takes the place of three or four dogs."

"And this other one?"

"He is one of the most beautiful greyhounds."

"And this third [sic] one?"

"A setter. I cannot tell you anything about him: will he be docile, will he not? will he have good scent, will he not? It is a matter of race."

"And this fourth [sic] one?"

"He promises to be a very beautiful hound."

"They are all dogs?"

"Yes."

"And, tell me. I have an excellent gamekeeper, he will do everything I wish; could I not order him to make a brach out of the basset, a greyhound out of the brach, a field dog out of the greyhound, a hound out of the field dog, and a barbet out of the hound?"

"Do nothing of the kind."

"And why?...They have just been born, they are nothing; fit for everything,

rearing will dispose of them at my will."

"You are making fun of me."

"M. Helvetius, you are right. But what if there should be in the human species the same variety of individuals as there is in the canine race, what if each had his own gait and game?"

"Réfutation de Helvétius," Diderot, *Oeuvres Complètes,* ed. J. Assézat (Paris: Garnier Frères, 1875), II, 243–44, 406–7. Trans. Henry R. Winkler.

D. Jefferson. Natural Goodness More Evident Among Farmers than Merchants, 1786

How happens it that Rhode Island is opposed to every useful proposition?

Her geography accounts for it, with the aid of one or two observations. The cultivators of the earth are the most virtuous citizens, and possess most of the *amor patriæ.* Merchants are the least virtuous, and possess the least of the *amor patriæ.* The latter reside principally in the seaport towns, the former in the interior country. Now, it happened that of the territory constituting Rhode Island and Connecticut, the part containing the seaports was erected into a State by itself, called Rhode Island, and that containing the interior country was erected into another State called Connecticut. For though it has a little seacoast, there are no good ports in it. Hence it happens that there is scarcely one merchant in the whole State of Connecticut, while there is not a single man in Rhode Island who is not a merchant of some sort. Their whole territory is but a thousand square miles, and what of that is in use is laid out in grass farms almost entirely. Hence they have scarcely any body employed in agriculture. All exercise some species of commerce. This circumstance has decided the characters of these two States. The remedies to this evil are hazardous. One would be to consolidate the two States into one. Another would be to banish Rhode Island from the Union. A third, to compel her submission to the will of the other twelve. A fourth, for the other twelve to govern themselves according to the new propositions, and to let Rhode Island go on by herself according to the ancient articles. But the dangers and difficulties attending all these remedies are obvious.

Thomas Jefferson, "Answers to Questions Propounded by M. de Meusnier," in S. K. Padover, ed., *The Complete Jefferson* (New York: Duell, Sloan & Pearce, Inc., 1943), pp. 43–44.

E. Franklin. From Poor Richard, 1753–58

He's a fool that makes his doctor his heir.

Men and melons are hard to know.

Where there's marriage without love, there will be love without marriage.

A learned blockhead is a greater blockhead than an ignorant one.

The ancients tell us what is best; but we must learn of the moderns what is fittest.

Sin is not hurtful because it is forbidden, but it is forbidden because it is hurtful.

Beware of little expences; a small leak will sink a great ship.

A man without ceremony has need of great merit in its place.

Philosophy as well as foppery often changes fashion.

The wit of conversation consists more in finding it in others, than shewing a great deal yourself.

In a corrupt age, the putting the world in order would breed confusion; then e'en mind your own business.

To serve the publick faithfully, and at the same time please it entirely is impracticable.

Men often mistake themselves, seldom forget themselves.

The Writings of Benjamin Franklin, ed. A. H. Smyth (New York: The Macmillan Company, 1905–1907).

F. Lichtenberg, Aphorisms, ca. 1790

Many conclusions about men's characters could perhaps be drawn from their dreams, if they would report them exactly. But quite a few would be needed, not just one.

I commend dreams again; we live and feel as much dreaming as waking and are the one as much as the other. It is one of the superiorities of man that he dreams *and knows it.* We have hardly made the right use of this yet. Dream is a life which, combined with the rest of us, makes up what we call human life. Dreams gradually merge into our waking; we cannot say where man's waking state begins.

We often strive to subdue some vicious emotion, and try at the same time to preserve all of our good ones. This comes from our method of describing man: we fail to see his character as a very neatly constructed totality, which can be rearranged only by changing the relative position of its various parts. Rather, we regard his emotions as adhesive beauty-patches, which we may shift or throw away at will. Many such errors derive from the languages indispensable in describing the emotions. Thus we always think of the most ordinary meaning the moment we neglect, to the slightest degree, the particular association. Therefore, if a general system of characterization is to be invented, a proper language must first be found.

Everyone should study at least enough philosophy and *belles lettres* to make his sexual experience more delectable.

If an angel were to tell us about his philosophy, I believe many of his statements might well sound like "$2 \times 2 = 13$."

Truth has to overcome a thousand obstacles to get on paper undamaged, and back from the paper to the mind. Liars are its weakest enemies. The star-gazing writer, who holds forth about all matters and views all matters as other honest people do when they have had a drop too much; the supersubtle, affected "judge of human nature," who sees and wants to see a man's whole life mirrored in each of his acts; the good, pious man who believes in every instance because he is respectful, who examines none of the things he learned before his fifteenth year and builds up the little bit he has examined of an unexamined base—these are enemies of truth.

Because of his obscure sense of his own perfectibility, man still thinks himself far from the goal even when he has reached it; and reason does not sufficiently enlighten him. What he finds easy, he thinks bad, and so he strains from the bad to the good, and from the good to a type of the bad which he thinks better than good.

The progress of the good and the purposeful in the world. If, for instance, it is rooted in human nature that ultimately the Christian religion will perish again some day, it will happen whether people oppose this or not. Going against the stream and obstructing it for a little while makes only an infinitely small bend in the line. Only it is too bad that *we* have to be the spectators and not some other generation; no one can blame us for working as hard as we can to shape our times according to our own minds.

I always think that we on this sphere

serve a purpose whose fulfillment a conspiracy of the whole human race cannot prevent. In just the same way a good book will go down to posterity even if all the critical judges should combine to cast suspicion on it—not by satire but with the mien of the innocent lamb and the accent of the lover of truth—even if they should keep absolute silence about it. If it contains a dozen new truths, stated well and vigorously, if the expert in human nature appears in the rest of the work, then a legion of witty magazine writers will be as little able to block its course to eternity as I could fan back the storm or the rising flood with a playing card. A man can condemn a good book through envy, lack of judgment, or foolishness, but Man cannot.

It would be worth-while to investigate whether it isn't harmful to devote too much care to bringing up children. We don't yet know man well enough to relieve chance completely of this function. I believe that if our pedagogues succeed in their intention—I mean, if they bring it about that the children are shaped completely by their influence—there won't be a single really great man produced from now on.

A book is a mirror: when a monkey looks in, no apostle can look out.

If a later generation were to reconstruct the man of today from our sentimental writings, they would believe he had been a heart with testicles.

Just as one says someone "holds an office," while actually the office holds him.

I am convinced that a person doesn't only love himself in others; he also hates himself in others.

Materialism is the asymptote of psychology.

In a machine as complicated as this world, we are all, I think, gambling in a lottery as far as the essentials are concerned, even though we may have a slight part in determining events.

As soon as people know that someone is blind, they think they can tell it from behind.

We don't devour each other; we merely slaughter each other.

There is something in every person's character that cannot be broken—the bony structure of his character. Wanting to change it is the same as teaching a sheep to retrieve.

The myths of the physicists.

Sense is order; and order is, in the last analysis, harmony with our own nature. When we speak reasonably, we speak only from our essence and our nature. In order to incorporate something in our memory, therefore, we always try to supply sense or another sort of ordering. Therefore *genera* and *species* among plants and animals, as well as other similarities, including rhyme. In just that category, our hypotheses also belong; we must have some, because otherwise we could not remember things. This has been said very long ago, but one comes back to it again from all directions.

Thus we try to bring sense into the physical world. But the question is whether we can really make sense of everything. Certainly, by much testing and reflection, a meaning can be brought into something which is not sensible for us, or not sensible at all. Thus one sees in the sand faces, landscapes, etc., which certainly are not the intention of these patterns. Symmetry belongs here too; silhouette in the blot of ink, etc. Also the scale in the range of creatures—all that is *not in the things but in us*. Generally one forgets too easily that when we observe nature, we always observe only ourselves, especially our orderings.

Man is a creature who searches for causes; he could be named the cause-searcher within the hierarchy of minds. Other minds perhaps conceive things under other categories, incomprehensible to us.

The Lichtenberg Reader. Trans. and ed. by Franz H. Mautner and Henry Hatfield (Boston: Beacon Press, 1959), pp. 43–100 *passim.*

G. Pope. "The Proper Study...," 1733

Know then thyself, presume not God
  to scan,
The proper study of mankind is Man.
Placed on this isthmus of a middle
  state,
A being darkly wise and rudely great:
With too much knowledge for the
  Sceptic side,
With too much weakness for the Stoic's
  pride,
He hangs between, in doubt to act or
  rest;
In doubt to deem himself a God or
  Beast;
In doubt his mind or body to prefer;
Born but to die, and reas'ning but to
  err;
Alike in ignorance, his reason such,
Whether he thinks too little or too
  much;
Chaos of thought and passion, all con-
  fused;
Still by himself abused or disabused;
Created half to rise, and half to fall;
Great lord of all things, yet a prey
  to all;
Sole judge of truth, in endless error
  hurl'd;
The glory, jest, and riddle of the world!
Go, wondrous creature! mount where
  Science guides;
Go, measure earth, weigh air, and state
  the tides;
Instruct the planets in what orbs to
  run,
Correct old Time, and regulate the sun;
Go, soar with Plato to th' empyreal
  sphere,
To the first good, first perfect, and first
  fair;
Or tread the mazy round his followers
  trod,
And quitting sense call imitating God;
As eastern priests in giddy circles run,
And turn their heads to imitate the sun.
Go, teach Eternal Wisdom how to
  rule—
Then drop into thyself, and be a fool!

Alexander Pope, *An Essay on Man*, Epistle II.

IV. Individual Liberty or Collective Authority: Political Ultimates

The last phase of our general problem of what the thinkers of the Enlightenment really meant in their great debate over the nature of man and the state is more specifically political. These thinkers made frequent use of terms like "social contract"—by which they meant at bottom that government is, or should be, founded on the consent of the governed; and "natural law"—by which they meant at bottom that there are principles of justice, of right and wrong, which men can learn to know and agree on, to which actual existing laws (which they commonly called "civil law") ought to conform. Under this natural law, men had "natural rights." But these terms are highly technical, and rewarding though their study is, call for special training in formal political theory and in jurisprudence. We shall try here to go behind these terms to a central problem most important to us: were these thinkers seeking to promote the freedom of the individual citizen, his "right" to do as he likes subject to a minimum of restraint from government; or were they rather seeking to impose on men—for their own greater good, indeed, as these thinkers saw it—a more enlightened, more efficient, and perhaps even more rigid system of government than the existing ones? Were these thinkers on the side of liberty or of authority? Did they want a society edging toward anarchism, or did they want a kind of authoritarianism, even totalitarianism, an "enlightened despotism?" Did they trust the common man or did they distrust him? The problem is especially acute in what is perhaps the most famous political writing of the age, Rousseau's *Social Contract* (1762). Some have seen in this work a defense of individual freedom; others have seen in it a defense of collective authority. The problem, which is a very knotty one indeed, can perhaps be put with undue simplicity: are liberty and equality, coupled as ideals in the great democratic documents of the time, at bottom incompatible? If so, toward which side did the thinkers of the Enlightenment lean, or what compromises did they advocate? To an excerpt from Rousseau we have added selections which illustrate the range of thought on this problem in our period. William Godwin was the English philosophical anarchist whose ideas considerably influenced the youthful writings of Wordsworth, Coleridge, and Shelley. The passage quoted is from his best-known work, *Political Justice*. Maximilien de Robespierre, the "Incorruptible," was the principal leader of revolutionary France during the days of the Terror in 1793 and 1794. His position on the question of liberty and equality appears in a speech delivered in 1793. Thomas Jefferson, finally, is the author of the letter which contains our concluding selection.

A. French Declaration of the Rights of Man and the Citizen, 1789

The representatives of the French people, organized in National Assembly, considering that ignorance, forgetfulness, or contempt of the rights of man are the sole causes of public misfortunes and of the corruption of governments, have resolved to set forth in a solemn declaration the natural, inalienable, and sacred rights of man, in order that such declaration, continually before all members of the social body, may be a perpetual reminder of their rights and duties; in order that the acts of the legislative power and those of the executive power may constantly be compared with the aim of every political institution and may accordingly be more respected; in order that the demands of the citizens, founded henceforth upon simple and incontestable principles, may always be directed towards the maintenance of the Constitution and the welfare of all.

Accordingly, the National Assembly recognizes and proclaims, in the presence and under the auspices of the Supreme Being, the following rights of man and citizen.

1. Men are born and remain free and equal in rights; social distinctions may be based only upon general usefulness.

2. The aim of every political association is the preservation of the natural and inalienable rights of man; these rights are liberty, property, security, and resistance to oppression.

3. The source of all sovereignty resides essentially in the nation; no group, no individual may exercise authority not emanating expressly therefrom.

4. Liberty consists of the power to do whatever is not injurious to others; thus the enjoyment of the natural rights of every man has for its limits only those that assure other members of society the enjoyment of those same rights; such limits may be determined only by law.

5. The law has the right to forbid only actions which are injurious to society. Whatever is not forbidden by law may not be prevented, and no one may be constrained to do what it does not prescribe.

6. Law is the expression of the general will; all citizens have the right to concur personally, or through their representatives, in its formation; it must be the same for all, whether it protects or punishes. All citizens, being equal before it, are equally admissible to all public offices, positions, and employments, according to their capacity, and without other distinction than that of virtues and talents.

7. No man may be accused, arrested, or detained except in the cases determined by law, and according to the forms prescribed thereby. Whoever solicit, expedite, or execute arbitrary orders, or have them executed, must be punished; but every citizen summoned or apprehended in pursuance of the law must obey immediately; he renders himself culpable by resistance.

8. The law is to establish only penalties that are absolutely and obviously necessary; and no one may be punished except by virtue of a law established and promulgated prior to the offence and legally applied.

9. Since every man is presumed inno-

cent until declared guilty, if arrest be deemed indispensable, all unnecessary severity for securing the person of the accused must be severely repressed by law.

10. No one is to be disquieted because of his opinions, even religious, provided their manifestation does not disturb the public order established by law.

11. Free communication of ideas and opinions is one of the most precious of the rights of man. Consequently, every citizen may speak, write, and print freely, subject to responsibility for the abuse of such liberty in the cases determined by law.

12. The guarantee of the rights of man and citizen necessitates a public force; such a force, therefore, is instituted for the advantage of all and not for the particular benefit of those to whom it is entrusted.

13. For the maintenance of the public force and for the expenses of administration a common tax is indispensable; it must be assessed equally on all citizens in proportion to their means.

14. Citizens have the right to ascertain, by themselves or through their representatives, the necessity of the public tax, to consent to it freely, to supervise its use, and to determine its quota, assessment, payment, and duration.

15. Society has the right to require of every public agent an accounting of his administration.

16. Every society in which the guarantee of rights is not assured or the separation of powers not determined has no constitution at all.

17. Since property is a sacred and inviolable right, no one may be deprived thereof unless a legally established public necessity obviously requires it, and upon condition of a just and previous indemnity.

John Hall Stewart, *A Documentary Survey of the French Revolution* (New York: The Macmillan Company, 1951), pp. 113–15.

B. Rousseau. Forcing a Man To Be Free, 1762

CHAPTER VI: The Social Contract

I suppose men to have reached the point at which the obstacles in the way of their preservation in the state of nature show their power of resistance to be greater than the resources at the disposal of each individual for his maintenance in that state. That primitive condition can then subsist no longer; and the human race would perish unless it changed its manner of existence.

But, as men cannot engender new forces, but only unite and direct existing ones, they have no other means of preserving themselves than the formation, by aggregation, of a sum of forces great enough to overcome the resistance. These they have to bring into play by means of a single motive power, and cause to act in concert.

This sum of forces can arise only where several persons come together: but, as the force and liberty of each man are the chief instruments of his self-preservation, how can he pledge them without harming his own interests, and neglecting the care he owes to himself? This difficulty, in its bearing on my present subject, may be stated in the following terms—

"The problem is to find a form of association which will defend and protect with the whole common force the person and goods of each associate, and in which each, while uniting himself with all, may still obey himself alone, and remain as free as before." This is the fundamental problem of which the *Social Contract* provides the solution.

The clauses of this contract are so determined by the nature of the act that the slightest modification would make them vain and ineffective; so that, although they have perhaps never been formally set forth, they are everywhere the same and everywhere tacitly admitted and recognised, until, on the violation of the social compact, each regains his original rights and resumes his natural liberty, while losing the conventional liberty in favour of which he renounced it.

These clauses, properly understood, may be reduced to one—the total alienation of each associate, together with all his rights, to the whole community; for, in the first place, as each gives himself absolutely, the conditions are the same for all; and, this being so, no one has any interest in making them burdensome to others.

Moreover, the alienation being without reserve, the union is as perfect as it can be, and no associate has anything more to demand: for, if the individuals retained certain rights, as there would be no common superior to decide between them and the public, each, being on one point his own judge, would ask to be so on all; the state of nature would thus continue, and the association would necessarily become inoperative or tyrannical.

Finally, each man, in giving himself to all, gives himself to nobody; and as there is no associate over whom he does not acquire the same right as he yields others over himself, he gains an equivalent for everything he loses, and an increase of force for the preservation of what he has.

If then we discard from the social compact what is not of its essence, we shall find that it reduces itself to the following terms—

"Each of us puts his person and all his power in common under the supreme direction of the general will, and, in our corporate capacity, we receive each member as an indivisible part of the whole."

At once, in place of the individual personality of each contracting party, this act of association creates a moral and collective body, composed of as many members as the assembly contains votes, and receiving from this act its unity, its common identity, its life and its will. This public person, so formed by the union of all other persons, formerly took the name of *city*, and now takes that of *Republic* or *body politic;* it is called by its members *State* when passive, *Sovereign* when active, and *Power* when compared with others like itself. Those who are associated in it take collectively the name of *people*, and sever-

ally are called *citizens*, as sharing in the sovereign power, and *subjects*, as being under the laws of the State. But these terms are often confused and taken one for another: it is enough to know how to distinguish them when they are being used with precision.

CHAPTER VII: The Sovereign

This formula shows us that the act of association comprises a mutual undertaking between the public and the individuals, and that each individual, in making a contract, as we may say, with himself, is bound in a double capacity; as a member of the Sovereign he is bound to the individuals, and as a member of the State to the Sovereign. But the maxim of civil right, that no one is bound by undertakings made to himself, does not apply in this case; for there is a great difference between incurring an obligation to yourself and incurring one to a whole of which you form a part. . . .

In fact, each individual, as a man, may have a particular will contrary or dissimilar to the general will which he has as a citizen. His particular interest may speak to him quite differently from the common interest: his absolute and naturally independent existence may make him look upon what he owes to the common cause as a gratuitous contribution, the loss of which will do less harm to others than the payment of it is burdensome to himself; and, regarding the moral person which constitutes the State as a *persona ficta*, because not a man, he may wish to enjoy the rights of citizenship without being ready to fulfil the duties of a subject. The continuance of such an injustice could not but prove the undoing of the body politic.

In order then that the social compact may not be an empty formula, it tacitly includes the undertaking, which alone can give force to the rest, that whoever refuses to obey the general will shall be compelled to do so by the whole body. *This means nothing less than that he will be forced to be free;** for this is the condition which, by giving each citizen to his country,

---

* Note: italics not in original.

secures him against all personal dependence. In this lies the key to the working of the political machine; this alone legitimises civil undertakings, which, without it, would be absurd, tyrannical, and liable to the most frightful abuses. . . .

BOOK IV

CHAPTER II: Voting

. . .There is but one law which, from its nature, needs unanimous consent. This is the social compact; for civil association is the most voluntary of all acts. Every man being born free and his own master, no one, under any pretext whatsoever, can make any man subject without his consent. To decide that the son of a slave is born a slave is to decide that he is not born a man.

If then there are opponents when the social compact is made, their opposition does not invalidate the contract, but merely prevents them from being included in it. They are foreigners among citizens. When the State is instituted, residence constitutes consent; to dwell within its territory is to submit to the Sovereign.

Apart from this primitive contract, the vote of the majority always binds all the rest. This follows from the contract itself. But it is asked how a man can be both free and forced to conform to wills that are not his own. How are the opponents at once free and subject to laws they have not agreed to?

I retort that the question is wrongly put. The citizen gives his consent to all the laws, including those which are passed in spite of his opposition, and even those which punish him when he dares to break any of them. The constant will of all the members of the State is the general will; by virtue of it they are citizens and free. When in the popular assembly a law is proposed, what the people is asked is not exactly whether it approves or rejects the proposal, but whether it is in conformity with the general will, which is their will. Each man, in giving his vote, states his opinion on that point; and the general will is found by counting votes. When therefore the opinion that is contrary to my own prevails, this proves neither more nor less than that I was mistaken, and that what I thought to be the general will was not so. If my particular opinion had carried the day I should have achieved the opposite of what was my will; and it is in that case that I should not have been free.

This presupposes, indeed, that all the qualities of the general will still reside in the majority: when they cease to do so, whatever side a man may take, liberty is no longer possible.

J. J. Rousseau, *The Social Contract*, trans. by G. D. H. Cole, Everyman's ed. (New York: E. P. Dutton & Co., n. d.), pp. 14–18, 93–94.

C. Godwin. Toward Individual Freedom? 1793

. . .It is. . .necessary before we enter upon the subject carefully to distinguish between society and government. Men associated at first for the sake of mutual assistance. They did not foresee that any restraint would be necessary to regulate the conduct of individual members of the society towards each other or towards the whole. The necessity of restraint grew out of the errors and perverseness of a few. An acute writer has expressed this idea with peculiar felicity. "Society and government," says he, "are different in themselves and have different origins. Society is produced by our wants, and government by our wickedness. Society is in every state a blessing; government even in its best state but a necessary evil."[1]

. . .If there be any truth more unquestionable than the rest, it is that every man is bound to the exertion of his faculties in the discovery of right and to the carrying into effect all the right with which he is acquainted. It may be granted that an infallible standard, if it could be discovered, would be considerably beneficial. But this infallible standard itself would be of little

---

[1] [Thomas Paine] *Common Sense*, p. 1.

use in human affairs unless it had the property of reasoning as well as deciding, of enlightening the mind as well as constraining the body. If a man be in some cases obliged to prefer his own judgment, he is in all cases obliged to consult that judgment before he can determine whether the matter in question be of the sort provided for or no. So that from this reasoning it ultimately appears that no man is obliged to conform to any rule of conduct farther than the rule is consistent with justice.

Such are the genuine principles of human society. Such would be the unconstrained concord of its members in a state where every individual within the society and every neighbour without was capable of listening with sobriety to the dictates of reason. We shall not fail to be impressed with considerable regret if, when we descend to the present mixed characters of mankind, we find ourselves obliged in any degree to depart from so simple and grand a principle. The universal exercise of private judgment is a doctrine so unspeakably beautiful that the true politician will certainly resolve to interfere with it as sparingly and in as few instances as possible. Let us consider what are the emergencies that may be thought to demand an exception. They can only be briefly stated in this place, each of them requiring to be minutely examined in the subsequent stages of the enquiry.

In the first place then it seems necessary for some powerful arbitrator to interfere where the proceedings of the individual threaten the most injurious consequences to his neighbours, and where the instant nature of the case will not accord with the uncertain progress of argument and conviction addressed to the mind of the offender. . . . [But all punishment, even when necessary is evil.]

Notwithstanding all these objections, it would be difficult to find a country respecting which we could say that the inhabitants might with safety be dismissed from the operation of punishment. So mixed is human character, so wild are its excursions, so calamitous and detestable are the errors into which it occasionally falls, that something more than argument seems necessary for their suppression. Human beings are such tyros in the art of reasoning that the wisest of us often prove impotent in our attempts where an instant effect was most powerfully wanted. While I stand still to reason with the thief, the assassin or the oppressor, they hasten to new scenes of devastation, and with unsparing violence confound all the principles of human society. I should obtain little success by the abolition of punishment unless I could at the same time abolish those causes that generate temptation and make punishment necessary. Meanwhile the arguments already adduced may be sufficient to show that punishment is always an evil, and to persuade us never to recur to it but from the most evident necessity.

The remaining cases in which it may seem requisite to have recourse to the general will of the society and to supersede the private judgment of individuals are when we are called upon to counteract the hostilities of an internal enemy or to repel the attacks of a foreign invader. Here, as in the former instance, the evils that arise from an usurpation upon private judgment are many and various. It is wrong that I should contribute in any mode to a proceeding, a war for example, that I believe to be unjust. Ought I to draw my sword when the adversary appears to me to be employed in repelling a wanton aggression? The case seems not to be at all different if I contribute my property, the produce it may be of my personal labour, though custom has reconciled us to the one rather than the other.

The consequences are a degradation of character and a relaxation of principle in the person who is thus made the instrument of a transaction which his judgment disapproves. In this case, as has been already stated generally, the human mind is compressed and unnerved till it affords us scarcely the semblance of what it might otherwise have been. And in addition to the general considerations in similar cases, it may be observed that the frequent and obstinate wars which at present desolate the human race would be nearly extirpated if they were supported only by the voluntary contributions of those by whom their principle was approved.

The objection which has hitherto been permitted practically to supersede these reasonings is the difficulty of conducting an affair in the success of which millions may be interested upon so precarious a support as that of private judgment. The men with whom we are usually concerned in human society are of so mixed a character, and a self-love of the narrowest kind is so deeply rooted in many of them, that it seems nearly unavoidable upon the scheme of voluntary contribution that the most generous would pay a very ample proportion, while the mean and avaricious, though they contributed nothing, would come in for their full share of the benefit. He that would reconcile a perfect freedom in this respect with the interest of the whole, ought to propose at the same time the means of extirpating selfishness and vice. How far such a proposal is feasible will come hereafter to be considered.

BOOK III

CHAPTER II: Of the Social Contract

Upon the first statement of the system of a social contract various difficulties present themselves. Who are the parties to this contract? For whom did they consent, for themselves only or for others? For how long a time is this contract to be considered as binding? If the consent of every individual be necessary, in what manner is that consent to be given? Is it to be tacit or declared in express terms?

Little will be gained for the cause of equality and justice if our ancestors, at the first institution of government, had a right indeed of choosing the system of regulations under which they thought proper to live, but at the same time could barter away the understandings and independence of all that came after them to the latest posterity. But if the contract must be renewed in each successive generation, what periods must be fixed on for that

purpose? And if I be obliged to submit to the established government till my turn comes to assent to it, upon what principle is that obligation founded? Surely not upon the contract into which my father entered before I was born?

Secondly, what is the nature of the consent in consequence of which I am to be reckoned the subject of any particular government? It is usually said that acquiescence is sufficient, and that this acquiescence is to be inferred from my living quietly under the protection of the laws. But if this be true, an end is as effectually put to all political science, all discrimination of better and worse, as by any system invented by the most slavish sycophant that ever existed. Upon this hypothesis every government that is quietly submitted to is a lawful government, whether it be the usurpation of Cromwell or the tyranny of Caligula. Acquiescence is frequently nothing more than a choice on the part of the individual of what he deems the least evil. In many cases it is not so much as this, since the peasant and the artisan, who form the bulk of a nation, however dissatisfied with the government of their country, seldom have it in their power to transport themselves to another. It is also to be observed upon the system of acquiescence that it is in little agreement with the established opinions and practices of mankind. Thus what has been called the law of nations lays least stress upon the allegiance of a foreigner settling among us, though his acquiescence is certainly most complete; while natives removing into an uninhabited region are claimed by the mother country, and removing into a neighbouring territory are punished by municipal law if they take arms against the country in which they were born. Now surely acquiescence can scarcely be construed into consent while the individuals concerned are wholly unapprised of the authority intended to be rested upon it.

Mr. Locke, the great champion of the doctrine of an original contract, has been aware of this difficulty, and therefore observes that "a tacit consent indeed obliges a man to obey the laws of any government as long as he has any possessions or enjoyment of any part of the dominions of that government; but nothing can make a man a member of the commonwealth but his actually entering into it by positive engagement, and express promise and compact." A singular distinction; implying upon the face of it that an acquiescence such as has just been described is sufficient to render a man amenable to the penal regulations of society, but that his own consent is necessary to entitle him to its privileges.

A third objection to the social contract will suggest itself as soon as we attempt to ascertain the extent of the obligation, even supposing it to have been entered into in the most solemn manner by every member of the community. Allowing that I am called upon, at the period of my coming of age for example, to declare my assent or dissent to any system of opinions or any code of practical institutes; for how long a period does this declaration bind me? Am I precluded from better information for the whole course of my life? And if not for my whole life, why for a year, a week or even an hour? If my deliberate judgment or my real sentiment be of no avail in the case, in what sense can it be affirmed that all lawful government is founded in my consent?

But the question of time is not the only difficulty. If you demand my assent to any proposition, it is necessary that the proposition should be stated simply and clearly. So numerous are the varieties of human understanding in all cases where its independence and integrity are sufficiently preserved that there is little chance of any two men coming to a precise agreement about ten successive propositions that are in their own nature open to debate. What then can be more absurd than to present to me the laws of England in fifty volumes folio and call upon me to give an honest and uninfluenced vote upon their whole contents at once?

But the social contract, considered as the foundation of civil government, requires more of me than this. I am not only obliged to consent to all the laws that are actually upon record, but to all the laws that shall hereafter be made. It was under this view of the subject that Rousseau, in tracing the consequences of the social contract, was led to assert that "the great body of the people, in whom the sovereign authority resides, can neither delegate nor resign it. The essence of that authority," he adds, "is the general will; and will cannot be represented. It must either be the same or another; there is no alternative. The deputies of the people cannot be its representatives; they are merely its attorneys. The laws that the community does not ratify in person are no laws, are nullities."

...Lastly, if government be founded in the consent of the people, it can have no power over any individual by whom that consent is refused. If a tacit consent be not sufficient, still less can I be deemed to have consented to a measure upon which I put an express negative. This immediately follows from the observations of Rousseau. If the people, or the individuals of whom the people is constituted, cannot delegate their authority to a representative, neither can any individual delegate his authority to a majority in an assembly of which he is himself a member. The rules by which my actions shall be directed are matters of a consideration entirely personal, and no man can transfer to another the keeping of his conscience and the judging of his duties. But this brings us back to the point from which we set out. No consent of ours can divest us of our moral capacity. This is a species of property which we can neither barter nor resign, and of consequence it is impossible for any government to derive its authority from an original contract.

William Godwin, *An Enquiry Concerning Political Justice and Its Influence on General Virtue and Happiness,* ed. R. A. Preston (New York: Alfred A. Knopf, Inc., 1926), I, 39, 78–86, 92–96. Reprinted by permission of Appleton-Century-Crofts.

D. Robespierre. Toward Authoritarian Collectivism? 1793

What is the purpose, what is the goal for which we strive? We wish a peaceful enjoyment of freedom and equality, the rule of that eternal justice whose laws are graven not in marble or in stone, but in in the hearts of all men. We wish a social order that shall hold in check all base and cruel passions, which shall awaken to life all benevolent and noble impulses, that shall make the noblest ambition that of being useful to our country, that shall draw its honorable distinctions only from equality, in which the generality shall safeguard the welfare of the individual, and in which all hearts may be moved by any evidence of republican spirit. . . . We want morality in the place of egotism, principles in the place of mere habit, the rule of reason in the place of the slavery of tradition, contempt for vice in the place of contempt for misfortune, the love of glory in the place of avarice. Honest men instead of "good society," truth instead of empty show, manly greatness instead of the depravity of the great, a sublime, powerful, victorious and happy people!

The splendor of the goal pursued by our Revolution is simultaneously the source of our strength and our weakness. It is the source of our weakness, because it unites all the perfidious and vicious individuals, all the advocates of tyranny who think of plunder, who think to find in the Republic a booty. Thus we may explain the disaffection of many persons who began the struggle together with us, but who have left us when our path was but half accomplished, because they did not pursue the objects we were pursuing. . . .

You are surrounded beyond the boundaries; at home, all the friends of the tyrants conspire, and will continue to conspire, so long as treason still has a hope. We must stifle the domestic and foreign enemies of the Republic, or we must be destroyed with the Republic. And therefore, under the present circumstances, the principle of our Republic is this: to influence the people by the use of reason, to influence our enemies by the use of terror.

In times of peace, virtue is the source from which the government of the people takes its power. During the Revolution, the sources of this power are virtue and terror: virtue, without which terror will be a disaster; and terror, without which virtue is powerless. But terror is nothing more nor less than swift, severe and indomitable justice. . . .

It has been said that terror is the means by which a despotic government rules. Has your rule anything in common with such a government? Yes, indeed, but only in the sense that the sword in hands of the protagonists of liberty resembles the sword in the hands of the champion of tyranny. When despots rule because their subjects are terrified, the despots are justified—as despots. You put down all the enemies of freedom by means of terror, and you are justified—as founders of the Republic. *The government of the Revolution is the despotism of liberty against tyranny.** Must might be used only in order to protect crime? . . .

If tyranny prevails for but a single day, all the patriots will have been wiped out by the next morning. And yet some persons dare declare that despotism is justice and that the justice of the people is despotism and rebellion. . . .

Either we or our enemies must succumb. "Show consideration for the Royalists!" shout some persons; "have compassion with the criminal!" "No, I tell you; you have compassion with innocence, compassion with the weak, and compassion with humanity! . . ."

The whole task of protecting the Republic is for the advantage of the loyal citizen. In the Republic, only republicans may be citizens. The Royalists and conspirators are foreigners to us, enemies. Is not the terrible war in which we now are involved a single indissoluble struggle? Are

---

* Note: italics not in original.

the enemies within not the allies of those who attack us from without? The murderers who rend the flesh of their country at home; the intriguers who seek to purchase the conscience of the representatives of the people; the traitors who sell themselves; the pamphleteers who besmirch us and are preparing for a political counter-revolution by means of a moral counter-revolution;—are all these individuals any less dangerous than the tyrants whom they serve? All those who would intervene between these criminals and the sword of justice are like unto those who would throw themselves between the bayonets of our soldiers and the troops of the enemy, and the enthusiasm of their false feelings amounts in my eyes only to sighs directed toward England and Austria!

Maximilien de Robespierre, *Speeches: Voices of Revolt,* I (New York: International Publishers, 1927), 72–75.

E. Jefferson. On the Need for Revolution, 1816

Some men look at constitutions with sanctimonious reverence, and deem them like the ark of the covenant, too sacred to be touched. They ascribe to the men of the preceding age a wisdom more than human, and suppose what they did to be beyond amendment. I knew that age well; I belonged to it, and labored with it. It deserved well of its country. It was very like the present, but without the experience of the present; and forty years of experience in government is worth a century of book-reading; and this they would say themselves, were they to rise from the dead. I am certainly not an advocate for frequent and untried changes in laws and constitutions. I think moderate imperfections had better be borne with; because, when once known, we accommodate ourselves to them, and find practical means of correcting their ill effects. But I know also, that laws and institutions must go hand in hand with the progress of the human mind. As that becomes more developed, more enlightened, as new discoveries are made, new truths disclosed, and manners and opinions change with the change of circumstances, institutions must advance also, and keep pace with the times. We might as well require a man to wear still the coat which fitted him when a boy, as civilized society to remain ever under the regimen of their barbarous ancestors. It is this preposterous idea which has lately deluged Europe in blood. Their monarchs, instead of wisely yielding to the gradual change of circumstances, of favoring progressive accommodation to progressive improvement, have clung to old abuses, entrenched themselves behind steady habits, and obliged their subjects to seek through blood and violence rash and ruinous innovations, which, had they been referred to the peaceful deliberations and collected wisdom of the nation, would have been put into acceptable and salutary forms. Let us follow no such examples, nor weakly believe that one generation is not as capable as another of taking care of itself, and of ordering its own affairs. Let us, as our sister States have done, avail ourselves of our reason and experience, to correct the crude essays of our first and unexperienced, although wise, virtuous, and well-meaning councils. And lastly, let us provide in our constitution for its revision at stated periods. What these periods should be, nature herself indicates. By the European tables of mortality, of the adults living at any one moment of time, a majority will be dead in about nineteen years. At the end of that period then, a new majority is come into place; or, in other words, a new generation. Each generation is as independent of the one preceding, as that was of all which had gone before. It has then, like them, a right to choose for itself the form of government it believes most promotive of its own happiness; consequently, to accommodate to the circumstances in which it finds itself, that received from its predecessors; and it is for the peace and good of mankind, that a solemn opportunity of doing this every nineteen or twenty years, should be provided by the constitution; so that it may be handed on, with periodical repairs, from generation to generation, to the end of time, if anything human can so long endure. It is now forty years since the constitution of Virginia was formed. The same tables inform us, that, within that period, two-thirds of the adults then living are now dead. Have then the remaining third, even if they had the wish, the right to hold in obedience to their will, and to laws heretofore made by them, the other two-thirds, who, with themselves, compose the present mass of adults? If they have not, who has? The dead? But the dead have no rights. They are nothing; and nothing cannot own something. Where there is no substance, there can be no accident. This corporeal globe, and everything upon it, belong to its present corporeal inhabitants, during their generation. They alone have a right to direct what is the concern of themselves alone, and to declare the law of that direction; and this declaration can only be made by their majority. That majority, then, has a right to depute representatives to a convention, and to make the constitution what they think will be the best for themselves. But how collect their voice? This is the real difficulty. If invited by private authority, or county or district meetings, these divisions are so large that few will attend; and their voice will be imperfectly, or falsely pronounced. Here, then, would be one of the advantages of the ward divisions I have proposed. The mayor of every ward, on a question like the present, would call his ward together, take the simple yea or nay of its members, convey these to the country court, who would hand on those of all its wards to the proper general authority, and the voice of the whole people would be thus fairly, full, and peaceably expressed, discussed, and decided by the common reason of the society. If this avenue be shut to the call of sufferance, it will make itself heard through that of force, and we shall go on, as other nations are doing, in the endless circle of oppression, rebellion, reformation; and oppression, rebellion, reformation, again; and so on forever.

Thomas Jefferson, "Government by the People" (letter to Samuel Kercheval, July 12, 1816), in S. K. Padover, ed., *The Complete Jefferson, op. cit.,* pp. 291–93.

10

The French Revolution and Napoleon

JOHN HALL STEWART

Western Reserve University

In 1789 there burst upon France a tremendous cataclysm—the French Revolution—which, as we shall see in the first part of this problem, had been developing for three-quarters of a century. Change was long overdue in many parts of the French institutional structure. In other parts, whether absolutely necessary or not, it was desired by numerous sections of the populace. Need and desire for change became coupled with the growth of an ideology, the essence of which was the theory of the natural rights of man. This idea gave momentum to the demand for change, especially on the part of the middle class, which wished political power and social status concomitant with the economic influence that it already possessed.

Had France been dominated by a "benevolent despot" such as the late Frederick the Great of Prussia, it is possible that the unfortunate circumstances might not have evolved—or if they *had,* their solution doubtless would have been provided with speed and efficiency. But France was not to experience enlightened despotism. Instead of intelligent and competent leadership, it had only the indifferent government of Louis XV. When he died in 1774, after a relatively inglorious reign of nearly 60 years, he was succeeded by his grandson, Louis XVI, who, although decidedly more virtuous, was no more effective a sovereign than his predecessor. Louis XVI had the misfortune to inherit a position and responsibilities for which he was not fitted by either training or temperament. It was during the later years of his reign that matters reached a crisis which resulted in the metamorphosis of French institutional life known as the French Revolution.

Stemming immediately from financial distress, which neither Louis nor his ministers could (or were permitted to) solve, the first step towards the Revolution took the form of the summoning of the Estates General. This outmoded agency had not met for 175 years, and it was now revived essentially as a financial expedient when all others had failed. Constituted, as previously, of representatives of the two privileged orders (the clergy and the nobles) and the "unprivileged" third estate, the Estates General of 1789 differed from its predecessors, however, in one vital respect: the commoners had as many delegates as the nobles and clergy combined. Granted as a sort of compromise, this circumstance resulted, in a few short weeks, in a momentous accomplishment. Owing to the inertia and vacillation of the king, the commoners were able to enlist the support of the more progressive aristocrats and clerics, to defy the royal authority, to gain control of the Estates General, and to transform it into a National Assembly, the avowed purpose of which was to provide France with a constitution and a program of reforms.

During the ensuing six years, this assembly and two succeeding ones—the Legislative Assembly (1791–1792) and the National Convention (1792–1795)—managed to achieve many of the objectives contemplated by the leaders of 1789. Politically, France received not only one constitution, but, after the virtually inevitable fall of the monarchy in 1792, two others. Both of these latter ones provided for a republican form of government. The first, in 1793, was more democratic in form, but because of critical conditions it was never put into effect; the second, in 1795, was less democratic in character, but endured until 1799, by which time (as we shall see) the Revolution had "ended," and the destinies of France had passed into other hands. The French people also received (at least on paper) certain guarantees of personal liberties, and they were permitted some experience in practical politics. The legal system underwent a thorough and progressive reorganization. Religious liberty was established, and the Roman Church, the church of the majority of Frenchmen, became, at least for a time, substantially a department of the state. The entire economy was recast in a new mold of "free enterprise." The social structure was re-established on bases of equality and "careers open to talents." Even the cultural aspects of life were revitalized by plans for universal education, encouragement of the arts, and such accomplishments as the creation of the metric system.

The foregoing items represent but a suggestion of the fundamental change which France underwent, the *real* revolution. As might be expected, this revolution was not achieved without a struggle. First came the conflict between revolutionaries and *anti*-revolutionaries. In time this was augmented by quarrels among the revolutionaries themselves, the moderates and the radicals. As seems to be the case in most revolutions, the radicals triumphed, and for a brief period in 1793 and 1794 they dominated the situation through means that we know as

"The Reign of Terror." The circumstances were complicated by the outbreak of foreign war with the states of Europe which viewed the Revolution as a danger to European stability and wished to suppress it. Paradoxically, despite all that the revolutionary leaders were able to achieve in the face of seemingly insurmountable obstacles, they never did solve the problem of finances, the problem which had precipitated the entire movement in 1789. In the end it was met, as is too often the case in revolutions, by a forced currency, which rapidly depreciated in value, and by repudiation of the bulk of national obligations. The fact remains, however, that, for good or ill, within an astonishingly short period of time, a tremendous amount had been achieved, and France had been transformed into a modern state.

The years from 1795 to 1799 in the history of France (the period of the "Directory") represent, at one and the same time, three different things. First, it was during this time that the second republican constitution was given an opportunity to function and many of the essential features of the Revolution were brought to completion. Second, it was the period during which there rose to power the man who was to take charge of events in 1799, namely, Napoleon Bonaparte. (Accordingly, these years may be considered as the last phase of the French Revolution and the first phase of the Napoleonic Era.) Third, and this is most significant, it represents the phase of transition between the two epochs. By 1799 France was weary—of terror, of internal conflict, of foreign war, of financial and economic unsettlement. The time was ripe for a "strong man" to assume control of events. And, as is usually the case, such a man was on hand, ready and eager to meet the emergency. The years that follow, from 1799 to 1815, present not only the history of the "fate" of the Revolution in the hands of a dictator; they also portray the life of one of the most striking figures in the entire story of the human race.

An obscure Corsican, Napoleon Bonaparte experienced much hardship and frustration during his early years—a most fitting background for a potential dictator. Entering the army, he took advantage of every opportunity to advance himself. In 1795, when the heirs of the "Terror" were faced with the necessity of employing force to perpetuate themselves in power, Napoleon had the good fortune to be selected as the man to direct the action—which he did with great dispatch. Possibly fearing that he might endeavor to capitalize upon his newly acquired prominence, the executive "Directors" of the new government gave him a dubious reward in the form of the command of the French Army of Italy. So, a general at the age of 26, Napoleon embarked upon his career. Transforming what had long been a graveyard of military reputations into a scene of brilliant victories and diplomatic triumphs, Napoleon returned to France in 1797 in a cloud of glory, to find the government even more deeply in his debt. Two years later, despite an ill-fated Egyptian expedition which, had the full truth of it been known, might have ruined his chances, once again he was in the right place at the right time. The faltering government of the Directory, dispossessed by a clever *coup d'état*, yielded to Bonaparte.

From 1799 to 1814, and again briefly in 1815, Napoleon Bonaparte ruled France. This period is the famed "Napoleonic Era." At first maintaining a pretense of governing through a republican constitution as "First Consul" (nominally for ten years), he soon acquired the title and status of "Consul for Life." By 1804 he had established himself as "Emperor of the French," with the inheritance vested in his family. These achievements alone are suggestive of the character and tactics of the man. The acquisition of power, however, is only one of the significant features of Napoleon's régime. With regard to France itself, he consolidated and modified the principal gains of the Revolution in such a way that it is difficult to determine to which period France today is more deeply indebted. Suffice it to say that the legal system, local government, educational institutions, and many other features of modern France bear the unmistakable marks of Napoleon's endeavors.

As with most dictators, Napoleon's path soon led to war (after a brief interlude of "pacification"), war with a series of European coalitions over ten long and bloody years. Successful at the outset, Napoleon gained control of more European territory than had been in the hands of a single state or individual since the days of Charlemagne. Throughout his vast empire he disseminated the ideas and institutions of revolutionary France in a manner which was to have profound effects upon the future of Europe. Age, illness, war-weariness, and an exaggerated sense of his own destiny proved, however, in the long run, to be Napoleon's undoing. Between 1812, when he staged a disastrous invasion of Russia, and 1814, when a desperate and overwhelming European coalition brought him to his knees, his doom was sealed. He was shipped off to the little island of Elba to reign over a "comic kingdom." Meanwhile, representatives of the great powers convened at Vienna to attempt to restore Europe to its pre-Revolutionary, pre-Napoleonic status, and to devise ways and means of maintaining such a restoration.

Napoleon's escape from Elba, and his recapturing of France by the force of his personality, were only portions of an anticlimax which was settled in a few months on the decisive field of Waterloo. This time he was destined to be sentenced to isolation on St. Helena, a rocky island in mid-Atlantic, a "prison" from which escape was to be provided only by death, in 1821—in his fifty-second year! Part Three of this section is designed to suggest something of the character and achievements of the man.

Thus in 1815 apparently ended the Age of the French Revolution and Napoleon, an age during which the oldest and most civilized of European states had been turned inside out, and Western Europe as a whole had been turned upside down. It would seem, in view of the brief summary of the epoch, that it well merits the special attention which historians have given it. On the other hand, as is suggested in Part Two of this section, opinions are by no means unanimous concerning the significance of the French Revolution.

Time and space preclude the possibility of dealing with more than a few aspects of the French Revolution and Napoleon in this book. Accordingly, we shall approach them through three problems, each of which represents a basic feature of their study. The result may suggest to the reader something of the complexity of one of the most important periods in the history of modern Europe. Attempts at solving these problems will doubtless produce more or less definite conclusions concerning at least three aspects of the French Revolution and Napoleon. Obviously, however, these are not enough—they must be supplemented by further conclusions, not only about other phases of these historical phenomena, but also about each of them as a whole. Unless additional problems are sought and solved, any comprehension of this period of European history will remain sketchy to say the least. Nor would one have any idea of what ultimately came of it.

What additional type of problem will serve as a means of suggesting the breadth of these topics—perhaps also as an introduction to subsequent problems in this book? To what extent did the French Revolution *actually* effect fundamental change in French institutions; in other words, how was the France of 1799 different from and still similar to that of 1789? By what processes were these changes brought about—by legislation or by fiat, by accident or by necessity, by peaceful or by violent action? Why did the "Terror" develop; and was it, in its various forms, unavoidable? To what extent did the changes represent the wishes of the people of France as a whole? Did the aims and objectives of the revolutionaries change during the decade from 1789 to 1799; and if so, how and why? Who were the leaders of the Revolution during its several phases, what type of men were they, and what were their contributions? Why was Napoleon able to take control of the situation in 1799? To what extent did he retain the gains of the Revolution intact; to what extent did he alter them? How and why was Napoleon able to dominate the European scene as he did, for so many years? Why at least did he and his empire fall; or did they really *fall?* And why have both the French Revolution and Napoleon continued to fascinate both the casual and the serious student of history these many generations? Above all, did the French Revolution and the Napoleonic Era come to a full stop in 1815? Or did they both continue to affect the course of French and European history in the years that followed?

I. *What Caused the French Revolution?*

One of the most important factors in the study of history is causation—the reasons why things happen. It is especially significant in the study of revolutions in general and the French Revolution in particular. A revolution, strictly speaking, is any movement which results in *fundamental* change. What causes such movements? Obviously, dissatisfaction with things as they are must have something to do with it. If everyone were satisfied, there would be neither need nor demand for change. Dissatisfaction, however, is apparently never enough in itself to effect change. In order to produce results, it must be made active, through the leadership of individuals who hope for better things. Peculiarly, these persons usually belong to a group which is en-

joying enough benefits to make it desirous of more. They seldom represent the downtrodden elements in the population.

In time the leaders develop or adopt an ideology, which serves as a justification for their demands and provides patterns for their plans. This is where ideas enter the scene. But, no matter how much dissatisfaction, leadership, or ideology, the change is seldom achieved until the existing regime breaks down and provides the "revolutionaries" with an opportunity to assume control of the situation. Then the revolution begins.

Here the problem consists of examining evidence, both primary and secondary, with a view to determining why a revolution came to France, why it came there rather than elsewhere, why it came when it did and in the form which it assumed.

The Evidence of Contemporaries

In dealing with contemporary evidence, certain factors must always be taken into consideration: the authenticity of the evidence; the qualifications of the writer; the extent to which he was an observer or a participant; the degree to which he was motivated by self-interest or prejudice. Here we have accounts by an observer (Young), a participant (Sieyes), and a man who, in a sense, belongs in both categories (Weber). To what extent do these excerpts indicate what contemporaries thought the causes of the French Revolution were?

A. Arthur Young

Unsuccessful as a practical farmer, nevertheless the Englishman Arthur Young (1741–1820) was among the foremost agricultural enthusiasts, authorities, and writers of the eighteenth century. Observant, understanding, and a fine reporter, he set down in *Travels in France* one of the best descriptions of conditions in France prior to the Revolution.

Peasantry in Guienne (10 June, 1787)

Pass Payrac, and meet many poor beggars, which we had not done before. All the country, girls and women, are without shoes or stockings; and the ploughmen at their work have neither sabots nor feet to their stockings. This is a poverty that strikes at the root of national prosperity; a large consumption among the poor being of more consequence than among the rich: the wealth of a nation lies in its circulation and consumption; and the case of poor people abstaining from the use of manufactures of leather and wool ought to be considered as an evil of the first magnitude. It reminded me of the misery of Ireland. . . .

Peasantry in Béarn (12 August, 1787)

A succession of many well built, tight, and COMFORTABLE farming cottages, built of stone, and covered with tiles, . . . and young trees nursed up with such care, that nothing but the fostering attention of the owner could effect anything like it. To every house belongs a farm, perfectly well inclosed, with grass borders mown and neatly kept around the corn fields, with gates to pass from one inclosure to another. . . . There are some parts of England. . . that resemble this country of Bearne; but we have very little that is equal to what I have seen in this ride of twelve miles from Pau to Moneng. It is all in the hands of little proprietors, without the farms being so small as to occasion a vicious and miserable population. It is visible in their new built houses and stables; . . . even in the coops for their poultry, and the sties for their hogs. A peasant does not think of rendering his pig comfortable, if his own happiness hangs by the thread of a nine year lease. . . .

(Paris, 17 October, 1787)

. . .One opinion pervaded the whole company, that they are on the eve of some great revolution in the government: that everything points to it: the confusion in the finances great; with a *deficit* impossible to provide for without the states-general of the kingdom, yet no ideas formed of what would be the consequence of their meeting: no minister existing, or to be looked to in or out of power, with such decisive talents as to promise any other remedy than paliative ones: a prince on the throne, with excellent dispositions, but without the resources of a mind that could govern in such a moment without ministers: a court buried in pleasure and dissipation; and adding to the distress instead of endeavouring to be placed in a more independent situation: a great ferment amongst all ranks of men, who are eager for some change, without knowing what to look to or to hope for: and a strong leaven of liberty, increasing every hour since the American revolution; altogether form a combination of circumstances that promise e'er long to ferment into motion if some master hand of very superior talents and inflexible courage, is not found at the helm to guide events, instead of being driven by them. It is very remarkable that such conversation never occurs but a bankruptcy is a topic: the curious question on which is, *would a bankruptcy occasion a civil war, and a total overthrow of the government?* The answers that I have received to this question appear to be just: such a measure conducted by a man of abilities, vigour, and firmness would certainly not occasion either one or the other. But the same measure, attempted by a man of a different character, might possibly do both. All

agree that the states of the kingdom cannot assemble without more liberty being the consequence; but I meet with so few men that have any just ideas of freedom that I question much the species of this new liberty that is to arise. They know not how to value the privileges of THE PEOPLE: as to the nobility and the clergy, if a revolution added anything to their scale I think it would do more mischief than good. . . .

Arthur Young, *Travels During the Years 1787, 1788, and 1789. Undertaken More Particularly with a View of Ascertaining the Cultivation, Wealth, Resources, and National Prosperity of the Kingdom of France* (London, 1792), pp. 18, 41–42, 66.

B. Abbé Sieyès

The career of Abbé Emmanuel Joseph Sieyès (1748–1836) spanned the Old Régime, the Revolution, the Napoleonic Era, and the Restoration. In public life almost continuously from 1789 to 1815, he first gained recognition through the publication, in 1789, of his provocative pamphlet, "What Is the Third Estate?"

The plan of this pamphlet is very simple. We have three questions to ask:

1st. What is the third estate? Everything.
2nd. What has it been heretofore in the political order? Nothing.
3rd. What does it demand? To become something therein. . . .

CHAPTER I: THE THIRD ESTATE IS A COMPLETE NATION

What are the essentials of national existence and prosperity? *Private* enterprise and *public* functions.

Private enterprise may be divided into four categories: 1st. Since earth and water furnish the raw material for man's needs, the first category will comprise all families engaged in agricultural pursuits. 2nd. Between the original sale of materials and their consumption or use, further workmanship. . .adds to these materials a second value. . .Human industry thus succeeds in improving the benefits of nature

and in increasing the gross produce. . . . Such is the work of the second class. 3rd. Between production and consumption, as well as among the different degrees of production, a group of intermediate agents. . .comes into being; these are the dealers and merchants. . . . 4th. In addition to these three classes of industrious and useful citizens. . .a society needs many private undertakings and endeavors which are *directly* useful or agreeable to the *individual*. This fourth class includes from the most distinguished scientific and liberal professions to the least esteemed domestic services. Such are the labors which sustain society. Who performs them? The third estate.

Public functions likewise. . .may be classified under four well-known headings: the Sword, the Robe, the Church, and the Administration. It is unnecessary to discuss them in detail in order to demonstrate that the third estate everywhere constitutes nineteen-twentieths of them, except that it is burdened with all that is really arduous, with all the tasks that the privileged order refuses to perform. Only the lucrative and honorary positions are held by members of the privileged order. . . .

It suffices here to have revealed that the alleged utility of a privileged order to public service is only a chimera: that without it, the higher positions would be infinitely better filled; that they naturally ought to be the lot of and reward for talents and recognized services; and that if the privileged classes have succeeded in usurping all the lucrative and honorary positions, it is both an odious injustice to the majority of citizens and an act of treason against the state.

Who, then, would dare to say that the third estate has not within itself all that is necessary to constitute a complete nation?...If the privileged order were abolished, the nation would not be something less but something more. Thus, what is the third estate? Everything; but an everything shackled and oppressed. What would it be without the privileged order? Everything; but an everything free and flourishing. Nothing can progress without it; everything would proceed infinitely better without the others....

What is a nation? a body of associates living under a *common* law and represented by the same *legislature*.

Is it not exceedingly clear that the noble order has privileges, exemptions, even rights separate from the rights of the majority of citizens? Thus it deviates from the common order, from the common law. Thus its civil rights already render it a people apart in a great nation....

Also, it enjoys its political rights separately. It has its own representatives, who are by no means charged with representing the people. Its deputation sits apart; ... it is foreign to the nation in principle, since its mandate does not emanate from the people, and in aim, since its purpose is to defend not the general but a special interest.

The third estate, then, comprises everything that appertains to the nation; and whatever is not the third estate may not be regarded as being of the nation. What is the third estate? Everything!

John Hall Stewart, *A Documentary Survey of the French Revolution* (New York: The Macmillan Company, 1951), pp. 42–44.

C. Joseph Weber

Joseph Weber was the foster brother of Marie Antoinette. He was born in 1755, but the place and date of his death remain unknown. He lived at the French Court, and hence witnessed many of the leading events of the Revolution. In the light of modern scholarship, his analysis of revolutions is unusual.

...Thirty different writers might assign thirty different causes for this shock which the world has experienced, and each render his explanation plausible.

The truth is that there are numerous causes of which one may say, "Without that the Revolution would not have happened"; but there is not one which could be put forward as the sole cause of the Revolution.

...I...recognize three primary and immediate causes of the French Revolution: the disorder in the finances, the state of mind, and the war in America.

If order had reigned in the treasury; if the equilibrium between expenditure and

receipts had been perfect; then the ideas of independence, which filled all minds, would have been vented in private circles, in academic sessions, or in a few parliamentary remonstrances; ...

If the general disposition of mind had been, under Louis XVI, what it had been under Louis XIV, or even under half the reign of Louis XV, the disorder of the finances would not have led to any political catastrophe....

...if...there had been no war in America; and there had been sixteen millions less in the national debt; then the disposition of mind would not have suddenly carried theories of peaceful independence to the convulsions and excesses of an actual revolt.

To have prevented the French Revolution, then, one of these three things was necessary: to arrange the finances, to control the trend of thought, or to abandon the American insurgents. By avoiding one of these three causes of disturbance, the other two would have been rendered powerless. Instead, all three were united when they were most potent. A Leopold, a Frederick, a Gustavus might still have found a way to triumph over these; but Louis XVI was born to be the father of a submissive people, and not to be the master of rebellious subjects; the Providence which had destined him to be a great example had given him the constancy of martyrs rather than the courage of heroes, ...

...The character of the unfortunate Louis XVI, and the variance between his particular virtues and the requirements of events, have obviously contributed so much to the success of the Revolution, that I ought perhaps to present them here as a fourth primary cause.... But beyond that, ... lacking one personage, another would have come forward. Whenever, in a great state, the sources of the public treasury have dried up; when the old restraints of rank and subordination are broken down, and there is no firm hand to impose new ones immediately, then it must be expected that vices, passions, and even virtues will enter into a fermentation whose effects will be incalculable.... There will be enthusiasts, dangerous by the very purity of their intentions, and corrupt beings who will willingly cause public misfortune to further their personal interests. There will be youth, avid for novelties, drunk with presumption, and disdaining the experience of centuries; old men, bowed down by the yoke of routine, and understanding nothing except that which exists no longer; ...One will see those ambitious for power and for riches seize, some without discernment and others, without scruple, all means of satiating the passion which torments them. Into this tumult, already so terrible, the discontented, the vindictive, the envious, the ingrate will throw themselves. At first, they will all belong to the classes superior in rank, in fortune, or in education. Soon each will devote all his efforts to move what one calls the brute mass of society, in order to detach some portion of it, and use it against his rivals. Once put into movement, this mass will overwhelm everything, men and projects, opposition and counsel, enemies and leaders.

That is a general description of the French Revolution; it is that of every revolution which breaks out under like circumstances and with like principles.

E. L. Higgins, *The French Revolution as Told by Contemporaries* (Boston: Houghton Mifflin Company, 1938), pp. 1–2. The excerpt comes from Joseph Weber, *Mémoires de Weber concernant Marie Antoinette*, 2 vols. (Paris, 1822), 1, 75–79 (originally published 1804), being vols. 55 and 56 of *Collection des mémoires relatifs à la Révolution francaise...*, ed. Saint-Albin Berville and Jean Francois Barriere, 56 vols. (Paris, 1820–1828).

The Verdict of Historians

Evaluation of verdicts of historians necessitates consideration of their competence and prejudices. It also requires a knowledge of their nationality, their remoteness from the events, the sources available and the extent to which they utilized them, and the possibility that the circumstances of their own time may have motivated their work. The following verdicts come from two French historians, one writing more than a half-century after the events, the other viewing the situation from a distance of a century and a half. How do they compare with each other and with the contemporary evidence? What answer or answers do they provide to the question, "What caused the French Revolution?"

A. Alexis de Tocqueville

In 1855 Alexis de Tocqueville (1805–1859) published perhaps the first serious scholarly analysis of the causes of the Revolution. Influenced by his study of democracy in America, and probably likewise by the fate of the Second Republic, Tocqueville's work indicated a belief in history as a process of continual evolution.

Let it be borne in mind that France was the only country in which the feudal system had preserved its injurious and irritating characteristics, while it had lost all those which were beneficial or useful; and it will seem less surprising that the Revolution which was to abolish the old constitution of Europe should have broken out there rather than elsewhere.

Let it also be borne in mind that France was the only feudal country in which the nobility had lost its old political rights, . . . but had nevertheless retained and even largely increased its pecuniary indemnities and the individual privileges of its members; . . . and it will at once be understood why its privileges seemed so inexplicable and detestable to the French. . . .

Let it be borne in mind, finally, that the nobility was separated from the middle classes, which it had eschewed, and from the people, whose affections it had lost; that it stood alone in the midst of the nation, seemingly the staff of an army, really a group of soldierless officers; and it will be easy to conceive how, after an existence of a thousand years, it was overthrown in a single night.

. . . The royal government abolished the provincial liberties, usurped the place of the local authorities in three fourths of the kingdom, and monopolized public business, great and small; . . . Paris consequently became of necessity the master of the country instead of the capital . . . These two facts, which were peculiar to France, would alone suffice to show how a revolt could achieve the overthrow of a monarchy which had endured so violent shocks during so many centuries . . .

Political life had been so long and so thoroughly extinguished in France—individuals had so entirely lost the habit of mixing in public affairs, of judging for themselves, of studying popular movements, and even understanding the people at all, that the French quite naturally drifted into a terrible revolution without seeing it—the very parties who had most to fear from it taking the lead, and undertaking to smooth and widen the way for its approach.

In the absence of free institutions, and, consequently, of political classes, active political bodies, or organized parties, the duty of leading public opinion, when it revived, naturally fell to the lot of philosophers. Hence it might be expected that the Revolution would be conducted less in view of specific facts than in conformity with abstract principles and general theories. It might be conjectured that, instead of assailing specific laws, it would attack all laws together, and would assume to substitute for the old Constitution of France a new system of government which these writers had conceived.

The Church was mixed with all the old institutions that were to be destroyed. Hence it was plain that the Revolution would shake the religious while it overthrew the civil power; and this done, and men's minds set free from all the restraints which religion, custom, and law impose on reformers, it was impossible to say to what unheard-of lengths of boldness it might not go. . . .

. . . The old government had deprived the French of the power and the desire to help each other. When the Revolution broke out, there were not ten men in the greater part of France who were in the habit of acting in concert, in a regular manner, and providing for their own defense; everything was left to the central power. And so, when that power made way for an irresponsible sovereign assembly, and exchanged its former mildness for ferocity, there was nothing to check or delay it for an instant. The same cause which had overthrown the monarchy had rendered every thing possible after its fall. . . .

To comprehend the contrast between the benign theories and the violent acts of the Revolution, one must remember that it was prepared by the most civilized classes of the nation, and executed by the roughest and unpolished. The former having no bond of mutual union, no common understanding among themselves, no hold on the people, the latter assumed the whole direction of affairs when the old authorities were abolished. Even where they did not govern they inspired the government; and a glance at the way they had lived under the old regime left no room for doubt as to what they would prove. . . .

The careful student of France during the eighteenth century must have noticed. . . the birth and development of two leading passions, which were not coeval, and not always similar in their tendencies.

One—the deepest and most solidly rooted—was a violent, unquenchable hatred of inequality. . . .

The other—of more recent date, and less solidly rooted—prompted men to seek to be free as well as equal.

Toward the close of the old regime these two passions were equally sincere, and apparently equally active; they met at the opening of the Revolution, and, blending together into one, they took fire from contact, and inflamed the whole heart of France.

Alexis C. M. H. C. de Tocqueville, *The Old Regime and the Revolution*, trans. John Bonner (New York: Harper and Brothers, 1856), pp. 246–51.

B. George Lefebvre

Former incumbent of the Professorship of the French Revolution at the Sorbonne, George Lefebvre (1874–1959) was one of the most distinguished scholars in his field. Of his numerous writings, many consider *Quatre-Vingt-Neuf* (1939) one of his most significant contributions, and the best analysis of the causes of the Revolution since Tocqueville. The excerpt is from the English translation of this work.

The ultimate cause of the French Revolution of 1789 goes deep into the history of France and of the western world. At the end of the eighteenth century the social structure of France was aristocratic. It showed the traces of having originated at a time when land was almost the only form of wealth, and when the possessors of land were the masters of those who needed it to work and to live. It is true that in the course of age-old struggles. . . the king had been able gradually to deprive the lords of their political power and subject nobles and clergy to his authority. But he had left them the first place in the social hierarchy. . . .

Meanwhile the growth of commerce and industry had created, step by step, a new form of wealth, mobile or commercial wealth, and a new class, called in France the bourgeoisie, which since the fourteenth century had taken its place as the Third Estate in the General Estates of the kingdom. This class had grown much stronger with the maritime discoveries of the fifteenth and sixteenth centuries and the ensuing exploitation of new worlds, and also because it proved highly useful to the monarchical state in supplying it with money and competent officials. In the eighteenth century commerce, industry and finance occupied an increasingly important place in the national economy. It was the bourgeoisie that rescued the royal treasury in moments of crisis. From its ranks were recruited most members of the liberal professions and most public employees. It had developed a new ideology which the "philosophers" and "economists" of the time had simply put into definite form. The role of the nobility had correspondingly declined; and the clergy, as the ideal which it proclaimed lost prestige, found its authority growing weaker. These groups preserved the highest rank in the legal structure of the country, but in reality economic power, personal abilities and confidence in the future had passed largely to the bourgeoisie. . . . The Revolution of 1789 restored the harmony between fact and law. . . .

But this deeper cause of the French Revolution does not explain all its distinctive features. In England, though there have been political revolutions, social evolution has gone on in relative calm. The French Revolution was realized by violence. . . . In France the Third Estate liberated itself. Hence the older aristocracy long preserved more wealth and influence in other countries than in France. These special features of the Revolution in France arose from its immediate causes, and especially from the collapse of the central power which in other countries was able to keep events under control.

There would have been no French Revolution—such as actually took place— if the king, "handing in his resignation," had not convoked the Estates General. The immediate cause lay in a government emergency for which Louis XVI could find no other solution. But the Third Estate was by no means the first to profit from the emergency, contrary to the general opinion, taken over from the Revolutionists themselves, who declared *ad nauseam* that "the people rose up and overthrew despotism and aristocracy." No doubt it did end that way. But the people were not the original motive force. The bourgeoisie, having no legal means of expression, was in no position to force the king to appeal to the nation. Still less were the peasants and the working classes. The privileged groups did have the necessary means: the clergy in its Assembly, the nobility in the Parliaments and the Provincial Estates. It is these bodies that forced the king's hand. ...The first act of the Revolution, in 1788, consisted in a triumph of the aristocracy, which, taking advantage of the government crisis, hoped to reassert itself and win back the political authority of which the Capetian dynasty had despoiled it. But, after having paralyzed the royal power which upheld its own social preeminence, the aristocracy opened the way to the bourgeois revolution, then to the popular revolution in the cities and finally to the revolution of the peasants—and found itself buried under the ruins of the Old Regime. ...

Georges Lefebvre, *The Coming of the French Revolution,* trans. R. R. Palmer (Princeton: Princeton University Press, 1947), pp. 1–3.

II. Was the French Revolution a "Good Thing" or a "Bad Thing"?

Ordinarily professional historians are but little concerned with the "goodness' or "badness" of the events which they record and interpret. Most observers, writers, and readers, however, are apt to view historical movements (especially such comprehensive movements as the French Revolution) as harmful or beneficial—to some people, to some places, at the time, or subsequently. In this part of our problem we have adequate evidence to suggest that few are immune to prejudice of one sort or another.

In the Eyes of Contemporaries

The factors to be considered in examining the opinions of persons contemporaneous with the events they are discussing have already been indicated. Whether the two contemporaries whose works are presented here were right or wrong, it is indeed possible to decide what each of them thought of the Revolution and of each other's evaluation of it. Their words also suggest that British opinion on the Revolution was by no means unanimous.

A. Edmund Burke

A Protestant Irishman, Edmund Burke (1729–1797) was a leading statesman, orator, and political theorist in Great Britain. Perhaps his greatest work was *Reflections* (1790), attacking the French Revolution, provoking replies from Mackintosh and Paine, and considered by many the most influential political pamphlet ever written.

...Abstractedly speaking, government, as well as liberty, is good; yet could I, in common sense, ten years ago, have felicitated France on her enjoyment of a government...without inquiry what the nature of that government was, or how it was administered? Can I now congratulate the same nation upon its freedom?...

...I must be tolerably sure, before I venture publicly to congratulate men upon a blessing, that they have really received one....I should therefore suspend my congratulations on the new liberty of France, until I was informed how it had been combined with government; with publick force; with the discipline and obedience of armies; with the collection of an effective and well-distributed revenue;

with morality and religion; with solidity and property; with peace and order; with civil and social manners. All these (in their way) are good things too; and, without them, liberty is not a benefit whilst it lasts, and is not likely to continue long. The effect of liberty to individuals is, that they may do what they please; we ought to see what it will please them to do, before we risk congratulations, which may be soon turned into complaints.... liberty, when men act in bodies, is power. Considerate people, before they declare themselves, will observe the use which is made of *power;* and particularly of so trying a thing as *new* power in *new* persons, of whose principles, tempers, and dispositions they have little or no experience, and in situations, where those who appear the most stirring in the scene may possibly not be the real movers....

...from Magna Charta to the Declaration of Right, it has been the uniform policy of our constitution to claim and assert our liberties, as an *entailed inheritance* derived to us from our forefathers, and to be transmitted to our posterity; as an estate specially belonging to the people of this kingdom, without any reference whatever to any other more general or prior right. By this means our constitution preserves a unity in so great a diversity of its parts....

...A spirit of innovation is generally the result of a selfish temper, and confined views. People will not look forward to posterity, who never look backward to their ancestors.... the idea of inheritance furnishes a sure principle of conservation, and a sure principle of transmission; without at all excluding a principle of improvement.... by preserving the method of nature in the conduct of the state, in what we improve, we are never wholly new; and in what we retain, we are never wholly obsolete. By adhering in this manner and on those principles to our forefathers, we are guided not by the superstition of antiquarians, but by the spirit of philosophick analogy....

Compute your gains: ... France has bought undisguised calamities at a higher price than any nation has purchased the most unequivocal blessings! France has bought poverty by crime! ... France, when she let loose the reins of regal authority, doubled the licence of a ferocious dissoluteness in manners, and of an insolent irreligion in opinions and practices; and has extended through all ranks of life ...all the unhappy corruptions that usually were the disease of wealth and power. This is one of the new principles of equality in France.

...Laws overturned; tribunals subverted; industry without vigour; commerce expiring; the revenue unpaid, yet the people impoverished; a church pillaged, and a state not relieved; civil and military anarchy made the constitution of the kingdom; everything human and divine sacrificed to the idol of publick credit, and national bankruptcy the consequence; and, to crown all, the paper securities of new, precarious, tottering power, the discredited paper securities of impoverished fraud and beggared rapine, held out as a currency for the support of an empire...

Were all these dreadful things necessary? Were they the inevitable results of the desperate struggle of determined patriots, compelled to wade through blood and tumult, to the quiet shore or a tranquil and prosperous liberty? No! nothing like it. The fresh ruins of France, which shock our feelings wherever we can turn our eyes, are not the devastation of civil war; they are the sad but instructive monuments of rash and ignorant counsel in time of profound peace....

...those who attempt to level, never equalise. In all societies, consisting of various descriptions of citizens, some descriptions must be uppermost. The levellers, therefore only change and pervert the natural order of things; ...

It is said that twenty-four millions ought to prevail over two hundred thousand. True; if the constitution of a kingdom be a problem of arithmetick.... to men who *may* reason calmly, it is ridiculous....

...In denying their false claims of right, I do not mean to injure those which are real, and are such as their pretended rights would totally destroy.... Men... have a right to do justice, as between their fellows...They have a right to the fruits of their industry; and to the means of making their industry fruitful. They have a right to the acquisitions of their parents; to the nourishment and improvement of their offspring; to instruction in life, and to consolation in death. Whatever each man can separately do, without trespassing upon others, he has a right to do for himself; and he has a right to a fair portion of all which society, with all its combinations of skill and force, can do in his favour. In this partnership all men have equal rights; but not to equal things. He that has but five shillings in the partnership, has as good a right to it, as he that has five hundred pounds has to his larger proportion. But he has not a right to an equal dividend in the product of the joint stock; and as to the share of power, authority, and direction which each individual ought to have in the management of the state, that I must deny to be amongst the direct original rights of man in civil society; ...

Government is not made in virtue of natural rights, which may and do exist in total independence of it; and exist in much greater clearness, and in a much greater degree of abstract perfection: but their abstract perfection is their practical defect. By having a right to everything they want everything. Government is a contrivance of human wisdom to provide for human *wants*. Men have a right that these wants should be provided for by this wisdom. Among these wants is to be reckoned the want, out of civil society, of a sufficient restraint upon their passions.... In this sense the restraints on men, as well as their liberties, are to be reckoned among their rights. But as the liberties and the restrictions vary with times and circumstances, and admit of infinite modifications, they cannot be settled upon any abstract rule; and nothing is so foolish as

to discuss them upon that principle....

The science of constructing a commonwealth, or renovating it, or reforming it, is, like every other experimental science, not to be taught *a priori*. Nor is it a short experience that can instruct us in that practical science; ... The science of government being therefore so practical in itself, and intended for such practical purposes, a matter which requires experience, ... it is with infinite caution that any man ought to venture upon pulling down an edifice which has answered in any tolerable degree for ages the common purposes of society, or on building it up again, without having models and patterns of approved utility before his eyes....

I do not know under what description to class the present ruling authority in France. It affects to be a pure democracy, though I think it in a direct train of becoming shortly a mischievous and ignoble oligarchy. But for the present I admit it to be a contrivance of the nature and effect of what it pretends to. I reprobate no form of government merely upon abstract principles. There may be situations in which the purely democratick form will become necessary. There may be some...where it would be clearly desirable. This I do not take to be the case of France, or of any other great country. Until now, we have seen no examples of considerable democracies. The ancients were better acquainted with them.... If I recollect rightly, Aristotle observes, that a democracy has many striking points of resemblance with a tyranny. Of this I am certain, that in a democracy, the majority of the citizens is capable of exercising the most cruel oppression upon the minority, whenever strong divisions prevail in that kind of polity, as they often must; and that oppression of the minority will extend to far greater numbers, and will be carried on with much greater fury, than can almost ever be apprehended from the dominion of a single sceptre....

Edmund Burke, *Reflections on the Revolution in France, and on the Proceedings in Certain Societies in London Relative to that Event. In a Letter Intended To Have Been Sent to a Gentleman in Paris* (1790), in *The Works of the Right Honourable Edmund Burke,* 8 vols. (Boston: Wells and Lilly, 1826–27), III, 24, 25, 50, 51, 55, 67, 70, 77, 78–80, 145–47.

B. Thomas Paine

Migrating from England to America in 1774, Thomas Paine (1737–1809) became a leading republican propagandist. In 1787 he returned to his native land, and in 1791–1792 published *Rights of Man* as a reply to Burke. Forced to flee to France, he became a member of the Convention. He died in America.

1. (Preface to the French edition)

The astonishment which the French Revolution has caused throughout Europe should be considered from two different points of view: first as it affects foreign peoples, secondly as it affects their governments.

The cause of the French people is that of all Europe, or rather of the whole world; but the governments of all those countries are by no means favorable to it. It is important that we should never lose sight of this distinction. We must not confuse the peoples with their governments; especially not the English people with its government.

The government of England is no friend to the revolution of France. . . .

The English nation, on the contrary, is very favorably disposed towards the French Revolution, and to the progress of liberty in the whole world; . . .

2. (Rights of Man)

There never did, there never will, and there never can, exist a Parliament, or any description of men, or any generation of men, in any country, possessed of the right or the power of binding and controlling posterity to the *"end of time,"* or of commanding forever how the world shall be governed, or who shall govern it; . . . Every age and generation must be as free to act for itself, *in all cases,* as the ages and generations which preceded it. The vanity and presumption of governing beyond the grave is the most ridiculous and insolent of all tyrannies. . . . It is the living, and not the dead, that are to be accommodated. . . .

I am not contending for nor against any form of government, nor for nor against any party, here or elsewhere. That which a whole nation chooses to do, it has a right to do. Mr. Burke says, No. Where, then, does the right exist? I am contending for the rights of the *living,* and against their being willed away, and controlled and contracted for, by the manuscript assumed authority of the dead; and Mr. Burke is contending for the authority of the dead over the rights and freedom of the living. . . .

It was not against Louis XVIth but against the despotic principles of the Government, that the nation revolted. These principles had not their origin in him, but in the original establishment; many centuries back: and they were become too deeply rooted to be removed, and the Augean stables of parasites and plunderers too abominably filthy to be cleansed by anything short of a complete and universal Revolution. . . .

Mr. Burke does not attend to the distinction between men and principles, and, therefore, he does not see that a revolt may take place against the despotism of the latter, while there lies no charge of despotism against the former. . . .

. . . There were . . . a thousand despotisms to be reformed in France, which had grown up under the hereditary despotism of the monarchy, and became so rooted as to be in a great measure independent of it. . . . But Mr. Burke, by considering the king as the only possible object of a revolt, speaks as if France was a village, in which everything that passed must be known to its commanding officer, and no oppression could be acted but what he could immediately control. . . .

. . . Man did not enter into society to become *worse* than he was before, nor to have fewer rights than he had before, but to have those rights better secured. His natural rights are the foundation of all his civil rights. . . .

. . . Natural rights are those which appertain to man in right of his existence. Of this kind are all the intellectual rights, or rights of the mind, and also those rights of acting as an individual for his own comfort and happiness, which are not injurious to the natural rights of others. Civil rights are those which appertain to man in right of his being a member of society. Every civil right has for its foundation some natural right pre-existing in the individual, but to the enjoyment of which his individual power is not, in all cases, sufficiently competent. Of this kind are all those which relate to security and protection. . . .

It was the error of. . . all those who were unacquainted with the affairs of France to confound the French nation with the French Government. The French nation, in effect, endeavoured to render the late Government insolvent for the purpose of taking government into its own hands: and it reserved its means for the support of the new Government. . . .

There is a general enigma running through the whole of Mr. Burke's book. He writes in a rage against the National Assembly; but what is he enraged about? If his assertions were as true as they are groundless, and that France by her Revolution, had annihilated her power, and become what he calls a *chasm*, it might excite the grief of a Frenchman. . . and provoke his rage against the National Assembly; but why should it excite the rage of Mr. Burke? Alas! it is not the nation of France that Mr. Burke means, but the Court; and every Court in Europe, dreading the same fate, is in mourning. He writes neither in the character of a Frenchman nor an Englishman, but in the fawning character of that creature known in all countries, and a friend to none—a courtier. . . . Nothing can be more terrible to a Court or Courtier than the Revolution of France. . . .

From the Revolutions of America and France, and the symptoms that have appeared in other countries, it is evident that the opinion of the world is changing with respect to systems of Government, and that revolutions are not within the compass of political calculations. The progress of time and circumstances, which men assign to the accomplishment of great changes, is too mechanical to measure the force of the mind, and the rapidity of reflection, by which revolutions are gen-

erated: All the old governments have received a shock from those that already appear, and which were once more improbable, and are greater subject of wonder, than a general revolution in Europe would be now.

When we survey the wretched condition of man, under the monarchical and hereditary systems of Government, . . . it becomes evident that those systems are bad, and that a general revolution in the principle and construction of Governments is necessary.

What is government more than the management of the affairs of a Nation? It is not, and from its nature cannot be, the property of any particular man or family, but of the whole community, at whose expence it is supported; and though by force and contrivance it has been usurped into an inheritance, the usurpation cannot alter the right of things. Sovereignty, as a matter of right, appertains to the Nation only, and not to any individual; and a Nation has at all times an inherent indefeasible right to abolish any form of Government it finds inconvenient, and to establish such as accords with its interest, disposition and happiness. . . .

When men think of what Government is, they must necessarily suppose it to possess a knowledge of all the objects and matters upon which its authority is to be exercised. In this view of Government, the republican system, as established by America and France, operates to embrace the whole of a Nation; and the knowledge necessary to the interest of all the parts, is to be found in the center, which the parts by representation form: But the old Governments are on a construction that excludes knowledge as well as happiness; . . . .

What were formerly called Revolutions, were little more than a change of persons, or an alteration of local circumstances. . . . But what we now see in the world, from the Revolutions of America and France, are a renovation of the natural order of things, a system of principles as universal as truth and the existence of man, and combining moral with political happiness and national prosperity....

As it is not difficult to perceive, from the enlightened state of mankind, that hereditary Governments are verging to their decline, and that Revolutions on the broad basis of national sovereignty and Government by representation, are making their way in Europe, it would be an act of wisdom to anticipate their approach, and produce Revolutions by reason and accommodation, rather than commit them to the issue of convulsions.

From what we now see, nothing of reform in the political world ought to be held improbable. It is an age of Revolutions, in which everything may be looked for....

Thomas Paine, *Rights of Man; Being an Answer to Mr. Burke's Attack on the French Revolution,* ed. Moncure Daniel Conway (New York: G. P. Putnam's Sons, 1895), p. 272, 273, 277, 278, 283–85, 306, 379, 381, 385, 386, 389.

In the Eyes of "Classic" Historians

A "classic" historian is more than one who has enjoyed great popularity but is now seldom read. He is a writer whose works are of value more for the opinions they present and the manner in which they reflect trends in historical writing than for the data they contain. Frequently written to justify or to denounce something, these books were often based on inadequate research—if only because the sources were not available. "Classic" historians of the French Revolution are legion, especially in France. In general their efforts represent attempts to evaluate the Revolution in the light of its extension into the history of France during the first three quarters of the nineteenth century. The two presented here are suggestive of the diverse points of view of the movement. What were the attitudes held by these men? Why did they hold them?

A. François Mignet

Scholar, journalist, liberal, François Mignet (1796–1884) left his native Provence for Paris in 1821. Three years later he published his history of the Revolution, one of the first formal studies of the movement, as a critique of the reactionary Bourbon monarchy of Charles X. The work long enjoyed popularity.

...This revolution not only modified the political power, but it entirely changed the internal existence of the nation.... France was in an utter confusion of arbitrary administration, of class legislation and special privileges to special bodies. For these abuses the revolution substituted a system more conformable with justice, and better suited to our times. It substituted law in the place of arbitrary will, equality in that of privilege; delivered men from the distinctions of classes, the land from the barriers of provinces, trade from the shackles of corporations and fellowships, agriculture from feudal subjection and the oppression of tithes, property from the impediment of entails, and brought everything to the condition of one state, one system of law, one people.

In order to effect such mighty reformation as this, the revolution had many obstacles to overcome, involving transient excesses with durable benefits. The privileged sought to prevent it, Europe to subject it; and thus forced into a struggle, it could not set bounds to its efforts, or moderate its victory. Resistance from within brought about the sovereignty of the multitude, and aggression from without, military domination. Yet the end was attained, in spite of anarchy and in spite of despotism: the old society was destroyed during the revolution, and the new one became established under the empire....

The constitution of 1791...was, however, less democratic than that of the United States, which had been practicable, despite the extent of the territory, proving that it is not the form of institutions, but the assent which they obtain, or the dissent which they excite, which permits or hinders their establishment. In a new country, after a revolution of independence, as in America, any constitution is possible; there is but one hostile party, that of the metropolis, and when that is overcome, the struggle ceases, because defeat leads to its expulsion. It is not so with social revolutions among nations who have long been in existence. Changes attack interests, interests form parties, parties enter into contest, and the more victory spreads the greater grows opposition. This is what happened in France. The work of the constituent assembly perished less from its defects than from the attacks of faction. Placed between the aristocracy and the multitude, it was attacked by the one and invaded by the other. The latter would not have become sovereign, had not civil war and the foreign coalition called for its intervention and aid. To defend the country, it became necessary that it should govern it; then it effected its revolution, as the middle class had effected its own. . . .

The French Revolution. . .had two wholly distinct objects; that of a free constitution, and that of a more perfect state of civilization. . . . The privileged classes wished to establish their régime against the court and the bourgeoisie, by preserving orders and the states-general; the bourgeoisie sought to establish its régime against the privileged classes and the multitude, by the constitution of 1791; and the multitude wished to establish its régime against all the others by the constitution of 1793. Not one of these governments could become consolidated, because they were all exclusive. But during their attempts each class, in power for a time, destroyed of the higher classes all that was intolerant or calculated to oppose the progress of modern civilization.

When the directory succeeded the convention the struggle between the classes was greatly weakened. The higher ranks of each formed a party which still contended for the possession and for the form of government; but the mass of the nation, which had been so profoundly agitated from 1789 to 1795, longed to become settled again, and to arrange itself according to the new order of things. This period witnessed the end of the movement for liberty, and the beginning of the movement towards civilization. The revolution now took its second character, its character of order, foundation, repose, after the agitation, the immense toil, and system of complete demolition of its early years.

This second period was remarkable, inasmuch as it seemed a kind of abandonment of liberty. . . . it was liberal under the directory and at the commencement of the Consulate, and military at the close of the Consulate and under the empire. . . . after having made a nation of sectaries it made a nation of working men, and then it made a nation of soldiers.

Many illusions were already destroyed; men had passed through so many different states, had lived so much in so few years, that all ideas were confounded and all creeds shaken. The reign of the middle class and that of the multitude had passed away. . . . They were far from that France of the 14th of July, with its deep conviction, its high morality, its assembly exercising the all-powerful sway of liberty and of reason. . . . They were far from the more sombre and more tempestuous France of the 10th of August, when a single class held the government and society, and had introduced therein its language, manners, and costume, the agitation of its fears, the fanaticism of its ideas, the distrust of its position. Then private life entirely gave place to public life; the republic presented, in turn, the aspect of an assembly and of a camp; the rich were subject to the poor; the creed of democracy combined with the gloomy and ragged administration of the people. At each of these periods men had been strongly attached to some idea; first to liberty and constitutional monarchy, afterwards, to equality, fraternity, and the republic. But at the beginning of the directory there was belief in nothing; . . .

François A. M. A. Mignet, *History of the French Revolution from 1789 to 1814,* trans. from the French (London: G. Bell and Sons, 1885) [Bohn's Standard Library], p. 1–3, 313–15.

B. Hippolyte A. Taine

Following a treatise on the Old Régime (1875), Hippolyte A. Taine (1828–1892), scholar extraordinary, produced three volumes on the Revolution (1878–1884). "Scientific" in approach, analytical rather than narrative, his work reflects an attempt to explain the misfortunes of France at the close of the Second Empire.

...In several of its laws...it [the Constituent Assembly] planted good seed. But in all that relates to political institutions and social organization its proceedings are those of an academy of Utopians, and not those of practical legislators.... it carried out its principle to the end, the principle of Rousseau. It deliberately refused to consider man as he really was under its own eyes, and persisted in seeing nothing in him but the abstract being created in books.... the Assembly destroyed on the one hand the time-honoured, spontaneous, and lasting societies formed by geographical position, history, common occupations and interests, and on the other, those natural chiefs whose name, repute, education, independence, and earnestness designated them as the best qualified to occupy high positions. In one direction it despoils and permits the ruin and proscription of the superior class.... In another it dispossesses and breaks up all historic or natural corporations.... Nothing remains but individual particles, twenty-six millions of equal and disconnected atoms. Never was so much disintegrated matter, less capable of resistance, offered to hands undertaking to mould it.... As awkward in destruction as it is in construction, it invents for the restoration of order in a society which is turned upside down a machine which would, of itself, create disorder in a tranquil society.... The masterpiece of ideal abstractions and of practical absurdities is perfected; spontaneous anarchy, by means of the Constitution, becomes legalized anarchy....

...Whatever the grand terms of liberty, equality, and fraternity may be, with which the Revolution graces itself, it is, in its essence, a *transfer of property;* in this alone consists its chief support, its enduring energy, its primary impulse and its historical significance....

The worst feature of anarchy is not so much the absence of the overthrown government as the rise of new governments of an inferior grade. Every fallen State produces bands which conquer and which are sovereign;...born enemies of work, of subordination, and of the law—form leagues for breaking down the worm-eaten barriers which still surround the sheep-like masses; and as they are unscrupulous, they slaughter on all occasions. On this foundation their authority rests;...their government, in keeping with its brutal masters, consists in robbery and murder; nothing else can be looked for from barbarians and brigands.

But never are they so dangerous as when, in a great State recently fallen, a sudden revolution places the central power in their hands; for they then regard themselves as the legitimate inheritors of the shattered government, and, under this title, they undertake to manage the commonwealth.... The important and dominant personage, the one whose ideas prevail,... is here the subordinate Jacobin, the pillar of the club, the maker of motions, the street rioter,...the faubourg cannoneer, the drinking market-porter who elaborates his political conceptions in the interval between his hiccoughs.—For information he has the rumours circulating in the streets which assign a traitor to each domicile, and for other acquisitions the club bombast, through which he becomes the leader of the great machine. This machine so vast, so complex,...transcends his limited comprehension;...In his narrow brain, perverted and turned topsy-turvy by the disproportionate notions put into it, only one idea suited to his gross instincts and aptitudes finds a place there, and that is the desire to kill his enemies; and these are also the State's enemies, however open or concealed, present or future, probable or even possible. He carries this savagery and bewilderment into politics, and hence the evil arising from his usurpation....

...The rulers of the country have brought with them into power the prejudices and sensibilities of the epoch; under the empire of the prevailing dogma they have deferred to the will of the multitude and, with too much faith in the rights of man, they have had too little in the rights of the magistrate; moreover, through humanity, they have abhorred bloodshed and, unwilling to repress, they have allowed themselves to be repressed.... while their constitutions, so many unhealthy products of theory and fear, have done no more than transform spontaneous anarchy into legal anarchy.... On the strength of this a faction arises which ends in becoming an organized band: under its clamorings...the majorities are all silenced, while the minorities vote, decree, and govern;... Of all the garrisons of the central citadel...not one has been able to defend itself, to refashion the executive instrument, to draw the sword and use it in the streets: on the first attack, often at the first summons, all have surrendered, and now the citadel, with every other public fortress, is in the hands of the Jacobins.

This time, its occupants are of a different stamp. Aside from the great mass of well-disposed people fond of a quiet life, the Revolution has sifted out and separated from the rest all who are fanatical, brutal or perverse enough to have lost respect for others; these form the new garrison.... None of this class are scrupulous concerning human life or property; for...they have shaped the theory to suit themselves, and reduced popular sovereignty to their sovereignty. The commonwealth, according to the Jacobin, is his;...everything belongs to him; the fact of being a Jacobin makes him legitimately czar and pope....his mandate does not emanate from a vote; it descends to him from aloft, conferred on him by Truth, by Reason, by Virtue. As he alone is enlightened, and the only patriot, he alone is worthy to take command, while resistance, according to his imperious pride, is criminal. If the majority protests it is because the majority is imbecile or corrupt; in either case, it merits a check, and a check it shall have. Accordingly, the Jacobin does nothing else from the outset;...there is no outrage not committed by him....if he hesitates he knows he is lost; to save himself from the scaffold he has no refuge but in a dictatorship....

Hippolyte A. Taine, *The French Revolution*, trans. John Durand, 3 vols. (New York: Henry Holt and Co., 1878–1885), I, 214–16; II, 196–98; III, 2–3.

In the Eyes of Modern Historians

Despite the beginnings of the "scientific" study of the French Revolution in the latter part of the nineteenth century, modern historians of the movement are apt to be quite as subjective in their judgments as were their "classic" predecessors. Particularly is this true of Frenchmen, to whom the Revolution is still a living thing. To conservatives it appears to have been a great mistake. To liberals it is apt to be considered an uncompleted mission. To radicals it may seem something which was only begun, and the fulfillment of which lies far ahead. Hence French writers still differ in their interpretations of the Revolution. What points of view may be discerned in the excerpts which follow? How are they similar to or different from those of the "classic" historians? What kind of account of the Revolution might be written by combining these "modern" approaches with those of their "classic" counterparts?

A. Alphonse Aulard

Alphonse Aulard (1849–1928) was the first holder of the Professorship of the French Revolution at the Sorbonne. A prodigious worker and exceptionally erudite, he completed his general history of the Revolution in 1901. This represented a new, authoritative statement of the "political" aspects of the movement.

(Preface)

...I propose to show how the principles of the Declaration of Rights were, between 1789 and 1804, put into operation by the institutions of the time; or interpreted by speeches, by the press, by the policies of the various political parties, and by the manifestations of public opinion. Two of these principles, the principle of the equality of rights, and the principle of national sovereignty, were those most often invoked in the elaboration of the new state politic. They are, historically, the essential principles of the Revolution;... The chief object of this book is the narration of the vicissitudes which these two principles underwent.

In other words, I wish to write the political history of the Revolution from the point of view of the origin and the development of Democracy and Republicanism.

Democracy is the logical consequence of the principle of equality. Republicanism is the logical consequence of the principle of national sovereignty....

(Conclusion)

Had I a historical thesis to sustain, or a train of reasoning to develop, in order to demonstrate the truth of a proposition, a logical conclusion would have been necessary. But I have merely attempted to narrate, objectively, and without any preconceived idea, the political history of the Revolution, from the point of view of the origin and development of democracy and the Republic....

I wish...not to write a conclusion..., but to suggest a few ideas which are too general in their nature to have found a fitting place at any particular point of the narrative, but which disengage themselves only from the whole mass of facts.

1. It is a mistake to say that the French Revolution was effected by a few distinguished individuals, by a few supermen...no individual emerges from the history of the ten years between 1789 and 1799 as the master of events:... Can we say that the French nation was the hero, the true super-man of the French Revolution? Yes; if we see the French nation not as a multitude, but in a condition of organized groups....

2. The Revolution was realised only partly and for a time. It was even suspended, and appeared to be abolished, during the rule of Napoleon I;...Why?—because the French people were not sufficiently educated to wield its own sovereignty....

3. It has been said that the generation which performed such great and terrible deeds was a generation of giants; or, to be more literal, that it was a more competent and remarkable generation than that which preceded it or that which followed. This is a retrospective illusion. The citizens who formed the various groups...by which the Revolution was effected, do not seem to have been superior either in talent or in enlightenment to the Frenchmen of the time of Louis XV or that of Louis-Philippe.... The generation of 1789 and 1793 was neither superior nor inferior; it was an average generation. Perhaps we may safely say that when first the guillotine and then proscription had deprived it of its most distinguished individuals it fell somewhat below the average; and that this was one of the circumstances which allowed Bonaparte to dominate it and cast it into slavery....

4. ...People used to denote, by the same phrase, both the principles which constitute the French Revolution and the actions consistent with those principles, and the period during which the Revolution was effected, with all the actions, consistent with or in contradiction to those principles, performed during that period. This confusion was as harmful to the truth as it was useful to the supporters of the retrograde policy, as it allowed one to attribute to the Revolution, considered as a sort of historical personage, the most grievous or even the most anti-revolutionary laws or actions.... This abusive manner of speaking—"The Revolution did or didn't do so-and-so"—has had the result that many people see in the Revolution a

kind of incoherent power; capricious, violent and sanguinary. It has been attempted thus to discredit the very principles of the Revolution; especially by the pains and to the profit of those who regard these principles as *satanic*, and who would govern society by the reverse of these principles. For the rest, all the political parties of the nineteenth century have pleaded their cause by means of arguments drawn from anything or everything that happened between 1789 and 1799; and these facts, taken at random or ingeniously selected, they have called *the French Revolution*. Now, I fancy, matters are clearer: the Revolution consists in the Declaration of Rights drafted in 1789 and completed in 1793, and the attempts made to realise that declaration; the counter-Revolution consists in the attempts made to prevent the French from acting in conformity with the principles of the Declaration of Rights; that is to say, according to reason, elucidated by history.

The French Revolution is, so to speak, a political, social, and rational ideal, which Frenchmen have attempted partially to realise, and which historians have attempted to confound either with its application, often incoherent, as far as it was effected, or with the events provoked by the very enemies of that ideal, with a view to abolishing or obscuring it. This book will, I hope, have contributed to dissipate this dangerous ambiguity.

5. The Imperial despotism arrested the Revolution, and marked a retrogression towards the principles of the *ancien régime;* provisionally abolishing liberty and partially abolishing equality. But they were rather the political results of the Revolution than the social which were thus suppressed.... and this it is that explains why, after its fall, when these results were contested by the returned royalists, that very Napoleon Bonaparte who disorganized the political work of the Revolution as completely as he possibly could, appeared to be, and was able to call himself, "the man of the Revolution."

François Victor Alphonse Aulard, *The French Revolution, A Political History, 1789–1804,* trans. Bernard Miall, 4 vols. (New York: Charles Scribner's Sons, 1910), I, 9; IV, 277–82. Reprinted with the permission of Charles Scribner's Sons.

B. Pierre Gaxotte

Pierre Gaxotte (born 1895) published his interpretation of the Revolution in 1928. Providing an interesting comparison with Taine, it must be viewed in the light of Gaxotte's attitude towards the Third Republic as the heir of the Revolution, and his concern with communism as part of the inheritance.

The France of the old regime was a very great and ancient structure in building which fifty generations had been engaged for more than fifteen centuries.... taking it all in all, the total effect was rich, the faccade was imposing, and those who lived in it were better off and more numerous than elsewhere....

Distress may cause riots, but cannot produce revolutions. These latter are due to more deep-lying causes, and in 1789 the French were not in distress. On the contrary,... the country had considerably increased in wealth since the middle of the century and..., with the exception of the country gentry, the material condition of all classes of society had sensibly improved....

Before the Revolution France was not unhappy. She had reason to complain, but not to revolt. Of the two great problems which demanded her attention—the abolition of the relics of feudalism and financial reform—neither would have been insoluble if the soul of France had not been stirred to its depths by an intellectual and moral crisis. This complicated the slightest conflicts and rendered a situation which was merely difficult, first disquieting and then desperate.

The tragedy of the eighteenth century lies, indeed, not in its wars nor in the "days" (*journées*) of the Revolution, but in the dissolution and reversal of the ideas which had illumined and dominated the seventeenth. Riots and massacres were but the bloody and signal expression of this fact; for, long before these happened, the real harm had already been done.

...The writers, reacting on the societies, and the societies on the writers, it came about that the unconscious band of brothers found themselves carried away by an increasingly rapid movement "towards the advent of a certain intellectual and moral type which no one had foreseen, of which everyone would disapprove, yet for which all were preparing the way": the socialistic Jacobin of 1793.

This evolution was hastened by the revolt of the American colonies against Great Britain....

The trial of the King is one of the most moving tragedies in all history.... But for those who are interested in the sequence of events it is above all necessary to throw light on the political reasons for his prosecution and punishment. The reasoning of the Montagnards was terrible in its simplicity: it was necessary to guillotine the King in order to make regicide the emblem and proof of republican sincerity. The question of whether or no the King was to die would divide the deputies and show the numbers on either side. Those who rejected the death penalty were to be accused of royalism, treason, and commerce with the *émigrés* and Austrians. Those who voted for it would remain indissolubly united by fear of a reaction.... The trial of the King was to mark the end of the *bourgeois* Republic, just as the declaration of war had meant the end of the Constitutional Monarchy....

...The more firmly the Revolutionary Government was established, the more sanguinary it became, and the more actively the guillotine was kept at work.... The Terror was of the very essence of the Revolution, because the Revolution was not merely a change in the system of government, but a social revolution, an attempt at expropriation and extermination.

While the armies, under pressure from the enemy, recovered the normal conditions of effective action..., France was subjected at home to a communistic experiment which was to leave her bled white, ruined, and ready to surrender to the first saviour who would present himself....

Communism was inconceivable without an unexampled display of coercion and force, and it was this which was the real significance of the Terror, and explained its development and duration. The terrorist dictatorship was connected with the social laws, and not with military events.... the Terror was organized at the very time when the danger from abroad was diminishing. It was reduced to a code when the frontiers had been cleared of the enemy, and it reached its high-water mark when the French arms were victorious....

The despotism of Liberty, the dogmatism of Reason—such were the names given by the revolutionists to the system of government which they had set up.... Let us say, more simply, that it was the reign of the Social Contract—"the handing over of the individual, with all his rights, to the community," in strict accordance with the rule laid down by Rousseau....

For forty years the clubs and societies had been elaborating their ideas and purging themselves of the dissident elements, and their work was now accomplished. In accordance with strict logic their doctrines had developed, through successive stages, from anarchic Liberalism to Communist dictatorship....

Communism, being a regime contrary to nature, could engender nothing but distress and ruin. The whole system of regulation, bureaucracy, inquisition, coercion, tribunals and the guillotine was bankrupt, completely and absolutely bankrupt. Never had so many and such terrible expedients been adopted to attain so piteous and humiliating an end—a France reduced to famine and living only by fraud or on succour from abroad....

...In the course of ten years the Revolution had falsified all calculations and disappointed all hopes. The benefits which had been expected of it were an ordered and stable government, sound finance, wise laws, peace abroad, and tranquillity at home. Instead of which there had been anarchy, war, communism, the Terror, insolvency, famine, and two or three bankruptcies. The Napoleonic dictatorship reconciled the need for authority with democratic ideology. It was an expedient of

theorists at their wits' end. The doctrinaires of 1789 had aimed at regenerating humanity and reconstructing the world. In order to escape the Bourbons, the doctrinaires of 1799 were reduced to trusting to the sword.

Pierre Gaxotte, *The French Revolution,* trans. Walter Alison Phillips (New York: Charles Scribner's Sons, 1932), p. 2, 21, 38, 40, 53, 54, 235, 288, 289, 303, 306, 307, 314, 410. Reprinted by permission of Charles Scribner's Sons.

III. What Is Napoleon's Claim to Greatness?

Whereas persons may understandably disagree over the interpretation of an historical era or movement, such as the French Revolution, differences of opinion invariably become more pronounced (and more acrimonious) when the biographical element enters into the discussion. Especially is this true if the individual in question happens to be a dynamic and enigmatic person such as Napoleon Bonaparte. And the problem becomes more complex when we consider that few persons have had as much written about them as has Napoleon I; few have been praised or denounced in as many ways or in as many languages. One thing is certain, we cannot avoid viewing him as a person, nor can we ignore his claim to greatness on the basis of achievement.

As a Person

The difficulties in evaluating Napoleon as a person are many. Here we have attempted to simplify them somewhat by seeking answers in the opinions held by one of his associates and by a French historian writing during the reign of the Emperor's nephew, Napoleon III. What are their impressions of the man? How and why do these writers differ in their attitudes? To what extent must their analyses be discounted? What manner of man emerges when we blend their accounts?

A. Judged by Louis Bourrienne

In many respects the most important and most useful memoirs about Napoleon are those of Louis Antoine Fauvelet de Bourrienne (1769–1834). Schoolmate, friend, secretary,

and diplomatic representative, Bourrienne ultimately lost favor because of peculation. He was in an unusually favorable position to observe and record the habits of Napoleon.

My long and intimate connection with Bonaparte from boyhood, my close relations with him when General, Consul, and Emperor, enabled me to see and appreciate all that was projected and all that was done during that considerable and momentous period of time. I not only had the opportunity of being present at the conception and the execution of the extraordinary deeds of one of the ablest men nature ever formed, but...I found means to employ the few moments of leisure which Bonaparte left at my disposal in making notes, collecting documents, and in recording for history facts respecting which the truth could otherwise with difficulty be ascertained...

Bonaparte had two ruling passions, glory and war. He was never more gay than in the camp, and never more morose than in the inactivity of peace. Plans for the construction of public monuments also pleased his imagination, and filled up the void caused by the want of active occupation. He was aware that monuments form part of the history of nations...

...In all his actions he lost sight of the present moment, and thought only of futurity;...

Before he fought a battle, Bonaparte thought little about what he should do in case of a success, but a great deal about what he should do in case of a reverse of fortune....

He did not esteem mankind, whom, indeed, he despised more and more in proportion as he became acquainted with them. . . .

One of Bonaparte's greatest misfortunes was, that he neither believed in friendship nor felt the necessity of loving. . . .

In his social relations Bonaparte's temper was bad; but his fits of ill-humour passed away like a cloud, and spent themselves in words. His violent language and bitter imprecations were frequently premeditated. . . .

. . . He possessed every requisite for being what is called in society an agreeable man, except the will to be so. His manner was imposing rather than pleasing, and those who did not know him well experienced in his presence an involuntary feeling of awe. . . .

He often talked a great deal, and sometimes a little too much; but no one could tell a story in a more agreeable and interesting way. His conversation rarely turned on gay or humourous subjects, and never on trivial matters. He was so fond of argument that in the warmth of discussion it was easy to draw from him secrets which he was most anxious to conceal. . . .

Bonaparte had no faith in medicine. He spoke of it as an art entirely conjectural, and his opinion on this subject was fixed and incontrovertible. His vigorous mind rejected all but demonstrative proofs.

He had little memory for proper names, words, or dates, but he had a wonderful recollection of facts and places. . . .

Bonaparte was insensible to the charms of poetic harmony. He had not even sufficient ear to feel the rhythm of poetry, and he never could recite a verse without violating the metre; yet the grand ideas of poetry charmed him. . . .

Gallantry to women was by no means a trait in Bonaparte's character. He seldom said anything agreeable to females, and he frequently addressed to them the rudest and most extraordinary remarks. . . .

On the subject of religion Bonaparte's ideas were very vague. . . . He was very fond of talking of religion. . . . He readily yielded up all that was proved against religion as the work of men and time: but he would not hear of materialism. . . . He

was perfectly tolerant towards every variety of religious faith. . . .

. . . Bonaparte was neither malignant nor vindictive. . . . None but those who are blinded by fury will call him a Nero or a Caligula. . . . He was very fond of children, a trait which seldom distinguishes a bad man. In the relations of private life, to call him amiable would not be using too strong a word, and he was very indulgent to the weakness of human nature. . . . To judge impartially, we must take into account the influence which time and circumstances exercise on men; and distinguish between the different characters of the Collegian, the General, the Consul, and the Emperor. . . .

. . . He had no idea of power except in direct force. All benevolent men who speculate on the amelioration of human society were regarded by Bonaparte as dangerous, because their maxims and principles were diametrically opposed to the harsh and arbitrary system he had adopted. . . . he always said that men were only to be governed by fear and interest. . . . Bonaparte held the liberty of the press in the greatest horror; . . . Great man as he was, he was sorely afraid of little paragraphs. . . .

The historian of these times ought to put no faith in the bulletins, despatches, notes, and proclamations which have emanated from Bonaparte, or passed through his hands. . . .

The bulletins always announced what Bonaparte wished to be believed true; but to form a proper judgment on any fact, counter-bulletins must be sought for and consulted. It is well-known, too, that Bonaparte attached great importance to the place whence he dated his bulletins; . . .

The official documents were almost always incorrect. There was falsity in the exaggerated descriptions of his victories, and falsity again in the suppression or palliation of his reverses and losses. A writer, if he took his materials from the bulletins and the official correspondence of the time, would compose a romance rather than a true history. . . .

. . . the slight estimation in which he held literary men. . . . he called them mere manufacturers of phrases. He could not pardon them for excelling him in a pursuit   in which he had no claim to distinction. . . .

Louis Antoine Fauvelet de Bourrienne, *Memoirs of Napoleon Bonaparte,* ed. and trans. Ramsay W. Phipps, new ed, rev., 4 vols. (New York: Charles Scribner's Sons, 1889); I, xxvi, xxvii, 313, 315, 316, 317, 319, 320, 322, 323, 324, 327, 328, 367; II, 112, 113, 233 (originally published 1829).

B. Judged by Pierre Lanfrey

Pierre Lanfrey (1828–1877) was a French journalist, historian, and critic of the Second Empire. His writings included studies of the Church in the eighteenth century, the French Revolution, and Napoleon. The last named (5 vols., 1867–1875) is still important because of its highly controversial approach to the subject.

In all times the true and distinctive mark of political genius has been aptitude for founding a solid and durable work, adapting it to the deep needs of a people and an epoch. The incomparable elements that Bonaparte possessed to realize such a work he only employs to astonish and to dazzle men. He tries to strike their imagination, not to satisfy their reason or their interests. The fate of his country is only a secondary object in comparison with the apotheosis which he dreams of for himself. Beyond this purely personal idea of glorification, we fail to discover in him any persistent or definite spring of action. It is almost impossible for him to stop at a determined end: he has no sooner advanced a step than he goes further still, again still further, without ever waiting till the ground is firm under his feet. For him, a conquest is a stepping-stone for a fresh conquest. Hence the hasty, feverish, impromptu character of his political creations, at home as well as abroad. All that he does in this respect, with the impatience and rapidity of an ambition greedy enough to devour a world, is in his mind only a transition, a beginning capable of an indefinite extension. Consequently everything remains unfinished, in a state of outline and experiment. He never acts with the idea of the definite, he wishes to retain to the last the power of changing everything according to opportunity, and above all things according to the humour of his insatiable cravings. He never aims at stability, but at size, at splendour; grandeur does not satisfy him, he must have the immeasurable, the gigantic; and beyond this perilous domain, something else attracts him still more; it is the unknown and the marvellous. Under the sting of this irresistible disquietude, he forgets the road to follow and the end to attain in the movement itself. He cares less about the final result than about the means that he will display, and the prodigious effect that he will produce. It matters little to him whether the work is ephemeral, provided he finds in it more activity, more noise, more glory. The task to accomplish and the means necessary to insure success are trifles beside the grand adventures for which they furnish him the opportunity or the pretext. This infatuation was so much the more terrible that it had taken possession of a cold and positive mind, whose most chimerical dreams clothed forms of mathematical rigour, and had at their service a military genius without equal. With enthusiastic temperaments exaltation is only temporary; but the studied frenzy of a calculating mind is without remedy, because it does not depend on a sentiment but on the very form of the intellect itself. . . .

. . . If there is, in fact, a striking and characteristic trait in the innumerable conversations which have been preserved by men who approached him most familiarly, it is the absence of all effusion or unreserved confidence. He was always engrossed with the endeavour either to penetrate the views of his interlocutor or so to work upon his mind as to bring him round to a calculated object; we look in vain for anything like sympathy, enthusiasm, or a moment of frank confidence about himself or about others. Even when he gave way to that coquettishness of feline grace of which his contemporaries have so often described the seduction, he never lost sight of the effect he wished to produce; he calculated everything, even his imprudence in language. He was as reserved with his own relations as with strangers. In short, we cannot find in his whole life a single instance of that philosophical irony which charms us so in a Caesar or a Frederick, because it shows that the man is superior to his part, that he knows his own value, that he is not the dupe of his own fortune. . . . Napoleon, on the contrary, is always on the stage, constantly thinking of himself; . . . he had not that supreme greatness of the man who has a just appreciation of his worth; he remained, by his incurable infatuation, on a level with narrow minds; . . .

The *régime* inaugurated under the name of Empire was no other than pure Caesarism. . .

. . . In order to create this power . . . it was necessary to do violence to the spirit of the people no less than to the spirit of the times; in order to preserve it, it was necessary to hinder this people from recovering a consciousness of its own existence . . .

. . . This transformation of the Consulate into an Empire . . . was inspired by a puerile vanity, for which real power was no longer enough if it was not accompanied by that external homage invented and brought to perfection by so many centuries of monarchical superstition. In this Bonaparte was very inferior to Cromwell, of whom he spoke with so much disdain; in the English statesman there was more seriousness, more sense, more manliness. . . . Bonaparte's genius is prodigious, but within narrow limits. He was endowed with an extraordinary penetration, and yet he had no foresight; he was calculating, and yet he was incapable of governing himself. . . . He made great political interests subservient to a miserable satisfaction of self-love. Never did the innate littleness of his soul betray itself more visibly than in the feverish haste with which he adopted all the forms of ancient etiquette. What did he care for the perils which this petty ambition was going to create for us, provided that he, the son of the obscure lawyer of Ajaccio, could call kings "our dearly-beloved brother"—provided that he could sign his letters to the Pope, "Your devoted son"—provided that he could say, "My good town of Paris, my subjects, my people, my ministers, my palace, my forest of Fontainebleau"?

Pierre Lanfrey, *The History of Napoleon the First,* trans. from the French, 2nd ed., 4 vols. (New York: The Macmillan Company, 1886), II, 150–53, 431, 433, 434.

As a Man of Achievement

In the last analysis, a man's claim to greatness cannot rest upon an understanding of his personality alone—however much his character may have had to do with what he accomplished. Rather we must seek the answer in the man's actual achievements. How many of these were of significance during his own time? How many of them endured? How have they affected mankind? What do we learn when we ask these and comparable questions about Napolen I?

Napoleon's career was many-sided, but above all he was concerned with war and statecraft. It would seem advisable, therefore, to examine what has been said by two experts —one in military history, the other in the Napoleonic Era as a whole—with respect to these aspects of his endeavors. At the same time, we must remember that not all the opinions come from experts; that many of them, in fact, are proffered by persons whose approach is an emotional rather than a rational historical one. The last two examples cited —one by a novelist turned historian, one by a lawyer turned publicist—should provide many more interesting questions concerning the manner in which people arrive at their conclusions about distinguished historical figures. What are we to do about such opinions? What place do we give them in our study of history?

A. Judged by Theodore A. Dodge

American army officer and historian, Theodore Ayrault Dodge (1842–1909) wrote widely on military affairs. The following excerpt is taken from a series of six lectures in which he evaluated the careers of Alexander the Great, Hannibal, Julius Caesar, Gustavus Adolphus, Frederick the Great, and Napoleon I.

...In certain respects Napoleon was the greatest of all soldiers. He had, to be sure, the history of other great captains to profit by; he had not to invent; he had only to improve. But he did for the military art what constitutes the greatest advance in any art, he reduced it to its most simple, most perfect form;...

Napoleon's career is a notable example of the necessity of coexistent intellect, character, and opportunity to produce the greatest success in war. His strength distinctly rose through half his career, and as distinctly fell during the other half. His intellectual power never changed. The plan of the Waterloo campaign was as brilliant as any which he ever conceived. His opportunity here was equal to that of 1796. But his execution was marred by weakening physique, upon which followed a decline of that decisiveness which is so indispensable to the great captain....

The men of the Revolution had cut loose from eighteenth century methods of warfare by rising *en masse* and putting the personal element into the scale. But it was reserved for Napoleon to substitute a new method for the old.... He made himself independent of magazines, as Frederick had done but rarely. With a smaller army he always had more men at point of contact. This was Napoleon's strongest point. He divined what his enemy would do, not from his tent but from the saddle, seeing with his own eyes and weighing all he saw and heard. He was every day and all day long in motion; he rode unheard-of distances. He relied on no one but himself, as, with his comparatively small army, he could well do; and correctly seeing and therefore correctly gauging circumstances, he had the courage to act upon his facts. He sought battle as the result of every manoeuvre. The weight of his intellect and his character were equally thrown into all he did. And his abnormal ambition drove him to abnormal energy....

...Napoleon's success came from study of the situation. His art was founded on an intimate knowledge of all the facts, coupled with such reasoning power as enabled him to gauge correctly what his enemy was apt to do. Without the art the study would be useless. But the art could not exist apart from study....

There is a magnificence of uncertainty and risk, and corresponding genius in the management of the battles of Napoleon; but for purely artistic tactics they do not appeal to us as do Frederick's. The *motif* of Alexander's battles is more akin to Napoleon's; that of Hannibal's to Frederick's.

It has been said that Napoleon never considered what he should do in case of failure. The reverse is more exact. Before delivering a battle, Napoleon busied himself little with what he would do in case of success. That was easy to decide. He busied himself markedly with what could be done in case of reverse.

Like all great captains, Napoleon preferred lieutenants who obeyed instead of initiating. He chafed at independent action. This was the chief's prerogative. But as his armies grew in size he gave his marshals charge of detail under general instructions from himself. Dependence on Napoleon gradually sapped the self-reliance of more than one of his lieutenants, and though there are instances of noble ability at a distance from control, most of his marshals were able tacticians, rather than great generals. Napoleon grew impatient of contradiction or explanation; and he sometimes did not learn or was not told of things he ought to know. He was no longer so active. Campaigning was a hardship. His belief in his destiny became so strong that he began to take greater risks. Such a thing as failure did not exist for him. His armies were increasing in size.... The difficulties he had to contend with were growing fast.

These things had the effect of making Napoleon's military plans more magnificent, more far-reaching. But all the less could be pay heed to detail, and from now on one can, with some brilliant exceptions, perceive more errors of execution. In the general conception he was greater than ever, and this balanced the scale. His ability to put all his skill into the work immediately in hand was marvellous. But with a vast whole in view, the parts were, perhaps of necessity, lost sight of. . . .

In making his plans, Napoleon never began by "What can the enemy do?" but he first sought to place his army in the best position, and then asked, "What now can the enemy do?" This gave him the initiative. But his plan was always elastic enough to bend to what the enemy might do. He never made plans colored by the enemy's possibilities. He chose his own plan intelligently, according to the geography, topography, and existing conditions, and made it elastic enough to be equal to the enemy's. . . .

In Napoleon's battles, tactical details are made to yield to strategic needs. Frederick generally chose his point of attack from a strictly tactical standpoint. Napoleon did not appear to consider that there were such things as tactical difficulties. He always moved on the enemy as seemed to him strategically desirable, and with his great masses he could readily do so. The result of Napoleon's battles was so wonderful, just because he always struck from such a strategic direction as to leave a beaten enemy no kind of loophole. But Napoleon would have been more than human if his extraordinary successes had not finally damaged his character. It is but the story of Alexander with a variation. In the beginning he was, after securing strategic value, strenuous to preserve his tactical values. By and by he began to pay less heed to these; stupendous successes bred disbelief in failure; carelessness resulted, then indecision. Those historians who maintain that Napoleon succumbed solely to the gigantic opposition his status in Europe had evoked, can show good reasons for their belief, for Napoleon's task was indeed immense. But was he overtaxed more than Hannibal, Caesar, or Frederick? . . .

The secret of Napoleon's power lay in his clear eye for facts, his positive mind. . . . Napoleon said of himself that he was most of all a slave of men, obliged to obey a heartless master, the calculation of circumstances and the nature of things. Coupled with this were a reliance on facts, rare capacity for divination, and an immense power of imagination. But finally the latter overran the other qualities. His successes convinced him that he could do anything; he forgot what his success had been grounded on, and he began to neglect facts. . . . Napoleon believed himself able to accomplish all things, until his accuracy of judgment was lost in his refusal to look facts in the face. He ceased to be slave of the nature of things. He deserted belief in facts for belief in his destiny. Finally facts became for him not what they were, but what he wished them to be. He refused credit to what did not suit his theory of how things ought to turn.

Napoleon had what rarely coexists,— an equally clear head on the map and in the field. On the map he was able in both theory and practice. His theories were text-books; his letters are treatises. No higher praise can be spoken than to say that every one of Napoleon's fourteen campaigns was, in a military sense, properly planned.

Napoleon showed the value of masses in strategy as well as tactics. In former times the worth of troops was of greater value than numbers. Today worth of itself is less essential than it was. Napoleon founded his calculations on the equality of thousands. It is he who collated all that was done by the other great captains, clothed it in a dress fit for our own days, and taught the modern world how to make war in perfect form. . . .

Theodore Ayrault Dodge, *Great Captains: A Course of Six Lectures Showing the Influence on the Art of War of the Campaigns of Alexander, Hannibal, Caesar, Gustavus Adolphus, Frederick, and Napoleon* (Boston: Houghton Mifflin Company, 1889), pp. 178–79, 184–85, 188–89, 191–93, 197, 200–201, 213, 214.

B. Judged by H. A. L. Fisher

Herbert Fisher (1865–1940) was a distinguished British scholar and public servant. Of his numerous highly successful ventures into Napoleonic history, one of the most significant was the essay from which the following paragraphs are selected.

It will probably be admitted, even by the most strenuous opponent of French imperialism, that with two exceptions Napoleon has exercised a greater influence upon the political and social state of Europe than any other single man. Nothing in the achievements of the Consulate and the Empire was fraught with such tremendous consequence for the future of European civilization as the conquest of Gaul by Julius Caesar or the assumption of the imperial crown by Charlemagne; but then we must remember that Caesar and Charlemagne were operating upon political conditions which were still comparatively simple and susceptible of receiving a deep and durable impress from a powerful will, while Napoleon, living many centuries afterwards, suffered the penalty of time. He was brought up against complex masses of tradition, political, social, and ecclesiastical, which had been hardened by ages of settled European life and were protected by the great vested interests of an old community. He affronted many things which Europeans were wont to consider respectable and even holy, monarchical sentiment, aristocratic caste, the Catholic Church, the sentiment of nationality. Much of his work was immediately undone upon his fall. All of it was compressed within a period of twenty years. But when all deductions have been made for ill-calculated plans, transitional expedients, and policies triumphantly cancelled by his opponents, there remains a residuum of durable political influences so great as immeasurably to overshadow any which can be ascribed to any other modern ruler of a European state.

In saying this we do not mean to imply that there have not been minds in Europe of finer, higher, and more original quality.

The most durable and successful features of Napoleon's statesmanship are not those parts which one might be tempted to call extravagantly Napoleonic, but those which seem to satisfy deep-seated needs and to crown long processes of historical development. Again, there have been many influences in Europe, on the religious and moral side, which have made more difference to the lives of ordinary men and women than the career of Napoleon.... The system of Napoleon did not start full-fledged from his brain, and was indeed not so much a system as a series of brilliant improvisations made in response to the stress of fortune...he adapted the ideas of his age to the needs of the situation.

This really comes to saying that Napoleon was a statesman. It is not the business of a statesman to be original. It is his business to measure the human forces about him, to take stock of the conflicting traditions, the complex interests, the hidden currents and open water-ways of thought and feeling, and so to contrive his political and constitutional formulae as to rally for their support the best and highest energies of his people. Exactly in proportion as he is successful in doing this, his work will stand the test and strain of time.

The great transfiguring ideas in politics, even where they originate with men of action, can seldom be safely used until they have survived some controversy and become the familiar property of political thought. It is therefore no more a condemnation of Napoleon's genius to observe that he merely worked with the ideas of the French Revolution than to say that he breathed the air and trod the earth. The supreme proof of his genius lies, on the contrary, in the fact that he harnessed the wild living spirit of the Revolution to his own career.

These observations will prepare us to consider the general question of Napoleon's legacy to Europe. We should naturally expect to find that those parts of his work would be most permanent which are founded upon common sense, and might therefore have occurred to any man of ordinary high abilities on a survey of the political situation, and that those parts are least permanent which could only have come from Napoleon and are stamped by the peculiar idiosyncracy of his temperament. This is in the main true. The civil work of the Consulate, the Codes, the Concordat, the Prefects, the Legion of Honour, together with the Imperial University and the Lycées—this is the work for which the previous history of France was fitting prolusion, so that being adjusted to the needs of the country it was able to endure through a century of factious strife and revolutionary upheaval. The Grand Empire on the other hand perished, for it belonged to the peculiar temperament of Napoleon to imagine a monster which almost everything in its previous history had prepared Europe to reject.

The true greatness of Napoleon as a civil ruler lies in the fact, firstly that he saved for France the most valuable conquests of the French Revolution, social equality and industrial freedom, secondly that he brought to a conclusion the difficult operation of securing for the remodelled state the sanction and support of the Church, and thirdly that he gave to France a code of laws and a system of administration which remain substantially unchanged today. He saved equality which was a fierce national passion, and sacrificed liberty which had become a disease. The Code Napoléon, which he regarded as his main title to glory, is, so to speak, the last testament of the French Revolution....

Modern France is still very much as the Consulate left it. Parliamentary government has taken root, the Concordat has been denounced after an uneasy life of a hundred years, and some measure of decentralization has been effectually introduced into local government and the fabric of the University. The ideal of the lay state has become more widely held with the lapse of time, and is embodied in the scheme of compulsory secular education which the Third Republic owes to the oratory of Gambetta and the strenuous powers of Ferry. These changes, however important though they be, have neither transformed the political spirit of France nor swept away the main blocks of Napoleonic granite, the Prefects, the Codes, the Legion of Honour, the Lycée. The most serious innovation is the Parliamentary system, introduced during the Hundred Days in deference to the public opinion of Paris and without faith in its merits by Napoleon himself, and accepted as the unpleasant necessity of vulgar times by the restored Bourbons.... However mutable may be the balances of parliamentary power, the tradition of a cogent civil service, an inquisitorial police, and a special body of administrative law has been handed down from the days of Napoleon.

One change, not of institutions but of political spirit, is certainly notable. France is no longer the firebrand of Europe. For fifty good years after the battle of Waterloo she continued to be tormented by the shade of Napoleon summoning her to redeem the frontier of the Rhine and to reverse the work of the Congress of Vienna. It may be open to question how far this survival of the Bonapartist spirit was a wholesome element in European political life, how far a virulent poison. A spirit of empty, vainglorious, military imperialism, chafing under the lassitude of enforced peace and the ignominy of frontiers restricted in the general interests of Europe, does not command much natural sympathy. But it was part of the singular history of the Napoleonic memory that it became associated with liberal ideas in France and with national hopes in Italy and Poland. When Europe was given over to the autocrats, the faults of Napoleon were forgotten and his merits called to mind. Over and against the petty conventions of court and caste he stood out as the supreme type of unaided human energy mounting to the highest pinnacle of fortune, and moulding the destiny of the world. It was forgotten that he had tried to manufacture a new nobility, that he had introduced privileged entails, that he had married an Austrian Archduchess, and copied the stiff ceremonials of Spain in Italy and of the Ancien Régime in France.

In the sentiment of the common people he remained the Little Corporal sprung from nowhere, of the same humble clay as themselves, an everlasting proof that for the highest tasks of war and government it is not blue blood that is wanted, but the brain, heart, and nerve of the heroic man. So conceived the Napoleonic memory was at once a valuable safeguard against a possible reaction to the *Ancien Régime* and an important auxiliary to liberal ideas. The mischief was that this democratic and wholesome sentiment did not exhaust the content of the Imperial tradition, but was allied in it with the evil precedents of domestic tyranny and military expansion....

Outside the frontiers of France the system of Napoleon seemed to be most firmly secured in the Piedmontese, Rhenish, and Belgian departments of the Grand Empire. Of these territories, the first became, after the cataclysm, the scene of a reaction so stupid and violent that all the good results of the French period were swept away, so that the work of liberalisation had to be done over again almost from the beginning...In the Rhenish departments the seeds sown by the French Revolution were not so easily uprooted, and a numerous and prosperous peasant proprietary continued to testify to the enduring benefits conferred by twenty years of government under the French law. The third case is even more important....

It is usual to attach great importance to the encouragement which Napoleon gave to the idea of Polish nationality, and to find in this phase of imperial policy the secret not only of the close sympathy between France and Poland which subsisted until the fall of the Second Empire, but also of some influences working in the Polish revolutions of the nineteenth century. We have no wish to underrate the spell which Napoleon cast upon Poland, or the reality of the hopes excited by the creation of the short-lived Grand Duchy of Warsaw; but the case must not be overstated. The alliance between France and Poland was a diplomatic tradition of the *Ancien Régime* and, had Napoleon never been born, a Frenchman would still have been more acceptable to a Pole than a Prussian, a Russian, or an Austrian. By force of circumstances revolutionary France, attacked by the autocratic powers of the East, was the natural ally of revolutionary Poland....Every blow struck for the French Revolution was a blow struck for Polish liberty. What Napoleon did then was not to create a new sentiment of friendship, but to give to this inherent connexion of interest a certain amount of additional and palpable support...

With the southern Slavs the influence of the Emperor has been still more decisive. Napoleon was never in Croatia, but with the possible exception of Belgium there is no outlying part of the Grand Empire which has felt in a more effective and enduring way the power of his person and his policy....

The Empire then was most permanently effective where it cooperated with national sentiment or was brought into contact with rude peoples still in that tribal stage of civilization which made the barbaric world so pliant to the impress of Imperial Rome. One of the most curious revenges of history is the fact that the revolutionary movement in Russia took its origin from the victorious entrance of Russian troops into Paris in 1814. Here in the capital of Napoleon these half-barbarian visitors...beheld for the first time the spectacle of a progressive state, a well-appointed government, and a liberal civilization. The ferment did its work and the Decembrist revolution of 1825 was the result. From this curious military disturbance...we may date that active and continuous working of Western political ideas in the Muscovite world...

It is only natural to expect that the Napoleonic influence would be specially strong in the Latin countries....He made the Revolution a vital thing in Italy, and without a revolutionary party Italian unity would never have been achieved....

...The Peninsular War created Spanish liberalism and was the means of disseminating, especially in the more forward maritime provinces, the doctrines of progress, equality, and popular sovereignty. . . .

The place of the Teutonic race in Europe and therefore in the whole world has been decisively altered by the career and policy of Napoleon. . . . The larger consequences of his masterful intervention in German affairs were the disappearance of the Holy Roman Empire coupled with an immense simplification in the political geography of that composite and cumbrous state; and when these changes are coupled with the great series of reforms accomplished in Prussia under the stress of the Jena disaster and with the general spread of pan-German feeling in the War of Liberation, it becomes clear that Napoleon must rank as one of the makers of modern Germany.

It is needless to say that nothing was further from Napoleon's intention than to go down to history in such a role. His intention was precisely the opposite—to denationalize the Germans, to fix upon them French laws and institutions, and to harness them to the ambitions of the French Empire. . . .

Herbert A. L. Fisher, "Thoughts on the Influence of Napoleon," in *Studies in History and Politics* (Oxford: The Clarendon Press, 1920), pp. 198–213 *passim*.

C. Judged by H. G. Wells

An English novelist and student of social problems, Herbert George Wells (1866–1946) entered the field of historical writing after World War I. His much-sold and doubtless widely read *Outline of History* (1920) was designed to direct mankind toward an era of wisdom in which war might be avoided. The objectivity with which his *Outline* began yielded to a pronounced subjectivity as Mr. Wells drew nearer to his own time; and this is painfully apparent in his brief estimate of Napoleon I. But, as one of his critics remarked, it is much easier to be dispassionate about the Java Ape-Man, who left only a jaw-bone as evidence, than it is to avoid bias about a man who left thirty volumes of letters.

. . . The old order of things was dead or dying; strange new forces drove through the world seeking form and direction; the promise of a world republic and an enduring world peace whispered in a multitude of startled minds. Had this man any profundity of vision, any power of creative imagination, had he been accessible to any disinterested ambition, he might have done work for mankind that would have made him the very sun of history. All Europe and America, stirred by the first promise of a new age, was waiting for him. Not France alone. France was in his hand, his instrument, to do with as he pleased, willing for peace, but tempered for war like an exquisite sword. There lacked nothing to this great occasion but a noble imagination. And failing that, Napoleon could do no more than strut upon the crest of this great mountain of opportunity like a cockerel on a dunghill. The figure he makes in history is one of almost incredible self-conceit, of vanity, greed, and cunning, of callous contempt and disregard of all who trusted him, and of a grandiose aping of Caesar, Alexander, and Charlemagne which would be purely comic if it were not caked over with human blood. Until, as Victor Hugo said in his tremendous way, "God was bored by him," and he was kicked aside into a corner to end his days, explaining and explaining how very clever his worst blunders had been. . .

The career and personality of Napoleon I bulks disproportionately in the nineteenth-century histories. He was of little significance to the broad onward movement of human affairs; he was an interruption, a reminder of latent evils, a thing like the bacterium of some pestilence. Even regarded as a pestilence, he was not of supreme rank; he killed far fewer people than the influenza epidemic of 1918, and produced less political and social disruption than the plague of Justinian.

H. G. Wells, *The Outline of History, Being a Plain History of Life and Mankind,* rev. ed. (New York: The Macmillan Company, 1921), pp. 898–99, 922. By permission of Doubleday & Company, Inc. © 1920 H. G. Wells, Published by Doubleday & Company, Inc., and Cassell & Company, Ltd. By permission of the Executors of H. G. Wells estate.

D. *Judged by Robert G. Ingersoll*

Flamboyant in appearance, in speech, and in writing, Robert G. Ingersoll (1833–1899) was one of the most colorful American figures of the late nineteenth century. The son of a Congregational minister and a lawyer by profession, he came to devote most of his time and energy to denouncing organized Christianity. One of his few excursions into historical analysis took the form of the following eloquent "Soliloquy on Viewing the Tomb of Napoleon Bonaparte."

A little while ago, I stood by the grave of the old Napoleon—a magnificent tomb of gilt and gold, fit almost for a dead deity—and gazed upon the sarcophagus of rare and nameless marble, where rest at last the ashes of that restless man. I leaned over the balustrade and thought about the career of the greatest soldier of the modern world.

I saw him walking upon the banks of the Seine, contemplating suicide. I saw him at Toulon—I saw him putting down the mob in the streets of Paris—I saw him at the head of the army of Italy—I saw him crossing the bridge of Lodi with the tri-color in his hand—I saw him in Egypt in the shadows of the pyramids—I saw him conquer the Alps and mingle the eagles of France with the eagles of the crags. I saw him at Marengo—at Ulm and Austerlitz. I saw him in Russia, where the infantry of the snow and the cavalry of the wild blast scattered his legions like winter's withered leaves. I saw him at Leipsic in defeat and disaster—driven by a million bayonets back upon Paris—clutched like a wild beast—banished to Elba. I saw him escape and retake an empire by the force of his genius. I saw him upon the frightful field of Waterloo, where Chance and Fate combined to wreck the fortunes of their former king. And I saw him at St. Helena, with his hands crossed behind him, gazing out upon the sad and solemn sea.

I thought of the orphans and widows he had made—of the tears that had been shed for his glory, and of the only woman who ever loved him, pushed from his heart by the cold hand of ambition. And I said I would rather have been a French peasant and worn wooden shoes. I would rather have lived in a hut with a vine growing over the door, and the grapes growing purple in the kisses of the autumn sun. I would rather have been that poor peasant with my loving wife by my side, knitting as the day died out of the sky—with my children upon my knees and their arms about me—I would rather have been that man and gone down to the tongueless silence of the dreamless dust, than to have been that imperial impersonation of force and murder known as "Napoleon the Great."

Robert G. Ingersoll, "The Liberty of Man, Woman and Child," *The Writings of Robert G. Ingersoll* Dresden edition, 12 v. (New York, 1908), I, 369–71.

11

The
New Industrial
and Social Order

HARRY H. KIMBER

Michigan State University

In the middle years of the nineteenth century there came to a climax in Great Britain a series of changes in the methods by which man satisfied his basic economic needs of food, clothing, and shelter. As time went on, these changes not only increased in complexity and refinement but spread among the nations on the continent of Europe and across the seas to the New World, and, as the century came to a close, increasingly to the Orient as well. The life and civilization of Western man, and ultimately of the whole world, was affected more radically by these changes than by any other series of events in history. Historians have given the name of Industrial Revolution—an analogy with political change which overturns the government of states—to this profound and complicated movement which affects the very constitution of society. In order better to indicate the broad scope as well as the basic character of the changes involved, the term Economic Revolution is sometimes preferred. These changes have yet to run their course; in fact, implicit in them is the principle of change itself, change which makes the idea of a final end realized in a static world almost incomprehensible to the contemporary mind.

Five basic factors of change revolutionized Western society in the nineteenth century. Machinery came to replace hand work throughout whole industries. This was increasingly accompanied by the application on a large scale of power, at first water power and steam power, to machinery. New ways and means of transportation were brought into existence by the development of canal systems and new kinds of roads and the application of the steam engine to transport. The application of scientific knowledge and of machinery to farming brought about equally revolutionary changes in agriculture. Another kind of revolutionary change that was an integral part of the Industrial Revolution was the development of new forms in the methods and character of business organization, or in the means by which the capital required to carry on manufacture and trade under the new system was amassed from many sources, and the development of new methods by which the great enterprises characteristic of the new order were owned, controlled, and directed.

The changes represented by the Industrial Revolution constitute an interrelated complex of consequences, none of which stands in isolation. A great social change brought about by industrialization was the concentration of the manufacturing and trading population in great urban centers of enormous size and complexity: the modern city. To support these urban populations the supply of food on an unprecedented scale was essential; this made possible by equally revolutionary changes in methods of agriculture. The revolution in transportation, by land and by sea, was indispensable to the mass delivery of foodstuffs and to the supply of raw materials and the exchange of goods. The economic changes mentioned above not only resulted in a new economic order, but they brought about social changes which were in themselves revolutionary in scope and result. Such changes spread into virtually every area of society, modifying old and creating new social groupings, bringing into being new classes in society, and calling forth new forms of government, however much their newness was concealed by the preservation of accustomed forms and usages. In short, a new civilization was born.

The new civilization of the nineteenth century posed for its contemporaries many problems. Rising out of the foundations of Western Europe, it was inextricably bound up with the culture pattern of the past at the same time that it was essentially a new thing upon the earth. Greek, Roman, and Christian ideals dominated the minds of men, but they were now of necessity applied to a contemporary social and intellectual world that in points of difference was further from Queen Anne's England than the people of that age were from the Romans of Caesar's time.

The new order posed questions in at least three major areas: the economic, the social, and the political. The readings which follow are not intended to summarize in any degree of completeness the many and various facets which these questions presented in the course of the century, but they are rather to be regarded as introductions to the nature of the questions faced by the people of the nineteenth century, stated in the terms in which they appeared and reappeared in the economic, social, and political conflicts of the day. Since most of these problems were posed first in Great Britain, most of our materials are taken from the writings and speeches of Englishmen of the period.

In the group of readings on "The New Society" the problem of the new economic order is discussed by John Stuart Mill, Friedrich Engels, and Leo XIII in terms of the right of private property and its corollary, competition. Under the heading of "The Myth of Progress" Thomas Malthus and Robert Owen debate the basic question posed by the secularist view of society: Can man by the exercise of reason alone progress toward the perfection of a social order? In the third section two members of Parliament and a political philosopher deal with the problem of the new political balance created by the rise, in the age of capitalism, of the working man to an increasingly dominant position in the body politic.

I. The New Society

The nineteenth century in England was marked by a new and vigorous concern for social ethics. This concern for the social question—the Condition of England Question, as it was then called—was evidenced not only in the writings of intellectuals and men of letters, but also in the popular movements of protest and reform which arose from among the working classes. Under the Industrial Revolution the standard of living of the working classes had so far improved as to make them more sensitive to injustice and more capable of imagining a better ordering of society than had been the case with their semifeudal predecessors of the previous century. There was violence and lawlessness in the eighteenth century, but it was the violence of fanatical or ignorant men, and the lawlessness of gin and hysteria; the trades union movement, the agitation for parliamentary reform preceding the passage of the Bill of 1832, Chartism in its various phases, the rise of Socialism, all strike a different note. The great popular movements of the nineteenth century reflect "the resentment of men convinced that there is something false and degrading in the arrangement and justice of their world." [J. L. and Barbara Hammond, *The Bleak Age* (London, New York, and Toronto: Longmans, Green & Co., 1934), p. 3.]

This is in short the social question. A new social order was gradually arising upon the ruins of the old—the old order based on the land economy of the Middle Ages, the new order the result of the industrialization of the modern world. In the readings that follow there are presented aspects of three of the basic ideas involved in the nineteenth-century debate on social issues: the idea of private property and free competition, a criticism of the competitive system of capitalism, and a statement of economic and social rights and responsibilities from a Christian point of view.

A. John Stuart Mill Defends Economic Liberalism

John Stuart Mill (1806–1873) is one of the great exponents of nineteenth-century liberalism, perhaps best known for his defense of individual freedom in the classic *Essay on Liberty* (1859). Mill belonged to the school of thought known as the Philosophical Radicals, which professed to accept no socio-political institution on the basis of authority or custom but subjected all things to the scrutiny of reason in the light of the criterion of utility as set forth in the writings of Jeremy Bentham.

In writing the *Principles of Political Economy*, Mill was aware of the problems posed by the new order, the condition of the workers, the rise of the capitalist class, and the remedies proposed by early Socialists and Communists. In the following passages he goes to the heart of the matter, the place of the individual in society. He defends private property and the principle of competition on utilitarian grounds. From the right of private property and the workings of competition in economic life there arises the highest value of civilized social order, the freedom of the individual.

Private property, in every defence made of it, is supposed to mean, the guarantee to individuals of the fruits of their own labour and abstinence. The guarantee to them of the fruits of the labour and abstinence of others, transmitted to them without any merit or exertion of their own, is not of the essence of the institution, but a mere incidental consequence, which when it reaches a certain height, does not promote, but conflicts with the ends which render private property legitimate. To judge of the final destination of the institution of property, we must suppose everything rectified, which causes the institution to work in a manner opposed to that equitable principle, of proportion between remuneration and exertion, on which in every vindication of it that will bear the light, it is assumed to be grounded. We must also suppose two conditions realized, without which neither Communism nor any other laws or institutions could make the condition of the mass of mankind other than degraded and miserable. One of these conditions is, universal education; the other, a due limitation of the numbers of the community. With these, there could be no poverty even under the present social institutions: and these being supposed, the question of Socialism is not, as generally stated by Socialists, a question of flying to the sole refuge against the evils which now bear down humanity; but a mere question of comparative advantages, which futurity must determine. We are too ignorant either of what individual agency in its best form, or Socialism in its best form, can accomplish, to be qualified to decide which of the two will be the ultimate form of human society.

If a conjecture may be hazarded, the decision will probably depend mainly on one consideration, viz. which of the two systems is consistent with the greatest amount of human liberty and spontaneity. After the means of subsistence are assured, the next in strength of the personal wants of human beings is liberty; and (unlike the physical wants, which as civilization advances become more moderate and more amenable to control) it increases instead of diminishing in intensity, as the intelligence and the moral faculties are more developed. ... The restraints of Communism would be freedom in comparison with the present condition of the majority of the human race. The generality of labourers in this and most other countries, have as little choice of occupation or freedom of locomotion, are practically as dependent on fixed rules and on the will of others, as they could be on any system short of actual slavery; to say nothing of the entire domestic subjection of one half the species, to which it is the signal honour of Owenism and most other forms of Socialism that they assign equal rights, in all respects, with those of the hitherto dominant sex. But it is not by comparison with the present bad state of society that the claims of Communism can be estimated; nor is it sufficient that it should promise greater personal and mental freedom than is now enjoyed by those who have not enough of either to deserve the name. The question is, whether there would be any asylum left for individuality of character; whether public opinion would not be a tyrannical yoke; whether the absolute dependence of each on all, and surveillance of each by all, would not grind all down into a tame uniformity of thoughts, feelings, and actions. This is already one of the glaring evils of the existing state of society, notwithstanding a much greater diversity of education and pursuits, and a much less absolute dependence of the individual on the mass, than would exist in the Communistic régime. No society in which eccentricity is a matter of reproach, can be in a wholesome state. It is yet to be ascertained whether the Communistic scheme would be consistent with that multiform development of human nature, those manifold unlikenesses, that diversity of tastes and talents, and variety of intellectual points of view, which not only form a great part of the interest of human life, but by bringing intellects into stimulating collision, and by presenting to each innumerable notions that he would not have conceived of himself, are the mainspring of mental and moral progression. ...

The institution of property, when limited to its essential elements, consists in the recognition, in each person, of a right to the exclusive disposal of what he or she have produced by their own exertions, or received either by gift or by fair agreement, without force or fraud, from those who produced it. The foundation of the whole is, the right of producers to what they themselves have produced. It may be objected, therefore, to the institution as it now exists, that it recognises rights of property in individuals over things which they have not produced. For example (it may be said) the operatives in a manufactory create, by their labour and skill, the whole produce; yet, instead of its belonging to them, the law gives them only their stipulated hire, and transfers the produce to some one who has merely supplied the funds, without perhaps contributing anything to the work itself, even in the form of superintendence. The answer to this is, that the labour of manufacture is only one of the conditions which must combine for the production of the commodity. The labour cannot be carried on without materials and machinery, nor without a stock of necessaries provided in advance, to maintain the labourers during the production. All these things are the fruits of previous labour. If the labourers were possessed of them, they would not need to divide the produce with any one; but while they have them not, an equivalent must be given to those who have, both for the antecedent labour, and for the abstinence by which the produce of that labour, instead of being expended on indulgences, has been reserved for this use. The capital may not have been, and in most cases was not, created by the labour and abstinence of the present possessor; but it was created by the labour and abstinence of some former person, who may indeed have been wrongfully dispossessed of it, but who, in the present age of the world, much more probably transferred his claims to the present capitalist by gift or voluntary contract: and the abstinence at least must have been continued by each successive owner, down to the present. If it be said, as it may with truth, that those who have inherited the savings of others have an advantage which they may have in no way deserved, over the industrious whose predecessors have not left them anything;

I not only admit, but strenuously contend, that this unearned advantage should be curtailed, as much as is consistent with justice to those who thought fit to dispose of their savings by giving them to their descendants. But while it is true that the labourers are at a disadvantage compared with those whose predecessors have saved, it is also true that the labourers are far better off than if those predecessors had not saved. They share in the advantage, though not to an equal extent with the inheritors. The terms of co-operation between present labour and the fruits of past labour and saving, are a subject for adjustment between the two parties. Each is necessary to the other. The capitalist can do nothing without labourers, nor the labourers without capital. If the labourers compete for employment, the capitalists on their part compete for labour, to the full extent of the circulating capital of the country. Competition is often spoken of as if it were necessarily a cause of misery and degradation to the labouring class; as if high wages were not precisely as much a product of competition as low wages. The remuneration of labour is as much the result of the law of competition in the United States, as it is in Ireland, and much more completely so than in England. . . .

Instead of looking upon competition as the baneful and antisocial principle which it is held to be by the generality of Socialists, I conceive that, even in the present state of society and industry, every restriction of it is an evil, and every extension of it, even if for the time injuriously affecting some class of labourers, is always an ultimate good. To be protected against competition is to be protected in idleness, in mental dullness; to be saved the necessity of being as active and as intelligent as other people; and if it is also to be protected against being underbid for employment by a less highly paid class of labourers, this is only where old custom or local and partial monopoly has placed some particular class of artizans in a privileged position as compared with the rest; and the time has come when the interest of universal improvement is no longer promoted by prolonging the privileges of a few. If the slop-sellers and others of their class have lowered the wages of tailors, and some other artizans, by making them an affair of competition instead of custom, so much the better in the end. What is now required is not to bolster up old customs, whereby limited classes of labouring people obtain partial gains which interest them in keeping up the present organization of society, but to introduce new general practices beneficial to all; and there is reason to rejoice at whatever makes the privileged classes of skilled artizans feel, that they have the same interests, and depend for their remuneration on the same general causes, and must resort for the improvement of their condition to the same remedies, as the less fortunately circumstanced and comparatively helpless multitude. . . .

John Stuart Mill, *Principles of Political Economy,* from the 5th London ed. (New York: Appleton-Century-Crofts, 1865), I, 268–71, 278–80.

B. Friedrich Engels Attacks Competition

Friedrich Engels (1820–1895) was, with Karl Marx, a co-founder of modern or "scientific" Socialism. Engels' association with Marx began shortly after the writing of the book from which the following passages are taken. This description of the condition of the English working class was first published in Germany in 1845, and appeared in an American edition forty years later. The book was to some extent the result of Engels's own observations while in England on business, but in the main its material is drawn from evidence presented before government commissions of inquiry. Not only does the book present something less than a balanced picture of the good and evil which flowed from the Industrial Revolution and the rise of capitalism, but in a later edition the author himself makes the point that the things described are largely matters of the past. Improvement in the standards of life and labor of the mass of the people should not, however, he warns his readers, lead us into justifying an economic system based on private wealth and competition. Concessions to justice and philanthropy are made only to speed capital concentration in the hands of the few by crushing the smaller competitors who could not afford to grant such amenities to their employees. The major grievance is the capitalistic system itself.

The capitalistic system gradually destroyed the old society of landowners, agricultural laborers, and petty bourgeoisie, and erected in its place a social structure dominated by two classes, the capitalist and the proletariat.

The old medieval culture of status, weakened by Renaissance emphasis upon individualism, was now dissolved by the facts of urban life in the age of the Industrial Revolution. Engels describes the workings of individualism in the following words:

"The brutal indifference, the unfeeling isolation of each in his private interest becomes the more repellant and offensive, the more these individuals are crowded together, within a limited space. And, however much one may be aware that this isolation of the individual, this narrow self-seeking is the fundamental principle of our society everywhere, it is nowhere so shamelessly barefaced, so self-conscious as just here in the crowding of the great city. The dissolution of mankind into monads, of which each one has a separate principle, the world of atoms, is here carried out to its utmost extreme. Hence it comes, too, that the social war, the war of each against all, is here openly declared. . . .People regard each other only as useful objects; each exploits the other, and the end of it all is, that the stronger treads the weaker under foot, and that the powerful few, the capitalists, seize everything for themselves, while to the weak many, the poor, scarcely a bare existence remains." [Friedrich Engels, *The Condition of the Working-Class in England in 1844* (London: George Allen & Unwin, Ltd., 1950), p. 24.]

Competition is the completest expression of the battle of all against all which rules in modern civil society. This battle, a battle for life, for existence, for everything, in case of need a battle of life and death, is fought not between the different classes of society only, but also between the individual members of these classes. Each is in the way of the other, and each seeks to crowd out all who are in his way, and to put himself in their place. The workers are in constant competition among themselves as the members of the bourgeoisie among themselves. The power-loom weaver is in competition with the hand-loom weaver, the unemployed or ill-paid hand-loom weaver with him who has work or is better paid, each trying to supplant the other. But this competition of the workers among themselves is the worst side of the present state of things in its effect upon the worker, the sharpest weapon against the proletariat in the hands of the bourgeoisie. Hence the effort of the workers to nullify this competition by associations, hence the hatred of the bourgeoisie towards these associations, and its triumph in every defeat which befalls them. . . .

Fine freedom, where the proletarian has no other choice than that of either accepting the conditions which the bourgeoisie offers him, or of starving, of freezing to death, of sleeping naked among the beasts of the forest! A fine "equivalent" valued at pleasure by the bourgeoisie! And if one proletarian is such a fool as to starve rather than agree to the equitable propositions of the bourgeoisie, his "natural superiors," another is easily found in his place; there are proletarians enough in the world, and not all so insane as to prefer dying to living.

Here we have the competition of the workers among themselves. If *all* the proletarians announced their determination to starve rather than work for the bourgeoisie, the latter would have to surrender its monopoly. But this is not the case—is, indeed, a rather impossible case—so that the bourgeoisie still thrives. To this competition of the worker there is but one limit; no worker will work for less than he needs to subsist. If he must starve, he will prefer to starve in idleness rather than in toil. . . .

From this it is evident what the minimum of wages is. The maximum is deter-

mined by the competition of the bourgeoisie among themselves; for we have seen how they, too, must compete with each other. The bourgeois can increase his capital only in commerce and manufacture, and in both cases he needs workers. Even if he invests his capital at interest, he needs them indirectly; for without commerce and manufacture, no one would pay him interest upon his capital, no one could use it. So the bourgeois certainly needs workers, not indeed for his immediate living, for at need he could consume his capital, but as we need an article of trade or a beast of burden,—as a means of profit. The proletarian produces the goods which the bourgeois sells with advantage. When, therefore, the demand for these goods increases so that all the competing working-men are employed, and a few more might perhaps be useful, the competition among the workers falls away, and the bourgeoisie begin to compete among themselves. The capitalist in search of workmen knows very well that his profits increase as prices rise in consequence of the increased demand for his goods, and pays a trifle higher wages rather than let the whole profit escape him. He sends the butter to fetch the cheese, and getting the latter, leaves the butter ungrudgingly to the workers. So one capitalist after another goes in chase of workers, and wages rise; but only as high as the increasing demand permits. If the capitalist, who willingly sacrificed a part of his extraordinary profit, runs into danger of sacrificing any part of his ordinary average profit, he takes very good care not to pay more than average wages.

From this we can determine the average rate of wages. Under average circumstances, when neither workers nor capitalists have reason to compete, especially among themselves, when there are just as many workers at hand as can be employed in producing precisely the goods that are demanded, wages stand a little above the minimum. How far they rise above the minimum will depend upon the average needs and the grade of civilisation of the workers. If the workers are accustomed to eat meat several times in the week, the capitalists must reconcile themselves to paying wages enough to make this food attainable, not less, because the workers are not competing among themselves and have no occasion to content themselves with less; not more, because the capitalists, in the absence of competition among themselves, have no occasion to attract working-men by extraordinary favours.

This standard of the average needs and the average civilisation of the workers has become very complicated by reason of the complications of English industry, and is different for different sorts of workers, as has been pointed out. Most industrial occupations demand a certain skill and regularity, and for these qualities which involve a certain grade of civilisation, the rate of wages must be such as to induce the worker to acquire such skill and subject himself to such regularity. Hence it is that the average wages of industrial workers are higher than those of mere porters, day labourers, etc., higher especially than those of agricultural laborers, a fact to which the additional cost of the necessities of life in cities contributes somewhat. In other words, the worker is, in law and in fact, the slave of the property-holding class, so effectually a slave that he is sold like a piece of goods, rises and falls in value like a commodity. If the demand for workers increases, the price of workers rises; if it falls, their price falls. If it falls so greatly that a number of them become unsaleable, if they are left in stock, they are simply left idle; and as they cannot live upon that, they die of starvation. For, to speak in the words of the economists, the expense incurred in maintaining them would not be reproduced, would be money thrown away, and to this end no man advances capital; and, so far, Malthus was perfectly right in his theory of population. The only difference as compared with the old, outspoken slavery is this, that the worker of to-day seems to be free because he is not sold once for all, but piecemeal by the day, the week, the year, and because no one owner sells him to another, but he is forced to sell himself

in this way instead, being the slave of no particular person, but of the whole property-holding class. For him the matter is unchanged at bottom, and if this semblance of liberty necessarily gives him some real freedom on the one hand, it entails on the other the disadvantage that no one guarantees him a subsistence; he is in danger of being repudiated at any moment by his master, the bourgeoisie, and left to die of starvation, if the bourgeoisie ceases to have an interest in his employment, his existence. The bourgeoisie, on the other hand, is far better off under the present arrangement than under the old slave system; it can dismiss its employees at discretion without sacrificing invested capital, and gets its work done much more cheaply than is possible with slave labour, as Adam Smith comfortingly pointed out.

Hence it follows, too, that Adam Smith was perfectly right in making the assertion: "That the demand for men, like that for any other commodity, necessarily regulates the production of men, quickens it when it goes on too slowly, and stops it when it advances too fast." *Just as in the case of any other commodity!* If there are too few labourers at hand, prices, i.e. wages, rise, the workers are more prosperous, marriages multiply, more children are born and more live to grow up, until a sufficient number of labourers has been secured. If there are too many on hand, prices fall, want of work, poverty, and starvation, and consequent diseases arise, and the "surplus population" is put out of the way. And Malthus, who carried the foregoing proposition of Smith farther, was also right, in his way, in asserting that there are always more people on hand than can be maintained from the available means of subsistence. Surplus population is engendered rather by the competition of the workers among themselves, which forces each separate worker to labour as much each day as his strength can possibly admit. If a manufacturer can employ ten hands nine hours daily, he can employ nine if each works ten hours, and the tenth goes hungry. And if a manufacturer can force the nine hands to work an extra hour daily for the same wages by threatening to discharge them at a time when the demand for hands is not very great, he discharges the tenth and saves so much wages. This is the process on a small scale, which goes on in a nation on a large one. The productiveness of each hand raised to the highest pitch by the competition of the workers among themselves, the division of labour, the introduction of machinery, the subjugation of the forces of nature, deprive a multitude of workers of bread. These starving workers are then removed from the market, . . . and so it goes on, always the same old round, or rather, so it would go if other circumstances did not intervene. The introduction of the industrial forces already referred to for increasing production leads, in the course of time, to a reduction of prices of the articles produced and to consequent increased consumption, so that a large part of the displaced workers finally, after long suffering, find work again. If, in addition to this, the conquest of foreign markets constantly and rapidly increases the demand for manufactured goods, as has been the case in England during the past sixty years, the demand for hands increases, and, in proportion to it, the population. Thus, instead of diminishing, the population of the British Empire has increased with extraordinary rapidity, and is still increasing. Yet, in spite of the extension of industry, in spite of the demand for working-men which, in general, has increased, there is, according to the confession of all the official political parties (Tory, Whig, and Radical), permanent surplus, superfluous population; the competition among the workers is constantly greater than the competition to secure workers.

Whence comes this incongruity? It lies in the nature of industrial competition and the commercial crises which arise from them. In the present unregulated production and distribution of the means of subsistence, which is carried on not directly for the sake of supplying needs, but for profit, in the system under which every one works for himself to enrich himself, disturbances inevitably arise at every moment. For example, England supplies a number of countries with most diverse goods. Now, although the manufacturer may know how much of each article is consumed in each country annually, he cannot know how much is on hand at every given moment, much less can he know how much his competitors export thither. He can only draw most uncertain inferences from the perpetual fluctuations in prices, as to the quantities on hand and the needs of the moment. He must trust to luck in exporting his goods. Everything is done blindly, as guess-work, more or less at the mercy of accident. Upon the slightest favourable report, each one exports what he can, and before long such a market is glutted, sales stop, capital remains inactive, prices fall, and English manufacture has no further employment for its hands. In the beginning of the development of manufacture, these checks were limited to single branches and single markets; but the centralising tendency of competition which drives the hands thrown out of one branch into such other branches as are most easily accessible, and transfers the goods which cannot be disposed of in one market to other markets, has gradually brought the single minor crises nearer together and united them into one periodically recurring crisis. Such a crisis usually recurs once in five years after a brief period of activity and general prosperity; the home market, like all foreign ones, is glutted with English goods, which it can only slowly absorb, the industrial movement comes to a standstill in almost every branch, the small manufacturers and merchants who cannot survive a prolonged inactivity of their invested capital fail, the larger ones suspend business during the worst season, close their mills or work short time, perhaps half the day; wages fall by reason of the competition of the unemployed, the diminution of working-time and the lack of profitable sales; want becomes universal among the workers, the small savings, which individuals may have made, are rapidly consumed, the philanthropic institutions are overburdened, the poor-rates are doubled, trebled, and still insufficient, the number of the starving increases, and the whole multitude of "surplus" population presses in terrific numbers into the foreground. This continues for a time; the "surplus" exist as best they may, or perish; philanthropy and the Poor Law help many of them to a painful prolongation of their existence. Others find scant means of subsistence here and there in such kinds of work as have been least open to competition, are most remote from manufacture. And with how little can a human being keep body and soul together for a time! Gradually the state of things improve; the accumulations of goods are consumed, the general depression among the men of commerce and manufacture prevents a too hasty replenishing of the markets, and at last rising prices and favourable reports from all directions restore activity. Most of the markets are distant ones; demand increases and prices rise constantly while the first exports are arriving; people struggle for the first goods, the first sales enliven trade still more, the prospective ones promise still higher prices; expecting a further rise, merchants begin to buy upon speculation, and so to withdraw from consumption the articles intended for it, just when they are most needed. Speculation forces prices still higher, by inspiring others to purchase, and appropriating new importations at once. All this is reported to England, manufacturers begin to produce with a will, new mills are built, every means is employed to make the most of the favourable moment. Speculation arises here, too, exerting the same influence as upon foreign markets, raising prices, withdrawing goods from consumption, spurring manufacture

in both ways to the highest pitch of effort. Then come the daring speculators working with fictitious capital, living upon credit, ruined if they cannot speedily sell; they hurl themselves into this universal, disorderly race for profits, multiply the disorder and haste by their unbridled passion, which drives prices and production to madness. It is a frantic struggle, which carries away even the most experienced and phlegmatic; goods are spun, woven, hammered, as if all mankind were to be newly equipped, as though two thousand million new consumers had been discovered in the moon. All at once the shaky speculators abroad, who must have money, begin to sell, below market price, of course, for their need is urgent; one sale is followed by others, prices fluctuate, speculators throw their goods upon the market in terror, the market is disordered, credit shaken, one house after another stops payments, bankruptcy follows bankruptcy, and the discovery is made that three times more goods are on hand or under way than can be consumed. The news reaches England, where production has been going on at full speed meanwhile, panic seizes all hands, failures abroad cause others in England, the panic crushes a number of firms, all reserves are thrown upon the market here, too, in the moment of anxiety, and the alarm is still further exaggerated. This is the beginning of the crisis, which then takes precisely the same course as its predecessor, and gives place in turn to a season of prosperity. So it goes on perpetually,—prosperity, crisis, prosperity, crisis, and this perennial round in which English industry moves is, as has been before observed, usually completed once in five or six years.

Friedrich Engels, *The Condition of the Working-Class in England in 1844* (London: George Allen & Unwin, Ltd., 1950), pp. 75–84.

C. Pope Leo XIII Asserts the Right of Private Property

The pontificate of Pope Leo XIII extended from 1878 to 1903. The whole Christian world

was confronted by the Industrial Revolution with a situation in which that scheme of social ethics which had been developed in the predominantly agrarian and static social order of the Middle Ages was often unrealistic and sometimes reactionary. Unchanging in its view of the nature of man and of society and uncompromising in its assertion of right principles of Christian conduct, in the face of industrialism, nationalism, and democracy, the Church required a restatement of its position in modern terms. In *Rerum Novarum* (1891) and in other encyclicals Pope Leo XIII applied Christian principles to the social problems that were arising out of the new economic order. He taught that all power must be exercised with regard to the demands of justice, that the dignity of labor, derived as a means of the accomplishment of the supernatural destiny of man, must not be violated; and, in contrast to the Marxian theory of inevitable class struggle, he preached the peaceful ordering of society through the mutual recognition of the moral rights and the spiritual responsibilities of both Capital and Labor.

The encyclicals of Leo helped to effect a reconciliation between the ancient Church and the modern age, and assumed for the Christian religion a place of leadership in the solution of the social question and the reconstruction of society. Other papal pronouncements on social and economic issues followed, the latest being the *Mater et Magistra* of John XXIII. The Roman Catholic Church was not alone, of course, in addressing itself to the problem of Christian implications of the new social issues. In one place or another, the questions raised in *Rerum Novarum* have been faced by almost all of the Christian churches time and again in the nineteenth and twentieth centuries.

1. It is not surprising that the spirit of revolutionary change, which has so long been predominant in the nations of the world, should have passed beyond politics and made its influence felt in the cognate field of practical economy. The elements of a conflict are unmistakable: the growth of industry, and the surprising discoveries of science; the changed relations of masters and workmen; the enormous fortunes of individuals, and the poverty of the masses; the increased self-reliance and the closer mutual combination of the working population; and, finally, a general moral deterioration. The momentous seriousness of the present state of things just now fills every mind with painful apprehension; wise men discuss it; practical men propose schemes;

popular meetings, legislatures, and sovereign princes, all are occupied with it—and there is nothing which has a deeper hold on public attention.

2. Therefore, Venerable Brethren, as on former occasions, when it seemed opportune to refute false teaching, We have addressed you in the interest of the Church and of the common weal, and have issued Letters on Political Power, on Human Liberty, on the Christian Constitution of the State, and on similar subjects, so now We have thought it useful to speak on the CONDITION OF LABOR. It is a matter on which We have touched once or twice already. But in this Letter the responsibility of the Apostolic office urges Us to treat the question expressly and at length, in order that there may be no mistake as to the principles which truth and justice dictate for its settlement. The discussion is not easy, nor is it free from danger. It is not easy to define the relative rights and the mutual duties of the wealthy and of the poor, of capital and of labor. And the danger lies in this, that crafty agitators constantly make use of these disputes to pervert men's judgments and to stir up the people to sedition.

3. But all agree, and there can be no question whatever, that some remedy must be found, and quickly found, for the misery and wretchedness which press so heavily at this moment on the large majority of the very poor. The ancient workmen's Guilds were destroyed in the last century, and no other organization took their place. Public institutions and the laws have repudiated the ancient religion. Hence by degrees it has come to pass that Working-Men have been given over, isolated and defenseless, to the callousness of employers, and the greed of unrestrained competition. The evil has been increased by rapacious Usury, which, although more than once condemned by the Church, is nevertheless, under a different form but with the same guilt, still practiced by avaricious and grasping men. And to this must be added the custom of working by contract, and the concentration of so many branches of trade in the hands

of a few individuals, so that a small number of very rich men have been able to lay upon the masses of the poor a yoke little better than slavery itself.

4. To remedy these evils the *Socialists,* working on the poor man's envy of the rich, endeavor to destroy private property, and maintain that individual possessions should become the common property of all, to be administered by the State or by municipal bodies. They hold that, by thus transferring property from private persons to the community, the present evil state of things will be set to rights, because each citizen will then have his equal share of whatever there is to enjoy. But their proposals are so clearly futile for all practical purposes, that if they were carried out the working-man himself would be among the first to suffer. Moreover they are emphatically unjust, because they would rob the lawful possessor, bring the State into a sphere that is not its own, and cause complete confusion in the community.

5. It is surely undeniable that, when a man engages in remunerative labor, the very reason and motive of his work is to obtain property, and to hold it as his own private possession. If one man hires out to another his strength or his industry, he does this for the purpose of receiving in return what is necessary for food and living; he thereby expressly proposes to acquire a full and real right, not only to the remuneration, but also to the disposal of that remuneration as he pleases. Thus, if he lives sparingly, saves money, and invests his savings, for greater security, in land, the land in such a case is only his wages in another form; and consequently, a working-man's little estate thus purchased should be as completely at his own disposal as the wages he receives for his labor. But it is precisely in this power of disposal that ownership consists, whether the property be land or movable goods. The *Socialists,* therefore, in endeavoring to transfer the possessions of individuals to the community, strike at the interests of every wage-earner, for they deprive him of the liberty of disposing of his

wages, and thus of all hope and possibility of increasing his stock and of bettering his condition in life.

6. What is of still greater importance, however, is that the remedy they propose is manifestly against justice. For every man has by nature the right to possess property as his own. This is one of the chief points of distinction between man and the animal creation. For the brute has no power of self-direction, but is governed by two chief instincts, which keep his powers alert, move him to use his strength, and determine him to action without the power of choice. These instincts are self-preservation and the propagation of the species. Both can attain their purpose by means of things which are close at hand; beyond their surroundings the brute creation cannot go, for they are moved to action by sensibility alone, and by the things which sense perceives. But with man it is different indeed. He possesses, on the one hand, the full perfection of animal nature, and therefore he enjoys, at least as much as the rest of the animal race, the fruition of the things of the body. But animality, however perfect, is far from being the whole of humanity, and is indeed humanity's humble handmaid, made to serve and obey. It is the mind, or the reason, which is the chief thing in us who are human beings; it is this which makes a human being human, and distinguishes him essentially and completely from the brute. And on this account—viz., that man alone among animals possesses reason—it must be within his right to have things not merely for temporary and momentary use, as other living beings have them, but in stable and permanent possession; he must have not only things which perish in the using, but also those which, though used, remain for use in the future.

7. This becomes still more clearly evident if we consider man's nature a little more deeply. For man, comprehending by the power of his reason things innumerable, and joining the future with the present—being, moreover, the master of his own acts—governs himself by the

foresight of his counsel, under the eternal law and the power of God, Whose Providence governs all things; wherefore it is in his power to exercise his choice not only on things which regard his present welfare, but also on those which will be for his advantage in time to come. Hence man not only can possess the fruits of the earth, but also the earth itself; for of the products of the earth he can make provision for the future. Man's needs do not die out, but recur; satisfied today, they demand new supplies to-morrow. Nature, therefore, owes to man a storehouse that shall never fail, the daily supply of his daily wants. And this he finds only in the inexhaustible fertility of the earth.

8. Nor must we, at this stage, have recourse to the State. Man is older than the State; and he holds the right of providing for the life of his body prior to the formation of any State. And to say that God has given the earth to the use and enjoyment of the universal human race is not to deny that there can be private property. For God has granted the earth to mankind in general; not in the sense that all without distinction can deal with it as they please, but rather that no part of it has been assigned to any one in particular, and that the limits of private possession have been left to be fixed by man's own industry and the laws of individual peoples. Moreover the earth, though divided among private owners, ceases not thereby to minister to the needs of all; for there is no one who does not live on what the land brings forth. Those who do not possess the soil, contribute their labor; so that it may be truly said that all human subsistence is derived either from labor on one's own land, or from some laborious industry which is paid for either in the produce of the land itself or in that which is exchanged for what the land brings forth.

9. Here, again, we have another proof that private ownership is according to nature's law. For that which is required for the preservation of life, and for life's well-being, is produced in great abundance by the earth, but not until man has brought it into cultivation and lavished upon it his care and skill. Now, when man thus spends the industry of his mind and the strength of his body in procuring the fruits of nature, by that act he makes his own that portion of nature's field which he cultivates—that portion on which he leaves, as it were, the impress of his own personality; and it cannot but be just that he should possess that portion as his own, and should have a right to keep it without molestation.

10. These arguments are so strong and convincing that it seems surprising that certain obsolete opinions should now be revived in opposition to what is here laid down. We are told that it is right for private persons to have the use of the soil and the fruits of their land, but that it is unjust for anyone to possess as owner either the land on which he has built or the estate which he has cultivated. But those who assert this do not perceive that they are robbing man of what his own labor has produced. For the soil which is tilled and cultivated with toil and skill utterly changes its condition; it was wild before, it is now fruitful; it was barren, and now it brings forth in abundance. That which has thus altered and improved it becomes so truly part of itself as to be in great measure indistinguishable and inseparable from it. Is it just that the fruit of a man's sweat and labor should be enjoyed by another? As effects follow their cause, so it is just and right that the results of labor should belong to him who has labored.

11. With reason, therefore, the common opinion of mankind, little affected by the few dissentients who have maintained the opposite view, has found in the study of nature, and in the law of Nature herself, the foundation of the division of property, and has consecrated by the practice of all ages the principle of private ownership, as being pre-eminently in conformity with human nature, and as conducing in the most unmistakable manner to the peace and tranquility of human life. The same principle is confirmed and enforced by the civil laws—laws which, as

long as they are just, derive their binding force from the law of nature. The authority of the Divine Law adds its sanction, forbidding us in the gravest terms even to covet that which is another's:—*Thou shalt not covet thy neighbor's wife; nor his house, nor his field, nor his manservant, nor his maidservant, nor his ox, nor his ass, nor anything which is his.*

12. The rights here spoken of, belonging to each individual man, are seen in a much stronger light if they are considered in relation to man's social and domestic obligations.

13. In choosing a state of life, it is indisputable that all are at full liberty either to follow the counsel of Jesus Christ as to virginity, or to enter into the bonds of marriage. No human law can abolish the natural and primitive right of marriage, or in any way limit the chief and principal purpose of marriage, ordained by God's authority from the beginning: *Increase and multiply.* Thus we have the Family; the "society" of a man's own household; a society limited indeed in numbers, but a true "society," anterior to every kind of State or nation, with rights and duties of its own, totally independent of the commonwealth.

14. That right of property, therefore, which has been proved to belong naturally to individual persons, must also belong to a man in his capacity of head of a family; nay, such a person must possess this right so much the more clearly in proportion as his position multiplies his duties. For it is a most sacred law of nature that a father must provide food and all necessaries for those whom he has begotten; and, similarly, nature dictates that a man's children, who carry on, as it were, and continue his own personality, should be provided by him with all that is needful to enable them honorably to keep themselves from want and misery in the uncertainties of this mortal life. Now, in no other way can a father effect this except by the ownership of profitable property, which he can transmit to his children by inheritance. A family, no less than a State, is, as We have said, a true society,

governed by a power within itself, that is to say by the father. Wherefore, provided the limits be not transgressed which are prescribed by the very purposes for which it exists, the Family has at least equal rights with the State in the choice and pursuit of those things which are needful to its preservation and its just liberty....

20. Let it be laid down, in the first place, that humanity must remain as it is. It is impossible to reduce human society to a level. The *Socialists* may do their utmost, but all striving against nature is vain. There naturally exist among mankind innumerable differences of the most important kind; people differ in capability, in diligence, in health, and in strength; and unequal fortune is a necessary result of inequality in condition. Such inequality is far from being disadvantageous either to individuals or to the community; social and public life can only go on by the help of various kinds of capacity and the playing of many parts; and each man, as a rule, chooses the part which peculiarly suits his case. As regards bodily labor, even had man never fallen from *the state of innocence,* he would not have been wholly unoccupied; but that which would then have been his free choice and his delight, became afterwards compulsory, and the painful expiation of his sin. *Cursed be the earth in thy work; in thy labor thou shalt eat of it all the days of thy life.* In like manner, the other pains and hardships of life will have no end or cessation on this earth; for the consequences of sin are bitter and hard to bear, and they must be with man as long as life lasts. To suffer and to endure, therefore, is the lot of humanity; let men try as they may, no strength and no artifice will ever succeed in banishing from human life the ills and troubles which beset it. If any there are who pretend differently—who hold out to a hardpressed people freedom from pain and trouble, undisturbed repose, and constant enjoyment—they cheat the people and impose upon them, and their lying promises will only make the evil worse than

before. There is nothing more useful than to look at the world as it really is—and at the same time to look elsewhere for a remedy to its troubles.

21. The great mistake that is made in the matter now under consideration is to possess one's self of the idea that class is naturally hostile to class; that rich and poor are intended by nature to live at war with one another. So irrational and so false is this view, that the exact contrary is the truth. Just as the symmetry of the human body is the result of the disposition of the members of the body, so in a state it is ordained by nature that these two classes should exist in harmony and agreement, and should, as it were, fit into one another, so as to maintain the equilibrium of the body politic. Each requires the other; capital cannot do without labor, nor labor without capital. Mutual agreement results in pleasantness and good order; perpetual conflict necessarily produces confusion and outrage. Now, in preventing such strife as this, and in making it impossible, the efficacy of Christianity is marvelous and manifold. First of all, there is nothing more powerful than Religion (of which the Church is the interpreter and guardian) in drawing rich and poor together, by reminding each class of its duties to the other, and especially of the duties of justice. Thus Religion teaches the laboring man and the workman to carry out honestly and well all equitable agreements freely made; never to injure capital, or to outrage the person of an employer; never to employ violence in representing his own cause, or to engage in riot or disorder; and to have nothing to do with men of evil principles, who work upon the people with artful promises, and raise foolish hopes which usually end in disaster and in repentance when too late. Religion teaches the rich man and the employer that their work people are not their slaves; that they must respect in every man his dignity as a man

and as a Christian; that labor is nothing to be ashamed of, if we listen to right reason and to Christian philosophy, but is an honorable employment, enabling a man to sustain his life in an upright and creditable way; and that it is shameful and inhuman to treat men like chattels to make money by, or to look upon them merely as so much muscle or physical power. Thus, again, Religion teaches that, as among the workman's concerns are Religion herself and things spiritual and mental, the employer is bound to see that he has time for the duties of piety; that he be not exposed to corrupting influences and dangerous occasions; and that he be not led away to neglect his home and family or to squander his wages. Then, again, the employer must never tax his work people beyond their strength, nor employ them in work unsuited to their sex or age. His great and principal obligation is to give to every one that which is just. Doubtless before we can decide whether wages are adequate, many things have to be considered; but rich men and masters should remember this—that to exercise pressure for the sake of gain upon the indigent and the destitute, and to make one's profit out of the need of another is condemned by all laws, human and divine. To defraud any one of wages that are his due is a crime which cries to the avenging anger of Heaven. *Behold, the hire of the laborers....which by fraud hath been kept back by you, crieth; and the cry of them hath entered into the ears of the Lord of Sabaoth.* Finally, the rich must religiously refrain from cutting down the workman's earnings, either by force, by fraud, or by usurious dealing; and with the more reason because the poor man is weak and unprotected, and because his slender means should be sacred in proportion to their scantiness.

22. Were these prospects carefully obeyed and followed, would not strife die out and cease?

From the encyclical letter "Rerum Novarum" addressed to the Roman Catholic world in 1891 by Pope Leo XIII, in Henry George, *The Condition of Labor, an Open Letter to Pope Leo XIII* (New York: United States Book Co., 1891), pp. 121–32.

II. *The Myth of Progress*

The changing society of the nineteenth century was the product not alone of the economic changes effected by the Industrial Revolution; it was also in large part the adolescent child of the Enlightenment, and, as such, was apt to manifest a brash rejection of ancient wisdom. Calvinistic doctrine, influential in English thinking long after the restoration of King and Church, although tending to encourage political democracy, was apt to dull the edge of religion as an instrument of social reform. Earthly prosperity was regarded as the evidence of grace and the reward of virtue; earthly poverty became the consequence of imprudence or the penalty for vice. Now came Rousseau's doctrine of the essential goodness of man and from this root grew many branches, among them the Socialism of Saint-Simon and the Positivism of Comte. The mists of old beliefs were swept away, and unaided by Divine Providence, man sought to find in the laws governing the social world the key to his own way to perfection. The "Myth" of Redemption was replaced by the Myth of Progress. The ultimate end of the cycle in the twentieth century was not the good society but crashing catastrophe, and so the question remains with us: Can man by his own unaided efforts create a perfect world?

The following selections represent two points of view taken in the debate. Malthus, the pessimist, asserts on scientific grounds the proposition that mankind is doomed, by the operation of natural laws irresistible except by moral means, to limits to self-improvement. Owen, the optimist, expresses the view that by education in right principles the perfect society can be established among men.

A. *Thomas Malthus Describes the Principle of Population*

Thomas Robert Malthus (1766–1834) was a parish priest of the Church of England who later relinquished parochial duties in favor of a teaching post. Few men have had a more continuous and pervasive influence upon the discussion of a public question than has had Malthus upon the problem of social improvement. Against the optimism of those who held that if reason adduces right principles and education inculcates character in accordance with knowledge, society can be improved, Malthus interposed the view that population increases disproportionately to the supply of food, and that misery and want are natural devices to keep it in check.

The great and unlooked for discoveries that have taken place of late years in natural philosophy; the increasing diffusion of general knowledge from the extension of the art of printing; the ardent and unshackled spirit of inquiry that prevails throughout the lettered, and even unlettered world; the new and extraordinary lights that have been thrown on political subjects, which dazzle, and astonish the understanding; and particularly that tremendous phenomenon in the political horizon, the French revolution, which, like a blazing comet, seems destined either to inspire with fresh life and vigour, or to scorch up and destroy the shrinking inhabitants of the earth, have all concurred to lead many able men into the opinion, that we were touching on a period big with the most important changes, changes that would in some measure be decisive of the future fate of mankind.

It has been said, that the great question is now at issue, whether man shall henceforth start forwards with accelerated velocity towards illimitable, and hitherto unconceived improvement; or be condemned to a perpetual oscillation between happiness and misery, and after every effort remain still at an immeasurable distance from the wished-for goal.

Yet, anxiously as every friend of mankind must look forwards to the termination of this painful suspense; and, eagerly as the inquiring mind would hail every ray of light that might assist its view into futurity, it is much to be lamented, that the writers on each side of this momentous question still keep far aloof from each other. Their mutual arguments do not meet with a candid examination. The question is not brought to rest on fewer points; and even in theory scarcely seems to be approaching to a decision.

The advocate for the present order of things, is apt to treat the sect of speculative philosophers, either as a set of artful and designing knaves, who preach up ardent benevolence, and draw captivating pictures of a happier state of society, only the better to enable them to destroy the present establishments, and to forward their own deep-laid schemes of ambition: or, as wild and mad-headed enthusiasts, whose silly speculations, and absurd paradoxes, are not worthy the attention of any reasonable man.

The advocate for the perfectibility of man, and of society, retorts on the defender of establishments a more than equal contempt. He brands him as the slave of the most miserable, and narrow prejudices; or, as the defender of the abuses of civil society, only because he profits by them. He paints him either as a character who prostitutes his understanding to his interest; or as one whose powers of mind are not of a size to grasp any thing great and noble; who cannot see above five yards before him; and who must therefore be utterly unable to take in the views of the enlightened benefactor of mankind.

In this unamicable contest, the cause of truth cannot but suffer. The really good arguments on each side of the question are not allowed to have their proper weight. Each pursues his own theory, little solicitous to correct, or improve it, by an attention to what is advanced by his opponents.

The friend of the present order of things condemns all political speculations in the gross. He will not even condescend to examine the grounds from which the perfectibility of society is inferred. Much less will he give himself the trouble in a fair and candid manner to attempt an exposition of their fallacy.

The speculative philosopher equally offends against the cause of truth. With eyes fixed on a happier state of society, the blessings of which he paints in the most captivating colours, he allows himself to indulge in the most bitter invectives against every present establishment, without applying his talents to consider the best and safest means of removing abuses, and without seeming to be aware of the tremendous obstacles that threaten, even in theory, to oppose the progress of man towards perfection.

It is an acknowledged truth in philosophy, that a just theory will always be confirmed by experiment. Yet so much friction, and so many minute circumstances occur in practice, which it is next to impossible for the most enlarged and penetrating mind to foresee, that on few subjects can any theory be pronounced just, that has not stood the test of experience. But an untried theory cannot fairly be advanced as probable, much less as just, till all the arguments against it, have been maturely weighed, and clearly and consistently refuted.

I have read some of the speculations on the perfectibility of man and of society, with great pleasure. I have been warmed and delighted with the enchanting picture which they hold forth. I ardently wish for such happy improvements. But I see great, and, to my understanding, unconquerable difficulties in the way to them. These difficulties it is my present purpose to state; declaring, at the same time, that so far from exulting in them, as a cause of triumph over the friends of innovation, nothing would give me greater pleasure than to see them completely removed.

The most important argument that I shall adduce is certainly not new. The principles on which it depends have been explained in part by Hume, and more at large by Dr. Adam Smith. It has been advanced and applied to the present subject, though not with its proper weight, or in the most forcible point of view, by Mr. Wallace: and it may probably have been stated by many writers that I have never met with. I should certainly therefore not think of advancing it again, though I mean to place it in a point of view in some degree different from any that I have hitherto seen, if it had ever been fairly and satisfactorily answered.

The cause of this neglect on the part of the advocates for the perfectibility of mankind, is not easily accounted for. I cannot doubt the talents of such men as Godwin and Condorcet. I am unwilling to doubt their candour. To my understanding, and probably to that of most others, the difficulty appears insurmountable. Yet these men of acknowledged ability and penetration, scarcely design to notice it, and hold on their course in such speculations, with unabated ardour, and undiminished confidence. I have certainly no right to say that they purposely shut their eyes to such arguments. I ought rather to doubt the validity of them, when neglected by such men, however forcibly their truth may strike my own mind. Yet in this respect it must be acknowledged that we are all of us too prone to err. If I saw a glass of wine repeatedly presented to a man, and he took no notice of it, I should be apt to think that he was blind or uncivil. A juster philosophy might teach me rather to think that my eyes deceived me, and that the offer was not really what I conceived it to be.

In entering upon the argument I must premise that I put out of the question, at present, all mere conjectures; that is, all suppositions, the probable realization of which cannot be inferred upon any just philosophical grounds. A writer may tell me that he thinks man will ultimately become an ostrich. I cannot properly contradict him. But before he can expect to bring any reasonable person over to his opinion, he ought to shew, that the necks of mankind have been gradually elongating; that the lips have grown harder, and more prominent; that the legs and feet are daily altering their shape; and that the hair is beginning to change into stubs of feathers. And till the probability of so wonderful a conversion can be shewn, it is surely lost time and lost eloquence to expatiate on the happiness of man in such a state; to describe his powers, both of running and flying; to paint him in a condition where all narrow luxuries would be contemned; where he would be employed only in collecting the necessaries of life; and where, consequently, each man's share of labour would be light, and his portion of leisure ample.

I think I may fairly make two postulata.

First, That food is necessary to the existence of man.

Secondly, That the passion between the sexes is necessary, and will remain nearly in its present state.

These two laws ever since we have had any knowledge of mankind, appear to have been fixed laws of our nature; and, as we have not hitherto seen any alteration in them, we have no right to conclude that they will ever cease to be what they now are, without an immediate act of power in that Being who first arranged the system of the universe; and for the advantage of his creatures, still executes, according to fixed laws, all its various operations.

I do not know that any writer has supposed that on this earth man will ultimately be able to live without food. But Mr. Godwin has conjectured that the passion between the sexes may in time be extinguished. As, however, he calls this part of his work, a deviation into the land of conjecture, I will not dwell longer upon it at present, than to say, that the best arguments for the perfectibility of man, are drawn from a contemplation of the great progress that he has already made from the savage state, and the difficulty of saying where he is to stop. But towards the extinction of the passion between the sexes, no progress whatever has hitherto been made. It appears to exist in as much force at present as it did two thousand, or four thousand years ago. There are individual exceptions now as there always have been. But, as these exceptions do not appear to increase in number, it would surely be a very unphilosophical mode of arguing, to infer merely from the existence of an exception, that the exception would, in time, become the rule, and the rule the exception.

Assuming then, my postulata as granted, I say, that the power of population is indefinitely greater than the power in the earth to produce subsistence for man.

Population, when unchecked, increases in a geometrical ratio. Subsistence increases only in an arithmetical ratio. A slight acquaintance with numbers will shew the immensity of the first power in comparison of the second.

By that law of our nature which makes food necessary to the life of man, the effects of these two unequal powers must be kept equal.

This implies a strong and constantly operating check on population from the difficulty of subsistence. This difficulty must fall some where; and must necessarily be severely felt by a large portion of mankind.

Through the animal and vegetable kingdoms, nature has scattered the seeds of life abroad with the most profuse and liberal hand. She has been comparatively sparing in the room, and the nourishment necessary to rear them. The germs of existence contained in this spot of earth, with ample food, and ample room to expand in, would fill millions of worlds in the course of a few thousand years. Necessity, that imperious all pervading law of nature, restrains them within the prescribed bounds. The race of plants, and the race of animals shrink under this great restrictive law. And the race of man cannot, by any efforts of reason, escape from it. Among plants and animals its effects are waste of seed, sickness, and premature death. Among mankind, misery and vice. The former, misery, is an absolutely necessary consequence of it. Vice is a highly probable consequence, and we therefore see it abundantly prevail; but it ought not, perhaps, to be called an absolutely

necessary consequence. The ordeal of virtue is to resist all temptation to evil.

This natural inequality of the two powers of population, and of production in the earth, and that great law of our nature which must constantly keep their effects equal, form the great difficulty that to me appears insurmountable in the way to the perfectibility of society. All other arguments are of slight and subordinate consideration in comparison of this. I see no way by which man can escape from the weight of this law which pervades all animated nature. No fancied equality, no agrarian regulations in their utmost extent, could remove the pressure of it even for a single century. And it appears, therefore, to be decisive against the possible existence of a society, all the members of which, should live in ease, happiness, and comparative leisure; and feel no anxiety about providing the means of subsistence for themselves and families.

Consequently, if the premises are just, the argument is conclusive against the perfectibility of the mass of mankind.

Thomas Robert Malthus, *First Essay on Population*, 1798, reprinted for the Royal Economic Society from the 1798 ed. (London: Macmillan & Co., Ltd., 1926), pp. 1–17.

B. Robert Owen Prescribes Education for the New World

Robert Owen (1771–1858), a significant figure in the development of the new social order in England, is typical of what is sometimes called the Utopian school of Socialism because he believed in the essential goodness of man, regarded religion as a universal force, rather than as a delusion foisted by the exploiters on the exploited, and looked to education and improvement of the social environment as means to reform. Owen was a philanthropist. He rejected, on the one hand, competition as a principle of social order, and, on the other hand, the theory of history as the product of materialistic forces, while struggle or war between classes as the inevitable outcome of the march of progress had no place in his theories and methods of reform.

As proprietor of the mills at New Lanark,

Scotland, Owen created a model factory community, introduced labor reforms, and established a school for the cultivation of a spirit of universal benevolence. He believed that environment determined character, that social ills were due to social wrongs, and that education provided the means by which a controlled environment would pour the characters of men in a mold suitable for "the New Society."

In order to create a community based on good will he bought a 30,000-acre estate in the New World, and at New Harmony, Indiana, established his pioneer co-operative community. New Harmony was soon rent with dissention and three years after its establishment, Owen withdrew with a loss of nearly his entire fortune. Upon his return to England, Owen was instrumental in establishing Cooperative Societies, set up an exchange system whereby workmen sold to one another the products of their own labors, and became actively associated with the organization of workmen into labor unions.

Whatever the failures and futilities of his life, Robert Owen has had a potent influence on English and American social attitudes and thought. Here, in contrast to Malthus, is his prescription for the improvement of the lot of man.

Those who have duly reflected on the nature and extent of the mental movements of the world for the last half century, must be conscious that great changes are in progress; that man is about to advance another important step towards that degree of intelligence which his natural powers seem capable of attaining. Observe the transactions of the passing hours; see the whole mass of mind in full motion; behold it momentarily increasing in vigour, and preparing ere long to burst its confinement. But what is to be the nature of this change? A due attention to the facts around us, and to those transmitted by the invention of printing from former ages, will afford a satisfactory reply.

From the earliest ages it has been the practice of the world, to act on the supposition that each individual man forms his own character, and that therefore he is accountable for all his sentiments and habits, and consequently merits reward for some, and punishment for others. Every system which has been established among men has been founded on these erroneous principles. When, however, they shall be brought to the test of fair examination, they will be found not only unsupported, but in direct opposition to all experience, and to the evidence of our senses. This is not a slight mistake which involves only trivial consequences; it is a fundamental error of the highest possible magnitude; it enters into all our proceedings regarding man from his infancy, and will be found to be the true and sole origin of evil. It generates and perpetuates ignorance, hatred, and revenge, where, without such error, only intelligence, confidence, and kindness would exist. It has hitherto been the Evil Genius of the world. It severs man from man throughout the various regions of the earth; and makes enemies of those who, but for this gross error, would have enjoyed each other's kind offices and sincere friendship. It is, in short, an error which carries misery in all its consequences.

This error cannot much longer exist; for every day will make it more and more evident THAT THE CHARACTER OF MAN IS, WITHOUT A SINGLE EXCEPTION, ALWAYS FORMED FOR HIM; THAT IT MAY BE, AND IS CHIEFLY, CREATED BY HIS PREDECESSORS; THAT THEY GIVE HIM, OR MAY GIVE HIM, HIS IDEAS AND HABITS, WHICH ARE THE POWERS THAT GOVERN AND DIRECT HIS CONDUCT. MAN, THEREFORE, NEVER DID, NOR IS IT POSSIBLE HE EVER CAN, FORM HIS OWN CHARACTER. . . .

Had not mankind been misinstructed from infancy on this subject, making it necessary that they should unlearn what they have been taught, the simple statement of this truth would render it instantaneously obvious to every rational mind. Men would know that their predecessors might have given them the habits of ferocious cannibalism, or of the highest known benevolence and intelligence: and by the acquirement of this knowledge they would soon learn that, as parents, preceptors, and legislators united, they possess the means of training the rising generations to either of those extremes; that they may with the greatest certainty make them the conscientious worshippers of Juggernaut, or of the most pure spirit possessing the essence of every excellence which the human imagination can conceive; that they may train the young to become effeminate, deceitful, ignorantly selfish, intemperate, revengeful, murderous,—of course ignorant, irrational, and miserable; or to be manly, just, generous, temperate, active, kind, and benevolent,—that is, intelligent, rational, and happy. The knowledge of these principles having been derived from facts which perpetually exist, they defy ingenuity itself to confute them; nay, the most severe scrutiny will make it evident that they are utterly unassailable.

Is it then wisdom to think and to act in opposition to the facts which hourly exhibit themselves around us, and in direct contradiction to the evidence of our senses? Inquire of the most learned and wise of the present day, ask them to speak with sincerity, and they will tell you that they have long known the principles on which society has been founded to be false. Hitherto, however, the tide of public opinion in all countries has been directed by a combination of prejudice, bigotry, and fanaticism, derived from the wildest imaginations of ignorance; and the most enlightened men have not dared to expose those errors which to them were offensive, prominent, and glaring.

Happily for man, this reign of ignorance rapidly approaches to dissolution; its terrors are already on the wing, and soon they will be compelled to take their flight, never more to return. For now the knowledge of the existing errors is not only possessed by the learned and reflecting, but it is spreading far and wide throughout society; and ere long it will be fully comprehended even by the most ignorant.

Attempts may indeed be made by individuals, who through ignorance mistake their real interests, to retard the progress of this knowledge; but as it will prove itself to be in unison with the evidence of our senses, and therefore true beyond the possibility of disproof, it cannot be impeded, and in its course will overwhelm all opposition.

These principles, however, are not more true in theory than beneficial in practice whenever they are properly applied. Why, then, should all their substantial advantages be longer withheld from the mass of mankind? Can it, by possibility, be a crime to pursue the only practical means which a rational being can adopt to diminish the misery of man, and increase his happiness?

These questions, of the deepest interest to society, are now brought to the fair test of public experiment. It remains to be proved, whether the character of man shall continue to be formed under the guidance of the most inconsistent notions, the errors of which for centuries past have been manifest to every reflecting rational mind; or whether it shall be moulded under the direction of uniformly consistent principles, derived from the unvarying facts of the creation; principles, the truth of which no sane man will now attempt to deny.

Robert Owen, *A New View of Society,* a facsimile reproduction of the 3rd ed. printed in London in 1817 (New York: Free Press of Glencoe, Inc, n.d.), pp. 90–95.

III. *The New State*

The Industrial Revolution, creating as it did new forms of wealth and correspondingly new social classes, shifted the political balance in the state. The earlier phase of this shift in power was reflected in the English Constitution by the Parliamentary Reform Act of 1832, whereby the virtual monopoly of power in the legislature—which controlled the executive—hitherto enjoyed by landed wealth, was gradually destroyed, and the new middle classes, together with the better-off artisans, were permitted to share in the control of the state. Bitterly disappointed at this limited extension of the franchise, the working classes, whose agitation had helped to accomplish the passage of the Act of 1832, continued to press for more radical reform. The Chartist movement went through its several phases. A combination of repression, years of prosperity, and the distraction of other movements, drained off enthusiasm and support for further extension of the franchise.

But the urbanization of culture which accompanied the growth of the factory system had gradually raised the material standards of living of the working classes; increased both the need and the opportunity for education; and made the "lower orders" of society more conscious of their standard of living, more articulate in the definition of their rights, and more sophisticated in the choice of means to achieve them than ever before in history. The working-class leaders looked to legislation for relief and to political reform for legislation. By the mid-sixties the demand for further extension of the representative base of Parliament revived and, as events proved, could no longer be ignored.

With the exception of a few Philosophical Radicals, such as J. S. Mill, responsible men in both the Conservative and Liberal parties repudiated any intention of creating a "democratic" England. It became increasingly obvious, however, that once the aristocratic principle was repudiated no logical stopping place for the extension of political power could be found; in the end the parties vied with each other for the partisan advantage of being the first to accomplish the inevitable. The Liberal Reform Bill of 1866 proposed a moderate extension of the franchise, but it was defeated by a combination of the anti-democratic Liberals with the Conservative opposition. The Conservatives, thereby brought into office, passed in 1867 a bill far more radical in its effects than the Liberal bill would have been. By the Reform Act of 1867, which enfranchised the "rate-paying householder," the urban working classes were given the right to vote for members of the House of Commons. The balance of political power was shifted to the working man and the democratic era was ushered in.

The question of political democracy, the prospects of a state based on a popular franchise rather than a restricted one, was one of the great questions of the nineteenth century. Was the course that was chosen the wisest one? How far and to what extent have the predictions, the hopes and the fears, of both the proponents and opponents of the democratic state been realized in fact? For the greatest good of the state, should votes be weighed as well as counted?

A. *Robert Lowe Warns Against Democracy*

Robert Lowe (1811–1892), born the son of an Anglican clergyman, was educated at Winchester School and Oxford University, became a lawyer, emigrated to Australia, and while there served in the Legislative Council of New South Wales. Returning to England, he became an editorial writer for *The Times* and then, entering English political life, was elected to the House of Commons in 1852.

He held ministerial rank under Palmerston and played a considerable role in educational reform. He was not included in the Russell Ministry of 1865, and led the fight against the Liberal Reform Bill of 1866. He was likewise a prominent opponent of the Conservative Reform Bill of 1867. It is from his speech delivered in the course of the debate on this bill that the passages which follow are taken. Later Lowe held the important post of Chancellor of the Exchequer in the Gladstone Cabinet of 1868, going to the Home Office in 1873. In 1880 he retired to the House of Lords as Viscount Sherbrooke.

Lowe is best remembered today for his frank and vitriolic opposition to the progress of democracy. He was a man of great integrity. The views which he expresses on the extension of the franchise were widely shared among the leading political and literary figures of his day. They must not be supposed to represent mere reactionism or blind obstruction to progress. "I have been a Liberal all my life," said Lowe in a debate on a similar issue in 1865, "I was a Liberal at a time and in places where it was not so easy to make professions of Liberalism as in the present day; I suffered for my Liberal principles but I did so gladly because I had confidence in them.... But...because I am a Liberal, and know that by pure and clear intelligence alone can the cause of true progress be promoted, I regard as one of the greatest dangers with which the country can be threatened a proposal to subvert the existing order of things, and to transfer power from the hands of property and intelligence, and to place it in the hands of men whose whole life is necessarily occupied in daily struggles for existence." [Parliamentary Debates, Commons, third series, Vol. 178, cols. 1439–40.]

...I should have thought that, before we handed our Constitution over, as I have said, to persons who are more numerous probably than the present constituency, and before we effected a complete and absolute transfer of power, we ought to have had some little inquiry. The hon. and learned Member for Edinburgh (Mr. Moncreiff) has told us that the notion, which every statesman in England has held up to the present time, that property and intelligence ought to be represented in this House as well as numbers, is one of those platitudes that has long since been buried. I only wish that all other platitudes were buried with it. As it is, things are daily said which make me hardly able to believe my ears. Scotland, it is said, is a highly-favoured country; and England is an ill-used country; because, in Scotland, according to the declaration made the other night, a greater amount of proverty and ignorance will be admitted into the constituencies than in England. The hon. and learned Member for Sheffield (Mr. Roebuck) is congratulated beyond measure. He is happy above all the children of men, because he is to have 28,000 electors let loose upon him in addition to and below his present constituency. On the other hand, the hon. Member for Birmingham (Mr. Bright) has been treated with the most cruel ingratitude by the House, because it has withheld from his embraces 36,000 men of Birmingham who are burning to record their votes for somebody. People are happy according to the proportion of poverty and ignorance they are allowed to represent, and are miserable in proportion to the prevalence in their constituencies of those elements which used to be sovereign in this country—property and intelligence. I should like to bury that platitude with the rest. In like manner words have faded from our recollection. Nobody could get up last year without making use of the strong vernacular expression—"swamping." Who talks of "swamping" now? The only idea now is to see how many persons we can enfranchise, to take care that they shall be as poor and ignorant as possible, to adopt, indeed, a principle like household suffrage—occupation of a house being, no doubt, in the abstract, some proof of respectability—but then to strain that principle until you do away with the respectability by bringing in the dregs of the house-occupying class to control the respectable householders. That seems to be the idea on which we are acting. Lamenting this as I do, I must beg the House to consider for a few moments what will follow. . . .

You are going to transfer power mainly to the non-electors, who are more numerous than the present constituencies. Now, what do you know of the non-electors of this country? What are their politics? What are their views? What will be their influence for good or for evil upon our institutions? Last year my right hon. Friend, the Member for South Lancashire, wished to enfranchise skilled labour, the *élite* of the working class. That has dropped out of our discussions. Nobody talks of skilled labour. The object of this Bill, so far as I understand it, or except as it may be modified in some degree by the lodger franchise, is to enfranchise unskilled labour. We know what the politics of skilled labour are. I confess they are not much to my taste. Trade unions, mechanics' institutes, and the gregarious life which working men lead, have helped to form a school of opinion which I will not examine, because we have got past it. The question now is not what is the opinion of the *élite* of the working classes, but what is the opinion of the unskilled labour class. For instance, in the borough I represent you will, I rather think, give us some Wiltshire labourers with 8s. a week wages. Will any Gentleman favour me with a *précis* of the politics of these men? (*Laughter*.) But it is really no joke. You are handing over to new and untried persons the institutions of this country, and everything, which is dear to us as Englishmen, and it is well that we should know something about them. The fact is, that the great mass of those you are going to enfranchise are people who have no politics at all. Their politics are yet to be learnt. It has not been worth anybody's while to teach them or to agitate them because they have had no vote, and they are unacquainted with even the rudiments of political instruction. You are about to take away the management of affairs from the upper and middle classes, who have managed affairs since the Reform Bill, as I think with some little success, and you are about to place it in the hands of people of whose politics you know nothing, for the best of all possible reasons—because they do not know what their politics are themselves. But they will not be always without politics; and what will they be? What must be the politics of people who are struggling hard to keep themselves off the parish—whose every day is taken up with hard, unskilled labor, and who are always on the verge of pauperism? With every disposition to speak favourably of them, their politics must take one form —socialism. What other aspect can politics bear in their eyes? What can be their view of a state of society in which all the good things are given to others, and all the evil things are given to them? They know nothing of the laws that regulate the distribution of wealth. They attribute to society the inequalities of society. Unless they are absolute angels, they will suppose that they are being treated with great harshness and great cruelty. What man will speak acceptably to them except the man who promises somehow or other to re-distribute the good things of this world more equally, so that the poor will get more, and the rich and powerful will get less? Is it possible to suppose that any other language will be acceptable to them? It would be idle to deceive ourselves. Once give them power, and the use they will make of it will be to try to remedy evils which no doubt grind them very sorely, and which, I suppose, we should all like to remedy if we could, but which most of us believe to be beyond the reach of legislation. Do you suppose that the working classes will not take any steps in this direction? We are going to make a revolution, and on the Continent when a revolution is made (a thing of which we have no experience from 1688 till today) the first step is always to take the duties off spirituous liquors. That is the first flight which young freedom has always taken. "Why," it will be said, "why should your beer, your sugar, your tea, and spirits be taxed when there are so many rich people who can pay these taxes perfectly well." And will not all this come with the force of absolute conviction to the minds of these people? "Why," it will be said, "should the comforts and luxuries of the poor man be taxed? Let the duties

be taken off these things and put upon the rich. Where is the difficulty of imposing a graduated income tax? Is is not monstrous that while you are paying £20,000,000 a year upon sugar, tea, spirits, tobacco, and so forth, here is a great nobleman with a house full of the most valuable pictures, plate, jewels, statuary— all sorts of what the French call 'dead values'—upon which he pays no tax at all? Put a tax upon these things and relieve yourselves from the heavy taxes which you bear." Do not you see that the first step after the enfranchisement of the unskilled labour class must necessarily be to turn indirect taxation into direct taxation, so assessed as to fall mainly upon the upper classes? Are you so "soft" as to suppose that, when you have stripped yourselves of political power and transferred it to these people—and they have twenty times the motive to use it that you have, for their necessity is sorer and the stake to them greater—they will consider political questions fairly, and will not consider first of all how they can benefit themselves? Of course they will....

There is a feeling among hon. Gentlemen opposite that something will be gained for party by their measure. They think that the middle classes have been uniformly hostile to them, and that something may be gained if they get to a lower class—that one will counteract the other. I have faith in no such speculation. We have inaugurated a new era in English politics this Session, and depend upon it the new fashion will henceforth be the rule and not the exception. This Session we have not had what we before possessed—a party of attack and a party of resistance. We have instead two parties of competition, who, like Cleon and the Sausage-seller of Aristophanes, are both bidding for the support of Demos. Do not suppose this is the mere product of the Reform Bill, and that when you get a new Parliament this unwelcome symptom will disappear. This will be a permanent condition of things. It is the condition of things in America. There the old condition of things has vanished. You have now no

Conservative party there—the very tradition of such a thing is forgotten. You have two parties' candidates for popular favour, seeking to outbid each other. Each of them is willing to do anything in the world to secure popular favour— the only difficulty is to find out what the people want; and the difference between them is that one calculates well and the other makes mistakes and does not succeed in doing what the people desire. As to not immediately setting themselves to do what the people desire, because what they desire is wrong or foolish, that never enters their heads. As to the working man, for instance—no sooner does he show a disposition to go very near socialism, than a party and press immediately start up to advocate and develop his views. This is what we are coming to....

Have you so totally unlearnt the simplest lessons of experience as to believe that it is by diving into the depths of ignorance and poverty you can find wisdom to manage the delicate and weighty affairs of this great Empire?...I took upon myself two years ago—only two years—to make a prophecy. I said that if we embarked on the course of democracy we should either ruin our party or our country. Sir, I was wrong, as prophets very often are. It is not a question of alternatives; we are going to ruin both.

Parliamentary Debates, Commons, third series, Vol. 187, cols. 786–99.

B. A Minister Defends Extension of the Franchise

Sir Austen Henry Layard (1817–1894) was Under-Secretary of State for Foreign Affairs in the Russell Cabinet at the time that the Reform Bill of 1866 was under consideration. Layard's interests and accomplishments ranged from law to archaeology and from domestic politics to diplomacy. Educated on the Continent, he later worked in a London law office, traveled in Turkey and Persia, and became a political agent of the British ambassador to Turkey, by whom he was commissioned to undertake excavations in Assyria. His archaeological activities were later sponsored by the British Museum. In 1852 he entered Parliament as member for Aylesbury, in 1860 shifting his constituency to Southwark. Later on in his career he was knighted and became British ambassador to the Sublime Porte (Turkey).

In the speech which follows, Layard takes up point by point the major arguments which had been advanced against the extension of the franchise to the working classes. In considering this issue as a historical question, it always must be borne in mind that it is the climate of opinion of the nineteenth century which is relevant to the issue—not twentieth-century ideas of democracy.

I will now endeavour to meet the principal arguments and objections which, as I understand, have been urged against the Bill of the Government....

Now, as regards the first objection, that the working classes are already sufficiently represented, and that by admitting a larger number of them to the franchise we should be running the risk of swamping and overpowering other classes, which have an equal right to representation....

Until we have men in this House who are of the working classes themselves, who are in constant association with them, who have that intimate knowledge of their habits of thought, their necessities, their real or imagined grievances, and their views, and who can consequently state them to the House of Commons in a manner which will be satisfactory to the artizans themselves, I contend that the working classes are not properly represented in Parliament....

The rest of my noble Friend the Member for Haddingtonshire seems to be disturbed by nightmares of Mr. Odger, and he is haunted by visions of Mr. Potter and the Trades Unions. But I confess that I should feel no alarm at seeing those Gentlemen amongst us. On the contrary I think their presence here would be of great advantage to us and to those whom they represent. If the grievances of which they complain on behalf of the working classes are just grievances, they would be listened to; and if redress were possible, I cannot doubt but that the justice of the House of Commons would seek to give that redress. If those grievances were ill founded, or were attributable to causes over which legislation had no control, the truth would appear after impartial and open discussion, and I have sufficient confidence in the good sense and fairness of the working classes to feel convinced that they would yield to argument and admit themselves wrong. We have nothing to fear from fair public debate of these delicate and important social questions which affect and agitate the working classes; but we have everything to fear from the effect which a sense of injustice produces upon those classes when they think that they have not a fair hearing, and when they believe that the House of Commons refuses to listen to and to remedy what they consider, whether erroneously or not is beside the question, their just grievances.

But allowing that the reduction of the franchise as proposed by the Government would admit a far larger number than 25 per cent of the working classes to the register, there is no chance whatever that such men as I have mentioned would be elected to Parliament in any sufficient numbers to affect the balance of classes in this House in the slightest imaginable degree. I will go further and say, that if we were to adopt the most extreme democratic views, and have universal suffrage, there are no statistics to show that the working classes, as opposed to the agricultural and other classes, would obtain such a majority in the constituencies of the country as seriously to affect the character and composition of the House of Commons, and through it the institutions of the country. The alarm felt lest the workingmen should obtain such an ascendancy in the constituencies as to be able to return a House composed of a majority of their own body, is surely a mere delusion. It is founded upon an assumption which is quite baseless, viz. that but one set of opinions upon political and social questions exists amongst the working classes, and that they are at all times prepared to act and vote together. Now my experience of the working classes proves to me the contrary. I believe that the political opinions of those who compose them differ as much as the political opinions of any other classes in this country. . . .

But then we are told that the working classes might take advantage of the disunion amongst other classes or amongst political parties, and give their support to one side or the other, first exacting promises and conditions favourable to their designs, and that by thus commanding the majority they could secure the objects they had in view. It appears to me that this argument also has been fully answered by the Member for Westminster (Mr. Mill) when he pointed out that in the face of great public interests a minority never could be a majority, and that it was the most improbable of all things that if the working classes, in an absolute minority, were to put forward views and claims which were dangerous to the real interests of the other classes, they would be able to carry them in Parliament. The truth of this has been proved over and over again. . . .

Let me now turn to the second objection—that the working classes are from various causes not fitted for the exercise of the franchise. I have no desire to recur again to the words of the right hon. Member for Calne (Mr. Lowe), which have been the subject of such frequent comment in this House and elsewhere, and have made so deep an impression on the working classes throughout the country. The right hon. Gentleman has endeavoured to explain away the meaning of those words; I leave it to the country to decide with what success. But I wish to show that, supposing those words bore the interpretation placed upon them by the Chancellor of the Exchequer and by the working classes, they would only express an opinion upon the condition of those classes, and upon their unfitness to be admitted to political rights, which has more than once been expressed by the right hon. Gentleman. . . .

There is an argument which has been advanced more than once in this debate against the working classes, grounded upon the charge against them of "impulsiveness," which ought not, I think, to be left unnoticed or unanswered. I mean the argument, or rather the assertion, that if they had any preponderating influence in this House, and in the government of the country, they would soon plunge this country into war.... Let us test the validity of this argument by the facts. Let us look at the annals of the last Parliament, and see whether motions in this House and opinions outside of this House in favour of war have been supported by the working classes or by hon. Gentlemen opposite and those whom they represent....

Whilst the civil war was raging in America, what classes in this country called upon the Government to take steps which would have inevitably involved us in war with the United States? Was it the working classes?...It is a fact not to be forgotten—and it is one, I think, which furnishes a complete answer to the charge made against the working classes of their readiness to drive the Government into war—that during all the suffering entailed upon a great body of the working men of this country by the suspension of their labour in consequence of the cotton famine, not a single petition was presented to this House by them asking for any interference in the affairs of the United States; and that, with the sole exception of Liverpool, every constituency in this kingdom in which the working classes have any influence, most warmly and cordially supported the Government in their determination to maintain strict neutrality during the civil war in America.

Having now disposed, so far as I am able, of objections to the lowering of the franchise founded upon the impulsiveness of the working classes, let me say a few words on the charge of venality brought against them. This accusation has been urged by several Members of the House during the debate, but by none with greater force and eloquence than my right hon. Friend the Member for Hertfordshire (Sir E. Bulwer-Lytton) in his great speech of the other evening. He described, in his telling manner, the con-

test for the vote of the working man between Smith with the £5 note and Brown with the rights of man, in which Smith, of course, prevailed....

Sir, I say that until this House is prepared, until society itself is prepared, to condemn and punish him who corrupts, it has no right to condemn and punish him who is corrupted. Nor have we any right to exclude from the franchise a large portion of our fellow-countrymen, whose honesty as a class I will venture to declare will bear comparison with that of any other class, because we can show that some of them have been corrupted.

I now come to the next objection, viz. that the working classes do not pay direct taxes, and have not sufficient stake in the country to entitle them to a larger share in its government. The best answer has already been given to that objection by the Chancellor of the Exchequer, when he showed that the aggregate incomes of the working classes amount to almost as much as the aggregate incomes of all other classes of the community; that is to say, that it is nearly half the actual income of the country....

I may further point out this remarkable fact—one most deserving of attention, and in my opinion reflecting the highest credit upon the working men—that theirs is the only class which, as a class, provides for the poor, the needy, the sick, and the suffering, by an organised and regular saving from individual incomes—by the daily putting by of something which leads to an actual privation and sacrifice.... We impose no such self-denial upon ourselves. I say, Sir, that with all that other classes may give in charity—and no one will deny the charity of our middle and upper classes—none make so great a daily uninterrupted sacrifice....

Have the working classes then no stake in the country, as it has been asserted? Would their property, large as I have shown it to be, be less affected, less liable to loss, than that enjoyed by any other portion of the community, in the event of foreign war or domestic commotion? They know as well as we do how sensitive credit is, how the funds rise and fall, how mis-government, how any interruption to the public peace can lower the value of all property. I will go further, and maintain that they have even a greater stake in the country than other classes have, and would feel more acutely than any other class any derangement in the public credit or any event which might check the prosperity of the nation. To us a decrease in the value of our property or of our incomes means a luxury the less; with them it means a necessity the less: with us reduced rent means food and clothing less luxurious, less costly; with them reduced wages or no wages at all means too often no food and no clothing at all. And will any one say in the face of these facts, that the working classes have no interest in the well-being, prosperity, and peace of the country?

I will now come to another argument against the Bill to which I have alluded, viz. that by lowering the franchise and increasing the size of and lowering constituencies, you render it impossible for any but rich men and demagogues to enter the House of Commons. . . .

For my part, Sir, I believe the time will come when all the legitimate expenses of elections will be met by a county and borough rate, and when all expenses not absolutely necessary and legitimate will be prohibited by laws which we shall be prepared to enforce, and when those who incur illegal expenses will be duly punished. Until the corruption of voters is not only a punishable offence, but is considered to be disgraceful by this House and by society, and until this House and society unmistakably mark their sense of the conduct of those who have engaged in such practices, corruption and bribery will never be put an end to. You have no right to throw it in the teeth of the working men that they are unfit to exercise the franchise because they are corrupt, whilst you are their corruptors. . . .

But now let me turn to the second part of the objection, that besides wealthy men only demagogues, who would pander to the passions and prejudices of the mob,

would be returned to this House. This again is an assertion which can be tested by facts, and I venture to say that facts are entirely opposed to it. In the first place no constituency in which the working classes at this time have a decided influence at elections return a "demagogue," or any Member who can be considered as bearing any resemblance to that character; nor, as far as I am aware, has any "demagogue" offered himself for election to any such constituency. That was not so thirty or forty years ago, when men who would certainly be now thought demagogues of the most violent character were returned to this House. In truth, as you trust the working classes, as you extend to them their just rights, men of this kind have less influence over them, and are less likely to become sufficiently important to command the support of any number of working men. . . .

And all this dread of democracy—all these predictions of terrible results to the Constitution—are founded upon the supposition that a certain number of the working classes must be admitted by the Government Bill to the franchise. Have you, then, so much fear of the working classes—do you think that their admission to a share in the Government of the country would be productive of such vast evils?

You now declare that you do not doubt their individual fitness, if character and conduct are to be the tests of fitness, to exercise the franchise. You now repudiate the description of their habits and their vices which you cheered not long ago. You go further; you now praise them, and declare that you have unbounded faith in them. I do not doubt the generous sympathy felt by the right hon. Baronet the Member for Hertfordshire (Sir E. Bulwer-Lytton) for the working man; and few who heard his speech will forget the noble words in which he described the aspirations of the working man as "the eternal link between the aims of educated labour and the dreams of philosophy and genius." But it is of little use to talk of sympathy for the working classes, and to admit their fitness for the enjoyment of the franchise, whilst at the same time you refuse to put any trust in them, and to give the franchise to them. Your opinion of our duty to the working man somewhat resembles the view which the Scotch pedagogue took of our duty towards our neighbour, which his pupil had described to be, "to fear him, to love him, and to trust him." "You may fear him and love him as much as you like," said he, "but you must not trust him." As long as the working man is just what you wish him to be, you will say a good word in his favour; but he must be the model working man after your own notion. He must have all the virtues of his own class and of all other classes put together. If he pays his rent punctually for twenty years, brings up respectably a large family of children, has never been seen at the beerhouse, and is unknown to the relieving officer, he shall receive a prize of 10s., presented to him by a great peer, or by an illustrious man of letters. He will be allowed to read newspapers, to study history, and to attend lectures at the institute. All this he may do, and a great deal more; but if he attempts to apply the principles that he has learned —if he attempts to put into practice the lessons of political economy which he has been taught—if he begins to think that he is entitled to make the most of the sweat of his brow and the labour of his hand— if it dawns upon him that he has as much right to combine with his fellow-men to obtain a fair price for his work as the owners of capital have a right to combine against him for the regulation of his wages —then, indeed, the benevolent admirers of the working classes, and the dispensers of so many good things to him, lift up their hands in amazement, stand aghast at his audacity and his ingratitude, and behold the flood of democracy about to sweep over the land, and to wash away, even to the very last vestiges, the glorious institutions of this country. . . .

I appeal to the justice, not to the liberality, of the House of Commons. If you will only do justice to the working classes, if you will only place confidence in them, depend upon it that they will not show themselves unworthy of that confidence, but that they will give you even greater proofs than they have hitherto given of the love they bear to the Throne, the institutions, and the greatness of their country.

Parliamentary Debates, Commons, third series, Vol. 182, cols. 1434–59.

C. Sir Henry Maine Evaluates the New Order

Sir Henry James Summer Maine (1822–1888) is one of the great nineteenth-century writers on the history and philosophy of political institutions. Regius Professor of Civil Law at Cambridge University, he later held posts of increasing honor and responsibility in both the political and the academic world. His most notable and still influential book on *Ancient Law* was published in 1861. Among his other books are *Village Communities in East and West*, 1871; *Early History of Institutions*, 1875; *Early Law and Custom*, 1883; and the book from which the following passage is taken, *Popular Government*, 1885. Limitations of space have required the deletion of extensive passages in which Maine supports and illustrates his argument by numerous examples and copious allusions drawn from his rich store of historical data. Produced in the intellectual climate of the eighties, the argument of *Popular Government* has distinct Darwinian overtones, just as earlier writers on social science were apt to sound a Malthusian note.

The real fear of democracy that lay at the root of the opposition of such men as Maine to universal suffrage was, however, a fear of the tyranny of the majority. Such an extension of political power to the mass of the people would lead, so they believed, to a repression of individual rights and become a barrier to true progress. It was in the constitutional safeguards against precipitate popular action that Maine found strength in the American Constitution. "On the whole," he wrote, "there is only one country in which the question of the safest and most workable form of democratic government has been adequately discussed, and the results of discussion tested by experiment. This is the United States of America. American experience has, I think, shown that, by wise Constitutional provisions thoroughly thought out beforehand, Democracy may be made tolerable. The public powers are carefully defined; the mode in which they are to be exercised is fixed; and the amplest securities are taken that none of the more important Constitutional arrangements shall be altered without every guarantee of caution and every opportunity for deliberation."

Political liberty, said Hobbes, is political power. When a man burns to be free, he is not longing for the "desolate freedom of the wild ass"; what he wants is a share of political government. But, in wide democracies, political power is minced into morsels, and each man's portion of it is almost infinitesimally small. One of the first results of this political comminution...is that two of the historical watchwords of Democracy exclude one another, and that, where there is political liberty, there can be no Equality.

"The man who can sweep the greatest number of fragments of political power into one heap will govern the rest. The strongest man in one form or another will always rule. If the government is a military one, the qualities which make a man a great soldier will make him a ruler. If the government is a monarchy, the qualities which kings value in counsellors, in administrators, in generals, will give power. In a pure democracy, the ruling men will be the Wire-pullers and their friends; but they will be no more on an equality with the people than soldiers or Ministers of State are on an equality with the subjects of a Monarchy.... In some ages, a powerful character, in others cunning, in others power of transacting business, in others eloquence, in others a good hold upon commonplaces and a facility in applying them to practical purposes, will enable a man to climb on his neighbours' shoulders and direct them this way or that; but under all circumstances the rank and file are directed by leaders of one kind or another who get the command of their collective force."

There is no doubt that, in popular gov-

ernments resting on a wide suffrage, either without an army or having little reason to fear it, the leader, whether or not he be cunning, or eloquent, or well provided with commonplaces, will be the Wire-puller. The process of cutting up political power into petty fragments has in him its most remarkable product. The morsels of power are so small that men, if left to themselves, would not care to employ them....

The Wire-puller is not intelligible unless we take into account one of the strongest forces acting on human nature—Party feeling. Party feeling is probably far more a survival of the primitive combativeness of mankind than a consequence of conscious intellectual differences between man and man. It is essentially the same sentiment which in certain states of society leads to civil, intertribal, or international war; and it is as universal as humanity....

It is through this great natural tendency to take sides that the Wire-puller works. Without it he would be powerless. His business is to fan its flame; to keep it constantly acting upon the man who has once declared himself a partisan; to make escape from it difficult and distasteful. His art is that of the Nonconformist preacher, who gave importance to a body of commonplace religionists by persuading them to wear a uniform and take a military title, or of the man who made the success of a Temperance Society by prevailing on its members to wear always and openly a blue ribbon. In the long-run, these contrivances cannot be confined to any one party, and their effects on all parties and their leaders, and on the whole ruling democracy, must be in the highest degree serious and lasting. The first of these effects will be, I think, to make all parties very like one another, and indeed in the end almost indistinguishable, however leaders may quarrel and partisan hate partisan. In the next place, each party will probably become more and more homogeneous; and the opinions it professes, and the policy which is the outcome of those opinions, will less and less reflect the individual mind of any leader, but only the ideas which seem to that mind to be most likely to win favour with the greatest number of supporters. Lastly, the wire-pulling system, when fully developed, will infallibly lead to the constant enlargement of the area of suffrage. What is called universal suffrage has greatly declined in the estimation, not only of philosophers who follow Bentham, but of the *a priori* theorists who assumed that it was the inseparable accompaniment of a Republic, but who found that in practice it was the natural basis of a tyranny. But extensions of the suffrage, though no longer believed to be good in themselves, have now a permanent place in the armoury of parties, and are sure to be a favourite weapon of the Wire-puller. The Athenian statesmen who, worsted in a quarrel of aristocratic cliques, "took the people into partnership," have a close parallel in the modern politicians who introduce household suffrage into towns to "dish" one side, and into counties to "dish" the other.

Let us now suppose the competition of Parties, stimulated to the utmost by the modern contrivances of the Wire-puller, to have produced an electoral system under which every adult male has a vote, and perhaps every adult female. Let us assume that the new machinery has extracted a vote from every one of these electors. How is the result to be expressed? It is, that the average opinion of a great multitude has been obtained, and that this average opinion becomes the basis and standard of all government and law. There is hardly any experience of the way in which such a system would work, except in the eyes of those who believe that history began since their own birth. The universal suffrage of white males in the United States is about fifty years old; that of white and black is less than twenty. The French threw away universal suffrage after the Reign of Terror; it was twice revived in France, that the Napoleonic tyranny might be founded on it; and it was introduced into Germany, that the personal power of Prince Bismarck might be confirmed. But one of the strangest of vulgar ideas is that a very wide suffrage could or would promote progress, new ideas, new discoveries and inventions, new arts of life. Such a suffrage is

commonly associated with Radicalism; and no doubt amid its most certain effects would be the extensive destruction of existing institutions; but the chances are that, in the long-run, it would produce a mischievous form of Conservatism. . . .

A moment's reflection will satisfy any competently instructed person that this is not too broad a proposition. Let him turn over in his mind the great epochs of scientific invention and social change during the last two centuries, and consider what would have occurred if universal suffrage had been established at any one of them. Universal suffrage, which to-day excludes Free Trade from the United States, would certainly have prohibited the spinning-jenny and the power-loom. It would certainly have forbidden the threshing-machine. It would have prevented the adoption of the Gregorian Calendar; and it would have restored the Stuarts. It would have proscribed the Roman Catholics with the mob which burned Lord Mansfield's house and library in 1780, and it would have proscribed the Dissenters with the mob which burned Dr. Priestley's house and library in 1791.

There are possibly many persons who, without denying these conclusions in the past, tacitly assume that no such mistakes will be committed in the future, because the community is already too enlightened for them, and will become more enlightened through popular education. But without questioning the advantages of popular education under certain aspects, its manifest tendency is to diffuse popular commonplaces, to fasten them on the mind at the time when it is most easily impressed, and thus to stereotype average opinion. It is of course possible that universal suffrage would not now force on governments the same legislation which it would infallibly have dictated a hundred years ago; but then we are necessarily ignorant what germs of social and material improvement there may be in the womb of time, and how far they may conflict with the popular prejudice which hereafter will be omnipotent. . . .

It is perfectly possible, I think, as Mr.

Herbert Spencer has shown in a recent admirable volume, to revive even in our day the fiscal tyranny which once left even European populations in doubt whether it was worth while preserving life by thrift and toil. You have only to tempt a portion of the population into temporary idleness by promising them a share in a fictitious hoard lying (as Mill puts it) in an imaginary strong-box which is supposed to contain all human wealth. You have only to take the heart out of those who would willingly labour and save, by taxing them *ad misericordiam* for the most laudable philanthropic objects. For it makes not the smallest difference to the motives of the thrifty and industrious part of mankind whether their fiscal oppressor be an Eastern despot, or a feudal baron, or a democratic legislature, and whether they are taxed for the benefit of a corporation called Society, or for the advantage of an individual styled King or Lord. Here then is the great question about democratic legislation, when carried to more than a moderate length. How will it affect human motives? What motives will it substitute for those now acting on men? The motives, which at present impel mankind to the labour and pain which produce the resuscitation of wealth in ever-increasing quantities, are such as infallibly to entail inequality in the distribution of wealth. They are the springs of action called into activity by the strenuous and never-ending struggle for existence, the beneficent private war which makes one man strive to climb on the shoulders of another and remain there through the law of the survival of the fittest.

These truths are best exemplified in the part of the world to which the superficial thinker would perhaps look for the triumph of the opposite principle. The United States have justly been called the home of the disinherited of the earth; but, if those vanquished under one sky in the struggle for existence had not continued under another the same battle in which they had been once worsted, there would have been no such exploit performed as the cultivation of the vast American territory from

end to end and from side to side. There could be no grosser delusion than to suppose this result to have been attained by democratic legislation. It has really been obtained through the sifting out of the strongest by natural selection. The Government of the United States, which I examine in another part of this volume, now rests on universal suffrage, but then it is only a political government. It is a government under which coercive restraint, except in politics, is reduced to a minimum. There has hardly ever before been a community in which the weak have been pushed so pitilessly to the wall, in which those who have succeeded have so uniformly been the strong, and in which in so short a time there has arisen so great an inequality of private fortune and domestic luxury. And at the same time, there has never been a country in which, on the whole, the persons distanced in the race have suffered so little from their ill-success. All this beneficent prosperity is the fruit of recognising the principle of population, and the one remedy for its excess in perpetual emigration. It all reposes on the sacredness of contract and the stability of private property, the first the implement, and the last the reward, of success in the universal competition. These, however, are all principles and institutions which the British friends of the "artisan" and "agricultural labourer" seem not a little inclined to treat as their ancestors did agricultural and industrial machinery. The Americans are still of the opinion that more is to be got for human happiness by private energy than by public legislation. The Irish, however, even in the United States, are of another opinion, and the Irish opinion is manifestly rising into favour here. But on the question, whether future democratic legislation will follow the new opinion, the prospects of popular government to a great extent depend. There are two sets of motives, and two only, by which the great bulk of the materials of human subsistence and comfort have hitherto been produced and reproduced. One has led to the cultivation of the territory of the Northern States of the American Union, from the Atlantic to the Pacific. The other had a considerable share in bringing about the industrial and agricultural progress of the Southern States, and in old days it produced the wonderful prosperity of Peru under the Incas. One system is economical competition; the other consists in the daily task, perhaps fairly and kindly allotted, but enforced by the prison or the scourge. So far as we have any experience to teach us, we are driven to the conclusion, that every society of men must adopt one system or the other, or it will pass through penury to starvation.

I have thus shown that popular governments of the modern type have not hitherto proved stable as compared with other forms of political rule, and that they include certain sources of weakness which do not promise security for them in the near or remote future. My chief conclusion can only be stated negatively. There is not at present sufficient evidence to warrant the common belief, that these governments are likely to be of indefinitely long duration. There is, however, one positive conclusion from which no one can escape who bases a forecast of the prospects of popular government, not on moral preference or *a priori* assumption, but on actual experience as witnessed to by history. If there be any reason for thinking that constitutional freedom will last, it is a reason furnished by a particular set of facts, with which Englishmen ought to be familiar, but of which many of them, under the empire of prevailing ideas, are exceedingly apt to miss the significance. The British Constitution has existed for a considerable length of time, and therefore free institutions generally may continue to exist. I am quite aware that this will seem to some a commonplace conclusion, perhaps as commonplace as the conclusion of M. Taine, who, after describing the conquest of all France by the Jacobin Club, declares that his inference is so simple, that he hardly ventures to state it. *"Jusqu'à présent, je n'ai guère trouvé qu'un (Principe) si sim-ple qu'il semblera puéril et que j'ose à peine l'énoncer. Il consiste tout entier dans cette remarque, qu'une société humaine, surtout une société moderne, est une chose vaste et compliquée."* This observation, that "a human society, and particularly a modern society is a vast and complicated thing," is in fact the very proposition which Burke enforced with all the splendour of his eloquence and all the power of his argument; but as M. Taine says, it may now seem to some too simple and commonplace to be worth putting into words. In the same way, many persons in whom familiarity has bred contempt, may think it a trivial observation that the British Constitution, if not (as some call it) a holy thing, is a thing unique and remarkable. A series of undesigned changes brought it to such a condition, that satisfaction and impatience, the two great sources of political conduct, were both reasonably gratified under it. In this condition it became, not metaphorically but literally, the envy of the world, and the world took on all sides to copying it. The imitations have not been generally happy. One nation alone, consisting of Englishmen, has practised a modification of it successfully, amidst abounding material plenty. It is not too much to say, that the only evidence worth mentioning for the duration of popular government is to be found in the success of the British Constitution during two centuries under special conditions, and in the success of the American Constitution during one century under conditions still more peculiar and more unlikely to recur. Yet, so far as our own Constitution is concerned, that nice balance of attractions, which caused it to move evenly on its stately path, is perhaps destined to be disturbed. One of the forces governing it may gain dangerously at the expense of the other; and the British political system, with the national greatness and material prosperity attendant on it, may yet be launched into space and find its last affinities in silence and cold.

Sir Henry Sumner Maine, *Popular Government* (New York: Henry Holt & Co., 1886), pp. 29–55.

12

Liberalism
and Nationalism
in the Mid-Nineteenth Century

EVALYN A. CLARK

Vassar College

Students of liberalism and nationalism in the mid-twentieth century may find it easier to understand mid-nineteenth-century attitudes towards these phenomena than could their predecessors of the pre-World War II period. For to a degree the pendulum has swung again.

In the period from 1815 to 1880, liberals—especially liberal intellectuals—ordinarily took it for granted that nationalism was progressive, even radical, that it was humanitarian and the foe of reaction and autocracy. Indeed, liberalism and nationalism were to them the opposite sides of the same coin. Hence national independence of oppressed minorities from the ancient, reactionary empires of Hapsburg, Czar, and Sultan, was the essential first step towards achieving liberal reforms within a national state. This was the position of Giuseppe Mazzini, John Stuart Mill, and the prevalent belief of most nineteenth-century liberals. Mill, perhaps the best exponent of liberal nationalism, defined nationality in liberal, even democratic, terms as the feeling of common sympathies, the desire to form a nationality, to live under a government of one's own choosing, not primarily in the romantic or traditionalist terms of race, descent, geography, or language. In a famous passage in his *Considerations on Representative Government,* he wrote: "It is in general a necessary condition of free institutions

415

that the boundaries of governments should coincide, in the main, with those of nationalities." It is clear that Mill, in a country long unified, was liberal enough to subordinate the quest for national independence to the struggle for human liberty, as many continental liberals were not, especially in lands that lacked both.

The revolutions of 1848 were certainly warning enough that nations or groups that have gained liberty may not grant it to others, that Germans and Hungarians in the course of their struggle for freedom might come to despise and oppress Czechs, Poles, Serbs, and Croatians; and that some of these minorities, doubly oppressed, might in desperation prefer to return to their ancient oppressor. John Stuart Mill was not the only one to raise his voice against the dangers of this type of liberalism. Lord Acton, Alexis de Tocqueville, and Richard Cobden warned that crusades for liberty as a philosophical ideal—what we now call ideological wars—intervention in other countries' affairs, or forcing peoples to be free, could destroy the desired aims of liberty and peace. They warned that the idea of a national mission expressed by Michelet, Palmerston, Mazzini, and Kossuth might mean merely the old "divine right" transferred to "the people," and that it might thus become as absolute and hostile to individual liberty as was its hated ancestor. Which was more important, the freedom of man or the freedom of states? This then was the dilemma posed by the revolutions of 1848, and even more by Bismarck's subsequent rise to power in Germany and by the unification of Italy. In all of these, the struggle for individual liberty frequently came into conflict with the quest for national independence and unity. In 1848, neither won. But in the 1860s and 1870s, the liberal cause was defeated in Germany as elsewhere in Central Europe, leaving nationalism, its earlier ally, the victor. Though in France and Italy by 1870, both liberals and nationalists were nominally successful, it is perhaps fair to say that only in liberal England was the partnership an equal one.

Conflicts within the liberal camp itself still further complicated the situation. Should liberals pursue their aims to the point of violence or revolution, or should they rely on majority rule and the slow growth of parliamentary democracy? This question arose intermittently throughout the century, and as might be expected, became particularly acute during the 1848 revolutions. Many liberals, especially in England, in the earlier half of the century had rejected, whether for romantic or for rational and "Manchesterian" reasons, the bloodshed and tyranny of war and revolution. Liberalism to them meant not only peace, but hatred of military force. It stood for free trade in international affairs and for peaceful internal reforms—a moderate extension of the suffrage, parliamentary responsibility, broader educational opportunities, and orderly legislation to assure freedom of speech, assembly, and religion. To other liberals, however, especially those who disliked the despotic and feudal character of the central and eastern European empires, the struggles of oppressed nationalities to preserve their own culture and to free themselves became the chief goal. As the cultural nationalism of the first half-century grew increasingly political, the revolutionary character of the ideal of self-determination—if it were to succeed in certain countries—showed more clearly. Mill's and Mazzini's ideal of national states could only be achieved by overturning every government east of the Rhine, which was, in fact, just what the revolutions of 1848 proceeded to do. Hence the pacifist liberal, from the decade of the 1820s, more and more often had to face the moral question whether or not he should support and intervene in such wars and insurrections as those of the Greeks, Poles, Germans, Czechs, Hungarians, Serbians, and Italians. Some liberals were forced to face the problem in their own country; with others it was a question of supporting a foreign policy of intervention. Poland particularly, in 1830, 1848, and again in 1863, became almost a test case, and a difficult one, to the nineteenth-century liberal conscience. Some turned to nationalism and preferred national freedom—their own or others—to peace, or even to individual freedom. Some turned from liberalism to radicalism because they thought the liberals were too cautious in their pacifist neutrality. Indeed, one of the striking developments of the period was the rise of the more radical advocates of the policy of intervention— Auguste Blanqui and Louis Blanc in 1848 and 1871, Gustav Struve and the German Republicans of 1848—who would even stage insurrections against their own moderate governments on such issues as "Aid to Poland," "No peace with the Danes," and "No peace with the Germans," "No peace with Austria," while we find Mazzini and Garibaldi speaking of a "holy war" to free oppressed nationalities.

Prior to 1848, liberal, socialistic, radical-republican, and national ideals and movements were often blended and their future conflicts concealed by common aims and common enemies. The bloody events of 1848 and 1849 revealed the latent antagonism of what were becoming increasingly uneasy alliances—not only of nationalism and liberalism, but of liberalism and democracy and even of democracy and socialism. Many liberals came to feel as Ernest Renan did in 1849, after his initial sympathy with the social revolution, that "the revolutionary philosophy, great and liberating as it was, contained the hidden poison of belief in violence, and an idea of justice based on a materialistic conception of property and a neglect of individual rights —all these carry the seeds of destruction." (*Essais de morale et de critique,* Paris, 1859, p. x.) This dilemma of the liberals over the "social question" may well be compared with the twentieth-century debate over the relation of democracy to socialism, and to communism.

The disappointment of all participants in the revolutions of 1848 contributed largely to the reaction against the earlier romantic and liberal-national ideals and to the success of the realist cult. The postrevolutionary nationalist differs markedly from the optimistic idealist of the prerevolutionary years. Since the thinkers and talkers appeared to have failed, it was felt that men of action and power, practical politicians and generals—the Bismarcks and Cavours—were necessary.

After 1870, the glorification of racial differences, imperial greatness, military strength, and the intolerant treatment of minorities in the name of national unity became increasingly the concomitants of nationalism. There were, moreover, new instruments and techniques at hand to aid in the spread of those ideas. The telegraph, railroad, and steamship may not impress a generation accustomed to jets, radio, television, and Telstar, but together with cheap newspapers and postal service, they provided their age with new and greater means of mass communication and propaganda than had ever been known before.

Under their impact, and accompanied by such movements as popular education, universal suffrage, urbanization, the decline in religion, and military conscription, the nationalist movements tended to become mass movements, and in general to grow more intolerant and illiberal. Liberals consequently came to distrust equally the chauvinism of the Left, as seen in the Paris Commune, and of the Right as seen in Napoleon III, Bismarck, and the Russian Pan-Slavs.

By the beginning of the last quarter of the century, Germany and Italy had finally achieved their unity and independence by war and forceful unification. France and England, the oldest nations in terms of unity, had gained many liberal reforms. Even some of the oppressed Slavic peoples had achieved independence or autonomy, though the Poles, Czechs, and South Slavs were still bitterly resentful of their oppression.

But as the century closed, liberals with their eyes on reform tended more and more to think of nationalism as foe rather than friend, while the Right came more and more to claim a monopoly of patriotism and the Left to turn against it with disillusioned diatribes. The Paris Commune, the Second International, the rise of anarchism and the Dreyfus case produced a reversal of partners. The radical and socialist Left became antipatriotic, antimilitarist, and international—"the worker has no fatherland." The Right became the self-appointed defenders of the shrines of *Revanche*, of Pan-German, Pan-Slavic, and anti-Semitic movements. They became shrill advocates of the creeds of militarism and imperialism. Only in countries like England, France, and America where both were long established did liberalism remain a friend of nationalism. This kinship was evident in 1917 when Woodrow Wilson expressed the war aims of the Allies both in terms of "national self-determination" and "making the world safe for democracy." But when the war was over, the rise of the postwar dictators, who were non-liberals but arch-nationalists, and growing doubt regarding the real identification of the two ideals led to a widespread disillusionment of liberals with nationalism. It was with World War II and the growing claims of emergent nations in Asia, Africa, and elsewhere, that the pendulum began to swing back again, leaving us face to face with a situation not too dissimilar to that of the nineteenth century. For it is a situation in which the peoples of those states which are fighting for independence, and their sympathizers elsewhere, once again identify nationalism with freedom and progress. For this reason, the following nineteenth century extracts illustrating the ideas and point of view of men who were involved in the struggles of those years may have a familiar ring to many mid-twentieth-century readers accustomed to contemporary headlines that equate liberalism with national aspirations.

I. Years of Crisis: 1848 and 1849

The year 1848 has been called by G. M. Trevelyan "the turning point at which modern history failed to turn" from despotism to freedom. Or perhaps we may borrow Winston Churchill's expressive phrase, "the hinge of fate," for these crucial years in the movements of liberalism and nationalism. Many of the problems of our own day were then given a decisive turn—the "problem of Germany," the perpetual instability of French governments, the hostility of Czechs to Germans and of Hungarians and Germans to

Slavs, the relations of Russia and the West, the hostility of conservatism and of revolutionary socialism to reforming liberalism, and the growing estrangement of liberalism and nationalism.

In 1848, when revolutionary uprisings blazed their way across most of Europe, the three great problems of the day were the "social question," the "national question," and the "political question." The "political question" could comprise the striving for a republic, a constitution, and universal suffrage, singly or in combination, but these aims were often grouped together by the conservatives under the opprobrious label of "republicanism." Actually, Cavour, for example, was a monarchist, while Mazzini cared little about a constitution. All three of these problems were intertwined in the revolutions of 1848, but the political and social questions remained uppermost in France, while in the Austrian Empire the national question soon came to overshadow everything else.

A. The French Republic—Liberal or Social?

In France with its revolutionary and republican traditions the revolutionists in the beginning agreed on a republic. They disagreed on whether it was to be a "liberal" or a "democratic and social" republic. The Provisional Government, established after the overthrow of Louis Philippe, proved from the very first to be an uneasy compromise, when the ministers chosen by the Chamber of French deputies had to accept two socialists as the price of their confirmation by the people of Paris at the Hotel de Ville. The resultant fusion of rival groups had little authority and less unity.

The majority of the Provisional Government were moderate republicans who were really in the tradition of 1789, favoring private property and as much laissez faire as possible, but willing to accept universal suffrage and the republic.

The leader of the majority was Alphonse de Lamartine, the poet-statesman and historian of the Girondists. Catapulted into power and popularity by the February Revolution, he thought of himself as the savior of France. As real head of the Provisional Government, though officially Minister for Foreign Affairs, he tried to reconcile the republican factions within the creaking Provisional Government in the name of national unity. But Lamartine in his attempt at reconciling all, at least all the republicans, only succeeded in winning the distrust of all. His "Manifesto to Europe" of March, 1848, issued when he was Minister for Foreign Affairs, tried to pacify the apprehensions of European chancelleries. They had feared that the revolutionary Republic might continue the military and propagandist interventionism of the First Republic by declaring a crusading war on Prussia, Austria, and Russia to free the Poles and the Italians or tear up the frontiers of 1815. Yet it breathed forth the resurgent glory of France and warned against any aggression against France or other nations who wanted to be free. Palmerston shrewdly noted that this Manifesto was designed for internal consumption as well and was Lamartine's attempt to satisfy both the bellicose and pacifist groups of the French republicans. The emotional appeal of revolutionary intervention in favor of oppressed nations was expressed in the marching cry "Long live Poland" shouted by the insurgent workmen and students as they invaded the National Assembly on May 15. In their brief moment of power they decreed war on the Russian and German monarchs unless Poland were immediately freed.

Lamartine opposed the extreme antibourgeois Left whether inside the Provisional Government or outside in the revolutionary clubs. He also opposed the attempts of the socialists to take over the revolution and to make the red flag the flag of the new republic. Yet he tried to keep both the Robespierrist Ledru-Rollin and the socialist Louis Blanc inside the government by supporting Blanc's demands for the "right to work," and expressing sympathy for the people. But Lamartine meant by "the people" all Frenchmen, whereas Louis Blanc meant all workers and Blanqui meant a minority of professional revolutionists. In June, when the clash of concepts became clear, Lamartine had to choose to fight for the Republic against the Paris populace. By then he had also earned the distrust of the moderate republicans such as Tocqueville as well as of the resurgent Right by his denunciations of the bourgeoisie and his wooing of the Left.

The very presence of Ledru-Rollin and of Louis Blanc in the Provisional Government is indicative of its disunity and instability. Alexandre Auguste Ledru-Rollin, in the key post of Minister of the Interior, was a Jacobin or Montagnard republican who thought himself a second Robespierre and aroused the fears of the provinces and the bourgeoisie by his leanings toward socialism and his demands for continuing the tradition of 1793. He defended the Terror of the past, but shrank from it in the present.

Louis Blanc, the socialist leader forced into the Provisional Government by the workers, was usually allied with the Jacobins to form the Left minority in the government. He was the idol of the people of Paris—an uncompromising enemy of laissez faire, a preacher of gradual transition to socialism through producers' cooperatives financed by the state. His ideal was a democratic republic, based on the principle of association of all workers and achieved by political measures, rather than by armed force or the dictatorship of a minority. In this ideal republic all would work as a moral duty and there would be no social distinctions and privileges of inherited wealth: "From each according to his ability, to each according to his need." Though Louis Blanc steadfastly denied any responsibility for the May 15 insurrection or the June Days, which put a bloody end to the uneasy truce of February, the workers grew more insurrectionary and listened more to his bitter attacks on capitalism and privilege than to his pleas for moderation and political maturity.

Moreover the Paris workers were not in a mood to make fine distinctions between the theoretically peaceful preachings of a Louis Blanc and those declarations of class war and unrelenting hostility to the bourgeois state preached by Auguste Blanqui and other revolutionary militants outside the government. Blanqui, one of the greatest revolutionaries of the nineteenth century, was the dread of all governments, democratic as well as reactionary. But despite the fact that he spent most of his life in prison, he managed to take part in the French revolutions of 1830, 1848, and the Commune of 1871. His proclaimed aims were the dictatorship of the workers over Paris and of Paris over the provinces. These were to be achieved by a *coup d'état,* the confiscation of property, and the destruction of existing social and political institutions. Through his control over the largest of the revolutionary clubs, the Central Republican Society, usually called the Blanqui Club, he was able to stir up constant insur-

rections or threats of insurrections against the government. He was as hostile to the Jacobin and socialist minority of the Provisional Government or National Assembly as he was to the moderate republican majority. He has often been compared to Lenin in his intransigent temperament and his techniques of revolution.

As in the great Revolution, a crucial role was played by the revolutionary clubs of various shades of radicalism who exerted pressure on the weak government. These clubs became more socialist as their membership came to include more unemployed workers. They grew increasingly hostile to the parliamentary republic and turned to violence after the resounding defeat of the radicals in the April elections to the National Assembly. It was the clubs led by Blanqui and the Robespierrist Barbès who precipitated the May 15 insurrection which invaded the Assembly, for a few hours overturned the government, and replaced it by a provisional government of leaders of the revolutionary clubs. This insurrection alarmed not only the Rightist Party of Order and the moderates in the National Assembly but even the Montagnards like Ledru-Rollin. It fatally compromised the mediating influence of Louis Blanc, since both workers and deputies suspected him, probably unjustly, of betraying them. Henceforth the Assembly and the workers of Paris moved to an open split, Blanqui and Barbès were imprisoned, and Louis Blanc narrowly escaped. The aroused Assembly forced the government to close the National Workshops, set up as a pretended concession to Louis Blanc, which had become centers of social ferment. The Paris workers rose in desperate armed revolt and the bloody June Days of civil war brought terrible defeat to the leaderless revolutionaries but also fatal discredit and disunion to the republicans.

After the June Days, the moderate republicans, disunited even in their own ranks, succumbed before Louis Napoleon's drive for power and the bitter hostility of the workers against the Republic. The Center lost most of its supporters who moved either to the extreme Left or Right. Louis Napoleon became the rallying point of all those discontented with the domestic and foreign policy of the Republic, from extreme Left to extreme Right. The embittered workmen cheered him as the heir of the great Revolution. The Right hailed him as the foe of the Revolution and the restorer of order and past glory.

Louis Napoleon could be all things to all men more successfully than Lamartine.

Did the Left defeat liberalism by frightening the peasants and middle class with their premature radicalism and chauvinism? Or were the liberals themselves too timid and too fearful of democracy and social reforms? Were they too inexperienced in practical politics or too stagestruck in re-enacting the romantic and heroic drama of the Great Revolution? Or perhaps the democratic faith in the panacea of universal suffrage and republicanism was too optimistic for the historical circumstances. Certainly Tocqueville's unheeded warning to the National Assembly that direct election of the President by universal suffrage of an illiterate and inexperienced people could lead to dictatorship of a demagogue was only too soon and too thoroughly vindicated.

1. ALPHONSE DE LAMARTINE:
LIBERAL REPUBLIC LEADER

France is a Republic. The French Republic does not need to be recognized in order to exist; it *is* by natural right and by national might. It is the will of a great nation authorized by itself alone. However, since the French Republic wishes to enter into the family of established nations as a regular power and not as a force disruptive of European order, it is fitting that you should promptly make known to the governments to which you are accredited the principles and policies which hereafter will govern the foreign policies of the French government.

The proclamation of the French Republic is not an act of aggression against any form of government anywhere in the world. The diversity of forms of government is just as legitimate as is the diversity of character, geographical situation and intellectual, moral and material development among peoples. Nations, like individuals, are not all the same age; the principles which govern them pass through successive phases. Monarchic, aristocratic, constitutional and republican forms of government express the varying degrees of maturity of the mind of the people. They demand more liberty in proportion to their readiness for it; they demand more equality and democ-

racy as they become more animated by justice and love towards fellow man. It is a question of time. A people is as much lost by setting ahead the clock of this maturity as it would be dishonored by failing to profit by it. Monarchies and the republics do not, in the eyes of true statesmen, represent absolute principles locked in a death struggle; rather they are contrasting facts which can coexist providing they have mutual respect and understanding.

War, then, is not now one of the principles of the French Republic as it was its fatal and glorious necessity in 1792. Between 1792 and 1848 lies half a century. To go back, after this half century, to the principles of 1792, to the period of Empire and conquest, would not be advancing but regressing. Yesterday's revolution [February, 1848] was a step forward, not backward. We and the world alike wish to go forward in brotherhood and peace....

In 1792, the nation was not united, two peoples existed on the same soil.... Today there are no longer any distinct and unequal classes, all are enfranchised by liberty, all are leveled by equality before the law.... There is not a single French citizen, whatever his political belief, who does not put his fatherland first and who, by this very unity, makes her impregnable in the face of attempted invasion....

In 1792 neither France nor Europe was ready to understand and accept a harmonious interrelation of nations with its resultant of benefits to mankind.... Fifty years' freedom of thought, freedom of speech, freedom of the press have had their effect; books, newspapers and speeches have propagated European enlightenment. Reason, shining over all, passing over national boundaries, has given men's minds a fatherland of the spirit which will be the crowning achievement of the French Revolution and the establishment of international brotherhood throughout the world.

In 1792, liberty was a novelty, equality a scandal, the Republic a problem.... [Thrones and peoples] will realize that there is such a thing as conservative liberty; that there may exist in a Republic not only a better system but also that there is more true order in government by all for all than in government by and for a few.

Make no mistake, however. These ideas which the Government charges you to present to the European powers as a pledge of European security are not to be taken as suing for forgiveness by the Republic for daring to be born, still less as a humble petition for the right to exist as a great state. . . .

The French people will declare war on no one; needless to say, she would accept the challenge were she to be attacked. The thoughts of those now governing France run as follows: France would be fortunate, in case war should be imposed upon her, thus forcing her to grow in strength and glory despite her moderation. France would be guilty were she to declare war without being forced to do so. . . .

Although the French Republic proclaims that the treaties of 1815 no longer exist except as facts to be modified by mutual consent, and that it is her right and her duty to bring about this modification, legally and peacefully, nevertheless, the good sense, moderation, conscientiousness, and prudence of the Republic exist and these are, for Europe, a better and more honorable guarantee than the letter of those treaties which have been frequently violated or modified.

Endeavor, Sir, to achieve comprehension and acceptance of the Republic's emancipation from the treaties of 1815 and, at the same time, show that this freedom is not irreconcilable with the peace of Europe. Thus, we proclaim it aloud, were Providence to decree that the hour of reconstruction of certain oppressed European nations had struck—were Switzerland, our faithful ally since the days of Francis I, either hindered or threatened in her political progress. . . , were Italy's independent states to be invaded, their internal transformation to be limited or thwarted, or were these states to be forcibly prevented from joining in the formation of an Italian nation, then the French Republic would believe she had the right to take arms herself in order to protect these legitimate movements of state growth and nationality.

The Republic, you see, in one bound has passed by the age of proscription and dictatorships. She is equally resolved never to let liberty be veiled at home nor her democratic principles be obscured abroad. Let no man place his hand between the peaceful radiance of her liberty and the eyes of mankind. She declares herself to be allied by heart and mind to all rights, progress and legitimate development of the institutions of all nations who wish to live by the same principles as her own. Never will she carry on hidden and inflammatory propaganda among her neighbors. Well she knows that the only liberties which endure are those which spring from their native soil. Nonetheless, she will strive, by the example of order and peace she sets to the world to indulge in the only real and honest propagandizing, that of winning admiration and sympathy. This is no war, it is nature; this is no agitation of Europe, it is life; this is no torch to set the world aflame, it is a beacon light to summon and guide the peoples of the world! . . .

These three words [Liberty, Equality and Fraternity] in their application to our foreign affairs mean this: setting France free from the chains which outrage her principles and her dignity; restoration of the position she should hold among the great European powers; finally, the proclamation of her alliance and amity with all peoples. If France is aware of her role in the liberal, civilizing mission of this century, no one of these words means war. If Europe is wise and just, there is not one which does not say peace.

Manifesto to Europe or *Circular of the Minister of Foreign Affairs to the Diplomatic Agents of the French Republic,* in *Le Moniteur universel,* March 4, 1848, pp. 544–45, in part, trans. E. A. Clark.

2. ALEXIS DE TOCQUEVILLE: A LIBERAL REPUBLICAN CRITIC

I had spent the best days of my youth amid a society which seemed to increase in greatness and prosperity as it increased in liberty; I had conceived the idea of a balanced, regulated liberty, held in check by religion, custom and law; the attractions of this liberty had touched me; it had become the passion of my life; I felt that I could never be consoled for its loss, and that I must renounce all hope of its recovery.

I had gained too much experience of mankind to be able to content myself with empty words; I knew that, if one great revolution is able to establish liberty in a country, a number of succeeding revolutions make all regular liberty impossible for very many years. . . .

I began to pass in review the history of our last sixty years, and I smiled bitterly when I thought of the illusions formed at the conclusion of each period in this long revolution.

The Constitutional Monarchy had succeeded the *Ancien Régime*; the Republic, the Monarchy; the Empire, the Republic; the Restoration, the Empire; and then came the Monarchy of July. After each of these successive changes it was said that the French Revolution, having accomplished what was presumptuously called its work, was finished; this had been said and it had been believed. Alas! I myself had hoped it under the Restoration, and again after the fall of the Government of the Restoration; and here is the French Revolution beginning over again, for it is still the same one. As we go on, its end seems farther off and shrouded in greater darkness. Shall we ever—as we are assured by other prophets, perhaps as delusive as their predecessors—shall we ever attain a more complete and more far-reaching social transformation than our fathers foresaw and desired, and than we ourselves are able to foresee; or are we not destined simply to end in a condition of intermittent anarchy, the well-known chronic and incurable complaint of old races?

All the deputies who came to Paris [for the National Assembly in early May] with the desire to put down the excesses of the Revolution and to combat the demagogic party regarded him [Lamartine] beforehand as their only possible leader, and looked to him unhesitatingly to place himself at their head to attack and overthrow the Socialists and demagogues. They soon discovered that they were deceived, and that Lamartine did not see the part he was called upon to play in so simple a light. It must be confessed that his was a very complex and difficult position. It was forgotten at the time, but he could not himself forget, that he had contributed more than any other to the success of the Revolution of February. . . .

He was then following the tortuous road that was so soon to lead him to his ruin, struggling to dominate the Mountain without overthrowing it, and to slacken the revolutionary fire without extinguishing it, so as to give the country a feeling of security strong enough for it to bless him, not strong enough to cause it to forget him. . . .

The nation saw in Ledru-Rollin the bloody image of the Terror; it beheld in him the genius of evil as in Lamartine the genius of good, and it was mistaken in both cases. . . .

Lamartine, who had seen nothing but Paris during the last two months, and who had there, so to speak, lived in the very heart of the revolutionary party, exaggerated the power of the Capital and the inactivity of the rest of France. He overestimated both. But I am not sure that I, on my side, did not strain a point on the other side. . . . In any case, I am led to believe that it was Lamartine's tergiversations and his semiconnivance with the enemy that saved us, while it ruined him. Their effect was to amuse the leaders of the Mountain and to divide them. The Montagnards of the old school, who were retained in the Government, separated themselves from the Socialists, who were excluded from it. . . .

Lamartine saw these dangers more

closely and clearly than I, and I believe today that the fear of arousing a mortal conflict influenced his conduct as much as did his ambition. . . .

It was then [at the May 15 uprising against the National Assembly on the pretext of demonstrations of sympathy for the Prussian repression of Polish riots] that I saw appear, in his turn, in the tribune a man whom I have never seen since, but the recollection of whom has always filled me with horror and disgust. He had wan, emaciated cheeks, white lips, a sickly, wicked and repulsive expression, a dirty pallor, the appearance of a mouldy corpse; he wore no visible linen; an old black frock-coat tightly covered his lean, withered limbs; he seemed to have passed his life in a sewer and to have just left it. I was told it was Blanqui.

Blanqui said one word about Poland; then, turning sharply to domestic affairs, he asked for revenge for what he called the massacres of Rouen, recalled with threats the wretchedness in which the people had been left, and complained of the wrongs done to the latter by the Assembly. After thus exciting his hearers, he returned to the subject of Poland and, like Raspail, demanded an immediate vote. . . .

A long interval passed; at last Barbès darted up and climbed, or rather leapt, into the tribune. He was one of those men in whom the demagogue, the madman and the knight-errant are so closely intermingled that it is not possible to say where one ends or the other commences, and who can only make their way in a society as sick and troubled as ours. . . .

"I demand," said he, in panting, jerking tones, "that, immediately and before rising, the Assembly shall vote the departure of an army for Poland, a tax of a milliard upon the rich, the removal of the troops from Paris, and shall forbid the beating to arms; if not, the representatives to be declared traitors to the country.". . .

The whole time elapsing between the [insurrections of May] and the days of June was filled with the anxiety caused by the approach of these latter days. . . . The National Assembly was so constantly pos-

sessed by this thought that one might have said that it read the words "Civil War" written on the four walls of the House. . . .

The danger was perceived afar off as well as near at hand. The provinces grew indignant and irritated with Paris; for the first time for sixty years they ventured to entertain the idea of resisting it. . . . The ruin of commerce, universal war, the dread of Socialism made the Republic more and more hateful in the eyes of the provinces. This hatred manifested itself especially beneath the secrecy of the ballot. The electors were called upon to re-elect in twenty-one departments; and in general they elected the men who in their eyes represented the Monarchy in some form or other. . . .

It was then that suddenly, for the first time, the name of Louis Napoleon came into notice. The Prince was elected at the same time in Paris and in several departments. Republicans, Legitimists and demagogues gave him their votes; for the nation at that time was like a frightened flock of sheep, which runs in all directions without following any road. . . .

I come at last to the insurrection of June, the most extensive and the most singular that has occurred in our history, and perhaps in any other. . . .

What distinguished it also, among all the events of this kind which have succeeded one another in France for sixty years, is that it did not aim at changing the form of government, but at altering the order of society. It was not, strictly speaking, a political struggle, in the sense which until then we had given to the word, but a combat of class against class, a sort of Servile War. It represented the facts of the Revolution of February in the same manner as the theories of Socialism represented its ideas; or rather it issued naturally from these ideas, as a son does from his mother. We behold in it nothing more than a blind and rude, but powerful, effort on the part of the workmen to escape from the necessities of their condition, which had been depicted to them as one of unlawful oppression, and to open up by main force a road towards that imaginary comfort with which they had been deluded. It was this mixture of greed and false theory which first gave birth to the insurrection and then made it so formidable. These poor people had been told that the wealth of the rich was in some way the produce of a theft practised upon themselves. They had been assured that the inequality of fortunes was as opposed to morality and the welfare of society as it was to nature. Prompted by their needs and their passions, many had believed this obscure and erroneous notion of right, which, mingled with brute force, imparted to the latter an energy, a tenacity and a power which it would never have possessed unaided.

It must also be observed that this formidable insurrection was not the enterprise of a certain number of conspirators, but the revolt of one whole section of the population against another. . . .

Such were the days of June, necessary and disastrous days. They did not extinguish revolutionary ardour in France, but they put a stop, at least for a time, to what may be called the work appertaining to the Revolution of February. They delivered the nation from the tyranny of the Paris workmen and restored it to possession of itself.

Socialist theories continued to penetrate into the minds of the people in the shape of envious and greedy desires, and to sow the seed of future revolutions; but the socialist party itself was beaten and powerless. The Montagnards, who did not belong to it, felt that they were irrevocably affected by the blow that had struck it. The moderate Republicans themselves did not fail to be alarmed lest this victory had led them to a slope which might precipitate them from the Republic, and they made an immediate effort to stop their descent, but in vain. Personally I detested the Mountain, and was indifferent to the Republic; but I adored Liberty, and I conceived great apprehensions for it immediately after these days. I at once looked upon the June fighting as a necessary crisis, after which, however, the temper of the nation would undergo a certain change. The love of independence was to be followed by a dread of, and perhaps a distaste for, free institutions; after such an abuse of liberty a return of this sort was inevitable. This retrograde movement began, in fact, on the 27th of June. At first very slow and invisible, as it were, to the naked eye, it grew swifter, impetuous, irresistible. Where will it stop? I do not know.

Alexis de Tocqueville, *Recollections,* trans. Alexander Teixeira de Mattos (New York: The Macmillan Co., 1896), pp. 85–87, 145–46, 149–54, 163–65, 180–83, 187–88, 230–31.

3. LOUIS BLANC: FOR A SOCIAL AND DEMOCRATIC REPUBLIC

The cry of our days is: "LAISSEZ FAIRE, LAISSEZ PASSER! To the strongest the reward of their strength." That means: Woe to the weaker, woe to the loser. For in a society where the conditions are unequal, individualism is not liberty—it is war!

We are entering now upon fateful days. Will society be destroyed or transformed? And note well that I do not speak solely as representative of one faction or even one class. No—progress exists, for me, only on condition that everyone profits from it— everyone without exception. Progress, to

me, means solidarity recognized and realized by all interests. Do you know why I have declared, in my heart, war to the death against the principle of antagonism? Not only because it is the misfortune of the worker; it is also frequently the misfortune of the employer; because it merely shifts tyranny, when it does not make it permanent. Now, whatever the source, tyranny is odious to me. Therefore, I believe in the happiness of all by the association of all, in accord with the noble motto inscribed on our flag, that motto created by our ancestors, the most glorious advance of the human spirit: Liberty, Equality, Fraternity.

Beware, gentlemen, of that dangerous doctrine: "We wish *laissez faire, laissez passer* because we wish liberty." Liberty cannot, in fact, exist for all, when their forces are completely unequal. I have written before and I repeat here confidently: Look now, in all honesty, is the worker free not to die from hunger who in the universal disorder created by unlimited competition cannot find the work which alone can give him bread? Is the vagabond who has no refuge free not to sleep on the street pavement, I ask you? Or is he even free to sleep on the street since he is punished for the crime of vagrancy?...

I address myself to your heart, to your patriotism....

We have a glorious mission to perform.

To France, now a republic, falls the eternal honor of inaugurating in the world the principle of association. Let us hasten to establish it in order to cut short all cause and pretext of hatred in our midst; in order to produce for a known market, in order that nothing in our destiny be given over to chance, to the unforeseen, to blind and brutal force; in order that we may turn away in wholesome fear from these paths which lead to civil war; in order that we may prepare for our fatherland by common effort, the place we desire.

The solution we are looking for is this, and I say it from the bottom of my heart: to make an end of revolutions—Progress; to end wars—Justice!

Address of the President of the Government Commission on Labor at the Luxembourg Palace, meeting of March 17, *Le Moniteur universel*, (no. 79) March 19, 1848, p. 639, trans. E. A. Clark.

M. Louis Blanc: "Until now, my friends, power has always been on one side and the nation on the other. These two forces, instead of interpenetrating and comprehending one another, always consider themselves enemies. That is why until now society has always lived between power by oppression and liberty by revolt. Now all this is going to change! Till now power has been resistance, we have been movement. Till now, power has distrusted the people, because it had the insolence to believe itself above them. Now we lend all our strength, all our hopes, in the confidence that the people gives us and that we have in the people, because we are sure that our heart beats in unison with theirs. Yes, fraternal accord between those who compose society and those who are called to the honor of leadership—fraternal accord, permanent, indestructible, for henceforth power can only be the union of good men, elected by their equals, to guide and

regulate the march of mankind toward liberty." (Prolonged acclamations: Long live Louis Blanc, long live the Republic!)

The delegates begin to leave the room when Louis Blanc returns suddenly, his face shining with joy, and stops them on the stairs with these words: "My friends, return! I have great news for you!" Everyone immediately rushes into the hall. M. Louis Blanc: "Two words only!" Profound silence.

"The Republic we have proclaimed is going to triumph over all of Europe. I have just learned from my honorable colleague M. de Lamartine, Minister of Foreign Affairs, who has just received the news, that Austria has revolted. (Explosion of applause. Cries of joy.)

"Austria has revolted and Metternich has fled!" (Immense enthusiasm. From all sides: "Long live the Republic! Long live the universal Republic!")

[Stenographic report of the meeting of March 19, when members of the Provisional Government were acclaimed by the Commission.] *Ibid.*, March 20, p. 645, trans. E. A. Clark.

Certainly no one admires more than I the genius of M. Lamartine, his integrity, the chivalrous character of his attempts

and the splendor of his imagination so well supported by the brilliance of his style. But these very qualities had a fatal side, seeming to veil both to himself and others the nature of his faults. Gifted with a prodigious power of illusion, he imagined that he had suddenly given France the Republic he had so long rejected as impossible; dragged at the end of the movement, he thought he was its head and imagined it would be easy to master it. . . . He dreamed of his role, with the passion of the man of letters—it can be summed up in two words—to be applauded. . . . He coveted the support of all, he was sympathetic to all opinions, he sought to place himself at the point of intersection of all parties. With equal ardor he pursued the approbation of the salon and the revolutionary clubs. . . .

His natural generosity leads me to suppose that M. Lamartine was aiming to achieve general reconciliation. But he yielded also to an inner reason which he probably did not admit to himself—the human heart is so ready to deceive itself. . . . It was one of the faults and misfortunes of M. Lamartine that for the sake of his own vanity and glory he would flatter and connive with intelligent and strong characters like M. Barbès, but also with sharp wits, like M. Blanqui, who made use of him while he thought he was using them.

In any case, this calculated and superficial good will of M. Lamartine never extended to the Luxembourg when this palace of the aristocracy became the palace of the people. Why? Because M. de Lamartine knew nothing of real public opinion, because he could not forgive the Luxembourg for being the heart and soul of that February Revolution—all else was shadow and noise—because, finally, he was afraid of socialism, that great reality, as children are afraid of phantoms.

If it were only a question of loving the People with a poetic love, he could have done that certainly, and no one more willingly than he would have lavished on human sufferings the treasures of a sentimentality gushing forth in metaphors. But to espouse boldly the cause of the poor and oppressed against the strong, to brave with the valor of an indomitable soul, injustice armed with a sword, or even injustice crowned with flowers; to expose oneself, for the sake of eternal truth, to being misunderstood, wronged, vilified, ridiculed, stung to the quick by myriad vipers; to endure the hatred of the dishonest in order to keep one's inner peace, to be willing to make adversaries of the whole world if necessary—that is what he lacks. M. Lamartine defied death nobly with the courage of a soldier; he trembled at detractors, with the weakness of a poet. He did not know how to make mortal enemies. This explains why he had on his side all parties for a day. He went to bed thinking he had France on his bedside table. He fell asleep in self-intoxication. He dreamed of dictatorship. He woke up and he was alone.

Louis Blanc, *Histoire de la Révolution de 1848*, 2 vols. (Paris: Flammarion, 1880), II, 63–65, trans. E. A. Clark.

4. THE REVOLUTIONARY RADICALS: THE CLUBS AND COMMITTEES

This Society has for its object—first, to defend the rights of the people, the exercise of which has been restored to them by the Revolution of February; secondly, to draw from this Revolution all its social consequences. As its point of departure, the Society takes the Declaration of the Rights of Man as laid down in 1793 by Robespierre. It ensues that, in a political point of view, the Republic, one and indivisible, comprehends the inalienable laws of the people. In a social point of view, the old constitution is abolished; and that which is called to replace it must rest on equality and fraternity, the fundamental principles of the new social compact. Consequently, the social revolution, now at its commencement, places itself between the Pariahs and the Privileged of the ancient state of society. To the first it says—Be united, but calm; for in this lies your strength. Your number is such that it must suffice to manifest your will, and make you obtain all you desire. It is also such that you cannot desire anything but what is just. Your voice and your will are the voice and the will of God. To the others it says—The old social form has disappeared. The reign of privilege and exploitation is past. In the point of view of the ancient social form, if the privileges with which you were invested were acquired in a legal manner, do not avail yourselves of them: these laws were your own work; the immense majority of your brethren were strangers to them, and, therefore, are not bound to respect them. Rally, then, together, for you have need of the pardon of those whom you have so long sacrificed. If, in spite of this promise of pardon, you persist in remaining isolated in order to defend the old social form, you will find in the vanguard, on the day of conflict, our sections organized: and your brethren will no longer hold towards you the language of pardon, but that of justice. [The Members of the Central Committee: Villain, Lebon, Huber, Chipron, Barbès]

Placard of the Society of the Rights of Man and of the Citizen (April 29), *The Annual Register, or a View of the History and Politics of the Year 1848* (London, 1849), pp. 262–63.

B. The Revolutions of 1848 in Central Europe: Nationalist Antagonisms

All over Europe, both during the 1848 revolutions and afterward, the forces of liberalism were so divided over the "political question" and the "social question" that they furnished no strong center coalition to resist the crossfire of the extreme right of autocratic rulers—Napoleon III, the Czar, the Hapsburg Emperor, the Prussian King—or the extreme left of the revolutionary radicals.

In continental Europe outside France, it was the "national question" that came to dominate the revolutions of 1848. Mazzini's ideal of liberal nationalism, which held that the nations must achieve their own freedom, and at the same time work fraternally for a common ideal transcending all nations, that is, an internationalism based on republican, liberal, and pacific policies and institutions, was badly betrayed by the events of 1848–49. This was particularly the case in Central Europe, especially in the Hapsburg Empire. There after a brief March honeymoon of liberal declarations of fraternity among the oppressed nationalities, came the increasing bitterness and strife of nationality against nationality. In a few months these national animosities combined with Russian arms and Hapsburg politics to bring defeat to both national and liberal aims in the polyglot Empire. The mutual suspicion, rivalry, and accusations of Slav, Magyar, and German that culminated in World War I and are still a force in Europe crystallized in 1848–49.

When the news of the Paris Revolution of late February reached Vienna, it set off a chain reaction of uprisings and revolutionary events all over the Austrian Empire and indeed over most of continental Europe. Appropriately enough, the dramatic events centered around the Ides of March. Louis Kossuth's speech in the Hungarian Diet demanded freedom and a constitution for all the Empire. Meetings of Czechs and Germans in Prague demanded autonomy for Bohemia, and Croats demanded the same from Hungary. There were uprisings in Berlin and in North Italy. And in Vienna on March 13, students and workers joined forces in a revolt that toppled Metternich overnight and forced the Emperor to promise a constitution to his dominions. Yet these predominantly national revolutions in the Hapsburg Empire contained the same divisive, self-defeating hatreds as the political and social revolution in France. The German radicals in Vienna and Bohemia hoped for the merging of German Austria, including Bohemia, in a united Germany. Kossuth, the Hungarian leader, supported this on condition that the Magyars should keep their ascendancy over the Slavs in Hungary. The Slavs, however, in both Austria and Hungary, hoped for Slav autonomy. The Czechs of Bohemia, especially the most literate, liberal, and Western of the Slavic minorities in the Hapsburg Empire, hoped for a transformation of the Austrian monarchy into a group of national states under the personal monarchy of the House of Austria. This would achieve at least Slav equality with the Germans and Magyars, or perhaps eventually Slav predominance, since they formed the great majority of the inhabitants of the Empire. This policy of Austroslavism, as it was called later, seemed to most of them their only hope. They knew they were too weak as individual states to resist the growing threat of German unity and of Russian despotism. The unity of all Germany dreamed of by the Frankfurt Congress was defeated partly by the Slavs' rival claims. The call for a Slav Congress to be held at Prague in June, 1848, to counterbalance the German Congress declared that such a move to unite Germany "would not only destroy the unity of Austria but would annihilate also the union of the Slavic races, whose national independence would be threatened."

This warning had first been sounded by Frantisek Palacky, Czech historian and an advocate of Austrian federalism, in April. He wrote to the Committee of Fifty at Frankfurt declining to take part in the planning of the German National Assembly on the ground that Bohemia was a Slav kingdom, not a province of Greater Germany. It was he who uttered the famous phrase, "Assuredly, if the Austrian state had not existed for ages, it would have been necessary, in the interests of Europe and of humanity, for us to invent it."

The Czech moderates were neither separatists nor Russophiles. Palacky indeed justified the existence of Austria as a necessary bulwark against the "ever accelerated expansion of the Russian monarchy," which threatened western civilization and the cause of freedom by a "universal monarchy, that is to say, an infinite and inexpressible evil." His ideal was a Danubian federation of equal nationalities gathered around a liberal and reformed Austria. Such a grouping would unite the whole area between the Russian Empire and the German Confederation and thus preserve peace and liberty for the Slavs and for Europe.

The Slav Congress, then, was called by the Czech moderates to counteract Magyarizing and Germanizing centralization and to declare the rights and the brotherhood of the Slav peoples long submerged beneath German and Magyar. It was in no sense intended as a revolt against the Hapsburgs. Though the Czechs demanded and obtained an autonomous government in April, the moderates declared their loyalty to Austria at the Slav Congress in June. But the insurrection of a Czech radical minority of students and workers discredited the Slav Congress. It brought swift military reprisal in Prague from the imperial government and shattered Czech dreams of freedom. Yet the Czechs still felt they needed protection against the Germans, as their brother Slavs needed it against the Magyars, so they perforce supported the imperial government.

Ironically, it was the liberal emancipation of the peasants in the Hapsburg Empire that led to the emergence of the Slavs as a political force and set the Germans and Magyars, who were landowners and bourgeois, against the Slavs, who were overwhelmingly peasants. Extension of the suffrage and the constitutional equality of the Slav majority with the Magyar and German minorities originated as liberal reforms but led to nationalistic struggles for predominance. In the end everyone lost, but the chief victim was liberalism.

1. THE SLAVIC VIEWPOINT: THE CZECHS

. . . The Slavs, among whom liberty was ever cherished the more fervently as they showed little aspiration for conquest and dominion, and among whom the desire for independence always prevented the formation of a higher central power of any kind, fell in the course of the ages, people after people, under alien dominion. A policy which has long been condemned, as it should be condemned, in the eyes of the world, has most recently of all deprived the heroic Polish nation, our noble kinsmen, of their independence as a State. The whole great Slavonic world, it seemed, found itself in bondage for all time when the ready servants of that system of bondage did not hesitate to deny to the Slavs the very capacity to be free. . . . Now the long under-yoked Slav is again raising his head, he is scaring violence away from his presence, and with lusty emphasis is claiming his ancient heritage, his liberty. Strong in feeling, stronger still in will-power and his newly acquired fraternal unanimity, he remains none the less true to his natural character and the principles of his forefathers. He demands neither conquest nor dominion, but he asks for liberty for himself and for all others: he demands that liberty shall be unconditionally recognized as the most sacred right that man possesses. Therefore we Slavs reject and hold in abhorrence all dominion based on main force and evasion of the law; we reject all privileges and prerogatives as well as all political differentiation of classes; we demand unconditional equality before the law, an equal measure of rights and duties for all. Where a single slave is born among millions, true liberty does not exist in that place. Yes, liberty, equality, fraternity for all who live in the State is our watchword today, as it was a thousand years ago.

Nor is it only for the individuals in the State that we lift up our voices and put forward our demands. Not less sacred to us than man in the enjoyment of his natural rights is the nation, with its sum total of spiritual needs and interests. Even if history has attributed a more complete human development to certain nations than to others, it has none the less always been seen that the capacity of those other nations for development is in no way limited. Nature in and for herself draws no distinction between nations as though some were noble and others ignoble; she has not called any one nation to dominate over others, nor set aside any nation to serve another as an instrument for that other's ends. . . . Yet the German threatens many a Slavonic people with violence if it will not agree to assist in the upbuilding of the political greatness of Germany, and thus the Magyar is not ashamed to arrogate to himself exclusive national rights in Hungary. We Slavs utterly decry all such pretensions; and we reject them the more emphatically the more they are wrongfully disguised in the garb of freedom. Faithful, however, to our natural character, and declining to seek revenge for wrongs done us in the past, we extend a brotherly hand to all neighboring nations who are prepared to recognise and effectively champion with us the full equality of all nations, irrespective of their political power or size.

Similarly we reprehend and hold in abhorrence that policy which claims to deal with lands and nations as mere material, subject to a ruling power, to take, to change, to partition at pleasure or fancy irrespective of the race, the language, the customs and the inclinations of the nations,

and regardless of their natural connection or of the independence which is their right. . . .

Taking our stand on the conviction that the mighty current of thought of today demands new political formations and that the State must be reconstructed, if not within new bounds at least upon new foundations, we have proposed to the Austrian Emperor, under whose constitutional rule the majority of us live, that the imperial State be converted into a federation of nations all enjoying equal rights, whereby regard would be paid not less to the different needs of these nations than to those of the united Monarchy. We see in such a federal union not only our own salvation but also liberty, enlightenment and humanity generally; and we are confident that civilised Europe would readily contribute to the realisation of that union. In any case we are determined to ensure for our nationality in Austria, by all the means available to us, a full recognition of the same rights in the State as the German and Magyar nations already enjoy, and in this we rely upon the powerful demand for all genuine rights which wells up warmly in every truly free breast.

The enemies of our nationality have succeeded in terrifying Europe with the bogy of political Panslavism which, they have declared, threatens to destroy all that has been won anywhere for freedom, enlightenment and humanity. We, however, are acquainted with the one magic word which of itself suffices to lay that bogy; and for the sake of freedom, enlightenment and humanity we do not desire to keep it secret from the nations disquieted by the pricks of their own conscience. That word is justice, justice towards the Slavonic nations generally and justice towards its oppressed branches in particular. . . . We raise our voices emphatically on behalf of our unhappy brethren the Poles, whom malicious violence has robbed of independence; we ask the governments concerned finally to remedy this old sin, this curse which has descended as a burdensome heritage upon their Cabinet policy, and in this matter we rely upon the sympathies of all Europe. . . . We look to the Governments of Prussia and Saxony to abandon at long last the systematic denationalisation of the Slavs in...East and West Prussia, which they have carried on up till now; we demand of the Hungarian Ministry that without delay they cease to employ inhuman and violent methods against the Slavonic peoples in Hungary, in particular the Serbs, the Croats, the Slovaks and Ruthenians, and that the national rights which are their due shall be fully assured them as speedily as possible.

We, the youngest but by no means the weakest, in entering once more the political arena of Europe, propose that a general European Congress of Nations be summoned for the discussion of all international questions; being thoroughly convinced that free nations will more easily come to agreement than paid diplomats. May this proposal meet with due consideration before the reactionary policy of the individual Courts causes the nations, incited by hatred and malice, mutually to destroy one another!

In the name of liberty, equality and fraternity of all nations. František Palacký, President of the Slavonic Congress.

"Manifesto of the First Slavonic Congress to the Nations of Europe, June 12, 1848," *The Slavonic and East European Review*, XXVI (April 1948), 309–13, trans. Dr. William Beardmore.

2. THE MAGYAR VIEW: LOUIS KOSSUTH'S SPEECH OF THE 11TH JULY, 1848

Gentlemen, the country is in danger. Perhaps it would suffice to say thus much; for, with the dawn of liberty, the dark veil has dropped from the nation. You know what the condition of our country is; you know that besides the troops of the line, a militia of about twelve thousand men has been organized; you know that the authorities have been empowered to place corps of the National Guard on a war footing, in order to establish an effective force to defend the country, and to punish sedition, which is rife on our frontiers. This command found an echo in the nation.

Under such circumstances we took the reins of government, menaced by treachery, rebellion, reactionary movements, and by all those passions which the policy of Metternich leagued to us as a cursed inheritance. Scarcely had we assumed the government—nay, not all of us had even assembled—when we already received the most authentic information that the Panslavonic agitation had no other object than to excite the whole of the upper provinces to open rebellion, and that even the day had been fixed when the outbreak should take place....

Croatia is in open rebellion! Many years have elapsed, gentlemen, when not only one or the other, but numbers, called the attention of the government to the fact, that in encouraging—I say not forgiving, but encouraging—the Illyric agitation, it would nourish a serpent in its bosom which would compass the ruin of the dynasty. And since the revolutionary state in which we find Europe shaking on her foundations, the gentlemen in those parts fancied they might with impunity break out in open rebellion. Had Hungary given any cause whatever for this rebellion, she would, without considering the fact that there is a revolution, ask you to be just to Croatia, and to subdue the revolt, not with the force of arms, but with the sacred name of justice.

Where is a reason to be found that, even if we take up arms to quell the disturbance, we should feel in our own hearts the conviction of having ourselves provoked the disturbance? I say, no! The rights we have acquired for ourselves, we have likewise acquired for Croatia; the liberty that was granted to the people, was likewise granted to the Croats; we extended the indemnity allowed by us to our nobility, at our own expense, to Croatia—for that country is too small and powerless to raise herself the indemnity.

With regard to nationality, Croatia entertained apprehensions—though produced by various conceptions and by erroneous ideas—for the Parliament has expressly decreed that in public life the Croats should have the fullest right to make use of their own language in accordance with their own statutes; and thus their nationality has been sanctioned, by this public recognition. Their municipal rights the Parliament has not only not impaired, but extended and augmented. . . .

In one word, we have not neglected anything whatever which, within the limits of integrity, of liberty, and of the rights of the people, we could do to pacify their minds. We, gentlemen, can not, therefore, admit that on the part of the cabinet the slightest cause has been given to provoke the Croatian rebellion.

If a people think the liberty they possess too limited, and take up arms to conquer more, they certainly play a doubtful game—for a sword has two edges. Still I can understand it. But if a people say, Your liberty is too much for us, we will not have it if you give it us, but we will go and bow under the old yoke of Absolutism —that is a thing which I endeavor in vain to understand.

The case, however, stands nearly thus: in the so-called petition which was sent to his majesty by the Conventicle of Agram, they pray that they may be allowed to separate from Hungary—not to be a self-consistent, independent nation, but to submit to the Austrian ministry. . . . I do not, indeed, ascribe to the sentiment of freedom so great an influence on the masses, as not to be persuaded that even this sham loyalty, in its awkward affectation, is but an empty pretext under which other purposes are concealed. On the part of the leaders it covers the reactionary tendency; but on the other hand, this idea is connected with the plan of erecting an Austro-Slavonian monarchy. They say: "Let us send deputies to Vienna; let us procure the majority for the Slavonian element, and Austria will cease to be a German empire; and what with the Bohemians, and our people down here, a new Slavonian empire will rise." This is a rather hazardous game, and Europe will probably soon decide on the question; for if we should

not master these affairs, they will become a European question. This much is certain, that this combination (if of any consequence at all) will doubtless involve the ruin of the Austrian dynasty. There can be no doubt about it.

The Viennese ministers have thought proper, in the name of the Austrian emperor, to declare to the cabinet of the King of Hungary, that unless we make peace with the Croats at any price, they will act in opposition to us. This is as much as to say, that the Austrian emperor declares war to the King of Hungary, or to his own self. Whatever opinion you, gentlemen, may have formed of the cabinet, I believe you may so far rely on our patriotic feelings and on our honor, as to render it superfluous on my part to tell you that we have replied to this menace in a manner becoming the dignity of the nation.

The Austrian relations, the affairs of the countries on the Lower Danube, the Servian disturbances, the Croation rebellion, Panslavonian agitators, and the reactionary movements—all these circumstances, taken together, cause me to say the nation is in danger, or rather, that it will be in danger unless our resolution be firm!

The danger, therefore is great, or rather, a danger threatening to become great gathers on the horizon of our country, and we ought, above all, to find in ourselves the strength for its removal. That nation alone will live which in itself has sufficient vital power; that which knows not to save itself by its own strength, but only by the aid of others, has no future. I therefore demand of you, gentlemen, a great resolution. Proclaim that, in just appreciation of the extraordinary circumstances on account of which the Parliament has assembled, the nation is determined to bring the greatest sacrifices for the defense of its crown, of its liberty, and of its independence, and that, in this respect, it will at no price enter with any one into a transaction which even in the least might injure the national independence and liberty, but that it will be always ready to grant all reasonable wishes of everyone. But in order to realize this important resolution, either by mediating, if possible, an honorable peace, or by fighting a victorious battle, the government is to be authorized by the nation to raise the effective strength of the army to two hundred thousand men, and for this purpose to equip immediately forty thousand men, and the rest as the protection of the country and the honor of the nation may demand. . . .

Gentlemen, what I meant to say is, that this request on the part of the government ought not be considered as a vote of confidence. No; we ask for your vote for the preservation of the country! And I would ask you, gentlemen, if anywhere in our country a breast sighs for liberation, or a wish waits for its fulfillment, let that breast suffer yet a while, let that wish have a little patience, until we have saved the country. (Cheers.) This is my request! You all have risen to a man, and I bow before the nation's greatness! If your energy equals your patriotism, I will make bold to say, that even the gates of hell shall not prevail against Hungary!

W. H. Stiles, *Austria in 1848–49* (New York: Harper and Brothers, 1852), II, 384–94.

II. A Foreign Policy for Liberal Nationalism

The dilemma of the liberal in international affairs is well illustrated by a famous debate that took place in the British House of Commons in 1850. Occasioned by Palmerston's high-handed conduct of what came to be known as the Don Pacifico affair, it revealed the deep-seated conflicts that lay within the liberal camp then emerging from a realignment of the old Whigs and Tories—Manchester, Palmerstonian, Peelite, Gladstonian. They were all liberals of a sort, but were by no means of one mind on all issues.

Viscount Palmerston, England's Secretary of State for Foreign Affairs, had entered Parliament at the age of twenty-three, hence had a lifetime of experience in cabinets and the House of Commons. Starting as a Conservative and follower of William Pitt, he came to accept moderate parliamentary reform and entered the Foreign Office under Earl Grey, the Whig leader. He was a disciple of Canning in maintaining that a strong foreign policy would lead to peace. This meant upholding the power and prestige of England, and defending British interests by intervention at times or by secret diplomacy at other times. He sympathized with oppressed nationalities and constitutionalism, but not to the extent of quixotic adventures that would sacrifice British interests, as the Hungarians, Poles, and Italians found to their cost in 1849.

When the Tories were split in 1846 by Sir Robert Peel's defection to the Free Traders, Lord John Russell and the Whigs came into power and Palmerston again returned to the Foreign Office to preside through the stormy years of revolution on the Continent.

What triggered the Parliamentary explosion over the Don Pacifico affair was Palmerston's arbitrary ordering of the British fleet to Greece to force a settlement of the undoubtedly exaggerated claims of Don Pacifico, a Portuguese Jew from Gilbraltar and therefore a British subject, against the Greek government for property damages inflicted by a Greek mob in 1847. Palmerston's willingness to risk war with France and Russia, the co-guarantors of Greek independence, led to alarmed protest both inside and outside of his own party.

The debate began with a motion of confidence in Palmerston by one of his supporters in the House of Commons, in answer to the House of Lords' condemnation of Palmerston's moves in the Don Pacifico incident. It was moved: "That the principles which have hitherto regulated the foreign policy of Her Majesty's Government are such as were required to preserve untarnished the honor and dignity of this country, and in times of unexampled difficulty the best qualified to maintain peace between England and the various countries of the world." The ensuing debate ranged widely over Palmerston's quarrels with the French constitutional monarchy and republic, and his stormy interventions and retreats on the Continent during the revolutions of 1848–49. It reflected the cross-currents and realignments of English opinion and policy during the revolutions, when practically every vital question of British relations with the Continent came to the fore, not only with the major powers of France, Prussia, Austria, and Russia, but with all the smaller powers and submerged nations as well.

In England nationalism was seldom a conscious and articulate doctrine even among the intellectuals, but nationalist feeling had penetrated so deeply all levels of the population that Palmerston could appeal to uninformed public opinion and the popular newspapers to support his flamboyant statement of British national interest. The debate resulted in a resounding victory in his favor both in the House of Commons and in public acclaim, all the more notable because of the opposition of *The Times,* the leaders of most of the Parliamentary groups, the Queen and the Prince Consort, and even his own divided cabinet. It is doubtful, however, if even he could have succeeded if he had not tempered what some opponents have labeled chauvinism and bullying by his appeal to justice, generosity, and individual rights.

The divisions within liberal thought are shown by the Parliamentary critics and supporters of Palmerston. William Ewart Gladstone, like Palmerston, had begun as a Conservative, but was on the path that led to his emergence as a Liberal and the formation of the Liberal Party. The following was his first major speech on foreign policy in the House of Commons. John Bright and Richard Cobden were the leaders of the Manchester liberals who believed that free trade, disarmament, and nonintervention would lead to peace, internationalism, and the true prestige of England. Alexander Cockburn, who had just entered the House of Commons a year before as a rising lawyer, gained an opportunity for distinction by the legal and forensic ability manifested in this decisive speech and in consequence became Palmerston's Attorney-General.

The inconsistency of the liberals was gleefully pointed out by Henry Drummond, a Tory of the old school, who was elected to the House for the first time in 1847. He did not enter politics until he was in his sixties and remained an independent and sarcastic observer, portrayed by Carlyle as "a singular mixture of all things."

The basic question for the liberals was: Should England follow the reformist pledge of 1830 by the Whig Earl Grey, "Peace, nonintervention, and retrenchment," or should it actively intervene by political or military means to advance the cause of liberalism and national independence? Was Palmerston at heart a crusader or an opportunist pursuing the balance of power for England's benefit? What should be England's reaction to the Continent—"splendid isolation" or participation? These were questions Gladstone himself and successive governments of Britain have had to face, and that Britain is still facing in the mid-twentieth century.

The Great Debate Over British Intervention: The Don Pacifico Affair

A. Palmerston Defends His Foreign Policy

When I say that this is an important question, I say it in the fullest expression of the term. It is a matter which concerns not merely the tenure of office by one individual, or even by a Government; it is a question that involves principles of national policy, and the deepest interests as well as the honour and dignity of England.

With regard to our policy with respect to Italy, I utterly deny the charges that have been brought against us, of having been the advocates, supporters, and encouragers of revolution. It has always been the fate of advocates of temperate reform and of constitutional improvement to be run at as the fomentors of revolution. It is the easiest mode of putting them down, it is the received *formula.* It is the established practice of those who are the advocates of arbitrary government to say, "Never mind real revolutionists; we know how to deal with them; your dangerous man is the moderate reformer; he is such a plausible man; the only way of getting rid of him, is to set the world at him, by calling him a revolutionist."

Now, there are revolutionists of two kinds in this world. In the first place, there are those violent, hotheaded, and unthinking men who fly to arms, who overthrow established Governments; and who recklessly, without regard to consequences, and without measuring difficulties and comparing strength, deluge their country with blood, and draw down the greatest calamities on their fellow-countrymen. These are the revolutionists of one class. But there are revolutionists of another kind; blind-minded men, who, animated by antiquated prejudices, and daunted by ignorant apprehensions, dam up the current of human improvement; until the irresistible pressure of accumulated discontent breaks down the opposing barriers, and overthrows and levels to the earth, those very institutions which a timely application of renovating means would have rendered strong and lasting. Such revolutionists as these are the men who call us revolutionists. It was not to make revolutions that the Earl of Minto went to Italy, or that we, at the request of the Governments of Austria and Naples, offered our mediation between contending parties. . . .

I believe that the principles on which we have acted are those which are held by the great mass of the people of this country. I am convinced these principles are calculated, so far as the influence of England may properly be exercised with respect to the destinies of other countries, to conduce to the maintenance of peace, to the advancement of civilisation, to the welfare and happiness of mankind. . . .

It is a noble thing to be allowed to guide the policy and to influence the destinies of such a country; and, if ever it was an object of honourable ambition, more than ever must it be so at the moment at which I am speaking. For while we have seen . . . the political earthquake rocking Europe from side to side—while we have seen thrones shaken, shattered, levelled; institutions overthrown and destroyed—while in almost every country of Europe the conflict of civil war has deluged the land with blood, from the Atlantic to the Black Sea, from the Baltic to the Mediterranean; this country has presented a spectacle honourable to the people of England, and worthy of the admiration of *mankind*.

We have shown that liberty is compatible with order; that individual freedom is reconcilable with obedience to the law. We have shown the example of a nation, in which every class of society accepts with cheerfulness the lot which Providence has assigned to it; while at the same time every individual of each class is constantly striving to raise himself in the social scale—not by injustice and wrong, not by violence and illegality—but by persevering good conduct, and by the steady and energetic exertion of the moral and intellectual faculties with which his Creator has endowed him. To govern such a people as this, is indeed an object worthy of the ambition of the noblest man who lives in the land; and therefore I find no fault with those who may think any opportunity a fair one, for endeavouring to place themselves in so distinguished and honourable a position. But I contend that we have not in our foreign policy done anything to forfeit the confidence of the country. . . . I maintain that the principles which can be traced through all our foreign transactions, as the guiding rule and directing spirit of our proceedings, are such as deserve approbation. I therefore fearlessly challenge the verdict which this House, as representing a political, a commercial, a constitutional country, is to give on the question now brought before it; whether the principles on which the foreign policy of Her Majesty's Government has been conducted, and the sense of duty which has led us to think ourselves bound to afford protection to our fellow subjects abroad, are proper and fitting guides for those who are charged with the Government of England; and whether, as the Roman, in days of old, held himself free from indignity, when he could say *Civis Romanus sum* [I am a Roman citizen]; so also a British subject, in whatever land he may be, shall feel confident that the watchful eye and the strong arm of England, will protect him against injustice and wrong.

Parliamentary Debates, Commons, third series, Vol. 112, June 25, 1850 cols. 380, 432–33, 443–44.

B. Gladstone's Criticism

Sir, I am well prepared, following the example of other and more distinguished men, to bear my share in the abuse which, I doubt not, may attend the part which we shall take on this occasion. I am prepared to hear it said that we are espousing the cause, as against England, of countries other than our own; that we cabal against the noble Lord because he is the protector of Englishmen domiciled abroad. Sir, I deny that he has truly protected Englishmen by the course he has pursued. I hold that no Minister in his place can really give to Englishmen resident in foreign lands either an effectual or a permanent protection, except by a careful observance of the principles that have been consecrated by the universal assent of mankind for governing the conduct of nation to nation. In vain do you talk to us of a knot of foreign conspirators against the noble Lord,...[it] is the combined opinion of civilised Europe....

Sir, great as is the influence and power of Britain, she cannot afford to follow, for any length of time, a self-isolating policy. It would be a contravention of the law of nature and of God, if it were possible for any single nation of Christendom to emancipate itself from the obligations which bind all other nations, and to arrogate, in the face of mankind, a position of peculiar privilege. And now I will grapple with the noble Lord on the ground which he selected for himself, in the most triumphant portion of his speech, by his reference to those emphatic words, *Civis Romanus sum* [I am a Roman citizen]. He vaunted, amidst the cheers of his supporters, that under his administration an Englishman should be, throughout the world, what the citizen of Rome had been. What then, Sir, was a Roman citizen? He was the member of a privileged caste; he belonged to a conquering race, to a nation that held all others bound down by the strong arm of power. For him there was to be an exceptional system of law; for him principles were to be asserted, and by him rights were to be enjoyed that were denied to the rest of the world. Is such, then, the view of the noble Lord, as to the relation that is to subsist between England and other countries? Does he make the claim for us, that we are to be uplifted upon a platform high above the standing-ground of all other nations? It is, indeed, too clear, not only from the expressions, but from the whole spirit of the speech of the noble Viscount, that too much of this notion is lurking in his mind; that he adopts in part that vain conception, that we, forsooth, have a mission to be the censors of vice and folly, of abuse and imperfection, among the other countries of the world; that we are to be the universal schoolmasters; and that all those who hesitate to recognise our office, can be governed only by prejudice or personal animosity, and should have the blind war of diplomacy forthwith declared against them.... What, Sir, ought a Foreign Secretary to be? Is he to be like some gallant knight at a tournament of old, pricking forth into the lists, armed at all points, confiding in all his sinews and his skill, challenging all comers for the sake of honour, and having no other duty than to lay as many as possible of his adversaries sprawling in the dust? If such is the idea of a good Foreign Secretary, I, for one, would vote to the noble Lord his present appointment for his life. But, Sir, I do not understand the duty of a Secretary for Foreign Affairs to be of such a character. I understand it to be his duty to conciliate peace with dignity. I think it to be the very first of all his duties studiously to observe, and to exalt in honour among mankind, that great code of principles which is termed the law of nations which...I find...a great and noble monument of human wisdom, founded on the combined dictates of reason and experience....

Sir, the English people, whom we are here to represent, are indeed a great and noble people; but it adds nothing to their greatness or their nobleness, that when we assemble in this place we should trumpet forth our virtues in elaborate panegyrics, and designate those who may not be wholly of our mind as a knot of foreign conspirators. When, indeed, I heard the hon. and learned Gentleman the Member for Sheffield [Mr. Roebuck, supporter of Palmerston] glorifying us, together with the rest of the people of this country, and announcing that we soared in unapproachable greatness, and the like, I confess I felt that eulogies such as those savoured somewhat of bombast; and thought it much to the honour of this House that the praises thus vented seemed to fall so flat; that the cookery of the hon. and learned Gentleman was evidently seasoned beyond the capacity and relish of our palates. It is this insular temper, and this self-glorifying tendency, which the policy of the noble Lord, and the doctrines of his supporters, tend so much to foment, and which has given to that policy the quarrelsome character that marks some of their speeches; for, indeed, it seems as if there lay upon the noble Lord an absolute necessity for quarrelling. No doubt it makes a difference, what may be the institutions of one country or another. If he can, he will quarrel with an absolute monarchy. If he can not find an absolute monarchy for the purpose, he will quarrel with one which is limited. If he cannot find even that, yet, sooner than not quarrel at all, he will quarrel with a republic. He has lately shown us this in the case of France; he showed it once before in the case of America. . . .

Sir, I say the policy of the noble Lord tends to encourage and confirm in us that which is our besetting fault and weakness, both as a nation and as individuals. Let an Englishman travel where he will as a private person, he is found in general to be upright, highminded, brave, liberal, and true; but with all this, foreigners are too often sensible of something that galls them in his presence, and I apprehend it is because he has too great a tendency to self-esteem—too little disposition to regard the feelings, the habits, and the ideas of others. Sir, I find this characteristic too plainly legible in the policy of the noble Lord. I doubt not that use will be made of our present debate to work upon this peculiar weakness of the English mind. The people

will be told that those who oppose the Motion are governed by personal motives, have no regard for public principle, no enlarged ideas of national policy. . . but, Sir, let the House of Commons be warned —let it warn itself—against all illusions. There is in this case also a course of appeal. There is an appeal, such as the hon. and learned Member for Sheffield has made, from the one House of Parliament to the other. There is a further appeal from this House of Parliament to the people of England; but, lastly, there is also an appeal from the people of England to the general sentiment of the civilised world; and I, for my part, am of opinion that England will stand shorn of a chief part of her glory and her pride if she shall be found to have separated herself, through the policy she pursues abroad, from the moral supports which the general and fixed convictions of mankind afford— if the day shall come in which she may continue to excite the wonder and the fear of other nations, but in which she shall have no part in their affection and their regard.

No, Sir, let it not be so: let us recognise, and recognise with frankness, the equality of the weak with the strong; the principles of brotherhood among nations, and of their sacred independence. When we are asking for the maintenance of the rights which belong to our fellow-subjects resident in Greece, let us do as we would be done by, and let us pay all the respect to a feeble State and to the infancy of free institutions, which we should desire and should exact from others towards their maturity and their strength. Let us refrain from all gratuitous and arbitrary meddling in the internal concerns of other States, even as we should resent the same interference if it were attempted to be practised towards ourselves. If the noble Lord has indeed acted on these principles, let the Government to which he belongs have your verdict in its favour; but if he has departed from them, as I contend, and as I humbly think and urge upon you that it has been too amply proved, then the House of Commons must not shrink from the performance of its duty, under whatever expectations of momentary obloquy or reproach, because we shall have done what is right; we shall enjoy the peace of our own consciences, and receive, whether a little sooner or a little later, the approval of the voice of the public, for having entered our solemn protest against a system of policy which we believe...must of necessity in its final results be unfavourable even to the security of British subjects resident abroad...unfavourable to the dignity of the country...and equally unfavourable to that other great and sacred object...the maintenance of peace with the nations of the world.

Ibid., cols. 586–90.

C. A Manchester Liberal's Criticism: Richard Cobden

...But what would Earl Grey have said to the doctrine of the hon. and learned Gentleman, that we have no prospect of peace with the countries of Europe till they have adopted constitutional Governments? What sort of constitutional Governments? Is it our own? Why, even if they came so far as this, and suppose they adopt our form of government, might not hon. Members in the Assembly at Washington get up and say, "We will have no peace till we make the world republican." The hon. and learned Gentleman seems to have set out with the doctrine that we ought to interfere with the forms of government of the nations of Europe; and, judging from the noble Lord's speech, I must say he appears to be no unwilling pupil in that school of policy. If the House of Commons votes its approbation of such sentiments, and the noble Lord acts on them, I think the Foreign Office will have undertaken the reform and constitutionalising of every country on the face of the earth. But do you think the people of this country, when they get cool, will see the wisdom of carrying out such a course?...

If you claim the right of intervention in your Government, you must tolerate it in other nations also. With what face could you get up and denounce the Emperor of Russia for invading Hungary after the doctrine advocated by the hon. and learned Member to-night, had been adopted by this country? I say, if you want to benefit nations struggling for their freedom, establish as one of the maxims of international law the principle of non-intervention. If you want to give a guarantee for peace, and, as I believe, the surest guarantee for progress and freedom, lay down this principle and act on it—that no foreign State has a right by force to interfere with the domestic concerns of another State, even to confer what you conceive to be a benefit upon it, against its own consent....

But I come back to the principle. Do you want to benefit the Hungarians? I will tell you the sentiments of the leading Hungarians. I have seen them all, and I must say that, much as I admired them during their noble struggle, what I have seen of them in adversity has entitled them to still greater respect, for I never saw men endure adversity with more manly fortitude and dignified self-respect. They have avoided all expressions of sympathy from public meetings, and (loathing the idea of being dependent on the charity of others) have sought, by emigration to America and elsewhere, an opportunity of subsisting by the labour of their own hands. These men say, "We don't ask you to help us, or to come to our assistance. Establish such a principle as shall provide we shall not be interfered with by others." And what do the Italians say? They don't want the English to interfere with them or to help them. "Leave us to ourselves," say they. "Establish the principle that we shall not be interefered with by foreigners." [Mr. Roebuck: Hear, hear!] I will answer the hon. and learned Gentleman's cheer. He seems to ask, how will you keep out Austria from Italy, and Russia from Hungary? Why, by setting a good example ourselves, and then, if necessary, by protesting against the violation of the principle by others. I will give him an illustration of what I mean. Does he remember when Kossuth took refuge in Turkey, and Austria and the Emperor of Russia demanded him back? I beg him to understand that that illustrious refugee was not saved by any intervention of the Foreign Secretary. Has it not been admitted that the Emperor of Russia gave up his claim before the courier arrived from England? What was it then that liberated him? It was the universal outburst of public opinion and public indignation in Western Europe. And why had public opinion this power? Because this demand for the extradition of political offenders was a violation of the law of nations, which declares that persons who have committed political offences in one State shall find a sanctuary in another, and ought not to be delivered up. . . . Let us begin and set the example to other nations of non-intervention. I have no doubt that our example and protest would influence the Governments of Austria and Russia; but what possible moral influence can this country have with those States when the Government goes abroad to interfere with the domestic affairs of other countries? It is said, however, that the noble Lord the Foreign Secretary goes abroad as the champion of liberalism and constitutionalism. But I cannot fall into this delusion. I cannot trace this battle that we are taught to believe is going on under the noble Viscount's auspices between liberalism and despotism abroad. I do not think that the noble Lord is more democratic than his colleagues. . . . I do not find that the noble Lord has taken up any great question of constitutional freedom abroad. Did he ever protest against the invasion of Hungary by Russia? He made a speech against Austria, I remember, on one occasion, but he did not breathe a syllable against Russia. The only allusion he made to Russia was in the nature of an apology, uttered in a sense that seemed to justify the part taken by Russia rather than otherwise. . . .

I believe the progress of freedom depends more upon the maintenance of peace, the spread of commerce, and the diffusion of education, than upon the labours of cabinets and foreign offices. And if you prevent those perturbations which have recently taken place abroad in consequence of your foreign policy, and if you will leave other nations in greater tranquillity, those ideas of freedom will continue to progress, and you need not trouble yourself about them. . . . In private life we no longer find it necessary to carry arms for our protection, as did our forefathers. There has been the discontinuance of the practice of duelling; and something should be done to carry the same spirit into the intercourse of nations.

Ibid., cols. 670, 671–74.

D. A Radical Supporter of Palmerston Defends Intervention: Mr. Cockburn

I admit that to those hon. Gentlemen who consider that peace is the great end and aim of existence, and that to peace all else is to be sacrificed—who hold that man was created by Heaven for the sole purpose of producing, and manufacturing, and consuming cotton—who recognise no nobler aspirations, no impulses of humanity—I admit to them, that peace is of the greatest importance to this country—not merely peace between this country and foreign Governments, but peace between foreign Governments and the people who are subjected to those Governments. I admit to them that peace is essential to the development of our industry, and to the progress of our manufactures. But I tell those men that every revolution and struggle in Europe is fatal to our interests, and I tell them that as matters now are, such things will frequently occur. Mark my words, unless the relations between the governors and the governed be placed on a more satisfactory basis, you may secure peace for the day, as men have before now bought peace at the price of their independence; but that is an unsafe and an uncertain condition of things. You had far better obtain peace, based and founded on principles which are likely to endure; otherwise you only put off the evil day. You may execute the leaders, and imprison their followers. You may decimate by military executions—it matters not. The time will come when the struggle will be renewed and renewed, over and over again, till freedom is at last secured. It would be far better to settle it at once, and to settle it as it can only be settled, by inducing arbitrary monarchs to act righteously by their subjects—by inducing the people to accept the counsels of mediation and peace....

...When the right hon. Gentleman the Member for the University of Oxford [Gladstone] says we are a byword and a scorn among nations, and that 'Englishman" is a hated name, he says what is utterly incorrect. He identifies a nation with its arbitrary rulers. I tell him that the nations, that is, the people of Europe, do not dislike the English, but, on the contrary, our policy for the last few years has endeared us to them. They know the difficulties of our position, they make all allowance for the Government, they know it cannot interfere by force of arms, but they know that constitutional liberty in every quarter of the world has the sympathy of the minds and hearts of the British people, and they know that the Government exhibits the faithful echo of these sympathies. We have now arrived at a most momentous epoch in the history of this country—aye, and of the world. We are called upon to take our choice between two great antagonistic principles. Is the foreign policy of this country to be the foreign policy which the noble Lord and the Government have pursued—that middle policy between absolutism and republicanism, encouraging constitutional governments, but not interfering to establish them by military force; using only our moral influence, and taking the proud position as the head of the constitutional nations of the world? The arbitrary rulers of foreign nations may endeavour to destroy Her Majesty's Government; but rest assured of this—when the nations of the Continent have at length succeeded in establishing constitutional governments, and in securing free institutions for themselves, and when their voices can speak out, they will look back gratefully to the sympathy we have shown them in their time of suffering and distress; and the influence which we shall maintain amongst them will be commensurate with that sympathy.

Ibid., cols. 638, 642–43.

E. A Tory Criticism of All Liberalism: Mr. Drummond

The present Ministry was founded on agitation originally, and is supported by agitation now; and it is impossible that a Government which is the creature of agitation at home, can be the promoters of peace abroad. Amongst the chief supporters of the Government are the Manchester School, the heads of which have openly declared the ultimate object that they have in view. The hon. Member for Manchester [John Bright] declared lately at a public meeting—

"We live in an age of agitation. I am one of those who greatly approve of this state of things, and rejoice at it. There is a party in this country rapidly moving onward towards a peaceable, wide, and enduring democracy. The glorious constitution of Crown, Lords, and Commons, is in fact an imposture, which it is part of my duty to expose."

Another speaker of the same class said—

"If the working classes will but join the middle classes in right good earnest, the upper classes, the corinthian capital of the column, would soon begin to crumble;

and fall they must, for they are rotten at the core."

I am at a loss to discover any difference between these principles and those enunciated by the noble Lord the other night at the conclusion of his speech. I was lately looking at a bed of red roses; many were of different shades, some deep red, and called the Black Prince, and some quite light, and rejoicing in the name of the Maiden's Blush. I am willing to conclude that Her Majesty's Ministers are of the delicate tint of the maiden's blush; but still they are all red: some darker and some lighter, but all alike red; and I am totally unable to discover any difference between them and the red republicans, save as one red rose differs from another. . . .

It is absurd to suppose that we can

adopt agitation as a political principle at home, and make tranquillity the principle of our transactions abroad. The principle of the Government from first to last has been to keep up a system of political agitation; and the Ministers are only the stormy petrels, the harbingers of universal European convulsion. I have no doubt that they will so continue, and that nothing will stop them. But I deprecate any attempt to overturn the Government so long as the country is unconvinced of the delusiveness of the path which we are pursuing—a path which I am convinced can lead but to one result, which is the involving of all the countries in Europe in one scene of universal bloodshed. . . .

. . . I will not consent to overthrow one set of men merely to uphold another equally culpable with themselves.

Ibid., cols. 593–96.

III. The Making of a Nation—
Two Liberal Nationalists
Who United Italy

The stormy history of "the making of Italy" in the mid-nineteenth century was centered on two liberal nationalists, yet two who were at opposite poles temperamentally and politically—Giuseppe Mazzini and Count Camillo Cavour.

Mazzini, as a student of sixteen, dedicated his life to the crusade for Italy's national freedom and unity. In typically romantic fashion he swore always to wear black until all Italy was a free republic ruled by "God and the People," with Austria expelled, the Pope deprived of his secular power, and Rome the capital of a united Italy. He wore black till his death in 1872 though Italy was united by 1870—an intransigent republican, romantic idealist, and exiled conspirator to the end.

After the failure of the 1831 revolution Mazzini, from his exile in Marseilles, founded "Young Italy." This was a secret society of young men dedicated to setting Italy aflame by political propaganda smuggled in by exiles and to organizing insurrections which they hoped would lead to nationwide revolution and the establishment of an Italian republic. The Metternichian system forced the young and politically inexperienced Italian patriots into

isolated groups which developed a mentality of conspiratorial secrecy. Consequently, Mazzini and Young Italy were filled with a messianic idealism, and while noble and self-sacrificing were frequently unrealistic in the choice of the means to achieve their ends. Their chief contribution was their romantic literary appeal to the greatness of Italy's and of Rome's heroic past, and their ethical appeal for faith, for self-sacrificing resistance to Austrian oppression, and fraternal love of all Italians and of mankind. Their chief weakness was their lack of political realism. This was manifested in their conspiratorial, abortive uprisings, their romantic faith in popular action and the "religion of humanity," and in their fanatical determination that "Italy shall go it alone" without reliance on other countries.

This was a determination shared by the new King of Sardinia, Charles Albert of the House of Savoy. Savoy, Piedmont, Sardinia, and Genoa comprised the little kingdom of Sardinia which was to become the nucleus of a united Italy in the years 1848–70. The revolutionary years of 1848–49 were crucial ones for Italy. Charles Albert took the flight of Metternich in the March revolutions of 1848 as a heaven-sent chance to wage a war for Italian independence against Austria. The new pope, Pius IX, who started as a liberal reformer, at first blessed the crusade for Italian freedom. All of Upper Italy declared for unification under the House of Savoy, to the dismay of the rigidly republican Mazzini. Austria's unexpected recovery and catastrophic military defeat of Charles Albert led to his abdication and death and to the apparent crushing of Italy's attempt at independence.

Yet the revolutions of 1848–49 were a turning point in Italian history as in the rest of the Continent. The constitution granted by Charles Albert was maintained by the new monarch, Victor Emmanuel, despite Austrian pressure. The young king was clothed with the glory of Charles Albert's martyrdom for Italy and the renown of the constitution that provided parliamentary government. Moreover, Piedmont's enlightened educational program, her new railroads, her growing commercial prosperity built on free trade made her a natural leader in the unification movement. Important too was the defeat of the republican and papal-federalist movements after 1848. The timid retreat of the papal government from liberal reforms and the growing realism of temper throughout Italy weakened both of these movements. Mazzini's influence after 1848 was largely supplanted or rivaled by the rise of Cavour.

Count Camillo Cavour, who is generally taken as the political architect of Italian unification, emerged as the leading Italian statesman after 1848. He was a liberal nationalist of quite a different stamp from Mazzini, and the two were constantly at odds on the means to free and unify Italy. Cavour was a Piedmontese noble, a moderate, practical man with experience in military, industrial, financial, and agricultural affairs, widely traveled, and the editor of the liberal newspaper *Il Risorgimento*, which urged Italian independence and constitutional monarchy.

Elected to the first Piedmontese Chamber of Deputies he entered the cabinet and became prime minister in 1852. He was responsible for Piedmont's remarkable economic and political progress in the decade of the 1850s and for the turn of Italian opinion to "Italy and Victor Emmanuel." He was a parliamentarian par excellence but a man of action as well, and a European statesman in his outlook. Cavour's policy was one of diplomacy, not conspiracy—of gaining an alliance with France, securing the friendship of the English government and winning over English public opinion by disavowing Mazzini's revolutionary uprisings and by proving Italian

capacity for economic progress and parliamentary self-government. He was aware of the demands of power politics but also of the power of public opinion and made "the Italian question" a burning one for the conscience of European liberals. With the often unreliable help of Napoleon III he maneuvered Austria into war and defeat in 1859 and freed Upper Italy except Venice. He won over all the republican leaders except Mazzini and backed up secretly the daring capture of Sicily, Southern Italy, and the Papal States by Garibaldi and his redshirted "Thousand" volunteers.

In October 1860, by national plebiscite, Italy became united and Victor Emmanuel became King of all Italy except Rome and Venice, which were freed by 1870, again by a combination of war and diplomacy. In 1861 the first national Parliament met, but Cavour was stricken and died within three months. He has been compared with Lincoln in his statesmanlike defense of national unity in the midst of protracted war and in his tragic death at the start of difficult national reconstruction.

Mazzini may then be taken as the literary, religious, ethical spokesman of the romantic liberal nationalism which was influential before 1848, Cavour as the more rational, power-political statesman of the organized national movements after 1848.

A. Mazzini on Duties Toward Your Country

Your first duties—first as regards importance—are, as I have already told you, towards Humanity. You are *men* before you are either citizens or fathers. If you do not embrace the whole human family in your affection, if you do not bear witness to your belief in the Unity of that family, consequent upon the Unity of God, and in that fraternity among the peoples which is destined to reduce that unity to action; if, wheresoever a fellow-creature suffers, or the dignity of human nature is violated by falsehood or tyranny—you are not ready, if able, to aid the unhappy, and do not feel called upon to combat, if able, for the redemption of the betrayed or oppressed—you violate your law of life, you comprehend not that Religion which will be the guide and blessing of the future.

But what can each of you, singly, *do* for the moral improvement and progress of Humanity?...You cannot attempt united action, distinct and divided as you are in language, customs, tendencies, and capacity. The individual is too insignificant, and Humanity too vast. The mariner of Brittany prays to God as he puts to sea: *Help me, my God! my boat is so small and thy ocean so wide!* And this prayer is the true expression of the condition of each one of you, until you find the means of infinitely multiplying your forces and powers of action.

This means was provided for you by God when he gave you a country; when, even as a wise overseer of labour distributes the various branches of employment according to the different capacities of the workmen, he divided Humanity into distinct groups or nuclei upon the face of the earth, thus creating the germ of Nationalities. Evil governments have disfigured the divine design. Nevertheless you may still trace it, distinctly marked out—at least as far as Europe is concerned—by the course of the great rivers, the direction of the higher mountains, and other geographical conditions. They have disfigured it by their conquests, their greed, and their jealousy even of the righteous power of others; disfigured it so far that, if we except England and France—there is not perhaps a single country whose present boundaries correspond to that design.

These governments did not, and do not recognise any country save their own families or dynasty, the egotism of caste. But the Divine design will infallibly be realized. Natural divisions, and the spontaneous, innate tendencies of the peoples, will take the place of the arbitrary divisions sanctioned by evil governments. The map of Europe will be re-drawn. The countries of the Peoples, defined by the vote of free men, will arise upon the ruins of the countries of kings and privileged castes, and between these countries harmony and fraternity will exist. And the common work of Humanity, of general

amelioration and the gradual discovery and application of its Law of life, being distributed according to local and general capacities, will be wrought out in peaceful and progressive development and advance. Then may each one of you, fortified by the power and the affection of many millions, all speaking the same language, gifted with the same tendencies, and educated by the same historical tradition, hope, even by your own single effort, to be able to benefit all Humanity.

O my brothers, love your Country! Our Country is our Home, the house that God has given us, placing therein a numerous family that loves us, and whom we love; a family with whom we sympathise more readily, and whom we understand more quickly than we do others; and which, from its being centred round a given spot, and from the homogeneous nature of its elements, is adapted to a special branch of activity. Our country is our common workshop, whence the products of our activity are sent forth for the benefit of the whole world; wherein the tools and implements of labour we can most usefully employ are gathered together: nor may we reject them without disobeying the plan of the Almighty, and diminishing our own strength.

In labouring for our own country on the right principle, we labour for Humanity. Our country is the fulcrum of the lever we have to wield for the common good. If we abandon that fulcrum, we run the risk of rendering ourselves useless not only to humanity but to our country itself. Before men can *associate* with the nations of which humanity is composed, they must have a National existence. There is no true association except among equals. It is only through our country that we can have a recognised *collective* existence....

Country is not a mere zone of territory. The true country is the Idea to which it gives birth; it is the Thought of love, the sense of communion which unites in one all the sons of that territory.

So long as a single one amongst your brothers has no vote to represent him in the development of the national life, so long as there is one left to vegetate in ignorance where others are educated, so long as a single man, able and willing to work, languishes in poverty through want of work to do, you have no country in the sense in which country ought to exist—the country of all and for all.

Education, labour, and the franchise, are the three main pillars of the nation. Rest not until you have built them strongly up with your own labour and exertions. Never deny your sister nations. Be it yours to evolve the life of your country in loveliness and strength; free from all servile fears or sceptical doubts; maintaining as its basis the People; as its guide the consequences of the principles of its Religious Faith, logically and energetically applied; its strength, the united strength of all; its aim, the fulfilment of the mission given to it by God.

And so long as you are ready to die for Humanity, the life of your country will be immortal.

Giuseppe Mazzini, *On the Duties of Man*, Ch. 5, "Duties toward Your Country," 1858, from E. A. Venturi, *Joseph Mazzini, a Memoir, with Two Essays by Mazzini, "Thoughts on Democracy" and "The Duties of Man,"* 2nd ed. (London: Henry S. King & Co., 1877), pp. 312–17.

B. Cavour Writes on the Difficulties of Preserving Italian Liberty in 1860

Italy is now in a very crucial situation. It is rather disconcerting to be following the path of diplomacy while Garibaldi is going his own way opposite. I am still hopeful that we will emerge from this crisis and that we will succeed in establishing our nation on a solid basis of order and liberty, in spite of the obstinacy of the reactionaries and the foolish behavior of the Republicans....

As for me, I have no trust in dictatorships, and most of all none in civilian dictatorships. I am convinced that it is possible to achieve with a Parliament what cannot be done by absolute power. My thirteen years of experience have convinced me that an honest, vigorous government, which need not fear exposure by demagogues and is not easily frightened by party turbulence, can greatly profit by parliamentary battles. It is only when Parliament is closed that I have ever felt myself weak. And certainly I cannot disregard my own experience nor renounce the principles I have held all my life. I am the son of Liberty; it is to her I owe all that I am. If a veil must be drawn over the statue [of Liberty], I am not the one to do it. If the Italians could be convinced that they need a dictator, they would choose Garibaldi, not me—and rightly. But the parliamentary road is the safer one, though it is the longer one.

Letters of Cavour to the Countess de Circourt in Switzerland, written at Turin, September 23 and December 29, 1860. *Le Comte de Cavour et la Comtesse de Circourt, Lettres inédites,* publiées par le Comte Nigra (Turin: Roux, 1894), pp. 103, 107, trans. E. A. Clark.

IV. The Franco-Prussian War and the Annexation of Alsace-Lorraine

The decades following the revolutions of 1848 witnessed a disillusionment with idealism and liberalism. The Czechs, the Poles, and the South Slavs fell into a sullen resentment under renewed oppression by the old absolute monarchies, while the Hungarians, the Germans, and the Italians achieved political power under "realistic" political leaders who were willing to sacrifice freedom to power and unity.

The War of 1870 between France and Germany is often taken as the beginning of "contemporary history" because it proved a repercussions, in both thought and action. of the two chief rivals but in its international repercussions, in both thought and action. The new age of power politics was marked by the trend to forceful, illiberal, and aggressive nationalism in much of the Continent, especially in Central and Eastern Europe.

Heinrich von Treitschke's career epitomizes the evolution of a liberal nationalist to one who, dropping his liberal tendencies, became an apologist for Prussia's and Bismarck's policy of unification by "blood and iron." His early opposition to Bismarck's unconstitutional defiance of the Reichstag was changed to passionate support with Bismarck's success in the Danish War of 1864 and the Austro-Prussian War of 1866. By 1870 Treitschke at the age of thirty-six was one of the most influential political writers and speakers in Germany. His forceful journalism and widely attended university lectures on politics and history at Heidelberg made him a power to reckon with. In 1871 he began his career in the Reichstag and shortly after he was appointed to the University of Berlin.

The article here quoted in part was written August 30, 1870, just before the decisive Prussian victory at Sedan, and in a widely read pamphlet popularized Bismarck's demand for the annexation of Alsace-Lorraine as punishment for France's alleged war guilt. The arguments are a kind of recapitulation of all the stages of the evolution of Treitschke's—and Germany's—nationalism. Side by side, often in contradiction, like successive geological layers confused by rough excavation, appear arguments of the successive stages, romantic, liberal, and Bismarckian.

His French contemporary, the philosopher Ernest Renan, resisted this realistic and Darwinian approach to nationalism, and warned of its dangers. Renan was one of the leading Germanophile intellectuals, venerating the idealism of Kant, Fichte, Herder, and Goethe, as did Michelet and Victor Hugo. He recognized the German theologian and philosopher David Strauss, author of the agnostic and controversial *Life of Jesus*, as his "master," and was carrying on a warm correspondence with him as the war began. Renan had cherished as the great ideal of his life "the intellectual, moral, and political alliance of Germany and France, including England, which should constitute a force capable of governing the world and directing it in the ways of a liberal civilization, equally distant from the uninformed blind order of democracy and from the childish yearnings to return to a dead past." (*La reforme intellectuelle et morale*, Paris 1884, 4th ed. [first published 1871], preface, p. v.). He expected Strauss to maintain the same Olympian internationalism and dislike of militarism, whether of the Prussian or the French variety. His two open letters, published at the beginning and after the war in response to two open letters published by Strauss challenging him to speak for France, reveal his tragic but not bitter disillusionment at the passionate Prussianism of the German intellectuals whom he had admired and had defended at the cost of considerable unpopularity during the war. He came to believe there were "two opposite poles of the German character," the gentle and liberal one he had idealized and the "man of iron."

The problems of war guilt, peace terms, national character, self-determination, and national security were focused in the impassioned arguments for and against the annexation of Alsace-Lorraine.

The depth of the passions aroused by the annexation can be seen in the subsequent *"Revanche"* policies of the French Rightist nationalists and the issue of Alsace-Lorraine in World War I. The very bitterness of this French-German animosity renders all the more striking the attempt at reconciliation of France and Germany after World War II. The same problems are still there, yet basically Adenauer and de Gaulle were echoing Renan, not Treitschke.

A.   *Heinrich von Treitschke*

Wherever Germans live, as far as the remote colonies beyond the seas, the flags are flying from every window, and the clanging of bells and the thunder of cannon are proclaiming victory after victory. All of us know that after three more frightful struggles—at Metz, at Strassburg, at Paris—the war will be gloriously closed. To him who remembers at this moment the bitter shame which we have hidden in our hearts for so many years since the day of Olmütz, it must often appear as if all this were a dream. . . .

The thought, however, which, after first knocking timidly at our doors as a shamefaced wish, has, in four swift weeks, grown to be the mightly war-cry of the nation, is no other than this: "Restore what you stole from us long ago: give back Alsace and Lorraine."

Were I to marshal the reasons which

make it our duty to demand this, I should feel as if the task had been set me to prove that the world is round. What can be said on the subject was said after the battle of Leipzig, in Ernst Moritz Arndt's glorious tract, "The Rhine the German River, not the German Boundary"; said exhaustively, and beyond contradiction, at the time of the Second Peace of Paris, by all the considerable statesmen of non-Austrian-Germany—by Stein and Humboldt, by Munster and Gagern. . . . If a reckless, robber-war like this is to cost that people nothing more than a war indemnity, the cynical jesters, who worship chance and fortune as the only governing powers among the nations, and laugh at the rights of States as a dream of kind-hearted ideologues, would be proved to be in the right. The sense of justice to Germany demands the lessening of France. . . .

What is demanded by justice is, at the same time, absolutely necessary for our security. . . .

Every State must seek the guarantees of its security in itself alone. The silly fancy, that gratitude and magnanimity could secure the German countries against a defeated France, has, twice over, been its own fearful punishment. What German can read without rage the account of those peace proceedings at Paris in which victor and vanquished exchanged parts, and a respectful attention was paid to all the prejudices of France, while nobody thought of the feelings of Germany? . . . If the France of 1815, which still possessed a great treasure of moral forces, fell back so soon on greedy dreams of conquest, what have we to expect from the society of the Second Empire, which has lost all its faith in the ideal treasures of life. . . ? The nation is our enemy, not this Bonaparte, who rather obeyed than led it. . . .

The distracted world already foresees a whole brood of wars springing out of the bloody seed of this. We owe it some guarantee of permanent peace among the nations. . . . The statesmen of the present day, whenever they have realised the altered equilibrium of the Powers, will feel that the strengthening of the boundaries of Germany contributes to the security of the peace of the world. We are a peaceful nation. The traditions of the Hohenzollerns, the constitution of our Army, the long and difficult work before us in the upbuilding of our united German States, forbid the abuse of our warlike power. . . .

In view of our obligation to secure the peace of the world, who will venture to object that the people of Alsace and Lorraine do not want to belong to us? The doctrine of the right of all the branches of the German race to decide on their own destinies, the plausible solution of demagogues without a fatherland, shiver to pieces in presence of the sacred necessity of these great days. These territories are ours by the right of the sword, and we shall dispose of them in virtue of a higher right—the right of the German nation, which will not permit its lost children to remain strangers to the German Empire. We Germans, who know Germany and France, know better than these unfortunates themselves what is good for the people of Alsace. . . . Against their will we shall restore them to their true selves. We have seen with joyful wonder the undying power of the moral forces of history, manifested far too frequently in the immense changes of these days, to place much confidence in the value of a mere popular disinclination. The spirit of a nation lays hold, not only of the generations which live beside it, but of those which are before and behind it. We appeal from the mistaken wishes of the men who are there to-day to the wishes of those who were there before them. We appeal to all those strong German men who once stamped the seal of our German nature on the language and manners, the art and the social life, of the Upper Rhine. Before the nineteenth century closes the world will recognise that . . . we were only obeying the dictates of national honour when we made little account of the preferences of the people who live in Alsace to-day.

When Alsace fell under the dominion of the French our Empire lay powerless on the ground. The fire of the German spirit, which had once flamed through the whole world, seemed extinguished. Germany bowed herself before the conquering policy and the victorious culture of France.... We have broken with the rules of their Art, and we can confidently challenge comparison between the free movement of our scientific and religious life and the spiritual culture of France. We have succeeded in giving our richer and stronger language such a freedom and delicacy that it need no longer fear the rivalry of French. Even the advantage of their elder culture, the fine tone and polish of social intercourse, is passing away....

At all times the subjection of a German race to France has been an unhealthy thing; today it is an offence against the reason of History—a vassalship of free men to half-educated barbarians....

When our united strength has won that outwork of the German State, which is now in such mortal peril, the nation will have pledged its soul to the idea of unity. The resistance of the new province will strengthen the impulse of our policy towards unity, and constrain all sensible men to range themselves in disciplined loyalty behind the Prussian throne. The advantage is all the greater as it is still possible that some new Republican attempt in Paris might tempt the moonstruck glance of the German radicals once more to turn gradually towards the West....

A politico-economical consideration may be added.... Nature has dealt with our country much more like a stepmother than a mother. The singularly barren outline of our shore coast-line on the North Sea, and the course of most of our German rivers and hill-chains, are just as unfavorable to political unity as they are to commerce. Only a few strips of our German soil can compare in natural fertility with wealthy Normandy, the luxurious plains of England, and the teeming cornfields of the interior of Russia. But here, in Alsace, there is a real German district, the soil of which, under favoring skies, is rich with blessings....

...We are not now so exhausted in money and in men as not to be able to defy the opposition of the whole of Europe.

The neutral Powers might have stopped this French attempt at robbery by one strong and timely word. They failed to utter it, and they cannot complain to-day because we alone decide what we shall take as the prize of the victory which we alone have won. We owe it to the clear-sighted audacity of Count Bismarck that this war was begun at the right time—that the Court of the Tuileries was not allowed the welcome respite which would have permitted it to complete the web of its treacherous devices. And as the war began as a work of clear and statesmanlike calculation, so it will end....

We desire to renew the power and glory of the Hohenstaufens and the Ottos, but not their World-Empire. Our new State owes its strength to the national idea.... For this reason it finds its western frontier indicated to it by the language and manners and life of the rural population. Every State is kept fresh and young from below. New forces never cease to arise out of the healthy depths of the peasant class....

...It is not the business of a wise national policy to go very far beyond this extent of territory; but, at the same time, such a policy ought not to cling with *doctrinaire* obstinacy to the boundary of language as a limit which must in no case be crossed. There is no perfect identity between the political and the national frontier in any European country. Not one of the Great Powers, and Germany no more than the rest of them, can ever subscribe to the principle that "language alone decides the formation of States." It would be impossible to carry that principle into effect. From a military point of view the German territory in France is secured by two strongholds [Metz and Belfort], which lie a few miles beyond the line of language....

The German territory which we demand is ours by nature and by history... [of the time of the Nibelungs, the Hohenstaufens, the Hanseatic League, the Meistersingers, the Reformation, the Holy Roman Empire]. In the tempests of the great Revolution the people of Alsace, like all the citizens of France, learned to forget their past. . . .

Most assuredly, the task of reuniting there the broken links between the ages is one of the heaviest that has ever been imposed upon the political forces of our nation. . . .

Perverse obstinacy, and a thousand French intrigues creeping in the dark, will make every step on the newly conquered soil difficult for us: but our ultimate success is certain, for on our side fights what is stronger than the lying artifices of the stranger—nature herself and the voice of common blood.

Heinrich von Treitschke, *"Was Fordern Wir von Frankreich,"* ["What We Demand from France,"] *Preussische Jahrbücher,* (26) 1870, 367 ff., reprinted in *Zehn Jahre deutscher Kämpfe,* 3e Auflage (Berlin, 1897), translated into English in *Germany, France, Russia and Islam* (New York: G. P. Putnam's Sons, 1915), pp. 96–99, 101–21, 134–39, 154, 158.

B. Ernest Renan

Your fiery Germanists allege that Alsace is a German territory unjustly detached from the German Empire. Take note that all nationalities are imperfect arrangements; if you start applying such logic to the ethnography of each district, you will be paving the way for wars without end. Many a fair province linguistically French, does not form a part of France and this is an advantage even for France itself. There are Slavic lands which belong to Prussia. . . . Is it worthy of Germany to take over by force a province which, already rebellious and irritable, has become irreconcilable since the destruction of Strasbourg? The mind sometimes stands aghast before the audacity of your statesmen. The King of Prussia seems to be on the point of taking on the heavy task of settling the French problem, of giving—and consequently guaranteeing —a government to France. Could anyone lightheartedly assume such a burden? How can you fail to see the result of this policy would be the necessity of occupying France forever with some three or four hundred thousand men? . . .

I am amazed that your best minds do not see this and especially that they are opposed to European intervention on these questions. Peace cannot, it seems to me, be concluded directly between France and Germany; it can only be the work of Europe, which condemned the war and must wish that no member of the European family of nations be seriously weakened. You speak with good right of guarantees against the return of dreams of aggression; but what guarantee would be worth that of Europe consecrating anew the present frontiers and forbidding everyone without exception to dream of upsetting the boundaries fixed by ancient treaties? All other solutions will leave the door open to vengeance without end. Let Europe do this and she will have sown the seed for the future of the most fruitful institution—a central authority, a sort of congress of the United States of Europe, judging the nations, exercising control over them and correcting the principle of nationality by the principle of federation.

Ernest Renan, "Lettre à M. Strauss," September 13, 1870, *Journal des Débats,* September 16, 1870, reprinted in *La Réforme intellectuelle et morale,* 4th ed. (Paris: Calmann Levy, 1884), pp. 180–82, trans. E. A. Clark.

We were evidently wrong in our belief that the nineteenth century had ushered in an era of civilization, peace, and popular sovereignty. "How can you declare that the shifting of human beings is a crime and a shame when previously such transfers were acceptable to races as noble as your own and were even profitable to you," you may ask. Let us look at the dates. Today's concept of justice is not that of yesterday. The sentiment of nationalism is not a hundred years old. . . . In those days [before the Revolution] the transfer of a province simply meant the assignment of real estate from one prince to another; the people themselves usually remained indifferent. This consciousness of nationality has been given the world by our own Revolution; it is we who have given it to those whom we have fought (and often fought unjustly); it is our own doctrine. That is why we French liberals were in favor of the Venetians, for the Milanese against Austria; for Bohemia, for Hungary against Viennese centralization; for Poland against Russia; for the Greeks and the Slavs in Turkey against the Turks. We were also in favor of the Romans against the Pope or rather against the foreign coercion which kept these vassals of the Pope in spite of themselves; we were unwilling to concede that a population could, against its will, be subjugated to a religious idea which asserted its need of territory in order to exist. . . .

Wars would continue without end unless there is some limit set for revenge for past violence. Lorraine certainly did once form part of the German Empire but so also did Holland, Switzerland, even Italy (down to Benevento), and—if you go beyond the treaty of Verdun—all of France with Catalonia thrown in! Nowadays Alsace is a Germanic land both by language and by race, but before it was overrun by the Germanic peoples, Alsace was a Celtic land as was also part of South Germany. Now we do not conclude from this that South Germany ought to be French; but let no one come tell us that by ancient right Metz and Luxembourg ought to be German! There is no end to such archaeology! In almost every case where the fiery patriots of Germany set up German claims we could just as easily set up a Celtic claim to antedate them; before the Celtic period—so they say—were non-Aryan Finns and Lapps; before the Lapps there were cavemen and before cavemen there were orangoutangs! If one carries out this historical philosophy the

only legitimate rights would be those of the orangoutangs unjustly dispossessed by the perfidy of civilized men!

Let us be less arbitrary; alongside of the rights of the dead, let us pay some attention to the rights of the living. The treaty of 843 [Verdun], a pact of division of territory between the barbarian chieftains who certainly were only concerned with their personal convenience, cannot everlastingly be a cornerstone of national rights. . . .

The European nations, as history has made them, are like peers in one great senate where each member is inviolable. Europe is a confederation of states held together by their common concept of civilization. The individuality of each nation is, doubtless, formed by race, language, history, and religion but also by something much more tangible: the determination of different provinces of a state to live united. . . . Alsace is German linguistically and racially but she has no desire to be a part of the German state; that settles the question. We hear talk of the rights of France, the rights of Germany; these abstractions are far less important to us than is the right of the Alsatians, living creatures of flesh and blood, to obey that power to which they have consented.

Do not blame our French liberals for considering that the right of peoples not to be transferred without their own consent amounts almost to divine right. For those who, like us, no longer admit the dynastic principle, which bases the unity of the state on the personal rights of the sovereign, there is no other right of nations. . . [than the principle of nationality].

Our policy is based on the rights of nations, yours is based on the theory of racism. Overemphasis on humanity's division into races, aside from the fact that it is based on scientific error, since very few countries possess a race which is really pure, can only result in wars of extermination, "zoological" wars if I may say so, similar to those waged by the different species of carnivorous animals in their struggle for survival. It would be the end of that fruitful mingling of numerous and essential elements which we call humanity. You have raised aloft in the world the banner of archaeological and ethnographical politics in place of that of liberal politics; this system will be fatal for you. Comparative philology which you have created and which you have mistakenly transported into the realm of politics is going to do you a bad turn. The Slavs have taken it up with passion; every Slav schoolmaster is your enemy, a termite which will bring down your house. How can you believe that the Slavs will not do to you what you have done to others, they who follow your lead in every respect, follow step by step? Each assertion of Pan-Germanism is at the same time an assertion of Pan-Slavism, each of your moves towards concentration is at the same time a catalytic agent "precipitating" the Slav, setting him apart as a separate entity. A glance at the affairs of Austria emphasizes this fact. In fifty years, the Slav will recognize that it is you who have made his name synonymous with *slave;* he will see the long historical exploitation of his race by yours; the number of Slavs is twice yours, the Slav, like the dragon of the Apocalypse whose tail swept away a third of the stars, will one day bring the hordes of Central Asia in his wake, those former followers of Genghis Khan and Tamerlane. How much better it would have been had you kept for that day appeals to reason, to morality, to love of principle. Think what a weight will be thrown into the balance of the world on that day when Bohemia, Moravia, Croatia, Serbia, all the Slav peoples of the Turkish Empire—peoples surely destined for liberation, races heroic and warlike still, needing only a leader, gather around that Moscow-centered conglomeration; which already unites so many different elements into a Slav matrix and which may well be the appointed kernel for future Slav unity just as Macedonia, only partially Greek, Piedmont partially Italian, Prussia partially German, were the focal points for Greek, Italian and German unity. And you are too wise to

count on any gratitude from Russia. One of the hidden causes of Prussian ill will toward us is that part of their culture is due to us. One of Russia's grievances, one day, will be that she was civilized by the Germans. They may deny it but at the same time they will prove it by their very denial and this memory will irritate them. The Academy of St. Petersburg will, one day, feel resentful towards the Academy of Berlin for its own Germanness just as the Academy of Berlin holds it against us that it used to be half French. Our century is the century of the triumph of the serf over the master: in certain respects the Slav is still your serf.

Now, on the day of the Slav victory we are going to be worth more than you are, just as Athens, under the Roman Empire, still played a leading part whereas Sparta no longer played any role.

Watch out for ethnography or rather do not apply it too much to politics. Under the pretense of German etymology you take over for Prussia such and such a village of Lorraine. The name of Vienna (Vindobona), Worms (Borbitomagus), Mainz (Mogontiacum) are Gallic; we are never going to claim these towns; but if, one fine day, the Slavs put in a claim for Prussia, Pomerania, Silesia, Berlin on the ground that their names are Slav; if they did along the Elbe and the Oder what you have done along the Moselle, if they started pointing out on the map villages formerly settled by Slavic tribes, what would you have to say? A nation and a race are not synonymous. Little Switzerland, so solidly built, has three languages, three or four races, two religions. A nation is an association, centuries old but not eternal, between provinces partly of common origin serving as a kernel and others which group themselves around it; the whole bound together by common interests or by ancient actions which have been accepted and transformed into interests. England which is the most perfect of nations is the most mixed, judged ethnographically and historically: pure Bretons, Romanized Bretons, Irish, Scotch, Anglo-Saxons, Danes, pure Normans, French Normans, all blend together.

But I stop; these days it would be naïve to speak of moderation, justice, fraternity, of the gratitude and consideration which peoples owe each other. The way you will have to behave in those provinces annexed against their wish will finally demoralize you. You will have to give the lie to all your principles, to treat as criminals men whom you should respect (men who will have done nothing but what you did so nobly after Jena); all moral ideas will be perverted. Our whole system of European equilibrium and concert will be banished to cloud-cuckoo land; our liberal tenets will be an out-of-date jargon. Because of the action of Prussian statesmen, France for many a day will have only one objective: winning back the lost provinces. Stirring up the ever-growing hate of the Slavs for the Germans, favoring Pan-Slavism, truckling to every Russian ambition, dazzling the eyes of the Catholic party everywhere with the re-establishment of the Pope in Rome; in domestic affairs, yielding to the legiti-mist clerical party of the West since it alone is intensely fanatical; these are the policies necessitated by such a situation. It is just the opposite of what we dreamed of!...but, what can we do? We would, on the other hand, be culpable were we to attempt, by advocating even now, generous and disinterested pursuits, to prevent the country from listening to the voice of two million Frenchmen crying out for the assistance of their former Fatherland.

France is on the point of saying, like your Herwegh, "Enough of love, now let us try hate." I have no intention of following her in this new experiment—whose success one may, moreover, question since the resolve France finds it the most difficult to follow is that of hate. In any case life is too short to waste time and strength in such a sorry pursuit. In my modest way, I have worked for friendship between France and Germany; if the time has come "to leave off kissing," I shall withdraw. I shall not advocate hate after having preached love; I shall be silent.

"Nouvelle Lettre à M. Strauss," September 15, 1871, *ibid.*,   pp. 193–202, 207–9.

13

Imperialistic Rivalries
Before World War I

LOWELL RAGATZ

The Ohio State University

Up to the close of the Napoleonic era modern European wars were largely dynastic in nature. They arose through conflict between rulers, each of whom sought narrow private benefits from the struggles. The concept of the nation in arms did not emerge until the period of international upheaval attending the spread of the French Revolution. After 1815, wars increasingly came to be waged between national states rather than between monarchs. The stakes became higher, although they were much the same in character—control of outlying lands, commonly overseas, coveted by two or more powers in the national interest. In this dynamic age, as the individual began closely to associate himself with the nation at large, "national interests" were more and more identified as his own interests. As a result, the power politics of the old dynastic struggles now emerged as a peculiarly personal matter for the individual in state after state.

Rivalry for control of remote African, Asiatic, and Pacific areas, and the economic opportunity it afforded, became an increasingly disturbing factor in international relations. Clashing extra-European ambitions led to rising strife, particularly among the various powers of Europe. The importance of the imperialist rivalries of the period is attested by the fact that virtually every one of the major international

452

conferences of 1815–1914 dealt with problems raised by such conflict. Most of the leading treaties of the time sought to adjust these imperialist problems in one way or another.

To illustrate these developments, we can turn to some of the highlights in the international affairs of the century after 1815. Opposing Levantine interests occasioned bitter controversy between France and Great Britain in the late 1830s and early 1840s, bringing them dangerously close to war. When, however, Russia began active encroachments in the Holy Land in the 1850s, the old enemies, who regarded the Near East as their particular preserve, joined forces against her in the Crimean War (1853–56) and rejuvenated the Turk, "the sick man of Europe," to hold the Romanovs in check. Similarly, when the Austro-Prussian War of 1866 terminated Austria's leadership in Germanic affairs, Hapsburg interest turned to southeastern Europe where the Austrians soon were at swords' points with the Russians. Russia, for her part, capitalized on Ottoman atrocities against restless Christian minorities in Bulgaria by unleashing a war against the Turks. She apparently emerged with hegemony over the Balkans by the Treaty of San Stefano in 1878, but this result of her military triumph was denied her. Thoroughly aroused, Britain and Austria-Hungary summoned the powers to the Congress of Berlin, where they collectively deprived the tsarist regime of the spoils of victory. The Russians, therefore, sought compensation in eastern and southwestern Asia where they promptly collided with rising Japan and India-conscious Britain.

These developments only begin to tell the story of the impact of imperialism on the international relations of the modern world. From 1878 to 1914, as in the earlier period, the struggle for colonies, or for strategic bases, or for commercial rights in various parts of the world, was at the very forefront of the intercourse of the major powers. Thus, although they had helped to block Russian expansion in the Near East at Ottoman expense, the Austrians in 1878 themselves began an administration of Turkey's northwest Balkan provinces, Bosnia and Herzegovina, which ended in ultimate annexation. The British, also in 1878, established a protectorate over Turkey's insular possession Cyprus. Four years later, the British began a military occupation of Turkey's Nile dependency, Egypt, in order presumably to safeguard the interests of various European nationals. Originally intended as a temporary measure, the occupation was still in force when World War I broke out.

The Franco-Prussian War of 1870–71, which upset the European diplomatic balance by wresting continental leadership from France and according it to the newly united German Empire, was a strictly European affair, but it soon had important overseas repercussions. Republican leaders in defeated France sought to regain prestige by creating a new empire in Africa and Asia. Through a series of shrewdly conceived moves in 1884 and 1885, German patriots, arguing that colonial possessions symbolized greatness, forced Count Otto von Bismarck, the Chancellor who had united Germany, reluctantly to accept control over extensive lands in Africa and over a portion of New Guinea. Germany's sudden emergence as a colonial power, coupled with rapid expansion of German trade in traditional British areas of exploitation, in turn brought Germany into rivalry with Great Britain. When the imperious new German Emperor, William II (r. 1888–1918), later encouraged a naval building program which challenged British supremacy on the seas, the traditional Anglo-German friendship came to an abrupt close.

Meanwhile, on the Continent, Bismarck, ever fearful of French vengeance, sought to divert France by supporting her adventures in Africa and Asia. At the same time, he worked to safeguard the German Empire by creating the Three Emperors' League of 1872, designed to ensure peace between Germany, Austria-Hungary, and Russia should any of them become involved in war. Unhappily for Germany, Balkan rivalries drew the Romanovs and Hapsburgs steadily apart, another evidence of the role of imperialism in the international politics of the period. The unstable Three Emperors' League was relegated to the background in 1879 by a more logical German and Austrian alliance, aimed primarily at Russia.

Bismarck, none the less, with amazing adroitness, maneuvered a renewal of the League in 1881. When this renewal finally lapsed six years later, he devised the German-Russian Reinsurance Treaty of 1887 which, unknown to Austria, recognized Russia's dominant position in the eastern Balkan lands. But William II refused to renew the Reinsurance Treaty in 1890, holding that it was incompatible with the Dual Alliance of Germany and Austria-Hungary.

This Teutonic alignment was expanded into a Triple Alliance in 1882. Again, the major impelling factor was an imperialistic one. Italy, embittered over France's recent seizure of Tunisia, which she herself coveted, sought admission to the fold. Soon a second armed camp appeared. In 1894, after some years of gestation, a Franco-Russian Alliance aimed at Germany, the common foe sandwiched between the two partners, was born. This agreement with Germany's western rival was Russia's answer to the Kaiser's failure to continue the Reinsurance Treaty.

Britain, standing alone among the European Great Powers, now found herself in dangerous isolation. She sought first to improve her position by a close understanding with the United States. In the Hay-Pauncefote Treaty of 1901 she yielded her joint right under the Clayton-Bulwer Treaty of 1850 to construct a trans-Isthmian canal. When her ardent wooing of the United States proved unavailing because of ingrained American opposition to entangling alliances, she reversed her centuries-old anti-French policy. The Entente Cordiale of 1904 halted bitter Anglo-French colonial rivalries in Africa, Asia, America, and the Pacific by a more rational policy of compromise. This agreement soon made it possible for Britain to act in concert with France against Germany, from whom both powers felt a threat as the twentieth century progressed. Finally, the Anglo-Russian Entente of 1907 resolved colonial rivalries in three Asiatic spheres—Persia, Afghanistan, and Tibet—and the Triple Entente now confronted the Triple Alliance. Colonial questions had been a major determinant of the structure of both groups.

Meanwhile, Japan, treading the path of empire in the wake of the Western Powers, was checked in her ambitious project of annexing China's outlying province, Manchuria. At the close of the first Sino-Japanese War (1894–95), Japan had seized the Liaotung Peninsula in lower Manchuria from China. In 1895, Russia, Germany, and France forced Japan to return this territory to China and accept an additional cash indemnity instead. Three years later, these powers, joined by Britain, forced a disintegrating China to grant them long-term leases to strategic areas. To complete the irony, Russia herself then acquired the Liaotung Peninsula. Such duplicity led Japan to accept an alliance with Britain clearly aimed at Russia, then the common foe. Shortly thereafter, Japan defeated Russia in the war of 1904–1905 and at length acquired the Liaotung Peninsula. Afterwards, in the decade before World War I, Japan steadily increased her pressure designed to achieve control of large parts of a China which was deep in the throes of civil war and revolution.

As the various diplomatic alliances among the major powers began to take shape in the twentieth century, the imperialist struggles provided a further testing ground of their strength. The Algeciras Conference of 1906, the Bosnian crisis of 1908, the Agadir crisis of 1911, the Turko-Italian War of 1911–12, and finally the Balkan Wars of 1912–13 not only evidenced the imperialistic strife of the period, but influenced profoundly the diplomacy of all the powers. Certainly this ceaseless conflict became a dominant factor conditioning the European mind to accept a great war. It is less evident that it formed the basic cause of the war, and its influence in that connection has been keenly debated by scholars and laymen. Our problem here, in any event, is to assess the nature of imperialism, to study the various points of view with regard to its reason for being, and to examine at least one facet of its relation to the coming of World War I. The selections which follow will enable the reader to understand some of the issues involved and give him a start toward grasping the complicated interrelations between pre-1914 imperialism and the eruption of the first great twentieth-century world war.

I. Origins and Nature of Imperialism

"Imperialism" is a word of many meanings. The term is highly elastic and, as one writer phrases it, "so elusive of definition and covers practices and procedures of such variant and even contradictory character, that it has become a downright nuisance." (Jacob Viner, in the review section of the *Journal of Political Economy*, December, 1929, pp. 745ff.) Adjectives such as agricultural, ancient, commercial, cultural, economic, industrial, military, modern, open door, and religious are frequently employed to make it less nebulous and are commonly encountered in contemporary writing.

"Imperialism" is, however, most commonly used in the sense of extending economic and political control over outlying lands and people—in modern times, empire building carried out by national states. While operating freely before 1815, imperialism has been a dominant force in European life only during the nineteenth and twentieth centuries. With Nationalism, Democracy, and Industrialization, it has given Old World history its distinctive pattern and has underlain many of the most important developments of the period.

Imperialism arose through the need for industrial raw materials, for markets for surplus manufactures, and for outlets for oversupplies of capital. At times, too, expansion was viewed as a means of relieving overpopulation. It appeared at different times in different countries, roughly paralleling their economic development, always raised both ardent champions and bitter foes, and regularly became a hotly contested domestic issue in each country coming under its sway.

Its importance in shaping foreign relations cannot be overemphasized. Since 1815, it extended European rule over most of Africa and over vast portions of Asia and Oceania, led to European financial penetration of all quarters of the earth, and made Europe the world's workshop. If Europe gained paramount economic, political, and social position in global affairs between 1815 and 1914, if the world was, literally, Europe's oyster in the Age of Middle Class Democracy, this was due largely to the play of imperialism.

There can be no real understanding of Old World events and extra-European happenings since 1815 without according overseas expansion careful consideration. Imperialism provides a key to world affairs following the collapse of the Napoleonic regime and today forms one of the most important branches of historical studies.

A. Variant Causal Theories

With mounting realization of imperialism's major role in twentieth-century world affairs, keen interest has developed in its origins, its development, and its many ramifications. Outstanding in its historical presentation of the subject is a slender volume little-known in America, *The Foundations of Imperialist Policy*, published in England in 1922 under the name "Michel Pavlovitch."

Mikhail Weltmann (1871–1927), who deemed it expedient to conceal his German extraction under this pseudonym, was a pre-revolutionary agitator of some twenty years' standing who early found an important niche in the Communist hierarchy. A participant in the agonizing negotiations culminating in the humiliating Brest-Litovsk Treaty (1918), he became the Soviet's chief adviser on Eastern affairs and operated numerous indoctrination centers, as at Tashkent, capital of old Tsarist Turkistan, aimed at fomenting anti-British sentiment in Asia. He later served as rector of Moscow's Oriental Institute, chairman of the Society of Asiatic Revolutionaries in the capital city and, from 1922–27, edited *The New East*, a propaganda journal. A prolific writer, he is best remembered today for his dispassionate *Foundations of Imperialist Policy*, embracing a series of lectures delivered before the staid British General Staff Academy over the fall and winter of 1918–19 when international relations were still in flux. This admirably summarizes major theories, including his own, respecting what imperialism is and how it came into being. The salient portions are presented here.

The term "imperialism" is little un-

derstood....A series of theories have arisen regarding [it]...I divide all the existing theories...into three groups: the philosophical..., the historical and [the] Marxian....

The French writer, Romain Rolland (1866–1944),...in one of his novels, *The Burning Bush* (1913), uses the word imperialism as a synonym for the ideas of murder, theft, violence....The well-known French writer, Ernest Seyère, has...a... four-volumed work on *The Philosophy of Imperialism*, in which the chief intellectual representatives and inspirers of imperialism are represented as being...Count Joseph Gobineau (1816–1882), the exponent of Nordic supremacy;...Friedrich Nietzsche (1844–1900), the philosopher; ...Jean-Jacques Rousseau (1712–1778), the political theorist; Pierre Proudhon (1809–1865), the social reformer; and finally Karl Marx (1818–1883), the father of Scientific Socialism....

Gobineau [in his *The Inequality of Human Races*, 1855] affirmed that the Aryan race...is destined to dominate all other races....Nietzsche recognized the right of the separate personality excelling in any kind of talent...to dominate... the whole sphere surrounding it....This theory of "individual imperialism" grants the right to a Napoleon,...to a Caesar or Alexander..., to dominate over the masses....

In Jean-Jacques Rousseau, Seyère sees a representative of "plebian imperialism"..., the domination of the bourgeoisie over the other classes. Finally, in Karl Marx, aiming at the dictatorship of the proletariat, Seyère sees the theoretician of class imperialism....

Seyère discovers imperialism in the efforts for advancement of separate individuals in racial or national struggles, in the endeavors of one class to dominate another....Followers...have gone even further. Thus some of his pupils discover imperialism...in all phenomena of organic and even inorganic life....When one ant makes war on another...it is a manifestation of imperialist tendencies....When an oak in its growth...does not allow the young shrubs to develop, it consummates plant imperialism.... With Seyère and his followers the term "imperialism" is a substitute for the conception of "the struggle for existence"....

Seyère's theory... has... enjoyed... respect and prestige in professional circles... [because] it justifies the whole existing structure of society....Seyère's followers have deduced that imperialism is an eternal law of life; that..., consequently, the struggle against imperialism and its accompanying phenomena..., wars, militarism, navalism and so on, are doomed to fail....But...Seyère's theory is unscientific because it throws into one heap the most varied phenomena....Apart from this, it is reactionary, for it represents an apologia for imperialism....

Many...understand by the word "imperialism" a foreign policy...of a combative and conquering character. This is not altogether correct....Imperialism implies robbery and violence, but it is not robbery and violence alone.... *Imperialism is a definite economic phenomenon arising at a definite stage of economic development....[It] is the last stage in the development of capitalism....*Every historical mode of production, every phase in the development of the productive forces of society, has... *its own special forms of foreign policy.*...Imperialism is a special stage in the development of the foreign policy appertaining to a particular economic era....[It] is the policy of a state aiming at world-supremacy, at the extension of its influence outside the limits of its national frontiers, at the consolidation of its hegemony not only within the limits of one continent, but over the whole earth....

Bismarck was...the most brilliant representative of the robber policy of the nineteenth century....The wars led by Bismarck were murderous, robber wars, but they were not imperialist wars. *The idea of world-supremacy was foreign to Bismarck.* He thought that if Germany had extended her frontiers on the European continent within certain definite limits this was quite sufficient....Bismarck, that assassin, that bandit, was the representative of the era of the birth of capitalism in Germany....But in proportion as...industry began to develop... the position began to change radically.... [With] industry...choking within its existing limits,...there appears a new foreign policy, new people come on to the political arena who demand for Germany the hegemony of the whole world....The wars of 1866 and 1871 were *national* wars...whereas the war of 1914–1918 was ...an imperialist war...for world-hegemony....

From the point of view...of the Marxian school, imperialism represents...the highest stage of capitalist production, a stage...only...reached...at the end of the nineteenth century. In Marxian literature there are various theories regarding ...imperialism. The theories of Karl Kautsky (1854–1938), Rudolf Hilferding (1877–1941) and Vladimir Lenin (1870–1924) deserve special attention.

How does Kautsky[1] define the essence of imperialist policy? "Imperialism... consists in the endeavor of every industrial capitalist nation to...annex a greater and greater number of agrarian districts, no matter to what nationality...[these] might belong."

An industrial country produces... many commodities...it is quite incapable of using up within its own national bound-

---

[1] One of Germany's most distinguished Socialist leaders. A close friend and a disciple of Marx, he played a key role in formulation of the Erfurt Program (1891), in which Marxist preachment of revolution as the means to social justice triumphed over advocacy by Ferdinand Lassalle (1825–64) of state action to the same end. Kautsky likewise led the resistance to Eduard Bernstein (1850–1932) who, in 1898, precipitated a revisionist movement by denying the inevitability of both mounting class struggle and world revolution. He adopted a pacifist stand in 1914 and, three years later, helped launch the Independent Socialist Party. In 1919, he co-edited German documents purportedly establishing the Kaiser's war guilt.

aries....Imperialism manifests itself in the endeavor to conquer agrarian countries so as to sell to them the surplus goods.... Thus, from Kautsky's point of view, the fundamental feature of imperialism is the tendency to seize agrarian, economically backward districts. But this theory...is incomplete and incorrect....[Actually], imperialist policy consists in the endeavor of every industrial capitalist country to subject and annex not only districts of an agrarian nature, but also the most industrially developed provinces, belonging to the neighboring state. Agrarian districts are seized before others only because it is easier to conquer them....The object for which the [First] World War broke out was the endeavor to seize, not backward provinces, but...neighboring industrial districts....An *extension* on the European continent...was of greater importance than the most magnificent acquisitions in the African or Asiatic continents....

Hilferding,[2] a conspicuous Marxist, dedicated his well-known book, *Finance Capital* (1910), to the question of imperialism....The essense of Hilferding's theory consists in the following:...In the first stages of the development of... banks,...the bankers simply occupied themselves in supplying money at interest. When a manufacturer wanted to extend his business,...he went to a banker...and the banker...[loaned him] money without in the least interesting himself in the business of production....But...as excess money began to be amassed..., the banks accumulated enormous capital....[They] then...ceased to content themselves with the role of usurers and became the directors of...industry....Finance capital is bank capital penetrating into industry, directing and controlling...it....

According to Hilferding's theory, imperialism is the policy of...finance capital. Finance capital...pursues a robber policy of conquest [and]...aims at the seizure of new and ever fresh territory....According to Hilferding, the aggressive policy of modern capitalist States on the eve of the [First] World War is to be explained by the needs of finance capital driving the States...to the conquest of all parts of the earth not yet partitioned out....

The export of commodities was the characteristic feature of the old capitalism. For modern capitalism, the characteristic feature is the export of capital.... It is a characteristic feature of the export of capital, as distinct from that of goods, that for the former there is really no limit....This is why finance capital is endeavoring to seize even such regions as would not have been looked at by industrial capital. Hence, finance capital is the ...motive force of the most frenzied policy of conquest....Finance capital has no limits to its extension...and...there is no limit to its policy of conquest....Thus... finance capital is a fundamental cause of imperialism and of the policy of conquest of the modern era.

Under the influence of...Hilferding's book, Kautsky changed his views on imperialism. Formerly Kautsky affirmed... that imperialism is expressed in the endeavor of industrial countries to conquer agricultural, economically backward regions....Kautsky's new theory [is] that finance capital represents the opposite of industrial capital. Whilst industrial capital ...is peace-loving or pacifist, finance capital...supports a robber policy of conquests....

A considerable step forward in the development of the theory of finance

---

2 This Viennese-born physician entered politics in 1907 and, as political director of *Vorwärts*, emerged one of the Social Democratic Party's most able publicists. Becoming a citizen of the German Republic by naturalization after World War I, he edited *Freiheit*, the Majority Socialist Party organ, and fiercely battled communism. In 1923, he served as Finance Minister in the Stresemann Cabinet. Having vigorously opposed Hitler, he fled to France a decade later and, hunted down there by Nazi military police during the 1940 invasion, allegedly committed suicide in prison.

capital is made by Comrade Lenin's[3] theory... [according to which] the fundamental feature of the modern capitalist order...is...monopoly. Whilst the previous economic stage is characterized by the gigantic growth of...productive forces and the lowering of...prices..., the present stage of monopoly...is characterised by a halt in the development of industry ...and...in the fall of...prices.... This ...is pointed out with particular force... in his work *Imperialism, the Highest Stage of Capitalism* (1916).... Lenin...continues:

"If it were necessary to give the briefest possible definition of imperialism, we should have to say that imperialism is the monopoly stage of capitalism. Such a definition would include what is most important, for, on the one hand, finance capital is the bank capital of a few very big monopolist banks, merged with the capital is the bank capital of a few very dustrialists; and, on the other hand, the division of the world is the transition from a colonial policy which has extended without hindrance to territories unseized by any capitalist power, to a colonial policy of monopolistic possession of the territory of the world which has been completely divided up...."[4]

One can formulate Lenin's theory in short by means of the following definition: "Imperialism is monopolist capitalism." This short definition Lenin completes by indicating the following fundamental features of imperialism: (1) The concentration of production and capital having reached such a state of development that it has given rise to monopoly, which plays a deciding role in economic life. (2) The fusion of bank capital with industrial capital and the creation on this basis of finance capital.... (3) The export of capi-

tal as distinct from the export of commodities attains particularly great importance. (4) There are formed international monopolist alliances of capitalists who divide out the world between them. (5) The partition of the earth by the great capitalist Power is complete....

A very important side of imperialism is, according to Lenin, parasitism.... Modern imperialism leads to the growth of the class of...stockholders, that is,... people who live exclusively on cutting their coupons.... A stockholder...neither sows nor reaps,...plays the role of a parasite, and nevertheless gets all he needs.... Whilst in the preceding epoch the industrial bourgeoisie...directed industry, trying to raise the profit of the factories and to increase the productivity of the country..., the...capitalist entrepreneur...is lost in a sea of parasites....

In such an order of society, when the country lives on the export of capital,... parasitism cannot but infect...all classes of the population.... The French worker or peasant who held a few Russian or Moroccan loan shares began to value the alliance with Russia, and...had an interest in the success of French policy regarding Morocco.... On the eve of the [1914] war, thousands...of workers and peasants were...interested in imperialist policy, in colonial adventures. This...made its mark on the psychology...of the peasants... [and]...workers and the latter were therefore no longer people with a purely proletarian psychology....

The modern structure of society has a decomposing influence on the bourgeoisie.... In the period preceding the World War the bourgeoisie were degenerating, and the main cause of this decadence was the parasitism appertaining to imperialism....

---

[3] Following two periods of exile in Siberia, this foremost revolutionist (born V. I. Ulyanov) had settled in London, where, in 1803, he precipitated a split of the Russian Social Democratic Party into two groups, the radical Bolsheviks, which he headed, and the moderate Mensheviks. Back home at the time of the 1905 revolution, he had returned to exile two years later and was living in Switzerland during World War I.

[4] *Selected Works* (2 vols. in 4 parts, Moscow, 1950–51), I, part 2, 524.

[In many writings, I personally have] emphasized the...dominating role of the metallurgical industry in home economics and in the foreign policy of modern states and...formulated the essence of imperialism in the following way. Imperialism is the modern form of the policy of conquest dictated...by the interests of the metallurgical industry, which now...plays a colossal role in the foreign policy of the modern States....This epoch is characterised by the *transference of the center of gravity of economic life of the capitalist countries from the textile to the metallurgical industry*....This transposition... is the most important fact of contemporary evolution of capital, and...in the long run,...is the fundamental cause of the extraordinarily rapid growth of militarism, navalism and of...the modern policy of conquest,...the imperialism of the first-class Powers of the twentieth century.

Whilst the center of gravity of the capitalist economy of a given country lay in the textile industry..., the bourgeoisie ...[was opposed to] an aggressive foreign policy...[and] colonial adventures which would...augment the National Debt, increase the burden of taxation...[and] decrease...the buying abilities of the home market....The fundamental reason for the peace-loving proclivities of the textile manufacturers...was...[their] complete dependence...on the...uninterrupted import of raw materials from overseas....

Present-day civilization...is based to a considered extent on iron....It is...more adaptable than other industries to... fusion into mighty national and international capitalist associations....This circumstance...[brought about] the domination of the metallurgical industry in the whole system of capitalist economy.... [The] metallurgical industry...is the most ruthless enemy of...peace between the...Powers. Metallurgy...is interested in militarism and navalism....One year of war gives the metallurgical industry more...profits than many years of a peaceful period....Imperialism...was the product of the transference of the center of gravity of the whole capitalist economy...to metallurgical industry. Only in the communist order of society will metallurgy cease to play the role...of the main factor in international conflicts, and... then serve exclusively for the good of the laboring masses.

Michel Pavlovitch, *The Foundations of Imperialist Policy* (London: The Labour Publishing Company, 1922), pp. 7 ff.

B. Imperialism's Atavistic Nature

A striking new view on the roots of imperialism was offered on the Continent in 1919, shortly after Pavlovitch's London lectures, by Joseph Alois Schumpeter (1883–1950), an economist serving on Austrian and German university faculties between 1909 and 1932 with an interim as Minister of Finance in his native Austria in 1919–20. Specializing in the entrepreneur's role in the capitalistic system, he was brought to Harvard as professor of economics in 1932 and enjoyed a distinguished career in his adopted country until his death eighteen years later. His appraisal of imperialism, in an essay, "Zur Soziologie der Imperialismen," published in the *Archiv für Sozialwissenschaft und Sozialpolitik* in 1919 (Vol. XLVI, 1 ff. and 275 ff.), was soon known to specialists, but did not attract popular attention until 1951 when a translation under the title, "The Sociology of Imperialism," was included in a posthumous volume, *Imperialism and Social Classes*, edited by a former student, Paul M. Sweezy. Excerpts covering its basic principles follow.

Aggressive attitudes on the part of states...can be explained...only in part by the real and concrete interests of the people....The interest that actually explains a warlike act need not...be openly admitted....There must be a reason for the declaration of war. But that *reason* is not the *cause*....A concrete interest *must be present*....The conduct of the state... must be calculated to *promote* this interest....This interest...is actually the *political driving force* behind the action. The three...conditions are frequently not fulfilled. Whenever such is the case, a problem arises. And among the problems of this nature is the problem of imperialism.

No one calls it imperialism when a state, no matter how brutally and vigorously, pursues concrete interests of its own.... The word "imperialism" has been abused as a slogan to the point where it threatens to lose all meaning but,... whenever the word...is used, there is always the implication...of an aggressiveness, the true reasons for which do not lie in the aims which are temporarily being pursued.... This...is our definition: imperialism is the objectless disposition on the part of a state to unlimited forcible expansion.

Now it may be possible...to give an "economic explanation" for this phenomenon.... An attempt can be made...to derive imperialistic tendencies from the economic-structural influences that shape life in general.... Again, the attempt may be made to reduce imperialist phenomena to economic class *interests*.... This is precisely what neo-Marxist theory does. Briefly, it views imperialism simply as the reflex of the interests of the capitalist upper stratum, at a given stage of capitalist development.... There is much truth in it.... But...it does not, of logical necessity, follow from the economic interpretation of history.... We propose to analyze...imperialism by means of historical examples.... A common basic trait emerges in every case, making a single sociological problem of imperialism in all ages, though there are substantial differences among the individual cases. Hence the plural, "imperialisms," in the title.

["Imperialism" is often made a catch phrase to serve party ends.] Disraeli's speech in the Crystal Palace in 1872 marked the birth of imperialism as the catch phrase of domestic policy. It was put in the form of "Imperial Federation." The colonies, of which Disraeli, in 1852, had written: "These wretched colonies... are a millstone round our necks,"...were

to become autonomous members in a unified empire. This empire was to form a customs union.... The appeal to national sentiment, the battle cry against "Liberal" cosmopolitanism,...emerged.... The "Imperial Federation" plan..., because [of] its protective tariff, its militarist sentiments, its ideology of a unified "Greater Britain" . . . foreshadowed . . . aggressive trends.... That it was not without value as a slogan is shown by the very fact that...it never vanished..., becoming a stock weapon in the political arsenal of English Conservatism, usurped even by many Liberals....

It was, in truth, a fascinating vision which was unfolded before the provincial mind.... But...this imperialism is no more than a phrase.... Disraeli *spoke* but did not *act*.... He did not even try to follow through.... [He] was quite right in not taking a single step in the direction of practical imperialism.... The masses of the British electorate would never have sanctioned an imperialist policy, would never have made sacrifices for it. As a toy, as a political arabesque, they accepted imperialism, just so long as no one tried it in earnest.... England...condemned the Boer War, did everything in its power to "undo" it, proving that it was merely a chance aberration from the general trend.... The rejection of imperialism meant the rejection of all the interests and arguments on which the movement was based....

The imperialist wave that in recent decades has been beating against the mainland of social evolution in England did not rise from the true depths of that evolution but was rather a temporary reaction of political sentiment and of threatened individual interests. Aggressive nationalism..., the instincts of dominance and war derived from the distant past and alive down to the present...do not die overnight. From time to time they seek to come into their own.... But where, as in England, there is a lack of sufficiently powerful interests with which those trends might ally themselves,... they are condemned to political impotence.... In England imperialism will remain a playing of politics for a long time to come. But in terms of *practical* politics, there is no room left for it....

What imperialism looks like when it is not mere words, and what problems it offers, can best be illustrated by examples from antiquity.... [In] the Egyptian, Assyrian and Persian empires and...from a more recent period of history we...find... one basic trait common to all, even the most modern brand of imperialism—a trait which for that reason alone cannot very well be the product of modern economic evolution. ... Imperialism ... appears in history when a people has acquired a warlike disposition and a corresponding social organization *before* it has had an opportunity to be absorbed in the peaceful exploitation of its definite area of settlement. Peoples who were so absorbed...never of themselves develop imperialist tendencies .... Peoples...who were formed into a warlike pattern by their environment before they settled permanently...remain natural-born imperialists until centuries of peaceful work wear down that warlike disposition and undermine the corresponding social organization....

"Objectless" tendencies toward forcible expansion...play a very large role in the history of mankind.... Numberless wars ...have been waged without...reasonable interest.... The explanation lies...in... situations that molded peoples...into warriors...to avoid extinction and in the fact that psychological dispositions and social structures..., once firmly established, tend to...continue in effect long after they have lost their meaning and their life-preserving function.... The orientation toward war is mainly fostered by the domestic interests of ruling classes, but also by the influence of all those who stand to gain individually from a war policy, whether economically or socially. Both groups of factors are generally overgrown by elements of an altogether different character, not only in terms of political phraseology, but also of psychological motivation. Imperialisms differ greatly in detail, but they all have at least these traits in common, turning them into a single phenomenon in the field of sociology as we noted....

Imperialism is atavistic in character. It falls into that large group of surviving features from earlier ages that play such an important part in every concrete social situation.... It is an element that stems from the living conditions...of the past.... It is an atavism in the social structure, in individual, psychological habits of emotional reaction. Since the vital needs that created it have passed away for good, it too must gradually disappear...as...the structure that brought it to the fore goes into a decline, giving way...to other structures that have no room for it and eliminate the power factors that supported it. It tends to disappear as an element of habitual emotional reaction, because of the progressive rationalization of life and mind, a process in which old functional needs are absorbed by new tasks, in which heretofore military energies are functionally modified.... Cases of imperialism should decline in intensity the later they occur in the history of a people and of a culture....

It is from absolute autocracy that the present age has taken over what imperialistic tendencies it displays. And the imperialism of absolute autocracy flourished before the Industrial Revolution that created the modern world....

Capitalism began to shape society and impress its stamp on every page of social history only with the second half of the eighteenth century.... Not until...the Industrial Revolution did the working masses ...overcome...the environment of peasantry, guild and aristocracy.... A transformation in the basic economic factors... created the objective opportunity for the production of commodities, for large-scale industry, working for a market of customers whose individual identities were unknown, operating solely with a view to maximum financial profit. It was this opportunity that created an economically oriented leadership—personalities whose field of achievement was the organization of such commodity production in the form of capitalist enterprise.... Capitalist entrepreneurs fought the former ruling circles for a share in state control.... Their mode of life, their cast of mind became increasingly important elements on the social scene.... This applied primarily to the industrial and financial leaders.... But soon it applied also to the working masses which this movement created and placed in an altogether new class situation.... In the course of the nineteenth century...competitive capitalism...kept on raising the demand for labor and thus the economic level and social power of the workers, until this class too was able to assert itself in a political sense....

Capitalist society...created the industrial and financial bureaucrat [and] the journalist and...opened up new vistas to the jurist and physician. The "professional" of capitalistic society arose as a class type.... The rentier, the beneficiary of industrial loan capital, is also a creature of capitalism. All these types are shaped by the capitalist mode of production, and... tend...to bring other types—even the peasant—into conformity with themselves.

These new types were now cast adrift from the fixed order of earlier times.... They were removed from the old world, engaged in building a new...specialized, mechanized world. Thus they were all inevitably democratized, individualized and rationalized.... We must therefore anticipate finding...the imperialistic impulse ...which rests on the primitive contingencies of physical combat, gradually disappearing, washed away by new exigencies of daily life.... The competitive system absorbs the full energies of most of the people at all economic levels.... What excess energy there is flows largely into industry itself...and for the rest is applied to art, science and the social struggle.... Wars of conquest and adventurism in foreign policy in general are bound to be regarded as troublesome distractions,... a diversion from the accustomed and therefore "true" task. A purely capitalistic world therefore can offer no fertile soil to imperialistic impulses.

That does not mean that it cannot still maintain an interest in imperialistic expansion.... The point is that its people are likely to be essentially of an unwarlike disposition. Hence we must expect that anti-imperialist tendencies will show themselves wherever capitalism penetrates the economy.... Throughout the world of

capitalism...there has arisen a fundamental opposition to war, expansion, cabinet diplomacy, armaments and socially entrenched professional armies.... Modern pacificism...is unquestionably a phenomenon of the capitalistic world. Wherever capitalism penetrated, peace parties of such strength arose that virtually every war meant a political struggle on the domestic scene....

In the distant past, imperialism had needed no disguise whatever, and in the absolute autocracies only a very transparent one; but today imperialism is carefully hidden from public view.... No ruling class today can openly afford to regard war as...a normal element in the life of nations.... Today it must be characterized as an abnormality and a disaster. True, war is still glorified. But glorification...unleashes such a storm of indignation that every practical politician carefully disassociates himself from such things.... Popular attitude ... makes a policy of imperialism more and more difficult—indeed, the very word imperialism is applied only to the enemy, in a reproachful sense.... The type of industrial worker created by capitalism is always vigorously anti-imperialist. . . . No initiative for a forcible policy of expansion ever emanates from this quarter. On this point official socialism unquestionably formulates not merely the interests but also the conscious will of the workers. Even less than peasant imperialism is there any such thing as socialist or other working class imperialism....

The capitalist age has seen the development of methods for preventing war, for the peaceful settlement of disputes between states.... The trend can be explained only from the mentality of capitalism as a mode of life. It definitely limits the opportunities imperialism needs if it is to be a vital force.... Among all capitalist economies, that of the United States is least burdened with precapitalist elements, survivals, reminiscences, and power factors.... Among all countries the United States is likely to exhibit the weakest imperialist trend.... The case is particularly instructive, because the United States has seen a particularly strong emergence of capitalist interests in an imperialist direction.... Nevertheless the United States was the first advocate of disarmament and arbitration....

Capitalism is by nature anti-imperialist. Hence we cannot readily derive from it such imperialist tendencies as actually exist, but must...see them only as alien elements, carried into the world of capitalism from the outside.... Expansive interests within it are likely to ally themselves with imperialist tendencies flowing from non-capitalist sources, to use them.... And from this union the picture of modern imperialism is put together.... It is in the nature of a capitalist economy...that many people stand to gain economically in any war.... But...the national economy as a whole, of course, is impoverished by the tremendous excess in consumption brought on by war.... The gain of the capitalists as a class cannot be a motive for war.... At most, an interest in expansion may make the capitalists allies of those who stand for imperialist trends.... Where free trade prevails *no* class has an interest in forcible expansion as such.... Economic interest in forcible expansion on the part of a people or a class is not necessarily a product of capitalism....

Protective tariffs alone...do not basically change this situation as it affects interests.... The basic alignment of interests remains essentially what it was under free trade.... Protective tariffs...harm... both workers and capitalists—in contrast to entrepreneurs—not only in their role as consumers, but also as producers.... As for entrepreneurs, they are benefited only by the tariff that happens to be levied on their own product.... Today the protective tariff confers its...benefits...only on the large landowners....

It is not true that the capitalist system as such must collapse from immanent necessity, that it necessarily makes its continued existence impossible by its own growth and development. Marx's line of reasoning on this point shows serious defects....

[Free-trade countries reap little benefit from conquest.] But it is a different matter with countries that function in a monopolist role *vis a vis* their colonies [or in subjugated] advanced capitalist countries. ....We have here...a strong, undeniable economic interest in...an aggressive economic policy, an aggressive foreign policy generally, and...wars of expansion with a typically imperialist character.... But the real interest in export monopolism...is limited to the entrepreneurs and their ally, high finance.... The balance sheet of export monopolism is anything but a brilliant success, even for the entrepreneurs....

It is a basic fallacy to describe imperialism as a necessary phase of capitalism, or even to speak of the development of capitalism into imperialism.... The mode of life of the capitalist world does not favor imperialist attitudes.... The alignment of interests in a capitalist economy...by no means points unequivocally in the direction of imperialism.... Modern imperialism...does not *coincide* with nationalism and militarism, though it *fuses* with them by supporting them as it is supported by them. It too is—not only historically, but also sociologically—a heritage of the autocratic state, ... the outcome of precapitalist forces which the autocratic state has reorganized.... It would never have been evolved by the "inner logic" of capitalism itself.... Export monopolism... is not...imperialism. And even if it had been able to arise without protective tariffs, it would never have developed into imperialism in the hands of an unwarlike bourgeoisie. If this did happen, it was only because the heritage included the war machine...and because a class oriented toward war maintained itself in a ruling position. This class clung to its domestic interest in war, and the pro-military interests among the bourgeoisie were able to ally themselves with it. This alliance... led to social conditions that...cannot be explained from capitalist production methods alone....

The precapitalist elements in our social life may still have great vitality...but in the end the climate of the modern world must destroy them.... Their props...are not of the most durable material. Whatever opinion is held concerning the vitality of capitalism, ... it is bound to withstand the onslaughts of its enemies and its own irrationality much longer than essentially untenable export monopolism.... Export monopolism may perish in revolution, or it may be peacefully relinquished; this may happen soon, or it may take some time and require desperate struggle; but one thing is certain—it *will* happen.... Warlike instincts...and organizational forms oriented toward war...will be politically overcome in time.... And with them, imperialisms will wither and die....

Joseph A. Schumpeter, *Imperialism and Social Classes* trans. Heinz Norden, ed. Paul M. Sweezy (New York: Augustus M. Kelley, Inc., 1951), *passim*. By permission of the President and Fellows of Harvard College.

C. Imperialism, Militarism, and Nationalism

With mounting realization of imperialism's great role in recent and contemporary world affairs, great interest has developed in its origins, its development, and its many ramifications. Outstanding among books on the subject has been *The Pattern of Imperialism*, by Earle M. Winslow (1896–   ), from which the following selection has been excerpted.

The story of Imperialism and Militarism constitutes the history of power as it has been exercised by one group over another.... "Imperialism" and "Militarism"...are coeval terms, representing the same general pattern of thought and behavior in the ordering of human relationships. It makes little difference whether we speak of "Militarism and war" or "Imperialism and war." A nation that is militaristic is likely to want to give its militarism an aggressive outlet, which can only mean an attitude of belligerency and an act of hostility towards some other nation. Imperialism is only a more concrete term for the same behavior; it suggests not only ability and willingness to use military power, but also the territory on and against which such power must be employed. It is not a synonym for Colonialism —many colonies have been established by people innocent of imperialistic aggression, in places empty of other people against whom aggression needed to be used in order to make the settlement a success. Even where the intruders fought the natives, as so often...happened in the colonization of the Americas, the conflict was rarely waged primarily as an expedition of military or naval power....

We have come to regard...this colonial activity and conflict as Colonialism rather than as Imperialism. The latter term quite properly suggests something more organized, more military, more self-consciously aggressive, bent on objectives above and beyond the mere occupation of virgin territory in which conflict was incidental... and subordinate to the desire of Europeans to find a new place to live. We readily associate Imperialism with what the Romans did in Gaul and elsewhere and what Napoleon, Hitler and Mussolini were up to; with British policies in India, French and Dutch policies in Africa, Asia and the Pacific and Japanese policies in China. And we must not be too modest—we Americans are accused, and we accuse ourselves, of following imperialistic policies in Latin America, in the Caribbean, in the Philippines and in other parts of the world too numerous to mention. Soviet Russia, despite the protests of Marxists that Communism is incapable of following an imperialistic policy, appears to the more imaginative to be no less imperialistic than the so-called capitalist powers, which the critics of Capitalism have long regarded as the only groups capable of committing the sin of Imperialism....

The theory of Imperialism in some form or other has long been almost a monopoly of the radicals—Socialists, Communists, Marxists or other critics of Capitalism who ascribe modern Imperialism to the workings of the private enterprise economy.... But there are other theories, hypotheses, explanations and interpretations of Imperialism, which have not had their origin in radical or Marxian thought, which . . . range from almost-Socialistic theories to a complete denial of the view that Capitalism or any economic system can be a cause of Imperialism, accompanied by the affirmation . . . that the causes must be looked for in behavior patterns which are far older than Capitalism.

One of the common assumptions of those who undertake to interpret History is that Nationalism...reflects on the political side what Capitalism reflects in the economic sphere, and that Nationalism and Capitalism combine to produce "economic imperialism"....It is only comparatively recently that History has been told in terms of Nationalism and Internationalism; in terms, that is, of conflict as well as peaceful intercourse between nations, with emphasis sometimes on international trade, international co-operation and international peace, and again on economic Nationalism, international rivalries and international war.

But it is important to make clear at the beginning that...Imperialism...is not an extension or expansion of Nationalism. . . . Nationalism . . . did not emerge until the eighteenth century, when the French Revolution brought its first real manifestation. It developed simultaneously with Democracy and Industrialism and the phenomenon which marked all three movements was the overthrow of absolute monarchic forms of government by the ideas and realities of popular sovereignty....

To all this, Imperialism is entirely foreign....Consciousness of belonging to an empire...is completely subordinate to the consciousness of belonging to a nationality. ...The modern nation contains no foreigners, except as a transient phenomenon. But empires always contain "foreigners"— people alien to the mother or ruling country. And these foreigners are universally regarded...either as objects of charity and solicitude (the White Man's Burden, the recipients of a civilizing mission, etc.) or as slaves, never quite as equals. This is clearly a much more ancient attitude than that expressed in Nationalism or nationality.

No—Nationalism does not necessarily lead to Imperialism; it may be the road to Internationalism. On the other hand, Imperialism never leads to Interimperialism. Nationalism has within it the same feeling as has Democracy, that of mutuality, but Imperialism is an exclusive concept. Wherever the spirit of exclusiveness creeps into a nation, as it well may, it is a sign that that nation is losing the attributes of Nationalism, Internationalism and Democracy and is setting forth on the ancient business of telling "foreigners" what to do and what not to do, which is the path of empire....

Many people have [regarded]...Nationalism...and Imperialism as almost synonymous, or at least merely as different stages in the same process, with Nationalism paving the way to Imperialism. But nation-building and empire-building by no means involve the same set of attitudes; in fact, they involve attitudes which are essentially opposed to each other, and which find their opposite expressions in popular rather than scholarly reactions....The greater part of the popular reaction to... Imperialism and Militarism has been emotional, favorable or unfavorable according to whether the person concerned was on the giving or the receiving end of the process or in the favored or exploited class.... No explanation has been more widespread than that based on the view that human selfishness and cupidity...constitute the source of Imperialism and war. This is a modern development of thought, but its beginnings can be detected wherever men have spoken of their desires which express themselves in terms of property and gain.

Earle M. Winslow, *The Pattern of Imperialism* (New York: Columbia University Press, 1948), pp. 3–8.

D. Expansion the Major Cause of World Unrest

One school of writers regards overseas rivalry between acquisitive nations as the basic factor behind mounting global tensions since 1815, and Imperialism as the force giving birth to World Politics. Among the more able exponents of these views has been Parker T. Moon (1892–1936), sometime Professor of International Relations at Columbia, who wrote the most widely used treatise in the field.

The American public is barely beginning to realize the significance of... present-day Imperialism. . . . Of ancient Imperialism...we have heard much and of Napoleon's spectacular exploits every schoolboy has read. But the realms conquered by military emperors of past ages were baubles...compared with the far-flung dominions which have been won...in our own supposedly prosaic generation....

Little as the general public may realize the fact, Imperialism is the most impressive achievement and the most momentous world-problem of our age.... More than half of the world's land surface and more than a billion human beings are included in the colonies and "backward countries" dominated by a few imperialist nations. Every man, woman and child in Great Britain has ten colonial subjects, black, brown and yellow. For every acre in France there are twenty in the French colonies and protectorates. Italy is one-sixth as large as her [ex-] colonies; Portugal, one twenty-third; Belgium, one-eightieth. The nations of western Europe are dwarfs beside their colonial possessions.

How prevalent Imperialism was in Europe before the [First World] War, and still remains, it is difficult for Americans to appreciate, since the "average" American has been accustomed...to think that seizure of territory was somewhat akin to theft, that Militarism and aggressive war were out of date among democratic nations, that conquest was contrary to the normal principles of international morality....

This, however,...has not been the attitude of the imperialist nations of Europe or of Europeanized Japan. French statesmen have vehemently declared the conquest of colonies to be...imperative for France and the Third Republic has won almost five million square miles. Italian patriots...proclaimed it a sacred duty and Italy...[at one time held] almost a million square miles. Englishmen have regarded it, in Kipling's words, as "the White Man's Burden" which civilized peoples dare not shirk; and in the last half-century four million square miles have been added to the British Empire, besides many a veiled protectorate and sphere of influence not formally annexed. Germany at first, under Bismarck's cautious guidance, abstained from...empire-building, but at length plunged into World Politics ...to appropriate a million square miles in Africa and the East Indies, to dominate the rich Asiatic empire of the Ottoman sultans; and finally to stake all and lose all in the titanic conflict of 1914. Austria-Hungary, as lesser partner in the Central European coalition, strove to master the Balkans. Russian tsars...stretched acquisitive hands into Central Asia, Persia, Manchuria and Mongolia and looked hungrily on Turkey, Tibet and Afghanistan. Japan ...took Formosa, Korea, part of Manchuria, Shantung, German islands in the Pacific and . . . attempted . . . to make . . . China...a Japanese protectorate. All the Great Powers save the United States boldly and frankly set themselves to the epic task, in the nineteenth century, of carving out stupendous colonial empires; and even the United States, feeling the same urge to action, reached into the Pacific and into the Caribbean for modest parcels of colonial territory.

Nor were the Great Powers more imperialist than several of the smaller nations. Belgium, with her vast property in Central Africa; Portugal, with colonies larger than the German Kaiser's; Spain, clinging tenaciously to a strip of Morocco together with pitiable fragments of her former colonial grandeur; and Holland glorying in a magnificent East-Indian island empire, have vied with stronger states in seeking the rewards which all hoped to win in the stirring game of World Politics.

"World Politics"—it is a phrase to conjure with! Imperialism has given birth to world-wide empires, to world-wide diplomacy. Great Britain is not, in truth, a European nation, but the nucleus of a universal power. The tricolor of France flies in the Congo jungle, on Sahara's sands, above Indo-Chinese rice-fields. European diplomatists act the drama of international relations on a stage as broad as earth.... Such is the meaning of World Politics. And Imperialism is the root and *raison d'être* of World Politics.

If, from this commanding standpoint, one reviews the recent history of international relations, the alliances, ententes, crises and wars reveal a new meaning. Almost without exception, they were but surface manifestations of the swift, deep current of Imperialism. When France and England trembled on the verge of war in 1898, during the Fashoda Crisis, imperialist rivalry for a million or so square miles of the African Sudan was the cause. The German Emperor's celebrated telegram to President Kruger, congratulating him on having repulsed a British invasion, was... a revelation of tense imperialist competition in South Africa and as such it both angered and alarmed British statesmen. The Moroccan "crises" of 1905 and 1911, which so nearly embroiled all Europe in war, were not unique results of some peculiarly German—or peculiarly French—aggressiveness; rather, they were two of the innumerable explosions which have been caused when the aims of imperialist nations happened to cross.

The South African War of 1899... would never have been fought had English Imperialism not been active in South Africa; nor would the Spanish-American War have occurred if there had been no American interests in Cuba. The greatest war the twentieth century had witnessed before 1914 was the purely imperialist Russo-Japanese struggle for Korea and Manchuria.... [In World War I, the] alignment of European powers was dictated by Imperialism, not by race or democracy

or kinship of culture. Germany, Austria-Hungary and Turkey were allied by Teutonic domination in the Near East. Republican France and monarchist England were bound together by the far-reaching imperialist bargain of 1904; liberal England and tsarist Russia by an agreement of 1907 regarding imperialist interests in Persia, Afghanistan and Tibet....

The climax has not yet been reached; the dénouement is still uncertain. Never was imperialist rivalry so keen as after the... [First World] War. We are now entering a period of intensified international economic competition in which the problem of Imperialism is becoming all the more acute because most of the backward areas available for colonies have already been appropriated. Competition is stimulated by scarcity.... Moreover, tariff barriers are being erected in hitherto open colonies; governments are...officially participating in the international scramble for oil, railway and mining concessions; the tide of immigrant "surplus population" from Europe and Asia is being turned back ...by American restrictions...[and is seeking] new outlets; backward peoples are fast becoming educated to the point of providing a really important and rapidly increasing market for manufactures; raw materials are becoming more and more the stakes of diplomacy. [Imperialism has thus become the greatest force making for unrest in the post-World War I era.]

Parker T. Moon, *Imperialism and World Politics* (New York: The Macmillan Company, 1926), pp. 1–5.

E. Empire Builders— Missionaries of Civilization

The seamy side of imperialism was most conspicuous and was most commonly discussed. There was, however, another aspect to the problem, and occasional writers lauded expansion as an instrument of human betterment in backward regions. Such appraisers viewed a given country's effort in perspective, regarding it as part of a common undertaking for the benefit of mankind, and developed a strong sense of group achievement in which

there was no place for national rivalry. Prominent among such writings was an article by the editors of *The Edinburgh Review* (1802–1929) appearing in 1907.

Let us...say boldly that the modern European movement of expansion is not ...primarily a colonizing movement. It is not a movement merely in favor of annexing territory, of opening up new countries, of settling on the soil and bringing backwoods and prairies under cultivation. It is much more a movement towards organizing, directing and controlling where organization, direction and control are needed and are lacking. What pushes us on in Egypt, and France on in Morocco, is not so much the lust of dominion and desire for acquiring fresh possessions, as the sense that we...can restore order where there is chaos, and fertility where there is sterility. Our Cromers [British Agent and Consul-General in Egypt, 1883–1907, and "the maker of modern Egypt"] and Willcockses [builder of the Aswan Dam in the 1890s, irrigating vast areas in the Nile valley] and Garstins [the engineer who cleared the upper Nile of vegetable growth and opened it to navigation] act not from narrowly selfish motives of personal or even national aggrandizement. They act because they are charged with certain ideas and capacities which, in the sphere where they are called upon to work, are precisely the ideas and capacities of which there is most urgent need....

But...these ideas of government and these applications of science...are not the special property of the English nation.... The idea of a Government and administration honestly devoted to the welfare of society, which has proved such a blessing to the Egyptian people, the idea of a scientific knowledge and skill applied to the practical affairs of life, which has so marvellously extended the productivity of the Nile Valley, are in truth European ideas. They are ideas which the Western races have spent centuries in testing, analyzing and perfecting, and they in fact constitute the main elements in what we call in the lump European civilization.

Europe had absorbed these political and scientific ideas until she was full to bursting with them when the greatly increased facilities in locomotion resulting from her own practical science brought her into contact with regions where these ideas had never been heard of, and where life in consequence was lived under conditions of anarchy, with none of its possibilities realized and resources developed. The result of this contact has been a lively recognition on the part of Europe of the field for effective action thus opened to her and

an overmastering desire to bring her political and scientific ideas to bear on these new scenes of social anarchy and wasted opportunity. Nothing is easier than, in the way this desire has been carried out, to see only shallow and selfish motives at work; but there could be no more infallible proof of intellectual inferiority and second-rateness than is implied in the resting satisfied with such explanations. Under the selfish rivalries and jealousies which are apt to distort and color a national application of European ideas there has always been the deeper motive at work, the consciousness of possessing the powers and the knowledge most needed and which could be most favorably exercised.

This deeper European motive has been stronger than the selfish national motive. We have profited by the work we have done in India, and shall profit perhaps by the work we are doing in Egypt. France has on the whole profited by the work she has done in Algeria and Tunisia, and will probably profit some day by the work that awaits her in Morocco. But the work was not done for the profit.... It was done... because those who did it...were acting, not on behalf of England or on behalf of France, but on behalf of European ideas and European science.... Even the South African [Boer] War was...not the selfish and sordid business that many people represent it to have been. It was not the selfish and sordid motive that aroused popular enthusiasm and excitement here in England, but the belief that Kruger's government was inefficient, corrupt and oppressive beyond all bearing.... With the general public, the European motive was throughout the strongest.

Most of us, probably, are ready enough to admit our own disinterestedness. We are no greedy landgrabbers, but the apostles of an idea, the missionaries of Western civilization. We make that claim for ourselves, and we make it also for those with whom we are in friendship and sympathy. We make it for France. France, introducing order into chaos, transforming a pirates' den into a beautiful and prosperous city, and reviving by her wells and springs the date palms of a thousand perishing oases, is also a missionary of Western civilization. Her action, like ours, is to be accounted for, not by selfish and sordid motives, but by an appreciation of the great opportunities that have been set before her for bringing European ideas and European science to bear upon regions which most need their influence....

Germany's share in Europe civilization is equal to England's share or France's. Germany, as much as England or France, believes in and lives by the great political and scientific ideals which have inspired that civilization; and, this being so, is it not evident that...when she builds her new railway [direct to Baghdad] she too will be actuated by the desire...to apply Western ideas to the conditions of life where they are most needed? Whether the new railway will ever profit her much it is impossible to say, but whether it does or not, it will not have been undertaken mainly for mere profit. It will have been undertaken mainly because the anarchy and ignorance of Asia Minor and Mesopotamia are a perpetual challenge to the ideas and capacities of which Germany is full....

We have no wish here to enforce Germany's claims to be the chosen instrument for the carrying out of this task. There is, however, one characteristic of her Turkish policy which the Baghdad railway so forcibly illustrates that it is impossible not to refer to it. We English have been so accustomed to calculate quite openly upon the speedy decline and disintegration of the Turkish Empire, and even to hurry the process by plucking off such fragments as were most accessible or as seemed ripe for the operation, that we have a difficulty in understanding the directly contrary hypothesis that Turkish affairs may be mended ...by infusing into the Turkish Government and administration certain qualities which have hitherto been lacking to them and so building them up and strengthening them from within....

The Baghdad railway is a kind of hypodermic syringe for the infusion of these ideas into the Turkish system. But it is not the only means Germany is employing. She is working to the same end in many other ways. German engineers for several years have been mapping out the Turkish railway systems of Syria and Arabia; and...[are about]...to survey the section to Medina. This southern railway system, extending to the Holy Cities, may...prove as strengthening an influence ...as the Baghdad railway itself to the Turkish Empire. In conception and execution it has been throughout a German work. Similarly, in matters of revenue and finance, German counsel is attended to.... In all other departments of the Turkish government, especially in the instruction, organization and equipment of the Turkish army, we find the same prevalence of German activity, the same aid and advice constantly proffered and accepted; the same instilling, everywhere, through German channels, of European ideas of order and efficiency.

Already this stiffening of Turkish counsels has produced a marked effect.... Although the good resolutions of an Abdul Hamid, with only his own shifty Oriental impulses to depend upon, may be of negligible importance,... the good resolutions of an Abdul Hamid, steadied by German tenacity and common sense,... [are] of a different value and worthy of a quite different consideration.

"The Benefits of the Baghdad Railway," *The Edinburgh Review,* October, 1907, pp. 371 ff.

II.   The Great Debate : Pros and Cons of Empire

There had been a lull in empire building following the break-up of the old overseas domains between 1775 and 1825. Renewed interest appeared about 1850 and led to the rapid creation of second empires commonly larger and more widely scattered than the first.

Distinct interests in almost every western country sought to further expansion as a national enterprise. Such groups had widely divergent objectives and not all were primarily activated by self-interest. Conspicuously pro-colonial were the great industrialists (especially the textile, ceramic, liquor, and armaments manufacturers), import-export houses, investors, bankers, promoters, shipbuilders, army officers, big navy groups, church leaders, exponents of "the White Man's Burden," militant patriots, and rabble-rousing politicians. Collectively, they exercised tremendous influence in shaping public thinking and at times succeeded in forcing a reluctant government's hands.

Conversely, intellectuals, agrarian interests, "Little Germans" and their counterparts in other lands, Socialists, and Communists offered vigorous opposition. Vociferous Colonial Nationalism, so widespread in our own day, had not yet emerged to lend force to their arguments. The debate progressed from country to country and went on intermittently to 1914 with little variation in argument and with the imperialists normally emerging triumphant.

A. Overseas Possessions Ensure National Greatness and Strength

An early vehement demand for German colonies appears in Friedrich List's *National System of Political Economy*, a renowned exposition of protectionist doctrines published in 1841. The author (1789–1846), a distinguished figure in the free-trade controversy of the day, regarded the acquisition and exploitation of overseas possessions as the certain and best means for any country to attain a commanding economic position.

The highest means of development of the manufacturing power, of the internal and external commerce proceeding from it, of any considerable coast and sea navigation, or extensive sea fisheries and consequently of a respectable naval power, are *colonies*.

The mother nation supplies the colonies with manufactured goods and obtains in return their surplus produce of agricultural products and raw materials; this interchange gives activity to its manufactures,

augments thereby its population and the demand for its internal agricultural products and enlarges its mercantile marine and naval power. The superior power of the mother country in population, capital and enterprising spirit obtains through colonization an advantageous outlet, which is again made good with interest by the fact that a considerable portion of those who have enriched themselves in the colony bring back the capital which they have acquired there and pour it into the lap of the mother nation, or expend their income in it.

Agricultural nations, which...need... colonies, ...do not possess the power of utilizing and maintaining them. What the colonies require cannot be offered by them, and what they can offer, the colony itself possesses.

The exchange of manufactured goods for natural products is the fundamental condition on which the position of the present colonies continues. On that account, the United States of North America seceded from England as soon as they felt the necessity and the power of manufacturing for themselves [and] of carrying on for themselves navigation and commerce with the countries of the torrid zone. On that account, Canada will also secede after she has reached the same point. On that account, independent agricultural-manufacturing-commercial states will also arise in the countries of temperate climate in Australia in the course of time.

But this exchange between the countries of the temperate zone and the countries of the torrid zone is based upon natural causes, and will be so for all time. Hence India has given up her manufacturing power with her independence to England; hence all Asiatic countries of the torrid zone will pass gradually under the dominion of the manufacturing-commercial nations of the temperate zone; hence all the islands of the torrid zone which are at present dependent colonies can hardly ever liberate themselves from that condition; and the states of South America will always remain dependent to a certain degree on the manufacturing-commercial nations.

England owes her immense colonial possessions solely to her surpassing manufacturing power. If the other European nations wish also to partake of the profitable business of cultivating waste territories and civilizing barbarous nations, or nations once civilized but which are again sunk in barbarism, they must commence with the development of their own internal manufacturing powers, of their mercantile marine and of their naval power. And should they be hindered in these endeavors by England's manufacturing, commercial and naval supremacy, in the union of their powers lies the only means of reducing such unreasonable pretensions to reasonable ones.

Friedrich List, *National System of Political Economy,* trans. Sampson Lloyd (London: Longmans, Green and Company, 1904), pp. 216–17.

B. Colonies a Bread-and-Butter Proposition

W. T. Stead (1849–1912) was a world-famous journalist and social reformer. Imperialism was one of his many enthusiasms and he found a great hero in Cecil Rhodes (1853–1902), leading British exponent of an "all red" African domain from Cairo to the Cape. In the late 1890s, Stead wrote *A History of the Mystery,* a fictionalized account of the Jameson Raid into Transvaal—an attempt at conquest (1895) and a provocative prelude to the Boer War (1899–1902). This became a best-seller. Rhodes here appears thinly disguised as "Mr. Cecil," a highly vocal imperialist voicing a telling contemporary British argument for expansion.

"So you really saw a genuine meeting of the unemployed in London's East End last night?" [queried Stirling.]

"Yes," said Cecil, very soberly. "Mark my words, Stirling, you will be eating each other before very long on these islands. . . . It weighs on me like a nightmare, and the meeting last night, the wild speeches, which were nothing but semi-articulate wails for bread, and the hungry look on the faces of those present, gave me a bad turn. . . . And your Little Englanders. . . are such fools they do not see it. It makes me mad to think of it sometimes, and you who know what traitors these people are, . . . speak to them. . . [and] meet them at dinner instead of treating them as they deserve—as traitors to their country."

Stirling said nothing, while Cecil paced backwards and forwards.

"Oh, you are all alike," he said savagely. . . . "You are all so full of the politics of the parish pump, you have never a thought for the great problem which over-shadows everything. They call it an Imperial question; a bread-and-butter question it is, or rather a bread-without-butter question for the people, as you will find out before very long. . . .

"Never was I so convinced as last night, when I walked home from that meeting, . . . that the very existence of your people depends upon us beyond the seas. How many are there of you here? Forty millions in these little islands, and in another twenty or thirty years, how many will there be? Twenty or thirty millions more. What are you to feed them on? Your trade, your foreign trade. You could not feed your people. . . for six months but for that, and yet who thinks about it?

"I suppose what these people would like would be for me to take my money . . . and break it up into sixpences and give it away to your forty millions as. . . [one gives] sixpences to the children in the workhouse at Christmas. Sixpence a head all round for your forty millions would just wipe out a million; and what better would you be. . . a week after the sixpences had been distributed? The million would be gone and all its potentialities of usefulness, but your forty millions of people would remain without any prospect of getting anything more to eat because they had sixpence a head last week. . . .

"A great fortune that is frittered away in doles is like a shower of rain falling in the desert; but a great fortune that is devoted to hewing out a channel for enterprise and industry is like the creation of a river on whose banks generations yet unborn shall find sustenance and prosperity.... In order to keep your forty millions here from eating each other for lack of other victuals, we beyond the seas must keep open as much of the surface of this planet as we can for the overflow of your population to inhabit and...create markets where you can dispose of the produce of your factories and of your mines. The Empire, I am always telling you, is a bread-and-butter question. If you have not to be cannibals, you have got to be Imperialists."

W. T. Stead, *A History of the Mystery.* The Masterpiece Library, Penny Popular Novels No. 58. Abridged (London: The Reviews Office, 1897), pp. 3–4.

C. The German People Must Have "Lebensraum"!

The spectacle of German youth flocking from their homes and being lost to the Fatherland was abhorrent to Heinrich von Treitschke (1834–1896), the "patriotic" historian glorifying the House of Hohenzollern and Prussia. A major force in molding the minds of the rising generation, he became a strong advocate of overseas expansion and made Young Germany world-empire conscious. As a leading German Imperialist, he was bitterly hostile to Great Britain which he regarded as a nation of insolent shopkeepers. His essay, "First Attempts at German Colonization," appearing on the eve of the Berlin Conference of 1884–85 on African affairs, is a classic in the literature of imperialism.

Without any pressure from authority, there has risen from the people...a spontaneous demand for German colonies.... By the persistent endeavors of our brave travellers, missionaries and merchants, the first attempt at German colonization[1] has ...been rendered possible. Germany's modest gains on the [West] African Coast ...aroused attention in the world at large, because everyone knew that they were not due, as in the case of the colonizing experiments of the Electorate of Brandenburg,[2]

to the bold idea of a great mind, but because a whole nation greeted them with a joyful cry, "At last! At last!"

For a nation that suffers from continual over-production, and sends yearly 200,000 of her children abroad, the question of colonization is vital. During the first years which followed the restoration of the German Empire [in 1871], well-meaning people began to hope that the constant draining away of Germany forces into foreign countries would gradually cease, together with the political persecutions, the discontent and the petty domestic coercive laws of the good old times. This hope was disappointed, and was doomed to be so, for those political grievances were not the only, nor even the most important causes of German emigration.

In the short time since the establishment of the Empire, the population has increased by a full eighth, and this rapid growth, in spite of all the misery which it involves, is nevertheless the characteristic of a healthy national life.... Our population...must, in no distant future, rise to a hundred millions and more, ... [and] their fatherland... [will then] be too narrow for the Germans.... According to all appearance, German emigration will still, for a long while, remain an unavoidable necessity, and it becomes a new duty for

---

[1] In German Southwest Africa, Togo, and Kamerun, where protectorates were proclaimed in 1884.

[2] In the late seventeenth century, the Elector of Brandenburg, which later developed into Prussia, tried to break into the lucrative slave trade by opening a trading post at Cape Three Points and a distribution center in the Caribbean. Brandenburg was in no economic position to press the venture, and it collapsed early in the 1700s. The experiment is of historical significance only because it represented the first attempt at overseas activity by a German state.

the motherland to take care that her wandering children remain true to their nationality and open new channels for her commerce. This is...more important than our political control of the lands we colonize. A state whose frontiers march with those of three Great Powers, and whose seaboard lies open towards a fourth, will generally only be able to carry on great national wars and must keep its chief military forces carefully collected in Europe. The protection of a remote, easily-threatened colonial empire would involve it in embarrassments and not strengthen it....

The German emigrants in North America are completely lost to our State and our nationality. Set in the midst of a certainly less intellectual but commercially more energetic people, the nationality of the German minority must inevitably be suppressed by that of the majority.... The German emigration to North America is an absolute loss for our nation—a present given to a foreign country without any equivalent compensation.... Therefore it is quite justifiable on the ground of national self-preservation...[to] seek for ways and means to divert the stream of German emigrants into lands where they run no danger of losing their nationality. Such a territory has been already found in the south of Brazil. There, unassisted and sometimes not even suspected by the motherland, German nationality remains quite intact...and our rapidly increasing export trade with [this area]...shows that the commerce of the old home profits greatly by the loyalty of her emigrant children. Other such territories will also be discovered if our nation enters with prudence and boldness on the new era now opening to the colonizing energy of Europeans.

With the crossing of Africa begins the last epoch of great discoveries. When once the center of the Dark Continent lies open, ...it will be our turn to show what we can do; in those remote regions, the power of the state can only follow the free action of the nation and not precede it. In this new world it must be seen whether the trivial pedantry of an unfortunate past...

has at last been overcome forever, and whether the German trader has enough self-confidence to venture on rivalry with the predominant financial strength of England.

The future will show whether the founding of German agricultural colonies is possible in the interior of Africa; there will certainly be an opportunity for founding mercantile colonies which will yield a rich return. After destiny has treated us badly for so many centuries, we may well count for once on the favor of fortune. In South Africa also circumstances are decidedly favorable for us. English colonial policy, which has been successful everywhere else, has not been fortunate at the Cape. The civilization which flourishes there is Teutonic and Dutch. The attitude of England, wavering between weakness and violence, has evoked among the brave Dutch Boers a deadly ineradicable hatred. ... [We may well], in some form or other, undertake the protectorate of the Teutonic population of South Africa and succeed as heirs of the English in a neglected colony which, since the opening of the Suez Canal, has little more value for England.

If our nation dares decidedly to follow the new path of an independent colonial policy, it will inevitably become involved in a conflict of interests with England. It lies in the nature of things that the new Great Power of central Europe must come to an understanding with all the other Great Powers. We have already made our reckoning with Austria, with France and with Russia; our last reckoning, that with England, will probably be the most tedious and the most difficult; for here we are confronted by a line of policy which for centuries, almost unhindered by the other Powers, aims directly at maritime supremacy....

England's state policy since the days of William III has never been anything else than a remarkably shrewd and remarkably conscienceless commercial policy. The extraordinary successes of this state-policy have been purchased at a high price, consisting in the first place of a number of sins and enormities. The history of the

English East India Company is the most defiled page in the annals of the modern European nations, for the shocking vampirism of this merchant-rule sprang solely from greed. . . .

A still more serious factor in the situation is that, owing to her transatlantic successes, England has lost her position as a European Great Power; in negotiations on the continent her voice counts no longer. . . . The worst consequence, however, of British commercial policy is the immense and well-justified hatred which all nations have gradually been conceiving towards England. From the point of view of international law England is today the place where barbarism reigns. . . . [Her] national policy, like every policy which aims at the unreasonable goal of world supremacy, always reckoned, as its foundation principle, on the misfortunes of all other nations.

England's commercial supremacy had its origin in the discords on the continent and, owing to her brilliant successes, which were often gained without a struggle, there has grown up in the English people a spirit of arrogance, for which "chauvinism" is too mild an expression. Sir Charles Dilke, the well known Radical member of Mr. Gladstone's Cabinet, in his book, *Greater Britain*, . . . claims as necessary acquisitions for "Greater Britain," China, Japan, Chili, Peru, the La Plata States, the tablelands of Africa—in short, the whole world.

In spite of the outrageous ill-usage of Ireland, and the bestial coarseness of the London mob, he calls Great Britain the land which from the earliest time exhibits the greatest amount of culture and insight, together with the least intermixture of ignorance and crime. He looks confidently forward to the time when Russia and France will only be pigmies by the side of England. In only three passages does he deign to make a cursory mention of the Germans. One of them is when he indignantly asks whether we really wish to be so selfish as to decline to support with German money the Euphrates Railway [planned as a precursor to the later German-constructed Baghdad line] which is indispensable to Greater Britain. Thus, then, the manifold glories of the world's history, which commenced with the empire of the monosyllabic Chinese, are to conclude their melancholy cycle with the empire of the monosyllabic British! . . .

German policy is national and cosmopolitan at the same time; it counts, otherwise than British policy does, on the peaceful prosperity of her neighbors. We can rejoice without reserve at each advance of the Russians in Central Asia and each French success in Tonkin. Our ambition only reaches thus far, that in the still uncolonized quarters of the earth, wind and sun should be fairly divided between the civilized nations. . . .

The great German seaport towns. . . have the prospect of a new period of revival; it is from the Hansa [Baltic] towns that the bold pioneers of our nation in Africa come. What Schiller at the commencement of the nineteenth century wrote about the greedy polyplike arms of England is not out of date today; but we hope that when the twentieth century dawns the transatlantic world will have already learned that the Germans today no longer, as in Schiller's day, escape from the stress of life into the still and holy places of the heart.

Adolf Hausrath, *Treitschke: His Doctrine of German Destiny and of International Relations* (New York: G. P. Putnam's Sons, 1914), pp. 205–16.

D. Counterviews

Great Britain was the dominant colonial power in the world after the close of the Napoleonic Wars. There a large-scale controversy centering about the retention of overseas possessions was in full swing by mid-century following the triumph of free-trade doctrines. Now that colonies no longer existed for the exclusive advantage of the Motherland, had they not become a liability rather than an asset? Precisely the same arguments were used in other countries in turn almost to the outbreak of World War I. A penetrating article by the editors, in *The Edinburgh Review* for April 1851, admirably summarizes the views of both imperialists and anticolonists.

In former times, and under the old mercantile system, we valued our colonies as outlets for our manufactures, and as sources of supply for needful products which we could not obtain, or could not obtain so cheaply or so well, elsewhere. We valued them as the principal and the surest channels for that commerce which we felt to be the lifeblood of the nation. They were secure, increasing and favored markets for those articles of British produce which other nations excluded as far as they could by severe and prohibitory tariffs; and they produced for us exclusively those valuable raw materials and articles of luxury which we wished to debar other nations from procuring.

In conformity with these ideas, we bound them to the mother country in the bands of a strict and mutually favoring system of customs' duties: we compelled them to trade with us exclusively; to take from us exclusively all the articles with which we could supply them; and to send to us exclusively all the produce of their soil. In return, we admitted their produce to our markets at lower rates than that of other countries or excluded the produce of other countries altogether. This was a consistent, intelligible and mutually fair system. Under it our colonies were *customers who could not escape us* and vendors who could sell to us alone.

But a new system has risen up, not only differing from the old one, but based upon radically opposite notions of commercial policy. We have discovered that under this system our colonies have cost us, in addition to the annual estimate for their civil government and their defence, a sum amounting to many millions a year in the extra price which we have paid for their produce beyond that at which other countries could have supplied it to us. In obedience to our new and wiser commercial

policy, we have abolished all discriminating and protective duties; we have announced to our colonies that we shall no longer favor their productions and, as a necessary and just corollary, that we shall no longer compel them to favor ours—that we shall supply ourselves with our sugar, coffee, cotton and indigo wherever we can buy them cheapest and that they are at liberty to follow the same principle in the purchase of their calicoes, silks and woollens. They are therefore to us now, in a commercial point of view, friendly trading communities and nothing more. The very object for which we founded, governed, defended and cherished them, has been abandoned: why, then, should we any longer incur the cost of their maintenance?

Being, then, on the footing of independent states as far as their tariffs are concerned, they yield us nothing and benefit us in nothing as colonies that they would not yield us and serve us were they altogether independent. Nay, they are even less serviceable to us; for the experience of the United States has shown us how immeasurably faster colonies advance in population, in enterprise, in agriculture and in commerce—in everything which makes them valuable as customers—when separated from the mother country than when still attached to it by the bonds of allegiance and the clumsy fetters of remote and injudicious control. . . .

In the next place, our colonies used to be regarded as inexhaustible storehouses of waste and fertile land and as outlets for our dense and often-suffering population; and it is in this view, perhaps, that most persons are still disposed especially to value them. But what is the fact? Have we not the plainest indications that even in this respect they would be more valuable if they were independent and that even now the United States, because independent, are preferred by our emigrants? According to Sir William Molesworth's statement in 1848, of 1,673,600 persons who had emigrated during the preceding twenty years, 825,564 went direct to the United States, and how many more went indirectly through Canada we can only guess....

Again—we used to make some of our colonies serviceable as prisons for our convicts—distant and safe receptacles for the disposal of our metropolitan villany and filth—places for "burying our dead out of our sight." *Now* we can use them as such no longer. Our colonies have one and all remonstrated; have refused to receive the sweepings of our gaols any longer; have threatened to rebel if we persist in sending them; and we have ourselves, on more than one occasion, admitted the system to be an indefensible one and have announced our determination to abandon it.

We have been taught to believe that our colonial empire, "on which the sun never sets," is about the most important element in our national greatness and that these vast dominions in every part of the world add incalculably, though in some mysterious way, to our imperial dignity and strength.... [Now we are told] that this "prestige of empire" is a hollow show...; that outlying dependencies which require to be garrisoned in time of peace and protected in time of war draft off from this country the forces which are needed for our defence at home; dissipate our army and navy...; and waste the funds which should be devoted to the protection of the mother country.

It is idle, [we learn,] to pretend that a system which gives us such a vast additional territory to defend without giving us any additional means of defending it can be other than a source of dangerous weakness; that if we had no dependencies, we should be impregnable and invulnerable at home; and that half our navy and a fourth of our army would suffice for the protection of our hearths and homes. If, indeed, the colonies paid tribute into our treasury, if they furnished contingents to our military force and supplied a fixed quota of ships and stores toward the augmentation of our navy, the case might be different. But they do nothing of all this. ... Our colonial empire costs us at least £4,000,000 a year—a sum nearly equal to

the income-tax, ... the malt tax... [or] the sugar tax; any one of which might be repealed, to the infinite relief of our people, in case our colonies were abandoned.

Lastly, we govern them ill.... They are perpetual sources of difficulty and dispute; they are always quarrelling with us and complaining of us, and not unfrequently breaking out into open rebellion; they yearn for independence and would gladly purchase immunity from our vexatious interference and ignorant control by encountering all the risks and difficulties to which a severance of the imperial connection might expose them. Since, then, the colonies are commercially as free as America or Spain; since they are no longer favored or enforced customers for our productions; since they would be at least as available to our emigrants if independent as if still subject to our rule; since they refuse to help us by relieving us of our convict population; since they are sources of weakness and not of strength to us in times of peril or of war; since they pay no part of the expenses of the mother country and only a small portion of their own; since we mismanage their affairs and impede their progress; and since they themselves wish to be set free from a fettering and galling yoke; what argument, which will bear the test of close investigation can be adduced to warrant our retaining them in tutelage?

Such is...the reasoning we have to meet.... The position is undoubtedly a strong one: nevertheless, we hold that there are sufficient grounds for maintaining inviolate the connection actually existing between the colonies and the mother country.... Since...there is no foundation for the idea that we need to abandon our colonies from sheer inability to retain them, we may proceed to point out a few of the reasons which may be urged for preserving the connection inviolate....

In the first place, not a single one of our colonies is inhabited by a homogeneous population. In none is the British race the sole one; in scarcely any is it the most numerous. Some of the dependencies have been taken from savage tribes; others have been conquered from other European nations. . . . With what show of decency or justice could England abandon to their own guidance and protection countries peopled by such various, heterogeneous and often hostile races, even if any considerable number of their inhabitants were unwise enough to wish it? What inevitable injustice such a step must entail upon one or other section of the colonists, what certain peril to the interests of them all and of humanity at large! . . .

Colonies with mixed and aboriginal populations. . . we simply could *not* abandon; colonies with a population exclusively or overwhelmingly British come under a different category. But even with these we think it is not difficult to see that the interests of civilization will be far more effectually served by their retention than by their abandonment, by still maintaining them as integral portions of the British Empire than by casting them adrift to run the chances of a hazardous voyage unassisted and alone. They would "go ahead" far faster, we are told, if independent than if still subject to the hampering rule of the mother country; and the example of the United States is triumphantly appealed to in confirmation of the assertion. We reply that we can well believe that they would go ahead far faster if free than if fettered, but not than they will now, when colonial legislatures have been created and endowed with the powers of managing all strictly colonial concerns. There is scarcely an advantage, conferrable by freedom, possessed by the United States since their separation from Britain, that will not now be enjoyed in an equal degree by our North American and our Australian dependencies. . . .

If, indeed, it were true, as is often ignorantly alleged, that the colonies hated Great Britain and were anxious to cast off their allegiance to her, much might be urged against the policy of retaining unwilling and therefore troublesome and dangerous dependencies. But we believe the statement to be the reverse of true. They may hate the Colonial Office: they do not hate England. They are often

indignant, and sometimes we think they have been so with justice, at the vexatious interference, the injudicious control, the irritating vacillations, the sad mistakes of the authorities at home; they often bluster and sometimes rebel; they nurture in their bosom, as does every community, a noisy knot of turbulent and disaffected men; they talk largely at times of their desire of independence, and occasionally even forget themselves so far as to hint at "annexation." But this is the mere effervescence of political excitement. . . .

If, in an evil hour, the counsels of the counterfeit economists were to prevail, and England were to resign her children to the vanity and feebleness of independence, we feel certain that the very first peril they encountered from without, the very first time they were menaced either with insult or with conquest by a foreign Power, they would instinctively and undoubtingly appeal to England for assistance and protection; and England would respond to their confidence with the most prompt and generous aid. . . . We should have to bear the expense of defending them from attack without having any control over their conduct in incurring it.

Finally: there is one other consequence which would ensue from the abandonment of our colonial Empire which demands to be most deliberately weighed. . . . If we emancipate our colonies and cast them on their own unaided resources both for self-government and self-defence, they will of course immediately look about them for the means of securing these primary objects. However economically they may manage, . . . they can neither govern themselves, nor defend themselves, without a considerable revenue. . . . How [can this] revenue be raised?

There are three sources from the combination of which it might be derived: the sale of waste lands, direct taxation or customs duties on imported articles. The first of these sources could never produce much. . . . Direct taxation is always burdensome, irritating and unwelcome. . . . In colonies where the population is scanty and scattered, there would arise peculiar and insuperable obstacles in the way of levying a capitation-tax, a land-tax or an income-tax. . . . The source of indirect taxation alone remains; and from this accordingly we should find that the revenue of the emancipated colonies would inevitably be raised. A further option has to be made in the choice between import and export duties; . . . the former, among a commercially educated people, will obviously be the most popular and will certainly be adopted. . . .

In a densely populated and luxurious country like England, moderate duties suffice to procure a large revenue . . . but this could not be the case in a thinly peopled colony; a low scale of duties could never raise an ample or adequate revenue; the money must be obtained, and objectionable and burdensome as such a way of obtaining it would be, . . . it would be adopted as a matter of course. The first effect, then, of our proclaiming the independence of our colonies, must inevitably be the enactment by them of a high tariff on all imported commodities; and as the commodities required by new countries are, by the nature of the case, articles of manufactured rather than of agricultural produce, and as England is the chief manufacturing country in the world, it would be chiefly on our productions that this high tariff would press. . . . [This would effectively close to us] the markets we ourselves have planted in the wilderness. . . .

We hope we have succeeded in making it clear that our colonies are far too valuable portions of our Empire to be lightly laid down or put away. . . . Many of them, in simple justice to the native population or to those British subjects who have settled there on the faith of the imperial connection, we could not possibly abandon. Others the interests of civilization and humanity compel us to retain. All of them ought to be, and will be if we govern them aright, sources of strength and pride to us. The very interests of that free and enlightened commercial policy for which we have fought so long and sacrificed so much forbid us to entertain the thought of severing the time-hallowed connection between Great Britain and the communities which have gone forth from her bosom. . . .

The cost of our colonies . . . we could easily sustain were it twice as great; the affection of the colonists it is easy to preserve or to recover where, through misjudgment or misunderstanding, it has been shaken or impaired. By ruling them with forbearance, steadiness and justice; by leading them forward in the path of freedom with an encouraging but cautious hand; by bestowing on them the fullest powers of self-government wherever the infusion of British blood is large enough to warrant such a course . . . we may secure the existence and rivet the cohesion of a vast dominion blest with the wisest, soberest, most beneficial form of liberty which the world has yet enjoyed, and spread to distant lands and future ages the highest, most prolific, most expansive development of civilization which Providence has ever granted to humanity. . . .

To cast our colonial Empire to the winds . . . [to save some millions] a year is a line of policy which, we sincerely think, is worthy only of a narrow and a niggard school which will be counselled only by men who are merchants rather than statesmen and whose mercantile wisdom even is confined, short-sighted and unenlightened; one which, we feel assured, can never be adopted by England till the national spirit which has made her what she is shall have begun to wane and fade away.

"Shall We Retain Our Colonies?" *The Edinburgh Review,* April, 1851, pp. 475 ff.

III. Does Imperialism Pay ?

Empire building is costly business, involving heavy expenditures in men and money. Returns on investments are generally not immediate and normally continue low for long periods. Taxpayers view attendant drains upon the public treasury with apprehension and soon begin to query, "What is there in it for *us*?" and then, "What am *I* getting out of this?"

Expansionists seek to curb such critical tendencies by fostering pride in empire and a feeling of partnership in a national enterprise predestined to pay off handsomely. Conversely, anti-imperialists seek to demonstrate either that there is no gain whatsoever in colonial undertakings or that, while every citizen shares in the staggering cost, the huge profits fill the pockets of only a few who chance to be strategically placed. The debate arises in every country venturing upon the path of empire and periodically breaks out anew without any final decision ever being reached.

A. An Affirmative American Opinion

The Spanish-American War (1898) unexpectedly brought a new colonial empire into being and the United States was suddenly confronted with the many problems attendant upon overseas expansion. The public at large was entirely unprepared for this startling development and the pros and cons of imperialism were avidly argued East, West, North, and South. The question most commonly put by the practical down-to-earth citizen was "Is there money in it?" O. P. Austin (1848–1933), Chief of the United States Bureau of Statistics and a popular writer, sought to show that it was indeed a profitable venture and (hoping to allay the doubts of timorous souls opposing the extension of alien rule upon moral grounds) that it at the same time bestowed incalculable benefits upon the inhabitants of the area involved. His article today stands as the foremost popular exposition of these views.

Does colonization pay? This is a question which Americans are now asking. . . . The best answer is provided by the experience of those other nations that long ago reached the point where such a step was found necessary. . . .

The three modern colonizing powers from whose experience we are able to draw lessons are Great Britain, France and Spain. Germany has so recently begun to colonize that her experiments have not yet sufficiently advanced to justify us in including her colonies in this study. Great Britain is the largest and by far the most successful of the colonizing powers; France comes next in order; Spain's colonial experiments are generally conceded to have been unsuccessful.

A study of these three groups of colonies shows that all those of Great Britain (except Canada and Australia), like those of France and Spain, were established with a view to their commercial usefulness rather than as permanent homes for any considerable percentage of the population of the governing country. Great Britain's principal colonies, named in the order of their imports from the governing country, are: India, Australasia, British Africa, Canada, British Asia and the British West Indies. Canada absorbs less than 7 per cent of the goods which England sends to her colonies but sells to England vastly more than she buys from her. Australasia absorbs 26 per cent of Great Britain's exports to her colonies and supplies 31 per cent of Great Britain's imports from the colonies. Canada has become practically self-supporting in the way of meeting her own requirements and those which she cannot meet she can secure more conveniently from the United States. Therefore, as a market, she is of comparatively little value to the United Kingdom. For many years Australasia will continue to be an important market for British manufactures: she also supplies raw materials to Great Britain. Of the total commerce of Great Britain with her colonies, a large proportion is with those established and maintained because of advantage to her commerce.

The points to be considered in determining the somewhat mercenary question, "Does colonization pay?" as viewed with regard to the interests of the colonizing country, are (1) the market that the colonies afford for the goods which the colonizing country has to sell and whether control gives to the mother country a larger share of the market than she would have without that control; (2) the supplies the colonies are able to furnish for use in the mother country and whether the purchase of these supplies from the colonies proves more advantageous to the mother country than if they should be purchased from other parts of the world; (3) the advantages, if any, which accrue to the native population of the country controlled.

The commercial ambitions of countries which have reached a stage of development to warrant them in entering the field of modern colonization are...(1) to enlarge the markets for their manufactures; (2) to obtain reliable supplies of the materials which their people must consume for food or use in manufacturing and (3), in obtaining them, to give some share of the profit of production or transportation to the people of the home country. With these cold business considerations in view, let us study...the commerce of the countries whose modern colonial experiences seem likely to prove instructive along these lines.

In 1897, Great Britain's exports of domestic produce and manufactures amounted to $1,135,970,000, of which $391,274,000, or 34.4 per cent, was sent to her colonies.... Here is a market found by Great Britain in her colonies, during 1897, for nearly $400,000,000 worth of goods, all of which are the product of labor; and all are of a kind for which the producers and manufacturers of the United States are now seeking a market....Great Britain's sales of manufactures to her colonies alone in 1897 [were] 40 per cent greater than our total sales of manufactures to the entire world in that year.

"But," the objector will say, "would not Great Britain have made these same sales if the countries had not held colonial relations with her, especially since the tariff laws of her colonies at that time made no discrimination in favor of products from the mother country?" Let us see.

In 1897, the total imports of the world, exclusive of the United Kingdom, were $8,172,000,000, of which $962,000,000 was taken by the British colonies; leaving the total imports of the non-British world

during that year $7,210,000,000. In that year, Great Britain's exports...to the non-British world amounted to $1,005,000,000 or...14 per cent of the total.... [Of the] total importations of the British colonies in that year,...the United Kingdom supplied $391,000,000 or 41 per cent....

Even to the United States, an English-speaking country from which her purchases are enormous, she supplied in that year less than 22 per cent of the total imports.

It will thus be seen that...the colonizing country...sells to her colonies a much larger percentage of what they buy than she is able to sell to countries with which she does not have this relation—even under the most favorable conditions. ...A study of the exports of France to the whole world and to her colonies shows even more strikingly the advantage in her colonial trade over that with other parts of the world. The imports of the non-French world, in 1897, amounted to $9,-249,000,000, of which 9.33 per cent was supplied by France; the total imports of the French colonies were $111,157,000, and of this $68,685,000 or 62 per cent was supplied by France. In 1897, Spain's exports to the whole world amounted to $208,382,000, of which $71,962,000 or 35 per cent went to her colonies.

A further study of the commerce of 1897 shows that the total exports of the non-British world were in round terms $8,245,000,000, of which the United Kingdom took...about 21 per cent, [and that] the total exports from the British colonies ...[were] $80,250,000, of which the United Kingdom took...57 per cent.... How much her own people were benefited by her giving so large a proportion of her trade to her own colonies cannot be statistically determined; though the estimate made by distinguished British writers that the investment of British capital in the colonies today is more than $2,000,000,000 shows that a considerable percentage of this benefit must have accrued to her citizens, directly or indirectly. To the profits must be added those of the carrying trade between the United Kingdom and her colonies, which is almost exclusively in the hands of her vessel owners.

In attempting, then, to answer the question, "Does colonization pay the colonizing country?" we find that [in the case of] Great Britain, the colonial relationship brought her from the colonies a market for merchandise valued at fully $250,000,000,000 in excess of that which she would have sold had they belonged to the non-British...world. Most of this accrues to the benefit of home labor....On the other hand, she expended among them ...about $460,000,000, by which she must have materially benefited not only her people residing in those colonies, but those of her home citizens having [investments] in the colonies....

The development of modern commerce and of the carrying trade makes the interchange of commodities and natural products between the great sections of the globe much greater today than ever before; and every year's developments add to the facilities for quick and inexpensive interchange. The older and well-developed countries, especially those in a temperate climate, require three classes of articles from other parts of the world: (1) foodstuffs of a class which they cannot produce at home; (2) materials for use in manufacturing and (3) certain lines of manufactured articles not convenient to be produced at home. On the other hand, the newer countries, especially those in the tropical zone, where manufacturing has not developed, require chiefly two classes of imports: (1) foodstuffs of the class which they cannot produce at home and (2) manufactures which they cannot produce.

The well-developed countries of the temperate zone require sugar, coffee, tea, silks, tropical fruits, spices [and] fibres for use in manufacturing—all of which are produced in the tropical countries freely and with less expenditure of labor than they could be produced if grown in the temperate zones. On the other hand, the articles which the tropical countries require —bread-stuffs, meats, clothing, manufactures of iron and steel, machinery and the various classes of household and business conveniences which modern igenuity offers them—are all produced abundantly and cheaply in the temperate zone and by the very people who want and require the products of the tropical countries.

Thus the great colonizing countries, all lying in the temperate zones, are dependent upon territory lying near the equator for certain lines of products which they must have; while the tropical countries are dependent upon those of the temperate zone for other and equally important lines of products. It is...due to this fact...that the drift has been so rapid during this century toward the control of tropical territory by governments located in the temperate zone.

To put it in homely form, and with no intention to put it offensively, it may be said that the disposition of modern progressive nations lying in the temperate zone is to control "garden spots" in the tropics, where there may be produced, under their direction and through the operation of their accumulated wealth, the articles of tropical growth which their citizens require and, in return, to furnish to the people occupying those garden spots the foodstuffs and manufactures which they require; to develop for them their territory by the construction of roads, canals, railways and telegraphs and by the establishment of schools [and] newspapers; and to give them the benefit of other blessings of civilization which they have not the facilities for creating.

Now let us apply the foregoing facts to the United States and to the islands which the events of the past year have brought into closer relationship with us. The United States has become a great manufacturing as well as producing and consuming nation. Her manufacturers supply the home market and send abroad more than a million dollars' worth per day of their product. In doing this, however, they require constantly increasing quantities of tropical materials; and the people who are cooperating with them in developing the higher stages of her progress, whether in the factory, on the farm, in the mines or forests, require also a constantly increasing quantity of tropical productions.... These articles these islands can produce, while on the other hand they now import, under normal conditions, $100,000,000 worth of foodstuffs and manufactures of the class which we produce and desire to sell. They will double or treble that demand when internal transportation and invested capital will develop within them new areas of production and consumption and stimulate those already existing.

O. P. Austin, "Does Colonization Pay?" *The Forum,* January, 1900, pp. 621 ff.

B. *Three Tragic Fallacies Attending Empire Building*

Expansionists have always laid special emphasis upon the value of colonies as (1) yielders of huge commercial profits, (2) outlets for surplus population, and (3) sources of supply for essential raw products. These doctrines have been resoundingly challenged by Professor Grover Clark (1891–1938), Far Eastern journalist and sometime professor of economics at the University of Denver, in his famed *A Place in the Sun,* and his elaborate parallel statistical study, *The Balance Sheets of Empire.* The latter contains an admirable summary of his dispassionate findings.

Western expansion in the past four centuries, culminating in the swiftly moving drive during the three decades which just preceded the [First] World War, undoubtedly has brought certain substantial advantages to the Western peoples. But, especially in the decades just before and since the [First] World War, this expansion also brought heavy costs in money, in lives and in...antagonisms. These costs are the debit entries which must be made in the ledger of Imperialism.

For the three centuries up to 1800 the record, if it were available (as it is not, except in very general terms), probably would show a cash profit to the Western governments and taxpayers, provided no money value were put on the lives lost in the taking as well as in the taken countries.

For the eight decades preceding the new drive for colonies which started in the 1880's, the governments as such spent considerably more on expansion than they received directly from it. These losses ultimately fell on the taxpayers. But private interests were making good profits on trade with the overseas territories and the governmental expenditures were much less than they came to be later. Perhaps the private profits roughly equalled the governments' losses. In any case, between 1800 and 1880, the balance for the people as a whole in the colony-holding countries was not large on either the debit or the credit side of the ledger.

Since 1880, however, the cash costs to the countries which have used force to get or keep control of colonies unquestionably have been very substantially more than any possible cash profits derived from the trade with the territories controlled. Germany and Italy have spent more directly on their colonies than the total value of the trade with them; Italy's margin of expense over trade value was very large even before the...drive into Ethiopia started. Japan has not spent as much directly on getting and keeping her colonies as the total value of her trade with them, but considerably more than the possible profits on that trade. The direct colonial expenses for France and Britain probably have been some, but not much, more than the profits on the trade with the overseas territories, especially if the trade with the Dominions be counted in the British total.

For all these countries, however, the direct expenditures on the colonies are only a part of the real colonial costs. A part of the general naval and military defence expenses must be charged against the colonies since not one of these nations would feel required to maintain such expensive armed forces if it did not have the overseas territories. If a conservatively estimated share of the general expenditures for defence be allocated to the colonies as their proper share of the overhead expenses of keeping up the nation's armed forces, the ledgers of the colonies show a large red ink balance for every one of the principal colony-holding countries. And this debit balance for the cash accounts includes no portion of the expenses of the [First] World War, even though the jealousies aroused by the drive for colonies were so important a factor in bringing that war about.

The record shows, too, that the gains in other than direct money terms which frequently are claimed to result from the possession of colonies have not been anything like enough to compensate for the heavy cash losses which the ledger records.

In spite of all that was said about the value of colonies as outlets for population, and as places to which people could go without being lost to the fatherland, the number of those who left all Europe permanently to live in the overseas territories controlled by European governments (which does not include the British Dominions) in the past half century has been extremely small compared either with the increase in population at home or with the migration to regions which were completely independent or, like the Dominions, practically so. Europe's population in this period has increased about 173 millions. The net emigration from Europe has been about 19.3 millions. The net emigration to the territories controlled from Europe has been about 500,000, which is less than 0.3 per cent of the population increase in Europe and only 2.6 per cent of all the permanent emigrants.

In spite, too, of the insistently repeated assertion that the possession of colonies and the consequent control of raw materials in them materially increases a nation's security in time of war and gives it substantial advantages in time of peace, the records show that this claim, like the claims that colonies provide important outlets for population and yield large and profitable trade to the holding country, is fundamentally fallacious.

The wartime situation is obvious enough. Access to the sources of raw materials depends on the ability to keep communications open with those sources, not on the presence or absence of political control over the territories where the sources are.

In times of peace, substantial advantages can be derived from ownership of the source of any particular raw material, in insuring either supplies or large profits for the owning country's nationals, only to the extent that something approaching monopoly control can be maintained of all the sources of supply. But, through the development of new sources or of substitute products for all the important raw materials, whether agricultural or mineral, it has become practically impossible for any country today to keep anything like monopoly control of any raw material. The tendency...is strongly toward rather than away from increased competition in the world's raw materials markets.

Furthermore, the fallacy of the claim that a country really can make itself materially less dependent on foreign sources of supply and on foreign markets by adding to the territory under its control is strikingly demonstrated by the actual trade record of the colony-holding countries.

Not one of them does as much as a fourth of its trade with its colonies. Japan has the best record in this respect, but even she,...in 1929–1934, when her trade with her colonies was at its highest in proportion of her total trade, did only 22 per cent of her external business with the lands under her control. Even if all the British trade with the Dominions be included, the United Kingdom, even since the Ottawa Agrements of 1932 [which accorded nearly all Dominion produce free entry into Great Britain and gave increased preferential rates to British manufactures entering the Dominions], has done with all the British countries just over a third of her external trade, and the share with the British territories under London's control has been only 15 per cent of the total.

Nor does one of the colony-holding countries get from the overseas territories which it controls as much as a fifth of the raw materials and the foodstuffs which it requires, or sell to these regions as much as a third of the products of its factories. Even including the trade with the independent Dominions, the United Kingdom gets only a little more than a third of its food and raw materials imports from within the British Commonwealth, and sells less than half its exported manufactured goods to the British countries.

In brief, every country depends far more on foreign sources of supply and foreign markets than it does on overseas territories and sources under its own control, in spite of all the claims that have been made to justify the taking of colonies and in spite of all the money and lives that have been spent to get and keep colonies.

Moreover, no country gets *all* of its trade with its colonies, or with any colony, *because* it has political control. Control gives some advantages in getting trade, but the very fact that all the colonies trade with other countries than the one in control demonstrates that the controlling country could and probably would get a fair amount of trade with the regions which make up its colonies even if it did not have control.

Obviously it is impossible to determine precisely what proportion of the trade, in any particular case, goes to the holding country because it has control. But it is interesting to observe the British record in this connection. In the past half century, the share which the territories controlled from London have had in the trade of the United Kingdom has decreased, while that of the self-governing Dominion areas has increased. The record of the overseas countries tells the same story: the share of the United Kingdom in the trade of the regions which it controls has fallen off, while that in the trade of the Dominions has increased. On its face, this record suggests that the trade importance of the British overseas countries has been in inverse, not direct, ratio to the amount of political control. But to draw that conclusion would be to give far more weight to the influence of political control in determining the movement of trade than the facts warrant.

Stated briefly, these are the conclusions which are inescapable from a careful analysis of the record for the past half century of what their colonies actually have meant to the principal colony-holding countries. The three main arguments for possessing colonies turn out to be three great fallacies, and they are seen to be dangerous as well as costly fallacies when account is taken of the results of the struggle for colonies not only or even primarily in cash but in lives lost, in wars caused and in the pyramided hatreds which so gravely threaten new wars.

Grover Clark, *The Balance Sheets of Imperialism* (New York: Columbia University Press, 1936), pp. 3–5.

C. A Few Gain But the Nation Loses

Imperialism, by J. A. Hobson (1858–1940), distinguished British economist and journalist, appeared in 1902, at the close of the Boer War. It created a tremendous sensation and gave birth to anti-expansionist movements in many lands. Democrats in the United States and Socialists and Communists in Europe, in particular, drew ammunition from its devastating pages and used Hobson's arguments with telling effect.

Most spectacular of his charges was that, while empire building was carried on at public expense, huge profits accrued to members of narrowly restricted groups and that the nation as a whole gained little if anything. This scholarly study continues the classic indictment of imperialism in our own day.

. . . Imperialism . . . is clearly condemned as a business policy in that, at enormous expense, it has procured a small, bad, unsafe increase of markets and has jeopardized the entire wealth of the nation in rousing the strong resentment of other nations. . . . [This being the case], we may ask, "How is the British nation induced to embark upon such unsound business?" The only possible answer is that the business interests of the nation as a whole are subordinated to those of certain sectional interests that usurp control of the national resources and use them for their private gain. . . .

Although . . . Imperialism has been bad business for the nation, it has been good business for certain classes and certain trades within the nation. The vast expenditure on armaments, the costly wars, the grave risks and embarrassments of foreign policy, the checks upon political and social reforms within Great Britain, though fraught with great injury to the nation, have served well the present business interests of certain industries and professions. . . .

What is the direct economic outcome of Imperialism? A great expenditure of public money upon ships, guns, military and naval equipment and stores, growing and productive of enormous profits when a war, or an alarm of war, occurs; new public loans and important fluctuations in the home and foreign bourses; more posts for soldiers and sailors and in the diplomatic and consular services; improvement of foreign investments by the substitution of the British flag for a foreign flag; acquisition of markets for certain classes of export and some protection and assistance for British trades in these manufactures; employment for engineers, missionaries, speculative miners, ranchers and other emigrants.

Certain definite business and professional interests feeding upon imperialistic expenditure, or upon the results of that expenditure, are thus set up in opposition to the common good and, instinctively feeling their way to one another, are found united in strong sympathy to support every new imperialist exploit. . . . Some . . . , especially the shipbuilding, boilermaking and gun and ammunition making trades, are conducted by large firms with immense capital whose heads are well aware of the uses of political influence for trade purposes.

These men are Imperialists by conviction; a pushful policy is good for them.

With them stand the great manufacturers for export trade who gain a living by supplying the real or artificial wants of the new countries we annex or open up. Manchester, Sheffield, Birmingham, to name three representative cases, are full of firms which compete in pushing textiles and hardware, engines, tools, machinery, spirits, guns, upon new markets. The public debts which ripen in our colonies, and in foreign countries that come under our protectorate or influence, are largely loaned in the shape of rails, engines, guns and other materials of civilization made and sent out by British firms. The making of railways, canals and other public works, establishment of factories, the development of mines, the improvement of agriculture in new countries, stimulate a definite interest in important manufacturing industries which feeds a very firm imperialist faith in their owners.

The proportion which such trade bears to the total industry of Great Britain is not great, but some of it is extremely influential and able to make a definite impression upon politics through chambers of commerce, parliamentary representatives and semi-political, semi-commercial bodies like the Imperial South African Association or the China Society.

The shipping trade has a very definite interest which makes for Imperialism. This is well illustrated by the policy of state subsidies now claimed by shipping firms as a retainer and in order to encourage British shipping for purposes of imperial safety and defence.

The services are, of course, imperialist by conviction and by professional interest and every increase of the army, navy and air force enhances the political power they exert. . . . To the military services we may add the Indian Civil Service and the numerous official and semi-official posts in our colonies and protectorates. Every expansion of the Empire is also regarded by these same classes as affording new openings for their sons as ranchers, planters, engineers or missionaries. . . . From this standpoint our colonies [are] a vast system of outdoor relief for the upper classes.

In all the professions, military and civil, the army, diplomacy, the church, the bar, teaching and engineering, Greater Britain serves for an overflow, relieving the congestion of the home market and offering chances to more reckless or adventurous members, while it furnishes a convenient limbo for damaged characters and careers. . . .

By far the most important economic factor in Imperialism is the influence relating to investments. . . . In dealing with . . . foreign investments we are facing the most important factor in the economics of Imperialism. Whatever figures we take, two facts are evident. First, that the income derived as interest upon foreign investments enormously exceeded that derived as profits upon ordinary export and import trade. Secondly, that while our foreign and colonial trade, and presumably the income from it, were growing but slowly, the share of our import values representing income from foreign investments was growing very rapidly. . . .

The modern foreign policy of Great Britain has been primarily a struggle for profitable markets of investment. To a larger extent every year Great Britain has been becoming a nation living upon tribute from abroad, and the classes who enjoy this tribute have had an ever-increasing incentive to employ the public policy, the public purse and the public force to extend the field of their private investments and to safeguard and improve their existing investments. This is, perhaps, the most important fact in modern politics and the obscurity in which it is wrapped has constituted the gravest danger to our State.

What was true of Great Britain was true likewise of France, Germany, the United States and of all countries in which modern Capitalism has placed large surplus savings in the hands of a plutocracy or of a thrifty middle class. . . .

Aggressive Imperialism, which costs the taxpayer so dear, which is of so little value to the manufacturer and trader, which is fraught with such grave incalculable peril to the citizen, is a source of great gain to the investor who cannot find at home the profitable use he seeks for his capital and insists that his Government should help him to profitable and secure investments abroad.

If, contemplating the enormous expenditure on armaments, the ruinous wars, the diplomatic audacity or knavery by which modern governments seek to extend their territorial power, we put the plain, practical question, *Cui bono?*, the first and most obvious answer is the investor. . . . The big money-lender and speculator . . . [are] determinants of imperial policy. They have the largest definite stake in the business of Imperialism and the amplest means of forcing their will upon the policy of nations. . . .

Such is the array of distinctively economic forces making for Imperialism—a large loose group of trades and professions seeking profitable business and lucrative employment from the expansion of military and civil services and from the expenditure on military operations, the opening up of new tracts of territory and trade with the same and the provision of new capital which these operations require, all these finding their central guiding and directing force in the power of the general financier.

The play of these forces does not openly appear. They are essentially parasites upon patriotism and they adapt themselves to its protecting colors. In the mouths of their representatives are noble phrases, expressive of their desire to extend the area of civilization, to establish good government, promote Christianity, extirpate slavery and elevate the lower races. Some of the business men who hold such language may entertain a genuine, though usually a vague, desire to accomplish these ends, but they are primarily engaged in business and they are not unaware of the utility of the more unselfish forces in furthering their ends. Their true attitude of mind was expressed by Mr. Rhodes in his famous description of Her Majesty's Flag as "the greatest commercial asset in the world."

J. A. Hobson, *Imperialism* (London, 1938), pp. 46–61. Used by permission of George Allen & Unwin, Ltd., publishers.

14

The
Advance of Communism

R. V. BURKS

Radio Free Europe

Considered as a historical epoch, the twentieth century has been especially characterized by the emergence of totalitarian ideologies. These ideologies, in particular fascism and communism, have dominated both the century's politics and its war-making. It is therefore not astonishing that those especially concerned with the fate of mankind should be profoundly interested in the forces which have spawned the aggressive faith which is world communism.

The advance of communism has been swift. In the early years of the century it was hardly more than a curious Russian sect, an offshoot of the main body of Marxian socialism. In 1917, a tiny minority of Communists managed, in the conditions of chaos and collapse produced by the defeat of the tsarist armies in World War I, to seize control of the Russian government; thereafter by a miracle compounded of discipline, propaganda, and luck they succeeded in consolidating their hold over the Russian one-sixth of the land surface of the glove. Once firmly in the saddle, the Communists through systematic terror, the enslavement of the peasantry, and the sacrifice of five million human lives managed to industrialize Russia and make of her a first-class military power, able to contend on more or less even terms with Nazi Germany; this industrial transformation of Russia the Communists accomplished in the short space of thirteen years (1928–41). Meantime communism had become a world movement with a satellite regime in Outer Mongolia and with adherents and parties in almost every country of the world looking to the holy city of Moscow for guidance and support.

Having come to power in Russia during World War I, communism made its next great advance as a consequence of World War II. In the course of destroying the Nazi empire, Soviet troops came to occupy most of eastern Europe. Between 1944 and 1948, Communist governments were established in eight additional countries: in Poland, East Germany, Czechoslovakia, Hungary, Romania, Bulgaria, Yugoslavia, and Albania. At approximately the same time, armies of Chinese Communists, fighting essentially as guerrillas, succeeded in defeating the armed forces of the established government and finally ensconced themselves in 1949 as masters of China. Communist regimes also emerged in the northern halves of Korea and Vietnam. Only by dint of hard fighting were the anti-Communist forces able in the forties, fifties, and sixties to prevent the Communists from overrunning South Korea and South Vietnam, and from setting up regimes of their own in Laos, Malaya, and Greece. In the early sixties appeared the first Communist regime not located on the Eurasian land mass, that is, the first regime overseas: the revolutionary Cuban government of Fidel Castro. With this development, communism had in less than one-half century conquered or established 14 of approximately 111 states, had come to rule over 35 per cent of the world's population of two and one-half billion, and held in its grasp about 29.2 per cent of the land surface of the globe.

The recitation of these well-known but essential facts brings to mind several historic parallels, of which perhaps the most striking is that of the rise and spread of the fighting faith of Islam. Between the death of the prophet Mohammed at Mecca in 632 and the crucial defeat of his followers at Tours in France exactly a century later, Islam made itself master of roughly the southern half of the Mediterranean world and, in the bargain, conquered Persia and a part of northern India. In so doing, Islam produced a civilization and a world order of its own which competed on better than even terms with the Christian Frankish state in the northwest Mediterranean area, and the Christian Byzantine Empire in the northeast.

Aside from the speed and the scope of this advance, what makes the parallel with communism particularly apt is the element of fanatical belief. The Moslems knew themselves to be endowed with a revelation of ultimate and absolute truth whose final triumph was preordained, as a gateway to the perfect social order. The faith of the Communists is secular rather than otherworldly. It keeps heaven as the terminal point in the historical process, but places this heaven on earth as a utopia characterized primarily by the absence of social classes. It views the history which leads to this utopia as an unending struggle between the forces of good and the forces of evil, but it defines "good" not as the army of those who follow Allah but as the legion of the industrial proletariat, and "evil" not as the host of the unbelievers but as the handful of factory-owning exploiters and their minions. If with Islam the struggle is ethical, a battle for men's souls, with communism the struggle is economic, a war between those who own and those who operate the instruments of production. In communism, finally, the Mohammedan hell of fire and brimstone is replaced with an alternating and ever more insistent rhythm of war and economic crisis, which is located within history, rather than after it, and precedes the emergence of the classless utopia. Thus, despite their obvious differences, both Islam and communism are teleological and apocalyptic.

There are other interesting points of similarity between the two movements. In each case there is geographic contiguity. Islam spread roughly throughout a great semiarid arc beginning with the Atlas Mountains in northwestern Africa and ending with the Hindu Kush in northeastern Iran. This is an area of deserts, dry plateaus and mountains occasionally interrupted by flood plains, fertile coastal strips, and oases. As someone has said, Islam failed to conquer beyond the line where the olive tree would grow. Communism, on the other hand, except for its new overseas venture in Cuba, is so far a solid red patch in the center of the Eurasian land mass. It is an isolated, continental phenomenon. The seas to which Communist countries so far have access are either landlocked (Black) or icebound (White) or dominated by near-lying and hostile islands (Taiwan) or archipelagoes (Japanese). Because of its geography, communism has a major transportation problem: enormous distances through terrain which either because of climate or soil or demography is relatively unfruitful.

At the cultural level, too, there are suggestive parallels. Both Islam and communism originated in backward areas: Islam in the Arabian desert, communism (officially the doctrine of the urban proletariat) in pre-industrial and illiterate Russia. The emergence and expansion of each was peculiarly the work of a single people, of the Arabs in the case of Islam, of the Russians in the case of communism; this was expressed in the fact that in each instance the language of the bearer-folk became both the *lingua franca* and the *lingua sacra* of the movement. Each movement could also be viewed as a process by which the people in question built an empire for itself and laid claim to a dominant position in the civilized world. Perhaps most striking of all is the fact that the adoption of the new faith by another major people, one with a great past and a complex culture, led ultimately to schism and heresy. In Islam the division was between the Shi'ites and the Sunnites, the former being a heretical movement based primarily on the Persians and reflecting their will to independent greatness. In communism a deep-going and open schism emerged between the orthodox and the revisionists, between those parties which wished to promote world revolution even at serious risk of nuclear war, and those prepared to compromise. The orthodox were led by the Chinese, the moderates by the Russians.

However striking these parallels, there are also many important differences between Islam and communism. Perhaps the most obvious is the secular character of communism, which stoutly denies the existence of another world and concentrates all its energies on this one. It is not that communism is less religious, but that its religious energy is concentrated on the construction of a man-made, earthly heaven. A more important difference is the fact that communism is one embodiment of the technological revolution which is a central feature of our twentieth century. In comparison with this technological revolution, Islam, for all its advances in medicine and mathematics, had little to offer. The technological revolution is essentially a series of break-throughs in man's understanding of and control over nature (e.g., atomic energy, synthetic raw materials). Aside from claiming the inside track in the technological revolution, communism provides a method for applying the revolution to underdeveloped and backward areas in a systematic and rapid way, so that they may make a great leap forward, from the darkness of the Middle Ages to the golden twentieth century within the span of a man's life. It is for this reason that communism has spread from backward Russia to countries even less developed, in contrast to Islam, which came out of the desert to overwhelm much more advanced cultures. It is interesting that so far communism has been unable to seize control of any of the advanced countries of the West. In the most advanced, those with the highest living standards, communism has remained little more than a ridiculous sect. It is the association of communism with the technological revolution which makes of this ideology a world-embracing threat, one which even spills over into interplanetary space. Islam threatened only the Mediterranean world of early medieval times and did not menace the cultures of the Far East.

Above all, communism is different from Islam in possessing what Lenin called a party of the new type. This party is the engine and the motor force of the movement. It is a combination, to employ imperfect but essential analogies, of religious order, military unit, and political elite. The party believes not only that it can foresee but also that it can control the future course of human history. The nearest equivalent in Islam would be perhaps the Ulema, or body of men learned in the lore of Islam—judges, teachers, readers of the sacred script, and the like. But the Ulema did not constitute a hierarchy, nor was it under military discipline, nor did it have responsibility for military affairs (except the proclamation of the *jihad,* or holy war), nor for the rule of subject peoples. The Ulema taught, interpreted, and preserved the law of Islam, which it regarded as both unchanging and perfect. It is almost true to say that, far from believing that it could control history, the Ulema did not believe in history, at least not in history as a man-made process.

This comparison of seventh-century Islam and twentieth-century communism gives us an idea of the order of historical significance which we must assign to communism. It also makes it easier to understand that, just as Islam was opposed in its advance by Christianity, so in our own day communism must overcome the opposition of democracy. Some time after 1917, western scholars began to realize that democracy, too, had its religious characteristics. In a much less dogmatic way than communism, democracy attempted to interpret the nature of history and divine the destiny of man. For example, democracy hoped for and believed in the emergence in the future of a truly democratic and uninterruptedly prosperous society in which war would be eliminated by some form of world government, poverty by the machine, and disease by modern medicine. For the believer in democracy, history was not so much a struggle between social classes as a duel between ignorance and enlightenment, between ancient superstition and modern science; a race, as it were, between education and nuclear catastrophe. Democracy, like communism, also tried to channel change in the direction of utopia, though this meant not the waging of war or revolution, but support of the United Nations, financial contribution to cancer research, and the organization of a Peace Corps. One of the first to realize the religious character of democratic belief was the historian Carl L. Becker, who presented the idea in a fascinating little book entitled *The Heavenly City of the Eighteenth-Century Philosophers* (New Haven: Yale University Press, 1932).

At the same time the confrontation of communism and democracy had a practical feature. Just as the doctrine of communism was embodied in the Union of Soviet Socialist Republics, so the United States of America assumed (rather unwillingly at first) the costly and burdensome role of champion of freedom. With the final defeat in 1945 of Nazi Germany, the palladin of fascism, there began a long struggle between the U.S. and the U.S.S.R., a struggle for prestige and influence, a conflict of propaganda and crisis, a battle over military bases and armaments. The stakes in this struggle were high, and the use of violence by the Communists a continuing feature. Moreover, the two giants have organized their associates into military blocs (Warsaw Pact versus NATO), fostered supranational economic organizations in support of their military power (Comecon versus Common Market), competed in the development of weapons of a destructiveness hitherto unimagined, and engaged in an undisguised race for the mastery of outer space.

Faced with this growing threat to world peace and western civilization, western scholars have become deeply concerned with the causes of communism as a world movement. What accounts for its dynamism? What inner need brings so many men to such a fanatical belief? What, if any, combination of force, persuasion, and economic aid will bring the movement to a halt, or at the least reduce its rate of expansion within acceptable limits?

The Communists of course explain their movement as the inevitable result of industrialization. According to their doctrine the coming of capitalism brings with it a ruthless exploitation of the new urban working class by a handful of enormously wealthy capitalist families. In their suffering the proletarians gradually turn to communism as their beacon and salvation, and under its guidance overthrow their oppressors. This is a story of much pathos. But unfortunately it stands in open contradiction to the facts. As we pointed out in comparing it with Islam, communism has had its greatest success in backward, that is to say, preindustrial, countries. The order of events is the reverse of that predicted by the Communists. The Communist party first seizes power, then uses police terror together with centralized planning to force the development of industry at a rapid pace, in the process creating an urban proletariat which before did not exist, or existed only on a minor scale.

Communism is thus an act of faith consummated in defiance of the facts. Communist doctrine tells us only what Communists believe; it does not explain why they believe or how they came to believe. The fact that the acts of a Communist may be traced to his faith in a classless society does not elucidate why the man believes in such a society. The problem is to find the factors or forces operating in world history which produce this desperate act of faith among so many millions.

To attack this problem we present, first, three writers who have set themselves the formidable task of understanding how communism came to Russia. Were the Russians merely the first victims of an international conspiracy of totalitarian crackpots, or did they turn to communism because it promised fulfillment of their ancient messianic myth of world imperium? Then a second triad of authors deals with the related problem of explaining why communism has spread beyond Russia. Is the appeal of communism due to the fact that it offers an apparently rapid and successful method of industrialization; or is it rather that its religious character makes it available as a vehicle for the frenetic nationalism of awakening peoples? Or is the advance of Communism due to some combination of these factors?

I. *Communism Conquers Russia*

In Marxist theory, communism should not have come to Russia first, but to one of the advanced industrial countries, such as Germany. Marx had said that the revolution would occur first where the evils of capitalism had made the urban proletariat most desperate; only when capitalism had matured could a revolutionary situation be anticipated. Back in 1903, the Russian Marxists had split on this very issue. One faction, the Mensheviks under Plekhanov, argued that many decades must pass before peasant Russia could become an industrial nation; meantime Russian Marxists should devote themselves to the purity of the faith and the education of the tiny working class. An opposing faction, the Bolsheviks under Lenin, did not wish to wait. Lenin declared in effect that by organizing a party of the new type (i.e., the Communist party, as it came to be called) one could seize power at a revolutionary moment, when the apparatus of the tsarist state was paralyzed by some external blow, such as defeat in war. The world revolution might well begin, Lenin argued, at the weakest link in the imperial chain, in a country such as backward Russia.

In 1917, Lenin was proved to have been right. He and his followers nonetheless continued to believe that the essential element in the success of revolution would be an upheaval in Germany. And even after it had become apparent that the revolutionary tide was ebbing, the Bolsheviks clung to the idea that the next great advance would take place in an industrial country; throughout the twenties, they gave special attention to the German party. With Lenin's death, in 1924, a new factional dispute arose. The Trotskyites wished to push forward with world revolution at all costs, advocating the so-called theory of permanent revolution on the ground that if the capitalists were given time to recover, they would league together against revolutionary Russia and destroy her. The Stalinists argued to the contrary that the Bolsheviks should consolidate the position they had won by using the authority of the state to industrialize Russia in a hurry and make of her a great power, ready for the next upheaval. This was the doctrine of building socialism in one country. Thus it was that the Communist leaders themselves came to place industrialization *after* the revolution rather than before it.

A. *Burnham: Communism as an International Conspiracy Incidentally Based on Russia*

Our first writer, James Burnham, is an American and a professor of philosophy. In his view, communism is a dangerous world conspiracy which, as a matter of historical accident, first came to power in Russia. As a consequence, communism has acquired some Russian traits, just as it would have acquired German traits if the Communists had first seized power in Germany, or British traits if Britain had been first. The fact that the power base of communism is Russia has also made for a certain continuity of tsarist and Soviet foreign policy. But all this is deceptive and misleading. The Russian people, so far from approving of, or believing in, communism, are in fact its first victims. They are in their vast majority bitterly opposed to the Communists and their policy. This is shown by the fact that the Communists were able to consolidate their power only by the use of terror, purges, censorship, and slave labor camps. Instead of having amalgamated with Russian nationalism, communism is taking over and absorbing and replacing not only Russian nationalism, but Georgian, Kazak, Ukrainian, and Chinese nationalism as well. Communism accomplishes this fact by granting to each conquered nationality everything it desires—the national language, industrialization, mass education—except the crucial gift of political power. It is a grave mistake to think of communism as merely a more virulent form of Russian imperialism. The Communists say that Russia is their base of operations and that they mean to conquer the world. In Burnham's view, they mean what they say. Possession of the Russian base, with its immense reservoirs of population and raw material, together with the penetration so far achieved in the countries of the free world, give the Communists better than an even chance. If the democracies do not destroy communism, both at home and abroad, then communism will in the end destroy the democracies and rule the world. This is why Burnham entitles his book *The Struggle for the World*.

During recent years there has been much dispute about the question: has Communism taken over Russia, or Russia taken over Communism? Are we to understand Communism as primarily an international movement, acknowledging no fatherland, that happens to have had its chief local success to date in Russia; or are we to believe, as many analysts contend, that Communism is, or has become, no more than a new outward form for the older nationalism and imperialism of Russia?

These two views seem incompatible; and there seems at hand much evidence, especially from the last decade, for the second. It is a fact that the Russian communists control the world Communist movement. It is a fact that during the past ten years there has been within the Soviet Union a revival of Russian nationalist tradition. The cult of the traditional heroes of Russian history, tsars and soldiers and even legendary figures, has reappeared with official approval. Literature and the arts express pride in Russian themes. Tsarist military decorations, uniforms and even modes of address have been reinstated. The Orthodox Church has been permitted to resume a less hampered activity. During the war, internal propaganda stressed the patriotic defense of the holy motherland. In addition, many of the aims of Soviet foreign policy, both those achieved and those still in process, are seen to be continuations of the foreign policies of imperial Russia. . . .

The Communist world movement first came to complete power in the great and populous Russian empire. There is nothing surprising in the subsequent result that the Russian Communists became dominant in the world movement. This would have been true of the German Communists, if Germany had been the first nation conquered; or of the British Communists if it had been England. And the succeeding stage of Communist development would then have had a German or an English bias. Since 1917 the Russian Communists have had at their immediate disposal the greater percentage of the material substance of power—human beings, funds, lands, factories, armies. Naturally, so backed, their voices have been louder in international Communist councils than those of any others. Naturally, also, when it came to choices on international policy —in connection with Germany or China or Austria or Argentina—they would tend to support a decision which would be favorable to their own special interests, even if that decision meant difficulty for Communists in Germany or China or Argentina. The Russian Communists discovered, moreover, that to control the masses of the Russian people, to get them to endure uninterrupted sufferings and to die in wars, the symbols of Russian nationalism and even Russian religion were useful instruments.

But to conclude from this that international Communism is only "the Russian state party," an extension throughout the world of the Russian foreign office, and that Communism is "nothing but Russian imperialism," would be a disorienting mistake.

From the point of view of Communists themselves, Communist Russia is not a "national fatherland" in the ordinary sense, but a "fortress of the world revolution," just as a conquered trade union in a non-Communist country might be considered a pillbox, or a Communist cell in the State Department, a sentry post. The dispute between Trotsky and Stalin, so far as it was more than a struggle for personal power, was not over "world revolution" versus nationalism. Both Trotsky and Stalin, like all Communists, believed in both world revolution and the defense of a Communist Russia. The principal issue between them was a purely tactical problem. What percentage of Communist resources and energies should be assigned directly to the Russian fortress, and what to operations in the still unconquered sections of the earth? Trotsky argued for a faster pace, and for a bigger allotment to the non-Communist hinterland. Stalin wanted more time, and a relatively greater share given to increasing the armaments and strengthening the walls of the fortress already won.

The internal consolidation of the proletarian dictatorship in the U.S.S.R., the success achieved in the work of socialist construction, the growth of the influence and authority of the U.S.S.R. among the masses of the proletariat and the oppressed peoples of the colonies signify the continuation, intensification and expansion of the *international social revolution.* . . . The U.S.S.R. inevitably becomes the base of the world movement of all oppressed classes, the center of international revolution, the greatest factor in world history. In the U.S.S.R., the world proletariat for the first time acquires a country that is really its own. . . . The U.S.S.R. is the only fatherland of the international proletariat, the principal bulwark of its achievements and the most important factor for its international emancipation. . . .

These words are not from Trotsky, but from the 1928 Program of the Communist International, written under the direct supervision of Stalin.

Soviet patriotism, with its Russian component, is therefore not merely consistent with Communist internationalism, but obligatory upon genuine Communists. When the Communists conquered power in one nation, the strategy of the world Communist struggle for a monopoly of world power was thereby necessarily altered. Before that, Communists were against the governments of all nations, and for their overthrow. Thereafter the Communists had an existing state of their own; and every extension of the power or boundaries of that state became automatically an extension of world Communism. . . .

Soviet "neo-Russian" imperialism is thus identical with "revolutionary emancipation." Nor is it surprising that there is a continuity between Soviet imperialism and tsarist imperialism, since the general lines of both are in considerable part dictated by evident geopolitical considerations. Soviet state policy is identical with world Communist policy. That is why we can get light on Soviet policy by reading the New York *Daily Worker* and observing the activities of American Communists, just as we get light on American Communists by noting what the Soviet government is doing. . . .

Within the Soviet domain, there are, it is true, especially among the youth, some millions of total believers, whose minds and souls are shaped absolutely by the Communist myth. But there is every reason to think that this is not true of the majority of the people. The outside world may be led to believe that workers rule in Russia; but the Russian workers know by life that they are serfs and slaves. Comfortable American journalists can believe that Stalin liquidated counter-revolutionary kulaks as a class; but Russian peasants know that he tortured and killed and robbed their families and starved [their] neighbors. English and American preachers and diplomats can accept the confessions at the Moscow trials and complacently explain them as expressions of the peculiarities of the Russian soul; but Russians who knew and worked with the defendants understand that the confessions are fables of the N.K.V.D. [Soviet secret police]. French poets can rejoice at the unanimity of will shown by a Soviet election; but Russians know how that unanimity is obtained....

Let us ask: why are the secret police, the purges, and the prohibition of foreign travel considered necessary by the regime, and not merely admitted publicly in the controlled press, but constantly and spectacularly emphasized, especially in internal propaganda? The only possible explanation is that the regime recognizes the existence of profound mass discontent, however inarticulate and unorganized. If everyone, or nearly everyone, liked the regime, why would it be necessary to have the enormous secret police apparatus operating in every social, cultural, economic and political institution? Why would it be necessary to institute the periodic purges which, by the official accounts, involve hundreds of thousands, even millions, of persons, and often sweep away the entire staffs of magazines, theaters, movie trusts, factories, farms, party committees, commissariats, and so on, which in many cases, have been praised a few months before as the best defenders of the revolution? If the masses of the people believe Stalin to be the messiah that is described by our own fellow-travellers (exercising their decadent right of free speech from their vantage point of another continent), why, we may wonder, does Stalin need to make the attempt to get away from him a criminal offense?

The regime confronts here an insoluble dilemma. In order to propagate the Communist myth in the non-Communist world, it must swamp the ether, the newsstands and the bookstalls of all countries with the story of the happy, contented land of socialism. In order to terrorize its own unhappy subjects into submission, it must fill the columns of *Pravda, Izvestia,* and *Red Star* with denunciations of wrecking, sabotage, graft, "diversions," plots and deviations, on a scale so huge that it would

seem to indicate a belief by the regime that nine-tenths of the population must be criminals and traitors. Both versions are lies, but the second, in its own indirect way, informs us very plainly about the true relation between the regime and the people....

The internationalism of earlier Communism—of Communism while it was still comparatively weak, still a relatively isolated sect—was doctrinaire, abstract. It was based upon a presumed identity of international "class forces," independent of all national divisions. The Communists proclaimed that the masses had no true fatherland, that nationalism was just a trick whereby the class enemy forged heavier chains, that the main enemy was always one's own government, that sentiments of patriotism were shameful treachery to the revolution. These ideas were at variance both with reality and more especially with the deep traditional feelings of the masses. Consequently, this earlier internationalism, or rather anti-nationalism, often found itself crashing head on against the powerful sweep of national sentiment, which, far from subsiding, has reached a new intensity in our times. Potential recruits or followers of the Communists were offended and repelled by [this] anti-nationalism; it was a difficult barrier between Communism and "the mind of the masses."

Social Democracy, in accordance with Marx's own precepts, was also originally internationalist in this same doctrinaire sense, and met the same troubles. In 1914, at the outbreak of the First World War, Social Democracy ended the dilemma by succumbing to nationalism. Within each of the warring nations, the Socialists abandoned their previous abstract formulas about the unity of the workers of the world, the duty of opposing "their own" governments and fighting against "imperialist wars," and so on. They decided to be patriotic citizens and soldiers, fighting for their respective governments against the national enemies. The end result of this solution has been the disintegration of Social Democracy as an independent historical force. Social Democracy (called simply "socialism" in the United States), in any crisis such as war or revolution, henceforth became subordinated to one or another national state. Thus the Socialist parties in many of the Allied powers in the Second World War became the governmental leaders in the fight for national survival. After the war the British (Socialist) Labor party or the French Socialist party is first of all English or French, and only secondarily Socialist.

Communism has taken a different path, of far greater historical weight. It is not succumbing to nationalism, but absorbing nationalism, and thereby integrating into one movement two of the greatest—perhaps the two greatest—historical forces of the present age. There is here a typical "triumph of Stalinist realism." The Stalinist method has always been to try, as far as possible, to swim with the tide, never directly counter to it, but always to keep on top of the water, not to be dragged under. Since nationalist sentiments do exist, let us not weaken and isolate ourselves by bucking them, but rather let us exploit them, let us make them an avenue of approach to the masses instead of a wall of separation.

A decade ago the national flag, in each country, began to appear on party platforms along with the Red banner; comrades sang "The Star-Spangled Banner" or "God Save the King" as well as "The Internationale"; the portraits of the traditional patriotic heroes were hung beside those of Marx, Lenin and Stalin; the Communist school in New York was re-named "The Jefferson School," and the N.K.V.D. recruited a contingent for the Spanish civil war as "The Abraham Lincoln Brigade." The Red army, during the war, organized Czech divisions and Polish divisions and Hungarian and Spanish, and for that matter German divisions. Communism becomes a kind of world political chameleon, more American than Washington or Lincoln ("Communism is [twentieth-century] Americanism"), more French than Joan of Arc, more Chinese than Sun-Yat-sen, more German than Frederick—and, needless to say, more Russian than Peter the Great....

Stalin has written several tens of thousands of words about the national question; and on these there have been many million words of commentary. His "solution" of the national question, however, boils down to a very simple formula: grant nationalities everything expedient except power. Let them keep native costumes, songs, language, food, dances (it is all these that make big conferences in Moscow so colorful); anything so long as they do not have power. Power, under the Communist system, is a monopoly; that is the constant. The method was gradually worked out for the nationalities within the borders of the twelve original Soviet republics; it was extended to the four new republics formed during the war; and it is being used, with suitable adaptations and at various stages, for the nationalities that are brought under the expanding Communist influence. Many puzzling and seemingly irreconcilable features of present-day Communist policy make ready sense when they are understood in terms of multi-nationalism. It would, moreover, be a grave mistake to underestimate the power of this remarkable hybrid. Its career is not ended, but only beginning....

Part III of the Program of the International has as its title: "The ultimate aim of the Communist international—world Communism." The official *History of the Communist Party,* required reading for all Communists everywhere, declares: "Study of the history of the Communist party strengthens the certainty of the final victory of the great task of the Lenin-Stalin party: the victory of Communism in the whole world."

The fact that this is the Communists' belief, that world conquest is, in their own minds, their goal, is not, by itself, particularly important. There have been, and still are, other groups and even individuals who have believed in this same goal of world conquest. Several such individuals can be found in almost any insane asylum. There the belief is not taken seriously in objective terms. It is regarded as a delusion which, far from being coherently related to the total behavior of the maniac, is symptomatic of the breach between his diseased mind and its social environment.

The situation is analogous when this goal is professed, as it has often been, by small and weak sects. Then, too, it can be treated as a more or less troublesome delusion. It is not materially possible for the sect to do anything about the goal, and the rest of the world does not have to be concerned. Often the actions of the sect, in spite of the professed goal, do not have any positive relation to it; the grandiose goal is no more than an inverted answer to some obscure psychotic need. Implicit in at least one interpretation of the doctrines of Mohammedanism, Judaism, and even Calvinism is a goal of world conquest, but none of these groups is acting in practice to realize the goal; and none of them is in a material position to have a chance in this historical period to achieve it, even if they should attempt to do so. Therefore, in these cases also, the goal may be disregarded.

When, however, we find that a belief in the goal of world conquest is combined with both sufficient means to give a chance of achieving it, and actions which in fact work toward it, then the purpose must be taken quite literally, at face value. This was the case with Nazism; and it seems also to have been true of at least one section of the Shintoist-militarist Japanese leadership. It is much more obviously true of Communism. In Communist doctrine, there is not the slightest ambiguity about the goal of world conquest. In action, Communists work always and everywhere toward that goal. And at the present time the means at their disposal, in numbers, material resources, and psychological influence, are enough to give them a very substantial probability of reaching it.

However often this plain truth is repeated, very few of the leaders and citizens of the Democratic nations really believe it. They do not believe it, I suppose, because they do not want to believe it. It is, we may grant, an uncomfortable belief, putting a pistol to the will, and demanding just Yes or No as an answer. Nevertheless, and in spite of however many exorcisms by Henry Wallace or the Dean of Canterbury, it is true, and will continue to be true, until the issue is decided. . . .

Even if world empire were not the positive goal of Communism, it would, from the Communist standpoint, be a necessary aim as a defensive measure. The Communists believe, and have always believed, that there are only two alternatives for modern society: Communism or capitalism. In spite of what people may "subjectively" think, they are all "objectively" lined up on one side or the other: there is no in-between. When, therefore, Communism became a serious world force by conquering a large section of the earth and its inhabitants, an inescapable historical dilemma was presented. Either capitalism would destroy the new Communist world, or Communism would conquer the remainder of capitalism. (Somewhat paradoxically, the Communists hold the latter result to be in the long run "inevitable.") The showdown might be drawn out or for a while postponed, but it cannot be avoided. . . .

The Communist objectives in relation to the United States may be summed up as follows:

First, to try to prevent interference by the United States with the Communist plans for the consolidation of Fortress Eurasia, and even to gain United States assistance in fulfilling those plans.

Second, to weaken, undermine and demoralize the United States to the maximum extent possible prior to the open war struggle.

Third, to become imbedded within the social fabric of United States life in order to be ready for direct action—espionage, sabotage, stimulation of riots and revolts, etc.—when open war begins.

These objectives are furthered, of course, by Communist activities and propaganda throughout the world. Within the United States and its dependencies they are promoted by a powerful and complex network. Many Americans, understanding nothing of totalitarian politics, dismiss the

Communists as "a negligible force in American life," because the Communist party gets few votes in elections. For Communists, elections—particularly the vote one gets in elections—are among the most minor of political exertions. It might be recalled that in 1917, at the beginning of the Russian revolution, the Russian Bolshevik faction, which became the Communist party, numbered only about 25,000 members. In general it is a law of politics that a small minority, tightly organized and disciplined, knowing in advance what it wants and planning consciously how to get it, has far greater weight than loose, amorphous majorities. . . .

It is of course true that many of these rifts, or potential rifts, exist, independently of Communism, within the fabric of our society. There would be a Negro problem, a labor problem, a religious problem, a Jewish problem, if there were no Communist movement. It is further true that many good citizens, non-Communists and anti-Communists, concern themselves with these problems. Their concern, however, is to try to solve them. What they do not grasp is that the concern of the Communists—with whom they so often join their activities, frequently without themselves knowing of the united front into which they enter—is not to solve them but to make them insoluble. They do not understand that the Communists do not want to mend the nation, but to smash it beyond repair. The good citizen is glad to find Communist allies when he seeks, say, a fair trial for a Negro; he does not know that the Communist will use him for the precise purpose, not of helping the Negro, but of embittering and poisoning race relationships. The good citizen joins a committee to support, perhaps, the families of strikers; he does not know that the Communists in the committee have as their objective not the well-being of labor but the hopeless exaggeration of class conflicts, and the undermining of the American economy. Or the good citizen, as a humanitarian, joins some committee "for Soviet-American friendship," equally unaware that the function of the committee is to protect and defend not the peoples of Russia and the United States, but the Communist dictatorship today crushing the Russian people and tomorrow aiming for the people of America.

So, if all goes according to plan, the full war will open with the United States so isolated, and so internally weakened, divided, demoralized, that it will be unable even to make a good showing in the struggle. Meanwhile, in the war itself, with public Communist activities limited or abolished, the infiltrated divisions will be in a position to take direct action to break down the industrial and military machine, and the morale of the nation.

The downfall of the United States will remove the last great obstacle. The Communist world empire will begin.

B. Berdyaev: Communism as a New Version of Russian Orthodoxy, Autocracy, and Nationalism

We have next an exiled Russian whose approach to communism is diametrically opposed to that of Burnham. Nicholas Berdyaev was probably the most significant Orthodox theologian of the first half of the twentieth century; he also played a role in the existentialist school of philosophy after he took up residence in the West in 1922. In his *Origin of Russian Communism*, an excerpt of which is given below, Berdyaev expounds the thesis that communism, although it came to Russia from the West, was transformed by its Russian adherents into something more Russian than western. In the beginning, Marxism made little sense in Russia, for the industrial proletariat of which it spoke hardly existed there. But when Lenin, the organizer of the Bolshevik party, replaced the traditional but outworn Russian myth of the Third Rome with the new messianic myth of the international working class, and when he replaced a discredited tsarist autocracy with the dictatorship of the proletariat, he was able to reestablish a tottering and demoralized tsardom on a new, and firm, religious base. Thus for Berdyaev the ideological doctrine and the governmental practice of Soviet Russia are only secondarily Marxist or Communist. They derive mainly from the Russian past. The connection between communism and Russia is so far from being accidental that we can in fact affirm that the Soviet Union is old Russia writ large.

And in actual fact Russian Marxism, since it had arisen in a country still not industrialized and with no developed proletariat, was bound to be torn by a moral self-contradiction which weighed upon the conscience of many Russian socialists. How is it possible to desire the growth of capitalism, to welcome this growth, and at the same time to regard capitalism as an evil and a moral wrong against which every socialist is called to fight? This complicated question gives rise to moral conflict. The growth of capitalist industry in Russia presupposed the turning of the peasantry into a proletariat, depriving them of their means of production, i.e. reducing a considerable part of the nation to a condition of beggary.

This double-mindedness in assigning the values of capitalism and the bourgeoisie is to be seen in Marxism in its most classical form. Marx, in so far as he took his stand upon the evolutionary point of view and recognized the existence of various stages in history, to which different values are to be assigned, set a high value upon the mission of the bourgeoisie in the past and the role of capitalism in the development of the material strength of mankind. The whole conception of Marxism is very much dependent on the growth of capitalism and adjusts the messianic idea of the proletariat—which has nothing in common with science—to capitalist industry. Marxism believes that the factory, and the factory alone, will create

the new man.... But the first Russian Marxists were faced with a moral problem and a problem of cognition, and it set up a moral and logical conflict. We shall see that this moral conflict was decided only by Lenin and the Bolsheviks. It is precisely the Marxist Lenin who will assert the possibility of establishing socialism in Russia independently of the development of capitalism and before a working class of any great size was organized.

Plekhanov [the leader of the Mensheviks] declared himself against confusing the revolution which was to overthrow the absolute monarchy with the social revolution. He was opposed to a revolutionary socialist seizure of power, i.e. to the Communist revolution in the course it actually took. The social revolution must be waited for. The liberation of the workers should be the work of the workers themselves, not of a revolutionary clique. This needs an increase in the number of workers, the development of their consciousness; it presupposes a greater development of industry. Plekhanov was fundamentally the enemy of Bakuninism, which he regarded as a mixture of Fourier and Stenka Razin. He was opposed to sedition and conspiracy, to Jacobinism and belief in committees. A dictatorship can achieve nothing unless the working class has been prepared for revolution. He stresses the reactionary character of the peasant commune as a hindrance to economic development. One must rely upon the objective social process. Plekhanov did not accept the Bolshevik revolution, because he was always opposed to the seizure of power for which neither strength nor consciousness had been prepared. What is needed above all is the revolutionizing of thought, not an elemental upheaval, and a revolutionizing of the thought of the working class itself, not of a partisan organized minority.

But with such an application of Marxist principles to Russia, there would be long to wait for the social revolution. The very possibility of direct socialist activity in Russia would be made a matter of doubt. The revolutionary will might be finally crushed by intellectual theory. Thus, the more revolutionary-minded Russian Marxists were obliged to interpret Marxism in some other way and to set up other theories of the Russian revolution, to work out other tactics. In this wing of Russian Marxism, the revolutionary will overcame the intellectual theories and the armchair interpretation of Marxism. There occurred unnoticed a combination of the traditions of revolutionary Marxism with those of the old revolutionary outlook which had no desire to tolerate a capitalist stage in the development of Russia, with Chernishevsky, Bakunin, Nechaev, Tkachev. This time it was not Fourier but Marx who was united with Stenka Razin. The Marxists who were Bolsheviks stood much more clearly in the line of Russian tradition than those who were Mensheviks. On the basis of the evolutionary determinist interpretation of Marxism it is impossible to justify a proletarian socialist revolution in a peasant country, industrially backward and with a feebly developed working class. With such an understanding of Marxism one must rely first of all on a bourgeois revolution, on the development of capitalism and then, when the time comes, bring about the socialist revolution. This was not very favorable to the stimulation of the revolutionary will. . . .

This "orthodox" [Leninist] Marxism, which was in actual fact Marxism which had been changed by being given a Russian form, adopted primarily not the determinist, evolutionary scientific side of Marxism, but its messianic myth-creating religious side, which gave scope to the stimulation of the revolutionary will, and assigned a foremost place to the proletariat's revolutionary struggle as controlled by an organized minority, which was inspired by the conscious proletariat idea. This orthodox totalitarian Marxism always insisted on the preaching of materialist belief, but it contained strong idealist elements also. It showed how great was the authority of an idea over human life, if it is an integrated idea, and answers to the instincts of the masses. In Bolshevist Marxism the proletariat ceased to be an empir-

ical reality, for as an empirical reality the proletariat was a mere nothing; it was above all the idea of a proletariat that mattered, and those who became vehicles for the expression of this idea might be an insignificant minority. If this insignificant minority is entirely possessed by the gigantic idea of the proletariat, if its revolutionary will is stimulated, if it is well organized and disciplined, then it can work miracles; it can overpower the determinism which normally controls social life. And Lenin proved in practice that this is possible. He brought about the revolution in Marx's name, but not in Marx's way. The Communist revolution was brought about in Russia in the name of totalitarian Marxism—Marxism as the religion of the proletariat, but it was a contradiction of everything that Marx had said about the development of human society. It was not revolutionary *narodnichestvo* [a utopian peasant socialism], but orthodox totalitarian Marxism which succeeded in achieving the revolution, in which Russia skipped that stage of capitalist development which to the first Russian Marxists had appeared so unavoidable. And it was clear that this agreed with Russian tradition and the instincts of the people.

At that time the illusions of the revolutionary *narodnichestvo* had already been outlived; the myth about the peasantry had collapsed. The people had not accepted a revolutionary intelligentsia. A new revolutionary myth was needed. And the myth about the people was changed into the myth about the proletariat. Marxism broke up the conception of the people as an integral organism; it analysed it into classes with opposed interests. But in the myth of the proletariat, the myth of the Russian people arose in a new form. There took place, as it were, an identification of the Russian people with the proletariat, and of Russian messianism with proletarian messianism. The Soviet Russia of workers and peasants came into being. In it the notion of the people as a peasantry was combined with the idea of it as a proletariat, and that in spite of everything that had been said by Marx, who regarded the peasantry as a petty-bourgeois, reactionary class. Orthodox totalitarian Marxism forbade any reference to the opposition between the interests of the proletariat and those of the peasantry. That was the rock on which Trotsky struck, desiring as he did to be true to classical Marxism. The peasantry was declared to be a revolutionary class, although the Soviet Government had constantly to fight it, sometimes very bitterly. Lenin turned anew to the old tradition of Russian revolutionary thought. He pronounced that the industrial backwardness of Russia, the rudimentary character of its capitalism, is a great asset for the social revolution.

There will be no need to deal with a strong, organized bourgeoisie. There Lenin was obliged to repeat what Tkachev had said, and by no means what Engels had said. Bolshevism is much more traditional than is commonly supposed. It agreed with the distinctive character of the Russian historical process. There had taken place a Russification and orientalizing of Marxism. . . .

Lenin's purpose, which he followed up with unusual logical consistency, was the formation of a strong party representing a well organized and iron disciplined minority and relying upon the strength of its integrated revolutionary Marxist outlook. The party had to have a doctrine in which nothing whatever is to be changed and it had to prepare for dictatorship over life as a complete whole. The very organization of the party, which was centralized in the extreme, was a dictatorship on a small scale. Every member of the party was subjected to this dictatorship of the center. The Bolshevik party which Lenin built up in the course of many years was to provide the pattern of the future organization of the whole of Russia, and in actual fact Russia was organized on the pattern of the Bolshevik party organization. The whole of Russia, the whole Russian people, was subjected not only to the dictatorship of the Communist party but also to the dictatorship of the Communist dictator, in thought and in conscience. Lenin denied freedom within the party and this denial

of freedom was transferred to the whole of Russia.

This is indeed the dictatorship of a general outlook for which Lenin had prepared. He was able to do this only because he combined in himself two traditions: the tradition of the Russian revolutionary intelligentsia in its most maximalist tendency, and the tradition of Russian Government in its most despotic aspect. The Social Democrat Mensheviks and the Socialist Revolutionaries remained in the stream of the first tradition only, and that in a mitigated form. But combining in himself traditions which in the nineteenth century had been in mortal conflict, Lenin was able to fashion a scheme for the organization of a Communist state and to realize it. However paradoxical it may sound, still Bolshevism is the third appearance of Russian autocratic imperialism; its first appearance being the Muscovite Tsardom and its second the Petrine Empire. Bolshevism stands for a strong centralized state. A union was achieved of the will to social justice and the will to political power, and the second will was the stronger. Bolshevism entered into Russian life as a power which was militarized in the highest degree, but the old Russian state also had always been militarized.

The problem of power was fundamental with Lenin and all his followers; it distinguished the Bolsheviks from all other revolutionaries. They too created a police state, in its methods of government very like the old Russian state. But to organize government, to subject to it the laboring and peasant masses, could not be a matter of the use of armed force alone, or of sheer coercion. An integrated doctrine was needed, a consistent general outlook, and symbols which held the state together were required. In the Muscovite Tsardom and in the empire the people were held together by a unity of religious faith; so also a new single faith had to be expressed for the masses in elementary symbols. Marxism in its Russian form was wholly suitable for this. . . .

Lenin did not believe in man. He recognized in him no sort of inward principle;

he did not believe in spirit and the freedom of the spirit, but he had a boundless faith in the social regimentation of man. He believed that a compulsory social organization could create any sort of new man you like, for instance, a completely social man who would no longer need the use of force. Marx believed the same thing, that the new man could be manufactured in factories. This was Lenin's utopianism, but it was a utopianism which could be and was realized. One thing he did not foresee; he did not foresee that class oppression might take an entirely different form, quite unlike its capitalist form. The dictatorship of the proletariat, having increased the power of the state, is developing a colossal bureaucracy which spreads like a network over the whole country and brings everything into subjection to itself. This new Soviet bureaucracy is more powerful than that of the tsarist regime. It is a new privileged class which can exploit the masses pitilessly. This is happening. An ordinary workman very often receives 75 roubles a month, but a Soviet civil servant, a specialist, gets 1,600 roubles a month, and this portentous inequality exists in a Communist state. Soviet Russia is a country of state capitalism which is capable of exploitation no less than private capitalism. The transitional period may be drawn out indefinitely. Those who are in power in it acquire a taste for power and desire no changes, which are unavoidable for the final realization of Communism. The will-to-power becomes satisfying in itself and men will fight for it as an end and not as a means.

All this was beyond Lenin's view. In this he was particularly utopian and very naive. The Soviet state has become like any other despotic state. It uses the same methods of falsehood and violence. It is first and foremost a state of the military police kind. Its international politics are as like the diplomacy of bourgeois states as two peas. The Communist revolution was distinctively Russian, but the miraculous birth of the new life did not take place. The old Adam has remained and continues to act, if in another form. . . .

Bolshevism made use of everything for its own triumph. It made use of the weakness of the Liberal Democratic government [of 1917], of the unsuitability of its watchwords to weld the insurgent masses together. It made use of the objective impossibility of carrying on the war any longer when the spirit of it was hopelessly lost by the unwillingness of the soldiers to go on fighting, and it proclaimed peace. It made use of the disorganization and discontent of the peasantry and divided all the land among the peasants, destroying what was left of feudalism and the dominance of the nobility. It made use of the Russian traditions of government by imposition, and instead of an unfamiliar Democracy of which they had had no experience it proclaimed a dictatorship which was more like the old rule of the tsar. It made use of the characteristics of the Russian spirit in all its incompatibility with a secularized bourgeois society. It made use of its religious instinct, its dogmatism and maximalism, its search after social justice and the kingdom of God upon earth, its capacity for sacrifice and the patient bearing of suffering, and also of its manifestations of coarseness and cruelty. It made use of Russian messianism, which still remained, though in an unconscious form, and of the Russian faith in Russia's own path of development. It made use of the historic cleavage between the masses and the cultured classes, of the popular mistrust of the intelligentsia, and it easily destroyed such of the intelligentsia as did not submit to it.

It absorbed also the sectarian spirit of the Russian intelligentsia and Russian *narodnichestvo* while transforming them in accordance with the requirements of a new epoch. It fitted in with the absence among the Russian people of the Roman view of property and the bourgeois virtues; it fitted in with Russian collectivism which had its roots in religion; it made use of the breakdown of patriarchal life among the people and the dissolution of the old religious beliefs. It also set about spreading the new revolution by methods of violence from above, as Peter had done in his time;

it denied human freedom, which had been unknown to the masses before, and had been the privilege of the upper cultured classes of society, and for which the masses had certainly not been roused to fight. It proclaimed the necessity of the integral totalitarian outlook of a dominant creed, which corresponded with the habits, experience and requirements of the Russian people in faith and in the dominating principles of life. The Russian spirit is not prone to scepticism, and a sceptical liberalism suits it less than anything. The spirit of the people could very readily pass from one integrated faith to another integrated faith, from one orthodoxy to another orthodoxy which embraced the whole of life. Russia passed from the old Middle Ages to the new Middle Ages, avoiding the ways of the new history with its secularization, its differentiation of various fields of culture, with its liberalism, its individualism, its triumph of the bourgeoisie and of capitalism.

The old consecrated Russian empire fell and a new one was formed, also a consecrated empire, an inverted theocracy. Marxism, itself so un-Russian in origin and character, assumed a Russian style, an oriental style approaching Slavophilism. Even the old Slavophil's dream of transferring the capital from St. Petersburg to Moscow, to the Kremlin, was realized by the Red Communists, and Russian Communism proclaimed anew that old idea of the Slavophils and Dostoyevsky—*ex Oriente lux*. Light proceeds from Moscow, from the Kremlin, a light to lighten the bourgeois darkness of the West. At the same time Communism creates a despotic and bureaucratic state, called into being to dominate the whole life of the people, not only in body but also in soul, in accord with the traditions of Ivan the Terrible and the rule of the tsars. Marxism in its Russian form proclaims the dominance of politics over economics, the power of the government to change the life of the country in any way it likes. In its grandiose schemes which were always on a world-wide scale, Communism makes use of the Russian disposition for making plans and castle-building which had hitherto had no scope for realization or practical application. Lenin desired to overcome Russian sloth, the product of the life of the gentry and of serfdom, to conquer Oblomov and Rudin, the "superfluous people," and in this positive task it seems he was successful.

A metamorphosis had taken place, i.e. an Americanization of the Russian people, the production of a new type of practical man with whom daydreaming and castle-building passed into action and constructiveness, of a technician, a bureaucrat of a new type. But here also the special characteristics of the Russian spirit had their say. The faith of the people was given a new direction, the Russian peasants now reverence the machine as a totem. Technical undertakings are not the ordinary matter-of-fact customary affair that they are to Western people; they have been given a mystic character and linked on with plans for an almost cosmic revolution. . . .

The Russian people [had] not realized their messianic idea of Moscow the Third Rome. The ecclesiastical schism of the seventeenth century revealed that the Muscovite tsardom is not the Third Rome: still less, of course, was the Petersburg empire a realization of the idea of the Third Rome. In it a final cleavage took place. The messianic idea of the Russian people assumed either an apocalyptic form or a revolutionary; and then there occurred an amazing event in the destiny of the Russian people. Instead of the Third Rome in Russia, the Third International was achieved, and many of the features of the Third Rome pass over to the Third International. The Third International is also a consecrated realm, and it also is founded on an orthodox faith. The fact that the Third International is not international but a Russian national idea is very poorly understood in the West. Here we have the transformation of Russian messianism. Western Communists, when they join the Third International, play a humiliating part; they do not understand that in joining the Third International they are joining the Russian people and the realizing its messianic vocation.

I have heard that at a French Communist meeting a French Communist asserted, "Marx said that the workmen have no fatherland. This used to be true, but now it is no longer true; they have a fatherland, that is, Russia, Moscow, and the workers should defend their fatherland." This is absolutely true and ought to be understood by everybody. Something has happened which Marx and the Western Marxists could not have foreseen, and that is a sort of identification of the two messianisms, the messianism of the Russian people and the messianism of the proletariat. The Russian working class and peasantry are a proletariat; and the proletariat of the whole world from France to China is becoming the Russian people—a unique people in the world; and the messianic consciousness of the working class

and proletariat is bringing about an almost Slavophil attitude towards the West. The West is always identified with the bourgeoisie and capitalism. The nationalization of Russian Communism, to which all bear witness, has its course in the fact that Communism has come into existence in only one country, in Russia, and the Communist realm is surrounded by bourgeois capitalist states. A Communist revolution in a single country inevitably leads to nationalism and a nationalist standpoint in political relations with other countries.... In Soviet Russia now they talk about the socialist fatherland and they want to defend it; they are ready to sacrifice their lives for it. But the socialist fatherland is still the same Russia, and in Russia perhaps popular patriotism is coming into being for the first time....

Nicholas Berdyaev, *The Origin of Russian Communism*, trans. R. M. French, new ed. (London: Geoffrey Bles, Ltd., 1948), pp. 102–4, 106–7, 117–21, 127–28, 140–42, 144–45. By permission of Geoffrey Bles, Ltd., and The University of Michigan Press.

C. Toynbee: Communism as Russian Weapon Against a Technologically Superior West

To the presentations of Burnham and Berdyaev we now add a third point of view. For the noted British historian Arnold Toynbee, communism is neither an international conspiracy, accidentally based on Russia, nor a modernized form of Russian messianic nationalism and imperialism. Communism is rather a spiritual weapon which Russia has found useful in fighting (or fighting off) the West. The conflict between Russia and the West goes back to the Middle Ages. It has been marked, in the first place, by constant western aggression against Russia and, in the second, by the standing technological inferiority of the power attacked. To preserve their independence against the West, the Russians have had to put up with a tyrannical government capable of mobilizing the whole of the national resources in the defense of the fatherland and of trying to keep up with western technology by forced marches. This last has proved difficult, for the West has continued to put itself through more and more complex

technological revolutions, successively replacing the musket with the machine gun, and the machine gun with the thermonuclear missile. Only when the Russians found an ideological weapon of great force did the battle proceed on more or less even terms. By the adoption of the western heresy we call communism, Russia has finally offset the technological superiority of the West. This heresy disorients the West by the acerbity and accuracy of its criticism; it appeals to the discontented and the deprived and thus brings about the formation of fifth columns within the advanced states of the West; and it attracts the former colonial peoples of the free world, who fear imperialism and resent the wealth of the West.

Let us begin with Russia's experience, for Russia is part of the world's great non-Western majority. Though the Russians have been Christians and are, many of them, Christians still, they have never been Western Christians. Russia was converted not from Rome, as England was, but from Constantinople; and, in spite of their common Christian origins, Eastern and Western Christendom have always been foreign to one another, and have often been mutually antipathetic and hostile, as Russia and the West unhappily still are today, when each of them is in what one might call a "post-Christian" phase of its history.

This on the whole unhappy story of Russia's relations with the West did, though, have a happier first chapter; for, in spite of the difference between the Russian and the Western way of life, Russia and the West got on fairly well with one another in the early Middle Ages. The peoples traded, and the royal families intermarried. An English King Harold's daughter, for instance, married a Russian prince. The estrangement began in the thirteenth century, after the subjugation of Russia by the Tatars. The Tatars' domination over Russia was temporary, because the Tatars were nomads from the steppes who could not ever make themselves at home in Russia's fields and forests. Russia's lasting losses as a result of this temporary Tatar conquest were, not to her Tatar conquerors, but to her Western neighbors; for these took advantage of Russia's prostration in order to lop off, and annex to Western Christendom, the western fringes of the Russian world in White Russia and in the western half of the Ukraine. It was not till 1945 that Russia recaptured the last piece of these huge Russian territories that were taken from her by Western powers in the thirteenth and fourteenth centuries.

These Western conquests at Russia's expense in the late Middle Ages had an effect on Russia's life at home, as well as on her relations with her Western assailants. The pressure on Russia from the West did not merely estrange Russia from the West; it was one of the hard facts of Russian life that moved the Russians to submit to the yoke of a new native Russian power at Moscow which, at the price of autocracy, imposed on Russia the political unity that she now had to have if she was to survive. It was no accident that this newfangled autocratic centralizing government of Russia should have arisen at Moscow; for Moscow stood in the fairway

of the easiest line for the invasion of what was left of Russia by a Western aggressor. The Poles in 1610, the French in 1812, the Germans in 1941, all marched this way. Since an early date in the fourteenth century, autocracy and centralization have been the dominant notes of all successive Russian regimes. This Moscovite Russian political tradition has perhaps always been as disagreeable for the Russians themselves as it has certainly been distasteful and alarming to their neighbors; but unfortunately the Russians have learned to put up with it, partly perhaps out of sheer habit, but also, no doubt, because they have felt it to be a lesser evil than the alternative fate of being conquered by aggressive neighbors.

This Russian attitude of resignation towards an autocratic regime that has become traditional in Russia is, of course, one of the main difficulties, as we Westerners see it, in the relations between Russia and the West today. The great majority of people in the West feel that tyranny is an intolerable social evil. At a fearful cost we have put down tyranny when it has raised its head among our Western selves in the forms of Fascism and National Socialism. We feel the same detestation and distrust of it in its Russian form, whether this calls itself tsarism or calls itself Communism. We do not want to see this Russian brand of tyranny spread; and we are particularly concerned about this danger to Western ideals of liberty now that we Franks find ourselves thrown upon the defensive for the first time in our history since the second Turkish siege of Vienna in 1682–3. Our present anxiety about what seems to us to be a post-war threat to the West from Russia is a well-justified anxiety in our belief. At the same time, we must take care not to allow the reversal in the relation between Russia and the West since 1945 to mislead us into forgetting the past in our natural preoccupation with the present. When we look at the encounter between Russia and the West in the historian's instead of the journalist's perspective, we shall see that, over a period of several centuries ending in 1945, the Russians have had the same reason for looking askance at the West that we Westerners feel that we have for looking askance at Russia today.

During the last few centuries, this threat to Russia from the West, which has been a constant threat from the thirteenth century till 1945, has been made more serious for Russia by the outbreak, in the West, of a technological revolution which has become chronic and which does not yet show any signs of abating.

When the West adopted fire-arms, Russia followed suit, and in the sixteenth century she used these new weapons from the West to conquer the Tatars in the Volga valley and more primitive peoples in the Urals and in Siberia. But in 1610 the superiority of the Western armaments of the day enabled the Poles to occupy Moscow and to hold it for two years, while at about the same time the Swedes were also able to deprive Russia of her outlet on the Baltic sea at the head of the Gulf of Finland. The Russian retort to these seventeenth-century Western acts of aggression was to adopt the technology of the West wholesale, together with as much of the Western way of life as was inseparable from Western technology.

It was characteristic of the autocratic centralizing Muscovite regime that this technological and accompanying social revolution in Russia at the turn of the seventeenth and eighteenth centuries should have been imposed upon Russia from above downwards, by the fiat of one man of genius, Peter the Great. Peter is a key figure for an understanding of the world's relations with the West not only in Russia but everywhere; for Peter is the archetype of the autocratic Westernizing reformer who, during the last two and a half centuries, has saved the world from falling entirely under Western domination by forcing the world to train itself to resist Western aggression with Western weapons. Sultans Selim III and Mahmud II and President Mustafa Kemal Atatürk in Turkey, Mehmed 'Ali Pasha in Egypt, and "the Elder Statesmen," who made the Westernizing revolution in Japan in the

eighteen-sixties, were, all of them, following in Peter the Great's footsteps consciously or unconsciously.

Peter launched Russia on a technological race with the West which Russia is still running. Russia has never yet been able to afford to rest, because the West has continually been making fresh spurts. For example, Peter and his eighteenth-century successors brought Russia close enough abreast of the Western world of the day to make Russia just able to defeat her Swedish Western invaders in 1709 and her French Western invaders in 1812; but, in the nineteenth-century Western industrial revolution, the West once more left Russia behind, so that in the First World War Russia was defeated by her German Western invaders as she had been defeated, two hundred years earlier, by the Poles and the Swedes. The present Communist autocratic government was able to supplant the tsardom in Russia in consequence of Russia's defeat by an industrial Western technology in 1914–17; and the Communist regime then set out, from 1928 to 1941, to do for Russia, all over again, what the Tsar Peter had done for her about 230 years earlier.

For the second time in the modern chapter of her history Russia was now put, by an autocratic ruler, through a forced march to catch up with a Western technology that had once more shot ahead of hers; and Stalin's tyrannical course of technological Westernization was eventually justified, like Peter's, through an ordeal by battle. The Communist technological revolution in Russia defeated the German invaders in the Second World War, as Peter's technological revolution had defeated the Swedish invaders in 1709 and the French invaders in 1812. And then, a few months after the completion of the liberation of Russian soil from German Western occupation in 1945, Russia's American Western allies dropped in Japan an atom bomb that announced the outbreak of a third Western technological revolution. So today, for the third time, Russia is having to make a forced march in an effort to catch up with a Western technology that, for the third time, has left her behind by shooting ahead. The result of this third event in the perpetual competition between Russia and the West still lies hidden in the future; but it is already clear that this renewal of the technological race is another of the very serious difficulties now besetting the relations between these two ex-Christian societies.

Technology is, of course, only a long Greek name for a bag of tools; and we have to ask ourselves: What are the tools that count in this competition in the use of tools as means to power? A power-loom or a locomotive is obviously a tool for this purpose, as well as a gun, an aeroplane, or a bomb. But all tools are not of the material kind; there are spiritual tools as well, and these are the most potent that man has made. A creed, for instance, can be a tool; and, in the new round in the competition between Russia and the West that began in 1917, the Russians this time threw into their scale of the balances a creed that weighed as heavily against their Western competitors' material tools as, in the Roman story of the ransoming of Rome from the Gauls, the sword thrown in by Brennus weighed against the Roman gold.

Communism, then, is a weapon; and, like bombs, aeroplanes, and guns, this is a weapon of Western origin. If it had not been invented by a couple of nineteenth-century Westerners, Karl Marx and Friedrich Engels, who were brought up in the Rhineland and spent the best part of their working lives in London and in Manchester respectively, Communism could never have become Russia's official ideology. There was nothing in the Russian tradition that could have led the Russians to invent Communism for themselves; and it is certain that they would never have dreamed of it if it had not been lying, ready-made, there in the West, for a revolutionary Russian regime to apply in Russia in 1917.

In borrowing from the West a Western ideology, besides a Western industrial revolution, to serve as an anti-Western weapon, the Bolsheviki in 1917 were making a great new departure in Russian history; for this was the first time that Russia had ever borrowed a creed from the West. We have already noticed that Christianity had come to Russia, not from the West, but from Byzantium, where Christianity had a distinctive, non-Western form and spirit; and a fifteenth-century Western attempt to impose Western Christianity on Russia had been a failure. In A.D. 1439, at an ecclesiastical council held at Florence, representatives of the Eastern Orthodox Church in what then still remained of the Byzantine empire had unwillingly recognized the ecclesiastical supremacy of the Roman see in the hope that, in return, the Western world would save Constantinople from conquest by the Turks. The metropolitan archbishop of Moscow, who was a suffragan of the Greek patriarch of Constantinople, had been attending the Council, and he had voted the same way as his brethren who were representing the Greek Orthodox church; but when he came home to Moscow, his recognition of the pope's supremacy was repudiated there and he himself was deposed.

Two hundred and fifty years later, when Peter the Great went to the West to learn the "know-how" of Western technology, there was no longer any question of Russia's being required to adopt a Western form of Christianity as the price of being initiated into the secrets of Western technological efficiency. Before the end of the seventeenth century there had been a revulsion in the West, not merely against religious fanaticism, but against religion itself, in consequence of the West's weariness of its own domestic wars of religion. The Western world, whose apprentice Russia became in Peter's day, was thus an irreligious world, and the sophisticated minority of Russians who became the agents of the Westernization of Russia followed the example of their sophisticated Western contemporaries by turning lukewarm towards the Russian form of Christianity without adopting any Western form of Christianity instead. So, in adopting Communism in 1917, Russia was making a breach with her traditions by taking up a Western creed for the first time in her history.

The reader will also have noticed that this Western creed, which Russia did take up in 1917, was one that was particularly well suited to serve Russia as a Western weapon for waging an anti-Western spiritual warfare. In the West, where Communism had arisen, this new creed was a heresy. It was a Western criticism of the West's failure to live up to her own Christian principles in the economic and social life of this professedly Christian society; and a creed of Western origin which was at the same time an indictment of Western practice was, of course, just the spiritual weapon that an adversary of the West would like to pick up and turn against its makers. With this Western spiritual weapon in her hands, Russia could carry her war with the West into the enemy's country on the spiritual plane. Since Communism had originated as a product of uneasy Western consciences, it could appeal to other uneasy Western consciences when it was radiated back into the Western world by a Russian propaganda. And so now, for the first time in the modern Western world's history since the close of the seventeenth century, when the flow of Western converts to Islam almost ceased, the West has again found itself threatened with spiritual disintegration from inside, as well as with an assault from outside. In thus threatening to undermine the Western civilization's foundation on the West's own home ground, Communism has already proved itself a more effective anti-Western weapon in Russian hands than any material weapon could ever be.

Communism has also served Russia as a weapon for bringing into the Russian camp the Chinese quarter of the human race, as well as other sections of that majority of mankind that is neither Russian nor Western. We know that the outcome of the struggle to win the allegiance of these neutrals may be decisive for the outcome of the Russo-Western conflict as a whole, because this non-Western and non-Russian majority of mankind may prove to hold the casting vote in a com-petition between Russia and the West for world power. Now Communism can make a twofold appeal to a depressed Asian, African, and Latin American peasantry when it is the voice of Russia that is commending Communism to them. The Russian spokesman can say to the Asian peasantry first: "If you follow the Russian example, Communism will give you the strength to stand up against the West, as a Communist Russia can already stand up against the West today." The second appeal of Communism to the Asian peasantry is Communism's claim that it can, and that private enterprise neither can nor would if it could, get rid of the extreme inequality between a rich minority and a poverty-stricken majority in Asian countries. Discontented Asians, however, are not the only public for whom Communism has an appeal. Communism also has an appeal for all men, since it can claim to offer mankind the unity which is our only alternative to self-destruction in an atomic age.

It looks as if, in the encounter between Russia and the West, the spiritual initiative, though not the technological lead, has now passed, at any rate for the moment, from the Western to the Russian side. We Westerners cannot afford to resign ourselves to this, because this Western heresy—Communism—which the Russians have taken up, seems to the great majority of people in the West to be a perverse, misguided, and disastrous doctrine and way of life. A theologian might put it that our great modern Western heresiarch Karl Marx has made what is a heretic's characteristic intellectual mistake and moral aberration. In putting his finger on one point in orthodox practice in which there has been a crying need for reform, he had lost sight of all other considerations and therefore has produced a remedy that is worse than the disease.

The Russians' success in capturing the initiative from us Westerners by taking up this Western heresy called Communism and radiating it out into the world in a cloud of anti-Western poison-gas does not, of course, mean that Communism is destined to prevail. Marx's vision seems, in non-Marxian eyes, far too narrow and too badly warped to be likely to prove permanently satisfying to human hearts and minds. All the same, Communism's success, so far as it has gone, looks like a portent of things to come. What it does tell us is that the present encounter between the world and the West is now moving off the technological plane on to the spiritual plane. . . .

Arnold Toynbee, *The World and the West* (London: Oxford University Press, 1953), pp. 4–16.

II. *Communism Spreads Outside Russia*

The great advances of communism have come in the aftermath of war. Communism appeared in Russia as the immediate consequence of the breakdown of the tsarist military effort in World War I. For a few years thereafter communism threatened the European countries adjacent to Russia, but by the early 1920s it was apparent that, for the time being, victory would be limited to Russia and to Outer Mongolia, which turned Communist in 1924.

The second great advance of communism was closely associated with the forward movement of the Soviet armies at the conclusion of World War II, although three states, Estonia, Latvia and Lithuania, had acquired formal status as Soviet republics in the early months of the war. In Europe the line of Communist advance turned out to be almost identical with the area of Soviet military occupation. Attempts to push across this line, as in the guerrilla war in Greece, ended in failure. In Asia the decisive fact was the victory of communism in mainland China which came as the result of years of war and civil war, in which the Russians had a negligible role. This victory was followed by Chinese-inspired guerrilla efforts in Vietnam, Malaya. and the Philippines; in time even the Soviet-established Communist regime of North Korea came under Chinese influence.

After the experience of two world wars it seemed reasonable for Communists to believe that a third would bring the final triumph. Certainly such a proposition was in accordance with what Marx had taught. In the late 1950s, however, the Russians undertook to revise the traditional doctrine. They argued that with the advent of thermonuclear weapons, which even the great Lenin could not have foreseen, warfare had become so destructive as to make the cost of final victory through war prohibitively high. Nor could Lenin, the Russians argued, have foreseen that the emergence of a mighty Socialist camp would slowly shift the balance of power so that the capitalist states would be forced by the logic of events to surrender one key position after another until their power had finally crumbled. Victory would come through the waging of cold war. The Chinese, on the other hand, stood by the traditional doctrine, and accused the Russian comrades of the grievous sins of revisionism, underestimation of the revolutionary masses, overestimation of the enemy, and plain cowardice. This difference of view over the best strategy for the further spread of communism was one of the major issues in the great schism in the Bloc and movement. Thus the Communists themselves could no longer agree on how the final triumph was to be achieved.

In the wake of World War II some fifteen states were, as we have already pointed out, added to the Communist roster by one device or other. There were an additional seven or eight cases (perhaps equally interesting from our point of view) in which the Communists attempted to seize power but failed. With so many successes and so many failures in such widely disparate areas to choose from, we have selected the three revolutions which have had the greatest influence on the movement as a whole. In Yugoslavia the Communists have developed a special brand of communism frequently referred to as "national." This was after they had been expelled from the Socialist camp in 1948, and declared heretical. In a mood of defiance, bolstered by substantial doses of western aid, the Yugoslav Communists developed a regime widely divergent from the Muscovite pattern, with an independent foreign policy, a private agriculture, a semi-market economy, and something resembling the rule of law. This deviant Yugoslav regime became a major bone of contention between the Chinese and the Russians, particularly as the latter tended after 1955 to imitate some of Yugoslavia's heretical practices.

Chinese communism has been selected because it is the communism of the second major country to have joined the camp. In little more than a decade China ended by forming a camp of her own, orthodox, anti-Soviet, and propagating (if you please!) a poor man's communism, if not a colored man's communism, not only in Asia but throughout the world. It is difficult to foresee the role which China will play over the long run in the advance of communism; if in forty years this nation of nearly a billion people, the most populous on earth, were to become as highly industrialized as Soviet Russia, the effect on the balance of international power would be little less than revolutionary.

Finally, we have chosen the case of communism in Cuba, which involves a number of important "firsts." Cuba was the first country whose communism could not be attributed to the immediate aftermath of war. It was the first instance of a country overseas, i.e. not located on the Eurasian land mass in close proximity to other Communist states, developing a Communist regime. It was also the first time a successful Communist revolution had taken place without the Communist party having played a major role: Castro first seized power and then turned to the Soviet bloc for support, in the process converting his regime to the "people's democratic" variety of socialism. It is plain that the Cuban case can add a new dimension to our understanding of the dynamics of communism.

A. Burks: Yugoslav Communism as a Resolution of Ethnic Conflict

In his *Dynamics of Communism in Eastern Europe,* R. V. Burks, an American historian, has attempted to assemble the evidence concerning the social origins and character of the Communist parties and movements in the area of the People's Democracies. In his treatment of Yugoslavia, Burks argues that the Communist movement, far from representing an almost nonexistent working class, had its roots in a variety of factors not foreseen by either Marx or Lenin. For one thing, there was communism among the Yugoslavs because of a traditional sympathy for the Russians, a fellow Slavic people to whom the numerically weaker South Slavs had frequently looked for assistance in their age-long battle against foreign oppressors. For another thing, after 1943, it was clear that Soviet Russia was on the winning side and would

have a major voice in whatever political settlement was to emerge from the Yugoslav civil war being fought in the midst of Axis occupation. Most importantly, however, communism fed on the conflict between the Serbs, who dominated the state apparatus and the army, and such dissident national groups as the Croats, the Montenegrins, and the Slavo-Macedonians. In the interwar underground, communism became a vehicle for resistance to Serb rule, and in the conditions of Axis occupation, it became a platform for the development of a new Yugoslav nationalism, one which included all South Slavs as equals and which, at least for the period of guerrilla fighting, overcame the traditional animosities between the variegated ethnic groups who make up the population of Yugoslavia. It was the resolution of ethnic conflict as much as any other factor, Burks suggests in the following passage, which accounts for the triumph of communism in Yugoslavia. The student will ponder the connection between a Communist movement which by war's end incorporated a new brand of nationalism, and the development of a national deviation by the Tito regime after 1948.

Yugoslavia was overrun in April; Russia was invaded in June. In July there was a guerrilla rising in the hills of Serbia. The Germans were taken by surprise. In this uprising, the joint product of a simmering hatred for the Germans and a stormy outburst of sympathy for the Russians (and a glowing pride in them), there were two guerrilla armies. One was commanded by a Serbian officer of the line, Draza Mihailovic; the other by a professional revolutionary of mixed Croatian and Slovenian ancestry, Josip Broz. In the early weeks of fighting, the guerrillas achieved notable success, but by November they were fighting each other as well as the Germans; when the latter brought up reinforcements, both the Partisans of Tito and the Chetniks of Mihailovic were badly beaten.

Draza Mihailovic drew from this defeat the lesson that active resistance against the Axis did not pay. Open acts of resistance led inevitably to German reprisals against the civilian population; the Serbs could easily be decimated and so lose their numerical preponderance and their political hegemony within Yugoslavia. The outcome of the war would not be decided in the backwoods of the Balkans, a minor theater at best. As time progressed, and Tito began to receive assistance from the Western allies, Mihailovic began to fear that allied victory would mean the triumph of Communism in Yugoslavia and the end of Serb rule. The Serbian leader therefore came to collaborate with the Germans and the Italians, hoping to achieve a local decision which the advancing Russians would not be able to reverse. That in this policy Mihailovic had the tacit assent of the population of Serbia is indicated by the fact that, until the very last months of the war, the Partisan movement in Serbia proper was insignificant.

Upon the defeat of the 1941 uprising in Serbia, Tito withdrew his battered forces into the highlands of Bosnia. His theatre of action from 1941 to 1944 was in fact the zone of the Dinaric Alps, a food deficit area whose population had a long tradition of guerrilla resistance against the Turk. He and his shoeless, ragged, half-starved warriors, only some 20,000 strong during the worst of the fighting, marched from Montenegro to the bleak hills of northwestern Bosnia and back south again, fighting not only the Germans and Italians but the Croatian *Ustashe* and the Serbian Chetniks as well.

In contrast to Mihailovic, who fought for the interests of the Serbs, as he understood those interests, Tito campaigned on a platform of pan-South Slav nationalism. At a time when Yugoslavia had been broken up more or less into her component ethnic parts, the federalist doctrine of the Communists created a haven in which the idea of Yugoslav nationalism could take refuge. Meeting at Jajce (central Bosnia) in November 1943, Tito's Anti-Fascist Council of National Liberation proclaimed:

"1. The peoples of Yugoslavia do not recognize and never have recognized the partition of Yugoslavia by Fascist imperialists, but have proved in the common armed struggle their firm will to remain united in Yugoslavia.

"2. In order to carry out the principle of sovereignty of the nation of Yugoslavia and in order that Yugoslavia may be the true home of all its people, and no longer an arena for the machinations of reactionary influences, Yugoslavia is being built up on a federal principle which will ensure full equality for the nations of Serbia, Croatia, Slovenia, Macedonia, Montenegro, Bosnia, and Herzegovina."

The envoy of Prime Minister Winston Churchill to the Partisans, Fitzroy Maclean, was astonished by the strength of the national feeling which animated these men, by their faith in the rebirth of Yugoslavia. Maclean wondered whether the Communist Tito disguised himself as a nationalist in order to impose his social extremism, or whether his Communism was only an instrument for the realization of a national front dominating all particularisms. The struggle between Tito and Mihailovic, between Partisan and Chetnik, had come to revolve around the alternative of Serbian hegemony versus a Communist Yugoslav nationalism.

The Partisan army

Ethnically speaking, who were the men who fought under Tito's banner? During the 1941 rising, they were primarily *Srbijanci*, Serbs of Serbia, composed mainly of townsfolk from Belgrad. As the defeated Partisans retreated from Serbia into Bosnia, they were met by a stream of *prechani*[1] refugees fleeing massacres organized by the new Croatian Poglavnik, Ante Pavelic, and carried out by a special police bearing the name of Pavelic's old terrorist organization, the *Ustasha*. The object of the massacres was the physical extermination of the Serbian minority in Bosnia and Croatia, so as to make the new enlarged Croatian state Croatian in majority. At the time of the July 1941 rising, the *prechani* of Bosnia and Croatia had

---

[1] Serbs resident in Bosnia, Croatia and other Yugoslav territories never belonging to the traditional kingdom of Serbia.

put Chetnik units into the field. But the forces of Mihailovic were concentrated in Serbia proper, while the Partisans were in Bosnia. Tito welcomed the surviving *prechani,* fed and armed them. (He also deliberately provoked the Germans to reprisals on the civilian population, because the fanaticized survivors sought refuge in his ranks.)

Of the 27 Partisan divisions organized before the end of 1943, approximately 15 appear to have been made up of Serbs, primarily *prechani.* (A Partisan division was little better than a regiment in size and contained approximately 3,500 men.) There were the First and Second proletarian divisions, whose nucleus was the *Srbijanci* of the July 1941 insurrection. The most significant element in these two elite divisions was Communist youth from the University of Belgrad and from provincial lycees. In the capital, the Communist unit at the university had persuaded the Ministry of Defense to provide it with regular military instruction in view of the German threat; now the trainees were to play key roles, not in the Royal but in the Partisan army. The First and Second were cadre divisions, providing officer complements for the newer divisions as these were formed. There were five divisions from the *prechani* area of northwestern Bosnia, where the first fury of the *Ustasha* had been vented, and five from other parts of Bosnia (which may have contained some representation from the Croatian minority in Bosnia). There were two further divisions from Croatian Slavonia, made up primarily from the Serbian minority of that region, and a division from the Voivodina composed of the survivors of Serb massacres perpetrated by the Hungarian occupying forces there. If we add the division of Montenegrin Partisans, we can assert that, up to this point, the composition of Tito's forces was not too different from that of Mihailovic's army. The difference would be that in the Chetnik ranks the *Srbijanci* were the predominant element, whereas among the Partisans the *prechani* were easily the most numerous.

In contrast with the Chetniks, how-ever, the Partisan army in the days of its greatest trials contained important non-Serb and non-Montenegrin elements. There were, for example, the five Partisan divisions from Dalmatia, composed almost entirely of Croatians. Dalmatia had been annexed by Italy, whom the Dalmatians regarded as their hereditary enemy. The fact that the local Serb minority sided with the enemy, that the local Chetniks collaborated with the occupying forces, helped to drive the Croatian majority into the Partisan camp. The Chetniks indiscriminately slaughtered the Croatians in Dalmatia in retaliation for the *Ustasha* massacres in Bosnia. There were also five Slovenian divisions, reflecting perhaps the partition of the country between Italy and Greater Germany, so that even a Yugoslavia organized along Communist federal lines seemed a lesser evil. Finally, there was the Herzegovinian division, one of the last to be organized before the end of 1943, made up of Bosniaks, the Serbo-Croatian-speaking Moslem minority in Bosnia. The Bosniaks had at first tended to sympathize with the Pavelic regime, which treated them as Croatians of Moslem faith. They had even produced an SS division of their own. But now, as the struggle turned, they began to throw in their lot with the Communists.

Thus by a rough calculation, two-fifths of Tito's forces by the end of 1943 represented Slavic elements simply not to be found in Mihailovic's command: Croatians, Slovenians, Bosniaks. This ethnic distribution is also reflected in the composition of the Partisan Anti-Fascist Council of National Liberation (AVNOJ) at its foundation in November 1942. Of AVNOJ's 70 members, 35 were Serbs, 17 Montenegrins, 13 Croats, 4 Moslems, and 1 was a Jew.

In 1944, as it became clear that ultimate Partisan triumph was certain, a further 27 Partisan divisions were formed. Seven of the new divisions bore familiar names, or came from the old areas; they represented fresh recruitment from the populations who had supported Tito from the beginning. The other 20 were organized in areas where Partisan strength had hitherto been scanty. Who was climbing on the band wagon?

Of the 20 divisions recruited in new territory, 5 came from Croatia proper. By 1943 Tito had brought under his control a goodly section of the new Croatian state. Pavelic's towns were short of food, owing to the disruption of communications. There were as yet no renegades among the *Ustasha*, but the Croatian *Domobran*, or militia, began to desert to the Partisans when it got a chance. By 1944, however, even *Ustasha* units were going over to Tito *en masse*, under the Partisan policy of amnesty.

Of the 20 divisions formed in 1944 another 9 were organized in Serbia proper. In May 1944 Mihailovic's commander for central and southeast Serbia went over to the Partisans, thus setting the pattern for mass defection. It is worth noting that, at the very last, Mihailovic himself was forced to come out in favor of a federal Yugoslavia. A Chetnik congress at Ba, a little village not far from Belgrad, adopted a resolution in favor of federalism, constitutional monarchy, and economic reform. At the last Mihailovic made overtures to the Croatian peasant party, offered the hand of friendship to those Bosniaks who had survived the Chetnik counter-massacres, and even made a working alliance with the clerical party in Slovenia.

Lastly, in addition to Croatians from Croatia, and Serbians from Serbia, the 20 divisions formed in 1944 included 6 made up of Macedonians. As we have seen, the Macedonians had at first collaborated with the Bulgarian occupiers, and the Macedonian Communists had refused to cooperate with Tito in the development of resistance activities. By 1944 not only had the Macedonians become irked with Bulgarian rule, but it had also become apparent to them that the Bulgars would end up on the losing side.

Thus, by the end of 1944, Tito's army included a representation from each of the Yugoslav peoples, as the accompanying table shows. According to the table the non-Slavs, the *Srbijanci*, and the Slavo-Macedonians were grossly underrepresented, whereas the Montenegrins and the Bosniaks were heavily overrepresented. Nonetheless, it is clear that the new Yugoslav ruling class (some 92 per cent of Partisan officers were party members by 1948) was not what its predecessor had been, primarily a Serbian affair.

Tito's principal party lieutenants were ethnically as many-hued as were his Partisan officers. There was Tito himself, of mixed Croatian and Slovenian descent. There were two Slovenians, E. Kardelj and B. Kidric; two Montenegrins, M. Djilas and S. Vukmanovic-Tempo; two Serbs, S. Zujovic and A. Rankovic; one Croatian, H. Hebrang; and one Jew, M. Pijade....

We do not have to be Communists to recognize that the history of the CPY has about it the excitement and the drama of a Balkan folk epic. If we seek the characterize this epic in political terms, we can say that the struggle within the Yugoslav party paralleled the struggle within the Yugoslav state, except that the outcome was reversed. In both the party and the

Ethnic Derivation of a sample of 438 Partisan Officers

Ethnic Group	Per cent in Yugoslav Population in 1921	Per cent Among Partisan Officers
Croats	27.6	27.9
Srbijanci	22.4	13.3
Prechani	16.8	18.5
Non-Slavs	12.5	.0
Slovenes	8.8	12.3
Slavo-Macedonians	5.6	.9
Bosniaks	4.9	10.0
Montenegrins	1.4	17.1
	100.0	100.0

state there was a basic conflict between the Serbs and the non-Serbs over the question of Serbian hegemony. In the national politics of the interwar period the Serbs won; in the underground politics of the party the non-Serbs were victorious. The German occupation brought the issue to civil war. In this bloody conflict the party became the paladin of a Yugoslav if Communist-formulated nationalism. It defended this Communist nationalism against both the hegemonist nationalism of the *Srbijanci* and the separatist nationalism of the Croats.

If we ask ourselves what provides the operational connection between Communist ideology and Yugoslav nationalism we must answer from the evidence available that it is probably the religious character of Communism. Nationality in the Balkans has long been more definable by the religious than by other differences. This tendency to identify religion and nationality dates back at least to the days of Turkish rule and the millet system of governing subject peoples. The Turks thought of religion and law as inseparable if not identical. Most of what we would today regard as functions of local government they turned over to the alien and heretical clergy. The infidel should be governed by his own (inferior) law. This is why, until recently, the Moslem peoples of the Balkans tended to think of themselves as Turks, even when this was not ethnically true.

In the Yugoslav case, Serbo-Croatian is a single language. There are neither Serb nor Croat dialects. Dialects exist, but they are spoken by both peoples. It is almost true to say that a Croat may be defined as a Catholic Serb, a Serb as an Orthodox Croat, and a Bosniak as a Moslem Serbo-Croat. During the *Ustasha* massacres—which frequently involved burning down the local Orthodox church with the parish population jammed inside—those who would abjure their Orthodoxy and accept conversion to Catholicism were usually spared.

Thus Communism provided a bridge by which Croats, Serbs, and Bosniaks could all become Yugoslavs in a national sense. Communism replaced the religious faiths which had helped make them different nationalities. It gave them a common faith, a common view of the world and the meaning of existence in it. And if this faith could bridge the gap between Serbs and Croats, it could also serve to bind the Slovenes to the Slavo-Macedonians as parts of the same greater whole.

The Yugoslav Communists were making strict local use of what passed for universal truth. It was in this fashion that Communist doctrine became the mid-wife of a new and truly Yugoslav nationalism.

R. V. Burks, *The Dynamics of Communism in Eastern Europe* (Princeton, N.J.: Princeton University Press, 1961), pp. 119–26, 129–30. Reprinted by permission of Princeton University Press.

B. Mehnert: The Chinese Party: A By-product of Chinese Tradition?

Klaus Mehnert is a prominent German journalist and professor of political science who resided for many years in both Russia and China, speaks their languages and, more recently, has succeeded in traveling widely on their territories. One product of this most unusual background is a comparative study of the two regimes published in German as *Peking und Moskau*. Mehnert's approach is institutional and comparative. He first compares Chinese with Russian society in pre-revolutionary times, then the two revolutionary movements; and finally he traces the history of the relationship between the two nations, down to the eve of the great schism. In all this Mehnert is concerned to explain to himself and to his reader how far communism became Sinified in the process of conquering China, and how far China and Chinese institutions have been Communized or Russified in this process. He wishes through the technique of comparative analysis to understand the origin and nature of Chinese communism. In the following passages Mehnert deals with the Chinese cadres, the bearers of the revolution. He discusses their social composition, their special use of "criticism and self-criticism," their relationship to the traditional Chinese ruling class, or gentry, and the influence upon them of the guerrilla experience. The Soviet cadre is of course brought in by way of comparison and the question is raised whether the Chinese comrades will not, with the industrialization of their homeland, acquire the bureaucratic and managerial outlook which characterizes their Soviet counterparts. Or are these differences more deeply rooted?

In China there was a similar trend, but with some slight differences. In the revolutionary groups, which may be regarded as the forerunners of the subsequent Communist Party of China, the most active men were professors and students, and here the respect due to one's teacher in Asia created particularly strong bonds of loyalty. After the founding of the Party in 1921, the proportion of non-academic members in the Party's leadership did, it is true, increase, but only a small minority came from the working class. This shrank even further when the center of gravity of the struggle shifted from the cities to the provinces. A study of the Communist leading class at the beginning of the forties shows the following: only 17 per cent might be called proletarian even if we use the term in its widest sense; 70 per cent were intellectuals from non-proletarian families. In other words, the old Chinese tradition whereby the leaders of peasant revolts were often intellectuals was apparent in the Communist revolution also.

Symptomatic of this are the men who have led the CPC since its foundation: Ch'en Tu-hsiu (1921–27) was a professor at the National University of Peking and a journalist; Ch'ü Ch'iu-pai (1927–28) was a typical intellectual, from an impoverished upper class family and the grandson of a high official; Li Li-san (1928–30) who as a student in 1920 had founded a Communist cell in France with Chou En-lai, had from his earliest youth been an organizer and functionary, i.e. one

of those professional revolutionaries spoken of by Lenin; Wang Ming (alias Ch'en Shao-yu, 1930–32), the son of a well-to-do peasant, was for a time a student in Moscow and a true *apparatchik* in the way he occupied his post; even Mao Tse-tung (the *de facto* leader of the CPC since Wang Ming's resignation) came, as we have seen, from a prosperous peasant family and was a student and political organizer.

A look at the men who went to make up the Central Committee which was elected at the Eighth Party Congress in September 1956 is also very revealing. Of the ninety-seven members of the CC who together occupied the 585 principal official posts in China, we know something about eighty-one, and of this number only seven were workers. Of the remaining seventy-four, fifty-five came from the country: twenty-eight from well-to-do peasant families, and four from poor ones; the rest have merchant (ten), civil service (five), and teacher (four) family backgrounds. Thirty-nine have studied abroad, the greater part of them in the Soviet Union and the rest (in this order) in France, Japan, Germany, and the United States. At the time they joined the Party, a total of fifty members of the Eighth CC were students. As recently as 1961 Foreign Minister Ch'en Yi, a veteran Communist, stated: "Among the leading comrades of the Party Central Committee there are many who come from families of higher social standing and there are not many who come from worker and peasant families. . . ."

However, we are struck by a difference of another kind between Mao and Stalin. Mao has devoted a great deal of energy—including his own personal energy—to the education of his cadres, to their "rectification" (the Chinese Communists' own translation for their word for this process—*ch'eng feng*). Outwardly this process of his recalls the original bloodless purges in the Soviet Union in which Party members were examined on their ideological knowledge. (Elsewhere I have related how in Moscow early in the thirties I once for

my own amusement took part in the preliminary test for one of these examina-
tions.) But the intensity with which these
rectification campaigns—especially the best
known one, from 1942 to 1944—were
carried on far exceeded anything to be
found in similar manifestations in the
USSR.

The first Communist cells in China,
early in the twenties, were study groups,
and even today one of the chief duties of
the cell (*hsiao tsu*=small group) is still
that of becoming a "study group" (*hsüeh
hsi hsiao tsu*). Not only the CPC, but the
great majority of the population, with its
hundreds of millions of people, is divided
up into study groups averaging ten members which meet frequently, sometimes
daily, to discuss prescribed topics under
the direction of the group leader. There is
nothing which cannot serve as a topic,
from the most intimate details of private
life to new Party resolutions. On my
travels through China in 1957 I often came
across study groups of this kind. Once in
a small rural clinic I found the entire staff,
from the doctor in charge to the cleaning
woman, sitting around a table studying
Mao's speech "On Contradictions." The
method devised by the Bolsheviks called
"criticism and self-criticism" has been
greatly intensified in China, and the main
principle in its application seems to be to
keep each cell member alternating between
two states: bliss at being accepted or fear
of being rejected. . . .

Does this intellectual and pseudo-
intellectual activity on the part of the
kan pu (from *kan*=to work, and *pu*=
component part; i.e. working part, or
"activist") or cadres mean that this body
of Party functionaries is to be regarded
as a resurrected gentry? A fleeting glance
might indeed detect some parallels. Both
gentry and *kan pu* belong to a privileged
group in society which is sharply distinguished from the rest of the population;
its members, whether or not they occupy
government posts, form the backbone of
the administration, one might even say of
the State as a whole. The road to this
position is open to every citizen—in

theory, at least, and to some extent also
in fact. It is true that this road to the
gentry was barred to persons of certain
occupations which were considered dishonorable and the promotion to cadre
status is obstructed by certain social backgrounds. It is also true that in both cases
admission presupposed adherence to the
dominant ideology—Confucian or Marxist
—rather than occupational training, thus
enabling the State to use these people in
almost any required position. A comprehensive Western work on Chinese intellectual history comes after nearly a thousand
pages to the following conclusion:

> Despite important ideological differences,
> the new Communist elite resembles the old
> one in its combination of ideological and
> political authority, in its identification with
> a specific intellectual orthodoxy, and in its
> claim to quality for leadership by conforming
> to a rigorous code of conduct.

Continuing this line of thought one
might be tempted to explain the differences
between the Bolshevik Party functionary
and his Chinese counterpart—for example, the greater independence and higher
authority of the *kan pu*—by saying that
the *kan pu* carries on the tradition of the
gentry, which performed its duties without
detailed instructions from the capital and
to which the population reverently kow-
towed. It may indeed be true that the *kan
pu* is benefiting today from such residue
of the authority of the old élite as may
still remain after all these years of confusion and upheaval.

Yet similarities of this kind are superficial and fortuitous. The differences and
contrasts are far more significant. A member of the gentry was the upholder and
guardian of ancient tradition, the per-
sonification of Chinese culture, the symbol
of stability in the flux of time. The *kan
pu*, on the other hand, through the denial
and complete overthrow of the old order,
rose to power as the champion of a fresh
young ideology, an ideology, moreover,
which was born in the westernmost corner
of the Eurasian continent. A member of
the gentry was considered an ideal official

when, as a true disciple of Confucius, he governed as little as possible and left people to themselves and their non-government associations, particularly the clans. In the name of the State and the Party, the *kan pu* must continually interfere, exhort, threaten, punish, and drive the people to actions and forms of behavior which, if left to themselves, they would not contemplate. In his person a member of the gentry united the realms of the intellect and the State—in normal periods of Chinese history, an unbeatable combination. The *kan pu* (apart from a few specimens for display purposes) is anything but an intellectual; he is much more likely to be a coarse, shirt-sleeved type whose contrast to the intellectual élite is but thinly veiled and who is far more inclined to regard it as consisting of weeds rather than flowers. A member of the gentry was imbued with a highly humanistic ideology in which the art of government meant the discreet adjustment of personal relationships, the elimination of friction, the promotion of balance and harmony, here and now. The *kan pu* is obliged to serve the attainment of a goal which lies in the distant future and to this end continually has to release new forces, but at the same time new friction, imbalance, and discord. Hence the *kan pu* class is the antithesis of the gentry rather than its spiritual descendant. The most one could say is that its ancestors were the anti-Confucian "legalists" whose brief appearance on the Chinese scene we noted in Chapter III.

Actually it is the "veteran fighters" of a very recent past who today still determine the *kan pu* type. Some three and a half million of the total of seventeen million Party members joined the Party in the period before the founding of the Chinese People's Republic, i.e. before 1949. From their ranks come not only the entire top Party leadership but the bulk of the intermediate ranks. They were molded in the twenty years of guerrilla fighting; in thousands of little partisan units—often existing for years on end with no personal contact with headquarters—they waged war on Chiang and the Japanese.

It is here that the natural explanation for the differences between the Chinese and Soviet functionary is to be found. The school through which this guerrilla Communist, as we may call him, passed was a completely different one from that of the Russian Communist. The latter's struggle against Tsarism had been of a conspiratorial nature—underground work in urban settlements, the organizing of strikes and demonstrations, years as *émigrés* in the editorial offices of illegal papers and in the coffee houses of Vienna and Zürich, when they suddenly found themselves (after the brief interlude of the civil war) faced with the task of ruling the largest country in the world. And even that happened over forty years ago, years in which a clearly discernible type has emerged: that of the manager who is part of a tightly organized hierarchy. At the same time, many of the most talented have switched from a purely Party career to that of industrial management, primarily because they found greater possibilities of development in this area due to the "one-man leadership" in the economic field (*yedinonachalie*) introduced by Stalin in 1929. For years Khrushchev has been trying to lead the Party out of rigid Stalinist bureaucratism, to imbue it with fresh vigor, to bring it into closer contact with the masses. He has decentralized and again centralized the economy, increased the Party's supervisory functions in industrial concerns and agriculture, and handed over certain government tasks (such as dealing with juvenile delinquency and the black market) to mass organizations run by the Party. But he does not seem to have been particularly successful in these efforts.

The Chinese Party leadership, on the other hand, has so far managed to keep the Party more flexible and to preserve its position of power, in economic life as well. The "one-man leadership" adopted in industrial concerns in the early days in imitation of the Soviet pattern has been done away with; the role of the *kan pu* in the economy has been strengthened. Elements of guerrilla Communism were revived, especially during the phrase of the Great Leap; Party members were encouraged to indulge in independent thinking and to make their own decisions—within the framework, of course, of the "small study groups," where problems which could be solved on the spot were discussed and dealt with.

Such differences in style are not to be dismissed lightly, although it will not be possible to assess their importance for another ten or twenty years. For what will happen when Mao, that embodiment of guerrilla Communism, is no longer alive, when the "veteran fighters" no longer form a fifth of the Party, but only a tenth or a twentieth? When Chinese industry has reached the same stage of development and differentiation as Soviet industry had at the time when "one-man leadership" was put into effect throughout Russia's economy? Only then we will be in a position to judge whether the CPC is fundamentally different from the CPSU, or whether here too the differences are merely temporal ones due to varying levels of development.

Klaus Mehnert, *Peking and Moscow,* trans. Leila Vennewitz (New York: G. P. Putnam's Sons, 1963), pp. 212–13, 216, 222–25. © 1963 by Weidenfeld & Nicolson and D. P. Putnam's Sons. Reprinted by permission.

C. Draper: Cuban Communism as a Phenomenon of the Middle Class

Theodore Draper is an American journalist who has specialized in Castro's Cuban revolution. He argues in the following passage that Cuban communism—as indeed communism in underdeveloped countries generally—is a product of the petty bourgeoisie. Where industrialization has succeeded, says Draper, the proletariat has manifested little interest in communism, and where industrialization has failed or only begun, discontented elements of the middle class seize upon communism as a creed because it permits them the unlimited use of state power to change the social order and, at the same time, justifies their unlimited control over the governmental machinery. Thus Castro's revolution, far from liberating the industrial proletariat, has set about to industrialize the peasantry. The motive force of the revolution is not so much the ideal of socialism as it is the idea of national liberation from a foreign and presumably imperial influence. Unlike all his predecessors, Castro turned Communist after achieving power. To maintain himself he needed an anti-American ideology, disciplined cadres, and international support; these things only communism could provide him. Thus it was that the university-educated son of a Cuban landowner became the ruler of a peasant country in the name of an urban proletariat which had little love for him or the doctrine he espoused.

To begin with, what truth is there in Castro's "peasant revolution"? The core of the eighty-two men under Castro who invaded Cuba from Mexico in December, 1956, and the twelve who found their way to the mountainous Sierra Maestra at the eastern end of the island came from the middle class. At first, the peasants were hostile, and the original twelve dwindled at one time to only nine. Then in March, 1957, Frank Pais, the underground leader in Santiago de Cuba, sent fifty-eight recruits to the Sierra Maestra, many of them armed with weapons stolen from the U.S. naval base at Guantanamo. These reinforcements, overwhelmingly middle class in character, gave Castro his second wind. Castro himself was their ideal representative—son of a rich landowner, university graduate, lawyer. The *guajiros,* or peasants, in the mountains were utterly alien to most of them. . . .

For over a year, Castro's fighting force was so small that he did not expect to overthrow Batista from the mountains. . . . Victory was foreseen through the vastly larger resistance movement in the cities, overwhelmingly middle class in composition. This calculation was behind the ill-fated general strike of April 9, 1958. Castro's manifesto of March 12, 1958, read in part: "2. That the strategy of the final stroke should be based on the general revolutionary strike, to be seconded by military action..." It failed because the middle class could not carry off a general strike. Only the workers and trade unions could do so, and they refused mainly for two reasons: They were doing too well under Batista to take the risk, and the official Cuban Communists deliberately sabotaged the strike because they had not been consulted and no attempt was made to reach an agreement with them in advance....

In the mountains at this time.... the armed men under Castro numbered only about 300. Four months later, in August, 1958, the two columns commanded by Majors Guevara and Camilo Cienfuegos, which had been entrusted with the mission of cutting the island in two—the biggest single rebel operation of the entire struggle—amounted, according to Guevara, to 220 men.... Sartre was told that the total number of *barbudos* in Cuba during the whole campaign was only 3,000.[1] Castro's fighting force was until the end so minute that it hardly deserves to be called an army, let alone a "peasant army," and even the influx of the last four or five months failed to give it anything like a mass character. In any case, the character of an army is established by its leadership and cadres, which remained almost exclusively middle class throughout, and not by its common soldiers—or every army in the world would similarly be an army of the peasantry and proletariat.[2]

How could such a small band "defeat" Batista's army of over 40,000?

The answer is that it did not defeat Batista's army in any military sense. It succeeded in making Batista destroy himself. Until the spring of 1958, life in most of Cuba went on much as usual. But the fiasco of the April strike forced Castro to change his tactics. Disappointed in his hopes of a mass uprising, he shifted over to full-scale guerrilla warfare—bombings, sabotage, hit-and-run raids. Batista's answer to the terror was counterterror. The army and secret police struck back blindly, indiscriminately, senselessly. The students, blamed as the main troublemakers, were their chief victims. It became safer for young men to take to the hills than to walk in the streets. The orgy of murders, tortures, and brutalities sent tremors of fear and horror through the entire Cuban people and especially the middle-class parents of the middle-class students.

The universal revulsion in the last six months of Batista's rule penetrated and permeated his own army and made it incapable of carrying out the offensive it launched in May against Castro's hideout.... Batista's army "just evaporated." The engagements between the two sides were so few and inconclusive that Batista's abdication caught Castro by surprise. The real victor in this struggle was not Castro's "peasant army" but the entire Cuban people. The heaviest losses were suffered by the largely middle-class urban resistance movement, which secreted the political and psychological acids that ate into Batista's fighting force; Sartre was told that Batista's army and police killed 1,000 *barbudos* in the last clashes in the mountains and 19,000 in the urban resistance movement. ...It was the desertion of the middle class—on which Batista's power was based —that caused his regime to disintegrate from within and his army to evaporate....

The inner history of Castro's regime remains to be told. Its main lines, however, have become increasingly clear. Fidel Castro—as much demagogue as idealist, as much adventurer as revolutionary, as

---

[1] Even this figure may be vastly inflated. The true number was probably closer to 1,000 than to 3,000. But even Sartre's figure serves to make the point.

[2] The cream of the jest is that Guevara is authority for the statement that the *campesinos* of the Sierra Maestra, from whom the rebel army was first recruited, "came from that part of this social class which shows most aggressively its love for the land and its possession, that is to say, which expresses most perfectly the spirit which can be characterized as petty bourgeois" (*Verde Olivo,* April 9, 1961). Thus, the rebel army was initially made up of the urban and rural petty bourgeoisie, at least in spirit!

much anarchist as Communist or anything else—was suddenly and unexpectedly catapulted into power without a real party, a real army, or a real program. In the struggle for power, he had put forward no original economic or political ideas and had stayed well within the limits of traditional democratic reform and idiom in Cuba. He differed from Batista's other enemies chiefly in the tactics he was willing to employ, in his faith in armed struggle and his willingness to organize it. But once power came into his hands, he refused to permit anything that might lessen or restrict it. He would not tolerate the functioning of a government that was not the façade of his personal rule or of a party that might develop a life of its own. His power and his promises were from the first incompatible, and this contradiction forced him to seek a basis for his regime wholly at variance with that of the anti-Batista revolution. He did not have the disciplined and experienced cadres, the ideology, and the international support to switch revolutions in full view of the audience. Only the Cuban and Russian Communists could make them available to him. . . .

Castro's self-analysis on December 1, 1961, was, in essence, not very different from this interpretation. In the main, he sought to blame his former disagreements and frictions with the Communists on his class prejudices, his lack of understanding of Marxism, his susceptibility to imperialist and reactionary propaganda, his "ingenuousness." His real conversion to Communism, he implied, had come *after* he had taken power, when he realized that he was trying to make "a socialist revolution without socialists" and needed the "experienced cadres" of the PSP. More than once he took pains to acknowledge that the Communist old-timers—Juan Marinello, Anibal Escalante, Blas Roca, and Carlos Rafael Rodriguez, especially the latter, who seems to have become his latest mentor—had known more about the revolution

than he had known, and that he had merely become a "student" of Marxism-Leninism.[3] Despite the backing and filling in this speech, Castro's professions of inadequacy and inferiority rang true to me. . . .

Marxian socialism was predicated not merely on a nationalized economy but on the harmonious development of several factors. The achievement of economic democracy by the socialist revolution pressuposed the achievement of political democracy by the bourgeois-democratic revolution. For this reason, the classical Marxists took political democracy for granted, as we no longer can, and they assumed that economic democracy would be built on it. They conceived of socialism as the culmination of capitalist development, without which the prerequistes of socialism—an advanced industrial economy and a preponderant, impoverished, class-conscious proletariat—could not be fulfilled.

History has not worked out that way. Where capitalism has been successful, the prerequisite of a preponderant, impoverished, class-conscious proletariat has not been fulfilled; and where capitalism has not been successful, the prerequisite of an advanced industrial economy has also not been fulfilled. Either the middle class has not been strong enough to achieve a viable capitalist economy, or it has been strong enough to bar the way to a socialist economy.

This familiar dilemma of modern socialism has spawned all sorts of bastard and spurious "socialisms." Instead of the proletariat, they issue out of the middle class, but of that part in revolt against the shortcomings of the middle class. These sons and daughters of the bourgeoisie gravitate irresistibly toward the ideology of socialism but they can make use only of those aspects of socialism which conditions permit them to utilize. They cannot be faithful to the fundamental ideas of the socialist tradition—that the proletariat should liberate itself, that there are pre-

---

[3] Not yet an advanced student, as his reference to Engels, who lived on the profits of textile mills, as a *comerciante* ("merchant") would indicate.

requisites of socialism, especially an advanced industrial economy, and that socialism must fulfill and complement political democracy.

But there is one aspect of socialism on which they can seize without delay or restraint. They can find in Marxism an ideological sanction for the unrestricted and unlimited use of the state to change the social order, and they can find in Leninism a sanction for *their* unrestricted and unlimited power over the state. In classical Marxism, the role of the socialist state was conditioned by the stage of development at which it was put into effect and by the class relationships that governed its realization. In this caricature of socialism, however, the only prerequisite that really matters is the seizure of power, no matter by whom, how, when, or where. Thus we live in a time not only of "Cuban socialism" but of "Indonesian socialism" and even of "African socialism."

This phenomenon indicates that we are badly in need of new words to assume some of the burden that has been thrust on socialism. The order of development cannot be inverted—first the revolution, then the prerequisites of socialism—without resulting in a totally different kind of social order, alien to the letter and, infinitely more, to the spirit of socialism. These inverted revolutions from above belong to what, for want of a better word, we must call the Communist family of revolutions, which, in practice, serve to industrialize the peasantry rather than to liberate the proletariat. But even this family has grown so large and now covers so much ground that its name does not necessarily guarantee full understanding.

For about thirty years, the only Communism was Russian Communism and, in effect, Communism was whatever the Russians said it was. Then, in 1948, came the Titoist variant—a small Communist state in rebellion against Russian domination—and, at the end of 1949, the Chinese variant—a Communist state so vast that it could rival Soviet Russia in power. But both the Yugoslav and Chinese Communist leaderships derived from a common

source, the Comintern, which from 1919 to 1943 was tightly controlled by and wholly dependent on the Russian Communists. Thus far the line of descent was clear and direct.

Now a new branch of the family has begun to emerge. It is related to the national-revolutionary movements, which the world Communist movement long before Khrushchev had recognized as a distinct force and with which it had sometimes collaborated and sometimes competed. As late as 1954, the Soviet press attacked Ghana's President Kwame Nkrumah and his party as a "screen" for British imperialism. Under Khrushchev, however, the pendulum has swung over to the outermost limits of collaboration. This policy, apparently one of the points at issue between the Russian and Chinese Communist Parties, reflects the undeniable fact of the last few years that no Communist has been a match for Nkrumah in Ghana, Sékou Touré in Guinea, or Fidel Castro in Cuba. The local Communists were, therefore, advised to bide their time and achieve their goal in two stages instead of one. First the national-revolutionary movement could win power, then the Communists could win power in the national-revolutionary movement.

This strategy owes its success to a shrewd assessment of the national-revolutionary movements. They are far more capable than the Communists of achieving national unity against the common enemy. But the common enemy, not a social and political program, gives them their *raison d'être*. As a result, they are much more inspiring and effective before taking power than they are afterward. Filling the political and social vacuum the day after the revolution gives the Communists greater opportunities than they had during the revolution. Above all, the nationalist leaders are usually men whose magnetic mass appeal is combined with intellectual fuzziness, adventurist temperaments, and insatiable egos. Their strong appeal makes them indispensable, and their weak points make them vulnerable, to the Communists. They serve the Communists only on condition that the Communists should appear to be serving them. Their political school was nothing like the Comintern, and they represent a variant still further away from the Russian prototype than Marshal Tito or Mao Tse-tung.

This variant has gone further in Cuba than anywhere else, though the story is far from finished there, too. For this reason, Fidel Castro has cast such a large shadow from such a small island.

The phenomenon of Fidel Castro has, as yet, received little serious study. His revolution may not be the one that he promised to make, but it is for all that a genuine revolution. It is related to other upheavals in countries with similar national and social resentments and inequalities. It cannot be dismissed as nothing more than a diabolical aberration because it is not what it claims to be. It belongs to a new type of system, neither capitalist nor socialist, that emerges where capitalism has not succeeded and socialism cannot

succeed. In most pro- and anti-Castro propaganda, the revolution that brought him into power is so ruthlessly distorted that his entire political development begins and ends in fantasy. The serious student will seek answers to questions that the mythologists of "Left" and "Right" do not even ask. How could a revolution basically middle class in nature be turned against that class?[4] How could a revolution made without the official Communists, and for the most part despite them, become so intimately linked with them? How, in short, could Fidel Castro promise one revolution and make another, and what consequences flowed from this revolutionary schizophrenia?

The answers, as I have suggested, take us into territory that has been as yet hardly explored. For the Communists and the *Fidelistas* to meet, *both* had to travel some distance from their starting points. . . .

Theodore Draper, *Castro's Revolution—Myths and Realities* (New York: Frederick A. Praeger, Inc., 1962), pp. 11–15, 23, 48–53, 56–57, 155–56.

---

[4] I do not use "middle class" in the classical Marxian sense of an antifeudal bourgeois revolution. I use "middle class" in the more ordinary sense of a leadership that derived from middle-class families and followed a middle-class way of life. Cuba had already had its bourgeois revolution, but it was a partially unfulfilled one. This is no place for an extended "class" analysis of the Cuban revolution, if one can as yet be made. My own view, in brief, is that the main drive in the struggle for power came from the middle class, especially its younger generation, with other classes providing additional mass support. After the seizure of power, however, the formerly pro-Castro middle-class adherents and sympathizers divided so much that the mass basis changed, though the "class" character of the leadership did not. Boris Goldenberg, who observed the Cuban scene at close range for twenty years, has proposed what may be a particularly fruitful type of analysis. He has called the 26th of July Movement "a group of youths of middle-class origin, with a heroic leader, much faith and little ideological clarity." He considers it "erroneous to characterize the Cuban revolution as the expression of a particular social class," but "it does not for that reason lack a sociological base. This latter is formed by the enormous and heterogeneous mass of the economically 'rootless' "—from all classes ("El desenvolvimiento de la revolucion cubana," *Cuadernos*, January-February, 1961, pp. 34–35). In a forthcoming book on the Cuban revolution in relation to the development of Latin America as a whole, Mr. Goldenberg has worked out his views in greater detail.

15

The Disintegration
of the Versailles Settlement
and the Road
to World War II

HENRY R. WINKLER

Rutgers University

As in the case of other major conflicts, the outcome of World War I bore little relationship to the issues which had precipitated the conflict. The long years of bitter struggle had unleashed forces whose impact brought into being an almost entirely new international order. On the European continent, the three great eastern empires had collapsed. In Germany, a fledgling republic, established partly as a result of Allied demands, reluctantly faced the consequences of the defeat of the Hohenzollern armies. In central Europe, independent succession states, with indeterminate boundaries, mutually exclusive claims, and little prospect of stable economic foundations, sprang into existence as the Hapsburg monarchy broke up like a ship on the rocks. Russia, in control of the Bolsheviks but deep in the throes of civil war and intervention, was almost completely isolated from the international affairs of the rest of Europe. In large parts of Europe starvation threatened, and the specter of further revolution was more than the fearful nightmare of timid men.

These were some of the circumstances which faced the ·representatives of the victorious Allies who gathered in Paris to plan for the reconstruction of the war-torn world. If the result did not usher in the bright new future of wartime aspiration, these difficulties must be considered in assessing the settlement finally achieved. The postwar treaties were attempts to accomplish a number of ends: to "punish" those responsible for the war, to guarantee insofar as possible the right of national self-determination, to establish machinery for the pacific conduct of international relations. Almost from the beginning, these treaties became the focus of an impassioned debate, which reflected conflicting judgments of the conditions under which a peaceful future might be assured. The first part of our problem, therefore, calls for an assessment of the major element in the postwar settlement, the treaty of Versailles designed to cope with the "German question."

Once the Paris Conference had completed its tasks, Europe settled down to a decade of comparative quiet. But it was a calm that concealed fundamental weaknesses in the international situation. Nothing had been done to deal with the problem of Bolshevist Russia. The Soviet State remained isolated and hostile on the flank of a shattered continent. Perhaps equally serious was the withdrawal of the United States from participation in the "affairs of Europe." Woodrow Wilson's dream of a League of Nations had come to fruition, but the League that was established was little more than a rump in the absence of half of the major Powers. Not only the U.S.S.R. and the United States but Germany also (until 1926) was absent from the councils of the League. As a result, from the beginning Great Britain and France were its key members. It is one of the tragedies of the interwar years that they should have differed so sharply in their approach to the problems of this critical decade.

The major concern of France, understandably enough, was with the danger of a German revival. French statesmen for the most part acknowledged the importance of Germany to the economic life of Europe, but their fears of Germany aggression tended to compel them to make economic considerations secondary to strategic questions in the determination of policy. They supported the League with varying degrees of enthusiasm, but in virtually every case they regarded it as merely one of the instruments to ensure French security against aggression from the east. Meanwhile, parallel with the untested guarantees of the League, they proceeded to organize a system of alliances with the states of central and eastern Europe. At the same time, they insisted on a rigid adherence to the military and economic terms of Versailles in order to redress the balance, based on a larger population and a greater industrial potential, favoring Germany in her relations with France.

As for Great Britain, her policy reflected cleavages deeply rooted in British political life. The Conservative governments which were in office for the greater part of this period were reluctant to commit themselves to a policy which might involve automatic military support of the European *status quo*. In particular, they refused to accept the French thesis that an attempt by Germany to upset the settlement in eastern Europe was as great a threat to the interests of the western powers as an attack across the Rhine. As a consequence, they were willing to guarantee the Franco-German border, but rejected any direct responsibility for the maintenance of the territorial arrangements in the east. In contrast, a substantial core of the Labour and Liberal opposition insisted that a peaceful and prosperous European order could only be established within the framework of a strengthened League of Nations. Some recognized that their position implied adequate military guarantees to make the League effective and to temper French fears of aggression. Others, strongly influenced by pacifist revulsion from the horrors of war, thought of the League as a substitute for military sanctions, placing their hopes in the gradual development of a general spirit of international collaboration.

Whatever the merits of these respective positions, the decade of the twenties seemed to offer the possibility that Europe would settle down to a peaceful future. The signature of the Locarno treaties in 1925, guaranteeing the critical frontiers of western Europe and providing for arbitration agreements between Germany and Poland and Czechoslovakia, was followed by Germany's entrance into the League of Nations. Europe experienced a certain measure of economic prosperity which augured well for future stability and the "spirit of Locarno" appeared to be a backdrop for further triumphs in the establishment of a real international peace. But the hopes of the twenties were transmuted by the great depression into the fears and tensions of the thirties. Democracy, which had seemed to be taking root in central and eastern Europe, collapsed under the pressure of economic crisis. In Britain and France the economic catastrophe created circumstances which made it difficult for those countries to take a firm lead at a period when the times demanded a complete rethinking of the bases of previous policies. Above all, unrest in Germany, always a problem, reached new heights and finally brought Adolf Hitler into power.

The triumph of Hitler's National Socialism was another victory for the totalitarian opponents of European democracy. Russian communism and Italian fascism had already been established for over a decade. Now the Nazi version of fascism came to fruition among a people whose achievements in science, in music, in philosophy, in literature could be matched by very few. Yet eventually the Nazis were brutally to slaughter some six million Jews, an act of barbarism unprecedented in modern history. As their justification, they appealed to ideological postulates—doctrines of race, of primitive tribalism, of the purifying virtues of war—and many, if not a majority of the German people, accepted these doctrines. Why? Rejecting its ideology yet seeking to discover the nondoctrinal origins of Nazism, students of the movement have differed in their assessment of its character. The second part of our problem, therefore, has to do with three of the major interpretations which have been offered to explain the nature of Germany fascism.

Italy, Japan, and Germany, to say nothing of Soviet Russia, were all dissatisfied with the international situation. In the 1930s, the first three of these powers were determined to rewrite the terms of Paris and redraw the frontiers of 1919—by arms if necessary. The weaknesses and vacillations of the western states played directly into their hands. The Japanese invasion of Manchuria in 1931 was the first major attempt to change the *status quo* by force. When the League of Nations failed to halt the Japanese in their seizure of Chinese territory, the signal was given for an outburst of aggression that led finally to the renewed horror of war in 1939.

In Europe, the festering pressure of Germany, once the National Socialist party had triumphed in 1933, became the chief touchstone of international relations. Faced with a Nazi threat to its own territory, the Soviet Union shifted from its dogmatic isolationism and emerged as the advocate of "collective security" against aggression. Conversely, during the next three years, Fascist Italy moved from an uneasy opposition to German ambitions in central Europe to an equally uneasy partnership with the Nazis in the so-called Rome-Berlin Axis. As for the western powers, they stood by while Adolf Hitler built up German power and undermined the resistance of his future victims. Hitler's abandonment of the League and his open program of large-scale rearmament should perhaps have been their cue for effective action. But France was so ideologically divided—and so defensively minded—that her leaders failed to take any real initiative in crushing the ambitions of Germany. With the United States still aloof from European affairs, leadership inevitably fell to Great Britain. Here too there were factors which blocked a firm stand against the Nazi menace. The fear of war, a strong current of pacifism, mistrust of Russian collaboration, the belief that Germany would be satisfied when her "legitimate grievances" were removed—these were some of the elements in the picture. From 1933 to 1939, Britain witnessed an impassioned debate over the respective merits of "appeasing" the dictators or of uniting with other nations to resist their attacks upon the European order.

For the most part, the advocates of appeasement were the formulators of western policy. Whether their policy was correct or whether "collective security" would have been more successful in curbing aggression and perhaps even avoiding war is the implied question in our third part. From 1935, the dictators moved from triumph to triumph. The Italian seizure of Abyssinia was followed by German reoccupation of the demilitarized Rhineland. In Spain, the Nazis and Fascists shared with General Franco victory in a war that seemed to foreshadow the ideological alignments of a future European struggle. After Germany, Italy, and Japan had drawn together in an Anti-Comintern Pact, Hitler began to tighten the screws against Germany's neighbors. When he annexed Austria in March, 1938, the democratic powers stood helplessly by. A few months later, it was the turn of Czechoslovakia. Hitler's ever growing claims for the German minority in Czechoslovakia brought demands for a strong stand from the advocates of collective security, in the West and in Russia. But, as we have seen, their opponents determined the policy that was followed. At Munich in September, 1938, Hitler was given all that he demanded—under the threat of precipitating war if his requirements were not met. The conflicting interpretations of the Munich policy and its consequences appear in the third part of this problem.

After Munich, events in Europe rushed to a rapid climax. In March, 1939, Hitler seized the rump Czecho-Slovak State that had survived the surgery of Munich. Almost immediately, the Nazi leader began to demand that Poland come to heel, but this time the western powers reacted differently. Britain gave a military guarantee—which could hardly be implemented—to Poland, the first basic change in her East European policy since 1919. But it was clear that without Russian participation any alliance against Nazi Germany would have difficulty defending Poland or preventing Nazi hegemony in central and eastern Europe. Through the summer of 1939, negotiations were carried on by Britain and France for an agreement with the Russians. Mutual suspicion, and the fears of Poland, the Baltic countries, and Romania, all contributed to the slow pace of these conversations. Suddenly, on August 23, came the announcement that Russia and Germany had signed a Non-Aggression Pact. The outbreak of war was now inevitable, since Germany, freed of the threat of Russian intervention, was prepared to invade Poland. In the last part of this problem, we turn to the Anglo-French-Russian negotiations to examine the conflicting western and Russian positions and then study the implications of the Nazi-Soviet Pact as it is analyzed in various quarters. There, on the eve of a second world conflict, we leave the problem of international diplomacy between the wars.

The attempt to achieve peace and security between 1919 and 1939 is a chronicle of failure. Why it failed is as vital a question today as it was in 1939. There are no easy answers. But it may be hoped that the conflicting views presented in the course of this chapter will at least illustrate the complexity of a problem upon whose solution in our time depends perhaps the future of all mankind.

I. The Carthaginian Peace?

Throughout our period, the Treaty of Versailles was a symbol in many quarters of all that was wrong with the postwar world. As early as 1919, the influential pen of John Maynard Keynes produced an indictment of the treaty, and his charges affected the attitudes of a large segment of western opinion. *The Economic Consequences of the Peace* presented an interpretation which held that the Allied Powers intended deliberately to reduce the German people to servitude. German nationalism was not slow in elaborating the charges. Perhaps the chief weapon in Adolf Hitler's arsenal was his constant fulmination against the iniquities of Versailles. As time went on, observers began to wonder. In 1944, for example, a young Frenchman, Etienne Mantoux, wrote an answer to Keynes which argued, first, that the major problems of the postwar era were the outcome of the war itself and not of the treaty, and secondly, that the terms of Versailles were proper and could have been implemented if there had been the will to do so in the West and the desire, in Germany, to live peacefully with her neighbors. Whatever the merits of the argument, it is clear that the stereotype of Versailles—what men thought it was—had a profound effect on the international policies pursued during the two decades under discussion in this chapter.

A. Versailles For and Against

The following selections illustrate the two conflicting theses which were developed during the debate on the Versailles Treaty. Both statements, made on the morrow of the signature of the treaty, reflect arguments which continued to be used in the years that followed. The first excerpt is from the official defence of the treaty made before the British House of Commons by David Lloyd George. Prime Minister of Great Britain, he had shared with Georges Clemenceau of France and Woodrow Wilson of the United States the major responsibility for deciding upon the terms of the settlement. He had certain reservations about the document, but in this statement to Parliament he emphasizes the two main justifications for a stern peace—Germany's responsibility for unleashing the war and the need for guarantees that it "would not happen again." In contrast with this view was the attitude of the British Labour party. From the beginning it was a major opponent of the treaty. It branded the settlement as punitive, vindictive, grasping, and above all, certain to fail completely. All of this appears in our second selection, which is taken from a pamphlet published by the Labour party in 1919. Its author, Arthur Henderson, was secretary of the Labour party and at this time was serving as its leader as well. He had represented Labour in the coalition cabinet set up by Lloyd George during the war and was to be an influential figure on the international scene in the years that followed Versailles.

1. LLOYD GEORGE

The last time I had the opportunity of addressing the House upon this Treaty, its main outlines had been settled. I ventured then to call it a "stern, but a just Treaty." I adhere to that description. The terms are in many respects terrible terms to impose upon a country. Terrible were the deeds which it requites. Terrible were the consequences that were inflicted upon the world. Still more terrible would have been the consequences had they succeeded. What do these terms mean to Germany? Let us look at the matter quite frankly.... I am not minimising the terms. If hon. Members want to exercise their imagination to realise what the terms mean, they have only to apply the terms to Great Britain, and they will begin to realise what they mean. There is no doubt that they are stern. Are they just? Let us examine separately those which have been challenged.

Take the Territorial terms. In so far as territories have been taken away from Germany, it is a restoration. Alsace-Lorraine—forcibly taken away from the land to which its population were deeply attached. Is it an injustice to restore them to their country? Schleswig-Holstein—the meanest of the Hohenzollern frauds; robbing a poor, small, helpless country, with a pretense that you are not doing it, and then retaining that land against the wishes of the population for fifty or sixty years. I am glad the opportunity has come for restoring Schleswig-Holstein. Poland— torn to bits, to feed the carnivorous greed of Russian, Austrian, and Prussian autocracy. This Treaty has reknit the torn flag of Poland, which is now waving over a free and a united people; and it will have to be defended, not merely with gallantry, but with wisdom. For Poland is indeed in a perilous position, between a

Germany shorn of her prey and an unknown Russia which has not yet emerged. All these territorial adjustments of which we have heard are restoration. Take Danzig—a free city, forcibly incorporated in the Kingdom of Prussia. They are all territories that ought not to belong to Germany, and they are now restored to the independence of which they have been deprived by Prussian aggression....

I come now to the question of reparation. Are the terms we have imposed unjust to Germany? If the whole cost of the War, all the costs incurred by every country that has been forced into war by the action of Germany, had been thrown upon Germany, it would have been in accord with every principle of civilised jurisprudence in the world. There was but one limit to the justice and the wisdom of the reparation we claimed, and that was the limit of Germany's capacity to pay. The experts of all the great Allied countries examined with very close attention that question, and they arrived with fair unanimity at the approximate limits of the reparation which could be recovered from Germany, and under the Treaty we have never exceeded nor fallen short of their verdict. We have set out certain categories of damage which Germany has to repair; damage to property on land and sea; damage for loss of life amongst civilians— that includes the damage sustained by the relatives of those gallant sailors who lost their lives in the merchant shipping of this country; damage for the loss of shipping and of cargoes; and also the damage which is represented by the pensions and the separation allowances paid by each country in respect of casualties in the War. Is there anything unjust in imposing upon Germany those payments? I do not believe anyone could claim it to be unjust. Certainly no one could claim that it was unjust unless he believed that the justice of the War was on the side of Germany.

I come to another condition—disarmament. Having regard to the use which Germany made of her great army, is there anything unjust in scattering that army, disarming it, making it incapable of repeating the injury which it has inflicted upon the world?...

Then I am told, "Oh, yes, take them individually and they may be quite fair, but the cumulative effect is so crushing that you ought to have taken that into account." [Hon. Members: "Hear, hear!"] I will deal with that. That is a criticism, and I am prepared to meet it. They say it may be just, but is it wise? I agree that justice ought to be guided by wisdom. If these conditions do not meet that test, I agree they fail, although we could defend each individual decision upon its merits. Let us examine them. There were three alternative methods of dealing with Germany, bearing in mind her crime. What was that crime? Germany not merely provoked, but planned the most devastating war the earth has ever seen. She planned it and prepared for it for years. She deliberately embarked upon it, not to defend herself against assailants, but to aggrandise herself at the expense of her neighbours. I cannot think of a worse crime, certainly in the conditions of Europe as they were. They knew there were millions of armed men in other lands, and they deliberately hurled 4,000,000 of their own youth against millions in France, millions in Russia, and possibly millions in the United Kingdom. They knew not how far it would extend. They lit a fire: They knew not what it would devour, what it would scorch, what it would burn, what sufferings would be caused, or what would be the desolation. They recked it not....

There are three ways of dealing with that crime. One was to say, "You tried, you failed; go, and sin no more." [An Hon. Member: "Hear, hear."] Hon. Members may think that that is a good way of doing it, but let use see what it means. I am not afraid of examining that. Do not let us imagine, because it looks ridiculous, that there are not people who believe in it—I mean outside this House. [An Hon. Member: "And inside it too."] You have got to answer it. Had that happened, you must remember that Germany suffered less than her victims. Louvain is not in Prussia. France is not in Pomerania, the devastated territories are not in Brandenburg. Look at that land of desolation and wilderness. I have traversed it pretty well from one end to the other. I felt it my duty to do so, in order to know with what I was dealing. That is not across the Rhine. Go across the Rhine. There are no devastated cities and no scorched plains there. The country is whole; the factories are there, the machinery is there—their own and other peoples—and if you had done that Germany would have been better off than the people she had victimised. The cost of the War would have been less, because she would have had a perfect military machine. She would have said, "Look at the triumph of militarism! We have kept all this devastation from you. France is paying more now than we are!" Why, to have done that would have been to put a premium on militarism. The point I do not think is worth arguing.

Let us take the second. The second is to go to the other extreme—to treat Germany as Rome treated Carthage, or, may I say, Prussia treated Poland—destroy her national existence, tear her to pieces, fling one piece to one conqueror, another to another, and a third to another. Fling the bits to the winds of heaven, and have done with them. That is how Prussia treated Poland. It was not merely a crime, it was a blunder, and after a century and a half Poland reappears a formidable and bitter foe. She had 20,000,000 population; Germany had 60,000,000. It is not merely that it would have been wrong and an injustice, but it would have been a folly, and I am glad that we have not soiled our hands with Prussian methods in dealing with Prussia.

What is the third method? To compel Germany, in so far as it is in her power to restore, to repair, to redress. Yes, and to take every possible precaution of every kind that is in our power against the recurrence of another such crime—to make such an example as will discourage ambitious rulers—yea, and ambitious peoples—from ever attempting to repeat this infamy. That is not vengeance. It is discouragement. This crime must be marked. The world cannot take these risks again. I said that Germany failed. I shudder to think how near she got to success. When you are thinking of the terms of peace you must think of making it impossible for any country to repeat an experiment of this kind without running the most terrible risks to her destiny. Every delegate entering the Council felt in his heart the supreme need for imposing terms that would make not merely rulers, but nations, shrink from attempting a crime of this kind again. That was the principle upon which we proceeded.

But it is said, "Are you not punishing Germany for the crime of her rulers?" Well, I am sorry to have to answer this, but I must. If Germany had been commited to this War against the will of her people, I say at once we ought to have taken that into account in the terms of peace. But was that so? [Hon. Members: "No, no!"] The nation approved, the nation applauded; the nation had been taught to approve and to applaud. From the Baltic to the Boden Sea the nation was united and enthusiastic behind the enterprise. It was not like the unity and enthusiasm of France to repel an invader on French soil. It was an enthusiasm which was at its highest when German troops were marching through Belgium. . . . I should have been glad had it been possible to say that this was a war which had been entered into against the will of the German people. But it was not, and therefore it is essential that nations must know, if they enter into unprovoked wars of aggression against their neighbours, what may lie in store for them when defeat falls upon their arms. I therefore have no hesitation in challenging anyone, either inside or outside this House, to point to a single Clause in this Treaty that is not in accordance with the stern and highest demands of justice and fair play. . . .

Parliamentary Debates, Commons, fifth series, Vol. 117, July 3, 1919, cols. 1213–16, 1218–22.

2. HENDERSON

The Treaty is obviously based on a principle which President Wilson has repeatedly repudiated, namely, that peace will best be secured by the mere destruction of German military power and the punishment of the German people. It responds in this to the theory naturally popular in war time—and in which we are apt to acquiesce as a perhaps necessary part of war moral—that the main obstacle to permanent peace and a better organisation of the world was German military power and the special wickedness of the German race.

But the actual situation of the world which confronts us now, after the utter and complete destruction of German military power, assuredly proves the inadequacy of such a theory. Although German power has disappeared with a completeness that is one of the most astounding dramas of history, we have neither peace nor disarmament nor the prospect of these things. New wars in which Russians, Italians, Jugo-Slavs, Hungarians, Japanese, and Chinese are likely to be involved; a new naval rivalry which may create a gulf between ourselves and the Americans; vast new campaigns stretching from Archangel to the Caspian Sea; conscription for the purpose of military occupation of millions of square miles of territory; costly military interventions to prevent the trying by other peoples of political experiments of which we do not approve—it is these things which have followed that destruction of German militarism which was to give us permanent peace and a more rational world order.

The fact of itself condemns the whole principle and spirit upon which the Treaty is based. For although the theory of establishing peace by preponderant military power has been so tragically exploded by the results which have followed the German collapse, the democracies are asked to believe that, if only the new German Republic is treated with sufficient severity, if its territory, or much of it, is occupied militarily by half a dozen different countries; if this section of the German race is handed over to the Poles, that to the French, the other to the Czecho-Slovaks, some more to the Italians; if the sources of Germany's wealth are taken from her; if the population, especially the younger part of it, and more particularly the children, are exposed to conditions so severe as to amount to the employment of what Mr. Churchill calls "the weapon of starvation," the world will have peace. Beyond this merely negative and repressive method the Treaty does not in fact go. European history has no meaning if there were the slightest chance of such methods succeeding.

The settlement is supported on the ground that it is and should be punitive; that militarism needs an "example." Such a plea is prompted by the application of a false analogy of persons to states and nations, and is irreconcilable with justice, humanity, or expediency. It is morally bad for two main reasons:

1. The chief punitive measures—the blockade or economic restrictions—creating want and suffering, will fall mainly upon those who have no possible responsibility whatever for the war: those who are now children or who were unborn when the offences were committed; and upon the politically uninstructed mass of workers who, owing to the control of the press by the Government, were honestly convinced that they were going into a defensive war, and were doing nothing less than their duty. These groups will suffer much more punishment than the official and wealthy classes who have the largest share of the guilt. Starvation or restriction will not touch the latter; it will the former. Such a result, far from creating a sense of guilt and predisposing to repentance and reform, will create a profound sense of injustice fatal to any "conversion" of the German people, which alone could justify punishment.

2. Even if we accept the idea of 70 millions of men, women, children, invalids, decrepit, all being equally guilty, we know from our experience in dealing with the individual criminal that if no provision is made for enabling him to earn an honest living—his offence once purged—he cannot be won from crime, but must remain an outlaw to the common danger. If the law does not protect even the criminal in his just rights it compels the criminal to protect himself; to take the law, that is, into his own hands. This Treaty makes no constructive provision whatever. As it stands, it justifies the plea of the German militarist that a Germany which is not preponderantly powerful will be crushed by her enemies, and that her only security is in her own strength.

The Treaty is based upon utterly inconsistent principles. The principles of justice and the League of Nations and the 14 points are, it is true, included in the document, but only in the form of generalisations, aspirations, and vague formulae. Most of the actualities created by the terms, down to the minutest details, are governed by the idea of punishment, of strategy, or the snatching of some economic or territorial advantage for one or the other of the Allies. The result of such a settlement can be predicted with certainty.

Many of its provisions are patently unenforceable, e.g., the indemnity. The history of the Treaty of Berlin shows that the existence of impossible obligations guaranteed by the Great Powers is a perpetual source of unrest and of danger to the peace of the world. In so far as the conditions are enforceable, they can only be enforced by the permanent military subjection of Germany or a permanent threat of starvation. No nation of 60 millions can be expected to acquiesce in the violations of nationality and the economic servitude imposed by this Treaty. The Allied Governments and the new League of Nations will therefore have to devote all their energies to the task of "keeping Germany down," and the peoples of the world will live under the shadow of a renewal of the war at the first favorable opportunity.

Even if Germany and Russia are not driven into an alliance, every international dispute among the Allied Powers—the question of Fiume proves this—will attain a dangerous and exaggerated importance as opening an opportunity to upset the unjust terms of this peace, in the shadow of the settlement. Then the conditions now exposed must have important effects upon the internal situation in Germany. Political and economic chaos is threatening to engulf the whole of Europe east of the Rhine. The recovery of stability and order depends largely upon what happens in Germany during the next six or twelve months. A peace, such as this, which offers the German people no possibility of economic recovery, no guarantee of justice or equality, plays straight into the hands of the reactionaries on the one side and the extremists on the other. The complete economic ruin of Germany will inevitably bring the downfall of the moderates, and a struggle for power between the militarist reactionaries and the extremists. The only certainty with regard to the issue of such a struggle is that it would be fatal to the peace and recovery of Europe.

Even if we view the Treaty only from the limited standpoint of our own nation, without reference to its wide implications for the world as a whole, there is sufficient cause to fear its effects upon the British people. It is difficult, if not impossible, to see how it could be carried out except by the permanent militarisation of the Allied peoples, the continuance of conscription in this country, the lasting organisation of Europe as an armed camp, with all the economic and social results which the predominance of the military over the civil power involves for this country. If there is a hope that these effects will not follow their causes contained in the Treaty, it is because its provisions are unworkable as well as unjust, and because its speedy revision after it has been signed is not merely desirable, but also inevitable as soon as its implications are fully ascertained. The Brest-Litovsk peace was indefensible and merited the unstinted condemnation it received from world democracy. From the beginning it was obvious it could not stand, and the same must be said of the Peace of Paris, for it also in many respects does violence to the fundamental principles of an enduring and just peace.

Arthur Henderson, *The Peace Terms* (London: Labour party, [1919]), pp. 6–9.

II. *The Character of German Fascism*

With the signature of the postwar treaties, Europe faced the task of organizing the peace. From the start, conflicting views were evident as to how best this might be accomplished. There is no clear-cut pattern to be traced, for within most countries champions of virtually every proposed road to peace were to be found. With sweeping oversimplification, nevertheless, we may say that the major split was between those who saw disarmament and conciliation as the avenues to European security. and those who thought in terms of maintaining superior military power against any threat to the postwar settlement. The first view found its most active advocates in Great Britain; the second in France. On the whole, the British proponents of national disarmament were also the outstanding supporters of the League of Nations as a sub-

stitute for "power politics." Frenchmen, for the most part, considered the League as the armed guarantor of the European *status quo*, particularly after the failure of the American and British governments to ratify a tripower guarantee treaty, originally projected by Woodrow Wilson. Within these broad positions, however, there was substantial variation. Some of the "League of Nations group" in Britain agreed with the French insistence on armed superiority, but for the League rather than for any nation or group of nations. Others rejected force completely. The argument for disarmament, which became in the eyes of many almost a symbol of goodwill, had its critics. That it was rejected by the conventional supporters of Allied preponderance goes without saying. But it was also questioned by those who argued that any system based on international law would be a sham without some provision for its enforcement. Throughout the twenties, these arguments eddied in a world in which a major problem was the return of Germany to the mainstream of European affairs. Weak though the new German Republic might be, it appeared on the whole to promise that reintegration could gradually be achieved. But with the success of Nazism in 1933, the assumptions upon which policy was based required the most serious re-examination. Approaches to peace while German democracy was slowly being established might be totally unrealistic if the new system represented a fundamental change in Germany's orientation. In 1933, men differed as to the origins and intentions of Nazism and they have subsequently continued to differ. Here we can only show some of the interpretations of the Nazi movement, but the selections below may give an indication of the importance of understanding its meaning for the history of the twentieth century.

A. Nazism as an Outgrowth of German History

J. E. Spenlé, a Frenchman who has specialized in the history of German thought, here argues that there is an intimate connection between the Lutheran Reformation and the Nazi movement. The effect of Luther's teaching, he asserts, was to subordinate the church to the state, so that heretical ideas acquired a treasonable character; to separate public from private morality, so that the state was freed of any moral restrictions; to represent God as an arbitrary despot, so that there was no approach to Him, or to any other problem by way of human reason; and finally to foster a religious imperialism which, in secular dress, has become the essence of German patriotism. Spenlé does not insist that the Lutheran Reformation was the only development in German history predisposing the Germans to Nazism, but his analysis of this particular factor suggests the type of argument used by those who regard Nazism as pre-eminently a national movement.

The attempt to find in Luther's doctrine an anticipation of the idea of freedom of conscience is badly mistaken. Traditional Lutheran theology has been all too often confused with a certain watered-down Protestantism, of more or less liberal tendencies, completely reshaped by the philosophy of the eighteenth century. The freedom which Luther claims for the believer is solely the freedom to come in touch with God directly, without any human being as intermediary, by means of reading and pondering Holy Scripture. In the place of the authority of tradition and of the hierarchy of the Catholic Church, Luther puts the infallible authority of the written Word, of a Bible conceived of as literally inspired; but the principle of authority remains. It is merely transferred. Traditional "theocracy" gives way to Lutheran "Bibliocracy," which ends up as an "orthodoxy" much more dogmatic than the orthodoxy of the living and adaptable tradition of the [Catholic] Church.

Even more erroneous is the opinion of those who have found in Luther's Reformation a doctrine which is favorable to modern Liberalism or Democracy. Exactly the opposite is the case. The reformer was indeed faced with a difficult problem. After having proclaimed the "priesthood of all believers" and after having abolished the hierarchy of the Roman Church, he should logically have arrived at an entirely free and, if we may say so, democratic organization of the religious community. The individual congregation should at least have had the right to choose its pastor and the duty of covering the expenses of worship, of religious education, and of poor relief. The idea of Democracy could thus have been derived from the theological premises of the Reformation, as in fact happened in those countries where the Calvinist type of Protestantism was victorious. But this was not the case in Lutheran Germany. Rather Luther entrusted the task of judging souls, of defending the faith, and of organizing the new rites to the worldly power of the German princes, to the *Weltliche Obrigkeit* [secular authority] (whom the Apostle Paul called the magistrate). . . .

[Luther] lives in a period when the [Holy Roman] Empire is declining, when there are wild outbursts of passion and all kinds of revolts. Worse yet: mutinous peasants and anarchist sectarians all take his preachments, the doctrines of "evangelical freedom" and the "priesthood of all believers," which he has proclaimed, as points of departure. Had he not said that he recognized no authority other than that of the Bible? But it is on the authority of Biblical texts and Biblical prophecy that the rebellious peasantry claim to base the famous "Twelve Articles" containing their revolutionary demands, and on this same authority that Thomas Muenzer's Anabaptists base themselves in order to establish, arms in hand, the Kingdom of God on earth in the form of a theocratic communism. Luther flies into a rage when he sees his work of reformation so badly botched by the Bolsheviks of his age. He throws the helm sharply to the right. He thunders against all these partisans of anarchy and appeals to the only force for order existing in the Empire, a force which he has already partly won for his work of reform: the German princes.

As a consequence of this fact, the relationship between church and state, between the religious and the political communities, or, in the words of the middle ages, between the spiritual and the secular powers, will be profoundly modified. In the middle ages the Church is independent of the state; she has her own organization, her own hierarchy, her canon law, her own taxation system. And furthermore she is a *universal* institution. She stands above the diverse nationalities and the changing, temporal sovereignties. The Lutheran Church, on the other hand, will acquire a "territorial" and a "confessional" character. She finds herself under the tutelage of the state, which organizes worship, exercises the right of censorship, appoints and pays the church personnel, and protects the faith. The right to reform—*jus reformandi*—and the episcopal authority—*jus episcopale*—are delegated to the sovereign princes, who exercise them within their territorial frontiers. These princes are subject to no judge except their own consciences and are responsible to God alone. There is, above them, no higher spiritual authority. They are not even obliged to

be practicing Lutherans or to have a spiritual confessor; of the thunderbolt of excommunication they need have no fear. If it is a question of defining a dogma or of finding some formula which will establish religious peace and harmony, then it is they, the lay princes, who deliberate, as in the diet at Augsburg. They seek advice in matters of faith from the theologians, that is to say, from the professors of theology, whom they call to this religious tribunal. Thus the University, or at least the faculty of Protestant theology, thanks to Lutheranism, will play a preponderant role in German religious file. Doubtless there continues to exist, theoretically, the fiction of a universal church, of an "invisible" community of believers. But in fact there can be seen only a diversity of religious confessions entrenched behind their particular territorial frontiers. Thus the Lutheran Reformation replaces the principle of Catholic universalism with the principle of confessionalism and territorialism. The superiority of the spiritual over the secular is replaced with the principle of princely absolutism.

For this absolutism has, in Luther's eyes, a mystical character. Absolutism is of divine origin. *Alle Obrigkeit kommt von oben* ("All authority comes from God"). Not indeed because recognized and sanctified by the Church, but rather because ordained directly, and outside the Church, by God himself for the realization of His creative plan for the world. The Lutheran Reformation emphasizes the divine authority of the sovereign, a *direct* creation of the will of God. Politics has its own requirements, its own principles, its own rules, yes even its own ethics, and in these matters religion is not to intervene. What determines the divine character of the sovereign is not that he represents law, justice, or love, but rather that he is the possessor of power. In place of the word "power" Luther prefers to use the word "sword"—the sword which God has placed in the hands of the princes in order to fight the devil, that is, to chastise dissension, rebellion, anarchy. Now a sword is never something merciful. It is by definition something hard and trenchant. The Christian church, it is true, preaches love, forgiveness of sins, and peace. But the state for its part must impose peace and it can do so only by compulsion, with the sword, by means of war. If the state is belligerent, if it appears to be hard and despotic, that is not its fault, but the fault of the corrupt condition in which the world finds itself. As a believer, the Christian lives, then, in an invisible kingdom of grace; he follows the ethics of love and forgiveness. But as member of the state, or rather as the subject of authority, his attitude ought to be that of absolute submission, of unconditional obedience to the source of authority established by God. As a subject he knows no other morality than the strict fulfillment of his duty, of his function, of his *"Beruf"* [calling], be he prince, magistrate, soldier, or hangman. There is no place here for "conscientious objection." Well known is the famous epistle of Luther's, in which he fulminates against the "murderous and pillaging bands of rebellious peasants" and advises the German princes what to do. Let them try yet once more to bring the erring rebels to their senses. But if this effort fails, let them resort to the most severe reprisals. The Evangel enjoins it. "Lay about with the sword, slaughter, strangle as many as you can. If you thereby lose your life, so much the better for you—never could a more beautiful death befall you, for you will die as a consequence of your faith in the word of God and in the service of the love of your fellow man.". . .

And in consequence his theology is basically anti-rational and anti-humanistic. Between the world of reason and the world of faith there looms up an eternal abyss. It is not rational intellect, it is not search for divine truth which makes the Christian, but *faith alone* (*sola fides*). But faith is by no means the rational acceptance of a truth; it is a living force, which is derived from a need for salvation, and from a deep-going moral pessimism. The "theoretical" optimism of reason is for God an annonyance. If reason were sufficient, the divine work of salvation would then be superfluous. As a consequence, Luther saw in Aristotle his great enemy, he who had usurped *cathedra Christi* [the throne of Christ]. "I believe," so he wrote in 1518, "that it is impossible to reform the church if one does not begin by pulling up by the roots all the *canones* and *decretales*, the whole body of scholastic theology, together with philosophy and logic, such as today are held in great esteem, in order to replace them with something else." The certainty and security which reason provides are misleading. God is not concerned with being known. He is all-powerful and absolutely despotic. He is unfathomable—more obscure than the deepest abyss. Man must become aware of his absolute misery, of his utter worthlessness, in order that he may hear God's call, which is an entirely *personal* call and in no way an impersonal verity. What so sharply distinguishes the Lutheran faith is that it makes itself master of God. God exists for mankind. Christ died *for* mankind. "If God were seated like a bump on a log alone in heaven," Luther said, "He would not be God." For if man is nothing in comparison with God, so God on the other hand would not be God without man—just as the master is no master without servants and the father no father without children.

"The German," writes Thomas Mann, "comes to God only after having abandoned dogma and after having overcome the misery of his own nothingness; he finds his balance in social life only when he has traversed the abyss of loneliness; he achieves health only after he has explored the extremes of sickness and death." We have here a dialectic entirely characteristic of the German manner of thinking and which proceeds by opposites, as a consequence of some internal crisis, fetching affirmation from negation, transforming want into abundance, misery into triumph, sinfulness into innocence, painful anxiety into unshakable confidence. This is precisely the miracle of the Lutheran faith; it is also the secret of that "transmutation of values" of which Nietzsche will later speak. And if we take a closer look, this Lutheran faith is even beyond morality. *"Peccate fortiter"* ["sin brave-ly"], wrote Luther to the wise and timor-ous Melanchthon. It is not so much a matter of wisely avoiding evil (for evil is perhaps as indispensable to salvation and to God's plan for the world as the good) but rather of freeing ourselves once and for all of this oppressive and unbearable antithesis between good and evil, between the divine law and sin, which denotes that we are not yet perfect in the faith, that we are not yet completely one with the will of God and with His grace, and do not share in His grace and His creative power.

This is what distinguishes the the-ology of faith from the theology of love. The two are not mutually exclusive, but the first is superior to the second. Luther himself gave both of these aspects of Chris-tianity formulation in the two basic prop-ositions which he inscribed at the begin-ning of his essay *"On Christian Freedom"*:

"The Christian," we read, "is lord and master of all things and subject to none." This is the definition of faith.

"The Christian," we read further, "is the obedient servant of all and subject to everyone." And that is the principle of love.

But the reformer obviously prefers the first to the second proposition. For faith alone raises us to the heavenly and the divine, while love holds us down to the earthly and the human and binds us to the thousand attachments and the thou-sand dependencies of daily life. "I do not stop repeating," Luther says, "that faith makes masters (*Herren*) of us, while love makes slaves (*Knechte*) of us. I would go so far as to say: through faith we become gods." It is precisely the kingdom, the dominion, the empire which is the final goal. Faith makes us victorious over all our enemies and, at the same time, frees us from all earthly bonds. And is it not this religious imperialism which breaks out in Luther's famous hymn? Let us recall the last verse of the last stanza:

"Take they then our life, goods, fame, child, and wife. When their worst is done, they yet have nothing won: *the Empire ours remaineth.*

"Das Reich muss uns doch bleiben!"

What messianic power [is contained] in this Lutheran mysticism, whose song of triumph peals out like a provocation thrown into the face of the whole world! Luther set going the great religious war which shattered the world-wide univer-sality of the [Catholic] Church and of the [Holy Roman] Empire. But the German faith endures. And it will not in the future prove compatible with the ideas of reason, law or humanity which were developed by the Renaissance. . . . The spirit of the Lu-theran Reformation has from the begin-ning been amalgamated with German na-tional feeling. German nationalism is secu-larized Lutheranism transferred to the political sphere.

Jean Edouard Spenlé, *La Pensée allemande de Luther à Nietzsche,* trans. R. V. Burks, 3rd ed. (Paris: Librairie Armand Colin, 1942), pp. 15–19, 22–25.

B. Fascism as a Phase of Monopoly Capitalism

Frederick L. Schuman is an American political scientist who has specialized in the study of international politics. He views fas-cism as the disease of a sick society, bred of petty-bourgeois neuroses, and fostered by the propertied classes in order to protect and en-large their monopolistic industrial concerns. Fascism appears first in marginal states, where a slight dislocation will stagger the whole economy, but it can appear anywhere that capitalism exists, because it is intimately as-sociated with the latest, or monopoly, stage of capitalism, a stage in which warfare, and warfare alone, remains an economically prof-itable activity. By this reading, Nazism is not merely an outgrowth of German national-ism, but an international phenomenon stem-ming from the breakdown of the economic system itself. Another great depression may well bring America, or Britain, to the same pass. The student should bear in mind that Schuman wrote the following passage in 1936.

Fascism is the social philosophy and

the state-form of the bourgeoisie in the monopolistic epoch of late capitalism. It emerges first, not in the lands where monopolistic enterprise has reached its highest point of development, but rather where the deprivations produced by the dilemma of an economy strangling for lack of markets first manifest themselves most acutely. The dictatorship of the proletariat arrived first, not in Great Britain or the United States, where capitalism was oldest (and therefore in Marxist theory most ripe for the revolutionary transition to socialism), but in backward Russia. Here the moneyed elite was feeblest. Here the proletariat was most bitterly exploited and oppressed and at the same time most revolutionary, most disciplined, most unified. Here above all, impact of the First Imperialist War [1914–18] produced the most disastrous social and economic consequences, shattering the power of the state and of the ruling classes and opening the way for the seizure of power by the Bolshevists.

Similarly the dictatorship of Fascism arrived first, not where monopolistic industry had evolved most elaborately, but in backward Italy. The Italian elite in 1920–23 felt itself most acutely menaced by proletarian and peasant social revolution—whether justifiably or not is irrelevant. The Italian petty bourgeoisie was numerous, poor, embittered. In Italy the impact of the Great War led to a degradation of national symbols and to painful frustrations of patriotic expectations. Italy had "won the war, but lost the peace." Mass paranoia and megalomania, combined with the fear and desperation of the ruling classes, enabled the black-shirts of Mussolini to seize power.

A decade later Germany succumbed to the same disease of a sick society. Here trusts, monopolies, and cartels had long been features of industrial organization. Even before 1914 acute observers—for example, Brentano and Rathenau—were noting that industrial combinations were becoming more powerful than the state and were assuming state functions. During the blood-bath which followed Sarajevo,

the state, the general staff, heavy industry, and the landed nobility were so closely integrated as to become one. After 1919 the industrial and landed elite was obliged to rule through a tepid, imported democracy for which it had scant respect. The loyalty of the masses to Weimar was destroyed by the inflation and by the diplomatic and military impotence of the republic. The *Kleinbuergertum* [petty bourgeoisie] had long since begun to exhibit neurotic symptoms of a class suffering chronically from material and psychic insecurities. These insecurities were enormously multiplied by the economic consequences of military defeat. Here, as in Italy, poverty in natural resources made the margin between prosperity and depression a narrow one and caused economic and social maladjustments to reflect themselves more immediately in psychological and political disorders than where comfortable reserves of wealth can be drawn upon in a crisis—for example, the United States. Germany, like Italy, was economically a "marginal" state. Here Fascism blossomed into full flower as a demagogic movement bred of petty-bourgeois neuroses and as an instrument of power used by the ruling classes to serve their purposes. Here the Fascist state is most clearly the coercive and co-ordinating agency of the plutocracy in the age of monopolistic capitalism.

It is worthy of note, moreover, that Fascism appears first not only in "marginal" nations, but in "marginal" classes and "marginal" industries. It is nurtured by the social groups which are affected first and most severely by the maladjustments of a diseased economy. The petty bourgeoisie is everywhere in the West the least sharply defined and the most insecure segment of the social hierarchy. Its social status is most ambiguous. Its defences against pressure from above and below are weakest. Its identification with the symbols of nationalism is most intimate and its psychic frustrations are most acute when these symbols are debased. On the other hand, investment banking and heavy industry—that is, iron, steel, shipbuilding, armaments, and construction—are the economic activities which are first affected by down swings of the business cycle and the last to recover in up swings. These are the most sensitive centers of financial and industrial power in highly developed capitalistic societies. Bankers and heavy industrialists are most prosperous when capitalistic economy is expanding and least prosperous when it is contracting. It is here that competition first becomes destructive with the shrinking of the market. Here governmental aid, foreign markets, protective tariffs are demanded first and most insistently. Here trusts, cartels, holding companies, interlocking directorates, and all the other devices of monopoly first become general. Both Mussolini and Hitler were heavily subsidized by the powers of iron and steel, banking and investment. Thyssen and Krupp, Schroeder and Schacht constituted the liaison between those powerful but "marginal" business groups and the NSDAP [Nazi Party]. Without this alliance the Fascist state would never have come into being.

The seeds of Fascism are obviously falling upon fertile soil in other nations similarly afflicted with the dilemma of late capitalism. In Japan "economic planning," state control of business, militant nationalism, and belligerent imperialism marched hand in hand with industrial capitalism from the beginning. Japan effected the transition from an indigenous feudalism to an indigenous Fascism without the intervening phase of Democratic Liberalism. In the Britain, the France, the America of the Great Depression heavy industry and investment banking are likewise prostrate. Here, too, the lower middle classes are reduced to desperation, while workers and farmers suffer unemployment and impoverishment and sink to a level of misery which paralyzes all will to action. In all of the Western states Democratic governments continue to wrestle with the problems of depression by the application of half-hearted, tentative, and "temporary" policies which have been carried to their logical conclusion by Fascism: business codes, price-fixing, production quotas, import and export quotas, restriction of competition, subsidies to agriculture, work-creation schemes, and the like.

In all of the Western states the failure of such steps to effect a restoration of prosperity has bred incipient Fascist movements which need for their rapid development only financial support from business and a further disintegration of Democratic ideology among the masses. The spread of Fascism in these states has not been thwarted save in France by any greater powers of resistance on the part of the proletariat, but only by the greater antiquity and stability of the Democratic tradition. The temporary success of the new experiments, such as the NRA [New Deal law for the control of industry under government leadership], or another "automatic" up swing of the business cycle in spite of the new experiments, may delay the advent of Fascism in the Western Democracies for a considerable period. But if the analysis of the genesis and import of Fascism here essayed has any validity, these developments will not prevent the adoption by the ruling classes of such political and economic techniques as are necessary for the preservation of capitalistic economy in the epoch of business contraction and monopoly. Neither will they prevent the emergence of political ideologies and state-forms comparable in fact, if not in name, to those of Italy and Germany.

Even in this event, however, the slow descent of the Fascist societies toward the new mediaevalism can by no means be forecast with any degree of certainty. The continuity of economic and cultural retrogression is far more likely to be interrupted by the advent of the Second Imperialist War. In the Third Reich the aristocracy is driven toward conquest by hunger for land and glory. The plutocracy is driven toward conquest by the shrinking of its markets, by the diminution of its profits through the impoverishment of domestic consumers, by the bright prospects of gain to be got by forging the weapons of war and by using them to conquer new markets in the East. The neurotic middle-class masses are driven toward conquest by nationalist megalomania, by morbid longings for murder and suicide bred of the insecurities and tensions of a diseased society. The Nazi leaders are driven toward conquest by all these pressures and by the exigencies of internal politics in a dictatorship which must become increasingly unstable and insecure with the further disintegration of the economic and social order of monopolistic capitalism. Salvation is to be had only through economic expansion in new markets. New markets are to be had only by the military subjugation of the Danube basin and of such portions of the Soviet Union as can be conquered from Communism.

Fascism is driven toward war by its own ideology and by the tightening ropes of economic strangulation in which its ruling classes are entangled. Fascism was born of the trauma of the First Imperialist War. It may perish in the trauma of the Second Imperialist War. War again on a world-wide scale would doubtless bring irremediable catastrophe in its wake. Neither Britain nor the United States could long remain aloof if Russia were attacked or if two continental coalitions fell upon one another's throats. Japan would seek to seize Siberia and to oust America from the western Pacific. The U.S.S.R., if compelled to fight, would fight with all possible weapons, including colonial revolt and proletarian revolution organized by the Comintern. Finally might come a long and bloody descent into chaos for Western civilization—or world-wide social revolution—or both....

The prospect may give pause to the preachers of war. But for the ruling classes of the West war is still profitable. Conquest may still be lucrative after all other economic activity has ceased to pay dividends. When the armed pilgrims on Fascism's road reach this goal, when pathological hatreds, lusts, and longings for extinction create the means of their own satisfaction, the great guns will again thunder their doom, the terror of the skies will sow fire over the earth, and the shells will shriek their dirge over a world in agony. Fascism itself will be consumed by its war-made sons....

Frederick L. Schuman, *The Nazi Dictatorship. A Study in Social Pathology and the Politics of Fascism,* 2nd. ed., rev., pp. 501–5. Copyright 1935, 1936 by Alfred A. Knopf, Inc., New York. Reprinted by permission of the publisher.

C. Fascism as Modernized Tyranny

Wilhelm Roepke, a renowned German economist who was deprived of his professorial chair by Hitler in 1933 and shortly thereafter fled into exile, sees fascism and communism as cut from the same cloth. They are both collectivist or totalitarian movements which constitute a twentieth-century, mechanized revival of a very ancient phenomenon, that of political tyranny. The intellectual progenitors of totalitarianism are to be found in all western countries and the partisans of the movement are those dregs of society, criminals, crackpots, and perverts, who band together and, by a cunning mixture of deceit and violence, manage to seize control of the state. They then vent their insane fury, first on their own, afterwards on neighboring peoples. Only the use of force will stop them, and the western democracies must bear a heavy share of the responsibility for the destruction wrought by the Fascists because they did not intervene when it became clear that the German anti-Fascists were unable to halt the march of the Brown Shirts. Instead the western democracies approved and applauded the new tyranny until the day when fascism, having got a firm grip on the German people, launched a vicious assault on the democracies themselves.

It did indeed call for no exceptional clarity of vision to recognize Nazism as a frightful barbarian invasion of the laboriously hedged garden of civilization. But why was there general blindness to this in Germany, as later in the rest of the world, and why, in both cases, were men's eyes opened only when it was too late, when Germany had suffered the catastrophe of tyranny, and the world the catastrophe of war? The main reason lay in the *weakening of the moral reflexes.* That was what prevented so many people, faced with a barbarism that in the preceding generation would have made its perpetrators utterly impossible in the civilized world, from taking up the only proper attitude of flaming and uncompromising indignation, and nipping the evil in the bud. People were blind because they were determined to be blind. But that determination in face of unprecedented barbarism proved the serious weakening of the moral sense, of which the world had already given a first sign in the case of Fascist Italy when men praised the punctuality of the trains and the improvement of tourist travel, but forgot what that regime meant for the Italians.

Thus the failure to recognize the true features of Nazism was in the last resort a moral failure, which men sought to cover up with all sorts of theories by way of excuse, euphemism, or even justification, and with state witticisms. *But this is a responsibility the world must share in full with the Germans.* There was certainly a good deal in this National Socialism that was anything but edifying, and certainly its victims deserved sympathy and assistance. But, on the other hand, had not Germany been given order and discipline? Were not the *Autobahnen,* the motor roads, perfect? Was not the economic and social policy of the Third Reich a thoroughly interesting experiment, perhaps worth emulating? Was it really so monstrous for the Third Reich to repudiate the limitations on its armaments (they could not be maintained forever), to claim full sovereignty over the Rhineland, to work for reunion with the Germans of Austria and perhaps even of Sudeten, and to treat Danzig more and more openly as a German city under its rule?...

One of these questions of ours had reference to the fact that one ground for coming to terms with Nazism was the idea that it was an efficient bulwark against Bolshevism, or at least was, in comparison with Bolshevism, the lesser evil. In this belief there was all too ready acceptance of the Nazi propaganda claim that the *coup d'etat* of 1933 saved Germany from a Communist revolution. That theory was indeed one of the trump cards played by National Socialism against unfavorable world opinion—we know with what success. At the outset and for a long time very few realized that this was no more than casting out devils through Beelzebub, and that the differences between the Red collectivism and the Brown totalitarianism could not remove from the world the essential similarity of their principles of structure....

It remains a serious fault that the world should have allowed itself to be so led astray in its judgment and its moral susceptibilities by this playing off of Communism against National Socialism. How grave is this fault and how ready our times show themselves to submit to this mental and emotional confusion is shown by the fact that today we see the same unsureness and denseness in regard to Communism. Nobody who actively defends Communism or even finds excuses for it has any right to be indignant with the people for its seduction by the Brown collectivism, and a world that today shows the same attitude to National Socialism, an attitude of palliation and of appeasement, if not of actual encouragement, proves to us that it is in a moral and mental condition that might have made it an accomplice in Nazism.

This play between Fascism (National Socialism) and Communism was facilitated by a certain interpretation of National Socialism. We refer to the idea that National Socialism, like Fascism, was fundamentally simply a spurious and insincere collectivism, with the aid of which "capitalism" was trying to maintain its position in a last desperate struggle against genuine collectivism, without troubling too much about the methods of government or the ideologies to be worked off on the masses who were to be fooled. Such a theory was well adapted to make the fundamental opponents of collectivism more ready to come to terms with National Socialism, if it did not actually throw them into its arms, while winning the allegiance of the others for "true" collectivism. One side was persuaded in this way to see in National Socialism an ally in the struggle against collectivism, and the other to see in collectivism an ally against Nazism. One side thus became partisans or promoters of Nazism and the other of Communism.

We may feel the latter to be less unattractive than the former, but this does not prevent the two sides from both being wrong, because the interpretation of Nazism from which both proceed is untenable. It is an altogether primitive sociological principle, although, unfortunately, propagated by Marxism, that a government is simply the executive organ of the "ruling class." "The class that in truth rules politically is the class of the rulers, with their religious, philosophic, or moral ideas, whatever these may be," but not a group that stands for any sort of common economic interests. It is cheap romanticism to suppose that the leaders of a state are marionettes, dancing at the ends of wires pulled by the "capitalists." The idea is completely untenable, even though there are actually "capitalists" who themselves entertained it. In Germany itself it was mainly "capitalists" who were so stupid as cynically to promote Hitler's rise to power, and later one of them, when the National Socialism he had supported had driven him into emigration, was actually simple enough to publish a book describing the wretched part he had played, instead of keeping a shamed silence. All these "capitalists" were driven long ago to the painful conclusion that Nazism was an entirely genuine collectivism, and was determined to rule by its own uncontrolled power. Thus those socialists who still adhered to the theory that National Socialism was a last desperate struggle of "monopoly capitalism" and was a pseudo-collectivism made the same mistake in their theories that the "capitalists" of the type of Fritz Thyssen had made earlier in practice. . . .

Thus intellectual confusion and moral obtuseness united to clear away the obsta-cles in the path of the Nazis—obstacles that otherwise would soon have made an end of their dominance. We who knew what Nazism meant had assumed in those critical years after the *coup d'état* of 1933 that the conclusions we had drawn must force themselves upon the whole world. We took it for granted that at the very outset the Third Reich must come to grief through the resistance of the outer world, after the internal resistance had proved inadequate. We imagined the world's reactions and power of decision to be still more or less normal, so that we could not believe that the Nazi regime would last long. We thought the object lesson the Nazis had given in Germany would be sufficient to open the eyes of the rest of the world; the failure in Germany would increase the resolution abroad; since the battle had been lost in Germany, in the international field the determination not to lose it could not, we thought, but increase accordingly.

It had been impossible for us to make any mistake in our estimate of National Socialism; but unfortunately we were entirely mistaken in our estimate of the world outside Germany. We had not expected such inertia, indecision, and lack of unity. Indeed, time after time, from 1933 to this day the points were set wrongly with such incredibly mistaken instinct that disaster rushed upon us all like an express train. Thus we had the depressing spectacle of the representatives of foreign countries willingly shaking hands with murderers, liars, Reichstag-burners, torturers, blackmailers, sexual perverts, and such fry, hurrying to attend Nazi festivals, and taking pains to make it seem that these figures from the dregs of society were entitled to consideration. . . .

During the first years of the regime it would have been child's play to make an end of the monstrous thing, and in all probability even in 1936 the simple mobilization of France would have sufficed to turn the treaty-breaking reoccupation of the Rhineland from a triumph into an annihilating political defeat of Hitler. When in 1938 Austria was violated, nobody stirred, and when in the autumn of that same year the same game of extortion and menace was played against Czechoslovakia, in the Munich capitulation world policy in regard to the Third Reich descended to the uttermost extreme of weakness. During the whole period countless Germans had set their last desperate hopes on a firm attitude on the part of the great powers, but again and again they had to witness the triumph of their hated tyrants over a spineless world. Finally, Russia too made concessions to Hitler in the Molotov-Ribbentrop agreement, enabling Hitler at last to let loose war and, with the support of Russian deliveries, to carry it on successfully for a considerable time. The dismal picture is completed by the sudden chorus of praise from the Communists of all countries of the coalition of Nazism and Communism against the "imperialist and capitalist world."

If we consider all this soberly and with scientific objectivity, we can no longer doubt that *the world-wide catastrophe of today is the gigantic price the world has to pay for its deafness to all the warning signals that prophesied with ever increasing shrillness from 1930 to 1939 the hell the satanic forces of National Socialism were to let loose, first against Germany herself and then against the rest of the world. The horrors of the war correspond exactly with those that the world permitted Germany to suffer, while it actually maintained normal relations with the Nazis and organized with them international festivals and congresses. . . .*

Today it seems almost incredible that the world should have been able for so long to harbor the illusion that the Nazis might treat foreign countries better than they treated their own people; its doing so is inexcusable. Today, however, it should be clear to everybody that Nazism began its march of conquest in Germany itself, that the Germans were the first victims of that barbarian invasion which poured over them from below, that they were the first to be overwhelmed by terrorism and by mass hypnosis, and that all that the occupied countries had later to endure was

suffered first by the Germans themselves, including the worst fate of all, that of being impressed or seduced into becoming tools of further conquests and oppression. . . .

It would be a misjudgment of the German problem if we were pharisaically to ignore the share of guilt that has to be borne by the world outside Germany; and this guilt is at the same time an offense against that section of the German people which stood out against Nazism. . . . But it would also be an error to see in Nazism nothing more than the sudden madness of a single nation in the midst of an entirely healthy world, and to forget that it was the special German form of a tendency that was of an international character. The Third Reich was the German form of the social and administrative system that we know as totalitarianism; and just as that system is not the mark of a nation but of a period, it came into existence in Germany owing to conditions that can be shown to have existed throughout the civilized world. For reasons peculiar to Germany, she succumbed to germs of disease from which other countries were not free, but against which they were able to set greater powers of resistance. The disease obtained an exceptional hold over Germany because in that country national characteristics, international infection, and the exceptional circumstances of the time made up a particularly dangerous combination. The world could not have had so appalling a degree of complicity in German totalitarianism and its career if it had not already been itself infected.

Some years ago the great French historian and sociologist Elie Halévy coined the phrase "era of tyrannies," which has since become famous. But long before this it had become clear that those state systems of which the first had made its appearance in Russia in 1917, and which then appeared in several other countries in a great variety of forms, have essential traits common to all of them, later comprehended under the name "totalitarianism." Whether in Bolshevism, Fascism, or Nazism, we meet continually with the forcible and ruthless usurpation of the power of the state by a minority drawn from the masses, resting on their support, flattering them and threatening them at the same time; a minority led by a "charismatic [divinely endowed] leader" (Max Weber) and brazenly identifying itself with the state. It is a tyranny that does away with all the guarantees of the constitutional state, constituting as the only party the minority that has created it, furnishing that party with far-reaching judicial and administrative functions, and permitting within the whole of the nation no groups, no activities, no opinions, no associations or religions, no publications, no educational institutions, no business transactions that are not dependent on the will of the government. . . .

If National Socialism is essentially a particular form of totalitarianism, the story of its intellectual birth must to that extent be also that of totalitarianism. It is a specially complicated story, and this is not the place for its detailed narration. But the very circumstance that German totalitarianism was preceded by the Russian and Italian forms shows to how great an extent Nazism took over and worked out with German thoroughness ideas that were by no means of German origin. It would be wearisome to compile the names that mark the various stages passed through by the ideology of the totalitarian state. But if we merely mention the chief writers, such as the Frenchman Georges Sorel (who by their own acknowledgment strongly influenced both Lenin and Mussolini) and the Italian Pareto, and if we add how deeply the theorists and practicians alike both of Russian Bolshevism and of Italian Fascism influenced the German National Socialists, we have made it easy to see that the outer world worked just as ardently on the building of the intellectual foundations of the Third Reich as did Germany herself.

Even the racial mania that seems to be an exclusive domain of German totalitarianism was presented to the Germans by foreigners—particularly by the French writer Gobineau, who himself simply elaborated the idea that dates back to the eighteenth century. The racial delusion may be described as a cross between those foreign germs and the specifically German ethical romanticism that will occupy us later. While these and other precursors of the Nazi racial doctrine have nothing in common with the appalling delusionary character of that doctrine, the fact remains that that is the abyss into which we are inevitably plunged in the end if we once pursue the mistaken path of the biologism of which Darwin and his school laid the foundations. The Nazi racial doctrine is the final putrid product of the decay of an intellectual process by which in the course of the nineteenth century man was degraded, with the zeal of a misunderstood science, to a subject of zoology and stud farming; but in this process all the principal countries of the West took part. The death chambers of Auschwitz and Maidanek are the final gruesome result of certain scientific ideas having ultimately found their way in the course of a century to the morally and mentally lowest levels of humanity, to a group that then, through a social catastrophe of inconceivable dimensions, became the rulers of a great people. . . .

The all-important thing we must always keep in mind is the incontrovertible fact that *the National Socialists did not come into power by the clear will of a majority of the German nation, but by the disreputable backstairs method of the coup d'état.* At the beginning of the Third Reich the majority of the German nation was opposed to Nazism, and the importance of this fundamental fact is in no way diminished because, by the iron logic of totalitarianism, the nation that had become its victim suffered on top of all else immeasurable injury to its soul and was brought down to the acceptance of its own servitude. And was the development different in Italy or in the Communistic countries? Have the Poles, the Rumanians, the Latvians, or the Yugoslavs, all, or even a majority of them, become Communists, simply because the ruthless machinery of totalitarianism has descended upon them? And is even the case of Russia so unambiguous that we may identify the Russians with Communism, or more precisely with Stalinism? Is not the answer obvious?...

There are people who say that the Germans ought to have made a more courageous stand against Nazism and its atrocities, and we fully share this opinion. But ought we not, in order to be quite just, also bear in mind that diabolical hostage system of the Nazis, which threatened the family of every rebel with a cruel death? How far was a man entitled to show courage at the expense of his wife and children?

Who, again, can judge the way the soul of man reacts to an unceasing flow of subtle monopolist propaganda, shutting out all other information? It may be admitted that the German, for reasons we shall consider later, is particularly easily influenced and particularly lacking in judgment in all political questions; but we do not know how the experiment would have worked out with any other nation that was unable, like the occupied countries of Europe, to draw strength from resistance, from the patriotic revolt against the impudent pretensions of an alien conqueror speaking another language. The whipping up of the German's patriotism, on the contrary, bound him all the more strongly to his own tyrannical government....

But how can we get over the appalling fact that the Germans, wherever they carried their conquests, committed the most horrible crimes and hair-raising cruelties, that the German name is associated with the cold-blooded extermination of millions, with the infliction of indescribable tortures, with unfeeling destruction of irreplaceable values, and with causing infinite mental torment? All those of us who learned with boundless indignation and the deepest horror of these crimes know how near we were to wishing for that execrable country the fate of Sodom and Gomorrah. And yet the National Socialists would have attained one of the aims they were probably pursuing with their atrocities if we allowed ourselves to be carried away by our anger into identifying Germany with Nazism. This is the very point at which our sense of justice is subjected to its

hardest test and must not fail us. The test is very hard even if we recall that unfortunately this is not the first time in history that terror, mass murder, and the most appalling cruelties have made their appearance in the midst of a nation; that in England Henry VIII delivered seventy thousand to the hangman, that in Soviet Russia millions of peasants have been "liquidated" in cold blood, and that a few decades ago millions of Armenians were cruelly murdered in Turkey....

If we probe to the bottom of the question, we shall probably come up against the following general truth: Every society, however civilized and Phaeacian it may seem to us, conceals in its depth a sewer of subhuman types, which must be kept firmly closed like the fisherman's bottle in the *Arabian Nights*. In other words, the powers of evil lurk everywhere, awaiting their chance from some earthquake or conflagration, revolution or war. Bore into these depths and it will be seen how masses of the dregs of humanity are hurled into the air. Ask the French with their bloodthirsty militia of the Laval regime, the Norwegians with their *hirden*, the Dutch, the Croats, the Hungarians, or the Austrians, and let not the Englishman or American be too sure that "it can't happen here." Instead, let them be glad that they have been spared that experience so far. And we will not be so tactless as to ask how things are in Russia.

The upheaval of society by totalitarianism must of necessity bring the worst elements to the top. That is a general law, which has only been confirmed by Nazism and is of universal application all over the world. Whenever anything resembling the Nazi upheaval has happened (as in Russia, in Italy, or elsewhere), the biggest blackguards have regularly set the tone, dragging the honor of their country through the mire. Thus what happened in Germany was simply that such men as the execrable von Papen and his backers, who can never do adequate penance for their stupidity and perversity, opened up the sewers of the German community, a process that some of them, by unpardonable stupidity, even mistook for the fresh-water supply....

Wilhelm Roepke, *The Solution of the German Problem,* trans. E. W. Dickes (New York: G. P. Putnam's Sons, 1947), pp. 6–11, 13–14, 17–18, 25–26, 32–34, 42–43, 45–46. By permission of George Allen & Unwin, Ltd.

III. Appeasement and the Munich Settlement

In the wake of the great depression came a tragic deterioration in European relations. The depression was by no means the sole force behind the increase in international tension, but it served as a precipitant of aggression on the part of the "revisionist" powers, in Asia as well as Europe. A major turning point in the history of the western world was September, 1931. The Japanese seizure of Manchuria ushered in an almost unbroken series of successes for the enemies of the existing international order. Japan, Italy, and above all Germany moved step by step to achieve their purposes, not by negotiation, discussion, and compromise, but by force and the threat of force. The specter of war settled heavily over a western society that had dreamed briefly of an international future based on law instead of force. The vision was dissipated by the strident and menacing demands of the Fascist powers and their supporters. Into the hands of the governments of the western European democracies, above all into those of Great Britain, fell the task of dealing with these new challenges to the stability of Europe and of the world. They retreated almost continually. By 1937, when Neville Chamberlain became the British Prime Minister, they had erected their retreat into a system. "Appeasement" did not begin in 1937—it had been urged in the twenties by the very groups which castigated it in the thirties. But its positive virtues, in the face of naked aggression, were proclaimed most systematically after Chamberlain took over the reins of government. It reached its culmination at Munich in the autumn of 1938, where Chamberlain and Edouard Daladier, the French Premier, agreed finally to the Nazi seizure of a part of Czechoslovakia in order to avert the possibility of war. Was the policy of retreat before the aggressors wise? Was it inevitable in the light of the European situation? What were the alternatives? In the debate centering about the German-Czech crisis can be found the basic approaches to the whole problem of aggression in the disastrous era of the 1930s, the era of appeasement.

A. The Grand Alliance

The threatening growth of German power under the Nazis brought Winston Churchill into the lists as the outstanding champion of British rearmament and European collective opposition to the pressures of Hitler's Reich. The following except illustrates the nature of Churchill's position as the Nazis swallowed Austria and turned their attention to Czechoslovakia. Neville Chamberlain's views of the Churchill proposal can be seen in a selection from a letter to his sister, published in 1946 by his biographer.

1. CHURCHILL

Our affairs have come to such a pass that there is no escape without running risks.

On every ground of prudence as well as of duty I urge His Majesty's Government to proclaim a renewed, revivified, unflinching adherence to the Covenant of the League of Nations. What is there ridiculous about collective security? The only thing that is ridiculous about it is that we have not got it. Let us see whether we cannot do something to procure a strong element of collective security for ourselves and for others. We have been urged to make common cause in self-defense with the French Republic. What is that but the beginning of collective security? I agree with that. Not so lightly will the two great liberal democracies of the West be challenged, and not so easily, if challenged, will they be subjugated. That is the beginning of collective security. But why stop there? Why be edged and pushed farther down the slope in a disorderly expostulating crowd of embarrassed States? Why not make a stand while there is still a good company of united, very powerful countries that share our dangers and aspirations? Why should we delay until we are confronted with a general landslide of those small countries passing over, because they have no other choice, to the overwhelming power of the Nazi regime?

If a number of States were assembled around Great Britain and France in a solemn treaty for mutual defense against aggression; if they had their forces marshaled in what you may call a Grand Alliance; if they had their Staff arrangements concerted; if all this rested, as it can honourably rest, upon the Covenant of the League of Nations, in pursuance of all the purposes and ideals of the League of Nations; if that were sustained, as it would be, by the moral sense of the world; and if that were done in the year 1938—and, believe me, it may be the last chance there will be of doing it—then I say that you might even now arrest this approaching war. Then perhaps the curse which overhangs Europe would pass away. Then per-

haps the ferocious passions which now grip a great people would turn inwards—and not outwards in an internal rather than an external explosion, and mankind would be spared the deadly ordeal towards which we have been sagging and sliding month by month. I have ventured to indicate a positive conception, a practical and realistic conception, and one which I am convinced will unite all the forces of this country without whose help your armies cannot be filled or your munitions made. Before we cast away this hope, this cause and this plan, which I do not at all disguise has an element of risk, let those who wish to reject it ponder well and earnestly upon what will happen to us if, when all else has been thrown to the wolves, we are left to face our fate alone.

Parliamentary Debates, Commons, fifth series, Vol. 333, March 4, 1938, cols. 99–100.

2. CHAMBERLAIN

...with Franco winning in Spain by the aid of German guns and Italian planes, with a French government in which one cannot have the slightest confidence and which I suspect to be in closish touch with our Opposition, with the Russians stealthily and cunningly pulling all the strings behind the scenes to get us involved in war with Germany (our Secret Service doesn't spend all its time looking out of the window), and finally with a Germany flushed with triumph, and all too conscious of her power, the prospect looked black indeed. In face of such problems, to be badgered and pressed to come out and give a clear, bold, and unmistakable lead, show "ordinary courage," and all the rest of the twaddle, is calculated to vex the man who has to take the responsibility for the consequences. As a matter of fact, the plan of the "Grand Alliance," as Winston calls it, had occurred to me long before he mentioned it.... I talked about it to Hali-

fax, and we submitted it to the chiefs of the staff and the F. O. experts. It is a very attractive idea; indeed, there is almost everything to be said for it until you come to examine its practicability. From that moment its attraction vanishes. You have only to look at the map to see that nothing that France or we could do could possibly save Czechoslovakia from being overrun by the Germans, if they wanted to do it. The Austrian frontier is practically open; the great Skoda munition works are within easy bombing distance of the German aerodromes, the railways all pass through German territory, Russia is 100 miles away. Therefore we could not help Czechoslovakia —she would simply be a pretext for going to war with Germany. That we could not think of unless we had a reasonable prospect of being able to beat her to her knees in a reasonable time, and of that I see no sign. I have therefore abandoned any idea of giving guarantees to Czechoslovakia, or the French in connection with her obligations to that country.

Keith Feiling, *The Life of Neville Chamberlain* (London: Macmillan & Co., Ltd., 1946), pp. 347–48, by permission of Macmillan & Co., Ltd., St. Martin's Press, Inc., The Macmillan Company of Canada, Limited, and Mrs. Neville Chamberlain.

B. Munich and After

In Britain, as elsewhere in the world, the Munich settlement was greeted with relief: war had been averted. Among many, however, relief was accompanied by fear for the kind of a future it portended for the peoples of Europe, to say nothing of the Czechs themselves. Neville Chamberlain's defense of Munich, made in the British Parliament immediately after the pact was signed, appears in the first selection below. From the many criticisms leveled at it during the debate in the House of Commons, portions of the biting indictment by Clement Attlee, leader of the Labour party, are selected to indicate the position of those who felt that it did not mean "peace in our time."

1. CHAMBERLAIN

Before I come to describe the Agreement which was signed at Munich in the small hours of Friday morning last, I would like to remind the House of two things which I think it very essential not to forget when those terms are being considered. The first is this: We did not go there to decide whether the predominantly German areas in the Sudetenland should be passed over to the German Reich. That had been decided already. Czechoslovakia had accepted the Anglo-French proposals. What we had to consider was the method, the conditions and the time of the transfer of the territory. The second point to remember is that time was one of the essential factors. All the elements were present on the spot for the outbreak of a conflict which might have precipitated the catastrophe. We had populations inflamed to a high degree; we had extremists on both sides ready to work up and provoke incidents; we had considerable quantities of arms which were by no means confined to regularly organised forces. Therefore, it was essential that we should quickly reach a conclusion, so that this painful and difficult operation of transfer might be carried out at the earliest possible moment and concluded as soon as was consistent, with orderly procedure, in order that we might avoid the possibility of something that

might have rendered all our attempts at peaceful solution useless. . . .

Before giving a verdict upon this arrangement, we should do well to avoid describing it as a personal or a national triumph for anyone. The real triumph is that it has shown that representatives of four great Powers can find it possible to agree on a way of carrying out a difficult and delicate operation by discussion instead of by force of arms, and thereby they have averted a catastrophe which would have ended civilisation as we have known it. The relief that our escape from this great peril of war has, I think, everywhere been mingled in this country with a profound feeling of sympathy—[Hon. Members: "Shame."] I have nothing to be ashamed of. Let those who have, hang their heads. We must feel profound sympathy for a small and gallant nation in the hour of their national grief and loss.

Mr. Bellenger: It is an insult to say it.

The Prime Minister: I say in the name of this House and of the people of this country that Czechoslovakia has earned our admiration and respect for her restraint, for her dignity, for her magnificent discipline in face of such a trial as few nations have ever been called upon to meet. . . .

I pass from that subject, and I would like to say a few words in respect of the various other participants, besides ourselves, in the Munich Agreement. After everything that has been said about the German Chancellor today and in the past, I do feel that the House ought to recognise the difficulty for a man in that position to take back such emphatic declarations as he had already made amidst the enthusiastic cheers of his supporters, and to recognise that in consenting, even though it were only at the last moment, to discuss with the representatives of other Powers those things which he had declared he had already decided once for all, was a real and a substantial contribution on his part. . . .

In my view the strongest force of all, one which grew and took fresh shapes and forms every day was the force not of any one individual, but was that unmistakable sense of unanimity among the peoples of the world that war must somehow be averted. The peoples of the British Empire were at one with those of Germany, of France and of Italy, and their anxiety, their intense desire for peace, pervaded the whole atmosphere of the conference, and I believe that that, and not threats, made possible the concessions that were made. I know the House will want to hear what I am sure it does not doubt, that throughout these discussions the Dominions, the Governments of the Dominions, have been kept in the closest touch with the march of events by telegraph and by personal contact, and I would like to say how greatly I was encouraged on each of the journeys I made to Germany by the knowledge that I went with the good wishes of the Governments of the Dominions. They shared all our anxieties and all our hopes. They rejoiced with us that peace was preserved, and with us they look forward to further efforts to consolidate what has been done.

Ever since I assumed my present office my main purpose has been to work for the pacification of Europe, for the removal of those suspicions and those animosities which have so long poisoned the air. The path which leads to appeasement is long and bristles with obstacles. The question of Czechoslovakia is the latest and perhaps the most dangerous. Now that we have got past it, I feel that it may be possible to make further progress along the road to sanity.

My right hon. Friend has alluded in somewhat bitter terms to my conversation last Friday morning with Herr Hitler. I do not know why that conversation should give rise to suspicion, still less to criticism. I entered into no pact. I made no new commitments. There is no secret understanding. Our conversation was hostile to no other nations. The objects of that conversation, for which I asked, was to try to extend a little further the personal contact which I had established with Herr Hitler and which I believe to be essential in modern diplomacy. We had a friendly and entirely non-committal conversation, car-

ried on, on my part, largely with a view to seeing whether there could be points in common between the head of a democratic Government and the ruler of a totalitarian State. We see the result in the declaration which has been published, in which my right hon. Friend (Mr. Duff Cooper) finds so much ground for suspicion. . . .

I believe that there are many who will feel with me that such a declaration, signed by the German Chancellor and myself, is something more than a pious expression of opinion. In our relations with other countries everything depends on there being sincerity and good will on both sides. I believe that there is sincerity and good will on both sides in this declaration. That is why to me its significance goes far beyond its actual words. If there is one lesson which we should learn from the events of these last weeks it is this, that lasting peace is not to be obtained by sitting still and waiting for it to come. It requires active, positive efforts to achieve it. No doubt I shall have plenty of critics who will say that I am guilty of facile optimism, and that I should disbelieve every word that is uttered by rulers of other great States in Europe. I am too much of a realist to believe that we are going to achieve our paradise in a day. We have only laid the foundations of peace. The superstructure is not even begun.

For a long period now we have been engaged in this country in a great programme of rearmament, which is daily increasing in pace and volume. Let no one think that because we have signed this agreement between these four Powers at Munich we can afford to relax our efforts in regard to that programme at this moment. Disarmament on the part of this country can never be unilateral again. We have tried that once, and we very nearly brought ourselves to disaster. If disarmament is to come it must come by steps, and it must come by the agreement and the active co-operation of other countries. Until we know that we have obtained that co-operation and until we have agreed upon the actual steps to be taken, we here must remain on guard. . . .

While we must renew our determination to fill up the deficiencies that yet remain in our armaments and in our defensive precautions, so that we may be ready to defend ourselves and make our diplomacy effective—(Interruption)—yes I am a realist—nevertheless I say with an equal sense of reality that I do see fresh opportunities of approaching this subject of disarmament opening up before us, and I believe that they are at least as hopeful today as they have been at any previous time. It is to such tasks—the winning back of confidence, the gradual removal of hostility between nations until they feel that they can safely discard their weapons, one by one, that I would wish to devote what energy and time may be left to me before I hand over my office to younger men.

Parliamentary Debates, Commons, fifth series, Vol. 339, October 3, 1938, cols. 41–42, 45, 47–50.

2. ATTLEE

We all feel relief that war has not come this time. Every one of us has been passing through days of anxiety; we cannot, however, feel that peace has been established, but that we have nothing but an armistice in a state of war. We have been unable to go in for carefree rejoicing. We have felt that we are in the midst of a tragedy. We have felt humiliation. This has not been a victory for reason and humanity. It has been a victory for brute force. At every stage of the proceedings there have been time limits laid down by the owner and ruler of armed force. The terms have not been terms negotiated; they have been terms laid down as ultimata. We have seen today, a gallant, civilised and democratic people betrayed and handed over to a ruthless despotism. We have seen something more. We have seen the cause of democracy, which is, in our view, the cause of civilisation and humanity, receive a terrible defeat. . . .

I fear that the House is faced with this, that the real outstanding problem in this business, the real big issue, the central fact of the situation, is that the map of Europe has been forcibly altered by the threat of war. Herr Hitler has successfully asserted the law of the jungle. He has claimed to do what he will by force and in doing so has struck at the roots of the life of civilised peoples. In doing this to one nation he threatens all, and if he does this, and he has with impunity, there is no longer any peace in the world even although there may be a pause in actual warfare. The whole of Europe is now under the constant menace of armed force. That is why many people cannot feel very happy about the present situation. They feel that there has been an immense victory for force and wrong. Ever since the last War people have realised that if peace is to be preserved there must be something above the will of the individual ruler of an armed State. That is the whole basis of the League of Nations and many people are surprised today to be under this menace— people who have grown to political consciousness in the years from 1918 to 1932, because between those years there was peace. Now we have gone back.

I say we are witnessing a degeneration of the world due to two things. The first thing is the failure to deal with the political and economic questions arising out of the follies of the Peace Treaties, and arising out of the widespread injustice and maladjustments of the economic system. The other thing is the failure to deal with force, the failure to restrain aggression. . . .

When the National Government overthrew the whole policy of collective security and abandoned it and the League, we told this House over and over again that we were entering on a very dangerous course. We realised that we were back in 1914 with all its dangers, and we knew that sooner or later a challenge would come to this country; and that is what has happened. The real pity of it is that, having decided to leave the League system which we practised and in which we believed, and to embark on a policy of alliances and power politics, instead of strengthening the people whose natural interests were with ours, we have had nothing but constant flirtations with this and that dictator. The Prime Minister has been the dupe of the dictators, and I say that today we are in a dangerous position.

...We are left isolated. The Union of Soviet Socialist Republic [sic] may well hold aloof in future when it considers what little trust can be placed on our Western democracies, and we shall be left alone with France; all our potential allies have gone; and France, which in my view has the greatest responsibility for this debacle of policy, finds herself in the position of a second-class State.

And what have we got in place of the alliances and covenants and collective security and all the rest of it which buttressed this country in the past? We are left with two promises, one from Signor Mussolini and one from Herr Hitler. That is really all that we have got. We have to walk by faith—the faith of the Prime Minister in Signor Mussolini and his faith in Herr Hitler. The Prime Minister has said how difficult it was for Herr Hitler to recede from a statement which he had once made. I have five pages of statements made by Herr Hitler, from every one of which he has receded. I need not go through them; you know them—pages of them; but the Prime Minister says against all experience that he has faith in Herr Hitler's promise, grounded on two or three interviews—a pretty flimsy support for this country.

I ask, what is to happen next? What reason have we to think that Herr Hitler will stop now? Suppose he does not. What will happen?...

...The real question that faces us in this Debate is not just a review of the past, not just our apprehensions of the present; it is, What can we do for the future of the human race?

Parliamentary Debates, Commons, fifth series, Vol. 339, October 3, 1938, cols. 51, 55–56, 62–64, 66.

IV. The Coming of the War

After Munich, the Nazis moved quickly toward their next objectives. In March, 1939, they brutally put an end to the fiction of Czech independence. Immediately, the familiar campaign of hysterical vituperation—this time against Poland—began. Now, however, the western reaction had changed. The British government gave an outright guarantee of support to Poland. More realistically, perhaps, it joined with its French ally in opening negotiations looking toward an Anglo-French-Soviet pact against Nazi aggression. The negotiations dragged on through the summer. The western democracies were unwilling to meet Soviet demands with regard to the defence of the Baltic states. The Russian leaders, apparently mistrusting western intentions, refused proposals which in their view would have committed them to "pulling British and French chestnuts out of the fire." The western statesmen did not fully grasp the urgency of their problem, for meanwhile the Soviet leaders, with spectacular disregard of ideological questions, were in touch with the Nazi hierarchy. On August 23, the Russians cast their lot—temporarily at least—with the Nazis. In a treaty, whose secret clauses gave them a free hand to seize parts of Poland and Romania, they pledged in essence to remain neutral in the event of a war over Poland. Soviet motives in these tangled negotiations leading up to the bombshell of August 23 are of prime importance in considering how World War II was precipitated. This last part, therefore, contains material which aid the student to understand the nature of the situation on the eve of conflict.

A. Anglo-French-Soviet Negotiations

Two views of the Anglo-French-Soviet conversations follow. The problem as seen by the West is explained to the British House of Commons by Neville Chamberlain on May 19, 1939. At this juncture, the negotiations seemed to have stalled completely. The western powers were unwilling to accede to the Soviet demand that the three signatories guarantee the defence of the Baltic states against aggression, whether those states wanted to be defended or not. The governments of these countries feared the Soviet Union as much as they did Nazi Germany. The British and French governments, for their part, had little confidence in the motives of the Soviet Union. But even if they wanted a pact against Nazi aggression, they had to decide whether the Soviet conditions were immutable or whether they were merely counters to be used in bargaining. The information available seems to indicate that neither Britain nor France ever really decided how to assess the Soviet position until it was too late to conclude an agreement. Something of the feeling of western indecision and ambiguity, of the failure of the British and French governments to realize how urgent their problem actually was, can be sensed in Chamberlain's speech. As for the Soviet leaders, their suspicion of the West was no less marked than the western distrust of the Soviet Union. By June, 1939, when Andrey A. Zhdanov, an important member of the Soviet Politburo, published a strong denunciation of the western position, the Soviet leaders had already begun secret conversations with the Nazi regime. Whether the Zhdanov article was an attempt to bring Britain and France to terms or a preparatory justification for the future pact with Germany, its appearance in the official newspaper *Pravda* gave it the stamp of an important policy statement by the Soviet leadership.

1. CHAMBERLAIN

...I turn to the discussions with the Government of the Soviet Union.... We are not concerned at all with Russian internal doctrine. We are concerned with the best method of building up what my right hon. Friend for Warwick and Leamington (Mr. Eden) has called a peace front. If we can evolve a method by which we can enlist the co-operation and assistance of the Soviet Union in building up that peace front, we welcome it; we want it; we attach value to it. The suggestion that we despise the assistance of the Soviet Union is without foundation. Without accepting any view of an unauthorised character as to the precise value of the Russian military forces, or the way in which they would best be employed, no one would be so foolish as to suppose that that huge country, with its vast population and enormous resources, would be a negligible factor in such a situation as that with which we are confronted....

The House may remember a recent statement by M. Stalin, that it was the policy of the Soviet Union "to support States which might be victims of aggression, provided that they were prepared to defend their independence." That is our own point of view, and it appeared to indicate that the Soviet Union might be prepared to collaborate in carrying this aim into effect. But we were also aware... that the direct participation of the Soviet Union in this matter might not be altogether in accordance with the wishes of some of the countries for whose benefit, or on whose behalf, these arrangements were being made. We would desire to have the collaboration of all these countries, and we do not want to have any division among them. Accordingly, we suggested to the Soviet Government that they should make a declaration with regard to Poland and Rumania similar to the one which had been made by ourselves and France, namely, that if Great Britain and France should be involved in conflict in consequence of undertakings which we had given to those countries, or either of them, the Soviet Union express its readiness to lend its assistance to Poland or Rumania, as the case might be, always provided, of course, that their assistance was desired.... The British Government have never desired to ask the Soviet Government to do anything which they were not prepared to do themselves. They have always wanted the arrangement to be reciprocal.... If it be argued that it did not provide for the case of a direct attack on the Soviet Union, agreed; but it did not provide for the case of a direct attack on this country.... It may be argued that it did not cover the case of certain States, other than Poland and Rumania, which are neighbours of Russia, and through which perhaps she might be attacked. Again, I say, it is quite true that it did not cover that, but, on the other hand, it equally did not apply to certain western

States which, if attacked, might cause us ultimately to be involved in war.... Our suggestion did not contemplate that the Soviet Government should intervene irrespective of whether Great Britain and France did so—although, as a matter of fact, our own commitments which follow upon the assurances we have given are irrespective of whether the Soviet Union come in. Therefore, if there be an inequality between the two States in the proposals which have been made, the inequality was in favour of the Soviet Union and not of this country....

Nevertheless, since the proposal was not acceptable to the Soviet Union, we tried again. What we, above all, were anxious for was, that we should be able to come to an agreement quickly, and it is always easy to come to an agreement quickly if you accept everything that the other side puts up. [An Hon. Member: "That is what you did at Munich."] No doubt that is what some would have done. I do ask the House to remember that in this matter we are trying to build up, not an alliance between ourselves and other countries, but a peace front against aggression, and we should not be succeeding in that policy if, by ensuring the co-operation of one country, we rendered another country uneasy and unwilling to collaborate with us. Therefore, I suggest...that in this matter, which is one of great difficulty and delicacy, a certain amount of caution is necessary, caution arising not out of ideological differences, not out of pure obstinacy, not even because we think that one course serves narrow British interests better than another, but because the object of our policy is to build up this peace front. We would rather delay for a few days longer than hastily take a step which might result in the work that we have

already done crumbling before our very eyes.

We thought that perhaps the Soviet Government might have been willing to declare its agreement with us on those matters on which we could agree, and that it would be prepared to let us discuss further, and at greater leisure, the subjects on which difficulties still existed. That, in our view, would have been a wise course to take to show agreement and I cannot help thinking that, if we agreed even on a part of the policy to be pursued, it would have made it easier to come to a complete agreement on the rest. I cannot help saying how much I regret the decision of the Soviet Government not to let M. Potemkin go to Geneva. My Noble Friend [the Foreign Secretary] will, therefore, be deprived of the opportunity of discussing personally with him these matters, which I think, might have been valuable for both of us.... This is one of the cases in which I cannot help feeling that there is a sort of veil, a sort of wall between the two Governments which it is extremely difficult to penetrate, and that if only that opportunity had been afforded us we might have, perhaps, managed to shake hands across the gap....

I have nothing more to say except this. Throughout this matter we have been in close touch with the Government of France, with whom we are happy to have collaboration and counsel. There is no difference between us.... I do trust that ...it may be found possible to overcome these obstacles which have hitherto prevented us from reaching an agreement with the Government of the Soviet Union, and that we shall be able in due course to report to the House that we have at last made a final agreement with them.

Parliamentary Debates, Commons, fifth series, Vol. 347, May 17, 1939, cols. 1836–40.

2. ZHDANOV

The Anglo-Franco-Soviet negotiations on the conclusion of an effective pact of mutual assistance against aggression have reached a deadlock. Despite the utmost clarity of the position of the Soviet Government, despite all efforts of the Soviet Government aimed at the earliest conclusion of a pact of mutual assistance, no substantial progress is discernible in the course of the negotiations. In the present international situation this fact cannot but be of serious importance. It encourages the hopes of the aggressors and all enemies to peace in the possibility of the disruption of agreement among the democratic states against aggression and it impels aggressors to the further unleashing of aggression.

A question arises in this connection: What is the reason for the delay in the negotiations whose favourable termination is impatiently and hopefully awaited by all pacific nations and all friends of peace?

I permit myself to express my personal opinion in this matter, although my friends do not share it. They still think that when beginning the negotiations on a pact for mutual assistance with the U.S.S.R. the English and French Governments had serious intentions to create a powerful barrier against aggression in Europe. I believe, and shall try to prove it by facts, that the English and French Governments had no wish for an equal treaty with the U.S.S.R., that is, for the only kind of treaty to which a self-respecting state can agree, and that is precisely what has caused the state of stagnation into which the negotiations have entered.

What are these facts?

Anglo-Soviet negotiations in the direct sense of this word, that is, since we were presented on 15 April with the first British proposals, have been going on for seventy-five days. Of these, the Soviet Government took sixteen days in preparing answers to the various English projects and proposals while the remaining of fifty-nine have been consumed by delays and procrastination on the part of the English and French. The question is: Who, in such a case, if not the English and French, bears responsibility for such slow progress in the negotiations?

Further, it is well known, from the practice of concluding international agreements similar to the Anglo-Franco-Soviet one, that this same England concluded pacts of mutual assistance with Turkey and Poland within a very short space of time. Hence it follows that when England *desired* to conclude treaties with Turkey and Poland she was able to secure the necessary speed for the negotiations. The impermissible delays and endless procrastination in negotiations with the U.S.S.R. permit doubts in the sincerity of the real intentions of England and France and compel us to put the question as to what exactly forms the basis of such policy: Is it a serious endeavour to ensure a peace front or a desire to utilize the negotiations as well as the delay in the negotiations for some different purposes having nothing in common with the creation of a front of pacific powers?

This question suggests itself all the more in that in the course of the negotiations the English and French Governments pile up artificial difficulties, make it appear that serious differences exist between England and France on the one hand and the U.S.S.R. on the other, questions which, given goodwill and sincere intention by England and France, could be solved without delay or hindrance. It is known, for instance, that the question of a tripartite guarantee of immediate assistance to Latvia, Estonia and Finland, in the event of violation of their neutrality by aggressors, forms just such an artificially invented "stumbling block" in the negotiations. Statements to the effect that the said Baltic states do not desire those guarantees and that precisely this circumstance allegedly hinders England and France from accepting the Soviet proposal, are obviously unsubstantial and could only be inspired by one intention; to hamper the negotiations in order to disrupt them. In any case facts are known to us which show that when, for instance, England believes it to be in her interest to guarantee some country or other, she finds proper ways for it without waiting for these countries themselves to demand guarantees.

The English newspaper, the *Sunday Times,* in its issue of 4 June this year, states that "Poland...agreed that if Great Britain was drawn into war on account of the invasion of Holland she would come to Britain's assistance" and that "Great Britain agreed that if Poland was drawn into war on account of the invasion of Danzig or Lithuania she would come to Poland's assistance." Thus Poland and Great Britain give a guarantee simultaneously both to Lithuania and Holland. I do not know whether Lithuania and Holland were asked about this bilateral guarantee. In any case, the press reported nothing to this effect. Moreover, as far as I know, both Holland and Lithuania deny the existence of such guarantees. Still, the *Sunday Times* reports a pact of bilateral guarantee for these countries has already, in the main, been concluded, and it is no secret for anyone that the *Sunday Times* report has not been denied anywhere.

Not, long ago, in an interview with a certain French journalist, the Polish Minister for Foreign Affairs, Beck, declared quite unequivocally that Poland neither demanded nor requested from the U.S.S.R. anything in the sense of granting her any guarantees whatever and that she was fully satisfied with the fact that Poland and the U.S.S.R. recently concluded a trade agreement. Wherein then differs the position of Poland from the position of the ruling circles of the three Baltic states? In nothing whatsoever. However, this does not prevent England and France from demanding from the U.S.S.R. guarantees not only for Poland and four other states of whose desire to receive a guarantee from the U.S.S.R. we know nothing, but also for Holland and Switzerland, with whom the U.S.S.R. does not even maintain ordinary diplomatic relations.

All this shows that the English and French do not desire a treaty with the U.S.S.R. that is based on principles of equality and reciprocity, although they vow every day, that they too are for "equality." They desire a treaty in which the U.S.S.R. would play the labourer shouldering the entire burden of obligations. But no self-respecting country will agree to such a treaty if it does not wish to become a plaything in the hands of people who like others to pull their chestnuts out of the fire for them. Still less can the U.S.S.R. agree to such a treaty, whose strength, power and dignity are known to the whole world.

It seems to me that the English and French desire not a real treaty acceptable to the U.S.S.R., but only talks about a treaty in order to speculate before public opinion in their countries on the alleged unyielding attitude of the U.S.S.R. and thus make easier for themselves the road to a deal with the aggressors.

The next few days must show whether this is so or not.

Pravda, June 29, 1939, in *Documents on International Affairs 1939–1946* (London: Oxford University Press, 1951), Vol. I, pp. 418–20. Issued under the auspices of the Royal Institute of International Affairs.

B. The Nazi-Soviet Pact

The meaning of the Russo-German agreement on August 23 was debated bitterly at the time, and has continued to be argued since. Was it a defensive maneuver by the Soviets, designed to gain time to prepare for a German attack considered inevitable? Or was it a move to embroil all of Europe in an exhausting conflict, the major beneficiary of which would be a Communist regime nursing its strength in neutral isolation? Or did it represent a typical imperialist bargain directed toward the cold-blooded division of eastern Europe between German and Russian masters? Here is a series of conflicting views. Vyacheslav Molotov was the Soviet Commissar for Foreign Affairs. His speech to the Supreme Soviet of the U.S.S.R. is the official Russian explanation of the Pact. Waclaw Gryzbowski, the Polish Ambassador to Moscow at the time, sees in the agreement a cynical green light to Germany, the signal for the unleashing of a world conflict. His acid comments, it should be noted, were made before the secret articles of the pact, providing among other things for the partition of Poland, became known to the world. Two other excerpts have been added to throw some light on the reaction to the pact in the West. While official comment was guarded, individual figures were outspoken. To illustrate how sharply divided was their response, we quote from two speeches in the British House of Commons, both by members of the more extreme "left." John McGovern, a member of the tiny Independent Labour party, had at one time been a strong sympathizer of the Communist "experiment" in Russia. He had become disillusioned with the Soviet regime, and a recent trip around the Continent had convinced him of its single-minded intention to promote the expansion of Russian power. His analysis of the pact reflects this view of Soviet policy. Ellen Wilkinson, who was once described as the "most vigorous man in the Labour party," was usually well to the left of the more moderate leadership of that party. Vehemently opposed to the policy of Neville Chamberlain's National Government, she tended to lay the blame for what had happened at its feet rather than at those of the Soviet leaders. Her speech in the House of Commons, made like McGovern's the day after the announcement of the pact, reflects some of the bitterness with which she responded to the collapse of the common East-West front against Nazi aggression.

1. MOLOTOV

...What is the root of these contradictions in the position of Great Britain and France? In a few words, it can be put as follows:

On the one hand the British and French Governments fear aggression, and for that reason would like to have a pact of mutual assistance with the Soviet Union, in so far as it would strengthen them—Great Britain and France. But on the other hand the British and French Governments are afraid that the conclusion of a real pact of mutual assistance with the U.S.S.R. may strengthen our country—the Soviet Union —which it appears does not answer their purpose. One cannot but see that these fears outweighed other considerations. Only in this way can we understand the position of Poland, which has been acting on the instructions of Great Britain and France.

I shall now go on to the Soviet-German Non-Aggression Pact.

The decision to conclude a non-aggression pact between the U.S.S.R. and Germany was adopted after military negotiations with France and Great Britain had reached an impasse owing to the insuperable difficulties I have mentioned. As the negotiations had shown that the conclusion of a pact of mutual assistance could not be expected, we could not but explore other possibilities of ensuring peace and eliminating the danger of war between Germany and the U.S.S.R. If the British and French Governments refused to reckon with this, that is their affair. *It is our duty to think of the interests of the Soviet people, the interests of the Union of Soviet Socialist Republics*—all the more because we are firmly convinced that the interests of the U.S.S.R. coincide with the fundamental interests of the peoples of other countries.

But that is only one side of the matter. Another circumstance was required before the Soviet-German Non-Aggression Pact could come into existence. It was necessary that in her foreign policy Germany should make a turn towards good neighbourly relations with the Soviet Union. Only when this second condition was fulfilled, only when it became clear to us that the German Government desired to change its foreign policy so as to secure an improvement of relations with the U.S.S.R., was a basis found for the conclusion of the Soviet-German Non-Aggression Pact. Everybody knows that during the last six years, ever since the National-Socialists came into power, political relations between Germany and the U.S.S.R. have been strained. Everybody also knows that, despite the differences of outlook and political systems, the Soviet Government had endeavoured to maintain normal business and political relations with Germany....

Since 1926 the political basis of our relations with Germany has been the Treaty of Neutrality which was prolonged by the present German Government in 1933. This Treaty of Neutrality remains in force to this day. The Soviet Government considered it desirable even before this to take a further step towards improving political relations with Germany, but circumstances have been such that this has become possible only now.

It is true that, in the present case, we are dealing *not with a pact of mutual assistance*, as in the case of the Anglo-French-Soviet negotiations, but *only with a non-aggression pact*. Nevertheless, conditions being what they are it is difficult to over-estimate the international importance of the Soviet-German pact. That is why we favoured the visit of the German Minister for Foreign Affairs, Herr von Ribbentrop, to Moscow.

August 23, 1939, the day the Soviet-German Non-Aggression Pact was signed, is to be regarded as a date of great historical importance. The non-aggression pact between the U.S.S.R. and Germany marks a turning point in the history of Europe, and not of Europe alone. Only yesterday German Fascists were pursuing a foreign policy hostile to us. Yes, only yesterday we were enemies in the sphere of foreign relations. Today, however, the situation has changed and we are enemies no longer.

The art of politics in the sphere of foreign relations does not consist in increasing the number of enemies for one's country. On the contrary, the art of politics in this sphere is to reduce the number of such enemies and make the enemies of yesterday good neighbours, maintaining peaceable relations one with the other. History has shown that enmity and wars between our country and Germany have been to the detriment of our countries, not to their benefit.

The countries which suffered most of all in the war of 1914–18 were Russia and Germany. Therefore, the interests of the peoples of the Soviet Union and Germany do not lie in mutual enmity. On the contrary, the peoples of the Soviet Union and Germany stand in need of peaceable relations. The Soviet-German Non-Aggression Pact puts an end to the enmity between Germany and the U.S.S.R. and this is in the interests of both countries. The fact that our outlooks and political systems differ must not and cannot be an obstacle to the establishment of good political relations between both States, just as like differences are no impediment to the good political relations which the U.S.S.R. maintains with other non-Soviet capitalist countries.

Only the enemies of Germany and the U.S.S.R. can strive to create and foment enmity between the peoples of these countries. We have always stood for amity between the peoples of the U.S.S.R. and Germany, and for the growth and development of friendship between the peoples of the Soviet Union and the German people.

The chief importance of the Soviet-German Non-Aggression Pact lies in the fact that the two largest States of Europe have agreed to put an end to enmity between them, to eliminate the menace of war and to live at peace one with the other, making narrower thereby the zone of possible military conflicts in Europe....

V. Molotov, *Soviet Foreign Policy, Four Speeches* (London: Lawrence and Wishart, 1941), pp. 9–20, in *Documents on International Affairs 1939–1946, op. cit.*, pp. 439–42.

2. GRYZBOWSKI

...(c) At the beginning of May M. Litvinov himself vanished from the political scene. Today we realize that the Soviet's imperialistic plans must have been already sufficiently formulated for them to retain a final and decisive understanding with Chancellor Hitler as a trump card in their policy of instigation of war. It is obvious that such an understanding could not be negotiated by M. Litvinov....

M. Molotov took over the Commissariat for Foreign Affairs on May 5th....

Some days later...I gave M. Molotov a résumé of our attitude.

We could not accept a one-sided guarantee. Nor could we accept a mutual guarantee, because in the event of a conflict with Germany our forces would be completely engaged, and so we would not be in any position to give help to the Soviets.

Also we could not accept collective negotiations, and made our adoption of a definite attitude conditional on the results of the Anglo-French negotiations. We rejected all discussion of matters affecting us other than by the bilateral method. Our alliance with Rumania, being purely defensive, could not in any way be regarded as directed against the U.S.S.R.

In addition I indicated our favourable attitude to the Anglo-Franco-Soviet negotiations, and once more emphasized our entire loyalty in relation to the Soviets. In the event of conflict we by no means rejected specified forms of Soviet aid, but considered it premature to determine them definitely. We considered it premature to open bilateral negotiations with the Soviets before the Anglo-Franco-Soviet negotiations had achieved a result. M. Molotov made no objection whatever....

It has to be borne in mind that so long as the Anglo-French negotiations lasted it was almost impossible for us to go beyond a waiting attitude. We felt no optimism whatever in regard to the result of those negotiations. It was difficult to expect that the Soviets would do anything in the direction of preventing a conflict or even rendering its outbreak difficult. We observed rather that their tactics aimed at the exact opposite.

The German-Soviet Pact of Non-Aggression justly made a deep impression. The fact that two mutually contradictory sets of negotiations had been carried on simultaneously was a true measure of the cynicism of Soviet policy. The conclusion of the pact was beyond all doubt an encouragement to Germany to make war. The scope of the obligations undertaken, the extent of the understanding between the Soviets and Germany remained vague.

The Soviets endeavored to give it the appearance of a pact assuring them peace, but not effecting any fundamental change in their policy. In this regard M. Molotov even appealed to Poland's example.

The undefined character of the obligations resulting from the pact was emphasized by M. Voroshilov's interview given a few days later. Evidently influenced by news emanating from Berlin and London of the conversations between the British Ambassador and Chancellor Hitler, Marshal Voroshilov gave the Soviet Press an interview, in which he stated that the Anglo-Franco-Soviet negotiations were only suspended, and that their renewal would not be in contradiction with the Soviet-German pact.

Moreover, Marshal Voroshilov simultaneously stated that the supply of raw material and war material to Poland in the event of a conflict was a "commercial matter," equally not in contradiction with the pact.

The warning was understood in Berlin....

Polish White Book, no. 184, in *Documents on International Affairs 1939–1946, op. cit.*, pp. 435–37.

3. MCGOVERN

...I am not disappointed with the Russian Pact. I am one who believes in knowing who are your friends and who are your enemies, and while I could not assist any campaign which would involve the world in strife for purposes which I do not approve, at the same time I have no use for treachery or double-dealing of any kind. I am sure that at this moment it must give great pleasure to Torgler and Thaelmann in the concentration camps and to Dimitroff who was accused of the Reichstag fire, as well as to Goering who made such a great outburst of physical violence against him, to see von Ribbentrop flying in Hitler's aeroplane over what is regarded as the sacred soil of Russia. It must be gratifying to them to see the Nazis who have brutally maltreated and murdered thousands of communists in Germany, exchanging handshakes of friendship with the Russians. It must be gratifying to them to see the Russian entertaining those brutal people who have done to death so many men in the concentration camps and back streets of Germany....

I think the leaders of this nation are entitled to realise where they stand, and this pact between Germany and Russia does at least remove any doubt from the minds of the people of this country as regards counting on assistance which cannot be obtained. I took the view last year rightly or wrongly—and there was reason and evidence behind it—that the one country in the world which desired war was Russia. I took that view strongly. At that time I cycled from Prague to Vienna and from Vienna to Berlin spending a week in each city and developing contacts with well-informed quarters. I took the view that Russia wanted the major Powers to be involved in conflict. The Russians did not want a short war. They wanted a prolonged struggle in which the conditions would be suitable for world revolt, or, if they did not secure world revolt, they wanted at least to weaken those nations who were dominant and were feared by them. I say, honestly and sincerely, that I believe the leaders at the Kremlin were prepared to sacrifice 20,000,000 or 30,000,-000 lives in that gamble for themselves.

...In relation to Russia's aim I disagreed—not because I wanted to—with members of both the Labour party and the Liberal Party about the aid that Russia would give in a war. I know there are people who have both misinterpreted and misunderstood my point of view, but I had it clearly in mind. Even if you did conclude a pact with Russia it would, in my estimation, give no real aid. Russia is like the man who goes to sea and proclaims that he is going in to bathe, but only paddles his feet in the water. That is all Russia would have done. She fans the flames. She would bring about that extended period of war, to which I have referred.

Today we have the position that the Swastika and the Hammer and Sickle fly side by side and that the free democratic nations are left to see the realisation of this policy on the part of Russia. I leave that to the apologists of the Communist party. No doubt they can apologize for that as they can for almost anything under the sun....

Parliamentary Debates, Commons, fifth series, Vol. 351, August 24, 1939, cols. 37–41.

4. WILKINSON

...There is one feature of our Debate which is rather curious, and that is that everybody has spoken as though this Russo-German pact was such a tremendous triumph for Hitler. But is it? After all, he has had to swallow almost everything he has said, and in fact has got what might be described as "The German Munich." He has had to send Ribbentrop, of all people, to Moscow, on a penance to Canossa, though he went in a Nazi-decorated aeroplane instead of a white sheet. Really, is that a sign of such internal strength as could cause that bogy-bogy speech which has just been made by the right hon. Member for Sparkbrook? The big mistake that has been made is that this country has steadily under-estimated the Russian strength. Whatever else can be

said of Herr Hitler he has tended to put a much higher valuation upon it than we have....

One of the tragedies of the policy of this country has been continually to under-estimate what really was happening in that enormous country of Russia, covering one-sixth of the surface of the globe and the only country—certainly in Europe and, I believe, taking the United States into consideration—that can be self-sufficient in war production. We have treated that country with studied insult for as long as Members on the other side have been in power in this country. There was no insult too foul for them to repeat in the old days. I accept unhesitatingly the Prime Minister's word that in the last few weeks or days—since the beginning of August—he has done everything in his power to get conclusions through the Military Mission sent to Russia, but you cannot alter the effect of years and years of insult when, because you are obviously in a tight corner, you are prepared to go a long way to meet the point of view of the other people. Really, that had got to be said.

An attitude of high moral propriety has been taken in this House. There has been the suggestion that in some way or another it was Russia's moral right to save the British Empire. Why? Was it a moral obligation and a right and a duty which she owed to the human race to save the British Empire? To do Russia justice—if we can in this House—she has never proclaimed her affection for either the British Empire or for the present Government. What Russia has done on certain occasions is to make concrete offers of help to this country. There was, first, the concrete offer of general disarmament, and when that was laughed out of court there were concrete proposals of assistance provided that the alliance, or pact, or whatever you like, was to be a concrete reality. That has been done again and again. I would refer hon. Members to the columns of their daily Bible, the "Times," for proof of that. Each one of those offers has been either coldly ignored or laughed at. If we behave like that to a country when we are in a tight corner we cannot really complain if she does not hasten to our assistance. . . .

The right hon. Gentleman over and over again has said at that Box that he did not wish to see Europe divided into two ideological blocs. He has got his way. Europe is no longer divided into ideological blocs, because Russia and Germany are now on the same side. There was a time when he could have had that division, which would have meant that the whole of the armed forces of the democracies, not only Russia but the Oslo group and America—I for one find it difficult to recognise it as a democracy. . . .

Viscountess Astor: Is Russia a democracy?

Miss Wilkinson: It is very much so. The point I want to get out is that Russia was supremely concerned, as an anti-Fascist democracy at that time, to try everything she could to get an anti-Fascist group. The Prime Minister said: "We will not have this ideological grouping." Very well, he has seen what Herr Hitler calls potentially the greatest force in the world swing over probably to the other side—we do not as yet know for certain. I suggest that it is about time that we got to an ideological grouping. Men will not fight for the Bank of England, Montagu Norman and the City of London, but they will fight for something they consider is supremely worth fighting for. . . .

Parliamentary Debates, Commons, fifth series, Vol. 351, August 24, 1939, cols. 46–48, 51.

16

The Aftermath
of World War II

JAMES L. GODFREY

University of North Carolina

War solves some problems; others it postpones or makes worse. During the fighting, governments and people have the task of achieving victory, and problems are resolved within the comparatively simple frame of that imperative necessity. With the cessation of open hostilities, nations confront the problems of peace. These are more difficult to solve, for there is no clearly defined and generally accepted goal as clearly mandatory upon all as that of victory in war. Unity of will gives way to diffusion of purpose, haste to procrastination, and suspicion thrives where cooperation once grew.

During the course of World War II, the danger from a common enemy ensured a measure of somewhat uneasy collaboration between Great Britain and the United States on the one hand and the Soviet Union on the other. At Teheran in 1943, at Yalta and Potsdam in 1945, the principal Allied leaders met to discuss certain obviously vital postwar issues—the establishment of an organization to promote international peace and security, the treatment of the defeated powers, the future of countries freed from German and Japanese control. Even before the Potsdam discussions, the United Nations Charter, signed in the closing weeks of the war, appeared to offer added evidence that the victorious Allies could work together in relative harmony and for common purposes.

In a few short years, however, wartime hopes gave way to postwar tensions. A basic and continuing problem to emerge was the antagonism and incompatibility of the Soviet zone of influence and that of western Europe and the United States. The circumstances of the war had made allies of western and eastern Europe; the coming of peace removed the compulsion that had forced them together and permitted the resumption of rivalry on a more intense level than that of prewar years. This was not simply a rivalry between "capitalism" and "communism." In fact, the economies of western Europe had or were in the process of receiving infusions of socialism. The competition involved very wide sections of the total culture—political organization and moral systems as well as the economic systems of the two countries. While Europe was the center for much of this, the struggle went on in many parts of the world. Men fought and died in Israel, in Greece, in Hungary, in Indo-China, in a score of other places scattered over the globe. Yet because no full-scale international holocaust broke out, the struggle, somewhat ironically, came to be labeled the "cold war."

The European (and American, for the United States became the pivot of the western group) manifestations of the cold war concern us here, and we shall take a look at two ways in which it has expressed itself. One is the sharp confrontation of East and West in the eastern Mediterranean, a confrontation precipitated after enunciation of the so-called Truman Doctrine by the President of the United States on March 12, 1947. The other is the stalemate in Berlin which has come to be most enduring and has been taken to symbolize the most significant feature of the struggle between the Soviet system and that of the free world.

Next we shall turn to non-Communist Europe and examine a development which most observers would have considered quite unlikely immediately after the world conflict. To many, the most exciting phenomenon in contemporary Europe is the change that is taking place in its patterns of economic organization and growth. And the movement for economic integration of western Europe has raised political questions whose solutions may be even more important for the future of Europe as a whole. From the beginning, the problems posed by European integration were many. Britain, for example, was a European nation, the center of a vast and vague Commonwealth, and had separate relations with the United States as well. Was her move toward the European Common Market a positive good, a necessary evil, or something to be avoided at all costs? Could her relatively planned economy—her agricultural system above all—remain protected if she became one of the European states in fact as in name? Did, indeed, the Common Market states welcome the prospect of British membership? These were some of the issues posed in the postwar world, and we shall look at materials which illuminate them.

Just as the United States must be central to any understanding of the postwar history of Europe, so increasingly must account be taken of the Communist regime in China. For a few years after the Chinese Communists had triumphed in their country, it was assumed that Chinese and Soviet Communists were the closest of allies. But in the 1950s and especially in the 1960s, the general solidarity within the

Communist world began to show evidences of internal strains and fissures. Historians began to conjecture that both Russia and China might well be more nationalistic than they were Communist. They felt that it could be, though it was by no means certain that it would be, that a Russo-Chinese struggle for dominance of the Communist world would emerge as one of the central facts of the twentieth century. In any case, the conflicting Russian and Chinese positions in this emerging struggle merit attention in the pages that follow.

Outside of Europe, particularly in Africa and Asia, other changes have come with bewildering rapidity. The great colonial nations have seen their former charges launch with varying success upon national careers for themselves. The circumstances in which these new nations have been founded represent such wide differences and their independence is so recent that little of general validity can be said beyond a recognition of the overwhelming importance to Europe of a fundamental shift in the relations of the European and non-European worlds. On all of our problems, and on numerous others not even mentioned, there is no shortage of documents in the modern world; they settle about us like the leaves of autumn. Perhaps those selected may be considered as representative, giving us a few fleeting clues to three or four of the problems in the history of postwar Europe.

I. The Truman Doctrine

By early 1947, clashes had broken out between the Soviet Union and the West over the German and Austrian settlement, over Persia and Turkey, over China. The wartime alliance was already succumbing to the tensions of the developing cold war. It was over Greece that the rift became complete. Since 1944, British troops had intervened there to prevent the Communists from seizing the country. A complicated civil war, in which Communist guerrillas were aided from Yugoslavia, Albania, and Bulgaria, dragged on despite Greek appeals to the United Nations. Finally, the British, themselves in a desperate financial and economic plight, turned to the United States for help in supporting the Greek regime. On March 12, 1947, President Harry S. Truman recommended military and economic assistance to Greece—and to Turkey as well. In so doing, he challenged the Soviet Union in an area close to some of her most vital interests. The words with which the President supported his actions heralded the beginning of a policy of "containing" future Communist expansion and of negotiating with the Russians in the future from "positions of strength." Together with the subsequent Marshall Plan, which offered economic aid in the recovery of non-Communist Europe, the Truman Doctrine set the tone for American

—and to a somewhat lesser extent western European—policy for at least a decade after its proclamation. Needless to say, it was castigated by spokesmen for the Soviet Union who rejected every American argument and charged that the United States was imposing its will upon smaller states as it sought expansion under a smokescreen of altruism. The conflicting points of view may be followed in a selection from President Truman's message to Congress and in a response which appeared in the Soviet newspaper *Izvestia*.

A. Truman's Message to Congress, March 12, 1947

Mr. President, Mr. Speaker, Members of the Congress of the United States:

The gravity of the situation which confronts the world today necessitates my appearance before a joint session of the Congress.

The foreign policy and the national security of this country are involved.

One aspect of the present situation, which I wish to present to you at this time for your consideration and decision, concerns Greece and Turkey.

The United States has received from

the Greek Government an urgent appeal for financial and economic assistance. Preliminary reports from the American Economic Mission now in Greece and reports from the American Ambassador in Greece corroborate the statement of the Greek Government that assistance is imperative if Greece is to survive as a free nation.

I do not believe that the American people and the Congress wish to turn a deaf ear to the appeal of the Greek Government. . . .

The very existence of the Greek state is today threatened by the terrorist activities of several thousand armed men, led by Communists, who defy the Government's authority at a number of points, particularly along the northern boundaries. A commission appointed by the United Nations Security Council is at present investigating disturbed conditions in northern Greece and alleged border violations along the frontier between Greece on the one hand and Albania, Bulgaria, and Yugoslavia on the other.

Meanwhile, the Greek Government is unable to cope with the situation. The Greek Army is small and poorly equipped. It needs supplies and equipment if it is to restore authority to the Government throughout Greek territory.

Greece must have assistance if it is to become a self-supporting and self-respecting democracy.

The United States must supply that assistance. We have already extended to Greece certain types of relief and economic aid, but these are inadequate.

There is no other country to which democratic Greece can turn.

No other nation is willing and able to provide the necessary support for a democratic Greek Government. . . .

The future of Turkey as an independent and economically sound state is clearly no less important to the freedom-loving peoples of the world than the future of Greece. The circumstances in which Turkey finds itself today are considerably different from those of Greece. Turkey has been spared the disasters that have beset Greece. And during the war the United States and Great Britain furnished Turkey with material aid.

Nevertheless, Turkey now needs our support.

Since the war Turkey has sought additional financial assistance from Great Britain and the United States for the purpose of effecting that modernization necessary for the maintenance of its national integrity.

That integrity is essential to the preservation of order in the Middle East.

The British Government has informed us that, owing to its own difficulties, it can no longer extend financial or economic aid to Turkey.

As in the case of Greece, if Turkey is to have the assistance it needs, the United States must supply it. We are the only country able to provide that help.

I am fully aware of the broad implications involved if the United States extends assistance to Greece and Turkey, and I shall discuss these implications with you at this time.

One of the primary objectives of the foreign policy of the United States is the creation of conditions in which we and other nations will be able to work out a way of life free from coercion. This was a fundamental issue in the war with Germany and Japan. Our victory was won over countries which sought to impose their will, and their way of life upon other nations.

To insure the peaceful development of nations, free from coercion, the United States has taken a leading part in establishing the United Nations. The United Nations is designed to make possible lasting freedom and independence for all its members. We shall not realize our objectives, however, unless we are willing to help free peoples to maintain their free institutions and their national integrity against aggressive movements that seek to impose upon them totalitarian regimes. This is no more than a frank recognition that totalitarian regimes imposed upon free peoples, by direct or indirect aggression, undermine the foundations of international peace and hence the security of the United States.

The peoples of a number of countries of the world have recently had totalitarian regimes forced upon them against their will. The Government of the United States had made frequent protests against coercion and intimidation, in violation of the Yalta agreement, in Poland, Rumania, and Bulgaria. I must also state that in a number of other countries there have been similar developments.

At the present moment in world history nearly every nation must choose between alternative ways of life. The choice is too often not a free one.

One way of life is based upon the will of the majority, and is distinguished by free institutions, representative government, free elections, guaranties of individual liberty, freedom of speech and religion, and freedom from political oppression.

The second way of life is based upon the will of a minority forcibly imposed upon the majority. It relies upon terror and oppression, a controlled press and radio, fixed elections, and the suppression of personal freedoms.

I believe that it must be the policy of the United States to support free peoples who are resisting attempted subjugation by armed minorities or by outside pressures.

I believe that we must assist free peoples to work out their own destinies in their own way.

I believe that our help should be primarily through economic and financial aid which is essential to economic stability and orderly political processes.

The world is not static, and the *status quo* is not sacred. But we cannot allow changes in the *status quo* in violation of the Charter of the United Nations by such methods as coercion, or by such subterfuges as political infiltration. In helping free and independent nations to maintain their freedom, the United States will be giving effect to the principles of the Charter of the United Nations.

It is necessary only to glance at a map to realize that the survival and integrity of the Greek nation are of grave importance in a much wider situation. If Greece should fall under the control of an armed minority, the effect upon its neighbor, Turkey, would be immediate and serious. Confusion and disorder might well spread throughout the entire Middle East.

Moreover, the disappearance of Greece as an independent state would have a profound effect upon those countries in Europe whose peoples are struggling against great difficulties to maintain their freedoms and their independence while they repair the damages of war.

It would be an unspeakable tragedy if these countries, which have struggled so long against overwhelming odds, should lose that victory for which they sacrificed so much. Collapse of free institutions and loss of independence would be disastrous not only for them but for the world. Discouragement and possibly failure would quickly be the lot of neighboring peoples striving to maintain their freedom and independence.

Should we fail to aid Greece and Turkey in this fateful hour, the effect will be far-reaching to the West as well as to the East.

We must take immediate and resolute action.

I therefore ask the Congress to provide authority for assistance to Greece and Turkey in the amount of $400,000,000 for the period ending June 30, 1948. In requesting these funds, I have taken into consideration the maximum amount of relief assistance which would be furnished to Greece out of the $350,000,000 which I recently requested that the Congress authorize for the prevention of starvation and suffering in countries devastated by the war.

In addition to funds, I ask the Congress to authorize the detail of American civilian and military personnel to Greece and Turkey, at the request of those countries, to assist in the tasks of reconstruction, and for the purpose of supervising the use of such financial and material assistance as may be furnished. I recommend that authority also be provided for the instruction and training of selected Greek and Turkish personnel.

Finally, I ask that the Congress provide authority which will permit the speediest and most effective use, in terms of needed commodities, supplies, and equipment, of such funds as may be authorized.

If further funds, or further authority, should be needed for purposes indicated in this message, I shall not hesitate to bring the situation before the Congress. On this subject the Executive and Legislative branches of the Government must work together.

This is a serious course upon which we embark.

I would not recommend it except that the alternative is much more serious.

The United States contributed $341,-000,000,000 toward winning World War II. This is an investment in world freedom and world peace.

The assistance that I am recommending for Greece and Turkey amounts to little more than one tenth of one percent of this investment. It is only common sense that we should safeguard this investment and make sure that it was not in vain.

The seeds of totalitarian regimes are nurtured by misery and want. They spread and grow in the evil soil of poverty and strife. They reach their full growth when the hope of a people for a better life has died.

We must keep that hope alive.

The free peoples of the world look to us for support in maintaining their freedoms.

If we falter in our leadership, we may endanger the peace of the world—and we shall surely endanger the welfare of our own Nation.

Great responsibilities have been placed upon us by the swift movement of events.

I am confident that the Congress will face these responsibilities squarely.

Department of State Bulletin, March 23, 1947, pp. 534–37.

B. Russian Criticism of the Truman Doctrine

On March 12, President Truman addressed a message to the U.S. Congress asking for 400 million dollars to be assigned for urgent aid to Greece and Turkey, and for authority to send to those countries American civil and military personnel, and to provide for the training by Americans of specially picked Greek and Turkish personnel.

Greece, said Truman, was in a desperate economic and olitical situation. Britain was no longer able to act as trustee for the Greeks. Turkey had requested speedy American aid. Turkey, unlike Greece, had not suffered from the Second World War, but she needed financial aid from Britain and from the U.S.A. in order to carry out that modernisation necessary for maintaining her national integrity. Since the British Government, on account of its own difficulties, was not capable of offering financial or other aid to the Turks, this aid must be furnished by the U.S.A.

Thus Congress was asked to do two "good deeds" at once—to save Greece from internal disorders and to pay for the cost of "modernising" Turkey.

The pathetic appeal of the Tsaldaris Government to the U.S.A. is clear evidence of the bankruptcy of the political regime in Greece. But the matter does not lie solely with the Greek Monarchists and their friends, now cracked up to American Congressmen as the direct descendants of the heroes of Thermopylae: it is well known that the real masters of Greece have been and are the British military authorities.

British troops have been on Greek territory since 1944. On Churchill's initiative, Britain took on herself the responsibility for "stabilising" political conditions in Greece. The British authorities did not confine themselves to perpetuating the rule of the reactionary, anti-democratic forces in Greece, making no scruple in supporting ex-collaborators with the Germans. The entire political and economic activities under a number of short-lived Greek Governments have been carried on under close British control and direction.

Today we can see the results of this policy—complete bankruptcy. British troops failed to bring peace and tranquillity to tormented Greece. The Greek people have been plunged into the abyss of new sufferings, of hunger and poverty. Civil war takes on ever fiercer forms.

Was not the presence of foreign troops on Greek territory instrumental in bringing about this state of affairs? Does not Britain, who proclaimed herself the guardian of Greece, bear responsibility for the bankruptcy of her charge?

The American President's message completely glosses over these questions. The U.S.A. does not wish to criticise Britain, since she herself intends to follow the British example. Truman's statement makes it clear that the U.S.A. does not intend to deviate from the course of British policy in Greece. So one cannot expect better results.

The U.S. Government has no intention of acting in the Greek question as one might have expected a member of UNO, concerned about the fate of another member, to act. It is obvious that in Washington they do not wish to take into account the obligations assumed by the U.S. Government regarding UNO. Truman did not even consider it necessary to wait for the findings of the Security Council Commission specially sent to Greece to investigate the situation on the spot.

Truman, indeed, failed to reckon either with the international organisation or with the sovereignty of Greece. What will be left of Greek sovereignty when the "American military and civilian personnel" gets to work in Greece by means of the 250 million dollars brought into that country? The sovereignty and independence of Greece will be the first victims of such singular "defence."

The American arguments for assisting Turkey base themselves on the existence of a threat to the integrity of Turkish territory—though no-one and nothing actually threatens Turkey's integrity. This "assistance" is evidently aimed at putting this country also under U.S. control.

Some American commentators admit this quite openly. Walter Lippmann, for example, frankly points out in the *Herald-Tribune* that an American alliance with Turkey would give the U.S.A. a strategic position, incomparably more advantageous than any other, from which power could be wielded over the Middle East.

Commenting on Truman's message to Congress, *The New York Times* proclaims the advent of "the age of American responsibility." Yet what is this responsibility but a smokescreen for expansion? The cry of saving Greece and Turkey from the expansion of the so-called "totalitarian states" is not new. Hitler used to refer to the Bolsheviks when he wanted to open the road for his own conquests. Now they want to take Greece and Turkey under their control, they raise a din about "totalitarian states." This seems all the more attractive since, in elbowing in itself, the U.S.A. is pushing non-totalitarian Britain out of yet another country or two.…

We are now witnessing a fresh intrusion of the U.S.A. into the affairs of other states. American claims to leadership in international affairs grow parallel with the growing appetite of the American quarters concerned. But the American leaders, in the new historical circumstances, fail to reckon with the fact that the old methods of the colonisers and die-hard politicians have out-lived their time and are doomed to failure. In this lies the chief weakness of Truman's message.

Soviet News, March 15, 1947.

II. Berlin

The "cold war" for some time maintained its warmest temperature in the city of Berlin. After the war, Germany had been divided into zones of occupation administered by the Russians, British, French, and Americans. All were agreed in principle upon the denazification and demilitarization of Germany and the introduction of democratic institutions. But in practice, agreement broke down. France opposed the formation of a central German administration. More importantly, Russian policy in the Allied Control Council which had been set up diverged sharply from that of the British and Americans. Gradually the latter attempted to ensure—and France eventually concurred—that in their western zone Germany should be made self-sufficient and a contributor to the recovery of Europe. They laid plans for a constituent assembly to draw up a constitution for a Federal German Government subject to the limitations of an occupation statute. And in June, 1948, they promulgated a currency reform in the western zones which elicited violent Russian protests.

In reaction to the currency regulations, the Soviet authorities, having already withdrawn from the Allied Control Council, now walked out of the Berlin Kommandatura, a miniature Control Council for the joint administration of Berlin, the position of which, surrounded as it was by the Soviet Zone, was most precarious. Meanwhile, they imposed a blockade on Berlin which was broken by the western powers after almost a year by the determined use of a massive air lift to fly in supplies and keep open access to the city.

But with the Berlin blockade, the pattern of the "German problem" began to emerge. Step by step, the western powers promoted the establishment of an independent Federal German Republic which came into existence in 1949. Despite French and British misgivings, the new West German Republic also became a participant in the military defense of the West under the North Atlantic Treaty Organization. For their part, the Russians turned their zone of occupation into the German Democratic Republic, whose government, in the eyes of the West, was nothing more than a Soviet satellite. As for Berlin, it too was divided into an eastern and western zone, at the end of the 1950s, indeed, by an actual wall which had been built by the East German Communists to seal off the eastern part of the city from any but minimal contact with the West.

The struggle for Berlin, then, was part of an even broader struggle for Germany as a whole—and with it perhaps the future of all of Europe. The two documents below sum up the controversy and throw light on the conflicting positions over Berlin and Germany. On November 27, 1958, the Soviet Union declared its intention to consider Berlin as a free city and stated that if a four-power agreement had not been reached prior to May 27, 1959, it would transfer its control power in Eastern Germany to the Communist government of the German Democratic Republic. On December 31, 1958, the British Government, in accord with those of France and the United States, presented its reply setting forth the western view of the fundamental issues of the Berlin problem.

A. Note from the Soviet Government Regarding the Question of Berlin, 27 November 1958

...The question of Berlin, which lies in the centre of the German Democratic Republic but the western part of which is severed from the German Democratic Republic as a consequence of foreign occupation, profoundly affects not only the national interests of the German people but also the interests of all peoples wishing to establish a lasting peace in Europe. There, in the historic capital of Germany, two worlds are in direct contact and barricades of the "cold war" exist at every step. A situation of constant friction and tension has prevailed for many years in the city, which is divided into two parts. Berlin, which witnessed the greatest triumph of the joint struggle of our countries against fascist aggression, has now become a dangerous centre of contradictions between the great powers which were allies in the last war. Its role in the relations between the powers can be compared with a slow-burning fuse leading to a barrel of gunpowder. Incidents arising there, even if they seem to be of local significance, in a situation of heated passions, suspicion and mutual apprehension may cause a conflagration which it will be difficult to put out.

This is the dismal finale, reached after 13 postwar years, to the once joint, concerted policy of the four powers—the U.S.S.R., the United States, the United Kingdom and France—towards Germany.
. . .

Expressing the will of the peoples who made incalculable sacrifices for the sake of smashing the Hitler aggressors, the governments of the four powers solemnly pledged themselves to extirpate German militarism and nazism, to prevent forever their resurgence and to take all measures to ensure that Germany would never again threaten her neighbours or the preservation of world peace. The participants in the Potsdam Conference expressed their determination to prevent any fascist and militarist activity or propaganda. They also pledged themselves to permit and encourage all democratic political parties in Germany. With the aim of destroying the economic foundations of German militarism, it was resolved to eliminate the excessive concentration in the economy of Germany, represented in the form of cartels, syndicates, trusts and other monopoly organisations which had ensured the assumption of power by fascism and the preparation and carrying out of Hitler aggression.

The Potsdam Agreement contained important provisions whereby Germany was to be regarded as a single economic whole during the occupation period. The agreement also provided for the setting up of central German administrative departments. The Council of Foreign Ministers, set up by decision of the Potsdam Conference, was instructed to prepare a peace settlement for Germany.

The implementation of all these measures should have enabled the German people to effect a fundamental reconstruction of their life and to ensure the establishment of a united, peaceloving and democratic German state.

Such are the main provisions of the Potsdam Agreement, which ensured a just combination of the interests both of the peoples who had fought against Germany and the fundamental interests of the German people themselves, and at the same time created a sound foundation for carrying through a concerted policy of the four powers on the German question, and consequently, for extensive and fruitful cooperation among them on European questions in general.

However, further developments did not follow the course laid down at Potsdam. The relations between the U.S.S.R. and the three western powers increasingly deteriorated and there was a growth of mutual distrust and suspicion, which have now already developed into unfriendly relations. . . .

The relations of the United States, and also of the United Kingdom and France, with the Soviet Union took a particularly sharp turn when those powers began carrying through in Germany a policy contrary to the Potsdam Agreement. The first violation of the Potsdam Agreement was the refusal of the governments of the United States, the United Kingdom and France to honour their commitments under this agreement regarding the transfer to the Soviet Union of the agreed amount of industrial equipment from Western Germany as partial compensation for the destruction and damage inflicted on the national economy of the U.S.S.R. by the aggression of Hitler Germany.

But that was not all, and the governments of the United States and the United Kingdom, with every passing year, further abandoned the principles underlying the Potsdam Agreement. . . .

Two states thus came into being in Germany. Whereas in Western Germany, whose development was directed by the United States, the United Kingdom and France, a government took office whose representatives do not conceal their hatred of the Soviet Union and often openly advertise the similarity of their aspirations with the plans of the nazi aggressors, in Eastern Germany a government was created which broke forever with Germany's aggressive past. State and public affairs in the German Democratic Republic are regulated by a constitution that is fully in keeping with the principles of the Potsdam Agreement and the finest progressive traditions of the German people. The domination of the monopolies and *junkers* was abolished forever in the German Democratic Republic, nazism was extirpated, and a number of other social and economic transformations were carried out which prevented the possibility of a revival of militarism and made the German Democratic Republic an important factor for peace in Europe. The government of the German Democratic Republic solemnly proclaimed that it would fulfil its commitments under the Potsdam Agreement to the letter, which, by the way, the government of the Federal Republic of Germany is obstinately avoiding doing. The inclusion of the Federal Republic of Germany in the North Atlantic bloc impelled the Soviet Union to take retaliatory measures, since the obligations binding the Soviet Union, the United States, the United Kingdom and France, had been broken by the three western powers who had united with Western Germany, and previously with Italy, against the Soviet Union, which had borne the brunt of the struggle against the fascist aggressors. This restricted military grouping likewise created a threat to other countries. Such a situation impelled the Soviet Union and a number of other European countries that had suffered from aggression by German and Italian fascism, to establish their own defensive organisation, concluding for this purpose the Warsaw Treaty, to which the German Democratic Republic also acceded.

There is only one conclusion to be drawn from the foregoing: The Potsdam Agreement has been grossly violated by the western powers. It looks now like the trunk of a tree, once mighty and fruit-bearing, but now mangled and with its core cut out. The lofty aims for which the Potsdam Agreement was concluded, have long since been thrown away by the western powers, and their practical activity in Germany is

diametrically opposed to what the Potsdam Agreement envisaged. . .

The Soviet Union, like other countries concerned to strengthen peace in Europe, supports the proposals of the German Democratic Republic for the peaceful unification of Germany. The government of the U.S.S.R. is sorry to note that none of the efforts made in this direction have so far produced any positive result, since the governments of the United States and the other N.A.T.O. countries—and, above all, the government of the Federal Republic of Germany—are, in point of fact, doing nothing towards the conclusion of a peace treaty, or the uniting of Germany.

Consequently, the policies of the United States, the United Kingdom and France, directed as they are towards the militarisation of Western Germany and involving her in the military bloc of the western powers, have prevented the enforcement of those provisions of the Potsdam Agreement which deal with Germany unity. . . .

The fact that Germany still has no peace treaty is, above all, the fault of the governments of the United States, the United Kingdom and France, which have never seemed to like the idea of drafting such a treaty.

It is well known that the governments of the three powers have reacted negatively to every approach the Soviet government has made to them for the preparation of a peace treaty with Germany.

At the moment, the United States, the United Kingdom and France—as follows from their Notes of September 30 last— are opposed to the latest proposals for a peaceful settlement with Germany, put forward by the Soviet Union and the German Democratic Republic, while making no proposals of their own on this subject, just as they have made none at any time during the postwar period. In point of fact, the recent Note of the United States government is a restatement of a position shown to be utterly unrealistic, whereby Germany's national unity would be re-established by the U.S.S.R., the United

States, Britain and France, instead of by the German states which are to unite. Another fact revealed by the United States government's Note is that it is once again avoiding negotiations with the Soviet Union and the other interested countries for the drafting of a peace treaty with Germany. The result really is a vicious circle: The government of the United States objects to the drafting of a German peace treaty on the grounds of the absence of a united German state—while, at the same time, it hampers the reunification of Germany by rejecting the only feasible chance of solving this problem through agreement between the two German states.

Are not the western powers sticking to this line on the preparation of a peace treaty so as to preserve their privileges in Western Germany and to maintain the occupation regime in West Berlin interminably?

It is become increasingly clear that this is precisely the situation. . . .

Anxious to live in peace and friendship with the whole German people, the Soviet Union has established and is maintaining normal diplomatic relations with both German states. It maintains close friendly relations with the German Democratic Republic. These relations have been anchored in the treaty which the Soviet Union and the German Democratic Republic concluded on September 20, 1955. In conformity with that treaty, relations between the two states are based on the principles of complete equality, respect for each other's sovereignty and non-interference in one another's domestic affairs. These, too, are the principles by which the Soviet government is guided in its relations with the other German state—the Federal Republic of Germany. . . .

A patently absurd situation has arisen, therefore, in which the Soviet Union supports and maintains, as it were, favourable conditions for activity by the western powers directed against the U.S.S.R. and its Warsaw Treaty allies. It is clearly obvious that the Soviet Union, and the other parties to the Warsaw Treaty, can no

longer tolerate this state of affairs. For the occupation regime in West Berlin to continue would be tantamount to recognising something like a privileged position for the N.A.T.O. countries, a privileged position for which, of course, there is no justification.

Can anyone really seriously believe that the Soviet Union will help the forces of aggression to develop subversive activities against the socialist countries, let alone to prepare an attack on them? It must be clear to everyone of sound mind that the Soviet Union cannot maintain a situation in West Berlin which is detrimental to its legitimate interests, to its security and to the security of the other socialist countries. It would be well to remember that the Soviet Union is not a Jordan or an Iran, and that is will never allow methods of pressure to be applied to it, in order to force on it conditions suiting the powers belonging to the opposing N.A.T.O. military bloc. But this is just what the western powers want from the Soviet Union, since they seek to retain their occupation rights in West Berlin.

Can the Soviet government afford to disregard all these facts, which affect the basic security interests of the Soviet Union, and its ally, the German Democratic Republic, and of all the signatories of the Warsaw Defence Treaty? Why, of course not! The Soviet government can no longer consider itself bound by that part of the Allied agreements on Germany which has assumed an unequal character and is being used for the maintenance of the occupation regime in West Berlin and for interference in the domestic affairs of the German Democratic Republic.

In view of this, the government of the U.S.S.R. hereby notifies the government of the United States that the Soviet Union regards as null and void the "Protocol of the Agreement between the Governments of the Union of Soviet Socialist Republics, the United States of America and the United Kingdom, on the Occupation Zones of Germany and on the Administration of Greater Berlin," dated September 12,

1944; and the associated supplementary agreements, including the Agreement on the Control Mechanism in Germany concluded between the governments of the U.S.S.R., the United States, the United Kingdom and France on May 1, 1945—that is, to say, the agreements which were to be effective during the first years following the surrender of Germany. . . .

The best way to solve the Berlin question would be for a decision to be taken, based on the enforcement of the Potsdam Agreement on Germany. But this would be possible only if the three western powers resumed, in common with the U.S.S.R., a policy towards Germany which would accord with the spirit and the principles of the Potsdam Agreement. In the present circumstances, this would mean the withdrawal of the Federal Republic of Germany from N.A.T.O., with the simultaneous withdrawal of the German Democratic Republic from the Warsaw Treaty Organisation, and the achievement of an agreement whereby, in accordance with the principles of the Potsdam Agreement, neither of the two German states would have any armed forces in excess of those needed to maintain law and order at home and to guard their frontiers. . .

An independent solution to the Berlin problem must be found in the very near future, since the western powers are refusing to take part in the drafting of a peace treaty with Germany, and the government of the Federal Republic of Germany, supported by the same powers, is pursuing a policy of obstructing Germany's unification. It is necessary to prevent West Berlin from being used any longer for intensified espionage, wrecking or any other subversive activities against the socialist countries, against the German Democratic Republic, the U.S.S.R., or, to quote the leaders of the United States government, to prevent it from being used for "indirect aggression" against the countries of the socialist camp.

Essentially speaking, the only interest the United States, the United Kingdom and France have in West Berlin consists in using this "frontline city," as it is vociferously called in the West, as a vantage point from which to carry on hostile activity against the socialist countries. This is the only benefit the western powers are deriving from their presence in Berlin as occupationists. The ending of the legally unjustified occupation of West Berlin would do no harm either to the United States, or to the United Kingdom, or to France. It would, on the other hand, go far towards improving the international atmosphere in Europe and setting people's minds at rest in all countries.

Conversely, the only conclusion one can draw from the western powers persisting in preserving their occupation of West Berlin is that "indirect aggression" against the German Democratic Republic and the Soviet Union is not the only aim they are pursuing, and that there must be some plans for a yet more dangerous use of West Berlin. . . .

The most correct and natural way to solve the problem would, of course, be for the western part of Berlin, which is virtually detached from the German Democratic Republic, to be reunited with its eastern part and for Berlin to become a single united city within the state on whose land it is situated.

However, the Soviet government, taking into account the present unrealistic policy of the United States, and also of the United Kingdom and France, with regard to the German Democratic Republic, cannot fail to see the difficulties the western powers have in contributing to such a solution of the Berlin problem. At the same time it is guided by concern to prevent the process of abolishing the occupation regime from involving anything like a painful disruption of the ways which have become entrenched in the life of the population of West Berlin.

One cannot, of course, fail to take into account the fact that the political and economic development of West Berlin, during its occupation by the three western powers, has differed from that of East Berlin and the German Democratic Republic, with the result that the way of life in the two parts of Berlin is entirely different at the present time. The Soviet government considers that upon the ending of foreign occupation, the population of West Berlin should be given the right to establish a way of life of its own choosing. Should the inhabitants of West Berlin desire to preserve the present way of life, based on private capitalist ownership, it is up to them to do so. The U.S.S.R., for its part, will respect any choice the West Berliners may make.

On the strength of all these considerations, the Soviet government finds it possible for the question of West Berlin to be settled for the time being by making West Berlin an independent political entity— a free city—without any state, including either of the existing German states, interfering in its life. It might be possible, in particular, to agree on the territory of the free city being demilitarised and having no armed forces on it. The free city of West Berlin could have its own government and could run its own economy and its administrative and other affairs.

The four powers, which shared in the administration of Berlin after the war, could, as could the two German states, undertake to respect the status of West Berlin as a free city, just as has been done by the four powers, for instance, with regard to the neutral status which has been adopted by the Austrian Republic.

For its part, the Soviet government would have no objection to the United Nations also sharing, in one way or another, in observing the free-city status of West Berlin. . . .

It should, of course, be borne in mind that the consent of the German Democratic Republic to the setting up of such an independent political organism as the free city of West Berlin within its territory would be a concession, a definite sacrifice by the German Democratic Republic for the sake of strengthening peace in Europe, for the sake of the national interests of the German people as a whole.

The Soviet government, for its part, has resolved to carry out measures designed to abolish the occupation regime in Berlin, guided by the desire to normalise the situation in Berlin, in the interests of European peace, and in the interests of the peaceful and independent development of Germany. It hopes that the government of the United States will show a proper understanding of these motives and adopt a realistic attitude on the Berlin issue.

At the same time the Soviet government is ready to open negotiations with the governments of the United States and other countries concerned, on granting West Berlin the status of a demilitarised free city. If this proposal is not acceptable to the United States government, there is no topic left for talks on the Berlin question by the former occupying powers. . . .

In view of this the Soviet government proposes to make no changes in the present procedure for military traffic of the United States, the United Kingdom and France from West Berlin to the Federal Republic of Germany for half a year. It regards this period as quite adequate for finding a sound basis for a solution to the problems connected with the change in the position of Berlin and for preventing the possibility of any complications if, of course, the governments of the western powers do not deliberately work for such complications.

During this period the sides will have the possibility of proving, by settling the Berlin issue, their desire for a relaxation of international tension.

If the above period is not used for reaching an appropriate agreement, the Soviet Union will effect the planned measures by agreement with the German Democratic Republic.

It is envisaged that the German Democratic Republic, like any other independent state, must fully control questions concerning its space, that is to say, exercise its sovereignty on land, on water and in the air. At the same time there will be an end to all the contacts still maintained between representatives of the armed forces and other officials of the Soviet Union in Germany and corresponding representatives of the armed forces and other officials of the United States, the United Kingdom, and France on questions relating to Berlin.

Voices are being raised in the capitals

of some western powers claiming that these powers do not recognise the Soviet Union's decision to discard the functions of maintaining the occupation status in Berlin. How can such a question be raised? Anyone who today speaks of non-recognition of the steps planned by the Soviet Union would obviously like to speak of it, not the language of reason and well-founded argument, but in the language of brute force, forgetting that the Soviet people are not affected by threats or intimidation. If, behind the word 'non-recognition,' there really lies the intention to resort to force and draw the world into a war over Berlin, the advocates of such a policy should take into consideration the fact that they are assuming a very grave responsibility before the peoples and before history for all the consequences of that policy.

Anyone who brandishes weapons in connection with the situation in Berlin once again exposes his interest in maintaining the occupation regime in Berlin for aggressive purposes. The government of the Soviet Union would like to hope that the problem of normalising the situation in Berlin, which life itself raises before our states as an imperative necessity, will in any case be solved in accordance with the considerations of statesmanship, in the interests of peace among the peoples, without any unnecessary tension or aggravation of the 'cold war'. . . .

Soviet News, November 28, 1958.

B. Note from the United Kingdom Government to the Government of the Soviet Union regarding Berlin, 31 December 1958

. . .The Soviet Government's Note. . . deals at some length with the question of the Potsdam Agreement. Her Majesty's Government do not accept the argument that the status of Berlin depends upon that agreement. Their view of the purely juridical position of Berlin is set forth in later passages of this Note. Nevertheless they consider it useful to comment on certain of the observations in the Soviet Government's Note on the subject of the Potsdam Agreement.

2. As the Soviet Government correctly states, the Potsdam Agreement provided for Germany to be regarded as a single economic whole. But the Soviet Government made no attempt to fulfil this vital provision of the Agreement. From the beginning of the occupation the Soviet Government carried out an independent economic policy in its Zone, which was progressively stripped of assets and equipment for the sole benefit of the Soviet Union. In addition the Soviet Government while maintaining its own claims to reparations persistently refused to agree to any of the measures, such as common import-export programmes for Germany as a whole, which were specifically called for under the Potsdam Agreement.

3. The Soviet Government further contends that the Western Powers, in contravention of the Potsdam Agreement, 'brought to life and strengthened the very forces which had forged the Hitlerite military machine.' Her Majesty's Government would recall in this connexion the measures of re-militarisation which the Soviet Government carried out in its Zone of Germany. The most important of these was the creation of *Bereitschaften* ('Alert Squads') to which Her Majesty's Government drew the attention of the Soviet Government in a Note of May 25, 1950:

'In that part of Germany subject to Soviet control, a police force has been created which, by reason of its organisation, training and equipment, has the character of an army. . . . It is known. . .to be organised on the basis of *Bereitschaften* under the control of the *Hauptverwaltung fuer Ausbildung* (Training Department) and to consist of nearly 50,000 men. They are embodied in military formations, which include artillery, tank and infantry battalions. They receive basic military training and are not employed on normal police duties. They are equipped with military weapons including, in some units, machine guns, anti-tank guns, anti-aircraft guns, mortars and tanks. A number of high-ranking German army officers are employed in the force.'

4. The Soviet Government also alleges that the Western Powers have violated those provisions of the Potsdam Agreement aimed at securing the unity of Germany as a peace-loving democratic State. The word "democratic" would seem to-day to be susceptible of many interpretations. In the West, it still denotes a social system in which freedom of religion, speech, voting and the press are permitted. As the Soviet Government is aware, specific provision for the establishment of such freedoms was made in the Potsdam Agreement, as well as for the formation of free trade unions. None of these freedoms exists in East Germany. If it is suggested that this is a matter of opinion Her Majesty's Government would recall that some two million Germans have left East Germany in recent years rather than endure any longer the social system which exists there. These are facts, not theories.

5. Her Majesty's Government's object in drawing attention to these considerations is simply to correct the impression presented by the Soviet Government in that part of its Note dealing with the Potsdam Agreement. As stated above, however, Her Majesty's Government do not admit the relevance of the Potsdam Agreement to the question of Berlin, which is the question immediately at issue. . . .

The Berlin situation of which the Soviet Government complains and which it considers abnormal is a result of the very nature of the German problem as it has existed since 1945. When Hitler's Reich collapsed the Western allies were in military possession of more than one-third of the area which was then occupied by the Soviet authorities. The Soviet Union was in possession of Berlin. As a result of the Agreements of September 12, 1944, and May 1, 1945, the Western Allies withdrew and permitted the Soviet occupation of large parts of Mecklenburg, Saxony, Thuringia and Anhalt. In consequence of the same Agreements, the three Western Powers moved into their sectors in West Berlin.

2. The Soviet Union has directly and through the regime which it refers to as the German Democratic Republic consolidated its hold over the large areas which the Western allies relinquished to it. It now demands that the Western allies should relinquish their rights in Berlin which were provided for in the above Agreements. But Agreements made by the Four Powers cannot be considered obsolete because one of them, having obtained the full advantage therefrom, now considers that the time has come to cancel them. These Agreements are binding upon all of the signatories so long as they have not been replaced by other agreements following free negotiation.

3. In any case however the right of the three Western Powers to be in Berlin rests, not on the agreements referred to above, but on the unconditional surrender of Germany and the assumption by the victorious Powers of supreme authority in Germany. They are not prepared to relinquish this right, upon the continued exercise of which the freedom of West Berlin will depend as long as there is no settlement of the German problem.

4. So far as the Potsdam Agreement is concerned, the status of Berlin does not depend upon that Agreement and it is the Soviet Union that bears responsibility for the fact that the Potsdam Agreement was not implemented.

5. The Soviet memorandum purports formally to repudiate the Agreements of September 12, 1944, and May 1, 1945. This repudiation in fact involves other and more recent engagements. Her Majesty's Government would refer in this connexion to the Four Power Agreement of June 20, 1949, whereby, among other things, the Soviet Union assumed "an obligation" to assure the normal functioning of transport and communication between Berlin and the Western zones of Germany. This "obligation" the Soviet Union now purports to

shed. Her Majesty's Government would also refer to the "Summit" Agreement of July 23, 1955, whereby the Four Powers recognised 'their common responsibility for the settlement of the German question,' a phrase which necessarily includes the problem of Berlin. Apparently the Soviet Union now attempts to free itself from these agreed responsibilities and obligations.

6. Her Majesty's Government note that the Soviet Government wishes to terminate its own authority in the quadripartite regime in the sector which it occupies in the City of Berlin. However that may be Her Majesty's Government will not and do not in any way accept a unilateral denunciation of the Agreements of 1944 and 1945, nor are they prepared to relieve the Soviet Union of the obligations which it assumed in June 1949. Such action on the part of the Soviet Government would have no legal basis since the Agreements can only be terminated by mutual consent. Her Majesty's Government will accordingly continue to hold the Soviet Government directly responsible under existing Agreements, for the discharge of its obligations undertaken with respect to Berlin. The French and United States Governments and Her Majesty's Government have the right to maintain garrisons in their sectors of Berlin and to have free access thereto. Certain administrative procedures have been agreed with the Soviet authorities and are in operation at the present time. Her Majesty's Government will not accept a unilateral repudiation on the part of the Soviet Government of its obligations in respect of that freedom of access. Nor will they accept the substitution of the regime which the Soviet Government refers to as the German Democratic Republic for the Soviet Government in this respect.

7. The continued protection of the freedom of more than two million people of West Berlin is a right and responsibility solemnly accepted by the three Western Powers. Thus Her Majesty's Government cannot consider any proposal which would have the effect of jeopardising the freedom and security of these people. The rights of the Three Powers to remain in Berlin with

unhindered communications by land and air between that city and the Federal Republic of Germany are under existing conditions essential to the discharge of that right and responsibility. Hence the proposal for a so-called "free city" for West Berlin, as put forward by the Soviet Union, is unacceptable.

8. In the view of Her Majesty's Government there can be no 'threat' to the Soviet Government or the regime which the Soviet Government refers to as the German Democratic Republic from the presence of the French, United States and British garrisons in Berlin. The forces of the three Western Powers in Berlin number about 10,000 men. The Soviet Government, on the other hand, is said to maintain some 350,000 troops in East Germany while the regime which the Soviet Government refer to as the German Democratic Republic is understood also to maintain over 200,000 men under arms. In these circumstances, the fear that the Western troops in Berlin may 'inflict harm' appears to be wholly unfounded. If Berlin has become a focus of international tension, it is because the Soviet Government has deliberately threatened to disturb the existing arrangements at present inforce there, arrangements to which the Soviet Government is itself a party. The inhabitants of West Berlin have recently reaffirmed in a free vote their overwhelming approval and support for the existing status of that city.

9. As is stated in the Soviet Government's Note of November 27, it is certainly not normal that thirteen years after the end of the war there should still remain in a part of German territory a system of occupation instituted in 1945. Her Majesty's Government deplore this fact and the fact that Germany has not yet been reunified so that Berlin might resume its rightful position as capital of a united Germany. For ten years the Western Powers have at numerous international meetings with the Soviet Union done everything in their power to bring about the signing of a Peace Treaty with a reunified Germany. But all their efforts have failed.

10. The form of government in Berlin, the validity of which the Soviet Government attempts to contest to-day, is only one aspect of the German problem. This problem, which has often been defined, involves the well-known questions of re-unification of Germany and European security as well as a Peace Treaty. Her Majesty's Government made clear their readiness to discuss these problems in their Note to the Soviet Government of September 30, 1958, in which it was stated:

'Her Majesty's Government are ready at any time to enter into discussions with the Soviet Government on the basis of these proposals (i.e., the Western proposals for free all-German elections and free decisions for an all-German Government) or of any other proposals genuinely designed to ensure the re-unification of Germany in freedom, in any appropriate forum. They regard the solution of the German problem as essential if a lasting settlement in Europe is to be achieved.' The Soviet Government has not yet replied to this Note.

11. Public repudiation of solemn engagements, formally entered into and re-peatedly reaffirmed, coupled with an ultimatum threatening unilateral action to implement that repudiation unless it be acquiesced in within six months, would afford no reasonable basis for negotiation between sovereign states. Her Majesty's Government could not embark on discussion with the Soviet Government upon these questions under menace. It is assumed that this is not the purpose of the Soviet Note of November 27 and that the Soviet Government, like themselves, is ready to enter into discussions in an atmosphere devoid of coercion or threats.

12. On this basis Her Majesty's Government would be glad to learn whether the Soviet Government is ready to enter into discussions of all these problems between the Four Powers concerned. In that event, it would be the object of Her Majesty's Government to discuss the question of Berlin in the wider framework of negotiations for a solution of the German problem as well as that of European security. Her Majesty's Government would welcome the views of the Soviet Government at an early date.

Command 634, pp. 24–27.

III. *The European Common Market*

While the cold war was splitting Europe into East and West, western Europe undertook a most significant search for new forms of integration. Primed by American aid, the nations of western Europe made a dramatic economic and psychological recovery after World War II. As the years passed, a series of institutions began to emerge which signalized the drive toward new European institutions and closer unity of the western European powers. Western European Union, the Council of Europe, Benelux, the European Coal and Steel Community, the European Atomic Energy Community—these were but a sample of the groupings which came into being during these years.

Most important of these institutions, in the eyes of many observers, was the European Economic Community, or Common Market, which was established in the Treaty of Rome (1957) and which envisaged a high degree of political as well as economic unity. Six nations—France, West Germany, Italy, Belgium, the Netherlands, Luxembourg—proposed "by establishing a common market and gradually removing differences between the economic policies of Member States, to promote throughout the Community the harmonious development of economic activities, continuous and balanced expansion, increased stability, a more rapid improvement in the standard of living and closer relations between its Member States."

From the beginning, there were basic differences of view among the Six. Germany, Italy, and the Benelux countries tended to favor continued negotiations to widen the scope of the European association. France, particularly after Charles de Gaulle resumed the presidency, appeared reluctant to look outward from the prospect of a tightly knit "little Europe" dominated by France and Germany. All this, in turn, reflected a concern from the major western European nation outside the Six, that is, Great Britain. At first, British governments favored a pragmatic, empirical approach to cooperation rather than more binding institutional arrangements. They preferred, as the first document below indicates, to establish a free trade area rather than the Common Market's customs union based on common external tariff arrangements. But the evident success of the Common Market and the halting progress of the free trade area led to a re-evaluation and, in 1961, the British government reversed its stand, not without serious domestic criticism, and applied for membership in the Common Market. Our second document indicates the British reasoning of that time.

The negotiations for British membership were of necessity complicated and delicate. As they went forward in Brussels they were accompanied by a fair amount of optimism and, although it was realized that possibility for failure was never out of the question, there was wide assumption that the negotiations would succeed. The collapse, brought on by French refusal to approve the new member, was all the more dramatic for the air of confidence which had prevailed and for the fact that interjected into the entire matter was the personality of Charles de Gaulle and his aspirations for France. Many saw in it not only a check to Great Britain but a shock to the entire concept of Western solidarity and a possible blow to the efficacy of NATO and the leadership of the United States.

The French position was given by de Gaulle on January 14, 1963 at a very large press conference in Paris. He had been given a question which appears below with his answer.

A. *Great Britain's Attitude in 1957*

1. Her Majesty's Goverment earnestly desire a successful outcome of the continued efforts in the post-war world to strengthen the cohesion and promote the prosperity of Western Europe. They have therefore given careful thought in recent months to the widely held view that our principal economic need in Europe is to remove existing barriers to trade and develop a single market for manufactured goods. With a population of 250 million, there is clearly a great opportunity which Europe can seize provided that the free circulations of goods is not impeded by tariffs and quantitative restrictions throughout Europe. The need to take large and constructive measures to remove these barriers to trade is the more urgent in view of the pace of technical development which increasingly demands larger markets in order that its full benefits may be obtained. During the past decade a great deal has been done in the Organisation for European Economic Co-operation and elsewhere to lower trade barriers in Europe, but her Majesty's Government believe that what is needed now is a much bolder approach.

2. With these considerations in mind Her Majesty's Government are glad that the negotiations which were set in train in June 1955 for the establishment of a Customs and Economic Union consisting of France, Germany, Italy, Belgium, Holland and Luxembourg are now approaching a successful conclusion. There are, however, substantial reasons why the United Kingdom could not become a member of such a Union. These arise in particular from the United Kingdom's interests and responsibilities in the Commonwealth. If the United Kingdom were to join the Customs and Economic Union, the United Kingdom tariff would be replaced by a single common tariff with the other member countries against the rest of the world. This would mean that goods entering the United Kingdom from the Commonwealth would have to pay duty at the same rate as goods coming from any other third country not a member of the Customs and Economic Union, while goods from the Union would be admitted free of duty. Her Majesty's Government could not contemplate entering arrangements which would in principle make it impossible for the United Kingdom to treat imports from the Commonwealth at least as favourably as those from Europe.

3. At the same time it is of great importance in the view of Her Majesty's Government to establish free trade over as wide an area as possible within Western Europe. It was for this reason that Her Majesty's Government strongly supported the decision taken by the Council of O.E.E.C. in July 1956 that a study should

be made urgently to discover whether other member countries of the Organisation could be associated with the Customs and Economic Union.

4. The possibility of such an association has now been examined by Working Party No. 17 of the Council. Her Majesty's Government believe, with the members of that Working Party, that it is fully practicable for the United Kingdom and many other O.E.E.C. countries, including the countries which are proposing to create a Customs and Economic Union, to enter a Free Trade Area. The members of this Free Trade Area would undertake to eliminate, in respect of each other's products, protective duties and other restrictive regulations of commerce, including quantitative restrictions. They would be free to keep their own separate and different tariffs on imports from outside the Area, except that the countries which were also members of the Customs and Economic Union would in due course establish a common external tariff; they would also be able to vary these tariffs, subject to any international agreements by which they are bound from time to time.

5. Her Majesty's Government's own examination of this problem had led to the conclusion that, provided foodstuffs were excluded from its scope, a Free Trade Area in Europe could be established. On 26th November 1956 the Government informed the House of Commons of their intention to enter into negotiations in O.E.E.C. with this in view. Now that the practicability of a European Free Trade Area has been confirmed by the Working Party, Her Majesty's Government hope that other countries will also declare, either before or in the course of the forthcoming meeting of O.E.E.C., their willingness to negotiate on these lines.

6. Her Majesty's Government recognise the desirability of associating with the development of the Free Trade Area as many countries in Europe as possible. At the same time it is of the essence of the Free Trade Area that the obligations undertaken by its members progressively to remove tariffs over the whole field of trade which it includes should be reciprocal. Accordingly it is the view of Her Majesty's Government that the Free Trade Area should be open to all the members countries of O.E.E.C. who were prepared to accept its obligations. The position of any such countries which felt unable to accept the obligations of a Free Trade Area would need to be examined....

11. Her Majesty's Government's concept of the Free Trade Area differs in some important respects from that of the Customs and Economic Union now contemplated by the Messina Powers. The arrangements proposed for the Customs and Economic Union involve far-reaching provisions for economic integration and harmonisation of financial and social policies, and for mutual assistance in the financing of investment. These arrangements are to be effected within an appropriate institutional framework. Her Majesty's Government envisage the Free Trade Area, on the other hand, as a concept related primarily to the removal of restrictions on trade such as tariffs and quotas. Nevertheless, Her Majesty's Government recognise that co-operation in the field of economic policy is of great and continuing importance. In practice an appreciable movement towards closer economic cooperation may be expected to take place among the members of a Free Trade Area over a period of years, either as a matter of deliberate policy or as a spontaneous development.

A European Free Trade Area (London: HMSO, 1957).

B. Great Britain's Attitude in 1961

THE PRIME MINISTER (MR. HAROLD MAC-MILLAN): With permission, I wish to make a statement on the policy of Her Majesty's Government towards the European Economic Community.

The future relations between the European Economic Community, the United Kingdom, the Commonwealth and the rest of Europe are clearly matters of capital importance in the life of our country and, indeed, of all the countries of the free world.

This is a political as well as an economic issue. Although the Treaty of Rome is concerned with economic matters it has an important political objective, namely, to promote unity and stability in Europe which is so essential a factor in the struggle for freedom and progress throughout the world. In this modern world the tendency towards larger groups of nations acting together in the common interest leads to greater unity and thus adds to our strength in the struggle for freedom.

I believe that it is both our duty and our interest to contribute towards that strength by securing the closest possible unity within Europe. At the same time, if a closer relationship between the United Kingdom and the countries of the European Economic Community were to disrupt the long-standing and historic ties between the United Kingdom and the other nations of the Commonwealth the loss would be greater than the gain. The Commonwealth is a great source of stability and strength both to Western Europe and to the world as a whole, and I am sure that its value is fully appreciated by the member Governments of the European Economic Community. I do not think that Britain's contribution to the Commonwealth will be reduced if Europe unites. On the contrary, I think that its value will be enhanced.

On the economic side, a community comprising, as members or in association, the countries of free Europe could have a very rapidly expanding economy supplying, as eventually it would, a single market of approaching 300 million people. This rapidly expanding economy could, in turn, lead to an increased demand for products from other parts of the world and so help to expand world trade and improve the prospects of the less developed areas of the world.

No British Government could join the European Economic Community without prior negotiation with a view to meeting the needs of the Commonwealth countries, of our European Free Trade Association partners, and of British agriculture consistently with the broad principles and purpose which have inspired the concept of European unity and which are embodied in the Rome Treaty.

As the House knows, Ministers have recently visited Commonwealth countries to discuss the problems which would arise if the British Government decided to negotiate for membership of the European Economic Community. We have explained to Commonwealth Governments the broad political and economic considerations which we have to take into account. They, for their part, told us their views and, in some cases, their anxieties about their essential interests. We have assured Commonwealth Governments that we shall keep in close consultation with them throughout any negotiations which might take place.

Secondly, there is the European Free Trade Association. We have treaty and other obligations to our partners in this Association and my right hon. Friends have just returned from a meeting of the European Free Trade Association Ministerial Council, in Geneva, where all were agreed that they should work closely together throughout any negotiations. Finally, we are determined to continue to protect the standard of living of our agricultural community.

During the past nine months, we have had useful and frank discussions with the European Economic Community Governments. We have now reached the stage where we cannot make further progress without entering into formal negotiations. I believe that the great majority in the House and in the country will feel that they cannot fairly judge whether it is possible for the United Kingdom to join the European Economic Community until there is a clearer picture before them of the conditions on which we could join and the extent to which these could meet our special needs.

Article 237 of the Treaty of Rome envisages that the conditions of admission of a new member and the changes in the Treaty necessitated thereby should be the subject of an agreement. Negotiations must, therefore, be held in order to establish the conditions on which we might join. In order to enter into these negotiations it is necessary, under the Treaty, to make formal application to join the Community, although the ultimate decision whether to join or not must depend on the result of the negotiations.

Therefore, after long and earnest consideration, Her Majesty's Government have come to the conclusion that it would be right for Britain to make a formal application under Article 237 of the Treaty for negotiations with a view to joining the Community if satisfactory arrangements can be made to meet the special needs of the United Kingdom, of the Commonwealth and of the European Free Trade Association.

If, as I earnestly hope, our offer to enter into negotiations with the European Economic Community is accepted we shall spare no efforts to reach a satisfactory agreement. These negotiations must inevitably be of a detailed and technical character, covering a very large number of the most delicate and difficult matters. They may, therefore, be protracted and there can, of course, be no guarantee of success. When any negotiations are brought to a conclusion then it will be the duty of the Government to recommend to the House what course we should pursue.

No agreement will be entered into until it has been approved by the House after full consultation with other Commonwealth countries by whatever procedure they may generally agree.

Parliamentary Debates, House of Commons, July 31, 1961 vol. 645, cols. 928–31.

C. The French Riposte

"Could you define explicitly France's position towards Britain's entry into the Common Market and the political evolution of Europe?"

A very clear question, to which I shall endeavour to reply clearly. When you talk about economics—and much more so when you practise them—what you say and what you do must conform to realities, because without that you can get into impasses and sometimes even land yourself in ruin. In this very great affair of the European Economic Community, and also in that of the eventual adhesion of Great Britain, it is the facts that must first be considered. Feelings, favourable though they might be and are, cannot be invoked against the real facts of the problem. What are these facts?

The Treaty of Rome was concluded between six continental States—States which are, economically speaking, one may say, of the same nature. Indeed, whether it be a matter of their industrial or agricultural production, their external exchanges, their habits or their commercial clientele, their living or working conditions, there is between them much more resemblance than difference. Moreover, they are adjacent, they inter-penetrate, they are an extension of each other through their communications.

The fact of grouping and linking them in such a way that what they have to produce, buy, sell, and consume is produced, bought, sold, and consumed in preference among themselves is therefore in conformity with realities. Moreover, it must be added that from the point of view of their economic development, their social progress, their technical capacity, they are keeping pace. They are marching in similar fashion.

It so happens, too, that there is between them no kind of political grievance, no frontier question, no rivalry in domination or power. On the contrary, they are joined in solidarity, first of all because of the consciousness they have of together constituting an important part of the sources of our civilization; and also as concerns their security, because they are continentals and have before them one and the same menace from one extremity to the other of their territorial entity (*ensemble*). Then, finally, they are in solidarity through the fact that not one among them is bound abroad by any special political or military agreement.

Thus it was psychologically and materially possible to create an economic community of the Six, though not without difficulties. When the Treaty of Rome was signed in 1957, it was after long discussions; and when it was concluded, it was necessary—in order to achieve something —that we French put in order our economic, financial, and monetary affairs..., and that was done in 1959. From that moment the Community was in principle viable...

However, this treaty, which was precise and complete enough concerning industry, was not at all so on the subject of agriculture, and for our country this had to be settled. Indeed, it is obvious that agriculture is an essential element in our national activity as a whole. We cannot conceive of a Common Market in which French agriculture would not find outlets in keeping with its production. And we agree further that, of the Six, we are the country on which this necessity is imposed in the most imperative manner.

This is why when, last January, consideration was given to the setting in motion of the second phase of the treaty—in other words a practical start in its application—we were led to pose the entry of agriculture into the Common Market as a formal condition. This was finally accepted by our partners, but very difficult and very complex arrangements were needed and some rulings are still outstanding.

Thereupon Great Britain posed her candidature to the Common Market. She did it after having earlier refused to participate in the Communities which we were building, as well as after creating a sort of Free Trade Area with six other States, and finally—I may well say it as the negotiations held at such length on this subject will be recalled—after having put some pressure on the Six to prevent a real beginning being made in the application of the Common Market.

England thus asked in turn to enter, but on her own conditions. This poses without doubt to each of the six States, and poses to England, problems of a very great dimension. England in effect is insular, she is maritime, she is linked through her exchanges, her markets, her supply

lines to the most diverse and often the most distant countries; she pursues essentially industrial and commercial activities, and only slight agricultural ones. She has in all her doings very marked and very original habits and traditions. In short, the nature, the structure, the very situation that are England's differ profoundly from those of the continentals.

What is to be done so that England, as she lives, produces, and trades, can be incorporated into the Common Market, as it has been conceived and as it functions? For example, the means by which the people of Great Britain are fed, and which are in fact the importation of foodstuffs bought cheaply in the two Americas and in the old Dominions while at the same time considerable subsidies are given to English farmers? These methods are obviously incompatible with the system which the Six have established quite naturally for themselves.

The system of the Six consists of making a whole of the agricultural products of the entire Community, strictly fixing their prices, prohibiting subsidies, organizing their consumption between all the participants, and imposing on each participant the payment to the Community of saving which they would achieve in fetching their food from outside instead of eating what the Common Market has to offer. Once again, what is to be done to bring England, as she is, into this system?

One might sometimes have believed that our English friends, in posing their candidature to the Common Market, were agreeing to transform themselves to the point of applying all the conditions which are accepted and practised by the Six.... But the question is to know whether Great Britain can now place herself, like the Continent and with it, inside a tariff which is genuinely common, to renounce all Commonwealth preferences, to cease any pretence that her agriculture be privileged, and, more than that, to treat her engagements with other countries of the Free Trade Area as null and void. That question is the whole question. It cannot be said that it is yet resolved. Will it be so one day? Obviously only England can answer.

The question is even further complicated, since after England other States, which are linked to her through the Free Trade Area, would like or wish to enter the Common Market for the same reasons as Britain. It must be agreed that first the entry of Great Britain, and then of these States, will completely change the whole of the adjustments, the agreements, the compensation, the rules which have already been established between the Six, because all these States, like Britain, have very important peculiarities. It will then be another Common Market whose construction ought to be envisaged. But this Market, which would be increased to 11 and then 13 and then perhaps 18, would without any doubt no longer resemble the one which the Six built.

Further, this Community, expanding in such fashion, would see itself faced with problems of economic relations with all kinds of other States, and first with the United States. It can be foreseen that the cohesion of its members, who would be very numerous and diverse, would not endure for long, and that finally it would appear as a colossal Atlantic community under American domination and direction which would quickly have absorbed the European Community. It is a hypothesis which in the eyes of some can be perfectly justified, but it is not at all what France wanted to do or is doing—and which is a properly European construction.

Yet it is possible that one day England might be able to transform herself sufficiently to become part of the European Community, without restriction, without reserve, and in preference to anything else, and in that event the Six would open the door to her and France would raise no obstacle, although obviously the very fact of England's participation in the Community would considerably change its nature and its volume.

It is possible, too, that England might not yet be so disposed, and this is certainly what seems to emanate from the long, long Brussels conversations. But if that is the case, there is nothing dramatic about it. First, whatever decision England takes in this matter there is no reason, as far as we are concerned, for the relations we have with her to be changed. The consideration and the respect which are due to this great country, this great people, will not thereby be in the slightest impaired.

What England has done across the centuries and in the world is recognized as immense, although there have often been conflicts with France. Britain's glorious participation in the victory which crowned the First World War—we French shall always admire it. As for the role England played in the most dramatic and decisive moment of the Second World War, no one has the right to forget it. In truth, the destiny of the free world, and first of all ours and even that of the United States and Russia, depended in a large measure on the resolution, the solidity, and the courage of the English people, as Churchill was able to harness them. Even at the present moment no one can contest British capacity and worth.

Moreover, I repeat, even if the Brussels negotiations were shortly not to succeed, nothing would prevent the conclusion between the Common Market and Great Britain of an agreement of association designed to safeguard exchanges, and nothing would prevent close relations between England and France from being maintained, nor the pursuit and development of their direct cooperation in all kinds of fields, notably the scientific, technical, and industrial—as the two countries have just proved by deciding to build together the supersonic aircraft *Concorde*.

Lastly, it is very possible that Britain's own evolution, and the evolution of the universe, might bring the English towards the Continent, whatever delays this achievement might demand. For my part, that is what I readily believe, and that is why, in my opinion, it will in any case have been a great honour for the British Prime Minister, my friend Harold Macmillan, and for his Government, to have discerned that goal in good time, to have had enough political courage to have proclaimed it, and to have led their country the first steps along the path which one day, perhaps, will lead it to moor alongside the Continent.

Keesing's Contemporary Archives, pp. 19197–98.

IV. *Ideological Controversy Between Soviet and Chinese Communists*

If western Europe faced serious "internal" differences and if the West as a whole was ranged in sharply drawn hostility to the Communist world, that Communist world appeared to many to remain virtually monolithic in its solidarity. But reality belied appearances. As Communist China emerged as a major factor in the postwar world, differences between the Soviet Union and China became pronounced. Those differences took an ideological form and centered, in addition to such specific issues as Soviet policy toward Albania and Yugoslavia or Chinese aggression in India, about the general question of peaceful coexistence with the West. Yet it was possible perhaps to interpret the quarrel as the clash of conflicting nationalisms expressing itself in the vocabulary of Communist theory and polemics. The Russo-Chinese split was felt sharply throughout the Communist world. Most Communist parties supported the Soviet position, but active minorities continued to support the more aggressive stand of the Chinese leadership. And as the quarrel deepened between 1960 and 1965, it appeared possible that a Russo-Chinese struggle for dominance of the Communist world would emerge as one major determinant of the course of twentieth century history. In any event the two documents below, selected from among many, will give something of the flavor of the struggle as seen by the two major protagonists.

A. *The Chinese Position. Letter of June 14, 1963*

(1) For several years there have been differences within the international Communist movement.... The central issue is ...whether or not to accept the fact that the people still living under the imperialist and capitalist system...need to make revolution, and whether or not to accept the fact that the people already on the Social-

ist road...need to carry their revolution forward to the end....

(2) The revolutionary principles of the 1957 declaration and the 1960 statement ...may be summarized as follows:... Workers of the world, unite with the oppressed peoples;...bring the proletarian world revolution step by step to complete victory; and establish a new world without imperialism, without capitalism, and without the exploitation of man by man....

(3) If the general line of the international Communist movement is one-sidedly reduced to "peaceful co-existence," "peaceful competition," and "peaceful transition," this is to violate the revolutionary principles of the 1957 declaration and the 1960 statement....

(4) The fundamental contradictions in the contemporary world...are: the contradiction between the Socialist camp and the imperialist camp; the contradiction between the proletariat and the bourgeoisie in the capitalist countries; the contradiction between the oppressed nations and imperialism; and the contradictions among imperialist countries and among monopoly capitalist groups....

(5) The following erroneous views should be repudiated...:(a) the view which blots out the class content of the contradiction between the Socialist and imperialist camps...; (b) the view which recognizes only the contradiction between the Socialist and imperialist camps...; (c) the view which maintains...that the contradiction between the proletariat and the bourgeoisie can be resolved without a proletarian revolution in each country and that the contradiction between the oppressed nations and imperialism can be resolved without revolution...; (d) the view which denies that the development of the inherent contradictions in the contemporary capitalist world inevitably leads to

a new situation in which the imperialist countries are locked in an intense struggle, and asserts that the contradictions among the imperialist countries can be reconciled or even eliminated by 'international agreements among the big monopolies'; and (e) the view which maintains that the contradiction between the two world systems of Socialism and capitalism will automatically disappear in the course of 'economic competition,'. . .and that a 'world without wars,' a new world of 'all-round co-operation,' will appear. . . .

(6) Now that there is a Socialist camp consisting of 13 countries—Albania, Bulgaria, China, Cuba, Czechoslovakia, the German Democratic Republic, Hungary, the Democratic People's Republic of Korea, Mongolia, Poland, Rumania, the Soviet Union, and the Democratic Republic of Vietnam—. . .the touchstone of proletarian internationalism is whether or not it resolutely defends the whole of the Socialist camp.

If anybody. . .does not defend the unity of the Socialist camp but on the contrary creates tension and splits within it, or even follows the policies of the Yugoslav revisionists, tries to liquidate the Socialist camp, or helps capitalist countries to attack fraternal Socialist countries, he is betraying the interests of the entire international proletariat. . . .

If anybody, following in the footsteps of others, defends the erroneous opportunist line and policies pursued by a certain Socialist country instead of upholding the correct Marxist-Leninist line. . .he is departing from Marxism-Leninism and proletarian internationalism.

(7) The 1960 statement points out: . . .'U. S. imperialism is the main force of aggression and war.'. . .To make no distinction between enemies, friends, and ourselves, and to entrust the fate of the people and of mankind to collaboration with U.S. imperialism, is to lead people astray. . . .

(8) Certain persons in the international Communist movement are now taking a passive or scornful or negative attitude towards the struggles of the oppressed nations for liberation. . . .The attitude taken towards the revolutionary struggles of the people in the Asian, African, and Latin American countries is an important criterion for differentiating those who want revolution from those who do not. . . .

(9) The oppressed nations and peoples of Asia, Africa, and Latin America are faced with the urgent task of fighting imperialism and its lackeys. . . . In these areas extremely broad sections of the population refuse to be slaves of imperialism. They include not only the workers, peasants, intellectuals, and petty bourgeoisie, but also the patriotic national bourgeoisie and even certain kings, princes, and aristocrats. . . . The proletariat and its party must. . .organize a broad united front against imperialism. . . . The proletarian party should maintain its ideological, political, and organizational independence and insist on the leadership of the revolution. The proletarian party and the revolutionary people must learn to master all forms of struggle, including armed struggle. . . . The policy of the proletarian party should be. . .to unite with the bourgeoisie, in so far as they tend to be progressive, anti-imperialist, and anti-feudal, but to struggle against their reactionary tendencies to compromise and collaborate with imperialism and the forces of feudalism. . . .

(10) In the imperialist and capitalist countries the proletarian revolution and the dictatorship of the proletariat are essential. . . . It is wrong to refuse to use parliamentary and other legal forms of struggle when they can and should be used. However, if a Marxist-Leninist party falls into legalism or parliamentary cretinism, confining the struggle within the limits permitted by the bourgeoisie, this will inevitably lead to renouncing the proletarian revolution and the dictatorship of the proletariat.

(11) Marx and Lenin did raise the possibility that revolutions may develop peacefully. But, as Lenin pointed out, the peaceful development of revolution is an opportunity 'very seldom to be met with in the history of revolution.' As a matter of fact, there is no historical precedent for peaceful transition from capitalism to So-

cialism.... The proletarian party must never base its thinking, its policies for revolution, and its entire work on the assumption that the imperialists and reactionaries will accept peaceful transformation....

(12) If the leading group in any party adopt a non-revolutionary line and convert it into a reformist party, then Marxist-Leninists inside and outside the party will replace them and lead the people in making revolution.... There are certain persons who assert that they have made the greatest creative contributions to revolutionary theory since Lenin and that they alone are correct. But it is very dubious... whether they really have a general line for the international Communist movement which conforms with Marxism-Leninism....

(13) Certain persons have one-sidedly exaggerated the role of peaceful competition between Socialist and imperialist countries in their attempt to substitute peaceful competition for the revolutionary struggles of the oppressed peoples. According to their preaching, it would seem that imperialism will automatically collapse in the course of this peaceful competition, and that the only thing the oppressed peoples have to do is to wait quietly for the advent of this day. What does this have in common with Marxist-Leninist views?

Moreover, certain persons have concocted the strange tale that China and some other Socialist countries want to "unleash wars" and to spread Socialism by 'wars between States.' As the statement of 1960 points out, such tales are nothing but imperialist and reactionary slanders. To put it bluntly, the purpose of those who repeat these slanders is to hide the fact that they are opposed to revolutions by the oppressed peoples and nations of the world and opposed to others supporting such revolutions.

(14) Certain persons say that revolutions are entirely possible without war.... If they are referring to a war of national liberation or a revolutionary civil war, then this formulation is, in effect, opposed to revolutionary wars and to revolution. If they are referring to a world war, then

they are shooting at a non-existent target. Although Marxist-Leninists have pointed out, on the basis of the history of the two World Wars, that world wars inevitably lead to revolution, no Marxist-Leninist ever has held or ever will hold that revolution must be made through world war.

Marxist-Leninists take the abolition of war as their ideal and believe that war can be abolished. But how can war be abolished?... Certain persons now actually hold that it is possible to bring about "a world without weapons, without armed forces, and without wars" through "general and complete disarmament" while the system of imperialism and of the exploitation of man by man still exists. This is sheer illusion....

If one regards general and complete disarmament as the fundamental road to world peace, spreads the illusion that imperialism will automatically lay down its arms, and tries to liquidate the revolutionary struggles of the oppressed peoples and nations on the pretext of disarmament, then this is deliberately to deceive the people of the world and help the imperialists in their policies of aggression and war.... World peace can be won only by the struggles of the people in all countries and not by begging the imperialists for it....

(15) The complete banning and destruction of nuclear weapons is an important task in the struggle to defend world peace. We must do our utmost to this end. ... However, if the imperialists are forced to accept an agreement to ban nuclear weapons, it decidedly will not be because of their 'love for humanity,' but because of the pressure of the people of all countries and for the sake of their own vital interests....

The emergence of nuclear weapons does not and cannot resolve the fundamental contradictions in the contemporary world, does not and cannot alter the law of class struggle, and does not and cannot change the nature of imperialism and reaction. It cannot, therefore, be said that with the emergence of nuclear weapons the possibility and the necessity of social and national revolutions have disappeared, or that the basic principles of Marxism-Leninism, and especially the theories of proletarian revolution and the dictatorship of the proletariat, ...have become outmoded....

(16) It was Lenin who advanced the thesis that it is possible for the Socialist countries to practise peaceful co-existence with the capitalist countries.... The People's Republic of China, too, has consistently pursued the policy of peaceful co-existence with countries having different social systems, and it is China which initiated the Five Principles of Peaceful Co-existence.

However, a few years ago certain persons suddenly claimed Lenin's policy of peaceful co-existence as their own 'great discovery.' They maintain that they have a monopoly in the interpretation of this policy. They treat 'peaceful co-existence' as if it were an all-inclusive, mystical book from heaven, and attribute to it every success the people of the world achieve by struggle. What is more, they label all who disagree with their distortions of Lenin's views as opponents of peaceful co-existence. ...

Lenin's principle of peaceful co-existence...designates a relationship between countries with different social systems.... It should never be extended to apply to the relations between oppressed and oppressor nations, between oppressed and oppressor countries, or between oppressed and oppressor classes, and never be described as the main content of the transition from capitalism to Socialism. Still less should it be asserted that peaceful co-existence is mankind's road to Socialism.

The general line of the foreign policy of the Socialist countries should have the following content: to develop relations of friendship, mutual assistance, and cooperation among the countries of the Socialist camp in accordance with the principle of proletarian internationalism; to strive for peaceful co-existence on the basis of the Five Principles with countries having different social systems, and oppose the imperialist policies of aggression and war; and to support and assist the revolutionary

struggles of all the oppressed peoples and nations. These three aspects are inter-related and indivisible, and not a single one can be omitted.

(17) For a very long historical period after the proletariat takes power, class struggle continues.... To deny the existence of class struggle in the period of the dictatorship of the proletariat and the necessity of thoroughly completing the Socialist revolution on the economic, political, and ideological fronts...violates Marxism-Leninism.

(18) The fundamental thesis of Marx and Lenin is that the dictatorship of the proletariat will inevitably continue for the entire historical period of the transition from capitalism to Communism.... If it is announced, half-way through, that the dictatorship of the proletariat is no longer necessary...this would lead to extremely grave consequences and make any transition to Communism out of the question....

Is it possible to replace the State of the dictatorship of the proletariat by a 'State of the whole people'? This is not a question of the internal affairs of any particular country, but a fundamental problem involving the universal truth of Marxism-Leninism....In calling a Socialist State the 'State of the whole people,' is one trying to replace the Marxist-Leninist theory of the State by the bourgeois theory of the State? Is one trying to replace the State of the dictatorship of the proletariat by a State of a different character?...

(19) Is it possible to replace the party which is the vanguard of the proletariat by a 'party of the entire people'? This, too, is not a question of the internal affairs of any particular party, but a fundamental problem involving the universal truth of Marxism-Leninism.... What will happen if it is announced half-way before entering the higher stage of Communist society that the party of the proletariat has become a 'party of the entire people' and if its proletarian class character is repudiated?...Does this not disarm the proletariat and all the working people, organizationally and ideologically, and is it not tantamount to helping to restore capitalism? ...

(20) Over the past few years certain persons have violated Lenin's integral teachings about the interrelationship of leaders, party, class, and masses, and raised the issue of 'combating the personality cult'; this is erroneous and harmful. . . . To raise the question of 'combating the personality cult' is actually to counterpose the leaders to the masses, undermine the party's unified leadership, which is based on democratic centralism, dissipate its fighting strength, and disintegrate its ranks. . . .

While loudly combating the so-called personality cult, certain persons are in reality doing their best to defame the proletarian party and the dictatorship of the proletariat. At the same time, they are enormously exaggerating the role of certain individuals, shifting all errors on to others, and claiming all credit for themselves. What is more serious is that, under the pretext of 'combating the personality cult,' certain persons are crudely interfering in the internal affairs of other fraternal parties and fraternal countries, and forcing other fraternal parties to change their leadership in order to impose their own wrong line on these parties. What is this if not Great-Power chauvinism, sectarianism, and splittism? . . .

(21) Relations between Socialist countries, whether large or small, and whether more developed or less developed economically, must be based on the principles of complete equality. . .Every Socialist country must rely mainly on itself for its construction. . . . If, proceeding only from its own partial interests, any Socialist country unilaterally demands that other fraternal countries submit to its needs, and uses the pretext of opposing what they call 'going it alone' and 'nationalism' to prevent other fraternal countries from applying the principle of relying mainly on their own efforts in their construction and from developing their economies on the basis of independence, or even goes to the length of putting economic pressure on other fraternal countries—then these are pure manifestations of national egoism. . . . In relations among Socialist countries it would be preposterous

to follow the practice of gaining profit for oneself at the expense of others, . . .or go so far as to take the 'economic integration' and the 'Common Market' which monopoly capitalist groups have instituted for the purpose of seizing markets and grabbing profits, as examples which Socialist countries ought to follow in their economic co-operation and mutual assistance.

(22) If the principle of independence and equality is accepted in relations among fraternal parties, then it is impermissible for any party to place itself above others, to interfere in their internal affairs, and to adopt patriarchal ways in relations with them. If it is accepted that there are no 'superiors' and 'subordinates' in relations among fraternal parties, then it is impermissible to impose the programme, resolutions, and line of one's own party on other fraternal parties as the 'common programme' of the international Communist movement.

If the principle of reaching unanimity through consultation is accepted in relations between fraternal parties, then one should not emphasize 'who is in the majority' or 'who is in the minority,' and bank on a so-called majority in order to force through one's own erroneous line and carry out sectarian and splitting policies. If it is agreed that differences between fraternal parties should be settled through inter-party consultation, then other fraternal parties should not be attacked publicly and by name at one's own party congress or other party congresses, in speeches by party leaders, resolutions, statements, etc.; and still less should the ideological differences among fraternal parties be extended into the sphere of State relations. . . .

In the sphere of relations among fraternal parties and countries, the question of Soviet-Albanian relations is an outstanding one at present. . . . How to treat the Marxist-Leninist fraternal Albanian Party of Labour is one question. How to treat the Yugoslav revisionist clique of traitors to Marxism-Leninism is quite another question. These two essentially different questions must on no account be placed on a par.

Your letter says that you 'do not relinquish the hope that the relations between the C.P.S.U. and the Albanian Party of Labour may be improved,' but at the same time you continue to attack the Albanian comrades for what you call 'splitting activities.' Clearly this is self-contradictory and in no way contributes to resolving the problem of Soviet-Albanian relations.

Who is it that has taken splitting actions in Soviet-Albanian relations? Who is it that has extended the ideological differences between the Soviet and Albanian parties to State relations? Who is it that has brought the divergences between the Soviet and Albanian parties and between the two countries into the open before the enemy? Who is it that has openly called for a change in the Albanian party and State leadership? All this is plain and clear to the whole world... We once again express our sincere hope that the leading comrades of the C.P.S.U. will observe the principles guiding relations among fraternal parties and countries and take the initiative in seeking an effective way to improve Soviet-Albanian relations....

The comrades of the C.P.S.U. state in their letter that 'the Communist Party of the Soviet Union has never taken and will never take a single step that could sow hostility among the peoples of our country toward the fraternal Chinese people or other peoples.' Here we do not desire to enumerate the many unpleasant events that have occurred in the past; we only wish that the comrades of the C.P.S.U. will strictly abide by this statement in their future actions. During the past few years our party members and our people have exercised the greatest restraint in the face of a series of grave incidents which were in violation of the principles guiding relations among fraternal parties and countries.... The spirit of proletarian internationalism of the Chinese Communists and the Chinese people has stood a severe test....

(23) Certain persons are now attempting to introduce the Yugoslav revisionist clique into the Socialist community and the international Communist ranks. This is openly to tear up the agreement unanimously reached at the 1960 meeting of the fraternal parties and is absolutely impermissible.

Over the past few years...the many experiences and lessons of the international Communist movement have fully confirmed the correctness of the conclusion in the (Moscow) declaration and the statement that revisionism is at present the main danger, or that dogmatism is no less dangerous than revisionism.... Genuine Marxist-Leninist parties...must not barter away principles, approving one thing today and another tomorrow....

It is necessary at all times to adhere to the universal truth of Marxism-Leninism. Failure to do so will lead to right opportunist or revisionist errors. On the other hand, it is always necessary to proceed from reality,...and independently work out and apply policies and tactics suited to the conditions of one's own country. Errors of dogmatism will be committed if one fails to do so, if one mechanically copies the policies and tactics of another Communist Party, submits blindly to the will of others, or accepts without analysis the programme and resolutions of another Communist Party as one's own line. Some people are now violating this basic principle.... On the pretext of 'creatively developing Marxism-Leninism' they cast aside the universal truth of Marxism-Leninism. Moreover, they describe as "universal Marxist-Leninist truths" their own prescriptions, which are based on nothing but subjective conjecture..., and they force others to accept these prescriptions unconditionally. That is why so many grave phenomena have come to pass in the international Communist movement....

(24) If a party is not a proletarian revolutionary party but a bourgeois reformist party; if it is not a Marxist-Leninist party but a revisionist party;... if it is not a party that can use its brains to think for itself...., but instead is a party that parrots the words of others, copies foreign experience without analysis, runs hither and thither in response to the

baton of certain persons abroad, and has become a hodgepodge of revisionism, dogmatism, and everything but Marxist-Leninist principle; then such a party is absolutely incapable of leading the proletariat and the masses in revolutionary struggle. . . .

(25) The public polemics in the international Communist movement have been provoked by certain fraternal party leaders and forced on us. Since a public debate has been provoked, it ought to be conducted on the basis of equality among fraternal parties. . .and by presenting the facts and reasoning things out. . . . Since certain party leaders have published innumerable articles attacking other fraternal parties, why do they not publish in their own Press the articles those parties have written in reply?

Latterly, the Communist Party of China has been subjected to preposterous attacks. . . . We have published these articles and speeches attacking us in our own Press. . . . Between Dec. 15, 1962, and March 8, 1963, we wrote seven articles in reply to our attackers. . . . Presumably you are referring to these articles when towards the end of your letter of March 30 you accuse the Chinese Press of making 'groundless attacks' on the C.P.S.U. It is turning things upside down to describe articles replying to our attackers as 'attacks.'

Since you describe our articles as 'groundless' and as so very bad, why do you not publish all seven of these "groundless attacks" in the same way as we have published your articles, and let all the Soviet comrades and Soviet people think for themselves and judge who is right and who wrong? You are of course entitled to make a point-by-point refutation of these articles you consider 'groundless attacks.' Although you call our articles "groundless" and our arguments wrong, you do not tell the Soviet people what our arguments actually are. This practice can hardly be described as showing a serious attitude towards the discussion of problems by fraternal parties, towards the truth, or towards the masses. . . .

Keesing's Contemporary Archives, pp. 19567–69.

B. The Soviet Position. Reply of July 14, 1963

The frankly hostile actions of the C.P.C. leaders, their persistent striving to sharpen polemics in the international Communist movement, the deliberate distortion of the positions of our party, and the incorrect interpretation of the motives for which we refrained temporarily from publishing the letter impel us to publish the letter of the C.P.C. central committee of June 14, 1963, and to give our appraisal of this document. All who read the letter of the C.P.C. central committee will see, behind the bombastic phrases about unity and cohesion, unfriendly and slanderous attacks on our party and our country. . . .

The document is crammed with charges —overt and covert—against the C.P.S.U. and the Soviet Union. The authors of the letter permit themselves unworthy fabrications, insulting to Communists, about 'the betrayal of the interests of the whole international proletariat and all the peoples of the world,' and 'a departure from Marxism-Leninism and proletarian internationalism.' They hint at 'cowardice in face of the imperialists,' at 'a step back in the course of historic development,' and even at 'the organizational and moral disarming of the proletariat and all working people,' which is tantamount to 'helping to restore capitalism' in our country. . . .

At a first glance many theses in the (Chinese) letter may seem puzzling. Whom are the Chinese comrades actually arguing with? Are there Communists who, for instance, object to Socialist revolution or who do not regard it as their duty to fight against imperialism and to support the national liberation movement? . . . The Chinese comrades first ascribe to the C.P.S.U. and other Marxist-Leninist parties views which they have never expressed and which are alien to them; secondly, by paying lip-service to formulae and positions borrowed from the documents of the Communist movement, they try to camouflage their erroneous views. . . .

In point of fact, however, the questions which bear on vital interests of the peoples are in the centre of the dispute. These are the questions of war and peace, the role and development of the world Socialist system, the struggle against the ideology and practice of the personality cult, the strategy and tactics of the world labour movement, and the national liberation struggle. . . .

The world Communist movement, in the declaration and statement, set before Communists as a task of extreme importance that of struggling for peace and averting a nuclear world catastrophe. . . . Though the nature of imperialism has not changed and the danger of the outbreak of war has not been averted, in modern conditions the forces of peace, of which the mighty community of Socialist States is the main bulwark, can by their joint efforts avert a new world war. . . .

The nuclear rocket weapons which have been created. . .possess an unprecedented devastating force. . . . Have Communists the right to ignore this danger? Must we tell the people the whole truth about the consequences of nuclear war? We believe that, without question, we must. This cannot have a 'paralysing' effect on the masses, as the Chinese comrades asert. On the contrary, the truth about modern war will mobilize the will and energy of the masses in the struggle for peace and against imperialism. . . .

What is the position of the C.P.C. leadership? What do the theses that they propagate mean—that an end cannot be put to war so long as imperialism exists?; that peaceful co-existence is an illusion?; that it is not the general line of the foreign policy of Socialist countries?; that the peace struggle hinders the revolutionary struggle?. . . They do not believe in the possibility of preventing a new world war; they underestimate the forces of peace and Socialism and overestimate the forces of imperialism; in fact, they ignore the mobilization of the

masses for the struggle against the war danger. . . .

The Chinese comrades obviously underestimate the whole danger of nuclear war. 'The atomic bomb is a paper tiger, it is not terrible at all.' they contend. The main thing is to put an end to imperialism as quickly as possible, but how and with what losses this will be achieved seems to be a secondary question. To whom, it is right to ask, is it secondary? To the hundreds of millions of people who are doomed to death in the event of the unleashing of a nuclear war? To the States that will be erased from the face of the earth in the very first hours of such a war?. . .

Some responsible Chinese leaders have also declared that it is possible to sacrifice hundreds of millions of people in war. 'On the ruins of destroyed imperialism,' asserts *Long Live Leninism,* which was approved by the C.P.C. central committee, 'the victorious peoples will create with tremendous speed a civilization a thousand times higher than the capitalist system, and will build their bright future.' Is it permissible to ask the Chinese comrades if they realize what sort of ruins a nuclear world war would leave behind?. . . They say frankly, "On the ruins of a destroyed imperialism" —in other words, as a result of the unleashing of war—'a bright future will be built.' If we agree to this, then indeed there is no need for the principle of peaceful co-existence. . . .

We ourselves produce the nuclear weapon and have manufactured it in sufficient quantity. We know its destructive force full well. If imperialism starts a war against us we shall not hesitate to use this formidable weapon against the aggressor; but if we are not attacked, we shall not be the first to use this weapon. . . .

We would like to ask the Chinese comrades who suggest building a 'bright future' on the ruins of the old world destroyed by a nuclear war whether they have consulted the working class of the countries where imperialism dominates? . . . The nuclear bomb does not distinguish between the imperialists and working people. . . .

The posing of the question in this way

by the Chinese comrades may give rise to the well-justified suspicion that this is no longer a class approach in the struggle for the abolition of capitalism, but has entirely different aims. If both the exploiters and the exploited are buried under the ruins of the old world, who will build the 'bright future'? In this connexion it is impossible not to note the fact that instead of the internationalist class approach expressed in the call "Workers of the world, unite,' the Chinese comrades propagate the slogan, which is devoid of any class meaning, 'The wind from the east prevails over the wind from the west.'. . .

The Chinese comrades allege that in the period of the Caribbean crisis we made an 'adventurist' mistake by introducing rockets into Cuba and then 'capitulated' to American imperialism when we removed the rockets from Cuba. Such assertions utterly contradict the facts. What was the actual state of affairs? The C.P.S.U. central committee and the Soviet Government possessed trustworthy information that an armed aggression by U.S. imperialism against Cuba was about the take place. . . . Proceeding from the need to defend the Cuban revolution, the Soviet Government and the Cuban Government reached agreement on the delivery of missiles to Cuba. . . . Such a resolute step on the part of the Soviet Union and Cuba was a shock to the American imperialists, who felt for the first time in their history that if they were to undertake an armed invasion of Cuba, a shattering retaliatory blow would be dealt against their own territory.

Inasmuch as the point in question was not simply a conflict between the United States and Cuba, but a clash between the two major nuclear Powers, the crisis in the Caribbean area would have turned from a local into a world one. A real danger of nuclear war arose. There was one alternative in the prevailing situation; either to . . .embark upon a course of unleashing a world nuclear war, or, profiting from the opportunity offered by the delivery of missiles, to take all steps to reach an agreement on a peaceful solution of the crisis and to prevent aggression against Cuba. As

is known, we chose the second path. . . . Agreement to remove the missile weapons in return for the U.S. Government's commitment not to invade Cuba. . .made it possible to frustrate the plans of the extreme adventurist circles of American imperialism. . . .

The Chinese comrades regard our statement that the Kennedy Government also displayed a certain reasonableness and a realistic approach in the Cuban crisis as 'prettifying imperialism.' Do they really think that all bourgeois Governments lack all reason in everything they do?. . .The Chinese comrades argue that the imperialists cannot be trusted in anything, that they are bound to cheat. But this is not a case of good faith, but rather one of sober calculation. Eight months have passed since the elimination of the Caribbean crisis, and the U.S. Government is keeping its word—there has been no invasion of Cuba. We also assumed a commitment to remove our missiles from Cuba, and we have fulfilled it. It should not, however, be forgotten that we have also given a commitment to the Cuban people: if the U.S. imperialists do not keep their promise but invade Cuba, we shall come to the assistance of the Cuban people. . . .

What are the Chinese leaders dissatisfied with? Is it perhaps the fact that it was possible to prevent the invasion of Cuba and the unleashing of a world war?. . .

The true position of the C.P.C. leadership is demonstrated very clearly. . .in its complete underestimation and, what is more, deliberate ignoring of the struggle for disarmament. They try to prove that general disarmament is possible only when Socialism triumphs all over the world. Must the Marxists sit on their hands, waiting for the victory of Socialism all over the world, while mankind suffocates in the clutches of the arms race?. . .One can repeat *ad infinitum* that war is inevitable, claiming that such a viewpoint is evidence of one's 'revolutionary spirit.' In fact, this approach merely indicates lack of faith in one's strength and fear of imperialism. . . .

The C.P.C. central committee accuses the Communist parties of extending peaceful co-existence between States with different social systems to relations between the exploiters and the exploited, between the oppressed and the oppressing classes, between the working masses and the imperialists. This is a truly monstrous fabrication.... When we speak of peaceful co-existence we mean the inter-State relations of the Socialist countries with the countries of capitalism. The principle of peaceful co-existence, naturally, can in no way be applied to relations between the antagonistic classes inside the capitalist States....

The C.P.C. leaders have taken on themselves the role of defenders of the personality cult, of propagators of Stalin's wrong ideas. They are trying to thrust upon other parties the practices, ideology, ethics, and forms and methods of leadership which flourished in the period of the personality cult. The letter went on to quote statements made in 1956 by Mao Tse-tung, Liu Shao-chi, and Teng Ksiaoping fully supporting the decisions of the 20th congress of the C.P.S.U., including its condemnation of the personality cult, and commented that they have made a turn of 180 degrees in evaluating the 20th congress of our party....

The atmosphere of fear, suspicion, and uncertainty which poisoned the life of the people in their period of the personality cult has gone.... Ask the people whose fathers and mothers were victims of the reprisals in the period of the personality cult what it means for them to obtain recognition that their fathers, mothers, and brothers were honest people, and that they themselves are not outcasts in our society....

Soviet people find it strange and outrageous that the Chinese comrades should be trying to smear the C.P.S.U. programme. Alluding to the fact that our party proclaims as its task the struggle for a better life for the people, the C.P.C. leaders hint at some sort of 'bourgeoisification' and 'degeneration' of Soviet society. To follow their line of thinking, it seems that if a people walk in rope sandals and eat watery soup out of a common bowl, that is Communism, and if a working man lives

well and wants to live even better tomorrow, that is almost tantamount to the restoration of capitalism!...

The next important question on which we differ is that of ways and methods of the revolutionary struggle of the working class. As depicted by the Chinese comrades, the differences on this question appear as follows: one side—they themselves—stands for world revolution, while the other—the C.P.S.U., the Marxist-Leninist parties—have forgotten the revolution and even fear it, and instead of revolutionary struggle are concerned with things unworthy of a real revolutionary, such as peace, the economic development of the Socialist countries, the improvement of the living standards of their peoples, and the struggle for the democratic rights and vital interests of the working people of the capitalist countries....

Lenin taught that 'we exert our main influence on the international revolution by our economic policy'...But now it turns out that there are comrades who have decided that Lenin was wrong. What is this—lack of faith in the ability of the Socialist countries to defeat capitalism in economic competition? Or is it the attitude of persons who, on meeting with difficulties in building Socialism, have become disappointed and do not see the possibility of exerting the main influence on the international revolutionary movement by their economic successes? . . . They want to achieve the revolution sooner, by other and what seem to them shorter ways. But the victorious revolution can consolidate its successes and prove the superiority of Socialism over capitalism by the work, and only by the work, of the people.

The Chinese comrades, in a haughty and abusive way, accuse the Communist parties of France, Italy, the United States, and other countries of nothing less than opportunism and reformism, of 'parliamentary cretinism,' even of slipping down to 'bourgeois Socialism.' On what grounds do they do this? On the grounds that these Communist parties do not put forward the slogan of an immediate proletarian revolution, although even the Chinese leaders must realize that this cannot be done without the existence of a revolutionary situation. . . .

The Chinese comrades have also disagreed with the world Communist movement on the forms of the transition of different countries to Socialism. . . . The Chinese comrades regard as the main criterion of revolutionary spirit recognition of the armed uprising. . . . (They) are thereby in fact denying the possibility of using peaceful forms of struggle for the victory of the Socialist revolution, whereas Marxism-Leninism teaches that Communists must master all form of revolutionary class struggle, both violent and non-violent.

Yet another important question is that of the relationship between the struggle of the international working class and the national liberation movement of the peoples of Asia, Africa, and Latin America.

These are the great forces of our epoch Correct co-ordination between them constitutes one of the main prerequisites for victory over imperialism.

How do the Chinese comrades solve this problem? This is seen from their new theory, according to which the main contradiction of our time is not between Socialism and imperialism, but between the national liberation movement and imperialism. The decisive force in the struggle against imperialism, the Chinese comrades maintain, is not the world system of Socialism, not the struggle of the international working class, but the national liberation movement.

In this way the Chinese comrades apparently want to win popularity among the peoples of Asia, Africa, and Latin America by the easiest possible means. But let no one be deceived by this theory. Whether the Chinese theoreticians want it or not, this theory in essence means isolating the national liberation movement from the international working class and its creation, the world system of Socialism. . . . The Chinese comrades . . . want to amend Lenin and prove that it is not the working class but the petty bourgeoisie or the national bourgeoisie, or even "certain patriotically minded kings, princes, and

aristocrats," who must be the leaders of the world struggle against imperialism. . . .

The question arises, what is the explanation for the incorrect propositions of the C.P.C. leadership on the basic problems of our time? It is either the complete divorcement of the Chinese comrades from actual reality—a dogmatic, bookish approach to problems of war, peace, and revolution; their lack of understanding of the concrete conditions of the present epoch—or the fact that behind the rumpus about the 'world revolution' raised by the Chinese comrades there are other goals, which have nothing in common with revolution. . . .

The formula of 'building Socialism mainly by our own forces' conceals the concept of creating self-sufficient national economies for which economic contacts with other countries are restricted to trade alone. The Chinese comrades are trying to impose this approach on other Socialist countries. . . . It can not be regarded otherwise than as an attempt to undermine the unity of the Socialist commonwealth. . . .

[The letter also accused the Chinese leadership of organizing and supporting various anti-party groups of renegades, including dissident Communist groups in Belgium, the U.S.A., Brazil, Australia, Italy, India, and Ceylon; alleged that the Trotskyist Fourth International was trying to use the Chinese party's position to further its own ends; and said that the Chinese leaders had published in many languages abusive attacks on the Soviet, French, Italian, Indian, and U.S. Communist parties, and were trying to subordinate other fraternal parties to their influence and control. . . .]

Differences on a number of ideological questions of principle continue to remain between the C.P.S.U. and the League of Communists of Yugoslavia. But it would be wrong to 'excommunicate' Yugoslavia from Socialism on these grounds. . . . At the present time there are 14 Socialist countries in the world. . . . The range of questions encountered by the fraternal parties which stand at the helm of State is increasing, and besides this each of the fraternal parties is working in different conditions. It is not surprising that in these circumstances the fraternal parties may develop different approaches to the solution of this or that problem. . . .

If we were to follow the example of the Chinese leaders, because of our serious differences with the leaders of the Albanian Party of Labour we should long since have proclaimed Albania to be a non-Socialist country. But that would be a wrong and subjective approach. In spite of our differences with the Albanian leaders, the Soviet Communists regard Albania as a Socialist country, and for their part do everything in their power to prevent Albania from being split away from the Socialist community. . . .

A meeting of the delegations of the C.P.S.U. and the C.P.C. is being held in Moscow at the present time. Unfortunately the C.P.C. representatives are continuing to worsen the situation. In spite of this, the delegation of the C.P.S.U. are displaying the utmost patience and self-control, working for a successful outcome to the negotiations. The very near future will show whether the Chinese comrades will agree to build our relations on the basis of what united us and not what divides us. . . .

Keesing's Contemporary Archives, pp. 19570–72.

Index